By Richard M. Langworth and
The Editors of Consumer Guide®

# Encyclopedia of
# American
# Cars
# 1940~1970

BEEKMAN HOUSE

NEW YORK

# Contents

Manufactured in the United States of America
1 2 3 4 5 6 7 8 9 10

Published by:
Beekman House
A Division of Crown Publishers, Inc.
One Park Avenue
New York, N.Y. 10016

Library of Congress Catalog Card Number: 80–81314
ISBN: 0–517–294648

Chief Contributing Author: Richard M. Langworth
Contributing Authors: Alden Jewell, R. Perry Zavitz
Editorial Assistant: Barbara F. Langworth
Photo Credits: Applegate & Applegate Collection, Asa E. Hall, Alden Jewell, Richard Quinn
Cover Photos: David Gooley, Mel Winer
Book Designer: Frank E. Peiler

# Contents

## Acknowledgements

It would be impossible to list in this short space the numerous members of the automotive industry and the old-car avocation whose kind assistance and research over the past 20 years contributed in some way to the material in this book. We can offer them all only a general, but very sincere, thanks. We would be remiss, however, if we failed to single out those whose assistance has been particularly important:

**Collections and Libraries:** Henry Austin Clark, Jr. and the Long Island Automotive Museum, Southampton, New York; James J. Bradley and the National Automotive History Collection, Detroit, Michigan; John Conde, Randy Mason, and G. Donald Adams of the Henry Ford Museum and Greenfield Village, Dearborn, Michigan; Michael Moore and the Library of Harrah's Automobile Collection, Reno, Nevada; Briggs S. Cunningham and John Burgess of the Briggs Cunningham Automotive Museum, Costa Mesa, California; Brooks Stevens and the Brooks Stevens Automotive Museum,

Mequon, Wisconsin; G. N. Georgano and the National Motor Museum, Beaulieu, Hampshire, England.

**Editors and Publications:** David Brownell, Michael Lamm, and the editors of *Special-Interest Autos* magazine, Bennington, Vermont; Donald R. Peterson and the editors of *Car Collector* magazine, Norcross, Georgia; Graham Robson and the editors of *Autocar* and *Thoroughbred and Classic Car,* London, England.

**Individual Researchers:** Pete Booz, Hudson; Alex Burr, Hudson; George E. Domer, American Bantam and Kaiser-Frazer; Jim Dunne, Buick and Pontiac; John A. Conde, American Motors; Sam Folz, Corvette; Fred K. Fox, Studebaker; Jeffrey I. Godshall, Graham, Kaiser-Frazer, Hupmobile; Walter Gosden, Cadillac; Harold Hagen, Kaiser-Frazer; Asa Hall, Studebaker and Avanti II; George L. Hamlin, Packard; William B. Hamlin, Tucker; Maurice D. Hendry, Cadillac and Lincoln; Rick Kopec, Shelby; Paul McLaughlin, Ford Mustang; David Newell, Chevrolet Corvair; Jan P. Norbye, Buick and Pontiac; James Petrik, Ford Thunderbird; Richard C. Ryan, Ford Thunderbird; Rich Taylor, sports cars; W. William Tilden, Willys.

# Introduction

About 10 years ago, a fairly small minority of automotive writers realized that the focus of interest in old cars had shifted—or was shifting—dramatically. To editorial colleagues reared in a different age, they preached that the emphasis of coverage should move away from the antiques and Classics of the pre-World II years, and toward the more interesting of the postwar cars. Generally, these pleas fell on deaf ears: the "postwar fanatics" were dismissed as a gaggle of dirty-fingernailed upstarts without taste or understanding.

No longer.

Take any random sample of car enthusiasts today, and ask them to pick their favorite 30-year period in automotive history. The vast majority will probably select a span bounded roughly by 1940 and 1970. Today, there are more cars from 1940-70 being preserved and restored (and more clubs devoted to them) than from all previous years put together. Publications that haughtily dismissed post-1940 models as unworthy 10 years ago are now struggling to regain readers lost to other publications that responded faster and earlier to the surging interest in postwar cars. Today, the prewar-oriented car book is the exception, instead of the rule.

The reason for the prominence of the 1940-70 era has little to do with the period's technological significance. The automobile as we know it today was developed largely during the *1930s,* not the '40s or '50s. (The closest contemporary equivalent to a '30s-style revolution in car design started in the late 1970s, as the U.S. industry began a massive move toward high-efficiency engineering with the emphasis on better space utilization and fuel economy through smaller size, lighter weight, and greater attention to vehicle aerodynamics.) One automotive writer has characterized the 1940-70 period as Part III in a three-part drama. In Part I (1900 through World War I), we experimented with all manner of approaches to personal transportation, using engines running on electricity and steam as well as gasoline. In Part II (roughly, the "between-the-wars" period), we settled on the internal-combustion engine, and then proceeded to perfect it and the components around it. In Part III (1940–1970), we didn't create anything fundamentally new at all—only better and better versions of basic concepts laid down in the '30s.

Why then all the fuss about these later cars? The cause of this sociological quirk is uncommonly apparent: nostalgia. The millions who grew up with these cars are now at their peak earning level—which means discretionary income. A person with fond memories of a 1940 LaSalle, a 1950 Kaiser, or a 1960 Studebaker will find it infinitely more fascinating—and desirable as a collector's item—than a 1930 Pierce-Arrow or a 1920 Peerless.

Call it a temporary fad if you like. But there is evidence to suggest this is *not* the passing craze antique cars were in the '30s and '40s, or Classics were in the '40s and early '50s. The advent of government regulations and the increasing automotive sameness that resulted mean relatively few cars of the 1970s will be worth remembering—or saving—in the future. Of course, there were interesting cars, even great cars, built during that decade. Some are still around today, and others will no doubt appear in the future. But the broad spectrum of interest that surrounds the cars of 1940-70 is missing. One indication is today's younger enthusiasts, who are looking even farther back in time than their fathers for automotive excitement. Young people not yet born when the last '57 Chevy rolled off the line are finding their passion in a fuel-injected Bel Air coupe, for example. The Milestone Car Society, devoted to recognizing the finer automobiles of the post-1945 period, has cut off its consideration of cars built after 1967—the last year before federal regulations took hold.

Writing this book has been gratifying for those of us who were part of that small, vocal minority ten years back. We believed that what were then called "special-interest cars" deserved a place in history. This book provides such a place. Yet, while its publication fulfills that goal, this book is also something we welcome out of necessity. As writers and researchers, and as enthusiasts, having all these facts at hand in one volume will perhaps be the greatest reward of all.

## Genesis of an Era

Ironically, the styling and engineering developments of 1940-70 were almost wholly the result of lessons learned during the greatest economic disaster in mod-

ern history. The Depression may have meant the end for many automobile producers, but it forced the survivors to think, plan, and invent. In so doing, they altered the shape of the American automobile almost completely.

During the 1930s, the industry parted company with clumsy, unsynchronized manual transmissions; complicated sleeve-valve engines; ancient wood-and-fabric bodies; mechanical brakes; and solid front axles. In their place came synchromesh gears, semi-automatic and fully automatic transmissions, side-valve and overhead-valve engines, all-steel bodies composed of fewer and larger panels welded together, hydraulic brakes, and independent front suspension. As roads improved, buyers demanded more speed, so higher-revving engines were needed. This led to now foundry and engine-building techniques that guaranteed high-rpm reliability. Cars could then be geared higher to travel faster. The advent of automatic shiftless transmissions made it less important to gear and "cam" a car so the lazy driver could pull away from a crawl without changing out of "High." As we learned how independent front suspensions and rubber engine mounts could help absorb road shocks, we were able to design stiffer chassis, which made overall construction tighter and more solid. Compared to its 1930 forebear—an upright box on artillery wheels wheezing along on four or six small cylinders—the automobile of 1940 was a sleek torpedo on slotted steel wheels, with more room inside, a longer wheelbase, and a vibration-free, rubber-mounted engine—and it was a good 20 mph faster.

In the process of thinning out industry ranks, the Depression years largely determined the nature of the major producers as we know them today—and selected those independents strong enough to survive. Ever since its founding by W. C. Durant in 1908, General Motors had been striving for managerial and creative decentralization through its division structure. While Henry Ford ruled his strongly centralized company almost singlehandedly, the division concept put GM ahead in production during the early 1920s. Only after Henry Ford II took over his grandfather's troubled firm in 1945 did Ford begin to decentralize—and to rebuild.

Walter P. Chrysler was an old GM man, and saw the light very early on. Although Chrysler Corporation was founded in the '20s, it came of age during the '30s. Following a division structure not unlike GM's, Chrysler built the second largest car company in the nation during the decade, and it remained so until the early 1950s.

By 1940, only a few independent manufacturers were left. After the war there were just four, all with high hopes: Nash, Hudson, Packard, Studebaker. Together with newcomer Kaiser-Frazer and later joined by Crosley and Willys, the independents enjoyed as much as a 15-percent market share in the late '40s and early '50s. But it didn't last. Nash's president George Mason was the only high-ranking executive among the independents who could envision the benefits of merger. He had managed to add Hudson to his empire in 1954, thus forming American Motors, but died before he could

meld in Packard and Studebaker. One by one, the other independents vanished, though Studebaker-Packard lasted longer than most. Only AMC is still hanging on, and seems destined to survive as a producer of "specialty" models not offered by the "Big Three."

## The 1940s

Although classic four-square styling was largely abandoned after World War II, some of its finest expressions appeared in 1940-42: the senior Packards, the Hupp Skylark and Graham Hollywood, and the last production LaSalle. Other cars, like the sleek Fords and Mercurys of 1940, offered near-perfection in line and form. Chrysler's 1949 products, boxy and upright, symbolized that corporation's concern for ample interior space within compact exterior dimensions.

The modern V8 engine was perhaps the most significant engineering development of the decade. Of course, V8s had been around for years—at Cadillac since 1915, and at Ford since 1932. But these were relatively heavy, long-stroke, low-compression engines, known for smoothness rather than performance. In 1949, Cadillac and Oldsmobile pioneered a new generation of V8s, the forerunners of the powerplants found in most large US cars today. America's light, efficient, and powerful V8 soon became famous worldwide for its performance and reliability.

The '40s also offered traditionally designed engines for those who preferred them. Packard's magnificent 356 cubic-inch straight eight and Cadillac's 346 V8 were L-head units known for quietness and smooth operation. Both are highly prized by today's collectors and enthusiasts.

Most engines of the 1940s, however, were plain side-valve inline sixes and eights that may not have been revolutionary, but were dependable and economical. The 230- and 170-cid sixes sold by Plymouth and Studebaker, respectively, served their makers well right on through the '50s, and were well-known for thriftiness. Studebaker's powerplant was a traditional winner in the Mobilgas Economy Run.

Racing was not emphasized by the industry as a whole during the '40s, but many individuals recorded performances that indicated the competition potential of certain production models. The supercharged Graham of 1940-41 was among the fastest cars powered by a conventional side-valve six. The Hudson Super Six, the Graham's postwar counterpart, could reach speeds that far exceeded what was normally expected from six cylinders. Oldsmobile and Cadillac achieved early competition success with their overhead-valve V8s. Cadillac scored an unbelieveable 10th- and 11th-place finish at the grueling 24 hours of Le Mans in 1950. Oldsmobile's fast, lightweight 88 dominated stock-car racing from 1949 through 1951.

Another extremely important engineering highlight of the '40s was the increasing use of the modern automatic transmission. Before, there had been only semi-

# Introduction

automatics. Oldsmobile offered one in 1937, then dropped it in 1938 for Hydra-Matic—the most successful completely shift-free transmission of all time. Chrysler enthusiastically marketed its Fluid Drive (which eliminated most shift motions) well into the 1950s. Ford was conservative, and stayed with the manual gearshift (both with and without overdrive) for all 1940-49 Fords and Mercurys. It offered the GM-built Hydra-Matic for the 1949 Lincoln, but did not manufacture an automatic of its own until 1951. Nash and Kaiser-Frazer stayed with stickshifts until 1950, then gave in and purchased Hydra-Matic, too. Hudson also bought the GM transmission, but not until 1951.

Two independents that did strike out with automatics of their own were Packard and Studebaker. Packard's Ultramatic was the only such unit developed entirely by an independent without any help from a transmission firm. It was a smooth-shifting gearbox, but not amenable to the extra power delivered by later Packard engines. Studebaker teamed up with Detroit Gear to create a fine three-speed automatic, but it didn't arrive until 1950.

GM really had the automatic market to itself in the 1940s. Cadillac began offering Hydra-Matic in 1948; Buick debuted its Dynaflow Drive the same year. Though smooth in operation, Dynaflow was not in the same performance league as Hydra-Matic.

The '40s were years of attrition and false starts for the smaller automakers. American Bantam, Hupmobile, and Graham all ceased production well before World War II—and did not return afterward. Willys-Overland, which offered conventional passenger cars through the 1942 model year, came back after the war with an interesting line of Jeep-like vehicles. These included the unique Jeepster that appeared for 1948—the last true touring car in the American industry. The decade's best-known failure was the Tucker—a brilliant concept that nevertheless saw no more than a few dozen copies. For years, the assumption was that the Tucker had been killed—prematurely—by General Motors and its cohorts. Yet even though its admirable design caused the big manufacturers a bit of concern, it was not actually a serious threat to them. Whether the car could have been realistically produced at the price Preston Tucker claimed will probably never be known.

## The 1950s

A lot of people think the cars of the '50s are responsible for the sorry state of the automotive scene today. Critics tell us they were heavy, ungainly, dumb-looking beasts with no—or at best few—redeeming virtues. Yet, they were nowhere near as uniformly bad as skeptics like to insist. In fact, several important advances were made between 1950 and 1960.

Consider, for example, torsion bar suspension, short-stroke V8s, efficient automatic transmissions, and unit construction—which we tried and liked—and air suspension, tailfins, and pushbutton transmissions—which we tried, disliked, and discarded. Notwithstanding the emphasis on chrome-laden gimmickry, the 1950s also brought some innovative new body styles such as the two- and four-door pillarless hardtop, and the all-steel station wagon that became (for the first time in its history) more like a car than a truck.

If these years are remembered for some of the industry's worst styling excesses, they also were marked by some of the finest automotive designs of all time: the Studebaker "Loewy coupes," the Continental Mark II, the Darrin-styled Kaisers, the two-seat Thunderbirds. Finally—and this may come as a surprise—American cars of this decade are considered by many experts to have been safer than cars had ever been before. Maybe the seatbelts, padded dashes, and dished steering wheels weren't merely sales gimmicks after all.

There's something else about these automobiles that even their admirers often fail to mention, perhaps because it's so obvious. These cars have an intrinsic character—a special appeal—which the industry somehow lost in the late '60s. They were different—vastly different—from the cars of today. This was probably the last decade when a manufacturer dared sell something clearly unique, like the "Step-down" Hudson, the tiny Nash Metropolitan, or the fiberglass Woodill Wildfire. Cars of the '50s were also built differently: interiors were trimmed in comfortable mohair or genuine leather; bodies were made of heavy-gauge steel. Their makers shunned things like plastic, cardboard, and decals. While the average family car of 1950-59 probably handled as sloppily as everyone said it did, it was also built with more pure integrity than its more nimble successors. Every piece of trim met every other piece precisely where intended. Each door, trunklid, and hood closed with a resounding clunk, swinging shut on vault-like hinges. Collectors still discover rust-free examples with six-figure mileage, and interiors, paint, and mechanical components in approximately the same shape as when the car left the factory a quarter century ago. And this, despite the industry's reputation for haphazard assembly quality in the latter years of the decade.

## The 1960s

The '60s do not really seem that long ago, and headlines from that turbulent era are still fresh in many memories. It's not at all difficult to remember the cars: the 18-foot-long luxury hardtops, the bucket-seat sporty compacts, the personal cars, the ponycars, and the muscle cars of 1960-69. An incredible assortment of types streamed out of the factory gates in those years. There was a car for every taste and budget—anything from the $1700 Metropolitan to the $18,500 Crown Imperial limousine.

Government demands that the industry clean up exhaust emissions and make cars safer were good ideas, even if the legislation that followed was often controversial. But the mandates that took effect in the late

'60s also guaranteed an end to the uninhibited experimentation that characterized the early years of the decade.

In a way, the public had as much to do with the decline of innovation as the government. What incentive was there for automakers to develop something really new or different when buyers seemed interested mainly in performance, styling, and "pizzazz?" Consider the record. After generating high initial interest, the sophisticated Corvair was soon forgotten—long before Ralph Nader came along. Buyers yawned at the first Pontiac Tempest, not sure what to make of its all-independent suspension and rear-mounted transaxle. The Tempest sold well, but it might have done even better with a more ordinary drivetrain. In 1966, Oldsmobile introduced its radical, superbly engineered front-wheel-drive Toronado—which was consistently outsold by the conventionally designed Buick Riviera. Pontiac's overhead-cam six of 1966, an engine that offered as good a balance between economy and performance as any engine on the market, was almost completely ignored as most customers insisted on big-block V8s.

Sales records aside, there is something significant about the technological tours de force of the '60s: nearly all of them came from General Motors. There are many reasons for this. The decline of the independents after World War II (the mergers and demise of Nash and Hudson, Packard and Studebaker, plus the disappearance of Kaiser and Willys) radically altered the nature of the industry. Soon, the high-volume manufacturers discovered there were not just one or two kinds of buyers, but six or eight. The result was a raft of new sizes and concepts designed for distinct segments of the market—and new categories like compact, sporty-compact, intermediate, standard, luxury, and personal-specialty. Yet ironically, all this variety gradually blurred the distinction in price or status between makes. What had happened was that the market had subdivided after about 1955, but hadn't really expanded. This can be seen in the production figures. Chevrolet, for example, wasn't actually turning out any more cars in 1970 than it did in 1960, but it was building a far greater variety of models.

General Motors was best able to adapt to this new situation. Ford had its successes—the Mustang, the Continental Mark III, and the Torino—but they were triumphs of packaging or marketing, not technology. But GM had grown so large by the mid-'60s that it could just as easily produce either unusual, technically interesting designs like the Corvair or Toronado or boringly ordinary cars like the Chevy II or Impala.

Despite the domination of the market by GM and Ford, a few specialty manufacturers operated profitably during the '60s by appealing to small but significant groups of buyers overlooked by the industry giants. The Avanti II has continued to occupy its own market niche up to the present day, long after its parent company fell apart. The original Shelby GT-350 was little more than a re-engineered Mustang designed by a former racer who believed there was a tiny—but vocal—market for all-out performance. Checker still sells 6000 cars a year to practical folk looking for taxicab toughness and simplicity. Brooks Stevens found that others shared his dream of driving a "modern classic," and would buy an Excalibur.

Buyers did not always react enthusiastically to important engineering advances in the 1960s, but they did become more discriminating in their judgments of gimmicky or useless features. As the decade began, the public almost immediately started rejecting such things as tailfins, pushbutton transmissions, retractable hardtops, and chrome-encrusted super-cruisers. Rapidly, new models appeared from the likes of Pontiac, Lincoln, Dodge, and Chevrolet—cars that illustrated that good design means more than a five-pound hood ornament. The early compacts proved that the industry could still build practical cars—and that they could be designed to sell—after a generation of offering impractical ones. The sporty compacts brought home a point the Europeans had long accepted: the *best* car is not necessarily the biggest. Heading into the 1970s, it was clear that America's automotive values were slowly beginning to change. As events were to prove, the changes couldn't have been more timely.

**Today and Tomorrow**

Few in the American automobile industry are prepared to predict where we go from here. On the one hand, there is the threat of foreign competition, chiefly from Japan. At its worst it could leave the United States in the same position as Great Britain: dependent on imports, and without a native industry able to respond quickly enough to changing conditions. On the other hand, there is the possibility that the events of the '70s—fuel shortages, inflation, the near-deaths of AMC and Chrysler—may have taught Americans a lesson. Already it is evident that government regulation in all phases of life enjoys far less public support than it did 10 years ago. That applies to the cars we drive as much as anything else. Ten years from now, we may well find ourselves blazing a new trail of plenty, instead of roaming around on the rim of disaster. Time and the degree of common sense we choose to apply will be the decisive factors.

This book makes no prediction about the future. It does, however, succinctly describe where we've been and what we've done—the mistakes, the successes, the good cars, the great cars, the awful cars. If certain decisions had been different, would the outcomes have been altered? They might have been, but hindsight is cheap and far too easily indulged. In this context, it is perhaps well to recall the admonition of George Santayana—that those who ignore the mistakes of the past are bound to relive them.

# Qualifications and Exceptions

Even the best system of terminology and classification has its exceptions. For the major makes section, the intent was to include every volume manufacturer that did business in America between 1940 and 1970. Thus, Graham and Hupmobile, for example, are listed even though both were active only briefly in 1940, and produced just a handful of cars. Similarly, there is a listing for AMC, activated as a separate nameplate in 1965, though it didn't become American Motors' only make until 1970.

Several makes usually considered "minor" by the industry are the first exceptions. Avanti II, Checker, Excalibur, and Shelby are all treated as major makes, even though their production was a mere fraction of total industry volume. The reasoning was partly subjective, and tempered by present conditions. Avanti II, Checker, and Excalibur are still in business today. Though their volume isn't likely to increase, any make still in production 10 or more years since 1970 warranted more than a mere notation among the "minors," in our view. As for Shelby, that make expired in 1970, but in some years its volume was quite considerable for a tiny company—not to mention the impact of the cars themselves.

Canadian-built cars are not included here, but again there is an exception: the 1965-66 Studebaker, which was nominally a Canadian product in those years. This decision was made on the grounds that Studebaker had been too much a part of the American scene in previous years to leave out its last cars. The problem, of course, is that if Canadian Studebakers are listed, then Canadian Plymouths, for example, should be included, too. An argument, though perhaps lame, can be made for the 1965-66 Studebakers, because including them effectively caps a story; lumping in Canadian Plymouths would only have exceeded the basic scope of this book.

A different problem arises in deciding how to treat major *models* of certain makes—cars substantially different in technology or character from the company's usual products. For improved clarity and coverage, the unique rear-engined Corvair and the singular Corvette sports car have their own chapters apart from "Chevrolet." Likewise, the Ford Mustang and Thunderbird appear separately from "Ford." But this led to more exceptions: the Kaiser Darrin is not listed separately from Kaiser, for example. Another reason for treating Corvair, Corvette, Mustang, and Thunderbird individually is that the main Chevrolet and Ford entries were already enormous.

The Nash Metropolitan involved two more exceptions. Because of its individual character, many authorities consider it distinct from other Nash models. Yet, it was labeled a Nash until 1958, when that nameplate disappeared and Metropolitan became a make in its own right. For convenience, all the Metropolitans are grouped in one place as a second chapter after Nash. On the other hand, there was no need to do the same thing with Hudson's compact Jet, or the Valiant (officially, a separate make in 1960, and a Plymouth model from 1961). Though smaller than their relatives in the Hudson and Plymouth lines, the Jet and Valiant were not, in our view, "substantially different" enough, either technically or in character, to warrant such treatment. In other cases, industry terminology is followed. The 1956 Clipper, for example, has its own entry as a make because Studebaker-Packard registered it as such, and created separate Clipper franchises that year. The 1956 Clipper was nearly identical to the 1955 version except that it was, strictly speaking, not a Packard. So, all non-1956 Clippers are found under Packard.

Continental was also a distinct make in 1956-60, and again with release of the Mark III in 1968. Although its modern-day status is vague, there was no problem separating appropriate models from Lincoln in the period covered.

With AMC (the make, not the corporation), the same principle applies. American Motors used the nameplate "Rambler" almost exclusively from 1957 through 1965; the 1965 Ambassador and Marlin both bore Rambler script and emblems. In 1966-67, however, these models had new "AMC" identification. In 1968, the Rebel, AMX, and Javelin also appeared as AMC products and not as Ramblers. In 1970, the Rambler name disappeared entirely in favor of AMC. Thus, the reader will

find the 1965 Marlin, for example, discussed under "Rambler," and the 1966-67 Marlins under "AMC."

The editors were fairly groggy by the time they arrived at Willys, but unfortunately this make posed some of the most serious problems encountered. Officially, the Willys passenger car ended after 1955 with the expiration of the domestic Aero-based models. But a steel-bodied station wagon continued to be offered through 1961—variously called a Willys, a Kaiser Jeep, and a Jeep. From 1960 on, Jeep Corporation marketed the four-wheel-drive Wagoneer much like a passenger model, and in 1967 new owner American Motors released the Jeepster 2, designed in the image of the 1948 original.

Most industry sources and the collector hobby consider the 1948-51 Jeepster a passenger car, but none list the Jeep wagons, Wagoneer, or Jeepster 2 as such. They are all defined as "trucks." Including the original Jeepster might seem to imply including the wagons, Wagoneer, and Jeepster 2 as well. The problem was that by leaving in those models, the book would be opened up to similar contemporary competitors like the Ford Bronco or International Scout, which were definitely beyond our scope. Ultimately, it was decided to make two more exceptions: the original Jeepster and Aero passenger cars are the only Willys models discussed.

## Chapter Texts

The general text for each entry presents a detailed account of each make's history. There is, we think, sound reason for this even in a reference work. Too often "encyclopedias" simply report statistics. But to understand what was done, it is essential to know how and why it was done, and what the result was. Therefore, a cumulative total of 40 years' research has been surveyed for information on the designers, engineers, and executives who shaped these cars; the reasons why they did what they did; the alternative plans they rejected; and the successes or failures that followed. Each chapter is intended to offer a concise, yet complete, description of each major manufacturer—a basic outline for the casual user, a quick education for the uninitiated, and a solid review for the expert. In the process of writing these entries, the authors and contributors have attempted to puncture many hoary automotive legends — that the Corvair was torpedoed by Ralph Nader, for example, or that Studebaker was a victim of a plot at Ford. So much ignorance has been prepetuated by inexpert or poorly researched accounts in the past that the temptation to set down reliable facts was too great to resist.

## Photographs

Selecting photographs for a work like this can be more difficult than editing text. Limited space and the great variety of cars offered by the larger companies mean it is not always possible to provide a truly representative sample for each model year over such a broad time span. While this book cannot contain the detailed photographic references of a single-make history, the most important and influential models are shown.

Unlike some other automotive encyclopedias, this one includes pictures of selected prototypes, experimentals, and show cars as well as production models—all clearly labeled as such. The reasons are the inordinate interest in such non-production designs among today's enthusiasts, and the importance of these proposals as benchmarks. While there are hundreds, even thousands, of styling studies for each model and model year among most of the major makes, there are those interesting or key design ideas that either evolved into production or were abruptly dismissed. The prototypes selected represent the industry at its best and its worst in line with the major goal of this book: to present a broad, clear, and factual account of the American automobile industry.

## Tables

At the end of each chapter is a series of tables listing every model and body style offered by each make in the 1940–1970 period. Of all the elements in a book like this, charts are the most time consuming, and pose the greatest problems of style and accuracy. Space naturally plays a part in the choice of material to be included. The object was to provide, at a glance, the data most readers would be likely to require in a hurry: models, wheelbases, body styles, weights, prices, model year production, and engine availability. In using the tables, the reader should keep the following in mind:

### Series or Model Entries

Each group of body styles is listed under a series or model heading. This indicates the factory model or series code number (where applicable), name, and wheelbase (in inches). Code numbers posed many problems. On several occasions, it was unclear whether a code applied to the series or model as a whole, or to specific body styles—or both. In rare instances where they were misleading or irrelevant, the code numbers were omitted. Where a code applies to both model/series and body style, the first part is shown with the model/series and the second with the body style. An example is Dodge from 1959 onward. Officially, the 1959 Coronet six-cylinder club sedan was designated by the factory as MD1-L21, but "MD1-L" applied to *all* Coronet sixes, and "21" only to the club sedan. The number is divided accordingly.

In the '60s, some code systems became more complex, so numbers are listed as the situation required. In 1961, for example, codes for the Dodge Lancer follow 1959 practice because there was only one of each. But

# Qualifications and Exceptions

the 1961 Dart Six series consisted of Seneca, Pioneer, and Phoenix sub-series. In this case, only the series number "RD3" is shown in the heading, the rest of the designation appearing alongside each individual body style. In reality, a 1961 Dart six Phoenix hardtop coupe was RD3-H434; it is shown as model RD3, body style H434.

## Body Styles

For best readability, it was important to limit each entry to one line. To do this the following standard abbreviations were adopted:

| abbreviation | meaning |
| --- | --- |
| A/S | auxiliary seats |
| bus cpe | business coupe |
| cpe | coupe |
| comm | commercial, as in special-order chassis |
| conv cpe | two-door convertible coupe |
| conv sdn | four-door convertible sedan |
| div | division window, as for limousines |
| fstbk | fastback, torpedo |
| form | formal, as in sedan |
| htp cpe | two-door hardtop (pillarless) |
| htp sdn | four-door hardtop (pillarless) |
| htp wgn | hardtop wagon (two- or four-doors) |
| J/B | jet-back, early form of fastback |
| limo | limousine |
| proto | prototype |
| rdstr | two-door, two-seat roadster |
| sdn 2d | two-door sedan |
| sdn 4d | four-door sedan |
| spt cpe | sport coupe |
| spt sdn | sport sedan |
| T/B | trunk-back or notchback sedan |
| util | utility, as in sedan (two-door) |
| wgn 2d | two-door station wagon |
| wgn 4d | four-door station wagon |

The reader should assume that all body styles except sports cars and small models like American Bantams are of five- or six-passenger capacity. Exceptions are specified. There were also cases, Cadillac in particular, where it was necessary to indicate the number of side windows to differentiate between otherwise identical body styles. These various abbreviations are as follows:

| abbreviation | meaning |
| --- | --- |
| P (7P, 8P, etc.) | number of passengers (maximum) |
| S (2S, 3S, etc.) | number of seats (used mainly for wagons) |
| W (4W, 6W) | number of side windows |

Engine designations follow a consistent pattern of one letter and one digit (except for Corvair). The letter is for configuration, the digit, for the number of cylinders:

| abbreviation | meaning |
| --- | --- |
| L (L6, L8, etc.) | inline or "straight" engine |
| V (V6, V8, etc.) | V-type engine |

Manufacturers often differed in treating engine options. Some grouped both standard and extra-cost engines under the same model code; others listed engines separately and even gave them separate model numbers. The charts follow the practice each manufacturer used for a given model year. Pontiac sixes and eights, for example, were always separate models and are shown as such. Plymouth engines were usually different options within the same model, and are combined. This difference is emphasized by spelling out and capitalizing the words "Six" and "Eight" in cases like Pontiac, or using the abbreviations "L6" and "V8" in a case like Plymouth.

Where engine options are combined, prices shown are for six-cylinder models only. Production figures are for the total number of that model built, regardless of engine.

## Weight

The column marked "wght" shows the initial advertised curb weight (not adjusted for passengers, fuel, or cargo) for each body style, as shown by industry sources, usually the National Automobile Dealers Association (NADA). The reader may expect these figures to differ slightly from other published figures, because weights varied depending on equipment fitted, or even the scales used.

It is important to note, however, that when more than one engine was offered, the curb weight has been *averaged*. For example, the 1955 Chevrolet Bel Air convertible weighed 3315 pounds as a six and 3285 pounds as a V8. Our listed weight is the average: 3300 pounds. Usually the choice of engine did not change curb weight by more than 100-150 pounds. Averaging was deemed necessary for maximum readability.

## Prices

Figures shown in the price column are based on initial advertised delivered prices according to NADA and similar comtemporary sources. Like weights, prices varied during most model years. When more than one standard engine was available, however, prices were *not averaged*. Instead, the least expensive standard version (usually a six) is shown.

## Model Yea Production

The question most often asked about older cars (and one of the most important for a reference work) is: "How many did they make?" The answer is not always clear-cut, as production figures have been the subject of research—and some dispute—among automotive

historians for several decades. The figures listed, however, have been thoroughly researched and cross-checked.

Note that only *model year* production figures, *not* calendar year figures are used throughout this book in both the tables and the text. The reason for this is that calendar year totals always include some portion of at least two model years, which creates confusion when comparing one make with another. Model year figures normally represent production of only a single line of cars marketed as the 1949, 1959, 1969, etc. models.

Comparing production figures strictly on a model year basis reveals some surprises. For example, Ford outproduced Chevrolet in model year terms more often than is commonly thought—and Plymouth nearly passed Ford as number-two producer on at least three occasions. A summary of model year production (quantities of 1000 cars or more) is found at the end of the major makes section.

Production by make received long and painstaking analysis. Too often in the past, lists of production figures have been based solely on company handouts, which are often misleading and sometimes inaccurate. The 1953 Buick Skylark, for example, is listed by Buick (and at least one other source) as the "Roadmaster Anniversary Convertible." The contradictions and false trails of factory lists were fully explored, and compared to other lists from a dozen different sources. Sometimes, it was discovered that there were cars built that weren't "officially" listed; in other cases, models were listed but not actually produced.

There were a few cases where it was possible to go beyond known information by estimating, such as where a company listed a combined total for two or three model years. Such lumping serves nobody. Where we felt confident to do so, production was proportioned over individual model years. The usual standard for these breakdowns was calendar year output in cases where it very nearly coincided with model year output (usually when a model year began in January rather than September or October).

In some instances, available factory figures included non-production models, usually styles intended for production but not produced in volume. These are included in the charts and are clearly labeled as non-production. While not all companies include non-production models, the ones available are shown for completeness.

There were a few cases where even estimating proved impossible, or where a large group of models or body styles were lumped together. It is hoped that future editions of this book will be able to make some of these figures more specific.

## Engine

Under each set of model year listings is a list of standard (S) and optional (O) engines and their model or series availability. Other basic information provided includes configuration (L or V), number of cylinders, displacement (to the nearest 0.1 cubic inch), bore and stroke (to the nearest .01 inch), and SAE gross horsepower. In cases where there was more than one standard engine, all are shown as "S."

### Additions and Corrections

Much care has been taken in compiling this book to insure a high degree of accuracy. Nevertheless, additional research may yield data or conclusions other than those presented here. The publishers welcome additions and suggestions. They may be addressed to Richard M. Langworth, Box 385, Contoocook, New Hampshire 03229, or to CONSUMER GUIDE® magazine, 3841 West Oakton Street, Skokie, Illinois 60076.

—Richard M. Langworth

## BOOKS

Butler, Don: *The Plymouth-DeSoto Story*
Chappell, Pat: *The Hot One, Chevrolet 1955-1957*
Consumer Guide, Editors of: *The American Sports Car; Cars of the 40s; Cars of the 50s; Cars of the 60s; Corvette, America's Only True Sports Car; Mustang, The Car That Started the Ponycar Stampede; Cadillac, Standard of Excellence*
Dammann, George: *Illustrated History of Ford, Seventy Years of Buick, Sixty Years of Chevrolet*
Dawes, Nathaniel E.: *The Packard, 1942-1962*
Deutsch, Jan G.: *Selling the People's Cadillac*
Dunne, Jim and Norbye, Jan P.: *Buick, The Postwar Years; Pontiac, The Postwar Years*
Georgano, G. N.: *The Complete Encyclopedia of Motorcars*
Heasley, Jerry: *The Production Book for U.S. Cars*
Hendry, Maurice D.: *Cadillac, Lincoln*
Kopec, Rick: *The Shelby-American Guide*
Langworth, Richard M.: *Chrysler, The Postwar Years; Hudson, The Postwar Years; Kaiser-Frazer, Last Onslaught on Detroit; Oldsmobile, The First Seventy-five Years (Part 2); Personal Luxury, The Thunderbird Story; Studebaker, The Postwar Years*
Ludvigsen, Karl E.: *Corvette, America's Star-Spangled Sports Car*
MacPherson, Thomas E.: *The Dodge Story*
Martin, Terry; Bradley, James; Langworth, Richard; Weber, Don; Grayson, Stan; Yost, L. Morgan; Leslie, C. A. Jr.; Phillips, Richard; Hamlin, George; Heinmuller, Dwight: *Packard, A History of the Motorcar and the Company*
Narus, Don: *Town & Country, Chrysler's Wonderful Woodie*
Norbye, Jan P. and Dunne, Jim: *Buick, The Postwar Years; Pontiac, The Postwar Years*
Pearson, Charles T.: *The Indomitable Tin Goose*
Ritch, O'Cee: *The Lincoln Continental*
Schneider, Roy: *Cadillacs of the Forties*

## PERIODICALS

*Autocar, Automobile Connoisseur, Automobile Quarterly, Automotive News, Car and Driver, Car Classics, Car Collector, Cars & Parts, Mechanix Illustrated, Motor, Motor Trend, Official National Market Reports Blue and Red Books, Official N.A.D.A. Used Car Guide, Popular Mechanics, Popular Science, Road & Track, Special-Interest Autos, Sports Car Graphic, Sports Cars Illustrated, Wards Automotive Yearbook, Wards Monthly*

# Allstate
**Sears, Roebuck & Co.**
**Chicago, Illinois**

Theodore V. Houser, Sears vice-president for merchandising, had a seat on the board of Kaiser-Frazer. In 1949, Houser discussed with K-F the possibility of offering one of Willow Run's automobiles under the Allstate name. Sears wanted to sell a complete car, along with parts and accessories for it, at the new auto shops then opening up adjacent to its retail stores. A hookup with Kaiser-Frazer was a natural. At the time, Houser was buying Homart enamelware from Kaiser Metals Company, in which Sears held a 45-percent share.

The first Allstate proposals were simply the large 1949 K-F cars bearing different logos. Until the compact Henry J arrived for 1951, Sears remained dubious. The Henry J, however, was exactly what T. V. Houser had been looking for—a low-priced, uncomplicated, easy-to-service car.

Kaiser-Frazer president Edgar F. Kaiser managed to convince his dealers to accept a department store as a competitor, and the Allstate was announced in November 1951. It was the only new make for 1952, and the first car offered by Sears since its high-wheeler of 1912. In an apparent attempt to feel out the market with a pilot program, Sears concentrated Allstate promotion on the Southeast, although the car was available nationally through the 1952 Sears catalog.

Based strictly on the Henry J, the Allstate featured a distinctive front-end treatment by designer Alex Tremulis, special Allstate badges, and a major interior upgrading that followed Sears' practice of improving on proprietary products. K-F's interior specialist, Carleton Spencer, used quilted saran plastic combined with a coated paper fiber encapsulated in vinyl—a material he'd discovered in use on the transatlantic telegraph cable. It seemed impervious to normal wear, and was superior to the upholstery material used in most Henry Js.

The cars wore Sears-Allstate tires and tubes, bat-

1952 Deluxe two-door sedan

Allstate proposal based on a large K-F model

1952 Deluxe two-door sedan

1952 Deluxe interior

February 1952 proposal by Brooks Stevens for Allstate wagon

teries, and spark plugs, each with the appropriate guarantee: 18 months for the tires, 24 months for the battery, and 90 days or 4000 miles for the whole car (the standard K-F warranty). Allstates were usually fitted with trunklids and dashboard gloveboxes, items that were found less often on Henry Js. The basic and standard models lacked the opening trunk. The more expensive Deluxe Six had armrests and a horn ring, which were not available or optional on the lower-priced versions.

Sears aggressively marketed the Allstate with five trim variations (against four for the Henry J) and two different L-head engines—a six and a four. The lowest-priced 1952 Allstate (the basic Four) was priced just below the standard Henry J.

For 1953, there was little change. A full-width rubber-covered pad was added across the instrument panel, and the taillights were relocated to the rear fenders. The line was reduced to just three models—two Fours and the Six.

But the idea failed. Whether it failed because people didn't take to buying cars in department stores, or because of the narrow marketing approach in the Southeast, is difficult to determine. Both factors probably contributed. Only 1566 Allstates were built for 1952; the count was 797 when Sears canceled the project in early 1953. Exact model-by-model production figures are no longer available, so the figures shown in the tables are estimates based on reliable sources.

The Allstate's demise killed Sears' plans for future models. Among these were two proposals for a two-door station wagon, one by industrial designer Brooks Stevens, the other by Gordon Tercey of K-F Styling.

Today, Allstates are extremely rare, and are considered more desirable than comparable Henry Js because of this. In 1971, Allstate Insurance purchased one of the Sears' cars for historical purposes. In the '60s it would have been hard to convince the folks at Sears parts counters that the car had ever existed.

# Allstate Specifications

## 1952

### A2304 Four (wb 100.0)

| | | Wght | Price | Prod |
|---|---|---|---|---|
| 110 | basic sdn 2d | 2,300 | 1,395 | 200 |
| 111 | std sdn 2d | 2,300 | 1,486 | 500 |
| 113 | Deluxe sdn 2d | 2,300 | 1,539 | 200 |

### A2404 Six (wb 100.0)

| | | Wght | Price | Prod |
|---|---|---|---|---|
| — | basic sdn 2d | 2,325 | 1,594 | 200 |
| 115 | Deluxe sdn 2d | 2,325 | 1,693 | 466 |

### 1952 Engines

| | bore×stroke | bhp | availability |
|---|---|---|---|
| L4, 134.2 | 3.11×4.38 | 68 | S-Allstate Four |
| L6, 161.0 | 3.13×3.50 | 80 | S-Allstate Six |

## 1953

### A3304 Four (wb 100.0)

| | | Wght | Price | Prod |
|---|---|---|---|---|
| 210 | std sdn 2d | 2,405 | 1,528 | 200 |
| 213 | Deluxe sdn 2d | 2,405 | 1,589 | 225 |

### A3404 Six (wb 100.0)

| | | Wght | Price | Prod |
|---|---|---|---|---|
| 215 | Deluxe sdn 2d | 2,455 | 1,785 | 372 |

### 1953 Engines

| | bore×stroke | bhp | availability |
|---|---|---|---|
| L4, 134.2 | 3.11×4.38 | 68 | S-Allstate Four |
| L6, 161.0 | 3.13×3.50 | 80 | S-Allstate Six |

# American Bantam

American Bantam Car Co.
Butler, Pennsylvania

Americans have rarely bought really tiny cars in great numbers. Of the various firms that have tried to make a go of minicars, the one that lasted the longest was American Austin, which became American Bantam in 1935.

Sir Herbert Austin came to America from Britain in 1929, seeking a company to build his famous Austin Seven under license. He met with the city fathers of Butler, Pennsylvania, who were looking for new industry—and Butler became the Austin's home. Although Detroit was already the mecca of the American automotive industry, Sir Herbert chose Butler because of its advantages for a small operation. It was close to the East Coast, so getting imported components from dock to factory would be easy. It also had a solid labor force. (Austin also considered an early feeler from Manchester, New Hampshire.) By 1930, Austin had set up shop in a factory that had once housed the Standard Steel Car Company.

American Austins were produced through 1934, but the company's first year was by far its best. About 8500 cars left the assembly line in 1930. After that, production never exceeded 5000. The firm was troubled by precarious finances and several reorganizations. Despite claims that 180,000 initial orders had been received, officials probably never expected to reach Detroit-style production levels. The original minimum figure Sir Herbert set—for the first 10 years of operation—was only 50,000 cars, and the firm did average that many cars during its first five years.

But in 1934, American Austin went into receivership; it had not been able to recover from the Depression. For almost two years it looked like the car from Butler would be history. Then Roy S. Evans, a hard-driving salesman who earlier had sold 8 percent of the firm's production, bought the company. He looked for a novel trademark to symbolize his car's durability and ruggedness, and chose the bantam rooster. The American Austin was duly renamed the American Bantam.

While American Austins were close copies of their British cousins, the Bantams were quite different. Alexis de Sakhnoffsky created the Bantam's handsome styling: a horizontal-bar grille painted body color, pontoon fenders, a smooth rear apron, and an attractively restyled dash. For his work, de Sakhnoffsky charged a fee of only $300, and Roy Evans tooled the entire Bantam line for a total cost of only $7000.

The original Austin engine was also altered for the Bantam. Babbit bearings replaced the earlier car's more expensive roller bearings, and full-pressure lubrication with mechanical pump feed was used. Drivetrain modifications included a sturdy new three-speed gearbox with synchromesh on second and third gears. The rear axle was a semi-floating Hotchkiss type with spiral bevel gears. Ross cam-and-lever steering was a marked improvement over the old-fashioned Austin steering. The frame and cross members were heavier than the Austin's, and the clutch was revised for smoother operation.

Initial production comprised roadsters and coupes only. A later addition was the Boulevard Delivery. This style mated the front end of the roadster with its dropped beltline to a square-cut panel box trimmed with tiny carriage lamps. This car was "open drive,"

1940 American Bantam Panel Delivery

1940-41 American Bantam convertible sedan

1939-40 American Bantam Boulevard Delivery

that is, it had a snap-on top for covering the driver's compartment in inclement weather. Another interesting creation was Alex Tremulis' Riviera drophead convertible. It began as a custom built for Roy Evans and ended up in limited production. (Neither model made the "official" list, though they were available.)

Unfortunately, these novel creations were not enough to brake a long slide, and the early '40s were American Bantam's last years as a car producer. The most important feature for the 1940 line was me-

chanical. A three-main-bearing crankshaft replaced the old two-bearing design. This significantly improved reliability at high speeds. The engine was also enlarged slightly by increasing the stroke. The company quoted a 0–30 mph time of only 5.5 seconds, and was not exaggerating. When the Bantam's light weight is taken into account, it's easy to see why it was so quick.

Other changes for 1940 included improved mechanical brakes with no brake anchor pins. This eliminated feedback without increasing pedal effort. Monroe hydraulic shocks were added, plus Goodyear airfoam seat cushions in deluxe models. A less desirable change affected the headlamps. From a conventional position between the hood and fenders, they moved outboard to the tops of the fenders—an aesthetically displeasing position.

There were slightly fewer offerings in the 1940 line than the year before. Three coupes, a roadster, a convertible, and a wagon were listed. Panel trucks, Rivieras, and the Boulevard Delivery were also sold in small quantities. But a mere 800 American Bantams were sold for 1940. The 1941 line, with only 138 estimated sales, was a continuation of the 1940 models.

What saved American Bantam was World War II. In late 1939, the company successfully adapted its Pennsylvania National Guard scout car to the Army's GP (General Purpose) specification. The result was a go-anywhere four-wheel-drive vehicle weighing only 1300 pounds. Working prototypes of what would be known as the Jeep were on the road by 1940. Though Bantam wouldn't make as many of them as Ford and Willys-Overland, it does get the credit for the Jeep's original design. (Willys-Overland lost a court case in which it claimed to have been the inventor.)

When the war ended, Roy S. Evans left the company, after deciding not to resume civilian car production—in retrospect, a wise move. The firm built trailers until 1956, when the plant was sold to the Armco Steel Corporation.

## American Bantam Specifications

### 1940

**Series 65 (wb 75.0)—800 built**

| | | Wght | Price | Prod |
|---|---|---|---|---|
| 65 | cpe | 1,261 | 399 | — |
| 65 | Master cpe | 1,275 | 449 | — |
| 65 | conv cpe | 1,340 | 525 | — |
| 65 | Master rdstr | 1,211 | 449 | — |
| 65 | conv sdn | 1,296 | 549 | — |
| 65 | wgn 2d | 1,400 | 565 | — |

| 1940 Engine | bore×stroke | bhp | availability |
|---|---|---|---|
| L4, 50.1 | 2.26×3.13 | 22 | S-all |

### 1941

**Series 65 (wb 75.0)—138 built**

| | | Wght | Price | Prod |
|---|---|---|---|---|
| 65 | cpe | 1,261 | 399 | — |
| 65 | Master cpe | 1,275 | 449 | — |
| 65 | conv cpe | 1,340 | 525 | — |
| 65 | Master rdstr | 1,211 | 449 | — |
| 65 | conv sdn | 1,296 | 549 | — |
| 65 | wgn 2d | 1,400 | 565 | — |

| 1941 Engine | bore×stroke | bhp | availability |
|---|---|---|---|
| L4, 50.1 | 2.26×3.13 | 22 | S-all |

# AMC
## American Motors Corp.
## Kenosha, Wisconsin

American Motors first marketed cars with the AMC label in 1966, when the "Rambler" prefix for the Ambassador and Marlin was dropped. In 1968, the Rebel lost its Rambler name too, and the new AMX and Javelin were added to the company's stable. The Rambler nameplate appeared for the last time in 1969 on the final edition of the Rambler American design that had appeared in 1964. In 1970, this was replaced by the Hornet and Gremlin.

The top-of-the-line 1966 Ambassador was a facelifted version of the redesigned 1965 Rambler Ambassador. It was one of the better efforts from the studios of Richard A. Teague, AMC vice-president for styling. A graceful-looking car, it rode a wheelbase four inches longer than the 1964 Ambassador's. A special model for '66 was the elegantly appointed DPL hardtop, which had reclining bucket seats, fold-down center armrests, pile carpeting, and an extensive list of accessories. Officially, the DPL was a model in its own right, not an Ambassador. It became the Ambassador DPL in 1967.

Ranked below the DPL were the regular Ambassador sedans, wagons, hardtops, and one convertible, available in the 880 and 990 series. All were offered with the long-running "Typhoon" 232-cid six, or with a choice of two optional V8 engines, in 287- and 327-cid sizes. Only the 270-bhp 327 V8 required premium gasoline.

Although most Ambassadors were ordered with automatic transmission, a few were equipped with a three-speed manual transmission or AMC's "Twin Stick" overdrive. A four-speed synchromesh gearbox was also marketed for the Ambassador 990 and DPL.

The big Ambassador evolved nicely through the late '60s. For 1967, wheelbase was lengthened and semi-fastback styling with slightly rounder body contours was adopted. In 1968, the hood was refined and a new model sequence appeared: Ambassador, Ambassador DPL, and Ambassador SST. New frontal styling, which included a sculptured hood, plastic grille, and horizontal quad headlights, arrived in 1969. The 1970 version was restyled with new rear fenders and taillamps on sedans and hardtops, and new roof panels and taillamps on wagons. By 1969, the Ambassador's wheelbase had grown to 122 inches, and air conditioning was standard.

AMC made an unsuccessful try at the booming personal-car market with the radically styled 1965 Rambler Marlin, renamed AMC Marlin for 1966-67. Styled by Teague, the Marlin was a huge fastback based on the intermediate Rambler Classic chassis of '65–'66 and borrowing some of its front-end sheetmetal. It featured rakishly shaped rear side windows and C-pillar styling. The '66 model was changed only slightly. It had a new

1966 Ambassador DPL hardtop coupe

1967 Ambassador DPL hardtop coupe

1966 Ambassador 990 convertible

1966 Ambassador 990 station wagon

1967 Marlin fastback coupe

1967 Marlin fastback coupe

1968 Rebel SST convertible

1968 Javelin fastback coupe

grille, a sway bar was adopted for six-cylinder models, and an optional black vinyl-covered roof treatment was offered. The 1967 Marlin was the last of the line. It was fully restyled and a much more handsome car because of its longer wheelbase shared with that year's Ambassador. Measuring 6.5 inches longer than 1965-66 Marlins, it was perhaps the nicest-looking of the three. But it remained a very low-production item. Fewer than 5000 and 3000 Marlins were built for 1966 and 1967, respectively. Marlin offered some sports car features (optional four-speed transmission, tachometer, bucket seats, and engines ranging up to 280 bhp), but it lacked a sports car's taut, precise handling and small, efficient size.

A more successful innovation was the 1968 Javelin, a ponycar in the Mustang image. It was beautifully shaped and exciting. More important, it was successful: over 56,000 units were built that year, helping AMC recover from a four-year sales slump. With its standard 232 six, the Javelin cruised at 80 mph; with the optional 290 V8, it could do 100 mph. The Javelin's optional "Go Package" included a 343 V8 with four-barrel carburetor, dual exhausts, power front disc brakes, heavy-duty suspension, and wide tires. So equipped, the car would run from 0 to 60 mph in eight seconds, and approach 120 mph maximum. The Javelin was roomier, larger, and longer than its Mustang, Camaro, and Barracuda rivals. Its styling was cleaner, too.

The Javelin was facelifted for 1969 with a slightly altered grille. In 1970, it received a "twin-venturi" grille, revised wheel covers, and a new hood with simulated air scoops. Sales were not as impressive in 1969-70 as they were in 1968 because of additional competition in the ponycar market—notably a sleek new Camaro.

An exciting mid-1968 introduction was the AMX, a

two-seat coupe based on the Javelin bodyshell and riding a special shorter wheelbase. AMC introduced a new 390-cid V8 for the AMX with 315 bhp and 425 foot-pounds of torque. It included a forged-steel crankshaft and connecting rods. The standard engine was a 290 V8, and the 343 was available as an option. The AMX's

1968 Javelin SST fastback coupe

1968 Javelin fastback coupe

1968 AMX two-seat fastback coupe

1968 Rebel SST convertible

1968 Ambassador SST four-door sedan

1968 Rebel SST hardtop coupe

1968 Ambassador SST hardtop coupe

1969 Rebel SST hardtop coupe

tight suspension, comprehensive instrumentation, bucket seats, and optional four-speed gearbox made it a genuine sports car, and it did well in competition. As with the Marlin, the AMX's best styling came in its last year. The 1970 models were smoothly integrated and looked the part of a serious sports car. Production was, however, much lower than management had expected. The car never sold well, and production for all three years failed to top 20,000 units. As good as it was, American Motors was probably the wrong company to sell a performance car like the AMX. (The company has revived the AMX name from time to time for its sporty models in the 1970s.)

Another new AMC make for 1968 was the Rebel, introduced the year before as a Rambler model taking over from the Classic. Rebel was AMC's intermediate

with a 114-inch wheelbase. A variety of six-cylinder and V8 engines was offered. Prices were competitive, starting at around $2500. Sedans, hardtops, wagons, and a convertible were available in three series. Rebel was the only AMC line to offer a convertible in 1968, but few were built: only 377 in the 550 series and another 823 in SST guise. In fact, these would be AMC's last convertibles. The 1969 lineup was trimmed to two series—basic and SST. A wider track and a new grille, plus a restyled rear deck and taillights, were the only changes of note.

For 1970, Rebel sedans and hardtops were lengthened two inches to accommodate redesigned roof panels and rear fenders, and new taillights appeared. In addition to the basic and SST series, AMC again went after the performance crowd with "The Machine"—a

1969 Ambassador SST four-door sedan

1969 Javelin SST fastback coupe

1970 AMX two-seat fastback coupe

1970 Javelin fastback coupe

1970 Hornet two-door sedan

1970 Gremlin two-door sedan

Rebel with a difference. This car packed the company's most potent V8, a four-speed Hurst-linkage transmission, and a 3.54:1 rear axle ratio. The two-door hardtop body featured a Ram-Air hood scoop, a special red-white-and-blue paint treatment, and 15-inch mag wheels with raised-white-letter tires. An 8000-rpm tachometer, dual exhausts, low-back-pressure mufflers, and a definite front-end rake completed this expensive package. Although The Machine certainly had a performance image, the racing honors went to the Javelin. Mark Donohue drove a Javelin SST to the Trans-Am championship that year.

American Motors spent $40 million, a million man-hours, and three years to design its new compact for 1970. The car was dubbed Hornet, the first time that time-honored name had been seen since the last Hudsons in 1957. Entirely new from the ground up, the Hornet came as a two- or four-door sedan on a 108-inch wheelbase, and both six and V8 engines were available. Hornet sales for the year were 92,458—a strong showing that helped the company's sagging finances. But on the whole, Kenosha still lost money that year—$58.2 million on sales of over $1 billion.

In April 1970, another new model arrived, intriguingly named the Gremlin. As the first ''subcompact'' introduced by an American automaker it sold well, and over 26,000 moved out before the short model year ended in mid-1970. The Gremlin carried AMC's most economical six-cylinder engine and attractive prices. Its styling was based on the Hornet's. Ahead of the B-pillar, the two cars were quite similar, but the Gremlin had a truncated rear end. Overall, the car's appearance was controver-

1970 Rebel SST hardtop coupe

1970 Ambassador DPL four-door sedan

sial. Stylist Teague insisted the Gremlin's unorthodox design was the only way to go. "Nobody would have paid it any attention if it had looked like one of the Big Three," he said.

With the Hornet and Gremlin, American Motors began to switch from being a "full-line" automaker to a specialty producer of compact and subcompact cars. This was the approach that had been so profitable for the firm in the early '60s. The Rebel and AMX appeared

for the last time in 1970. Though the company dallied with the low-selling Ambassador and the Rebel's Matador replacement for most of the '70s, it soon reached the conclusion that it could not compete model-for-model with the Big Three. Further specialization—which meant dropping the Javelin, Matador, and Ambassador and introducing the later Pacer, Concord, Spirit, and Eagle models—marked AMC's slow climb back toward profitability in the '70s.

# AMC Specifications

## 1966

| Marlin (wb 112.0) | | Wght | Price | Prod |
|---|---|---|---|---|
| 6659-7 | fstbk cpe | 3,050 | 2,601 | 4,547 |

| Ambassador 880 (wb 116.0)* | | Wght | Price | Prod |
|---|---|---|---|---|
| 6685-2 | sdn 4d | 3,006 | 2,455 | — |
| 6686-2 | sdn 2d | 2,970 | 2,404 | — |
| 6688-2 | wgn 4d | 3,160 | 2,759 | — |

| Ambassador 990 (wb 116.0)* | | Wght | Price | Prod |
|---|---|---|---|---|
| 6685-5 | sdn 4d | 3,034 | 2,574 | — |
| 6687-5 | conv cpe | 3,462 | 2,968 | — |
| 6688-5 | wgn 4d | 3,180 | 2,880 | — |
| 6689-5 | htp cpe | 3,056 | 2,600 | — |

| DPL (wb 116.0)* | | Wght | Price | Prod |
|---|---|---|---|---|
| 6689-7 | htp cpe | 3,090 | 2,756 | — |

| 1966 Engines | bore×stroke | bhp | availability |
|---|---|---|---|
| L6, 232 | 3.75×3.50 | 145 | S-Marlin |
| L6, 232 | 2.75×3.50 | 155 | S-Ambassador |
| V8, 287 | 3.75×3.25 | 198 | O-all |
| V8, 327 | 4.00×3.25 | 250/270 | O-all |

*Total 1966 calendar year 279,225; includes Rambler American and Classic models and early 1967 production.

## 1967

| Marlin (wb 118.0) | | Wght | Price | Prod |
|---|---|---|---|---|
| 6759-7 | fstbk cpe | 3,342 | 2,963 | 2,545 |

| Ambassador 880 (wb 118.0)* | | Wght | Price | Prod |
|---|---|---|---|---|
| 6785-2 | sdn 4d | 3,279 | 2,657 | — |
| 6786-2 | sdn 4d | 3,310 | 2,519 | — |
| 6788-2 | wgn 4d | 3,486 | 2,962 | — |

| Ambassador 990 (wb 118.0)* | | Wght | Price | Prod |
|---|---|---|---|---|
| 6785-5 | sdn 4d | 3,324 | 2,776 | — |
| 6788-5 | wgn 4d | 3,545 | 3,083 | — |
| 6789-5 | htp cpe | 3,376 | 2,803 | — |

| Ambassador DPL (wb 118.0)* | | Wght | Price | Prod |
|---|---|---|---|---|
| 6787-7 | conv cpe | 3,434 | 3,143 | — |
| 6789-7 | htp cpe | 3,394 | 2,958 | — |

| 1967 Engines | bore×stroke | bhp | availability |
|---|---|---|---|
| L6, 232 | 3.75×3.50 | 145 | S-Marlin |
| L6, 232 | 3.75×3.50 | 155 | S-Ambassador; O-Marlin |
| V8, 290 | 3.75×3.28 | 200 | S-Amb. conv; O-others |
| V8, 343 | 4.08×3.28 | 235 | O-all |
| V8, 343 | 4.08×3.28 | 280 | O-all |

*Total 1967 calendar year 229,058; includes Rambler American and Rebel models and early 1968 production.

## 1968

| Rebel 550 (wb 114.0)* | | Wght | Price | Prod |
|---|---|---|---|---|
| 6815 | sdn 4d | 3,062 | 2,443 | — |
| 6817 | conv 2d | 3,195 | 2,736 | 377 |
| 6818 | wgn 4d | 3,301 | 2,729 | — |
| 6819 | htp cpe | 3,117 | 2,454 | — |

| Rebel 770 (wb 114.0)* | | Wght | Price | Prod |
|---|---|---|---|---|
| 6815-5 | sdn 4d | 3,074 | 2,542 | — |
| 6818-5 | wgn 4d | 3,306 | 2,854 | — |

| | | Wght | Price | Prod |
|---|---|---|---|---|
| 6819-5 | htp cpe | 3,116 | 2,556 | — |

**Rebel SST (wb 114.0)***

| | | | | |
|---|---|---|---|---|
| 6817-7 | conv cpe | 3,427 | 2,999 | 823 |
| 6819-7 | htp cpe | 3,348 | 2,775 | — |

**AMX (wb 97.0)***

| | | | | |
|---|---|---|---|---|
| 6839-7 | fstbk cpe 2S | 3,097 | 3,245 | 6,725 |

**Javelin (wb 109.0)—56,462 built**

| | | | | |
|---|---|---|---|---|
| 6879-5 | fstbk cpe | 2,826 | 2,482 | — |
| 6879-7 | SST fstbk cpe | 2,836 | 2,587 | — |

**Ambassador (wb 118.0)***

| | | | | |
|---|---|---|---|---|
| 6885-2 | sdn 4d | 3,193 | 2,820 | — |
| 6889-2 | htp cpe | 3,258 | 2,892 | — |

**Ambassador DPL (wb 118.0)***

| | | | | |
|---|---|---|---|---|
| 6885-5 | sdn 4d | 3,265 | 2,920 | — |
| 6888-5 | wgn 4d | 3,475 | 3,207 | — |
| 6889-5 | htp cpe | 3,321 | 2,947 | — |

**Ambassador SST (wb 118.0)***

| | | | | |
|---|---|---|---|---|
| 6885-7 | sdn 4d | 3,496 | 3,151 | — |
| 6889-7 | htp cpe | 3,530 | 3,172 | — |

*Total 1968 calendar year 268,439; includes Rambler American and early 1969 production.

| 1968 Engines | bore×stroke | bhp | availability |
|---|---|---|---|
| L6, 232 | 3.75×3.50 | 145 | S-Javelin, Rebel exc SST |
| L6, 232 | 3.75×3.50 | 155 | S-Amb exc SST |
| V8, 290 | 3.75×3.28 | 200 | S-Rebel SST, Amb SST; O-all |
| V8, 290 | 3.75×3.28 | 225 | S-AMX; O-Javelin |
| V8, 343 | 4.08×3.28 | 235 | O-Rebel, Ambassador |
| V8, 343 | 4.08×3.28 | 280 | O-AMX Javelin, Rebel, Amb |
| V8, 390 | 4.17×3.57 | 315 | O-all |

# 1969

**Rebel (wb 114.0)***

| | | Wght | Price | Prod |
|---|---|---|---|---|
| 6915 | sdn 4d | 3,062 | 2,484 | — |
| 6918 | wgn 4d | 3,301 | 2,817 | — |
| 6919 | htp cpe | 3,117 | 2,496 | — |

**Rebel SST (wb 114.0)***

| | | | | |
|---|---|---|---|---|
| 6915-7 | sdn 4d | 3,074 | 2,584 | — |
| 6918-7 | wgn 4d | 3,306 | 2,947 | — |
| 6919-7 | htp cpe | 3,140 | 2,598 | — |

**AMX (wb 97.0)***

| | | | | |
|---|---|---|---|---|
| 6939-7 | fstbk cpe 2S | 3,097 | 3,297 | 8,293 |

**Javelin (wb 109.0)—40,675 built**

| | | | | |
|---|---|---|---|---|
| 6979-5 | fstbk cpe | 2,826 | 2,512 | — |
| 6979-7 | SST fstbk cpe | 2,836 | 2,633 | — |

**Ambassador (wb 122.0)***

| | | | | |
|---|---|---|---|---|
| 6985-2 | sdn 4d | 3,276 | 2,914 | — |

**Ambassador DPL (wb 122.0)***

| | | | | |
|---|---|---|---|---|
| 6985-5 | sdn 4d | 3,358 | 3,165 | — |
| 6988-5 | wgn 4d | 3,561 | 3,504 | — |
| 6989-5 | htp cpe | 3,403 | 3,182 | — |

**Ambassador SST (wb 122.0)***

| | | | | |
|---|---|---|---|---|
| 6985-7 | sdn 4d | 3,508 | 3,605 | — |
| 6988-7 | wgn 4d | 3,732 | 3,998 | — |
| 6989-7 | htp cpe | 3,566 | 3,622 | — |

*Total 1969 calendar year 242,898; includes Rambler American and early 1970 production.

| 1969 Engines | bore×stroke | bhp | availability |
|---|---|---|---|
| L6, 232 | 3.75×3.50 | 145 | S-Javelin, Rebel |
| L6, 232 | 3.75×3.50 | 155 | S-Amb, Amb DPL; O-Rebel |
| V8, 290 | 3.75×3.28 | 200 | S-Amb SST; O-Amb, Reb, Jav |
| V8, 290 | 3.75×3.28 | 225 | S-AMX; O-Javelin |
| V8, 343 | 4.08×3.28 | 235 | O-Rebel, Ambassador |
| V8, 343 | 4.08×3.28 | 280 | O-AMX, Jav, Rebel, Amb |
| V8, 390 | 4.17×3.57 | 315 | O-AMX, Jav SST, Amb SST |

# 1970*

**Hornet (wb 108.0)**

| | | Wght | Price | Prod |
|---|---|---|---|---|
| 7005-0 | sdn 4d | 2,748 | 2,072 | — |
| 7006-0 | sdn 2d | 2,677 | 1,994 | — |

**Hornet SST (wb 108.0)**

| | | | | |
|---|---|---|---|---|
| 7005-7 | sdn 4d | 2,766 | 2,137 | — |
| 7006-7 | sdn 2d | 2,705 | 2,144 | — |

**Rebel (wb 114.0)**

| | | | | |
|---|---|---|---|---|
| 7015-0 | sdn 4d | 3,129 | 2,636 | — |
| 7018-0 | wgn 4d | 3,356 | 2,766 | — |
| 7019-0 | htp cpe | 3,148 | 2,660 | — |

**Rebel SST (wb 114.0)**

| | | | | |
|---|---|---|---|---|
| 7015-7 | sdn 4d | 3,155 | 2,684 | — |
| 7018-0 | wgn 4d | 3,375 | 3,072 | — |
| 7019-7 | htp cpe | 3,206 | 2,718 | — |

**Rebel Machine (wb 114.0)**

| | | | | |
|---|---|---|---|---|
| 7019-0 | htp cpe | 3,650 | 3,475 | — |

**AMX (wb 97.0)**

| | | | | |
|---|---|---|---|---|
| 7039-7 | fstbk cpe 2S | 3,126 | 3,395 | — |

**Gremlin (wb 96.0)**

| | | | | |
|---|---|---|---|---|
| 7046-0 | sdn 2d | 2,497 | 1,879 | — |
| 7046-5 | sdn 2d | 2,557 | 1,959 | — |

**Javelin (wb 109.0)**

| | | | | |
|---|---|---|---|---|
| 7079-5 | fstbk cpe | 2,845 | 2,720 | — |
| 7079-7 | SST fstbk cpe | 2,863 | 2,848 | — |
| 7079-7 | SST/Trans-Am fstbk cpe | 3,340 | 3,995 | — |

**Ambassador (wb 122.0)**

| | | | | |
|---|---|---|---|---|
| 7085-2 | sdn 4d | 3,328 | 3,020 | — |

**Ambassador DPL (wb 122.0)**

| | | | | |
|---|---|---|---|---|
| 7085-5 | sdn 4d | 3,523 | 3,588 | — |
| 7088-5 | wgn 4d | 3,817 | 3,946 | — |
| 7089-5 | htp cpe | 3,555 | 3,605 | — |

**Ambassador SST (wb 122.0)**

| | | | | |
|---|---|---|---|---|
| 7085-7 | sdn 4d | 3,557 | 3,722 | — |
| 7088-5 | wgn 4d | 3,852 | 4,122 | — |
| 7089-5 | htp cpe | 3,606 | 3,739 | — |

*Total 1970 calendar year 276,110; includes early 1971 production.

| 1970 Engines | bore×stroke | bhp | availability |
|---|---|---|---|
| L6, 199 | 3.75×3.00 | 128 | S-Hornet, Gremlin |
| L6, 232 | 3.75×3.50 | 145 | S-Hornet SST, Rebel, Javelin; O-Hornet, Gremlin |
| L6, 232 | 3.75×3.50 | 155 | S-Amb; O-Hornet, Rebel |
| V8, 304 | 3.75×3.44 | 210 | S-DPL, SST; O-all exc AMX |
| V8, 360 | 4.08×3.44 | 245 | O-Rebel, Amb, Jav |
| V8, 360 | 4.08×3.44 | 290 | S-AMX; O-Reb, Amb, Jav |
| V8, 390 | 4.17×3.57 | 325 | O-AMX, Jav, Reb SST, Amb SST |
| V8, 390 | 4.17×3.57 | 340 | S-Rebel Machine; O-all |

# Avanti II

**Avanti Motor Corp.**
**South Bend, Indiana**

Studebaker fled to Canada in 1963. Leo Newman and the late Nathan Altman had been partners in one of the oldest Studebaker dealerships in the country. Two years later, Newman and Altman resurrected the Avanti, Studebaker's greatest car of the '60s.

The Studebaker Avanti, designed by a team of stylists working under Raymond Loewy, had been a failure in the marketplace. But it was loved by hardcore Studebaker enthusiasts—the only Studebaker in two generations to have inspired such interest. Before it was phased out by Studebaker, the Avanti had captured virtually every major U.S. Auto Club speed record, including a 170.78-mph flying-mile at Bonneville. Newman and Altman decided the Avanti was too good to lose. So, they bought the name, the production rights, and the tooling for it, along with a portion of Studebaker's abandoned factory in South Bend. Production of a revised version called the Avanti II commenced in late 1965. The goal was an output of 300 cars a year. That figure was never achieved, but production has been adequate and consistent ever since.

Unlike its predecessor, the Avanti II has been a commercial success. The car's fiberglass body panels insured there would be no expensive sheetmetal dies to maintain. Construction could be done by hand on a miniature assembly line so each car could be built carefully and tailored to each customer's personal specifications. Altman, a born salesman, reveled in the Avanti II business. Visitors to the factory would frequently find him with telephone in hand, talking long-distance to an affluent customer about individualizing his car.

The Avanti II is still in production today, though its base price at this writing has soared to about $23,000. In the 1960s, it was a far better buy: prices began at $6550. And in those days, even the most dedicated devotee of high living would have been hard put to push the price of a tailor-made Avanti II past $10,000, though Newman and Altman tried their best to help. The option list included a Hurst four-speed shifter, power steering, air conditioning, electric window lifts, tinted windshield and rear window, AM/FM radio, Eppe fog or driving lights, limited-slip differential, Magnum 500 chromed wheels, and a variety of Firestone and Michelin bias-ply and radial tires. The basic Avanti II came with vinyl trim, but textured "Raphael vinyl" could be ordered for $200 extra. Genuine leather seats and door panel trim cost $300, and full leather trim went for $500. Paint color could be ordered to suit any preference.

Although early Avanti IIs used the same modified Studebaker convertible frame as the original Avanti, they were not powered by Studebaker V8s. The supply had dried up when Studebaker left South Bend. Instead, the factory switched to the Chevrolet 327 cubic-inch V8 in Corvette tune. Displacement was later enlarged to 350 cid. Buyers could choose either a fully synchronized Borg-Warner four-speed manual transmission or Avanti's "power-shift" automatic, designed to permit manual selection of first and second gears. All these mechanical changes were hidden from view under a body that was almost identical with that of the original

**1966 Avanti II sport coupe**

22

Avanti. The main visual clues for identifying the new model were its more level stance (Altman's customers disliked the original's noticeable front-end rake), the addition of a Roman numeral II to the Avanti script, and reduced-radius wheel openings.

The Corvette engine provided excellent performance for the aerodynamic four-place grand tourer. A typical 0-60 mph acceleration time for an Avanti II with automatic was under nine seconds; with a 3.54:1 rear axle ratio, the car could achieve 125 miles per hour. The Chevy V8 was lighter than the old Studebaker engine, and this improved front/rear weight distribution from the 59/41 of the original car to 57/43 for the Avanti II. The new car still understeered, but final oversteer could be induced by a judicious poke at the throttle. The front-disc/rear-drum brakes resisted fade, and provided nearly 1 G deceleration from 80 mph in a panic stop. Obviously Newman and Altman cared about safety as much as straight-line performance.

The Avanti II sold to a somewhat different clientele than Studebaker's version. In the 1960s, its $6500 base price was Cadillac Eldorado money. The original Avanti had sold for $4445, which was Chrysler territory. Newman and Altman realized this difference meant a change in market appeal. Accordingly, their promotion

1968 Avanti II sport coupe

was aimed at the customer interested more in "personal-luxury" than performance.

On the open road, the Avanti II was in its element. Road testers gave it points for safety, quietness, structural rigidity, and a ride that was firm but comfortable. "In this day of great concern over automotive safety," wrote John R. Bond in 1966, "the Avanti II should make new friends, for obviously there was more thought given to safety in its conception than in most American cars. Good brakes, sensible interior design and decent handling impart security to the driver . . . It's a better car than it was three years ago."

# Avanti II Specifications

## 1965

| (wb 109.0) | | | Wght | Price | Prod |
|---|---|---|---|---|---|
| | opt cpe | | 3,217 | 6,550 | 21 |

| 1965 Engine | bore×stroke | bhp | availability |
|---|---|---|---|
| V8, 327.0 | 4.00×3.25 | 300 | S-all |

## 1966

| (wb 109.0) | | | Wght | Price | Prod |
|---|---|---|---|---|---|
| | spt cpe | | 3,181 | 7,200 | 77 |

| 1966 Engine | bore×stroke | bhp | availability |
|---|---|---|---|
| V8, 327.0 | 4.00×3.25 | 300 | S-all |

## 1967

| (wb 109.0) | | | Wght | Price | Prod |
|---|---|---|---|---|---|
| | spt cpe | | 3,217 | 7,200 | 60 |

| 1967 Engine | bore×stroke | bhp | availability |
|---|---|---|---|
| V8, 327.0 | 4.00×3.25 | 300 | S-all |

## 1968

| (wb 109.0) | | | Wght | Price | Prod |
|---|---|---|---|---|---|
| | spt cpe | | 3,217 | 6,645 | 89 |

| 1968 Engine | bore×stroke | bhp | availability |
|---|---|---|---|
| V8, 327.0 | 400×3.25 | 300 | S-all |

## 1969

| (wb 109.0) | | | Wght | Price | Prod |
|---|---|---|---|---|---|
| | spt cpe | | 3,217 | 7,145 | 103 |

| 1969 Engines | bore×stroke | bhp | availability |
|---|---|---|---|
| V8, 327.0 | 4.00×3.25 | 300 | S-all |
| V8, 350.0 | 4.00×3.48 | 300 | O-all |

## 1970

| (wb 109.0) | | | Wght | Price | Prod |
|---|---|---|---|---|---|
| | spt cpe | | 3,342 | 7,500 | 111 |

| 1970 Engine | bore×stroke | bhp | availability |
|---|---|---|---|
| V8, 350.0 | 4.00×3.48 | 300 | S-all |

# Buick

**Buick Division, General Motors Corp.**
**Flint, Michigan**

During the 1940s, Buick was GM's number-two producer after Chevrolet, and usually fourth in the industry behind the "Big Three"—Chevy, Ford, and Plymouth. The division normally turned out upwards of 300,000 cars a year. After the war, as GM endured an extended strike, Buick took awhile to regain momentum, but by 1949 it was producing nearly 400,000 cars. In 1950, it would top half a million.

"Valve in Head—Ahead in Value" was Buick's slogan, and the cars reflected that characteristic throughout the '40s. They were big, but only slightly ostentatious. For those who felt status was everything, there was always Cadillac. Buick's buyers were, for the most part, professional people, a loyal group that returned to the cars from Flint time and time again. The prewar line was one of the widest in Buick's history, one that wouldn't be matched in scope until well into the 1950s.

For 1940, the Buick lineup was divided into four series, bearing names as well as numbers. The Series 40 Special ranged from simple sedans to spectacular open styles. The Series 50 Super comprised a smaller number of models, including a wood-bodied estate wagon.

1940 Series 80 Limited Streamlined formal sedan

1941 Series 90 Limited eight-passenger sedan

1941 Series 70 Roadmaster convertible phaeton

1941 Series 60 Century business coupe

1941 Series 60 Century four-door sedan

1941 Series 70 Roadmaster four-door sedan

Specials and Supers rode a 121-inch wheelbase, and were powered by the 248 cubic-inch Buick five-main-bearing straight eight, a smooth and respected powerplant.

The larger cars were the Series 60 Century, Series 70 Roadmaster, and the Series 80 and 90 Limiteds, all powered by a 320.2-cid engine, also with five main bearings. The long sedans and limousines used a 140-inch wheelbase.

A number of interesting special bodies were offered for 1940, some of them for the last time. The crop of convertible sedans had started to thin out by the start of the decade, and the last in the Century line appeared that year. The Super and Roadmaster versions continued for one more season. In the Limited series, Buick built just 14 Streamlined Sedans, with fastback styling reminiscent of the Lincoln-Zephyr. More popular was the Limited convertible sedan or phaeton, which had conventional "trunkback" styling and sold for $1952. Buick sold just seven streamlined phaetons and 250 trunkbacks. Similar body alternatives were offered for the formal sedans.

Custom bodies occasionally appeared in 1940, but not as regular catalog offerings. Rakish town cars from Brewster, one of which rode the Series 90 chassis, were not identified as Buicks at all. But the Series 90 Brewster Buick was the first to earn coveted "Classic" status from the Classic Car Club of America. Buffalo's Brunn Company also designed custom models, including a fairly conventional town car body on the Roadmaster chassis—strictly a one-off.

Buick had a banner year in 1941. Model year production totaled 374,000 units. Leading the line was a beautiful series of opulent customs by Brunn on the Limited chassis. These included a phaeton, town car, landau brougham, and full landau. Most flamboyant was the Brunn convertible coupe, offered to dealers for $3500. At that price, only the prototype was sold. The car was significant because of its "sweep-spear" side motif, which prefigured a postwar production styling trademark.

The Roadmaster lineup continued unchanged in 1941, while the Century series was trimmed of its convertible, convertible sedan, and club coupe. The station wagon shifted from the Super to the Special series, but nevertheless sold for about $200 more than its 1940 counterpart. Specials were split into two sub-series: the 40, which rode a 118-inch wheelbase, and the 40A on a 121-inch span.

The 1941 Special/Super 248-cid engine featured a new piston design that provided better compression of the fuel/air mixture before combustion and a corresponding increase in horsepower. Available for the 40A Special touring sedan and sedanet was Compound Carburetion, two carburetors with a progessive linkage, which further boosted horsepower to 125. Compound Carburetion was standard on other models, resulting in 165 bhp for the Century, Roadmaster, and Limited. The 1941 chassis design was a carryover for all

Harley Earl's Y-Job show car

1942 Series 70 Roadmaster convertible coupe

but the Limited, which used a new X-member frame. No Buick was yet available with automatic transmission.

Styling was evolutionary, marked mainly by a bolder, heavier grille and revised ports along the sides of the hood. One new idea was the fastback, offered as the 40A Special and Century touring sedan, business coupe, and sedanet. It did away with anachronisms of the "trunkback" age. Apparently it appealed to the public: over 100,000 Special fastback touring sedans were sold.

World War II came at the wrong time for Buick. Car production ended after February 2, 1942. The new models had been completely restyled along the lines of Harley Earl's Y-Job show car, and were much sleeker than any that had gone before. A wide, low, vertical-bar grille arrived, and would be continued on postwar models through 1954. Fastback, or "torpedo," styling was more popular than ever. The Century put in its last appearance until 1954, and was available in only two styles, both fastbacks. The streamlined models continued to dominate Special sales, and also appeared as sedanets in the Super and Roadmaster Series.

Most '42 Buicks featured Harley Earl's new "Airfoil" front fenders, which swept back through almost the entire length of the car to meet the leading edge of the rear fenders. Limiteds and Specials lacked the full-sweep treatment, but their fenders extended back well into the doors. Streamlining had truly arrived in Flint.

Cars built after January 1, 1942 used painted metal instead of plated parts, as per government order. On Specials and Supers, cast-iron pistons were used in place of aluminum ones. Base horsepower dropped to 110 bhp (118 with Compound Carburetion). By the time production ground to a halt, more than 92,000 of the

# Buick

1942 models had been built. Production would not begin again until October 1945.

When cars started rolling off the Flint lines again, there were no exotic Brunn customs. Only standard production bodies were offered. Buick built a mere 2482 cars in the closing months of 1945. But production picked up the following year when more than 150,000 units were built. Naturally, the postwar cars were warmed-over '42s, but were available in a few new body styles: sedans and sedanets in Special, Super, and Roadmaster guise; Super and Roadmaster convertibles; and a Super estate wagon. Styling was cleaned up. Most models bore single instead of double side moldings, a simpler grille, and the first of Buick's distinctive "gunsight" hood ornaments. Wheelbase choices, now without a Limited in the field, were restricted to 121 inches for the Special, 124 for the Super, and 129 for Roadmaster. Compound Carburetion was not offered, so Specials and Supers were both rated at 110 bhp. This combination of models, wheelbases, and engines would endure through 1948 with only minor changes in horsepower.

Undoubtedly, Buick's production potential in the early postwar years was left unexploited. The Special, which would set many records in the 1950s, actually accounted for the smallest number of sales in this period. Supers were the most popular. The Special did not outstrip the Super in production until 1950, when it became Buick's biggest success story. By 1954, it would help the division surpass Plymouth.

Styling changes for the 1947-48 models were minimal, since GM planned to introduce its first all-new postwar cars for 1949. The '47 Buicks were marked by a wing-top grille that gave them a very low look. A new, more elaborate crest appeared above it. In 1948, Specials received a full-length belt molding; Supers and Roadmasters acquired chrome fender nameplates. Instrument panel gauges were gold-colored, and steering wheels were three-spoke, flexible types with semi-circular horn rings. The most important news in 1948 was Dynaflow, Buick's excellent automatic transmission. It was offered as a $244 option on the Roadmaster only. Demand for this torque-converter automatic was so high the division had to double its planned production. By 1950, Dynaflow was being fitted to 85 percent of all Buicks sold.

The long-awaited 1949 design helped model year production surge to 324,276 units, right behind the Chevy-Ford-Plymouth trio. The '49s were sleek and graceful compared to their predecessors, and re-

**1946 Roadmaster sedanet**

**1946 Special sedanet**

**1947 Roadmaster convertible coupe**

**1949 Roadmaster Riviera hardtop coupe**

**1950 Special sport coupe**

viewers agreed they were worth all the attention they got. Harley Earl's Art & Colour Studio had successfully adapted aircraft fuselage lines to an automobile. Only a hint of the separate rear fender remained on the Super and Roadmaster (the Special retained 1948 fender styling). The new bodies featured the first of Buick's now-legendary portholes, an idea inspired by Ned Nickles of Earl's staff. Easily, the most eye-catching model was the Roadmaster Riviera. Together with Cadillac's Coupe deVille and Oldsmobile's Holiday, it was the first mass-production hardtop in the modern sense, and ushered in a new trend that would eventually make the convertible obsolete. Roadmaster Rivieras were good looking, luxurious cars with beautiful pillarless roof-lines. They were available with either conventional straight side moldings or with sweep-spear trim. The latter quickly became another Buick trademark.

With the emphasis mainly on styling, the '49 Buicks were much the same mechanically as the earlier postwar models. The Special's horsepower remained at 110 bhp, the Super's at 115. Supers equipped with Dynaflow also got higher 6.9:1 compression heads for an output of 120 bhp. The Roadmaster had been raised to 150 bhp in 1948, and it continued in that form with Dynaflow Drive standard. Bodies remained unaltered for the most part. The woody wagon was reworked to fit the new styling. Although the result was very pleasing, the wagon sold in small numbers.

Thanks to the 1942 redesign, Buick emerged from the war in fine fettle. While nearly all manufacturers were forced to stay with their prewar designs, Flint's styling was technically only one year old in 1945 and still fairly fresh. Packard, by contrast, was left with a two-year-old design in its very handsome Clipper, and felt obliged to undertake a severe facelift by 1948. Buick was able to stretch out its '42 tooling through the 1949 Special—and come back with a brand-new model for 1950. One year makes a difference.

Three different styling periods, a 50th anniversary, and the advent of V8 engines marked Buick history in the '50s. Throughout the decade, Buicks were big, powerful, and sometimes garish cars. They reflected what could be considered as either the best contemporary thinking—or the worst depravity of those glittery years before the advent of compacts, pollution controls, and safety regulations. Buicks of the '50s were very different from the division's present-day cars. Yet both generations share a tradition of quality, high performance in their class, and product lines carefully orchestrated to fit the times and the market.

The 1949 restyling adopted by all General Motors lines resulted in the lowest, sleekest Buicks in history. But there was more to come in 1950. If '49 had been the Year of the Porthole, 1950 was the Year of the Sweepspear. Through 1953, the lineup comprised the Special, Super, and Roadmaster series. The Special was sleekly styled and competitively priced, designed to catch third-place Plymouth in the production race. Yet it began the decade as a rather utilitarian series. Attractive,

1950 Roadmaster four-door sedan

1950 Super Riviera hardtop coupe

1951 Super Deluxe two-door sedan

1951 Special sport coupe

LeSabre show car of 1951

sporty hardtops and convertibles were added later. The pioneering two-door Riviera hardtop of 1949 continued in Super and Roadmaster trim, and was extended to the Special by 1951. The Riviera name was also applied to a very well-proportioned four-door sedan in the Super and Roadmaster series riding a special extended

1952 Special Riviera hardtop coupe

1953 Skylark convertible coupe

1953 Roadmaster four-door sedan

1954 Century four-door sedan

wheelbase. There were also two woody wagons offered with wooden body parts made of mahogany and white ash. They were big, expensive haulers: the 1953 Roadmaster estate wagon cost $4031 and weighed 4315 pounds.

For all 1950-52 models and the '53 Special, Buick continued to rely on its aging but proven valve-in-head straight eight. Displacement, compression, and horsepower varied from model to model. The base Special engine of 1950 produced 115 bhp, or 120 bhp with Dynaflow automatic. Supers and the 1951-53 Specials offered up to 143 bhp. Roadmasters used a hefty 320-cid version that put out 170 bhp at 3800 rpm by 1952.

Dynaflow Drive (some called it "Dyna-slush") had been introduced as a standard Roadmaster item in late 1947. It became increasingly popular on other models at around $200 extra. Its torque converter system depended on induced rotation of a drive turbine through an oil bath by a facing crankshaft-driven turbine. Dynaflow was smooth, but none too exciting in performance. The Twin-Turbine Dynaflow of 1953 was more positive in operation. By the end of the decade, an even better Triple-Turbine setup was offered across the board as a $296 option. But Dynaflow in all its forms couldn't deliver acceleration like Hydra-Matic, and was therefore handicapped in an age of horsepower and hot rods.

Golden Anniversary year 1953 was significant. It saw the arrival of power steering, a 12-volt electrical system, and a fine new overhead-valve V8 for the Super and Roadmaster. The engine was an oversquare design of 322 cid developing up to 188 bhp thanks to an industry-topping 8.5:1 compression ratio.

That year also saw the debut of the limited-edition Skylark sports convertible, a car for flashy Hollywood types and Texas oil barons. Buick made only 1690 of them, priced at an extraordinary $5000 each. Many custom features were standard, including wraparound windshield and special bodywork.

Skylark was another of those Harley Earl styling projects for which GM had long been famous. Typical of company thinking, it was designed for the broadest possible appeal. Instead of being a two-seat sports car—which accounted for only 0.27 percent of the market in 1953—it was a luxurious, sporty "personal" four-seater like Ford's post-1957 Thunderbirds and Buick's own Riviera of the '60s. Like the similar Oldsmobile Fiesta and Cadillac Eldorado, the Skylark was a large chopped-and-sectioned convertible. Four inches were removed from windshield height, and the top was correspondingly lower. Skylark was much cleaner-looking than standard Buicks. It had no portholes and no hubcaps, but sported the Kelsey-Hayes chrome wire wheels that were coming into fashion throughout the industry by 1953.

Skylark was back again the following year, but the '54 version was much less radical and sold for only $4483. It arrived with tack-on tailfins and huge, chrome-plated, die-cast taillight housings. Its full circular wheel cutouts approximated those of the Wildcat II show car. But

apparently, the '54 Skylark was less impressive than the '53, for only 836 were sold and the model was discontinued for 1955.

Buick's show cars of the '50s were among the wildest in the industry. Led by the XP-300 and the LeSabre of 1951, they were rolling laboratories—test vehicles for a number of unique ideas.

Both the XP-300 and the LeSabre used an experimental 215-cid aluminum V8. This was *not* a forerunner of the 215 V8 of the early '60s, but rather a very special job, exactly square with 3.25-inch bore-and-stroke dimensions. It boasted a 10:1 compression ratio and over 300 bhp. Induction was boosted by a Roots-type supercharger. All this meant a combination of methanol and gasoline had to be used for fuel.

Styling on these two showpieces was radical. On a 116-inch wheelbase, LeSabre sported the wraparound windshield and "Dagmar" bumpers that would be featured on production models a few years later. The XP-300 sat on a 115-inch-wheelbase chassis and featured a concave grille and mesh-backed headlamp nacelles that would be seen on the '54s.

Meanwhile, Buick production was pushing relentlessly toward the industry's number-three spot. The division broke an all-time record in calendar year 1950 with more than 550,000 cars. Flint built 531,000 units in 1954, and found itself trailing only Chevrolet and Ford—a position it had not held since 1930. In 1955, output hit 781,000, another record and nearly 50 percent higher than the previous best figure. This success was based largely on the Special, which had become one of the industry's best sellers.

Special sales began to take off with the arrival of a 264-cid V8 in 1954. In the industry's banner year of 1955, Specials were everywhere. Over 380,000 were made, including 155,000 Riviera two-door hardtops, the single most popular model of the day. The entire Buick line had been restyled in 1954, with a longer, squarer body style and wraparound windshield. That only helped keep sales booming.

Buicks became really fast cars in 1954, too. The Century series reappeared with a 195-bhp V8 in the smaller, lighter Special bodyshell. It immediately became the "hot" Buick.

Four-door and two-door Rivieras joined the Special and Century series in 1955, followed by Super and Roadmaster versions in 1956. The rest of the industry had to play catch-up while Buick dealers enjoyed unprecedented success.

The mild 1956 facelift left the line relatively unchanged, and the cars didn't sell as well as the year before. The division added model year designation to exterior nameplates beginning in '56. This practice was later abandoned after customers complained it made last year's model obsolete even sooner than without it. With the horsepower race in full swing, the '56s were the most powerful Buicks yet. The Special delivered 220 bhp, the rest of the line had 255. A '56 Century could leap from 0 to 60 mph in 10.5 seconds and top 110

mph—and every model in the line could do at least 100 mph.

The line was fully restyled again in 1957. Ed Ragsdale, Buick's general manager, never said how much the retooling had cost, but it must have run several hundred million. Yet, despite the most sweeping alterations since 1949, the '57s didn't sell particularly well, possibly because Buick's rivals were pressing hard. At

**1955 Century convertible coupe**

**Centurion show car of 1956**

**1956 Roadmaster Riviera hardtop sedan**

**1956 Special four-door sedan**

1957 Century Caballero hardtop wagon

1957 Roadmaster convertible coupe

1958 Limited hardtop coupe

1959 Electra 225 convertible

1959 LeSabre hardtop sedan

Chrysler, Virgil Exner's tailfinned "Forward Look" had been introduced. Highland Park was selling almost as many 1956 cars as it had sold in 1955, and Plymouth was forging its way back into third place. But the '57 Buicks were clean, well-styled automobiles. Model additions were few but interesting: the four-door hardtop Caballero station wagon in the Century and Special series, and a Series 75 Roadmaster based on the Series 70, offering every possible accessory except air conditioning as standard. Series 75s came with Dynaflow, power steering, power brakes, flexible-spoke steering wheel, dual exhausts, automatic windshield washers and wide-angle wipers, backup lights, clock, special interior with deep-pile carpeting, and a host of other features. Though 1957 was a good year for Buick, it was even better for Plymouth, which knocked Flint out of third place for the first time in three years.

In those days, the answer to sales problems was to pile on more chrome. Thus, the ugliest Buicks in history materialized for 1958. From a monstrous grille that contained 160 chrome squares within a huge shell, to hastily contrived chrome-draped tailfins, it was a ghastly looking machine(and the revived Limited series in particular). It didn't sell, but the '58 recession was probably more to blame than the awful styling. Buick production dropped to 240,000 units, and the division slipped behind Oldsmobile to fifth place. Air suspension was offered, but seldom ordered. Altogether, '58 was a very bad year.

So was 1959. But while the '58 design had been tasteless, the '59 went the other way in a peak year for Buick styling. Though dominated by the now-omnipresent tailfin, the new design was at least smooth, clean, and fairly dignified (the grille had fewer chrome squares, too). Buick now shared the corporate A-body with other GM lines, but it wasn't obvious. Gone were the traditional model names: the Special was renamed LeSabre, the Century became Invicta, the Super and Roadmaster were dubbed Electra and Electra 225. At the bottom end, LeSabre and Invicta retained the old Special/Century body styles. The hardtop wagon, which hadn't sold well, was dropped. The two Electras were priced down quite a bit from 1958, and rode slightly shorter wheelbases. Buick was called 1959's most changed car, and the change was for the better.

There were some new mechanical developments that year: a 401-cid V8 with 325 bhp was offered for the upper three models, a 364 V8 for the LeSabre. Power brakes and steering were standard on Electras, a $150 option for the other series. Air conditioning was a $430 extra. Air suspension, for the rear only, was still not popular.

Significantly, Buick dealers were selling more Opels in 1959 than ever before. The captive German import assigned to Buick in 1958 grabbed an increasing number of customers as people saw penalties in oversize, overweight automobiles. But Buick Division was already planning its own compact, the 1961 Special/Skylark, and its star would rise again.

1960 LeSabre four-door sedan

1961 Special four-door sedan

1961 LeSabre hardtop sedan

1962 Special Deluxe convertible coupe

1962 Electra 225 hardtop coupe

1963 Wildcat hardtop sedan

For Buick, the 1960s were very successful years. The division built about 250,000 cars in 1960, ranking ninth in the industry. For the 1969 model year Buick built more than 665,000 units, and enjoyed a tight hold on fifth place. The improvement was due in part to the debut of the Special and Skylark, and in part to increased production of the larger models. For example, some 56,000 Electras came off the lines in 1960; nearly 159,000 in 1969. LeSabre production was about 152,000 units in 1960, and nearly 198,000 in '69. The Wildcat, which replaced the Invicta in 1964, began at the 35,000 level but almost doubled that figure by 1969.

The 1961 Special was one of the "second-wave" GM compacts—the Buick-Oldsmobile-Pontiac cars that followed the 1960 Chevrolet Corvair. The Special's first engine was a 215-cid aluminum-block V8 that was light, smooth-running, efficient, and economical. This quiet, powerful engine would have a long life. After GM sold manufacturing rights to British Leyland, it went on in modified form to power Rover sedans in the late '60s through the 1976 3500 sedan and V8 Land-Rover of 1980.

To profit from the sporty-car market pioneered in 1960 by the Corvair Monza, Buick introduced the mid-1961 Special Deluxe Skylark. This coupe had bucket seats, deluxe trim, vinyl-covered roof, and a 185-bhp version of the aluminum V8. More than 12,000 were sold before the end of the model year. In 1962, Buick introduced a Skylark convertible and an optional Borg-Warner four-speed transmission—and watched sales increase to more than 42,000.

In the early part of the decade, the big Buicks changed dramatically. The 1960 LeSabre, Invicta, Electra, and Electra 225—sedans, station wagons, two-door and four-door hardtops, and convertibles—were heavy iron objects of dubious styling merit, basically face-lifted '59s. Their 1961 replacements had shorter wheelbases, weighed 100 to 200 pounds less, and looked much cleaner. In 1962, the Wildcat appeared as a specialty model based on the Invicta. It was a two-ton, 123-inch-wheelbase luxury hardtop priced at nearly $4000, equipped with bucket seats, vinyl roof, and distinctive exterior trim. It was well received and returned for 1963. Fewer that 31,500 Invictas were sold that year. From 1964 on, Wildcat was Buick's middle full-size series.

Production of the top-of-the-line Electra steadily increased throughout the '60s. Buick offered two Electras in '61—the basic model, and the longer, more luxurious

31

1963 Riviera hardtop coupe

1964 Wildcat hardtop coupe

1964 Riviera hardtop coupe

1965 LeSabre Custom hardtop coupe

Electra 225 (named for its overall length). In 1962, the base model was dropped, and all Electras became "225s"; the division then concentrated on fewer offerings. Electras were powered by Buick's largest engine, the 401-cid V8. Its output was 325 bhp at 4400 rpm for 1960-63.

During these years, Buick styling was hardly exceptional. But the 1963 Riviera, a personal-luxury sports coupe, changed the division's stodgy image almost overnight. Many people felt that Bill Mitchell, chief of GM styling, had created one of the best automotive shapes of all time.

The Riviera's origins can be found in Mitchell's project to revive the LaSalle, Cadillac's low-priced cousin, which had disappeared after 1940. Numerous renderings and clay models had been completed—notably, an experimental convertible shown at the 1955 Motorama featuring a LaSalle-type grille. Designed by Buick stylist Ned Nickles, it was named LaSalle II. Although it never went into production, it encouraged GM to build a "personal-luxury" competitor to Ford's Thunderbird. Ultimately, management tapped Buick to design and build it. Cadillac didn't have the facilities, Chevrolet was enjoying record sales, and Oldsmobile and Pontiac were occupied with other things. Buick sales needed a shot in the arm, though. The name Riviera was a natural, having been associated with the make since 1949.

The Riviera borrowed some of its design features from various sources. For example, English custom coachwork inspired its razor-edged body styling. But the finished product was handsome and individual. The final clay model was approved by early 1961, and a production run of 40,000 was scheduled for the 1963 model year. Riding a 117-inch wheelbase, Riviera was about 14 inches shorter than other Buicks. The 325-bhp 401 V8 was standard in its debut year. A 425-cid powerplant with up to 360 bhp was a 1964 option. Transmission was two-speed Turbine Drive in '63; three-speed Twin-Turbine Hydra-Matic was used from 1964 on.

The Riviera's handling was well up to its performance. Standing quarter-mile time was 16 seconds at 85 mph with the standard V8; 15.5 seconds and 90-plus mph with the 360-bhp engine.

In 1964, Buick's compact line was restyled and enlarged. Wheelbases went up to 115 inches for sedans, 120 inches for station wagons. There were new engines, too: a 225-cid V6 with 155 bhp and a 300-cid V8 with 210 bhp. The plush Skylark was now considered part of the Special series, though it is listed individually in our model year production charts. People liked the luxury it offered. By 1964, Skylark was rapidly becoming Buick's most popular compact. The production ratio of Skylarks to Specials was about 9 to 10 in 1964. From 1965 on, Skylark pulled away. By 1969, Buick was building nearly five Skylarks to every one Special.

The large Buicks—LeSabre, Wildcat, and Electra—were lengthened for 1964, although there was no change in wheelbase. The LeSabre's standard engine became a 300-cid V8. Wildcats were the hot rods of the

family, since they carried the 401-cid Electra engine in the lighter, shorter LeSabre chassis. As such, the Wildcat was Buick's performance model, much like the Century had been in the '50s. Riviera, meanwhile, remained basically unchanged, though a 425-cid V8 was added to the option list.

In the first half of the decade, Buick production rose by 50 percent, the division climbing from ninth to fifth place. And instead of a limited lineup of large cars priced just below Cadillac, Buick offered full-size and intermediate models, plus the unique Riviera. Riviera sales consistently ran at 35,000 to 40,000 units a year. In 1965, Riviera's headlights were hidden behind the grille, and the taillights were integrated with the rear bumper.

The year 1965 was significant in other ways, too. Numerous trim and model variations were offered so the buyer could custom-build his Buick. There were standard, Deluxe, and Skylark versions of the compact Special, with V6 or V8 engines, priced from about $2350 to $3000; and V8 Special Sportwagons in the $3000–$3200 range. The Wildcat was offered with standard, deluxe, and Custom trim packages as a sedan, hardtop sedan, and coupe, and as a deluxe and Custom convertible. LeSabres and Electra 225s came in standard and Custom versions. The most expensive Buick was the Electra 225 Custom convertible, priced at $4440. LeSabres were fitted with the 300-cid V8; Wildcats and Electras had the big 401.

An important performance option for '65 was the Gran Sport package for Riviera and Skylark. Gran Sports were equipped with $250 worth of roadability improvements. Fitted with oversize tires, Super-Turbine 300 automatic transmission, and the Wildcat 401 engine, the Skylark Gran Sport was every inch a grand touring car. The Riviera version was, of course, even grander. Using the 425-cid engine, it could reach 125 mph on the straight. *Motor Trend* magazine pronounced it superb in every category: "It goes and handles better than before, and that's quite an improvement."

There were many changes for the 1966-67 Riviera. Although the crisp, razor-edged body was now much more massive, it rode a wheelbase only two inches longer than that of the 1965 model. The second-generation model's smooth sheetmetal, clean hidden-headlight grille, and large windows melded to create an impressive effect. Yet it sold for only about $4400—an amount that seems unbelievably low today.

Riviera was Buick's main news in '66 because the rest of the line was mostly a carryover. Modest facelifts of grilles, side trim, and taillights were the only alterations again in '67. Riviera got a new grille with a horizontal crossbar and redesigned parking lights. Specials and Skylarks, which continued with the 225 V6 or the 300 V8, were distinguished by different grilles.

For 1967, Buick introduced one of its largest engines ever: the 430-cid V8 standard on Wildcat, Electra, and Riviera. It had no more horsepower than previous engines, but it ran more smoothly and quietly. Also new

Riviera Silver Arrow show car of 1965

1966 Electra 225 hardtop coupe

1966 Special Deluxe four-door sedan

1967 Riviera GS hardtop coupe

1967 Special Deluxe four-door sedan

1968 LeSabre convertible

1968 Electra 225 hardtop coupe

1968 Skylark Custom hardtop sedan

1969 Riviera hardtop coupe

was a 400-cid cast-iron V8 for the Special/Skylark chassis. This powerplant appeared in a sporty series with bucket seats dubbed GS400, offered as a convertible, hardtop, or pillared coupe. An identical hardtop with the 340 engine appeared as the GS340. Sales were excellent. Model year production came to over 560,000 units, and the division ranked fifth in the industry.

In 1968, Skylark dominated sales among the "small" Buicks, although by then it had grown from compact to intermediate size. A record number were built for the model year. The junior editions used three different wheelbases: 112 inches for Special and Skylark two-

1969 Sportwagon four-door station wagon

1969 GS400 hardtop coupe

1969 Wildcat Custom hardtop coupe

1969 Electra 225 hardtop coupe

doors, 116 inches for four-doors and Special Deluxe station wagons, and 121 inches for Sportwagons. Again, a group of Gran Sport models was fielded. They were the GS350 hardtop, and the GS400 hardtop and convertible. Capacity of the V6 was upped to 250 cid, but compression was lowered to meet emissions requirements. There was a new 350-cid V8 with 280 bhp for the GS350. It also powered LeSabres, which rode the wheelbase length they'd had in 1960. The 430 was still reserved for Wildcat, Electra, and Riviera.

Buick's restyling for its 1968 big cars included new divided grilles, altered rear bumpers, and concealed windshield wipers. Skylarks and Specials were given a down-sloped side contour line and new grilles. The Riviera got a much heavier divided grille and was not quite as clean-looking as it had been in 1966-67. The senior cars featured bodyside moldings somewhat reminiscent of the old sweep-spear of the '50s. Many Buicks kept with tradition in another way—stylized "ventiports," a design trademark dating from the '40s.

No engine changes were made for the record-breaking 1969 model year when Buick produced more than 665,000 cars—its highest output for any year in the 60's. The Electra 225, Wildcat, and LeSabre were given new bodies with ventless side glass and busier grilles. Gran Sports and Sportwagons, meanwhile, were all but separate models now. GS350 and GS400 hardtops and convertibles, plus Sportwagons with two or three bench seats, were offered as in 1968. LeSabres remained structurally unchanged, but the Wildcat was switched

back from the Electra chassis to the LeSabre's, and handling was improved.

With this hot-selling lineup, Buick stood pat for 1970. Skylark, Sportwagon, Gran Sports, Wildcat, Electra 225, and the inevitable Riviera were continued. A new model designation was the Estate Wagon, actually a pair of upper-class haulers designed to do battle with the likes of the Chrysler Town & Country. The full-size line received new grilles, bumpers, and lights. Intermediates were restyled with a longer hood, shorter deck, and different grilles for each series. The '70 Riviera had a thin-line vertical-bar grille extending below the bumper. The big hardtop also reverted to exposed headlamps and adopted a longer hood and wider rear window than in 1969. Altered bumpers completed the package.

Mechanically, the big news in 1970 was an enormous 455 V8, the largest ever, which gulped premium gas at the rate of 12 mpg and was offered with compression ratios of at least 10:1. The last mammoth V8 Buick would build, the 455 was available in three versions with up to 370 bhp. In one of these guises it was standard on the GS and LeSabre 455, Riviera, Electra 225, Wildcat, and both Estate wagons.

Buicks of the '60s and 1970 were remarkably consistent from year to year in both design and engineering. The division never needed sensational engineering or styling breakthroughs (other than the Riviera) to maintain its sales position—a tribute to the sound design and value of its cars.

1970 Estate Wagon four-door station wagon

1970 Riviera hardtop coupe

1970 GS455 hardtop coupe

1970 Wildcat Custom convertible

# Buick Specifications

## 1940

### Series 40 Special (wb 121.0)

| | | Wght | Price | Prod |
|---|---|---|---|---|
| 41 | sdn 4d | 3,660 | 996 | 68,816 |
| 41C | spt phtn | 3,755 | 1,355 | 597 |
| 41T | taxi | 3,700 | 1,000 | 48 |
| 46 | bus cpe | 3,505 | 895 | 12,382 |
| 46C | conv cpe | 3,665 | 1,077 | 3,763 |
| 46S | spt cpe | 3,540 | 950 | 8,401 |
| 48 | sdn 2d | 3,605 | 955 | 20,768 |

### Series 50 Super (wb 121.0)

| | | | | |
|---|---|---|---|---|
| 51 | sdn 4d | 3,790 | 1,109 | 97,226 |
| 51C | spt phtn | 3,895 | 1,549 | 534 |
| 56C | conv cpe | 3,785 | 1,211 | 4,804 |
| 56S | spt cpe | 3,735 | 1,058 | 26,462 |
| 59 | wgn 4d | 3,870 | 1,242 | 501 |

### Series 60 Century (wb 126.0)

| | | | | |
|---|---|---|---|---|
| 61 | sdn 4d | 3,935 | 1,210 | 8,708 |
| 61C | spt phtn | 4,050 | 1,620 | 203 |
| 66 | bus cpe | 3,800 | 1,128 | 44 |
| 66C | conv cpe | 3,915 | 1,343 | 550 |
| 66S | spt cpe | 3,765 | 1,175 | 96 |

### Series 70 Roadmaster (wb 126.0)

| | | | | |
|---|---|---|---|---|
| 71 | sdn 4d | 4,045 | 1,359 | 13,733 |
| 71C | spt phtn | 4,195 | 1,768 | 238 |
| 76C | conv cpe | 4,055 | 1,431 | 612 |
| 76S | spt cpe | 3,990 | 1,277 | 3,972 |

### Series 80 Limited (wb 133.0)

| | | | | |
|---|---|---|---|---|
| 80C | Streamlined spt phtn | 4,540 | 1,952 | 7 |
| 81 | sdn 4d | 4,440 | 1,553 | 3,898 |
| 81C | T/B spt phtn | 4,540 | 1,952 | 250 |
| 81F | T/B form sdn | 4,455 | 1,727 | 270 |
| 87 | Streamlined spt sdn 4d | 4,380 | 1,553 | 14 |
| 87F | Streamlined form sdn | 4,455 | 1,727 | 7 |

### Series 90 Limited (wb 140.0)

| | | | | |
|---|---|---|---|---|
| 90 | sdn 4d, 8P, A/S | 4,645 | 2,096 | 828 |
| 90L | limo 8P, A/S | 4,705 | 2,199 | 634 |
| 91 | sdn 4d | 4,590 | 1,942 | 418 |

| 1940 Engines | bore×stroke | bhp | availability |
|---|---|---|---|
| L8, 248.0 | 3.09×4.13 | 107 | S-40, 50 |
| L8, 320.2 | 3.44×4.31 | 141 | S-60, 80, 90 |

## 1941

### Series 40 Special (wb 121.0)

| | | Wght | Price | Prod |
|---|---|---|---|---|
| 41 | sdn 4d | 3,730 | 1,052 | 92,528 |
| 41SE | sdn 4d | 3,790 | 1,134 | 13,402 |
| 46 | bus cpe | 3,630 | 935 | 9,201 |
| 46S | sedanet | 3,700 | 1,006 | 88,148 |
| 46SSE | sedanet | 3,690 | 1,063 | 9,614 |
| 49 | wgn 4d | 3,980 | 1,463 | 850 |

### Series 40A Special (wb 118.0)

| | | | | |
|---|---|---|---|---|
| 44 | bus cpe | 3,530 | 915 | 3,261 |
| 44C | conv cpe | 3,780 | 1,138 | 4,309 |
| 44S | spt cpe | 3,590 | 980 | 5,290 |
| 47 | sdn 4d | 3,670 | 1,021 | 14,139 |

### Series 50 Super (wb 121.0)

| | | | | |
|---|---|---|---|---|
| 51 | sdn 4d | 3,770 | 1,185 | 58,638 |
| 51C | conv phtn | 4,014 | 1,555 | 508 |
| 56 | bus cpe | 3,620 | 1,031 | 2,452 |
| 56C | conv cpe | 3,810 | 1,267 | 12,391 |
| 56S | spt cpe | 3,670 | 1,113 | 19,876 |

### Series 60 Century (wb 126.0)

| | | Wght | Price | Prod |
|---|---|---|---|---|
| 61 | sdn 4d | 4,025 | 1,288 | 15,136 |
| 66 | bus cpe | 3,870 | 1,195 | 222 |
| 66S | sedanet | 3,920 | 1,241 | 5,547 |

### Series 70 Roadmaster (wb 128.0)

| | | | | |
|---|---|---|---|---|
| 71 | sdn 4d | 4,010 | 1,364 | 10,553 |
| 71C | conv phtn | 4,469 | 1,775 | 326 |
| 76C | conv cpe | 4,045 | 1,457 | 1,869 |
| 76S | spt cpe | 3,920 | 1,282 | 2,834 |

### Series 90 Limited (wb 139.0)

| | | | | |
|---|---|---|---|---|
| 90 | sdn 4d, 8P, A/S | 4,680 | 2,360 | 906 |
| 90L | limo 8P, A/S | 4,760 | 2,465 | 669 |
| 91 | sdn 4d | 4,575 | 2,155 | 1,231 |
| 91F | form sdn, A/S | 4,665 | 2,310 | 296 |

| 1941 Engines | bore×stroke | bhp | availability |
|---|---|---|---|
| L8, 248.0 | 3.09×4.13 | 115 | S-40A, 40 exc SE |
| L8, 248.0 | 3.09×4.13 | 125 | S-50, 41SE, 46SSE |
| L8, 320.2 | 3.44×4.31 | 165 | S-60, 70, 90 |

## 1942

### Series 40A Special (wb 118.0)

| | | Wght | Price | Prod |
|---|---|---|---|---|
| 44 | util cpe | 3,510 | 990 | 461 |
| 44C | conv cpe | 3,790 | 1,260 | 1,788 |
| 47 | sdn 4d | 3,650 | 1,080 | 1,652 |
| 48 | bus sedanet | 3,555 | 1,010 | 559 |
| 48S | fam sedanet | 3,610 | 1,045 | 5,990 |

### Series 40B Special (wb 121.0)

| | | | | |
|---|---|---|---|---|
| 41 | sdn 4d | 3,760 | 1,120 | 17,397 |
| 41SE | sdn 4d | 3,785 | 1,200 | 2,288 |
| 46 | bus sedanet | 3,650 | 1,020 | 1,408 |
| 46S | fam sedanet | 3,705 | 1,075 | 11,856 |
| 46SSE | fam sedanet | 3,725 | 1,130 | 1,809 |
| 49 | wgn 4d | 3,925 | 1,450 | 327 |

### Series 50 Super (wb 124.0)

| | | | | |
|---|---|---|---|---|
| 51 | sdn 4d | 3,890 | 1,280 | 16,265 |
| 56C | conv cpe | 4,025 | 1,450 | 2,489 |
| 56S | sedanet | 3,800 | 1,230 | 14,629 |

### Series 60 Century (wb 126.0)

| | | | | |
|---|---|---|---|---|
| 61 | sdn 4d | 4,065 | 1,350 | 3,319 |
| 66S | sedanet | 3,985 | 1,300 | 1,232 |

### Series 70 Roadmaster (wb 129.0)

| | | | | |
|---|---|---|---|---|
| 71 | sdn 4d | 4,150 | 1,465 | 5,418 |
| 76C | conv cpe | 4,300 | 1,675 | 511 |
| 76S | sedanet | 4,075 | 1,395 | 2,475 |

### Series 90 Limited (wb 139.0)

| | | | | |
|---|---|---|---|---|
| 90 | sdn 4d, 8P, A/S | 4,710 | 2,445 | 150 |
| 90L | limo 8P, A/S | 4,765 | 2,545 | 250 |
| 91 | sdn 4d | 4,665 | 2,245 | 215 |
| 91F | form sdn | 4,695 | 2,395 | 85 |

| 1942 Engines | bore×stroke | bhp | availability |
|---|---|---|---|
| L8, 248.0 | 3.09×4.13 | 110 | S-40A, 40B exc SE |
| L8, 248.0 | 3.09×4.13 | 118 | S-50, 46SSE, 41SE |
| L8, 320.2 | 3.44×4.31 | 165 | S-60, 70, 90 |

## 1946

### Series 40 Special (121.0)

| | | Wght | Price | Prod |
|---|---|---|---|---|
| 41 | sdn 4d | 3,720 | 1,580 | 1,650 |
| 46S | sedanet | 3,670 | 1,522 | 1,350 |

### Series 50 Super (wb 124.0)

| | | | | |
|---|---|---|---|---|
| 51 | sdn 4d | 3,935 | 1,822 | 77,724 |
| 56C | conv cpe | 4,050 | 2,046 | 5,987 |

| | | Wght | Price | Prod |
|---|---|---|---|---|
| 56S | sedanet | 3,795 | 1,741 | 34,425 |
| 59 | wgn 4d | 4,170 | 2,594 | 748 |

### Series 70 Roadmaster (wb 129.0)

| | | Wght | Price | Prod |
|---|---|---|---|---|
| 71 | sdn 4d | 4,165 | 2,110 | 20,864 |
| 76C | conv cpe | 4,345 | 2,347 | 2,587 |
| 76S | sedanet | 4,095 | 2,014 | 8,292 |

| 1946 Engines | bore×stroke | bhp | availability |
|---|---|---|---|
| L8, 248.0 | 3.09×4.13 | 110 | S-40, 50 |
| L8, 320.2 | 3.44×4.31 | 144 | S-70 |

# 1947

### Series 40 Special (wb 121.0)

| | | Wght | Price | Prod |
|---|---|---|---|---|
| 41 | sdn 4d | 3,720 | 1,623 | 18,431 |
| 46S | sedanet | 3,760 | 1,611 | 14,603 |

### Series 50 Super (wb 124.0)

| | | | | |
|---|---|---|---|---|
| 51 | sdn 4d | 3,910 | 1,929 | 83,576 |
| 56C | conv cpe | 4,050 | 2,333 | 28,297 |
| 56S | sedanet | 3,795 | 1,843 | 46,917 |
| 59 | wgn 4d | 4,170 | 2,940 | 2,036 |

### Series 70 Roadmaster (wb 129.0)

| | | | | |
|---|---|---|---|---|
| 71 | sdn 4d | 4,190 | 2,232 | 47,152 |
| 76C | conv cpe | 4,345 | 2,651 | 12,074 |
| 76S | sedanet | 4,095 | 2,131 | 19,212 |
| 79 | wgn 4d | 4,445 | 3,249 | 529 |

| 1947 Engines | bore×stroke | bhp | availability |
|---|---|---|---|
| L8, 248.0 | 3.09×4.13 | 110 | S-40, 50 |
| L8, 320.2 | 3.44×4.31 | 144 | S-70 |

# 1948

### Series 40 Special (wb 121.0)

| | | Wght | Price | Prod |
|---|---|---|---|---|
| 41 | sdn 4d | 3,705 | 1,809 | 14,051 |
| 46S | sedanet | 3,635 | 1,735 | 11,176 |

### Series 50 Super (wb 124.0)

| | | | | |
|---|---|---|---|---|
| 51 | sdn 4d | 3,855 | 2,087 | 53,447 |
| 56C | conv cpe | 4,020 | 2,518 | 19,017 |
| 56S | sedanet | 3,770 | 1,987 | 33,819 |
| 59 | wgn 4d | 4,170 | 3,127 | 2,018 |

### Series 70 Roadmaster (wb 129.0)

| | | | | |
|---|---|---|---|---|
| 71 | sedan 4d | 4,160 | 2,418 | 47,569 |
| 76C | conv cpe | 4,315 | 2,837 | 11,503 |
| 76S | sedanet | 4,065 | 2,297 | 20,649 |
| 79 | wgn 4d | 4,460 | 3,433 | 350 |

| 1948 Engines | bore×stroke | bhp | availability |
|---|---|---|---|
| L8, 248.0 | 3.09×4.13 | 110 | S-40 |
| L8, 248.0 | 3.09×4.13 | 115 | S-50 |
| L8, 320.2 | 3.44×4.31 | 144 | S-70 |

# 1949

### Series 40 Special (wb 121.0)

| | | Wght | Price | Prod |
|---|---|---|---|---|
| 41 | sdn 4d | 3,695 | 1,861 | 5,940 |
| 46S | sedanet | 3,625 | 1,787 | 4,687 |

### Series 50 Super (wb 121.0)

| | | | | |
|---|---|---|---|---|
| 51 | sedan 4d | 3,835 | 2,157 | 136,423 |

### Series 40 Special (wb 121.0)

| | | | | |
|---|---|---|---|---|
| 56C | conv cpe | 3,985 | 2,583 | 22,110 |
| 56S | sedanet | 3,735 | 2,059 | 66,250 |
| 59 | wgn 4d | 4,100 | 3,178 | 1,847 |

### Series 70 Roadmaster (wb 126.0)

| | | Wght | Price | Prod |
|---|---|---|---|---|
| 71 | sdn 4d | 4,205 | 2,735 | 55,242 |
| 76C | conv cpe | 4,370 | 3,150 | 8,244 |
| 76R | Riviera htp cpe | 4,420 | 3,203 | 4,343 |
| 76S | sedanet | 4,115 | 2,618 | 18,537 |
| 79 | wgn 4d | 4,490 | 3,734 | 653 |

| 1949 Engines | bore×stroke | bhp | availability |
|---|---|---|---|
| L8, 248.0 | 3.09×4.13 | 110 | S-40 |
| L8, 348.0 | 3.09×4.13 | 115/120 | S-50 |
| L8, 320.2 | 3.44×4.31 | 150 | S-70 |

# 1950

### Series 40 Special (wb 121.5)

| | | Wght | Price | Prod |
|---|---|---|---|---|
| 41 | sdn 4d | 3,710 | 1,941 | 1,141 |
| 41D | DeLuxe sdn | 3,735 | 1,983 | 141,396 |
| 43 | J/B sdn 4d | 3,715 | 1,809 | 58,700 |
| 43D | DeLuxe J/B sdn, 4d | 3,720 | 1,952 | 14,335 |
| 46 | J/B cpe | 3,615 | 1,803 | 2,500 |
| 46D | DeLuxe J/B cpe | 3,665 | 1,899 | 76,902 |
| 46S | J/B sedanet | 3,655 | 1,856 | 42,935 |

### Series 50 Super (wb 121.5)

| | | | | |
|---|---|---|---|---|
| 51 | sdn 4d | 3,745 | 2,139 | 55,672 |
| 56C | conv cpe | 3,965 | 2,476 | 12,259 |
| 56R | Riviera htp cpe | 3,790 | 2,139 | 56,030 |
| 56S | J/B sedanet | 3,645 | 2,041 | 10,697 |
| 59 | wgn 4d | 4,115 | 2,844 | 2,480 |

### Series 50 Super (wb 125.5)

| | | | | |
|---|---|---|---|---|
| 52 | sdn 4d | 3,870 | 2,212 | 114,745 |

### Series 70 Roadmaster (wb 125.3; 72-130.3)

| | | | | |
|---|---|---|---|---|
| 71 | sdn 4d | 4,135 | 2,633 | 6,738 |
| 72 | Riviera sdn 4d | 4,220 | 2,738 | 54,212 |
| 75R | Riviera htp cpe | 4,135 | 2,633 | 2,300 |
| 76R | Riv DeLuxe htp cpe | 4,245 | 2,854 | 8,432 |
| 76C | conv cpe | 4,345 | 2,981 | 2,964 |
| 76S | J/B sedanet | 4,025 | 2,528 | 2,968 |
| 79 | wgn 4d | 4,470 | 3,407 | 420 |

| 1950 Engines | bore×stroke | bhp | availability |
|---|---|---|---|
| L8, 248.0 | 3.09×4.13 | 115/120 | S-40 |
| L8, 263.3 | 3.19×4.13 | 124/128 | S-50 |
| L8, 320.2 | 3.44×4.31 | 152 | S-70 |

# 1951

### Series 40 Special (wb 121.5)

| | | Wght | Price | Prod |
|---|---|---|---|---|
| 41 | sdn 4d | 3,605 | 2,139 | 999 |
| 41D | DeLuxe sdn 4d | 3,680 | 2,185 | 87,848 |
| 45R | Riviera sdn 2d | 3,645 | 2,225 | 16,491 |
| 46C | conv cpe | 3,830 | 2,561 | 2,099 |
| 46S | spt cpe | 3,600 | 2,046 | 2,700 |
| 48D | DeLuxe sdn 2d | 3,615 | 2,127 | 54,311 |

### Series 50 Super (wb 121.5; 52-125.5)

| | | | | |
|---|---|---|---|---|
| 51 | sdn 4d | 3,755 | 2,356 | 10,000 |
| 52 | Riviera sdn 4d | 3,845 | 2,437 | 92,886 |
| 56C | conv cpe | 3,965 | 2,728 | 8,116 |
| 56R | Riviera sdn 2d | 3,765 | 2,356 | 54,512 |
| 56S | DeLuxe sdn 2d | 3,685 | 2,248 | 1,500 |
| 59 | wgn 4d | 4,100 | 3,133 | 2,212 |

### Series 70 Roadmaster (wb 126.3; 72R-130.3)

| | | | | |
|---|---|---|---|---|
| 72R | Riviera sdn 4d | 4,240 | 3,044 | 48,758 |
| 76C | conv cpe | 4,355 | 3,283 | 2,911 |
| 76MR | Riviera htp cpe | 4,185 | 3,051 | 809 |

| | | Wght | Price | Prod |
|---|---|---|---|---|
| 76R | Riv htp cpe, hydraulic controls | 4,235 | 3,143 | 12,901 |
| 79R | wgn 4d | 4,470 | 3,780 | 679 |

| 1951 Engines | bore×stroke | bhp | availability |
|---|---|---|---|
| L8, 263.3 | 3.19×4.13 | 120/128 | S-40 |
| L8, 263.3 | 3.19×4.13 | 124/128 | S-50 |
| L8, 320.2 | 3.44×4.31 | 152 | S-70 |

## 1952

| Series 40 Special (wb 121.5) | | Wght | Price | Prod |
|---|---|---|---|---|
| 41 | sdn 4d | 3,650 | 2,209 | 137 |
| 41D | DeLuxe sdn 4d | 3,665 | 2,255 | 63,346 |
| 45R | Riviera htp cpe | 3,665 | 2,295 | 21,180 |
| 46C | conv cpe | 3,850 | 2,634 | 600 |
| 46S | spt cpe | 3,605 | 2,115 | 2,206 |
| 48D | sdn 2d | 3,620 | 2,197 | 32,684 |

| Series 50 Super (wb 121.5; 52-125.5) | | | | |
|---|---|---|---|---|
| 52 | sdn 4d | 3,825 | 2,563 | 71,387 |
| 56C | conv cpe | 3,970 | 2,869 | 6,904 |
| 56R | Riviera htp cpe | 3,775 | 2,478 | 55,400 |
| 59 | wgn 4d | 4,105 | 3,296 | 1,641 |

| Series 70 Roadmaster (wb 126.3;72R-130.3) | | | | |
|---|---|---|---|---|
| 72R | sdn 4d | 4,285 | 3,200 | 32,069 |
| 76C | conv cpe | 4,395 | 3,453 | 2,402 |
| 76R | Riviera htp cpe | 4,235 | 3,306 | 11,387 |
| 79R | wgn 4d | 4,505 | 3,977 | 359 |

| 1952 Engines | bore×stroke | bhp | availability |
|---|---|---|---|
| L8, 263.3 | 3.19×4.13 | 120/128 | S-40 |
| L8, 263.3 | 3.19×4.13 | 124/128 | S-50 |
| L8, 320.2 | 3.44×4.31 | 170 | S-70 |

## 1953

| Series 40 Special (wb 121.5) | | Wght | Price | Prod |
|---|---|---|---|---|
| 41D | DeLuxe sdn 4d | 3,710 | 2,255 | 100,312 |
| 45R | Riviera htp cpe | 3,705 | 2,295 | 58,780 |
| 46C | conv cpe | 3,815 | 2,553 | 4,282 |
| 48D | DeLuxe sdn | 3,675 | 2,197 | 53,796 |

| Series 50 Super (wb 121.5; 52-125.5) | | | | |
|---|---|---|---|---|
| 52 | Riviera sdn 4d | 3,905 | 2,696 | 90,685 |
| 56C | conv cpe | 4,035 | 3,002 | 6,701 |
| 56R | Riviera htp cpe | 3,845 | 2,611 | 91,298 |
| 59 | wgn 4d | 4,150 | 3,430 | 1,830 |

| Series 70 Roadmaster (wb 121.5; 72R-125.5) | | | | |
|---|---|---|---|---|
| 72R | Riviera sdn 4d | 4,100 | 3,254 | 50,523 |
| 76C | conv cpe | 4,250 | 3,506 | 3,318 |
| 76R | Riviera htp cpe | 4,125 | 3,358 | 22,927 |
| 76X | Skylark conv cpe | 4,315 | 5,000 | 1,690 |
| 79R | wgn 4d | 4,315 | 4,031 | 670 |

| 1953 Engines | bore×stroke | bhp | availability |
|---|---|---|---|
| L8, 263.3 | 3.19×4.13 | 125/130 | S-40 |
| V8, 322.0 | 4.00×3.20 | 164/170 | S-50 |
| V8, 322.0 | 4.00×3.20 | 188 | S-70 |

## 1954

| Series 40 Special (wb 122.0) | | Wght | Price | Prod |
|---|---|---|---|---|
| 41D | DeLuxe sdn 4d | 3,735 | 2,265 | 70,356 |
| 46C | conv cpe | 3,810 | 2,563 | 6,135 |
| 46R | Riviera htp cpe | 3,740 | 2,305 | 71,186 |
| 48D | DeLuxe sdn 2d | 3,690 | 2,207 | 41,557 |
| 49 | DeLuxe wgn 4d | 3,905 | 3,163 | 1,650 |

| Series 50 Super (wb 127.0) | | | | |
|---|---|---|---|---|
| 52 | Riviera sdn 4d | 4,105 | 2,711 | 41,756 |
| 56C | conv cpe | 4,145 | 2,964 | 3,343 |

| | | Wght | Price | Prod |
|---|---|---|---|---|
| 56R | Riviera htp cpe | 4,035 | 2,626 | 73,531 |

| Series 60 Century (wb 122.0) | | | | |
|---|---|---|---|---|
| 61 | sdn 4d | 3,805 | 2,520 | 31,919 |
| 66C | conv cpe | 3,950 | 2,963 | 2,790 |
| 66R | Riviera htp cpe | 3,795 | 2,534 | 45,710 |
| 69 | wgn 4d | 3,975 | 3,470 | 1,563 |

| Series 70 Roadmaster (wb 127.0) | | | | |
|---|---|---|---|---|
| 72R | Riviera sdn 4d | 4,250 | 3,269 | 26,862 |
| 76C | conv cpe | 4,355 | 3,521 | 20,404 |
| 76R | Riviera htp cpe | 4,215 | 3,373 | 3,305 |

| Series 100 Skylark (wb 122.0) | | | | |
|---|---|---|---|---|
| 100M | conv cpe | 4,260 | 4,483 | 836 |

| 1954 Engines | bore×stroke | bhp | availability |
|---|---|---|---|
| V8, 264.0 | 3.63×3.20 | 143/150 | S-40 |
| V8, 322.0 | 4.00×3.20 | 177/182 | S-50 |
| V8, 322.0 | 4.00×3.20 | 195/200 | S-60 |
| V8, 322.0 | 4.00×3.20 | 200 | S-70, 100 |

## 1955

| Series 40 Special (wb 122.0) | | Wght | Price | Prod |
|---|---|---|---|---|
| 41 | sdn 4d | 3,745 | 2,291 | 84,182 |
| 43 | Riviera htp sdn | 3,820 | 2,409 | 66,409 |
| 46C | conv cpe | 3,825 | 2,590 | 10,009 |
| 46R | Riviera htp cpe | 3,720 | 2,332 | 155,818 |
| 48 | sdn 2d | 3,715 | 2,233 | 61,879 |
| 49 | wgn 4d | 3,940 | 2,974 | 2,952 |

| Series 50 Super (wb 127.0) | | | | |
|---|---|---|---|---|
| 52 | sdn 4d | 4,140 | 2,876 | 43,280 |
| 56C | conv cpe | 4,280 | 3,225 | 3,527 |
| 56R | Riviera htp cpe | 4,075 | 2,831 | 85,656 |

| Series 60 Century (wb 122.0) | | | | |
|---|---|---|---|---|
| 61 | sdn 4d | 3,825 | 2,548 | 13,269 |
| 63 | Riviera htp sdn | 3,900 | 2,733 | 55,088 |
| 66C | conv cpe | 3,950 | 2,991 | 5,588 |
| 66R | Riviera htp cpe | 3,805 | 2,601 | 80,338 |
| 68 | sdn 2d | 3,795 | 2,490 | 270 |
| 69 | wgn 4d | 3,995 | 3,175 | 4,243 |

| Series 70 Roadmaster (wb 127.0) | | | | |
|---|---|---|---|---|
| 72 | sdn 4d | 4,300 | 3,349 | 31,717 |
| 76C | conv cpe | 4,415 | 3,552 | 4,739 |
| 76R | Riviera htp cpe | 4,270 | 3,453 | 28,071 |

| 1955 Engines | bore×stroke | bhp | availability |
|---|---|---|---|
| V8, 264.0 | 3.63×3.20 | 188 | S-40 |
| V8, 322.0 | 4.00×3.20 | 236 | S-50, 60, 70 |

## 1956

| Series 40 Special (wb 122.0) | | Wght | Price | Prod |
|---|---|---|---|---|
| 41 | sdn 4d | 3,790 | 2,416 | 66,977 |
| 43 | Riviera htp sdn | 3,860 | 2,528 | 91,025 |
| 46C | conv cpe | 3,880 | 2,740 | 9,712 |
| 46R | Riviera htp cpe | 3,775 | 2,457 | 113,861 |
| 48 | sdn 2d | 3,750 | 2,357 | 38,672 |
| 49 | wgn 4d | 3,945 | 2,775 | 13,770 |

| Series 50 Super (wb 127.0) | | | | |
|---|---|---|---|---|
| 52 | sdn 4d | 4,200 | 3,250 | 14,940 |
| 53 | Riviera htp sdn | 4,265 | 3,340 | 34,029 |
| 56C | conv cpe | 4,340 | 3,544 | 2,889 |
| 56R | Riviera htp cpe | 4,140 | 3,204 | 29,540 |

| Series 60 Century (wb 122.0) | | | | |
|---|---|---|---|---|
| 61 | sdn 4d | 3,930 | exp | 1 |
| 63 | Riviera htp sdn | 4,000 | 3,025 | 20,891 |

| | | Wght | Price | Prod |
|---|---|---|---|---|
| 63D | Riviera DeLuxe htp sdn | 4,000 | 3,041 | 35,082 |
| 66C | conv cpe | 4,045 | 3,306 | 4,721 |
| 66R | Riviera htp cpe | 3,890 | 2,963 | 33,334 |
| 69 | wgn 4d | 4,080 | 3,256 | 8,160 |

**Series 70 Roadmaster (wb 127.0)**

| | | Wght | Price | Prod |
|---|---|---|---|---|
| 72 | sdn 4d | 4,280 | 3,503 | 11,804 |
| 73 | Riviera htp sdn | 4,355 | 3,692 | 24,779 |
| 76C | conv cpe | 4,395 | 3,704 | 4,354 |
| 76R | Riviera htp cpe | 4,235 | 3,591 | 12,490 |

| 1956 Engines | bore×stroke | bhp | availability | |
|---|---|---|---|---|
| V8, 322.0 | 4.00×3.20 | 220 | S-40 | |
| V8, 322.0 | 4.00×3.20 | 255 | S-50, 60, 70 | |

# 1957

**Series 40 Special (wb 122.0)**

| | | Wght | Price | Prod |
|---|---|---|---|---|
| 41 | sdn 4d | 4,012 | 2,660 | 59,739 |
| 43 | Riviera htp sdn | 4,041 | 2,780 | 50,563 |
| 46C | conv cpe | 4,082 | 2,987 | 8,505 |
| 46R | Riviera htp cpe | 3,956 | 2,704 | 64,425 |
| 48 | sdn 2d | 2,596 | 2,596 | 23,180 |
| 49 | wgn 4d | 4,292 | 3,047 | 7,013 |
| 49D | Caballero wgn 4d | 4,309 | 3,167 | 6,817 |

**Series 50 Super (wb 127.5)**

| | | Wght | Price | Prod |
|---|---|---|---|---|
| 53 | Riviera htp sdn | 4,356 | 3,681 | 41,665 |
| 56C | conv cpe | 4,414 | 3,981 | 2,065 |
| 56R | Riviera htp cpe | 4,271 | 3,536 | 26,529 |

**Series 60 Century (wb 122.0)**

| | | Wght | Price | Prod |
|---|---|---|---|---|
| 61 | sdn 4d | 4,137 | 3,234 | 8,075 |
| 63 | Riviera htp sdn | 4,163 | 3,354 | 26,589 |
| 66C | conv cpe | 4,234 | 3,598 | 4,085 |
| 66R | Riviera htp cpe | 4,081 | 3,270 | 17,029 |
| 68 | sdn 2d | 4,080 | exp | 2 |
| 69 | Caballero wgn 4d | 4,423 | 3,706 | 10,186 |

**Series 70 Roadmaster (wb 127.5)**

| | | Wght | Price | Prod |
|---|---|---|---|---|
| 73 | Riviera htp sdn | 4,469 | 4,053 | 11,401 |
| 73A | Riviera htp sdn, 1-piece backlight | 4,455 | 4,066 | 10,526 |
| 76C | conv cpe | 4,500 | 4,066 | 4,363 |
| 76R | Riviera htp sdn | 4,374 | 3,944 | 3,826 |
| 76A | Riviera htp sdn, 1-piece backlight | 4,370 | 3,944 | 2,812 |

**Series 75 Roadmaster (wb 127.5)**

| | | Wght | Price | Prod |
|---|---|---|---|---|
| 75 | Riviera htp sdn | 4,539 | 4,483 | 12,250 |
| 75R | Riviera htp cpe | 4,427 | 4,373 | 2,404 |

| 1957 Engines | bore×stroke | bhp | availability | |
|---|---|---|---|---|
| V8, 364.0 | 4.13×3.40 | 250 | S-40 | |
| V8, 364.0 | 4.13×3.40 | 300 | S-50, 60, 70, 75 | |

# 1958

**Series 40 Special (wb 122.0)**

| | | Wght | Price | Prod |
|---|---|---|---|---|
| 41 | sdn 4d | 4,115 | 2,700 | 48,238 |
| 43 | Riviera htp sdn | 4,180 | 2,820 | 31,921 |
| 46C | conv cpe | 4,165 | 3,041 | 5,502 |
| 46R | Riviera htp cpe | 4,058 | 2,744 | 34,903 |
| 48 | sdn 2d | 4,063 | 2,636 | 11,566 |
| 49 | wgn 4d | 4,396 | 3,154 | 3,663 |
| 49D | Caballero htp wgn 4d | 4,408 | 3,261 | 3,420 |

**Series 50 Super (wb 127.5)**

| | | Wght | Price | Prod |
|---|---|---|---|---|
| 53 | Riviera htp sdn | 4,500 | 3,789 | 28,460 |
| 56R | Riviera htp cpe | 4,392 | 3,644 | 13,928 |

**Series 60 Century (wb 122.0)**

| | | Wght | Price | Prod |
|---|---|---|---|---|
| 61 | sdn 4d | 4,241 | 3,316 | 7,241 |

| | | Wght | Price | Prod |
|---|---|---|---|---|
| 63 | Riviera htp sdn | 4,267 | 3,436 | 15,171 |
| 66C | conv cpe | 4,302 | 3,680 | 2,588 |
| 66R | Riviera htp cpe | 4,182 | 3,368 | 8,100 |
| 68 | sdn 2d | 4,189 | exp | 2 |
| 69 | Caballero htp wgn 4d | 4,498 | 3,831 | 4,456 |

**Series 75 Roadmaster (wb 127.5)**

| | | Wght | Price | Prod |
|---|---|---|---|---|
| 75 | Riviera htp sdn | 4,668 | 4,667 | 10,505 |
| 75C | conv cpe | 4,676 | 4,680 | 1,181 |
| 75R | Riviera htp cpe | 4,568 | 4,557 | 2,368 |

**Series 700 Limited (wb 127.5)**

| | | Wght | Price | Prod |
|---|---|---|---|---|
| 750 | Riviera htp sdn | 4,710 | 5,112 | 5,571 |
| 755 | Riviera htp cpe | 4,691 | 5,002 | 1,026 |
| 756 | conv cpe | 4,603 | 5,125 | 839 |

| 1958 Engines | bore×stroke | bhp | availability | |
|---|---|---|---|---|
| V8, 364.0 | 4.13×3.40 | 250 | S-40 | |
| V8, 364.0 | 4.13×3.40 | 300 | S-50, 60, 75, 700 | |

# 1959

**4400 LeSabre (wb 123.0)**

| | | Wght | Price | Prod |
|---|---|---|---|---|
| 4411 | sdn 2d | 4,159 | 2,740 | 13,492 |
| 4419 | sdn 4d | 4,229 | 2,804 | 51,379 |
| 4435 | wgn 4d | 4,565 | 3,320 | 8,286 |
| 4437 | htp cpe | 4,188 | 2,849 | 35,189 |
| 4439 | htp sdn | 4,266 | 2,925 | 46,069 |
| 4467 | conv cpe | 4,216 | 3,129 | 10,489 |

**4600 Invicta (wb 123.0)**

| | | Wght | Price | Prod |
|---|---|---|---|---|
| 4619 | sdn 4d | 4,331 | 3,357 | 10,566 |
| 4635 | wgn 4d | 4,660 | 3,841 | 5,231 |
| 4637 | htp cpe | 4,274 | 3,447 | 11,451 |
| 4639 | htp sdn | 4,373 | 3,515 | 20,156 |
| 4667 | conv cpe | 4,317 | 3,620 | 5,447 |

**4700 Electra (wb 126.3)**

| | | Wght | Price | Prod |
|---|---|---|---|---|
| 4719 | sdn 4d | 4,557 | 3,856 | 12,357 |
| 4737 | htp cpe | 4,465 | 3,818 | 11,216 |
| 4739 | htp sdn | 4,573 | 3,963 | 20,612 |

**4800 Electra 225 (wb 126.3)**

| | | Wght | Price | Prod |
|---|---|---|---|---|
| 4829 | Riviera htp sdn | 4,632 | 4,300 | 6,324 |
| 4839 | htp sdn | 4,641 | 4,300 | 10,491 |
| 4867 | conv cpe | 4,562 | 4,192 | 5,493 |

| 1959 Engines | bore×stroke | bhp | availability | |
|---|---|---|---|---|
| V8, 364.0 | 4.13×3.40 | 250 | S-LeSabre | |
| V8, 401.0 | 4.19×3.64 | 325 | S-others | |

# 1960

**4400 LeSabre (wb 123.0)**

| | | Wght | Price | Prod |
|---|---|---|---|---|
| 4411 | sdn 2d | 4,139 | 2,756 | 14,388 |
| 4419 | sdn 4d | 4,219 | 2,870 | 54,033 |
| 4435 | wgn 4d, 2S | 4,568 | 3,386 | 5,331 |
| 4437 | htp cpe | 4,163 | 2,915 | 26,521 |
| 4439 | htp sdn | 4,269 | 2,991 | 35,999 |
| 4445 | wgn 4d, 3S | 4,574 | 3,493 | 2,222 |
| 4467 | conv cpe | 4,233 | 3,145 | 13,588 |

**4600 Invicta (wb 123.0)**

| | | Wght | Price | Prod |
|---|---|---|---|---|
| 4619 | sdn 4d | 4,324 | 3,357 | 10,839 |
| 4635 | wgn 4d, 2S | 4,644 | 3,841 | 3,471 |
| 4637 | htp cpe | 4,255 | 3,447 | 8,960 |
| 4639 | htp sdn | 4,365 | 3,515 | 15,300 |
| 4645 | wgn 4d, 3S | 4,679 | 3,948 | 1,605 |
| 4667 | conv cpe | 4,347 | 3,620 | 5,236 |

**4700 Electra (wb 126.3)**

| | | Wght | Price | Prod |
|---|---|---|---|---|
| 4719 | sdn 4d | 4,544 | 3,856 | 13,794 |

# Buick

| | | Wght | Price | Prod |
|---|---|---|---|---|
| 4737 | htp cpe | 4,453 | 3,818 | 7,416 |
| 4739 | htp sdn | 4,554 | 3,963 | 14,488 |

### 4800 Electra 225 (wb 126.3)

| | | Wght | Price | Prod |
|---|---|---|---|---|
| 4829 | Riviera htp sdn | 4,653 | 4,300 | 8,029 |
| 4839 | htp sdn | 4,650 | 4,300 | 5,841 |
| 4867 | conv cpe | 4,571 | 4,192 | 6,746 |

| 1960 Engines | bore×stroke | bhp | availability |
|---|---|---|---|
| V8, 364.0 | 4.13×3.40 | 235/250 | S-LeSabre |
| V8, 401.0 | 4.19×3.64 | 325 | S-others |

## 1961

### 4000 Special (wb 112.0)

| | | Wght | Price | Prod |
|---|---|---|---|---|
| 4019 | sdn 4d | 2,610 | 2,384 | 18,339 |
| 4027 | spt cpe | 2,579 | 2,330 | 4,232 |
| 4035 | wgn 4d | 2,775 | 2,681 | 6,101 |
| 4045 | wgn 4d, 3S | 2,844 | 2,762 | 798 |
| 4119 | Deluxe sdn 4d | 2,632 | 2,519 | 32,986 |
| 4135 | Deluxe wgn 4d | 2,794 | 2,816 | 11,729 |
| 4317 | Skylark spt cpe | 2,687 | 2,621 | 12,683 |

### 4400 LeSabre (wb 123.0)

| | | Wght | Price | Prod |
|---|---|---|---|---|
| 4411 | sdn 2d | 4,033 | 2,993 | 5,959 |
| 4435 | wgn 4d | 4,450 | 3,623 | 5,628 |
| 4437 | htp cpe | 4,054 | 3,152 | 14,474 |
| 4439 | htp sdn | 4,129 | 3,228 | 37,790 |
| 4445 | wgn 4d, 3S | 4,483 | 3,730 | 2,423 |
| 4467 | conv cpe | 4,186 | 3,382 | 11,951 |
| 4469 | sdn 4d | 4,102 | 3,107 | 35,005 |

### 4600 Invicta (wb 123.0)

| | | Wght | Price | Prod |
|---|---|---|---|---|
| 4637 | htp cpe | 4,090 | 3,447 | 6,382 |
| 4639 | htp sdn | 4,179 | 3,515 | 18,398 |
| 4667 | conv cpe | 4,206 | 3,620 | 3,953 |

### 4700 Electra (wb 126.0)

| | | Wght | Price | Prod |
|---|---|---|---|---|
| 4719 | sdn 4d | 4,298 | 3,825 | 13,818 |
| 4737 | htp cpe | 4,260 | 3,818 | 4,250 |
| 4739 | htp sdn | 4,333 | 3,932 | 8,978 |

### 4800 Electra 225 (wb 126.0)

| | | Wght | Price | Prod |
|---|---|---|---|---|
| 4829 | Riviera htp sdn | 4,417 | 4,350 | 13,719 |
| 4867 | conv cpe | 4,441 | 4,192 | 7,158 |

| 1961 Engines | bore×stroke | bhp | availability |
|---|---|---|---|
| V8, 215.0 | 3.50×2.80 | 155 | S-Special (Slylark 185 bhp) |
| V8, 364.0 | 4.13×3.40 | 235/250 | S-LeSabre |
| V8, 401.0 | 4.19×3.64 | 325 | S-others |

## 1962

### Special (wb 112.1)

| | | Wght | Price | Prod |
|---|---|---|---|---|
| 4019 | sdn 4d | 2,666 | 2,358 | 23,249 |
| 4027 | cpe | 2,638 | 2,304 | 19,135 |
| 4035 | wgn 4d | 2,876 | 2,655 | 7,382 |
| 4045 | wgn 4d, 3S | 2,896 | 2,736 | 2,814 |
| 4067 | conv cpe | 2,858 | 2,587 | 7,918 |
| 4119 | Del sdn 4d | 2,648 | 2,593 | 31,660 |
| 4135 | Del wgn 4d | 2,845 | 2,890 | 10,380 |
| 4167 | Del conv cpe | 2,820 | 2,879 | 8,332 |
| 4347 | Skylark htp cpe | 2,707 | 2,787 | 34,060 |
| 4367 | Skylark conv cpe | 2,871 | 3,012 | 8,913 |

### LeSabre (wb 123.0)

| | | Wght | Price | Prod |
|---|---|---|---|---|
| 4411 | sdn 2d | 4,041 | 3,091 | 7,418 |
| 4439 | stp sdn | 4,156 | 3,369 | 37,518 |
| 4447 | htp cpe | 4,054 | 3,293 | 25,479 |
| 4469 | sdn 4d | 4,104 | 3,227 | 56,783 |

### Invicta (wb 123.0)

| | | Wght | Price | Prod |
|---|---|---|---|---|
| 4435 | wgn 4d | 4,471 | 3,836 | 9,131 |

| | | Wght | Price | Prod |
|---|---|---|---|---|
| 4639 | htp sdn | 4,159 | 3,667 | 16,443 |
| 4645 | wgn 4d, 3S | 4,505 | 3,917 | 4,617 |
| 4647 | spt cpe | 4,077 | 3,733 | 10,335 |
| 4647 | Wildcat spt cpe | 4,150 | 3,927 | 2,000 |
| 4667 | conv cpe | 4,217 | 3,617 | 13,471 |

### Electra 225 (wb 126.0)

| | | Wght | Price | Prod |
|---|---|---|---|---|
| 4819 | sdn 4d | 4,304 | 4,051 | 13,523 |
| 4829 | Riviera htp sdn 6W | 4,390 | 4,448 | 15,395 |
| 4839 | htp sdn | 4,309 | 4,186 | 16,734 |
| 4847 | htp cpe | 4,235 | 4,062 | 8,992 |
| 4867 | conv cpe | 4,396 | 4,366 | 7,894 |

| 1962 Engines | bore×stroke | bhp | availability |
|---|---|---|---|
| V6, 198.0 | 3.63×3.20 | 135 | S-Special |
| V8, 215.0 | 3.50×2.80 | 155 | S-Special Deluxe |
| V8, 215.0 | 3.50×2.80 | 185 | S-Skylark |
| V8, 401.0 | 4.19×3.64 | 265/280 | S-LeSabre, Invicta |
| V8, 401.0 | 4.19×3.64 | 325 | S-Electra |

## 1963

### Special (wb 112.1)

| | | Wght | Price | Prod |
|---|---|---|---|---|
| 4019 | sdn 4d | 2,696 | 2,363 | 21,733 |
| 4027 | cpe | 2,661 | 2,309 | 21,886 |
| 4035 | wgn 4d | 2,866 | 2,659 | 5,867 |
| 4045 | wgn 4d, 3S | 2,903 | 2,740 | 2,415 |
| 4067 | conv cpe | 2,768 | 2,591 | 8,082 |
| 4119 | Del sdn 4d | 2,720 | 2,521 | 37,695 |
| 4135 | Del wgn 4d | 2,854 | 2,818 | 8,771 |
| 4347 | Skylark spt cpe | 2,757 | 2,857 | 32,109 |
| 4367 | Skylark conv cpe | 2,810 | 3,011 | 10,212 |

### LeSabre (wb 123.0)

| | | Wght | Price | Prod |
|---|---|---|---|---|
| 4411 | sdn 2d | 3,905 | 2,869 | 8,328 |
| 4435 | wgn 4d | 4,320 | 3,526 | 5,566 |
| 4439 | htp sdn | 4,007 | 3,146 | 50,420 |
| 4445 | wgn 4d, 3S | 4,340 | 3,606 | 3,922 |
| 4447 | htp cpe | 3,924 | 3,070 | 27,997 |
| 4467 | conv cpe | 4,052 | 3,339 | 9,975 |
| 4469 | sdn 4d | 3,970 | 3,004 | 64,995 |

### Wildcat (wb 123.0)

| | | Wght | Price | Prod |
|---|---|---|---|---|
| 4639 | htp sdn | 4,222 | 3,871 | 17,519 |
| 4647 | htp cpe | 4,123 | 3,849 | 12,185 |
| 4667 | conv cpe | 4,228 | 3,961 | 6,021 |

### Invicta (wb 123.0)

| | | Wght | Price | Prod |
|---|---|---|---|---|
| 4635 | wgn 4d | 4,397 | 3,969 | 3,495 |

### Electra 225 (wb 126.0)

| | | Wght | Price | Prod |
|---|---|---|---|---|
| 4819 | sdn 4d | 4,241 | 4,051 | 14,268 |
| 4829 | pillarless sdn | 4,284 | 4,254 | 11,468 |
| 4839 | htp sdn | 4,272 | 4,186 | 19,714 |
| 4847 | htp cpe | 4,153 | 4,062 | 6,848 |
| 4867 | conv cpe | 4,297 | 4,365 | 6,347 |

### Riviera (wb 117.0)

| | | Wght | Price | Prod |
|---|---|---|---|---|
| 4747 | spt cpe | 3,988 | 4,333 | 40,000 |

| 1963 Engines | bore×stroke | bhp | availability |
|---|---|---|---|
| V6, 198.0 | 3.63×3.20 | 135 | S-Special, Special Deluxe |
| V8, 215.0 | 3.50×2.80 | 155 | O-Special Deluxe, Skylark |
| V8, 215.0 | 3.50×2.80 | 200 | S-Skylark, O-all Specials |
| V8, 401.0 | 4.19×3.64 | 265/280 | S-LeSabre |
| V8, 401.0 | 4.19×3.64 | 325 | S-Invicta, Wildcat, Electra, Riviera |

## 1964

### Special (wb 115.0; wgns-120.0)

| | | Wght | Price | Prod |
|---|---|---|---|---|
| 4027 | cpe | 2,991 | 2,343 | 15,030 |

| | | Wght | Price | Prod |
|---|---|---|---|---|
| 4035 | wgn | 3,266 | 2,689 | 6,270 |
| 4067 | conv cpe | 3,108 | 2,605 | 6,308 |
| 4069 | sdn 4d | 3,008 | 2,397 | 17,983 |
| 4127 | Del cpe | 3,006 | 2,457 | 11,962 |
| 4135 | Del wgn 4d | 3,285 | 2,787 | 9,467 |
| 4169 | Del sdn 4d | 3,026 | 2,490 | 31,742 |
| 4337 | Skyl spt cpe | 3,057 | 2,680 | 42,356 |
| 4367 | Skyl conv cpe | 3,175 | 2,834 | 10,225 |
| 4369 | Skyl sdn 4d | 3,070 | 2,669 | 19,635 |
| 4255 | Skyl Spt Wgn | 3,557 | 2,989 | 2,709 |
| 4355 | Skyl Spt Wgn | 3,595 | 3,161 | 3,913 |
| 4265 | Skyl Spt Wgn 4d 3S | 3,689 | 3,124 | 2,586 |
| 4365 | Skyl Spt Wgn | 3,727 | 3,286 | 4,446 |

**LeSabre (wb 123.0)**

| | | | | |
|---|---|---|---|---|
| 4439 | htp sdn | 3,730 | 3,122 | 37,052 |
| 4447 | htp cpe | 3,620 | 3,061 | 24,177 |
| 4467 | conv cpe | 3,787 | 3,311 | 8,685 |
| 4469 | sdn 4d | 3,693 | 2,980 | 56,729 |
| 4635 | wgn 4d | 4,352 | 3,554 | 6,517 |
| 4645 | wgn 4d, 3S | 4,362 | 3,635 | 4,003 |

**Wildcat (wb 123.0)**

| | | | | |
|---|---|---|---|---|
| 4639 | htp sdn | 4,058 | 3,327 | 33,358 |
| 4647 | htp cpe | 4,003 | 3,267 | 22,893 |
| 4667 | conv cpe | 4,076 | 3,455 | 7,850 |
| 4669 | sdn | 4,021 | 3,164 | 20,144 |

**Electra 225 (wb 126.0)**

| | | | | |
|---|---|---|---|---|
| 4819 | sdn 4d | 4,212 | 4,059 | 15,968 |
| 4829 | pillarless sdn | 4,238 | 4,261 | 11,663 |
| 4839 | htp sdn | 4,229 | 4,194 | 24,935 |
| 4847 | htp cpe | 4,149 | 4,070 | 9,045 |
| 4867 | conv cpe | 4,280 | 4,374 | 7,181 |

**Riviera (wb 117.0)**

| | | | | |
|---|---|---|---|---|
| 4747 | htp cpe | 3,951 | 4,385 | 37,658 |

| 1964 Engines | bore×stroke | bhp | availability |
|---|---|---|---|
| V6, 225.0 | 3.75×3.40 | 155 | S-Special |
| V8, 300.0 | 3.75×3.40 | 210/250 | S-LeSabre 4400, Special |
| V8, 401.0 | 4.19×3.64 | 325 | S-LeS 4600, Wildcat, Elec |
| V8, 425.0 | 4.31×3.64 | 340(O–360) | S-Riv; O-LeS 4600, Wldct, Elec |

# 1965

**Special (wb 115.0)**

| | | Wght | Price | Prod |
|---|---|---|---|---|
| 43327 | cpe | 2,977 | 2,343 | 12,915 |
| 43335 | wgn 4d | 3,258 | 2,688 | 2,868 |
| 43367 | conv cpe | 3,087 | 2,605 | 3,357 |
| 43369 | sdn 4d | 3,010 | 2,397 | 13,828 |
| 43427 | cpe V8 | 3,080 | 2,414 | 5,309 |
| 43435 | wgn 4d | 3,365 | 2,759 | 3,676 |
| 43467 | conv cpe | 3,197 | 2,676 | 3,365 |
| 43469 | sdn 4d | 3,117 | 2,468 | 8,121 |
| 43535 | Del wgn 4d | 3,242 | 2,787 | 1,677 |
| 43569 | Del sdn 4d | 3,016 | 2,669 | 11,033 |
| 43635 | Del wgn 4d | 3,369 | 2,858 | 9,123 |
| 43669 | Del sdn 4d | 3,143 | 2,561 | 26,299 |

**Skylark (wb 115.0; wgns-120.0)**

| | | | | |
|---|---|---|---|---|
| 44255 | wgn 4d | 3,642 | 2,989 | 4,226 |
| 44265 | wgn 4d, 3S | 3,750 | 3,123 | 4,669 |
| 44327 | cpe | 3,035 | 2,537 | 4,195 |
| 44337 | htp cpe | 3,057 | 2,680 | 4,549 |
| 44367 | conv cpe | 3,149 | 2,834 | 1,181 |
| 44369 | sdn 4d | 3,086 | 2,669 | 3,385 |
| 44427 | cpe | 3,146 | 2,608 | 11,877 |
| 44437 | htp cpe | 3,198 | 2,751 | 47,034 |
| 44455 | Cus wgn 4d | 3,690 | 3,160 | 8,300 |
| 44465 | Cus wgn 3S | 3,802 | 3,285 | 11,166 |
| 44467 | conv cpe | 3,294 | 2,905 | 10,456 |
| 44469 | sdn 4d | 3,194 | 2,740 | 22,335 |

**LeSabre (wb 123.0)**

| | | Wght | Price | Prod |
|---|---|---|---|---|
| 45237 | htp cpe | 3,753 | 3,030 | 15,786 |
| 45239 | htp sdn | 3,809 | 3,090 | 18,384 |
| 45269 | sdn 4d | 3,788 | 2,948 | 37,788 |
| 45437 | Cus htp cpe | 3,724 | 3,100 | 21,049 |
| 45439 | Cus htp sdn | 3,811 | 3,166 | 23,394 |
| 45467 | Cus conv cpe | 3,812 | 3,325 | 6,543 |
| 45469 | Cus sdn 4d | 3,777 | 3,024 | 22,052 |

**Wildcat (wb 126.0)**

| | | | | |
|---|---|---|---|---|
| 46237 | htp cpe | 3,988 | 3,286 | 6,031 |
| 46239 | htp sdn | 4,089 | 3,346 | 7,499 |
| 46269 | sdn 4d | 4,058 | 3,182 | 10,184 |
| 46437 | Del htp cpe | 4,014 | 3,340 | 11,617 |
| 46439 | Del htp sdn | 4,075 | 3,407 | 13,903 |
| 46467 | Del conv cpe | 4,060 | 3,502 | 4,616 |
| 46460 | Del sdn 4d | 4,046 | 3,285 | 9,765 |
| 46637 | Cus htp cpe | 4,047 | 3,566 | 15,896 |
| 46639 | Cus htp sdn | 4,160 | 3,626 | 14,878 |
| 46667 | Cus conv cpe | 4,087 | 3,727 | 4,398 |

**Electra 225 (wb 126.0)**

| | | | | |
|---|---|---|---|---|
| 48237 | htp cpe | 4,208 | 4,082 | 6,302 |
| 48239 | htp sdn | 4,284 | 4,206 | 12,842 |
| 48269 | sdn 4d | 4,261 | 4,071 | 12,459 |
| 48437 | Cus htp cpe | 4,228 | 4,265 | 9,570 |
| 48439 | Cus htp sdn | 4,344 | 4,389 | 29,932 |
| 48467 | Cus conv cpe | 4,325 | 4,440 | 8,505 |
| 48469 | Cus sdn 4d | 4,272 | 4,254 | 7,197 |

**Riviera (wb 117.0)**

| | | | | |
|---|---|---|---|---|
| 49447 | htp cpe | 4,036 | 4,408 | 34,586 |

| 1965 Engines | bore×stroke | bhp | availability |
|---|---|---|---|
| V6, 225.0 | 3.75×3.40 | 155 | S-Special, Skylark |
| V8, 300.0 | 3.75×3.40 | 210/250 | S-Special, Skylark, LeSabre |
| V8, 401.0 | 4.19×3.64 | 325 | S-Wildcat, Electra, Riviera |
| V8, 425.0 | 4.31×3.64 | 340/360 | O-Wildcat, Electra Riviera |

# 1966

**Special (wb 115.0; wgns-120.0)**

| | | Wght | Price | Prod |
|---|---|---|---|---|
| 43307 | cpe | 3,009 | 2,348 | 9,322 |
| 43335 | wgn 4d | 3,296 | 2,695 | 1,451 |
| 43367 | conv cpe | 3,092 | 2,604 | 1,357 |
| 43369 | sdn 4d | 3,046 | 2,401 | 8,797 |
| 43407 | cpe | 3,091 | 2,418 | 5,719 |
| 43405 | wgn 4d | 3,399 | 2,764 | 3,038 |
| 43467 | conv cpe | 3,223 | 2,671 | 2,036 |
| 43469 | sdn 4d | 3,148 | 2,471 | 9,355 |
| 43507 | Del cpe | 3,009 | 2,432 | 2,359 |
| 43517 | Del htp cpe | 3,038 | 2,504 | 2,507 |
| 43535 | Del wgn 4d | 3,290 | 2,783 | 824 |
| 43569 | Del sdn 4d | 3,045 | 2,485 | 5,573 |
| 43607 | Del cpe | 3,112 | 2,502 | 4,908 |
| 43617 | Del htp cpe | 3,130 | 2,574 | 10,350 |
| 43635 | Del wgn 4d | 3,427 | 2,853 | 7,592 |
| 43669 | Del sdn 4d | 3,156 | 2,555 | 27,909 |

**Skylark (wb 115.0; wgns - 120.0)**

| | | | | |
|---|---|---|---|---|
| 44255 | wgn 4d | 3,713 | 3,025 | 2,469 |
| 44265 | wgn 4d, 3S | 3,811 | 3,173 | 2,667 |
| 44307 | cpe V6 | 3,034 | 2,624 | 1,454 |
| 44317 | htp cpe | 3,069 | 2,687 | 2,552 |
| 44339 | htp sdn | 3,172 | 2,846 | 1,422 |
| 44367 | conv cpe | 3,158 | 2,837 | 608 |
| 44407 | cpe | 3,145 | 2,694 | 6,427 |
| 44417 | htp cpe | 3,152 | 2,757 | 33,326 |
| 44439 | htp sdn | 3,285 | 2,916 | 18,873 |
| 44455 | Cus wgn 4d | 3,720 | 3,155 | 6,964 |
| 44465 | Cus wgn 4d, 3S | 3,844 | 3,293 | 9,510 |
| 44467 | conv cpe | 3,259 | 2,904 | 6,129 |
| 44607 | GS cpe | 3,479 | 2,956 | 1,835 |

# Buick

| | | Wght | Price | Prod |
|---|---|---|---|---|
| 44617 | GS htp cpe | 3,428 | 3,019 | 9,934 |
| 44667 | GS conv cpe | 3,532 | 3,167 | 2,047 |

**LeSabre (wb 123.0)**

| | | Wght | Price | Prod |
|---|---|---|---|---|
| 45237 | htp cpe | 3,751 | 3,022 | 13,843 |
| 45239 | htp sdn | 3,828 | 3,081 | 17,740 |
| 45269 | sdn 4d | 3,796 | 2,942 | 39,146 |
| 45437 | Cus htp cpe | 3,746 | 3,109 | 18,830 |
| 45439 | Cus htp sdn | 3,824 | 3,174 | 21,914 |
| 45467 | Cus conv cpe | 3,833 | 3,326 | 4,994 |
| 45469 | Cus sdn 4d | 3,788 | 3,035 | 25,932 |

**Wildcat (wb 126.0)**

| | | Wght | Price | Prod |
|---|---|---|---|---|
| 46437 | htp cpe | 4,003 | 3,326 | 9,774 |
| 46439 | htp sdn | 4,108 | 3,391 | 15,081 |
| 46467 | conv cpe | 4,065 | 3,480 | 2,690 |
| 46469 | sdn 4d | 4,070 | 3,233 | 14,389 |
| 46637 | Cus htp cpe | 4,018 | 3,547 | 10,800 |
| 46639 | Cus htp sdn | 4,176 | 3,606 | 13,060 |
| 46667 | Cus conv cpe | 4,079 | 3,701 | 2,790 |

**Electra 225 (wb 126.0)**

| | | Wght | Price | Prod |
|---|---|---|---|---|
| 48237 | htp cpe | 4,176 | 4,032 | 4,882 |
| 48239 | htp sdn | 4,271 | 4,153 | 10,792 |
| 48269 | sdn 4d | 4,255 | 4,022 | 11,740 |
| 48437 | Cus htp cpe | 4,230 | 4,211 | 10,119 |
| 48439 | Cus htp sdn | 4,323 | 4,332 | 34,149 |
| 48467 | Cus conv cpe | 4,298 | 4,378 | 7,175 |
| 48469 | Cus sdn 4d | 4,292 | 4,201 | 9,368 |

**Riviera (wb 119.0)**

| | | Wght | Price | Prod |
|---|---|---|---|---|
| 49487 | htp cpe | 4,180 | 4,424 | 45,348 |

| 1966 Engines | bore×stroke | bhp | availability |
|---|---|---|---|
| V6, 225.0 | 3.75×3.40 | 160 | S-Special, Skylark |
| V8, 300.0 | 3.75×3.40 | 210 | O-Special, Skylark |
| V8, 340.0 | 3.75×3.85 | 220 | S-4440 wagon, LeSabre |
| V8, 401.0 | 4.19×3.64 | 325 | S-Skylark GS, Wildcat, Electra |
| V8, 401.0 | 4.19×3.64 | 340 | S-Riviera; O-Wildcat, Electra |

# 1967

**Special (wb 115.0; wgns-120.0)**

| | | Wght | Price | Prod |
|---|---|---|---|---|
| 43307 | cpe | 3,071 | 2,411 | 6,989 |
| 43335 | wgn 4d | 3,343 | 2,742 | 908 |
| 43369 | sdn 4d | 3,077 | 2,462 | 4,711 |
| 43407 | cpe | 3,173 | 2,481 | 8,937 |
| 43435 | wgn 4d | 3,425 | 2,812 | 1,688 |
| 43469 | sdn 4d | 3,196 | 2,532 | 5,793 |
| 43517 | Del htp cpe | 3,127 | 2,566 | 2,357 |
| 43569 | Del sdn 4d | 3,142 | 2,545 | 3,650 |
| 43617 | Del htp cpe | 3,202 | 2,636 | 14,408 |
| 43635 | Del wgn 4d | 3,317 | 2,901 | 6,851 |
| 43669 | Del sdn 4d | 3,205 | 2,615 | 26,057 |

**Skylark (wb 115.0; wgns-120.0)**

| | | Wght | Price | Prod |
|---|---|---|---|---|
| 34017 | GS340 htp cpe | 3,283 | 2,845 | 3,692 |
| 44307 | cpe V6 | 3,137 | 2,665 | 894 |
| 44407 | cpe V8 | 3,229 | 2,735 | 3,165 |
| 44417 | htp cpe | 3,199 | 2,798 | 41,084 |
| 44439 | htp sdn | 3,373 | 2,950 | 13,721 |
| 44455 | wgn 4d | 3,772 | 3,202 | 8,554 |
| 44465 | wgn 4d, 3S | 3,876 | 3,340 | 10,529 |
| 44467 | conv cpe | 3,335 | 2,945 | 6,319 |
| 44469 | sdn 4d | 3,324 | 2,767 | 9,213 |
| 44607 | GS400 cpe | 3,439 | 2,956 | 1,014 |
| 44617 | GS400 htp cpe | 3,500 | 3,019 | 10,659 |
| 44667 | GS400 conv cpe | 3,505 | 3,167 | 2,140 |

**LeSabre (wb 123.0)**

| | | Wght | Price | Prod |
|---|---|---|---|---|
| 45239 | htp sdn | 3,878 | 3,142 | 17,464 |
| 45269 | sdn 4d | 3,847 | 3,002 | 36,220 |

| | | Wght | Price | Prod |
|---|---|---|---|---|
| 45287 | htp cpe | 3,819 | 3,084 | 13,760 |
| 45439 | Cus htp sdn | 3,873 | 3,236 | 32,526 |
| 45467 | Cus conv cpe | 3,890 | 3,388 | 4,624 |
| 45469 | Cus sdn 4d | 3,855 | 3,096 | 27,930 |
| 45487 | Cus htp cpe | 3,853 | 3,172 | 22,666 |

**Wildcat (wb 126.0)**

| | | Wght | Price | Prod |
|---|---|---|---|---|
| 46439 | htp sdn | 4,069 | 3,437 | 15,110 |
| 46467 | conv cpe | 4,064 | 3,536 | 2,276 |
| 46469 | sdn 4d | 4,008 | 3,277 | 14,579 |
| 46487 | htp cpe | 4,021 | 3,382 | 10,585 |
| 46639 | Cus htp sdn | 4,119 | 3,652 | 13,547 |
| 46667 | Cus conv cpe | 4,046 | 3,757 | 2,913 |
| 46687 | Cus htp cpe | 4,055 | 3,603 | 11,871 |

**Electra 225 (wb 126.0)**

| | | Wght | Price | Prod |
|---|---|---|---|---|
| 48239 | htp sdn | 4,293 | 4,184 | 12,491 |
| 48257 | htp cpe | 4,197 | 4,075 | 6,845 |
| 48269 | sdn 4d | 4,246 | 4,054 | 10,787 |
| 48439 | Cus htp sdn | 4,336 | 4,363 | 40,978 |
| 48457 | Cus htp cpe | 4,242 | 4,254 | 12,156 |
| 48467 | Cus conv cpe | 4,304 | 4,421 | 6,941 |
| 48469 | Cus sdn 4d | 4,312 | 4,270 | 10,106 |

**Riviera (wb 119.0)**

| | | Wght | Price | Prod |
|---|---|---|---|---|
| 49487 | htp cpe | 4,189 | 4,469 | 42,799 |

| 1967 Engines | bore×stroke | bhp | availability |
|---|---|---|---|
| V6, 225.0 | 3.75×3.40 | 160 | S-Special, Skylark |
| V6, 300.0 | 3.75×3.40 | 210 | O-Special, Skylark |
| V8, 340.0 | 3.75×3.85 | 220/260 | S-4400 wgn, LeS; O-Skyl |
| V8, 401.0 | 4.19×3.64 | 340 | S-GS400 |
| V8, 430.0 | 4.19×3.90 | 360 | S-Wildcat, Electra, Riviera |

# 1968

**Special Deluxe (wb 116.0; 2d-112.0)**

| | | Wght | Price | Prod |
|---|---|---|---|---|
| 43327 | cpe | 3,185 | 2,513 | 21,988 |
| 43369 | sdn 4d | 3,277 | 2,564 | 16,571 |
| 43435 | wgn 4d | 3,670 | 3,001 | 10,916 |

**Skylark (wb 116.0; 2d-112.0)**

| | | Wght | Price | Prod |
|---|---|---|---|---|
| 43537 | htp cpe | 3,240 | 2,688 | 32,795 |
| 43569 | sdn 4d | 3,278 | 2,666 | 27,387 |
| 44437 | Cus htp cpe | 3,344 | 2,956 | 44,143 |
| 44439 | Cus htp sdn | 3,481 | 3,108 | 12,984 |
| 44467 | Cus conv cpe | 3,394 | 3,098 | 8,188 |
| 44469 | Cus sdn 4d | 3,377 | 2,924 | 8,066 |

**Sportwagon (wb 121.0)**

| | | Wght | Price | Prod |
|---|---|---|---|---|
| 44455 | wgn 4d | 3,975 | 3,341 | 10,530 |
| 44465 | wgn 4d, 3S | 4,118 | 3,499 | 12,378 |

**Gran Sport (wb 112.0)**

| | | Wght | Price | Prod |
|---|---|---|---|---|
| 43437 | GS350 htp cpe | 3,375 | 2,926 | 8,317 |
| 44637 | GS400 htp cpe | 3,514 | 3,127 | 10,743 |
| 44667 | GS400 conv cpe | 3,547 | 3,271 | 2,454 |

**LeSabre (wb 123.0)**

| | | Wght | Price | Prod |
|---|---|---|---|---|
| 45239 | htp sdn | 3,980 | 3,281 | 18,058 |
| 45269 | sdn 4d | 3,946 | 3,141 | 37,433 |
| 45287 | htp cpe | 3,923 | 3,223 | 14,992 |
| 45439 | Cus htp sdn | 4,007 | 3,375 | 40,370 |
| 45467 | Cus conv cpe | 3,966 | 3,504 | 5,257 |
| 45469 | Cus sdn 4d | 3,950 | 3,235 | 34,112 |
| 45487 | Cus htp cpe | 3,932 | 3,311 | 29,596 |

**Wildcat (wb 126.0)**

| | | Wght | Price | Prod |
|---|---|---|---|---|
| 46439 | htp sdn | 4,133 | 3,576 | 15,153 |
| 46469 | sdn 4d | 4,076 | 3,416 | 15,201 |
| 46487 | htp cpe | 4,065 | 3,521 | 10,708 |
| 46639 | Cus htp sdn | 4,162 | 3,791 | 14,059 |

| 46667 | Cus conv cpe | | | Wght | Price | Prod |
|---|---|---|---|---|---|---|
| 46667 | Cus conv cpe | | | 4,118 | 3,873 | 3,572 |
| 46687 | Cus htp cpe | | | 4,082 | 3,742 | 11,276 |

### Electra 225 (wb (126.0)

| 48239 | htp sdn | | | 4,270 | 4,330 | 15,376 |
|---|---|---|---|---|---|---|
| 48257 | htp cpe | | | 4,180 | 4,221 | 10,705 |
| 48269 | sdn 4d | | | 4,253 | 4,200 | 12,723 |
| 48439 | Cus htp sdn | | | 4,314 | 4,509 | 50,846 |
| 48457 | Cus htp cpe | | | 4,223 | 4,400 | 16,826 |
| 48467 | Cus conv cpe | | | 4,285 | 4,541 | 7,976 |
| 48469 | Cus sdn 4d | | | 4,304 | 4,415 | 10,910 |

### Riviera (wb 119.0)

| 49487 | htp cpe | | | 4,222 | 4,615 | 49,284 |
|---|---|---|---|---|---|---|

| 1968 Engines | bore×stroke | bhp | availability |
|---|---|---|---|
| V6, 250.0 | 3.88×3.53 | 155 | S-Special Del, Skylark |
| V8, 350.0 | 0.00×3.85 | 230 | S-Swgn, Sky Cus, LeS; O-Spec, Sky |
| V8, 350.0 | 3.80×3.85 | 280 | S-GS350; O-Sp Del, Sky, LeS, Swgn |
| V8, 401.0 | 4.19×3.64 | 340 | S-GS400, Sportwagon 400 |
| V8, 430.0 | 4.19×3.90 | 360 | S-Wildcat, Electra, Riviera |

# 1969

### Special Deluxe (wb 116.0; 2d-112.0)

| | | | | Wght | Price | Prod |
|---|---|---|---|---|---|---|
| 43327 | cpe | | | 3,216 | 2,562 | 15,268 |
| 43369 | sdn 4d | | | 3,182 | 2,613 | 11,113 |
| 43435 | wgn 4d | | | 3,736 | 3,092 | 2,590 |
| 43436 | luxury wgn 4d | | | 3,783 | 3,124 | 6,677 |

### Skylark (wb 116.0; 2d-112.0)

| 43537 | htp cpe | | | 3,240 | 2,736 | 38,658 |
|---|---|---|---|---|---|---|
| 43569 | sdn 4d | | | 3,270 | 2,715 | 22,349 |
| 44437 | Cus htp cpe | | | 3,341 | 3,009 | 35,639 |
| 44439 | Cus htp sdn | | | 3,477 | 3,151 | 9,609 |
| 44467 | Cus conv cpe | | | 3,398 | 3,152 | 6,552 |
| 44469 | Cus sdn 4d | | | 3,397 | 2,978 | 6,423 |

### Sportwagon (wb 121.0)

| 44456 | wgn 4d | | | 4,106 | 3,465 | 9,157 |
|---|---|---|---|---|---|---|
| 44466 | wgn 4d, 3S | | | 4,321 | 3,621 | 11,513 |

### Gran Sport (wb 112.0)

| 43437 | GS350 htp cpe | | | 3,406 | 2,980 | 4,933 |
|---|---|---|---|---|---|---|
| 44637 | GS400 htp cpe | | | 3,549 | 3,181 | 6,356 |
| 44667 | GS400 conv cpe | | | 3,594 | 3,325 | 1,776 |

### LeSabre (wb 123.2)

| 45237 | htp cpe | | | 3,936 | 3,298 | 16,201 |
|---|---|---|---|---|---|---|
| 45239 | htp sdn | | | 3,983 | 3,356 | 17,235 |
| 45269 | sdn 4d | | | 3,966 | 3,216 | 36,664 |
| 45437 | Cus htp cpe | | | 4,018 | 3,386 | 38,887 |
| 45439 | Cus htp sdn | | | 4,073 | 3,450 | 48,123 |
| 45467 | Cus conv cpe | | | 3,958 | 3,579 | 3,620 |
| 45469 | Cus sdn 4d | | | 3,941 | 3,310 | 37,136 |

### Wildcat (wb 123.2)

| 46437 | htp cpe | | | 3,926 | 3,596 | 12,416 |
|---|---|---|---|---|---|---|
| 46439 | htp sdn | | | 4,304 | 3,651 | 13,805 |
| 46469 | sdn 4d | | | 4,102 | 3,491 | 13,126 |
| 46637 | Cus htp cpe | | | 4,134 | 3,817 | 12,136 |
| 46639 | Cus htp sdn | | | 4,220 | 3,866 | 13,596 |
| 46667 | Cus conv cpe | | | 4,152 | 3,948 | 2,374 |

### Electra 225 (wb 126.2)

| 48239 | htp sdn | | | 4,294 | 4,432 | 15,983 |
|---|---|---|---|---|---|---|
| 48257 | htp cpe | | | 4,203 | 4,323 | 13,128 |
| 48269 | sdn 4d | | | 4,238 | 4,302 | 14,521 |
| 48439 | Cus htp sdn | | | 4,328 | 4,611 | 65,240 |
| 48457 | Cus htp cpe | | | 4,222 | 4,502 | 27,018 |
| 48467 | Cus conv cpe | | | 4,309 | 4,643 | 8,294 |
| 48469 | Cus sdn 4d | | | 4,281 | 4,517 | 14,434 |

### Riviera (wb 119.0)

| | | | | Wght | Price | Prod |
|---|---|---|---|---|---|---|
| 49487 | htp cpe | | | 4,199 | 4,701 | 52,872 |

| 1969 Engines | bore×stroke | bhp | availability |
|---|---|---|---|
| V6, 250.0 | 3.88×3.53 | 155 | S-SD cpe & sdn, Skylark |
| V8, 350.0 | 3.80×3.85 | 230 | S-SD wgn, Sky Cus, LeS |
| V8, 350.0 | 3.80×3.85 | 280 | S-GS350; O-LeS, SW, SD, Sky |
| V8, V8, 401.0 | 4.19×3.64 | 340 | S-GS400; O-Sportwagon |
| V8, 430.0 | 4.19×3.90 | 360 | S-Riviera, Electra, Wildcat |

# 1970

### Skylark (wb 116.0; 2d-112.0)

| | | | | Wght | Price | Prod |
|---|---|---|---|---|---|---|
| 43327 | cpe | | | 3,250 | 2,685 | 18,620 |
| 43369 | sdn 4d | | | 3,311 | 2,736 | 13,420 |
| 43537 | 350 htp cpe | | | 3,277 | 2,859 | 70,918 |
| 43569 | 350 sdn 4d | | | 3,320 | 2,880 | 30,201 |
| 44437 | Cus htp cpe | | | 3,435 | 3,132 | 36,367 |
| 44439 | Cus htp sdn | | | 3,565 | 3,220 | 12,411 |
| 44467 | Cus conv cpe | | | 3,499 | 3,275 | 4,954 |
| 44469 | Cus sdn 4d | | | 3,499 | 3,101 | 7,113 |

### Sportwagon (wb 116.0)

| 43435 | wgn 4d | | | 3,775 | 3,210 | 2,239 |
|---|---|---|---|---|---|---|
| 43436 | luxury wgn 4d | | | 3,898 | 3,242 | 10,002 |

### Gran Sport (wb 112.0)

| 43437 | htp cpe | | | 3,434 | 3,098 | 9,948 |
|---|---|---|---|---|---|---|
| 44637 | 455 htp cpe | | | 3,562 | 3,283 | 8,732 |
| 44667 | 455 conv cpe | | | 3,619 | 3,469 | 1,416 |

### LeSabre (wb 124.0)

| 45237 | htp cpe | | | 3,866 | 3,419 | 14,163 |
|---|---|---|---|---|---|---|
| 45239 | htp sdn | | | 4,018 | 3,477 | 14,817 |
| 45269 | sdn 4d | | | 3,970 | 3,337 | 35,404 |
| 45437 | Cus htp cpe | | | 3,921 | 3,507 | 35,641 |
| 45439 | Cus htp sdn | | | 3,988 | 3,571 | 43,863 |
| 45467 | Cus conv cpe | | | 3,947 | 3,700 | 2,487 |
| 45469 | Cus sdn 4d | | | 3,950 | 3,431 | 36,682 |
| 46437 | Cus 455 htp cpe | | | 4,066 | 3,675 | 5,469 |
| 46439 | Cus 455 htp sdn | | | 4,143 | 3,739 | 6,541 |
| 46469 | Cus 455 sdn 4d | | | 4,107 | 3,599 | 5,555 |

### Estate Wagon (wb 124.0)

| 46036 | wgn 4d | | | 4,691 | 3,923 | 11,427 |
|---|---|---|---|---|---|---|
| 46046 | wgn 4d, 3S | | | 4,779 | 4,068 | 16,879 |

### Wildcat Custom (wb 124.0)

| 46637 | htp cpe | | | 4,099 | 3,949 | 9,447 |
|---|---|---|---|---|---|---|
| 46639 | htp sdn | | | 4,187 | 3,997 | 12,924 |
| 46667 | conv cpe | | | 4,214 | 4,079 | 1,244 |

### Electra 225 (wb 127.0)

| 48239 | htp sdn | | | 4,296 | 4,592 | 14,338 |
|---|---|---|---|---|---|---|
| 48257 | htp cpe | | | 4,214 | 4,482 | 12,013 |
| 48269 | sdn 4d | | | 4,274 | 4,461 | 12,580 |
| 48439 | Cus htp sdn | | | 4,385 | 4,771 | 65,114 |
| 48457 | Cus stp cpe | | | 4,297 | 4,661 | 26,002 |
| 48467 | Cus conv cpe | | | 4,341 | 4,802 | 6,045 |
| 48469 | Cus sdn 4d | | | 4,283 | 4,677 | 14,109 |

### Riviera (wb 119.0)

| 49487 | htp cpe | | | 4,216 | 4,854 | 37,336 |
|---|---|---|---|---|---|---|

| 1970 Engines | bore×stroke | bhp | availability |
|---|---|---|---|
| V6, 250.0 | 3.88×3.53 | 155 | S-Skylark, Skylark 350 |
| V8, 350.0 | 3.80×3.85 | 260 | S-LeS, Sky Cus, SW; O-Sky |
| V8, 350.0 | 3.80×3.85 | 285 | O-LeS, Sky, Sportwagon |
| V8, 350.0 | 3.80×3.85 | 315 | S-GS; O-LeS, Sky, Swgn |
| V8, 455.0 | 4.31×3.90 | 350/360 | S-GS455 |
| V8, 455.0 | 4.31×3.90 | 370 | S-Wldct, Est Wgn, LeS 455, Elec, Riv |

# Cadillac

**Cadillac Motor Car Division, General Motors Corp. Detroit, Michigan**

Cadillac was founded in late 1902 by Henry Martyn Leland, a brilliant engineer with prior experience at Ford and Oldsmobile. The first cars were single-cylinder models. The four-cylinder Cadillac 30 was introduced in 1909, and remained in production until 1915. During this period, Leland's emphasis on parts standardization came to the notice of the young auto industry. In England, three Cadillacs were disassembled, their components mixed up, and three complete cars reassembled from the pieces. This won Cadillac its first Dewar Trophy, and was the source of its slogan, "Standard of the World."

In 1909, Cadillac became part of the fledgling General Motors Corporation. In those days, it was an upper middle-priced car, not directly competitive with Packard and Pierce-Arrow, but always a high-quality item. The company's pioneer V8 engine of 1915 set new standards for smoothness, compactness, power, and reliability. Sales increased through the late Teens and '20s. By 1930, Cadillac was competing directly with Packard at the top of the luxury class. That was the year it introduced the outstanding V16 engine. Later, a V12 was produced as well. The Depression led to several bad years after 1929. At one point, General Motors actually considered discontinuing its highest-priced car. But sales recovered by the mid-'30s, and by the start of the '40s Cadillac was firmly established as a leading American luxury make. Cadillac never built a middle-priced model like the Packard One Twenty—LaSalle was a Cadillac product, but did not carry its "parent's" name. Consequently, Cadillac outstripped Packard as a luxury-car builder by 1935, and has remained the nation's leading prestige make right on through to the present.

Some of Cadillac's most important engineering developments, as well as many of its most beautiful automobiles, made their debut in the '40s. The decade began with the last of the opulent V16s and no fewer than four variations of Bill Mitchell's brilliant 60 Special. Like Buick, Cadillac offered facelifted models in 1940 and '41, then brought out a completely restyled line for 1942. This put the division in a good position to resume civilian car production after World War II.

Most 1940 Cadillacs were relatively plain-looking—almost Chevrolet-like at the front end, with simple bar-type grilles. One exception was the V16 Series 90, which had an eggcrate grille that would inspire postwar styling. The V16 shared its 141-inch wheelbase (the longest for Cadillac up to that time) with the V8 Series

1940 Series 72 Fleetwood five-passenger formal sedan

1940 Series 60 Special four-door sedan

1940 Sixteen (Series 90) five-passenger town sedan

1940 Series 62 convertible sedan

1940 Series 75 Fleetwood convertible coupe

1941 Series 60 Special four-door sedan

75. The V12 models had been discontinued earlier. Except for their engines, the Series 90 and 75 offered an identical lineup of two coupes, a convertible, a touring sedan with and without divider window, a trunkback convertible sedan, formal sedans for five or seven passengers, and a variety of seven-passenger sedans. The big difference was price. A basic Series 75 five-passenger sedan sold for $2995, while the same car in V16 guise cost $5140. The price spread was not really justified by the powerplant, for the Cadillac 346 cubic-inch V8 was one of the smoothest engines anywhere. V16 sales were therefore low, and 1940 proved the last year for this exotic engine.

One step down from the 90 and 75 was the Series 72, mounted on a 138-inch wheelbase. The 72 would also be making its last appearance that year. It offered slightly fewer models priced between $2670 and $3695. The 72 was an impressive and well-designed automobile, but its market was limited due to competition from the more luxurious 75. Even counting 75s, Cadillac produced only a little over 2500 long-wheelbase models. In later years, when the 75 was mainly a limousine line, production often neared 5000 units per year.

The crisp 60 Special, with its thin door and window pillars and squared-off roofline, was the first direct evidence of young Bill Mitchell's talent. Later, in 1958, Mitchell would relieve the legendary Harley Earl as GM chief of styling; his rise to prominence is due directly to the success of this, his first production design.

The 60 Special came in many varieties for 1940. Both the town sedan and Imperial (division-window sedan) could be ordered with a sunroof; the town car was available with either painted metal or leather-covered rear roof. Only 15 town cars were built, however. The bulk of 60 Special production was the basic sedan, which accounted for 4472 units.

Least expensive of the 1940 Cadillacs was the 62, which came as a coupe, convertible, and convertible sedan or touring sedan, ranging in price from $1685 up to $2195. Mounted on a 129-inch wheelbase, the 62 accounted for the bulk of Cadillac sales, and was chiefly responsible for the division's success in 1940, as in later years. It was cleanly styled, lushly upholstered, and offered a broad variety of body styles designed to appeal to every buyer.

All Cadillacs except the Series 90 shared the 346-cid, 90-degree L-head V8 first seen in 1936. Using a unit block and cast-iron crankcase, it featured three main bearings with counterweights and dual downdraft carburetors. The 346 was heavy, but reliable and exceptionally smooth-running. It developed 135 horsepower for the 62 and 60 Special, and was tuned for 140 bhp on the 72 and 75.

The Cadillac V16 was also an L-head, but built on a narrow 135-degree angle. With 431 cid it delivered 185 bhp. Like the V8, it was made of cast iron and had dual carburetors. But it featured nine main bearings, and separate manifolding for each cylinder block. Each bank of cylinders also had its own water pump and distributor. It was a big, impressive engine, typical of motoring's classic age—but its best days were long past. Cadillac had not produced more than 300 V16s a year since 1931. After 1940, the V16 became dispensible.

A significant and attractive model change occurred for 1941. Cadillac's companion make, LaSalle, was replaced by the relatively low-priced Series 61. This was a marketing decision based on the success of Packard's contemporary One Ten/One Twenty and the Lincoln-Zephyr—but the 61 was every inch a Cadillac, and only moderately underpriced compared to the 62. Packard continued to build medium-priced models long after World War II, while Cadillac (and Lincoln) kept its cars

1941 Series 62 convertible sedan

# Cadillac

1941 Series 62 convertible coupe

strictly in the luxury bracket. As a result, Packard's reputation as fine-car builder diminished in the '40s, and disappeared entirely in the '50s.

The 1941 models wore a fresh face—a complex egg-crate grille with the central section most prominent. This remained a Cadillac styling tradition into the 1970s. Taillights were also made more prominent, and one of them concealed the gas filler cap—another long-running feature. All '41s used the 346 V8, rated at 150 bhp. The departure of the V16 and Series 72 allowed the division to reduce the number of chassis, and only three wheelbases were used. The 75 rode a 136-inch wheelbase, the 67 a 138, and all other models a 126. Three

axle ratios were offered: the 3.77 and 4.27 were standard, while the 3.36 was for Hydra-Matic on the short-wheelbase models. Higher compression and more horsepower meant that most '41 Cadillacs could achieve a genuine 100 mph. Their 0–60 mph acceleration times averaged around 14 seconds—impressive performance 40 years ago.

The formula of V8s only and a broad price span helped Cadillac reach all-time record production for calendar 1941—66,130 units. This was only 6700 units short of Packard, which was selling a much higher proportion of lower-priced models. Much of the increase, of course, was due to the new 61. But the 62 line was also up dramatically—and Cadillac had added a Series 63 four-door that accounted for another 5000 sales. The outstanding 60 Special scored a healthy 4100 units, even though it was offered only as a sedan or division-window town car.

The 1942 lineup was similar in specification but had a brand-new look. Long pontoon fenders appeared, running back into the front doors. Matching rear fenders were blended into the rear doors on four-door models. Fastback styling, which had appeared on the 1941 Series 61, was now extended to the 62. Before production was curtailed by the war, Cadillac built 16,511 cars. In February 1942, the firm converted to war work and made tanks, aircraft engines, and munitions until V-J Day.

1942 Series 63 four-door sedan

1946 Series 62 four-door sedan

1942 Series 60 Special four-door sedan

1947 Series 62 convertible

Resuming civilian operations took several months after the war ended. The division managed to build only 1000 Series 61 sedans before the end of that year. In all, just 31,944 of the 1946 models were made. These were only slightly changed in appearance from the 1942 versions, but model offerings were greatly reduced. The 63 and 67 series were eliminated, along with the division-window 60 Special. What remained were the fastback 61s, fastback or notchback 62s, 60 Special, and the 75. Hydra-Matic transmission had become optional in 1941. It remained optional through 1949 on all models.

For one more year, Cadillac continued to rely on its prewar styling, so the '47s were quite similar to the '46s. The main visual differences were round instead of rectangular parking lights, and script instead of block-letter fender nameplates. The 60 Special lacked the previous model's three vertical chrome louvers behind the rear side window; the 1947 Series 75 omitted the stainless-steel-trimmed running boards formerly used. Prices were $150 to $200 higher than in '46, mainly due to postwar inflation. Production had now regained its prewar stride, and nearly 60,000 units were built for the calendar year. In model year totals, the 62 carried most of the volume, with just under 40,000 units.

Then came 1948—the year of the tailfin. Cadillac designers Bill Mitchell, Harley Earl, Frank Hershey, and Art Ross had been inspired before the war by the then-secret P-38 Lockheed Lightning pursuit fighter. During the war, a skeleton crew played with ideas for postwar styling that would incorporate the plane's features—pontoon front fenders, pointed noses, cockpit-like curved windshields, and tailfins.

Besides Cadillac's tailfin, the P-38 influence would be seen at other GM divisions. Oldsmobile, for example, adopted an engine-scoop motif for the headlamp bezels of its "Futuramic" 1949 models. But the fin had the most lasting impact on Cadillac styling. Said Bill Mitchell: "From a design standpoint the fins gave definition to the rear of the car for the first time. They made the back end as interesting as the front, and established a longstanding Cadillac styling hallmark."

On the 1948 Cadillac, the tailfin was the finishing touch on a magnificent overall design package. At the front, the traditional grille shape was retained, made more aggressive by a larger eggcrate pattern and a more shapely hood. The lines of the roof and fenders were clean, curvaceous, and beautiful from every angle. Attention was given to the interior as well: the 1948 dashboard was dominated by a huge, ornate drum-type housing for the speedometer, minor gauges, and controls. This lasted only a year, because it was complicated and costly to produce. For 1949, it was replaced by a simplified dash duplicating the grille shape, a design followed closely for the next eight years.

Cadillac stayed with the '47 model and body style lineup for 1948, but there was a new addition the next year: the Coupe deVille. A $3497 entry in the 62 series, it joined Oldsmobile's Holiday and Buick's Riviera as

1948 Series 62 convertible

1948 Series 62 club coupe (sedanet)

1948 Fleetwood Series 60 Special four-door sedan (prototype)

1948 Fleetwood Series 75 seven-passenger imperial sedan

the first production hardtops. Cadillac sold 2150 of them in 1949—a higher percentage of production than either Holiday or Riviera. The idea was to combine the airiness of a convertible with the snugness of a closed car—and it succeeded admirably. It started a trend that, by the late '50s, would dominate industry body styles. (There was also one 60 Special Coupe deVille built on the 133-inch wheelbase strictly as an experimental model.)

Following Cadillac's styling revolution of 1948, the

1949 Series 6I club coupe (sedanet)

1949 Series 62 convertible

1949 Series 62 Coupe deVille hardtop coupe

1950 Series 6I four-door sedan

1950 Fleetwood Series 60 Special four-door sedan

exciting overhead-valve V8 of 1949 was the second punch in a potent one-two combination delivered directly to Packard, Lincoln, and Chrysler Imperial. Designed by Ed Cole, Jack Gordon, and Harry Barr, it was the product of ten years' concentrated research and experimentation. The goals had been to reduce weight and increase compression to take advantage of the higher-octane fuels promised after the war. This dictated the valve arrangement, a stroke shorter than the bore, wedge-shaped combustion chambers, and "slipper" pistons. The latter, developed by Byron Ellis, traveled low between the crankshaft counterweights, allowing for short connecting rods and low reciprocating weight.

The new V8 displaced 331 cid and developed 160 bhp. Although this was a mere 10 percent numerical increase over the old L-head engine, there were other factors in the ohv's favor. Though built of cast iron, it weighed nearly 200 pounds less than its predecessor. Compression ratio was just 7.5:1, yet it was capable of being pushed to as high as 12:1 should the fuel become available. It produced more torque and delivered 14 percent better fuel economy. It was durable and reliable. And it could be bored and stroked to much larger displacements. The relatively light 62 model with this powerplant could clock 0–60 mph times of around 13 seconds and easily top 100 mph.

Driven by Sam and Miles Collier, a 1950 Cadillac finished 10th overall at Le Mans—a performance unmatched by any other luxury make. Its speed down the Mulsanne Straight was around 120 mph; average speed was 81.5 mph. Briggs Cunningham also raced a Cadillac at Le Mans that year—a streamlined special. He was even faster than the Colliers, but lost top gear and slid in some corners, resulting in an 11th-place finish.

Another enthusiastic Cadillac booster was Edward Gaylord of Chicago, amateur racer, later co-designer of the Gaylord automobile. "I owned one of the 1950 61s with stickshift and 3.77 rear axle ratio," Gaylord said, "along with a new Jaguar XK-120. The Cadillac was the faster car up to about 90 mph. My Cadillac set what was then a stock-car record at the original quarter-mile drag races in Santa Ana, California . . . The only competition I had in acceleration was from the small 135-horsepower Olds 88 coupe, but the Cadillac engine was substantially more efficient both in performance and economy."

The best styling in the industry and the new V8 put Cadillac firmly atop the luxury-car field. So well did the V8 meet its needs that Cadillac retained the 331-cid size through 1955. But the V8 gained over 100 horsepower in the 1949-55 period—ultimately reaching 270 bhp in the '55 Eldorado.

The good styling didn't last. The most unfortunate aspect to '50s Cadillacs was the gradual decline from smooth design to chrome-laden glitter. The trend peaked in 1958-59; a return to more conservative architecture began in the 1960s. But the Earl/Mitch-

1951 Series 62 Coupe deVille hardtop coupe

1952 Series 62 convertible

1951 Series 62 convertible

1952 Series 62 four-door sedan

1951 Fleetwood Series 60 Special four-door sedan

1953 Series 62 convertible

ell/Hershey/Ross styling of 1948 was so good that not much facelifting was needed to keep it fresh. As Mitchell said, "a traditional look is always preserved. If a grille is changed, the tail end is left alone; if a fin is changed, the grille is not monkeyed with."

Through 1953, styling changes were fairly minor: a new grille and a one-piece windshield in 1950, small auxiliary grilles under the headlamps in 1951, a winged badge in that spot for 1952, "Dagmar" bumpers and a one-piece rear window in 1953.

The model lineup didn't change much either. The 62 series, accounting for most sales, comprised a four-door sedan, coupe, Coupe deVille (hardtop) and convertible; the 60 Special was a sedan with its own 130-inch wheelbase (down from 133 in 1949); the 75 limousine and sedan rode a wheelbase of 146.8 inches. The latter were updated for the first time in 1950; during 1948-49 the smaller Cadillacs had new styling, but the

75 retained prewar lines. Low production precluded early amortization of the prewar dies.

The Cadillac 61, on a short 122-inch wheelbase, was available in 1950-51 in sedan or sedanet (coupe) form. Manual shift was standard and the 61 was priced $575 less than the 62. But by 1952, the division no longer needed a price leader—sales of the "standard" model 62 were more than adequate. The 61 was accordingly dropped, never to appear again.

A feature at General Motors in 1953 was the ultra-expensive, Motorama-inspired limited edition: Buick's Skylark, Oldsmobile's Fiesta, and Cadillac's Eldorado. Only 532 of the latter were built, largely because each one sold for a towering $7750. Like Buick's Skylark, the Eldorado featured a custom interior and special cut-down panoramic windshield. A metal lid covered the top when lowered. It was indeed a striking car, and it prefigured many styling features of the near future.

1953 Fleetwood Series 60 Special four-door sedan

1954 Series 62 convertible

1953 Series 62 Eldorado convertible

1955 Series 62 Eldorado convertible

1954 Fleetwood Series 75 eight-passenger sedan

1955 Series 62 Coupe deVille hardtop coupe

1954 Fleetwood Series 60 Special four-door sedan

1956 Series 62 Sedan deVille hardtop sedan

Model year 1954 saw a major restyle—longer, lower, and wider cars with more power. Wheelbases were lengthened throughout the line, even on the Series 75. Power output on the V8 was up to 230 bhp. Cadillac reduced the price of an Eldorado to $4738 and made more of them—2150 units. Sales doubled for 1956, when the Eldorado line doubled to include the Seville coupe and Biarritz convertible, each priced at $6556. From 1955 onwards, Eldorados were distinctively styled with sharply pointed fins above round taillights. The rest of the line continued to use the small taillight-and-

fin design that had become a Cadillac tradition.

Division sales had topped 100,000 cars for the first time in 1950, and continued to improve through the middle years of the decade. In 1955, Cadillac sold 140,777 units, the highest ever. Even this was only a temporary plateau. Production would break 200,000 in the '60s, and 223,000 by 1969. Despite momentary challenges—a revitalized Imperial in 1957, a crisp new Lincoln Continental in 1961—Cadillac was never really threatened as the standard of the luxury-car world. Neither Lincoln nor Imperial ever built more than 40,000

1956 Series 62 Eldorado Seville hardtop coupe

1956 Series 62 four-door sedan

1957 Series 62 Eldorado Biarritz convertible

1957 Fleetwood Series 60 Special hardtop sedan

1957 Series 62 Eldorado Seville hardtop coupe

1957 Eldorado Brougham hardtop sedan

1957 Fleetwood Series 75 nine-passenger limousine

1958 Fleetwood Series 60 Special hardtop sedan

cars in one year; at Cadillac, that would be considered a good quarterly output.

The line was restyled again for 1957, this time inspired by the Eldorado Brougham and Park Avenue show cars. The production 1957 Eldorado Brougham sold for a princely $13,074. One of Cadillac's most interesting cars, it had descended from the Orleans, Park Avenue, and Brougham showmobiles of 1953-55. It was a pillarless sedan with center-opening doors and a brushed stainless-steel roof—the latter one of Harley Earl's favorite touches. The Brougham also featured

quad headlights—a first for the industry, shared with Nash and Lincoln that year.

Mechanically, the Brougham's most unique feature was its air suspension, designed by engineers Lester Milliken and Fred Dowin. Based on systems used for commercial vehicles since 1952, it employed an air "spring" at each wheel. The spring consisted of a dome air chamber, rubber diaphragm, and pistons. The domes were fed by a central air compressor, and were continually adjusted for load and road conditions by valves and solenoids. These devices kept the

1958 Series 62 Eldorado Seville hardtop coupe

Cadillac's futuristic Cyclone "dream car" from 1959

1959 Eldorado Brougham hardtop sedan (by Pininfarina)

1959 Series 62 hardtop coupe

1959 Series 62 six-window hardtop sedan

1959 Eldorado Biarritz convertible

Brougham level and smoothed its ride. The system differed from those offered optionally by other GM divisions because it was an open arrangement: it took in air from the outside.

But the cost and complexity of air suspension proved too high in relation to its benefits. The air domes leaked, and dealer replacements were frequent. In many Broughams the system was simply rooted out in favor of conventional coil springs. Four years later, air suspension was dropped.

The Brougham itself, after two years of production totaling 704 units, was completely restyled and final assembly farmed out to Pininfarina in Italy. Only 99 were built in 1959, 101 in 1960.

Styling for 1958 was typical of GM that year, and among the most garish ever seen. The cars were big, heavy, laden with brightwork, and far less memorable than, say, the 1953 Eldorado or the Eldorado Brougham. Sales were poor, due probably to the nationwide recession rather than the styling, which was, after all, in vogue. Production, at 121,778 units, was lower than it had been since 1954. The DeVille became a 62 sub-series, pillar sedans were temporarily

eliminated, and the 62 line was expanded by a special four-door with an extended deck.

Cadillac's durable V8, which had been bored out to 365 cid for 1956, was developing 310 bhp by 1958. All models that year were available with cruise control, high-pressure cooling system, two-speaker radio with automatic signal-seeking, and automatic parking brake release. There was even a special show Eldorado with a "thinking" convertible top that raised itself and the side windows when a sensor spotted raindrops.

The restyling for 1959 resulted in tailfins of near-ridiculous proportions, but there were some suspension improvements, a new 390-cid engine, and better power steering. The lineup included convertibles, hardtop two-doors, and four- and six-window hardtop sedans. This was the last year for the old 75 chassis, which was updated in 1960. Prices were generally higher than before, with 62s at around $5000 and Eldorados going for $7400 and up. But Cadillac built 138,000 cars for calender 1959, a fair improvement on its 1958 showing.

The line was facelifted for 1960, with a more restrained look than the chrome-laden '59. The grille was

1960 Fleetwood Series 60 Special hardtop sedan

1960 Eldorado Brougham hardtop sedan (by Pininfarina)

1961 Fleetwood Series 60 Special hardtop sedan

1961 Series 62 hardtop coupe

1962 six-window Sedan deVille hardtop sedan

1963 four-window Sedan deVille hardtop sedan

cleaner and the tailfins were reduced in height. A carry-over feature was a choice of rooflines on hardtop sedans in the 62 and DeVille series. Prices throughout the line were not changed from the year before. Nor were there any changes in mechanical specifications. The standard horsepower rating was still 325; the Eldorado offered 345. Cadillac had dropped to 10th place in production in 1958, but stayed 10th again in 1960. It would continue to hold 10th place—an impressive position for a luxury make—until 1965. Model year 1960 was the last for the limited-edition Eldorado Brougham. Management was already working on a successor that would sell in higher numbers and would, therefore, be more profitable.

In 1961, styling began showing the influence of William Mitchell, who favored a more chiseled look than Harley Earl and was not terribly enamored of chrome. The '61s were cleaner than any Cadillac had been in years. The grille was reduced in size to a modest grid between the headlights. The wraparound windshield was abandoned (except for the Series 75), yet Mitchell contrived to improve visibility. The model range also thinned: the Eldorado Seville was dropped along with the Brougham. The sole remaining Eldorado was the Biarritz convertible, but the '61 edition used the standard 325-bhp engine.

At General Motors, the early '60s was a period of little styling change: the corporation had found what it wanted and was holding on to it. Predictably, Cadillac changed little for '62. Tailfins were lowered, and cornering lights were added to the front fender. Detail trim changes included a slightly flashier grille and a thin bright metal molding low on the bodysides. The roofline was squared off on some models; backup, turn, and stop lights were combined in panels that showed white in the daylight. New models were the 62 Town Sedan and the DeVille Park Avenue, a pair of short-deck four-door hardtops. The engine remained unchanged, but a new dual braking system appeared with separate front and rear hydraulic lines. Cadillac produced about 160,000 cars, some 23,000 more than the previous year.

The long-running V8 was revised for 1963 for the first time in 14 years. Displacement, bore, and stroke were unchanged, as were valves, rocker arms, cylinder heads, and connecting rods. But everything else was

different. The new block was stiffer, but 50 pounds lighter, than its predecessor. There was a lighter, stronger crankshaft. Accessory mounting points were relocated for improved accessibility. The reworked engine added little to Cadillac's already top-class performance, but it was smoother and quieter by far. And performance was already of a high order. The 1963 models would reach 115–120 mph, do 0 to 60 mph in 10 seconds and 0 to 80 mph in 16 seconds, and return about 14 miles per gallon. Most impressive was their near-silence at high speed—many testers held them superior to Rolls-Royce in this respect.

The 1963 model was, generally, a departure from recent styling traditions. The fins were still there, but lower than ever; a bulkier full-width grille contained parking lights built into grille extensions under the headlamps. New body panels and side moldings created a more slab-sided look than past models. The rear end was more massive, with elongated vertical taillight and backup light housings.

Prices rose only slightly in 1963, and Cadillac remained an excellent buy for the money. Standard equipment included Hydra-Matic, power steering, power brakes, heater, remote-control outside mirror, and backup lights. A six-way power seat became standard on Eldorado; power windows were standard on all models except 62 sedans and coupes. Even power vent windows were offered. The specifications included self-adjusting brakes, cornering lights, and turn signal indicators atop the front fenders. Remarkably, the 62 still cost as little as $5026. Even the Eldorado Biarritz was only $6608. Production topped 164,000 in calendar 1963.

Revisions were minor for '64. New, lower tailfins—the last true Cadillac fins—created an unbroken beltline, accentuating length. There was a body-color horizontal

1964 Fleetwood Eldorado Biarritz convertible

1965 Calais hardtop coupe

1964 Series 62 hardtop coupe

1965 Fleetwood Eldorado convertible

1964 Fleetwood Series 75 nine-passenger limousine

1965 Sedan deVille hardtop sedan

grille divider bar, and new taillamp housings with the usual assortment of red and white lights. Cadillac's new Comfort-Control heating/air-conditioning system maintained a set temperature regardless of outside conditions. It has been on the Cadillac options sheet ever since. Sales were around 165,000, slightly higher than 1963 and still good for 10th place in the industry.

Cadillac had a resounding year in 1965, producing close to 200,000 cars. But it was a banner year for the rest of the industry too, and even this output was only good for 11th place. The Series 62, which had been around since 1940, was finally put to rest; its place was taken by the Calais. DeVille, Eldorado, 60 Special, and 75 were continued. The last three comprised the Fleetwood series. Each bore Fleetwood nameplates, a wreath-and-crest medallion, broad bright rocker panel and rear quarter moldings, and rectangular pattern rear appliqués. A new Fleetwood Brougham offered a vinyl

1966 Fleetwood Seventy-Five limousine

1966 Coupe deVille hardtop coupe

1966 Fleetwood Brougham four-door sedan

roof with "Brougham" script on the rear roof pillars.

The major styling change for 1965 was a longer, lower silhouette and the disappearance of tailfins. The 60 Special regained its customary 133-inch wheelbase, after using the standard 129.5-inch-wheelbase chassis from 1959. Rear styling consisted of a straight bumper and vertical lamp clusters. There was a new flush-top contour on the rear quarter panels, and curved-glass side windows. Horsepower was now up to 340 bhp, giving Cadillac the highest power-to-weight ratio in the industry. On all models except the 75 there was dual driving range Turbo Hydra-Matic and a perimeter-type frame. All Cadillacs featured a sonically balanced exhaust system. Prices were still remarkably stable. They'd risen only a few dollars since 1961.

In 1966, Cadillac had its first 200,000-car year. For the January–December period, 205,001 were assembled. The 1966 was a mild facelift of the '65 design, with new front bumper, new grille, and integrated vertical taillight housings. The perimeter frame was now adopted for the 75, which was fully restyled for the first time since 1959. Variable-ratio power steering, which provided maximum assist at low speed and minimum at cruising speed, was introduced for all models. Another new option was carbon-cloth seat heating pads. The Fleetwood Brougham moved up one step by adopting the 133-inch 60 Special wheelbase; it was more luxuriously trimmed, and priced about $320 higher.

Management changes occurred rapidly in 1965-66. Chief engineer Fred Arnold retired in 1965, after a long and rich career, succeeded by Carleton A. Rasmussen. The following year saw general manager Harold G. Warner retire in favor of Kenneth N. Scott. Scott was replaced six months later by Calvin J. Werner, who remained general manager until 1969. In July of that year, he was relieved by George R. Elges.

The new front-wheel-drive Eldorado of 1967 was the most significant single Cadillac model of the '60s. Based on the Oldsmobile Toronado, which had appeared the year before, it was a new concept in the luxury field. Front drive gave it outstanding roadability; Bill Mitchell gave it magnificent styling. In market orientation, it was the long-awaited replacement for the 1957-60 Eldorado Brougham. Six years of careful planning and research were behind it.

The Eldorado project began with a 1959 styling exercise code-named XP-727, which underwent several rethinks during 1960-62. By early 1962, it was decided that front-wheel drive would be used, and prototypes developed with that consideration in mind. For awhile, Cadillac considered calling the new car LaSalle, but ultimately picked Eldorado, a more current name with greater public recognition. Clay model XP-825, with razor-edged lines and a formal roofline, was the direct predecessor of the production front-drive Eldorado.

Compared with the Toronado, the new Eldorado's 1967 introduction was, in typical Cadillac fashion, very low-key. Cadillac preferred it that way, and it used the extra lead time to make some improvements on the

Toronado package. The Eldorado rode better than the Toronado, yet it handled at least as well. Its front suspension consisted of torsion bars, A-arms, and telescopic shocks; rear suspension was by semi-elliptic leaf springs with four shock absorbers—two horizontal, two vertical. The chassis featured self-leveling control and radially vented caliper front disc brakes.

On its own relatively compact 120-inch wheelbase, the Eldorado sold for $6277. Cadillac, orchestrating its debut with traditional precision, targeted the car for ten percent of total production, or about 20,000 units. The actual 1967 model year figure was 17,930. Sales held at over 23,000 in 1968, 1969, and 1970. The Eldorado quickly became established as a technological tour de force—the ultimate Cadillac. And, unlike the Eldorado Brougham before it, it made money from the day it appeared.

The remainder of the 1967 line was broken down into the usual Calais, DeVille, and Fleetwood series. Front ends were revised and given a forward-rake grille and fenders. Line-wide features were mylar printed circuits for the instrument panel, automatic level control (standard on all Fleetwoods), cruise control, and tilt steering wheel. Bolstered by the new Eldorado, Cadillac built 213,161 cars for the calendar year.

In 1968, the focus was on the engine again: an all-new 472-cid V8 with 375 bhp. Designed around government emission control requirements, the 472 was extensively proven, running the equivalent of 500,000 miles in laboratory testing. Other mechanical features for '68 were hidden windshield wipers and several new safety devices, most mandated by the government.

Major styling changes for the 1968 Eldorado were a new grille, longer hood, side marker lights, and larger taillights. Other models were also given a longer hood, along with a revised grille and a trunklid designed to in-

1967 Fleetwood Eldorado hardtop coupe

1968 DeVille convertible

1967 Fleetwood Brougham four-door sedan

1968 Hardtop Sedan deVille hardtop sedan

1967 Coupe deVille hardtop coupe

1968 Fleetwood Eldorado hardtop coupe

crease cargo capacity. The new engine was not as economical as the old one, but it was capable of propelling a Coupe deVille from 0 to 100 mph in 27.8 seconds.

In 1969, Cadillac broke back into the top ten producers with a record 266,798 units for the calendar year. It passed both Chrysler and American Motors, moving into ninth place. The Eldorado's front end was revised, its headlights no longer hidden as in 1967-68. The other models were completely restyled, with a new body and squarer roofline. Headlamps were now horizontal instead of vertical. Parking lights wrapped around at the front, the grille was new, and the hood was longer. A somewhat unpopular change was the elimination of front vent windows. Prices ranged from just over $5400 for the Calais to well over $10,000 for the 75 limousine.

Eldorado had a new engine for 1970, and a badge reading "8.2 litres" (500 cubic inches) to prove it. The largest production-car engine in the world, it developed 400 bhp and 550 pounds-feet of torque. Other models retained the 472 V8 with 375 bhp. New mechanical features included integral steering knuckle, bias-ply fiberglass-belted tires, a radio antenna imbedded in the windshield, and more safety features. All Cadillacs now came equipped with energy-absorbing steering column, pushbutton seatbelt buckles, shoulder harnesses, head restraints, hazard flashers, folding front seatback latches, backup lights, side marker lights, and reflectors. Cadillac offered an anti-theft ignition key warning buzzer, and anti-theft steering column/transmission lock with starter switch.

Stylewise, the major changes for 1970 were a new grille with bright vertical accents over a cross-hatch pattern, new horizontal chrome trim on parking lights, winged crests instead of "Vs" on hoods of the DeVille

Eldorado Biarritz Town Coupe show car, 1968

1969 Fleetwood Eldorado hardtop coupe

1969 Fleetwood Brougham four-door sedan

1969 Coupe deVille hardtop coupe

1970 Coupe deVille hardtop coupe

1970 Hardtop Sedan deVille hardtop sedan

and Calais, and new taillamps. The Eldorado grille was narrower and separate from the headlamps, while its taillamps were more slender than in 1969.

Cadillac's performance was disappointing in 1970. Calendar year output dropped over 100,000 units, putting the division back in 11th place behind Chrysler and AMC. Still, Cadillac had out-produced Lincoln 3-1 and Imperial 15-1 in a year that had been generally quiet for the industry as a whole. As before, Cadillac reigned supreme as America's number-one luxury car.

# Cadillac Specifications

## 1940

### Series 62 (wb 129.0)

| | | Wght | Price | Prod |
|---|---|---|---|---|
| 6219 | sdn 4d | 4,065 | 1,745 | 4,302 |
| 6227 | cpe 2–4P | 3,975 | 1,685 | 1,322 |
| 6229 | conv sdn | 4,265 | 2,195 | 75 |
| 6267 | conv cpe | 4,080 | 1,795 | 200 |
| 62 | chassis | — | — | 1 |

### Series 60 Special (wb 127.0)

| | | | | |
|---|---|---|---|---|
| 6019F | division sdn | 4,110 | 2,230 | 110 |
| 6019S | sdn 4d. | 4,070 | 2,090 | 4,472 |
| 6053LB | town car-leather back | 4,365 | 3,820 | 6 |
| 6053MB | town car-metal back | 4,365 | 3,465 | 9 |

### Series 72 (wb 138.0)

| | | | | |
|---|---|---|---|---|
| 7219 | sdn 4d | 4,670 | 2,670 | 455 |
| 7219F | division sdn | 4,710 | 2,740 | 100 |
| 7223 | sdn 4d, 7P | 4,700 | 2,785 | 305 |
| 7223L | livery sdn 7P | 4,700 | 2,690 | 25 |
| 7233 | imperial sdn 7P | 4,740 | 2,915 | 292 |
| 7233F | formal sdn 7P | 4,780 | 3,695 | 20 |
| 7233L | livery imp sdn 7P | 4,740 | 2,825 | 36 |
| 7259 | formal sdn | 4,670 | 3,695 | 18 |
| 72 | comm chassis (wb 165.0) | — | — | 275 |

### Series 75 (wb 141.3)

| | | | | |
|---|---|---|---|---|
| 7519 | sdn 4d | 4,900 | 2,995 | 155 |
| 7419F | division sdn | 4,940 | 3,155 | 25 |
| 7523 | sdn 4d, 7P | 4,930 | 3,210 | 166 |
| 7529 | conv sdn 7P, T/B | 5,110 | 3,945 | 45 |
| 7533 | imperial sdn 7P | 4,970 | 3,360 | 338 |
| 7533F | formal sdn 7P | 4,970 | 3,995 | 42 |
| 7539 | town sdn | 4,935 | 3,635 | 14 |
| 7553 | town car 7P | 5,195 | 5,115 | 14 |
| 7557 | cpe 2–4P | 4,785 | 3,280 | 15 |
| 7557B | cpe | 4,810 | 3,380 | 12 |
| 7559 | formal sdn, T/B | 4,900 | 3,995 | 48 |
| 7567 | conv cpe | 4,915 | 3,380 | 30 |
| 75 | chassis | — | — | 3 |
| 75 | comm chassis (wb 161.0) | — | — | 52 |

### Sixteen (wb 141.3)

| | | | | |
|---|---|---|---|---|
| 9019 | sdn 4d | 5,190 | 5,140 | 4 |
| 9023 | sdn 4d, 7P | 5,215 | 5,270 | 4 |
| 9029 | conv sdn, T/B | 5,265 | 6,000 | 2 |
| 9033 | imperial sdn 7P | 5,260 | 5,420 | 20 |
| 9033F | formal sdn 7P, T/B | 5,260 | 6,055 | 20 |
| 9039 | town sdn, T/B | 5,220 | 5,695 | 1 |
| 9053 | town car 7P, T/B | 5,330 | 7,175 | 2 |
| 9057 | cpe 2–4P | 4,830 | 5,340 | 2 |
| 9057B | cpe | 4,930 | 5,440 | 1 |
| 9059 | formal sdn, T/B | 5,190 | 6,055 | 2 |
| 9067 | conv cpe 2–4P | 4,970 | 5,440 | 2 |
| 90 | chassis | — | — | 1 |

### 1940 Engines

| 1940 Engines | bore×stroke | bhp | availability |
|---|---|---|---|
| V8, 346.0 | 3.50×4.50 | 135 | S-62, 60S |
| V8, 346.0 | 3.50×4.50 | 140 | S-72, 75 |
| V16, 431.0 | 3.25×3.25 | 185 | S-Sixteen |

## 1941

### Series 61 (wb 126.0)

| | | Wght | Price | Prod |
|---|---|---|---|---|
| 6109 | sdn 4d | 4,065 | 1,445 | 10,925 |
| 6109D | del sdn 4d | 4,085 | 1,535 | 3,495 |
| 6127 | cpe | 3,985 | 1,345 | 11,812 |
| 6127D | del cpe | 4,005 | 1,435 | 3,015 |
| 61 | chassis | — | — | 3 |

### Series 62 (wb 126.0)

| | | | | |
|---|---|---|---|---|
| 6219 | sdn 4d | 4,030 | 1,495 | 8,012 |
| 6219D | del sdn 4d | 4,050 | 1,585 | 7,850 |
| 6227 | cpe 2–4P | 3,950 | 1,420 | 1,985 |
| 6227D | del cpe 2–4P | 3,970 | 1,510 | 1,900 |
| 6229D | conv sdn | 4,230 | 1,965 | 400 |
| 6267D | conv cpe | 4,055 | 1,645 | 3,100 |
| 62 | chassis | — | — | 4 |
| 62 | comm chassis (wb 163.0) | — | — | 1,475 |

### Series 63 (wb 126.0)

| | | | | |
|---|---|---|---|---|
| 6319 | sdn 4d | 4,140 | 1,695 | 5,050 |

### Series 60 Special (wb 126.0)

| | | | | |
|---|---|---|---|---|
| 6019 | sdn 4d | 4,230 | 2,195 | 3,878 |
| 6019F | division sdn | 4,290 | 2,345 | 220 |
| 6053LB | town car | 4,485 | — | 1 |
| 60 | chassis | — | — | 1 |

### Series 67 (wb 138.0)

| | | | | |
|---|---|---|---|---|
| 6719 | sdn 4d | 4,555 | 2,595 | 315 |
| 6719F | division sdn | 4,615 | 2,745 | 95 |
| 6723 | sdn 4d, 7P | 4,630 | 2,735 | 280 |
| 6733 | imperial sdn 7P | 4,705 | 2,890 | 210 |

### Series 75 (wb 136.0)

| | | | | |
|---|---|---|---|---|
| 7519 | sdn 4d | 4,750 | 2,995 | 422 |
| 7519F | division sdn | 4,810 | 3,150 | 132 |
| 7523 | sdn 4d, 7P | 4,800 | 3,140 | 405 |
| 7523L | business sdn 9P | 4,750 | 2,895 | 54 |
| 7533 | imperial sdn 7P | 4,860 | 3,295 | 757 |
| 7533F | formal sdn 7P | 4,915 | 4,045 | 98 |
| 7533L | business imperial sdn 7P | 4,810 | 3,050 | 6 |
| 7559 | formal sdn | 4,900 | 3,920 | 75 |
| 75 | chassis | — | — | 5 |
| 75 | comm chassis (wb 163.0) | — | — | 150 |

### 1941 Engine

| 1941 Engine | bore×stroke | bhp | availability |
|---|---|---|---|
| V8, 346.0 | 3.50×4.50 | 150 | S-all |

## 1942

| Series 61 (wb 126.0) | | Wght | Price | Prod |
|---|---|---|---|---|
| 6107 | club cpe | 4,035 | 1,450 | 2,482 |
| 6109 | sdn 4d | 4,115 | 1,530 | 3,218 |

| Series 62 (wb 129.0) | | | | |
|---|---|---|---|---|
| 6207 | club cpe | 4,105 | 1,545 | 515 |
| 6207D | club cpe | 4,125 | 1,630 | 530 |
| 6267D | conv cpe | 4,365 | 1,880 | 308 |
| 6269 | sdn 4d | 4,185 | 1,630 | 1,780 |
| 6269D | sdn 4d | 4,205 | 1,705 | 1,827 |

| Series 63 (wb 126.0) | | | | |
|---|---|---|---|---|
| 6319 | sdn 4d | 4,115 | 1,745 | 1,750 |

| Series 60 Special (wb 133.0) | | | | |
|---|---|---|---|---|
| 6069 | sdn 4d | 4,310 | 2,265 | 1,684 |
| 6069L | division sdn | 4,365 | 2,415 | 190 |
| 60 | chassis | — | — | 1 |

| Series 67 (wb 138.0) | | | | |
|---|---|---|---|---|
| 6719 | sdn 4d | 4,605 | 2,700 | 200 |
| 6719F | division sdn | 4,665 | 2,845 | 50 |
| 6723 | sdn 7P | 4,680 | 2,845 | 260 |
| 6733 | imperial sdn 7P | 4,755 | 2,995 | 190 |

| Series 75 (wb 136.0) | | | | |
|---|---|---|---|---|
| 7519 | sdn 4d | 4,750 | 3,080 | 205 |
| 7519F | division sdn | 4,810 | 3,230 | 65 |
| 7523 | sdn 4d, 7P | 4,800 | 3,230 | 225 |
| 7523L | business sdn 9P | 4,750 | 2,935 | 29 |
| 7533 | imperial sdn 7P | 4,860 | 3,375 | 430 |
| 7533F | formal sdn 7P | 4,915 | 4,215 | 80 |
| 7533L | business imperial sdn 9P | 4,860 | 3,080 | 6 |
| 7559 | formal sdn | 4,900 | 4,060 | 60 |
| 75 | chassis | — | — | 1 |
| 75 | comm chassis (wb 163.0) | — | — | 425 |

| 1942 Engine | bore×stroke | bhp | availability | |
|---|---|---|---|---|
| V8, 346.0 | 3.50×4.50 | 150 | S-all | |

## 1946

| Series 61 (wb 126.0) | | Wght | Price | Prod |
|---|---|---|---|---|
| 6107 | club cpe | 4,145 | 2,052 | 800 |
| 6109 | sdn 4d | 4,225 | 2,176 | 2,200 |
| 61 | chassis | — | — | 1 |

| Series 62 (wb 129.0) | | | | |
|---|---|---|---|---|
| 6207 | club cpe | 4,215 | 2,284 | 2,323 |
| 6267D | conv cpe | 4,475 | 2,556 | 1,342 |
| 6269 | sdn 4d | 4,295 | 2,359 | 14,900 |
| 62 | chassis | — | — | 1 |

| Series 60 Special (wb 133.0) | | | | |
|---|---|---|---|---|
| 6069 | sdn 4d | 4,420 | 3,095 | 5,700 |

| Series 75 (wb 136.0) | | | | |
|---|---|---|---|---|
| 7519 | sdn 4d | 4,860 | 4,298 | 150 |
| 7523 | sdn 4d, 7P | 4,905 | 4,475 | 225 |
| 7523L | business sdn 9P | 4,920 | 4,153 | 22 |
| 7533 | imperial sdn 7P | 4,925 | 4,669 | 221 |
| 7533L | business imperial sdn 9P | 4,925 | 4,346 | 17 |
| 75 | comm chassis (wb 163.0) | — | — | 1,292 |

| 1946 Engine | bore×stroke | bhp | availability | |
|---|---|---|---|---|
| V8, 346.0 | 3.50×4.50 | 150 | S-all | |

## 1947

| Series 61 (wb 126.0) | | Wght | Price | Prod |
|---|---|---|---|---|
| 6107 | club cpe | 4,080 | 2,200 | 3,395 |
| 6109 | sdn 4d | 4,165 | 2,324 | 5,160 |

| Series 62 (wb 129.0) | | | | |
|---|---|---|---|---|
| 6207 | club cpe | 4,145 | 2,446 | 7,245 |
| 6267 | conv cpe | 4,455 | 2,902 | 6,755 |
| 6269 | sdn 4d | 4,235 | 2,523 | 25,834 |
| 62 | chassis | — | — | 1 |

| Series 60 Special (wb 133.0) | | | | |
|---|---|---|---|---|
| 6069 | sdn 4d | 4,370 | 3,195 | 8,500 |

| Series 75 (wb 136.0) | | | | |
|---|---|---|---|---|
| 7519 | sdn 4d | 4,875 | 4,471 | 300 |
| 7523 | sdn 4d, 7P | 4,895 | 4,686 | 890 |
| 7523L | business sdn 9P | 4,790 | 4,368 | 135 |
| 7533 | imperial sdn 7P | 4,930 | 4,887 | 1,005 |
| 7533L | business imperial sdn 9P | 4,800 | 4,560 | 80 |
| 75 | chassis | — | — | 3 |
| 75 | comm & bus chassis (wb 163.0) | — | — | 2,623 |

| 1947 Engine | bore×stroke | bhp | availability | |
|---|---|---|---|---|
| V8, 346.0 | 3.50×4.50 | 150 | S-all | |

## 1948

| Series 61 (wb 126.0) | | Wght | Price | Prod |
|---|---|---|---|---|
| 6107 | club cpe | 4,068 | 2,728 | 3,521 |
| 6169 | sdn 4d | 4,150 | 2,833 | 5,081 |
| 61 | chassis | — | — | 1 |

| Series 62 (wb 126.0) | | | | |
|---|---|---|---|---|
| 6207 | club cpe | 4,125 | 2,912 | 4,764 |
| 6267 | conv cpe | 4,449 | 3,442 | 5,450 |
| 6259 | sdn 4d | 4,179 | 2,996 | 23,997 |
| 62 | chassis | — | — | 2 |

| Series 60 Special (wb 133.0) | | | | |
|---|---|---|---|---|
| 6069 | sdn 4d | 4,356 | 3,820 | 6,561 |

| Series 75 (wb 136.0) | | | | |
|---|---|---|---|---|
| 7519 | sdn 4d | 4,875 | 4,779 | 225 |
| 7523 | sdn 4d, 7P | 4,878 | 4,999 | 499 |
| 7523L | business sdn 9P | 4,780 | 4,679 | 90 |
| 7533 | imperial sdn 7P | 4,959 | 5,199 | 382 |
| 7533L | bus imperial sdn 9P | — | — | 64 |
| 75 | chassis | — | — | 2 |
| 75 | comm chassis (wb 163.0) | — | — | 2,067 |

| 1948 Engine | bore×stroke | bhp | availability | |
|---|---|---|---|---|
| V8, 346.0 | 3.50×4.50 | 150 | S-all | |

## 1949

| Series 61 (wb 126.0) | | Wght | Price | Prod |
|---|---|---|---|---|
| 6107 | club cpe | 3,838 | 2,788 | 6,409 |
| 6169 | sdn 4d | 3,915 | 2,893 | 15,738 |
| 61 | chassis | — | — | 1 |

| Series 62 (wb 126.0) | | | | |
|---|---|---|---|---|
| 6207 | club cpe | 3,862 | 2,966 | 7,515 |
| 6237 | Coupe de Ville htp cpe | 4,033 | 3,497 | 2,150 |
| 6267 | conv cpe | 4,218 | 3,442 | 8,000 |
| 6269 | sdn 4d | 3,956 | 3,050 | 37,977 |
| 62 | chassis | — | — | 1 |

| Series 60 Special (wb 133.0) | | | | |
|---|---|---|---|---|
| 6037 | Coupe de Ville htp cpe | 4,200 | exp | 1 |
| 6069 | sdn 4d | 4,129 | 3,828 | 11,399 |

# Cadillac

## Series 75 (wb 136.0)

| | | Wght | Price | Prod |
|---|---|---|---|---|
| 7519 | sdn 4d | 4,579 | 4,750 | 220 |
| 7523 | sdn 4d, 7P | 4,626 | 4,970 | 595 |
| 7523L | business sdn 9P | 4,522 | 4,650 | 35 |
| 7533 | imperial sdn 7P | 4,648 | 5,170 | 626 |
| 7533L | business imperial sdn 9P | 4,573 | 4,839 | 25 |
| 75 | chassis | — | — | 1 |
| 86 | comm chassis (wb 163.0) | — | — | 1,861 |

| 1949 Engine | bore×stroke | bhp | availability | |
|---|---|---|---|---|
| V8, 331.0 | 3.81×3.63 | 160 | S-all | |

## 1950

### Series 61 (wb 122.0)

| | | Wght | Price | Prod |
|---|---|---|---|---|
| 6137 | club cpe | 3,829 | 2,761 | 11,839 |
| 6169 | sdn 4d | 3,822 | 2,866 | 14,931 |
| 61 | chassis | — | — | 2 |

### Series 62 (wb 126.0)

| | | Wght | Price | Prod |
|---|---|---|---|---|
| 6219 | sdn 4d | 4,012 | 3,234 | 41,890 |
| 6237 | club cpe | 3,993 | 3,150 | 6,434 |
| 6237D | Coupe de Ville htp cpe | 4,074 | 3,523 | 4,507 |
| 6267 | conv cpe | 4,316 | 3,654 | 6,986 |
| 62 | chassis | — | — | 1 |

### Series 60 Special (wb 130.0)

| | | Wght | Price | Prod |
|---|---|---|---|---|
| 6019 | sdn 4d | 4,136 | 3,797 | 13,755 |

### Series 75 (wb 146.8)

| | | Wght | Price | Prod |
|---|---|---|---|---|
| 7523 | sdn 4d, 7P | 4,555 | 4,770 | 716 |
| 7523L | business sdn 9P | 4,235 | exp | 1 |
| 7533 | imperial sdn 7P | 4,586 | 4,959 | 743 |
| 86 | comm chassis (wb 157.0) | — | — | 2,052 |

| 1950 Engine | bore×stroke | bhp | availability | |
|---|---|---|---|---|
| V8, 331.0 | 3.81×3.63 | 160 | S-all | |

## 1951

### Series 61 (wb 122.0)

| | | Wght | Price | Prod |
|---|---|---|---|---|
| 6137 | club cpe | 3,829 | 2,810 | 2,400 |
| 6169 | sdn 4d | 3,827 | 2,917 | 2,300 |

### Series 62 (wb 126.0)

| | | Wght | Price | Prod |
|---|---|---|---|---|
| 6219 | sdn 4d | 4,062 | 3,528 | 55,352 |
| 6237 | cpe | 4,081 | 3,436 | 10,132 |
| 6237D | Coupe De Ville htp cpe | 4,156 | 3,843 | 10,241 |
| 6267 | conv cpe | 4,377 | 3,987 | 6,117 |
| 62-126 | chassis | — | — | 2 |

### Series 60 Special (wb 130.0)

| | | Wght | Price | Prod |
|---|---|---|---|---|
| 6019 | sdn 4d | 4,234 | 4,142 | 18,631 |

### Series 75 (wb 146.8)

| | | Wght | Price | Prod |
|---|---|---|---|---|
| 7523 | sdn 4d, 8P | 4,621 | 5,200 | 1,090 |
| 7523L | business sdn 9P | 4,300 | exp | 30 |
| 7533 | imperial sdn 8P | 4,652 | 5,405 | 1,085 |
| 86 | comm chassis (wb 157.0) | — | — | 2,960 |

| 1951 Engine | bore×stroke | bhp | availability | |
|---|---|---|---|---|
| V8, 331.0 | 3.81×3.63 | 160 | S-all | |

## 1952

### Series 62 (wb 126.0)

| | | Wght | Price | Prod |
|---|---|---|---|---|
| 6219 | sdn 4d | 4,140 | 3,684 | 42,625 |
| 6237 | cpe | 4,173 | 3,587 | 10,065 |

| | | Wght | Price | Prod |
|---|---|---|---|---|
| 6237D | Coupe de Ville htp cpe | 4,203 | 4,013 | 11,165 |
| 6267 | conv cpe | 4,416 | 4,163 | 6,400 |

### Series 60 Special (wb 130.0)

| | | Wght | Price | Prod |
|---|---|---|---|---|
| 6019 | sdn 4d | 4,255 | 4,323 | 16,110 |

### Series 75 (wb 146.8)

| | | Wght | Price | Prod |
|---|---|---|---|---|
| 7523 | sdn 4d, 8P | 4,698 | 5,428 | 1,400 |
| 7533 | imperial sdn 8P | 4,733 | 5,643 | 800 |
| 8680S | comm chassis (wb 157.0) | — | — | 1,694 |

| 1952 Engine | bore×stroke | bhp | availability | |
|---|---|---|---|---|
| V8, 331.0 | 3.81×3.63 | 190 | S-all | |

## 1953

### Series 62 (wb 126.0)

| | | Wght | Price | Prod |
|---|---|---|---|---|
| 6219 | sdn 4d | 4,225 | 3,666 | 47,640 |
| 6237 | cpe | 4,320 | 3,571 | 14,353 |
| 6237D | Coupe de Ville htp cpe | 4,320 | 3,995 | 14,550 |
| 6267 | conv cpe | 4,500 | 4,144 | 8,367 |
| 6267S | Eldorado conv cpe | 4,800 | 7,750 | 532 |
| 62 | chassis | — | — | 4 |

### Series 60 Special (wb 130.0)

| | | Wght | Price | Prod |
|---|---|---|---|---|
| 6019 | sdn 4d | 4,415 | 4,305 | 20,000 |

### Series 75 (wb 146.8)

| | | Wght | Price | Prod |
|---|---|---|---|---|
| 7523 | sdn 4d, 8P | 4,830 | 5,408 | 1,435 |
| 7533 | imperial sdn 8P | 4,850 | 5,621 | 765 |
| 8680S | comm chassis (wb 157.0) | — | — | 2,005 |

| 1953 Engine | bore×stroke | bhp | availability | |
|---|---|---|---|---|
| V8, 331.0 | 3.81×3.63 | 210 | S-all | |

## 1954

### Series 62 (wb 129.0)

| | | Wght | Price | Prod |
|---|---|---|---|---|
| 6219 | sdn 4d | 4,370 | 3,933 | 34,252 |
| 6219S | DeVille htp sdn | — | proto | 1 |
| 6237 | htp cpe | 4,365 | 3,838 | 17,460 |
| 6237D | Coupe de Ville htp cpe | 4,405 | 4,261 | 17,170 |
| 6267 | conv cpe | 4,610 | 4,404 | 6,310 |
| 6267S | Eldorado conv cpe | 4,815 | 4,738 | 2,150 |
| 62 | chassis | — | — | 1 |

### Series 60 Special (wb 133.0)

| | | Wght | Price | Prod |
|---|---|---|---|---|
| 6019 | sdn 4d | 4,500 | 4,863 | 16,200 |

### Series 75 (wb 149.8)

| | | Wght | Price | Prod |
|---|---|---|---|---|
| 7523 | sdn 4d, 8P | 5,055 | 5,875 | 889 |
| 7533 | imperial sdn 8P | 5,105 | 6,090 | 611 |
| 8680S | comm chassis (wb 158.0) | — | — | 1,635 |

| 1954 Engine | bore×stroke | bhp | availability | |
|---|---|---|---|---|
| V8, 331.0 | 3.81×3.63 | 230 | S-all | |

## 1955

### Series 62 (wb 129.0)

| | | Wght | Price | Prod |
|---|---|---|---|---|
| 6219 | sdn 4d | 4,370 | 3,977 | 45,300 |
| 6237 | htp cpe | 4,358 | 3,882 | 27,879 |
| 6237D | Coupe de Ville htp cpe | 4,424 | 4,305 | 33,300 |
| 6267 | conv cpe | 4,627 | 4,448 | 8,150 |
| 6267S | Eldorado conv cpe | 4,809 | 6,286 | 3,950 |
| 62 | chassis | — | — | 7 |

| Series 60 Special (wb 133.0) | | Wght | Price | Prod |
|---|---|---|---|---|
| 6019 | sdn 4d | 4,540 | 4,728 | 18,300 |

| Series 75 (wb 149.8) | | | | |
|---|---|---|---|---|
| 7523 | sdn 4d, 8P | 5,020 | 6,187 | 1,075 |
| 7533 | limo 8P | 5,113 | 6,402 | 841 |
| 8680S | comm chassis (wb 158.0) | — | — | 1,975 |

| 1955 Engines | bore×stroke | bhp | availability |
|---|---|---|---|
| V8, 331.0 | 3.81×3.63 | 250 | S-62, 60S, 75 |
| V8, 331.0 | 3.81×3.63 | 270 | S-Eldorado |

## 1956

| Series 62 (wb 129.0) | | Wght | Price | Prod |
|---|---|---|---|---|
| 6219 | sdn 4d | 4,130 | 4,296 | 26,666 |
| 6237 | htp cpe | 4,420 | 4,201 | 26,649 |
| 6237D | Coupe de Ville htp cpe | 4,445 | 4,624 | 24,086 |
| 6237S | Eldorado Seville htp cpe | 4,665 | 6,556 | 3,900 |
| 6239D | Sedan de Ville htp cpe | 4,550 | 4,753 | 41,732 |
| 6267 | conv cpe | 4,645 | 4,766 | 8,300 |
| 6267S | Eldorado Biarritz conv cpe | 4,880 | 6,556 | 2,150 |
| 62 | chassis | — | — | 19 |

| Series 60 Special (wb 133.0) | | | | |
|---|---|---|---|---|
| 6019 | sdn 4d | 4,610 | 5,047 | 17,000 |

| Series 75 (wb 149.8) | | | | |
|---|---|---|---|---|
| 7523 | sdn 4d, 8P | 5,050 | 6,613 | 1,095 |
| 7533 | limo 8P | 5,130 | 6,828 | 955 |
| 8680S | comm chassis (wb 158.0) | — | — | 2,025 |

| 1956 Engines | bore×stroke | bhp | availability |
|---|---|---|---|
| V8, 365.0 | 4.00×3.63 | 285 | S-62, 60S, 75 |
| V8, 365.0 | 4.00×3.63 | 305 | S-Eldorado |

## 1957

| Series 62 (wb 129.5) | | Wght | Price | Prod |
|---|---|---|---|---|
| 6237 | htp cpe | 4,565 | 4,677 | 25,120 |
| 6237D | Coupe de Ville htp cpe | 4,620 | 5,116 | 23,813 |
| 6237S | Eldorado Seville htp cpe | 4,810 | 7,286 | 2,100 |
| 6239 | htp sdn | 4,595 | 4,781 | 32,342 |
| 6239D | Sedan de Ville htp sdn | 4,655 | 5,256 | 23,808 |
| 6239S | Eldorado Seville htp cpe | 4,810 | 7,286 | 4 |
| 6267 | conv cpe | 4,730 | 5,293 | 9,000 |
| 6267S | Eldorado Biarritz conv cpe | 4,930 | 7,286 | 1,800 |
| 62 | chassis & export sdn | — | — | 385 |

| Series 60 Special (wb 133.0) | | | | |
|---|---|---|---|---|
| 6039 | htp sdn | 4,735 | 5,614 | 24,000 |

| Series 70 Eldorado Brougham (wb 129.0) | | | | |
|---|---|---|---|---|
| 7059 | htp sdn | 5,315 | 13,074 | 400 |

| Series 75 (wb 149.8) | | | | |
|---|---|---|---|---|
| 7523 | sdn 4d, 8P | 5,340 | 7,440 | 1,010 |
| 7533 | limo 8P | 5,390 | 7,678 | 890 |
| 8680S | comm chassis (wb 156.0) | — | — | 2,169 |

| 1957 Engines | bore×stroke | bhp | availability |
|---|---|---|---|
| V8, 365.0 | 4.00×3.63 | 300 | S-62, 60S, 70 |
| V8, 365.0 | 4.00×3.63 | 325 | S-Eldorado |

## 1958

| Series 62 (wb 129.5) | | Wght | Price | Prod |
|---|---|---|---|---|
| 6237 | htp cpe | 4,630 | 4,784 | 18,736 |
| 6237D | Coupe de Ville htp cpe | 4,705 | 5,251 | 18,414 |
| 6237S | Eldorado Seville htp cpe | 4,910 | 7,500 | 855 |
| 6239 | htp sdn | 4,675 | 4,891 | 13,335 |
| 6239E | htp sdn (ext. deck) | 4,770 | 5,079 | 20,952 |
| 6239 | Sedan de Ville htp sdn | 4,855 | 5,497 | 23,989 |
| 6267 | conv cpe | 4,856 | 5,454 | 7,825 |
| 6267S | Eldorado Biarritz conv cpe | 5,070 | 7,500 | 815 |
| 62 | chassis & exp sdn | — | — | 206 |

| Series 60 Special (wb 133.0) | | | | |
|---|---|---|---|---|
| 6039 | htp sdn | 4,930 | 6,232 | 12,900 |

| Series 70 Eldorado Brougham (wb 126.0) | | | | |
|---|---|---|---|---|
| 7059 | htp sdn | 5,315 | 13,074 | 304 |

| Series 75 (wb 149.8) | | | | |
|---|---|---|---|---|
| 7523 | sdn 4d, 9P | 5,360 | 8,460 | 802 |
| 7533 | limo 9P | 5,425 | 8,675 | 730 |
| 8680S | comm chassis (wb 156.0) | — | — | 1,915 |

| 1958 Engine | bore×stroke | bhp | availability |
|---|---|---|---|
| V8, 365.0 | 4.00×3.63 | 310 | S-all |

## 1959

| Series 62 (wb 130.0) | | Wght | Price | Prod |
|---|---|---|---|---|
| 6229 | htp sdn 6W | 4,770 | 5,080 | 23,461 |
| 6237 | htp cpe | 4,690 | 4,892 | 21,947 |
| 6239 | htp sdn 9W | 4,835 | 5,080 | 14,138 |
| 6267 | conv cpe | 4,855 | 5,455 | 11,130 |
| 62 | export sdn | — | — | 60 |

| De Ville (wb 13.0) | | | | |
|---|---|---|---|---|
| 6329 | htp sdn 6W | 4,850 | 5,498 | 19,158 |
| 6337 | htp cpe | 4,720 | 5,252 | 21,924 |
| 6339 | htp sdn 4W | 4,825 | 5,498 | 12,308 |

| Eldorado (wb 130.0) | | | | |
|---|---|---|---|---|
| 6437 | Seville htp cpe | — | 7,401 | 975 |
| 6467 | Biarritz conv cpe | — | 7,401 | 1,320 |
| 6929 | Brougham htp sdn | — | 13,075 | 99 |

| Series 60 Special (wb 130.0) | | | | |
|---|---|---|---|---|
| 6039 | htp sdn | 4,890 | 6,233 | 12,250 |

| Series 75 (wb 149.8) | | | | |
|---|---|---|---|---|
| 6723 | sdn 4d, 9P | 5,490 | 9,533 | 710 |
| 6733 | limo 9P | 5,570 | 9,748 | 690 |
| 6890 | comm chassis (wb 156.0) | — | — | 2,102 |

| 1959 Engines | bore×stroke | bhp | availability |
|---|---|---|---|
| V8, 390.0 | 4.00×3.88 | 325 | S-62, DeVille, 60S, 75 |
| V8, 390.0 | 4.00×3.88 | 345 | S-Eldorado |

## 1960

| Series 62 (wb 130.0) | | Wght | Price | Prod |
|---|---|---|---|---|
| 6229 | htp sdn 6W | 4,805 | 5,080 | 26,824 |
| 6237 | htp cpe | 4,670 | 4,892 | 19,978 |
| 6239 | htp sdn 4W | 4,775 | 5,080 | 9,984 |
| 6267 | conv cpe | 4,850 | 5,455 | 14,000 |
| 62 | chassis & export sdn | — | — | 38 |

| DeVille (wb 130.0) | | | | |
|---|---|---|---|---|
| 6329 | htp sdn 6W | 4,835 | 5,498 | 22,579 |
| 6337 | htp cpe | 4,705 | 5,252 | 21,585 |
| 6339 | htp sdn 4W | 4,815 | 5,498 | 9,225 |

| Eldorado (wb 130.0) | | | | |
|---|---|---|---|---|
| 6437 | Seville htp cpe | — | 7,401 | 1,075 |

# Cadillac

| | | Wght | Price | Prod |
|---|---|---|---|---|
| 6467 | Biarritz conv cpe | — | 7,401 | 1,285 |
| 6929 | Brougham htp sdn | — | 13,075 | 101 |
| **Series 60 Special (wb 130.0)** | | | | |
| 6039 | htp sdn | 4,880 | 6,233 | 11,800 |
| **Series 75 (wb 149.8)** | | | | |
| 6723 | sdn 4d, 9P | 5,475 | 9,533 | 718 |
| 6733 | limo 9P | 5,560 | 9,748 | 832 |
| 6890 | comm chassis (wb 156.0) | — | — | 2,160 |

| 1960 Engines | bore×stroke | bhp | availability |
|---|---|---|---|
| V8, 390.0 | 4.00×3.88 | 325 | S-62, DeVille, 60S, 75 |
| V8, 390.0 | 4.00×3.88 | 345 | S-Eldorado |

## 1961

| Series 62 (wb 129.5) | | Wght | Price | Prod |
|---|---|---|---|---|
| 6229 | htp sdn 6W | 4,680 | 5,080 | 26,216 |
| 6237 | htp cpe | 4,560 | 4,892 | 16,005 |
| 6239 | htp sdn 4W | 4,660 | 5,080 | 4,700 |
| 6267 | conv | 4,720 | 5,455 | 15,500 |
| 62 | chassis | — | — | 5 |
| **DeVille (wb 129.5)** | | | | |
| 6239 | htp sdn 6W | 4,710 | 5,498 | 26,415 |
| 6337 | htp cpe | 4,595 | 5,252 | 20,156 |
| 6339 | htp sdn 4W | 4,715 | 5,498 | 4,847 |
| 6399 | Town Sedan htp 6W | — | 5,498 | 3,756 |
| **Eldorado (wb 129.5)** | | | | |
| 6367 | Biarritz conv cpe | — | 6,477 | 1,450 |
| **Series 60 Special (wb 129.5)** | | | | |
| 6039 | htp sdn | 4,770 | 6,233 | 15,500 |
| **Series 75 (wb 149.8)** | | | | |
| 6723 | sdn 4d, 9P | 5,390 | 9,533 | 600 |
| 6733 | limo 9P | 5,420 | 9,748 | 926 |
| 6890 | comm chassis (wb 156.0) | — | — | 2,204 |

| 1961 Engine | bore×stroke | bhp | availability |
|---|---|---|---|
| V8, 390.0 | 4.00×3.88 | 325 | S-all |

## 1962

| Series 62 (wb 129.5) | | Wght | Price | Prod |
|---|---|---|---|---|
| 6229 | htp sdn 6W | 4,640 | 5,213 | 16,730 |
| 6239 | htp sdn 4W | 4,645 | 5,213 | 17,314 |
| 6247 | htp cpe | 4,530 | 5,025 | 16,833 |
| 6267 | conv cpe | 4,630 | 5,588 | 16,800 |
| 6289 | Town Sedan htp sdn | 4,590 | 5,213 | 2,600 |
| **DeVille (wb 129.5)** | | | | |
| 6329 | htp sdn 6W | 4,660 | 5,631 | 16,230 |
| 6339 | htp sdn 4W | 4,675 | 5,631 | 27,378 |
| 6347 | htp cpe | 4,595 | 5,385 | 25,675 |
| 6389 | Park Avenue htp sdn | 4,655 | 5,631 | 2,600 |
| **Eldorado (wb 129.5)** | | | | |
| 6367 | Biarritz conv cpe | 4,620 | 6,610 | 1,450 |
| **Series 60 Special (wb 129.5)** | | | | |
| 6039 | htp sdn 6W | 4,710 | 6,366 | 13,350 |
| **Series 75 (wb 149.8)** | | | | |
| 6723 | sdn 4d, 9P | 5,325 | 9,722 | 696 |
| 6733 | limo 9P | 5,390 | 9,937 | 904 |
| 6890 | comm chassis (wb 156.0) | — | — | 2,280 |

| 1962 Engine | bore×stroke | bhp | availability |
|---|---|---|---|
| V8, 390.0 | 4.00×3.88 | 325 | S-all |

## 1963

| Series 62 (wb 129.5) | | Wght | Price | Prod |
|---|---|---|---|---|
| 6229 | htp sdn 6W | 4,610 | 5,214 | 12,929 |
| 6239 | htp sdn 4W | 4,595 | 5,214 | 16,980 |
| 6257 | htp cpe | 4,505 | 5,026 | 17,786 |
| 6267 | conv cpe | 4,545 | 5,590 | 17,600 |
| 62 | chassis | — | — | 3 |
| **DeVille (wb 129.5)** | | | | |
| 6329 | htp sdn 6W | 4,650 | 5,633 | 15,146 |
| 6339 | htp sdn 4W | 4,605 | 5,633 | 30,579 |
| 6357 | htp cpe | 4,520 | 5,386 | 31,749 |
| 6389 | Park Avenue htp sdn | 4,590 | 5,633 | 1,575 |
| **Eldorado (wb 129.5)** | | | | |
| 6367 | Biarritz conv cpe | 4,640 | 6,608 | 1,825 |
| **Series 60 Special (wb 129.5)** | | | | |
| 6039 | htp sdn | 4,690 | 6,366 | 14,000 |
| **Series 75 (wb 149.8)** | | | | |
| 6723 | sdn 4d, 9P | 5,240 | 9,724 | 680 |
| 6733 | limo 9P | 5,300 | 9,939 | 795 |
| 6890 | comm chassis (wb 156.0) | — | — | 2,527 |

| 1963 Engine | bore×stroke | bhp | availability |
|---|---|---|---|
| V8, 390.0 | 4.00×3.88 | 325 | S-all |

## 1964

| Series 62 (wb 129.5) | | Wght | Price | Prod |
|---|---|---|---|---|
| 6229 | htp sdn 6W | 4,575 | 5,236 | 9,243 |
| 6239 | htp sdn 4W | 4,550 | 5,236 | 13,670 |
| 6257 | htp cpe | 4,475 | 5,048 | 12,166 |
| 6267 | conv cpe | 4,545 | 5,612 | 17,900 |
| **DeVille (wb 129.5)** | | | | |
| 6329 | htp sdn 6W | 4,600 | 5,655 | 14,627 |
| 6339 | htp cpe 4W | 4,575 | 5,655 | 39,674 |
| 6357 | htp cpe | 4,495 | 5,408 | 38,195 |
| **Eldorado (wb 129.5)** | | | | |
| 6367 | Biarritz conv cpe | 4,605 | 6,630 | 1,870 |
| **Series 60 Special (wb 129.5)** | | | | |
| 6039 | htp sdn | 4,680 | 6,388 | 14,550 |
| **Series 75 (wb 149.8)** | | | | |
| 6723 | sdn 4d, 9P | 5,215 | 9,746 | 617 |
| 6733 | limo 9P | 5,300 | 9,960 | 808 |
| 6890 | comm chassis (wb 156.0) | — | — | 2,639 |

| 1964 Engine | bore×stroke | bhp | availability |
|---|---|---|---|
| V8, 429.0 | 4.13×4.00 | 340 | S-all |

## 1965

| Calais (wb 129.5) | | Wght | Price | Prod |
|---|---|---|---|---|
| 68239 | htp sdn | 4,500 | 5,247 | 13,975 |
| 68257 | htp cpe | 4,435 | 5,059 | 12,515 |
| 68269 | sdn 4d | 4,490 | 5,247 | 7,721 |
| **DeVille (wb 129.5)** | | | | |
| 68339 | htp sdn | 4,560 | 5,666 | 45,535 |
| 68357 | htp cpe | 4,480 | 5,419 | 43,345 |
| 68367 | conv cpe | 4,690 | 5,639 | 19,200 |
| 68369 | sdn 4d | 4,555 | 5,666 | 15,000 |
| **Eldorado (wb 129.5)** | | | | |
| 68467 | conv cpe | 4,660 | 6,738 | 2,125 |
| **Sixty Special (wb 133.0)** | | | | |
| 68069 | sdn 4d | 4,670 | 6,479 | 18,100 |

| Seventy-Five (wb 149.8) | | Wght | Price | Prod |
|---|---|---|---|---|
| 69723 | sdn 4d, 9P | 5,190 | 9,746 | 455 |
| 69733 | limo 9P | 5,260 | 9,960 | 795 |
| 69890 | comm chassis (wb 156.0) | — | — | 2,669 |

| 1965 Engine | bore×stroke | bhp | availability |
|---|---|---|---|
| V8, 429.0 | 4.13×4.00 | 340 | S-all |

# 1966

| Calais (wb 129.5) | | Wght | Price | Prod |
|---|---|---|---|---|
| 68239 | htp sdn | 4,465 | 5,171 | 13,025 |
| 68257 | htp cpe | 4,390 | 4,986 | 11,080 |
| 68269 | sdn 4d | 4,460 | 5,171 | 4,575 |

| DeVille (wb 129.5) | | | | |
|---|---|---|---|---|
| 68339 | htp sdn | 4,515 | 5,581 | 60,550 |
| 68357 | htp cpe | 4,460 | 5,339 | 50,580 |
| 68367 | conv cpe | 4,445 | 5,555 | 19,200 |
| 68369 | sdn 4d | 4,535 | 5,581 | 11,860 |

| Eldorado (wb 129.5) | | | | |
|---|---|---|---|---|
| 68467 | conv cpe | 4,500 | 6,631 | 2,250 |

| Sixty Special (wb 133.0) | | | | |
|---|---|---|---|---|
| 68069 | sdn 4d | 4,615 | 6,378 | 5,455 |
| 68169 | Fleetwood Brougham sdn 4d | 4,665 | 6,695 | 13,630 |

| Seventy-Five (wb 149.8) | | | | |
|---|---|---|---|---|
| 69723 | sdn 4d, 9P | 5,320 | 10,312 | 980 |
| 69733 | limo 9P | 5,435 | 10,521 | 1,037 |
| 69890 | comm chassis (wb 156.0) | — | — | 2,463 |

| 1966 Engine | bore×stroke | bhp | availability |
|---|---|---|---|
| V8, 429.0 | 4.13×4.00 | 340 | S-all |

# 1967

| Calais (wb 129.5) | | Wght | Price | Prod |
|---|---|---|---|---|
| 68247 | htp cpe | 4,447 | 5,040 | 9,085 |
| 68249 | htp sdn | 4,495 | 5,215 | 9,880 |
| 68269 | sdn 4d | 4,499 | 5,215 | 2,865 |

| DeVille (wb 129.5) | | | | |
|---|---|---|---|---|
| 68347 | htp cpe | 4,486 | 5,392 | 52,905 |
| 68349 | htp sdn | 4,532 | 5,625 | 59,902 |
| 68367 | conv cpe | 4,479 | 5,608 | 18,202 |
| 68369 | sdn 4d | 4,534 | 5,625 | 8,800 |

| Eldorado (wb 120.0) | | | | |
|---|---|---|---|---|
| 69347 | htp cpe | 4,500 | 6,277 | 17,930 |

| Sixty Special (wb 133.0) | | | | |
|---|---|---|---|---|
| 68069 | sdn 4d | 4,678 | 6,423 | 3,550 |
| 68169 | Fleetwood Brougham sdn 4d | 4,715 | 6,739 | 12,750 |

| Seventy-Five (wb 149.8) | | | | |
|---|---|---|---|---|
| 69723 | sdn 4d, 9P | 5,344 | 10,360 | 835 |
| 69733 | limo 9P | 5,436 | 10,571 | 965 |
| 68490 | comm chassis (wb 156.0) | — | — | 2,333 |

| 1967 Engine | bore×stroke | bhp | availability |
|---|---|---|---|
| V8, 429.0 | 4.13×4.00 | 340 | S-all |

# 1968

| Calais (wb 129.5) | | Wght | Price | Prod |
|---|---|---|---|---|
| 68247 | htp cpe | 4,570 | 5,315 | 8,165 |
| 68249 | htp sdn | 4,640 | 5,491 | 10,025 |

| DeVille (wb 129.5) | | | | |
|---|---|---|---|---|
| 68347 | htp cpe | 4,595 | 5,552 | 63,935 |
| 68349 | htp sdn | 4,675 | 5,785 | 72,662 |

| | | Wght | Price | Prod |
|---|---|---|---|---|
| 68367 | conv cpe | 4,600 | 5,736 | 18,025 |
| 68369 | sdn 4d | 4,680 | 5,785 | 9,850 |

| Eldorado (wb 120.0) | | | | |
|---|---|---|---|---|
| 69347 | htp cpe | 4,580 | 6,605 | 24,528 |

| Sixty Special (wb 133.0) | | | | |
|---|---|---|---|---|
| 68069 | sdn 4d | 4,795 | 6,583 | 3,300 |
| 68169 | Fleetwood Brougham sdn 4d | 4,805 | 6,899 | 15,300 |

| Seventy-Five (wb 149.8) | | | | |
|---|---|---|---|---|
| 69723 | sdn 4d, 9P | 5,300 | 10,629 | 805 |
| 69733 | limo 9P | 5,385 | 10,768 | 995 |
| 69890 | comm chassis (wb 156.0) | — | — | 2,413 |

| 1968 Engine | bore×stroke | bhp | availability |
|---|---|---|---|
| V8, 472.0 | 4.00×4.06 | 375 | S-all |

# 1969

| Calais (wb 129.5) | | Wght | Price | Prod |
|---|---|---|---|---|
| 68247 | htp cpe | 4,555 | 5,484 | 5,600 |
| 68349 | htp sdn | 4,630 | 5,660 | 6,825 |

| DeVille (wb 129.5) | | | | |
|---|---|---|---|---|
| 68347 | htp cpe | 4,595 | 5,721 | 65,755 |
| 68349 | htp sdn | 4,660 | 5,954 | 72,958 |
| 68367 | conv cpe | 4,590 | 5,905 | 16,445 |
| 68369 | sdn 4d | 4,640 | 5,954 | 7,890 |

| Eldorado (wb 120.0) | | | | |
|---|---|---|---|---|
| 69347 | htp cpe | 4,550 | 6,711 | 23,333 |

| Sixty Special (wb 133.0) | | | | |
|---|---|---|---|---|
| 68069 | sdn 4d | 4,765 | 6,779 | 2,545 |
| 68169 | Fleetwood Brougham sdn 4d | 4,770 | 7,110 | 17,300 |

| Seventy-Five (wb 149.8) | | | | |
|---|---|---|---|---|
| 69723 | sdn 4d, 9P | 5,430 | 10,841 | 880 |
| 69733 | limo 9P | 5,555 | 10,979 | 1,156 |
| 69890 | comm chassis (wb 156.0) | — | — | 2,550 |

| 1969 Engine | bore×stroke | bhp | availability |
|---|---|---|---|
| V8, 472.0 | 4.30×4.06 | 375 | S-all |

# 1970

| Calais (wb 129.5) | | Wght | Price | Prod |
|---|---|---|---|---|
| 68247 | htp cpe | 4,620 | 5,637 | 4,724 |
| 68249 | htp sdn | 4,680 | 5,813 | 5,187 |

| DeVille (wb 129.5) | | | | |
|---|---|---|---|---|
| 68347 | htp cpe | 4,650 | 5,884 | 76,043 |
| 68349 | htp sdn | 4,725 | 6,118 | 83,274 |
| 68367 | conv cpe | 4,660 | 6,068 | 15,172 |
| 68369 | sdn 4d | 4,690 | 6,118 | 7,230 |

| Eldorado (wb 120.0) | | | | |
|---|---|---|---|---|
| 69347 | htp cpe | 4,630 | 6,903 | 28,842 |

| Sixty Special (wb 133.0) | | | | |
|---|---|---|---|---|
| 68089 | sdn 4d | 4,830 | 6,953 | 1,738 |
| 68189 | Fleetwood Brougham sdn 4d | 4,835 | 7,284 | 16,913 |

| Seventy-Five (wb 149.8) | | | | |
|---|---|---|---|---|
| 69723 | sdn 4d, 9P | 5,530 | 11,039 | 876 |
| 69733 | limo 9P | 5,630 | 11,178 | 1,240 |
| 69890 | comm chassis (wb 156.0) | — | — | 2,506 |

| 1970 Engines | bore×stroke | bhp | availability |
|---|---|---|---|
| V8, 472.0 | 4.30×4.06 | 375 | S-all exc Eldorado |
| V8, 500.0 | 4.30×4.30 | 400 | S-Eldorado |

# Checker
### Checker Motors Corp.
### Kalamazoo, Michigan

Checker, the Kalamazoo builder of taxicabs and air-port limousines, began marketing passenger cars in 1960. The company's practical four-door, the Superba, had the same upright, tank-like styling that had become familiar to anyone who'd ever seen a taxi. Checker president Morris Markin was steadfast: there'd be no change to this utilitarian, but unattractive, design from year to year as long as there were customers who wanted a car with a taxi's reliability and durability. The Superba's design dated back to the A8 taxicab of 1956.

The engine used in Checkers of this era was of Continental Motor Company design, roughly the same as that used in Kaisers of the late-1940s and 1950s. It displaced 226 cubic inches, but was offered with either side or overhead valves. The side-valve version had a 7.3:1 compression ratio, and produced 80 horsepower at 3100 rpm. The ohv engine had an 8.0:1 compression ratio and an output of 122 bhp at 4000 rpm. Either engine could be ordered in 1960 for the same price.

The 1960 Checker Superba was available as a four-door sedan and a four-door station wagon, in standard or Special form. The Special came with upgraded interior trim. True to its taxicab heritage, the Superba sedan had a pair of jump seats in the rear compartment and could carry up to eight adults. The wagon's rear seat could be folded up or down by means of an electronic servo controlled from the dashboard. This gimmick, and its different bodywork, made the Checker wagon about $350 more expensive than the sedan.

For 1961, the Superba Special was renamed

1965 Marathon four-door sedan

1970 Marathon DeLuxe four-door sedan

Marathon. The sedan's 15-inch wheels were replaced by 14-inchers for a slightly lower ride height. The overhead-valve engine became standard on station wagons. Prices did not change. Air conditioning cost $411 extra; power steering was a $64 option. Like Checker cabs, the Superba and Marathon had a full bank of gauges, a spartan but well-padded interior, wide doors, and a spacious rear compartment.

The same four offerings were continued for 1962. The only change was a return to 15-inch wheels for the sedans. In 1963, ouput on the overhead-valve engine was increased to 141 bhp at 4000 rpm. Prices rose in 1964—about $100 across the board. Optimistically, Checker decided to introduce a $7500 Town Custom limousine on a 129-inch wheelbase in '62. In addition to a glassed-off driver's compartment, the limousine offered a full range of power options. Production was limited, probably because demand for this most expensive of taxis was low.

The Superba name was dropped in 1964, which was also the last year for the old 226-cid engine. Checker than switched to Chevrolet engines for 1965: a 230-cid six, a 283 V8, and a 327 V8. The Town Custom limousine was still offered, but only on special order. The optional 283 V8 cost $110 extra, automatic transmission was priced at $248, and overdrive cost $108.

The 1966 Checker added a deluxe sedan, and a lower-priced limousine at $4541, temporarily reestablishing its four-model lineup. These two models were dropped the following year. The deluxe sedan was revived for 1968, and the deluxe limousine reappeared for 1969.

Checkers became faster cars during these years as their Chevy V8s became increasingly more potent. The big 350 was producing 300 bhp when Checker introduced it as an option in 1969; emission controls cut output to 250 bhp in its 1970 form, however. Prices for the optional engines were usually low: In 1968, these were $108 for the 307 and $195 for the 327.

Sales were moderate for Checker in the '60s, although adequate to sustain the level of production the firm desired—6000 to 7000 units a year. Checker's best year of the decade was 1962, when 8173 cars were built. Most of these, of course, were sold as commercial taxis.

Morris Markin, Checker's founder, never waivered from his goal to build a tough taxicab. If he could also sell a few of them as passenger cars, so much the better. But the fickle public, he insisted, would never control Checker styling or engineering. (It isn't widely known, but Nathan Altman once made overtures to Checker as a possible builder of his Avanti II. Markin, however, said the Avanti was too ugly to sell.)

Markin died in 1970. His son David then took over the company's operations.

# Checker Specifications

## 1960—6,980 built, inc taxis

| Superba (wb 120.0) | Wght | Price | Prod |
|---|---|---|---|
| sdn 4d | 3,410 | 2,542 | — |
| Special sdn 4d | 3,410 | 2,650 | — |
| wgn 4d | 3,780 | 2,896 | — |
| Special wgn 4d | 3,780 | 3,004 | — |

| 1960 Engines | bore×stroke | bhp | availability |
|---|---|---|---|
| L6, 226.0 | 3.31×4.38 | 80 | S-all |
| L6, 226.0 | 3.31×4.38 | 122 | O-all |

## 1961—5,683 built, inc taxis

| Superba (wb 120.0) | Wght | Price | Prod |
|---|---|---|---|
| sdn 4d | 3,320 | 2,542 | — |
| wgn 4d | 3,570 | 2,896 | — |

| Marathon (wb 120.0) | Wght | Price | Prod |
|---|---|---|---|
| sdn 4d | 3,345 | 2,650 | — |
| wgn 4d | 3,615 | 3,004 | — |

| 1961 Engines | bore×stroke | bhp | availability |
|---|---|---|---|
| L6, 226.0 | 3.31×4.38 | 80 | S-all |
| L6, 226.0 | 3.31×4.38 | 122 | S-wgn; O-sdn |

## 1962—8,173 built, inc taxis

| Superba (wb 120.0) | Wght | Price | Prod |
|---|---|---|---|
| sdn 4d | 3,320 | 2,642 | — |
| wgn 4d | 3,570 | 2,991 | — |

| Marathon (wb 120.0) | Wght | Price | Prod |
|---|---|---|---|
| sdn 4d | 3,345 | 2,793 | — |
| wgn 4d | 3,615 | 3,140 | — |

| Town Custom (wb 129.0) | Wght | Price | Prod |
|---|---|---|---|
| limo 8P | 5,000 | 7,500 | — |

| 1962 Engines | bore×stroke | bhp | availability |
|---|---|---|---|
| L6, 226.0 | 3.31×4.38 | 80 | S-all |
| L6, 226.0 | 3.31×4.38 | 122 | O-all |

## 1963—7,050 built, inc taxis

| Superba (wb 120.0) | Wght | Price | Prod |
|---|---|---|---|
| sdn 4d | 3,485 | 2,642 | — |
| wgn 4d | 3,625 | 2,991 | — |

| Marathon (wb 120.0) | Wght | Price | Prod |
|---|---|---|---|
| sdn 4d | 3,485 | 2,773 | — |
| wgn 4d | 3,625 | 3,140 | — |

| Town Custom (wb 129.0) | Wght | Price | Prod |
|---|---|---|---|
| limo 8P | 5,000 | 7,500 | — |

| 1963 Engines | bore×stroke | bhp | availability |
|---|---|---|---|
| L6, 226.0 | 3.31×4.38 | 80 | S-all |
| L6, 226.0 | 3.31×4.38 | 141 | O-all |

## 1964—6,310 built, inc taxis

| Marathon (wb 120.0) | Wght | Price | Prod |
|---|---|---|---|
| sdn 4d | 3,625 | 2,814 | — |
| wgn 4d | 3,720 | 3,160 | — |

| Town Custom (wb 129.0) | Wght | Price | Prod |
|---|---|---|---|
| limo 8P | 5,000 | 8,000 | — |

| 1964 Engines | bore×stroke | bhp | availability |
|---|---|---|---|
| L6, 226.0 | 3.31×4.38 | 80 | S-all |
| L6, 226.0 | 3.31×4.38 | 141 | O-all |

## 1965—6,136 built, inc taxis

| Marathon (wb 120.0) | Wght | Price | Prod |
|---|---|---|---|
| sdn 4d | 3,360 | 2,793 | — |
| wgn 4d | 3,450 | 3,140 | — |

| Town Custom (wb 129.0) | Wght | Price | Prod |
|---|---|---|---|
| limo 8P | 4,800 | 8,000 | — |

| 1965 Engines | bore×stroke | bhp | availability |
|---|---|---|---|
| L6, 230.0 | 3.88×3.25 | 140 | S-all |
| V8, 283.0 | 3.88×3.00 | 195 | O-all |
| V8, 327.0 | 4.00×3.25 | 250 | O-all |

## 1966—1,056 built; 5,761 inc taxis

| Marathon (wb 120.0) | | Wght | Price | Prod |
|---|---|---|---|---|
| A12 | sdn 4d | 3,400 | 2,874 | — |
| A12F | Deluxe sdn 4d | 3,800 | 3,567 | — |
| A12E | limo 8P | 3,800 | 4,541 | — |
| A12W | wgn 4d | 3,500 | 3,500 | — |

| 1966 Engines | bore×stroke | bhp | availability |
|---|---|---|---|
| L6, 230.0 | 3.88×3.25 | 140 | S-all |
| V8, 327.0 | 4.00×3.25 | 250 | O-all |

## 1967—935 built; 5,822 inc taxis

| Marathon (wb 120.0) | | Wght | Price | Prod |
|---|---|---|---|---|
| A12 | sdn 4d | 3,400 | 2,874 | — |
| A12W | wgn 4d | 3,500 | 3,075 | — |

| 1967 Engines | bore×stroke | bhp | availability |
|---|---|---|---|
| L6, 230.0 | 3.88×3.25 | 140 | S-all |
| V8, 327.0 | 4.00×3.25 | 250 | O-all |

## 1968—992 built; 5,477 inc taxis

| Marathon (wb 120.0) | | Wght | Price | Prod |
|---|---|---|---|---|
| A12 | sdn 4d | 3,390 | 3,221 | — |
| A12E | Deluxe sdn 4d | 3,590 | 3,913 | — |
| A12W | wgn 4d | 3,480 | 3,491 | — |

| 1968 Engines | bore×stroke | bhp | availability |
|---|---|---|---|
| L6, 230.0 | 3.88×3.25 | 140 | S-all |
| V8, 307.0 | 3.88×3.25 | 200 | O-all |
| V8, 327.0 | 4.00×3.25 | 275 | O-all |

## 1969—760 built; 5,417 inc taxis

| Marathon (wb 120.0) | | Wght | Price | Prod |
|---|---|---|---|---|
| A12 | sdn 4d | 3,390 | 3,290 | — |
| A12W | wgn 4d | 3,480 | 3,560 | — |

| DeLuxe (wb 129.0) | | Wght | Price | Prod |
|---|---|---|---|---|
| A12E | sdn 4d | 3,590 | 3,984 | — |
| A12E | limo 8P | 3,802 | 4,969 | — |

| 1969 Engines | bore×stroke | bhp | availability |
|---|---|---|---|
| L6, 230.0 | 3.88×3.25 | 155 | S-all |
| V8, 327.0 | 4.00×3.25 | 235 | O-all |
| V8, 350.0 | 4.00×3.48 | 300 | O-all |

## 1970—397 built

| Marathon (wb 120.0) | | Wght | Price | Prod |
|---|---|---|---|---|
| A12 | sdn 4d | 3,268 | 3,671 | — |
| A12W | wgn 4d | 3,470 | 3,941 | — |

| Marathon DeLuxe (wb 129.0) | | Wght | Price | Prod |
|---|---|---|---|---|
| A12E | sdn 4d | 3,378 | 4,364 | — |
| A12E | limo 8P | 3,578 | 5,338 | — |

| 1970 Engines | bore×stroke | bhp | availability |
|---|---|---|---|
| L6, 230.0 | 3.88×3.25 | 155 | S-all |
| V8, 350.0 | 4.00×3.48 | 250 | O-all |

# Chevrolet

**Chevrolet Motor Division, General Motors Corp.
Detroit, Michigan**

General Motors' fastest-selling make had its first million-unit calendar year in 1927. The division produced 1,750,000 cars, overpowering Ford, which was in the throes of transferring from Model T to Model A. Ford recovered, but only briefly. In the Depression era, Chevy outsold its rival almost every year, and by 1939 was clearly established as America's number-one car. The pattern continued throughout the '40s. Chevrolet produced a million 1941 models; by model year 1950 it had almost topped 1.5 million.

Competitiveness was evident in the 1940 line. The cars were thoroughly facelifted with what Chevrolet called Royal Clipper styling. Though not a drastic change from the past, it was sufficiently fresh to make the cars much newer-looking than the '39s. A new Special DeLuxe series was created for the top of the line, and included a convertible that was not available the previous year. The soft-top was quite successful: nearly 12,000 copies were sold.

Special and Master DeLuxe lines came standard with Knee-Action, the independent front suspension developed in 1934 by Maurice Olley. Chevrolet had reintroduced a cheaper model with a solid front axle in 1935, and this remained available through 1940, when it was called the Master 85. Both Master series were available as business coupes and two- and four-door sedans; the Master 85 included a woody wagon. The top-line Special DeLuxe also came in wagon form. These wagons, of course, were far different from today's all-steel wagons. Wooden construction made them heavy, ungainly, and hard to maintain. Later, Chevrolet and Plymouth would lead the trend to all-steel station wagons.

The engine that powered all Chevrolets of the '40s had evolved from a design first seen in the 1920s, and helped Chevy dislodge Ford from the number-one spot. It was developed by Ormond E. Hunt from an earlier design by Henry Crane. A light L-head, it had originally produced 46 horsepower. It was nicknamed the "Stovebolt Six" for its slotted-head bolts or stove bolts. It was also known as the "Cast-Iron Wonder" because of its cast-iron pistons.

In 1934, this powerplant got the name Blue Flame Six along with a longer stroke that boosted horsepower to 80. The 1940 configuration arrived in 1937, when the Blue Flame was redesigned for nearly square cylinder dimensions. Improvements over earlier versions included four (instead of three) main bearings, shorter length, and better oil and water pumps. In 1941, the Blue Flame's output was boosted to 90 bhp at 3300 rpm, and this is how it remained through the '40s and into the '50s.

The Blue Flame Six gained an undeserved reputation as a sluggard. In reality, it was capable of surprising performance. One man who proved it was Juan Manuel Fangio, later one of the world's great Formula One drivers. In 1940, Fangio won the 5900-mile Buenos Aires-Lima road race in his Chevy coupe, averaging 53.6 mph. His car was seen again after the war, and took three more first-place victories.

In model year production, 1941 was also a million-car year for Chevrolet. The division fielded the body/chassis combination that would carry it through 1948: 116-inch wheelbase, Knee-Action on all models, 90-bhp six, and attractive new styling by Harley Earl's Art & Colour Studio. The Master 85 series was dropped. The Master DeLuxe and Special DeLuxe retained the 1940 body styles. The Fleetline four-door sedan was a special addition, and 34,000 were sold that year. It was distinguished by a new, more formal-looking roofline with closed-in rear quarters, a takeoff on styling ideas first seen on the Cadillac 60 Special. The engine's 90 bhp was obtained by means of a 6.5:1 compression head, new pistons, and reduced combustion chambers. Valves, rocker arms, and water pump were also reworked.

Further refinements to the '41 styling were made for '42: fenders were extended back into the front doors as on the more expensive GM cars; and a smart, clean grille replaced the somewhat busy '41 rendition. The model line stayed mostly the same, but new names were added: Stylemaster for the lower-priced Master DeLuxe coupes and sedans; Fleetmaster for the Special DeLuxe. An offshoot of the upper series was the Fleetline, comprising a new torpedo-style two-door Aerosedan and a conventionally styled four-door Sportmaster sedan. Both were distinguished by triple bands of brightwork on front and rear fenders.

Civilian car production stopped in February 1942. Chevrolet's model year total up to then was 254,885 units, of which only 45,472 were produced in calendar year 1942. In the Special DeLuxe series, only a handful of convertibles, wagons, and business coupes were built. Because they are so rare, 1942 Chevys are highly sought-after by collectors today.

Production at GM was hampered after the war by strikes and material shortages. If you count Chevy's tiny output in 1945 as a calendar year, it was outpaced by Ford by about three to one. But after that, Chevy was on top again, even though its 1946-48 cars were only slightly modified versions of the '42 design.

The differences were slight, but they were there. The '46s had fewer grille bars and a hood emblem with upright instead of horizontal wings. Parking lights were rectangular, fitted horizontally into the lower corners of the grille instead of vertically as before. The model line-up went unchanged, although the old Master series was simply called Stylemaster. This line comprised two- and four-door sedans, sport coupe, and business coupe.

Fleetmaster sedans, coupes, convertible and wagon, and the Fleetline Aerosedan and Sportmaster were all continued.

It was during this period that Chevrolet experimented with and rejected a new rear-engine small car code-named Cadet. The design team was led by Maurice Olley. Several different configurations were considered. After spending a few million dollars on development, management concluded there was no market for it. Ford had reached the same conclusion at about the same time. Neither of the two giants fielded a small car until 1960, when the Corvair and Falcon were introduced.

Styling for each of the next two model years was basically a rerun of 1946. There was no change in the line-up of four Stylemasters, five Fleetmasters, and two Fleetlines, except for increased prices. But there were detail appearance changes. For 1947, the horizontal

grille bars were wider, the nameplate went from the bottom to the top of the grille, the hood medallion was now horizontal, and side hood and beltline moldings were eliminated. For 1948, the grille acquired a central vertical bar rising to the base of the top horizontal molding with a small "Chevrolet" emblem near its top. The 1947-48 Fleetlines had horizontal chrome moldings on front and rear fenders; Sportmaster sedans had pivoting wind wings in the rear doors.

Although there was little visible change at Chevy during this period, the division that had written the industry's greatest success story was never known for standing pat, or for making wrong decisions. Management was changing, and new ideas were being discussed for the future: sports cars, hardtop convertibles, and all-steel station wagons.

In June 1946, Nick Dreystadt, former Cadillac general manager, replaced M. E. Coyle as general manager of

1940 Master DeLuxe four-door Sport Sedan

1946 Stylemaster four-door Sport Sedan

1941 Master DeLuxe two-door Town Sedan

1947 Fleetmaster four-door Sport Sedan

1942 Special DeLuxe Fleetmaster five-passenger coupe

1948 Fleetline two-door Aerosedan

# Chevrolet

Chevrolet. Dreystadt encouraged development of new models, and with a forceful engineering program brought new life to a make that had a rather stodgy image by then. But Dreystadt unexpectedly died two years later, and his successor, W. E. Armstrong, resigned early because of illness. Thomas H. Keating then stepped up. He followed Dreystadt's policies and spoke

1949 DeLuxe Styleline four-door Sport Sedan

1950 DeLuxe Styleline four-door Sport Sedan

1951 DeLuxe Styleline Bel Air hardtop coupe

1951 DeLuxe Styleline four-door sedan

bullishly about Chevrolet's future. Soon after Keating took over, Edward N. Cole joined the team as Chevy's chief engineer.

The first order of business after the war was to change Chevy's look completely. GM had scheduled its first corporate postwar redesign for the 1949 model year, and Chevy's version was among the most attractive. Although wheelbase was actually an inch shorter, the '49 was cleanly styled from nose to tail and looked much more streamlined than the 1948 model. Its two-piece windshield was curved and two inches lower; fenders swept back smoothly through the cowl and doors, while the rear fenders rolled forward. Suspension revisions and a lower center of gravity made the '49 one of the best-handling Chevrolets ever—probably superior to that year's Plymouth and Ford. The '49s were also beautifully put together. The precise fit of body panels, the way the shifter snicked cleanly through the gears, and the car's positive response to controls testified that engineers and production people had gone to extremes to make them "right."

For the first time in years, the model line was overhauled for 49. The less expensive Series 1500GJ comprised the Special Styleline and the fastback Special Fleetline sedans. The more luxurious Series 2100GK included the Deluxe Styleline models—two- and four-door sedans, a coupe, convertible, and two station wagons. One of the wagons was trimmed with wood, one was all-steel, both carried eight passengers. This series also offered a pair of fastback sedans named DeLuxe Fleetline, a two-door and a four-door. Initially, the fastbacks sold well, but as time went on they fell out of favor, and disappeared at the end of 1952.

In the 1950s, Chevrolet evolved from staid family car to hot performance machine. The division moved from dull sedans to fast, sporty cars. Chevy also dropped from number-one in the industry to number-two—but only briefly.

Most of Chevrolet's decisions between 1950 and '59 were the right ones. It was right to build the Bel Air, first as a single hardtop and later as a separate series. It was highly successful, dominating production by 1957. It was right to build the 265 and 283 cubic-inch V8s, the engines that changed Chevrolet's performance reputation almost overnight. And it was right to market the Impala, because it added strength to the top of the line. Chevrolet would no longer be just one of the "low-priced three": now, it was an alternative for those who previously would have bought Pontiacs, Dodges, or Mercurys.

The 1950-52 period saw the last of the traditional low-cost, low-suds Chevys; 1953-54 saw a transition; 1955 a revolution. In the early years, the Special accounted for about 15–20 percent of total production. The costlier DeLuxe accounted for the rest, and offered a wide variety of models. Specials came in two- or four-door sedans, coupes, and business coupes known as Stylelines, and two- and four-door fastback sedans called Fleetlines. The DeLuxe lineup had no business coupe,

but offered wagon, hardtop, convertible, and the Fleetline fastbacks.

Fleetlines did well enough in the seller's market of 1946-50, but the fastback fad had faded by the early '50s. Accordingly, Chevrolet phased them out. The last was a two-door in the '52 Deluxe series, and relatively few were made. As rapidly as the fastbacks disappeared, Bel Air hardtops took their place. Chevrolet was a year ahead of Ford and Plymouth in introducing a pillarless coupe, and sales were brisk. All 1950-52 Chevys were powered by the hoary old "stovebolt six." By this time, the 216.5-cid mill had been coaxed up to 92 bhp at 3400 rpm, or 105 bhp at 3600 when teamed with optional Powerglide two-speed automatic. Prices in those years were competitive and styling was consistent, varying only in minor details like grille, taillights, and side moldings.

In 1953, all GM cars got a major facelift, but Chevy and Pontiac looked newest. Chevy renamed the Special the One-Fifty and the Deluxe became the Two-Ten; the Bel Air was made a series in its own right with a full range of body styles. The big news that year was the Corvette, America's first postwar sports car (see separate chapter). The Blue Flame Six was revised again, with much higher compression giving up to 115 bhp. It was continued through the '50s and beyond, grinding out as much as 145 bhp. It was sound and reliable, but not very exciting. Ed Cole's V8 took care of that.

Without question, the 265-cid V8 that appeared for 1955 was one of the industry's milestone engines. Though designed to be efficient and cheap to build, it was really one of those "blue sky" projects of the type that comes along only once or twice in an engineer's career. Said Cole, "I had worked on V8 engines all my professional life. I had lived and breathed engines. [Motor engineer Harry F.] Barr and I were always say-

1952 DeLuxe Styleline four-door sedan

1953 Bel Air convertible

1952 DeLuxe Styline two-door sedan

1954 Bel Air four-door sedan

1953 Bel Air four-door sedan

1954's Nomad show car — forerunner of Nomad wagons

1955 Bel Air Nomad two-door station wagon

1955 Two-Ten hardtop coupe

1958 styling preview—Biscayne show car, 1955

1956 Bel Air hardtop sedan

1956 Bel Air Nomad two-door station wagon

1957 Bel Air convertible

ing how we would do it if we could ever design a new engine. You just know you want five main bearings—there's no decision to make. We knew that a certain bore-stroke relationship was the most compact. We knew we'd like a displacement of 265 cubic inches . . . And we never changed any of this. We released our engine for tooling direct from the drawing boards—that's how crazy and confident we were.''

Cole and Barr had reason to be enthusiastic. The 265 weighed even less than the six. It had low reciprocating mass, which allowed high rpm; die-cast heads with integral, interchangeable valve guides; aluminum slipper pistons; and a crankshaft of forged pressed-steel instead of alloy iron. It performed beautifully, putting out 162 bhp at 4400 rpm, or 180 bhp at 4600 with Power-pak (a four-barrel carburetor and dual exhausts). It became the basis of all the great Chevy engines of the immediate future: the 225-bhp '56 Corvette and the bored-out fuel-injected 283 of 1957, the first mass-production engine with one horsepower per cubic inch. Chevrolet developed a new 348-cid V8 as a big-car option for 1958, and it was a good one. But the 283 remained the

best-known, best-loved engine of the period, earning Chevy a reputation for performance it had never enjoyed with the sixes.

Powerglide automatic, a torque converter using the Dynaflow principle, was an increasingly popular option in those years at a price under $200. Smooth in operation, it was well-suited to all but the high-powered models. These were available with a manual or stick-over-drive, three-speed Turboglide automatic from 1957 on, and an all-synchromesh four-speed manual starting in 1959.

Styling was as much a part of the mid-1950s picture as engineering. Harley Earl's Chevy design team—Clare MacKichan, Chuck Stebbins, Bob Veryzer, Carl Renner, and others—worked under Earl's guideline: "Go all the way, then back off." Though the '55 didn't reach production looking the way it had in fanciful renderings, it wasn't far off. The beltline dip and wrap-around windshield had been inspired by the Cadillac Eldorado, Oldsmobile Fiesta, and Buick Skylark limited editions of 1953; the eggcrate grille had been inspired by Ferrari and was one of Earl's favorite touches. The

1957 Two-Ten four-door sedan

1957 One-Fifty two-door utility sedan

1957 Bel Air Nomad two-door station wagon

1958 Impala hardtop coupe

1958 Bel Air hardtop sedan

1958 Biscayne four-door sedan

grille was unpopular with the public though, so the '56 version was broader, brighter, and more conventional.

Carl Renner was the man responsible for a unique hardtop wagon called the Bel Air Nomad. Actually, it was too impractical as a wagon, too bulky as a hardtop. But it was the ideal stylistic blend of both. If it didn't sell well, it was more because two-door wagons were generally less popular than four-doors rather than lack of appeal. The Nomad was relatively expensive, but there had never been such a beautiful wagon. Had anybody else built it, the Nomad would probably be quite rare today. Volume, however, was relatively high: 8386 were built for 1955; 7886 for '56, 6103 for 1957.

A mild facelift came about for '56, another in '57. Both Ford and Plymouth were completely restyled in 1957, so Chevrolet suffered by comparison. Yet record market penetration of close to 28 percent was achieved in 1956, and the '57 facelift was a good one. The engines previously described had the go to match the looks. A '57 Bel Air four-door hardtop with the 270-bhp engine would streak from 0 to 60 mph in 9.9 seconds, do the quarter-mile in 17.5 seconds, and run up to well over 110 mph. The lighter One-Fifty with the injected V8 was even faster.

Properly equipped, the 1955-57 Chevy was, and is, a formidable competitor on the race track. Before the Automobile Manufacturers Association recommended the industry withhdraw from organized racing in 1957, Chevy did quite well on NASCAR and other circuits. At the 1957 Daytona Speed Weeks, it added more achievements. In Class 4 (213 to 259 cubic inches) Chevrolets won the first three places in the two-way flying-mile; in Class 5 (259 to 305 cubic inches) they took 33 out of 37 places, with the best car averaging 131.076 mpg. Chevy also won the Pure Oil Manufacturers Trophy in '57 with 574 points, against only 309 for runner-up Ford.

The effects of the racing ban didn't take long. For 1958, Chevy back-pedaled on performance with a line of softer, more luxurious cars. Most reviewers were unhappy. Said Tom McCahill of *Mechanix Illustrated,* "When an ad man can't write about his product's success at Pikes Peak, Daytona Beach or Darlington, or how fast it gets away from a traffic light, what's he got left? All he can do is tell about the hand-woven Indian

rugs on the floor, the Da Vinci sculptured door handles, or the 'ten miles per gallon' it averaged under the featherfoot of a professional economy jockey.''

McCahill was right. The '58 Chevys were longer, lower, wider, heavier . . . and slower. The division was reaching for a new market sector—the solid, substantial Pontiac-types it had never gone after before—with such cars as the Impala. People who bought Impalas, then as now, didn't care about performance or handling. They wanted size and comfort. The Impala delivered.

Despite a rough year for the U.S. economy in '58, Chevy managed to build over 1.1 million cars: 60,000 were Impalas. That was a decent showing for a new series consisting of only a hardtop and convertible. The One-Fifty was renamed Delray; Biscayne replaced the Two-Ten title. Bel Air was still top of the line, with Impala as a sub-series for '58 only. ''Station Wagon'' became a separate series with no fewer than five models: the two-door Yeoman; four-door Yeoman, Brookwood, and Nomad; and the nine-passenger Brookwood. The '58 Nomad wasn't the same car it had been in 1955-57. It was now just a conventional wagon, and it remained so through 1961, its last year.

Chevrolet probably deserves credit for bucking the tailfin trend in 1958, but the stylists made up for it the following year with an overdecorated bat-wing tail. The result was a rear deck, as Tom McCahill said, ''big enough to land a Piper Cub.'' It could have been worse. Carl Renner said one 1959 proposal called for an upright, Edsel-like grille and was one of the ugliest things

he'd ever seen. As it turned out, the front end of the '59 was relatively mild, but the rear was a thing from another world. This was the year Ford beat Chevy in calendar year production, so Chevrolet's rear end was a lot more subdued for 1960.

Delray disappeared in 1959, leaving the Biscayne, Bel Air, Impala, and Station Wagon in the lineup. All rode a 119-inch wheelbase, the longest in postwar history. The growth between 1957 and 1959 was amazing. Wheelbases were up by four inches, length by nearly eleven inches, width by seven inches, and weight increased by 300 pounds. The '59s were the first of the overstuffed generation that would live on for the next 15 years. Only recently has GM been weaning the public from these enormous vehicles. At the time, of course, they made a degree of sense. In order to compete, the low-priced three—Ford, Chevy and Plymouth—needed larger and larger dimensions, cars the size of Cadillacs and Lincolns that would sell at half the price. Chevy led; Ford and Plymouth followed suit.

During the 1960s, Chevrolet expanded into at least five new market areas: compacts with the Corvair and Chevy II, intermediates with the Chevelle, super stockers with the Malibu and Impala SS, luxury full-size models with the Caprice, and ''ponycars'' with the Camaro. (The Corvette and Corvair are different enough to be treated separately.) Each new product of the decade was carefully designed to fill a basic need. Nearly every one succeeded.

Moving into so many new markets would seem to imply increased production. The division did set some

1959 Biscayne two-door sedan

1960 Impala convertible

1959 Impala four-door sedan

1961 Impala two-door sedan

records during the decade. But it was only producing some 500,000 more cars at the end of the '60s than it had been at the beginning, despite introducing four new lines in different size categories. Actually, the market had been subdivided. The departure of the independent automakers and the rise of compacts, sporty compacts, and intermediates in the '60s generated more competition than there had been in the '50s. In many cases, Chevy was competing against itself or other GM divisions.

Chevrolet offered a wide range of cars by the end of the decade, built on just four wheelbases: 108 inches for the Corvair and Camaro, 110 for the Chevy II and Nova, 115 for the Chevelle, and 119 for the big Chevrolets. The only exception was the 1968-72 Chevelle. Like other GM compacts of those years, it used a 112-inch wheelbase for two-door models and a 116-inch wheelbase for the four-doors.

The big Chevrolet progressed from overstyled outrageousness to clean, crisp elegance. The '60 model was a facelift of the horrendously finned '59 edition. The fins were cropped and completely disappeared for '61. By 1963, there was a new sculptured body without a trace of the outlandish '50s. Without a change in wheelbase, the large Chevrolet grew bulkier in the last years of the decade, but was deftly styled nonetheless. Another complete restyle in 1965 brought flowing lines and a slight upward sweep to the rear quarter panels. This shape continued until 1969, when a new look was fashioned with elliptical wheel openings, emphasized by subtle bulges. The prettiest full-size Chevy of the period might be the 1962. It had straight, correct lines and interesting roof styling with "bow" sculpturing like a raised convertible top.

Biscayne was still the price leader, but buyer interest fell during the decade. The Bel Air had become the mid-priced big Chevrolet in 1959 but its sales also decreased in the '60s. The top-line Impala had rapidly become the most popular single model in the United States. Its best sales year of the decade was 1964, when 889,600 units were built.

One Impala worthy of particular attention is the performance-bred Super Sport of 1962-67. Like Corvair and Camaro, the Impala SS is already a collector's item.

The concept was simple: take the big, 119-inch standard-wheelbase chassis, add sporty styling touches, and offer options designed to enhance performance and handling. The Impala SS was available as either a two-door hardtop or convertible. A six-cylinder engine was offered, but only 3600 were equipped with one in 1965. The exterior featured special SS emblems and deleted the regular Impala's rocker panel brightwork. Vinyl bucket seats and a central gearshift console were standard. Tachometer and sport steering wheel were optional. Big-displacement V8s were offered, like the famous 409 that developed 425 bhp. Equipped with exciting handling options like stiffer springs and shocks, sintered metallic brake linings, four-speed gearbox, and ultra-quick power steering, the Impala SS was the

1962 Impala convertible

1962 Chevy II 300 two-door sedan

1963 Impala convertible

1963 Chevy II 100 two-door sedan

1964 Impala hardtop coupe

Prototype for 1964 Chevelle Malibu four-door sedan

1965½ Caprice hardtop sedan

1965 Impala hardtop coupe

1966 Caprice hardtop sedan

highest-performance big Chevy in history.

But it didn't last. Government regulations, a decline in demand for race-bred automobiles, and the increased popularity of smaller sporty cars all combined to do in the Impala SS after 1967. Production fell rapidly during the five model years. Meanwhile, Chevrolet had found a far more lucrative market by dolling up the Impala with the best grades of upholstery and trim, and calling it Caprice. This top-of-the-line Chevy arrived in 1965 and captured some 180,000 buyers in 1966.

Next in Chevrolet's size hierarchy of the '60s was the intermediate Chevelle, introduced in 1964 to compete against Ford's Fairlane. The Chevelle was conventional: front engine, rear drive, coil springs in front, leaf springs in the rear. It provided almost as much interior room as the Impala, but had a more sensibly sized exterior. In effect, it was a revival of the ideally proportioned, middle-wheelbase "classic" Chevrolet of 1955-57. Sales went nowhere but up, from 328,400 units in its first year to nearly 440,000 by 1969. The addition of numerous performance options and its own SS variations only enhanced Chevelle's appeal.

Third down the size scale was the 110-inch-wheelbase Chevy II. It had been rushed into production for 1962 as a stopgap against Ford's Falcon, which was handily trimming Corvair in the compact market. While Corvair appealed mainly to car enthusiasts, Falcon pleased the much broader range of average buyers. Chevy IIs were available with a 153-cid four-cylinder engine with 90 bhp, or a 194-cid 120-bhp six. (Falcons had only six-cylinder powerplants.)

Chevrolet hoped to outflank and outproduce Ford in this segment. But through 1966, Chevy IIs outnumbered Falcons only once, in 1963. Between 1963 and '64, sales dropped nearly 50 percent, due partly to competition from the Chevelle. A spate of Super Sport models didn't help. By the middle of the decade, Chevy II seemed destined for oblivion.

Then in 1968, Chevy gave its compact an all-new body with a 111-inch wheelbase for two-door coupes and four-door sedans. The new cars were known by the name of the previous top-line series, Nova. Backed by a strong ad campaign and competitive prices, the Chevy II Nova made a comeback. The division concentrated on just the two body styles, which sold as fast as they could be built. Sales were up to 201,000 units in 1968, the best year since '63. The Chevy II title was dropped, and the basic design continued as the Nova through 1979, when it was replaced by the front-wheel-drive Citation.

The Camaro is one of the more interesting Chevrolets of the '60s, and potentially the most collectible (aside from Corvettes). Introduced for 1967, it was an immediate hit. Production topped 220,000 cars the first year, followed by 235,100 for 1968, and 243,100 for 1969.

The Camaro was born out of a need to replace the ailing Corvair. Despite the beautiful styling and impressive performance of the all-new 1965 models, Corvair was no threat to Ford's incredibly successful Mustang in the burgeoning "ponycar" market. Furthermore, the Corvair was expensive to build; it was entirely different in concept and technology from mainstream Chevrolet models. Six months after the '65s arrived, division managers decided Corvair would be allowed to fade away. Its replacement would be a conventional front-engine sporty car—the ultimate solution to the Mustang.

The Camaro's design became the responsibility of William L. Mitchell, GM's vice-president of styling, and head of the corporation's Styling Staff. There was no better team of designers in the industry during this period. The look that resulted—flat nose, chiseled profile, chopped-off rear deck, and low roofline—was exactly right. The Camaro appealed to those who wanted a four-seater with handling to match its straight-line performance.

1967 Impala hardtop coupe

1967 Camaro hardtop coupe

1967 Chevy II Nova SS hardtop coupe

1968 Impala convertible

1968 Camaro convertible

1968 Chevy II Nova coupe

1968 Chevelle SS 396 hardtop coupe

1969 Chevelle SS 396 hardtop coupe

The Camaro was more than a new Chevrolet: it was a new concept. Mustang had pointed the way, and GM has never been reticent about borrowing a good idea. Some 81 factory options and 41 dealer-installed accessories were offered so the buyer could tailor the car to taste and budget. Prices started at $2466 f.o.b. for the 140-bhp six-cylinder coupe and $2704 for the convertible. The 155-bhp, 250-cid six cost $26 extra; the 210-bhp 327 V8 was an additional $106. Next on the list was a 350-cid V8 with 295 bhp, exclusive to Camaro in '67. (Later, it became the most popular Corvette powerplant.) To get it, the buyer had to order the Super Sports package.

The SS option cost $211 and included a tight suspension (stiff springs and shocks), D70-14 Firestone Wide Oval tires, modified hood with extra sound insulation, SS emblems, and special hood striping. Early in the model year, the L-35 Chevrolet 396-cid V8 and Turbo Hydra-Matic became available at a cost of nearly $400. Scores of other options tempted buyers: custom carpeting, bucket seats, fold-down back seat, a special interior group, full instrumentation, and console-mounted shifters for the Turbo Hydra-Matic, heavy-duty three speed manual or four-speed manual. For $105, the Rally Sport package added a hidden-headlight grille, special taillights and emblems, aluminum rocker panel moldings, black-painted rocker bottoms, and miscellaneous trim. There were five different wheels and wheel covers, three types of steering wheels, plus headrests, shoulder belts, tinted glass, radios, heater, air conditioning, clock, cruise control, and a vinyl-covered roof for hardtops. Mechanical options included

1969 Impala Custom hardtop coupe

1970 Monte Carlo hardtop coupe

1969 Nova coupe

1970 Nova coupe

1969 Camaro 2-28 hardtop coupe

1970 Chevelle SS 396 hardtop coupe

1970 Caprice hardtop coupe

1970 Camaro sport coupe

sintered metallic brake linings, ventilated front disc brakes, vacuum brake booster, power steering, fast-ratio manual steering, stiff suspension, Positraction, and a dozen different axle ratios. Without too much trouble, a Camaro's price could be boosted to $5000.

The Camaro wasn't significantly changed in 1968 or '69, although interim facelifts were proposed. The ultimate restyling was scheduled for 1970. The '68 model received a new horizontal grille texture, ventless side glass, and restyled taillights. For 1969 there were slimmer body contours, lower front and rear wheel openings, a V-shaped grille, and a new rear styling.

A successful competition Chevrolet of these years

was the Z-28 Camaro, which won 18 of 25 Sports Car Club of America Trans-Am races and was Trans-Am sedan class champion in 1968 and 1969. Vincent W. Piggins, veteran competition engineer, had convinced management a car should be built expressly for SCCA sedan racing. Piggins combined the 327 V8 block with the 283 crankshaft to get a bore and stroke of 4×3 inches for a displacement of 302.4 cubic inches. Officially, this engine delivered 290 bhp at 5800 rpm (actually it was more like 350) and 290 pounds-feet of torque at 4200 rpm. This engine was combined with heavy-duty suspension, front disc brakes, metallic-lined rear drums, 11-inch clutch, close-ratio four-speed

transmission with a 2.20:1 first gear, quick steering, and wide Corvette wheels. The hood was reworked to increase airflow to the carburetor.

The Z-28 name came from the package's option number (not from Zora Arkus-Duntov, the famed Corvette engineer). It was a whale of an automobile for about $3300. Few Z-28s were intended for the general public, of course; the object was to win the Trans-Am championship. But production quickly climbed, from 602 in 1967 to 7199 in 1968 and 19,014 in 1969. The Z-28s are the ultimate performance Camaros. A decade or two from now, they will be one of the ultimate collector's Chevys.

In 1970, Chevrolet entered the personal-luxury field with the Monte Carlo and fielded an all-new Camaro. A 65-day strike prevented the division from outproducing Ford for the calendar year, but the 12-month total of near 1.5 million cars was respectable nonetheless.

The cleanly styled Monte Carlo hardtop sat on the 116-inch wheelbase used for the Chevelle four-doors. Fitted with the 350-cid V8 as standard, it was available with a variety of luxury and performance options to suit every buyer. Numerous engine choices were offered,

up to the huge 454-cid V8. At a base price of nearly $3000, the Monte Carlo sold well: over 130,000 copies in its first year, against a mere 40,000 of Ford's Thunderbird. Of course, the T-Bird was considerably more costly, but the Monte Carlo must be judged a success.

Shorn of its Chevy II designation, the Nova was facelifted for 1970, receiving a fine-mesh grille and large front, side, and rear lights. The intermediate Chevelle was vastly altered, and now bore a family resemblance to the full-size models. It had a divided grille, sculptured sides, and was offered as both a hardtop and a fixed-pillar coupe. The big-car sales emphasis was still on the luxurious Impala and Caprice; Biscayne and Bel Air were reduced to one four-door sedan each, offered with either six or V8.

The brilliant new 1970 Camaro was introduced in the spring of that year; the 1969 model was sold through the previous December. The new Camaro brought dramatic European-inspired GT styling to the ponycar field. Over 143,000 examples were sold that year. Its styling was so good that it was still around with surprisingly few changes ten years later.

# Chevrolet Specifications

## 1940

| KB Master 85 (wb 113.0) | Wght | Price | Prod |
|---|---|---|---|
| bus cpe | 2,865 | 659 | 25,734 |
| Town Sedan 2d, T/B | 2,915 | 699 | 66,431 |
| Sport Sedan 4d, T/B | 2,930 | 740 | 11,468 |
| wgn 4d, 8P | 3,106 | 903 | 411 |

| KH Master DeLuxe (wb 113.0) | | | |
|---|---|---|---|
| bus cpe | 2,920 | 684 | 28,090 |
| Sport Coupe | 2,925 | 715 | 17,234 |
| Town Sedan 2d, T/B | 2,965 | 725 | 143,125 |
| Sport Sedan 4d, T/B | 2,990 | 766 | 40,924 |

| KA Special DeLuxe | | | |
|---|---|---|---|
| bus cpe | 2,930 | 720 | 25,537 |
| Sport Coupe | 2,945 | 750 | 46,628 |
| conv cpe | 3,160 | 898 | 11,820 |
| Town Sedan 2d, T/B | 2,980 | 761 | 205,910 |
| Sport Sedan 4d, T/B | 3,010 | 802 | 138,811 |
| wgn 4d, 8P | 3,158 | 934 | 2,493 |

| 1940 Engine | bore×stroke | bhp | availability |
|---|---|---|---|
| L6, 216.5 | 3.50×3.75 | 85 | S-all |

## 1941

| AG Master DeLuxe (wb 116.0) | Wght | Price | Prod |
|---|---|---|---|
| bus cpe | 3,020 | 712 | 48,763 |
| cpe | 3,025 | 743 | 79,124 |
| Town Sedan 2d | 3,050 | 754 | 219,438 |
| Sport Sedan 4d | 3,090 | 795 | 59,538 |

| AH Special DeLuxe (wb 116.0) | | | |
|---|---|---|---|
| bus cpe | 3,040 | 769 | 17,602 |
| cpe | 3,050 | 800 | 155,889 |
| conv cpe | 3,285 | 949 | 15,296 |
| Town Sedan 2d | 3,095 | 810 | 228,458 |
| Sport Sedan 4d | 3,127 | 851 | 148,661 |
| wgn 4d, 8P | 3,410 | 995 | 2,045 |
| Fleetline sdn 4d | 3,130 | 877 | 34,162 |

| 1941 Engine | bore×stroke | bhp | availability |
|---|---|---|---|
| L6, 216.5 | 3.50×3.75 | 90 | S-all |

## 1942

| BG Stylemaster (wb 116.0) | Wght | Price | Prod |
|---|---|---|---|
| cpe 2P | 3,055 | 760 | 8,089 |
| cpe 5P | 3,060 | 790 | 17,442 |
| Town Sedan 2d | 3,090 | 800 | 41,872 |
| Sport Sedan 4d | 3,110 | 840 | 14,093 |

| BH Fleetmaster (wb 116.0) | | | |
|---|---|---|---|
| cpe 2P | 3,070 | 815 | 1,716 |
| cpe 5p | 3,085 | 845 | 22,187 |
| conv cpe | 3,385 | 1,080 | 1,182 |

# Chevrolet

| | | Wght | Price | Prod |
|---|---|---|---|---|
| | Town Sedan 2d | 3,120 | 855 | 39,421 |
| | Sport Sedan 4d | 3,145 | 895 | 31,441 |
| | wgn 4d, 8P | 3,425 | 1,095 | 1,057 |

### BH Fleetline (wb 116.0)

| | | Wght | Price | Prod |
|---|---|---|---|---|
| | Aerosedan 2d | 3,105 | 880 | 61,885 |
| | Sportmaster sdn 4d | 3,165 | 920 | 14,530 |

| 1942 Engine | bore×stroke | bhp | availability |
|---|---|---|---|
| L6, 216.5 | 3.50×3.75 | 90 | S-all |

## 1946

### DJ Stylemaster (wb 116.0)

| | | Wght | Price | Prod |
|---|---|---|---|---|
| | Sport Sedan 4d | 3,175 | 1,205 | 75,349 |
| | Town Sedan 2d | 3,170 | 1,152 | 61,104 |
| | spt cpe | 3,130 | 1,137 | 19,243 |
| | bus cpe | 3,105 | 1,098 | 14,267 |

### DK Fleetmaster (wb 116.0)

| | | Wght | Price | Prod |
|---|---|---|---|---|
| | Sport Sedan 4d | 3,225 | 1,280 | 73,746 |
| | Town Sedan 2d | 3,190 | 1,225 | 56,538 |
| | spt cpe | 3,145 | 1,212 | 27,036 |
| | conv cpe | 3,445 | 1,476 | 4,508 |
| | wgn 4d, 8P | 3,465 | 1,712 | 804 |

### DK Fleetline (wb 116.0)

| | | Wght | Price | Prod |
|---|---|---|---|---|
| | Sportmaster sdn 4d | 3,240 | 1,309 | 7,501 |
| | Aerosedan 2d | 3,165 | 1,249 | 57,932 |

| 1946 Engine | bore×stroke | bhp | availability |
|---|---|---|---|
| L6, 216.5 | 3.50×3.75 | 90 | S-all |

## 1947

### EJ Stylemaster (wb 116.0)

| | | Wght | Price | Prod |
|---|---|---|---|---|
| | Sport Sedan 4d | 3,130 | 1,276 | 42,571 |
| | Town Sedan 2d | 3,075 | 1,219 | 88,534 |
| | spt cpe | 3,060 | 1,202 | 34,513 |
| | bus cpe | 3,050 | 1,160 | 27,403 |

### EK Fleetmaster (wb 116.0)

| | | Wght | Price | Prod |
|---|---|---|---|---|
| | Sport Sedan 4d | 3,185 | 1,345 | 91,440 |
| | Town Sedan 2d | 3,125 | 1,286 | 80,128 |
| | spt cpe | 3,090 | 1,281 | 59,661 |
| | conv cpe | 3,390 | 1,628 | 28,443 |
| | wgn 4d, 8P | 3,465 | 1,893 | 4,912 |

### EK Fleetline (wb 116.0)

| | | Wght | Price | Prod |
|---|---|---|---|---|
| | Sportmaster sdn 4d | 3,150 | 1,371 | 54,531 |
| | Aerosedan 2d | 3,125 | 1,313 | 159,407 |

| 1947 Engine | bore×stroke | bhp | availability |
|---|---|---|---|
| L6, 216.5 | 3.50×3.75 | 90 | S-all |

## 1948

### FJ Stylemaster (wb 116.0)

| | | Wght | Price | Prod |
|---|---|---|---|---|
| 1502 | Town Sedan 2d | 3,095 | 1,313 | 70,228 |
| 1503 | Sport Sedan 4d | 3,115 | 1,371 | 48,456 |
| 1504 | bus cpe | 3,045 | 1,244 | 18,396 |
| 1524 | spt cpe | 3,020 | 1,323 | 34,513 |

### FK Fleetmaster (wb 116.0)

| | | Wght | Price | Prod |
|---|---|---|---|---|
| 2102 | Town Sedan 2d | 3,110 | 1,381 | 66,208 |
| 2103 | Sport Sedan 4d | 3,150 | 1,439 | 93,142 |
| 2109 | wgn 4d, 8P | 3,430 | 2,013 | 10,171 |
| 2124 | spt cpe | 3,050 | 1,402 | 58,786 |

| | | Wght | Price | Prod |
|---|---|---|---|---|
| 2134 | conv cpe | 3,340 | 1,750 | 20,471 |

### FK Fleetline (wb 116.0)

| | | Wght | Price | Prod |
|---|---|---|---|---|
| 2113 | Sportmaster sdn 4d | 3,150 | 1,492 | 64,217 |
| 2144 | Aerosedan 2d | 3,100 | 1,434 | 211,861 |

| 1948 Engine | bore×stroke | bhp | availability |
|---|---|---|---|
| L6, 216.5 | 3.50×3.75 | 90 | S-all |

## 1949

### GJ Special Styleline (wb 115.0)

| | | Wght | Price | Prod |
|---|---|---|---|---|
| 1502 | Town Sedan 2d | 3,070 | 1,413 | 69,398 |
| 1503 | Sport Sedan 4d | 3,090 | 1,460 | 46,334 |
| 1504 | bus cpe | 3,015 | 1,339 | 20,337 |
| 1524 | spt cpe | 3,030 | 1,418 | 9,310 |

### GJ Special Fleetline (wb 115.0)

| | | Wght | Price | Prod |
|---|---|---|---|---|
| 1552 | sdn 2d | 3,060 | 1,413 | 58,514 |
| 1553 | sdn 4d | 3,095 | 1,460 | 36,317 |

### GK DeLuxe Styleline (wb 115.0)

| | | Wght | Price | Prod |
|---|---|---|---|---|
| 2102 | Town Sedan 2d | 3,100 | 1,492 | 147,347 |
| 2103 | Sport Sedan 2d | 3,125 | 1,539 | 191,357 |
| 2109 | wgn 4d, wood body | 3,485 | 2,267 | 3,342 |
| 2119 | wgn 4d, steel body | 3,465 | 2,267 | 6,006 |
| 2124 | spt cpe | 3,065 | 1,508 | 78,785 |
| 2134 | conv cpe | 3,375 | 1,857 | 32,392 |

### GK DeLuxe Fleetline (wb 115.0)

| | | Wght | Price | Prod |
|---|---|---|---|---|
| 2152 | sdn 2d | 3,100 | 1,492 | 180,251 |
| 2153 | sdn 4d | 3,135 | 1,539 | 130,323 |

| 1949 Engine | bore×stroke | bhp | availability |
|---|---|---|---|
| L6, 216.5 | 3.50×3.75 | 90 | S-all |

## 1950

### HJ Special Styleline (wb 115.0)

| | | Wght | Price | Prod |
|---|---|---|---|---|
| 1502 | Town Sedan 2d | 3,085 | 1,403 | 89,897 |
| 1503 | Sport Sedan 4d | 3,120 | 1,450 | 55,644 |
| 1504 | bus cpe | 3,025 | 1,329 | 20,984 |
| 1524 | spt cpe | 3,050 | 1,408 | 28,328 |

### HJ Special Fleetline (wb 115.0)

| | | Wght | Price | Prod |
|---|---|---|---|---|
| 1552 | sdn 2d | 3,080 | 1,403 | 43,682 |
| 1553 | sdn 4d | 3,115 | 1,450 | 23,277 |

### HK DeLuxe Styleline (wb 115.0)

| | | Wght | Price | Prod |
|---|---|---|---|---|
| 2102 | Town Sedan 2d | 3,100 | 1,482 | 248,567 |
| 2103 | Sport Sedan 4d | 3,150 | 1,529 | 316,412 |
| 2119 | wgn 4d, steel body | 3,460 | 1,994 | 166,995 |
| 2124 | spt cpe | 3,090 | 1,498 | 81,536 |
| 2134 | conv cpe | 3,380 | 1,847 | 32,810 |
| 2154 | Bel Air htp cpe | 3,225 | 1,741 | 76,662 |

### HK DeLuxe Fleetline (wb 115.0)

| | | Wght | Price | Prod |
|---|---|---|---|---|
| 2152 | sdn 2d | 3,115 | 1,482 | 189,509 |
| 2153 | sdn 4d | 3,145 | 1,529 | 124,287 |

| 1950 Engine | bore×stroke | bhp | availability |
|---|---|---|---|
| L6, 216.5 | 3.50×3.75 | 92 | S-all |

## 1951

### JJ Special Styleline (wb 115.0)

| | | Wght | Price | Prod |
|---|---|---|---|---|
| 1502 | sdn 2d | 3,095 | 1,540 | 75,566 |
| 1503 | sdn 4d | 3,130 | 1,595 | 63,718 |

| | | Wght | Price | Prod |
|---|---|---|---|---|
| 1504 | bus cpe | 3,040 | 1,460 | 17,020 |
| 1524 | spt cpe | 3,060 | 1,545 | 18,981 |

**JJ Special Fleetline (wb 115.0)**

| | | | | |
|---|---|---|---|---|
| 1552 | sdn 2d | 3,090 | 1,540 | 6,441 |
| 1553 | sdn 4d | 3,130 | 1,594 | 3,364 |

**JK DeLuxe Styleline (wb 115.0)**

| | | | | |
|---|---|---|---|---|
| 2102 | sdn 2d | 3,110 | 1,629 | 262,933 |
| 2103 | sdn 4d | 3,140 | 1,680 | 380,270 |
| 2119 | wgn 4d | 3,470 | 2,191 | 23,586 |
| 2124 | spt cpe | 3,115 | 1,647 | 64,976 |
| 2134 | conv cpe | 3,380 | 2,030 | 20,172 |
| 2154 | Bel Air htp cpe | 3,225 | 1,914 | 103,356 |

**JK DeLuxe Fleetline (wb 115.0)**

| | | | | |
|---|---|---|---|---|
| 2152 | sdn 2d | 3,125 | 1,629 | 131,910 |
| 2153 | sdn 4d | 3,155 | 1,680 | 57,693 |

| 1951 Engine | bore×stroke | bhp | availability | |
|---|---|---|---|---|
| L6, 216.5 | 3.50×3.75 | 92 | S-all | |

# 1952

**KJ Special Styleline (wb 115.0)**

| | | Wght | Price | Prod |
|---|---|---|---|---|
| 1502 | sdn 2d | 3,085 | 1,614 | 54,781 |
| 1503 | sdn 4d | 3,115 | 1,670 | 35,460 |
| 1504 | bus cpe | 3,045 | 1,530 | 10,359 |
| 1524 | spt cpe | 3,050 | 1,620 | 8,906 |

**KK DeLuxe Styleline (wb 115.0)**

| | | | | |
|---|---|---|---|---|
| 2102 | sdn 2d | 3,110 | 1,707 | 215,417 |
| 2103 | sdn 4d | 3,145 | 1,761 | 319,736 |
| 2119 | wgn 4d | 3,475 | 2,297 | 12,756 |
| 2124 | spt cpe | 3,100 | 1,726 | 36,954 |
| 2134 | conv cpe | 3,380 | 2,128 | 11,975 |
| 2154 | Bel Air htp cpe | 3,215 | 2,006 | 74,634 |

**KK DeLuxe Fleetline (wb 115.0)**

| | | | | |
|---|---|---|---|---|
| 2152 | sdn 2d | 3,110 | 1,707 | 37,164 |

| 1952 Engines | bore×stroke | bhp | availability | |
|---|---|---|---|---|
| L6, 216.5 | 3.50×3.75 | 92 | S-manual shift | |
| L6, 235.5 | 3.56×3.94 | 105 | S-Powerglide | |

# 1953

**150 Special (wb 115.0)**

| | | Wght | Price | Prod |
|---|---|---|---|---|
| 1502 | sdn 2d | 3,180 | 1,613 | 79,416 |
| 1503 | sdn 4d | 3,215 | 1,670 | 54,207 |
| 1504 | bus cpe | 3,140 | 1,524 | 13,555 |
| 1509 | Handyman wgn 4d | 3,420 | 2,010 | 22,408 |
| 1524 | club cpe | 3,140 | 1,620 | 6,993 |

**210 DeLuxe (wb 115.0)**

| | | | | |
|---|---|---|---|---|
| 2102 | sdn 2d | 3,215 | 1,707 | 247,455 |
| 2103 | sdn 4d | 3,250 | 1,761 | 332,497 |
| 2109 | Handyman wgn 4d | 3,450 | 2,123 | 18,258 |
| 2119 | Townsman wgn 4d, 8P | 3,495 | 2,273 | 7,988 |
| 2124 | club cpe | 3,190 | 1,726 | 23,961 |
| 2134 | conv cpe | 3,435 | 2,093 | 5,617 |
| 2154 | htp cpe | 3,295 | 1,967 | 14,045 |

**240 Bel Air (wb 115.0)**

| | | | | |
|---|---|---|---|---|
| 2402 | sdn 2d | 3,230 | 1,820 | 144,401 |
| 2403 | sdn 4d | 3,275 | 1,874 | 247,284 |
| 2434 | conv cpe | 3,470 | 2,175 | 24,047 |
| 2454 | htp cpe | 3,310 | 2,051 | 99,028 |

| 1953 Engines | bore×stroke | bhp | availability | |
|---|---|---|---|---|
| L6, 235.5 | 3.56×3.94 | 105 | S-manual shift | |
| L6, 235.5 | 3.56×3.94 | 115 | S-Powerglide | |

# 1954

**150 Special (wb 115.0)**

| | | Wght | Price | Prod |
|---|---|---|---|---|
| 1502 | sdn 2d | 3,165 | 1,680 | 64,855 |
| 1503 | sdn 4d | 3,210 | 1,623 | 32,430 |
| 1509 | Handyman wgn 4d | 3,455 | 2,020 | 21,404 |
| 1512 | Utility sdn 2d, 3P | 3,145 | 1,539 | 10,770 |

**210 DeLuxe (wb (115.0)**

| | | | | |
|---|---|---|---|---|
| 2102 | sdn 2d | 3,185 | 1,717 | 195,498 |
| 2103 | sdn 4d | 3,230 | 1,771 | 235,146 |
| 2109 | Handyman wgn 4d | 3,470 | 2,133 | 27,175 |
| 2124 | Delray cpe | 3,185 | 1,782 | 66,403 |

**240 Bel Air (wb 115.0)**

| | | | | |
|---|---|---|---|---|
| 2402 | sdn 2d | 3,220 | 1,830 | 143,573 |
| 2403 | sdn 4d | 3,255 | 1,004 | 248,750 |
| 2419 | Townsman wgn 4d, 8P | 3,540 | 2,283 | 8,156 |
| 2434 | conv cpe | 3,445 | 2,185 | 19,383 |
| 2454 | Sport Coupe htp cpe | 3,300 | 2,061 | 66,378 |

| 1954 Engines | bore×stroke | bhp | availability | |
|---|---|---|---|---|
| L6, 235.5 | 3.56×3.94 | 115 | S-manual | |
| L6, 235.5 | 3.56×3.94 | 125 | S-Powerglide | |

# 1955

**150 (wb 115.0)**

| | | Wght | Price | Prod |
|---|---|---|---|---|
| 1502 | sdn 2d | 3,145 | 1,685 | 66,416 |
| 1503 | sdn 4d | 3,150 | 1,728 | 29,898 |
| 1512 | Util sdn | 3,070 | 1,593 | 11,196 |
| 1529 | Handyman wgn 4d | 3,275 | 2,030 | 17,936 |

**210 (wb 115.0)**

| | | | | |
|---|---|---|---|---|
| 2102 | sdn 2d | 3,130 | 1,775 | 249,105 |
| 2103 | sdn 4d | 3,165 | 1,819 | 317,724 |
| 2109 | Townsman wgn 4d | 3,355 | 2,127 | 82,303 |
| 2124 | Delray cpe | 3,130 | 1,835 | 115,584 |
| 2129 | Handyman wgn 2d | 3,315 | 2,079 | 28,918 |
| 2154 | htp cpe | — | — | 11,675 |

**Bel Air (wb 115.0)**

| | | | | |
|---|---|---|---|---|
| 2402 | sdn 2d | 3,140 | 1,888 | 168,313 |
| 2403 | sdn 4d | 3,185 | 1,932 | 345,372 |
| 2409 | Beauville wgn 4d | 3,370 | 2,262 | 24,313 |
| 2429 | Nomad wgn 2d | 3,285 | — | 8,386 |
| 2434 | conv cpe | 3,300 | 2,206 | 41,292 |
| 2454 | Sport Coupe htp cpe | 3,180 | 2,067 | 185,562 |

| 1955 Engines | bore×stroke | bhp | availability | |
|---|---|---|---|---|
| L6, 235.5 | 3.56×3.94 | 123/136 | S-manual/Powerglide | |
| V8, 265.0 | 3.75×3.00 | 162/170 | O-manual/Powerglide | |
| V8, 265.0 | 3.75×3.00 | 180 | O-all | |

# 1956

**150 (wb 115.0)**

| | | Wght | Price | Prod |
|---|---|---|---|---|
| 1502 | sdn 2d | 3,154 | 1,826 | 82,384 |
| 1503 | sdn 4d | 3,196 | 1,869 | 51,544 |
| 1512 | Util sdn | 3,117 | 1,734 | 9,879 |
| 1529 | Handyman wgn 2d | 3,299 | 2,171 | 13,487 |

**210 (wb 115.0)**

| | | | | |
|---|---|---|---|---|
| 2102 | sdn 2d | 3,167 | 1,912 | 205,545 |
| 2103 | sdn 4d | 3,202 | 1,955 | 283,125 |
| 2109 | Townsman wgn 4d | 3,371 | 2,263 | 113,656 |
| 2113 | Sport htp sdn | 3,252 | 2,117 | 20,021 |
| 2119 | Beauville wgn 4d, 9P | 3,490 | 2,348 | 17,988 |
| 2124 | Delray cpe | 3,172 | 1,971 | 56,382 |
| 2129 | Handyman wgn 2d | 3,334 | 2,215 | 22,038 |
| 2154 | Sport htp cpe | 3,194 | 2,063 | 18,616 |

### Bel Air (wb 115.0)

| | | Wght | Price | Prod |
|---|---|---|---|---|
| 2402 | sdn 2d | 3,187 | 2,025 | 104,849 |
| 2403 | sdn 4d | 3,221 | 2,068 | 269,798 |
| 2413 | Sport htp sdn | 3,270 | 2,230 | 103,602 |
| 2419 | Beauville wgn 4d, 9P | 3,506 | 2,482 | 13,279 |
| 2429 | Nomad wgn 2d | 3,352 | 2,608 | 7,886 |
| 2434 | conv cpe | 3,330 | 2,344 | 41,268 |
| 2454 | Sport htp cpe | 3,222 | 2,176 | 128,382 |

| 1956 Engines | bore×stroke | bhp | availability |
|---|---|---|---|
| L6, 235.5 | 3.56×3.94 | 140 | S-all |
| V8, 265.0 | 3.75×3.00 | 162/170 | O-manual/Powerglide |
| V8, 265.0 | 3.75×3.00 | 205/225 | O-all |

## 1957

### 150 (wb 115.0)

| | | Wght | Price | Prod |
|---|---|---|---|---|
| 1502 | sdn 2d | 3,211 | 1,996 | 70,774 |
| 1503 | sdn 4d | 3,236 | 2,048 | 52,266 |
| 1512 | Util sdn 2d | 3,163 | 1,885 | 8,300 |
| 1529 | Handyman wgn 2d | 3,406 | 2,307 | 14,740 |

### 210 (wb 115.0)

| | | Wght | Price | Prod |
|---|---|---|---|---|
| 2102 | sdn 2d | 3,225 | 2,122 | 160,090 |
| 2103 | sdn 4d | 3,270 | 2,174 | 260,401 |
| 2109 | Townsman wgn 4d | 3,461 | 2,456 | 127,803 |
| 2113 | Sport htp sdn | 3,320 | 2,270 | 16,178 |
| 2119 | Beauville wgn 4d | 3,561 | 2,563 | 21,083 |
| 2124 | Delray cpe | 3,220 | 2,162 | 25,644 |
| 2129 | Handyman wgn 2d | 3,406 | 2,402 | 17,528 |
| 2154 | Sport htp cpe | 3,260 | 2,204 | 22,631 |

### Bel Air (wb 115.0)

| | | Wght | Price | Prod |
|---|---|---|---|---|
| 2402 | sdn 2d | 3,232 | 2,238 | 62,757 |
| 2403 | sdn 4d | 3,276 | 2,290 | 254,331 |
| 2409 | Townsman wgn 4d | 3,460 | 2,580 | 27,375 |
| 2413 | Sport htp sdn | 3,340 | 2,364 | 137,672 |
| 2429 | Nomad wgn 2d | 3,465 | 2,757 | 6,103 |
| 2434 | conv cpe | 3,409 | 2,511 | 47,562 |
| 2454 | Sport htp cpe | 3,278 | 2,299 | 166,426 |

| 1957 Engines | bore×stroke | bhp | availability |
|---|---|---|---|
| L6, 235.5 | 3.56×3.94 | 140 | S-all |
| V8, 265.0 | 3.75×3.00 | 162 | O-all w/manual shift |
| V8, 283.0 | 3.88×3.00 | 185 | S-all w/automatic |
| V8, 283.0 | 3.88×3.00 | 245/250 | O-all |
| V8, 283.0 | 3.88×3.00 | 270/283 | O-manual shift |

## 1958

### Delray (wb 117.5)—178,000* built

| | | Wght | Price | Prod |
|---|---|---|---|---|
| 1121 | Util sdn 2d, L6 | 3,351 | 2,013 | — |
| 1141 | sdn 2d, L6 | 3,396 | 2,101 | — |
| 1149 | sdn 4d, L6 | 3,439 | 2,155 | — |
| 1221 | Util sdn 2d, V8 | 3,156 | 2,120 | — |
| 1241 | sdn 2d, V8 | 3,399 | 2,208 | — |
| 1249 | sdn 4d, V8 | 3,442 | 2,262 | — |

### Biscayne (wb 117.5)—100,000* built exc 1541

| | | Wght | Price | Prod |
|---|---|---|---|---|
| 1541 | sdn 2d, L6 | 3,404 | 2,236 | 76,229 |
| 1549 | sdn 4d, L6 | 3,447 | 2,290 | — |
| 1641 | sdn 2d, V8 | 3,407 | 2,343 | — |
| 1649 | sdn 4d, V8 | 3,450 | 2,397 | — |

### Bel Air (wb 117.5)—592,000* built

| | | Wght | Price | Prod |
|---|---|---|---|---|
| 1731 | Sport htp cpe, L6 | 3,455 | 2,447 | — |
| 1739 | Sport htp sdn, L6 | 3,511 | 2,511 | — |
| 1741 | sdn 2d, L6 | 3,424 | 2,386 | — |

| | | Wght | Price | Prod |
|---|---|---|---|---|
| 1747 | Impala htp cpe, L6 | 3,458 | 2,586 | — |
| 1749 | sdn 4d, L6 | 3,467 | 2,440 | — |
| 1767 | Impala conv cpe, L6 | 3,522 | 2,734 | — |
| 1831 | Sport htp cpe, V8 | 3,458 | 2,554 | — |
| 1839 | Sport htp sdn, V8 | 3,514 | 2,618 | — |
| 1841 | sdn 2d, V8 | 3,427 | 2,493 | — |
| 1847 | Impala htp cpe, V8 | 3,459 | 2,693 | — |
| 1849 | sdn 4d, V8 | 3,470 | 2,547 | — |
| 1867 | Impala conv cpe, V8 | 3,523 | 2,841 | — |

### Station Wagon (wb 117.5)—187,063 built

| | | Wght | Price | Prod |
|---|---|---|---|---|
| 1191 | Yeoman 2d, L6 | 3,693 | 2,413 | — |
| 1193 | Yeoman 4d, L6 | 3,740 | 2,467 | — |
| 1291 | Yeoman 2d, V8 | 3,696 | 2,520 | — |
| 1292 | Yeoman 4d, V8 | 3,743 | 2,574 | — |
| 1593 | Brookwood 4d, 6P, L6 | 3,748 | 2,571 | — |
| 1594 | Brookwood 4d, 9P, L6 | 3,837 | 2,678 | — |
| 1693 | Brookwood 4d, 6P, V8 | 3,751 | 2,678 | — |
| 1694 | Brookwood 4d, 9P, V8 | 3,839 | 2,785 | — |
| 1793 | Nomad 4d, L6 | 3,768 | 2,728 | — |
| 1893 | Nomad 4d, V8 | 3,771 | 2,835 | — |

*To nearest 100. Impalas approximately 60,000.

| 1958 Engines | bore×stroke | bhp | availability |
|---|---|---|---|
| L6, 235.5 | 3.56×3.94 | 145 | S-six |
| V8, 283.0 | 3.88×3.00 | 185 | S-V8 |
| V8, 348.0 | 4.13×3.25 | 250 | O-all |

## 1959

### Biscayne (wb 119.0)—311,800* built

| | | Wght | Price | Prod |
|---|---|---|---|---|
| 1111 | sdn 2d, L6 | 3,535 | 2,247 | — |
| 1119 | sdn 4d, L6 | 3,605 | 2,301 | — |
| 1121 | Util sdn 2d, L6 | 3,480 | 2,160 | — |
| 1211 | sdn 2d, V8 | 3,530 | 2,365 | — |
| 1219 | sdn 4d, V8 | 3,600 | 2,419 | — |
| 1221 | Util sdn 2d, V8 | 3,490 | 2,278 | — |

### Bel Air (wb 119.0)—447,100* built

| | | Wght | Price | Prod |
|---|---|---|---|---|
| 1511 | sdn 2d, L6 | 3,515 | 2,386 | — |
| 1519 | sdn 4d, L6 | 3,600 | 2,440 | — |
| 1539 | Sport htp sdn, L6 | 3,660 | 2,556 | — |
| 1611 | sdn 2d, V8 | 3,510 | 2,504 | — |
| 1619 | sdn 4d, V8 | 3,615 | 2,558 | — |
| 1639 | Sport htp sdn, V8 | 3,630 | 2,674 | — |

### Impala (wb 119.0)—407,200* built exc 1867

| | | Wght | Price | Prod |
|---|---|---|---|---|
| 1719 | sdn 4d, L6 | 3,625 | 2,592 | — |
| 1737 | Sport htp cpe, L6 | 3,570 | 2,599 | — |
| 1739 | Sport htp sdn, L6 | 3,665 | 2,664 | — |
| 1767 | conv cpe, L6 | 3,660 | 2,849 | — |
| 1819 | sdn 4d, V8 | 3,620 | 2,710 | — |
| 1837 | Sport htp cpe, V8 | 3,580 | 2,717 | — |
| 1839 | Sport htp sdn, V8 | 3,670 | 2,782 | — |
| 1867 | conv cpe, V8 | 3,650 | 2,967 | 65,800 |

### Station Wagon (wb 119.0)—195,583 built exc 1215

| | | Wght | Price | Prod |
|---|---|---|---|---|
| 1115 | Brookwood 2d, L6 | 3,870 | 2,571 | — |
| 1135 | Brookwood 4d, L6 | 3,955 | 2,638 | — |
| 1215 | Brookwood, 2d, V8 | 3,860 | 2,689 | 18,800 |
| 1235 | Brookwood, 4d, V8 | 3,955 | 2,756 | — |
| 1535 | Parkwood 4d, L6 | 3,965 | 2,749 | — |
| 1545 | Kingswood, 4d, 9P, L6 | 4,020 | 2,852 | — |
| 1635 | Parkwood 4d, V8 | 3,970 | 2,867 | — |
| 1645 | Kingswood 4d, 9P, V8 | 4,015 | 2,970 | — |
| 1735 | Nomad 4d, L6 | 3,980 | 2,891 | — |
| 1835 | Nomad 4d, V8 | 3,975 | 3,009 | — |

*To nearest 100.

| 1959 Engines | bore×stroke | bhp | availability |
|---|---|---|---|
| L6, 235.5 | 3.56×3.94 | 135 | S-six |
| V8, 283.0 | 3.88×3.00 | 185 | S-V8 |
| V8, 348.0 | 4.13×3.25 | 250–315 | O-all |

## 1960

| Biscayne (wb 119.0)—287,700* built | | Wght | Price | Prod |
|---|---|---|---|---|
| 1111 | sdn 2d, L6 | 3,485 | 2,262 | — |
| 1119 | sdn 4d, L6 | 3,555 | 2,316 | — |
| 1121 | Util sdn 2d, L6 | 3,455 | 2,175 | — |
| 1211 | sdn 2d, V8 | 3,500 | 2,369 | — |
| 1219 | sdn 4d, V8 | 3,570 | 2,423 | — |
| 1221 | Util sdn 2d, V8 | 3,470 | 2,282 | — |

| Biscayne Fleetmaster (wb 119.0)—prod included with Biscayne | | | | |
|---|---|---|---|---|
| 1311 | sdn 2d, L6 | 3,480 | 2,230 | — |
| 1319 | sdn 4d, L6 | 3,545 | 2,284 | — |
| 1411 | sdn 2d, V8 | 3,495 | 2,337 | — |
| 1419 | sdn 4d, V8 | 3,560 | 2,391 | — |

| Bel Air (wb 119.0)—381,500* built | | | | |
|---|---|---|---|---|
| 1511 | sdn 2d, L6 | 3,490 | 2,384 | — |
| 1519 | sdn 4d, L6 | 3,565 | 2,438 | — |
| 1537 | Sport htp cpe, L6 | 3,515 | 2,489 | — |
| 1539 | Sport htp sdn, L6 | 3,605 | 2,554 | — |
| 1611 | sdn 2d, V8 | 3,505 | 2,491 | — |
| 1619 | sdn 4d, V8 | 3,500 | 2,545 | — |
| 1637 | Sport htp cpe, L6 | 3,530 | 2,596 | — |
| 1639 | Sport htp sdn, V8 | 3,620 | 2,661 | — |

| Impala (wb 119.0)—411,000* built exc 1867 | | | | |
|---|---|---|---|---|
| 1719 | sdn 4d, L6 | 3,575 | 2,590 | — |
| 1737 | Sport htp cpe, L6 | 3,530 | 2,597 | — |
| 1739 | Sport htp sdn, L6 | 3,625 | 2,662 | — |
| 1767 | conv cpe, L6 | 3,625 | 2,847 | — |
| 1819 | sdn 4d, V8 | 3,580 | 2,697 | — |
| 1837 | Sport htp cpe, V8 | 3,540 | 2,704 | — |
| 1839 | Sport htp sdn, V8 | 3,625 | 2,769 | — |
| 1867 | conv cpe, V8 | 3,635 | 2,954 | 100,000* |

| Station Wagon (wb 119.0)—212,700* built | | | | |
|---|---|---|---|---|
| 1115 | Brookwood 2d, L6 | 3,845 | 2,586 | — |
| 1135 | Brookwood 4d, L6 | 3,935 | 2,653 | — |
| 1215 | Brookwood 2d, V8 | 3,855 | 2,693 | — |
| 1235 | Brookwood 4d, V8 | 3,935 | 2,760 | — |
| 1535 | Parkwood 4d, L6 | 3,945 | 2,747 | — |
| 1545 | Kingswood, 4d, 9P, L6 | 3,990 | 2,850 | — |
| 1635 | Parkwood 4d, V8 | 3,950 | 2,854 | — |
| 1645 | Kingswood 4d, 9P, V8 | 4,000 | 2,957 | 9 |
| 1735 | Nomad 4d, L6 | 3,955 | 2,889 | — |
| 1835 | Nomad 4d, V8 | 3,960 | 2,996 | — |

*To nearest 100; model 1645 dropped.

| 1960 Engines | bore×stroke | bhp | availability |
|---|---|---|---|
| L6, 235.5 | 3.56×3.94 | 135 | S-six |
| V8, 283.0 | 3.88×3.00 | 170 | S-V8 |
| V8, 348.0 | 4.13×3.25 | 250–335 | O-all |

## 1961

| Biscayne (wb 119.0)—201,000* built | | Wght | Price | Prod |
|---|---|---|---|---|
| 1111 | sdn 2d, L6 | 3,415 | 2,262 | — |
| 1121 | Util sdn 2d, L6 | 3,390 | 2,175 | — |
| 1169 | sdn 4d, L6 | 3,500 | 2,316 | — |
| 1211 | sdn 2d, V8 | 3,425 | 2,369 | — |
| 1221 | Util sdn 2d, V8 | 3,395 | 2,282 | — |
| 1269 | sdn 4d, V8 | 3,505 | 2,423 | — |

| Biscayne Fleetmaster (wb 119.0) | | | | |
|---|---|---|---|---|
| 1311 | sdn 2d, L6 | 3,410 | 2,230 | ** |
| 1369 | sdn 4d, L6 | 3,495 | 2,284 | ** |
| 1411 | sdn 2d, V8 | 3,415 | 2,337 | 3,000 |
| 1469 | sdn 4d, V8 | 3,500 | 2,391 | |

| Bel Air (wb 119.0)—330,000* built | | Wght | Price | Prod |
|---|---|---|---|---|
| 1511 | sdn 2d, L6 | 3,430 | 2,384 | — |
| 1537 | Sport htp cpe, L6 | 3,475 | 2,489 | — |
| 1539 | Sport htp sdn, L6 | 3,550 | 2,554 | — |
| 1569 | sdn 4d, L6 | 3,515 | 2,438 | — |
| 1611 | sdn 2d, V8 | 3,435 | 2,491 | — |
| 1637 | Sport htp cpe, V8 | 3,480 | 2,596 | — |
| 1639 | Sport htp sdn, V8 | 3,555 | 2,661 | — |
| 1669 | sdn 4d, V8 | 3,520 | 2,545 | — |

| Impala (wb 119.0)—426,400* built exc 1867 | | | | |
|---|---|---|---|---|
| 1711 | sdn 2d, L6 | 3,445 | 2,536 | — |
| 1737 | Sport htp cpe, L6 | 3,485 | 2,597 | — |
| 1739 | Sport htp sdn, L6 | 3,575 | 2,662 | — |
| 1767 | conv cpe, L6 | 3,605 | 2,847 | — |
| 1769 | sdn 4d, L6 | 3,530 | 2,590 | — |
| 1811 | sdn 2d, V8 | 3,440 | 2,643 | — |
| 1837 | Sport htp cpe, V8 | 3,480 | 2,704 | — |
| 1839 | Sport htp sdn, V8 | 3,570 | 2,769 | — |
| 1867 | conv cpe, V8 | 3,600 | 2,954 | 64,600 |
| 1869 | sdn 4d, V8 | 3,525 | 2,697 | — |

| Station Wagon (wb 119.0)*** | | | | |
|---|---|---|---|---|
| 1135 | Brookwood 4d, L6 | 3,850 | 2,653 | — |
| 1145 | Brookwood 4d, 9P, L6 | 3,900 | 2,756 | — |
| 1235 | Brookwood 4d, V8 | 3,845 | 2,760 | — |
| 1245 | Brookwood 4d, 9P, V8 | 3,895 | 2,864 | — |
| 1535 | Parkwood 4d, L6 | 3,865 | 2,747 | — |
| 1545 | Parkwood 4d, 9P, L6 | 3,910 | 2,850 | — |
| 1635 | Parkwood 4d, V8 | 3,860 | 2,854 | — |
| 1645 | Parkwood 4d, 9P, V8 | 3,905 | 2,957 | — |
| 1735 | Nomad 4d, L6 | 3,885 | 2,889 | — |
| 1745 | Nomad 4d, 9P, L6 | 3,935 | 2,992 | — |
| 1835 | Nomad 4d, V8 | 3,880 | 2,996 | — |
| 1845 | Nomad 4d, 9P, V8 | 3,930 | 3,099 | — |

*To nearest 100.
**Included with Biscayne.
***Included with models above.

| 1961 Engines | bore×stroke | bhp | availability |
|---|---|---|---|
| L6, 235.5 | 3.56×3.94 | 135 | S-six |
| V8, 283.0 | 3.88×3.00 | 170 | S-V8 |
| V8, 348.0 | 4.13×3.25 | 250–335 | O-all |

## 1962

| Chevy II 100 (wb 110.0) | | Wght | Price | Prod |
|---|---|---|---|---|
| 0111 | sdn 2d, L4 | 2,410 | 2,003 | 11,500* |
| 0135 | wgn 4d, L4 | 2,665 | 2,399 | |
| 0169 | sdn 4d, L4 | 2,445 | 2,041 | |
| 0211 | sdn 2d, L6 | 2,500 | 2,063 | 35,500* |
| 0235 | wgn 4d, L6 | 2,755 | 2,399 | |
| 0269 | sdn 4d, L6 | 2,535 | 2,101 | |

| Chevy II 300 (wb 110.0) | | | | |
|---|---|---|---|---|
| 0311 | sdn 2d, L4 | 2,425 | 2,084 | — |
| 0345 | wgn 4d, 9P, L4 | 2,765 | 2,517 | — |
| 0369 | sdn 4d, L4 | 2,460 | 2,122 | — |
| 0411 | sdn 2d, L6 | 2,515 | 2,144 | 92,800* |
| 0445 | wgn 4d, 9P, L6 | 2,855 | 2,577 | |
| 0469 | sdn 4d, L6 | 2,550 | 2,182 | |

| Chevy II Nova 400, L6 (wb 110.0) | | | | |
|---|---|---|---|---|
| 0435 | wgn 4d | 2,775 | 2,497 | — |
| 0437 | Sport htp cpe | 2,550 | 2,254 | 59,586 |
| 0441 | sdn 2d | 2,540 | 2,198 | 44,390 |
| 0449 | sdn 4d | 2,575 | 2,336 | 139,004 |
| 0467 | conv cpe | 2,745 | 2,475 | 23,741 |

# Chevrolet

| Biscayne (wb 119.0)—160,000** built | | Wght | Price | Prod |
|---|---|---|---|---|
| 1111 | sdn 2d, L6 | 3,405 | 2,324 | — |
| 1135 | wgn 4d, L6 | 3,845 | 2,725 | — |
| 1169 | sdn 4d, L6 | 3,480 | 2,378 | — |
| 1211 | sdn 2d, V8 | 3,400 | 2,431 | — |
| 1235 | wgn 4d, V8 | 3,840 | 2,832 | — |
| 1269 | sdn 4d, V8 | 3,475 | 2,485 | — |
| **Bel Air (wb 119.0)—365,000** built** | | | | |
| 1511 | sdn 2d, L6 | 3,410 | 2,456 | — |
| 1535 | wgn 4d, L6 | 3,845 | 2,819 | — |
| 1537 | Sport htp cpe, L6 | 3,445 | 2,561 | — |
| 1545 | wgn 4d, 9P, L6 | 3,895 | 2,922 | — |
| 1569 | sdn 4d, L6 | 3,480 | 2,510 | — |
| 1611 | sdn 2d, V8 | 3,405 | 2,563 | — |
| 1635 | wgn 4d, V8 | 3,840 | 2,926 | — |
| 1637 | Sport htp cpe, V8 | 3,440 | 2,668 | — |
| 1645 | wgn 4d, 9P, V8 | 3,890 | 3,029 | — |
| 1669 | sdn 4d, V8 | 3,475 | 2,617 | — |
| **Impala (wb 119.0)—704,900** built (includes SS models)** | | | | |
| 1735 | wgn 4d, L6 | 3,870 | 2,961 | — |
| 1739 | Sport htp sdn, L6 | 3,540 | 2,734 | — |
| 1745 | wgn 4d, 9P, L6 | 3,925 | 3,064 | — |
| 1747 | Sport htp cpe, L6 | 3,455 | 2,669 | — |
| 1767 | conv cpe, L6 | 3,565 | 2,919 | — |
| 1769 | sdn 4d, L6 | 3,510 | 2,662 | — |
| 1835 | wgn 4d, V8 | 3,865 | 3,068 | — |
| 1839 | Sport htp sdn, V8 | 3,535 | 2,841 | — |
| 1845 | wgn 4d, 9P, V8 | 3,920 | 3,171 | — |
| 1847 | Sport htp cpe, V8 | 3,450 | 2,776 | — |
| 1867 | conv cpe, V8 | 3,560 | 3,026 | — |
| 1869 | sdn 4d, V8 | 3,505 | 2,769 | — |

*To nearest 100.
**Does not include wagons.

| 1962 Engines | bore×stroke | bhp | availability |
|---|---|---|---|
| L4, 153.0 | 3.88×3.25 | 90 | S-Chevy II 100, 300 |
| L6, 194.0 | 3.56×3.25 | 120 | S-Chevy II all |
| L6, 235.5 | 3.56×3.94 | 135 | S-Chevrolet |
| V8, 283.0 | 3.88×3.00 | 170 | S-Chevrolet |
| V8, 327.0 | 4.00×3.25 | 250/300 | O-V8-all Chev |
| V8, 409.0 | 4.31×3.50 | 380/409 | O-V8-all Chev |

## 1963

| Chevy II 100 (wb 110.0)—50,400* built | | Wght | Price | Prod |
|---|---|---|---|---|
| 0111 | sdn 2d, L4 | 2,430 | 2,003 | — |
| 0135 | wgn 4d, L4 | 2,725 | 2,338 | — |
| 0169 | sdn 4d, L4 | 2,455 | 2,040 | — |
| 0211 | sdn 2d, L6 | 2,520 | 2,062 | — |
| 0235 | wgn 4d, L6 | 2,810 | 2,397 | — |
| 0269 | sdn 4d, L6 | 2,545 | 2,099 | — |
| **Chevy II 300 (wb 110.0)—78,800* built** | | | | |
| 0311 | sdn 2d, L4 | 2,440 | 2,084 | — |
| 0345 | wgn 4d, 9P, L4 | 2,810 | 2,516 | — |
| 0369 | sdn 4d, L4 | 2,470 | 2,121 | — |
| 0411 | sdn 2d, L6 | 2,530 | 2,143 | — |
| 0445 | wgn 4d, 9P, L6 | 2,900 | 2,575 | — |
| 0469 | sdn 4d, L6 | 2,560 | 2,180 | — |
| **Chevy II Nova 400, L6 (wb 110.0)** | | | | |
| 0435 | wgn 4d | 2,835 | 2,494 | — |
| 0437 | Sport htp cpe | 2,590 | 2,267 | 87,415 |
| 0449 | sdn 4d | 2,590 | 2,235 | 58,862 |
| 0467 | conv cpe | 2,760 | 2,472 | 24,823 |
| **Biscayne (wb 119.0)—186,500* built** | | | | |
| 1111 | sdn 2d, L6 | 3,205 | 2,322 | — |
| 1135 | wgn 4d, L6 | 3,685 | 2,723 | — |

| 1169 | sdn 4d, L6 | 3,280 | 2,376 | — |
|---|---|---|---|---|
| 1211 | sdn 2d, V8 | 3,340 | 2,429 | — |
| 1235 | wgn 4d, V8 | 3,810 | 2,830 | — |
| 1269 | sdn 4d, V8 | 3,415 | 2,483 | — |
| **Bel Air (wb 119.0)—354,100* built** | | Wght | Price | Prod |
| 1511 | sdn 2d, L6 | 3,215 | 2,454 | — |
| 1535 | wgn 4d, L6 | 3,685 | 2,818 | — |
| 1545 | wgn 4d, 9P, L6 | 3,720 | 2,921 | — |
| 1569 | sdn 4d, L6 | 3,280 | 2,508 | — |
| 1611 | sdn 2d, V8 | 3,345 | 2,561 | — |
| 1635 | wgn 4d, V8 | 3,810 | 2,925 | — |
| 1645 | wgn 4d, 9P, V8 | 3,850 | 3,028 | — |
| 1669 | sdn 4d, V8 | 3,415 | 2,615 | — |
| **Impala (wb 119.)—832,600* built (includes SS models)** | | | | |
| 1735 | wgn 4d, L6 | 3,705 | 2,960 | — |
| 1739 | Sport htp sdn, L6 | 3,350 | 2,732 | — |
| 1745 | wgn 4d, 9P, L6 | 3,745 | 3,063 | — |
| 1747 | Sport htp cpe, L6 | 3,265 | 2,667 | — |
| 1767 | conv cpe, L6 | 3,400 | 2,917 | — |
| 1769 | sdn 4d, L6 | 3,310 | 2,661 | — |
| 1835 | wgn 4d, V8 | 3,835 | 3,067 | — |
| 1839 | Sport htp sdn, V8 | 3,475 | 2,839 | — |
| 1845 | wgn 4d, 9P, V8 | 3,870 | 3,170 | — |
| 1847 | Sport htp cpe, V8 | 3,390 | 2,774 | — |
| 1867 | conv cpe, V8 | 3,525 | 3,024 | — |
| 1869 | sdn 4d, V8 | 3,435 | 2,768 | — |

*To nearest 100; does not include wagons. Total wagons 187,600; Chevy II wagons 75,274.

| 1963 Engines | bore×stroke | bhp | availability |
|---|---|---|---|
| L4, 153.0 | 3.88×3.25 | 90 | S-Chevy II |
| L6, 194.0 | 3.56×3.25 | 120 | S-Chevy II |
| L6, 230.0 | 3.87×3.25 | 140 | S-Chevrolet |
| V8, 283.0 | 3.88×3.00 | 170 | S-Chevrolet |
| V8, 327.0 | 4.00×3.25 | 250/300 | O-Chevrolet |
| V8, 409.0 | 4.31×3.50 | 340–425 | O-Chevrolet |

## 1964

| Chevy II 100 (wb 110.0)—53,100 built* | | Wght | Price | Prod |
|---|---|---|---|---|
| 0110 | sdn 2d, L4 | 2,455 | 2,011 | — |
| 0169 | sdn, L4 | 2,495 | 2,048 | — |
| 0211 | sdn 2d, L6 | 2,540 | 2,070 | — |
| 0235 | wgn 4d, L6 | 2,840 | 2,406 | — |
| 0269 | sdn 4d, L6 | 2,580 | 2,108 | — |
| **Chevy II Nova 400, L6 (wb 110.0)—102,900* built (includes SS)** | | | | |
| 0411 | sdn 2d | 2,560 | 2,206 | — |
| 0435 | wgn 4d | 2,860 | 2,503 | — |
| 0437 | Sport htp cpe | 2,660 | 2,271 | — |
| 0469 | sdn 4d | 2,595 | 2,243 | — |
| **Chevy II Nova SS, L6 (wb 110.0)** | | | | |
| 0447 | Sport htp cpe | 2,675 | 2,433 | — |
| **Chevelle 300 (wb 115.0)—68,300* built** | | | | |
| 5311 | sdn 2d, L6 | 2,825 | 2,231 | — |
| 5315 | wgn 2d, L6 | 3,050 | 2,528 | — |
| 5335 | wgn 4d, L6 | 3,130 | 2,566 | — |
| 5369 | sdn 4d, L6 | 2,850 | 2,268 | — |
| 5411 | sdn 2d, V8 | 2,995 | 2,339 | — |
| 5415 | wgn 2d, V8 | 3,170 | 2,636 | — |
| 5435 | wgn 4d, V8 | 2,250 | 2,674 | — |
| 5469 | sdn 4d, V8 | 2,980 | 2,376 | — |
| **Chevelle Malibu (wb 115.0) 149,000* built** | | | | |
| 5535 | wgn 4d, L6 | 3,140 | 2,647 | — |
| 5537 | Sport htp cpe, L6 | 2,850 | 2,376 | — |
| 5545 | wgn 4d, 9P, L6 | 3,240 | 2,744 | — |

| | | Wght | Price | Prod |
|---|---|---|---|---|
| 5567 | conv cpe, L6 | 2,995 | 2,587 | — |
| 5569 | sdn 4d, L6 | 2,870 | 2,349 | — |
| 5635 | wgn 4d, V8 | 3,265 | 2,755 | — |
| 5637 | Sport htp cpe, V8 | 2,975 | 2,484 | — |
| 5645 | wgn 4d, 9P, V8 | 3,365 | 2,852 | — |
| 5667 | conv cpe, V8 | 3,120 | 2,695 | — |
| 5669 | sdn 4d, V8 | 2,996 | 2,457 | — |

**Chevelle Malibu SS (wb 115.0) —67,100* built**

| | | Wght | Price | Prod |
|---|---|---|---|---|
| 5737 | Sport htp cpe, L6 | 2,875 | 2,538 | — |
| 5767 | conv cpe, L6 | 3,020 | 2,749 | — |
| 5837 | Sport htp cpe, V8 | 3,000 | 2,646 | — |
| 5867 | conv cpe, V8 | 3,145 | 2,857 | — |

**Biscayne (wb 119.0)—173,900* built**

| | | Wght | Price | Prod |
|---|---|---|---|---|
| 1111 | sdn 2d, L6 | 3,230 | 2,363 | — |
| 1135 | wgn 4d, L6 | 3,700 | 2,763 | — |
| 1169 | sdn 4d, L6 | 3,300 | 2,411 | — |
| 1211 | sdn 2d, V8 | 3,365 | 2,471 | — |
| 1235 | wgn 4d, V8 | 3,820 | 2,871 | — |
| 1269 | sdn 4d, V8 | 3,430 | 2,524 | — |

**Bel Air (wb 119.0)—318,100* built**

| | | Wght | Price | Prod |
|---|---|---|---|---|
| 1511 | sdn 2d, L6 | 3,235 | 2,465 | — |
| 1535 | wgn 4d, L6 | 3,745 | 2,828 | — |
| 1545 | wgn 4d, 9P, L6 | 3,705 | 2,931 | — |
| 1569 | sdn 4d, L6 | 3,305 | 2,519 | — |
| 1611 | sdn 2d, V8 | 3,370 | 2,573 | — |
| 1635 | wgn 4d, V8 | 3,825 | 2,935 | — |
| 1645 | wgn 4d, 9P, V8 | 3,865 | 3,039 | — |
| 1669 | sdn 4d, V8 | 3,440 | 2,626 | — |

**Impala (wb 119.0)—889,600* built (includes SS)**

| | | Wght | Price | Prod |
|---|---|---|---|---|
| 1735 | wgn 4d, L6 | 3,725 | 2,970 | — |
| 1739 | Sport htp sdn, L6 | 3,370 | 2,742 | — |
| 1745 | wgn 4d, 9P, L6 | 3,770 | 3,073 | — |
| 1767 | conv cpe, L6 | 3,400 | 2,927 | — |
| 1769 | sdn 4d, L6 | 3,340 | 2,671 | — |
| 1835 | wgn 4d, V8 | 3,850 | 3,077 | — |
| 1839 | Sport htp sdn, V8 | 3,490 | 2,850 | — |
| 1845 | wgn 4d, 9P, V8 | 3,895 | 3,181 | — |
| 1847 | Sport htp cpe, V8 | 3,415 | 2,786 | — |
| 1867 | conv cpe, V8 | 3,525 | 3,035 | — |
| 1869 | sdn 4d, V8 | 3,460 | 2,779 | — |

**Impala SS (wb 119.0)**

| | | Wght | Price | Prod |
|---|---|---|---|---|
| 1347 | htp cpe, L6 | 3,325 | 2,839 | — |
| 1367 | conv cpe, L6 | 3,435 | 3,088 | — |
| 1447 | Sport htp cpe, V8 | 3,450 | 2,947 | — |
| 1467 | conv cpe, V8 | 3,555 | 3,196 | — |

*To nearest 100; does not include wagons. Wagon production: Chevy II 35,700; Chevelle 44,000; others 192,800.

| 1964 Engines | bore×stroke | bhp | availability |
|---|---|---|---|
| L4, 153.0 | 3.88×3.25 | 90 | S-Chevy II 100 |
| L6, 194.0 | 3.56×3.25 | 120 | S-Chevy II 100/400, Chevelle |
| L6, 230.0 | 3.87×3.25 | 140 | S-Chevrolet; O-others |
| L6, 230.0 | 3.87×3.25 | 155 | O-all |
| V8, 283.0 | 3.88×3.00 | 195 | S-V8 Chvlle, Chvrlet; O-Chevy II |
| V8, 283.0 | 3.88×3.00 | 220 | O-Chevelle |
| V8, 327.0 | 4.00×3.25 | 250/300 | O-Chevrolet |
| V8, 409.0 | 4.31×3.50 | 340–425 | O-Chevrolet |

# 1965

**Chevy II 100 (wb 110.0)**

| | | Wght | Price | Prod |
|---|---|---|---|---|
| 11111 | sdn 2d, L4 | 2,505 | 2,011 | 1,300* |
| 11169 | sdn 4d, L4 | 2,520 | 2,048 | |

| | | Wght | Price | Prod |
|---|---|---|---|---|
| 11311 | sdn 2d, L6 | 2,605 | 2,077 | 39,200* |
| 11335 | wgn 4d, L6 | 2,875 | 2,413 | |
| 11369 | sdn 4d, L6 | 2,620 | 2,115 | |

**Chevy II Nova 400, L6 (wb 110.0)—51,700* built**

| | | Wght | Price | Prod |
|---|---|---|---|---|
| 11535 | wgn 4d | 2,880 | 2,510 | — |
| 11537 | htp cpe | 2,645 | 2,270 | — |
| 11569 | sdn 4d | 2,645 | 2,243 | — |

**Chevy II Nova SS, L6 (wb 110.0)**

| | | Wght | Price | Prod |
|---|---|---|---|---|
| 11737 | htp cpe | 2,690 | 2,433 | 4,800* |

**Chevelle 300 (wb 115.0)—31,600* built**

| | | Wght | Price | Prod |
|---|---|---|---|---|
| 13111 | sdn 2d, L6 | 2,870 | 2,156 | — |
| 13115 | wgn 2d, L6 | 3,140 | 2,453 | — |
| 13169 | sdn 4d, L6 | 2,900 | 2,193 | — |
| 13211 | sdn 2d, V8 | 3,010 | 2,262 | — |
| 13215 | wgn 2d, V8 | 3,275 | 2,561 | — |
| 13269 | sdn 4d, V8 | 3,035 | 2,301 | — |
| 13311 | Del sdn 2d, L6 | 2,870 | 2,231 | — |
| 13335 | Del wgn 4d, L6 | 3,185 | 2,567 | — |
| 13369 | Del sdn 4d, L6 | 2,910 | 2,269 | — |
| 13411 | Del sdn 2d, V8 | 3,010 | 2,339 | — |
| 13435 | Del wgn 4d, V8 | 3,320 | 2,674 | — |
| 13469 | Del sdn 4d, V8 | 3,050 | 2,377 | — |

**Chevelle Malibu (wb 115.0) 152,200* built**

| | | Wght | Price | Prod |
|---|---|---|---|---|
| 13535 | wgn 4d, L6 | 3,225 | 2,647 | — |
| 13537 | htp cpe, L6 | 2,930 | 2,377 | — |
| 13567 | conv cpe, L6 | 3,025 | 2,588 | — |
| 13569 | sdn 4d, L6 | 2,945 | 2,250 | — |
| 13635 | wgn 4d, V8 | 3,355 | 2,755 | — |
| 13637 | htp cpe, V8 | 3,065 | 2,485 | — |
| 13667 | conv cpe, V8 | 3,160 | 2,696 | — |
| 13669 | sdn 4d, V8 | 3,080 | 2,458 | — |

**Chevelle Malibu SS (wb 115.0) —81,100* built**

| | | Wght | Price | Prod |
|---|---|---|---|---|
| 13737 | htp cpe, L6 | 2,980 | 2,539 | — |
| 13767 | conv cpe, L6 | 3,075 | 2,750 | — |
| 13837 | htp cpe, V8 | 3,115 | 2,647 | — |
| 13867 | conv cpe, V8 | 3,210 | 2,858 | — |

**Biscayne (wb 119.0)**

| | | Wght | Price | Prod |
|---|---|---|---|---|
| 15311 | sdn 2d, L6 | 3,305 | 2,363 | 107,700* |
| 15335 | wgn 4d, L6 | 3,765 | 2,764 | |
| 15369 | sdn 4d, L6 | 3,365 | 2,417 | |
| 15411 | sdn 2d, V8 | 3,455 | 2,470 | 37,600* |
| 15435 | wgn 4d, V8 | 3,900 | 2,871 | |
| 15469 | sdn 4d, V8 | 3,515 | 2,524 | |

**Bel Air (wb 119.0)**

| | | Wght | Price | Prod |
|---|---|---|---|---|
| 15111 | sdn 2d, L6 | 3,310 | 2,465 | 107,800* |
| 15535 | wgn 4d, L6 | 3,765 | 2,828 | |
| 15545 | wgn 4d, 9P, L6 | 3,810 | 2,931 | |
| 15569 | sdn 4d, L6 | 3,380 | 2,519 | |
| 15611 | sdn 2d, V8 | 3,460 | 2,573 | 163,000* |
| 15635 | wgn 4d, V8 | 3,905 | 2,936 | |
| 15645 | wgn 4d, 9P, V8 | 3,950 | 3,039 | |
| 15669 | sdn 4d, V8 | 3,530 | 2,626 | |

**Impala (wb 119.0)—803,400* built (includes Caprice pkg)**

| | | Wght | Price | Prod |
|---|---|---|---|---|
| 16335 | wgn 4d, L6 | 3,825 | 2,970 | — |
| 16337 | htp cpe, L6 | 3,385 | 2,678 | — |
| 16339 | htp sdn, L6 | 3,490 | 2,742 | — |
| 16345 | wgn 4d, 9P, L6 | 3,865 | 3,073 | — |
| 16367 | conv cpe, L6 | 3,470 | 2,943 | — |
| 16369 | sdn 4d, L6 | 3,460 | 2,672 | — |
| 16435 | wgn 4d, V8 | 3,960 | 3,078 | — |
| 16437 | htp cpe, V8 | 3,525 | 2,785 | — |
| 16439 | htp sdn, V8 | 3,630 | 2,850 | — |
| 16445 | wgn 4d, 9P, V8 | 4,005 | 3,181 | — |

| | | Wght | Price | Prod |
|---|---|---|---|---|
| 16467 | conv cpe, V8 | 3,605 | 3,051 | — |
| 16469 | sdn 4d, V8 | 3,595 | 2,779 | — |

**Impala SS (wb 119.0)—243,100\* built**

| | | Wght | Price | Prod |
|---|---|---|---|---|
| 16537 | htp cpe, L6 | 3,435 | 2,839 | — |
| 16567 | conv cpe, L6 | 3,505 | 3,104 | — |
| 16637 | htp cpe, V8 | 3,570 | 2,947 | — |
| 16667 | conv cpe, V8 | 3,655 | 3,212 | — |

\*To nearest 100; does not include wagons. Wagon production: Chevy II 21,500; Chevelle 37,600; others 184,400. Convertible production: Malibu 19,765; Impala SS 27,842.

| 1965 Engines | bore×stroke | bhp | availability |
|---|---|---|---|
| L4, 153.0 | 3.88×3.25 | 90 | S-Chevy II 100 |
| L6, 194.0 | 3.56×3.25 | 120 | S-Chevy II, Chevelle |
| L6, 230.0 | 3.87×3.25 | 140 | S-Chevrolet; O-others |
| V8, 283.0 | 3.88×3.00 | 195 | S-Chevrolet, Chevelle; O-Chevy II |
| V8, 283.0 | 3.88×3.00 | 220 | O-all |
| V8, 327.0 | 4.00×3.25 | 250/300 | O-all |
| V8, 327.0 | 4.00×3.25 | 350 | O-Chevelle |
| V8, 396.0 | 4.09×3.75 | 325/425 | O-Chevrolet, Chevelle |
| V8, 409.0 | 4.31×3.50 | 340/400 | O-Chevrolet |

# 1966

**Chevy II 100 (wb 110.0)**

| | | Wght | Price | Prod |
|---|---|---|---|---|
| 11111 | sdn 2d, L4 | 2,520 | 2,028 | |
| 11169 | sdn 4d, L4 | 2,535 | 2,065 | |
| 11311 | sdn 2d, L6 | 2,620 | 2,090 | 44,500* |
| 11335 | wgn 4d, L6 | 2,855 | 2,430 | |
| 11369 | sdn 4d, L6 | 2,635 | 2,127 | |
| 11411 | sdn 2d, V8 | 2,775 | 2,197 | |
| 11435 | wgn 4d, V8 | 2,990 | 2,536 | 2,500* |
| 11469 | sdn 4d, V8 | 2,790 | 2,234 | |

**Chevy II Nova (wb 110.0)**

| | | Wght | Price | Prod |
|---|---|---|---|---|
| 11535 | wgn 4d, L6 | 2,885 | 2,518 | |
| 11537 | htp cpe, L6 | 2,675 | 2,271 | 54,300* |
| 11569 | sdn 4d, L6 | 2,640 | 2,245 | |
| 11635 | wgn 4d, V8 | 3,010 | 2,623 | |
| 11637 | htp cpe, V8 | 2,830 | 2,377 | 19,600* |
| 11669 | sdn 4d, V8 | 2,800 | 2,351 | |

**Chevy II Nova SS (wb 110.0)**

| | | Wght | Price | Prod |
|---|---|---|---|---|
| 11737 | htp cpe, L6 | 2,740 | 2,430 | 6,700* |
| 11837 | htp cpe, V8 | 2,870 | 2,535 | 16,300* |

**Chevelle 300 (wb 115.0)**

| | | Wght | Price | Prod |
|---|---|---|---|---|
| 13111 | sdn 2d, L6 | 2,895 | 2,156 | 23,300* |
| 13169 | sdn 4d, L6 | 2,935 | 2,202 | |
| 13211 | sdn 2d, V8 | 3,040 | 2,271 | 5,300* |
| 13269 | sdn 4d, V8 | 3,080 | 2,308 | |
| 13311 | Del sdn 2d, L6 | 2,910 | 2,239 | |
| 13335 | Del wgn 4d, L6 | 3,210 | 2,575 | |
| 13369 | Del sdn 4d, L6 | 2,945 | 2,276 | |
| 13411 | Del sdn 2d, V8 | 3,060 | 2,345 | 37,600* |
| 13435 | Del wgn 4d, V8 | 3,350 | 2,681 | |
| 13469 | Del sdn 4d, V8 | 3,095 | 2,382 | |

**Chevelle Malibu (wb 115.0)—241,600\* built**

| | | Wght | Price | Prod |
|---|---|---|---|---|
| 13517 | htp cpe, L6 | 2,935 | 2,378 | — |
| 13535 | wgn 4d, L6 | 3,235 | 2,651 | — |
| 13539 | htp sdn, L6 | 3,035 | 2,458 | — |
| 13567 | conv cpe, L6 | 3,030 | 2,588 | — |
| 13569 | sdn 4d, L6 | 2,960 | 2,352 | — |
| 13617 | htp cpe, V8 | 3,075 | 2,484 | — |
| 13635 | wgn 4d, V8 | 3,375 | 2,766 | — |
| 13639 | htp sdn, V8 | 3,180 | 2,564 | — |
| 13667 | conv cpe, V8 | 3,175 | 2,693 | — |
| 13669 | sdn 4d, V8 | 3,110 | 2,456 | — |

**Chevelle Malibu SS, V8 (wb 115.0)·72,300\* built**

| | | Wght | Price | Prod |
|---|---|---|---|---|
| 13817 | htp cpe | 3,375 | 2,776 | — |
| 13867 | conv cpe, V8 | 3,470 | 2,984 | — |

**Biscayne (wb 119.0)**

| | | Wght | Price | Prod |
|---|---|---|---|---|
| 15311 | sdn 2d, L6 | 3,310 | 2,379 | |
| 15335 | wgn 4d, L6 | 3,770 | 2,772 | 83,200* |
| 15369 | sdn 4d, L6 | 3,375 | 2,431 | |
| 15411 | sdn 2d, V8 | 3,445 | 2,484 | |
| 15435 | wgn 4d, V8 | 3,895 | 2,877 | 39,200* |
| 15469 | sdn 4d, V8 | 3,519 | 2,537 | |

**Bel Air (wb 119.0)**

| | | Wght | Price | Prod |
|---|---|---|---|---|
| 15111 | sdn 2d, L6 | 3,315 | 2,479 | |
| 15535 | wgn 4d, 2S, L6 | 3,770 | 2,835 | 72,100* |
| 15545 | wgn 4d, 3S, L6 | 3,815 | 2,948 | |
| 15569 | sdn 4d, L6 | 3,390 | 2,531 | |
| 15611 | sdn 2d, V8 | 3,445 | 2,584 | |
| 15635 | wgn 4d, 2S, V8 | 3,895 | 2,940 | |
| 15645 | wgn 4d, 9P, V8 | 3,940 | 3,053 | 164,500* |
| 15669 | sdn 4d, V8 | 3,525 | 2,636 | |

**Impala (wb 119.0)**

| | | Wght | Price | Prod |
|---|---|---|---|---|
| 16335 | wgn 4d, 2S, L6 | 3,805 | 2,971 | |
| 16337 | htp cpe, L6 | 3,430 | 2,684 | |
| 16339 | htp sdn, L6 | 3,525 | 2,747 | 33,100* |
| 16345 | wgn 4d, 3S, L6 | 3,860 | 3,083 | |
| 16367 | conv cpe, L6 | 3,484 | 2,935 | |
| 16369 | sdn 4d, L6 | 3,435 | 2,678 | |
| 16435 | wgn 4d, 2S, V8 | 3,990 | 3,076 | |
| 16437 | htp cpe, V8 | 3,555 | 2,789 | |
| 16439 | htp sdn, V8 | 3,650 | 2,852 | 621,800* |
| 16445 | wgn 4d, 3S, V8 | 4,005 | 3,189 | |
| 16467 | conv cpe, V8 | 3,610 | 3,041 | |
| 16469 | sdn 4d, V8 | 3,565 | 2,783 | |

**Impala SS (wb 119.0)—119,300\* built**

| | | Wght | Price | Prod |
|---|---|---|---|---|
| 16737 | htp cpe, L6 | 3,460 | 2,842 | — |
| 16767 | conv cpe, L6 | 3,505 | 3,093 | — |
| 16837 | htp cpe, V8 | 3,585 | 2,947 | — |
| 16867 | conv cpe, V8 | 3,630 | 3,199 | — |

**Caprice, V8 (wb 119.0)—181,000\* built**

| | | Wght | Price | Prod |
|---|---|---|---|---|
| 16635 | wgn 4d, 2S | 3,970 | 3,234 | — |
| 16639 | htp sdn | 3,675 | 3,063 | — |
| 16645 | wgn 4d, 3S | 4,020 | 3,347 | — |
| 16647 | htp cpe | 3,600 | 3,000 | — |

\*To nearest 100; does not include wagons. Wagon production: Chevy II 21,400; Chevelle 31,900; others 185,500. Impala SS convertible cpe 15,872.

| 1966 Engines | bore×stroke | bhp | availability |
|---|---|---|---|
| L4, 153.0 | 3.88×3.25 | 90 | S-Chevy II 100 |
| L6, 194.0 | 3.56×3.25 | 120 | S-Chevy II, Chevelle |
| L6, 230.0 | 3.87×3.25 | 140 | S-Chevrolet; O-others |
| V8, 283.0 | 3.88×3.00 | 195 | S-Chevelle, Chevrolet; O-Chevy II |
| V8, 327.0 | 4.00×3.25 | 250/300 | O-all |
| V8, 327.0 | 4.00×3.25 | 350 | O-Chevelle, Chevy II |
| V8, 396.0 | 4.09×3.76 | 325 | S-Chvlle 396; O-Chvrlet, Chvlle |
| V8, 409.0 | 4.31×3.50 | 340/400 | O-Chevrolet |

# 1967

**Chevy II 100 (wb 110.0)**

| | | Wght | Price | Prod |
|---|---|---|---|---|
| 11111 | sdn 2d, L4 | 2,555 | 2,090 | |
| 11169 | sdn 4d, L4 | 2,560 | 2,120 | |
| 11311 | sdn 2d, L6 | 2,640 | 2,152 | 34,200* |
| 11335 | wgn 4d, L6 | 2,865 | 2,478 | |
| 11369 | sdn 4d, L6 | 2,650 | 2,182 | |
| 11411 | sdn 2d, V8 | 2,770 | 2,258 | |

| | | Wght | Price | Prod |
|---|---|---|---|---|
| 11435 | wgn 4d, V8 | 2,985 | 2,583 | 1,700* |
| 11469 | sdn 4d, V8 | 2,780 | 2,287 | |

**Chevy II Nova (wb 110.0)**

| | | Wght | Price | Prod |
|---|---|---|---|---|
| 11535 | wgn 4d, L6 | 2,890 | 2,566 | 34,400* |
| 11537 | htp cpe, L6 | 2,660 | 2,330 | |
| 11569 | sdn 4d, L6 | 2,660 | 2,298 | |
| 11635 | wgn 4d, V8 | 3,015 | 2,671 | 13,200* |
| 11637 | htp cpe, V8 | 2,790 | 2,435 | |
| 11669 | sdn 4d, V8 | 2,790 | 2,403 | |

**Chevy II Nova SS (wb 110.0)**

| | | Wght | Price | Prod |
|---|---|---|---|---|
| 11737 | htp cpe, L6 | 2,690 | 2,487 | 1,900* |
| 11837 | htp cpe, V8 | 2,820 | 2,590 | 8,200* |

**Camaro (wb 108.1) (includes 602 Z-28s)**

| | | Wght | Price | Prod |
|---|---|---|---|---|
| 12337 | htp cpe, L6 | 2,770 | 2,466 | 58,808 |
| 12367 | conv cpe, L6 | 3,025 | 2,704 | |
| 12437 | htp cpe, V8 | 2,920 | 2,572 | 162,109 |
| 12467 | conv cpe, V8 | 3,180 | 2,809 | |

**Chevelle 300 (wb 115.0)**

| | | Wght | Price | Prod |
|---|---|---|---|---|
| 13111 | sdn 2d, L6 | 2,935 | 2,221 | 19,900* |
| 13169 | sdn 4d, L6 | 2,955 | 2,250 | |
| 13211 | sdn 2d, V8 | 3,070 | 2,326 | 4,800* |
| 13269 | sdn 4d, V8 | 3,090 | 2,356 | |
| 13311 | Del sdn 2d, L6 | 2,955 | 2,295 | |
| 13335 | Del wgn 4d, L6 | 3,230 | 2,619 | 19,300* |
| 13369 | Del sdn 4d, L6 | 2,980 | 2,324 | |
| 13411 | Del sdn 2d, V8 | 3,090 | 2,400 | |
| 13435 | Del wgn 4d, V8 | 3,360 | 2,725 | 7,000* |
| 13469 | Del sdn 4d, V8 | 3,110 | 2,430 | |

**Chevelle Malibu (wb 115.0)**

| | | Wght | Price | Prod |
|---|---|---|---|---|
| 13517 | htp cpe, L6 | 2,980 | 2,434 | |
| 13535 | wgn 4d, L6 | 3,260 | 2,695 | |
| 13539 | htp sdn, L6 | 3,065 | 2,506 | 40,600* |
| 13567 | conv cpe, L6 | 3,050 | 2,637 | |
| 13569 | sdn 4d, L6 | 3,000 | 2,400 | |
| 13617 | htp cpe, V8 | 3,115 | 2,540 | |
| 13635 | wgn 4d, V8 | 3,390 | 2,801 | |
| 13639 | htp sdn, V8 | 3,200 | 2,611 | 187,200* |
| 13667 | conv cpe, V8 | 3,185 | 2,743 | |
| 13669 | sdn 4d, V8 | 3,130 | 2,506 | |

**Chevelle Concours (wb 115.0)**

| | | Wght | Price | Prod |
|---|---|---|---|---|
| 13735 | wgn 4d, L6 | 3,270 | 2,827 | 5,900 |
| 13835 | wgn 4d, V8 | 3,405 | 2,933 | 21,400 |

**Chevelle Super Sports (wb 115.0)—63,000* built**

| | | Wght | Price | Prod |
|---|---|---|---|---|
| 13817 | htp cpe | 3,415 | 2,825 | — |
| 13867 | conv cpe, V8 | 3,485 | 3,033 | — |

**Biscayne (wb 119.0)**

| | | Wght | Price | Prod |
|---|---|---|---|---|
| 15311 | sdn 2d, L6 | 3,335 | 2,442 | |
| 15335 | wgn 4d, L6 | 3,765 | 2,817 | 54,200* |
| 15369 | sdn 4d, L6 | 3,395 | 2,484 | |
| 15411 | sdn 2d, V8 | 3,465 | 2,547 | |
| 15435 | wgn 4d, V8 | 3,885 | 2,923 | 38,600* |
| 15469 | sdn 4d, V8 | 3,525 | 2,589 | |

**Bel Air (wb 119.0)**

| | | Wght | Price | Prod |
|---|---|---|---|---|
| 15111 | sdn 2d, L6 | 3,340 | 2,542 | |
| 15535 | wgn 4d, 2S, L6 | 3,770 | 2,881 | 41,500* |
| 15545 | wgn 4d, 3S, L6 | 3,825 | 2,993 | |
| 15569 | sdn 4d, L6 | 3,410 | 2,584 | |
| 15611 | sdn 2d, V8 | 3,470 | 2,647 | |
| 15635 | wgn 4d, 2S, V8 | 3,890 | 2,986 | |
| 15645 | wgn 4d, 9P, V8 | 3,940 | 3,098 | 138,200* |
| 15669 | sdn 4d, V8 | 3,535 | 2,689 | |

**Impala (wb 119.0)**

| | | Wght | Price | Prod |
|---|---|---|---|---|
| 16335 | wgn 4d, 2S, L6 | 3,805 | 3,016 | |
| 16339 | htp sdn, L6 | 3,540 | 2,793 | |
| 16345 | wgn 4d, 3S, L6 | 3,868 | 3,129 | 18,800* |
| 16367 | conv cpe, L6 | 3,515 | 2,991 | |
| 16369 | sdn 4d, L6 | 3,455 | 2,723 | |
| 16387 | htp cpe, L6 | 3,475 | 2,740 | |
| 16435 | wgn 4d, 2S, V8 | 3,920 | 3,122 | |
| 16439 | htp sdn, V8 | 3,660 | 2,899 | |
| 16445 | wgn 4d, 3S, V8 | 3,990 | 3,234 | 556,800* |
| 16467 | conv cpe, V8 | 3,625 | 3,097 | |
| 16469 | sdn 4d, V8 | 3,575 | 2,828 | |
| 16487 | htp cpe, V8 | 3,590 | 2,845 | |

**Impala SS (wb 119.0)**

| | | Wght | Price | Prod |
|---|---|---|---|---|
| 16767 | conv cpe, L6 | 3,535 | 3,149 | 400 |
| 16787 | htp cpe, L6 | 3,500 | 2,898 | |
| 16867 | conv cpe, V8 | 3,650 | 3,254 | 73,600* |
| 16887 | htp cpe, V8 | 3,615 | 3,003 | |

**Caprice, V8 (wb 119.0)—124,500* built**

| | | Wght | Price | Prod |
|---|---|---|---|---|
| 16635 | wgn 4d, 2S | 3,935 | 3,301 | — |
| 16639 | htp sdn | 3,710 | 3,130 | — |
| 16645 | wgn 4d, 3S | 3,990 | 3,413 | — |
| 16647 | htp cpe | 3,605 | 3,078 | — |

*To nearest 100; does not include wagons. Wagon production: Chevy II 12,900; Chevelle 27,300; others 155,100. Convertible production: Camaro 25,141; Impala SS 9,545.

| 1967 Engines | bore×stroke | bhp | availability |
|---|---|---|---|
| L4, 153.0 | 3.88×3.25 | 90 | S-Chevy II 100 sdns |
| L6, 194.0 | 3.56×3.25 | 120 | S-Chevy II |
| L6, 230.0 | 3.88×3.25 | 140 | S-Camaro, Chevelle |
| L6, 250.0 | 3.88×3.53 | 155 | S-Chevrolet exc Caprice; O-others |
| V8, 283.0 | 3.88×3.00 | 195 | S-all exc Camaro |
| V8, 327.0 | 4.00×3.25 | 210 | O-Camaro |
| V8, 327.0 | 4.00×3.25 | 275 | O-all |
| V8, 327.0 | 4.00×3.25 | 325 | O-Chevelle |
| V8, 350.0 | 4.00×3.48 | 295 | O-Camaro |
| V8, 396.0 | 4.09×3.76 | 325 | S-Chevelle 396; O-Chevrolet |
| V8, 396.0 | 4.09×3.76 | 350 | O-Chevelle 396 |
| V8, 427.0 | 4.25×3.76 | 385 | O-Chevrolet |

# 1968

| Chevy II Nova (wb 111.0)—201,000* built | | Wght | Price | Prod |
|---|---|---|---|---|
| 11127 | cpe L4 | 2,760 | 2,222 | — |
| 11169 | sdn 4d, L4 | 2,790 | 2,252 | — |
| 11327 | cpe L6 | 2,860 | 2,284 | — |
| 11369 | sdn 4d, L6 | 2,890 | 2,314 | — |
| 11427 | cpe, V8 | 2,995 | 2,390 | — |
| 11469 | sdn 4d, V8 | 3,025 | 2,419 | — |

**Camaro (wb 108.1) (includes 7,199 Z-28s)**

| | | Wght | Price | Prod |
|---|---|---|---|---|
| 12337 | htp cpe, L6 | 2,810 | 2,588 | 50,937 |
| 12367 | conv cpe, L6 | 3,110 | 2,802 | |
| 12437 | htp cpe, V8 | 2,955 | 2,694 | 184,178 |
| 12467 | conv cpe, V8 | 3,245 | 2,908 | |

**Chevelle 300 (wb 112.0; 4d-116.0)**

| | | Wght | Price | Prod |
|---|---|---|---|---|
| 13127 | cpe, L6 | 3,020 | 2,341 | 2,900* |
| 13135 | Nomad wgn 4d, L6 | 3,370 | 2,625 | |
| 13227 | cpe, V8 | 3,155 | 2,447 | 9,700* |
| 13235 | Nomad wgn 4d, V8 | 3,500 | 2,731 | |
| 13327 | Del cpe, L6 | 3,035 | 2,415 | |
| 13335 | Cus Nomad wgn 4d, L6 | 3,415 | 2,736 | |
| 13337 | Del htp cpe, L6 | 3,050 | 2,479 | 25,500* |
| 13369 | Del sdn 4d, L6 | 3,105 | 2,445 | |
| 13427 | Del cpe, V8 | 3,170 | 2,521 | |
| 13435 | Cus Nomad wgn 4d, V8 | 3,545 | 2,841 | |
| 13437 | Del htp cpe, V8 | 3,185 | 2,584 | 17,700* |
| 13469 | Del sdn 4d, V8 | 3,240 | 2,550 | |

| Chevelle Malibu (wb 112.0; 4d-116.0) | | Wght | Price | Prod |
|---|---|---|---|---|
| 13535 | wgn 4d, L6 | 3,440 | 2,846 | |
| 13537 | htp cpe, L6 | 3,070 | 2,558 | |
| 13539 | htp sdn, L6 | 3,185 | 2,629 | 33,100* |
| 13567 | conv cpe, L6 | 3,135 | 2,757 | |
| 13569 | sdn 4d, L6 | 3,125 | 2,524 | |
| 13635 | wgn 4d, V8 | 3,575 | 2,951 | |
| 13637 | htp cpe, V8 | 3,204 | 2,663 | |
| 13639 | htp sdn, V8 | 3,315 | 2,735 | 233,200* |
| 13667 | conv cpe, V8 | 3,260 | 2,863 | |
| 13669 | sdn 4d. V8 | 3,255 | 2,629 | |

| Chevelle Concours (wb 116.0) | | | | |
|---|---|---|---|---|
| 13835 | wgn 4d, V8 | 3,580 | 3,083 | |

| Chevelle SS 396 (wb 112.0) | | | | |
|---|---|---|---|---|
| 13837 | htp cpe | 3,550 | 2,899 | 60,499 |
| 13867 | conv cpe | 3,570 | 3,102 | 2,286 |

| Biscayne (wb 119.0) | | | | |
|---|---|---|---|---|
| 15311 | sdn 2d, L6 | 3,400 | 2,581 | |
| 15335 | wgn 4d, L6 | 3,790 | 2,957 | 44,500* |
| 15369 | sdn 4d, L6 | 3,465 | 2,623 | |
| 15411 | sdn 2d, V8 | 3,520 | 2,686 | |
| 15435 | wgn 4d, V8 | 3,900 | 3,062 | 37,600* |
| 15469 | sdn 4d, V8 | 3,585 | 2,728 | |

| Bel Air (wb 119.0) | | | | |
|---|---|---|---|---|
| 15511 | sdn 2d, L6 | 3,405 | 2,681 | |
| 15535 | wgn 4d, 2S, L6 | 3,800 | 3,020 | |
| 15545 | wgn 4d, 3S, L6 | 3,845 | 3,133 | 28,800* |
| 15569 | sdn 4d, L6 | 3,470 | 2,723 | |
| 15611 | sdn 2d, V8 | 3,525 | 2,786 | |
| 15635 | wgn 4d, 2S, V8 | 3,910 | 3,125 | |
| 15645 | wgn 4d, 3S, V8 | 3,955 | 3,238 | 123,400* |
| 15669 | sdn 4d, V8 | 3,590 | 2,828 | |

| Impala (wb 119.0) | | | | |
|---|---|---|---|---|
| 16339 | hpt sdn, L6 | 3,605 | 2,917 | |
| 16369 | sdn 4d, L6 | 3,520 | 2,846 | 11,400* |
| 16387 | htp cpe, L6 | 3,250 | 2,863 | |
| 16435 | wgn 4d, 2S, V8 | 3,940 | 3,245 | |
| 16439 | htp sdn, V8 | 3,715 | 3,022 | |
| 16445 | wgn 4d, 3S, V8 | 3,905 | 3,358 | |
| 16447 | Cus htp cpe, V8 | 3,645 | 3,021 | 699,500* |
| 16467 | conv cpe, V8 | 3,680 | 3,197 | |
| 16469 | sdn 4d, V8 | 3,630 | 2,951 | |
| 16487 | htp cpe, V8 | 3,630 | 2,968 | |

| Caprice (wb 119.0)—115,500* built | | | | |
|---|---|---|---|---|
| 16635 | wgn 4d, 2S | 3,950 | 3,458 | — |
| 16639 | htp sdn | 3,755 | 3,271 | — |
| 16645 | wgn 4d, 3S | 4,005 | 3,570 | — |
| 16647 | htp cpe | 3,660 | 3,219 | — |

*To nearest 100; does not include wagons. Wagon production: Chevelle 45,500; others 175,600. Chevy II Nova SS cpe 5,571; Camaro convertible cpe 20,440.

| 1968 Engines | bore×stroke | bhp | availability |
|---|---|---|---|
| L4, 153.0 | 3.88×3.25 | 90 | S-Chevy II |
| L6, 230.0 | 3.88×3.25 | 140 | S-Chevy II, Camaro, Chevelle |
| L6, 250.0 | 3.88×3.53 | 155 | S-Chevrolet; O-Camaro, Chevelle |
| V8, 307.0 | 3.88×3.25 | 200 | S-Chevy II, Chevelle, Chevrolet |
| V8, 327.0 | 4.00×3.25 | 210 | S-Camaro |
| V8, 327.0 | 4.00×3.25 | 250 | O-Chevrolet |
| V8, 327.0 | 4.00×3.25 | 275 | O-all |
| V8, 327.0 | 4.00×3.25 | 325 | O-Chevelle |
| V8, 350.0 | 4.00×3.48 | 295 | O-Chevy II, Camaro |
| V8, 396.0 | 4.09×3.76 | 325 | S-Chevelle 396; O-Camaro, Chevr |
| V8, 396.0 | 4.09×3.76 | 350 | O-Chevrolet |
| V8, 427.0 | 4.25×3.76 | 385 | O-Chevrolet |

## 1969

| Chevy II Nova (wb 111.0) | | Wght | Price | Prod |
|---|---|---|---|---|
| 11127 | cpe, L4 | 2,785 | 2,237 | 6,100* |
| 11169 | sdn 4d, L4 | 2,810 | 2,267 | |
| 11327 | cpe L6 | 2,895 | 2,315 | 10,200* |
| 11369 | sdn 4d, L6 | 2,920 | 2,345 | |
| 11427 | cpe, V8 | 3,035 | 2,405 | 89,900* |
| 11469 | sdn 4d, V8 | 3,065 | 2,434 | |

| Camaro (wb 108.1) (includes 19,014 Z-28s) | | | | |
|---|---|---|---|---|
| 12337 | htp cpe, L6 | 3,040 | 2,638 | 65,008** |
| 12367 | conv cpe, L6 | 3,160 | 2,852 | |
| 12437 | htp cpe, V8 | 3,050 | 2,726 | 178,087** |
| 12467 | conv cpe, V8 | 3,295 | 2,940 | |

Note: wagon designation "CT" refers to conventional tailgate, opening from top. Most wagons had dual-action tailgates, opening from top or from side, from 1969 onward.

| Chevelle Nomad (wb 116.0) | | | | |
|---|---|---|---|---|
| 13135 | wgn 4d, CT, L6 | 3,390 | 2,668 | — |
| 13136 | wgn 4d, L6 | 3,475 | 2,710 | — |
| 13235 | wgn 4d, CT, V8 | 3,515 | 2,758 | — |
| 13236 | wgn 4d, V8 | 3,600 | 2,800 | — |

| Chevelle 300 Del (wb 112.0; 4d-116.0) | | | | |
|---|---|---|---|---|
| 13327 | cpe, L6 | 3,035 | 2,458 | |
| 13337 | htp cpe, L6 | 3,075 | 2,521 | 11,000* |
| 13369 | sdn 4d, L6 | 3,100 | 2,488 | |
| 13427 | cpe, V8 | 3,165 | 2,548 | |
| 13437 | htp cpe, V8 | 3,205 | 2,611 | 31,000* |
| 13469 | sdn 4d, V8 | 3,230 | 2,577 | |

| Chevelle Greenbrier (wb 116.0) | | | | |
|---|---|---|---|---|
| 13335 | wgn 4d, CT, L6 | 3,445 | 2,779 | 7,400* |
| 13336 | wgn 4d, L6 | 3,530 | 2,821 | |
| 13435 | wgn 4d, CT, V8 | 3,585 | 2,869 | |
| 13436 | wgn 4d, 2S, V8 | 3,665 | 2,911 | 38,500* |
| 13446 | wgn 4d, 3S, V8 | 3,740 | 3,020 | |

| Chevelle Malibu (wb 112.0; 4d-116.0) | | | | |
|---|---|---|---|---|
| 13537 | htp cpe, L6 | 3,095 | 2,601 | |
| 13539 | htp sdn, L6 | 3,205 | 2,672 | 23,500* |
| 13567 | conv cpe, L6 | 3,175 | 2,800 | |
| 13569 | sdn 4d, L6 | 3,130 | 2,567 | |
| 13637 | htp cpe, V8 | 3,230 | 2,690 | |
| 13639 | htp sdn, V8 | 3,340 | 2,762 | |
| 13667 | conv cpe, V8 | 3,300 | 2,889 | 343,600* |
| 13669 | sdn 4d, V8 | 3,265 | 2,657 | |

| Chevelle Concours (wb 116.0) | | | | |
|---|---|---|---|---|
| 13536 | wgn 4d, L6 | 3,545 | 2,931 | — |
| 13636 | wgn 4d, 2S, V8 | 3,685 | 3,021 | — |
| 13646 | wgn 4d, 3S, V8 | 3,755 | 3,141 | — |
| 13836 | del wgn 4d, 2S, V8 | 3,680 | 3,153 | — |
| 13846 | del wgn 4d, 3S, V8 | 3,730 | 3,266 | — |

| Biscayne (wb 119.0) | | | | |
|---|---|---|---|---|
| 15311 | sdn 2d, L6 | 3,530 | 2,645 | |
| 15336 | wgn 4d, L6 | 4,045 | 3,064 | 27,400* |
| 15369 | sdn 4d, L6 | 3,590 | 2,687 | |
| 15411 | sdn 2d, V8 | 3,670 | 2,751 | |
| 15436 | wgn 4d, V8 | 4,170 | 3,169 | 41,300* |
| 15469 | sdn 4d, V8 | 3,725 | 2,793 | |

| Bel Air (wb 119.0) | | | | |
|---|---|---|---|---|
| 15511 | sdn 2d, L6 | 3,540 | 2,745 | |
| 15536 | wgn 4d, 2S, L6 | 4,045 | 3,127 | 17,000* |
| 15546 | wgn 4d, 3S, L6 | 4,100 | 3,240 | |
| 15569 | sdn 4d, L6 | 3,590 | 2,787 | |

| | | Wght | Price | Prod |
|---|---|---|---|---|
| 15611 | sdn 2d, V8 | 3,675 | 2,851 | |
| 15636 | wgn 4d, 2S, V8 | 4,175 | 3,232 | 139,700* |
| 15646 | wgn 4d, 3S, V8 | 4,230 | 3,345 | |
| 15669 | sdn 4d, V8 | 3,725 | 2,893 | |

**Impala (wb 119.0)**

| | | Wght | Price | Prod |
|---|---|---|---|---|
| 16337 | htp cpe, L6 | 3,650 | 2,927 | |
| 16339 | htp sdn, L6 | 3,735 | 2,981 | 8,700* |
| 16369 | sdn 4d, L6 | 3,640 | 2,911 | |
| 16436 | wgn 4d, 2S, V8 | 3,725 | 3,352 | |
| 16437 | htp cpe, V8 | 3,775 | 3,033 | |
| 16439 | htp sdn, V8 | 3,855 | 3,056 | |
| 16446 | wgn 4d, 3S, V8 | 4,285 | 3,465 | 768,300* |
| 16447 | Cus htp cpe, V8 | 3,800 | 3,085 | |
| 16467 | conv cpe, V8 | 3,835 | 3,201 | |
| 16469 | sdn 4d, V8 | 3,760 | 3,016 | |

**Caprice, V8 (wb 119.0)—166,900* built**

| | | | | |
|---|---|---|---|---|
| 16636 | wgn 4d, 2S | 4,245 | 3,565 | — |
| 16639 | htp sdn | 3,895 | 3,346 | — |
| 16646 | wgn 4d, 3S | 4,300 | 3,678 | — |
| 16647 | htp cpe | 3,815 | 3,294 | — |

*To nearest 100; does not include wagons.
**Includes 1970 extension of 1969 model. Wagon production: Chevelle 45,900; others 59,300. Chevy II Nova SS cpe 17,564; Camaro convertible cpe 17,573.

| 1969 Engines | bore×stroke | bhp | availability |
|---|---|---|---|
| L4, 153.0 | 3.88×3.25 | 90 | S-Chevy II |
| L6, 230.0 | 3.88×3.25 | 140 | S-Chevelle, Chevy II |
| L6, 250.0 | 3.88×3.53 | 155 | S-Chvr; O-Chvl, Chev II, Cam |
| V8, 307.0 | 3.88×3.25 | 200 | S-Chevy II, Chevelle |
| V8, 327.0 | 4.00×3.25 | 210 | S-Camaro |
| V8, 327.0 | 4.00×3.25 | 235 | S-Chevrolet |
| V8, 350.0 | 4.00×3.48 | 255 | O-all |
| V8, 350.0 | 4.00×3.48 | 300 | O-Chevr, Chevl, II SS, Cam SS |
| V8, 396.0 | 4.09×3.76 | 265 | S-Chevelle 396; O-Chevrolet |
| V8, 396.0 | 4.09×3.76 | 325 | O Chevelle 396, Camaro SS |
| V8, 396.0 | 4.09×3.76 | 350 | O-Chevelle |
| V8, 427.0 | 4.25×3.76 | 335/390 | O-Chevrolet |

Note: Station wagon engines—for wb 116 read Chevelle; for wb 119 read Chevrolet.

# 1970

**Nova (wb 111.0)—254,242* built**

| | | Wght | Price | Prod |
|---|---|---|---|---|
| 11127 | htp cpe, L4 | 2,820 | 2,335 | — |
| 11169 | sdn 4d, L4 | 2,843 | 2,365 | — |
| 11327 | cpe, L6 | 2,919 | 2,414 | — |
| 11369 | sdn 4d, L6 | 2,942 | 2,443 | — |
| 11427 | cpe, V8 | 3,048 | 2,503 | — |
| 11469 | sdn 4d, V8 | 3,071 | 2,533 | — |

**Camaro (wb 108.1) (includes 8,733 Z-28s)**

| | | | | |
|---|---|---|---|---|
| 12387 | spt cpe, L6 | 3,076 | 2,749 | 12,566 |
| 12487 | spt cpe, V8 | 3,190 | 2,839 | 112,323 |

**Chevelle (wb 112.0; 4d-116.0)—354,855 built (including Malibu)**

| | | | | |
|---|---|---|---|---|
| 13337 | htp cpe, L6 | 3,142 | 2,620 | — |
| 13369 | sdn 4d, L6 | 3,196 | 2,585 | — |
| 13437 | htp cpe, V8 | 3,260 | 2,710 | — |
| 13469 | sdn 4d, V8 | 3,312 | 2,679 | — |

**Chevelle Malibu (wb 112.0; 4d-116.0)**

| | | | | |
|---|---|---|---|---|
| 13537 | htp cpe, L6 | 3,197 | 2,719 | — |
| 13539 | htp sdn, L6 | 3,302 | 2,790 | — |

| | | Wght | Price | Prod |
|---|---|---|---|---|
| 13567 | conv cpe, L6 | 3,243 | 2,919 | — |
| 13569 | sdn 4d, L6 | 3,221 | 2,685 | — |
| 13637 | htp cpe, V8 | 3,307 | 2,809 | — |
| 13639 | htp sdn, V8 | 3,409 | 2,881 | — |
| 13667 | conv cpe, V8 | 3,352 | 3,009 | — |
| 13669 | sdn 4d, V8 | 3,330 | 2,775 | |

**Station Wagon (wb 116.0)**

| | | | | |
|---|---|---|---|---|
| 13136 | Nomad 4d, 2S, L6 | 3,615 | 2,835 | — |
| 13236 | Nomad 4d, 2S, V8 | 3,718 | 2,925 | — |
| 13336 | Greenbrier 4d, 2S, L6 | 3,644 | 2,946 | — |
| 13436 | Greenbrier 4d, 2S, V8 | 3,748 | 3,100 | — |
| 13446 | Greenbrier 4d, 3S, V8 | 3,794 | 3,213 | — |
| 13536 | Concours 4d, 2S, L6 | 3,687 | 3,056 | — |
| 13636 | Concours 4d, 2S, V8 | 3,794 | 3,210 | — |
| 13646 | Concours 4d, 3S, V8 | 3,836 | 3,323 | — |
| 13836 | Concours del wgn 4d, 2S, V8 | 3,821 | 3,342 | — |
| 13846 | Concours del wgn 4d, 3S, V8 | 3,880 | 3,455 | — |

**Biscayne (wb 119.0)**

| | | | | |
|---|---|---|---|---|
| 15369 | sdn 4d, L6 | 3,600 | 2,787 | — |
| 15469 | sdn 4d, V8 | 3,759 | 2,898 | — |

**Bel Air (wb 119.0)**

| | | | | |
|---|---|---|---|---|
| 15569 | sdn 4d, L6 | 3,604 | 2,887 | — |
| 15669 | sdn 4d, V8 | 3,763 | 2,998 | — |

**Impala (wb 119.0)—495,909 built exc 16467**

| | | | | |
|---|---|---|---|---|
| 16337 | htp cpe, L6 | 3,641 | 3,038 | — |
| 16369 | sdn 4d, L6 | 3,655 | 3,021 | — |
| 16437 | htp cpe, V8 | 3,788 | 3,149 | — |
| 16439 | htp sdn, V8 | 3,871 | 3,203 | — |
| 16447 | Cus htp cpe, V8 | 3,801 | 3,266 | — |
| 16467 | conv cpe, V8 | 3,843 | 3,377 | 9,562 |
| 16469 | sdn 4d, V8 | 3,802 | 3,132 | — |

**Caprice (wb 119.0)**

| | | | | |
|---|---|---|---|---|
| 16639 | htp sdn | 3,905 | 3,527 | — |
| 16647 | htp cpe | 3,821 | 3,474 | — |

**Monte Carlo (wb 116.0)**

| | | | | |
|---|---|---|---|---|
| 13857 | htp cpe | 3,460 | 3,123 | 130,657 |

**Station Wagon (wb 119.0)**

| | | | | |
|---|---|---|---|---|
| 15436 | Brookwood 4d, 2S | 4,204 | 3,294 | — |
| 15636 | Townsman 4d, 2S | 4,208 | 3,357 | — |
| 15646 | Townsman 4d, 3S | 4,263 | 3,469 | — |
| 16436 | Kingswood 4d, 2S | 4,269 | 3,477 | — |
| 16446 | Kingswood 4d, 3S | 4,329 | 3,589 | — |
| 16636 | Kingswood del 4d, 2S | 4,295 | 3,753 | — |
| 16646 | Kingswood del 4d, 3S | 4,361 | 3,886 | — |

*Includes 19,558 SS coupes.

| 1970 Engines | bore×stroke | bhp | availability |
|---|---|---|---|
| L4, 153.0 | 3.88×3.25 | 90 | S-Nova |
| L6, 230.0 | 3.88×3.25 | 140 | S-Camaro; O-Nova |
| L6, 250.0 | 3.88×3.53 | 155 | S-Chevrolet exc Caprice & Impala cpe, Chevelle; O-Nova, Camaro |
| V8, 307.0 | 3.88×3.25 | 200 | S-Nova, Camaro; O-Chevelle |
| V8, 350.0 | 4.00×3.48 | 250 | S-Chevr, MC; O-others |
| V8, 350.0 | 4.00×3.48 | 300 | O-Chevr, MC, Chevl, Cam, Nova SS |
| V8, 396.0 | 4.09×3.76 | 325 | O-Camaro |
| V8, 396.0 | 4.09×3.76 | 350 | O-Chevelle |
| V8, 400.0 | 4.12×3.75 | 265 | O-Chevrolet, Monte Carlo |
| V8, 400.0 | 4.12×3.75 | 330 | O-Monte Carlo, Chevelle |
| V8, 454.0 | 4.25×4.00 | 345 | O-Chevrolet |
| V8, 454.0 | 4.25×4.00 | 360 | O-Monte Carlo |
| V8, 454.0 | 4.25×4.00 | 390 | O-Chevrolet |

Note: Station wagon engines—for wb 116 read Chevelle; for wb 119 read Chevrolet.

# Chevrolet Corvair

**Chevrolet Motor Division, General Motors Corp.
Detroit, Michigan**

Chevrolet's work on a small rear-engine car began after World War II, with a stillborn prototype called the Cadet. But postwar buyers were so hungry for cars, even warmed-over prewar models, that the division saw no need to build Cadets. By the late 1950's, however, the situation had changed radically. Import makes, led by Volkswagen and Renault, were biting into the domestic market. The growing number of economy-car sales was becoming too large to ignore.

The first modern compact, Studebaker's 1959 Lark, was so successful that it temporarily halted Studebaker's slide into oblivion. The Lark soon had rivals. In Detroit, Ford had laid plans for the Falcon, Chrysler was ready with the Valiant, and both were introduced as 1960 models. In 1958-59, General Motors had stemmed the tide with its so-called "captive imports," the British Vauxhall and the German Opel. For 1960, GM pinned its small-car sales hopes on the Corvair.

Largely the work of Edward N. Cole, long-time GM engineer (and future GM president), the Corvair was a technician's car, by far the most radical of the Big Three's new compacts. Its powerplant was a flat six that developed 80 or 95 horsepower. Relatively complicated, it had two cylinder heads, six separate cylinder barrels, and a divided crankcase. Flat sixes were not common in automobiles; Corvair's powerplant might

have been inspired by Cole's interest in airplanes. Unfortunately, the production engine weighed 388 pounds, some 100 pounds more than the target weight. This miscalculation would have a negative effect on the car's handling.

The suspension of the 108-inch-wheelbase chassis was basic—perhaps too basic. Up front were wishbones and coil springs; in back were semi-trailing swing axles. There was no anti-sway bar, although GM had known this was one of several ways to achieve acceptable handling with swing axles in a car with a rear-end weight bias. Management's decision to reduce cost while maximizing ease of service and efficiency of assembly prevented the use of more sophisticated suspension components until 1962, when a regular production option including stiffer springs, shorter rear axle limit straps, and a front sway bar was made available. A major suspension improvement was made in 1964, when a transverse compensating spring was adopted.

It should be pointed out, however, that the 1960-63 Corvair's rather basic four-wheel independent suspension did not create a "dangerous, ill-handling car," as lawsuits claimed. The car did not oversteer, to be sure. But the oversteer was not excessive when the tires were inflated to the recommended pressures: 15 psi front, 26

1958 clay for 1960 Corvair

1961 700 Lakewood four-door station wagon

1960 prototype for production 1962 convertible

1962 700 four-door station wagon

psi rear. The point was argued for years, and was settled only by a congressional investigation, which found in the Corvair's favor.

The Corvair's 10-year production run can be divided into two segments: the first generation of 1960-64, and the second generation of 1965-69.

Corvairs were initially offered in three series. The 500 was the most basic package. The 700 was slightly better trimmed. Most interesting was the 900 Monza with its deluxe interior and bucket seats. When Chevy offered an optional four-speed gearbox in 1961, Monza sales caught fire. A new market had been uncovered almost by accident: the sporty, fun-to-drive, bucket-seat compact. This was fortunate, because the 500 and 700 series Corvairs were not competitive in price with the Falcon and were being outsold by it.

The most highly prized first-generation Corvair is the turbocharged Monza Spyder of 1962-64. Its 150-bhp engine, multi-gauge instrument panel, many handling and performance options, and choice of coupe and convertible models made it highly desirable. Unfortunately, it wasn't cheap: the price was about $2800 plus options. Production was limited to about 40,000 units over three years.

For 1961, the flat six was bored out to 145 cid and optional horsepower went up to 98. In 1964, the engine was stroked for a displacement of 164 cubic inches and 95 to 110 hp in nonsupercharged form.

Another interesting first-generation Corvair was the Lakewood station wagon, which appeared in 1961. The Lakewood offered a surprising amount of cargo space—58 cubic feet behind the front seat, and 10 more cubic feet under the hood. This was more than other compact wagons, and even more than some larger models. The wagon didn't sell well, however, and production barely topped 25,000 units in 1961. For 1962, the Lakewood name was dropped, but the wagon was offered in both the 700 and Monza series. The Monza wagon was plush, equipped with bucket seats and deluxe trim. Only about 6000 of the 1962 models were built before this body style was dropped entirely to make room on the assembly line for the hot Chevy II

The sleek 1965 Corvairs were a design revolution. Good-looking even from normally unflattering angles, they were a tribute to the fine edge honed on GM cars by then styling chief William L. Mitchell and his designers. The new Corvair looked almost like the work of an Italian coachbuilder. (In fact, Pininfarina built a specially bodied 1964 Corvair with similar lines.) It was nicely shaped and not overdone, with just the right amount of trim. The car was new under the skin also. The turbocharged engine produced 180 bhp at 400 rpm, making it the most powerful stock powerplant. But probably the best all-around Corvair engine was the new 140-bhp version. New cylinder heads, redesigned manifolds, and four progressively linked carburetors gave it its extra power.

The 1960 Corvair had been the first mass-produced American car to offer a swing-axle rear suspension. The 1965 Corvair was the first to offer fully independent suspension (aside from the Corvette). There was only one difference between the two: Corvette's suspension design used a transverse leaf spring while Corvair's had a coil spring at each wheel. The rest of the two systems were the same: upper and lower control arms were used at each rear wheel. The uppers were actually the axle half-shafts; the lowers were unequal length, nonparallel bars. These four arms controlled all lateral wheel motion. Small rubber-mounted rods extended from each arm to the main rear cross-member to absorb shocks from movement at the trailing-arm pivot points.

No longer was there any question of tricky handling on hard corners. The Corvair's cornering was now nearly neutral, tending toward mild understeer at high speeds. The rear wheels, remaining at a constant angle with the ground, took most of the car's weight and enabled it to be pushed around corners at great speeds. Attention was also given to the front suspension, which was tuned to complement the new rear-end design and to provide roll stiffness.

Of all second-generation Corvairs, the 1965-66 Corsa was the most desirable. It came as a sport coupe with a base price of $2519 and as a convertible at $2665, complete with a full set of instruments, special exterior trim (including an aluminum rear panel for instant identification), deluxe interior, and the 140-bhp engine. The turbocharged six was a $158 option. With it, the Corsa was definitely in the high-performance category. A typical 0–60 mph acceleration time was less than 11 sec-

1963 900 Monza Spyder convertible

1966 Corsa convertible

1967 Monza hardtop sedan

1969 Monza hardtop coupe

onds, and the car could do the standing-start quarter-mile in 18 seconds at 80 mph. The Corsa could hit 115 mph when given enough straightaway, yet deliver more than 20 miles per gallon at moderate highway speeds.

Unfortunately, the Corsa didn't sell particularly well against Ford's Mustang, which could better the Chevy's performance. Even more critical was a decline in Monza sales. This most popular Corvair rallied slightly in 1965, but the following year, production plunged to about one-third the '65 level. By that time, Ralph Nader's book *Unsafe at Any Speed* was having an effect on Corvair's sales. But, according to Karl Ludvigsen in his history of Corvair, the car's fate had already been sealed by a GM directive in April 1965: "No more development work," was the order.

When the Camaro was added to the sporty-car lists for 1967, the Corvair line was trimmed to just two series: the 500 sedan and coupe; and the Monza sedan, coupe, and convertible. It would be the last year for the hardtop sedans, which are collector's items today.

The 1968-69 Corvairs were the rarest of the breed, available in just three models—500 hardtop, Monza coupe, and Monza convertible. These cars are readily identifiable by their front side marker lights—clear lenses in 1968, amber ones in 1969. Monza convertibles were the scarcest of all.

It was obvious by 1968 that the Corvair was becoming an orphan. Some Chevrolet dealers wouldn't handle them, and others refused to service them. Cole's vision had faded, and Corvair died an undeserved death.

# Chevrolet Corvair Specifications

## 1960

### 500 (wb 108.0)

| | | | Wght | Price | Prod |
|---|---|---|---|---|---|
| 0527 | cpe | | 2,270 | 1,984 | 14,628 |
| 0569 | sdn 4d | | 2,305 | 2,038 | 47,683 |

### 700 (wb 108.0)

| | | | | | |
|---|---|---|---|---|---|
| 0727 | cpe | | 2,290 | 2,049 | 36,562 |
| 0769 | sdn 4d | | 2,315 | 2,103 | 139,208 |

### 900 Monza (wb 108.0)

| | | | | | |
|---|---|---|---|---|---|
| 0927 | cpe | | 2,280 | 2,238 | 11,926 |

| 1960 Engines | bore×stroke | bhp | availability | |
|---|---|---|---|---|
| flat 6, 140.0 | 3.38×2.60 | 80 | S-all | |
| flat 6, 140.0 | 3.38×2.60 | 95 | O-all | |

## 1961

### 500 (wb 108.0)

| | | | Wght | Price | Prod |
|---|---|---|---|---|---|
| 0527 | cpe | | 2,320 | 1,920 | 16,857 |

| | | | Wght | Price | Prod |
|---|---|---|---|---|---|
| 0535 | Lakewood wgn 4d | | 2,530 | 2,266 | 5,591 |
| 0569 | sdn 4d | | 2,355 | 1,974 | 18,752 |

### 700 (wb 108.0)

| | | | | | |
|---|---|---|---|---|---|
| 0727 | cpe | | 2,350 | 1,985 | 24,786 |
| 0735 | Lakewood wgn 4d | | 2,555 | 2,331 | 20,451 |
| 0769 | sdn 4d | | 2,380 | 2,039 | 51,948 |

### 900 Monza (wb 108.0)

| | | | | | |
|---|---|---|---|---|---|
| 0927 | cpe | | 2,395 | 2,201 | 109,945 |
| 0969 | sdn 4d | | 2,420 | 2,201 | 33,745 |

| 1961 Engines | bore×stroke | bhp | availability | |
|---|---|---|---|---|
| flat 6, 145.0 | 3.44×2.60 | 80 | S-all | |
| flat 6, 145.0 | 3.44×2.60 | 98 | O-all | |

## 1962

### 500 (wb 108.0)

| | | | Wght | Price | Prod |
|---|---|---|---|---|---|
| 0527 | cpe | | 2,350 | 1,992 | 16,245 |

### 700 (wb 108.0)

| | | | | | |
|---|---|---|---|---|---|
| 0727 | cpe | | 2,390 | 2,057 | 18,474 |
| 0735 | wgn 4d | | 2,590 | 2,407 | 3,716 |
| 0769 | sdn 4d | | 2,410 | 2,111 | 35,368 |

| 900 Monza (wb 108.0) | | Wght | Price | Prod |
|---|---|---|---|---|
| 0927 | cpe | 2,440 | 2,273 | 144,844 |
| 0927 | Spyder cpe | 2,465 | 2,636 | 6,894 |
| 0935 | wgn 4d | 2,590 | 2,569 | 2,362 |
| 0967 | conv cpe | 2,625 | 2,483 | 13,995 |
| 0967 | Spyder conv cpe | 2,650 | 2,846 | 2,574 |
| 0969 | sdn 4d | 2,455 | 2,273 | 48,059 |

| 1962 Engines | bore×stroke | bhp | availability |
|---|---|---|---|
| flat 6, 145.0 | 3.44×2.60 | 80 | S-all exc Spyder |
| flat 6, 145.0 | 3.44×2.60 | 98 | O-all exc Spyder |
| flat 6, 145.0 | 3.44×2.60 | 150 | S-Monza Spyder |

## 1963

| 500 (wb 108.0) | | Wght | Price | Prod |
|---|---|---|---|---|
| 0527 | cpe | 2,030 | 1,992 | 16,680 |

| 700 (wb 108.0) | | | | |
|---|---|---|---|---|
| 0727 | cpe | 2,355 | 2,056 | 12,378 |
| 0769 | sdn 4d | 2,385 | 2,110 | 20,684 |

| 900 Monza (wb 108.0) | | | | |
|---|---|---|---|---|
| 0927 | cpe | 2,415 | 2,272 | 117,917 |
| 0927 | Spyder cpe | 2,440 | 2,589 | 11,627 |
| 0967 | conv cpe | 2,525 | 2,481 | 36,693 |
| 0967 | Spyder conv cpe | 2,550 | 2,798 | 7,472 |
| 0969 | sdn 4d | 2,450 | 2,326 | 31,120 |

| 1963 Engines | bore×stroke | bhp | availability |
|---|---|---|---|
| flat 6, 145.0 | 3.44×2.60 | 80 | S-all exc Spyder |
| flat 6, 145.0 | 3.44×2.60 | 98 | O-all exc Spyder |
| flat 6, 145.0 | 3.44×2.60 | 150 | S-Monza Spyder |

## 1964

| 500 (wb 108.0) | | Wght | Price | Prod |
|---|---|---|---|---|
| 0527 | cpe | 2,365 | 2,000 | 22,968 |

| 600 Monza Spyder (wb 108.0) | | | | |
|---|---|---|---|---|
| 0627 | cpe | 2,470 | 2,599 | 6,480 |
| 0667 | conv cpe | 2,580 | 2,811 | 4,761 |

| 700 (wb 108.0) | | | | |
|---|---|---|---|---|
| 0769 | sdn 4d | 2,415 | 2,119 | 16,295 |

| 900 Monza (wb 108.0) | | | | |
|---|---|---|---|---|
| 0927 | cpe | 2,445 | 2,281 | 88,440 |
| 0967 | conv cpe | 2,555 | 2,492 | 31,045 |
| 0969 | sdn 4d | 2,470 | 2,335 | 21,926 |

| 1964 Engines | bore×stroke | bhp | availability |
|---|---|---|---|
| flat 6, 164.0 | 3.44×2.94 | 95 | S-all exc 600 |
| flat 6, 164.0 | 3.44×2.94 | 110 | O-all exc 600 |
| flat 6, 164.0 | 3.44×2.94 | 150 | S-600 |

## 1965

| 500 (wb 108.0) | | Wght | Price | Prod |
|---|---|---|---|---|
| 10137 | htp cpe | 2,385 | 2,066 | 36,747 |
| 10139 | htp sdn | 2,405 | 2,142 | 17,560 |

| Monza (wb 108.0) | | | | |
|---|---|---|---|---|
| 10537 | htp cpe | 2,440 | 2,347 | 88,954 |
| 10539 | htp sdn | 2,465 | 2,422 | 37,157 |
| 10567 | conv cpe | 2,675 | 2,493 | 26,466 |

| Corsa (wb 108.0) | | | | |
|---|---|---|---|---|
| 10737 | htp cpe | 2,475 | 2,519 | 20,291 |
| 10767 | conv cpe | 2,710 | 2,665 | 8,353 |

| 1965 Engines | bore×stroke | bhp | availability |
|---|---|---|---|
| flat 6, 164.0 | 3.44×2.94 | 95 | S-all exc Corsa |
| flat 6, 164.0 | 3.44×2.94 | 110 | O-all exc Corsa |
| flat 6, 164.0 | 3.44×2.94 | 140 | S-Corsa; O-others |
| flat 6, 164.0 | 3.44×2.94 | 180 | O-Corsa |

## 1966

| 500 (wb 108.0) | | Wght | Price | Prod |
|---|---|---|---|---|
| 10137 | htp cpe | 2,400 | 2,083 | 24,045 |
| 10139 | htp sdn | 2,445 | 2,157 | 8,779 |

| Monza (wb 108.0) | | | | |
|---|---|---|---|---|
| 10537 | htp cpe | 2,445 | 2,350 | 37,605 |
| 10539 | htp sdn | 2,495 | 2,424 | 12,497 |
| 10567 | conv cpe | 2,675 | 2,493 | 10,345 |

| Corsa (wb 108.0) | | | | |
|---|---|---|---|---|
| 10737 | htp cpe | 2,485 | 2,519 | 7,330 |
| 10767 | conv cpe | 2,720 | 2,662 | 3,142 |

| 1966 Engines | bore×stroke | bhp | availability |
|---|---|---|---|
| flat 6, 164.0 | 3.44×2.94 | 95 | S-all exc Corsa |
| flat 6, 164.0 | 3.44×2.94 | 110 | O-all exc Corsa |
| flat 6, 164.0 | 3.44×2.94 | 140 | S-Corsa; O-others |
| flat 6, 164.0 | 3.44×2.94 | 180 | O-Corsa |

## 1967

| 500 (wb 108.0) | | Wght | Price | Prod |
|---|---|---|---|---|
| 10137 | htp cpe | 2,435 | 2,128 | 9,257 |
| 10139 | htp sdn | 2,470 | 2,194 | 2,959 |

| Monza (wb 108.0) | | | | |
|---|---|---|---|---|
| 10537 | htp cpe | 2,465 | 2,398 | 9,771 |
| 10539 | htp sdn | 2,515 | 2,464 | 3,157 |
| 10567 | conv cpe | 2,695 | 2,540 | 2,109 |

| 1967 Engines | bore×stroke | bhp | availability |
|---|---|---|---|
| flat 6, 164.0 | 3.44×2.94 | 95 | S-all |
| flat 6, 164.0 | 3.44×2.94 | 110/140 | O-all |

## 1968

| 500 (wb 108.0) | | Wght | Price | Prod |
|---|---|---|---|---|
| 10137 | htp cpe | 2,470 | 2,243 | 7,206 |

| Monza (wb 108.0) | | | | |
|---|---|---|---|---|
| 10537 | htp cpe | 2,500 | 2,507 | 6,807 |
| 10567 | conv cpe | 2,725 | 2,626 | 1,386 |

| 1968 Engines | bore×stroke | bhp | availability |
|---|---|---|---|
| flat 6, 164.0 | 3.44×2.94 | 95 | S-all |
| flat 6, 164.0 | 3.44×2.94 | 110 | O-all |

## 1969

| 500 (wb 108.0) | | Wght | Price | Prod |
|---|---|---|---|---|
| 10137 | htp cpe | 2,515 | 2,528 | 2,762 |

| Monza (wb 108.0) | | | | |
|---|---|---|---|---|
| 10537 | htp cpe | 2,545 | 2,522 | 2,717 |
| 10567 | conv cpe | 2,770 | 2,641 | 521 |

| 1969 Engines | bore×stroke | bhp | availability |
|---|---|---|---|
| flat 6, 164.0 | 3.44×2.94 | 95 | S-all |
| flat 6, 164.0 | 3.44×2.94 | 110 | O-all |

# Chevrolet Corvette

**Chevrolet Motor Division, General Motors Corp. Detroit, Michigan**

Chevrolet's Corvette was America's first and only successful fiberglass sports car. It debuted in 1953, the product of a 30-month cooperative development program between Harley Earl's Art & Colour Studio and the Chevrolet Division Engineering Staff. A simple managerial decision to have a sports car in the Chevy lineup was all it took to get the Corvette project in motion. The decision was a brave one, since sales of imported sports cars in the middle-'50s amounted to less than one percent of the market.

The first-generation 1953-55 Corvette was marked by rounded, rather bulbous styling derived from a variety of Motorama show cars and studio sketches. With ex-

tended pod-type taillights, a busy front end, and the then-mandatory wraparound windshield, it was hardly a timeless design. Indeed, the Corvette almost expired after 1955 due to disappointing sales, which some blamed on its rather awkward combination of features. Dyed-in-the-wool driving enthusiasts found it hard to accept the Corvette's two-speed Powerglide automatic transmission, even though its modified Chevrolet six developed a commendable 150 horsepower. "Boulevardier" types, on the other hand, disliked the plastic side curtains, and would have preferred proper roll-down windows like those of regular passenger cars. A V8 finally arrived in 1955: the 265 cubic-inch Chevrolet

Corvette Motorama show car of 1953

Corvair fastback show car of 1954

1953 Corvette convertible roadster

1955 Corvette convertible roadster

Motorama hardtop showcar, 1954

1956 Corvette with optional hardtop

small-block created by Ed Cole, John Gordon, and others. This powerplant delivered vastly improved performance, and almost all Corvettes that year were V8-equipped. Still, total 1955 model year production failed to surpass 700 units.

Late in 1954, a decision was made to give the Corvette a reprieve, and a fully redesigned model was readied for 1956. It was a considerable improvement on the stubby look of the earlier cars. Harley Earl had developed a beautifully sculptured body featuring a curving, concave section just aft of the front wheel openings, and a "toothy" grille. Engine changes—the six was dropped completely after 1955—eventually put Corvette in the serious performance class. Earl's styling lasted a full seven years before it was replaced by Bill Mitchell's Sting Ray design in 1963. In the process, Corvette became America's favorite sports car. The '56–'62 series was aggressive-looking, which nicely matched its performance. Manual as well as Powerglide transmissions were available from 1956 on, and eventually a close-ratio four-speed joined the list.

For 1957, the 265-cid V8 was bored out to 283 cid, and fuel injection versions of this were offered. "Fuelie" Corvettes developed a phenomenal 250 to 283 bhp that year. Though they were thunderingly fast in a straight line, they were only moderately successful in road racing competition. There were three carbureted and two injected V8s offered through the end of the '50s, and handling options improved roadability of the later models. Though GM had begun deemphasizing racing with the rest of the industry in 1957, numerous private drivers continued to campaign Corvettes. By dint of their numbers, Chevy's sports car began piling up wins in road racing as well as on the dragstrips by the end of the decade.

For 1960, Corvette was substantially the same as it had been in 1958-59—flashy and fast. But there was an increase in the use of aluminum: in the clutch housing, the radiator, and the cylinder heads of fuel-injected engines. The 1960 model also featured anti-sway bars front and rear, which greatly improved ride and handling. It was the first use of a rear sway bar on an American car.

Also that year, Corvette achieved international recognition in the 24-hour race at Le Mans in France. Three cars entered by Briggs Cunningham in the GT class all performed exceptionally well: one hit 151 miles per hour on the long Mulsanne Straight. A Corvette finished eighth overall in that race, the toughest of all international endurance contests.

The 1960-61 period was the last for the 283 V8. During those two years, six variations were offered. They ranged from a single four-barrel-carburetor engine to a fuel-injected version with 315 bhp. A wide assortment of rear axle ratios and three transmission choices (three-speed and four-speed manual plus automatic) were available. It was now possible to tailor a Corvette to very specific requirements, from boulevard touring to all-out competition.

**1956 Corvette convertible roadster**

**1957 Corvette with optional hardtop**

**Racing show car from '57—Corvette SR-2**

**Sebring SS racer with Duntov at the wheel**

**1958 Corvette with optional hardtop**

1958 Corvette with optional hardtop

1959 Corvette convertible roadster

Mitchell's Sting Ray racer in "street" trim

XP-700 show car of 1958

Sting Ray racer in '61— officially a "Corvette"

Styling for 1961-62 was a mild facelift of the 1960 model, but it was highly effective. The cars retained the basic 1958-60 front end and midsection, but were completely restyled at the rear. By that time, Mitchell had relieved Harley Earl as GM styling chief, and the new rear-end treatment was his idea. A "ducktail" shape, it was derived from Mitchell's Stingray racer and the experimental XP-700.

Engine and gearbox options for 1961 were unchanged from 1960. More than 85 percent of Corvette buyers ordered manual transmission, and more than half of them requested the four-speed. The 315-bhp engine was most impressive when coupled to stump-pulling rear axle ratios. With the 4.11:1 gearset, for example, the car could accelerate from 0 to 60 mph in 5.5 seconds, and cover the standing quarter-mile in 14.2 seconds at 99 mph. Despite this short gearing, top speed could approach 130 mph.

For 1962, Mitchell further refined the Corvette's styling. De-emphasizing the concave bodyside "cove," he eliminated its chrome outline. He also replaced the "speed streaks" inside it with a vertical grid. The grille

was blacked out, and a decorative strip of anodized aluminum was added to the rocker panels. Also in '62, stiffer springs were brought back as an option. Dr. Richard Thompson won the Sports Car Club of America (SCCA) A-production championship that year with a Corvette so equipped.

After Semon E. "Bunkie" Knudsen became Chevrolet's general manager in 1962, Corvette was slated for increased production. The car had turned the profit corner in 1958, and the division was seeing an adequate return on its investment. Production continued to rise in the years that followed.

In 1962, a new 327-cid V8, created by enlarging the 283, was introduced. The fuel-injection system was also modified. A 3.08:1 final drive ratio was adopted for quieter cruising with the two lowest-horsepower engines.

The 327 remained the basic Corvette powerplant through 1968. With its improved torque, the 327 Corvette with 3.70:1 rear axle could run the quarter-mile in 15 seconds at more than 100 mph. And, with its new optional sintered metallic brake linings, Corvette could

1961 Corvette convertible roadster

1962 Corvette convertible roadster

1963 Corvette Sting Ray roadster with hardtop

1963 Corvette Sting Ray "split-window" coupe

'63 Sting Ray roadsters with and without tops

stop as well as it could go. In SCCA racing, it was now the undisputed champion in both A- and B-production classes, and it competed in good form at Sebring.

The 1963 Sting Ray was a revolution, a complete revision of Chevrolet's sports car, which had been mostly unchanged up to that point. The only items carried over from 1962 were the engines. In addition to the Sting Ray roadster, there was a beautiful new fastback grand touring coupe. More than 10,000 copies of each were sold, and both were unquestionably landmark designs.

Prototypes for what became the 1963 Corvette began appearing in late 1959. The first of these cars was the experimental XP-720. Based on the Mitchell-designed Stingray racer, this coupe featured a smooth fastback fuselage set off by a distinctive split rear window. That window was Mitchell's idea, but it stayed in production only one year, 1963. To his disgust, but for better visibility, it was replaced on the 1964 coupes by a one-piece window.

The XP-720 package was practical as well as attractive. Early alterations from the Stingray racer included hidden headlights, achieved through the use of pivot-

ing sections that lay flush with the creased front end. There was an attractive dip in the beltline at the upper trailing edges of the doors. The coupe's doors were cut into the roof. A new "dual cockpit" dashboard was a fresh approach that worked remarkably well.

After the XP-720 was firmed up, a roadster version was developed. A four-passenger Corvette was considered too, but the idea was dropped because it seemed out of character with the car's concept. Final prototypes were intensively evaluated. Wind tunnel tests were made to determine aerodynamics. Body engineers added as well as subtracted weight. As a result, the 1963 model had almost twice as much steel support in its central body structure as the 1962 Corvette and less fiberglass in its body.

The 1963 Sting Ray had a shorter wheelbase than the 1962 model, and its rear track was two inches narrower. Frontal area was reduced by one square foot. Interior space, however, was at least as good in every dimension. And, thanks to the added steel reinforcement, the cockpit was stronger and safer than before.

Compared to the '62 model, the '63 was a superior

car. There were no engine changes from the previous year, but the chassis was extensively reworked, primarily at the rear. Its most significant feature was the fully independent rear suspension, a three-link type with double-jointed open driveshafts at either side, control arms, and trailing radius rods. A single transverse leaf spring was mounted to the frame with rubber-cushioned struts. In accord with the wishes of leading Corvette engineer Zora Arkus-Duntov, the differential was bolted to the rear cross-member. The frame itself was a well-reinforced box. Weight distribution was 48/52, compared to the previous 53/47. As a result of all this, the '63's ride and handling were significantly better. A new recirculating-ball steering gear, combined with a dual-arm, three-link ball-joint front suspension made the steering quicker. The front brake drums were wider, and all brakes were self-adjusting. There was an alternator instead of a generator, positive crankcase ventilation, a smaller flywheel, and a new aluminum clutch

housing. Competition options included stiff suspension, metallic brake linings, cast-aluminum knock-off wheels, and a 36.5-gallon long-distance fuel tank.

Styling actually became cleaner during the five years of the Sting Ray's life. In 1964, the fake hood louvers were deleted, and the coupe's rear quarter vents were made functional. In 1965, the sculptured hood panel was smoothed out, and the front fender slots were opened up. By 1967, the car had reached its styling peak, and the only changes were an oblong back-up light, bolt-on instead of knock-off aluminum wheels, revised front fender louvers, and an optional vinyl covering for the roadster's removable hardtop.

Mechanically, important advancements were made through the mid-1960s. The new fuel-injected small-block engine of 1963 developed 1.15 bhp per cubic-inch. For 1965, Corvettes were equipped with disc brakes on all four wheels, and the new Mark IV engine that developed 425 bhp made its debut.

**1965 Corvette Sting Ray coupe**

**1964 Corvette Sting Ray coupe**

**1966 Corvette Sting Ray coupe**

**Mako Shark II show car from 1965**

**1966 Corvette Sting Ray roadster**

The first Mark IV displaced 396 cid, but this was increased to 427 in 1966. To handle its bruce force, Chevrolet used a stiffer suspension, extra-heavy-duty clutch, and a larger radiator and fan. With the 4.11:1 rear axle ratio, a 1966 Mark IV could go from 0 to 60 in less than five seconds, with a top-end maximum of more than 140 mph. Fuel injection was dropped after 1965 for the smaller-displacement engines. This was mainly due to its high production costs and low sales.

Chevrolet had considered building a mid-engine Corvette for 1968, but that was ruled out due to the high cost of making the transaxle that would be needed. Instead, there was a complete restyling, chiefly the work of the division's design studio under David Holls. The 1968 model was an aggressive, swoopy-looking car with an air dam at the front and a spoiler at the rear. Its aerodynamic properties, however, were not especially good. A roadster and a notchback hardtop were offered. Pop-up hidden headlights and concealed wind-

shield wipers were featured. The 1968 model retained the 1967 engine lineup. From 1967 on, buyers could specify the potent L88, a competition engine that produced up to a staggering 560 bhp. It had aluminum heads, and came with an extra-heavy-duty clutch. It was joined in 1969 by the ZL-1 racing engine, with a dry sump and aluminum block. The ZL-1 weighed 100 pounds less than the L88, but it cost $3000!

The Sting Ray name disappeared in 1968, only to return—as one word—for 1969. These cars were improved in detail. The exterior door handles were cleaner than before, black-painted grille bars replaced the chrome, and the back-up lights were integrated with the inner taillights. Handling was improved by wider wheels, and the frame was stiffened. The interior was revised to create more room for passengers and their belongings. The 327 engine was stroked to 350 cid and was offered in 300- and 350-bhp tune. Four 427 engines were also available, with an array of axle ratios

**1966 Corvette Sting Ray coupe**

**1966 Corvette Sting Ray coupe**

**1967 Corvette Sting Ray coupe**

**1968 Corvette coupe**

**1968 Corvette roadster**

**1968 Corvette roadster**

**1969 Corvette Stingray coupe**

# Chevrolet Corvette

**1970 Corvette Stingray convertible roadster**

from 4.56:1 to 2.75:1.

The 1968 package, however, was not received with unamimous praise, and debate surrounds it to this day. *Road & Track* magazine summed up the case for the opposition, saying that the car was "highly reminiscent of certain older Ferraris, laid around a chassis that seemed fairly modern in 1962 but is now quite dated by the march of progress ... We feel that the general direction of the change is away from sports car and toward image-and-gadget car."

The new body was seven inches longer than its 1967 predecessor, most of that in extra front overhang. The car's wheelbase was unchanged at 98 inches, but its interior was more cramped, and there was less luggage space. About 150 pounds had been added to what *Road & Track* called the "already gross avoirdupois." It was a great machine, the magazine said, "for those who like their cars big, flashy, and full of blinking lights and trap doors ... The connoisseur who values finesse, efficiency, and the latest chassis design will have to look, unfortunately, to Europe."

Although the 1963-67 Sting Ray is considered *the* classic Corvette of the '60s, the 1968-70 models were more successful with the public. The production peak was set in 1969, with 38,762 units—a record that would stand until 1976. They were longer, heavier, and clumsier than their predecessors, but they were still very fast and appealing. They remained America's only true sports cars. "Corvettes are for driving, by drivers," *Car Life* magazine said. "The Corvette driver will be tired of smiling long before he's tired of the car."

# Chevrolet Corvette Specifications

## 1953

| 290 (wb 102.0) | | Wght | Price | Prod |
|---|---|---|---|---|
| 2934 | conv rdstr | 2,705 | 3,513 | 315 |

| 1953 Engine | bore×stroke | bhp | availability |
|---|---|---|---|
| L6, 235.5 | 3.56×3.94 | 150 | S-all |

## 1954

| 290 (wb 102.0) | | Wght | Price | Prod |
|---|---|---|---|---|
| 2934 | conv rdstr | 2,705 | 3,523 | 3,640 |

| 1954 Engine | bore×stroke | bhp | availability |
|---|---|---|---|
| L6, 235.5 | 3.56×3.94 | 150 | S-all |

## 1955

| 290 (wb 102.0) | | Wght | Price | Prod |
|---|---|---|---|---|
| 2934 | conv rdstr | 2,650 | 2,799 | 674 |

| 1955 Engines | bore×stroke | bhp | availability |
|---|---|---|---|
| L6, 235.5 | 3.56×3.94 | 150 | S-all |
| V8, 265.0 | 3.75×3.00 | 162 | O-all |

## 1956

| 290 (wb 102.0) | | Wght | Price | Prod |
|---|---|---|---|---|
| 2934 | conv rdstr | 2,764 | 3,149 | 3,388 |

| 1956 Engine | bore×stroke | bhp | availability |
|---|---|---|---|
| V8, 265.0 | 3.75×3.00 | 225 | S-all |

## 1957

| 290 (wb 102.0) | | Wght | Price | Prod |
|---|---|---|---|---|
| 2934 | conv rdstr | 2,730 | 3,465 | 6,246 |

| 1957 Engines | bore×stroke | bhp | availability |
|---|---|---|---|
| V8, 283.0 | 3.88×3.00 | 220 | S-all |
| V8, 283.0 | 3.88×3.00 | 245/270 | O-all |
| V8, 283.0 | 3.88×3.00 | 250/283 | O-all (FI) |

## 1958

| (wb 102.0) | | Wght | Price | Prod |
|---|---|---|---|---|
| 867 | conv rdstr | 2,793 | 3,631 | 9,168 |

| 1958 Engines | bore×stroke | bhp | availability |
|---|---|---|---|
| V8, 283.0 | 3.88×3.00 | 230 | S-all |
| V8, 283.0 | 3.88×3.00 | 245/270 | O-all |
| V8, 283.0 | 3.88×3.00 | 250/290 | O-all (FI) |

## 1959

| (wb 102.0) | | Wght | Price | Prod |
|---|---|---|---|---|
| 867 | conv rdstr | 2,840 | 3,875 | 9,670 |

| 1959 Engines | bore×stroke | bhp | availability |
|---|---|---|---|
| V8, 283.0 | 3.88×3.00 | 230 | S-all |
| V8, 283.0 | 3.88×3.00 | 245/270 | O-all |
| V8, 283.0 | 3.88×3.00 | 250/290 | O-all (FI) |

## 1960

| (wb 102.0) | | Wght | Price | Prod |
|---|---|---|---|---|
| 0867 | conv rdstr | 2,840 | 3,872 | 10,261 |

| 1960 Engines | bore×stroke | bhp | availability |
|---|---|---|---|
| V8, 283.0 | 3.88×3.00 | 230 | S-all |
| V8, 283.0 | 3.88×3.00 | 245/270 | O-all |
| V8, 283.0 | 3.88×3.00 | 275/315 | O-all (FI) |

## 1061

| (wb 102.0) | | Wght | Price | Prod |
|---|---|---|---|---|
| 0867 | conv rdstr | 2,905 | 3,934 | 10,939 |

| 1961 Engines | bore×stroke | bhp | availability |
|---|---|---|---|
| V8, 283.0 | 3.88×3.00 | 230 | S-all |
| V8, 283.0 | 3.88×3.00 | 245/270 | O-all |
| V8, 283.0 | 3.88×3.00 | 275/315 | O-all (FI) |

## 1962

| (wb 102.0) | | Wght | Price | Prod |
|---|---|---|---|---|
| 0867 | conv rdstr | 2,925 | 4,038 | 14,531 |

| 1962 Engines | bore×stroke | bhp | availbllity |
|---|---|---|---|
| V8, 327.0 | 4.00×3.25 | 250 | S-all |
| V8, 327.0 | 4.00×3.25 | 300/340 | O-all |
| V8, 327.0 | 4.00×3.25 | 360 | O-all (FI) |

## 1963

| Sting Ray (wb 98.0) | | Wght | Price | Prod |
|---|---|---|---|---|
| 0837 | cpe | 2,859 | 4,252 | 10,594 |
| 0867 | conv rdstr | 2,881 | 4,037 | 10,919 |

| 1963 Engines | bore×stroke | bhp | availability |
|---|---|---|---|
| V8, 327.0 | 4.00×3.25 | 250 | S-all |
| V8, 327.0 | 4.00×3.25 | 300/340 | O-all |
| V8, 327.0 | 4.00×3.25 | 360 | O-all (FI) |

## 1964

| Sting Ray (wb 98.0) | | Wght | Price | Prod |
|---|---|---|---|---|
| 0837 | cpe | 2,960 | 4,252 | 8,304 |
| 0867 | conv rdstr | 2,945 | 4,037 | 13,925 |

| 1964 Engines | bore×stroke | bhp | availability |
|---|---|---|---|
| V8, 327.0 | 4.00×3.25 | 250 | S-all |
| V8, 327.0 | 4.00×3.25 | 300 | O-all |
| V8, 327.0 | 4.00×3.25 | 395 | O-all (FI) |

## 1965

| Sting Ray (wb 98.0) | | Wght | Price | Prod |
|---|---|---|---|---|
| 19437 | cpe | 2,975 | 4,321 | 8,186 |
| 19467 | conv rdstr | 2,985 | 4,106 | 15,376 |

| 1965 Engines | bore×stroke | bhp | availability |
|---|---|---|---|
| V8, 327.0 | 4.00×3.25 | 250 | S-all |
| V8, 327.0 | 4.00×3.25 | 300/350 | O-all |
| V8, 327.0 | 4.00×3.25 | 395 | O-all (FI) |
| V8, 396.0 | 4.09×3.75 | 425 | O-all |

## 1966

| Sting Ray (wb 98.0) | | Wght | Price | Prod |
|---|---|---|---|---|
| 19437 | cpe | 2,985 | 4,295 | 9,958 |
| 19467 | conv rdstr | 3,005 | 4,084 | 17,762 |

| 1966 Engines | bore×stroke | bhp | availability |
|---|---|---|---|
| V8, 327.0 | 4.00×3.25 | 300 | S-all |
| V8, 327.0 | 4.00×3.25 | 350 | O-all |
| V8, 427.0 | 4.25×3.76 | 390/425 | O-all |

## 1967

| Sting Ray (wb 98.0) | | Wght | Price | Prod |
|---|---|---|---|---|
| 19437 | cpe | 3,000 | 4,353 | 8,504 |
| 19467 | conv rdstr | 3,020 | 4,141 | 14,436 |

| 1967 Engines | bore×stroke | bhp | availability |
|---|---|---|---|
| V8, 327.0 | 4.00×3.25 | 300 | S-all |
| V8, 327.0 | 4.00×3.25 | 350 | O-all |
| V8, 427.0 | 4.25×3.76 | 390–435 | O-all |

## 1968

| (wb 98.0) | | Wght | Price | Prod |
|---|---|---|---|---|
| 19437 | cpe | 3,055 | 4,663 | 9,936 |
| 19467 | conv rdstr | 3,065 | 4,320 | 18,630 |

| 1968 Engines | bore×stroke | bhp | availability |
|---|---|---|---|
| V8, 327.0 | 4.00×3.25 | 350 | S-all |
| V8, 427.0 | 4.25×3.76 | 400–435 | O-all |

## 1969

| Stingray (wb 98.0) | | Wght | Price | Prod |
|---|---|---|---|---|
| 19437 | cpe | 3,140 | 4,781 | 22,154 |
| 19467 | conv rdstr | 3,145 | 4,438 | 16,608 |

| 1969 Engines | bore×stroke | bhp | availability |
|---|---|---|---|
| V8, 350.0 | 4.00×3.48 | 300 | S-all |
| V8, 350.0 | 4.00×3.48 | 350 | O-all |
| V8, 427.0 | 4.25×3.76 | 390–435 | O-all |

## 1970

| Stingray (wb 98.0) | | Wght | Price | Prod |
|---|---|---|---|---|
| 19437 | cpe | 3,184 | 5,192 | 10,668 |
| 19467 | conv rdstr | 3,196 | 4,849 | 6,648 |

| 1970 Engines | bore×stroke | bhp | availability |
|---|---|---|---|
| V8, 350.0 | 4.00×3.48 | 300 | S-all |
| V8, 350.0 | 4.00×3.48 | 350/370 | O-all |
| V8, 427.0 | 4.25×3.76 | 390/460 | O-all |

Note: 1967-70 racing engines not listed; see text.

# Chrysler

**Chrysler Division, Chrysler Corp.**
**Highland Park, Michigan**

Chrysler Corporation restyled all its cars for 1940, capping a decade of notable engineering advances. During the '30s, Chrysler had introduced fully flexible rubber engine mounts, optional overdrive, hydraulic brakes, Fluid Drive (hydraulic clutch), and a new low-friction engine machining process called Superfinish. Chryslers had always been engineers' cars. Kaufman Thuma Keller succeeded founder Walter Chrysler as president in 1935. Although he lacked a technical background, Keller continued to emphasize engineering with his top managers. The general manager of Chrysler Division, for example, was David A. Wallace, an inventor with 75 automotive patents to his credit.

The early '40s were good years for Chrysler Division. From dangerously low production in recession year 1938, the make rose steadily from 11th to eighth place in the industry between 1939 and '41. Its success was due partly to the 1940 line, which spanned a price scale ranging from $895 for the Royal coupe to $2445 for the Crown Imperial eight-passenger limousine.

Styling was not radical: notchbacked, smooth at the front and rear, individual fenders. The design work had been directed by Raymond H. Dietrich, the famed coachbuilder. Yet engineering prevailed over styling, and was supported wholeheartedly by Keller, an archconservative. The design that resulted, as one wag put it, "wouldn't knock your eyes out but wouldn't knock your hat off either." (Chrysler's radical Airflow had sold poorly in the 1930s, so the division had gone to quieter-looking cars in the '40s.)

The line was set up in six- and eight-cylinder ranks. Six-cylinder Royals and Windsors rode a 122.5-inch wheelbase, with a 139.5-inch wheelbase for the eight-passenger sedans and limousines. The eight-cylinder Traveler, New Yorker, and Saratoga rode a 128.5-inch wheelbase (the last two included formal sedans as well). A 145.5-inch wheelbase carried the Crown Imperial sedans and limousine. All of the upper models used a 323.5 cubic-inch eight that developed 135–143 bhp at 3400 rpm.

Adding a little class to the 1940 line were two striking show cars from the house of LeBaron—the Newport and Thunderbolt. Six of each were built. The Newport, designed by Ralph Roberts of LeBaron, was a dual-cowl phaeton built on the Imperial chassis. It had a rakish envelope body and smooth fenders. The Thunderbolt, designed by Alex Tremulis of Briggs, had a similar envelope body, but was a retractable hardtop with single bench seat mounted on the New Yorker chassis. Designed to wow the public at auto shows, these two dream cars would later inspire postwar styling.

After the war, Chrysler would continue to use separate fenders, even for the total redesign of 1949. More customs, one-offs mainly, were turned out by the Der-

ham Body Company. These included town cars and a dual-cowl phaeton. Chrysler itself built a custom formal sedan, and A. J. Miller of Ohio built a long-wheelbase limousine/hearse.

The most interesting new model of 1941 was Dave Wallace's unique Town & Country station wagon, the first of that body style for Chrysler. Unlike other woodies of the day, the Town & Country had a clean, rounded shape and "clamshell" type rear doors that opened from the center. Built on the Windsor chassis, Town & Country was available with six- or nine-passenger seating. It sold for a remarkably low price, and a to-

1940 Royal coupe

Thunderbolt show car by Le Baron

Newport phaeton show car by Le Baron

tal of 999 were built, mostly the nine-passenger variety.

Styling changes for the rest of the '41 line were minor, including simpler grilles and more ornate taillamps. The Traveler was eliminated. The Saratoga series was expanded from two models to include club and business coupes, two- and four-door sedans, and a town sedan. Chrysler also issued a wide variety of upholstery in '41. There was Highlander Plaid, a striking combination of Scots plaid and leatherette trim; Saran trim, a woven plastic and leatherette designed for certain open models; and Navajo, a pattern resembling the blankets of the Southwest Indians. One new mechanical feature was optional Vacamatic transmission, a self-shifter that operated between the two lower and two higher gears. Manual shifting was still required from the low to high ranges.

A significant front facelift marked the 1942 models. A smooth appearance was achieved by wrapping the grille's chrome bands right around to the front fenders. The hoodline looked sleeker than before, and opened from the front instead of the side. The running boards were hidden from view, concealed under flares at the bottoms of the doors. Highlander Plaid was optional; another special upholstery called Thunderbird also borrowed Indian motifs. The Town & Country wagon was moved to the Windsor series. The six-cylinder engine was bored out to yield 120 bhp at 3800 rpm. The eight, which remained at 323.5 cid, was rated at 140 bhp for other models.

Like other cars, Chryslers built after January 1, 1942 used painted trim instead of chrome. In early February, production ended altogether. In those two months, the firm built only 5292 cars. During the war, Chrysler built anti-aircraft guns, Wright Cyclone airplane engines, land mine detectors, radar units, marine engines, and Sea Mule harbor tugs. But tanks were its most famous wartime product.

When they could during the war, small teams of designers and engineers would work on postwar car ideas, most of which never reached production. Planned but not implemented were smoother versions of the 1940-42 styles, with fully wrapped bumpers and grilles, thinner A- and B-pillars, and skirted rear fenders. Ultimately, Chrysler produced warmed-over versions of its 1942 cars from 1946 through the first part of 1949. Even the full redesign of mid-1949 was conservative compared to rival makes.

For 1946, fender brightwork was reduced. The grille was given prominent vertical bars, which made it one of the most highly chromed in the industry. The four wheelbases were continued with the same body style offerings as before. The six- and eight-passenger Crown Imperial sedans were dropped, leaving only the limousine. The '46 Town & Country was no longer a wagon, but a three-car line consisting of six-cylinder and eight-cylinder sedans and convertibles. Originally, Chrysler had promised an array of non-wagon woodies, including two-door broughams, roadsters, and a hardtop, but only a handful were built.

1942 New Yorker four-door sedan

Prototype 1946 Town & Country hardtop coupe

1946 Town & Country four-door sedan

1946 Royal club coupe

1946 Windsor convertible coupe

1947 Crown Imperial eight-passenger limousine

1947 Windsor Traveler four-door sedan

Prototype Town & Country hardtop coupe for 1949

1949 Saratoga club coupe

There were seven hardtops in all, made by grafting an elongated coupe top onto a Town & Country convertible. The eight-cylinder Town & Country sedan was eliminated after a run of one hundred 1946 models. Prewar engines were carried over, but were detuned slightly.

Prices increased dramatically between 1942 and 1946, mainly as a result of wartime and postwar infla-

tion. A Chrysler Royal could be bought for a little more than $1000 in 1942; by '46, its minimum price had risen to nearly $1500. Prices would continue to rise through the rest of the decade, to the point where a Crown Imperial sold for nearly double its 1940 figure. Even so, Chrysler was back among the top ten in model year production in both 1947 and '48.

For 1947, there were only detail alterations to fender trim, hubcaps, colors, carburetion, wheels, and instruments. Between August and November, Goodyear low-pressure Super Cushion tires were adopted. One new model in the Windsor series was the Traveler, a luxury utility car with special paint and interior, and an attractive wooden luggage rack. Unlike the comparable DeSoto Suburban, the Traveler did not have fold-down triple seats or wooden floorboards in the rear, having a separate trunk compartment instead. The eight-cylinder series went unchanged, except for a new eight-passenger sedan in the Crown Imperial series.

Chrysler's extravagant "jukebox" dashboard was one of the flashiest in the immediate postwar period. Making use of solid or mottled plastics, it was a symmetrical affair with gauges at the left, a glovebox at the right, and a huge radio speaker and a bank of control knobs in the middle. The knobs were made of clear lucite; chrome plating was everywhere. The radio had a tone selector providing adjustment from "Mello" to "Speech," with its dial changing from blue to red in the process. The steering wheel was 18 inches in diameter, and had three spokes with an enormous chrome horn ring. Over on the far left, the umbrella-handle handbrake was a long reach, but it was highly effective. It operated on the driveshaft rather than the rear brake drums—a heavy-handed approach, but it worked.

The 1948 line was a continuation of the '47 model run. The six-cylinder Town & Country sedan was discontinued at mid-year, but the eight-cylinder convertible carried on. Eventually, 8569 would be built from 1946, including a handful reserialed for the first part of 1949.

Chrysler wasn't ready on time with its redesigned Silver Anniversary models for 1949, so from December to March the old models were offered again—without the Town & Country. Prices weren't changed, and none of the old-style "first series" cars were actually built that year.

Many ideas had been considered for a streamlined '49 design with integral, skirted fenders. None of them came to pass. Keller insisted on bolt-upright styling with vast interior space, and he got it—with some loss of sales appeal. The '49 Chrysler was ornate, with a massive chrome-laden grille, prominent brightwork on the sides, and curious vertical taillights ending in a little hump. (Only the Crown Imperial was spared those gaudy devices.) There was a new Imperial sedan and a convertible Town & Country. Along with the new styling came a host of gimmick names for certain desirable features: Safety-Level Ride, Hydra-Lizer shock absorbers, Safety-Rim wheels, Full-Flow oil filter, and Cycle-bonded brake linings.

An assortment of customs were built on Chrysler chassis in the late '40s, mainly by Derham of Pennsylvania. It offered a town limousine and a dual-cowl phaeton in the 1946-48 period, and tried the same padded-top treatment on the '49 New Yorker. But the wildest of all was a New Yorker promotion car with a midsection designed to look like a giant Zippo lighter.

As the 1950s began, Chrysler was a high-volume line comprising no fewer than seven different series and 22 models. When the decade ended, it had become an upper medium-price make with just 15 models in four basic series. The lineup shrank when Imperial became a separate make in 1955 and the Windsor sixes were dropped after 1954. But over the years, styling and engineering improved. The dowdy 1950 cars powered by plodding L-head engines would give way to performance machines with exciting styling by 1955. Eventually, Chrysler would have some of the best-looking tailfins of the age.

Those tailfins, which arrived in grafted-on form in 1956, were nicely integrated into the all-new '57 styling. They were the work of Virgil M. Exner, who joined Chrysler after leaving Studebaker in 1949. Exner's tastes ran to classic cars—meaning bold, upright radiator grilles, open-wheel designs, and rakish lines. On arriving at Chrysler he found the engineering-oriented boxes of K. T. Keller, who was then preparing for retirement. Unfortunately, people didn't want practical compact cars in the early '50s—at least, not the people who bought Chryslers. The division was having sales troubles, and before Exner was able to get any completely new designs into production, Chrysler sank from 180,000 units to barely 100,000.

For 1950, the boxy cars that had emerged as Chrysler's first new postwar design were largely carryovers. Several models were on their way out. The six-cylinder Royals, which sold for less than $2200, were dropped after that year. The exotic wood-decorated Town & Country series was down to one model—the Newport, a hardtop powered by the straight eight and equipped with four-wheel disc brakes. By then, it had outlived its purpose, to glamorize an unglamorous lineup by offering something vividly different, so the T & C hardtop was dropped for '51. After that, the Town & Country name was reserved for station wagons only. The Saratoga, also a peripheral seller, was dropped after 1952.

For a short time, there were standard and luxury versions of the Windsor and New Yorker. But by the time the "Hundred Million Dollar Look" arrived in 1955, the line was down to just two series sans Imperial, which had become a separate make in its own right.

It's easy to summarize the 1950-54 Chryslers because they were all so much alike. All except the Crown Imperial and the long-wheelbase Windsor sedan were built on 125.5- or 131.5-inch wheelbases. All were styled pretty much the same way.

The '50 models wore broad, chrome, eggcrate smiles; the 1951-52 models had a more conservative three-bar grille. There were no significant differences

1950 Crown Imperial limousine by Derham

1951 Windsor club coupe

1952 Saratoga eight-passenger sedan

between the '51s and '52s, (the firm didn't even keep separate production figures for those two years). The only way to tell them apart is by the taillights: the '52s had built-in backup lamps.

While it lasted, the Saratoga was the quickest Chrysler and a notable stock-car contender. It used a Hemi V8 in the shorter Windsor chassis. New Yorkers came in roughly the same form as Windsor DeLuxe models, but on the longer wheelbase. Imperials were built as sedans, club coupes, hardtops, convertibles, and long-wheelbase cars in those years. For 1950, there was a special Imperial sedan with custom interior.

Perhaps it was the plain styling of this period that gave rise to Chrysler's reputation for engineering. It was certainly the company's great strength in the early '50s. A change in powerplants was part of that emphasis. The Chrysler six had been a dominant seller for some years, so its disappearance after 1954 came as a

surprise to many. But in reality it was part of a broad-based plan, partly instigated by Keller's successor, Lester Lum "Tex" Colbert.

Colbert set several early goals, among which were the decentralization of divisional management, the total redesign of all passenger cars as soon as possible, and an ambitious program of plant expansion and financing. Giving the divisions freer rein meant that people closer to the sales level could take more control in mapping policy. At Chrysler Division, the only market sector available was the top one. DeSoto had staked out the lower ground.

When the hemi-head V8 arrived in 1951, the six was gradually de-emphasized. It had taken close to 100,000 sales in 1950, but dropped to 84,000 by 1953 and to 45,000 in 1954.

The 331-cid hemispherical-head V8 was first offered

Exner-styled C-200 show car by Ghia from 1952

1953 Custom Imperial four-door sedan

1953 New Yorker Deluxe Newport hardtop coupe

on the 1951 New Yorker and Imperial. Though not really a new idea at the time, the Hemi offered exceptionally good volumetric efficiency for truly outstanding performance. Also, it had a lower compression ratio and could therefore use lower-octane fuel than non-Hemis. Yet it was capable of producing as much power as a conventional engine with more displacement.

The Hemi's output was more than ample: one early demonstration version achieved 352 bhp on the dynamometer after minor modifications to the camshaft, carburetors, and exhaust. Drag racers would later get as much as 1000 horsepower from it. On the other hand, it was complex and costly, requiring double the number of rocker shafts, pushrods, and rockers. The heads were heavy and expensive to manufacture. As result, the Hemi was replaced for '59 by a more conventional 383 wedge-head V8. But while it was around, it wrote a great story.

A stock Saratoga Hemi would run from 0 to 60 mph in as little as 10 seconds and achieve close to 110 mph flat out. Bill Sterling won the Mexican Road Race stock-car class in a Saratoga and was third overall—behind two Ferraris—in 1951. Chryslers placed high in NASCAR racing, though they were eclipsed in 1952-54 by the remarkable Hudson Hornets. Briggs Cunningham began running his outstanding Chrysler-powered sports cars in European road races. In 1953, he drove his C-5R to third place at Le Mans, averaging 104.14 mph against 105.85 mph for the winning Jaguar C-Type.

Chrysler engineers had built four special Hemi engines for the 1953 Indianapolis 500, all of which developed over 400 horsepower using Hillborn fuel injection. But a displacement limit prevented them from reaching their full potential. Then came the Chrysler 300 in 1955, delivering 300 bhp from its stock Hemi. The 300 dominated NASCAR events in 1955-56, and probably would have done so for several more years had the Auto Manufacturers Association not agreed to de-emphasize racing in 1957.

The 300 was part of Virgil Exner's all-new 1955 line, which rallied Chrysler from a 100,000-unit year in 1954 to 150,000, and finally brought styling up to par with performance. Based on a long line of Ghia-bodied Exner show cars, the '55s were clean and aggressive-looking. Their 1956 successors were generally even better—something rare for a facelift during the '50s. The modestly grilled, gracefully finned Forward Look cars of 1957 were probably Exner's design pinnacle, and that year's 300C was a breathtaking machine—big and powerful, yet safe and controllable. It was available as a convertible for the first time.

For 1955-56, there was a second two-door hardtop in the Windsor and New Yorker lines called Nassau and St. Regis, respectively. They were more conservatively two-toned and offered slightly better interiors. There were six- and nine-passenger Town & Country station wagons from 1958 on. A hastily conceived item in '56, the new four-door hardtop sedan was especially pretty in its 1957 form.

Bubble-top Le Comte show car, 1954

Chrysler's Falcon show car from 1955

1955 Windsor four-door sedan

1956 300B hardtop coupe

1955 New Yorker Deluxe convertible

Exner's Dart show car by Ghia, 1956

1955 300 hardtop coupe

1957 Chrysler 300C convertible

The Saratoga returned for '57, and over 37,000 were sold that year. It again offered a performance premium—a 295-bhp version of the Hemi. PowerFlite two-speed automatic transmission had come along in 1953, evolving into the three-speed TorqueFlite for '57, one of the finest automatics ever built. In 1956, Chrysler automatics adopted the famous (or infamous) pushbutton controls, mounted in a handy pod to the left of the steering wheel.

While the 1957 styling was superb, Chrysler's rush to set the pace had a negative effect on overall quality. Workmanship was also hampered by a series of strikes.

No discussion of Chrysler in the '50s is complete without a mention of Torsion-Aire ride, offered from 1957 on. Torsion bars were not a new idea—Packard had introduced an excellent four-wheel system in 1955—but Torsion-Aire went a long way toward proving big American cars could handle decently. Instead of sending road shocks up into the car like coil or leaf springs did, torsion bars absorbed force by winding up

against their anchor points. The resultant twisting motion eliminated most of the upward force caused by road irregularities. Unlike Packard, Chrysler put torsion bars on the front wheels only. It's likely they were used mainly to provide more engine compartment space rather than to improve suspension geometry. Nevertheless, torsion bars must be regarded as a major step toward better handling. They were still used on Chrysler products into the '80s, an indication of how well they worked.

1957 Windsor hardtop sedan

1957 New Yorker hardtop coupe

1958 300D hardtop coupe

1959 New Yorker hardtop sedan

Partly as a result of buyer dissatisfaction with quality control, and partly because of a recession, 1958 was a terrible year for the division. There was no major styling change to enhance the line's allure. Higher hopes were pinned on Exner's restyle for '59. The result was less graceful, but the new soaring tailfins seemed to solve the sales problem anyway. The "lion-hearted" 1959 Chrysler scored close to 70,000 sales for the model year.

A Windsor convertible was added in 1958, but otherwise the '59 line stayed the same: Windsors rode the 122-inch wheelbase that had appeared the year before; other models kept the 126-inch wheelbase that had been used since 1955. The new wedge-head V8 wasn't as powerful as the Hemi, but it was much simpler to build, and would survive for a long time.

That year's 300E has been unduly criticized as a performance weakling compared to its Hemi-powered predecessors, but road tests do not bear this out. It was just as quick as the 300D before it. With 10.1:1 compression, TorqueFlite, and a 3.31:1 rear axle ratio, the E could accelerate from rest to 60 mph in less than 8.5 seconds; in 17.5 seconds, it would be doing 90. But production in 1959 was a record low for the 300 series.

During the '60s, Chrysler advertising had a strident, almost belligerent tone, as the company repeatedly declared there would never be a small Chrysler. (Of course there would be, when the time was right and the government would allow little else.) As rival manufacturers were rushing compacts into production, Chrysler cried out it would do no such thing. Let Dodge and Plymouth divisions handle the compacts; Chryslers would always be the large, brawny, luxurious cars they'd traditionally been. And so they remained through the end of the decade.

The 1960-61 Chryslers were Exner's last outlandishly plumed creations. In the vernacular of the stylist, they were clean—uncluttered by excess chrome—and fitted with lots of glass and aggressive, inverted trapezoid grilles. Detail improvements for 1960 included four-way hazard flashers and optional swivel seats that pivoted outward through an automatic latch release when a door was opened.

The Saratoga had its last year in 1960. The Windsor lasted through 1961, replaced by the attractive Newport that became Chrysler's volume car into the '70s. Newports were competitively priced at just under $3000 through 1964, a point emphasized in division advertising. Sales soared, exceeding 125,000 units by 1965. The larger-engine models comprised six varieties of the luxury New Yorker, which sold at a rate of about 20,000 units a year. It was priced just under Imperial, and was competitive with the larger Buicks.

The most exciting of all Chryslers in 1960 was the sixth edition of the "letter series" line, the 300F. It combined racy styling with a road-hugging suspension and an optional Pont-a-Mousson four-speed gearbox. A set of ram-induction manifolds boosted output of its 413-cid V8 to 375 bhp. The 300F would do the standing

Turbo-Flite gas turbine experimental, 1961

1962 300 hardtop coupe

1961 New Yorker hardtop sedan

1962 New Yorker hardtop sedan

quarter-mile in 16 seconds at 85 mph. It rode hard, but cornered better than any other car of its size. A half dozen different axle ratios could be ordered. (Using the 3.03 ratio, special tuning, and some streamlining, Andy Granatelli came close to 190 mph for the flying-mile.) Offered as a hardtop or convertible, the 300F wasn't cheap, but it offered a lot of performance for the money.

The 1960 models were significant in that they were the first Chryslers with unit body construction instead of the traditional body on frame attached with flexible mountings. Since unit bodies were held together more by welds than by nuts and bolts, they were not as prone to looseness or rattles, though they were more susceptible to rust.

The 1961 line was mostly a repeat of 1960, except for the advent of the Newport and the demise of the Saratoga. The Newport was equipped with a smaller engine, and that year's 300G did not use the F's optional four-speed French gearbox. The letter series also returned to 15-inch wheels for the first time since 1956. Two engines were offered with 375 and 400 bhp, both with ram-induction.

Management changes during 1961 had an immediate effect on Chrysler products. At the end of July, corporate president Lester Lum "Tex" Colbert retired under fire and turned over the presidency to his chosen successor, William Newberg. But Newberg quit after two months when he was found to have financial interests in several of Chrysler's suppliers. Lynn A. Townsend, former administrative vice-president, ultimately replaced Colbert. In 1967, Townsend became board chairman. Chrysler's president from January 1967 to January 1970 was Virgil Boyd.

This shakeup brought with it a new styling head. Exner departed after shaping the 1962-64 models. His replacement was Elwood Engle, the former Ford designer generally credited for the elegant 1961 Lincoln Continental. As a result, the mid-1960s were years of change for Chrysler styling. For 1962, the division fielded what Exner called the "plucked chicken": a repeat of the conservative '61 but without the fins. The 1963-64 models had what Chrysler called "the crisp, clean custom look." They were chiseled, chunky cars, the last designed by Exner before he departed. For 1965, Engle unveiled his smooth, concave-sided styling with fenders edged in bright metal, one of his trademarks. This shape continued through 1968, when Engle came up with more rounded, less bulky "fuselage" styling for '69.

For 1962, the Windsor name was dropped, replaced in the three-tier model lineup by the "non-letter" 300s. These were sporty-looking cars having fashionable features such as a center console and front bucket seats. Offered as hardtops or convertibles, they were quite popular.

The New Yorker rode a 126-inch wheelbase in '62; all other Chryslers had a wheelbase of 122 inches. For 1963-64, the shorter wheelbase was adopted across the board, making New Yorker the same general size as the less expensive models. This did not hamper New Yorker sales, which were strong in both years. Two special models in this period were the 300 Pace Setter, two-door hardtop and convertible; and the New Yorker Salon, a four-door hardtop sedan. The Pace Setter commemorated Chrysler's selection as pace car for the 1963 Indianapolis 500, and was identified by crossed

checkered-flag emblems and special trim. The Salon came with such standard luxury accessories as air conditioning; AM/FM radio; auto-pilot; power brakes, steering, seats, and windows; TorqueFlite automatic transmission; color-keyed wheel covers; and vinyl-covered roof. Chrysler stayed with the same basic line-up in 1964.

The 1963-64 300J and 300K (they skipped the letter "I" to avoid confusion with the number "1") were big, burly cars in the letter series tradition, offered only in hardtop form. Some 400 of the 300Js were built (an all-time low), but 300K production was increased considerably. The 1965 300L was the last of the true letter series cars, and the convertible was reinstated. The 1963-65 letter series 300s weren't quite the potent machines their predecessors had been, but they did have tight suspensions and were the most roadable Chryslers in the lineup. The series was discontinued after 1965 because of low volume; Chrysler had successfully attracted a sporty-car clientele with its "non-letter" 300.

**1964 Newport Town & Country hardtop wagon**

**1964 300K convertible**

**1966 Newport hardtop sedan**

**1967 300 hardtop coupe**

**1967 Newport Custom hardtop coupe**

**1968 Newport convertible**

**1968 300 hardtop coupe**

**1969 Town & Country Station wagon**

All models did well in 1965 and 1966. The division built over 125,000 Newports, nearly 30,000 300s, and almost 50,000 New Yorkers in '65. Sales were even better in '66. Production of 300s nearly doubled, and Newport climbed by 42,000 units.

The Engle Chryslers of 1965-69 were shorter than their predecessors, but just as big inside. Wheelbase on all models except wagons was 124 inches, up two inches from 1964. During the late 1960s, the lineup grew. The Newport was joined in '67 by a Newport Cus-

Concept 70X show car, 1969

1969 Newport Custom hardtop sedan

1970 Town & Country station wagon

1970 New Yorker hardtop coupe

tom, priced about $200 higher. Promoted as "a giant step in luxury, a tiny step in price," the Custom comprised two-door and four-door hardtops and a four-door sedan. Deluxe interiors were done in jacquard or textured vinyl upholstery and featured pull-down center armrests. The dash of a fully equipped Newport Custom had eight toggle switches, three thumbwheels, 16 pushbuttons, three sliding levers, and 12 other controls that, as Chrysler brochures proclaimed, "put you in charge of almost every option in the book." It was the ultimate in gadgetry. Vinyl-covered lift handles were used on the trunk.

Chrysler wagons went through many changes during the late '60s. The luxurious New Yorker Town & Country was dropped after 1965 (very few units were sold that year). During 1966-68, wagons carried the Newport name. All-vinyl upholstery was used instead of the cloth-and-vinyl in Newport sedans. Standard features included power steering, power brakes, and automatic transmission. Wagons also had a three-in-one front seat that looked like a conventional bench. Each half could be adjusted individually, and there was a reclining seatback on the passenger's side. For 1969, the Town & Country returned as a separate series in its own right.

Mid-year specials were the focus of the 1968 spring selling season. Sportsgrain simulated wood paneling (like that of the wagons) was offered as a $126 option for Newport hardtops and convertibles. Newport Special two-door and four-door hardtops were available with turquoise color schemes, later extended to the 300 series.

After record calendar year production in 1968, the fuselage-styled 1969s did almost as well. The '69s were handsome, with a combination bumper/grille, clean lines, and smooth contours. If not the most beautiful Chryslers of the decade, they were close rivals to the good-looking '62s and '65s. Wheelbase remained at 124 inches. Length kept growing, to almost 225 inches overall with width of nearly 80 inches—about as big as an American passenger car would get.

Mid-year 1970 saw the first Cordobas: hardtop coupes and hardtop sedans in the Newport line, painted gold with special vinyl roof and bodyside moldings, gold wheels and grille, and "Aztec Eagle" upholstery. Newports were now offered with the 440-cid V8. A special Newport 440 hardtop was listed, complete with TorqueFlite, vinyl roof, and special accessories.

Another flashy product that year was the 300-H, formally known as the 300-Hurst because of the floor-mounted shifter used for its automatic gearbox. Performance options were standard, including special road wheels and H70×15 white-letter tires, the 440 engine, and heavy-duty suspension. All this was set off by a gold-and-white paint job, customized hood, rear deck spoiler, special grille paint, pinstriping, and a custom interior.

Vast changes were evident in corporate administration by 1969-70. Quality control had become an end in

itself for the first time in history, as engineers struggled to correct the firm's reputation for poor body durability. The old centralized structure had been decentralized under Colbert. Townsend recentralized it, but retained some divisional identity between Chrysler-Plymouth and Dodge. Still, the Chrysler marque would face tough sledding in the 1970s, partly because of its decision not to produce a smaller car until the very last minute.

# Chrysler Specifications

## 1940

### Series C-25 (wb 122.5; 8P-139.5)

| | Wght | Price | Prod |
|---|---|---|---|
| Royal sdn 4d | 3,175 | 995 | 23,274 |
| Windsor sdn 4d | 3,210 | 1,025 | 28,477 |
| Royal sdn 2d | 3,150 | 960 | 9,851 |
| Windsor sdn 2d | 3,175 | 995 | |
| Royal bus cpe | 3,075 | 895 | 5,117 |
| Windsor bus cpe | 3,095 | 935 | |
| Royal cpe | 3,110 | 960 | 4,315 |
| Windsor cpe | 3,135 | 995 | |
| Windsor Highlander cpe | 3,135 | 1,020 | |
| Windsor conv cpe | 3,360 | 1,160 | 2,275 |
| Windsor Highlander conv cpe | 3,360 | 1,185 | |
| Royal sdn 4d, 8P | 3,550 | 1,235 | 439 |
| Windsor sdn 4d, 8P | 3,575 | 1,275 | |
| Royal limo | 3,640 | 1,310 | 98 |
| Windsor limo | 3,660 | 1,350 | |
| chassis | — | — | 152 |

### Series C-26 (wb 128.5)

| | Wght | Price | Prod |
|---|---|---|---|
| Traveler sdn 4d | 3,590 | 1,180 | 14,603 |
| New Yorker sdn 4d | 3,635 | 1,260 | |
| Saratoga sdn 4d | 3,790 | 1,375 | |
| Traveler cpe | 3,525 | 1,150 | 1,117 |
| New Yorker cpe | 3,570 | 1,230 | |
| New Yorker Highlander cpe | 3,570 | 1,255 | |
| Traveler bus cpe | 3,475 | 1,095 | 731 |
| New Yorker bus cpe | 3,490 | 1,175 | |
| Traveler sdn 2d | 3,555 | 1,150 | 275 |
| New Yorker sdn 2d | 3,610 | 1,230 | |
| New Yorker conv cpe | 3,775 | 1,375 | 845 |
| New Yorker Highlndr conv cpe | 3,775 | 1,400 | |

### Series C-27 Crown Imperial (wb 145.5)

| | Wght | Price | Prod |
|---|---|---|---|
| sdn 4d | 4,340 | 2,245 | 355 |
| sdn 4d, 8P | 4,330 | 2,345 | 284 |
| limo, 8P | 4,365 | 2,445 | 210 |
| chassis | — | — | 1 |

### 1940 engines

| | bore×stroke | bhp | availability |
|---|---|---|---|
| L6, 241.5 | 3.38×4.50 | 108 | S-Royal, Windsor |
| L8, 323.5 | 3.25×4.88 | 135 | S-Traveler, NY, Saratoga |
| L8, 323.5 | 3.25×4.88 | 143 | S-Crown Imperial |

## 1941

### Series C-28S Royal (wb 121.5; 8P-139.5)

| | Wght | Price | Prod |
|---|---|---|---|
| sdn 4d | 3,300 | 1,091 | 51,378 |
| club cpe | 3,260 | 1,085 | 10,830 |
| luxury brougham 2d | 3,270 | 1,066 | 8,006 |
| bus cpe | 3,170 | 995 | 6,846 |
| town sdn 4d | 3,320 | 1,136 | 1,277 |
| sdn 4d, 8P | 3,650 | 1,345 | 297 |
| limo 8P | 3,695 | 1,415 | 31 |
| chassis | — | — | 3 |

### C-28W Windsor (wb 121.5; 8P-139.5)

| | Wght | Price | Prod |
|---|---|---|---|
| sdn 4d | 3,300 | 1,165 | 36,396 |
| club cpe | 3,260 | 1,142 | 8,513 |
| conv cpe | 3,470 | 1,315 | 4,432 |
| luxury brougham 2d | 3,270 | 1,128 | 2,898 |
| town sdn 4d | 3,315 | 1,198 | 2,704 |
| bus cpe | 3,170 | 1,045 | 1,921 |
| Town & Country wgn 4d, 9P | 3,595 | 1,492 | 799 |
| Town & Country wgn 4d, 6P | 3,540 | 1,412 | 200 |
| sdn 4d, 8P | 3,575 | 1,410 | 116 |
| limo, 8P | 3,660 | 1,487 | 54 |

### C-30K/30N (wb 127.5)

| | Wght | Price | Prod |
|---|---|---|---|
| Saratoga sdn 4d | 3,755 | 1,320 | 15,868 |
| New Yorker sdn 4d | 3,775 | 1,389 | |
| Saratoga club cpe | 3,685 | 1,299 | 2,845 |
| New Yorker club cpe | 3,690 | 1,369 | |
| Saratoga town sdn 4d | 3,750 | 1,350 | 2,326 |
| New Yorker town sdn 4d | 3,785 | 1,399 | |
| Saratoga bus cpe | 3,600 | 1,245 | 771 |
| New Yorker bus cpe | 3,635 | 1,325 | |
| Saratoga luxury brougham 2d | 3,715 | 1,293 | 293 |
| New Yorker luxury brougham 2d | 3,745 | 1,369 | |
| New Yorker conv cpe | 3,945 | 1,548 | 1,295 |
| Town & Country wgn 4d | exp | proto | 1 |
| chassis | — | — | 9 |

### C-33 Crown Imperial (wb 145.5)

| | Wght | Price | Prod |
|---|---|---|---|
| sdn 4d | 4,435 | 2,595 | 179 |
| sdn 4d, 8P | 4,495 | 2,696 | 205 |
| limo 8P | 4,560 | 2,795 | 316 |
| special town sdn 4d* | 3,900 | 1,760 | 894 |
| chassis | — | — | 1 |

*C-30 body and chassis, C-33 engine and nameplates.

### 1941 Engines

| | bore×stroke | bhp | availability |
|---|---|---|---|
| L6, 241.5 | 3.38×4.50 | 112 | S-Royal, Windsor |
| L8, 323.5 | 3.25×4.88 | 137 | S-Saratoga, NY |
| L8, 323.5 | 3.25×4.88 | 143 | S-Crown Imperial |

## 1942

### Series C-34S Royal (wb 121.5; 8P-139.5)

| | Wght | Price | Prod |
|---|---|---|---|
| bus cpe | 3,331 | 1,075 | 479 |
| club cpe | 3,406 | 1,168 | 779 |
| brougham 2d | 3,431 | 1,154 | 709 |
| sdn 4d | 3,476 | 1,177 | 7,424 |
| town sdn 4d | 3,481 | 1,222 | 73 |
| sdn 4d, 8P | 3,854 | 1,535 | 79 |
| limo 8P | 3,895 | 1,605 | 21 |

### C-34W Windsor (wb 121.5; 8P-139.5)

| | Wght | Price | Prod |
|---|---|---|---|
| bus cpe | 3,351 | 1,140 | 250 |
| club cpe | 3,426 | 1,228 | 1,713 |
| conv cpe | 3,661 | 1,420 | 574 |
| brougham 2d | 3,441 | 1,220 | 317 |

| | Wght | Price | Prod |
|---|---|---|---|
| sdn 4d | 3,496 | 1,255 | 10,054 |
| town sdn, 4d | 3,506 | 1,295 | 479 |
| Town & Country wgn 4d, 6P | 3,614 | 1,595 | 150 |
| Town & Country wgn 4d, 9P | 3,699 | 1,685 | 849 |
| sdn 4d, 8P | 3,879 | 1,605 | 29 |
| limo 8P | 3,900 | 1,685 | 12 |

**C-36K Saratoga (wb 127.5)**

| | Wght | Price | Prod |
|---|---|---|---|
| bus cpe | 3,703 | 1,325 | 80 |
| club cpe | 3,788 | 1,380 | 193 |
| brougham 2d | 3,798 | 1,365 | 36 |
| sdn 4d | 3,833 | 1,405 | 1,239 |
| town sdn 4d | 3,843 | 1,450 | 46 |
| chassis | — | — | 2 |

**C-36N New Yorker (wb 127.5)**

| | Wght | Price | Prod |
|---|---|---|---|
| bus cpe | 3,728 | 1,385 | 158 |
| club cpe | 3,790 | 1,430 | 1,234 |
| conv cpe | 4,033 | 1,640 | 401 |
| brougham 2d | 3,798 | 1,440 | 62 |
| Town & Country wgn 4d, 9P | — | proto | 1 |
| sdn 4d | 3,873 | 1,475 | 7,045 |
| town sdn 4d | 3,893 | 1,520 | 1,648 |

**C-33 Crown Imperial (wb 145.5)**

| | Wght | Price | Prod |
|---|---|---|---|
| sdn 4d | 4,565 | 2,815 | 81 |
| sdn 4d, 8P | 4,620 | 2,915 | 152 |
| limo 8P | 4,685 | 3,065 | 215 |
| chassis | — | — | 2 |

| 1942 Engines | bore×stroke | bhp | availability |
|---|---|---|---|
| L6, 250.6 | 3.44×4.50 | 120 | S-Royal, Windsor |
| L8, 323.5 | 3.25×4.88 | 140 | S-others |

## 1946

**Series C-38S Royal (wb 121.5; 8P-139.5)***

| | Wght | Price | Prod |
|---|---|---|---|
| sdn 4d | 3,523 | 1,561 | — |
| sdn 2d | 3,458 | 1,526 | — |
| club cpe | 3,443 | 1,551 | — |
| bus cpe | 3,373 | 1,431 | — |
| sdn 4d, 8P | 3,997 | 1,943 | — |
| limo 8P | 4,022 | 2,063 | — |
| chassis | — | — | — |

**C-38W Windsor (wb 121.5; 8P-139.5)***

| | Wght | Price | Prod |
|---|---|---|---|
| sdn 4d | 3,528 | 1,611 | — |
| sdn 2d | 3,468 | 1,591 | — |
| club cpe | 3,448 | 1,601 | — |
| bus cpe | 3,383 | 1,481 | — |
| conv cpe | 3,693 | 1,861 | — |
| sdn 4d, 8P | 3,977 | 1,993 | — |
| limo 8P | 4,052 | 2,113 | — |
| Traveler sdn 4d | 3,610 | 1,746 | — |

**C-39K Saratoga (wb 127.5)***

| | Wght | Price | Prod |
|---|---|---|---|
| sdn 4d | 3,972 | 1,863 | — |
| sdn 2d | 3,932 | 1,838 | — |
| club cpe | 3,892 | 1,848 | — |
| bus cpe | 3,817 | 1,753 | — |

**C-39N New Yorker (wb 127.5)***

| | Wght | Price | Prod |
|---|---|---|---|
| sdn 4d | 3,973 | 1,963 | — |
| sdn 2d | 3,932 | 1,938 | — |
| club cpe | 3,897 | 1,948 | — |
| bus cpe | 3,837 | 1,853 | — |
| conv cpe | 4,132 | 2,193 | — |
| chassis | — | — | — |

**C-38/39 Town & Country (wb 121.5; L8-127.5)***

| | Wght | Price | Prod |
|---|---|---|---|
| sdn 4d, L6 | 3,917 | 2,366 | 4,049 |
| brougham 2d, L6 | — | proto | 1 |

| | Wght | Price | Prod |
|---|---|---|---|
| conv cpe, L6 | — | proto | 1 |
| sdn 4d, L8 | 4,300 | 2,718 | 100 |
| conv cpe, L8 | 4,332 | 2,743 | 2,124 |
| htp cpe, L8 | — | proto | 7 |

**C-40 Crown Imperial (wb 145.5)***

| | Wght | Price | Prod |
|---|---|---|---|
| limo 8P | 4,814 | 3,875 | — |

| 1946 Engines | bore×stroke | bhp | availability |
|---|---|---|---|
| L6, 250.6 | 3.44×4.50 | 114 | S-Royal, Windsor, T&C six |
| L8, 323.5 | 3.25×4.88 | 135 | S-others |

## 1947

**Series C-38S Royal (wb 121.5; 8P-139.5)***

| | Wght | Price | Prod |
|---|---|---|---|
| sdn 4d | 3,523 | 1,601 | — |
| sdn 2d | 3,458 | 1,626 | — |
| club cpe | 3,443 | 1,651 | — |
| bus cpe | 3,373 | 1,561 | — |
| sdn 4d, 8P | 3,997 | 2,043 | — |
| limo 8P | 4,022 | 2,163 | — |

**C-38W Windsor (wb 121.5; 8P-139.5)***

| | Wght | Price | Prod |
|---|---|---|---|
| sdn 4d | 3,528 | 1,711 | — |
| Traveler sdn 4d | 3,610 | 1,846 | — |
| sdn 2d | 3,468 | 1,691 | — |
| club cpe | 3,448 | 1,701 | — |
| bus cpe | 3,383 | 1,611 | — |
| conv cpe | 3,693 | 2,075 | — |
| sdn 4d, 8P | 3,977 | 2,093 | — |
| limo 8P | 4,052 | 2,213 | — |

**C-39K Saratoga (wb 127.5)***

| | Wght | Price | Prod |
|---|---|---|---|
| sdn 4d | 3,972 | 1,973 | — |
| sdn 2d | 3,900 | 1,948 | — |
| club cpe | 3,930 | 1,958 | — |
| bus cpe | 3,817 | 1,873 | — |

**C-39N New Yorker (wb 127.5)***

| | Wght | Price | Prod |
|---|---|---|---|
| sdn 4d | 3,987 | 2,073 | — |
| sdn 2d | 3,932 | 2,048 | — |
| club cpe | 3,940 | 2,058 | — |
| bus cpe | 3,837 | 1,973 | — |
| conv cpe | 4,132 | 2,447 | — |

**C-38/39 Town & Country (wb 121.5; L8-127.5)**

| | Wght | Price | Prod |
|---|---|---|---|
| sdn 4d, L6 | 3,955 | 2,713 | 2,751 |
| conv cpe, L8 | 4,332 | 2,998 | 3,136 |

**C-40 Crown Imperial (wb 145.5)***

| | Wght | Price | Prod |
|---|---|---|---|
| sdn 4d, 8P | 4,865 | 4,205 | — |
| limo 8P | 4,875 | 4,305 | — |

| 1947 Engines | bore×stroke | bhp | availability |
|---|---|---|---|
| L6, 250.6 | 3.44×4.50 | 114 | S-Royal, Windsor, T&C six |
| L8, 323.5 | 3.25×4.88 | 135 | S-others |

## 1948–1949 First Series

**Series C-38S Royal (wb 121.5; 8P-139.5)***

| | Wght | Price | Prod |
|---|---|---|---|
| sdn 4d | 3,523 | 1,955 | — |
| sdn 2d | 3,485 | 1,908 | — |
| club cpe | 3,475 | 1,934 | — |
| bus cpe | 3,395 | 1,819 | — |
| sdn 4d, 8P | 3,925 | 2,380 | — |
| limo 8P | 4,022 | 2,506 | — |

**C-38W Windsor (wb 121.5; 8P-139.5)***

| | Wght | Price | Prod |
|---|---|---|---|
| sdn 4d | 3,528 | 2,021 | — |
| Traveler sdn 4d | 3,610 | 2,163 | — |
| sdn 2d | 3,510 | 1,989 | — |

| | Wght | Price | Prod |
|---|---|---|---|
| club cpe | 3,475 | 2,000 | — |
| bus cpe | 3,395 | 1,884 | — |
| conv cpe | 3,693 | 2,414 | — |
| sdn 4d, 8P | 3,935 | 2,434 | — |
| limo 8P | 4,035 | 2,561 | — |

**C-39K Saratoga (wb 127.5)***

| | Wght | Price | Prod |
|---|---|---|---|
| sdn 4d | 3,972 | 2,291 | — |
| sdn 2d | 3,900 | 2,254 | — |
| club cpe | 3,930 | 2,265 | — |
| bus cpe | 3,817 | 2,165 | — |

**C-39N New Yorker (wb 127.5)***

| | Wght | Price | Prod |
|---|---|---|---|
| sdn 4d | 3,987 | 2,411 | — |
| sdn 2d | 3,932 | 2,374 | — |
| club cpe | 3,940 | 2,385 | — |
| bus cpe | 3,837 | 2,285 | — |
| conv cpe | 4,132 | 2,815 | — |

**C-38/39 Town & Country (wb 121.5; L8-127.5)**

| | Wght | Price | Prod |
|---|---|---|---|
| sdn 4d, L6 | 3,955 | 2,860 | 1,175 |
| conv cpe, L8 | 4,332 | 3,395 | 3,309 |

**C-40 Crown Imperial (wb 145.5)***

| | Wght | Price | Prod |
|---|---|---|---|
| sdn 4d, 8P | 4,865 | 4,662 | — |
| limo 8P | 4,875 | 4,767 | — |

| 1948 Engines | bore×stroke | bhp | availability |
|---|---|---|---|
| L6, 250.6 | 3.44×4.50 | 114 | S-Royal, Windsor, T&C six |
| L8, 323.5 | 3.25×4.88 | 135 | S-others |

Note: First Series 1949 models sold December 1948 through March 1949 identical in weight and price to 1948 models and comprised about 15% of total production.

*Factory combined production figures for 1946 through 1949 first series and breakdowns are not available from Chrysler archives. However, since the Town & Country figures have been obtained (by historian Donald Narus), it is very likely that breakdowns exist for other models.

## Combined 1946–1949 First Series Production:

**C-38S Royal (wb 121.5; 8P-139.5)**

| | Prod |
|---|---|
| sdn 4d | 24,279 |
| sdn 2d | 1,117 |
| club cpe | 4,318 |
| bus cpe | 1,221 |
| sdn 4d, 8P | 626 |
| limo 8P | 169 |
| chassis | 1 |

**C-38W Windsor (wb 121.5; 8P-139.5)**

| | Prod |
|---|---|
| sdn 4d | 161,139 |
| Traveler sdn 4d | 4,182 |
| sdn 2d | 4,034 |
| club cpe | 26,482 |
| bus cpe | 1,980 |
| conv cpe | 11,200 |
| sdn 4d, 8P | 4,390 |
| limo 8P | 1,496 |

**C-39K Saratoga (wb 127.5)**

| | Prod |
|---|---|
| sdn 4d | 4,611 |
| sdn 2d | 155 |
| club cpe | 765 |
| bus cpe | 74 |

**C-39N New Yorker (wb 127.5)**

| | Prod |
|---|---|
| sdn 4d | 52,036 |
| sdn 2d | 545 |
| club cpe | 10,735 |
| bus cpe | 701 |

| | Prod |
|---|---|
| conv cpe | 3,000 |
| chassis | 2 |

**C-38/39 Town & Country (wb 121.5; L8-127.5)**

| | Prod |
|---|---|
| sdn 4d, L6 | 7,975 |
| brougham 2d, L6 (proto) | 1 |
| conv cpe, L6 (proto) | 1 |
| sdn 4d, L8 | 100 |
| conv cpe, L8 | 8,569 |
| htp cpe, L8 (proto) | 7 |

**C-40 Crown Imperial (wb 145.5)**

| | Prod |
|---|---|
| sdn 4d, 8P | 750 |
| limo 8P | 650 |

## 1949 Second Series

**C-45-1 Royal (wb 125.5; 8P-139.5)**

| | Wght | Price | Prod |
|---|---|---|---|
| sdn 4d | 3,550 | 2,134 | 13,192 |
| club cpe | 3,495 | 2,114 | 4,849 |
| wgn 4d, 9P | 4,060 | 3,121 | 850 |
| sdn 4d, 8P | 4,200 | 2,823 | 185 |

**C-45-2 Windsor (wb 125.5; 8P-139.5)**

| | Wght | Price | Prod |
|---|---|---|---|
| sdn 4d | 3,681 | 2,329 | 55,879 |
| club cpe | 3,631 | 2,308 | 17,732 |
| conv cpe | 3,845 | 2,741 | 3,234 |
| sdn 4d, 8P | 4,290 | 3,017 | 373 |
| limo 8P | 4,430 | 3,144 | 73 |

**C-46-1 Saratoga (wb 131.5)**

| | Wght | Price | Prod |
|---|---|---|---|
| sdn 4d | 4,103 | 3,610 | 1,810 |
| club cpe | 4,037 | 2,585 | 465 |

**C-46-2 New Yorker (wb 131.5)**

| | Wght | Price | Prod |
|---|---|---|---|
| sdn 4d | 4,113 | 2,726 | 18,799 |
| club cpe | 4,048 | 2,700 | 4,524 |
| conv cpe | 4,277 | 3,206 | 1,137 |
| chassis | — | — | 1 |

**C-46-2 Town & Country (wb 131.5)**

| | Wght | Price | Prod |
|---|---|---|---|
| conv cpe | 4,630 | 3,970 | 1,000 |

**C-46-2 Imperial (wb 131.5)**

| | Wght | Price | Prod |
|---|---|---|---|
| sdn 4d | 4,300 | 4,665 | 50 |

**C-47 Crown Imperial (wb 145.5)**

| | Wght | Price | Prod |
|---|---|---|---|
| sdn 4d, 8P | 5,250 | 5,229 | 40 |
| limo 8P | 5,295 | 5,334 | 45 |

| 1949 Engines | bore×stroke | bhp | availability |
|---|---|---|---|
| L6, 250.6 | 3.44×4.50 | 116 | S-Royal, Windsor |
| L8, 323.5 | 3.25×4.88 | 135 | S-others |

## 1950

**C-48-1 Royal (wb 125.5; 8P-139.5)**

| | Wght | Price | Prod |
|---|---|---|---|
| sdn 4d | 3,610 | 2,134 | 17,713 |
| club cpe | 3,540 | 2,114 | 5,900 |
| Town & Country wgn 4d, wood | 4,055 | 3,163 | 599 |
| Town & Country wgn 4d, steel | 3,964 | 2,735 | 100 |
| sdn 4d, 8P | 4,190 | 2,855 | 375 |

**C-48-2 Windsor (wb 125.5; 8P-139.5)**

| | Wght | Price | Prod |
|---|---|---|---|
| sdn 4d | 3,765 | 2,329 | 78,199 |
| Traveler sdn 4d | 3,830 | 2,560 | 900 |
| club cpe | 3,670 | 2,308 | 20,050 |
| Newport htp cpe | 3,875 | 2,637 | 9,925 |
| conv cpe | 3,905 | 2,741 | 2,201 |
| sdn 4d, 8P | 4,295 | 3,050 | 763 |
| limo 8P | 4,400 | 3,176 | 174 |
| chassis | — | — | 1 |

| C-49-1 Saratoga (wb 131.5) | Wght | Price | Prod |
|---|---|---|---|
| sdn 4d | 4,170 | 2,642 | 1,000 |
| club cpe | 4,110 | 2,616 | 300 |

| C-49-2 New Yorker (wb 131.5) | Wght | Price | Prod |
|---|---|---|---|
| sdn 4d | 4,190 | 2,758 | 22,633 |
| club cpe | 4,110 | 2,732 | 3,000 |
| Newport htp cpe | 4,370 | 3,133 | 2,800 |
| conv cpe | 4,360 | 3,232 | 899 |
| wgn 4d, wood | — | proto | 1 |
| chassis | — | — | 2 |

| C-49-2 Town & Country (wb 131.5) | Wght | Price | Prod |
|---|---|---|---|
| Newport htp cpe | 4,670 | 4,003 | 700 |

| C-49-2 Imperial (wb 131.5) | Wght | Price | Prod |
|---|---|---|---|
| sdn 4d | 4,245 | 3,055 | 9,500 |
| Deluxe sdn 4d | 4,250 | 3,176 | 1,150 |

| C-50 Crown Imperial (wb 145.5) | Wght | Price | Prod |
|---|---|---|---|
| sdn 4d, 8P | 5,235 | 5,229 | 209 |
| limo 8P | 5,305 | 5,334 | 205 |
| chassis | — | — | 1 |

| 1950 Engines | bore×stroke | bhp | availability |
|---|---|---|---|
| L6, 250.6 | 3.44×4.50 | 116 | S-Royal, Windsor |
| L8, 323.5 | 3.25×4.88 | 135 | S-others |

## 1951

| C-51W Windsor (wb 125.5; 8P-139.5) | Wght | Price | Prod |
|---|---|---|---|
| sdn 4d | 3,527 | 2,390 | 10,151* |
| club cpe | 3,570 | 2,368 | 4,243* |
| Town & Country wgn 4d | 3,965 | 3,063 | 1,239* |
| sdn 4d, 8P | 4,145 | 3,197 | 399* |
| ambulance (sp. order) | — | — | 153 |
| Deluxe sdn 4d | 3,775 | 2,608 | 47,573* |
| Deluxe Traveler sdn 4d | 3,890 | 2,867 | 850 |
| Deluxe club cpe | 3,700 | 2,585 | 8,365 |
| Deluxe Newport htp cpe | 3,855 | 2,953 | 6,426* |
| Deluxe conv cpe | 3,945 | 3,071 | 2,646* |
| Deluxe sdn 4d, 8P | 4,295 | 3,416 | 720 |
| Deluxe limo 8P | 4,415 | 3,557 | 152 |

| C-55 Saratoga (wb 125.5; 8P-139.5) | Wght | Price | Prod |
|---|---|---|---|
| sdn 4d | 4,018 | 3,016 | 22,375* |
| club cpe | 3,948 | 2,989 | 5,355* |
| Newport htp cpe | — | proto | 1 |
| Town & Country wgn 4d | 4,310 | 3,681 | 818* |
| sdn 4d, 8P | 4,465 | 3,912 | 115* |
| ambulance (sp. order) | — | — | 1 |

| C-52 New Yorker (wb 131.5) | Wght | Price | Prod |
|---|---|---|---|
| sdn 4d | 4,260 | 3,378 | 25,461* |
| club cpe | 4,145 | 3,348 | 3,533 |
| Newport htp cpe | 4,330 | 3,798 | 3,654* |
| conv cpe | 4,460 | 3,916 | 1,386* |
| Town & Country wgn 4d (4 C51s) | 4,455 | 4,026 | 251 |
| chassis | — | — | 1 |

| C-54 Imperial (wb 131.5) | Wght | Price | Prod |
|---|---|---|---|
| sdn 4d | 4,350 | 3,674 | 13,678* |
| club cpe | 4,230 | 3,661 | 2,226* |
| Newport htp cpe | 4,380 | 4,042 | 749* |
| conv cpe | 4,570 | 4,402 | 650 |

| C-53 Crown Imperial (wb 145.5) | Wght | Price | Prod |
|---|---|---|---|
| sdn 4d, 8P | 5,360 | 6,573 | 227* |
| limo 8P | 5,450 | 6,690 | 213* |
| chassis | — | — | 2 |

| 1951 Engines | bore×stroke | bhp | availability |
|---|---|---|---|
| L6, 250.6 | 3.44×4.50 | 116 | S-Windsor |
| V8, 331.1 | 3.81×3.63 | 180 | S-others |

## 1952

| C-51W Windsor (wb 125.5; 8P-139.5) | Wght | Price | Prod |
|---|---|---|---|
| sdn 4d | 3,640 | 2,498 | 5,961* |
| club cpe | 3,550 | 2,475 | 2,492* |
| Town & Country wgn 4d | 4,015 | 3,200 | 728* |
| sdn 4d, 8P | 4,145 | 3,342 | 234* |
| Deluxe sdn 4d | 3,775 | 2,727 | 27,940* |
| Deluxe Newport htp cpe | 3,855 | 3,087 | 3,774* |
| Deluxe conv cpe | 3,990 | 3,210 | 1,554* |

| C-55 Saratoga (wb 125.5; 8P-139.5) | Wght | Price | Prod |
|---|---|---|---|
| sdn 4d | 4,010 | 3,215 | 13,141* |
| club cpe | 3,935 | 3,187 | 3,145* |
| Town & Country wgn 4d, 8P | 4,345 | 3,925 | 481* |
| sdn 4d, 8P | 4,510 | 4,172 | 68* |

| C-62 New Yorker (wb 131.5) | Wght | Price | Prod |
|---|---|---|---|
| sdn 4d | 4,205 | 3,530 | 14,954* |
| Newport htp cpe | 4,325 | 3,969 | 2,146* |
| conv cpe | 4,450 | 4,093 | 814* |

| C-54 Imperial (wb 131.5) | Wght | Price | Prod |
|---|---|---|---|
| sdn 4d | 4,315 | 3,839 | 8,033* |
| club cpe | 4,220 | 3,826 | 1,307* |
| Newport htp cpe | 4,365 | 4,224 | 440* |

| C-53 Crown Imperial (wb 145.5) | Wght | Price | Prod |
|---|---|---|---|
| sdn 4d, 8P | 5,395 | 6,872 | 133* |
| limo 8P | 5,430 | 6,994 | 125* |

| 1952 Engines | bore×stroke | bhp | availability |
|---|---|---|---|
| L6, 264.5 | 3.44×4.75 | 119 | S-Windsor |
| V8, 331.1 | 3.81×3.63 | 180 | S-others |

*As with other corporate makes, Chrysler combined model year production for 1951–52. However, production figures are known for several 1951-only body styles, making production estimates of remaining body styles (spanning both years) more accurate. In the above cases (*), estimates are based on the known percentages of the two-year run: 63% in 1951 and 37% in 1952.

## 1953

| C-60-1 Windsor (wb 125.5; 8P-139.5) | Wght | Price | Prod |
|---|---|---|---|
| sdn 4d | 3,660 | 2,462 | 18,879 |
| club cpe | 3,600 | 2,442 | 11,646 |
| Town & Country wgn 4d | 3,960 | 3,259 | 1,242 |
| sdn 4d, 8P | 4,170 | 3,403 | 425 |

| C-60-2 Windsor Deluxe (wb 125.5) | Wght | Price | Prod |
|---|---|---|---|
| sdn 4d | 3,775 | 2,691 | 45,385 |
| Newport htp cpe | 3,775 | 2,995 | 5,642 |
| conv cpe | 4,005 | 3,217 | 1,250 |

| C-56-1 New Yorker (wb 125.5; 8P-139.5) | Wght | Price | Prod |
|---|---|---|---|
| sdn 4d | 4,005 | 3,150 | 37,540 |
| club cpe | 3,925 | 3,121 | 7,749 |
| Newport htp cpe | 4,020 | 3,487 | 2,525 |
| Town & Country wgn 4d | 4,265 | 3,898 | 1,399 |
| sdn 4d, 8P | 4,510 | 4,334 | 100 |

| C-56-2 New Yorker Deluxe (wb 125.5) | Wght | Price | Prod |
|---|---|---|---|
| sdn 4d | 4,025 | 3,293 | 20,585 |
| club cpe | 3,925 | 3,264 | 1,934 |
| Newport htp cpe | 4,025 | 3,653 | 3,715 |
| conv cpe | 4,295 | 3,945 | 950 |
| chassis | — | — | 21 |

| C-58 Custom Imperial (wb 133.5; htp cpe-131.5) | Wght | Price | Prod |
|---|---|---|---|
| sdn 4d | 4,305 | 4,225 | 7,793 |
| town limo 6P | 4,525 | 4,762 | 243 |
| Newport htp cpe | 4,290 | 4,525 | 823 |

| C-59 Crown Imperial (wb 145.5) | Wght | Price | Prod |
|---|---|---|---|
| sdn 4d, 8P | 5,235 | 6,872 | 48 |

# Chrysler

| | Wght | Price | Prod |
|---|---|---|---|
| limo 8P | 5,275 | 6,994 | 111 |
| chassis | — | — | 1 |

| 1953 Engines | bore×stroke | bhp | availability |
|---|---|---|---|
| L6, 264.5 | 3.44×4.75 | 119 | S-Windsor |
| V8, 331.1 | 3.81×3.63 | 180 | S-others |

## 1954

| C-62 Windsor Del (wb 125.5; 8P-139.5) | Wght | Price | Prod |
|---|---|---|---|
| sdn 4d | 3,655 | 2,562 | 33,563 |
| club cpe | 3,565 | 2,541 | 5,659 |
| Newport htp cpe | 3,685 | 2,831 | 3,655 |
| conv cpe | 3,915 | 3,046 | 500 |
| Town & Country wgn 4d | 3,955 | 3,321 | 650 |
| sdn 4d, 8P | 4,185 | 3,492 | 500 |

| C-63-1 New Yorker (wb 125.5; 8P-139.5) | Wght | Price | Prod |
|---|---|---|---|
| sdn 4d | 3,970 | 3,229 | 15,788 |
| club cpe | 3,910 | 3,202 | 2,079 |
| Newport htp cpe | 4,005 | 3,503 | 1,312 |
| Town & Country wgn 4d | 4,245 | 4,024 | 1,100 |
| sdn 4d, 8P | 4,450 | 4,368 | 140 |

| C-63-2 New Yorker Deluxe (wb 125.5) | Wght | Price | Prod |
|---|---|---|---|
| sdn 4d | 4,065 | 3,433 | 26,907 |
| club cpe | 4,005 | 3,406 | 1,861 |
| Newport htp cpe | 4,095 | 3,707 | 4,814 |
| conv cpe | 4,265 | 3,938 | 724 |
| chassis | — | — | 17 |

| C-64 Custom Imperial (wb 133.5) | Wght | Price | Prod |
|---|---|---|---|
| sdn 4d | 4,355 | 4,260 | 4,324 |
| town limo 6P | 4,465 | 4,797 | 83 |
| special town limo 6P | 4,475 | — | 2 |
| Newport htp cpe | 4,345 | 4,560 | 1,249 |
| conv cpe | — | proto | 1 |
| chassis | — | — | 2 |

| C-66 Crown Imperial (wb 145.5) | Wght | Price | Prod |
|---|---|---|---|
| sdn 4d, 8P | 5,220 | 6,922 | 23 |
| limo 8P | 5,295 | 7,044 | 77 |

| 1954 Engines | bore×stroke | bhp | availability |
|---|---|---|---|
| L6, 264.5 | 3.44×4.75 | 119 | S-Windsor Deluxe |
| V8, 331.1 | 3.81×3.63 | 195 | S-NY |
| V8, 331.1 | 3.81×3.63 | 235 | S-others |

## 1955

| C-67 Windsor Deluxe (wb 126.0) | Wght | Price | Prod |
|---|---|---|---|
| sdn 4d | 3,925 | 2,660 | 63,896 |
| Nassau htp cpe | 3,930 | 2,703 | 18,474 |
| Newport htp cpe | 3,925 | 2,818 | 13,126 |
| conv cpe | 4,075 | 3,090 | 1,395 |
| Town & Country wgn 4d | 4,295 | 3,332 | 1,983 |

| C-68 New Yorker Deluxe (wb 126.0) | Wght | Price | Prod |
|---|---|---|---|
| sdn 4d | 4,160 | 3,494 | 33,342 |
| Newport htp cpe | 4,140 | 3,652 | 5,777 |
| St. Regis htp cpe | 4,125 | 3,690 | 11,076 |
| conv cpe | 4,285 | 3,924 | 946 |
| Town & Country wgn 4d | 4,430 | 4,209 | 1,036 |
| chassis | — | — | 1 |

| C-68 300 (wb 126.0) | Wght | Price | Prod |
|---|---|---|---|
| htp cpe | 4,005 | 4,110 | 1,725 |

| 1955 Engines | bore×stroke | bhp | availability |
|---|---|---|---|
| V8, 301.0 | 3.63×3.63 | 188 | S-Windsor Deluxe |
| V8, 331.1 | 3.81×3.63 | 250 | S-NY Deluxe |
| V8, 331.1 | 3.81×3.63 | 300 | S-300 |

## 1956

| C-71 Windsor (wb 126.0) | Wght | Price | Prod |
|---|---|---|---|
| sdn 4d | 3,900 | 2,870 | 53,119 |
| Newport htp sdn | 3,990 | 3,128 | 7,050 |
| Nassau htp cpe | 3,910 | 2,905 | 11,400 |
| Newport htp cpe | 3,920 | 3,041 | 10,800 |
| conv cpe | 4,100 | 3,336 | 1,011 |
| Town & Country wgn 4d | 4,290 | 3,598 | 2,700 |

| C-72 New Yorker (wb 126.0) | Wght | Price | Prod |
|---|---|---|---|
| sdn 4d | 4,110 | 3,779 | 24,749 |
| Newport htp sdn | 4,220 | 4,102 | 3,599 |
| Newport htp cpe | 4,175 | 3,951 | 4,115 |
| St. Regis htp cpe | 4,175 | 3,995 | 6,686 |
| conv cpe | 4,360 | 4,243 | 921 |
| Town & Country wgn 4d | 4,460 | 4,523 | 1,070 |

| C-72 300B (wb 126.0) | Wght | Price | Prod |
|---|---|---|---|
| htp cpe | 4,145 | 4,419 | 1,102 |

| 1956 Engines | bore×stroke | bhp | availability |
|---|---|---|---|
| V8, 331.1 | 3.81×3.63 | 225 | S-Windsor |
| V8, 331.1 | 3.81×3.63 | 250 | O-Windsor |
| V8, 354.0 | 3.94×3.63 | 280 | S-NY |
| V8, 354.0 | 3.94×3.63 | 340 | S-300B |

## 1957

| C-75-1 Windsor (wb 126.0) | Wght | Price | Prod |
|---|---|---|---|
| sdn 4d | 3,995 | 3,088 | 17,639 |
| htp sdn | 4,030 | 3,217 | 14,354 |
| htp cpe | 3,925 | 3,153 | 14,027 |
| Town & Country wgn 4d | 4,210 | 3,575 | 2,035 |

| C-75-2 Saratoga (wb 126.0) | Wght | Price | Prod |
|---|---|---|---|
| sdn 4d | 4,165 | 3,718 | 14,977 |
| htp sdn | 4,195 | 3,832 | 11,586 |
| htp cpe | 4,075 | 3,754 | 10,633 |

| C-76 New Yorker (wb 126.0) | Wght | Price | Prod |
|---|---|---|---|
| sdn 4d | 4,315 | 4,173 | 12,369 |
| htp sdn | 4,330 | 4,259 | 10,948 |
| htp cpe | 4,220 | 4,202 | 8,863 |
| conv cpe | 4,365 | 4,638 | 1,049 |
| Town & Country wgn 4d | 4,490 | 4,746 | 1,391 |

| C-76 300C (wb 126.0) | Wght | Price | Prod |
|---|---|---|---|
| htp cpe | 4,235 | 4,929 | 1,918 |
| conv cpe | 4,390 | 5,359 | 484 |

| 1957 Engines | bore×stroke | bhp | availability |
|---|---|---|---|
| V8, 354.0 | 3.94×3.63 | 285 | S-Windsor |
| V8, 354.0 | 3.94×3.63 | 295 | S-Saratoga |
| V8, 392.0 | 4.00×3.90 | 325 | S-NY |
| V8, 392.0 | 4.00×3.90 | 375 | S-300C |

## 1958

| LC-1-L Windsor (wb 122.0) | Wght | Price | Prod |
|---|---|---|---|
| sdn 4d | 3,895 | 3,129 | 12,861 |
| htp sdn | 3,915 | 3,279 | 6,254 |
| htp cpe | 3,860 | 3,214 | 6,205 |
| Town & Country wgn 4d, 9P | 4,245 | 3,803 | 862 |
| Town & Country wgn 4d, 6P | 4,155 | 3,616 | 791 |
| conv cpe | — | — | 2 |

| LC-2-M Saratoga (wb 126.0) | Wght | Price | Prod |
|---|---|---|---|
| sdn 4d | 4,120 | 3,818 | 8,698 |
| htp sdn | 4,145 | 3,955 | 5,322 |

| | | Wght | Price | Prod |
|---|---|---|---|---|
| | htp cpe | 4,045 | 3,878 | 4,466 |

**LC-3-H New Yorker (wb 126.0)**

| | | Wght | Price | Prod |
|---|---|---|---|---|
| | sdn 4d | 4,195 | 4,295 | 7,110 |
| | htp sdn | 4,240 | 4,404 | 5,227 |
| | htp cpe | 4,205 | 4,347 | 3,205 |
| | conv cpe | 4,350 | 4,761 | 666 |
| | Town & Country wgn 4d, 9P | 4,445 | 5,083 | 775 |
| | Town & Country wgn 4d, 6P | 4,435 | 4,868 | 428 |

**LC-3-S 300D (wb 126.0)**

| | | Wght | Price | Prod |
|---|---|---|---|---|
| | htp cpe | 4,305 | 5,173 | 618 |
| | conv cpe | 4,475 | 5,603 | 191 |

**1958 Engines**

| 1958 Engines | bore×stroke | bhp | availability |
|---|---|---|---|
| V8, 354.0 | 3.94×3.63 | 290 | S-Windsor |
| V8, 354.0 | 3.94×3.63 | 310 | S-Saratoga |
| V8, 392.0 | 4.00×3.90 | 310 | S-NY |
| V8, 392.0 | 4.00×3.90 | 380 | S-300D |
| V8, 392.0 | 4.00×3.90 | 390 | O-300D |

# 1959

**MC-1-L Windsor (wb 122.0)**

| | | Wght | Price | Prod |
|---|---|---|---|---|
| 512 | htp cpe | 3,830 | 3,289 | 6,775 |
| 513 | sdn 4d | 3,800 | 3,204 | 19,910 |
| 514 | htp sdn | 3,735 | 3,353 | 6,084 |
| 515 | conv cpe | 3,950 | 3,620 | 961 |
| 576 | Town & Country wgn 4d, 6P | 4,045 | 3,691 | 751 |
| 577 | Town & Country wgn 4d, 9P | 4,070 | 3,878 | 992 |

**MC-2-M Saratoga (wb 126.0)**

| | | Wght | Price | Prod |
|---|---|---|---|---|
| 532 | htp cpe | 3,970 | 4,026 | 3,753 |
| 533 | sdn 4d | 4,010 | 3,966 | 8,783 |
| 534 | htp sdn | 4,035 | 4,104 | 4,943 |

**MC-3-H New Yorker (wb 126.0)**

| | | Wght | Price | Prod |
|---|---|---|---|---|
| 552 | htp cpe | 4,080 | 4,476 | 2,434 |
| 553 | sdn 4d | 4,120 | 4,424 | 7,792 |
| 554 | htp sdn | 4,165 | 4,533 | 4,805 |
| 555 | conv cpe | 4,270 | 4,890 | 286 |
| 578 | Town & Country wgn 6P | 4,295 | 4,997 | 444 |
| 579 | Town & Country wgn 9P | 4,360 | 5,212 | 564 |
| — | chassis | — | — | 3 |

**MC-3-H 300E (wb 126.0)**

| | | Wght | Price | Prod |
|---|---|---|---|---|
| 592 | htp cpe | 4,290 | 5,319 | 550 |
| 595 | conv cpe | 4,350 | 5,749 | 140 |

**1959 Engines**

| 1959 Engines | bore×stroke | bhp | availability |
|---|---|---|---|
| V8, 383.0 | 4.03×3.75 | 305 | S-Windsor |
| V8, 383.0 | 4.03×3.75 | 325 | S-Saratoga |
| V8, 413.0 | 4.18×3.75 | 350 | S-NY |
| V8, 413.0 | 4.18×3.75 | 380 | S-300E |

# 1960

**PC-1-L Windsor (wb 122.0)**

| | | Wght | Price | Prod |
|---|---|---|---|---|
| 23 | htp cpe | 3,855 | 3,279 | 6,496 |
| 27 | conv cpe | 3,855 | 3,623 | 1,467 |
| 41 | sdn 4d | 3,815 | 3,194 | 25,152 |
| 43 | htp sdn | 3,850 | 3,343 | 5,897 |
| 46 | Town & Country wgn 4d, 6P | 4,235 | 3,733 | 1,120 |
| 46 | Town & Country wgn 4d, 9P | 4,390 | 3,814 | 1,026 |

**PC-2-M Saratoga (wb 126.0)**

| | | Wght | Price | Prod |
|---|---|---|---|---|
| 23 | htp cpe | 4,030 | 3,989 | 2,963 |
| 41 | sdn 4d | 4,010 | 3,929 | 8,463 |
| 43 | htp sdn | 4,035 | 4,067 | 4,099 |

**PC-3-H New Yorker (wb 126.0)**

| | | Wght | Price | Prod |
|---|---|---|---|---|
| 23 | htp cpe | 4,175 | 4,461 | 2,835 |

| | | Wght | Price | Prod |
|---|---|---|---|---|
| 27 | conv cpe | 4,185 | 4,875 | 556 |
| 41 | sdn 4d | 4,145 | 4,409 | 9,079 |
| 43 | htp sdn | 4,175 | 4,518 | 5,625 |
| 46 | Town & Country wgn 6P | 4,515 | 5,022 | 624 |
| 46 | Town & Country wgn 9P | 4,535 | 5,131 | 671 |

**PC-3-H 300F (wb 126.0)**

| | | Wght | Price | Prod |
|---|---|---|---|---|
| 23 | htp cpe | 4,270 | 5,411 | 964 |
| 27 | conv cpe | 4,310 | 5,841 | 248 |

**1960 Engines**

| 1960 Engines | bore×stroke | bhp | availability |
|---|---|---|---|
| V8, 383.0 | 4.03×3.75 | 305 | S-Windsor |
| V8, 383.0 | 4.03×3.75 | 325 | S-Saratoga |
| V8, 413.0 | 4.18×3.75 | 350 | S-NY |
| V8, 413.0 | 4.18×3.75 | 375 | 3-300F |

# 1961

**RC-1-L Newport (wb 122.0)**

| | | Wght | Price | Prod |
|---|---|---|---|---|
| 812 | htp cpe | 3,690 | 3,025 | 9,405 |
| 813 | sdn 4d | 3,710 | 2,964 | 34,370 |
| 814 | htp sdn | 3,730 | 3,104 | 7,789 |
| 815 | conv cpe | 3,760 | 3,442 | 2,135 |
| 858 | Town & Country wgn 4d, 6P | 4,070 | 3,541 | 1,832 |
| 859 | Town & Country wgn 4d, 9P | 4,155 | 3,622 | 1,571 |

**RC-2-M Windsor (wb 122.0)**

| | | Wght | Price | Prod |
|---|---|---|---|---|
| 822 | htp cpe | 3,710 | 3,303 | 2,941 |
| 823 | sdn 4d | 3,730 | 3,218 | 10,239 |
| 824 | htp sdn | 3,765 | 3,367 | 4,156 |

**RC-3-H New Yorker (wb 126.0)**

| | | Wght | Price | Prod |
|---|---|---|---|---|
| 832 | htp cpe | 4,065 | 4,175 | 2,541 |
| 833 | sdn 4d | 4,055 | 4,123 | 9,984 |
| 834 | htp sdn | 4,100 | 4,261 | 5,862 |
| 835 | conv cpe | 4,070 | 4,592 | 576 |
| 878 | Town & Country wgn 4d, 6P | 4,425 | 4,764 | 676 |
| 879 | Town & Country wgn 4d, 9P | 4,455 | 4,871 | 760 |

**RC-4-P 300G (wb 126.0)**

| | | Wght | Price | Prod |
|---|---|---|---|---|
| 842 | htp cpe | 4,260 | 5,411 | 1,280 |
| 845 | conv cpe | 4,315 | 5,841 | 337 |

**1961 Engines**

| 1961 Engines | bore×stroke | bhp | availability |
|---|---|---|---|
| V8, 361.0 | 4.12×3.38 | 265 | S-Newport |
| V8, 383.0 | 4.25×3.38 | 305 | S-Windsor |
| V8, 413.0 | 4.18×3.75 | 350 | S-NY |
| V8, 413.0 | 4.18×3.75 | 375 | S-300G |
| V8, 413.0 | 4.18×3.75 | 400 | O-300G |

# 1962

**SC1-L Newport (wb 122.0)**

| | | Wght | Price | Prod |
|---|---|---|---|---|
| 812 | htp cpe | 3,650 | 3,027 | 11,910 |
| 813 | sdn 4d | 3,690 | 2,964 | 54,813 |
| 814 | htp sdn | 3,715 | 3,106 | 8,712 |
| 815 | conv cpe | 3,740 | 3,399 | 2,051 |
| 858 | Town & Country wgn 4d, 6P | 4,060 | 3,478 | 3,271 |
| 859 | Town & Country wgn 4d, 9P | 4,090 | 3,586 | 2,363 |

**SC2-M 300 (wb 122.0)**

| | | Wght | Price | Prod |
|---|---|---|---|---|
| 822 | htp cpe | 3,750 | 3,323 | 11,341 |
| 823 | sdn 4d | — | — | 1,801 |
| 824 | htp sdn | 3,760 | 3,400 | 10,030 |
| 825 | conv cpe | 3,815 | 3,883 | 1,848 |

**SC3-H New Yorker (wb 126.0)**

| | | Wght | Price | Prod |
|---|---|---|---|---|
| 833 | sdn 4d | 3,925 | 4,125 | 12,056 |
| 834 | htp sdn | 4,005 | 4,263 | 6,646 |
| 878 | Town & Country wgn 4d, 6P | 4,225 | 4,766 | 728 |

# Chrysler

| 879 | Town & Country wgn 4d, 9P | Wght | Price | Prod |
|---|---|---|---|---|
| | | 4,455 | 4,873 | 793 |

### SC2-M 300H (wb 122.0)

| 842 | htp cpe | 4,010 | 5,090 | 435 |
|---|---|---|---|---|
| 845 | conv cpe | 4,080 | 5,461 | 123 |

| 1962 Engines | bore×stroke | bhp | availability | |
|---|---|---|---|---|
| V8, 361.0 | 4.12×3.38 | 265 | S-Newport | |
| V8, 383.0 | 4.25×3.38 | 305 | S-300 | |
| V8, 413.0 | 4.18×3.75 | 340 | S-NY | |
| V8, 413.0 | 4.18×3.75 | 380 | S-300H | |

## 1963

### TC1-L Newport (wb 122.0)

| | | Wght | Price | Prod |
|---|---|---|---|---|
| 812 | htp cpe | 3,760 | 3,027 | 9,809 |
| 813 | sdn 4d | 3,770 | 2,964 | 49,067 |
| 814 | htp sdn | 3,800 | 3,106 | 8,437 |
| 815 | conv cpe | 3,825 | 3,399 | 2,093 |
| 858 | Town & Country wgn 4d, 6P | 4,200 | 3,478 | 3,618 |
| 859 | Town & Country wgn 4d, 9P | 4,215 | 3,586 | 2,948 |

### TC2-M 300 (wb 122.0)

| 802 | Pace Setter htp cpe | 3,790 | 3,769 | 306 |
|---|---|---|---|---|
| 822 | htp cpe | 3,790 | 3,430 | 9,423 |
| 805 | Pace Setter conv cpe | 3,840 | 4,129 | 1,861 |
| 825 | conv cpe | 3,845 | 3,790 | 1,535 |
| 823 | sdn 4d | 3,790 | — | 1,625 |
| 824 | htp sdn | 3,815 | 3,400 | 9,915 |

### TC3-H New Yorker (wb 122.0)

| 833 | sdn 4d | 3,910 | 4,981 | 14,884 |
|---|---|---|---|---|
| 834 | htp sdn | 3,950 | 4,118 | 10,229 |
| 884 | Salon htp sdn | 4,290 | 5,860 | 593 |
| 878 | Town & Country wgn 4d, 6P | 4,350 | 4,708 | 950 |
| 879 | Town & Country wgn 4d, 9P | 4,370 | 4,815 | 1,244 |

### TC2-M 300J (wb 122.0)

| 842 | htp cpe | 4,000 | 5,184 | 400 |
|---|---|---|---|---|

| 1963 Engines | bore×stroke | bhp | availability | |
|---|---|---|---|---|
| V8, 361.0 | 4.12×3.38 | 265 | S-Newport | |
| V8, 383.0 | 4.25×3.38 | 305 | S-300 | |
| V8, 413.0 | 4.19×3.75 | 340 | S-NY, 300J; O-300 | |
| V8, 413.0 | 4.19×3.75 | 360 | O-300 | |
| V8, 413.0 | 4.19×3.75 | 390 | O-300J | |

## 1964

### VC1-L Newport (wb 122.0)

| | | Wght | Price | Prod |
|---|---|---|---|---|
| 812 | htp cpe | 3,760 | 2,962 | 10,579 |
| 813 | sdn 4d | 3,805 | 2,901 | 55,957 |
| 814 | htp sdn | 3,795 | 3,042 | 9,710 |
| 815 | conv cpe | 3,810 | 3,334 | 2,176 |
| 858 | Town & Country wgn 4d, 6P | 4,175 | 3,414 | 3,720 |
| 859 | Town & Country wgn 4d, 9P | 4,200 | 3,521 | 3,041 |

### VC2-M 300 (wb 122.0)*

| 822 | htp cpe | 3,850 | 3,443 | 18,379 |
|---|---|---|---|---|
| 824 | htp sdn | 3,865 | 3,521 | 11,460 |
| 823 | sdn 4d | — | — | 2,078 |
| 825 | conv cpe | 4,120 | 3,803 | 1,401 |

### VC3-H New Yorker (wb 122.0)

| 832 | htp cpe | — | — | 300 |
|---|---|---|---|---|
| 833 | sdn 4d | 4,015 | 3,994 | 15,443 |
| 834 | htp sdn | 4,035 | 4,131 | 10,887 |
| 878 | Town & Country wgn 4d, 6P | 4,385 | 4,721 | 1,190 |

| 879 | Town & Country wgn 4d, 9P | Wght | Price | Prod |
|---|---|---|---|---|
| 879 | Town & Country wgn 4d, 9P | 4,395 | 4,828 | 1,603 |
| 884 | Salon htp sdn | 4,280 | 5,860 | 1,621 |

### VC2-M 300K (wb 122.0)*

| 842 | htp cpe | 3,965 | 4,056 | 3,022 |
|---|---|---|---|---|
| 845 | conv cpe | 3,995 | 4,522 | 625 |

*Silver 300 models: 300—2,152; 300K series—255.

| 1964 Engines | bore×stroke | bhp | availability | |
|---|---|---|---|---|
| V8, 361.0 | 4.12×3.38 | 265 | S-Newport | |
| V8, 383.0 | 4.25×3.38 | 305 | S-300 | |
| V8, 413.0 | 4.19×3.75 | 340 | S-NY, 300K; O-300 | |
| V8, 413.0 | 4.19×3.75 | 360 | O-300, 300K | |
| V8, 413.0 | 4.19×3.75 | 390 | O-300K | |

## 1965

### AC1-L Newport (wb 124.0; wgns-121.0)

| | | Wght | Price | Prod |
|---|---|---|---|---|
| C12 | htp cpe | 4,035 | 3,070 | 23,655 |
| C13 | sdn 4d, 4W | 4,045 | 3,009 | 61,054 |
| C14 | htp sdn | 4,050 | 3,149 | 17,062 |
| C15 | conv cpe | 4,025 | 3,442 | 3,192 |
| C18 | town sdn 4d, 6W | 4,000 | 3,146 | 12,411 |
| C56 | Town & Country wgn 4d, 6P | 4,360 | 3,521 | 4,683 |
| C57 | Town & Country wgn 4d, 9P | 4,455 | 3,629 | 3,738 |

### AC2-M 300 (wb 124.0)

| C22 | htp cpe | 4,085 | 3,551 | 11,621 |
|---|---|---|---|---|
| C24 | htp sdn 4W | 4,150 | 3,628 | 12,452 |
| C25 | conv cpe | 4,140 | 3,911 | 1,418 |
| C28 | htp town sdn 6W | — | — | 2,187 |

### AC3-H New Yorker (wb 124.0; wgns-121.0)

| C32 | htp cpe | 4,270 | 4,161 | 9,357 |
|---|---|---|---|---|
| C34 | htp sdn | 4,295 | 4,238 | 21,110 |
| C38 | town sdn 4d, 6W | 4,265 | 4,104 | 16,239 |
| C76 | Town & Country wgn 4d, 6P | 4,650 | 4,827 | 1,368 |
| C77 | Town & Country wgn 4d, 9P | 4,745 | 4,935 | 1,697 |

### AC2-P 300L (wb 124.0)

| C42 | htp cpe | 4,245 | 4,153 | 2,405 |
|---|---|---|---|---|
| C45 | conv cpe | 4,170 | 4,618 | 440 |

| 1965 Engines | bore×stroke | bhp | availability | |
|---|---|---|---|---|
| V8, 383.0 | 4.25×3.38 | 270 | S-Newport; O-300 | |
| V8, 383.0 | 4.25×3.38 | 315 | S-300; O-Newport | |
| V8, 413.0 | 4.19×3.75 | 340 | S-NY | |
| V8, 413.0 | 4.19×3.75 | 360 | S-300L; O-300, NY | |

## 1966

### BC1-L Newport (wb 124.0; wgns-121.0)

| | | Wght | Price | Prod |
|---|---|---|---|---|
| 23 | htp cpe | 3,920 | 3,112 | 37,622 |
| 27 | conv cpe | 4,020 | 3,476 | 3,085 |
| 41 | sdn 4d, 4W | 3,875 | 3,052 | 74,964 |
| 42 | sdn 4d, 6W | 3,910 | 3,183 | 9,432 |
| 43 | htp sdn | 4,010 | 3,190 | 24,966 |
| 45 | wgn 4d, 6P | 4,370 | 4,086 | 9,035 |
| 46 | wgn 4d, 9P | 4,550 | 4,192 | 8,567 |

### BC2-M 300 (wb 124.0)

| 23 | htp cpe | 3,940 | 3,583 | 24,103 |
|---|---|---|---|---|
| 27 | conv cpe | 4,015 | 3,936 | 2,500 |
| 41 | sdn 4d | 3,895 | 3,523 | 2,353 |
| 43 | htp sdn | 4,000 | 3,659 | 20,642 |

### BC3-H New Yorker (wb 124.0)

| 23 | htp cpe | 4,095 | 4,157 | 7,955 |
|---|---|---|---|---|
| 42 | sdn 4d | 4,100 | 4,101 | 13,025 |

| | | Wght | Price | Prod |
|---|---|---|---|---|
| 43 | htp sdn | 4,140 | 4,233 | 26,599 |

| 1966 Engines | bore×stroke | bhp | availability | |
|---|---|---|---|---|
| V8, 383.0 | 4.25×3.38 | 270 | S-Newport | |
| V8, 383.0 | 4.25×3.38 | 325 | S-300; O-Newport | |
| V8, 440.0 | 4.32×3.75 | 350 | S-NY | |

## 1967

### CC1-E Newport (wb 124.0; wgns-122.0)

| | | Wght | Price | Prod |
|---|---|---|---|---|
| 23 | htp cpe | 3,920 | 3,219 | 26,583 |
| 27 | conv cpe | 3,970 | 3,583 | 2,891 |
| 41 | sdn 4d | 3,955 | 3,159 | 48,945 |
| 43 | htp sdn | 3,980 | 3,296 | 14,247 |
| 45 | wgn 4d, 6P | 4,495 | 4,264 | 7,183 |
| 46 | wgn 4d, 9P | 4,550 | 4,369 | 7,520 |

### CC1-L Newport Custom (wb 124.0)

| | | Wght | Price | Prod |
|---|---|---|---|---|
| 23 | htp cpe | 3,935 | 3,407 | 14,193 |
| 41 | sdn 4d | 3,975 | 3,347 | 23,101 |
| 43 | htp sdn | 3,995 | 3,485 | 12,728 |

### CC2-M 300 (wb 124.0)

| | | Wght | Price | Prod |
|---|---|---|---|---|
| 23 | htp cpe | 4,070 | 3,936 | 11,556 |
| 27 | conv cpe | 4,105 | 4,289 | 1,594 |
| 43 | htp sdn | 4,135 | 4,012 | 8,744 |

### CC3-H New Yorker (wb 124.0)

| | | Wght | Price | Prod |
|---|---|---|---|---|
| 23 | htp cpe | 4,170 | 4,264 | 6,885 |
| 41 | sdn 4d | 4,185 | 4,208 | 10,907 |
| 43 | htp sdn | 4,240 | 4,339 | 21,665 |

| 1967 Engines | bore×stroke | bhp | availability | |
|---|---|---|---|---|
| V8, 383.0 | 4.25×3.38 | 270 | S-Newport | |
| V8, 383.0 | 4.25×3.38 | 325 | O-Newport | |
| V8, 440.0 | 4.32×3.75 | 350 | S-300, NY; O-wgns | |
| V8, 440.0 | 4.32×3.75 | 375 | O-all exc wgns | |

## 1968

### DC1-E Newport (wb 124.0; wgns-122.0)

| | | Wght | Price | Prod |
|---|---|---|---|---|
| CE23 | htp cpe* | 3,840 | 3,366 | 36,768 |
| CE27 | conv cpe* | 3,910 | 3,704 | 2,847 |
| CE41 | sdn 4d | 3,850 | 3,306 | 61,436 |
| CE43 | htp sdn | 3,865 | 3,444 | 20,191 |
| CE45 | Town & Country wgn 4d, 6P | 4,340 | 4,418 | 9,908 |
| CE46 | Town & Country wgn 4d, 9P | 4,410 | 4,523 | 12,223 |

### DC1-L Newport Custom (wb 124.0)

| | | Wght | Price | Prod |
|---|---|---|---|---|
| CL23 | htp cpe | 3,890 | 3,552 | 10,341 |
| CL41 | sdn 4d | 3,855 | 3,493 | 16,915 |
| CL43 | htp sdn | 3,860 | 3,631 | 11,640 |

### DC2-M 300 (wb 124.0)

| | | Wght | Price | Prod |
|---|---|---|---|---|
| CM23 | htp cpe | 3,985 | 4,010 | 16,953 |
| CM27 | conv cpe | 4,050 | 4,337 | 2,161 |
| CM43 | htp sdn | 4,015 | 4,086 | 15,507 |

### DC3-H New Yorker (wb 124.0)

| | | Wght | Price | Prod |
|---|---|---|---|---|
| CH23 | htp cpe | 4,060 | 4,424 | 8,060 |
| CH41 | sdn 4d | 4,055 | 4,367 | 13,092 |
| CH43 | htp sdn | 4,090 | 4,500 | 26,991 |

*Sportsgrain models: htp cpe 965; conv cpe 175.

| 1968 Engines | bore×stroke | bhp | availability | |
|---|---|---|---|---|
| V8, 383.0 | 4.25×3.38 | 290 | S-Newport, T&C | |
| V8, 383.0 | 4.25×3.38 | 330 | O-Newport, T&C | |
| V8, 440.0 | 4.32×3.75 | 350 | S-300, NY; O-T&C | |
| V8, 440.0 | 4.32×3.75 | 375 | O-all exc T&C | |

## 1969

### EC-E Newport (wb 124.0)*

| | | Wght | Price | Prod |
|---|---|---|---|---|
| CE23 | htp cpe | 3,891 | 3,485 | 33,639 |
| CE27 | conv cpe | 4,026 | 3,823 | 2,169 |
| CE41 | sdn 4d | 3,941 | 3,414 | 55,083 |
| CE43 | htp sdn | 4,156 | 3,549 | 20,608 |

### EC-L Newport Custom (wb 124.0)

| | | Wght | Price | Prod |
|---|---|---|---|---|
| CL23 | htp cpe | 3,891 | 3,652 | 10,995 |
| CL41 | sdn 4d | 3,951 | 3,580 | 18,401 |
| CL43 | htp sdn | 3,971 | 3,730 | 15,981 |

### EC-P Town & Country (wb 122.0)

| | | Wght | Price | Prod |
|---|---|---|---|---|
| CP45 | wgn 4d, 6P | 4,435 | 4,583 | 10,108 |
| CP46 | wgn 4d, 9P | 4,485 | 4,660 | 14,408 |

### EC-M 300 (wb 124.0)

| | | Wght | Price | Prod |
|---|---|---|---|---|
| CM23 | htp cpe | 3,965 | 4,104 | 16,075 |
| CM27 | conv cpe | 4,095 | 4,450 | 1,933 |
| CM43 | htp sdn | 4,045 | 4,183 | 14,464 |

### EC-H New Yorker (wb 124.0)

| | | Wght | Price | Prod |
|---|---|---|---|---|
| CH23 | htp cpe | 4,070 | 4,539 | 7,539 |
| CH41 | sdn 4d | 4,135 | 4,487 | 12,253 |
| CH43 | htp sdn | 4,165 | 4,615 | 27,157 |

*Sportsgrain models 195.

| 1969 Engines | bore×stroke | bhp | availability | |
|---|---|---|---|---|
| V8, 383.0 | 4.25×3.38 | 290 | S-Newport, T&C | |
| V8, 383.0 | 4.25×3.38 | 330 | O-Newport, T&C | |
| V8, 440.0 | 4.32×3.75 | 350 | S-300, NY; O-T&C | |
| V8, 440.0 | 4.32×3.75 | 375 | O-all exc T&C | |

## 1970

### FC-E Newport (wb 124.0)

| | | Wght | Price | Prod |
|---|---|---|---|---|
| CE23 | htp cpe* | 4,030 | 3,589 | 21,664 |
| CE27 | conv cpe | 4,085 | 3,925 | 1,124 |
| CE41 | sdn 4d | 4,080 | 3,514 | 39,285 |
| CE43 | htp sdn* | 4,110 | 3,652 | 16,940 |

### FC-L Newport Custom (wb 124.0)

| | | Wght | Price | Prod |
|---|---|---|---|---|
| CL23 | htp cpe | 4,035 | 3,781 | 6,639 |
| CL41 | sdn 4d | 4,091 | 3,710 | 13,767 |
| CL43 | htp sdn | 4,125 | 3,861 | 10,873 |

### FC-P Town & Country (wb 122.0)

| | | Wght | Price | Prod |
|---|---|---|---|---|
| CP45 | wgn 4d, 6P | 4,490 | 4,738 | 5,686 |
| CP46 | wgn 4d, 9P | 4,555 | 4,824 | 9,583 |

### FC-M 300 (wb 124.0)

| | | Wght | Price | Prod |
|---|---|---|---|---|
| CM23 | htp cpe* | 4,135 | 4,234 | 10,084 |
| CM27 | conv cpe | 4,175 | 4,580 | 1,077 |
| CM43 | htp sdn | 4,220 | 4,313 | 9,846 |

### FC-H New Yorker (wb 124.0)

| | | Wght | Price | Prod |
|---|---|---|---|---|
| CH23 | htp cpe | 4,235 | 4,681 | 4,917 |
| CH41 | sdn 4d | 4,310 | 4,630 | 9,389 |
| CH43 | htp sdn | 4,335 | 4,761 | 19,903 |

*CE23 includes 1,868 Cordoba htp cpes; CE43 includes 1,873 Cordoba htp sdns; CM23 includes 400 300-H "Hurst" htp cpes.

| 1970 Engines | bore×stroke | bhp | availability | |
|---|---|---|---|---|
| V8, 383.0 | 4.25×3.38 | 290 | S-Newport, T&C | |
| V8, 383.0 | 4.25×3.38 | 330 | O-Newport auto, T&C | |
| V8, 440.0 | 4.32×3.75 | 350 | S-NY, 300; O-T&C | |
| V8, 440.0 | 4.32×3.75 | 375 | O-all exc T&C | |

# Clipper
**Packard-Clipper Division, Studebaker-Packard Corp.**
**Detroit, Michigan**

Marketing wizard James J. Nance became president of Packard in 1952. Immediately, he started to divorce the medium-priced 200 models from Packard's luxury lines, declaring that continued emphasis on cheaper models after World War II had been "bleeding the Packard name white." Accordingly, the 200 became the Packard Clipper in 1953. For 1956, Nance registered Clipper as a separate make. There were also separate Packard and Clipper dealer signs, and even the factory was renamed Packard-Clipper Division of Studebaker-Packard Corporation. The Packard name appeared nowhere on Clippers except for a tiny script on the decklid. Early production models didn't even have that.

Nance's aim was to distinguish the Clipper still further from the "senior" Packard. Plans for 1957 called for Clipper to use the larger Studebaker bodyshell while Packard would continue with one of its own. That never materialized, however, because lenders failed to commit sufficient funds for the corporation to finance its all-new 1957 line. Nance resigned in August 1956.

Studebaker-Packard received temporary reprieve by way of a management agreement with Curtiss-Wright Corporation, which needed S-P mainly as a tax loss. Under C-W management, the Packard name was saved for 1957's deluxe line of Studebaker-based cars. But these were called Packard Clippers, so Clipper disappeared as a distinct make after only a year.

The 1956 Clipper line comprised five models in DeLuxe, Super, and Custom series with a choice of two body styles. All shared a 122-inch wheelbase and an overhead-valve Packard V8. Clippers also featured Packard's innovative Torsion-Level suspension, although a conventional suspension was available on the bottom-line DeLuxe. Options included overdrive transmission ($110), Ultramatic transmission ($199), power steering, power brakes, and air conditioning.

Clippers were luxuriously trimmed and nicely styled, though their sales volume wasn't sufficient to help the

**1956 Super hardtop coupe**

**1956 Custom four-door sedan**

**1956 Deluxe four-door sedan**

company. The DeLuxe sedan was the best seller. The handsome Custom Constellation hardtop was rarest, accounting for fewer than 1500 units.

Making Clipper a separate make was a good idea, but it came too late. Had the firm begun this marketing approach in the huge seller's market of 1946, the story might have had a happier ending.

# Clipper Specifications

## 1956

| 5640 Deluxe-Super (wb 122.0) | | Wght | Price | Prod |
|---|---|---|---|---|
| 5622 | Deluxe sdn 4d | 3,745 | 2,731 | 5,715 |
| 5642 | Super sdn 4d | 3,800 | 2,866 | 5,173 |
| 5647 | Super htp cpe | 3,825 | 2,916 | 3,999 |

| 5660 Custom (wb 122.0) | | | | |
|---|---|---|---|---|
| 5662 | sdn 4d | 3,860 | 3,069 | 2,129 |
| 5667 | Constellation htp cpe | 3,860 | 3,164 | 1,466 |

| 1956 Engines | bore×stroke | bhp | availability |
|---|---|---|---|
| V8, 352.0 | 4.00×3.50 | 240 | S-Deluxe, Super |
| V8, 352.0 | 4.00×3.50 | 275 | S-Custom |

# Continental

Continental Division, Ford Motor Co.
Dearborn, Michigan

The Continental "Marks" of 1956-60 and 1968-on were, and are, not officially Lincolns. The first of these were products of a separate division at Ford, created with the goal of establishing the firm's dominance in the uppermost reaches of the market—even higher than Cadillac. Only one model was offered for 1956 and 1957: the flawlessly styled, beautifully crafted Mark II. It was priced at $10,000, and worth every penny. Yet Ford lost about $1000 on every Mark II it sold, because this was primarily an "image" car—more of an ego trip than a calculated profit-maker. An attempt was made to put Continental into the black with a lower-priced 1958-60 model based on the standard Lincoln, but it never sold particularly well. The separate division was gone by 1961, and the Continental name was applied to a new line of four-door hardtops and convertibles designed by Elwood Engle.

Ever since the demise of the original Lincoln Continental in 1948, Ford had been pressured by its dealers and customers to build a successor. In 1953, with profits looking up, the effort was begun. William Clay Ford, younger brother of Henry Ford II, was put in charge of a Special Products Division to come up with a design. He called in five outside consultants to submit their ideas

for comparison. Management reviewed 13 different proposals using front, side, rear, and ¾-front views, and unanimously selected the design from Special Products. Harley F. Copp, chief engineer of the Special Products Division, designed a unique chassis that dipped low between front and rear axles to permit high seating without a high roofline. The starkly simple cockpit and dash were inspired by aircraft and locomotive designs. The engines were Lincoln V8s specially selected from the assembly line and individually balanced. These were connected to Multi-Drive three-speed automatic transmissions and 3.07:1 rear axles. The sleek and timeless coupe measured 218.5 inches overall. It was greeted with wonderment on both sides of the Atlantic, and has been considered one of the all-time great design achievements ever since its debut. It was in a class by itself.

But the euphoria didn't last. Though the Continental Division was hoping to add a beautiful four-door berline and perhaps a convertible to the line for 1958, word from the sales department deflated those hopes. The Mark II had not had much impact on luxury-car production; General Motors was still the leader. A moneyed few were indeed buying Mark IIs, but the car was not

Mark II clay model

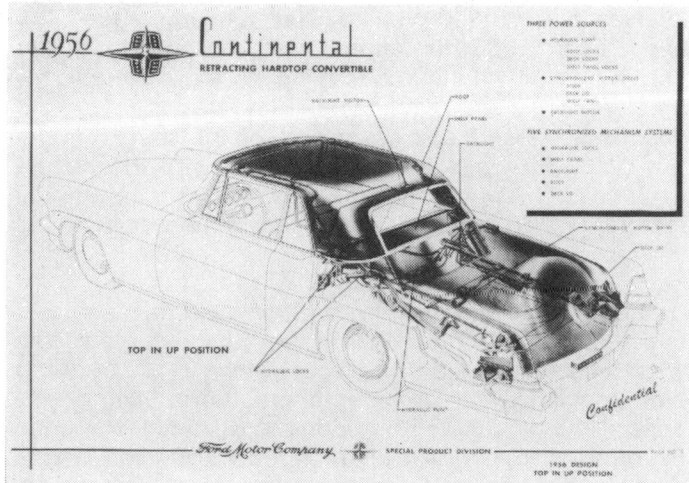

Proposed Mark II retractable hardtop

Chanelled Lincoln test mule for Mark II chassis

1956 Mark II hardtop coupe

1957 Mark II hardtop coupe

1958 Mark III convertible

1958 Mark III Landau hardtop sedan

1959 Mark IV town car (formal sedan)

1968 Mark III hardtop coupe

convincing those with slightly less cash to buy Lincolns instead of Cadillacs.

Accordingly, the $10,000 price of 1956-57 was cut to $5825 or $6283 for 1958. A Mercury cost expert was brought in, and a new Continental appeared, dubbed the Mark III. This Lincoln-based giant had a 131-inch wheelbase, with elongated fenders, large chrome appliques, huge tailfins, and canted quad headlamps. Four models were offered, and sales improved.

In 1959, the facelifted Mark IV arrived. A town car and limousine were added with extraordinary prices. A similar course was taken in 1960 with the Mark V. The Marks were then suspended, replaced by the smaller and more handsome Lincoln Continental in 1961. Continental Division quietly disappeared. Sales through 1960 were always far above the Mark II's level.

One Ford executive said years later that the Mark II program was, on balance, a tragedy. "For obvious reasons we don't like to talk about it," he said. "What we had going for us in the Mark II was literally a revival of the Duesenberg concept. What we ended up with was something much less—and even that didn't last long . . . It was a project that for a time broke Bill Ford's heart, and I guess you could say that in many ways it broke ours too."

Classic automobiles, it seems, are never quite forgotten. During the early '60s, Ford executives, engineers, stylists, and dealers longed for another Continental in the tradition of the Mark II. The answer was the 1968 Continental Mark III.

The new Continental, according to Ford Motor Company, was the car most closely linked to Henry Ford II. Just as his brother William Clay had influenced the early Mark II and his father Edsel had sponsored the "Mark I," Henry II insured that the '68 Mark III was a reflection of his personal taste. Why was the Mark III designation used again, instead of the more logical Mark VI? The reason is that Ford viewed the heavyweight 1958-60 cars as unworthy of the Continental marque. As a result, company promotion ballyhooed the new 1968 entry as a direct descendant of the Mark II.

The Mark III entered the product-planning stage in late 1965. From the beginning the goal was clear: this was to be a personal-luxury car with a long hood and short deck in the Continental tradition. Styling was supervised by design chief Eugene Bordinat. Hermann Brunn (namesake of the great coachbuilder) was a member of Bordinat's staff, and was larely responsible for the car's interior. Brunn designed large, comfort-

able bucket seats and a woodgrained dashboard with easy-to-reach controls. Henry II selected the car's final shape from a number of designs submitted by Ford stylists in early 1966.

The Mark III was ready by April 1968. Because of its late introduction, only a few thousand were built that year, but there was no question about the car's rightness for the market: in 1969 and 1970, more than 20,000 were sold.

The Mark III was set on a 117.2-inch wheelbase, some nine inches shorter than the Mark II's, and was the same length as the front-wheel-drive Cadillac Eldorado. Although the Eldorado was more technically advanced, the Continental seemed to have more magic in its name. In sales, it almost matched Eldorado during its four-year lifespan and never trailed by more than

2000 units a year. This was a significant achievement, because Lincoln's entire annual production had never come close to matching Cadillac's overall.

The Mark III was powered by a 460 cubic-inch V8 with 10.5:1 compression, one of the industry's largest engines. It was a good-looking car, with the longest hood —more than six feet—in the land. The buyer had a wide choice of luxury interiors and could choose from 26 exterior colors, including four special "Moondust" metallic paints. The 1969 and 1970 models increased in price but carried few changes. Standard features on all Mark IIIs included Select-Shift Turbo-Drive automatic transmission, power brakes (discs in front, drums in the rear), concealed headlights, ventless side windows, power seats, power windows, flow-through ventilation, and 150 pounds of sound-deadening insulation.

# Continental Specifications

## 1956

### Mark II (wb 126.0)

|  |  | Wght | Price | Prod |
|---|---|---|---|---|
| 60A | htp cpe | 4,825 | 9,695 | 1,325 |

| 1956 Engine | bore×stroke | bhp | availability |
|---|---|---|---|
| V8, 368.0 | 4.00×3.66 | 285 | S-all |

## 1957

### Mark II (wb 126.0)

|  |  | Wght | Price | Prod |
|---|---|---|---|---|
| 60A | htp cpe | 4,800 | 9,966 | 444 |

| 1957 Engine | bore×stroke | bhp | availability |
|---|---|---|---|
| V8, 368.0 | 4.00×3.66 | 300 | S-all |

## 1958

### Mark III (wb 131.0)

|  |  | Wght | Price | Prod |
|---|---|---|---|---|
| 54A | sdn 4d | 4,800 | 6,072 | 1,283 |
| 65A | htp cpe | 4,865 | 5,825 | 2,328 |
| 68A | conv cpe | 5,040 | 6,283 | 3,048 |
| 75A | Landau htp sdn | 4,965 | 6,072 | 5,891 |

| 1958 Engine | bore×stroke | bhp | availability |
|---|---|---|---|
| V8, 430.0 | 4.30×3.70 | 375 | S-all |

## 1959

### Mark IV (wb 131.0)

|  |  | Wght | Price | Prod |
|---|---|---|---|---|
| 23A | limo | 5,061 | 10,230 | 49 |
| 23B | form sdn | 5,190 | 9,208 | 78 |
| 54A | sdn 4d | 5,061 | 6,845 | 955 |
| 65A | htp cpe | 4,967 | 6,598 | 1,703 |
| 68A | conv cpe | 5,076 | 7,056 | 2,195 |
| 75A | htp sdn | 5,050 | 6,845 | 6,146 |

| 1959 Engine | bore×stroke | bhp | availability |
|---|---|---|---|
| V8, 430.0 | 4.30×3.70 | 350 | S-all |

## 1960

### Mark V (wb 131.0)

|  |  | Wght | Price | Prod |
|---|---|---|---|---|
| 23A | limo | 5,481 | 10,230 | 34 |
| 23B | form sdn | 5,272 | 9,208 | 136 |
| 54A | sdn 4d | 5,143 | 6,845 | 807 |
| 65A | htp cpe | 5,044 | 6,598 | 1,461 |
| 68A | conv cpe | 5,180 | 7,056 | 2,044 |
| 75A | htp sdn | 5,139 | 6,845 | 6,604 |

| 1960 Engine | bore×stroke | bhp | availability |
|---|---|---|---|
| V8, 430.0 | 4.30×3.70 | 315 | S-all |

## 1968

### Mark III (wb 117.2)

|  |  | Wght | Price | Prod |
|---|---|---|---|---|
| 89 | htp cpe | 4,739 | 6,585 | 7,770 |

| 1968 Engine | bore×stroke | bhp | availability |
|---|---|---|---|
| V8, 460.0 | 4.36×3.75 | 365 | S-all |

## 1969

### Mark III (wb 117.2)

|  |  | Wght | Price | Prod |
|---|---|---|---|---|
| 89 | htp cpe | 4,762 | 6,758 | 23,088 |

| 1969 Engine | bore×stroke | bhp | availability |
|---|---|---|---|
| V8, 460.0 | 4.36×3.75 | 365 | S-all |

## 1970

### Mark III (wb 117.2)

|  |  | Wght | Price | Prod |
|---|---|---|---|---|
| 89 | htp cpe | 4,675 | 7,281 | 21,432 |

| 1970 Engine | bore×stroke | bhp | availability |
|---|---|---|---|
| V8, 460.0 | 4.36×3.75 | 365 | S-all |

# Crosley

**Crosley Motors Inc.**
**Richmond-Marion, Indiana and Cincinnati, Ohio**

The Midwestern businessman who'd brought us radios and refrigerators in the '20s and '30s decided to get into the car business in 1939. Powel Crosley, Jr. offered a very small economy vehicle on an 80-inch wheelbase and carrying the lowest price in the land. In its first year, Crosley sold 2017 of them. To buy one, you visited your local hardware store or appliance shop—a novel if shortsighted marketing scheme. About 5000 Crosleys had been produced by 1942, when the war brought passenger-car production to a halt.

**1940 Series 2A convertible "sedan" coupe**

**1946 CC Four pickup**

**1948½ CC Four two-door sedan**

The 1940 Crosley line consisted of five models priced as low as $299. It included a standard and DeLuxe sedan with convertible top; station wagon; convertible; a "covered wagon" with full canvas top; plus several commercial bodies. Styling was basic, dominated by low, freestanding fenders and a prominent hood bulging out ahead of small horizontal grilles built into the front apron. Headlamps were attached to either side of the hood. Interiors were barren—just a central speedometer flanked by fuel and water gauges.

For its 1940-42 models, Crosley chose an air-cooled Waukeshaw two-cylinder engine with two main bearings. Performance wasn't quite as bad as the specifications suggest, since Crosleys were geared low at 5.14:1 and 5.57:1. Mechanical brakes, six-gallon fuel tank, disc wheels, and tiny 4.25 × 12-inch tires completed the economy package.

This design changed little for 1941. The same models were carried over, and the mechanical specifications were identical with the 1940 version. Prices were raised, however. The cars were now sold by separate automobile dealers besides Crosley's appliance outlets. The lineup was repeated for 1942.

During the war, Crosley developed the overhead-cam four-cylinder Cobra engine for a U.S. Navy project, using brazed copper and sheet steel for the block. This engine was selected to power the postwar civilian cars. This five-main-bearing engine had been fairly successful during the war in a variety of machines from truck refrigerators to Mooney Mite airplanes. It was less useful in its automotive application. The copper-steel block was subject to electrolysis, which caused holes to develop in cylinders and resulted in early rebuilds. Crosley soon rectified the fault by offering a cast-iron block that retained the original cylinder dimensions. Significantly, used-car price guides of the day gave a higher trade-in value for cars with the cast-iron engine, including 1946-48 models that had been retrofitted with the new unit.

The 1946 Crosley first appeared as a two-door four-seat sedan. Production began in June 1946. Later that year, a two-door convertible was added. A wagon and utility model followed by 1948. Commercial bodies were also offered, and in this period the future looked bright. After building almost 5000 cars in model year 1946, Crosley went on to produce 19,000 1947 models, and close to 29,000 of the 1948s. But this marked the end of prosperity. New designs from the Big Three, innovative new cars from the independents, and Crosley's growing reputation for engine problems combined to lower production drastically in model year 1949.

The sales slide was ironic in that the Crosley had become a much better car by 1949 than it had ever been before. New styling was introduced: a smooth hood,

1946-47 CC Four convertible and Powel Crosley

1949-50 CD Four two-door sedan and wagon

integral front fenders with sealed-beam headlights, remote-control door handles, and turn indicators on sedans and convertibles. In addition to the 80-inch wheelbase for sedan, delivery, convertible, and station wagon models, Crosley fielded an 85-inch wheelbase for its new Hotshot roadster.

The 1950 line comprised wagon, convertible, and sedan body styles in standard and Super trim, and a choice of two roadsters: the spartan, doorless Hotshot, and the slightly better-trimmed Super Sports (with conventional doors).

With its low prices Crosley was in a class by itself—but its engineering was also unique. For example, the 1949-50 model featured disc brakes. Along with Chrysler's 1950 Town & Country Newport, it was the first disc-braked car in series production. Unfortunately, Crosley's design proved troublesome, due to insufficient pre-production development. The brakes quickly deteriorated when exposed to road salt and grime, causing tremendous service woes. Since Crosley had only recently recovered from a rash of service difficulties with its unlamented sheetmetal engines, the disc brake problem was the last thing dealers wanted to hear about. Conventional drum brakes were reinstituted for 1951.

Though the Crosley roadster failed to sell, they were tremendous class competitors in racing. Right off the showroom floor, the little roadsters could do up to 90 mph. Their handling, thanks to semi-elliptic-and-coil-spring front suspension with quarter-elliptics at the rear, was outstanding. The Hotshot's greatest accomplishment was winning the Index of Performance at Sebring in 1951 after a fine showing in the 12-hour endurance race. Buyers were not impressed, however, and Crosley ended car production in mid-1952. The company merged with General Tire and Rubber, which quickly disposed of the automotive business. In all, the venture had cost Powel Crosley about $3 million.

1951 CD Four Hotshot roadster

Courtesy Henry Ford Museum

# Crosley Specifications

## 1940

| Series 2A (wb 80.0)—422 built | Wght | Price | Prod |
|---|---|---|---|
| sdn 2d | 975 | 349 | — |
| Deluxe sdn 2d | 975 | 359 | — |
| conv cpe | 950 | 299 | — |
| covered wgn 2d | 1,125 | 399 | — |
| wgn 2d | 1,160 | 450 | — |

| 1940 Engine | bore×stroke | bhp | availability |
|---|---|---|---|
| L2, 35.3 | 3.00×2.50 | 12 | S-all |

## 1941

| Series CB41 (wb 80.0)—2,289 built | Wght | Price | Prod |
|---|---|---|---|
| sdn 2d | 975 | 390 | — |
| Deluxe sdn 2d | 975 | 400 | — |
| conv cpe | 950 | 339 | — |
| covered wgn 2d | 1,125 | 441 | — |
| wgn 2d | 1,160 | 496 | — |

| 1941 Engine | bore×stroke | bhp | availability |
|---|---|---|---|
| L2, 35.3 | 3.00×2.50 | 12 | S-all |

## 1942

| Series CB42 (wb 80.0)—1,029 built | Wght | Price | Prod |
|---|---|---|---|
| sdn 2d | 975 | 468 | — |
| Deluxe sdn 2d | 1,050 | 516 | — |
| conv cpe | 975 | 413 | — |
| wgn 2d | 1,105 | 582 | — |

| 1942 Engine | bore×stroke | bhp | availability |
|---|---|---|---|
| L2, 35.3 | 3.00×2.50 | 7.5 | S-all |

## 1946

| CC Four (wb 80.0) | Wght | Price | Prod |
|---|---|---|---|
| sdn 2d | 1,145 | 905 | 4,987 |
| conv cpe | 1,150 | proto | 12 |

| 1946 Engine | bore×stroke | bhp | availability |
|---|---|---|---|
| L4, 44.0 | 2.50×2.25 | 26.5 | S-all; O-cast-iron block |

## 1947

| CC Four (wb 80.0) | Wght | Price | Prod |
|---|---|---|---|
| sdn 2d | 1,155 | 888 | 14,090 |
| conv cpe | 1,150 | 949 | 4,005 |
| wgn 2d | 1,305 | 929 | 1,249 |

| 1947 Engine | bore×stroke | bhp | availability |
|---|---|---|---|
| L4, 44.0 | 2.50×2.25 | 26.5 | S-all; O-cast-iron block |

## 1948

| CC Four (wb 80.0) | Wght | Price | Prod |
|---|---|---|---|
| sdn 2d | 1,280 | 869 | } 2,750 |
| Sport Utility sdn 2d | 1,160 | 799 | |
| conv cpe | 1,210 | 899 | 2,845 |
| wgn 2d | 1,305 | 929 | 23,489 |

| 1948 Engine | bore×stroke | bhp | availability |
|---|---|---|---|
| L4, 44.0 | 2.50×2.25 | 26.5 | S-all; O-cast-iron block |

## 1949

| CD Four (wb 80.0; rdstr-85.0) | Wght | Price | Prod |
|---|---|---|---|
| DeLuxe sdn 2d | 1,363 | 866 | 2,231 |
| conv cpe | 1,320 | 866 | 645 |
| wgn 4d | 1,403 | 894 | 3,803 |
| Hotshot rdstr | 1,175 | 849 | 752 |

| 1949 Engine | bore×stroke | bhp | availability |
|---|---|---|---|
| L4, 44.0 | 2.50×2.25 | 26.5 | S-all; O-cast-iron block |

## 1950

| CD Four (wb 80.0; rdstr-85.0) | Wght | Price | Prod |
|---|---|---|---|
| sdn 2d | 1,363 | 882 | } 1,367 |
| Super sdn 2d | 1,363 | 951 | |
| conv cpe | 1,320 | 882 | } 478 |
| Super conv cpe | 1,320 | 954 | |
| wgn 2d | 1,403 | 916 | } 4,205 |
| Super wgn 2d | 1,403 | 984 | |
| Hotshot rdstr | 1,175 | 872 | } 742 |
| Super Sports rdstr | 1,175 | 925 | |

| 1950 Engine | bore×stroke | bhp | availability |
|---|---|---|---|
| L4, 44.0 | 2.50×2.25 | 26.5 | S-all |

## 1951

| CD Four (wb 80.0; rdstr-85.0) | Wght | Price | Prod |
|---|---|---|---|
| bus cpe | 1,355 | 943 | } 1,077 |
| Super sdn 2d | 1,370 | 1,033 | |
| wgn 2d | 1,002 | 1,420 | } 9,500 |
| Super wgn 2d | 1,077 | 1,450 | |
| Super conv cpe | 1,035 | 1,310 | 391 |
| Hotshot rdstr | 1,180 | 952 | } 646 |
| Super Sports rdstr | 1,180 | 1,029 | |

| 1951 Engine | bore×stroke | bhp | availability |
|---|---|---|---|
| L4, 44.0 | 2.50×2.25 | 26.5 | S-all |

## 1952

| CD Four (wb 80.0; rdstr-85.0) | Wght | Price | Prod |
|---|---|---|---|
| Standard bus cpe | 1,355 | 943 | } 216 |
| Super sdn 2d | 1,400 | 1,033 | |
| Standard wgn 2d | 1,430 | 1,002 | } 1,355 |
| Super wgn 2d | 1,480 | 1,077 | |
| Super conv cpe | 1,400 | 1,035 | 146 |
| Hotshot rdstr | 1,240 | 952 | } 358 |
| Super Sports rdstr | 1,240 | 1,029 | |

| 1952 Engine | bore×stroke | bhp | availability |
|---|---|---|---|
| L4, 44.0 | 2.50×2.25 | 25.5 | S-all |

# DeSoto

**DeSoto Division, Chrysler Corp.
Detroit, Michigan**

In the '20s, when it seemed as if prosperity would go on forever, auto manufacturers looked upon expansion as the natural way of life. From GM and Chrysler, new makes proliferated. General Motors brought forth the Marquette, Viking, and Pontiac; Chrysler purchased Dodge, then created Plymouth and DeSoto.

As a lower-priced alternative to the big Chrysler with more prestige than Dodge, DeSoto found a market niche big enough to shelter it from the Depression, and moved smartly forward in the recovery years of 1939-41. From 1935, production kept increasing, with a slight hitch during the 1938 recession. In 1941, DeSoto Division built nearly 90,000 cars, and was running a solid 10th in the production race. Although it never rose quite that high after the war, DeSoto continued to contribute its share to Chrysler's profit picture in the late '40s.

DeSoto generally followed Chrysler in styling cycles and engineering innovations, and the '40s were no exception. It retained the '41 body past 1948 before the all-new postwar models debuted in March 1949.

Ever since 1933, DeSoto had used six-cylinder powerplants exclusively. The 1940 engine was a cast-iron L-head that developed 100 horsepower at 3600 rpm, or 105 bhp with high-compression aluminum head. A straightforward four-main-bearing design, it employed a Carter carburetor and AutoLite ignition. DeLuxe and Custom series were offered on two wheelbases: 122.5 inches standard, and 139.5 for long sedans and the limousine. A Custom convertible and limousine were also available. Among minor styling developments for 1940 were DeSoto's first sealed-beam headlamps, carried in the fenders instead of freestanding as before. Dashboards featured warning lights for low oil pressure and discharge, low fuel, and excessive water temperature. Like Chrysler's, DeSoto's speedometer gradually changed from green to red as speed increased. Altogether, it was a conventional lineup with less variety than Chrysler, aimed at a relatively small segment of the market.

Production soared with introduction of the '41s: good-looking cars with lower hoods and bolder front ends. Grilles featured the prominent vertical "teeth" that would be a DeSoto hallmark through 1955. Al-

1940 Custom coupe

1941 Custom four-door sedan

1941 Studio rendering for postwar DeSoto styling

1942 Sky-View taxicab

1942 Custom convertible coupe

1946 Custom Suburban eight-passenger sedan

1948 Custom club coupe

1949 Custom four-door sedan

though the division had produced only about 65,000 of the 1940 models, model year production reached nearly 100,000 on the strength of the new '41 line.

The standard-size cars lost an inch in wheelbase, but were 5.5 inches longer overall than the '40 models, as well as wider and lower. For the first time, DeSoto offered Fluid Drive, which greatly simplified gear changing. A new model was the Custom Town Sedan, a formal adaptation of the standard sedan with blind rear roof quarters. This very pretty car sold for about $50 more than the standard Custom four-door. DeSoto wooed the buyer with many optional extras, including an underseat heater, pushbutton radio, and streamlined fender skirts.

One of the more interesting model years was 1942, when the division adopted "Airfoil" hidden headlamps. They remained "out of sight, except at night." While not a first, they were the only hidden lamps in the industry that year, and imparted a clean look to the front end. Designers placed the entire grille on the lower half of the car's face. A sculpted lady was introduced as a hood mascot, and stayed into 1949.

Although the 1942 model line was identical with 1941's, there was a "squarer" L-head six. Somewhat detuned, it would power all DeSotos for the the rest of the decade. Stroked slightly, it would continue in production as the Powermaster Six through 1954—the last year for six-cylinder models.

There wasn't much time in 1942 for specials before civilian production ceased, but DeSoto did manage a plush Fifth Avenue version of the Custom Town Sedan. Distinguished on the exterior only by a nameplate, it sported a luxurious leather and Bedford cloth interior, and sold for about $75 more than the standard Town Sedan. Because production was so low, 1942 DeSotos are rare indeed. Fewer than 25,000 were built altogether, with fewer than 1000 of some styles.

When the division opened its doors again after World War II, the model lineup was cut, though the drivetrain and chassis combinations used for '42 were retained. The long-wheelbase DeLuxe was discontinued, and a convertible was substituted for the business coupe in the Custom series. Only three models rode the long wheelbase: a seven-passenger sedan, a limousine, and the intriguing DeSoto Suburban.

Desinged to provide the ultimate in stylish cargo hauling for hotels, airports, and well-heeled individuals, the Suburban featured a fold-down rear seat without trunk partition, providing a huge cargo hold. A metal-and-wood roof rack and beautifully fitted wooden interior panels completed the package. Not surprisingly, it was the most expensive model in the 1946 lineup, listing at nearly $100 more than the limousine.

The 1947 and '48 models were largely 1946 carryovers. Serial numbers are the only guide to model years. The '46 facelift had been mild: fenders flowed

1950 Custom wood-trimmed four-door station wagon

1952 Firedome four-door sedan

1951 Custom Sportsman hardtop coupe

1953 Firedome eight-passenger sedan

into the front doors, the grille was heavier and wider, medallions and parking lights were shuffled, and the rear fenders were deepened. Horsepower was listed at 109 for 1946-48, down 6 bhp from 1942. This was not a result of mechanical alterations, just a new rating method.

DeSoto built 11,600 taxicabs in 1946-48, making this the fifth most popular model in its line. Suburban production was also quite satisfactory: 7500 of the luxurious carryalls were built in the three-year period.

For 1949, the line was completely restyled, as was the rest of Chrysler Corporation. Standard models used a longer wheelbase, and DeSoto took on the boxy, upright styling typical of Chrysler products that year, which were conservative compared to their Ford and GM competition. The 236-cid six was continued with slightly more horsepower. Fluid Drive with "Tip-Toe hydraulic shift" became standard for Customs and a $121 option on DeLuxes. The front end sported a vertical-bar grille similar to that of the 1942-48 design. The lady mascot was replaced by a bust of Hernando DeSoto. Like all proper hood ornaments of those years, Hernando glowed brightly in the dark.

The 1949s appeared in March after a brief run of old-style models to fill the gap, and featured some interesting new utility vehicles. DeSoto's DeLuxe series included a new woody wagon priced at $2959. More significant was the all-steel Carry-All, similar to the

Suburban but on the standard wheelbase. The Carry-All's rear seat folded down to provide a long cargo bed.

In the Custom line, the long-wheelbase Suburban was continued on a chassis shared with an eight-passenger sedan. As before, the Suburban provided great cargo space and a rooftop luggage rack. It was also fitted with jump seats, giving it true nine-passenger capacity.

Of these three utility models, the Carry-All pointed the way of the future by handily selling 2690 copies. Woody wagon production was only 680; Suburban output, a mere 129. The woody continued only through 1950. Emphasis was then placed on the Carry-All.

Generally, 1949 had been a spectacular year for DeSoto. For the 1949 model year, it built three times as many Customs as DeLuxes, an indication of buyer preference for more luxurious, higher-priced cars. The division built its first V8 in 1952. But production declined to barely more than a trickle by the end of the '50s. Nevertheless, DeSoto had several good years during the decade. By the start of 1959, there was little indication the make would be phased out within 24 months.

In early 1950s, DeSoto still had six-cylinder cars with engines with up to 250.6 cid. They were still L-heads, providing up to 116 bhp for two series. The DeLuxe was utilitarian, while the Custom offered hardtops, convertibles, and long-wheelbase sedans. The 1950 model was boxy-looking, wearing more chrome up front than per-

haps any other Chrysler product. Stylist Virgil Exner brought in a somewhat sleeker style for '51.

For 1952, DeSoto introduced its version of the hemispherical-head V8, the 276.1-cid Firedome. Based on the larger Chrysler Hemi, it developed 160 bhp at 4400 rpm, and put DeSoto firmly in the horsepower race. Immediately, Firedome Eights accounted for nearly 50,000 sales. The six-cylinder Custom and DeLuxe series were combined in 1953 as the Powermaster Six, but sales didn't fare as well as the eight-cylinder models. By the end of 1953, Firedomes were outselling Powermasters by a margin of two to one. Both series included Sportsman hardtops.

Model year 1954 marked the debut of PowerFlite two-speed automatic transmission. Through that year, DeSotos came with three-speed manual transmission standard. Fluid Drive was the major gearbox option at $130, followed by overdrive at $96. That year also marked the end of the Powermaster and the long-wheelbase sedans. Two brilliantly engineered, good-looking 1955 series, the Firedome and the new top-of-the-line Fireflite, came with a 291-cid V8. With its

attractive two-tone color schemes, "gullwing" dash, and highly chromed front end, the '55 was just in time to save the division temporarily. Sales had been very poor in 1954—a nightmare period for all of Chrysler Corporation.

No '55 Chrysler product was really sedate in appearance, but DeSotos were possibly the most glittery of all. They appealed to buyers and sold well, putting the division over the 100,000 mark. The Firedome series offered a cheap Special hardtop at $110 less than the Sportsman; the Coronado sedan led the Fireflite series at a $100 premium over the $2800 standard sedan. The Coronado is a minor collector's item today. It is significant because it brought us one of the first three-tone paint jobs—turquoise, black, and white.

Horsepower went up to 230 and 255 bhp for 1956. The teeth were yanked out of the grille, replaced with a wire mesh. Unreadable gold-on-white instruments appeared, and DeSotos grew tailfins as did other Chrysler lines. Generally, this facelift produced questionable re-

*continued on page 145*

**1954 Firedome convertible**

**Adventurer I show car by Ghia, 1954**

**1955 Fireflite four-door sedan**

**1955 Fireflite convertible**

# The most imaginative vehicles from the early 40s to middle 50s.

# COLOR SHOWCASE I

1940 Buick Series 70 Roadmaster Sport Phaeton

1940 Mercury convertible

1941 Packard One Twenty club coupe

1940 LaSalle Series 50 four-door sedan

1941 Chevrolet Special Deluxe convertible

1941 Studebaker Commander Custom sedan coupe

1942 Chrysler Town & Country four-door station wagon

1946 Chrysler Town & Country four-door sedan

1947 Ford Super DeLuxe Sportsman convertible

1946 Ford Super DeLuxe four-door station wagon

1948 Chevrolet Fleetline two-door Aerosedan

1949 Buick Roadmaster Riviera hardtop coupe

1949 Packard Custom Eight convertible

1948 Tucker four-door sedan

1948 Willys Jeepster phaeton convertible

1950 Ford Custom convertible

1951 Kaiser Dragon four-door sedan

Third Excalibur prototype racing car, 1953-54

1953 Cunningham C3 touring coupe by Vignale

1952 Packard Patrician 400 four-door sedan

1953 Studebaker Commander Starlight coupe

1954 Mercury Monterey Sun Valley hardtop coupe

1954 Kaiser Darrin sports roadster

1954 Hudson Super Wasp Hollywood hardtop coupe

1955 Ford Thunderbird two-seat convertible

1955 Chevrolet Bel Air hardtop coupe

1955 Fireflite Sportsman hardtop coupe

1956 Adventurer hardtop coupe

continued from page 128

suits. A highlight, however was the new limited-edition Adventurer, a gold-bedecked two-door hardtop super-car. Equipped with a 341-cid, 320-bhp V8, it was part of the wild performance assortment that also included the Chrysler 300B, Plymouth Fury, and Dodge D-500.

One other introduction for '56 was DeSoto's first four-door hardtop. The Firedome version was called Seville, and appeared just as Cadillac was adopting that name for its two-door Eldorado hardtop. No legal entanglements developed.

DeSoto fared extremely well in 1956, while other Chrysler divisions suffered extensive production cut-backs. And 1957 proved to be another successful year. A low-cost Firesweep series on the 122-inch Dodge wheelbase joined the two upper lines in a last effort to extend DeSoto's market territory. It helped; customers could buy a Firesweep for only $2777 (the cheapest Firedome was $2958), and there was a full line of

1957 Fireflite Sportsman hardtop sedan

1957 Adventurer hardtop coupe

1957 Fireflite Sportsman hardtop coupe

1957 Fireflite Shopper six-passenger station wagon

1957 Firedome four-door sedan

sedans, hardtops, and wagons to choose from.

In 1957, DeSoto came as near as it ever did to passing Chrysler in production, ending up less than 8000 units behind. The '57s were big, heavy, powerful cars. The two upper series used a V8 with up to 290 bhp. The Firesweep engine was more conservative, producing about 260 bhp. An Adventurer soft-top now made its debut, offering 345 bhp.

Of all the Exner finned fantasies that arrived that year, DeSoto was the cleanest. Smooth rear panels, attractive taillights, simple but pleasant side moldings, and a front bumper unique to the division all helped give the '57 DeSotos first-rate styling. Yet, as good as they looked, the division would not be able to survive on looks alone. From a production level of 118,000 units in calendar year 1957, DeSoto fell to 50,000 the following year—the division's lowest output since 1938. The recession, a reputation for poor quality, and unwise marketing decisions all contributed to the downward spiral.

The 1958 models were basically the same as the '57s, except for a mild facelift. The grille became busier, and all models came with four lights. (As of 1957, some states still had not legalized "quadrilights," so DeSoto front fenders had been designed to accept either one or two headlamps.) Wagons and Sportsman hardtops proliferated along with four-door sedans; no fewer than four convertibles were offered. The Adventurer ragtop was the most expensive DeSoto in history, though Chrysler's corresponding 300D convertible cost $1300 more.

As ever, DeSotos were extremely quick. Fast-shifting TorqueFlite automatic transmission and torsion-bar suspension made them among the most roadworthy cars as well. A DeSoto Firedome with Turboflash V8 and the optional 305-bhp setup could accelerate from 0 to 60 in 7.7 seconds, to 80 mph in 13.5 seconds, and could reach 115 mph with little strain.

DeSoto said its towering tailfins of 1957-61 "added stability at speed," but this was advertising propaganda. Although they did little from an aerodynamic standpoint under 80 mph, they did make the cars look dramatically different from the opposition. The tailfins reached their height in 1959, the year that marked the beginning of the end.

DeSoto had joined the corporate switch to wedgehead engines in '58. For 1959, Firesweeps used the 361-cid unit, and other models got the more potent 383. Maximum horsepower—standard on the Adventurer—was 350 bhp at 5000 rpm. The wedge-heads gave away little to the Hemis in acceleration. As before, there was a wide choice of hardtops, wagons, sedans, and convertibles. The Adventurer became a regular series, and sales improved slightly. But it was hardly the kind of volume that had sustained DeSoto earlier in the decade.

DeSoto show cars in the '50s vied with those of the Chrysler label. They were built mainly by Ghia of Italy to Exner's designs. Adventurer I was the first, part of Exner's early series that began with the 1951 Chrysler

1958 Fireflite convertible

1959 Firedome Sportsman hardtop sedan

Cella I show car of 1959

K-310. Built in 1954, the Adventurer I rode a shortened 111-inch wheelbase, and accommodated four passengers. Its off-white coupe body was fitted with outside exhausts, wire wheels, and full instrumentation. It came closer to production than any other Exner special. "Had it been mass-produced," Exner said, "it would have been the first four-passenger sports car made in this country. It was better than a two-plus-two, and of course it had the DeSoto Hemi. It was my favorite car."

1959 Fireflite Sportsman hardtop coupe

1960 Adventurer hardtop coupe

1961 hardtop sedan

1961 hardtop coupe

Adventurer II followed in 1955. This standard-wheelbase, four-passenger coupe was designed more by Ghia's craftsmen than Exner. It was painted deep red, was fitted with wire wheels, and had no bumper. Adventurer II lacked the sleek integrated styling of its predecessor, and was not seriously considered for production.

DeSoto was discontinued in 1961 after 33 years of production. Its demise was hastened by a change in Chrysler's marketing approach. In the past there had been three types of dealers: Chrysler-Plymouth, DeSoto-Plymouth, and Dodge-Plymouth. The advent of Imperial as a separate make in 1955 prompted Chrysler Division to concentrate on the lower end of its market, while larger and more luxurious Dodge models increased that division's spread upward. Both Chrysler and Dodge ate into DeSoto's territory. Rumors of DeSoto's imminent demise were heard as early as 1959, and they naturally affected sales.

The statistics were ominous. Although 1959 calendar year production had increased slightly from 1958, the volume for both years was less than half that of 1957, when DeSoto built nearly 120,000 cars. The division was in the same kind of trouble as many other middle-priced cars, including Oldsmobile, Buick, and Mercury. But those rivals had higher volume and could stand to lose more money. Furthermore, all of them had smaller models ready for introduction in 1961. Although DeSoto's 1962 plans included downsized standard models, there was no program for a compact.

Initially, rumors of DeSoto's termination were strongly denied, and in 1959 a celebration was held to mark the division's two-millionth car. Press releases noted there were almost a million DeSotos still registered. The division announced $25 million would be invested in the engineering and styling of future cars, $7 million of which would be earmarked for the 1960 models. Officials said commitments had been made for 1961, and work on the 1962-63 line was in the development stage. It was also pointed out that Chrysler had regularly made a profit on DeSoto.

In 1960, however, Chrysler merged DeSoto and Plymouth into one division, with Valiant as an ostensibly separate make. Valiant did very well and Plymouth did fairly well, but DeSoto fared poorly. During the first two months of 1960, sales totaled 4746, or 0.51 percent of the industry total. This was down considerably from the first two months of 1959, when the figures were 6134 units and 0.72 percent. By the end of 1960, plans for the restyled 1962 models had been shelved, and the '61 DeSotos, announced in October, were taken off the market. Some DeSoto-Plymouth dealers became Chrysler-Plymouth agencies, much to the chagrin of existing Chrysler-Plymouth dealers nearby.

For 1960, the DeSoto line was reduced to two series, each with three body styles: sedan, hardtop sedan, and hardtop coupe. The Adventurer took the place of the Fireflite, though its price was a few hundred dollars less than the '59 Fireflite. The Fireflite was moved down into the $3000 area formerly occupied by the Firesweep, which was eliminated along with the mid-line Firedome. Station wagons and convertibles were also dropped. The most popular DeSoto was the Fireflite sedan, production of which failed to exceed 10,000.

All models rode the 122-inch wheelbase shared with Chrysler, and adopted the company's "unibody" construction, new that year. Adventurers used the Chrysler 383-cid V8 with the same compression, but 305 bhp at

4600 rpm. Automatic transmission, either PowerFlite or TorqueFlite, was optional on the Fireflite. Styling featured a blunt, trapezoidal grille similar to Chrysler's, composed of small horizontal bars and carried over a huge, curved bumper with rubber-capped bumper guards. Fins were as high as they'd ever been, and glass area was huge. Performance was mediocre. The Adventurer's specification duplicated the Chrysler Windsor's; the Fireflite's V8 was borrowed from Dodge. In a drag race, an Adventurer could stay with a Windsor, but would lose to a Saratoga or the lighter 383 Dodge Phoenix.

The '61 DeSoto's brief appearance resulted in very low production figures. No series names were used; the cars were simply "DeSotos." The four-door pillared sedan was eliminated. Publicity concentrated on the design's individuality. Odd might be a more apt description. The front displayed a curious double grille flanked by diagonally stacked headlights. A lattice-like lower grille was topped by a large, blunt oval bearing the name DeSoto in stylized letters against a fine mesh. Production tapered off by Christmas 1960, after which the few existing orders were filled mostly with Chrysler Windsors. It was a sad finale for a marque that had brought considerable prestige and profits to Chrysler for more than three decades.

# DeSoto Specifications

## 1940

### S-7S DeLuxe (wb 122.5; 7P-139.5)

|  | Wght | Price | Prod |
|---|---|---|---|
| bus cpe | 3,001 | 845 | 3,650 |
| cpe, A/S | 3,026 | 905 | 2,098 |
| sdn 2d | 3,066 | 905 | 7,072 |
| sdn 4d | 3,086 | 945 | 18,666 |
| sdn 4d, 7P | 3,490 | 1,175 | 142 |

### S-7C Custom (wb 122.5; 7P-139.5)

|  | Wght | Price | Prod |
|---|---|---|---|
| bus cpe | 3,024 | 885 | 1,898 |
| cpe, A/S | 3,044 | 945 | 2,234 |
| conv cpe | 3,329 | 1,095 | 1,085 |
| sdn 2d | 3,084 | 945 | 3,109 |
| sdn 4d | 3,104 | 985 | 25,221 |
| sdn 4d, 7P | 3,490 | 1,215 | 206 |
| limo 7P | 3,550 | 1,290 | 34 |
| chassis | — | — | 52 |

| 1940 Engines | bore×stroke | bhp | availability |
|---|---|---|---|
| L6, 228.1 | 3.38×4.25 | 100 | S-all |
| L6, 228.1 | 3.38×4.25 | 105 | O-all |

## 1941

### S-8S DeLuxe (wb 121.5; 7P-139.5)

|  | Wght | Price | Prod |
|---|---|---|---|
| bus cpe | 3,134 | 945 | 4,449 |
| club cpe | 3,219 | 1,025 | 5,603 |
| sdn 2d | 3,224 | 1,008 | 9,228 |
| sdn 4d | 3,254 | 1,035 | 26,417 |
| sdn 4d, 7P | 3,629 | 1,270 | 101 |

### S-8C Custom (wb 121.5; 7P-139.5)

|  | Wght | Price | Prod |
|---|---|---|---|
| bus cpe | 3,144 | 982 | 2,033 |
| club cpe | 3,239 | 1,080 | 6,726 |
| conv cpe | 3,494 | 1,240 | 2,937 |
| brougham 2d | 3,264 | 1,060 | 4,609 |
| sdn 4d | 3,269 | 1,085 | 30,876 |
| town sdn | 3,329 | 1,133 | 4,362 |
| sdn 4d, 7P | 3,649 | 1,310 | 120 |
| limo 7P | 3,700 | 1,390 | 35 |
| chassis | — | — | 1 |

| 1941 Engine | bore×stroke | bhp | availability |
|---|---|---|---|
| L6, 228.1 | 3.38×4.25 | 105 | S-all |

## 1942

### S-10S DeLuxe (wb 121.5; 7P-139.5)

|  | Wght | Price | Prod |
|---|---|---|---|
| bus cpe | 3,190 | 1,010 | 469 |
| club cpe | 3,270 | 1,092 | 1,968 |
| conv cpe | 3,500 | 1,250 | 79 |
| sdn 2d | 3,270 | 1,075 | 1,781 |
| sdn 4d | 3,315 | 1,103 | 6,463 |
| town sdn | 3,335 | 1,147 | 291 |
| sdn 4d, 7P | 3,705 | 1,455 | 49 |

### S-10C Custom (wb 121.5; 7P-139.5)

|  | Wght | Price | Prod |
|---|---|---|---|
| bus cpe | 3,205 | 1,046 | 120 |
| club cpe | 3,270 | 1,142 | 2,236 |
| conv cpe | 3,510 | 1,317 | 489 |
| sdn 2d | 3,305 | 1,142 | 913 |
| sdn 4d | 3,330 | 1,152 | 7,974 |
| town sdn | 3,365 | 1,196 | 1,084 |
| sdn 4d, 7P | 3,725 | 1,504 | 79 |
| limo 7P | 3,820 | 1,580 | 20 |

| 1942 Engine | bore×stroke | bhp | availability |
|---|---|---|---|
| L6, 236.6 | 3.44×4.25 | 115 | S-all |

## 1946

### S-11S DeLuxe (wb 121.5)*

|  | Wght | Price | Prod |
|---|---|---|---|
| bus cpe | 3,302 | 1,331 | — |
| club cpe | 3,392 | 1,451 | — |
| sdn 2d | 3,397 | 1,426 | — |
| sdn 4d | 3,427 | 1,461 | — |

### S-11C Custom (wb 121.5; 7–8P-139.5)*

|  | Wght | Price | Prod |
|---|---|---|---|
| club cpe | 3,378 | 1,501 | — |
| conv cpe | 3,618 | 1,761 | — |
| sdn 2d | 3,423 | 1,491 | — |
| sdn 4d | 3,433 | 1,511 | — |
| sdn 4d, 7P | 3,837 | 1,893 | — |

| | Wght | Price | Prod |
|---|---|---|---|
| limo 8P | 3,937 | 2,013 | — |
| Suburban sdn 4d, 8P | 4,012 | 2,093 | — |

| 1946 Engine | bore×stroke | bhp | availability |
|---|---|---|---|
| L6, 236.6 | 3.44×4.25 | 109 | S-all |

## 1947

| S-11S DeLuxe (wb 121.5)* | Wght | Price | Prod |
|---|---|---|---|
| bus cpe | 3,323 | 1,451 | — |
| club cpe | 3,413 | 1,541 | — |
| sdn 2d | 3,418 | 1,516 | — |
| sdn 4d | 3,448 | 1,551 | — |

| S-11C Custom (wb 121.5; 7–8P-139.5)* | Wght | Price | Prod |
|---|---|---|---|
| club cpe | 3,398 | 1,591 | — |
| conv cpe | 3,618 | 1,965 | — |
| sdn 2d | 3,443 | 1,581 | — |
| sdn 4d | 3,453 | 1,601 | — |
| sdn 4d, 7P | 3,837 | 1,983 | — |
| limo 7P | 3,995 | 2,013 | — |
| Suburban sdn 4d, 8P | 4,012 | 2,283 | — |

| 1947 Engine | bore×stroke | bhp | availability |
|---|---|---|---|
| L6, 236.6 | 3.44×4.25 | 109 | S-all |

## 1948

| S-11S DeLuxe (wb 121.5)* | Wght | Price | Prod |
|---|---|---|---|
| bus cpe | 3,285 | 1,699 | — |
| club cpe | 3,385 | 1,815 | — |
| sdn 2d | 3,375 | 1,788 | — |
| sdn 4d | 3,435 | 1,825 | — |

| S-11C Custom (wb 121.5; 7–9P-139.5)* | Wght | Price | Prod |
|---|---|---|---|
| club cpe | 3,389 | 1,874 | — |
| conv cpe | 3,599 | 2,296 | — |
| sdn 2d | 3,399 | 1,860 | — |
| sdn 4d | 3,439 | 1,892 | — |
| sdn 4d, 7P | 3,819 | 2,315 | — |
| limo 7P | 3,995 | 2,442 | — |
| Suburban sdn 4d, 9P | 3,974 | 2,631 | — |

| 1948 Engine | bore×stroke | bhp | availability |
|---|---|---|---|
| L6, 236.6 | 3.44×4.25 | 109 | S-all |

## 1949 First Series

| S-11S DeLuxe (wb 121.5)* | Wght | Price | Prod |
|---|---|---|---|
| bus cpe | 3,285 | 1,699 | — |
| club cpe | 3,385 | 1,815 | — |
| sdn 2d | 3,375 | 1,788 | — |
| sdn 4d | 3,435 | 1,825 | — |

| S-11C Custom (wb 121.5; 7–9P-139.5)* | Wght | Price | Prod |
|---|---|---|---|
| club cpe | 3,389 | 1,874 | — |
| conv cpe | 3,599 | 2,296 | — |
| sdn 2d | 3,399 | 1,860 | — |
| sdn 4d | 3,439 | 1,892 | — |
| sdn 4d, 7P | 3,819 | 2,315 | — |
| limo 7P | 3,995 | 2,442 | — |
| Suburban 4d, 9P | 3,974 | 2,631 | — |

| 1949(1) Engine | bore×stroke | bhp | availability |
|---|---|---|---|
| L6, 236.6 | 3.44×4.25 | 109 | S-all |

*Factory combined production figures for 1946 through 1949 First Series.

## Combined 1946–1949 First Series Production:

| S-11S DeLuxe (wb 121.5) | Prod |
|---|---|
| bus cpe | 1,950 |
| club cpe | 8,580 |
| sdn 2d | 12,751 |
| sdn 4d | 32,213 |

| S-11C Custom (wb 121.5; 7–9P-139.5) | Prod |
|---|---|
| club cpe | 38,720 |
| conv cpe | 8,100 |
| sdn 2d | 1,600 |
| sdn 4d | 126,226 |
| sdn 4d, 7P | 3,530 |
| limo 7P | 120 |
| Suburban 4d, 8–9P | 7,500 |
| chassis | 105 |

## 1949 Second Series

| S-13-1 DeLuxe (wb 125.5) | Wght | Price | Prod |
|---|---|---|---|
| club cpe | 3,455 | 1,976 | 6,807 |
| sdn 4d | 3,520 | 1,986 | 13,148 |
| Carry-All sdn 4d, 6P | 3,565 | 2,191 | 2,690 |
| wgn 4d, 9P | 3,915 | 2,959 | 680 |

| S-13-2 Custom (wb 125.5; 8–9P-139.5) | Wght | Price | Prod |
|---|---|---|---|
| club cpe | 3,585 | 2,156 | 18,431 |
| conv cpe | 3,785 | 2,578 | 3,385 |
| sdn 4d | 3,645 | 2,174 | 48,589 |
| sdn 4d, 8P | 4,200 | 2,863 | 342 |
| Suburban 4d, 9P | 4,410 | 3,179 | 129 |

| 1949(2) Engine | bore×stroke | bhp | availability |
|---|---|---|---|
| L6, 236.6 | 3.44×4.25 | 112 | S-all |

## 1950

| S-14-1 DeLuxe (wb 125.5; 8P-139.5) | Wght | Price | Prod |
|---|---|---|---|
| club cpc | 3,450 | 1,976 | 10,704 |
| sdn 4d | 3,525 | 1,986 | 18,489 |
| Carry-All sdn 4d, 5P | 3,600 | 2,191 | 3,900 |
| sdn 4d, 8P | 3,995 | 2,676 | 235 |
| chassis | — | — | 1 |

| S-14-2 Custom (wb 125.5; 8–9P-139.5) | Wght | Price | Prod |
|---|---|---|---|
| club cpe | 3,575 | 2,156 | 18,302 |
| Sportsman htp cpe | 3,735 | 2,489 | 4,600 |
| conv cpe | 3,815 | 2,578 | 2,900 |
| sdn 4d | 3,640 | 2,174 | 72,664 |
| wgn 4d (wood) | 4,035 | 3,093 | 600 |
| wgn 4d (steel) | 3,900 | 2,717 | 100 |
| sdn 4d, 8P | 4,115 | 2,863 | 734 |
| Suburban 4d, 9P | 4,400 | 3,179 | 623 |
| chassis | — | — | 2 |

| 1950 Engine | bore×stroke | bhp | availability |
|---|---|---|---|
| L6, 236.6 | 3.44×4.25 | 112 | S-all |

## 1951

| S-15-1 DeLuxe (wb 125.5; 8P-139.5)* | Wght | Price | Prod |
|---|---|---|---|
| club cpe | 3,475 | 2,215 | — |
| sdn 4d | 3,570 | 2,227 | — |
| Carry-All sdn 4d | 3,685 | 2,457 | — |
| sdn 4d, 8P | 4,045 | 3,001 | — |

| S-15-2 Custom (wb 125.5; 8–9P-139.5)* | Wght | Price | Prod |
|---|---|---|---|
| club cpe | 3,585 | 2,418 | — |
| Sportsman htp cpe | 3,760 | 2,761 | — |
| conv cpe | 2,862 | 2,840 | — |
| sdn 4d | 3,685 | 2,438 | — |
| wgn 4d | 3,960 | 3,047 | — |
| sdn 4d, 8P | 4,122 | 2,211 | — |
| Suburban 4d, 9P | 4,395 | 3,566 | — |

| 1951 Engine | bore×stroke | bhp | availability |
|---|---|---|---|
| L6, 250.6 | 3.44×4.50 | 116 | S-all |

## 1952

| S-15-1 DeLuxe (wb 125.5; 8P-139.5)* | Wght | Price | Prod |
|---|---|---|---|
| club cpe | 3,435 | 2,319 | — |
| sdn 4d | 3,540 | 2,333 | — |
| Carry-All sdn 4d | 3,650 | 2,572 | — |
| sdn 4d, 8P | 4,035 | 3,142 | — |

| S-15-2 Custom (wb 125.5; 8–9P-139.5)* | Wght | Price | Prod |
|---|---|---|---|
| club cpe | 3,565 | 2,531 | — |
| Sportsman htp cpe | 3,720 | 2,890 | — |
| conv cpe | 3,865 | 2,996 | — |
| sdn 4d | 3,660 | 2,552 | — |
| wgn 4d | 4,020 | 3,189 | — |
| sdn 4d, 8P | 4,155 | 3,362 | — |
| Suburban 4d, 9P | 4,370 | 3,734 | — |

| S-17 Firedome (wb 125.5; 8P-139.5) | Wght | Price | Prod |
|---|---|---|---|
| club cpe | 3,675 | 2,718 | 5,699 |
| Sportsman htp cpe | 3,850 | 3,078 | 3,000 |
| conv cpe | 3,950 | 3,183 | 850 |
| sdn 4d | 3,760 | 2,740 | 35,651 |
| wgn 4d | 4,080 | 3,377 | 550 |
| sdn 4d, 8P | 4,325 | 3,547 | 50 |

| 1952 Engines | bore×stroke | bhp | availability |
|---|---|---|---|
| L6, 250.6 | 3.44×4.50 | 116 | S-Deluxe, Custom |
| V8, 276.1 | 3.63×3.34 | 160 | S-Firedome |

*Factory combined 1951–1952 Deluxe and Custom production figures.

## 1951–1952 Deluxe and Custom Production:

| S-15-1 DeLuxe (wb 125.5; 8P-139.5) | Prod |
|---|---|
| club cpe | 6,100 |
| sdn 4d | 13,506 |
| Carry-All sdn 4d | 1,700 |
| sdn 4d, 8P | 343 |

| S-15-2 Custom (wb 125.5; 8–9P-139.5) | Prod |
|---|---|
| club cpe | 19,000 |
| Sportsman htp cpe | 8,750 |
| conv cpe | 3,950 |
| sdn 4d | 88,491 |
| wgn 4d | 1,440 |
| sdn 4d, 8P | 769 |
| Suburban 4d, 9P | 600 |

## 1953

| S-18 Powermaster (wb 125.5; 8P-139.5) | Wght | Price | Prod |
|---|---|---|---|
| club cpe | 3,480 | 2,334 | 8,063 |
| Sportsman htp cpe | 3,585 | 2,604 | 1,470 |
| sdn 4d | 3,535 | 2,356 | 33,644 |
| wgn 4d | 3,845 | 3,078 | 500 |
| sdn 4d, 8P | 4,080 | 3,251 | 225 |

| S-16 Firedome (wb 125.5; 8P-139.5) | Wght | Price | Prod |
|---|---|---|---|
| club cpe | 3,655 | 2,622 | 14,591 |
| Sportsman htp cpe | 3,740 | 2,893 | 4,700 |
| conv cpe | 3,990 | 3,114 | 1,700 |
| sdn 4d | 3,720 | 2,643 | 64,211 |
| wgn 4d | 3,995 | 3,351 | 1,100 |
| sdn 4d, 8P | 4,270 | 3,529 | 200 |

| 1953 Engines | bore×stroke | bhp | availability |
|---|---|---|---|
| L6, 250.6 | 3.44×4.50 | 116 | S-Powermaster |
| V8, 276.1 | 3.63×3.34 | 160 | S-Firedome |

## 1954

| S-20 Powermaster (wb 125.5; 8P-139.5) | Wght | Price | Prod |
|---|---|---|---|
| club cpe | 3,505 | 2,364 | 3,499 |
| Sportsman htp cpe (discont'd.) | 3,590 | 2,635 | 250 |
| sdn 4d | 3,570 | 2,386 | 14,967 |
| wgn 4d | 3,855 | 3,108 | 225 |
| sdn 4d, 8P | 4,100 | 2,381 | 263 |

| S-19 Firedome (wb 125.5; 8P-139.5) | Wght | Price | Prod |
|---|---|---|---|
| club cpe | 3,735 | 2,652 | 5,762 |
| Sportsman htp cpe | 3,815 | 2,923 | 4,382 |
| conv cpe | 4,015 | 3,144 | 1,025 |
| sdn 4d | 3,790 | 2,673 | 45,095 |
| wgn 4d | 4,045 | 3,381 | 946 |
| sdn 4d, 8P | 4,305 | 3,559 | 165 |
| chassis | — | — | 1 |

| 1954 Engines | bore×stroke | bhp | availability |
|---|---|---|---|
| L6, 250.6 | 3.44×4.50 | 116 | S-Powermaster |
| V8, 276.1 | 3.63×3.34 | 170 | S-Firedome |

## 1955

| S-22 Firedome (wb 126.0) | Wght | Price | Prod |
|---|---|---|---|
| Special htp cpe | 3,801 | 2,541 | 28,944 |
| Sportsman htp cpe | 3,805 | 2,654 | |
| conv cpe | 4,010 | 2,824 | 625 |
| sdn 4d | 3,870 | 2,498 | 46,388 |
| wgn 4d | 4,185 | 3,170 | 1,083 |

| S-21 Fireflite (wb 126.0) | Wght | Price | Prod |
|---|---|---|---|
| Sportsman htp cpe | 3,890 | 2,939 | 10,313 |
| conv cpe | 4,115 | 3,151 | 775 |
| sdn 4d (inc. Coronado) | 3,940 | 2,727 | 26,637 |

| 1955 Engines | bore×stroke | bhp | availability |
|---|---|---|---|
| V8, 291.0 | 3.72×3.34 | 185 | S-Firedome |
| V8, 291.0 | 3.72×3.34 | 200 | S-Fireflite |

## 1956

| S-23 Firedome (wb 126.0) | Wght | Price | Prod |
|---|---|---|---|
| Seville htp cpe | 3,800 | 3,734 | 19,136 |
| Seville htp sdn | 3,920 | 2,833 | 4,030 |
| Sportsman htp cpe | 3,835 | 2,854 | 4,589 |
| Sportsman htp sdn | 3,945 | 2,953 | 1,645 |
| conv cpe | 4,080 | 3,081 | 646 |
| sdn 4d | 3,780 | 2,678 | 44,909 |
| wgn 4d | 4,095 | 3,371 | 2,950 |

| S-24 Fireflite (wb 126.0) | Wght | Price | Prod |
|---|---|---|---|
| Sportsman htp cpe | 3,905 | 3,346 | 8,475 |
| Sportsman htp sdn | 3,970 | 3,431 | 3,350 |
| conv cpe | 4,075 | 3,544 | 1,385* |
| Pacesetter conv cpe | 4,070 | 3,615 | 100* |

| | | Wght | Price | Prod |
|---|---|---|---|---|
| | sdn 4d | 3,860 | 3,119 | 18,207 |
| | Adventurer htp cpe | 3,870 | 3,728 | 996 |

*Estimated; total conv cpes 1,485.

| 1956 Engines | bore×stroke | bhp | availability |
|---|---|---|---|
| V8, 330.4 | 3.72×3.80 | 230 | S-Firedome |
| V8, 330.4 | 3.72×3.80 | 255 | S-Fireflite exc Adventurer |
| V8, 341.4 | 3.78×3.80 | 320 | S-Adventurer |

## 1957

| S-27 Firesweep (wb 122.0) | | Wght | Price | Prod |
|---|---|---|---|---|
| | Sportsman htp cpe | 3,645 | 2,836 | 13,333 |
| | Sportsman htp sdn | 3,720 | 2,912 | 7,168 |
| | sdn 4d | 3,675 | 2,777 | 17,300 |
| | Shopper wgn 4d, 6P | 3,965 | 3,169 | 2,270 |
| | Explorer wgn 4d, 9P | 3,970 | 3,310 | 1,198 |

| S-25 Firedome (wb 126.0) | | Wght | Price | Prod |
|---|---|---|---|---|
| | Sportsman htp cpe | 3,910 | 3,085 | 12,179 |
| | Sportsman htp sdn | 3,960 | 3,142 | 9,050 |
| | conv cpe | 4,065 | 3,361 | 1,297 |
| | sdn 4d | 3,955 | 2,958 | 23,339 |

| S-26 Fireflite (wb 126.0) | | Wght | Price | Prod |
|---|---|---|---|---|
| | Sportsman htp cpe | 4,000 | 3,614 | 7,217 |
| | Sportsman htp sdn | 4,125 | 3,671 | 6,726 |
| | conv cpe | 4,085 | 3,890 | 1,151 |
| | sdn 4d | 4,025 | 3,487 | 11,565 |
| | Shopper wgn 4d, 6P | 4,290 | 3,982 | 837 |
| | Explorer wgn 4d, 9P | 4,250 | 4,124 | 934 |

| S-26A Adventurer (wb 126.0) | | Wght | Price | Prod |
|---|---|---|---|---|
| | htp cpe | 4,040 | 3,997 | 1,650 |
| | conv cpe | 4,235 | 4,272 | 300 |

| 1957 Engines | bore×stroke | bhp | availability |
|---|---|---|---|
| V8, 325.0 | 3.69×3.80 | 245 | S-Firesweep |
| V8, 325.0 | 3.69×3.80 | 260 | O-Firesweep |
| V8, 341.0 | 3.78×3.80 | 270 | S-Firedome |
| V8, 341.0 | 3.78×3.80 | 290 | S-Fireflite |
| V8, 345.0 | 3.80×3.80 | 345 | S-Adventurer |

## 1958

| LS1-L Firesweep (wb 122.0) | | Wght | Price | Prod |
|---|---|---|---|---|
| 23 | Sportsman htp cpe | 3,660 | 2,890 | 5,635 |
| 27 | conv cpe | 3,850 | 3,219 | 700 |
| 41 | sdn 4d | 3,660 | 2,819 | 7,646 |
| 43 | Sportsman htp sdn | 3,720 | 2,953 | 3,003 |
| 45A | Shopper wgn 4d, 6P | 3,955 | 3,266 | 1,305 |
| 45B | Explorer wgn 4d, 9P | 3,980 | 3,408 | 1,125 |

| LS2-M Firedome (wb 126.0) | | Wght | Price | Prod |
|---|---|---|---|---|
| 23 | Sportsman htp cpe | 3,825 | 3,178 | 4,325 |
| 27 | conv cpe | 4,065 | 3,489 | 519 |
| 41 | sdn 4d | 3,855 | 3,085 | 9,505 |
| 43 | Sportsman htp sdn | 3,920 | 3,235 | 3,130 |

| LS3-H Fireflite (wb 126.0) | | Wght | Price | Prod |
|---|---|---|---|---|
| 23 | Sportsman htp cpe | 3,920 | 3,675 | 3,284 |
| 27 | conv cpe | 4,105 | 3,972 | 474 |
| 41 | sdn 4d | 3,990 | 3,583 | 4,192 |
| 43 | Sportsman htp sdn | 3,980 | 3,731 | 3,243 |
| 45A | Shopper wgn 4d, 6P | 4,225 | 4,030 | 318 |
| 45B | Explorer wgn 4d, 9P | 4,295 | 4,172 | 609 |

| LS3-S Adventurer (wb 126.0) | | Wght | Price | Prod |
|---|---|---|---|---|
| 23 | htp cpe | 4,000 | 4,071 | 350 |
| 27 | conv cpe | 4,180 | 4,369 | 82 |

| 1958 Engines | bore×stroke | bhp | availability |
|---|---|---|---|
| V8, 350.0 | 4.06×3.38 | 280 | S-Firesweep |
| V8, 350.0 | 4.06×3.38 | 295 | O-Firesweep |
| V8, 361.0 | 4.13×3.38 | 295 | S-Firedome |
| V8, 361.0 | 4.13×3.38 | 305 | S-Fireflite; O-Firedome |
| V8, 361.0 | 4.13×3.38 | 345 | S-Adventurer |
| V8, 361.0 | 4.13×3.38 | 355 | O-Adventurer |

## 1959

| MS1-L Firesweep (wb 122.0) | | Wght | Price | Prod |
|---|---|---|---|---|
| 23 | Sportsman htp cpe | 3,625 | 2,967 | 5,481 |
| 27 | conv cpe | 3,840 | 3,315 | 596 |
| 41 | sdn 4d | 3,670 | 2,904 | 9,649 |
| 43 | Sportsman htp sdn | 3,700 | 3,038 | 2,875 |
| 45A | Shopper wgn 4d, 6P | 3,950 | 3,366 | 1,054 |
| 45B | Explorer wgn 4d, 9P | 3,980 | 3,508 | 1,179 |

| MS2-M Firedome (wb 126.0) | | Wght | Price | Prod |
|---|---|---|---|---|
| 23 | Sportsman htp cpe | 3,795 | 3,341 | 2,862* |
| 27 | conv cpe | 4,015 | 3,653 | 299* |
| 41 | sdn 4d | 3,840 | 3,234 | 9,171* |
| 43 | Sportsman htp sdn | 3,895 | 3,398 | 2,744* |

| MS3-H Fireflite (wb 126.0) | | Wght | Price | Prod |
|---|---|---|---|---|
| 23 | Sportsman htp cpe | 3,910 | 3,831 | 1,393 |
| 27 | conv cpe | 4,105 | 4,152 | 186 |
| 41 | sdn 4d | 3,920 | 3,763 | 4,480 |
| 43 | Sportsman htp sdn | 3,950 | 3,888 | 2,364 |
| 45A | Shopper wgn 4d, 6P | 4,170 | 4,216 | 271 |
| 45B | Explorer wgn 4d, 9P | 4,205 | 4,358 | 433 |

| MS3-S Adventurer (wb 126.0) | | Wght | Price | Prod |
|---|---|---|---|---|
| 23 | htp cpe | 3,980 | 4,427 | 590 |
| 27 | conv cpe | 4,120 | 4,749 | 97 |

*Includes Seville htp cpe, conv cpe, sdn 4d, and htp sdn, trim variation introduced in Spring 1959 to mark DeSoto's 30th anniversary.

| 1959 Engines | bore×stroke | bhp | availability |
|---|---|---|---|
| V8, 361.0 | 4.13×3.38 | 295 | S-Firesweep |
| V8, 383.0 | 4.25×3.38 | 305 | S-Firedome |
| V8, 383.0 | 4.25×3.38 | 325 | S-Fireflite |
| V8, 383.0 | 4.25×3.38 | 350 | S-Adventurer; O-others |

## 1960

| PS1-L Fireflite (wb 122.0) | | Wght | Price | Prod |
|---|---|---|---|---|
| 23 | htp cpe | 3,885 | 3,102 | 3,494 |
| 41 | sdn 4d | 3,865 | 3,017 | 9,032 |
| 43 | htp sdn | 3,865 | 3,167 | 1,958 |

| PS3-M Adventurer (wb 122.0) | | Wght | Price | Prod |
|---|---|---|---|---|
| 23 | htp cpe | 3,945 | 3,663 | 3,092 |
| 41 | sdn 4d | 3,895 | 3,579 | 5,746 |
| 43 | htp sdn | 3,940 | 3,727 | 2,759 |

| 1960 Engines | bore×stroke | bhp | availability |
|---|---|---|---|
| V8, 361.0 | 4.13×3.38 | 295 | S-Fireflite |
| V8, 383.0 | 4.25×3.38 | 305 | S-Adventurer |

## 1961

| (wb 122.0) | | Wght | Price | Prod |
|---|---|---|---|---|
| 612 | htp cpe | 3,760 | 3,102 | 911 |
| 614 | htp sdn | 3,820 | 3,167 | 2,123 |

| 1961 Engine | bore×stroke | bhp | availability |
|---|---|---|---|
| V8, 361.0 | 4.13×3.38 | 265 | S-all |

# Dodge

**Dodge Division, Chrysler Corp.**
**Detroit and Hamtramck, Michigan**

Chrysler bought the 14-year-old Dodge Brothers Corporation in 1928, and managed to produce 125,000 Dodge cars the following year before the Depression altered the economic climate. Yet, while other manufacturers were bottoming out in 1933 and 1934, the new division of Chrysler was producing an average of 100,000 units a year, running fourth in the industry behind Chevrolet, Ford, and Plymouth.

In its early years, Dodge had never made any pretense at sportiness. The Dodge brothers were traditional industrialists who believed in practicality and dollar-for-dollar value. Even in the 1940s, there was little about the marque that suggested the high-performance cars to come. Dodge was simply a solid, reliable, low-to-middle-priced car, the next step up from a Plymouth.

Dodge had built eight-cylinder engines in the early '30s, and would do so again in the '50s. But in the '40s, all models were powered by sixes. This was a cast-iron flathead unit with design roots going back to 1933. Since then, it had been enlarged to 217.8 cubic inches. For 1942, it was stroked for 230.2 cid, and its Stromberg carburetor was replaced by a Carter. In this form, it developed 105 bhp at 3600 rpm, and would be continued through 1949 and beyond.

Dodge retained the same body from 1940 through its "first series" 1949 models. The standard wheelbase was 119.5 inches. The car's 1940-41 styling was typical of Chrysler in that era: freestanding fenders; built-in headlamps; prominent, peaked radiator grille; high superstructure; limited glass area.

The 1940 line was grouped into Special and DeLuxe series. The Special comprised three body styles: a two-seat coupe, and two- and four-door sedans. The DeLuxe offered these plus a convertible, a larger coupe, and a seven-passenger sedan and limousine. DeLuxe prices ranged up to $1170 for the limousine. The running board was declining in popularity, so it was a $10 option for all models. Of about 195,000 cars built for 1940, 120,000 were DeLuxes, although only 1000 of these were on the long wheelbase. A feature that year was optional two-tone paint, with fenders, hood, and deck done in a contrasting shade. Predictably, it gave the car a taxicab look and was not popular.

In 1941, a clean facelift using a bold, horizontal grille greatly improved Dodge appearance. The DeLuxe name now designated the inexpensive three-model line. The new top-of-the-line series was labeled Custom. The 2–4 passenger coupe was replaced by a Town Sedan (with blind rear roof quarters); the two-door sedan was called the Brougham. Fluid Drive became an option, and the engine was boosted to 91 bhp through changes in compression. Parking lights were moved inboard to the grille. Turn indicators were housed in large chrome pods atop the fenders.

As it was for most manufacturers, 1941 was a banner year for Dodge. Model year production was one of the highest in the division's history: some 106,000 DeLuxes and 131,000 Customs were built. The new Town Sedan was a modest success. Long-wheelbase models continued to sell in small quantities. The division held seventh place in the industry, then crept ahead of sixth-place Oldsmobile in 1942.

When the federal government ordered car production halted in February 1942, Dodge had built only about 68,000 of its new models. They were good-looking cars—not quite as radical as the hidden-headlamp DeSotos, but nicely done throughout. Grilles were now full-width, heavier and wider than before, featuring a prominent eggcrate central section. Optional fender skirts carried bright moldings to blend with rear fender trim. Performance was improved by means of an enlarged engine that provided 105 bhp. A club coupe was added to the DeLuxe line. Production wasn't low enough to make the '42 Dodge as rare as some other makes that year. Of the standard wheelbase models, the convertible coupe—1185 units—is the scarcest.

After the war, Dodge got off to an especially slow start, and only 420 of the '46s were built before December 31, 1945. Wartime studies had produced a variety of interesting postwar styling proposals for the 1940-42 body. Among them were smooth grilles, wraparound bumpers, thin door pillars, and integral fenders. But body tooling was far from amortized in 1942, and Dodge's decision to produce a mildly facelifted version of its prewar designs for 1946-48 was typical of the postwar industry. Between January and December 1946, Dodge turned out these cars rapidly, finishing the year fourth behind the low-priced three.

Facelifting for the 1946-48 Dodges (which were physically identical except for serial numbers) was carried out by stylists A. B. Grisinger, John Chika, and Herb Weissinger—a trio later to win fame at Kaiser-Frazer. Allowed bolt-on alterations only, they opted for a new grille with very wide horizontal and vertical bars forming a pattern of rectangles. Parking lights were square, located at either side of the grille with the Dodge nameplate mounted above it. Mechanical changes included relocation of the starter from a foot pedal to a button on the dash, and front brakes equipped with double wheel cylinders. The transmission was also revised. An in-line fuel filter and full-flow oil filter became standard.

One part that is easy to change, despite carryover bodies, is the dashboard. This underwent continuous alteration at Dodge in the '40s. The 1940 edition was a relatively plain affair, flat and square, with instruments grouped under a big three-spoke steering wheel. In '41, the steering wheel came with two pairs of horizontal spokes and the dash was symmetrical: speedometer and large clock flanked a central radio-speaker panel,

with minor gauges positioned in a row to the left of the speedometer. In 1942, the dash got a woodgrain finish, and the steering wheel went back to three spokes. This pattern was retained for the 1946-48 models, with the addition of more brightwork. Dashboard symmetry was standard fare in the '40s—often at the expense of visibility. Dodge paid attention to practicality, however, by retaining needle gauges that were clear and readable.

After 1946, Fluid Drive was made standard for all models. This was an important selling point in an age when people were tiring of manual shift. Inaugurated in 1938, Fluid Drive was a complicated solution to a simple problem. Combining a conventional clutch with torque converter and electrical shifting circuits, it provided what one writer called a "full range of potential transmission trouble." But it did replace the conventional flywheel with a fluid-coupling torque converter. The converter performed the usual flywheel functions—storing energy, smoothing power impulses, and carrying the ring gear that meshed with the starter pinion.

Lacking a clutch plate contact, a clutch was mounted in tandem. The fluid coupling itself was a drum, filled with low-viscosity mineral oil. As the engine ran, a set of vanes attached to the inner casing rotated, throwing oil outward onto a facing runner that had another set of vanes. The oil turned the runner, allowing a smooth flow of power and avoiding any metal-to-metal contact.

There were two gear positions: Low for first and second; High for third and fourth. Low was used mainly for fast starts or towing situations. For normal driving, you simply shifted into High and pressed on the accelerator. At 14 mph when the accelerator was released, a "thump" announced the car had switched from third to fourth gear. Stops and starts were accomplished without any clutching or gear shifting at all. Fluid Drive eliminated 95 percent of gear shifting. The clutch was there, but it was used only to change between Low and High, or to back up.

Dodge's restyled 1949 models were not ready at new-car announcement time, so leftover '48s were sold as

1940 DeLuxe four-door sedan

1941 Custom convertible coupe

1940 Special two-door sedan

1942 DeLuxe club coupe

1941 Custom four-door sedan

1946 Deluxe three-passenger coupe

# Dodge

1949 Coronet four-door sedan

1949 Wayfarer roadster

A-227 front-wheel-drive prototype, 1949-50

1950 Coronet four-door sedan

1950 Wayfarer Sportabout roadster

'49s until April. The "second series" 1949, powered by a 103-bhp version of the old six, was entirely redesigned. First came the inexpensive Wayfarer series on a 115-inch wheelbase. It comprised a sedan, coupe, and a novel roadster with side curtains, in a price range of $1611 to $1738. The Meadowbrook and Coronet—the volume cars of the line—rode a 123.5-inch wheelbase. They were more luxuriously trimmed and available in a wider variety of body styles. The Coronet Town Sedan was a luxury trim option, about $85 more expensive than the standard model. It featured beautiful and luxurious Bedford cord upholstery. The Meadowbrook was a single four-door sedan, trimmed more simply and offered at about $75 less than the comparable Coronet.

The new squared-off body styling remained quite conservative. A bold eggcrate grille bore some resemblance to the 1946-48 design, but was more massive. Bolt-on rear fenders were capped by taillights visible from three sides. The slab-sided body was embellished by stainless-steel moldings. Collectors today agree that the Wayfarer roadster is the most desirable '49 Dodge, and many of these have been restored. By contrast, the 1949 woody wagon was not successful: only 800 unit sales were recorded for the model year. After 600 were sold in 1950, it was phased out. Dodge produced nearly 257,000 cars in 1949—a new record.

Dodge's image was transformed in the '50s. The cars began the decade as stodgy six-bangers, but soon became V8 track stars. Styling kept pace with performance. The division had its ups and downs in sales, however, as it deserted one kind of buyer for another.

The three-box '49 bodyshell got a major facelift for 1950 and a new Diplomat hardtop was added. Gyro-Matic drive, an improvement on standard Fluid Drive that eliminated gear changing, also appeared. All models were powered by the sturdy flathead six, which would serve Dodge through the decade. Two basic model lines were fielded. The D33 Wayfarer, including a winsome sport convertible, was priced just above the more expensive Plymouths. The D34 series comprised Meadowbrook and Coronet sedans and Coronet wagons, coupes, convertibles, and hardtops. Through 1952, Coronet would also be offered as a long-wheelbase sedan, Dodge's heaviest car, for taxi and limousine purposes.

Styling in the early '50s was pretty dull. But Dodge represented a step up in prestige for Plymouth owners in those years, and the cars did well. The division built over 340,000 in 1950, and 290,000 in 1951 to nail down seventh place in the industry. Dodge held onto seventh in 1952 by building only 206,000 cars, but dropped back to eighth for 1954 as production reached only 154,000 units.

Without a switch in wheelbases, styling became smoother and sleeker for 1951-52. A lower grille opening, clean flanks, and faired-in taillights gave a new look. The model lineup remained exactly as it had been in 1950. Wayfarers set the price pace; Coronets supplied the widest variety of body styles; and the Meadow-

brook filled the gap between them with a lone four-door sedan. Appearance changed only slightly for '52—the grille bar immediately above the bumper was painted.

For 1953, a major revamping was accompanied by the Red Ram V8 for the first Dodge performance cars of the decade. Originally, the Red Ram produced 140 bhp, though it was capable of much more than that. It was essentially a scaled-down version of the 331-cid Chrysler Hemi introduced in 1951. Chrysler had long been experimenting with hemispherical combustion chambers, and was now cashing in on what it had learned. The Hemi's advantages included smoother manifolding and porting, larger valves set farther apart, improved thermal efficiency, plenty of room for water passages, a more central spark plug location, and low heat rejection into coolant. Its main disadvantage was cost: engine for engine, Red Rams were more expensive to build than Chevy 265s, for example.

The 1953 Dodge was among the first production Chrysler automobiles styled by Virgil Exner, who had come from Studebaker a few years earlier. Surprisingly light, they handled well, and were known for economy as well as performance. A Dodge V8 scored 23.4 miles per gallon in the '53 Mobilgas Economy Run; the same year, other V8s broke 196 AAA stock-car records at Bonneville, and Danny Eames drove one to a record 102.62 mph at El Mirage dry lake in California. Dodge's V8 was a small-displacement, high-efficiency power-plant—unique in its hemi-head construction, reliable, and strong.

Only detail changes were made for '54. However, a new, luxurious Royal series appeared, joined at mid-year by the Royal 500 convertible, named for the Indianapolis race. Dodge had paced the Indiana classic that year, and a round of pace-car replicas seemed like a good idea. Included in the 500 package (at only $2632) were Kelsey-Hayes chrome wire wheels, a "continental" spare tire, special ornamentation, and a 150-bhp Red Ram V8. Dealers could even specify a four-barrel Offenhauser manifold that must have made the 500 a screamer, though Chrysler never quoted the actual horsepower.

Of the Royal convertibles sold in 1954, only 701 were 500s, but the package was far more successful than that

1952 Wayfarer two-door sedan

1952 Coronet four-door sedan

April 1950 proposal for 1953 Dodge restyle

1953 Coronet 500 convertible

1953 Coronet four-door sedan

Firearrow show car of 1954 by Ghia

figure suggests. The division had established itself as the "performance team" at Chrysler, and had begun to roll up victories. Lincoln is famous for its dominance in the Mexican Road Race of those years. What is not widely known is that Dodge overwhelmed the race's Medium Stock class, taking the 1-2-3-4-6-9 positions in the 1954 marathon.

Competition successes helped boost sales. In a generally poor year for Chrysler products, the Dodge sold well in '54. The division came back with another major restyling that was mainly the work of Exner staff member Murray Baldwin. Set on a new 120-inch wheelbase, the '55 Coronets, Royals, and Custom Royals offered engine options of up to 193 bhp. They were much larger, but nicely styled and well-built.

In 1956, all Chrysler products grew tailfins and Dodge was no exception. PowerFlite automatic transmission, which had arrived with gear lever control in '54, now had pushbuttons. Facelifted styling and new

interiors were enhanced by a new engine, the optional D-500 V8, which developed a hefty 260 bhp at 4400 rpm. Dodge also unveiled a four-door Lancer hardtop in all three series. In a declining year for the industry, the division built only 240,000 cars but still managed to hold onto eighth place. The following year, with torsion-bar suspension and all-new styling, Dodge climbed to seventh place, building nearly 290,000 units.

Exner's Forward Look was new from the ground up for 1957, yet it hadn't progressed to extremes. That year's Dodge was smoothly styled and aggressive-looking, with a massive bumper/grille, lots of glass, and still more power. An array of Hemi engines, ranging from the mild 325 to the top 354-cid D-500 with 340 bhp, offered performance enthusiasts much to choose from. Even the old six got a horsepower boost.

Dodge did not follow Chrysler, DeSoto, and Plymouth with a limited-edition "supercar" for '57. Instead, it offered the D-500 option across the board, even on the

1954 Royal V8 convertible

1955 Royal V8 four-door sedan

1955 Royal Lancer V8 hardtop coupe

1956 Custom Royal Lancer hardtop sedan

"La Femme" show car based on 1956 Custom Royal Lancer

1957 Royal Lancer hardtop coupe

plain Coronet two-door sedan. All D-500s were equipped with stiff shocks, stiff springs, and torsion bars for what *Motor Trend* magazine called "close liaison with the road." The soft ride of conventional Chrysler cars was replaced by firm suspension settings that put D-500s at the top of the class in handling. And with the 245-bhp engine, the car ran 0 to 60 in 9.4 seconds in the magazine's tests. The D-500 model continued in 1958-59, but its expensive Hemi engine was replaced with a wedge-head V8. Offered with optional fuel injection for 1958, the 361-cid wedge would produce 333 bhp at 4800 rpm—the highest power offered by Dodge that year.

Riding a 122-inch wheelbase in 1957, Dodge continued with the same body and chassis for 1958-59. The '58s got a mild but attractive facelift with four head-lamps and a less massive frontispiece. The model lineup was generally unchanged, but the Regal Lancer hardtop made its debut in February.

Fuel injection was a short-lived venture, marked by little success. Few buyers opted for it. More popular were the conventional V8s ranging up to 320 bhp. The old flathead six was still around, but was relegated to the Coronet series only and was not a wise buy. According to one tester: "It could be pretty much of a white elephant when you go to sell it." Dodge itself was somewhat of a white elephant in 1958, a disastrous year. Production plunged to 138,000 for the model year, barely enough to beat out Cadillac. Management remained calm—it was, after all, an abnormally poor year—and rebounded with a restyled 1959 line composed of the same basic models. The division built about 156,000 cars for its traditional eighth-place finish.

Fins went wild on most 1959 Chrysler Corporation cars, but remained fairly modest at Dodge. The front end was given a new look, the interior revised, and several interesting options premiered. Dodge and its companion divisions now had the popular swivel seat, a

1957 Custom Royal Lancer hardtop sedan

1957 Custom Royal convertible

1958 Regal Lancer hardtop coupe

1958 Custom Royal Lancer hardtop coupe

1959 Custom Sierra nine-passenger station wagon

1960 Matador hardtop sedan

# Dodge

semi-bucket affair that pivoted outward as the door opened. The twin four-barrel 383 V8 produced 1959's top horsepower—345 at 5000 rpm. Also available were 325 and 361 wedges, and the flathead six was marketed for the last time. Incidentally, the D-500 engines weren't cheap. The 383 with four-barrel cost $304 extra; the Super version with twin four-barrel cost $446. Both were thirsty, but it was the age of 30-cent gasoline. People were willing to spend extra money on the engines and gas to get the added performance.

Exner's Dodge show cars are worth mention. There was a Firearrow series beginning in 1953 with a mock-up roadster that was made road-ready the following year. In late 1954 came a Firearrow sport coupe and convertible. The latter inspired the limited-production Dual-Ghia of 1956. The Firearrow coupe was aerodynamically stable and achieved 143.44 mph on the banked oval at Chrysler's Proving Grounds.

Another show car was 1955's La Femme, a Custom Royal Lancer two-door hardtop painted pink and upholstered in white. Many custom accoutrements were featured, including a folding umbrella and fitted handbag stored in the backs of the front seats. La Femme was back again for the 1956 show route, and was all the rage. For awhile, it was considered for volume production, but no more than a handful were ultimately produced.

By 1970, Dodge was one of the leading names in high performance. In product orientation, the division had pushed upward into the market vacated by DeSoto, and downward into the compact and "ponycar" fields. As a result, volume increased rapidly. From 1964 through 1969, Dodge built an average of over half a million cars a year. In the industry's peak year of 1968, the division built a record 627,533 cars. But the competition was increasing output too, so Dodge's standing in the production race varied. In its best years, the division ranked fifth or sixth; in the worst 1961-63 period, it was eighth or ninth. The relatively poor showing in the early 1960s was temporary; Dodge quickly reoriented its product line and recovered rapidly. As Robert McCurry assumed the post of division president in the mid-1960s, Dodge achieved new status as a builder of hot cars.

Only one series on a fairly long wheelbase had been offered in 1959. For 1960, Dodge recognized the growing interest in smaller cars and added the new Dart line of sixes and V8s with a 118-inch wheelbase for sedans and hardtop and a 122-inch wheelbase for wagons. Darts were available in three series: Seneca, Pioneer, and Phoenix. The "senior" Matador and Polara rode the 122-inch wheelbase and were offered with V8s only.

Dart's six-cylinder engine was the larger of two excellent Chrysler Corporation slant sixes. Displacing 225 cid, it continued in various Dodge models on through the '70s. The Dart 318 V8 was another solid, reliable unit. Matadors used the Chrysler 361-cid V8; Polaras got the 383 V8, the latter offered optionally on Matador and Phoenix.

1960 Dart Phoenix hardtop coupe

1961 Dart Phoenix convertible

Unit body/chassis construction was new for 1960, accompanied by a complete restyling. The Dart and the large Dodges got "chrome-y" front ends, large blunt grilles, and reworked tailfins. On the big cars the fins ended ahead of the taillights; the Dart's ran all the way back. Despite the heavy-handed appearance, most models were relatively light and offered good performance with reasonable economy. The year brought an industry-wide recovery from the 1958-59 recession, and volume was up by over 200,000 units.

For 1961, Dodge was ready with its twin to the compact Valiant. Called Lancer, it used a modestly reworked version of the Valiant body/chassis. Lancers had a horizontal-bar grille, instead of Valiant's square one, and slightly better trim. There were two series, 170 and 770, each with sedans and wagons. The 770 also had a hardtop. Power came from a 170-cid slant six with 101 bhp. The Dart's 225-cid was optional.

The Dart was facelifted for 1961, with a full-width concave grille incorporating quad headlights, and reverse-slant tailfins. The six and V8 Seneca, Pioneer, and Phoenix models continued. The senior line was pared down to the Polara series only, though a convertible was added in the V8 Phoenix series. Darts and Polaras retained 1960's lineup of V8s. The top powerplant was the 383-cid D-500 with 330 bhp. Twin four-barrel carburetors and ram-induction were responsible for this outstanding output, and made the Polara extraordinarily fast, fully capable of 120 mph. Oversized Chrysler brakes and torsion-bar front suspension combined to make the D-500 as roadable as it was quick. Since the ram-induction engine was available on Darts

1961 Polara hardtop sedan

1962 Lancer GT hardtop coupe

1962 Custom 880 hardtop sedan

1963 Custom 880 hardtop sedan

as well as Polaras, Dodge also had an extremely rapid "intermediate." The D-500 Dart Phoenix had almost one horsepower for every 10 pounds of weight.

Sales dropped by over 25 percent in 1961, as a result of increased competition in the compact-car market, and an overall downtrend in the industry. Lancer did not sell well, but it was a temporary entry anyway. As development work progressed on its successor, Lancer returned for '62 with a busier grille as the only significant change.

Dart and Polara were treated to a brand-new body on a 116-inch wheelbase for 1962. Inspired by Virgil Exner, these cars were as much as 400 pounds lighter and six inches shorter than the '61s. If Americans like compacts, Exner reasoned, they'd also prefer downsized versions of standard-size models. Unfortunately, the designer was about 15 years ahead of his time: the '62s did not sell well. Most manufacturers enjoyed increased sales that year, but Dodge dropped. What

saved the division was a separate line of Chrysler-based large cars introduced at mid-year on a 122-inch wheelbase, the 880 and Custom 880. The year's performance news was marked by release of two 413-cid wedge engines, offering 410 and 420 bhp.

While Plymouth struggled on for another year with its shortened '62 design, Dodge increased standard wheelbase to 119 inches for 1963 and emphasized performance. The 413-cid wedge with 360 bhp was available for 880s. The performance version was punched out to 426 cid as the Ramcharger. With aluminum pistons and high-lift cam, it developed 415 or 425 bhp. Ramchargers were available in the light 330, 440, and Polara cars that won the 1962 National Hot Rod Association Championship for Dodge. The 330 reigned supreme on literally every dragstrip. They were also strong contenders at Daytona.

Also new for 1963 was the compact replacement for the Lancer. Dodge added five inches to the Valiant

1962 Polara 500 convertible

1964 Custom 880 convertible

**1964 Polara hardtop coupe**

**1964 Dart GT hardtop coupe**

**1965 Dart GT convertible**

**1965 Monaco hardtop coupe**

**1965 Coronet 500 hardtop coupe**

**1965 Coronet 500 hardtop coupe**

wheelbase for all models except wagons to create an all-new Dart. Hardtops, sedans, wagons, and convertibles were offered. Sales rebounded, and Dodge moved ahead of Rambler into seventh place.

The 1964 lineup was substantially the same as 1963's, distinguished by facelifts. Darts could be ordered with the 273-cid Valiant V8. The GT hardtop and convertible were snazzy, and priced remarkably low. The big Dodges came with the usual assortment of sixes and V8s. This year's Ramcharger was powered by the fabled Hemi, making its return to the performance wars. Dodge's Hemi-powered intermediates (and their Plymouth counterparts) dominated the NASCAR ovals that season, sweeping the Daytona 500, for example, 1-2-3. The 880 continued to satisfy big-car customers. Dodge climbed back into sixth place for the first time since 1960.

Dart received only a minor facelift for 1965. The division renamed its midrange line Coronet, which featured new styling and a 117-inch wheelbase for all models but the wagons, which rode a 116-inch wheelbase. A special 115-inch wheelbase Coronet Hemi-Charger was also offered, a two-door sedan weighing just 3165 pounds. The Hemi-Charger was perhaps one of the greatest performance bargains of the decade. It sold at a base price of $3165, which included heavy-duty springs and shocks, anti-roll bar, four-speed transmission, and strong "police" brakes. It could accelerate to 60 mph in seven seconds, and hit a top speed of 120 mph. In racing tune, developing up to 430 bhp, it ruled the tracks in 1965.

The '65 line also included the glamorous Coronet 500 hardtop and convertible with bucket seats and center console, plus a completely new 121-inch wheelbase line of Polaras, Custom 880s, and the sports/luxury Monaco hardtop. Aside from the wagons, the Monaco was the most expensive of the senior Dodges.

For 1966, the offerings continued to be six and V8 Darts; six and V8 Coronets in standard, Deluxe, 440, and 500 guise; V8 Polaras and Monacos; and a hardtop Monaco 500. The Custom 880 was dropped in favor of a full-line Monaco series. A bright new addition was the fastback Charger on the 117-inch wheelbase. Although it shared some sheetmetal with the Coronet, the Charger had a look all its own: hidden headlamps, fold-down split-back rear seat, a sporty interior. Standard power was the 318 V8, but the 361, 383, and 426 Hemi V8s were available as options. So were manual transmission, "Rallye" suspension, and long list of luxury equipment. A 383 Charger with TorqueFlite automatic could run 0–60 mph in about nine seconds and hit 110 mph.

Dodge restyled most of its models for 1967. Dart hardtops, sedans, and convertibles continued on the 111-inch wheelbase, but the wagons were dropped. The new body styling was good-looking and clean-lined. Monaco and Polara adopted the Chrysler Newport's styling and sleeker roofline for a much lower profile than their predecessors. The Charger retained its 1966

look, while the Coronet had a minor facelift and two new additions, the R/T (Road/Track) hardtop and convertible. Standard R/T equipment included the 440-cid 375-bhp engine, heavy-duty suspension, wide tires, and oversize brakes. The 426 Hemi V8 was again listed as an option for the Coronet R/T and the Charger.

The approach for 1968 was to facelift the Dart, Polara, and Monaco, and to completely restyle the Coronet and Charger. These were the best-looking Dodge intermediates of the decade, with a long, low, bullet-shaped fuselage; larger windows; a plain grille; and strong but light bumpers. The Charger featured hidden headlamps and a "flying buttress" roofline.

Several new variations appeared in the compact and intermediate lines. The Dart GTS comprised plush, grand touring hardtops and convertibles available with a new lightweight 340-cid V8. The Coronet Super Bee was a light, fast two-door coupe, equipped with a special 335-bhp version of the 383 engine. R/T equipment was made available for the Charger as well as the Coronet and resulted in a fine road car.

The Super Bee, Dart GTS, Coronet and Charger R/Ts

1966 Charger fastback hardtop coupe

1967 Dart GT hardtop coupe

1966 Coronet 500 hardtop coupe

1967 Coronet 500 hardtop coupe

1966 Dart GT convertible

1967 Monaco hardtop sedan

1966 Monaco 500 hardtop coupe

1968 Dart GTS hardtop coupe

composed what Dodge called its "Scat Pack," each denoted by bumble-bee stripes. These were among the most roadable machines in America during 1968. The R/T's ultimate engines, a 375-bhp Magnum 440 or a 425-bhp Hemi, made it a winning entry on the nation's dragstrips once again.

Like other Chrysler models that shared the same bodyshell, Polara and Monaco received all-new "fuse-lage" styling for 1969, but retained their 122-inch wheelbase. The Dart, Coronet, and Charger were face-lifted. Chargers were given a split grille; Coronet R/Ts and 500s sported full-width taillamps. The usual wide range of engines was offered. A new variation was the

Dart Swinger two-door hardtop, which came with special identifying trim, a bright aluminum grille, and a choice of 318- or 340-cid V8s.

The pride of the '69 fleet was the exotic Charger Daytona, built especially for the Daytona 500. It featured a wind-cheating bullet nose with hidden headlights, a front spoiler, an aerodynamic full-fastback roof, and a towering rear-deck stabilizer. Compared with the previous Charger 500 racing car, the Daytona was about 20 percent more aerodynamic, which gave it an advantage of 500 yards per lap. Dodge built only 505 Charger Daytonas—just enough to qualify the model as a production car for NASCAR racing. The list price was

1968 Monaco 500 hardtop coupe

1969 Charger hardtop coupe

1968 Coronet R/T hardtop coupe

1969 Charger Daytona hardtop coupe

1968 Coronet 440 hardtop coupe

1969 Polara 500 hardtop coupe

1968 Charger hardtop coupe

1969 Dart Swinger hardtop coupe

about $8000. A Daytona won the Talledega 500 in September 1969, but arch-rival Ford failed to show up. In 1970, the Daytonas and Plymouth's similar Superbird won 38 of 48 major NASCAR races.

For 1970, Dodge fielded its answer to the Mustang and Camaro ponycars, fittingly named Challenger. Like its Ford and GM rivals, Challenger was offered with both six-cylinder and V8 engines. There were three models: hardtop coupe, convertible, and the Special Edition. The latter was a coupe with a padded vinyl roof and smaller "formal" rear window. Priced attractively in the $3000-3500 range and offering a broad list of options, the Challenger sold extremely well. Six-cylinder

models outpaced the V8s. Hardtops were the most popular; only about 10,000 Special Edition coupes found buyers.

Though specifications and dimensions of the 1970 line largely duplicated those of 1969, some significant styling changes occurred. Darts and Coronets received a new split grille. The Dart was particularly well-executed, with a longer hood and new rear styling. The Charger, closely resembling its 1969 predecessor, had a full-width grille surrounded by a massive loop bumper and was offered in six-cylinder form for the first time. The exotic Daytona had proved its point on the race tracks and was dropped.

**1969 Coronet 500 hardtop coupe**

**1969 Coronet R/T hardtop coupe**

**1969 Charger 500 hardtop coupe**

**1970 Polara Custom hardtop coupe**

**1970 Dart Swinger 340 hardtop coupe**

**1970 Charger hardtop coupe**

**1970 Coronet 500 hardtop coupe**

**1970 Challenger R/T convertible**

The senior-series Polara and Monaco were restyled following the general '70 theme. Loop-type bumpers surrounded grille and taillights; side marker lights were set into the bumper ends. Ignition/steering column locks, fiberglass-belted tires, dual-action wagon tailgates, and a long list of federally mandated safety equipment completed the 1970 equipment package. With some 400,000 sales, the year proved encouraging.

## Dodge Specifications

### 1940

| D-17 Special (wb 119.5) | Wght | Price | Prod |
|---|---|---|---|
| bus cpe | 2,867 | 755 | 12,001 |
| sdn 2d | 2,942 | 815 | 27,700 |
| sdn 4d | 2,997 | 855 | 26,803 |

| D-14 DeLuxe (wb 119.5; 7P-139.5) | Wght | Price | Prod |
|---|---|---|---|
| bus cpe | 2,905 | 803 | 12,750 |
| cpe, A/S | 2,973 | 855 | 8,028 |
| conv cpe | 3,190 | 1,030 | 2,100 |
| sdn 2d | 2,990 | 860 | 19,838 |
| sdn 4d | 3,028 | 905 | 84,976 |
| sdn 4d, 7P | 3,460 | 1,095 | 932 |
| limo 7P | 3,500 | 1,170 | 79 |
| chassis | — | — | 298 |

| 1940 Engine | bore×stroke | bhp | availability |
|---|---|---|---|
| L6, 217.8 | 3.25×4.38 | 87 | S-all |

### 1941

| D-19 DeLuxe (wb 119.5) | Wght | Price | Prod |
|---|---|---|---|
| bus cpe | 3,034 | 862 | 22,318 |
| sdn 2d | 3,109 | 915 | 34,566 |
| sdn 4d | 3,149 | 954 | 49,579 |

| D-19 Custom (wb 119.5; 7P-137.5) | Wght | Price | Prod |
|---|---|---|---|
| club cpe | 3,154 | 995 | 18,024 |
| conv cpe | 3,384 | 1,162 | 3,554 |
| brougham 2d | 3,169 | 962 | 20,146 |
| sdn 4d | 3,194 | 999 | 72,067 |
| town sdn | 3,234 | 1,062 | 16,074 |
| sdn 4d, 7P | 3,579 | 1,195 | 604 |
| limo 7P | 3,669 | 1,262 | 50 |
| chassis | — | — | 20 |

| 1941 Engine | bore×stroke | bhp | availability |
|---|---|---|---|
| L6, 217.8 | 3.25×4.38 | 91 | S-all |

### 1942

| D-22 DeLuxe (wb 119.5) | Wght | Price | Prod |
|---|---|---|---|
| bus cpe | 3,056 | 895 | 5,257 |
| club cpe | 3,131 | 995 | 3,314 |
| sdn 2d | 3,131 | 958 | 9,767 |
| sdn 4d | 3,171 | 998 | 13,343 |

| D-22 Custom (wb 119.5; 7P-137.5) | Wght | Price | Prod |
|---|---|---|---|
| club cpe | 3,171 | 1,045 | 4,659 |
| conv cpe | 3,476 | 1,245 | 1,185 |
| brougham 2d | 3,171 | 1,008 | 4,685 |
| sdn 4d | 3,206 | 1,048 | 22,055 |
| town sdn | 3,256 | 1,105 | 4,047 |
| sdn 4d, 7P | 3,693 | 1,395 | 201 |

| | Wght | Price | Prod |
|---|---|---|---|
| limo 7P | 3,768 | 1,475 | 9 |

| 1942 Engine | bore×stroke | bhp | availability |
|---|---|---|---|
| L6, 230.2 | 3.25×4.63 | 105 | S-all |

### 1946

| D-24S DeLuxe (wb 119.5)* | Wght | Price | Prod |
|---|---|---|---|
| bus cpe | 3,146 | 1,229 | — |
| sdn 2d | 3,236 | 1,299 | — |
| sdn 4d | 3,256 | 1,339 | — |

| D-24C Custom (wb 119.5; 7P-137.5)* | Wght | Price | Prod |
|---|---|---|---|
| club cpe | 3,241 | 1,384 | — |
| conv cpe | 3,461 | 1,649 | — |
| sdn 4d | 3,281 | 1,389 | — |
| town sdn | 3,331 | 1,444 | — |
| sdn 4d, 7P | 3,757 | 1,743 | — |

| 1946 Engine | bore×stroke | bhp | availability |
|---|---|---|---|
| L6, 230.2 | 3.25×4.63 | 102 | S-all |

### 1947

| D-24S DeLuxe (wb 119.5)* | Wght | Price | Prod |
|---|---|---|---|
| bus cpe | 3,147 | 1,347 | — |
| sdn 2d | 3,236 | 1,417 | — |
| sdn 4d | 3,256 | 1,457 | — |

| D-24C Custom (wb 119.5; 7P-137.5)* | Wght | Price | Prod |
|---|---|---|---|
| club cpe | 3,241 | 1,502 | — |
| conv cpe | 3,461 | 1,871 | — |
| sdn 4d | 3,281 | 1,507 | — |
| town sdn | 3,331 | 1,577 | — |
| sdn 4d, 7P | 3,757 | 1,861 | — |

| 1947 Engine | bore×stroke | bhp | availability |
|---|---|---|---|
| L6, 230.2 | 3.25×4.63 | 102 | S-all |

### 1948

| D-24S DeLuxe (wb 119.5)* | Wght | Price | Prod |
|---|---|---|---|
| bus cpe | 3,146 | 1,587 | — |
| sdn 2d | 3,236 | 1,676 | — |
| sdn 4d | 3,256 | 1,718 | — |

| D-24C Custom (wb 119.5; 7P-137.5)* | Wght | Price | Prod |
|---|---|---|---|
| club cpe | 3,241 | 1,774 | — |
| conv cpe | 3,461 | 2,189 | — |
| sdn 4d | 3,281 | 1,788 | — |
| town sdn | 3,331 | 1,872 | — |
| sdn 4d, 7P | 3,757 | 2,179 | — |

| 1948 Engine | bore×stroke | bhp | availability |
|---|---|---|---|
| L6, 230.2 | 3.25×4.63 | 102 | S-all |

## 1949 First Series

| D-24S DeLuxe (wb 119.5)* | Wght | Price | Prod |
|---|---|---|---|
| bus cpe | 3,146 | 1,587 | — |
| sdn 2d | 3,236 | 1,676 | — |
| sdn 4d | 3,256 | 1,718 | — |

| D-24C Custom (wb 119.5; 7P-137.5)* | Wght | Price | Prod |
|---|---|---|---|
| club cpe | 3,241 | 1,774 | — |
| conv cpe | 3,461 | 2,189 | — |
| sdn 4d | 3,281 | 1,788 | — |
| town sdn | 3,331 | 1,872 | — |
| sdn 4d, 7P | 3,757 | 2,179 | — |

| 1949(1) Engine | bore×stroke | bhp | availability |
|---|---|---|---|
| L6, 230.2 | 3.25×4.63 | 102 | S-all |

*Factory combined production figures for 1946 through 1949 First Series.

## Combined 1946–1949 First Series Production:

| D-24S DeLuxe (wb 119.5) | Prod |
|---|---|
| bus cpe | 27,600 |
| sdn 2d | 81,399 |
| sdn 4d | 61,987 |

| D-24C Custom (wb 119.5; 7P-137.5) | Prod |
|---|---|
| club cpe | 103,800 |
| conv cpe | 9,500 |
| sdn 4d | 333,911 |
| town sdn | 27,800 |
| sdn 4d, 7P | 3,698 |
| limo 7P (proto) | 2 |
| chassis | 302 |

## 1949 Second Series

| D-29 Wayfarer (wb 115.0) | Wght | Price | Prod |
|---|---|---|---|
| cpe | 3,065 | 1,611 | 9,342 |
| sdn 2d | 3,180 | 1,738 | 49,058 |
| rdstr | 3,145 | 1,727 | 5,420 |

| D-30 (wb 123.5; 8P-137.5) | Wght | Price | Prod |
|---|---|---|---|
| Meadowbrook sdn 4d | 3,355 | 1,848 | 144,390 |
| Coronet sdn 4d | 3,380 | 1,927 | |
| Coronet club cpe | 3,325 | 1,914 | 45,435 |
| Coronet conv cpe | 3,570 | 2,329 | 2,411 |
| Coronet wgn 4d, 9P | 3,830 | 2,865 | 800 |
| chassis | — | — | 1 |

| 1949(2) Engine | bore×stroke | bhp | availability |
|---|---|---|---|
| L6, 230.2 | 3.25×4.53 | 103 | S-all |

## 1950

| D-33 Wayfarer (wb 115.0) | Wght | Price | Prod |
|---|---|---|---|
| bus cpe | 3,095 | 1,611 | 7,500 |
| sdn 2d | 3,200 | 1,738 | 65,000 |
| Sportabout rdstr | 3,155 | 1,727 | 2,903 |

| D-34 (wb 123.5; 8P-137.5) | Wght | Price | Prod |
|---|---|---|---|
| Meadowbrook sdn 4d | 3,395 | 1,848 | 221,791 |
| Coronet sdn 4d | 3,405 | 1,927 | |
| Coronet club cpe | 3,340 | 1,914 | 38,502 |
| Coronet conv cpe | 3,590 | 2,329 | 1,800 |
| Coronet Diplomat htp cpe | 3,515 | 2,233 | 3,600 |
| Coronet wgn 4d (wood) | 3,850 | 2,865 | 600 |
| Coronet Sierra wgn 4d (steel) | 3,726 | 2,485 | 100 |
| chassis | — | — | 1 |

| 1950 Engine | bore×stroke | bhp | availability |
|---|---|---|---|
| L6, 230.2 | 3.25×4.63 | 103 | S-all |

## 1951

| D-41 Wayfarer (wb 115.0) | Wght | Price | Prod |
|---|---|---|---|
| bus cpe | 3,125 | 1,795 | * |
| sdn 2d | 3,210 | 1,936 | * |
| Sportabout rdstr | 3,175 | 1,924 | 1,002 |

| D-42 (wb 123.5; 8P-137.5)* | Wght | Price | Prod |
|---|---|---|---|
| Meadowbrook sdn 4d | 3,415 | 2,059 | — |
| Coronet sdn 4d | 3,415 | 2,148 | — |
| Coronet club cpe | 3,320 | 2,132 | — |
| Coronet Diplomat htp cpe | 3,515 | 2,478 | — |
| Coronet conv cpe | 3,575 | 2,568 | — |
| Coronet Sierra wgn 4d | 3,750 | 2,768 | — |
| Coronet sdn 4d, 8P | 3,935 | 2,916 | — |

| 1951 Engine | bore×stroke | bhp | availability |
|---|---|---|---|
| L6, 230.2 | 3.25×4.63 | 103 | S-all |

## 1952

| D-41 Wayfarer (wb 115.0)* | Wght | Price | Prod |
|---|---|---|---|
| bus cpe | 3,053 | 1,886 | — |
| sdn 2d | 3,140 | 2,034 | — |

| D-42 (wb 123.5; 8P-137.5)* | Wght | Price | Prod |
|---|---|---|---|
| Meadowbrook sdn 4d | 3,355 | 2,164 | — |
| Coronet sdn 4d | 3,385 | 2,256 | — |
| Coronet club cpe | 3,290 | 2,240 | — |
| Coronet conv cpe | 3,520 | 2,698 | — |
| Coronet Diplomat htp cpe | 3,475 | 2,602 | — |
| Coronet Sierra wgn 4d | 3,735 | 2,908 | — |
| Coronet sdn 4d, 8P | 3,935 | 3,064 | — |

| 1952 Engine | bore×stroke | bhp | availability |
|---|---|---|---|
| L6, 230.2 | 3.25×4.63 | 103 | S-all |

*Factory combined 1951–1952 production.

## Combined 1951–1952 production:

| D-41 Wayfarer (wb 115.0) | Prod |
|---|---|
| bus cpe | 6,702 |
| sdn 2d | 70,700 |
| Sportabout rdstr (1951 only) | 1,002 |

| D-42 (wb 123.5; 8P-137.5) | Prod |
|---|---|
| Meadowbrook-Coronet sdn 4d | 329,202 |
| Coronet club cpe | 56,103 |
| Coronet conv cpe | 5,550 |
| Coronet Diplomat htp cpe | 21,600 |
| Coronet Sierra wgn 4d | 4,000 |
| Coronet sdn 4d, 8P | 1,150 |

## 1953

| D-46 (wb 119.0) | Wght | Price | Prod |
|---|---|---|---|
| Meadowbrook Special cpe | 3,100 | 1,958 | 36,766 |
| Meadowbrook cpe | 3,085 | 1,958 | |
| Coronet cpe | 3,155 | 2,084 | |
| Meadowbrook Special sdn 4d | 3,195 | 2,000 | 84,158 |
| Meadowbrook sdn 4d | 3,175 | 2,000 | |
| Coronet sdn 4d | 3,220 | 2,111 | |

| D-47 Meadowbrook Suburban (wb 114.0) | Wght | Price | Prod |
|---|---|---|---|
| wgn 2d | 3,190 | 2,176 | 15,751 |

| D-44 Coronet Eight (wb 119.0) | Wght | Price | Prod |
|---|---|---|---|
| club cpe | 3,325 | 2,198 | 32,439 |
| sdn 4d | 3,385 | 2,220 | 124,059 |

# Dodge

| D-48 Coronet Eight (wb 114.0) | Wght | Price | Prod |
|---|---|---|---|
| conv cpe | 3,438 | 2,494 | 4,100 |
| Diplomat htp cpe | 3,310 | 2,361 | 17,334 |
| Sierra wgn 2d | 3,425 | 2,503 | 5,400 |
| chassis | — | — | 1 |

| 1953 Engines | bore×stroke | bhp | availability |
|---|---|---|---|
| L6, 230.2 | 3.25×4.63 | 103 | S-D-46, D-47 |
| V8, 241.3 | 3.44×3.25 | 140 | S-D-44, D-48 |

## 1954

| D51-1 Meadowbrook L6 (wb 119.0) | Wght | Price | Prod |
|---|---|---|---|
| club cpe | 3,120 | 1,983 | 3,501 |
| sdn 4d | 3,195 | 2,025 | 7,894 |

| D50-1 Meadowbrook V8 (wb 119.0) | | | |
|---|---|---|---|
| club cpe | 3,335 | 2,154 | 750 |
| sdn 4d | 3,390 | 2,176 | 3,299 |

| D51-2 Coronet L6 (wb 119.0) | | | |
|---|---|---|---|
| club cpe | 3,165 | 2,109 | 4,501 |
| sdn 4d | 3,235 | 2,136 | 14,900 |

| D52 Coronet L6 (wb 119.0; 2d-114.0) | | | |
|---|---|---|---|
| Suburban wgn 2d | 3,185 | 2,229 | 6,389 |
| Sierra wgn 4d, 6P | 3,430 | 2,719 | 312 |
| Sierra wgn 4d, 8P | 3,435 | 2,790 | |

| D50-2 Coronet V8 (wb 119.0) | | | |
|---|---|---|---|
| club cpe | 3,345 | 2,223 | 7,998 |
| sdn 4d | 3,405 | 2,245 | 36,063 |

| D53-2 Coronet V8 (wb 114.0; 4d-119.0) | | | |
|---|---|---|---|
| Sport htp cpe | 3,310 | 2,380 | 100 |
| conv cpe | 3,505 | 2,514 | 50 |
| Suburban wgn 2d | 3,400 | 2,517 | 3,100 |
| Sierra wgn 4d, 6P | 3,605 | 2,960 | 988 |
| Sierra wgn 4d, 8P | 3,660 | 3,031 | |

| D50-3 Royal V8 (wb 119.0) | | | |
|---|---|---|---|
| club cpe | 3,365 | 2,349 | 8,900 |
| sdn 4d | 3,425 | 2,373 | 50,050 |

| D53-3 Royal V8 (wb 114.0) | | | |
|---|---|---|---|
| Sport htp cpe | 3,355 | 2,503 | 3,852 |
| conv cpe (prod inc 701 model 500) | 3,575 | 2,632 | 2,000 |
| chassis | — | — | 1 |

| 1954 Engines | bore×stroke | bhp | availability |
|---|---|---|---|
| L6, 230.2 | 3.25×4.63 | 110 | S-all 6s |
| V8, 241.3 | 3.44×3.25 | 140 | S-Meadowbrook V8 |
| V8, 241.3 | 3.44×3.25 | 150 | S-others (Offenhauser manifold available) |

## 1955

| D56-1 Coronet L6 (wb 120.0) | Wght | Price | Prod |
|---|---|---|---|
| sdn 2d | 3,235 | 2,013 | 13,277 |
| sdn 4d | 3,295 | 2,093 | 15,976 |
| Suburban wgn 2d | 3,410 | 2,349 | 3,248 |
| Suburban wgn 4d, 6P | 3,480 | 2,463 | 1,311 |
| Suburban wgn 4d, 8P | 3,595 | 2,565 | |

| D55-1 Coronet V8 (wb 120.0) | | | |
|---|---|---|---|
| sdn 2d | 3,360 | 2,116 | 10,827 |
| club sdn 2d | 3,235 | 2,124 | |
| sdn 4d | 3,395 | 2,196 | 30,098 |
| Lancer htp cpe | 3,375 | 2,281 | 26,727 |
| Suburban wgn 2d | 3,550 | 2,452 | 4,867 |
| Suburban wgn 4d, 6P | 3,590 | 2,566 | 4,641 |
| Suburban wgn 4d, 8P | 3,695 | 2,668 | |

| D55-2 Royal V8 (wb 120.0) | Wght | Price | Prod |
|---|---|---|---|
| sdn 4d | 3,425 | 2,310 | 45,323 |
| Lancer htp cpe | 3,425 | 2,395 | 25,831 |
| Sierra wgn 4d, 6P | 3,655 | 2,659 | 5,506 |
| Sierra wgn 4d, 8P | 3,730 | 2,761 | |

| D55-3 Custom Royal V8 (wb 120.0) | | | |
|---|---|---|---|
| sdn 4d | 3,485 | 2,473 | 55,503 |
| Lancer sdn 4d | 3,505 | 2,516 | |
| Lancer htp cpe | 3,480 | 2,543 | 30,499 |
| Lancer conv cpe | 3,610 | 2,748 | 3,302 |

| 1955 Engines | bore×stroke | bhp | availability |
|---|---|---|---|
| L6, 230.2 | 3.25×4.63 | 123 | S-all 6s |
| V8, 270.1 | 3.63×3.25 | 175 | S-all V8s exc Custom Royal |
| V8, 270.1 | 3.63×3.25 | 183 | S-Custom Royal |
| V8, 270.1 | 3.63×3.25 | 193 | O-Custom Royal |

## 1956

| D62 Coronet L6 (wb 120.0)—142,613 built (includes D63-1) | Wght | Price | Prod |
|---|---|---|---|
| sdn 2d | 3,250 | 2,194 | — |
| sdn 4d | 3,295 | 2,267 | — |
| Suburban wgn 2d | 3,455 | 2,491 | — |

| D63-1 Coronet V8 (wb 120.0) | | | |
|---|---|---|---|
| club sdn 2d | 3,380 | 2,302 | — |
| sdn 4d | 3,435 | 2,375 | — |
| Lancer htp sdn | 3,560 | 2,552 | — |
| Lancer htp cpe | 3,430 | 2,438 | — |
| conv cpe | 3,600 | 2,678 | — |
| Sierra wgn 4d, 6P | 3,600 | 2,716 | — |
| Sierra wgn 4d, 8P | 3,715 | 2,822 | — |
| Suburban wgn 2d | 3,605 | 2,599 | — |

| D63-2 Royal V8 (wb 120.0)—48,780 built | | | |
|---|---|---|---|
| sdn 4d | 3,475 | 2,513 | — |
| Lancer htp sdn | 3,625 | 2,697 | — |
| Lancer htp cpe | 3,505 | 2,583 | — |
| Sierra wgn 4d, 6P | 3,710 | 2,869 | — |
| Sierra wgn 4d, 8P | 3,800 | 2,974 | — |
| Suburban wgn 2d | 3,620 | 2,729 | — |

| D63-3 Custom Royal V8 (wb 120.0)—49,293 built | | | |
|---|---|---|---|
| sdn 4d | 3,520 | 2,623 | — |
| Lancer htp sdn | 3,675 | 2,807 | — |
| Lancer htp cpe | 3,505 | 2,693 | — |
| conv cpe | 3,630 | 2,913 | — |

| 1956 Engines | bore×stroke | bhp | availability |
|---|---|---|---|
| L6, 230.2 | 3.25×4.63 | 131 | S-all 6s |
| V8, 270.0 | 3.63×3.25 | 189 | S-Coronet V8 |
| V8, 315.0 | 3.63×3.80 | 218 | S-Royal, Custom Royal |
| V8, 315.0 | 3.63×3.80 | 260 | O-all |

## 1957

| D72 Coronet L6 (wb 122.0)—160,979 built (includes D66 and D501) | Wght | Price | Prod |
|---|---|---|---|
| club sdn 2d | 3,400 | 2,370 | — |
| sdn 4d | 3,470 | 2,451 | — |

| D66 Coronet V8 (wb 122.0) | | | |
|---|---|---|---|
| club sdn 2d | 3,530 | 2,478 | — |
| sdn 4d | 3,620 | 2,559 | — |
| Lancer htp sdn | 3,665 | 2,665 | — |
| Lancer htp cpe | 3,570 | 2,580 | — |
| conv cpe | 3,815 | 2,842 | — |

| D501 Coronet D-500 V8 (wb 122.0) | Wght | Price | Prod |
|---|---|---|---|
| club sdn 2d | 3,885 | 3,314 | — |
| conv cpe | 3,975 | 3,670 | — |

| D67-1 Royal V8 (wb 122.0)—40,999 built | Wght | Price | Prod |
|---|---|---|---|
| sdn 4d | 3,620 | 2,712 | — |
| Lancer htp sdn | 3,690 | 2,818 | — |
| Lancer htp cpe | 3,585 | 2,769 | — |

| D67-2 Custom Royal V8 (wb 122.0)—55,149 built | Wght | Price | Prod |
|---|---|---|---|
| sdn 4d | 3,690 | 2,881 | — |
| Lancer htp sdn | 3,750 | 2,991 | — |
| Lancer htp cpe | 3,670 | 2,920 | — |
| conv cpe | 3,810 | 3,146 | — |

| D70 Station Wagon V8 (wb 122.0)—30,481 built (includes D71) | Wght | Price | Prod |
|---|---|---|---|
| Sierra wgn 4d, 6P | 3,930 | 2,946 | — |
| Sierra wgn 4d, 9P | 4,015 | 3,073 | — |
| Suburban wgn 2d | 3,830 | 2,861 | — |

| D71 Custom Station Wgn V8 (wb 122.0) | Wght | Price | Prod |
|---|---|---|---|
| Sierra wgn 4d, 6P | 3,960 | 3,087 | — |
| Sierra wgn 4d, 9P | 4,030 | 3,215 | — |

| 1957 Engines | bore×stroke | bhp | availability |
|---|---|---|---|
| L6, 230.2 | 3.25×4.63 | 138 | S-D72 |
| V8, 325.0 | 3.69×3.80 | 245 | S-all exc D72, D67-2, D501 |
| V8, 325.0 | 3.69×3.80 | 260 | S-D67-2 |
| V8, 325.0 | 3.69×3.80 | 285/310 | O-all (D-500) |
| V8, 354.0 | 3.94×3.63 | 340 | O-all (D-500) |

## 1958

| LD-1 Coronet L6 (wb 122.0)—77,388 built (includes LD-2 Coronet) | Wght | Price | Prod |
|---|---|---|---|
| club sdn 2d | 3,360 | 2,449 | — |
| sdn 4d | 3,410 | 2,530 | — |
| Lancer htp cpe | 3,400 | 2,572 | — |

| LD-2 Coronet V8 (wb 122.0) | Wght | Price | Prod |
|---|---|---|---|
| club sdn 2d | 3,505 | 2,556 | — |
| sdn 4d | 3,555 | 2,637 | — |
| Lancer htp sdn | 3,605 | 2,764 | — |
| Lancer htp cpe | 3,540 | 2,679 | — |
| conv cpe | 3,725 | 2,942 | — |

| LD-2 Royal V8 (wb 122.0)—15,165 built | Wght | Price | Prod |
|---|---|---|---|
| sdn 4d | 3,570 | 2,797 | — |
| Lancer htp sdn 4d | 3,640 | 2,915 | — |
| Lancer htp cpe | 3,565 | 2,854 | — |

| LD-3 Custom Royal V8 (wb 122.0) | Wght | Price | Prod |
|---|---|---|---|
| sdn 4d | 3,640 | 3,030 | |
| Lancer htp sdn | 3,670 | 3,142 | |
| Lancer htp cpe | 3,610 | 3,071 | 23,949 |
| conv cpe | 3,785 | 3,298 | |
| Regal Lancer htp cpe | 3,650 | 3,245 | 1,163 |

| LD-3 Station Wagon V8 (wb 122.0)—20,196 built | Wght | Price | Prod |
|---|---|---|---|
| Sierra wgn 4d, 6P | 3,930 | 3,035 | — |
| Sierra wgn 4d, 9P | 3,990 | 3,176 | — |
| Suburban wgn 2d | 3,875 | 2,970 | — |
| Custom Sierra wgn 4d, 6P | 3,955 | 3,212 | — |
| Custom Sierra wgn 4d, 9P | 4,035 | 3,354 | — |

| 1958 Engines | bore×stroke | bhp | availability |
|---|---|---|---|
| L6, 230.2 | 3.25×4.63 | 138 | S-Coronet 6 |
| V8, 325.0 | 3.69×3.80 | 252 | S-Coronet V8 |
| V8, 325.0 | 3.69×3.80 | 265 | S-Royal V8 |
| V8, 350.0 | 4.06×3.38 | 285 | S-Cus Royal, wgns |
| V8, 361.0 | 4.12×3.38 | 305/333 | O-all (D-500) |

## 1959

| MD1-L Coronet L6 (wb 122.0)—96,782 built (includes MD2-L) | | Wght | Price | Prod |
|---|---|---|---|---|
| 21 | club sdn 2d | 3,375 | 2,516 | — |
| 23 | Lancer htp cpe | 3,395 | 2,644 | — |
| 41 | sdn 4d | 3,425 | 2,587 | — |

| MD2-L Coronet V8 (wb 122.0) | | Wght | Price | Prod |
|---|---|---|---|---|
| 21 | club sdn 2d | 3,565 | 2,636 | — |
| 23 | Lancer htp cpe | 3,590 | 2,764 | — |
| 27 | conv cpe | 3,775 | 3,089 | — |
| 41 | sdn 4d | 3,615 | 2,707 | — |
| 43 | Lancer htp sdn | 3,620 | 2,842 | — |

| MD3-M Royal V8 (wb 122.0)—14,807 built | | Wght | Price | Prod |
|---|---|---|---|---|
| 23 | Lancer htp cpe | 3,625 | 2,990 | — |
| 41 | sdn 4d | 3,640 | 2,934 | — |
| 40 | Lancer htp sdn | 3,690 | 3,069 | — |

| MD3-H Custom Royal V8 (wb 122.0)—21,206 built | | Wght | Price | Prod |
|---|---|---|---|---|
| 23 | Lancer htp cpe | 3,675 | 3,201 | — |
| 27 | conv cpe | 3,820 | 3,422 | — |
| 41 | sdn 4d | 3,660 | 3,145 | — |
| 43 | Lancer htp sdn | 3,745 | 3,270 | — |

| MD3-L Sierra V8 (wb 122.0)—23,590 built (includes Customs) | | Wght | Price | Prod |
|---|---|---|---|---|
| 45A | wgn 4d, 6P | 3,940 | 3,103 | — |
| 45B | Sierra wgn 4d, 9P | 4,015 | 3,224 | — |

| MD3-H Custom V8 (wb 122.0) | | Wght | Price | Prod |
|---|---|---|---|---|
| 45A | wgn 4d, 6P | 3,980 | 3,318 | — |
| 45B | wgn 4d, 9P | 4,020 | 3,439 | — |

| 1959 Engines | bore×stroke | bhp | availability |
|---|---|---|---|
| L6, 230.2 | 3.25×4.63 | 138 | S-Coronet 6 |
| V8, 326.0 | 3.95×3.31 | 255 | S-Coronet V8 |
| V8, 361.0 | 4.12×3.38 | 305 | S-all exc Coronet |
| V8, 383.0 | 4.25×3.38 | 320/345 | O-all (D-500, Super D-500) |

## 1960

| PD3 Dart L6 (wb 118.0; wgns-122.0) | | Wght | Price | Prod |
|---|---|---|---|---|
| L21 | Seneca sdn 2d | 3,385 | 2,278 | |
| L41 | Seneca sdn 4d | 3,420 | 2,330 | 93,167 |
| L45 | Seneca wgn 4d | 3,805 | 2,695 | |
| M21 | Pioneer sdn 2d | 3,375 | 2,410 | |
| M23 | Pioneer htp cpe | 3,410 | 2,488 | |
| M41 | Pioneer sdn 4d | 3,430 | 2,459 | 36,434 |
| M45A | Pioneer wgn 4d, 6P | 3,820 | 2,787 | |
| M45B | Pioneer wgn 4d, 9P | 3,875 | 2,892 | |
| H23 | Phoenix htp cpe | 3,410 | 2,618 | |
| H27 | Phoenix conv cpe | 3,460 | 2,868 | 6,567 |
| H41 | Phoenix sdn 4d | 3,420 | 2,595 | |
| H43 | Phoenix htp sdn | 3,460 | 2,677 | |

| PD4 Dart V8 (wb 118.0; wgns-122.0) | | Wght | Price | Prod |
|---|---|---|---|---|
| L21 | Seneca sdn 2d | 3,530 | 2,397 | |
| L41 | Seneca sdn 4d | 3,600 | 2,449 | 45,737 |
| L45 | Seneca wgn 4d | 3,975 | 2,815 | |
| M21 | Pioneer sdn 2d | 3,540 | 2,530 | |
| M23 | Pioneer htp cpe | 3,610 | 2,607 | |
| M41 | Pioneer sdn 4d | 3,610 | 2,578 | 74,655 |
| M45A | Pioneer wgn 4d, 6P | 4,000 | 2,906 | |
| M45B | Pioneer wgn 4d, 9P | 4,065 | 3,011 | |
| H23 | Phoenix htp cpe | 3,605 | 2,737 | |
| H27 | Phoenix conv cpe | 3,690 | 2,988 | |
| H41 | Phoenix sdn 4d | 3,610 | 2,715 | 66,608 |
| H43 | Phoenix htp sdn | 3,655 | 2,796 | |

| PD1-L Matador (wb 122.0)—27,908 built | | Wght | Price | Prod |
|---|---|---|---|---|
| 23 | htp cpe | 3,705 | 2,996 | — |
| 41 | sdn 4d | 3,725 | 2,930 | — |
| 43 | htp sdn | 3,820 | 3,075 | — |

| | | Wght | Price | Prod |
|---|---|---|---|---|
| 45A | wgn 4d, 6P | 4,045 | 3,239 | — |
| 45B | wgn 4d, 9P | 4,120 | 3,354 | — |

**PD2-H Polara (wb 122.0)—16,728 built**

| | | Wght | Price | Prod |
|---|---|---|---|---|
| 23 | htp cpe | 3,740 | 3,196 | — |
| 27 | conv cpe | 3,765 | 3,416 | — |
| 41 | sdn 4d | 3,735 | 3,141 | — |
| 43 | htp sdn | 3,815 | 3,275 | — |
| 45A | wgn 4d, 6P | 4,085 | 3,506 | — |
| 45B | wgn 4d, 9P | 4,220 | 3,621 | — |

| 1960 Engines | bore×stroke | bhp | availability |
|---|---|---|---|
| L6, 225.0 | 3.40×4.13 | 145 | S-Dart 6 |
| V8, 318.0 | 3.91×3.31 | 230 | S-Seneca, Pioneer V8 |
| V8, 318.0 | 3.91×3.31 | 255 | S-Phoenix V8 |
| V8, 361.0 | 4.12×3.38 | 295 | S-Matador; O-Pioneer, Phoenix |
| V8, 383.0 | 4.25×3.38 | 325 | S-Polara; O-Matador, Phoenix |
| V8, 383.0 | 4.25×3.38 | 330 | O-Polara, Matador, Phoenix |

## 1961

**RW1-L Lancer 170 (wb 106.5)—25,508 built**

| | | Wght | Price | Prod |
|---|---|---|---|---|
| 711 | sdn 2d | 2,585 | 1,979 | — |
| 713 | sdn 4d | 2,595 | 2,041 | — |
| 756 | wgn 4d | 2,760 | 2,354 | — |

**RW1-H Lancer 770 (wb 106.5)—49,268 built**

| | | Wght | Price | Prod |
|---|---|---|---|---|
| 723 | htp cpe | 2,595 | 2,164 | — |
| 731 | spt cpe | 2,643 | 2,075 | — |
| 733 | sdn 4d | 2,605 | 2,137 | — |
| 776 | wgn 4d | 2,775 | 2,449 | — |

**RD3 Dart L6 (wb 118.0; wgns-122.0)**

| | | Wght | Price | Prod |
|---|---|---|---|---|
| L411 | Seneca sdn 2d | 3,290 | 2,278 | |
| L413 | Seneca sdn 4d | 3,335 | 2,330 | 60,527 |
| L456 | Seneca wgn 4d | 3,740 | 2,695 | |
| M421 | Pioneer sdn 2d | 3,290 | 2,410 | |
| M422 | Pioneer htp cpe | 3,335 | 2,488 | |
| M423 | Pioneer sdn 4d | 3,335 | 2,459 | 18,214 |
| M466 | Pioneer wgn 4d, 6P | 3,740 | 2,787 | |
| M467 | Pioneer wgn 4d, 9P | 3,825 | 2,892 | |
| H432 | Phoenix htp cpe | 3,325 | 2,618 | |
| H433 | Phoenix sdn 4d | 3,350 | 2,595 | 4,273 |
| H434 | Phoenix htp sdn | 3,385 | 2,677 | |

**RD4 Dart V8 (wb 118.0; wgns-122.0)**

| | | Wght | Price | Prod |
|---|---|---|---|---|
| L511 | Seneca sdn 2d | 3,470 | 2,397 | |
| L513 | Seneca sdn 4d | 3,515 | 2,449 | 27,174 |
| L556 | Seneca wgn 4d | 3,920 | 2,815 | |
| M521 | Pioneer sdn 2d | 3,460 | 2,530 | |
| M522 | Pioneer htp cpe | 3,500 | 2,607 | |
| M523 | Pioneer sdn 4d | 3,510 | 2,578 | 39,054 |
| M566 | Pioneer wgn 4d, 6P | 3,940 | 2,906 | |
| M567 | Pioneer wgn 4d, 9P | 4,005 | 3,011 | |
| H532 | Phoenix htp cpe | 3,520 | 2,737 | |
| H533 | Phoenix sdn 4d | 3,535 | 2,715 | |
| H534 | Phoenix htp sdn | 3,555 | 2,796 | 34,319 |
| H535 | Phoenix conv cpe | 3,580 | 2,988 | |

**RD1-L Polara (wb 122.0)—14,032 built**

| | | Wght | Price | Prod |
|---|---|---|---|---|
| 542 | htp cpe | 3,690 | 3,032 | — |
| 543 | sdn 4d | 3,700 | 2,966 | — |
| 544 | htp sdn | 3,740 | 3,110 | — |
| 545 | conv cpe | 3,765 | 3,252 | — |
| 578 | wgn 4d, 6P | 4,115 | 3,294 | — |
| 579 | wgn 4d, 9P | 4,125 | 3,409 | — |

| 1961 Engines | bore×stroke | bhp | availability |
|---|---|---|---|
| L6, 170.0 | 3.40×3.13 | 101 | S-Lancer |
| L6, 225.0 | 3.40×4.13 | 145 | S-Dart 6; O-Lancer |
| V8, 318.0 | 3.91×3.31 | 230 | S-Dart V8 |

| | bore×stroke | bhp | availability |
|---|---|---|---|
| V8, 318.0 | 3.91×3.31 | 260 | O-Dart V8 |
| V8, 361.0 | 4.12×3.38 | 265 | S-Polara |
| V8, 361.0 | 4.12×3.38 | 305 | O-Dart V8 (D-500) |
| V8, 383.0 | 4.25×3.38 | 325 | O-Polara (D-500) |
| V8, 383.0 | 4.25×3.38 | 330 | O-Polara, Dart V8 (ram ind) |

## 1962

**SL1-L Lancer 170 (wb 106.5)—19,780 built**

| | | Wght | Price | Prod |
|---|---|---|---|---|
| 711 | sdn 2d | 2,495 | 1,951 | — |
| 713 | sdn 4d | 2,525 | 2,011 | — |
| 756 | wgn 4d | 2,685 | 2,306 | — |

**SL1-H Lancer 770 (wb 106.5)—30,888 built**

| | | Wght | Price | Prod |
|---|---|---|---|---|
| 731 | sdn 2d | 2,520 | 2,052 | — |
| 733 | sdn 4d | 2,540 | 2,114 | — |
| 776 | wgn 4d | 2,705 | 2,408 | — |

**SL1-P Lancer GT (wb 106.5)**

| | | Wght | Price | Prod |
|---|---|---|---|---|
| 742 | htp cpe | 2,560 | 2,257 | 13,683 |

**SD1 Dart L6 (wb 116.0)**

| | | Wght | Price | Prod |
|---|---|---|---|---|
| L401 | Fleet Special sdn 2d | 2,965 | 2,158 | |
| L403 | Fleet Special sdn 4d | 2,995 | 2,214 | |
| L411 | sdn 2d | 2,970 | 2,241 | 43,927 |
| L413 | sdn 4d | 3,000 | 2,297 | |
| L456 | wgn 4d | 3,270 | 2,644 | |
| M421 | 330 sdn 2d | 2,965 | 2,375 | |
| M422 | 330 htp cpe | 2,985 | 2,463 | 11,606 |
| M423 | 330 sdn 4d | 3,000 | 2,432 | |
| M466 | 330 wgn 4d | 3,275 | 2,739 | |
| H432 | 440 htp cpe | 3,025 | 2,606 | 3,942 |
| H433 | 440 sdn 4d | 3,045 | 2,584 | |

**SD2 Dart V8 (wb 116.0)**

| | | Wght | Price | Prod |
|---|---|---|---|---|
| L501 | Fleet Special sdn 2d | 3,130 | 2,316 | |
| L503 | Fleet Special sdn 4d | 3,165 | 2,372 | |
| L511 | sdn 2d | 3,135 | 2,348 | 17,981 |
| L513 | sdn 4d | 3,170 | 2,404 | |
| L556 | wgn 4d | 3,435 | 2,751 | |
| M521 | 330 sdn 2d | 3,135 | 2,482 | |
| M522 | 330 htp cpe | 3,155 | 2,570 | |
| M523 | 330 sdn 4d | 3,170 | 2,540 | 26,544 |
| M566 | 330 wgn 4d, 6P | 3,435 | 2,848 | |
| M567 | 330 wgn 4d, 9P | 3,500 | 2,949 | |
| H532 | 440 htp cpe | 3,185 | 2,713 | |
| H533 | 440 sdn 4d | 3,205 | 2,691 | |
| H534 | 440 htp sdn | 3,260 | 2,763 | |
| H535 | 440 conv cpe | 3,285 | 2,945 | 42,360 |
| H576 | 440 wgn 4d, 6P | 3,460 | 2,989 | |
| H577 | 440 wgn 4d, 9P | 3,530 | 3,092 | |

**SD2-P Polara 500 (wb 116.0)—12,268 built**

| | | Wght | Price | Prod |
|---|---|---|---|---|
| 542 | htp cpe | 3,315 | 3,019 | — |
| 544 | htp sdn | 3,360 | 2,960 | — |
| 545 | conv cpe | 3,430 | 3,268 | — |

**SD3-L Custom 880 (wb 122.0)—17,505 built**

| | | Wght | Price | Prod |
|---|---|---|---|---|
| 612 | htp cpe | 3,615 | 3,030 | — |
| 613 | sdn 4d | 3,655 | 2,964 | — |
| 614 | htp sdn | 3,680 | 3,109 | — |
| 615 | conv cpe | 3,705 | 3,251 | — |
| 658 | wgn 4d, 6P | 4,025 | 3,292 | — |
| 659 | wgn 4d, 9P | 4,055 | 3,407 | — |

| 1962 Engines | bore×stroke | bhp | availability |
|---|---|---|---|
| L6, 170.0 | 3.40×3.13 | 101 | S-Lancer |
| L6, 225.0 | 3.40×4.13 | 145 | S-Dart 6; O-Lancer |
| V8, 318.0 | 3.91×3.31 | 230 | S-Dart V8 |
| V8, 318.0 | 3.91×3.31 | 260 | O-Dart V8 |
| V8, 361.0 | 4.12×3.38 | 265 | S-Custom 880 |
| V8, 361.0 | 4.12×3.38 | 305 | S-Polara 500; O-Dart V8 |

## 1963

### TL1-L Dart 170 (wb 111.0; wgns-106.0)—58,536 built

| | | Wght | Price | Prod |
|---|---|---|---|---|
| 711 | sdn 2d | 2,605 | 1,983 | — |
| 713 | sdn 4d | 2,625 | 2,041 | — |
| 756 | wgn 4d | 2,710 | 2,309 | — |

### TL1-H Dart 270 (wb 111.0; wgns 106.0)—61,159 built

| | | | | |
|---|---|---|---|---|
| 731 | sdn 2d | 2,610 | 2,079 | — |
| 733 | sdn 4d | 2,635 | 2,135 | — |
| 735 | conv cpe | 2,740 | 2,385 | — |
| 776 | wgn 4d | 2,735 | 2,433 | — |

### TL1-P Dart GT (wb 111.0)—34,227 built

| | | | | |
|---|---|---|---|---|
| 742 | htp cpe | 2,690 | 2,289 | — |
| 745 | conv cpe | 2,765 | 2,512 | — |

### TD1-L 330 L6 (wb 119.0; wgns-116.0)—51,761 built

| | | | | |
|---|---|---|---|---|
| 401 | Fleet Special sdn 2d | 3,040 | 2,205 | — |
| 403 | Fleet Special sdn 4d | 3,065 | 2,261 | — |
| 411 | sdn 2d | 3,050 | 2,245 | — |
| 413 | sdn 4d | 3,070 | 2,301 | — |
| 456 | wgn 4d, 2S | 3,320 | 2,648 | — |
| 457 | wgn 4d, 3S | 3,380 | 2,749 | — |

### TD1-M 440 L6 (wb 119.0; wgns-116.0)—13,146 built

| | | | | |
|---|---|---|---|---|
| 421 | sdn 2d | 3,050 | 2,381 | — |
| 422 | htp cpe | 3,050 | 2,470 | — |
| 423 | sdn 4d | 3,075 | 2,438 | — |

### TD1-H Polara L6 (wb 119.0)—68,262 built

| | | | | |
|---|---|---|---|---|
| 432 | htp cpe | 3,105 | 2,624 | — |
| 433 | sdn 4d | 3,105 | 2,602 | — |

### TD2-L 330 V8 (wb 119.0; wgns 116.0)—33,602 built

| | | | | |
|---|---|---|---|---|
| 601 | Fleet Special sdn 2d | 3,310 | 2,313 | — |
| 603 | Fleet Special sdn 4d | 3,335 | 2,369 | — |
| 611 | sdn 2d | 3,220 | 2,352 | — |
| 613 | sdn 4d | 3,245 | 2,408 | — |
| 656 | wgn 4d, 2S | 3,490 | 2,756 | — |
| 657 | wgn 4d, 3S | 3,550 | 2,857 | — |

### TD2-M 440 V8 (wb 119.0; wgns 116.0)—49,591 built

| | | | | |
|---|---|---|---|---|
| 621 | sdn 2d | 3,215 | 2,489 | — |
| 622 | htp cpe | 3,245 | 2,577 | — |
| 623 | sdn 4d | 3,250 | 2,546 | — |
| 666 | wgn 4d, 2S | 3,495 | 2,854 | — |
| 667 | wgn 4d, 3S | 3,555 | 2,956 | — |

### TD2-H Polara V8 (wb 119.0)—40,323 built

| | | | | |
|---|---|---|---|---|
| 632 | htp cpe | 3,255 | 2,732 | — |
| 633 | sdn 4d | 3,275 | 2,709 | — |
| 634 | htp sdn | 3,330 | 2,781 | — |
| 635 | conv cpe | 3,340 | 2,963 | — |

### TD2-P Polara 500 V8 (wb 119.0)—7,256 built

| | | | | |
|---|---|---|---|---|
| 642 | htp cpe | 3,375 | 2,965 | — |
| 645 | conv cpe | 3,455 | 3,196 | — |

### TA3 880 V8 (wb 122.0)

| | | Wght | Price | Prod |
|---|---|---|---|---|
| E503 | sdn 4d | 3,800 | 2,815 | 9,831 |
| E556 | wgn 4d, 6P | 4,145 | 3,142 | |
| E557 | wgn 4d, 9P | 4,175 | 3,257 | |
| L512 | Custom htp cpe | 3,825 | 3,030 | 18,435 |
| L513 | Custom sdn 4d | 3,815 | 2,964 | |
| L514 | Custom htp sdn | 3,840 | 3,109 | |
| L515 | Custom conv cpe | 3,845 | 3,251 | |
| L558 | Custom htp wgn 4d, 2S | 4,160 | 3,292 | |
| L559 | Custom htp wgn 4d, 3S | 4,186 | 3,407 | |

### 1963 Engines

| | bore×stroke | bhp | availability |
|---|---|---|---|
| L6, 170.0 | 3.40×3.13 | 101 | S-Dart |
| L6, 225.0 | 3.40×4.13 | 145 | S-330/440/Polara 6; O-Dart |
| V8, 318.0 | 3.91×3.31 | 230 | S-330, 440, Polara V8 |
| V8, 361.0 | 4.13×3.38 | 265 | S-880, Custom 880 |
| V8, 383.0 | 4.25×3.38 | 305 | S-Polara 500; O-others exc Dart |
| V8, 383.0 | 4.25×3.38 | 230 | O-all exc Dart |
| V8, 413.0 | 4.19×3.75 | 360 | O-880, Custom 880 |
| V8, 426.0 | 4.25×3.75 | 415/425 | O-all exc Dart (ram ind) |

## 1964

### VL1-L Dart 170 (wb 111.0; wgns-106.0)

| | | Wght | Price | Prod |
|---|---|---|---|---|
| 711 | sdn 2d | 2,615 | 1,988 | L6: 74,625 |
| 713 | sdn 4d | 2,640 | 2,053 | V8: 2,509 |
| 756 | wgn 4d, 2S | 2,740 | 2,315 | |

### VL1-H Dart 270 (wb 111.0; wgns-106.0)

| | | | | |
|---|---|---|---|---|
| 731 | sdn 2d | 2,625 | 2,094 | L6: 58,972 |
| 733 | sdn 4d | 2,645 | 2,160 | V8: 7,097 |
| 735 | conv cpe | 2,735 | 2,389 | |
| 776 | wgn 4d, 2S | 2,745 | 2,414 | |

### VL1-P Dart GT (wb 111.0)

| | | | | |
|---|---|---|---|---|
| 742 | htp cpe | 2,670 | 2,318 | L6: 37,660 |
| 745 | conv cpe | 2,770 | 2,536 | V8: 12,170 |

### VD1-L 330 L6 (wb 119.0; wgns-116.0)—57,957 built

| | | | | |
|---|---|---|---|---|
| 411 | sdn 2d | 3,115 | 2,264 | — |
| 413 | sdn 4d | 3,145 | 2,317 | — |
| 456 | wgn 4d, 2S | 3,400 | 2,654 | — |
| 457 | wgn 4d, 3S | 3,475 | 2,755 | — |

### VD1-M 440 L6 (wb 119.0)—15,147 built

| | | | | |
|---|---|---|---|---|
| 421 | sdn 2d | 3,110 | 2,401 | — |
| 422 | htp cpe | 3,120 | 2,483 | — |
| 423 | sdn 4d | 3,145 | 2,454 | — |

### VD1-H Polara L6 (wb 119.0)—3,810 built

| | | | | |
|---|---|---|---|---|
| 432 | htp cpe | 3,135 | 2,637 | — |
| 433 | sdn 4d | 3,170 | 2,615 | — |

### VD2-L 330 V8 (wb 119.0; wgns-116.0)—46,438 built

| | | | | |
|---|---|---|---|---|
| 611 | sdn 2d | 3,285 | 2,372 | — |
| 613 | sdn 4d | 3,325 | 2,424 | — |
| 656 | wgn 4d, 2S | 3,570 | 2,762 | — |
| 657 | wgn 4d, 3S | 3,620 | 2,863 | — |

### VD2-M 440 V8 (wb 119.0; wgns-116.0)—68,861 built

| | | | | |
|---|---|---|---|---|
| 621 | sdn 2d | 3,280 | 2,508 | — |
| 622 | htp cpe | 3,295 | 2,590 | — |
| 623 | sdn 4d | 3,330 | 2,562 | — |
| 666 | wgn 4d, 2S | 3,585 | 2,861 | — |
| 667 | wgn 4d, 3S | 3,640 | 2,962 | — |

### VD2-H Polara V8 (wb 119.0)—66,988 built

| | | | | |
|---|---|---|---|---|
| 632 | htp cpe | 3,320 | 2,745 | — |
| 633 | sdn 4d | 3,365 | 2,722 | — |
| 634 | htp sdn | 3,395 | 2,794 | — |
| 645 | conv cpe | 3,435 | 2,994 | — |

### VD2-P Polara 500 V8 (wb 119.0)—discont'd—17,787 built

| | | | | |
|---|---|---|---|---|
| 642 | htp cpe | 3,340 | 2,978 | — |
| 645 | conv cpe | 3,550 | 3,227 | — |

### VA3 880 V8 (wb 122.0)

| | | | | |
|---|---|---|---|---|
| E513 | sdn 4d | 3,795 | 2,826 | 10,526 |
| E556 | wgn 4d, 6P | 4,165 | 3,155 | |
| E557 | wgn 4d, 9P | 4,185 | 3,270 | |
| L522 | Custom htp cpe | 3,765 | 3,043 | 21,234 |
| L523 | Custom sdn 4d | 3,825 | 2,977 | |
| L524 | Custom htp sdn | 3,860 | 3,122 | |
| L525 | Custom conv cpe | 3,850 | 3,264 | |
| L568 | Custom htp wgn 4d, 2S | 4,155 | 3,305 | |
| L569 | Custom htp wgn 4d, 3S | 4,185 | 3,420 | |

| 1964 Engines | bore×stroke | bhp | availability |
|---|---|---|---|
| L6, 170.0 | 3.40×3.13 | 101 | S-Dart |
| L6, 225.0 | 3.40×4.13 | 145 | S-330/440/Polara 6;O-Dart |
| V8, 273.5 | 3.63×3.31 | 180 | O-Dart |
| V8, 318.0 | 3.91×3.31 | 230 | S-330, 440, Polara V8 |
| V8, 361.0 | 4.13×3.38 | 265 | S-880, Custom 880 |
| V8, 383.0 | 4.25×3.38 | 305/ 330 | O-all exc Dart |
| V8, 426.0 | 4.25×3.75 | 365 | O-all exc Dart |
| V8, 426.0 | 4.25×3.75 | 415/425 | O-all exc Dart (ram ind) |

## 1965

**AL1-L Dart 170 (wb 111.0; wgns-106.0)— 86,013 built**

| | | Wght | Price | Prod |
|---|---|---|---|---|
| L11 | sdn 2d | 2,645 | 2,074 | — |
| L13 | sdn 4d | 2,660 | 2,139 | — |
| L56 | wgn 4d | 2,770 | 2,407 | — |

**AL1-H Dart 270 (wb 111.0; wgns 106.0)—78,245 built**

| L31 | sdn 2d | 2,650 | 2,180 | — |
|---|---|---|---|---|
| L32 | htp cpe | 2,675 | 2,274 | — |
| L33 | sdn 4d | 2,670 | 2,247 | — |
| L35 | conv cpe | 2,765 | 2,481 | — |
| L76 | wgn 4d | 2,770 | 2,506 | — |

**AL1-P Dart GT (wb 111.0)—45,118 built**

| L42 | htp cpe | 2,715 | 2,404 | — |
|---|---|---|---|---|
| L45 | conv cpe | 2,795 | 2,628 | — |

**AW1-L Coronet L6 (wb 117.0; wgns-116.0)\***

| W11 | Deluxe sdn 2d | 3,090 | 2,257 | — |
|---|---|---|---|---|
| W13 | Deluxe sdn 4d | 3,140 | 2,296 | — |
| W21 | sdn 2d | 3,070 | 2,217 | — |
| W23 | sdn 4d | 3,095 | 2,256 | — |
| W56 | Deluxe wgn 4d | 3,390 | 2,592 | — |

**AW2-H Coronet 440 L6 (wb 117.0; wgns-116.0)\***

| W32 | htp cpe | 3,100 | 2,403 | — |
|---|---|---|---|---|
| W33 | sdn 4d | 3,125 | 2,377 | — |
| W35 | conv cpe | 3,230 | 2,622 | — |
| W76 | wgn 4d | 3,395 | 2,674 | — |

**AW2-L Coronet V8 (wb 117.0; wgns-116.0)\***

| W01 | Hemi-Charger sdn 2d | 3,165 | — | — |
|---|---|---|---|---|
| W11 | Deluxe sdn 2d | 3,160 | 2,353 | — |
| W13 | Deluxe sdn 4d | 3,210 | 2,392 | — |
| W21 | sdn 2d | 3,145 | 2,313 | — |
| W23 | sdn 4d | 3,195 | 2,352 | — |
| W56 | Deluxe wgn 4d | 3,470 | 2,688 | — |

**AW2-H Coronet 440 V8 (wb 117.0; wgns-116.0)\***

| W32 | htp cpe | 3,180 | 2,499 | — |
|---|---|---|---|---|
| W33 | sdn 4d | 3,230 | 2,473 | — |
| W35 | conv cpe | 3,295 | 2,718 | — |
| W76 | wgn 4d, 6P | 3,490 | 2,770 | — |
| W77 | wgn 4d, 9P | 3,560 | 2,868 | — |

**AW2-P Coronet 500 V8 (wb 117.0)—32,745 built**

| W42 | htp cpe | 3,255 | 2,674 | — |
|---|---|---|---|---|
| W45 | conv cpe | 3,340 | 2,894 | — |

**AW2-L Polara V8 (wb 121.0)—12,705 built**

| D12 | htp cpe | 3,850 | 2,837 | — |
|---|---|---|---|---|
| D13 | sdn 4d | 3,905 | 2,806 | — |
| D14 | htp sdn | 3,965 | 2,913 | — |
| D15 | conv cpe | 3,940 | 3,131 | — |
| D23 | sdn 4d (318) | 3,847 | 2,730 | — |
| D56 | wgn 4d, 6P | 4,220 | 3,153 | — |
| D57 | wgn 4d, 9P | 4,255 | 3,259 | — |

**AD2-H Custom 880 V8 (wb 121.0)—44,496 built**

| D32 | htp cpe | 3,945 | 3,085 | — |
|---|---|---|---|---|
| D34 | htp sdn | 4,155 | 3,150 | — |

| | | Wght | Price | Prod |
|---|---|---|---|---|
| D35 | conv cpe | 3,965 | 3,335 | — |
| D38 | sdn 4d | 3,915 | 3,010 | — |
| D76 | wgn 4d, 6P | 4,270 | 3,422 | — |
| D77 | wgn 4d, 9P | 4,355 | 3,527 | — |

**AD2-P Monaco V8 (wb 121.0)**

| D42 | htp cpe | 4,000 | 3,355 | 13,096 |
|---|---|---|---|---|

*Combined L6 and V8 production: Coronet 71,880; Coronet 440 104,767.

| 1965 Engines | bore×stroke | bhp | availability |
|---|---|---|---|
| L6, 170.0 | 3.40×3.13 | 101 | S-Dart |
| L6, 225.0 | 3.40×4.13 | 145 | S-Coronet/440 6; O-Dart |
| V8, 273.5 | 3.63×3.31 | 180 | S-Coronet/440/500 V8s; O-Dart |
| V8, 273.5 | 3.63×3.31 | 235 | O-Coronet/440/500 V8s, Dart |
| V8, 318.0 | 3.91×3.31 | 230 | O-Coronet/440/500 V8s |
| V8, 361.0 | 4.12×3.38 | 265 | O-Coronet/440/500 V8s |
| V8, 383.0 | 4.25×3.38 | 315 | S-Monaco; O-Coronets |
| V8, 383.0 | 4.25×3.38 | 270 | S-Polara, Custom 880 |
| V8, 383.0 | 4.25×3.38 | 330 | O-Coronet, 440, 500 V8s |
| V8, 413.0 | 4.19×3.75 | 340 | O-Polara, Custom 880, Monaco |
| V8, 426.0 | 4.25×3.75 | 365 | S-Hemi-Charger; O-others |
| V8, 426.0 | 4.25×3.75 | 425 | S-Hemi-Charger 425 |

## 1966

**BLL Dart (wb 111.0; wgns-106.0)— 75,990 built**

| | | Wght | Price | Prod |
|---|---|---|---|---|
| 1-21 | sdn 2d, L6 | 2,670 | 2,094 | — |
| 2-21 | sdn 2d, V8 | 2,860 | 2,222 | — |
| 1-41 | sdn 4d, L6 | 2,695 | 2,158 | — |
| 2-41 | sdn 4d, V8 | 2,895 | 2,286 | — |
| 1-45 | wgn 4d, L6 | 2,780 | 2,436 | — |
| 2-45 | wgn 4d, V8 | 2,990 | 2,564 | — |

**BLH Dart 270 (wb 111.0; wgns 106.0)—69,996 built**

| 1-23 | htp cpe, L6 | 2,720 | 2,307 | — |
|---|---|---|---|---|
| 2-23 | htp cpe, V8 | 2,890 | 2,435 | — |
| 1-27 | conv cpe, L6 | 2,805 | 2,570 | — |
| 2-27 | conv cpe, V8 | 2,995 | 2,698 | — |
| 1-41 | sdn 4d, L6 | 2,680 | 2,280 | — |
| 2-41 | sdn 4d, V8 | 2,895 | 2,408 | — |
| 1-45 | wgn 4d, L6 | 2,795 | 2,533 | — |
| 2-45 | wgn 4d, V8 | 3,020 | 2,661 | — |

**BLP Dart GT (wb 111.0)—30,041 built**

| 1-23 | htp cpe, L6 | 2,735 | 2,417 | — |
|---|---|---|---|---|
| 2-23 | htp cpe, V8 | 2,915 | 2,545 | — |
| 1-27 | conv cpe, L6 | 2,830 | 2,700 | — |
| 2-27 | conv cpe, V8 | 2,995 | 2,828 | — |

**BWL Coronet (wb 117.0)—66,161 built**

| 1-21 | sdn 2d, L6 | 3,055 | 2,264 | — |
|---|---|---|---|---|
| 2-21 | sdn 2d, V8 | 3,215 | 2,358 | — |
| 1-41 | sdn 4d, L6 | 3,077 | 2,306 | — |
| 2-41 | sdn 4d, V8 | 3,245 | 2,396 | — |
| 1-21 | Deluxe sdn 2d, L6 | 3,050 | 2,303 | — |
| 2-21 | Deluxe sdn 2d, V8 | 3,215 | 2,391 | — |
| 1-41 | Deluxe sdn 4d, L6 | 3,075 | 2,341 | — |
| 2-41 | Deluxe sdn 4d, V8 | 3,240 | 2,435 | — |
| 1-45 | Deluxe wgn 2d, L6 | 3,480 | 2,631 | — |
| 2-45 | Deluxe wgn 2d, V8 | 3,595 | 2,725 | — |

**BWH Coronet 440 (wb 117.0)—128,998 built**

| 1-23 | htp cpe, L6 | 3,075 | 2,457 | — |
|---|---|---|---|---|
| 2-23 | htp cpe, V8 | 3,235 | 2,551 | — |
| 1-27 | conv cpe, L6 | 3,185 | 2,672 | — |
| 2-27 | conv cpe, V8 | 3,310 | 2,766 | — |
| 1-41 | sdn 4d, L6 | 3,095 | 2,432 | — |
| 2-41 | sdn 4d, V8 | 3,220 | 2,526 | — |
| 1-45 | wgn 4d, L6 | 3,515 | 2,722 | — |
| 2-45 | wgn 4d, 2S, V8 | 3,585 | 2,816 | — |

| | | Wght | Price | Prod |
|---|---|---|---|---|
| 2-46 | wgn 4d, 3S, V8 | 3,680 | 2,926 | — |

**BWP Coronet 500 (wb 117.0)—55,683 built**

| | | Wght | Price | Prod |
|---|---|---|---|---|
| 1-23 | htp cpe, L6 | 3,115 | 2,611 | — |
| 2-23 | htp cpe, V8 | 3,275 | 2,705 | — |
| 1-27 | conv cpe, L6 | 3,180 | 2,827 | — |
| 2-27 | conv cpe, V8 | 3,345 | 2,921 | — |
| 1-41 | sdn 4d, L6 | 3,120 | 2,586 | — |
| 2-41 | sdn 4d, V8 | 3,280 | 2,680 | — |

**BX2-P Charger (wb 117.0)**

| | | Wght | Price | Prod |
|---|---|---|---|---|
| 29 | htp cpe 4P | 3,499 | 3,122 | 37,344 |

**BD2-L Polara (wb 121.0)—107,832 built**

| | | Wght | Price | Prod |
|---|---|---|---|---|
| 23 | htp cpe | 3,820 | 2,874 | — |
| 27 | conv cpe | 3,885 | 3,161 | — |
| 41 | sdn 4d | 3,860 | 2,838 | — |
| 41 | sdn 4d (318) | 3,765 | 2,763 | — |
| 43 | htp sdn | 3,880 | 2,948 | — |
| 45 | wgn 4d, 2S | 4,265 | 3,183 | — |
| 46 | wgn 4d, 3S | 4,295 | 3,286 | — |

**BD2-H Monaco (wb 121.0)—49,773 built**

| | | Wght | Price | Prod |
|---|---|---|---|---|
| 23 | htp cpe | 3,855 | 3,107 | — |
| 41 | sdn 4d | 3,890 | 3,033 | — |
| 43 | htp sdn | 4,835 | 3,170 | — |
| 45 | wgn 4d, 2S | 4,270 | 3,436 | — |
| 46 | wgn 4d, 3S | 4,315 | 3,539 | — |

**BD2-P Monaco 500 (wb 121.0)**

| | | Wght | Price | Prod |
|---|---|---|---|---|
| 23 | htp cpe | 3,895 | 3,604 | 10,840 |

| 1966 Engines | bore×stroke | bhp | availability |
|---|---|---|---|
| L6, 170.0 | 3.40×3.13 | 101 | S-Dart 6s |
| L6, 225.0 | 3.40×4.13 | 145 | S-Coronet 6; O-Dart 6 |
| V8, 273.5 | 3.63×3.31 | 180 | S-Coronet V8, Dart V8 |
| V8, 273.5 | 3.63×3.31 | 235 | O-Dart V8 |
| V8, 318.0 | 3.91×3.31 | 230 | S-Chrgr; O-Cor V8, Pol 318 sdn 4d |
| V8, 361.0 | 4.13×3.38 | 265 | O-Charger, Coronet V8 |
| V8, 383.0 | 4.25×3.38 | 270 | S-Pol, Pol 500, Mon; O-Mon 500 |
| V8, 383.0 | 4.25×3.38 | 325 | S-Monaco 500; O-all exc Dart |
| V8, 426.0 | 4.25×3.75 | 425 | O-Charger (max perf cam avail) |
| V8, 440.0 | 4.32×3.75 | 350 | O-Pol, Pol 500, Mon, Mon 500 |

# 1967

**CLL Dart (wb 111.0)—53,043 built**

| | | Wght | Price | Prod |
|---|---|---|---|---|
| 1-21 | sdn 2d, L6 | 2,710 | 2,187 | — |
| 2-21 | sdn 2d, V8 | 2,895 | 2,315 | — |
| 1-41 | sdn 4d, L6 | 2,725 | 2,224 | — |
| 2-41 | sdn 4d, V8 | 2,910 | 2,352 | — |

**CLH Dart 270 (wb 111.0)—63,227 built**

| | | Wght | Price | Prod |
|---|---|---|---|---|
| 1-23 | htp cpe, L6 | 2,725 | 2,388 | — |
| 2-23 | htp cpe, V8 | 2,910 | 2,516 | — |
| 1-41 | sdn 4d, L6 | 2,735 | 2,362 | — |
| 2-41 | sdn 4d, V8 | 2,915 | 2,490 | — |

**CLP Dart GT (wb 111.0)—38,225 built**

| | | Wght | Price | Prod |
|---|---|---|---|---|
| 1-23 | htp cpe, L6 | 2,750 | 2,499 | — |
| 2-23 | htp cpe, V8 | 2,930 | 2,627 | — |
| 1-27 | conv cpe, L6 | 2,850 | 2,732 | — |
| 2-27 | conv cpe, V8 | 3,030 | 2,860 | — |

**CWE Coronet (wb 117.0)—4,933 built**

| | | Wght | Price | Prod |
|---|---|---|---|---|
| 1-45 | wgn 4d, L6 | 3,485 | 2,622 | — |
| 2-45 | wgn 4d, V8 | 3,650 | 2,716 | — |

**CWL Coronet Deluxe (wb 117.0)—29,022 built**

| | | Wght | Price | Prod |
|---|---|---|---|---|
| 1-21 | sdn 2d, L6 | 3,045 | 2,359 | — |
| 2-21 | sdn 2d, V8 | 3,210 | 2,453 | — |

| | | Wght | Price | Prod |
|---|---|---|---|---|
| 1-41 | sdn 4d, L6 | 3,070 | 2,397 | — |
| 2-41 | sdn 4d, V8 | 3,235 | 2,491 | — |
| 1-45 | wgn 2d, L6 | 3,495 | 2,693 | — |
| 2-45 | wgn 2d, V8 | 3,625 | 2,787 | — |

**CWH Coronet 440 (wb 117.0)—106,368 built**

| | | Wght | Price | Prod |
|---|---|---|---|---|
| 1-23 | htp cpe, L6 | 3,065 | 2,500 | — |
| 2-23 | htp cpe, V8 | 3,235 | 2,594 | — |
| 1-27 | conv cpe, L6 | 3,140 | 2,740 | — |
| 2-27 | conv cpe, V8 | 3,305 | 2,834 | — |
| 1-41 | sdn 4d, L6 | 3,060 | 2,475 | — |
| 2-41 | sdn 4d, V8 | 3,225 | 2,569 | — |
| 1-45 | wgn 4d, L6 | 3,495 | 2,771 | — |
| 2-45 | wgn 4d, 2S, V8 | 3,605 | 2,865 | — |
| 2-46 | wgn 4d, 3S, V8 | 3,705 | 2,975 | — |

**CWP Coronet 500 (wb 117.0)—39,260 built (includes R/T)**

| | | Wght | Price | Prod |
|---|---|---|---|---|
| 1-23 | htp cpe, L6 | 3,115 | 2,679 | — |
| 2-23 | htp cpe, V8 | 3,280 | 2,773 | — |
| 1-27 | conv cpe, L6 | 3,190 | 2,919 | — |
| 2-27 | conv cpe, V8 | 3,355 | 3,013 | — |
| 1-41 | sdn 4d, L6 | 3,075 | 2,654 | — |
| 2-41 | sdn 4d, V8 | 3,235 | 2,748 | — |

**CW2-P Coronet R/T (wb 117.0)**

| | | Wght | Price | Prod |
|---|---|---|---|---|
| 23 | htp cpe, V8 | 3,565 | 3,199 | — |
| 27 | conv cpe, V8 | 3,640 | 3,438 | — |

**CW2-P Charger (wb 117.0)**

| | | Wght | Price | Prod |
|---|---|---|---|---|
| 29 | htp cpe 4P, V8 | 3,480 | 3,128 | 15,788 |

**CD2-L Polara (wb 122.0)—69,798 built**

| | | Wght | Price | Prod |
|---|---|---|---|---|
| 23 | htp cpe | 3,870 | 2,953 | — |
| 27 | conv cpe | 3,930 | 3,241 | — |
| 41 | sdn 4d | 3,885 | 2,915 | — |
| 41 | sdn 4d (318) | 3,765 | 2,843 | — |
| 43 | htp sdn | 3,920 | 3,028 | — |
| 45 | wgn 4d, 2S | 4,440 | 3,265 | — |
| 46 | wgn 4d, 3S | 4,450 | 3,368 | — |

**CD2-M Polara 500 (wb 122.0)—5,606 built**

| | | Wght | Price | Prod |
|---|---|---|---|---|
| 23 | htp cpe | 3,880 | 3,155 | — |
| 27 | conv cpe | 3,940 | 3,443 | — |

**CD2-H Monaco (wb 122.0)—35,225 built**

| | | Wght | Price | Prod |
|---|---|---|---|---|
| 23 | htp cpe | 3,885 | 3,213 | — |
| 41 | sdn 4d | 3,895 | 3,138 | — |
| 43 | htp sdn | 3,945 | 3,275 | — |
| 45 | wgn 4d, 2S | 4,425 | 3,543 | — |
| 46 | wgn 4d, 3S | 4,475 | 3,646 | — |

**CD2-P Monaco 500 (wb 122.0)**

| | | Wght | Price | Prod |
|---|---|---|---|---|
| 23 | htp cpe | 3,970 | 3,712 | 5,237 |

| 1967 Engines | bore×stroke | bhp | availability |
|---|---|---|---|
| L6, 170.0 | 3.40×3.13 | 115 | S-Dart 6 |
| L6, 225.0 | 3.40×4.13 | 145 | S-Coronet 6; O-Dart 6 |
| V8, 273.5 | 3.63×3.31 | 180 | S-Dart V8, Coronet V8 |
| V8, 273.5 | 3.63×3.31 | 235 | O-Dart V8 |
| V8, 318.0 | 3.91×3.31 | 230 | S-Chrgr, Polara 318; O-Cor V8 |
| V8, 383.0 | 4.25×3.38 | 270 | S-Polara, Monaco; O-Cor, Mon 500 |
| V8, 383.0 | 4.25×3.38 | 325 | S-Mon 500; O-Cor, Chrgr, Pol, Mon |
| V8, 426.0 | 4.25×3.75 | 425 | O-Coronet R/T, Charger |
| V8, 440.0 | 4.32×3.75 | 350 | O-Polara, Monaco |
| V8, 440.0 | 4.32×3.75 | 375 | S-Cor R/T; O-Chrgr, Pol, Mon |

# 1968

**DLL Dart (wb 111.0)—60,250 built**

| | | Wght | Price | Prod |
|---|---|---|---|---|
| 1-21 | sdn 2d, L6 | 2,705 | 2,323 | — |
| 2-21 | sdn 2d, V8 | 2,875 | 2,451 | — |

| | | Wght | Price | Prod |
|---|---|---|---|---|
| 1-41 | sdn 4d, L6 | 2,725 | 2,360 | — |
| 2-41 | sdn 4d, V8 | 2,900 | 2,488 | — |
| **DLH Dart 270 (wb 111.0)—76,497 built** | | | | |
| 1-23 | htp cpe, L6 | 2,725 | 2,525 | — |
| 2-23 | htp cpe, V8 | 2,885 | 2,653 | — |
| 1-41 | sdn 4d, L6 | 2,710 | 2,499 | — |
| 2-41 | sdn 4d, V8 | 2,900 | 2,627 | — |
| **DLP Dart GT (wb 111.0)—26,280 built** | | | | |
| 1-23 | htp cpe, L6 | 2,715 | 2,637 | — |
| 2-23 | htp cpe, V8 | 2,895 | 2,675 | — |
| 1-27 | conv cpe, L6 | 2,790 | 2,831 | — |
| 2-27 | conv cpe, V8 | 2,970 | 2,959 | — |
| **DL2-S Dart GTS (wb 110.0)—8,745 built** | | | | |
| 23 | htp cpe, V8 | 3,065 | 3,189 | — |
| 27 | conv cpe, V8 | 3,150 | 3,383 | — |
| **DWL Coronet Deluxe (wb 117.0)—46,299 built** | | | | |
| 1-21 | cpe, L6 | 3,015 | 2,487 | — |
| 2-21 | cpe, V8 | 3,200 | 2,581 | — |
| 1-41 | sdn 4d, L6 | 3,035 | 2,525 | — |
| 2-41 | sdn 4d, V8 | 3,220 | 2,619 | — |
| 1-45 | wgn 4d, L6 | 3,455 | 2,816 | — |
| 2-45 | wgn 4d, V8 | 3,590 | 2,910 | — |
| **DWH Coronet 440 (wb 117.0)—116,348 built (includes Super Bee)** | | | | |
| 1-21 | cpe, L6 | 3,015 | 2,565 | — |
| 2-21 | cpe, V8 | 3,200 | 2,671 | — |
| 1-23 | htp cpe, L6 | 3,040 | 2,627 | — |
| 2-23 | htp cpe, V8 | 3,225 | 2,733 | — |
| 1-41 | sdn 4d, L6 | 3,035 | 2,603 | — |
| 2-41 | sdn 4d, V8 | 3,320 | 2,709 | — |
| 1-45 | wgn 4d, L6 | 3,450 | 2,924 | — |
| 2-45 | wgn 4d, 2S, V8 | 3,585 | 3,030 | — |
| 2-46 | wgn 4d, 3S, V8 | 3,680 | 3,140 | — |
| **DWH Coronet Super Bee (wb 117.0)** | | | | |
| M-21 | cpe, V8 | 3,395 | 3,027 | — |
| **DW2-P Coronet 500 (wb 117.0)—40,139 built** | | | | |
| 23 | htp cpe, V8 | 3,260 | 2,879 | — |
| 27 | conv cpe, V8 | 3,360 | 3,036 | — |
| 41 | sdn 4d, V8 | 3,240 | 2,912 | — |
| 45 | wgn 4d, 2S, V8 | 3,610 | 3,212 | — |
| 46 | wgn 4d, 3S, V8 | 3,700 | 3,322 | — |
| **DW2-S Coronet R/T (wb 117.0)—10,849 built** | | | | |
| 23 | htp cpe, V8 | 3,530 | 3,379 | — |
| 27 | conv cpe, V8 | 3,630 | 3,613 | — |
| **DX1-S Charger (wb 117.0)—96,108 built** | | | | |
| 1P-29 | htp cpe 4P, L6 | 3,100 | 2,934 | — |
| 2P-29 | htp cpe 4P, V8 | 3,305 | 3,040 | — |
| 2X-29 | R/T htp cpe, 4P, V8 | 3,575 | 3,506 | — |
| **DD2-L Polara (wb 122.0)—99,055 built** | | | | |
| 23 | htp cpe | 3,700 | 3,027 | — |
| 27 | conv cpe | 3,755 | 3,288 | — |
| 41 | sdn 4d | 3,735 | 3,005 | — |
| 43 | htp sdn | 3,755 | 3,100 | — |
| 45 | wgn 4d, 2S | 4,155 | 3,388 | — |
| 46 | wgn 4d, 3S | 4,210 | 3,454 | — |
| **DD2-M Polara 500 (wb 122.0)—4,983 built** | | | | |
| 23 | htp cpe | 3,740 | 3,226 | — |
| 27 | conv cpe | 3,780 | 3,487 | — |
| **DD2-H Monaco (wb 122.0)—37,412 built** | | | | |
| 23 | htp cpe | 3,845 | 3,369 | — |
| 41 | sdn 4d | 3,885 | 3,294 | — |

| | | Wght | Price | Prod |
|---|---|---|---|---|
| 43 | htp sdn | 3,910 | 3,432 | — |
| 45 | wgn 4d, 2S | 4,295 | 3,702 | — |
| 46 | wgn 4d, 3S | 4,360 | 3,835 | — |
| **DD2-P Monaco 500 (wb 122.0)** | | | | |
| 23 | htp cpe | 3,885 | 3,869 | 4,568 |

| 1968 Engines | bore×stroke | bhp | availability |
|---|---|---|---|
| L6, 170.0 | 3.40×3.13 | 115 | S-Dart 6 |
| L6, 225.0 | 3.40×4.13 | 145 | S-Coronet 6; O-Dart 6 |
| V8, 273.5 | 3.63×3.31 | 190 | S-Dart V8, Coronet V8 |
| V8, 318.0 | 3.91×3.31 | 230 | S-Chrgr, Pol; O-Dart V8, Cor V8 |
| V8, 340.0 | 4.04×3.31 | 275 | S-Dart GTS |
| V8, 383.0 | 4.25×3.38 | 300 | O-Dart GTS |
| V8, 383.0 | 4.25×3.38 | 290 | S-Mon; O-Cor V8, Chrgr, Pol |
| V8, 383.0 | 4.25×3.38 | 330 | O-Cor V8, Chrgr, Pol, Mon |
| V8, 383.0 | 4.25×3.38 | 335 | S-Coronet Super Bee |
| V8, 426.0 | 4.25×3.75 | 425 | O-Cor R/T, Chrgr R/T; S-Chrgr Dayt |
| V8, 440.0 | 4.32×3.75 | 350 | O-Polara & Monaco wgns |
| V8, 440.0 | 4.32×3.75 | 375 | S-Cor R/T, Chrgr R/T; O-Pol, Mon |

## 1969

| **LL Dart (wb 111.0)—106,329 built (includes Swinger 340)** | | Wght | Price | Prod |
|---|---|---|---|---|
| 23 | Swinger htp cpe | 2,795 | 2,400 | — |
| 41 | sdn 4d | 2,810 | 2,413 | — |
| **LM Dart Swinger 340 (wb 111.0)** | | | | |
| 23 | htp cpe | 3,097 | 2,836 | — |
| **LH Dart Custom (wb 110.0)—63,740 built** | | | | |
| 23 | htp cpe | 2,795 | 2,577 | — |
| 41 | sdn 4d | 2,810 | 2,550 | — |
| **LP Dart GT (wb 111.0)—20,914 built** | | | | |
| 23 | htp cpe | 2,800 | 2,672 | — |
| 27 | conv cpe | 2,905 | 2,865 | — |
| **LS Dart GTS V8 (wb 110.0)—6,702 built** | | | | |
| 23 | htp cpe | 3,105 | 3,226 | — |
| 27 | conv cpe | 3,210 | 3,419 | — |
| **WL Coronet Deluxe (wb 117.0)—23,988 built** | | | | |
| 21 | cpe | 3,067 | 2,554 | — |
| 41 | sdn 4d | 3,097 | 2,589 | — |
| 45 | wgn 4d | 3,552 | 2,922 | — |
| **WH Coronet 440 (wb 117.0)—105,882 built** | | | | |
| 21 | cpe | 3,067 | 2,630 | — |
| 23 | htp cpe | 3,097 | 2,692 | — |
| 41 | sdn 4d | 3,102 | 2,670 | — |
| 45 | wgn 4d, 2S | 3,557 | 3,033 | — |
| 46 | wgn 4d, 3S, V8 only | 3,676 | 3,246 | — |
| **WM Coronet Super Bee V8 (wb 117.0)—27,846 built** | | | | |
| 21 | cpe | 3,440 | 3,076 | — |
| 23 | htp cpe | 3,470 | 3,138 | — |
| **WP Coronet 500 V8 (wb 117.0)—32,050 built** | | | | |
| 23 | htp cpe | 3,171 | 2,929 | — |
| 27 | conv cpe | 3,306 | 3,069 | — |
| 41 | sdn 4d | 3,206 | 2,963 | — |
| 45 | wgn 4d, 2S | 3,611 | 3,280 | — |
| 46 | wgn 4d, 3S | 3,676 | 3,392 | — |
| **WS Coronet R/T (wb 117.0)—7,238 built** | | | | |
| 23 | htp cpe | 3,601 | 3,442 | — |
| 27 | conv cpe | 3,721 | 3,660 | — |
| **XP/XS Charger (wb 117.0)** | | | | |
| XP29 | htp cpe, L6 | 3,103 | 3,020 | 69,142 |
| XP29 | htp cpe, V8 | 3,256 | 3,126 | |

| | | Wght | Price | Prod |
|---|---|---|---|---|
| XS29 | R/T htp cpe, V8 | 3,646 | 3,592 | 20,057 |
| — | Daytona htp cpe, V8 | — | 4,000 | 505 |

**XX Charger 500 V8 (wb 117.0)***

| | | Wght | Price | Prod |
|---|---|---|---|---|
| XX29 | htp cpe | 3,671 | 3,860 | — |

**DL Polara (wb 122.0)—83,122 built**

| | | Wght | Price | Prod |
|---|---|---|---|---|
| 23 | htp cpe | 3,646 | 3,117 | — |
| 27 | conv cpe | 3,791 | 3,377 | — |
| 41 | sdn 4d | 3,701 | 3,095 | — |
| 43 | htp sdn | 3,731 | 3,188 | — |
| 45 | wgn 4d, 2S | 4,161 | 3,522 | — |
| 46 | wgn 4d, 3S | 4,211 | 3,629 | — |

**DM Polara 500 (wb 122.0)—5,564 built**

| | | Wght | Price | Prod |
|---|---|---|---|---|
| 23 | htp cpe | 3,681 | 3,314 | — |
| 27 | conv cpe | 3,801 | 3,576 | — |

**DH Monaco (wb 122.0)—38,566 built**

| | | Wght | Price | Prod |
|---|---|---|---|---|
| 23 | htp cpe | 3,811 | 3,528 | — |
| 41 | sdn 4d | 3,846 | 3,452 | — |
| 43 | htp sdn | 3,891 | 3,591 | — |
| 45 | wgn 4d, 2S | 4,306 | 3,917 | — |
| 46 | wgn 4d, 3S | 4,361 | 4,046 | — |

*Production included with XP 29 models

| 1969 Engines | bore×stroke | bhp | availability |
|---|---|---|---|
| L6, 170.0 | 3.40×3.13 | 115 | S-Dart |
| L6, 225.0 | 3.40×4.13 | 145 | S-Coronet Del/440; O-Dart |
| V8, 273.5 | 3.63×3.31 | 190 | S-Dart V8 |
| V8, 318.0 | 3.91×3.31 | 230 | S-Cor Del/440/500, Chrgr, Pol; O-Dart |
| V8, 340.0 | 4.04×3.31 | 275 | S-GTS, Swinger 340 |
| V8, 383.0 | 4.25×3.38 | 290 | S-Monaco; O-Polara, Chrgr, Coronet |
| V8, 383.0 | 4.25×3.38 | 330 | O-GTS, Cor V8, Mon, Pol, Chrgr |
| V8, 383.0 | 4.25×3.38 | 335 | S-Coronet Super Bee |
| V8, 426.0 | 4.25×3.75 | 425 | O-Coronet R/T, Charger R/T |
| V8, 440.0 | 4.32×3.75 | 350 | O-Monaco & Polara wgns |
| V8, 440.0 | 4.32×3.75 | 375 | O-Monaco & Polara exc wagons |

# 1970

**LL Dart (wb 111.0)**

| | | Wght | Price | Prod |
|---|---|---|---|---|
| 23 | Swinger htp cpe | 2,903 | 2,261 | 119,883 |
| 41 | sdn 4d | 2,900 | 2,308 | 35,499 |

**LH Dart Custom (wb 111.0)**

| | | Wght | Price | Prod |
|---|---|---|---|---|
| 23 | htp cpe | 2,898 | 2,463 | 17,208 |
| 41 | sdn 4d | 2,905 | 2,467 | 23,779 |

**LM Dart Swinger 340 (wb 111.0)**

| | | Wght | Price | Prod |
|---|---|---|---|---|
| 23 | htp cpe | 3,130 | 2,631 | 13,785 |

**JH Challenger (wb 110.0)**

| | | Wght | Price | Prod |
|---|---|---|---|---|
| 23 | htp cpe | 3,028 | 2,851 | 53,337 |
| 27 | conv cpe | 3,103 | 3,120 | 3,173 |
| 29 | S.E. htp cpe | 3,053 | 3,083 | 6,584 |

**JS Challenger R/T (wb 110.0)**

| | | Wght | Price | Prod |
|---|---|---|---|---|
| 23 | htp cpe (inc T/A) | 3,405 | 3,226 | 14,889 |
| 27 | conv cpe | 3,470 | 3,535 | 1,070 |
| 29 | S.E. htp cpe | 3,440 | 3,498 | 3,979 |

**WL Coronet Deluxe (wb 117.0)**

| | | Wght | Price | Prod |
|---|---|---|---|---|
| 21 | cpe | 3,150 | 2,669 | 2,978 |
| 41 | sdn 4d | 3,188 | 2,704 | 7,894 |
| 45 | wgn 4d | 3,675 | 3,048 | 3,694 |

**WH Coronet 440 (wb 117.0)**

| | | Wght | Price | Prod |
|---|---|---|---|---|
| 21 | cpe | 3,170 | 2,743 | 1,236 |
| 23 | htp cpe | 3,185 | 2,805 | 24,341 |
| 41 | sdn 4d | 3,190 | 2,783 | 33,258 |
| 45 | wgn 4d | 3,673 | 3,156 | 3,964 |
| 46 | wgn 4d | 3,775 | 3,368 | 3,772 |

**WM Coronet Super Bee (wb 117.0)**

| | | Wght | Price | Prod |
|---|---|---|---|---|
| 21 | cpe | 3,500 | 3,012 | 3,966 |
| 23 | htp cpe | 3,535 | 3,074 | 11,540 |

**WP Coronet 500 (wb 117.0)**

| | | Wght | Price | Prod |
|---|---|---|---|---|
| 23 | htp cpe | 3,235 | 3,048 | 8,247 |
| 27 | conv cpe | 3,345 | 3,188 | 924 |
| 41 | sdn 4d | 3,255 | 3,082 | 2,890 |
| 45 | wgn 4d, 2S | 3,715 | 3,404 | 1,657 |
| 46 | wgn 4d, 3S | 3,785 | 3,514 | 1,779 |

**WS Coronet R/T (wb 117.0)**

| | | Wght | Price | Prod |
|---|---|---|---|---|
| 23 | htp cpe | 3,545 | 3,569 | 2,319 |
| 27 | conv cpe | 3,610 | 3,785 | 296 |

**XH/XP Charger (wb 117.0)**

| | | Wght | Price | Prod |
|---|---|---|---|---|
| XH29 | htp cpe | 3,293 | 3,001 | 30,101 |
| XP29 | 500 htp cpe | 3,293 | 3,139 | |

**XS/XX Charger R/T (wb 117.0)**

| | | Wght | Price | Prod |
|---|---|---|---|---|
| XS29 | htp cpe | 3,610 | 3,711 | 10,337 |
| XX29 | Daytona htp cpe | 3,710 | 3,993 | |

**DE Polara (wb 122.0)***

| | | Wght | Price | Prod |
|---|---|---|---|---|
| 41 | sdn 4d, L6 | 3,775 | 2,960 | — |
| 45 | wgn 4d, 2S, V8 | 4,180 | 3,513 | — |
| 46 | wgn 4d, 3S, V8 | 4,235 | 3,621 | — |

**DL Polara "Deluxe" V8 (wb 122.0)**

| | | Wght | Price | Prod |
|---|---|---|---|---|
| 23 | htp cpe | 3,770 | 3,224 | * |
| 27 | conv cpe | 3,830 | 3,527 | 842 |
| 41 | sdn 4d | 3,805 | 3,222 | * |
| 43 | htp sdn | 3,850 | 3,316 | * |
| 45 | wgn 4d, 2S | 4,180 | 3,670 | * |
| 46 | wgn 4d, 3S | 4,235 | 3,778 | * |

**DM Polara Custom V8 (wb 122.0)***

| | | Wght | Price | Prod |
|---|---|---|---|---|
| 23 | htp cpe | 4,005 | 3,458 | — |
| 41 | sdn 4d | 3,975 | 3,426 | — |
| 43 | htp sdn | 3,925 | 3,528 | — |

**DH Monaco (wb 122.0)**

| | | Wght | Price | Prod |
|---|---|---|---|---|
| 23 | htp cpe | 3,950 | 3,679 | 3,522 |
| 41 | sdn 4d | 4,010 | 3,604 | 4,721 |
| 43 | htp sdn | 4,045 | 3,743 | 10,974 |
| 45 | wgn 4d, 2S | 4,420 | 4,110 | 2,211 |
| 46 | wgn 4d, 3S | 4,475 | 4,242 | 3,264 |

*Dodge combined production figures for most Polara models. Available figures are:

| 23 | htp cpe (DL, DM) | 15,243 |
|---|---|---|
| 27 | conv cpe (DL) | 842 |
| 41 | sdn 4d (DE, DL, DM) | 18,740 |
| 43 | htp sdn (DL, DM) | 19,223 |
| 45 | wgn 4d, 2S (DE, DL) | 3,074 |
| 46 | wgn 4d, 3s (DE, DL) | 3,546 |

| 1970 Engines | bore×stroke | bhp | availability |
|---|---|---|---|
| L6, 198.0 | 3.40×3.64 | 125 | S-Dart |
| L6, 225.0 | 3.40×4.13 | 145 | S-Chal/Cor/Chrgr/Polara 6s; O-Dart |
| V8, 318.0 | 3.91×3.31 | 230 | S-Dart exc Swngr 340, Chal, Cor, Chrgr, Pol |
| V8, 340.0 | 4.04×3.31 | 275 | S-Swngr 340; O-Chal |
| V8, 383.0 | 4.25×3.38 | 290 | S-Mon, Pol Cus; O-Chal/Cor/Chrgr/ Polara V8s |
| V8, 383.0 | 4.25×3.38 | 330 | O-Chal, Cor, Pol, Pol Cus, Monaco |
| V8, 383.0 | 4.25×3.38 | 335 | S-Super Bee, Chal R/T; O-Chal, Chrgr R/T |
| V8, 426.0 | 4.25×3.75 | 425 | O-Chal, Super Bee, Cor/Chrgr R/Ts |
| V8, 440.0 | 4.32×3.75 | 350 | O-Monaco, Polara, Polara Custom |
| V8, 440.0 | 4.32×3.75 | 375 | S-Chrgr/Coronet/Challenger R/Ts |
| V8, 440.0 | 4.32×3.75 | 390 | O-Chrgr/Cor/Chal R/Ts, Super Bee |

# Edsel
**Edsel Division, Ford Motor Co.
Dearborn, Michigan**

A comedy of errors, or a good idea at the wrong time? The Edsel was both—proof that even giant multinational corporations sometimes make mistakes. "Its aim was right," said a prominent auto historian, "but the target moved."

The Edsel was developed in 1955, when sales of lower-medium-price cars were booming. Pontiac, Buick, and Dodge were producing nearly two million vehicles combined. By the time Edsel appeared in late 1957, the market had bottomed out. New-car sales were in a slump generally, and the market share for medium-price cars had dropped from 25 percent to about 18 percent. Edsel Division started with a goal of selling 100,000 of the first-year 1958 models. It produced a little over 50,000 cars by the end of calendar 1957. From there it was all downhill. In calendar 1958, only 26,563 Edsels were built. Output was less than 30,000 units in 1959, and the line disappeared for good by the end of November that year.

The car was never intended to bear the name of Henry Ford's son, but it wasn't for lack of trying. Ford had recruited poetess Marianne Moore to name the new car and she came up with some stunners: "Mongoose Civique," "Turcotinga," and "Utopian Turtletop." Ranger, Pacer, Corsair, and Citation were the top finishers of the 6000 names considered by the ad agency. Ernest Breech, Ford Motor Company's chairman of the board, didn't like any of them, though they were adopted as series designations for 1958. When told that Henry Ford II was against calling the car Edsel, Breech replied, "I'll take care of Henry." And he did.

Ranger and Pacer came on a 116- or 118-inch wheelbase shared with the '58 Ford. Corsair and Citation rode Mercury's 124-inch wheelbase. Bodyshells were simi-

1958 Citation hardtop sedan

1959 Corsair hardtop sedan

1960 Ranger four-door sedan

1960 Ranger convertible

larly shared and Edsel offered a wide choice of body styles. Prices were about $500 downstream of comparable Mercurys. Along with its unique "horse-collar" grille and narrow horizontal taillights (which one cynic called the ingrown toenail), Edsel featured numerous gadgets. The "Teletouch" automatic transmission was controlled by pushbuttons recessed in the steering wheel hub; the speedometer was a rotating drum; and almost everything except the rearview mirror could be power-assisted.

Two V8s were offered. A 361 cubic-inch engine was fitted to the two lower series and station wagons; the 410-cid unit was installed in the Corsair/Citation. Edsels were quite rapid, especially when equipped with the big engine.

For 1959, with sales dropping to basement level, the lineup was radically cut. Only Rangers, Corsairs, and station wagons were offered on a single wheelbase.

The Corsair line disappeared for 1960.

The 1960 Edsel's standard engine was a 292-cid V8, but at no extra cost, a buyer could order Ford's 223-cid inline six. For $58 more, the customer could have the "Super Express" V8, which developed 300 horsepower. Cars so equipped were capable of 0–60 mph times of less than 10 seconds.

For 1960, the upright central grille was replaced by a horizontal motif, divided in the center, which looked suspiciously like the '59 Pontiac. Heavy chrome accents were used on the fenders and sides of the body, which was a mildly restyled version of the all-new 1960 Ford design. Two-speed or three-speed automatic transmission, power steering, and air conditioning were options. The Ranger convertible, equipped with air conditioning and other options, could run up to $3800. Extremely low production makes the 1960 model the rarest of Edsel's three model years.

# Edsel Specifications

## 1958

### Ranger (wb 118.0; wgns-116.0)

|    |                    | Wght  | Price | Prod  |
|----|--------------------|-------|-------|-------|
| 21 | sdn 2d             | 3,729 | 2,519 | 4,615 |
| 22 | sdn 4d             | 3,805 | 2,592 | 6,576 |
| 23 | htp cpe            | 3,724 | 2,593 | 5,546 |
| 24 | htp sdn            | 3,796 | 2,678 | 3,077 |
| 26 | Roundup wgn 2d     | 3,761 | 2,876 | 963   |
| 27 | Villager wgn 4d, 6P | 3,827 | 2,933 | 2,294 |
| 28 | Villager wgn 4d, 9P | 3,900 | 2,990 | 978   |

### Pacer (wb 118.0; wgns-116.0)

|    |                    | Wght  | Price | Prod  |
|----|--------------------|-------|-------|-------|
| 42 | sdn 4d             | 3,826 | 2,375 | 6,083 |
| 43 | htp cpe            | 3,773 | 2,805 | 6,139 |
| 44 | htp sdn            | 3,857 | 2,863 | 4,959 |
| 45 | conv cpe           | 3,909 | 3,028 | 1,876 |
| 47 | Bermuda wgn 4d, 6P | 3,853 | 3,190 | 1,456 |
| 48 | Bermuda wgn 4d, 9P | 3,919 | 3,247 | 779   |

### Corsair (wb 124.0)

|    |         | Wght  | Price | Prod  |
|----|---------|-------|-------|-------|
| 63 | htp cpe | 4,134 | 3,346 | 3,312 |
| 64 | htp sdn | 4,235 | 3,425 | 5,880 |

### Citation (wb 124.0)

|    |          | Wght  | Price | Prod  |
|----|----------|-------|-------|-------|
| 83 | htp cpe  | 4,136 | 3,535 | 2,535 |
| 84 | htp sdn  | 4,230 | 3,615 | 5,112 |
| 85 | conv cpe | 4,311 | 3,801 | 930   |

### 1958 Engines

|           | bore×stroke | bhp | availability        |
|-----------|-------------|-----|---------------------|
| V8, 361.0 | 4.05×3.50   | 303 | S-Ranger, Pacer     |
| V8, 410.0 | 4.20×3.70   | 345 | S-Corsair, Citation |

## 1959

### Ranger (wb 120.0)

|     |         | Wght  | Price | Prod   |
|-----|---------|-------|-------|--------|
| 57F | htp sdn | 3,682 | 2,756 | 2,352  |
| 58D | sdn 4d  | 3,774 | 2,684 | 12,814 |
| 63F | htp cpe | 3,591 | 2,691 | 5,474  |
| 64C | sdn 2d  | 3,547 | 2,629 | 7,778  |

### Corsair (wb 120.0)

|     |          | Wght  | Price | Prod  |
|-----|----------|-------|-------|-------|
| 57B | htp sdn  | 3,709 | 2,885 | 1,694 |
| 58B | sdn 4d   | 3,696 | 2,812 | 3,301 |
| 63B | htp cpe  | 3,778 | 2,819 | 2,315 |
| 76E | conv cpe | 3,790 | 3,072 | 1,343 |

### Station Wagon (wb 120.0)

|     |                     | Wght  | Price | Prod  |
|-----|---------------------|-------|-------|-------|
| 71E | Villager wgn 4d, 9P | 3,930 | 3,055 | 2,133 |
| 71F | Villager wgn 4d, 6P | 3,842 | 2,971 | 5,687 |

### 1959 Engines

|           | bore×stroke | bhp | availability              |
|-----------|-------------|-----|---------------------------|
| L6, 223.0 | 3.62×3.60   | 145 | O-Ranger, Station Wagon   |
| V8, 292.0 | 3.75×3.30   | 200 | S-Ranger, Station Wagon   |
| V8, 332.0 | 4.00×3.30   | 225 | S-Corsair; O-others       |
| V8, 361.0 | 4.05×3.50   | 303 | O-all                     |

## 1960

### Ranger (wb 120.0)

|     |          | Wght  | Price | Prod  |
|-----|----------|-------|-------|-------|
| 57A | htp sdn  | 3,718 | 2,770 | 135   |
| 58A | sdn 4d   | 3,700 | 2,697 | 1,288 |
| 63A | htp cpe  | 3,641 | 2,705 | 295   |
| 64A | sdn 2d   | 3,601 | 2,643 | 939   |
| 76B | conv cpe | 3,836 | 3,000 | 76    |

### Station Wagon (wb 120.0)

|     |                     | Wght  | Price | Prod |
|-----|---------------------|-------|-------|------|
| 71E | Villager wgn 4d, 9P | 4,046 | 3,072 | 59   |
| 71F | Villager wgn 4d, 6P | 4,029 | 2,989 | 216  |

### 1960 Engines

|           | bore×stroke | bhp | availability |
|-----------|-------------|-----|--------------|
| L6, 223.0 | 3.62×3.50   | 145 | O-all        |
| V8, 292.0 | 3.75×3.30   | 185 | S-all        |
| V8, 352.0 | 4.00×3.50   | 300 | O-all        |

# Excalibur
### SS Automobiles Inc.
### Milwaukee, Wisconsin

America's most successful builder of cars fashioned in the image of the great classics is Excalibur, the Milwaukee concern founded by industrial designer Brooks Stevens. Fastidiously assembled, the Excalibur is a superb road machine. It's also exclusive: there have never been enough of them to meet demand.

The Excalibur Series I, introduced in 1964, remained in its original form until it was replaced by the Series II in 1970. Its styling echoes the classic 1928 Mercedes-Benz SSK. Even Excalibur's sales literature was patterned after that of the prewar Mercedes. Careful engineering and clever design distinguished the Excalibur from a motley group of VW-powered replicas that followed it.

In 1964, Stevens was finishing four years of design consulting for the ill-fated Studebaker Corporation. Studebaker had ceased car production at its South Bend, Indiana plant in late 1963, but continued some operations at its Hamilton, Ontario factory. Stevens hoped production would go on. But he was unimpressed by the firm's mundane cars at the 1964 Chicago Auto Show, and was determined to build a more exciting Studebaker "special" for the New York show in April. So, he ordered up a Lark Daytona convertible chassis with power disc brakes and a 290-horsepower, supercharged 289 cubic-inch Avanti V8. Studebaker managers tentatively approved his plan to build "a modern classic" for their company's New York display.

The prototype Excalibur was created in just six weeks by Stevens and his two sons, David and William. No sooner had it left for New York than Studebaker officials

1965-69 Series I SSK roadster

1967-69 Series I phaeton

changed their minds. A "contemporary classic," they said, would conflict with the image of the "common-sense car" they wanted to create for Studebaker.

More than time and money was at stake for Stevens, and he refused to scrap the project. Through hurried phone calls to the show's management, he arranged to display the Excalibur on a separate stand. The car was a hit and in August 1964, Stevens and his sons founded SS Automobiles to manufacture it. Some 100 copies had been sold by the beginning of 1966.

Studebaker's demise ended the supply of 289 V8s after 1965, so Stevens went shopping for a new engine. The 327-cid Corvette unit was duly provided by Stevens' friends Ed Cole and Semon E. "Bunkie" Knudsen at General Motors. After 1966, Excaliburs were also offered with a Paxton-supercharged V8 rated at 400 bhp, and high-performance Corvette engines. With the standard 3.31:1 rear axle ratio, the car was claimed to have a 0–60 mph time of less than five seconds and a top speed in the area of 160 mph. This was a considerable improvement over the 289, which did 0 to 60 in about seven seconds.

The 109-inch wheelbase Studebaker Daytona convertible chassis was hardly modern, but it offered some advantages. Unlike concurrent torque-box frames, it was quite narrow as its frame rails were not spread as far apart as other chassis that had to accommodate more modern, wider body sills. This made it perfectly suited for the Excalibur's narrower, vintage-style body. As a convertible chassis it was firmly X-braced. But it needed considerable re-engineering to insure safe handling in a high-powered car that weighed at least 500 pounds less than a Corvette.

David Stevens was largely responsible for the Excalibur's engineering. The car's classic-style cowl forced him to lower the Studebaker steering column and control pedals, but this was just the beginning. It was also necessary to alter the suspension geometry drastically by decreasing the spring rates and changing caster and camber. This modified Studebaker chassis was retained for all Series I cars. Like all Excaliburs that followed, the 1965-69 models were fast on both curves and straights.

Brooks Stevens was responsible for the styling, which was a surprisingly accurate rendition of the fabulous SSK. To Stevens, outside exhaust pipes were mandatory, but no one in the United States could supply them. Ultimately, he bought the flexible tubing from the same German firm that had supplied it to Mercedes-Benz back in the 1920s. The bodies of the first few cars were made of hammered aluminum; SS soon switched to fiberglass, mainly for reasons of cost and practicality. The radiator was made of sheet brass on the prototype; production radiators were cast aluminum. The Mercedes three-pointed star sug-

gested the hood ornament, an Excalibur sword in a circle. This resembled, but did not compromise, the Mercedes emblem, of which the German firm is notoriously protective. French-built free-standing headlamps closely resembled the original SSK units. White-on-black instruments from the Studebaker Hawk were placed in an SSK-like engine-turned dash panel. The seats used were modified Studebaker buckets, covered in expanded vinyl (leather upholstery would be used later). The initial price was almost unbelievably low: $7250 for a hand-built car having one of the most competently engineered chassis in the business.

For 1966, SS Automobiles expanded its line by adding a more elaborate roadster. Unlike the aggressive-looking SSK, the roadster had full fenders and running boards. By 1967, the line also included a phaeton.

As prices went up, the equipment offered and materials used increased in variety and quality. Standard equipment by 1969 included air conditioning, heater and defroster, variable-ratio power steering, tilt steering wheel, power front disc brakes, Positraction rear axle, chrome-plated wire wheels, luggage rack, AM-FM stereo, leather seats, Turbo Hydra-

Matic transmission, twin side-mounted spare tires, all-weather hardtop, air horns, driving lights, steel-belted radial tires, and automatically controlled self-leveling rear shock absorbers. For 1970, the Series II was introduced on a longer wheelbase with a larger Corvette V8. The same three body styles were offered, each riding a redesigned box-section frame. The chassis made extensive use of Corvette suspension components. The four-speed "Muncie" manual gearbox was standard, while three-speed Turbo Hydra-Matic became optional. Independent suspension and four-wheel disc brakes combined with Goodyear Polyglas tires mounted on specially designed wire wheels to offer a fine balance between ride and handling. According to SS Automobiles, the Series II SSK would leap from 0 to 60 mph in six seconds flat and reach 150 mph.

The lithe, cycle-fendered SSK was the definitive Excalibur, and is the model most sought-after by collectors today. Though it was phased out in the early 1970s, it has not been forgotten. Brooks Stevens has since developed the Series III and the 1980 Series IV Excaliburs, which owe their stylistic inspiration to subsequent Mercedes-Benz models of the 1930s.

# Excalibur Specifications

## 1965

| Series I (wb 109.0)* | Wght | Price | Prod |
|---|---|---|---|
| SSK rdstr | 2,100 | 7,250 | — |

| 1965 Engine | bore×stroke | bhp | availability |
|---|---|---|---|
| V8, 289.0 | 3.56×3.62 | 290 | S-all |

## 1966

| Series I (wb 109.0)* | Wght | Price | Prod |
|---|---|---|---|
| SSK rdstr | 2,100 | 7,250 | — |
| rdstr | 2,500 | 8,000 | — |

| 1966 Engine | bore×stroke | bhp | availability |
|---|---|---|---|
| V8, 327.0 | 4.00×3.25 | 300 | S-all |

## 1967

| Series I (wb 109.0)* | Wght | Price | Prod |
|---|---|---|---|
| SSK rdstr | 2,100 | 8,000 | — |
| rdstr | 2,500 | 8,500 | — |
| phtn | 2,600 | 9,000 | — |

| 1967 Engines | bore×stroke | bhp | availability |
|---|---|---|---|
| V8, 327.0 | 4.00×3.25 | 300 | S-all |
| V8, 327.0 | 4.00×3.25 | 400 | O-all |

## 1968

| Series I (wb 109.0)* | Wght | Price | Prod |
|---|---|---|---|
| SSK rdstr | 2,300 | 9,000 | — |
| rdstr | 2,500 | 9,250 | — |
| phtn | 2,600 | 9,500 | — |

| 1968 Engines | bore×stroke | bhp | availability |
|---|---|---|---|
| V8, 327.0 | 4.00×3.25 | 300 | S-all |
| V8, 327.0 | 4.00×3.25 | 435 | O-all |

## 1969

| Series I (wb 109.0)* | Wght | Price | Prod |
|---|---|---|---|
| SSK rdstr | 2,400 | 10,000 | — |
| rdstr | 2,550 | 10,500 | — |
| phtn | 2,650 | 11,000 | — |

| 1969 Engines | bore×stroke | bhp | availability |
|---|---|---|---|
| V8, 327.0 | 4.00×3.25 | 300 | S-all |
| V8, 327.0 | 4.00×3.25 | 435 | O-all |

* Production 1965–69: SSK 168; rdstr 59; phtn 89.

## 1970

| Series II (wb 111.0) | Wght | Price | Prod |
|---|---|---|---|
| SSK rdstr | 2,750 | 12,000 | — |
| SS rdstr | 2,900 | 12,500 | — |
| SS phtn | 3,000 | 13,000 | — |

| 1970 Engine | bore×stroke | bhp | availability |
|---|---|---|---|
| V8, 350.0 | 4.00×3.48 | 300 | S-all |

# Ford

**Ford Division, Ford Motor Co.
Dearborn, Michigan**

**H**enry Ford was a crusty old man in the 1940s, distrustful of younger leaders, new ideas, and especially wary of organized labor. Even son Edsel, respected for his business acumen, was unable to influence his father's decisions. The old man was often inclined to trust the judgment of self-seeking associates who helped him rule with an iron hand. Ford cars suffered as a result of this conservatism. Until 1939, Henry had insisted on mechanical instead of hydraulic brakes. He had also opposed the idea of a six-cylinder engine, or a market gap filler like Mercury. The 1940 Ford, the third facelift of a late-1930s design, was one of the most beautiful in history. But designer Bob Gregorie, encouraged by Edsel, must be given more credit than Henry for its styling.

After the war, Henry would pass the reins of his company over at last—but not to his son. Edsel had died in 1943, at age 49. Henry had continued to manage his increasingly troubled firm until his family insisted on a change in 1945. Control then passed to grandson Henry Ford II. "HFII" retired in 1980 after 33 years at the helm, years marked by great success. Unlike his grandfather, he consistently sought and encouraged talented managers. However, he just as consistently encouraged their retirement when they reached a certain level of power. Though the family no longer owns a majority of common stock, Ford is still very much a family operation.

Styling of the first Ford of the '40s was good—so good that this car has become one of the most desirable single models made by any manufacturer. The hood was crisply pointed, meeting a handsome grille composed mainly of delicate horizontal bars, flowing smoothly back to a rakishly angled windshield. The headlamps, sealed-beams for the first time, were faired into neat fender nacelles. The fenders themselves were beautifully curved to complement the body contours, and were often skirted at the rear for the ultimate streamlined appearance.

On a 112-inch wheelbase, Ford mounted two different engines: 60- and 85-bhp L-head V8s. The V8/60, never very popular, was a price leader. The larger V8/85 came in a wider range of models and two trim stages—standard and DeLuxe.

When Mercury arrived in 1939, many dealers were disappointed, since they felt a six-cylinder Ford would have been a better seller. Edsel Ford promised them one, but then had to reckon with his father. Henry approved a six in one of those strange about-faces for which he was noted. Edsel went to work, and brought out an L-head six in 1941, the Ford Special. This car replaced the unpopular V8/60. Its well-built flathead displaced 226 cubic inches, 90 more than the small V8, for a horsepower increase of 50 percent. In 1941, it ac-

tually delivered more horsepower than the V8/85. A vast array of six and V8 Specials, DeLuxes, and Super DeLuxes was offered. Styling, if not entirely new in the middle, was altered at each end. There were wider and more integral front fenders, a busy grille composed of vertical bars, a chromed-up hood, and larger rear fenders.

None of these changes did much for Ford production. It remained about the same in '41 as it was in 1940: less than two-thirds of Chevrolet's output. Ford had surpassed Chevrolet just once in the '30s. Chevy would reign supreme throughout the '40s, except for model years 1946 and '49.

A more cohesive, lower grille was introduced for

**1940 V8/85 DeLuxe Fordor sedan**

**1940 V8/85 DeLuxe coupe**

**Wartime prototype for postwar Ford**

1942. Ford built only 43,000 cars from January 1 through February 2, when civilian production ended. The low-priced Specials were restricted to six cylinders only that year, but otherwise the model lineup was unchanged. Prices were increased about $100 throughout, making the convertible coupe the first Ford (aside from wagons) to sell for over $1000 since the Model A town cars of about 10 years earlier.

The elder Henry had been a renowned pacifist before Pearl Harbor. After the Japanese attack, he grasped the altered situation, and quickly converted to war production. Ford built a variety of military vehicles including Jeeps (with Willys-Overland and American Bantam) during the conflict. Ford also built the mile-long Willow Run plant near Detroit, which produced a variety of bombers through 1945. Young Henry II moved into car production fast after Japan surrendered. For model year 1946, the company was once again the industry leader. Chevrolet, however, was back in full swing by 1947, and led production totals that year.

The 1946 Ford used prewar dies and the old 114-inch wheelbase, but important mechanical changes were made and body offerings were revised. The six remained at 90 bhp, but the V8 was boosted to 100 bhp, the result of a bore increase that gave 239 cid. The Special series of low-priced sixes was eliminated, leaving the DeLuxe and Super DeLuxe with six- and eight-cylinder engines. There was no six-cylinder convertible, but there were two convertible V8s, the standard model and a novel variation called the Sportsman.

Developed from design sketches made by Gregorie during the war, the Sportsman featured white ash and mahogany trim over its doors, rear body panels, and deck like the Chrysler Town & Country. This was an attractive way to add something new to an old-fashioned design, and helped increase floor traffic at

1942 Super DeLuxe four-door station wagon

1946 Super DeLuxe Fordor sedan

1946 Super DeLuxe Sportsman convertible

1948 DeLuxe Fordor sedan

1948 Super DeLuxe convertible

1948 Super DeLuxe four-door sedan

**Clay proposal for 1949 station wagon**

**1949 Custom V8 station wagon**

**1949 Custom V8 Tudor sedan**

Ford dealerships. The Sportsman was quite expensive, however, some $500 more than the regular convertible. As such it did not sell in high numbers.

Little outward change marked the 1947-48 models. Alterations involved a shuffle of nameplates and lower-mounted round parking lights in 1947. No styling changes were made for '48. The six was now rated at 95 instead of 90 bhp. Responding to postwar inflation, prices were on the rise, increasing about $100 model for model in 1947 and again in '48.

In the booming postwar seller's market, no styling or engineering changes were really needed. Ford output exceeded 429,000 units in 1947, but was only 236,000 in '48. That drop did not indicate trouble in Dearborn, only an early end to 1948 model production. Ford management had realized that a new car was needed. Work on the all-new postwar design began in early 1946, and the '49s were introduced earlier than usual, in June 1948.

Styling for the '49s was a competitive operation, as Ford solicited ideas from freelance designers as well as from its own design department. One of the competitors was George Walker, who employed a young stylist named Dick Caleal. The Walker team developed a package incorporating integral fenders. However, as the deadline approached, Caleal ran into trouble with the front and rear styling. According to Robert Bourke, then chief designer for the Loewy Studios at Studebaker, Caleal approached Bourke and his assistant Bob Koto for help. The Loewy people agreed to lend their friend Caleal whatever expertise they could on their own time. Late-night sessions at the Caleal home in Mishawaka, Indiana found the three men concocting a smooth-looking clay model with a bullet or spinner-type grille reminiscent of the later '50 Studebaker. According to Bourke, the quarter-scale clay was submitted to Walker, who put it under his arm and took it to Dearborn. It was accepted almost without alteration. The only significant change was in the taillights: horizontal lenses were used instead of the vertical taillights the team had planned. The design, of course, had none of the Studebaker's radical lines. But it brought Ford a calendar year production level the likes of which the company hadn't seen since 1937. In 1955, Walker became design director at Ford, mainly on the strength of this contribution.

The 1949s used the 100-bhp V8, which made for a sprightly performer able to run circles around rival Chevys and Plymouths. If a '49 Ford couldn't actually achieve 100 mph, the modifications necessary to make it do so weren't that involved. Multiple carburetors, headers, dual exhausts, and other speed equipment were all available at local auto accessory stores.

The low-selling Sportsman was eliminated for 1949, but a wider range of body types was offered. Again prices increased. Overdrive was optional on all models at $97. Ford would not have its own automatic transmission until 1951, though it had tried hard to get one earlier. Studebaker had developed an excellent automatic for 1950, in association with Warner Gear. Ford tried to buy the rights to use it on its own cars, but Studebaker refused—much to its regret later.

The '49 Fords were without doubt worthy automobiles. They were the first tangible evidence of a new hand at the controls—Henry II, ably assisted by a team of youthful executives.

The 1950-53 Ford continued to offer sixes and the famous flathead V8 so popular with hot rodders. By 1953, this engine was pumping out 110 bhp at 3800 rpm. Ford replaced the flathead six with an overhead-valve unit in 1952. From 1951 on, all these engines were accompanied by an optional two-speed Ford-O-Matic shiftless transmission.

Through these early years of the decade Ford Motor Company experienced a revival, moving ahead of Chrysler into the number-two spot. The reason? Interesting cars that sold well.

A special confection for 1950-51 was the V8 Crestliner. This limited-edition two-door was distinguished by a vivid contrasting color sweep on its sides and a

1950 Custom Crestliner two-door sedan

1951 Custom Tudor sedan

1952 Crestline Sunliner convertible

1953 Customline Fordor sedan

1954 Crestline Skyliner hardtop coupe

1954 Crestline Country Squire station wagon

padded vinyl top. Only 26,304 were sold before the series was canceled in 1952, but the wildly colored cars remain collector's items to this day. The rest of the line was divided between DeLuxes and Customs, sixes and V8s, sedans and coupes, Custom wagons, and the Custom V8 convertible. Styling was rather high and wide compared to arch-rival Chevrolet, but was better than Plymouth's. Ford built over a million cars in model year 1950, its highest total since 1930.

For '51, the hardtop Victoria with the same styling as the rest of the line appeared in the Custom V8 series. This neat alteration of the two-door coupe sold much better than the Crestliner. A new bodyshell came in 1952, with a look that would be mostly untouched for the next several years. The cars were lower and wider on a longer 115-inch wheelbase. Mainline and Customline now replaced the Deluxe and Custom designations. The Crestline became a top-of-the-line V8 series comprising the Victoria hardtop, Sunliner convertible, and the posh Country Squire station wagon. The latter

was the first all-steel Ford wagon, with wood decal trim.

Though 1953 was Ford's Golden Anniversary year, no significant changes were made to celebrate the event—except for an increase in prices. Ford Division built 1.2 million cars that year—an output shattered in 1955 with nearly 1.5 million cars. Ford was closing in on Chevy, but was straining its dealers to do so. A Ford could be bought at "less than cost" in 1953-54 when the "Ford Blitz" reached its peak. Chevrolet was not seriously damaged by the onslaught, but the independents were. Unable to discount as much, Studebaker, American Motors, and Kaiser-Willys dealers were hit hard. The Ford Blitz is generally considered one of the most important factors in the decline of the independents in the mid-'50s.

Ford made headlines in 1954 when it introduced its new overhead-valve, "Y-block" V8 with 130 bhp. This was easily the hottest engine in the low-price field. Together with ball-joint front suspension, also new that year, the Y-block greatly narrowed the engineering gap

181

1955 Fairlane Crown Victoria hardtop coupe

1956 Fairlane Victoria hardtop sedan (prototype)

1957 Fairlane 500 Skyliner retractable hardtop

1957 Fairlane 500 Victoria hardtop sedan

between expensive and inexpensive cars. Though it displaced 239 cubic inches (exactly the same as its flathead predecessor), it was entirely different in bore and stroke with oversquare dimensions. The Y-block had a 7.2:1 compression ratio in standard trim, but could be upped to 12:1 if required.

In styling, 1954 was mainly the same story as '53 except for one noteworthy addition: the Crestline Skyliner hardtop, with a novel front roof section made of transparent plastic. The concept was developed by interior styling director L. David Ash. Its current counterpart is the moonroof, though these are made of glass and cover a smaller area.

The 1955 Ford, bearing some resemblance to the 1952-54 models, was a good design, clean if highly chromed, with a rakish look of motion. Frank Hershey was the man in charge of styling. (Hershey also gets most of the credit for the '55 Thunderbird, one of the most important Fords in history. See separate chapter.)

Ford retained its basic line for '56—Mainline, Customline, Fairlane, and Station Wagon. This year the company tried to make safety a selling point. Standard for all models were a dished steering wheel, breakaway rearview mirror, and crashproof door locks; padded dash and sunvisors cost $16 extra, and factory-installed seatbelts cost $9. The public took to safety in a modest way early in the model year. But the rush to install seatbelts overtaxed Ford's supplier, and only 20 percent of the cars were so equipped. Ford continued to stress safety for a few years, but after Ford failed to catch Chevrolet in 1956, a lot of dealers said performance was more important.

An interesting 1955-56 model was the two-door Crown Victoria, developed from the 1954 Skyliner. Some featured the transparent half-top. All had a broad, stainless-steel wrapover roof band that looked like a roll bar, but added little if any strength. The model was dropped for 1957. Altogether, Ford sold 13,344 plastic-roof cars for 1954, 1999 for '55; and only 603 for '56. Though attractive, they were expensive and the plastic roof made them hot on a summer day.

Ford met dealer demand with an all-new '57 line, offering a vast array of V8 engines from the 190-bhp "300" powerplant on up to the Thunderbird's supercharged 312 V8 with 300 bhp. Wheelbase grew slightly, and there were now two of them, 116 and 118 inches. The model lineup was rearranged accordingly. There were Customs, including a business sedan; Custom 300s; Fairlanes; Fairlane 500s, including a Sunliner convertible and a retractable hardtop convertible; and Station Wagons. All were available with six or V8 power. The new styling was particularly simple for the period. It featured a clean, full-width rectangular grille; rakish side moldings; and tiny tailfins. It was a good year for the division. Some statisticians showed Ford ahead of Chevrolet in calendar year output for the first time since 1935, but the final tabulation indicated Chevy ahead by 130 cars. In model year production, though, Ford scored a substantial victory.

The Skyliner retractable hardtop was a unique mid-1957 arrival based on earlier developmental engineering by Continental Division. (A Mark II retractable was considered, but not produced.) Ford sold 20,766 retractables in 1957, but production tapered off quickly. The Skyliner was complicated and expensive: in '57, it cost $350 more than a standard convertible.

Ford settled for a facelift in 1958, using a bumper/grille reminiscent of the '58 Thunderbird and quad headlights. The cheaper of the two Custom series was retained. A recession now slowed sales. Ford sold fewer cars than Chevrolet, but hadn't invested as much money that year and was still able to keep production near a million units.

In 1959, Chevrolet fielded its all-new line of radical bat-fin models that didn't strike the public's fancy. Ford passed Chevy by some 12,000 units for the 12 months. The '59 Ford used the basic '57 body with updated, though still conservative, styling. Bizarre two-toning and radical fins were avoided in favor of a squared-off grille with floating, starlike ornaments, and simple side moldings. A new Galaxie series with a T-Bird-like roofline was added. It included sedans, hardtops, and a convertible.

For Ford Motor Company as a whole, 1959 justified the strenuous efforts of Henry Ford II and board chairman Ernest Breech. They had assumed control of a third-rate company in 1945, and had turned it into something approaching General Motors in less than 15 years.

Ford's history in the '60s closely parallels Chevrolet's. When the decade ended, the division was producing about 100,000 more cars each year than in 1960. During the period, Ford expanded into several important new markets, including economy compacts and sportier versions of regular production models. And like Chevrolet, Ford built these diverse types on relatively few wheelbases. (The two most highly specialized Fords, Mustang and Thunderbird, are discussed separately.)

Management changed rapidly. Lee A. Iacocca arrived as division general manager in 1960. In 1961, George Walker left as chief stylist, and Eugene Bordinat became Ford's chief of automotive design. Iacocca soon put an end to Robert S. McNamara's concept of building mundane people-haulers. By 1970, Ford was offering some of the world's best road cars. For much of the decade, Fords were the cars to beat on the nation's racetracks. In fact, the 1968-69 Dodge Charger racing program was an all-out effort to halt the Ford super-stockers. In this period, the division also evolved from a "Chevy-follower" to a "Chevy-leader." Its compact Falcon outsold the Corvair; its 1962 Fairlane intermediate was a bit ahead of, and more popular than, the Chevy II; its Mustang changed the public's attitude toward compact cars and sent Chevrolet racing to the drawing boards to develop the Camaro.

Looking at the size of Ford's products is the best way to summarize its cars of the '60s. The smallest was the

1957 Fairlane four-door Town sedan

1958 Fairlane 500 Skyliner retractable hardtop

Prototype for 1959 Galaxie hardtop coupe

Falcon, which rode a 109.5-inch wheelbase through 1965, and longer wheelbases from 1966 on. Falcon production gradually decreased, largely because of competition from both inside and outside Ford Division, but the car was always a profit-maker. To many, it was the ultimate "throw-away" car—built to sell at a low price, and designed to be discarded within a few years. Compared with the Corvair, Falcon's conventional independent front suspension, beam-axle rear suspension, and ordinary six-cylinder engine were uninteresting. But they added up to a simple little car that rode well, stopped well, provided excellent space utilization, and delivered 20–25 miles per gallon.

Ford brought out the bucket-seated Falcon Futura coupe as an answer to the Corvair Monza in the spring of 1961. This sporty little car was restyled for '64 with a much less distinctive, squared-off shape. The ultimate collector's Falcon, however, is the Futura Sprint, introduced for 1963½. Offered as a convertible or hardtop, it

1962 Falcon Futura two-door coupe

1967 Falcon Futura Sports Coupe

1963 Falcon Futura Sprint hardtop coupe

1968 Falcon Futura four-door station wagon

1964 Falcon two-door sedan

1969 Falcon Futura Sports Coupe

was powered by the compact yet lively small-block Fairlane V8. It was one of the finest engines built, and one of the most economical. The 260 completely transformed the Falcon's performance without greatly affecting gas mileage. Sprints had special trim, bucket seats, console, and full instrumentation including a 6000-rpm tachometer. When equipped with optional four-speed transmission, they were great fun to drive.

In 1966, Falcon was restyled a third time. It received a longer wheelbase and long-hood/short-deck proportions like the Mustang's. It remained in this form through the rest of the '60s. Ford later enlarged the small-block V8 to 289 cid and it also became a Falcon option. In its last year before emission controls, the 289 "Stage 2" offered 225 bhp with four-barrel carburetors, and made Falcon Sprints very fast. For 1968, the 289 was detuned to 195 bhp, but the larger 302-cid V8 appeared as an option. Equipped with a two-barrel carburetor, the 302 ran on regular gas and developed 210 bhp. With the four barrel, it required premium fuel, but developed 230 bhp. Stringent emissions controls meant

the end of the four-barrel package by 1969.

Ford held pat in early 1970 with a Falcon identical to the '69 version. Then it brought out a new mid-year model using the intermediate Torino bodyshell. These were much larger cars, from 10 to 22 inches longer than their predecessors. Ultimately, Falcon was displaced by another new 1970 offering, the compact Maverick.

In 1962, Ford broke new ground with the "intermediate-size" Fairlane. The name (originally derived from Henry Ford's estate) had been lifted from a series in the large Ford line. In concept, the Fairlane was identical with Virgil Exner's downsized '62 Plymouths and Dodges. But unlike Chrysler, Ford retained its full-size cars—a wise move, even though Fairlane sold more than 297,000 units for 1962, and broke the 300,000-unit level in 1963.

The Fairlane was significant for reasons other than first-year sales. It was the first Ford to use the small-block V8, the basis for some of Ford's hottest performance models. Bored out to 289 cid as a 1963 option, it developed 271 bhp, almost one horsepower per cubic

1970 Falcon Futura four-door sedan

1968 Torino GT fastback hardtop coupe

1963 Fairlane 500 four-door sedan

1969 Torino Squire four-door station wagon

1967 Fairlane 500XL hardtop coupe

1969 Fairlane 500 convertible

inch. Stroked to 302 cid in 1968, it delivered 230 bhp when equipped with the special carburetion setup. Powerful and smooth, yet surprisingly economical, this engine in all three displacements was the definitive small V8. Tuned versions used in racing and sports cars like the Ford GT40 and the Shelby Cobra disproved the old saw about there being no substitute for cubic inches. The GT40 nearly took the world GT Manufacturers Trophy away from Ferrari in its first full year of competition, 1964. In 1966 and again in '67, it won the LeMans 24 Hours outright.

Initially, Fairlane rode a 115.5-inch wheelbase and offered only two-door and four-door sedan body styles. As time went on, the line got more exciting. Along with a number of station wagons, a new Fairlane 500 series was added for 1963. The best Fairlanes appeared in '66 with a completely restyled body mounted on a 116-inch wheelbase (113 inches for wagons). These were long, sleek cars with smooth lines, curved side glass, and vertical taillights. The top of the line that year was the bucket-seat 500XL series, a hardtop coupe and a con-

vertible in standard and GT trim. Although they could be ordered with the 120-bhp six, most were equipped with the 289 V8. The fastest were the GTs, powered by Ford's new 390 V8 as standard equipment. Rated at 335 horsepower, this potent powerplant had a 10.5:1 compression ratio that necessitated premium fuel. Since the 390 could be ordered on any Fairlane, racing drivers slotted it into the lighter two-door sedans that quickly earned respect for their competitive prowess. From 1964 on, Ford offered a growing assortment of handling and performance options, including shifter suspensions and four-speed gearboxes.

For 1968, Fairlane was again restyled and the Torino introduced as the top-line series. The base Torino came with the 115-bhp six, but the GTs were far more exciting, featuring bucket seats, center console, paint striping, and more performance options than a salesman could memorize.

For 1969, Torino was largely unchanged except for two new arrivals, the fastback and hardtop Torino Cobra. The name symbolized Ford's close relationship

with Carroll Shelby's muscular sports cars. The Cobra came with the 428-cid engine from the Mach I Mustang. This powerplant had first appeared in the 1968½ Mercury Cyclone, and was known as the Cobra Jet. A $133 option was "Ram-Air," a fiberglass hood scoop with a special air cleaner assembly that ducted incoming air directly into the carburetor through a valve in the air cleaner. Four-speed gearbox, competition suspension including stiff shocks and springs, and functional hood locking pins were all standard. One magazine was ac-

tually disappointed when its Torino Cobra ran from 0 to 60 in 7.2 seconds and the quarter-mile in 15 seconds at 98.3 miles per hour! On the other hand, just about everyone admitted that of all the '69 "supercars"—Plymouth GTX, Dodge Charger R/T, Pontiac GTO, Chevelle 396, and Buick GS 400—the Torino Cobra was the tightest, the best built, and the quietest.

Torinos were potent racing machines. Ford found that the styling of the Torino's Mercury counterpart, the Cyclone, was slightly more aerodynamic, and in 1969

1969 Torino GT fastback hardtop coupe

1961 Galaxie two-door sedan

1970 Torino Brougham hardtop coupe

1962 Galaxie two-door sedan

1970 Torino GT fastback hardtop coupe

1963 Galaxie 500 hardtop coupe

only Cyclones were run in races more than 250 miles long. Nevertheless, both the Torino and the Cyclone could achieve about 190 mph. Lee Roy Yarborough won the 1969 Daytona 500 in a Ford.

For 1970, the Fairlane name was applied to an off-shoot of the Torino line. There was all-new aero-dynamic styling on a one-inch longer wheelbase. Profiles were lower and five inches longer than in '69.

Despite the Falcon and Fairlane, Ford was still a determined producer of full-size cars in the 1960s. The big models—the Custom, pre-1962 Fairlane, Galaxie, Galaxie 500, 500 XL, and LTD—all used Ford's 119-inch wheelbase (increased to 121 inches for 1969). They were heavy and not particularly exciting to drive on anything other than a superhighway. But plenty of interesting variations developed that made these 3000–4000-pound cruisers surprisingly capable, even on winding roads.

The big-car lineup for 1960 comprised Custom, Fairlane, Galaxie, and station wagon models available with

1965 Galaxie 500 LTD hardtop sedan

1966 Country Squire four-door station wagon

1967 Galaxie 500XL hardtop coupe

1968 Galaxie 500 convertible

1968 LTD hardtop sedan

1969 Country Squire four-door station wagon

1969 Galaxie 500 fastback hardtop coupe

1969 LTD hardtop sedan

1970 XL convertible

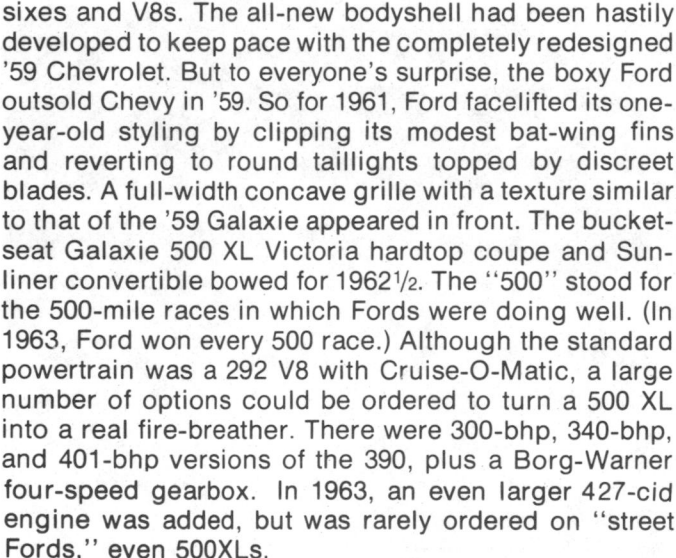

1970 Maverick two-door sedan

sixes and V8s. The all-new bodyshell had been hastily developed to keep pace with the completely redesigned '59 Chevrolet. But to everyone's surprise, the boxy Ford outsold Chevy in '59. So for 1961, Ford facelifted its one-year-old styling by clipping its modest bat-wing fins and reverting to round taillights topped by discreet blades. A full-width concave grille with a texture similar to that of the '59 Galaxie appeared in front. The bucket-seat Galaxie 500 XL Victoria hardtop coupe and Sun-liner convertible bowed for 1962½. The "500" stood for the 500-mile races in which Fords were doing well. (In 1963, Ford won every 500 race.) Although the standard powertrain was a 292 V8 with Cruise-O-Matic, a large number of options could be ordered to turn a 500 XL into a real fire-breather. There were 300-bhp, 340-bhp, and 401-bhp versions of the 390, plus a Borg-Warner four-speed gearbox. In 1963, an even larger 427-cid engine was added, but was rarely ordered on "street Fords," even 500XLs.

The 1963 Galaxie was a facelifted version of the chunky '62 styling. The line was augmented at mid-year by a set of 500 and 500XL sports hardtops with ultra-thin fastback rooflines. Both were available with 427 cubic-inch engines. For 1964, the big cars had more sculptured sheetmetal and a horizontal-bar grille, as well as a new roofline for four-door hardtops.

The 1964 lineup collectively won *Motor Trend* magazine's "Car of the Year" award on the basis of its "total performance" image. Performance was just what the big Fords delivered. A pair of Galaxie 500XLs tested by the magazine that year were truly impressive. The 390 V8 powered one of them from 0 to 60 mph in 9.3 sec-

onds; the 427 made that run in 7.4 seconds. The only complaints were the car's tendency to nosedive in panic stops and a slight roughness in the power brakes.

The 1965 Fords were completely restyled with longer, sleeker lines. They were also fitted with a new, sophisticated front suspension. Making their debut were the Galaxie LTD hardtop coupe and sedan, priced at about $3300. LTDs were favorably compared in quietness at speed to Rolls-Royces—at least in Ford advertising.

Ford held onto the '65 design through 1967, along with the 119-inch wheelbase. The 1968 models had new sheetmetal below the beltline, and concealed headlights on XL and LTD models. The '69 edition had new sheetmetal everywhere, a two-inch longer wheelbase, a tunneled backlight for SportsRoof (fastback) models, and ventless door glass on hardtops and convertibles. The LTD had become a separate series in 1967, and quickly became a strong sales contender. Ford built nearly 139,000 of them for '68, and more than twice that many for '69.

Throughout the decade, Ford production kept pace with Chevrolet's, often coming close to leading. In 1965, Ford enjoyed its first two-million-car year.

The full-size 1970 Fords had new grilles with a 'poke-through' center section on LTDs and XLs, new sheetmetal, and a new rear bumper with integral, horizontal taillamps. No less than five series were offered, with the LTD Brougham at the top of the line. A brand-new entry was the Maverick, a compact semi-fastback two-door sedan on a 103-inch wheelbase. Ideal for the '70s, Maverick took off in sales and succeeded the Falcon as the economy car in the lineup.

# Ford Specifications

## 1940—541,896 built

### 01A V8/85 (wb 112.0)

| | | Wght | Price | Prod |
|---|---|---|---|---|
| | cpe | 2,763 | 660 | — |
| | bus cpe | 2,801 | 681 | — |
| | Tudor sdn | 2,909 | 701 | — |
| | Fordor sdn | 2,936 | 747 | — |
| | wgn 4d | 3,249 | 875 | — |
| | DeLuxe cpe | 2,791 | 722 | — |
| | DeLuxe bus cpe | 2,831 | 742 | — |
| | DeLuxe conv cpe | 2,956 | 849 | — |
| | DeLuxe Tudor sdn | 2,927 | 762 | — |
| | DeLuxe Fordor sdn | 2,966 | 808 | — |
| | DeLuxe wgn 4d | 3,262 | 947 | — |

### 02A V8/60 (wb 112.0)

| | | Wght | Price | Prod |
|---|---|---|---|---|
| | cpe | 2,519 | 619 | — |
| | bus cpe | 2,549 | 640 | — |
| | Tudor sdn | 2,669 | 660 | — |
| | Fordor sdn | 2,696 | 706 | — |

| 1940 Engines | bore×stroke | bhp | availability |
|---|---|---|---|
| V8, 136.0 | 2.60×3.20 | 60 | S-V8/60 |
| V8, 221.0 | 3.06×3.75 | 85 | S-V8/85 |

## 1941—691,896 built

### 1GA Six (wb 114.0)

| | | Wght | Price | Prod |
|---|---|---|---|---|
| | Special cpe | 2,870 | 684 | — |
| | Special Tudor sdn | 2,975 | 720 | — |
| | Special Fordor sdn | 3,020 | 761 | — |
| | Deluxe cpe | 2,947 | 715 | — |
| | DeLuxe cpe, A/S | 2,970 | 746 | — |
| | DeLuxe Tudor sdn | 3,065 | 756 | — |
| | DeLuxe Fordor sdn | 3,100 | 797 | — |
| | DeLuxe wgn 4d | 3,395 | 946 | — |
| | Super DeLuxe cpe | 2,934 | 761 | — |
| | Super DeLuxe cpe, A/S | 2,974 | 792 | — |
| | Super DeLuxe sdn cpe | 3,030 | 833 | — |
| | Super DeLuxe conv cpe | 3,145 | 931 | — |
| | Super DeLuxe Tudor sdn | 3,096 | 802 | — |
| | Super DeLuxe Fordor sdn | 3,131 | 843 | — |
| | Super DeLuxe wgn 4d | 3,400 | 998 | — |

### 11A V8 (wb 114.0)

| | | Wght | Price | Prod |
|---|---|---|---|---|
| | Special cpe | 2,878 | 700 | — |
| | Special Tudor sdn | 2,983 | 736 | — |
| | Special Fordor sdn | 3,033 | 777 | — |
| | Deluxe cpe | 2,953 | 730 | — |
| | DeLuxe cpe, A/S | 2,981 | 761 | — |
| | DeLuxe Tudor sdn | 3,095 | 772 | — |
| | DeLuxe Fordor sdn | 3,121 | 813 | — |
| | DeLuxe wgn 4d | 3,412 | 962 | — |
| | Super DeLuxe cpe | 2,969 | 777 | — |
| | Super DeLuxe cpe, A/S | 3,001 | 807 | — |
| | Super DeLuxe sdn cpe | 3,052 | 849 | — |
| | Super DeLuxe conv cpe | 3,187 | 946 | — |
| | Super DeLuxe Tudor sdn | 3,110 | 818 | — |
| | Super DeLuxe Fordor sdn | 3,146 | 859 | — |
| | Super DeLuxe wgn 4d | 3,419 | 1,013 | — |

| 1941 Engines | bore×stroke | bhp | availability |
|---|---|---|---|
| L6, 226.0 | 3.30×4.40 | 90 | S-Six |
| V8, 221.0 | 3.06×3.75 | 85 | S-V8 |

## 1942—160,432 built

### 2GA Six (wb 114.0)

| | | Wght | Price | Prod |
|---|---|---|---|---|
| 70C | Special Tudor sdn | 3,053 | 815 | — |
| 73C | Special Fordor sdn | 3,093 | 850 | — |
| 77C | Special cpe | 2,910 | 780 | — |
| 70A | DeLuxe Tudor sdn | 3,122 | 840 | — |
| 72A | DeLuxe sdn cpe | 3,045 | 865 | — |
| 73A | DeLuxe Fordor sdn | 3,141 | 875 | — |
| 77A | DeLuxe cpe | 2,958 | 805 | — |
| 79A | DeLuxe wgn 4d, 8P | 3,405 | 1,035 | — |
| 70B | Super DeLuxe Tudor sdn | 3,136 | 885 | — |
| 72B | Super DeLuxe sdn cpe | 3,109 | 910 | — |
| 73B | Super DeLuxe Fordor sdn | 3,179 | 920 | — |
| 76 | Super DeLuxe conv cpe | 3,218 | 1,080 | — |
| 77B | Super DeLuxe cpe | 3,030 | 850 | — |
| 79B | Super DeLuxe wgn 4d, 8P | 3,453 | 1,115 | — |

### 21A V8 (wb 114.0)

| | | Wght | Price | Prod |
|---|---|---|---|---|
| 70A | DeLuxe Tudor sdn | 3,141 | 850 | — |
| 72A | DeLuxe sdn cpe | 3,065 | 875 | — |
| 73A | DeLuxe Fordor sdn | 3,161 | 885 | — |
| 77A | DeLuxe cpe | 2,978 | 815 | — |
| 79A | DeLuxe wgn 4d | 3,420 | 1,090 | — |
| 70B | Super DeLuxe Tudor sdn | 3,159 | 895 | — |
| 72B | Super DeLuxe sdn cpe | 3,120 | 920 | — |
| 73B | Super DeLuxe Fordor sdn | 3,200 | 930 | — |
| 76 | Super DeLuxe conv cpe | 3,238 | 1,090 | — |
| 77B | Super DeLuxe cpe | 3,050 | 860 | — |
| 79B | Super DeLuxe wgn 4d, 8P | 3,468 | 1,125 | — |

| 1942 Engines | bore×stroke | bhp | availability |
|---|---|---|---|
| L6, 226.0 | 3.30×4.40 | 90 | S-Six |
| V8, 221.0 | 3.06×3.75 | 90 | S-V8 |

## 1946

### 6GA Six (wb 114.0)*

| | | Wght | Price | Prod |
|---|---|---|---|---|
| 70A | DeLuxe Tudor sdn | 3,157 | 1,136 | — |
| 73A | DeLuxe Fordor sdn | 3,187 | 1,198 | — |
| 77A | DeLuxe cpe | 3,007 | 1,074 | — |
| 70B | Super DeLuxe Tudor sdn | 3,157 | 1,211 | — |
| 72B | Super DeLuxe cpe sdn | 3,107 | 1,257 | — |
| 73B | Super DeLuxe Fordor sdn | 3,207 | 1,273 | — |
| 77B | Super DeLuxe cpe | 3,007 | 1,148 | — |
| 79B | Super DeLuxe wgn 4d | 3,457 | 1,504 | — |

### 69A V8 (wb 114.0)*

| | | Wght | Price | Prod |
|---|---|---|---|---|
| 70A | DeLuxe Tudor sdn | 3,190 | 1,185 | — |
| 73A | DeLuxe Fordor sdn | 3,220 | 1,248 | — |
| 77A | DeLuxe cpe | 3,040 | 1,123 | — |
| 70B | Super DeLuxe Tudor sdn | 3,190 | 1,260 | — |
| 71 | Super DeLuxe Sprtsmn conv | 3,340 | 1,982 | 1,209 |
| 72B | Super DeLuxe cpe sdn | 3,140 | 1,307 | — |
| 73B | Super DeLuxe Fordor sdn | 3,240 | 1,322 | — |
| 76 | Super DeLuxe conv cpe | 3,240 | 1,488 | — |
| 77B | Super DeLuxe cpe | 3,040 | 1,197 | — |
| 79B | Super DeLuxe wgn 4d, 8P | 3,490 | 1,533 | — |

**\*Model Year Production by Body Style (Six/V8):**

### DeLuxe (wb 114.0)

| | | | | |
|---|---|---|---|---|
| | Tudor sdn | | | 74,954 |
| | Fordor sdn | | | 9,246 |

|  | Wght | Price | Prod |
|---|---|---|---|
| cpe |  |  | 10,670 |
| chassis |  |  | 86 |

### Super DeLuxe (wb 114.0)

|  | Wght | Price | Prod |
|---|---|---|---|
| Tudor sdn |  |  | 163,370 |
| Fordor sdn |  |  | 92,056 |
| sdn cpe |  |  | 70,826 |
| conv cpe |  |  | 16,359 |
| cpe |  |  | 12,249 |
| wgn 4d |  |  | 16,960 |
| chassis |  |  | 37 |

| 1946 Engines | bore×stroke | bhp | availability |
|---|---|---|---|
| L6, 226.0 | 3.30×4.40 | 90 | S-Six |
| V8, 239.4 | 3.19×3.75 | 100 | S-V8 |

## 1947

### 7GA Six (wb 114.0)*

|  | Wght | Price | Prod |
|---|---|---|---|
| DeLuxe Fordor sdn | 3,213 | 1,270 | — |
| DeLuxe Tudor sdn | 3,183 | 1,212 | — |
| Deluxe cpe | 3,033 | 1,154 | — |
| Super DeLuxe Fordor sdn | 3,233 | 1,372 | — |
| Super DeLuxe Tudor sdn | 3,183 | 1,309 | — |
| Super DeLuxe cpe sdn | 3,133 | 1,330 | — |
| Super DeLuxe cpe | 3,033 | 1,251 | — |
| Super DeLuxe wgn 4d, 8P | 3,487 | 1,893 | — |

### 79A V8 (wb 114.0)*

|  | Wght | Price | Prod |
|---|---|---|---|
| DeLuxe Fordor sdn | 3,246 | 1,346 | — |
| DeLuxe Tudor sdn | 3,216 | 1,288 | — |
| DeLuxe cpe | 3,066 | 1,230 | — |
| Super DeLuxe Fordor sdn | 3,266 | 1,440 | — |
| Super DeLuxe Tudor sdn | 3,216 | 1,382 | — |
| Super DeLuxe cpe sdn | 3,166 | 1,409 | — |
| Super DeLuxe conv cpe | 3,266 | 1,740 | 22,159 |
| Super DeLuxe Sprtsmn conv | 3,366 | 2,282 | 2,250 |
| Super DeLuxe wgn 4d, 8P | 3,520 | 1,972 | — |

*Model Year Production by Body Style (Six/V8):

### DeLuxe (wb 114.0)

|  | Wght | Price | Prod |
|---|---|---|---|
| Tudor sdn |  |  | 44,523 |
| Fordor sdn |  |  | 20 |
| cpe |  |  | 10,872 |
| chassis |  |  | 23 |

### Super DeLuxe (wb 114.0)

|  | Wght | Price | Prod |
|---|---|---|---|
| Tudor sdn |  |  | 136,126 |
| Fordor sdn |  |  | 116,744 |
| cpe sdn |  |  | 80,830 |
| wgn 4d, 8P |  |  | 16,104 |
| chassis |  |  | 23 |

| 1947 Engines | bore×stroke | bhp | availability |
|---|---|---|---|
| L6, 226.0 | 3.30×4.40 | 90 | S-Six |
| V8, 239.4 | 3.19×3.75 | 100 | S-V8 |

## 1948

### 87HA Six (wb 114.0)*

|  |  | Wght | Price | Prod |
|---|---|---|---|---|
| 70A | DeLuxe Tudor sdn | 3,183 | 1,212 | — |
| 77A | Deluxe cpe | 3,033 | 1,154 | — |
| 70B | Super DeLuxe Tudor sdn | 3,183 | 1,309 | — |
| 72B | Super DeLuxe cpe sdn | 3,133 | 1,330 | — |
| 73B | Super DeLuxe Fordor sdn | 3,233 | 1,372 | — |
| 79B | Super DeLuxe wgn 4d, 8P | 3,487 | 1,893 | — |

### 89A V8 (wb 114.0)*

|  |  | Wght | Price | Prod |
|---|---|---|---|---|
| 70A | DeLuxe Tudor sdn | 3,216 | 1,288 | — |

|  |  | Wght | Price | Prod |
|---|---|---|---|---|
| 77A | DeLuxe cpe | 3,066 | 1,230 | — |
| 70B | Super DeLuxe Tudor sdn | 3,216 | 1,382 | — |
| 71B | Super DeLuxe Sprtsmn conv | 3,366 | 2,282 | 28 |
| 72B | Super DeLuxe cpe sdn | 3,166 | 1,409 | — |
| 73B | Super DeLuxe Fordor sdn | 3,266 | 1,440 | — |
| 76B | Super DeLuxe conv cpe | 3,266 | 1,740 | 12,033 |
| 79B | Super DeLuxe wgn 4d, 8P | 3,520 | 1,972 | — |

*Model Year Production by Body Style (Six/V8):

### DeLuxe (wb 114.0)

|  | Wght | Price | Prod |
|---|---|---|---|
| Tudor sdn |  |  | 23,356 |
| cpe |  |  | 5,048 |

### Super DeLuxe (wb 114.0)

|  | Wght | Price | Prod |
|---|---|---|---|
| Tudor sdn |  |  | 82,161 |
| Fordor sdn |  |  | 71,358 |
| cpe sdn |  |  | 44,826 |
| wgn 4d, 8P |  |  | 8,912 |

| 1948 Engines | bore×stroke | bhp | availability |
|---|---|---|---|
| L6, 226.0 | 3.30×4.40 | 95 | S-Six |
| V8, 239.4 | 3.19×3.75 | 100 | S-V8 |

## 1949

### Standard (wb 114.0)

|  |  | Wght | Price | Prod |
|---|---|---|---|---|
| 70A | Tudor sdn | 2,965 | 1,425 | 126,770 |
| 72A | club cpe | 2,945 | 1,415 | 4,170 |
| 72C | bus cpe | 2,891 | 1,333 | 28,946 |
| 73A | Fordor sdn | 3,010 | 1,472 | 44,563 |
| — | chassis | — | — | 1 |

### Custom V8 (wb 114.0)

|  |  | Wght | Price | Prod |
|---|---|---|---|---|
| 70B | Tudor sdn | 2,968 | 1,511 | 433,316 |
| 72B | club cpe | 2,948 | 1,511 | 150,254 |
| 73B | Fordor sdn | 3,013 | 1,559 | 248,176 |
| 76 | conv cpe | 3,254 | 1,886 | 51,133 |
| 79 | wgn 2d, 8P | 3,543 | 2,119 | 31,412 |
| — | chassis | — | — | 18 |

| 1949 Engines | bore×stroke | bhp | availability |
|---|---|---|---|
| L6, 226.0 | 3.30×4.40 | 95 | S-Six |
| V8, 239.4 | 3.19×3.75 | 100 | O-V8 |

## 1950

### DeLuxe (wb 114.0)

|  |  | Wght | Price | Prod |
|---|---|---|---|---|
| D70 | Tudor sdn | 3,007 | 1,424 | 275,360 |
| D72C | bus cpe | 2,949 | 1,333 | 35,120 |
| D73 | Fordor sdn | 3,064 | 1,472 | 77,888 |

### Custom (wb 114.0)

|  |  | Wght | Price | Prod |
|---|---|---|---|---|
| C70 | Tudor sdn | 3,015 | 1,511 | 398,060 |
| C70C | Crestliner sdn 2d | 3,050 | 1,711 | 17,601 |
| C72 | club cpe | 2,981 | 1,511 | 85,111 |
| C73 | Fordor sdn | 3,078 | 1,558 | 247,181 |
| C76 | conv cpe | 3,263 | 1,948 | 50,299 |
| C79 | Country Squire wgn 2d | 3,511 | 2,028 | 22,292 |

| 1950 Engines | bore×stroke | bhp | availability |
|---|---|---|---|
| L6, 226.0 | 3.30×4.40 | 95 | S-all exc C70C, C76 |
| V8, 239.4 | 3.19×3.75 | 100 | S-C70C, C76; O-others |

## 1951

### DeLuxe (wb 114.0)

|  |  | Wght | Price | Prod |
|---|---|---|---|---|
| 70 | Tudor sdn | 3,043 | 1,417 | 146,010 |

| | | Wght | Price | Prod |
|---|---|---|---|---|
| 72C | bus cpe | 2,979 | 1,324 | 20,343 |
| 73 | Fordor sdn | 3,102 | 1,465 | 54,265 |

**Custom (wb 114.0)**

| | | Wght | Price | Prod |
|---|---|---|---|---|
| 60 | Victoria htp cpe | 3,188 | 1,925 | 110,286 |
| 70 | Tudor sdn | 3,043 | 1,505 | 317,869 |
| 70C | Crestliner sdn 2d | 3,065 | 1,595 | 8,703 |
| 72 | club cpe | 3,015 | 1,505 | 53,263 |
| 73 | Fordor sdn | 3,102 | 1,553 | 232,691 |
| 76 | conv cpe | 3,268 | 1,949 | 40,934 |
| 79 | Country Squire wgn 2d | 3,530 | 2,029 | 29,017 |

| 1951 Engines | bore×stroke | bhp | availability |
|---|---|---|---|
| L6, 226.0 | 3.30×4.40 | 95 | S-all exc 60, 70C, 76 |
| V8, 239.4 | 3.19×3.75 | 100 | S-60, 70C, 76; O-others |

## 1952

**Mainline (wb 115.0)**

| | | Wght | Price | Prod |
|---|---|---|---|---|
| 59A | Ranch Wagon 2d | 3,212 | 1,832 | 32,566 |
| 70A | sdn 2d | 3,111 | 1,485 | 79,931 |
| 72C | bus cpe | 3,035 | 1,389 | 10,137 |
| 73A | sdn 4d | 3,190 | 1,530 | 41,227 |

**Customline (wb 115.0)**

| | | Wght | Price | Prod |
|---|---|---|---|---|
| 70B | sdn 2d | 3,111 | 1,570 | 175,762 |
| 72B | club cpe | 3,116 | 1,579 | 26,550 |
| 73B | sdn 4d | 3,190 | 1,615 | 188,303 |
| 79C | Country Sedan wgn 4d, 6P | 3,617 | 2,060 | 11,927 |

**Crestline (wb 115.0)**

| | | Wght | Price | Prod |
|---|---|---|---|---|
| 60B | Victoria htp cpe | 3,274 | 1,925 | 77,320 |
| 76B | Sunliner conv cpe | 3,339 | 2,027 | 22,534 |
| 79B | Country Squire wgn 4d, 8P | 3,640 | 2,186 | 5,426 |

| 1952 Engines | bore×stroke | bhp | availability |
|---|---|---|---|
| L6, 215.3 | 3.56×3.60 | 101 | S-all exc 79C, Crestline (ohv) |
| V8, 239.4 | 3.19×3.75 | 110 | S-79C, Crestline; O-others |

## 1953

**Mainline (wb 115.0)**

| | | Wght | Price | Prod |
|---|---|---|---|---|
| 59A | Ranch Wagon 2d | 3,406 | 1,917 | 66,976 |
| 70A | sdn 2d | 3,092 | 1,497 | 152,995 |
| 72C | bus cpe | 3,018 | 1,400 | 16,280 |
| 73A | sdn 4d | 3,138 | 1,542 | 69,463 |

**Customline (wb 115.0)**

| | | Wght | Price | Prod |
|---|---|---|---|---|
| 70B | sdn 2d | 3,100 | 1,582 | 305,433 |
| 72B | club cpe | 3,084 | 1,591 | 43,999 |
| 73B | sdn 4d | 3,154 | 1,628 | 374,487 |
| 79B | Country Sedan wgn 4d, 6P | 3,539 | 2,076 | 37,743 |

**Crestline (wb 115.0)**

| | | Wght | Price | Prod |
|---|---|---|---|---|
| 60B | Victoria htp cpe | 3,250 | 1,941 | 128,302 |
| 76B | Sunliner conv cpe | 3,334 | 2,043 | 40,861 |
| 79C | Country Squire wgn 4d, 8P | 3,609 | 2,203 | 11,001 |
| — | chassis | — | — | 2 |

| 1953 Engines | bore×stroke | bhp | availability |
|---|---|---|---|
| L6, 215.3 | 3.56×3.60 | 101 | S-all exc 79B, Crestline |
| V8, 239.4 | 3.19×3.75 | 110 | S-79B, Crestline; O-others |

## 1954

**Mainline (wb 115.5)**

| | | Wght | Price | Prod |
|---|---|---|---|---|
| 59A | Ranch Wagon 2d | 3,399 | 2,029 | 44,315 |
| 70A | sdn 2d | 3,147 | 1,651 | 123,329 |

| | | Wght | Price | Prod |
|---|---|---|---|---|
| 72C | bus cpe | 3,082 | 1,548 | 10,665 |
| 73A | sdn 4d | 3,203 | 1,701 | 55,371 |

**Customline (wb 115.5)**

| | | Wght | Price | Prod |
|---|---|---|---|---|
| 59B | Ranch Wagon 2d | 3,405 | 2,122 | 36,086 |
| 70B | sdn 2d | 3,160 | 1,744 | 293,375 |
| 72B | club cpe | 3,141 | 1,753 | 33,951 |
| 73B | sdn 4d | 3,216 | 1,793 | 262,499 |
| 79B | Country Sedan wgn 4d, 6P | 3,574 | 2,202 | 48,384 |

**Crestline (wb 115.5)**

| | | Wght | Price | Prod |
|---|---|---|---|---|
| 60B | Victoria htp cpe | 3,245 | 2,055 | 95,464 |
| 60F | Skyliner htp cpe | 3,265 | 2,164 | 13,344 |
| 73C | sdn 4d | 3,220 | 1,898 | 99,677 |
| 76B | Sunliner conv cpe | 3,292 | 2,164 | 36,685 |
| 79C | Country Squire wgn 4d, 8P | 3,624 | 2,339 | 12,797 |

| 1954 Engines | bore×stroke | bhp | availability |
|---|---|---|---|
| L6, 223.0 | 3.62×3.60 | 115 | S-all exc 79B |
| V8, 239.4 | 3.50×3.10 | 130 | S-79B; O-others (ohv) |

## 1955

**Mainline (wb 115.5)**

| | | Wght | Price | Prod |
|---|---|---|---|---|
| 70A | sdn 2d | 3,119 | 1,707 | 76,698 |
| 70D | bus cpe | 3,081 | 1,606 | 8,809 |
| 73A | sdn 4d | 3,161 | 1,753 | 41,794 |

**Customline (wb 115.5)**

| | | Wght | Price | Prod |
|---|---|---|---|---|
| 70B | sdn 2d | 3,139 | 1,801 | 236,575 |
| 73B | sdn 4d | 3,181 | 1,845 | 235,417 |

**Fairlane (wb 115.5)**

| | | Wght | Price | Prod |
|---|---|---|---|---|
| 60B | Victoria htp cpe | 3,251 | 2,095 | 113,372 |
| 64A | Crown Victoria htp cpe | 3,313 | 2,202 | 33,165 |
| 64B | Crown Vic htp cpe, glass top | 3,321 | 2,272 | 1,999 |
| 70C | club sdn 2d | 3,155 | 1,914 | 173,311 |
| 73C | Town Sedan | 3,201 | 1,960 | 254,437 |
| 76B | Sunliner conv cpe | 3,315 | 2,224 | 49,966 |

**Station Wagon (wb 115.5)**

| | | Wght | Price | Prod |
|---|---|---|---|---|
| 59A | Ranch 2d, 6P | 3,376 | 2,043 | 40,493 |
| 59B | Custom Ranch 2d, 6P | 3,394 | 2,109 | 43,671 |
| 79B | Country Sedan 4d, 8P | 3,536 | 2,287 | 53,209 |
| 79C | Country Squire 4d, 8P | 3,538 | 2,392 | 19,011 |
| 79D | Country Sedan 4d, 6P | 3,460 | 2,156 | 53,075 |

| 1955 Engines | bore×stroke | bhp | availability |
|---|---|---|---|
| L6, 223.0 | 3.62×3.60 | 120 | S-all |
| V8, 272.0 | 3.62×3.30 | 162 | O-all |
| V8, 272.0 | 3.62×3.30 | 182 | O-all |

## 1956

**Mainline (wb 115.5)**

| | | Wght | Price | Prod |
|---|---|---|---|---|
| 70A | sdn 2d | 3,143 | 1,850 | 106,974 |
| 70D | bus sdn 2d | 3,088 | 1,748 | 8,020 |
| 73A | sdn 4d | 3,183 | 1,895 | 49,448 |

**Customline (wb 115.5)**

| | | Wght | Price | Prod |
|---|---|---|---|---|
| 64D | Victoria htp cpe | 3,202 | 1,985 | 33,130 |
| 70B | sdn 2d | 3,163 | 1,939 | 164,828 |
| 73B | sdn 4d | 3,203 | 1,985 | 170,695 |

**Fairlane (wb 115.5)**

| | | Wght | Price | Prod |
|---|---|---|---|---|
| 57A | Victoria htp sdn | 3,369 | 2,249 | 32,111 |
| 64A | Crown Victoria htp cpe | 3,289 | 2,337 | 9,209 |
| 64B | Crown Vic htp cpe, glass top | 3,299 | 2,407 | 603 |
| 64C | Victoria htp cpe | 3,274 | 2,194 | 177,735 |
| 70C | club sdn 2d | 3,179 | 2,047 | 142,629 |

| | | Wght | Price | Prod |
|---|---|---|---|---|
| 73C | Town Sedan | 3,219 | 2,093 | 224,872 |
| 76B | Sunliner conv cpe | 3,384 | 2,359 | 58,147 |

### Station Wagon (wb 115.5)

| | | Wght | Price | Prod |
|---|---|---|---|---|
| 59A | Ranch 2d, 6P | 3,402 | 2,185 | 48,348 |
| 59B | Custom Ranch 2d, 6P | 3,417 | 2,249 | 42,317 |
| 59C | Parklane 2d | 3,432 | 2,428 | 15,186 |
| 79B | Country Sedan 4d, 8P | 3,555 | 2,428 | 85,374 |
| 79C | Country Squire 4d, 8P | 3,566 | 2,533 | 23,221 |

| 1956 Engines | bore×stroke | bhp | availability | |
|---|---|---|---|---|
| L6, 223.0 | 3.62×3.60 | 137 | S-all | |
| V8, 272.0 | 3.62×3.30 | 173 | O-Mainline, Customline | |
| V8, 292.0 | 3.75×3.30 | 200 | O-Fairlane wgn, (202 bhp w/auto) | |
| V8, 312.0 | 3.80×3.44 | 215 | O-all (225 bhp w/auto) | |

## 1957

### Custom (wb 116.0)

| | | Wght | Price | Prod |
|---|---|---|---|---|
| 70A | sdn 2d | 3,211 | 1,991 | 116,963 |
| 70D | bus sdn 2d | 3,202 | 1,879 | 6,888 |
| 73A | sdn 4d | 3,254 | 2,042 | 68,924 |

### Custom 300 (wb 116.0)

| | | Wght | Price | Prod |
|---|---|---|---|---|
| 70B | sdn 2d | 3,224 | 2,105 | 160,360 |
| 73B | sdn 4d | 3,269 | 2,157 | 194,877 |

### Fairlane (wb 118.0)

| | | Wght | Price | Prod |
|---|---|---|---|---|
| 57B | Victoria htp sdn | 3,411 | 2,357 | 12,695 |
| 58A | Town Sedan 4d | 3,376 | 2,286 | 52,060 |
| 63B | Victoria htp cpe | 3,366 | 2,293 | 44,127 |
| 64A | club sdn 2d | 3,331 | 2,235 | 39,843 |

### Fairlane 500 (wb 118.0)

| | | Wght | Price | Prod |
|---|---|---|---|---|
| 51A | Skyliner retrac conv cpe | 3,916 | 2,942 | 20,766 |
| 57A | Victoria htp sdn | 3,426 | 2,404 | 68,550 |
| 58B | Town Sedan 4d | 3,384 | 2,286 | 193,162 |
| 63A | Victoria htp cpe | 3,381 | 2,339 | 183,202 |
| 64B | club sdn 2d | 3,346 | 2,281 | 93,756 |
| 76B | Sunliner conv cpe | 3,536 | 2,505 | 77,726 |

### Station Wagon (wb 116.0)

| | | Wght | Price | Prod |
|---|---|---|---|---|
| 59A | Ranch 2d, 6P | 3,455 | 2,301 | 60,486 |
| 59B | Del Rio 2d, 6P | 3,462 | 2,397 | 46,105 |
| 79C | Country Sedan 4d, 9P | 3,614 | 2,556 | 49,638 |
| 79D | Country Sedan 4d, 6P | 3,525 | 2,451 | 137,251 |
| 79E | Country Squire 4d, 9P | 3,628 | 2,684 | 27,690 |

| 1957 Engines | bore×stroke | bhp | availability | |
|---|---|---|---|---|
| L6, 223.0 | 3.62×3.60 | 144 | S-all exc 51A | |
| V8, 272.0 | 3.62×3.30 | 190 | S-51A; O-others | |
| V8, 292.0 | 3.75×3.30 | 212 | O-Fairlane, Fairlane 500, wgns | |
| V8, 312.0 | 3.80×3.44 | 245 | O-all | |

## 1958

### Custom (wb 116.0)

| | | Wght | Price | Prod |
|---|---|---|---|---|
| 70A | sdn 2d | 3,250 | 2,055 | 36,272 |
| 70D | bus sdn | 3,227 | 1,967 | 4,062 |
| 73A | sdn 4d | 3,278 | 2,109 | 27,811 |

### Custom 300 (wb 116.0)

| | | Wght | Price | Prod |
|---|---|---|---|---|
| 70B | sdn 2d | 3,300 | 2,305 | 137,169 |
| 73B | sdn 4d | 3,328 | 2,159 | 135,557 |

### Fairlane (wb 118.0)

| | | Wght | Price | Prod |
|---|---|---|---|---|
| 57B | Victoria htp sdn | 3,450 | 2,419 | 5,868 |
| 58A | Town Sedan 4d | 3,427 | 2,275 | 57,490 |
| 63B | Victoria htp cpe | 3,373 | 2,354 | 16,416 |
| 64A | club sdn 2d | 3,375 | 2,221 | 38,366 |

### Fairlane 500 (wb 118.0)

| | | Wght | Price | Prod |
|---|---|---|---|---|
| 51A | Skyliner retrac conv cpe | 4,069 | 3,163 | 14,713 |
| 57A | Victoria htp sdn | 3,488 | 2,499 | 36,509 |
| 58B | sdn 4d | 3,452 | 2,428 | 105,698 |
| 63A | Victoria htp cpe | 3,390 | 2,435 | 80,439 |
| 64B | club sdn 2d | 3,380 | 2,374 | 34,041 |
| 76B | Sunliner conv | 3,556 | 2,650 | 35,029 |

### Station Wagon (wb 116.0)

| | | Wght | Price | Prod |
|---|---|---|---|---|
| 59A | Ranch 2d, 6P | 3,552 | 2,397 | 34,578 |
| 59B | Del Rio 2d, 6P | 3,734 | 2,503 | 12,687 |
| 79A | Ranch 4d, 6P | 3,608 | 2,451 | 32,854 |
| 79C | Country Sedan 4d, 9P | 3,682 | 2,664 | 20,702 |
| 79D | Country Sedan 4d, 6P | 3,614 | 2,557 | 68,772 |
| 79E | Country Squire 4d, 9P | 3,718 | 2,794 | 15,020 |

| 1958 Engines | bore×stroke | bhp | availability | |
|---|---|---|---|---|
| L6, 223.0 | 3.62×3.60 | 145 | S-all exc 51A | |
| V8, 292.0 | 3.75×3.30 | 205 | S-51A; O-others | |
| V8, 332.0 | 4.00×3.30 | 240 | O-wgns (265 bhp w/auto) | |
| V8, 332.0 | 4.00×3.30 | 265 | O-all | |
| V8, 352.0 | 4.00×3.50 | 300 | O-all | |

## 1959

### Custom 300 (wb 118.0)

| | | Wght | Price | Prod |
|---|---|---|---|---|
| 58E | sdn 4d | 3,436 | 2,273 | 249,553 |
| 64F | sdn 2d | 3,360 | 2,219 | 228,576 |
| 64G | bus sdn | 3,334 | 2,132 | 4,084 |

### Fairlane (wb 118.0)

| | | Wght | Price | Prod |
|---|---|---|---|---|
| 58A | Town Sedan 4d | 3,466 | 2,411 | 64,663 |
| 64A | club sdn 2d | 3,382 | 2,357 | 35,126 |

### Fairlane 500 (wb 118.0)

| | | Wght | Price | Prod |
|---|---|---|---|---|
| 57A | Victoria htp sdn | 3,502 | 2,602 | 9,308 |
| 58B | sdn 4d | 3,468 | 2,530 | 35,670 |
| 63A | Victoria htp cpe | 3,416 | 2,537 | 23,892 |
| 64B | club sdn 2d | 3,388 | 2,476 | 10,141 |

### Galaxie (wb 118.0)

| | | Wght | Price | Prod |
|---|---|---|---|---|
| 51A | Skyliner retrac htp cpe | 4,064 | 3,346 | 12,915 |
| 54A | sdn 4d | 3,456 | 2,582 | 183,108 |
| 64H | club sdn 2d | 3,388 | 2,528 | 52,848 |
| 65A | Victoria htp cpe | 3,428 | 2,589 | 121,869 |
| 75A | Victoria htp sdn | 3,544 | 2,654 | 47,728 |
| 76B | Sunliner conv cpe | 3,578 | 2,839 | 45,868 |

### Station Wagon (wb 118.0)

| | | Wght | Price | Prod |
|---|---|---|---|---|
| 59C | Ranch 2d, 6P | 3,640 | 2,567 | 45,588 |
| 59D | Del Rio 2d, 6P | 3,664 | 2,678 | 8,663 |
| 71E | Country Sedan 4d, 9P | 3,818 | 2,829 | 28,811 |
| 71F | Country Sedan 4d, 6P | 3,768 | 2,745 | 94,601 |
| 71G | Country Squire 4d, 9P | 3,808 | 2,958 | 24,336 |
| 71H | Ranch 4d, 6P | 3,736 | 2,634 | 67,339 |

| 1959 Engines | bore×stroke | bhp | availability | |
|---|---|---|---|---|
| L6, 223.0 | 3.62×3.60 | 145 | S-all exc 51A | |
| V8, 292.0 | 3.75×3.30 | 200 | S-51A; O-others | |
| V8, 332.0 | 4.00×3.30 | 225 | O-all | |
| V8, 352.0 | 4.00×3.50 | 300 | O-all | |

## 1960

### Falcon (wb 109.5)

| | | Wght | Price | Prod |
|---|---|---|---|---|
| 58A | sdn 4d | 2,288 | 1,974 | 167,896 |
| 59A | wgn 2d | 2,540 | 2,225 | 27,552 |
| 64A | sdn 2d | 2,259 | 1,912 | 193,470 |
| 71A | wgn 4d | 2,575 | 2,287 | 46,758 |

| Custom 300 (wb 119.0) | | Wght | Price | Prod |
|---|---|---|---|---|
| 58F | sdn 4d | 3,576 | 2,284 | 572 |
| 64H | sdn 2d | 3,465 | 2,230 | 302 |

| Fairlane (wb 119.0) | | | | |
|---|---|---|---|---|
| 58E | sdn 4d | 3,656 | 2,311 | 109,801 |
| 64F | sdn 2d | 3,582 | 2,257 | 93,256 |
| 64G | bus sdn | 3,555 | 2,170 | 1,733 |

| Fairlane 500 (wb 119.0) | | | | |
|---|---|---|---|---|
| 58A | Town Sedan 4d | 3,663 | 2,388 | 153,234 |
| 64A | club sdn 2d | 3,586 | 2,334 | 91,041 |

| Galaxie (wb 119.0) | | | | |
|---|---|---|---|---|
| 54A | Town Sedan 4d | 3,684 | 2,603 | 104,784 |
| 62A | club sdn 2d | 3,603 | 2,549 | 31,866 |
| 63A | Starliner htp cpe | 3,617 | 2,610 | 68,461 |
| 76A | Victoria htp sdn | 3,692 | 2,675 | 39,215 |
| 76B | Sunliner conv cpe | 3,791 | 2,860 | 44,762 |

| Station Wagon (wb 119.0) | | | | |
|---|---|---|---|---|
| 59C | Ranch 2d, 6P | 3,881 | 2,586 | 27,136 |
| 71E | Country Sedan 4d, 9P | 4,058 | 2,837 | 19,277 |
| 71F | Country Sedan 4d, 6P | 4,012 | 2,752 | 59,302 |
| 71G | Country Squire 4d, 9P | 4,072 | 2,967 | 22,237 |
| 71H | Ranch 4d, 6P | 3,998 | 2,656 | 43,872 |

| 1960 Engines | bore×stroke | bhp | availability |
|---|---|---|---|
| L6, 144.3 | 3.50×2.50 | 90 | S-Falcon only |
| L6, 223.0 | 3.62×3.60 | 145 | S-all exc Falcon |
| V8, 292.0 | 3.75×3.30 | 185 | O-all exc Falcon |
| V8, 352.0 | 4.00×3.50 | 235 | O-all exc Falcon |
| V8, 352.0 | 4.00×3.50 | 300 | O-all exc Falcon |

# 1961

| Falcon (wb 109.5) | | Wght | Price | Prod |
|---|---|---|---|---|
| 58A | sdn 4d | 2,289 | 1,976 | 159,761 |
| 59A | wgn 2d | 2,525 | 2,227 | 32,045 |
| 62A | Futura cpe | 2,322 | 2,162 | 44,470 |
| 64A | sdn 2d (inc 50 Economy sdns) | 2,254 | 1,914 | 150,032 |
| 71A | wgn 4d | 2,558 | 2,270 | 87,933 |

| Custom 300 (wb 119.0) | | | | |
|---|---|---|---|---|
| 58F | sdn 4d | 3,516 | — | 303 |
| 64H | sdn 2d | 3,405 | — | 49 |

| Fairlane (wb 119.0) | | | | |
|---|---|---|---|---|
| 58E | sdn 4d | 3,634 | 2,317 | 96,602 |
| 64F | sdn 2d | 3,536 | 2,263 | 66,875 |

| Fairlane 500 (wb 119.0) | | | | |
|---|---|---|---|---|
| 58A | sdn 4d | 3,642 | 2,432 | 98,917 |
| 64A | sdn 2d | 3,551 | 2,378 | 42,468 |

| Galaxie (wb 119.0) | | | | |
|---|---|---|---|---|
| 54A | sdn 4d | 3,619 | 2,592 | 141,823 |
| 62A | sdn 2d | 3,537 | 2,538 | 27,780 |
| 63A | Starliner htp cpe | 3,566 | 2,599 | 29,669 |
| 65A | Victoria htp cpe | 3,594 | 2,599 | 75,437 |
| 75A | Victoria htp sdn | 3,637 | 2,664 | 30,342 |
| 76B | Sunliner conv cpe | 3,743 | 2,849 | 44,614 |

| Station Wagon (wb 119.0) | | | | |
|---|---|---|---|---|
| 59C | Ranch 2d, 6P | 3,865 | 2,588 | 12,042 |
| 71E | Country Sedan 4d, 9P | 4,011 | 2,858 | 16,356 |
| 71F | Country Sedan 4d, 6P | 3,983 | 2,754 | 46,311 |
| 71G | Country Squire 4d, 9P | 4,015 | 3,013 | 14,657 |
| 71H | Ranch 4d, 6P | 3,960 | 2,658 | 30,292 |
| 71J | Country Squire 4d, 6P | 3,969 | 2,943 | 16,961 |

| 1961 Engines | bore×stroke | bhp | availability |
|---|---|---|---|
| L6, 144.3 | 3.50×2.50 | 85 | S-Falcon |
| L6, 170.0 | 3.50×2.94 | 101 | O-Falcon |
| L6, 223.0 | 3.62×3.30 | 135 | S-all exc Falcon |
| V8, 292.0 | 3.75×3.30 | 175 | S-all exc Falcon |
| V8, 352.0 | 4.00×3.50 | 220 | O-all exc Falcon |
| V8, 390.0 | 4.05×3.78 | 300 | O-all exc Falcon |

# 1962

| Falcon (wb 109.5) | | Wght | Price | Prod |
|---|---|---|---|---|
| 58A | sdn 4d | 2,279 | 2,047 | 126,041 |
| 58B | Deluxe sdn 4d | 2,285 | 2,133 | |
| 59A | wgn 2d | 2,539 | 2,298 | 20,025 |
| 59B | Deluxe wgn 2d | 2,545 | 2,384 | |
| 62C | Futura cpe | 2,343 | 2,270 | 17,011 |
| 64A | sdn 2d | 2,243 | 1,985 | 143,650 |
| 64B | Deluxe sdn 2d | 2,249 | 2,071 | |
| 71A | wgn 4d | 2,575 | 2,341 | 66,819 |
| 71B | Deluxe wgn 4d | 2,581 | 2,427 | |
| 71C | Squire wgn 4d | 2,591 | 2,603 | 22,583 |

| Fairlane (wb 115.5) | | | | |
|---|---|---|---|---|
| 54A | sdn 4d | 2,848 | 2,216 | 45,342 |
| 62A | sdn 2d | 2,815 | 2,154 | 34,264 |
| 54B | 500 sdn 4d | 2,865 | 2,304 | 129,258 |
| 62B | 500 sdn 2d | 2,832 | 2,242 | 68,624 |
| 62C | 500 spt cpe | 2,928 | 2,403 | 19,628 |

| Galaxie (wb 119.0) | | | | |
|---|---|---|---|---|
| 54B | sdn 4d | 3,636 | 2,507 | 115,594 |
| 62B | sdn 2d | 3,554 | 2,453 | 54,930 |

| Galaxie 500 (wb 119.0) | | | | |
|---|---|---|---|---|
| 54A | sdn 4d | 3,650 | 2,667 | 174,195 |
| 62A | sdn 2d | 3,568 | 2,613 | 27,824 |
| 65A | Victoria htp cpe | 3,568 | 2,674 | 87,562 |
| 65B | XL Victoria htp cpe | 3,672 | 2,268 | 28,412 |
| 75A | Victoria htp sdn | 3,640 | 2,739 | 30,778 |
| 76A | Sunliner conv cpe | 3,730 | 2,924 | 42,646 |
| 76B | XL Sunliner conv cpe | 3,831 | 3,518 | 13,183 |

| Station Wagon (wb 119.0) | | | | |
|---|---|---|---|---|
| 71A | Country Squire 4d, 9P | 4,022 | 3,088 | 15,666 |
| 71B | Country Sedan 4d, 6P | 3,992 | 2,829 | 47,635 |
| 71C | Country Sedan 4d, 9P | 4,010 | 2,933 | 16,562 |
| 71D | Ranch 4d, 6P | 3,968 | 2,733 | 33,674 |
| 71E | Country Squire 4d, 6P | 4,006 | 3,018 | 16,114 |

| 1962 Engines | bore×stroke | bhp | availability |
|---|---|---|---|
| L6, 144.3 | 3.50×2.50 | 85 | S-Falcon |
| L6, 170.0 | 3.50×2.94 | 101 | O-Falcon |
| L6, 223.0 | 3.62×3.60 | 138 | S-all exc Falcon |
| V8, 221.0 | 3.50×2.87 | 145 | O-Fairlane |
| V8, 260.0 | 3.80×2.87 | 164 | O-Fairlane |
| V8, 292.0 | 3.75×3.30 | 170 | S-76B; O-all exc Falc, Fair |
| V8, 352.0 | 4.00×3.50 | 220 | O-all exc Falcon, Fairlane |
| V8, 390.0 | 4.05×3.78 | 300/340 | O-all exc Falcon, Fairlane |
| V8, 390.0 | 4.05×3.78 | 375/401 | O-all exc Falcon, Fairlane |

# 1963

| Series 0 Falcon (wb 109.5) | | Wght | Price | Prod |
|---|---|---|---|---|
| 54A | sdn 4d | 2,337 | 2,047 | 62,365 |
| 62A | sdn 2d | 2,300 | 1,985 | 70,630 |

| Series 10 Falcon Futura (wb 109.5) | | | | |
|---|---|---|---|---|
| 54B | sdn 4d | 2,345 | 2,161 | 31,736 |
| 62B | sdn 2d | 2,308 | 2,116 | 27,018 |

| | | Wght | Price | Prod |
|---|---|---|---|---|
| 63B | htp cpe | 2,438 | 2,198 | 28,496 |
| 63C | Sprint htp cpe | 2,438 | 2,320 | 10,479 |
| 76A | conv cpe | 2,645 | 2,470 | 31,192 |
| 76B | Sprint conv cpe | 2,645 | 2,600 | 4,602 |

### Series 20 Falcon Wagon (wb 109.5)

| | | Wght | Price | Prod |
|---|---|---|---|---|
| 59A | wgn 2d | 2,580 | 2,298 | 7,322 |
| 59B | Deluxe wgn 2d | 2,586 | 2,384 | 4,269 |
| 71A | wgn 4d | 2,617 | 2,341 | 18,484 |
| 71B | Deluxe wgn 4d | 2,623 | 2,427 | 23,477 |
| 71C | Squire wgn 4d | 2,639 | 2,603 | 8,269 |

### Series 30 Fairlane (wb 115.5)

| | | Wght | Price | Prod |
|---|---|---|---|---|
| 54A | sdn 4d | 2,930 | 2,216 | 44,454 |
| 62A | sdn 2d | 2,890 | 2,154 | 28,984 |
| 71B | Cus Ranch Wagon 4d | 3,298 | 2,613 | 29,612 |
| 71D | Ranch Wagon 4d | 3,281 | 2,525 | 24,006 |
| 71E | Squire Wagon 4d | 3,295 | 2,781 | 7,983 |

### Series 40 Fairlane 500 (wb 115.5)

| | | Wght | Price | Prod |
|---|---|---|---|---|
| 54B | sdn 4d | 2,945 | 2,304 | 104,175 |
| 62B | sdn 2d | 2,905 | 2,242 | 34,764 |
| 65A | htp cpe | 2,923 | 2,324 | 41,641 |
| 65B | htp cpe, bkt sts | 2,923 | 2,504 | 28,268 |

### Series 50 300 (wb 119.0)

| | | Wght | Price | Prod |
|---|---|---|---|---|
| 54E | sdn 4d | 3,627 | 2,378 | 44,142 |
| 62E | sdn 2d | 3,547 | 2,324 | 26,010 |

### Series 50 Galaxie (wb 119.0)

| | | Wght | Price | Prod |
|---|---|---|---|---|
| 54B | sdn 4d | 3,647 | 2,507 | 82,419 |
| 62B | sdn 2d | 3,567 | 2,453 | 30,335 |

### Series 60 Galaxie 500 (wb 119.0)

| | | Wght | Price | Prod |
|---|---|---|---|---|
| 54A | sdn 4d | 3,667 | 2,667 | 205,722 |
| 62A | sdn 2d | 3,587 | 2,613 | 21,137 |
| 63B | XL htp cpe, fstbk | 3,772 | 2,674 | 134,370 |
| 65A | htp cpe | 3,599 | 2,674 | 49,733 |
| 75A | htp sdn | 3,679 | 2,739 | 39,154 |
| 76A | Sunliner conv cpe | 3,757 | 2,924 | 29,713 |

### Series 70 Station Wagon (wb 119.0)

| | | Wght | Price | Prod |
|---|---|---|---|---|
| 71A | Country Squire 4d, 9P | 4,003 | 3,088 | 19,567 |
| 71B | Country Sedan 4d, 6P | 3,977 | 2,829 | 64,954 |
| 71C | Country Sedan 4d, 9P | 3,989 | 2,933 | 22,250 |
| 71E | Country Squire 4d, 6P | 3,991 | 3,018 | 20,359 |

| 1963 Engines | bore×stroke | bhp | availability |
|---|---|---|---|
| L6, 144.3 | 3.50×2.50 | 85 | S-Falcon |
| L6, 170.0 | 3.50×2.94 | 101 | O-Falcon |
| L6, 200.0 | 3.68×3.13 | 116 | S-Fairlane |
| L6, 223.0 | 3.62×3.60 | 138 | S-all exc Falcon, Fairlane |
| V8, 221.0 | 3.50×2.87 | 145 | O-Fairlane |
| V8, 260.0 | 3.80×2.87 | 164 | S-Falcon Sprint; O-others |
| V8, 289.0 | 4.00×2.87 | 271 | O-Fairlane |
| V8, 352.0 | 4.00×3.50 | 220 | O-all exc Falcon, Fairlane |
| V8, 390.0 | 4.05×3.78 | 300/330 | O-all exc Falcon, Fairlane |
| V8, 406.0 | 4.13×3.78 | 385/405 | O-all exc Falcon, Fairlane |
| V8, 427.0 | 4.23×3.78 | 410/425 | O-all exc Falcon, Fairlaine |

## 1964

### Series 0 Falcon (wb 109.5)

| | | Wght | Price | Prod |
|---|---|---|---|---|
| 01 | sdn 4d | 2,365 | 1,996 | 36,441 |
| 01 | Deluxe sdn 2d | 2,380 | 2,096 | 28,411 |
| 02 | sdn 4d | 2,400 | 2,058 | 27,722 |
| 02 | Deluxe sdn 4d | 2,420 | 2,158 | 26,532 |

### Series 10 Falcon Futura (wb 109.5)

| | | Wght | Price | Prod |
|---|---|---|---|---|
| 11 | htp cpe, bkt seats | 2,545 | 2,325 | 8,607 |
| 12 | conv cpe, bkt seats | 2,735 | 2,597 | 2,980 |
| 13 | Sprint htp cpe | 2,813 | 2,436 | 13,830 |

| | | Wght | Price | Prod |
|---|---|---|---|---|
| 14 | Sprint conv cpe | 3,008 | 2,671 | 4,278 |
| 15 | conv cpe | 2,710 | 2,481 | 13,220 |
| 16 | sdn 4d | 2,410 | 2,176 | 38,032 |
| 17 | htp cpe | 2,515 | 2,209 | 32,608 |
| 19 | sdn 2d | 2,375 | 2,127 | 16,833 |

### Series 20 Falcon Wagon (wb 109.5)

| | | Wght | Price | Prod |
|---|---|---|---|---|
| 21 | wgn 2d | 2,660 | 2,326 | 6,034 |
| 22 | wgn 4d | 2,695 | 2,360 | 17,779 |
| 24 | Deluxe wgn 4d | 2,715 | 2,446 | 20,697 |
| 26 | Squire wgn 4d | 2,720 | 2,622 | 6,766 |

### Series 30 Fairlane (wb 115.5)

| | | Wght | Price | Prod |
|---|---|---|---|---|
| 31 | sdn 2d | 2,855 | 2,194 | 20,421 |
| 32 | sdn 4d | 2,895 | 2,235 | 36,693 |
| 38 | Ranch wgn 4d | 3,290 | 2,531 | 20,980 |

### Series 40 Fairlane 500 (wb 115.5)

| | | Wght | Price | Prod |
|---|---|---|---|---|
| 41 | sdn 2d | 2,863 | 2,276 | 23,447 |
| 42 | sdn 4d | 2,910 | 2,317 | 86,919 |
| 43 | htp cpe | 2,925 | 2,341 | 42,733 |
| 47 | htp cpe, bkt sts | 2,945 | 2,502 | 21,431 |
| 48 | Ranch Cus wgn 4d | 3,310 | 2,612 | 24,962 |

### Series 50 Custom (wb 119.0)

| | | Wght | Price | Prod |
|---|---|---|---|---|
| 51 | 500 sdn 2d | 3,559 | 2,464 | 20,619 |
| 52 | 500 sdn 4d | 3,659 | 2,518 | 68,828 |
| 53 | sdn 2d | 3,529 | 2,361 | 41,359 |
| 54 | sdn 4d | 3,619 | 2,415 | 57,964 |

### Series 60 Galaxie 500 (wb 119.0)

| | | Wght | Price | Prod |
|---|---|---|---|---|
| 60 | XL htp sdn | 3,722 | 3,298 | 14,661 |
| 61 | sdn 2d | 3,574 | 2,624 | 13,041 |
| 62 | sdn 4d | 3,674 | 2,678 | 198,805 |
| 64 | htp sdn | 3,689 | 2,750 | 49,242 |
| 66 | htp cpe | 3,584 | 2,685 | 206,998 |
| — | Sunliner conv cpe | 3,759 | 2,947 | 37,311 |
| 68 | XL htp cpe | 3,622 | 3,233 | 58,306 |
| 69 | XL conv cpe | 3,687 | 3,495 | 15,169 |

### Series 70 Station Wagon (wb 119.0)

| | | Wght | Price | Prod |
|---|---|---|---|---|
| 72 | Country Sedan 4d, 6P | 3,973 | 2,840 | 68,578 |
| 74 | Country Sedan 4d, 9P | 3,983 | 2,944 | 25,661 |
| 76 | Country Squire 4d, 6P | 3,988 | 3,029 | 23,570 |
| 78 | Country Squire 4d, 9P | 3,998 | 3,099 | 23,120 |

| 1964 Engines | bore×stroke | bhp | availability |
|---|---|---|---|
| L6, 144.3 | 3.50×2.50 | 85 | S-Flcn exc conv, Sprnt, Del wgns |
| L6, 170.0 | 3.50×2.94 | 101 | S-Flcn conv, Sprnt, Del wgn; O-other Flcn |
| L6, 200.0 | 3.68×3.13 | 116 | S-Fairlane; O-Falcon |
| L6, 223.0 | 3.62×3.60 | 138 | S-all exc Fairlane, Falcon |
| V8, 260.0 | 3.80×2.87 | 116 | S-Flcn Sprnt, Fairlane; O-Flcn |
| V8, 289.0 | 4.00×2.87 | 195/271 | S-60, 68, 69; O-all exc Flcn |
| V8, 352.0 | 4.00×3.50 | 250 | O-all exc Falcon, Fairlane |
| V8, 390.0 | 4.05×3.78 | 300/330 | O-all exc Falcon, Fairlane |
| V8, 427.0 | 4.23×3.78 | 425 | O-all exc Falcon, Fairlane |

## 1965

### Series 0 Falcon (wb 109.5)

| | | Wght | Price | Prod |
|---|---|---|---|---|
| 01 | sdn 4d | 2,366 | 2,020 | 35,858 |
| 01 | Deluxe sdn 2d | 2,381 | 2,120 | 13,824 |
| 02 | sdn 4d | 2,406 | 2,082 | 30,186 |
| 02 | Deluxe sdn 4d | 2,426 | 2,182 | 13,850 |

### Series 10 Falcon Futura (wb 109.5)

| | | Wght | Price | Prod |
|---|---|---|---|---|
| 13 | Sprint htp cpe | 2,749 | 2,337 | 2,806 |
| 14 | Sprint conv cpe | 2,971 | 2,671 | 300 |
| 15 | conv cpe | 2,673 | 2,481 | 6,215 |
| 16 | sdn 4d | 2,413 | 2,192 | 33,985 |

| | | Wght | Price | Prod |
|---|---|---|---|---|
| 17 | htp cpe | 2,491 | 2,226 | 25,754 |
| 19 | sdn 2d | 2,373 | 2,144 | 11,670 |

**Series 20 Falcon Wagon (wb 109.5)**

| | | | | |
|---|---|---|---|---|
| 21 | wgn 2d | 2,611 | 2,333 | 4,891 |
| 22 | wgn 4d | 2,651 | 2,367 | 14,911 |
| 24 | Deluxe wgn 4d (Futura) | 2,667 | 2,506 | 12,548 |
| 26 | Squire wgn 4d | 2,669 | 2,665 | 6,703 |

**Series 30 Fairlane (wb 115.5)**

| | | | | |
|---|---|---|---|---|
| 31 | sdn 2d | 2,902 | 2,230 | 13,685 |
| 32 | sdn 4d | 2,954 | 2,271 | 25,378 |
| 38 | wgn 4d | 3,279 | 2,567 | 13,911 |

**Series 40 Fairlane 500 (wb 115.5)**

| | | | | |
|---|---|---|---|---|
| 41 | sdn 2d | 2,901 | 2,312 | 16,092 |
| 42 | sdn 4d | 2,959 | 2,353 | 77,836 |
| 43 | htp cpe | 2,973 | 2,377 | 11,100 |
| 47 | htp cpe, bkt sts | 2,984 | 2,538 | 15,141 |
| 48 | wgn 4d | 3,316 | 2,648 | 20,506 |

**Series 50 Custom (wb 119.0)**

| | | | | |
|---|---|---|---|---|
| 51 | sdn 2d | 3,336 | 2,464 | 49,034 |
| 52 | sdn 4d | 3,408 | 2,518 | 96,393 |
| 53 | 500 sdn 2d | 3,306 | 2,361 | 19,603 |
| 54 | 500 sdn 4d | 3,378 | 2,415 | 71,727 |

**Series 60 Galaxie 500 (wb 119.0)**

| | | | | |
|---|---|---|---|---|
| 60 | LTD htp sdn | 3,578 | 3,313 | 68,038 |
| 62 | sdn 4d | 3,440 | 2,678 | 181,183 |
| 64 | htp sdn | 3,480 | 2,765 | 49,982 |
| 65 | conv cpe | 3,592 | 2,950 | 31,930 |
| 66 | htp cpe | 3,380 | 2,685 | 157,284 |
| 67 | LTD htp cpe | 3,486 | 3,233 | 37,691 |
| 68 | XL htp cpe | 3,497 | 3,233 | 28,141 |
| 69 | XL conv cpe | 3,665 | 3,498 | 9,849 |

**Series 70 Station Wagon (wb 119.0)**

| | | | | |
|---|---|---|---|---|
| 71 | Ranch 4d, 6P | 3,869 | 2,763 | 30,817 |
| 72 | Country Sedan 4d, 6P | 3,879 | 2,855 | 59,693 |
| 74 | Country Sedan 4d, 9P | 3,893 | 2,959 | 32,344 |
| 76 | Country Squire 4d, 6P | 3,925 | 3,104 | 24,308 |
| 78 | Country Squire 4d, 9P | 3,937 | 3,174 | 30,502 |

| 1965 Engines | bore×stroke | bhp | availability |
|---|---|---|---|
| L6, 170.0 | 3.50×2.94 | 101 | S-Flcn exc Futura, Squire until 9/25/64 |
| L6, 200.0 | 3.68×3.13 | 120 | S-Futura/Squire, Fairlane; O-Flcn |
| L6, 240.0 | 4.00×3.18 | 150 | S-all exc Flcn, Fairlane, LTD, XL |
| V8, 289.0 | 4.00×2.87 | 200–271 | S-LTD, XL;O-others |
| V8, 352.0 | 4.00×3.50 | 250 | O-all exc Falcon, Fairlane |
| V8, 390.0 | 4.05×3.78 | 300/330 | O-all exc Falcon, Fairlane |
| V8, 427.0 | 4.23×3.78 | 425 | O-all exc Falcon, Fairlane |

# 1966

**Series 0 Falcon (wb 110.5; wgn-113.0)**

| | | Wght | Price | Prod |
|---|---|---|---|---|
| 01 | club cpe | 2,519 | 2,060 | 41,432 |
| 02 | sdn 4d | 2,559 | 2,114 | 34,685 |
| 06 | wgn 4d | 3,037 | 2,442 | 16,653 |

**Series 10 Falcon Futura (wb 110.9; wgn-113.0)**

| | | | | |
|---|---|---|---|---|
| 11 | club cpe | 2,527 | 2,183 | 21,997 |
| 12 | sdn 4d | 2,567 | 2,237 | 34,039 |
| 13 | spt cpe | 2,597 | 2,328 | 20,289 |
| 16 | wgn 4d | 3,045 | 2,553 | 13,574 |

**Series 30 Fairlane (wb 116; wgn 113.0)**

| | | | | |
|---|---|---|---|---|
| 31 | club cpe | 2,832 | 2,240 | 13,498 |
| 32 | sdn 4d | 2,877 | 2,280 | 26,170 |
| 38 | wgn 4d | 3,267 | 2,589 | 12,379 |

**Series 40 Fairlane 500 (wb 116; wgn-113.0)**

| | | Wght | Price | Prod |
|---|---|---|---|---|
| 40 | XL GT htp cpe, V8 | 3,493 | 2,843 | 33,015 |
| 41 | club cpe | 2,839 | 3,317 | 14,118 |
| 42 | sdn 4d | 2,884 | 2,357 | 68,635 |
| 43 | htp cpe | 2,941 | 2,378 | 75,947 |
| 44 | XL GT conv cpe | 3,070 | 3,068 | 4,327 |
| 45 | conv cpe | 3,169 | 2,603 | 9,299 |
| 46 | XL conv cpe | 3,184 | 2,768 | 4,560 |
| 47 | XL htp cpe | 2,969 | 2,533 | 23,942 |
| 48 | Deluxe wgn 4d | 3,277 | 2,665 | 19,826 |
| 49 | Squire wgn 4d | 3,285 | 2,796 | 11,558 |

**Series 50 Custom (wb 119.0)**

| | | | | |
|---|---|---|---|---|
| 51 | 500 sdn 2d | 3,397 | 2,481 | 28,789 |
| 52 | 500 sdn 4d | 3,466 | 2,533 | 109,449 |
| 53 | sdn 2d | 3,355 | 2,380 | 32,292 |
| 54 | sdn 4d | 3,455 | 2,432 | 72,245 |

**Series 60 Galaxie 500 (wb 119.0)**

| | | | | |
|---|---|---|---|---|
| 60 | LTD htp sdn | 3,649 | 3,278 | 69,400 |
| 61 | 7 Litre htp cpe | 3,914 | 3,621 | 8,705 |
| 62 | sdn 4d | 3,478 | 2,677 | 171,886 |
| 63 | 7 Litre conv cpe, V8 | 4,059 | 3,872 | 2,368 |
| 64 | htp sdn | 3,548 | 2,762 | 54,884 |
| 65 | conv cpe | 3,655 | 2,934 | 27,454 |
| 66 | htp cpe | 3,459 | 2,685 | 198,532 |
| 67 | LTD htp cpe | 3,601 | 3,201 | 31,696 |
| 68 | XL htp cpe | 3,616 | 3,231 | 25,715 |
| 69 | XL conv cpe | 3,761 | 3,480 | 6,360 |

**Series 70 Station Wagon (wb 119.0)**

| | | | | |
|---|---|---|---|---|
| 71 | Ranch 4d | 3,941 | 2,793 | 33,306 |
| 72 | Country Sedan 4d, 6P | 3,956 | 2,882 | 55,616 |
| 74 | Country Sedan 4d, 9P | 3,997 | 2,999 | 36,633 |
| 76 | Country Squire 4d, 6P | 4,026 | 3,182 | 27,645 |
| 78 | Country Squire 4d, 9P | 4,040 | 3,265 | 41,953 |

| 1966 Engines | bore×stroke | bhp | availability |
|---|---|---|---|
| L6, 170.0 | 3.50×2.94 | 105 | S-Falcon |
| L6, 200.0 | 3.68×3.13 | 120 | S-Flcn Futura/wgn, Fair exc GT, GTA; O-Flcn |
| L6, 240.0 | 4.00×3.18 | 150 | S-all exc Flcn, Fair; O-Flcn wgns |
| V8, 289.0 | 4.00×2.87 | 200/225 | S-XL, LTD; O-Flcn, Fair exc GT, GTA; 50, 60, 70 exc 7L |
| V8, 352.0 | 4.00×3.50 | 250 | O-all exc 7L, Fairlane, Falcon |
| V8, 390.0 | 4.05×3.78 | 265 | O-all exc 7L, Fair GT/GTA, Flcn |
| V8, 390.0 | 4.05×3.78 | 315 | O-all exc 7L, Fairlane, Falcon |
| V8, 390.0 | 4.05×3.78 | 335 | S-Fair GT/GTA; O-other Fair |
| V8, 427.0 | 4.23×3.78 | 410/425 | O-all exc 7L, 70, Fairlane, Flcn |
| V8, 428.0 | 4.13×3.98 | 345 | S-7L; O-others exc Fairlane, Flcn |

# 1967

**Falcon (wb 110.9; wgn-113.0)**

| | | Wght | Price | Prod |
|---|---|---|---|---|
| 10 | sdn 2d | 2,520 | 2,118 | 16,082 |
| 11 | sdn 4d | 2,551 | 2,167 | 13,554 |
| 12 | wgn 4d | 3,030 | 2,497 | 5,553 |

**Falcon Futura (wb 110.9; wgns-113.0)**

| | | | | |
|---|---|---|---|---|
| 20 | club cpe | 2,528 | 2,280 | 6,287 |
| 21 | sdn 4d | 2,559 | 2,322 | 11,254 |
| 22 | spt cpe | 3,062 | 2,437 | 7,053 |
| 23 | Squire wgn 4d | 2,556 | 2,609 | 4,552 |

**Fairlane (wb 116.0; wgns-113.0)**

| | | | | |
|---|---|---|---|---|
| 30 | sdn 2d | 2,832 | 2,297 | 10,628 |
| 31 | sdn 4d | 2,867 | 2,339 | 19,740 |
| 32 | Ranch wgn 4d | 3,283 | 2,643 | 10,881 |
| 33 | 500 club cpe | 2,840 | 2,377 | 8,473 |
| 34 | 500 sdn 4d | 2,887 | 2,417 | 51,522 |

| | | Wght | Price | Prod |
|---|---|---|---|---|
| 35 | 500 htp cpe | 2,927 | 2,439 | 70,135 |
| 36 | 500 conv cpe | 3,244 | 2,664 | 5,428 |
| 37 | Deluxe wgn 4d | 3,291 | 2,718 | 15,902 |
| 38 | Country Squire wgn 4d | 3,302 | 2,902 | 8,348 |
| **Fairlane 500XL (wb 116.0)** | | | | |
| 40 | htp cpe | 2,955 | 2,724 | 14,871 |
| 41 | conv cpe | 3,272 | 2,950 | 1,943 |
| 42 | GT htp cpe | 3,301 | 2,839 | 18,670 |
| 43 | GT conv cpe | 3,607 | 3,064 | 2,117 |
| **Series 50 Custom (wb 119.0)** | | | | |
| 50 | sdn 2d | 3,430 | 2,441 | 18,107 |
| 51 | sdn 4d | 3,488 | 2,496 | 41,417 |
| 52 | 500 sdn 2d | 3,482 | 2,553 | 18,146 |
| 53 | 500 sdn 4d | 3,490 | 2,595 | 83,260 |
| **Galaxie 500 (wb 119.0)** | | | | |
| 54 | sdn 4d | 3,500 | 2,732 | 130,063 |
| 55 | htp cpe | 3,503 | 2,755 | 197,388 |
| 56 | htp sdn | 3,571 | 2,808 | 57,087 |
| 57 | conv cpe | 3,682 | 3,003 | 19,068 |
| 58 | XL htp sdn | 3,594 | 3,243 | 18,174 |
| 59 | XL conv cpe | 3,794 | 3,493 | 5,161 |
| **LTD (wb 119.0)** | | | | |
| 62 | htp cpe | 3,626 | 3,362 | 46,036 |
| 64 | sdn 4d | 3,795 | 3,298 | 12,491 |
| 66 | htp sdn | 3,676 | 3,363 | 51,978 |
| **Station Wagon (wb 119.0)** | | | | |
| 70 | Ranch 4d, 6P | 3,930 | 2,836 | 23,932 |
| 71 | Country Sedan 4d, 6P | 3,943 | 2,935 | 50,818 |
| 72 | Country Sedan 4d, 9P | 4,023 | 3,061 | 34,377 |
| 73 | Country Squire 4d, 6P | 3,990 | 3,234 | 25,600 |
| 74 | Country Squire 4d, 9P | 4,030 | 3,359 | 44,024 |

| 1967 Engines | bore×stroke | bhp | availability |
|---|---|---|---|
| L6, 170.0 | 3.50×2.94 | 105 | S-Falcon exc Futura, wagons |
| L6, 200.0 | 3.68×3.13 | 120 | S-Flcn Futura/wgns, Fair exc GTs |
| L6, 240.0 | 4.00×3.18 | 150 | S-all exc Falcon, Fairlane |
| V8, 289.0 | 4.00×2.87 | 200 | S-Fair GT, 500XL, LTD; O-others |
| V8, 289.0 | 4.00×2.87 | 225 | O-Falcon |
| V8, 390.0 | 4.05×3.78 | 270 | O-Fairlane |
| V8, 390.0 | 4.05×3.78 | 315 | O-Cus, Gal, LTD, Station Wgn |
| V8, 390.0 | 4.05×3.78 | 320 | O-Fairlane |
| V8, 427.0 | 4.23×3.78 | 410/425 | O-all exc Falcon |
| V8, 428.0 | 4.13×3.98 | 345 | O-all exc Falcon, Fairlane |

## 1968

| Falcon (wb 110.9; wgn-113.0) | | Wght | Price | Prod |
|---|---|---|---|---|
| 10 | sdn 2d | 2,680 | 2,252 | 29,166 |
| 11 | sdn 4d | 2,714 | 2,301 | 36,443 |
| 12 | wgn 4d | 3,123 | 2,617 | 15,576 |
| **Falcon Futura (wb 110.9; wgn-113.0)** | | | | |
| 20 | sdn 2d | 2,685 | 2,415 | 10,633 |
| 21 | sdn 4d | 2,719 | 2,456 | 18,733 |
| 22 | spt cpe | 2,713 | 2,541 | 10,077 |
| 23 | wgn 4d | 3,123 | 2,728 | 10,761 |
| **Fairlane (wb 116.0; wgn-113.0)** | | | | |
| 30 | htp cpe | 3,028 | 2,456 | 44,683 |
| 31 | sdn 4d | 2,986 | 2,464 | 18,146 |
| 32 | wgn 4d | 3,333 | 2,770 | 14,800 |
| 33 | 500 htp cpe | 3,066 | 2,591 | 33,282 |
| 34 | 500 sdn 4d | 3,024 | 2,543 | 42,930 |
| 35 | 500 fstbk htp cpe | 3,080 | 2,566 | 32,452 |
| 36 | 500 conv cpe | 3,226 | 2,822 | 3,761 |
| 37 | 500 wgn 4d | 3,377 | 2,880 | 10,190 |

| Torino (wb 116.0; wgn-113.0) | | Wght | Price | Prod |
|---|---|---|---|---|
| 38 | Squire wgn 4d | 3,425 | 3,032 | 14,773 |
| 40 | htp cpe | 3,098 | 2,710 | 35,964 |
| 41 | sdn 4d | 3,062 | 2,688 | 17,962 |
| 42 | GT fstbk htp cpe | 3,208 | 2,747 | 74,135 |
| 43 | GT conv cpe | 3,352 | 3,001 | 5,310 |
| 44 | GT htp cpe | 3,194 | 2,772 | 23,939 |
| **Custom (wb 119.0)** | | | | |
| 50 | sdn 2d | 3,471 | 3,584 | 18,485 |
| 51 | sdn 4d | 3,498 | 2,642 | 45,980 |
| 52 | 500 sdn 2d | 3,460 | 2,699 | 8,983 |
| 53 | 500 sdn 4d | 3,511 | 2,741 | 49,398 |
| **Galaxie 500 (wb 119.0)** | | | | |
| 54 | sdn 4d | 3,516 | 2,864 | 117,877 |
| 55 | fstbk htp cpe | 3,534 | 2,881 | 69,760 |
| 56 | htp sdn | 3,562 | 2,936 | 55,461 |
| 57 | conv cpe | 3,679 | 3,108 | 11,832 |
| 58 | htp cpe | 3,540 | 2,916 | 84,332 |
| 60 | XL fstbk htp cpe | 3,588 | 2,985 | 50,048 |
| 61 | XL conv cpe | 3,745 | 3,214 | 6,066 |
| **LTD (wb 119.0)** | | | | |
| 62 | htp cpe | 3,679 | 3,153 | 54,163 |
| 64 | sdn 4d | 3,596 | 3,135 | 22,834 |
| 66 | htp sdn | 3,642 | 3,206 | 61,755 |
| **Station Wagon (wb 119.0)** | | | | |
| 70 | Ranch 4d, 6P | 3,925 | 3,000 | 18,237 |
| 71 | Ranch 500 4d, 6P | 3,935 | 3,063 | 18,181 |
| 72 | Ranch 500 4d, 9P | 3,981 | 3,176 | 13,421 |
| 73 | Country Sedan 4d, 6P | 3,944 | 3,184 | 39,335 |
| 74 | Country Sedan 4d, 9P | 4,001 | 3,295 | 29,374 |
| 75 | Country Squire 4d, 6P | 4,013 | 3,539 | 33,994 |
| 76 | Country Squire 4d, 9P | 4,059 | 3,619 | 57,776 |

| 1968 Engines | bore×stroke | bhp | availability |
|---|---|---|---|
| L6, 170.0 | 3.50×2.94 | 100 | S-base Falcon cpes, sdns |
| L6, 200.0 | 3.68×3.13 | 115 | S-Fair, Tor, Flcn Fut wgn; O-Flcn |
| L6, 240.0 | 4.00×3.18 | 150 | S-all exc Futura, Tor GT, LTD |
| V8, 289.0 | 4.00×2.87 | 195 | O-Falcon |
| V8, 302.0 | 4.00×3.00 | 210 | S-LTD, Tor GT; O-all exc Flcn |
| V8, 302.0 | 4.00×3.00 | 230 | O-Falcon, Fairlane, Torino |
| V8, 390.0 | 4.05×3.78 | 265 | O-all exc Falcon |
| V8, 390.0 | 4.05×3.78 | 315 | O-all exc Falcon, Fairlane |
| V8, 390.0 | 4.05×3.78 | 335 | O-Fairlane |
| V8, 427.0 | 4.23×3.78 | 390 | O-Fairlane/Torino htps |
| V8, 428.0 | 4.13×3.98 | 340 | O-all exc Falcon, Fairlane |

## 1969

| Falcon (wb 110.9; wgn-113.0) | | Wght | Price | Prod |
|---|---|---|---|---|
| 10 | sdn 2d | 2,700 | 2,283 | 29,262 |
| 11 | sdn 4d | 2,735 | 2,333 | 22,719 |
| 12 | wgn 4d | 3,100 | 2,660 | 11,568 |
| **Falcon Futura (wb 110.9; wgn-113.0)** | | | | |
| 20 | sdn 2d | 2,715 | 2,461 | 6,482 |
| 21 | sdn 4d | 2,748 | 2,498 | 11,850 |
| 22 | spt cpe | 2,738 | 2,598 | 5,931 |
| 23 | wgn 4d | 3,120 | 2,771 | 7,203 |
| **Fairlane (wb 116.0; wgn-113.0)** | | | | |
| 30 | htp cpe | 3,079 | 2,499 | 85,630 |
| 31 | sdn 4d | 3,065 | 2,488 | 27,296 |
| 32 | wgn 4d | 3,441 | 2,841 | 10,882 |
| 33 | 500 htp cpe | 3,090 | 2,626 | 28,179 |
| 34 | 500 sdn 4d | 3,082 | 2,568 | 40,888 |
| 35 | 500 fstbk htp cpe | 3,137 | 2,601 | 29,849 |
| 36 | 500 conv cpe | 3,278 | 2,851 | 2,264 |
| 37 | 500 wgn 4d | 3,469 | 2,951 | 12,869 |

| Torino (wb 116.0; wgn-113.0) | | Wght | Price | Prod |
|---|---|---|---|---|
| 38 | Squire wgn 4d | 3,503 | 3,107 | 14,472 |
| 40 | htp cpe | 3,143 | 2,754 | 20,789 |
| 41 | sdn 4d | 3,128 | 2,733 | 11,971 |
| 42 | GT fstbk htp cpe | 3,220 | 2,840 | 61,319 |
| 43 | GT conv cpe | 3,356 | 3,090 | 2,552 |
| 44 | GT htp cpe | 3,173 | 2,865 | 17,951 |

| Custom (wb 121.0) | | | | |
|---|---|---|---|---|
| 50 | sdn 2d | 3,605 | 2,649 | 15,439 |
| 51 | sdn 4d | 3,628 | 2,691 | 45,653 |
| 52 | 500 sdn 2d | 3,590 | 2,748 | 7,585 |
| 53 | 500 sdn 4d | 3,640 | 2,790 | 45,761 |
| 70 | Ranch wgn 4d | 4,089 | 3,091 | 17,489 |
| 71 | 500 wgn 4d, 6P | 4,102 | 3,155 | 16,432 |
| 72 | 500 wgn 4d, 9P | 4,152 | 3,268 | 11,563 |

| Galaxie 500 (wb 121.0) | | | | |
|---|---|---|---|---|
| 54 | sdn 4d | 3,690 | 2,914 | 104,606 |
| 55 | fstbk htp cpe | 3,700 | 2,930 | 63,921 |
| 56 | htp sdn | 3,725 | 2,983 | 64,031 |
| 57 | conv cpe | 3,860 | 3,159 | 6,910 |
| 58 | htp cpe | 3,655 | 2,982 | 71,920 |
| 73 | Country Sedan wgn 4d, 6P | 4,087 | 3,274 | 36,387 |
| 74 | Country Sedan wgn 4d, 9P | 4,112 | 3,390 | 27,517 |

| XL (wb 121.0) | | | | |
|---|---|---|---|---|
| 60 | fstbk htp cpe | 3,805 | 3,069 | 54,557 |
| 61 | conv cpe | 3,955 | 3,297 | 7,402 |

| LTD (wb 119.0) | | | | |
|---|---|---|---|---|
| 62 | htp cpe | 3,745 | 3,251 | 111,565 |
| 64 | sdn 4d | 3,745 | 3,209 | 63,709 |
| 66 | htp sdn | 3,840 | 3,278 | 113,168 |
| 75 | Country Squire wgn 4d, 6P | 4,202 | 3,661 | 46,445 |
| 76 | Country Squire wgn 4d, 9P | 4,227 | 3,738 | 82,790 |

| 1969 Engines | bore×stroke | bhp | availability |
|---|---|---|---|
| L6, 170.0 | 3.50×2.94 | 100 | S-Falcon exc Futura |
| L6, 200.0 | 3.68×3.13 | 115 | S-Futura |
| L6, 240.0 | 4.00×3.18 | 150 | S-all exc Flcn, Fair, Tor GT, LTD |
| L6, 250.0 | 3.68×3.91 | 155 | S-Fairlane, Tor exc GT, Cobra |
| V8, 302.0 | 4.00×3.00 | 220 | S-LTD, Tor GT; O-others |
| V8, 351.0 | 4.00×3.50 | 250 | O-Fairlane, Tor exc Cobra |
| V8, 351.0 | 3.00×3.50 | 290 | O-Fairlane, Tor exc Cobra |
| V8, 390.0 | 4.05×3.78 | 265 | O-full-size |
| V8, 390.0 | 4.05×3.78 | 320 | O-Fairlane, Tor exc Cobra |
| V8, 428.0 | 4.13×3.98 | 335* | S-Tor Cobra; O-Fairlane |
| V8, 429.0 | 4.36×3.59 | 320/360 | O-full-size |

*Available in standard and Ram Air versions.

# 1970

| Maverick (wb 103.0) | | Wght | Price | Prod |
|---|---|---|---|---|
| 91 | sdn 2d | 2,411 | 1,995 | 578,914 |

| Falcon (wb 110.9, wgn-113.0) | | | | |
|---|---|---|---|---|
| 10 | sdn 2d | 2,708 | 2,390 | 4,373 |
| 11 | sdn 4d | 2,753 | 2,438 | 5,301 |
| 12 | wgn 4d | 3,155 | 2,767 | 1,624 |

| Falcon Futura (wb 110.9; wgn-113.0) | | | | |
|---|---|---|---|---|
| 20 | sdn 2d | 2,727 | 2,542 | 1,129 |
| 21 | sdn 4d | 2,764 | 2,579 | 2,262 |
| 23 | wgn 4d | 3,191 | 2,878 | 1,005 |

| "1970½" Falcon (wb 117.0) | | | | |
|---|---|---|---|---|
| 26 | sdn 2d | 3,100 | 2,460 | 26,071 |
| 27 | sdn 4d | 3,116 | 2,500 | 30,443 |
| 40 | wgn 4d | 3,483 | 2,801 | 10,539 |

| Fairlane 500 (wb 117.0; wgn-114.0) | | Wght | Price | Prod |
|---|---|---|---|---|
| 28 | sdn 4d | 3,166 | 2,627 | 25,780 |
| 29 | htp cpe | 3,178 | 2,660 | 70,636 |
| 41 | wgn 4d | 3,558 | 2,957 | 13,613 |

| Torino (wb 117.0; wgn-114.0) | | | | |
|---|---|---|---|---|
| 30 | htp cpe | 3,223 | 2,722 | 49,826 |
| 31 | sdn 4d | 3,208 | 2,689 | 30,117 |
| 32 | htp sdn | 3,239 | 2,795 | 14,312 |
| 33 | Brougham htp cpe | 3,293 | 3,006 | 16,911 |
| 34 | fstbk htp cpe | 3,261 | 2,899 | 12,490 |
| 35 | GT htp cpe | 3,366 | 3,105 | 56,819 |
| 36 | Brougham htp sdn | 3,309 | 3,078 | 14,543 |
| 37 | GT conv cpe | 3,490 | 3,212 | 3,939 |
| 38 | Cobra fstbk htp cpe | 3,774 | 3,270 | 7,675 |
| 42 | wgn 4d | 3,603 | 3,164 | 10,613 |
| 43 | Brougham wgn 4d | 3,673 | 3,379 | 13,166 |

| Custom (wb 121.0) | | | | |
|---|---|---|---|---|
| 51 | sdn 4d | 3,545 | 2,850 | 42,849 |
| 52 | 500 htp cpe | 3,510 | 2,918 | 2,677 |
| 53 | 500 sdn 4d | 3,585 | 2,872 | 41,261 |
| 70 | Ranch wgn 4d | 4,079 | 3,305 | 15,086 |
| 71 | 500 wgn 4d, 6P | 4,049 | 3,368 | 15,304 |
| 72 | 500 wgn 4d, 9P | 4,137 | 3,481 | 9,943 |

| Galaxie 500 (wb 121.0) | | | | |
|---|---|---|---|---|
| 54 | sdn 4d | 3,601 | 3,026 | 101,784 |
| 55 | fstbk htp cpe | 3,610 | 3,043 | 50,825 |
| 56 | htp sdn | 3,672 | 3,096 | 53,817 |
| 58 | htp cpe | 3,611 | 3,094 | 57,059 |
| 73 | Country Sedan wgn 4d, 6P | 4,089 | 3,488 | 32,209 |
| 74 | Country Sedan wgn 4d, 9P | 4,112 | 3,600 | 22,645 |

| XL (wb 121.0) | | | | |
|---|---|---|---|---|
| 60 | fstbk htp cpe | 3,750 | 3,293 | 27,251 |
| 61 | conv cpe | 3,983 | 3,501 | 6,348 |

| LTD (wb 121.0) | | | | |
|---|---|---|---|---|
| 62 | htp cpe | 3,727 | 3,356 | 96,324 |
| 62 | Brougham htp cpe | 3,855 | 3,537 | |
| 64 | sdn 4d | 3,701 | 3,307 | 78,306 |
| 64 | Brougham sdn | 3,829 | 3,502 | |
| 66 | htp sdn | 3,771 | 3,385 | 90,390 |
| 66 | Brougham htp sdn | 4,029 | 3,579 | |
| 75 | Country Squire wgn 4d, 6P | 4,139 | 3,832 | 39,837 |
| 76 | Country Squire wgn 4d, 9P | 4,185 | 3,909 | 69,077 |

| 1970 Engines | bore×stroke | bhp | availability |
|---|---|---|---|
| L6, 170.0 | 3.50×2.94 | 105 | S-Maverick |
| L6, 200.0 | 3.68×3.13 | 120 | S-Falcon; O-Maverick |
| L6, 240.0 | 4.00×3.18 | 150 | S-full-size exc XL, LTD |
| L6, 250.0 | 3.68×3.91 | 155 | S-Tor exc GT, Brghm, Squire, Cobra |
| V8, 302.0 | 4.00×3.00 | 220 | S-Tor GT/Brghm/Squire, Cobra; O-others |
| V8, 351.0 | 4.00×3.50 | 250 | S-XL, LTD, big wgns; O-all exc Flcn, Cobra |
| V8, 351.0 | 4.00×3.50 | 300 | O-Torino exc Cobra |
| V8, 390.0 | 4.05×3.78 | 265 | O-all full-size |
| V8, 429.0 | 4.36×3.59 | 320 | O-all full-size |
| V8, 429.0 | 4.36×3.59 | 360 | S-Tor Cobra; O-Ford, Torino |
| V8, 429.0 | 4.36×3.59 | 370* | O-Torino exc wgns |
| V8, 429.0 | 4.36×3.59 | 375 | O-Torino, Cobra |

*Available in standard and Ram Air versions.

| 1970½ Engines | bore×stroke | bhp | availability |
|---|---|---|---|
| L6, 250.0 | 3.68×3.91 | 155 | S-Falcon |
| V8, 302.0 | 4.00×3.00 | 220 | O-Falcon |
| V8, 351.0 | 4.00×3.50 | 250/300 | O-Falcon |
| V8, 429.0 | 4.36×3.59 | 360 | O-Falcon |
| V8, 429.0 | 4.36×3.59 | 370 | O-Falcon (w/o Ram Air) |

# Ford Mustang

**Ford Division, Ford Motor Co.
Dearborn, Michigan**

The greatest single automotive success of the 1960s raised Ford volume by well over half a million cars, and set an all-time record for first-year sales of any new model. Between its April 1964 introductory date and January 1965, a total of 680,989 Mustangs were sold. Truck drivers drove through showroom windows staring at them, housewives entered contests to win them, and dealers auctioned them off because buyer demand exceeded supply by 15 to 1. America loved the Mustang.

This remarkable accomplishment can be credited to

Lee A. Iacocca, the engineer turned salesman, who worked his way from an obsure sales position to vice-president and general manager of Ford Division in five years. Later, Iacocca became president of Ford Motor Company and would go on to become chairman of the board at Chrysler Corporation.

Iacocca's idea was a new "personal car." In his early days as sales manager, people had pleaded with the firm to bring back the two-seat Thunderbird. Iacocca dreamed, doodled, and scribbled down thoughts in the little black book by which he governed his career. By

Mid-engine Mustang I experimental model

1965 2+2 fastback coupe

Mustang II show car of 1963

1965 hardtop coupe

1964½ convertible

1966 GT 2+2 fastback coupe

1961 he had a plan. His young-person's car would be inexpensive to build, but peppy and sporty-looking. It would sell for less than $2500. Projected volume was 100,000 units a year.

The first Mustang prototype was a low, mid-engine fiberglass two-seater on a 90-inch wheelbase, powered by a Ford Cardinal (soon to become the German Ford Taunus 12M) two-liter V4 with 90 horsepower. This Mustang I was pretty but impractical. When Iacocca looked at the people who gathered around it at a show, he said: "That's sure not the car we want to build, because it can't be a volume car. It's too far out." More prototypes followed, culminating in the four-seat, conventionally laid out, 108-inch-wheelbase production Mustang of 1964½. From a marketing standpoint, it

couldn't have been better.

For the 1965 through '68 model years, Mustang came in three basic forms: a hardtop, a convertible, and a semi-fastback coupe. Convertible sales started at the 100,000-unit annual level but had dropped to less than 15,000 a year by 1969. The crisp notchback hardtop was the sales leader. The coupe, known as the "2+2," was introduced with the rest of the Ford line in autumn 1964. It soon overtook the convertible in sales, and averaged about 50,000 units a year through 1970.

The standard Mustang engines during the first six months of production were the 170 cubic-inch Falcon and the 260 cid small-block V8. By fall, these had been replaced by Ford's 200-cid six and the bored-out 289 V8. In the last years of the '60s, before government reg-

**1966 hardtop coupe**

**1967 hardtop coupe**

**1967 GT 2+2 fastback coupe**

**GT/SC package on 1968 hardtop coupe**

**1967 convertible**

**1968 GT 2+2 fastback coupe**

# Ford Mustang

ulations put an end to Ford's "Total Performance" program, the company offered increasingly hairy engine options. For 1967, there was a 390 V8 with 320 bhp; for 1968, the most powerful engine was a 427 of 390 bhp; for 1969, a 335-bhp 428 was available. The 1970 Boss series included a 429 V8 with 375 bhp.

Part of Mustang's appeal lay in its myriad options, which enabled a customer to personalize the car. Careful use of the order form could result in anything from a cute economy car to a thunderingly fast drag racer or a deceptively nimble sporty car. Transmission choices comprised automatics, four-speeds, three-speeds, and stick-overdrive units. Handling packages, power steering, disc brakes, air conditioning, tachometer, and a clock were available. A Mustang could be ordered with bench seats instead of the standard buckets, though few people did so. For $170, the GT package offered a pleasant assortment of goodies, including front disc brakes, a full-gauge instrument panel, and special badges. A variety of interiors was available, along with accent stripes and special moldings for the exterior.

Mustang's shape was inspired, the work of Joe Oros, L. David Ash, and Gayle L. Halderman of the Ford Division styling studio. The long-hood/short-deck style was to fascinate many buyers in the '60s and early '70s. For the next several years, it was the only formula for what soon became known, in honor of Iacocca's brainchild, as the "ponycar." Styling was so good that it was

hardly changed at all during the first few years. The '66s were mostly unaltered; the '67s had a deeper grille and sculptured side panels that ended in twin simulated air scoops; the '68s had a new grille with an inner bright ring around the Mustang emblem. The 2+2 adopted full-fastback styling for '67. Only in 1969 was the package changed more extensively. The '69 version was lower, longer, and wider than earlier models, with ventless side glass and an eggcrate grille. A "SportsRoof" fastback with simulated air scoops and rear deck spoiler joined the line, along with the six or V8 Grandé hardtop coupe priced at $2866 to $2971, and the Mach I fastback at $3139. The Mach I had a 351 V8.

The 1970 Boss Mustang was even more unique than the '69—flashily painted, well-suspended, and fitted with the hottest engines ever. A competition shifter with Hurst linkage was new. Up the price scale was the Boss 429, powered by Ford's Cobra-Jet NASCAR engine with cast-magnesium rocker arm covers and semi-hemispherical combustion chambers.

Available Mach I engines for 1970 ranged from a 351 V8 to a 428-cid four-barrel unit with Ram Air. Mach I styling features included a special grille with driving lamps, a dull-finish black center hood section, functional hood scoop, quick-fill gas cap, and black honeycomb rear panel appliqué. The luxury Grandé was still offered with either six or V8 power. Like all Mustangs that year, it inherited the '69 Mach I's high-back front

**1969 Mach I fastback coupe**

**1969 Grande hardtop coupe**

**1969 convertible**

**1970 Boss 302 fastback coupe**

bucket seats. A landau-style black or white vinyl roof, racing-type mirrors, special identification, and bright wheelwell moldings completed the package.

There were still basic Mustangs in 1970, available with the standard six or 302 V8 in hardtop, convertible, and SportsRoof fastback styles. Like other models, they featured new front-end styling and reverted to single headlights. Recessed taillamps appeared at the rear.

Convertibles became much scarcer now; buyer preference for air conditioning and closed coupes had transformed the market, keeping ragtop production low.

In late 1970, Ford abandoned most of its Trans-Am, USAC, NASCAR, and international competition efforts, and also began to change the Mustang's character. After what Ford Division had called the "Sizzlin' '70s," later Mustangs would seem relatively tame.

# Ford Mustang Specifications

## 1965

| (wb 108.0) | | Wght | Price | Prod |
|---|---|---|---|---|
| 07 | htp cpe | 2,583 | 2,372 | 501,965 |
| 08 | conv cpe | 2,789 | 2,614 | 101,945 |
| 09 | fstbk cpe | 2,633 | 2,589 | 77,079 |

| 1965 Engines | bore×stroke | bhp | availability |
|---|---|---|---|
| L6, 170.0 | 3.50×2.94 | 101 | S-all through 9/24/64 |
| L6, 200.0 | 3.68×3.13 | 120 | S-all after 9/25/64 |
| V8, 260.0 | 3.80×2.87 | 164 | O-all through 9/25/64 |
| V8, 289.0 | 4.00×2.87 | 200 | O-all after 9/25/64 |
| V8, 289.0 | 4.00×2.87 | 225/271 | O-all |

## 1966

| (wb 108.0) | | Wght | Price | Prod |
|---|---|---|---|---|
| 01 | htp cpe | 2,488 | 2,416 | 499,751 |
| 02 | fstbk cpe | 2,519 | 2,607 | 35,698 |
| 03 | conv cpe | 2,650 | 2,653 | 72,119 |

| 1966 Engines | bore×stroke | bhp | availability |
|---|---|---|---|
| L6, 200.0 | 3.68×3.13 | 120 | S-all |
| V8, 289.0 | 4.00×2.87 | 200 | O-all |
| V8, 289.0 | 4.00×2.87 | 225/271 | O-all |

## 1967

| (wb 108.0) | | Wght | Price | Prod |
|---|---|---|---|---|
| 01 | htp cpe | 2,568 | 2,461 | 356,271 |
| 02 | fstbk cpe | 2,605 | 2,592 | 71,042 |
| 03 | conv cpe | 2,738 | 2,698 | 44,808 |

| 1967 Engines | bore×stroke | bhp | availability |
|---|---|---|---|
| L6, 200.0 | 3.68×3.13 | 120 | S-all |
| V8, 289.0 | 4.00×2.87 | 200 | O-all |
| V8, 289.0 | 4.00×2.87 | 225/271 | O-all |
| V8, 390.0 | 4.05×3.78 | 320 | O-all |

## 1968

| (wb 108.0) | | Wght | Price | Prod |
|---|---|---|---|---|
| 01 | htp cpe | 2,635 | 2,602 | 249,447 |
| 02 | fstbk cpe | 2,659 | 2,712 | 42,581 |
| 03 | conv cpe | 2,745 | 2,814 | 25,376 |

| 1968 Engines | bore×stroke | bhp | availability |
|---|---|---|---|
| L6, 200.0 | 3.68×3.13 | 115 | S-all |
| V8, 289.0 | 4.00×2.87 | 195 | O-all |
| V8, 302.0 | 4.00×3.00 | 230 | O-all |
| V8, 390.0 | 4.05×3.78 | 335 | O-all |
| V8, 427.0 | 4.23×3.78 | 390 | O-all |

## 1969

| (wb 108.0) | | Wght | Price | Prod |
|---|---|---|---|---|
| 01 | htp cpe | 2,798 | 2,635 | 128,458 |
| 02 | fstbk cpe | 2,822 | 2,635 | 61,980 |
| 02 | Boss 302 fstbk cpe, V8 | 3,210 | 3,588 | |
| 03 | conv cpe | 2,908 | 2,849 | 14,746 |
| 04 | Grande htp cpe | 2,873 | 2,866 | 22,182 |
| 05 | Mach I fstbk cpe | 3,175 | 3,139 | 72,458 |

| 1969 Engines | bore×stroke | bhp | availability |
|---|---|---|---|
| L6, 200.0 | 3.68×3.13 | 115 | S-all exc Mach I, Boss 302 |
| L6, 250.0 | 3.68×3.91 | 155 | O-all exc Mach I, Boss 302 |
| V8, 302.0 | 4.00×3.00 | 220 | O-all exc Mach I, Boss 302 |
| V8, 351.0 | 4.00×3.50 | 250 | S-Mach I; O-others exc Boss 302 |
| V8, 351.0 | 4.00×3.50 | 290 | O-all |
| V8, 390.0 | 4.05×3.78 | 320 | O-all |
| V8, 428.0 | 4.13×3.98 | 335 | O-Mach I (Ram Air avail) |

## 1970

| (wb 108.0) | | Wght | Price | Prod |
|---|---|---|---|---|
| 01 | htp cpe | 2,822 | 2,721 | 82,569 |
| 02 | fstbk cpe | 2,846 | 2,771 | 45,934 |
| 02 | Boss 302 fstbk cpe, V8 | 3,227 | 3,720 | |
| 03 | conv cpe | 2,932 | 3,025 | 7,673 |
| 04 | Grande htp cpe | 2,907 | 2,926 | 13,581 |
| 05 | Mach I cpe | 3,240 | 3,271 | 40,970 |

| 1970 Engines | bore×stroke | bhp | availability |
|---|---|---|---|
| L6, 200.0 | 3.68×3.13 | 115 | S-all exc Mach I, Boss 302 |
| L6, 250.0 | 3.68×3.91 | 155 | O-all exc Mach I, Boss 302 |
| V8, 302.0 | 4.00×3.00 | 220 | O-all exc Mach I, Boss 302 |
| V8, 351.0 | 4.00×3.50 | 250 | S-Mach I; O-others exc Boss 302 |
| V8, 351.0 | 4.00×3.50 | 300 | O-all |
| V8, 428.0 | 4.13×3.98 | 335 | O-Mach I (Ram Air avail) |
| V8, 429.0 | 4.36×3.59 | 375 | O-Mach 1, Boss |

# Ford Thunderbird
Ford Division, Ford Motor Co.
Dearborn, Michigan

The two-seat Thunderbird was a spectacular-looking newcomer in 1955, and still turns heads today. Initially, it was Ford's answer to the Chevrolet Corvette. Styling came from Ford Division designers working under Frank Hershey, and not directly from the George Walker consultant team as is often quoted. Also, it's not likely the project started with division general manager Lewis Crusoe admiring foreign sports cars at the 1951 Paris Automobile Show. Hershey and others say a two-seater was already in the works at Ford Styling well before that. Early market surveys had indicated a demand for a two-seater. But later, an even greater market was pinpointed for a four-seat model. As a result, the two-seaters planned for 1958 and beyond were dropped. T-Bird was enlarged and began stressing luxury over sportiness. It proved an intelligent move from a sales standpoint: the 1958 and later Thunderbirds handily outsold the Corvettes, and were always well ahead in sales of the 1955-57 two-seaters.

The 1955 Thunderbird was priced just below $3000 without options. Unlike the first Corvettes, manual and stick-overdrive transmissions were available as well as automatic. Power came from the 292-cid "Y-block" V8, and a detachable hardtop was offered as an option. For 1956, engine output was 202 bhp. Due to complaints about limited trunk space, Ford placed the spare tire outside, "continental" style, for the '56 edition. A popular no-cost option on '56-'57 hardtops was the famous T-Bird portholes, derived from vintage coachwork by Ford stylist Bill Boyer. Porthole hardtops outsold non-porthole versions heavily in 1956, and virtually all '57 Thunderbirds had them.

For 1957, the two-seater got what would be the only major restyle for its three-year design cycle. Modest tailfins were added, trailing back from midway on the body, and the front end featured a combination bumper/grille. Though basic stickshift models still came with the 292 V8, other versions had larger engines—all the way to a supercharged 312-cid unit with 300 bhp. With a base price still under $3500, the '57 T-Bird was an attractive buy. Because it remained in production through the end of the year, more '57s were built than either of the first two models.

The four-seater followed in 1958. It was a dramatic

1955 two-seat convertible with hardtop (pre-production)

1956 two-seat convertible with hardtop

1955 two-seat convertible (pre-production)

1956 two-seat convertible

1957 two-seat convertible with hardtop

1957 two-seat convertible

design with unibody construction, all-coil suspension, and rakish lowness. Crisp new styling popularized the square-cut "formal" hardtop roofline. The 113-inch wheelbase was compact, yet provided ample interior room for four. Both hardtop and convertible models were offered, though a rumored retractable hardtop model like the Ford Skyliner was canceled in the design stage.

With two models and room for four, the '58 Thunderbird was a solid success. Almost twice as many found buyers as any of the previous two-seaters. The

'59s changed only in detail: a horizontal instead of honeycomb pattern for grille, air scoop, and taillight panels; projectile-like door moldings; reworked Thunderbird script; a bird emblem for the hardtop's rear roof pillar instead of the '58's round emblem. Owing to production over a full model year, the '59 bested the '58 in sales.

The 1960 version was the last "squarebird" in the three-year styling cycle. It was substantially the same as its predecessor, but had a new grille with a main horizontal bar bisecting three vertical bars ahead of a grid

1958 hardtop coupe

1959 convertible

1960 hardtop coupe

1960 hardtop coupe

1961 hardtop coupe

1962 convertible

1963 Sports Roadster

1964 Landau hardtop coupe

1965 convertible

insert, new triple taillight clusters, and small trim changes. A 352-cid V8 was standard. The Lincoln Continental 430 V8 was optional. Hardtops outsold convertibles by nearly an eight to one ratio, indicating T-Bird customers wanted luxury first and sportiness second.

The 1961 model was entirely new, though a 113-inch wheelbase was retained. This styling and engineering would be continued through the 1963 model year. The bullet-shaped 61s had severely pointed front profiles, modest tailfins, and the traditional Ford circular taillights. Only one engine was now offered: the 390 V8 (created by stroking the old 352 a quarter-inch). In 1962, the 390 was offered with a powerpack option. With minor horsepower alterations, these two would be the basic Thunderbird powerplants through 1968, to be accompanied by big-block options in 1966-68.

Thunderbird engineering in the early and middle '60s was conservative but sound. Ford had considered front-wheel-drive for 1961, but felt it was too unorthodox for this market. Instead, engineers stressed quality control, solid construction, high ride standards, and minimum noise at speed. Extensive use of rubber bushings for the independent front suspension and leaf-spring rear suspension made the 1961-63 Thunderbirds among the best-riding cars of the day.

Styling for 1962 and 1963 was generally the same as for '61, but two new models were added. These were the Sports Roadster and the Landau.

The Sports Roadster was the only production four-seat car to become a two-seater. (There are many examples of the opposite, of course, including the 1958 Thunderbird.) The decision to build it was made by Lee A. Iacocca, Ford Division general manager, because dealers were beseiged with requests for another two-seater. Iacocca concluded there was no significant market for anything like the 1955-57 Thunderbird, but a semi-sports model wouldn't hurt.

The designer most responsible for the Sports Roadster was Bud Kaufman. He developed a fiberglass tonneau cover to hide the area behind the front seat. When fitted, the cover formed twin headrests for the front seats. Kaufman overcame fitting problems so the car's soft top could be raised and lowered with the cover in place. Kelsey-Hayes wire wheels were fitted to all Sports Roadsters. The stock rear fender skirts were left off because they wouldn't clear the pseudo knock-off hubcaps.

Limited demand made the Sports Roadster rare. The problem was price. It sold for about $650 more than the standard Thunderbird convertible. In 1964, dealers offered the tonneau cover and wire wheels as accessories. These are even scarcer today.

The Landau was more popular, because it cost only $77 more than the standard hardtop. It sported a vinyl-covered roof with a fake landau ("S") bar on each rear pillar. This distinctive touch made the Landau a hit. By 1966, it was outselling the unadorned hardtop, and composed the bulk of T-Bird production by 1969.

The 1963 model run also included 2000 examples of a

1966 Landau hardtop coupe

1967 hardtop coupe

1968 hardtop coupe

1968 Landau four-door sedan

1969 Landau four-door sedan

1969 Landau hardtop coupe

Limited Edition Landau, introduced in the spring of that year. It was identified by a special numbered plaque on the console, all-white background in the rear roof quarter, all-white interiors, and spinner wheel covers.

Thunderbird received completely new sheetmetal in 1964, along with a lot of bodyside sculpture. The third-generation four-seater, still on the original-length wheelbase, would be continued without major change through 1966. These were years of increasing emphasis on quiet, refined luxury. During this period, convertible sales declined noticeably. The last convertibles were run off for 1966, and accounted for only 7.5 percent of production.

Among features introduced on the '64–'66 cars were a cockpit-style passenger compartment and Silent-Flo ventilation (1964); front disc brakes (1965); full-width taillight housings including backup lights and sequential turn signals; and a "Town" (formal) roofline for the Landau and hardtop (1966). A popular accessory, which had first appeared in 1961, was the "Swing-Away" steering wheel. It shifted about 10 inches in-

board so the driver could be seated more easily.

Throughout the '60s, the pros and cons of offering a Thunderbird sedan were steadily debated by Ford officials. By 1965, Iacocca was satisfied that the sporting image was being handled by other Fords: he had launched the Mustang, and had an attractive array of Falcons and Fairlanes. Market surveys indicated that Thunderbird, now firmly entrenched as a personal-luxury car, no longer needed an image of sportiness. Accordingly, the car was completely restyled for 1967. In place of the convertible came a four-door Landau on a 117-inch wheelbase. The hardtop and two-door Landau were continued on a two-inch shorter wheelbase. The front featured a deeply recessed honeycomb grille with concealed headlamps. The front bumper was wrapped underneath. On two-door models, rear quarter windows retracted horizontally into the roof pillars.

This series was continued through 1970, despite the fact that the plain hardtop was a slow seller, as were other models in the line. Sales moved slowly but consistently downward in the last three years of the de-

# Ford Thunderbird

1970 Landau four-door sedan

1970 hardtop coupe

cade. The four-door Landau was not very practical; its rear doors seemed to detract from the formal roofline. It dropped in sales from almost 25,000 cars in 1967 to slightly more than 8400 for 1970.

Styling changes to distinguish the 1968 and 1969 Thunderbirds were minor. For 1968, an eggcrate grille pattern replaced the '67 honeycomb, and bodysill moldings were narrowed. For 1969, the grille texture was changed to horizontal louvers with three vertical dividers, and divided taillamps replaced the full-width cluster. The Landau coupe's rear quarter windows were eliminated. The '70 was restyled on the same wheel-

base; it received a longer hood and a more prominent, snout-like grille. Windshield wipers and radio antenna were concealed, and two-door models had a "faster" roofline.

Although Thunderbird had no performance image to uphold by now, the Ford slogan was "Total Performance." Big-block V8s were offered, but they did not sell well. The 1966-67 option was Ford's 428. For 1968-70, the 429 became standard. The 390 engine, which had powered Thunderbirds for eight years, was no longer offered although it was used in some Fairlanes, Torinos, Mustangs, and full-size Fords.

# Ford Thunderbird Specifications

## 1955

| (wb 102.0) | | | Wght | Price | Prod |
|---|---|---|---|---|---|
| 40A | conv 2S | | 2,980 | 2,944 | 16,155 |

| 1955 Engines | bore×stroke | bhp | availability |
|---|---|---|---|
| V8, 292.0 | 3.75×3.30 | 193 | S-stickshift |
| V8, 292.0 | 3.75×3.30 | 198 | S-automatic |

## 1956

| (wb 102.0) | | | Wght | Price | Prod |
|---|---|---|---|---|---|
| 40A | conv 2S | | 3,038 | 3,151 | 15,631 |

| 1956 Engines | bore×stroke | bhp | availability |
|---|---|---|---|
| V8, 292.0 | 3.75×3.30 | 202 | S-3-speed trans |
| V8, 312.0 | 3.80×3.44 | 215 | S-overdrive |
| V8, 312.0 | 3.80×3.44 | 225 | S-automatic |

## 1957

| (wb 102.0) | | | Wght | Price | Prod |
|---|---|---|---|---|---|
| 40 | conv 2S | | 3,145 | 3,408 | 21,380 |

| 1957 Engines | bore×stroke | bhp | availability |
|---|---|---|---|
| V8, 292.0 | 3.75×3.30 | 212 | S-3-speed trans |
| V8, 312.0 | 3.80×3.44 | 245 | S-overdrive, automatic |
| V8, 312.0 | 3.80×3.44 | 270/285 | O-all (3-speed briefly) |
| V8, 312.0 | 3.80×3.44 | 300 | O-auto; few od/3sp (superchgd) |

## 1958

| (wb 113.0) | | | Wght | Price | Prod |
|---|---|---|---|---|---|
| 63A | htp cpe | | 3,876 | 3,631 | 35,758 |
| 76A | conv cpe | | 3,944 | 3,929 | 2,134 |

| 1958 Engines | bore×stroke | bhp | availability |
|---|---|---|---|
| V8, 352.0 | 4.00×3.50 | 300 | S-all |
| V8, 430.0 | 4.30×3.70 | 350 | O-prod questionable |

## 1959

| (wb 113.0) | | | Wght | Price | Prod |
|---|---|---|---|---|---|
| 63A | htp cpe | | 3,813 | 3,696 | 57,195 |
| 76A | conv cpe | | 3,903 | 3,979 | 10,261 |

| 1959 Engines | bore×stroke | bhp | availability |
|---|---|---|---|
| V8, 352.0 | 4.00×3.50 | 300 | S-all |
| V8, 430.0 | 4.30×3.70 | 350 | O-all |

## 1960

| (wb 113.0) | | Wght | Price | Prod |
|---|---|---|---|---|
| 63A | htp cpe | 3,799 | 3,755 | 78,447 |
| 63B | htp cpe, gold top | 3,799 | 3,900* | 2,536 |
| 76A | conv cpe | 3,897 | 4,222 | 11,860 |

| 1960 Engines | bore×stroke | bhp | availability |
|---|---|---|---|
| V8, 352.0 | 4.00×3.50 | 300 | S-all |
| V8, 430.0 | 4.30×3.70 | 350 | O-all |

*Estimated.

## 1961

| (wb 113.0) | | Wght | Price | Prod |
|---|---|---|---|---|
| 63A | htp cpe | 3,958 | 4,172 | 62,535 |
| 76A | conv cpe | 4,130 | 4,639 | 10,516 |

| 1961 Engine | bore×stroke | bhp | availability |
|---|---|---|---|
| V8, 390.0 | 4.05×3.78 | 300 | S-all |

## 1962

| (wb 113.0) | | Wght | Price | Prod |
|---|---|---|---|---|
| 63A | htp cpe | 4,132 | 4,321 | 69,554* |
| 63B | Landau htp cpe | 4,144 | 4,398 | |
| 76A | conv cpe | 4,370 | 4,788 | 7,030* |
| 76B | Sports Roadster conv cpe | 4,471 | 5,439 | 1,427* |

*Some sources list total of 68,127 hardtops/Landaus and 9,884 convertibles.

| 1962 Engines | bore×stroke | bhp | availability |
|---|---|---|---|
| V8, 390.0 | 4.05×3.78 | 300 | S-all |
| V8, 390.0 | 4.05×3.78 | 340 | O-all |

## 1963

| Series 80 (wb 113.0) | | Wght | Price | Prod |
|---|---|---|---|---|
| 63A | htp cpe | 4,195 | 4,445 | 42,806* |
| 63B | Landau htp cpe | 4,203 | 4,548 | 14,139* |
| 76A | conv cpe | 4,322 | 4,912 | 5,913* |
| 76B | Sports Roadster conv cpe | 4,396 | 5,563 | 455* |

*Some sources list total of 59,000 hardtops/Landaus and 5,457 convertibles. Model 63B includes 2,000 Limited Edition Landaus with special trim; model 76B includes 37 units with 340-bhp engine.

| 1963 Engines | bore×stroke | bhp | availability |
|---|---|---|---|
| V8, 390.0 | 4.05×3.78 | 300 | S-all |
| V8, 390.0 | 4.05×3.78 | 340 | O-all |

## 1964

| Series 80 (wb 113.2) | | Wght | Price | Prod |
|---|---|---|---|---|
| 83 | htp cpe | 4,431 | 4,486 | 60,552 |
| 85 | conv cpe | 4,586 | 4,953 | 9,198 |
| 87 | Landau htp cpe | 4,441 | 4,589 | 22,715 |

| 1964 Engine | bore×stroke | bhp | availability |
|---|---|---|---|
| V8, 390.0 | 4.05×3.78 | 300 | S-all |

## 1965

| Series 80 (wb 113.2) | | Wght | Price | Prod |
|---|---|---|---|---|
| 83 | htp cpe | 4,470 | 4,486 | 42,652 |
| 85 | conv cpe | 4,588 | 4,953 | 6,846 |
| 87 | Landau htp cpe | 4,478 | 4,589 | 20,974 |
| 87 | Limited Ed Special Landau | 4,500 | 4,639 | 4,500 |

| 1965 Engine | bore×stroke | bhp | availability |
|---|---|---|---|
| V8, 390.0 | 4.00×3.78 | 300 | S-all |

## 1966

| Series 80 (wb 113.2) | | Wght | Price | Prod |
|---|---|---|---|---|
| 81 | Town Hardtop cpe | 4,359 | 4,483 | 15,633 |
| 83 | htp cpe | 4,388 | 4,426 | 13,389 |
| 85 | conv cpe | 4,496 | 4,879 | 5,049 |
| 87 | Landau htp cpe | 4,367 | 4,584 | 35,105 |

| 1966 Engines | bore×stroke | bhp | availability |
|---|---|---|---|
| V8, 390.0 | 4.00×3.78 | 315 | S-all |
| V8, 428.0 | 4.13×3.98 | 345 | O-all |

## 1967

| Series 80 (wb 114.7; 4d-117.2) | | Wght | Price | Prod |
|---|---|---|---|---|
| 81 | htp cpe | 4,248 | 4,603 | 15,567 |
| 82 | Landau htp cpe | 4,256 | 4,704 | 37,422 |
| 84 | Landau sdn 4d | 4,348 | 4,825 | 24,967 |

| 1967 Engines | bore×stroke | bhp | availability |
|---|---|---|---|
| V8, 390.0 | 4.00×3.78 | 315 | S-all |
| V8, 428.0 | 4.13×3.98 | 345 | O-all |

## 1968

| Series 80 (wb 114.7; 4d-117.2) | | Wght | Price | Prod |
|---|---|---|---|---|
| 83 | htp cpe | 4,366 | 4,716 | 9,977 |
| 84 | Landau htp cpe | 4,372 | 4,845 | 33,029 |
| 87 | Landau sdn 4d | 4,458 | 4,924 | 21,925 |

| 1968 Engines | bore×stroke | bhp | availability |
|---|---|---|---|
| V8, 390.0 | 4.05×3.78 | 315 | S-all |
| V8, 429.0 | 4.36×3.59 | 360 | O-all |

## 1969

| Series 80 (wb 114.7; 4d-117.2) | | Wght | Price | Prod |
|---|---|---|---|---|
| 83 | htp cpe | 4,348 | 4,824 | 5,913 |
| 84 | Landau htp cpe | 4,360 | 4,964 | 27,664 |
| 87 | Landau sdn 4d | 4,460 | 5,043 | 15,695 |

| 1969 Engine | bore×stroke | bhp | availability |
|---|---|---|---|
| V8, 429.0 | 4.36×3.59 | 360 | S-all |

## 1970

| Series 80 (wb 114.7; 4d-117.2) | | Wght | Price | Prod |
|---|---|---|---|---|
| 83 | htp cpe | 4,354 | 4,961 | 5,116 |
| 84 | Landau htp cpe | 4,630 | 5,104 | 36,847 |
| 87 | Landau sdn 4d | 4,464 | 5,182 | 8,401 |

| 1970 Engine | bore×stroke | bhp | availability |
|---|---|---|---|
| V8, 429.0 | 4.36×3.59 | 360 | S-all |

# Frazer
### Graham-Paige Motors/Kaiser-Frazer Corp.
### Willow Run, Michigan

**J**oseph Washington Frazer, a descendant of the Virginia Washingtons, was a high-born aristocrat who loved motorcars. Shunning the high society in which he would have blended nicely, he enrolled in a technical college, and learned salesmanship with Packard, Pierce-Arrow, and General Motors. He was one of many talented men who helped Walter Percy Chrysler build a great corporation in the 1920s. He even named the Plymouth in 1928. During the '30s, Frazer breathed new life into Willys-Overland. In the '40s, he and his associates acquired old-line Graham-Paige Motors with the idea of producing a postwar car. The Frazer was the result.

Early in 1945, Frazer was looking for a moneyed partner. Friends introduced him to Henry J. Kaiser, the West Coast sand-and-gravel tycoon and wartime builder of Liberty ships. Kaiser-Frazer Corporation was founded in July 1945.

Initially, Frazers were to be produced by Graham-Paige and Kaisers by Kaiser-Frazer under a joint tenancy agreement at Willow Run, the huge factory 17 miles outside Detroit that once had produced bombers. In early 1947, however, Graham-Paige was unable to sustain plant investment and sold its automotive interests to Kaiser-Frazer. J. W. Frazer was company president from 1945 to early 1949; Henry J. Kaiser was chairman of the board.

During the closing years of the war, Frazer had asked inventor William Stout and custom-car designer Howard Darrin to come up with ideas for the new postwar model. Stout's creation, called Project-Y, was derived from his novel rear-engined Scarab. It was too unorthodox and complicated for G-P to build. Darrin, however, designed a smooth-looking sedan body with flow-through fenders, a high and blunt hood, and acres of space inside. Although the end result was not all Darrin's work, it led directly to the production Frazer.

Built initially as a four-door sedan only, the Frazer of-

1947 Standard four-door sedan

1948 Manhattan four-door sedan

Joseph W. Frazer (left) and Henry J. Kaiser (right) with their cars in 1946

fered tremendous interior space. At 64 inches, its front seat was one of the widest in the industry. Well over 80 percent of its total width was available for passenger room. Frazer's six-cylinder powerplant was derived from the Continental "Red Seal" industrial engine, incorporating improvements for its automotive application. Most of the engines were built by Kaiser-Frazer; a few were assembled by Continental. Frazer had no automatic transmission until 1951. Up to then, a three-speed manual transmission was offered, with Borg-Warner overdrive an $80 option. The box-section chassis was equipped with a conventional suspension—coils and wishbones in front, a beam axle and semi-elliptic leaf springs at the rear.

Production began in June 1946, with a ratio of one Frazer to every two Kaisers. The base sedan was joined by the elegantly upholstered (and usually two-toned) Manhattan, priced about $400 higher.

In a market laden with prewar designs, the all-new Frazer was a refreshing standout. It was extremely clean, with no side trim to speak of and only a modest horizontal grille. It demonstrated Darrin's styling ideals

1951 Vagabond four-door utility sedan

in its lack of sheetmetal sculpture or decorative chrome. The long wheelbase provided a smooth ride, and the six-cylinder engine delivered excellent fuel economy. Some people thought these were shortcomings, however, and would have preferred eight cylinders and more chrome. Frazer ultimately offered optional hood ornaments and more glittery interiors, but was not able to provide an eight-cylinder engine, though several were considered.

The 1948 models were changed only in detail, such as redesigned nameplates. Prices increased. Despite the relatively tall prices, Frazer continued to do well in what was a seller's market. A total 48,071 cars were sold for 1948.

Kaiser-Frazer surprised the industry with its volume during those years. Observers had expressed a lack of confidence in the managerial combination. Henry Kaiser was a shipbuilder, they said, and didn't know an automobile from a motorboat. And Frazer had never built cars before; he'd only sold them. Yet, despite postwar material shortages, K-F succeeded. It formed a crack team of expeditors who foraged the country for everything from sheetmetal steel to copper wire. They usually got what they wanted—at a price. Thus, Kaiser-Frazer had the highest output of any independent in 1947-48, and a volume sufficient for ninth place in the industry production race.

The situation changed in 1949. Joseph Frazer realized this would be a facelift year for the company, and that its cars would be opposed by all-new designs from the Big Three and Nash. He recommended cutting back on production, but Henry Kaiser wanted even more output. The two were at loggerheads, so Frazer stepped down as president, taking the meaningless position of board vice-chairman. Kaiser's son Edgar assumed the presidency, tooled up for 200,000 cars—and sold only 58,000. The firm's downhill slide had begun.

The facelifted 1949 Frazers were well-built, good-looking cars. They adopted an egg-crate grille with prominent rectangular parking lamps and large, vertical, two-lens taillamps. A novel four-door convertible was added to the Manhattan series. It was a makeshift

**Clay models (original smaller) for 1947 Frazer**

**1949-50 Manhattan convertible sedan**

**1949-50 Manhattan four-door sedan**

1951 Manhattan hardtop sedan

Proposed 1952 Manhattan based on '51 Kaiser

job at best. Engineers John Widman and Ralph Is-brandt, directed to do or die, sheared the top off a sedan, put little glass panes where the door pillars were, and purchased beefed-up X-member frames for an inordinate price. Priced at over $3000, they simply weren't salable in large quantities.

Frazer's 1949 sales were generally disappointing. About 5000 leftovers were reserialed for the brief 1950 model run, which ended in the spring of that year.

Model year 1951 was cleanup time for Frazer. At that point, Kaiser had a brand-new body, but the Frazer was merely a restyled 1949-50 Kaiser. The restyling made the Frazers look radically different, however, and 50,000 orders were placed. Yet far fewer than that were delivered, and the marque came to an end as soon as all the old Kaiser bodies were used up.

For the abbreviated 1951 model year, the Frazer took on a new look. Leftover Kaiser utility sedans, with rear hatches and folding rear seat, were converted into Frazer Vagabonds; former Kaiser Virginian four-door hardtops became Manhattan sedans; pillared sedans were assigned to the standard Frazer series, but were trimmed similarly to the previous year's Manhattans. Altogether, 10,214 of the '51s were sold.

Kaiser-Frazer's styling department had created numerous renderings for future Frazers, based on the new 1951 Kaiser styling. However, with Joe Frazer out of the corporate picture, the Kaisers decided to discontinue the Frazer and concentrate on their new small car, the Henry J.

# Frazer Specifications

## 1947

**Standard (wb 123.5)**

| | | Wght | Price | Prod |
|---|---|---|---|---|
| F47 | sdn 4d | 3,340 | 2,295 | 36,120 |

**Manhattan (wb 123.5)**

| | | Wght | Price | Prod |
|---|---|---|---|---|
| F47C | sdn 4d | 3,375 | 2,712 | 32,655 |

| 1947 Engines | bore×stroke | bhp | availability |
|---|---|---|---|
| L6, 226.2 | 3.31×4.38 | 100 | S-all |
| L6, 226.2 | 3.31×4.38 | 112 | O-Manhattan |

## 1948

**F485 Standard (wb 123.5)**

| | | Wght | Price | Prod |
|---|---|---|---|---|
| 4851 | sdn 4d | 3,340 | 2,483· | 29,480 |

**F486 Manhattan (wb 123.5)**

| | | Wght | Price | Prod |
|---|---|---|---|---|
| 4861 | sdn 4d | 3,375 | 2,746 | 18,591 |

| 1948 Engines | bore×stroke | bhp | availability |
|---|---|---|---|
| L6, 226.2 | 3.31×4.38 | 100 | S-all |
| L6, 226.2 | 3.31×4.38 | 112 | O-Manhattan |

## 1949-50

**F495/505 Standard (wb 123.5)**

| | | Wght | Price | Prod |
|---|---|---|---|---|
| 4951/5051 | sdn 4d | 3,386 | 2,395 | 14,700* |

**F496/506 Manhattan (wb 123.5)**

| | | Wght | Price | Prod |
|---|---|---|---|---|
| 4961/5051 | sdn 4d | 3,391 | 2,595 | 9,950* |
| 4962/5052 | conv sdn | 3,726 | 3,295 | 70* |

*Estimated: actual total 24,923. Years were combined by factory; estimated breakdown 85% 1949, 15% 1950.

| 1949-50 Engine | bore×stroke | bhp | availability |
|---|---|---|---|
| L6, 226.2 | 3.31×4.38 | 112 | S-all |

## 1951

**F515 Standard (wb 123.5)**

| | | Wght | Price | Prod |
|---|---|---|---|---|
| 5151 | sdn 4d | 3,456 | 2,359 | 6,900* |
| 5155 | Vagabond util sdn 4d | 3,556 | 2,399 | 3,000* |

**F516 Manhattan (wb 123.5)**

| | | Wght | Price | Prod |
|---|---|---|---|---|
| 5161 | htp sdn | 3,771 | 3,075 | 152 |
| 5162 | conv sdn | 3,941 | 3,075 | 131 |

*Estimated from actual total of 9,931.

| 1951 Engines | bore×stroke | bhp | availability |
|---|---|---|---|
| L6, 226.2 | 3.31×4.38 | 115 | S-all |

# Graham
### Graham-Paige Motors Corp.
### Detroit, Michigan

The three Graham brothers—Joseph, Robert, and Ray—purchased the declining Paige Motor Company in 1927 to build their own car, in addition to a line of farm equipment. The car was called Graham-Paige through 1930 and simply Graham afterward, though Paige remained part of the company name. Production reached nearly 80,000 vehicles in 1929. Then came the Depression and company fortunes plunged. Graham-Paige lost money in every year of the '30s except 1933. Its attempt to rebound in 1938, dubbed "Spirit of Motion," was too radical for the public and was unsuccessful in the market.

Company president Joseph Graham had put a half-million dollars of his own money into the firm to keep it going. He realized a new model was needed, and quickly. In 1939 he was approached by Norman De Vaux, who'd once built his own cars and later was general manager of Hupmobile. Hupp was in similarly dire financial straits in '39, but De Vaux had an idea. He'd bought the tooling for the discontinued 1936-37 Cord Beverly sedan and wanted to build a Hupp version of it with rear-wheel drive instead of front drive. Graham said he'd agree to share the project's cost by building the bodies, provided his company could produce its own version with a Graham-Paige engine. The resulting Graham Hollywood had its own special "face" to distinguish it from Hupmobile's car, called the Skylark. But getting the line ready for production took many months, and the sleek new Hollywood sedans didn't roll out of the factory until May 1940.

The 1940 Graham line began with a slightly facelifted "Spirit of Motion" in two series, DeLuxe and Custom, available with or without supercharger. The blower was Graham's own centrifugal type, and was the only such unit available on a popularly priced car. Three body styles were offered: a combination coupe, and sedans with two or four doors. The powerplant, designed by Continental, developed 93 horsepower at 3800 rpm in

1938 Graham Standard two-door sedan

standard form, or 120 bhp at 4000 rpm with supercharger. A high numerical axle ratio of 4.27:1 gave excellent acceleration. But production was a mere 1000 units.

The Hollywood was first billed as a convertible and sedan, priced at $1380 and $1250. In fact, only one or two convertible prototypes were built. The sedan used the supercharged 120-bhp six and a 115-inch wheelbase, 10 inches shorter than the Cord's. To fit the tall Graham engine into the Beverly's body, engineers had to offset the carburetor and air cleaner that gave clearance for the Hollywood's low hoodline. The front end featured a pleasing two-grille combination with freestanding headlamps and delicately curved front fenders.

The big problem in using the old Cord dies was their complexity: it took seven separate pieces of metal to make a top, for example. Joseph Graham had hoped to simplify such matters, but assembly operations were hampered. Perhaps production wouldn't have been high in any case, because the public had lost confidence in Graham by 1940. The "Spirit of Motion" mod-

1937 Graham Supercharger Series 110 two-door sedan

1940 Graham Supercharger Custom four-door sedan

Rendering for 1940 Hollywood Custom Super four-door sedan

els sold in such small quantities that they were dropped from the 1941 line. After July 1940, only the Hollywood was listed.

For 1941, Graham increased horsepower and sold the Hollywood for $968; the supercharger cost an additional $97. The low prices didn't help, and in November the factory closed for good.

Graham-Paige's departure from the car business a year before U.S. entry into World War II proved to be beneficial. The company received $20 million worth of defense contracts and prospered through the war. Jo-

seph W. Frazer bought the firm in 1944, and built the Frazer as a G-P product in 1946-47 at Kaiser's Willow Run factory rather than G-P's old Detroit plant. In early 1947, Graham-Paige sold its automotive interests to Kaiser-Frazer, and in 1952 quit the farm product field as well. The firm then became a closed investment corporation, dropping the word 'Motors' from its title. Later, Graham-Paige operated Madison Square Garden and owned several professional New York athletic teams. All these non-automotive endeavors proved far more profitable than car making had ever been.

# Graham Specifications

## 1940

### 107 Supercharger (wb 120.0)— est. 1,000 built (includes Standard)

| | Wght | Price | Prod |
|---|---|---|---|
| Deluxe cpe | 3,245 | 1,160 | — |
| Deluxe sdn 2d | 3,250 | 1,135 | — |
| Deluxe sdn 4d | 3,250 | 1,160 | — |
| Custom cpe | 3,370 | 1,295 | — |
| Custom sdn 2d | 3,365 | 1,265 | — |
| Custom sdn 4d | 3,370 | 1,295 | — |

### 108 Standard (wb 120.0)

| | Wght | Price | Prod |
|---|---|---|---|
| Deluxe cpe | 3,190 | 1,020 | — |
| Deluxe sdn 2d | 3,195 | 995 | — |
| Deluxe sdn 4d | 3,195 | 1,015 | — |
| Custom cpe | 3,315 | 1,160 | — |
| Custom sdn 2d | 3,315 | 1,135 | — |
| Custom sdn 4d | 3,320 | 1,160 | — |

### Hollywood Custom Super (wb. 115.0)

| | Wght | Price | Prod |
|---|---|---|---|
| sdn 4d | 2,965 | 1,250 | * |

| | Wght | Price | Prod |
|---|---|---|---|
| conv cpe (prototype) | 3,075 | — | 1–2 |

| 1940 Engines | bore×stroke | bhp | availability |
|---|---|---|---|
| L6, 217.8 | 3.25×4.38 | 93 | S-unsupercharged |
| L6, 217.8 | 3.25×4.38 | 120 | S-supercharged |

## 1941

### 109 Custom Hollywood Schgd (wb 115.0)

| | Wght | Price | Prod |
|---|---|---|---|
| sdn 4d | 2,965 | 1,065 | * |

### 113 Custom Hollywood (wb 115.0)

| | Wght | Price | Prod |
|---|---|---|---|
| sdn 4d | 2,915 | 968 | * |

| 1941 Engines | bore×stroke | bhp | availability |
|---|---|---|---|
| L6, 217.8 | 3.25×4.38 | 95 | S-unsupercharged |
| L6, 217.8 | 3.25×4.38 | 124 | S-supercharged |

*Total 1940–41 Hollywood production 1,859.

# Henry J

**Kaiser-Frazer Corp.**
**Willow Run, Michigan**

Kaiser-Frazer was at the crossroads in 1949. The company had degenerated from healthy, record-high production in 1948 to just a skeleton the following year—from ninth place in the industry to fourteenth. Henry Kaiser, deciding to press on, borrowed $44 million from the Reconstruction Finance Corporation to maintain inventories, and tooled up for new models. This caused the abrupt departure of cofounder Joseph W. Frazer. Kaiser promised his lenders that part of the loan would go toward a new small car that all Americans could afford to buy: the Henry J.

Designer Howard "Dutch" Darrin had suggested a short-wheelbase compact related to his beautiful 1951 Kaiser, which was already locked up during Henry J planning. But Mr. Kaiser wanted something all-new. He settled on a prototype built by American Metal Products, a Detroit supplier of frames and springs for car seats. Darrin reluctantly tried to improve the styling of this ungainly little two-door sedan, applying his trademark "dip" in the beltline and little tailfins.

Henry Js were powered by Willys L-head fours and sixes of 134 and 161 cubic inches, respectively. Incredible economy was promised for the four, while the six-cylinder car turned out to be a hot rod, giving 0 to 60 times of around 14 seconds thanks to its light body. Though built on a 100-inch wheelbase, the Henry J could handle four passengers and a considerable amount of luggage. The basic four-cylinder model cost

K-F 1948 proposal for Henry J based on '51 Kaiser

1951 Standard (four) two-door sedan

1951 DeLuxe (six) two-door sedan

1952 Corsair DeLuxe (six) two-door sedan

1952 Corsair (four) two-door sedan

1952 Vagabond DeLuxe (six) two-door sedan

213

1953 Corsair (four) two-door sedan

1954 Corsair DeLuxe (six) two-door sedan

about $200 less than a Chevrolet.

K-F began its 1951 model year early, in March 1950. For a while, the Henry J was in demand: nearly 82,000 of the '51s were sold. Unfortunately, that saturated the market and sales were down sharply by the end of 1952.

The 1952-54 models received a mild facelift—a restyled full-width grille, repositioned taillights, and new interiors. An interim model, marketed in an effort to use up unwanted '51s, was the 1952 Vagabond. This was merely the previous year's model fitted with a "continental" outside spare tire, identifying script, and a

black-plastic-and-chrome hood ornament.

By 1954 when the last Henry Js (reserialed 1953s) were sold, it was evident the project had failed. Many felt the original approach was wrong. The austere, stripped 1951 models lacked gloveboxes, trunklids, and other features normally held essential—they were just too plain for most buyers. "I would have brought it out dressed up," said J. W. Frazer, "and undressed it later." Advance plans for hardtops, wagons, four-door sedans, and convertibles died with the last Henry J. Total production came to about 130,000 units.

# Henry J Specifications

## 1951

| K513 Standard (wb 100.0) | | Wght | Price | Prod |
|---|---|---|---|---|
| 5134 | sdn 2d | 2,293 | 1,363 | 38,500* |
| K514 DeLuxe (wb 100.0) | | | | |
| 5144 | sdn 2d | 2,341 | 1,499 | 43,400* |

| 1951 Engines | bore×stroke | bhp | availability |
|---|---|---|---|
| L4, 134.2 | 3.13×4.38 | 68 | S-K513 |
| L6, 161.0 | 3.13×3.50 | 80 | S-K514 |

## 1952

| K523 Vagabond (wb 100.0) | | Wght | Price | Prod |
|---|---|---|---|---|
| 5234 | sdn 2d | 2,365 | 1,407 | 3,000* |
| K524 Vagabond DeLuxe (wb 100.0) | | | | |
| 5244 | sdn 2d | 2,385 | 1,552 | 4,000* |
| K523 Corsair (wb 100.0) | | | | |
| 5234 | sdn 2d | 2,370 | 1,517 | 7,600* |
| K524 Corsair DeLuxe (wb 100.0) | | | | |
| 5244 | sdn 2d | 2,405 | 1,664 | 8,900* |

| 1952 Engines | bore×stroke | bhp | availability |
|---|---|---|---|
| L4, 134.2 | 3.13×4.38 | 68 | S-K523 |
| L6, 161.0 | 3.13×3.50 | 80 | S-K524 |

## 1953

| K533 Corsair (wb 100.0) | | Wght | Price | Prod |
|---|---|---|---|---|
| 5334 | sdn 2d | 2,395 | 1,399 | 8,500* |
| K534 Corsair DeLuxe (wb 100.0) | | | | |
| 5344 | sdn 2d | 2,445 | 1,561 | 8,100* |

| 1953 Engines | bore×stroke | bhp | availability |
|---|---|---|---|
| L4, 134.2 | 3.13×4.38 | 68 | S-K533 |
| L6, 161.0 | 3.13×3.50 | 80 | S-K534 |

## 1954

| K543 Corsair (wb 100.0) | | Wght | Price | Prod |
|---|---|---|---|---|
| 5434 | sdn 2d | 2,405 | 1,404 | 800* |
| K544 Corsair DeLuxe (wb 100.0) | | | | |
| 5444 | sdn 2d | 2,455 | 1,566 | 300* |

| 1954 Engines | bore×stroke | bhp | availability |
|---|---|---|---|
| L4, 134.2 | 3.13×4.38 | 68 | S-K543 |
| L6, 161.0 | 3.13×3.50 | 80 | S-K544 |

*Estimates based on highest serial numbers found. Total model year production:

| | |
|---|---|
| 1951 all | 81,942 |
| 1952 Vagabond | 7,017 |
| 1952 Corsair | 23,568 |
| 1953 all | 16,672 |
| 1954 all | 1,123 |

# Hudson

Hudson Motor Car Co.
Detroit, Michigan (1940-54)

American Motors Corp.
Kenosha, Wisconsin (1955-57)

Hudson produced some of America's finest, fleetest automobiles throughout its history, and usually placed high in the production race. The low-priced, four-cylinder Essex, introduced in 1919, brought the company up to third place behind Ford and Chevrolet by 1925. Hudson ranked third, fourth, or fifth in the industry through 1930. The company started to feel the Depression in '31. Production, which had topped 300,000 units in 1929, fell to barely 40,000 in 1933.

Roy D. Chapin, Sr., who had helped to found Hudson in 1910 and had been one of its leaders since that time, returned from temporary government service in 1933 to revive his ailing company. In 18 months he raised $6 million in loans and put most of the money into an Essex derivative called the Terraplane. This new model sold for as little as $425, went like a rocket, and brought new life to the company. Sales in 1936 tripled those of 1933, and production peaked at 123,266 units. But by then, Hudson had dropped to eighth place. Sales were cut in half due to the 1938 recession, and again the firm started to lose money.

Hudson had completely restyled its 1939 line, so the 1940 models were merely facelifted. The look was not innovative, but pleasing and clean: a rakishly pointed nose, a divided horizontal grille, and little side ornamentation. Hudson added another page to its book of endurance runs in 1940 by traveling over 20,000 miles at an average of 70.5 miles an hour, setting a new American Automobile Association record.

The 1940 line comprised seven distinct series, three wheelbases, and three different engines. On a 113-inch wheelbase were the Traveler and DeLuxe, offered as a convertible and convertible sedan powered by Hudson's smaller L-head six. A larger six powered the 118-inch-wheelbase Super, offered in a wide variety of body styles, and the 125-inch-wheelbase "Big Boy" series, made up of a carry-all and a seven-passenger sedan. The L-head eight was available for the 118-inch-wheelbase models, including some deluxe variants. The 125-inch-wheelbase eight-cylinder models formed the Country Club series. This consisted of two six-passenger sedans and one seven-passenger sedan. Registrations in 1940 did not exceed 80,000; the company lost about $1.5 million for the calendar year.

Another facelift was performed for 1941, several new models appeared, and Hudson's unit body was revised for new wheelbases: 116 inches for Traveler and DeLuxe Sixes, 121 and 128 inches for the larger Sixes and Eights. A new Commodore series debuted, listing a wide range of models on the two longer wheelbases. All the '41s had new parking lights mounted in large chrome housings atop the front fenders. Registrations were almost the same as in 1940, but the company made a profit of nearly $4 million. Credit this to defense

1940 Eight convertible coupe

1941 Super Six four-door sedan

1941 DeLuxe four-door sedan

1941 Commodore Eight convertible coupe

# Hudson

contracts, which began materializing in early 1941 and increased the company's total sales by 10 percent.

The defense bonus allowed Hudson a breather. The 1942 line, announced in August 1941, was one of the prettiest of all. Running boards were hidden, the grille was lowered and cleaned up, and the parking lights were moved off the fenders. Hudson's famous white triangle logo, placed on either side of the hood, was illuminated to add a touch of distinction after dark. The cars were soundly built and richly appointed. Again, the line began with the series of small sixes—coupes, sedans, and convertible sedans. Next was the Super Six, offering the same body choices plus a station wagon. At the top of the line were the Commodore Six and

Eight. Most of them rode the 121-inch wheelbase, though one long sedan was offered as well. The war put an end to all car production by February 2, so Hudson registered only 5396 cars in calendar year 1942.

During World War II, Hudson built Helldiver airplanes, Hudson Invader engines for landing craft, sections for B-29 bombers and Aircobras, and a variety of naval munitions. The company made a small profit in the war years, and jumped back into car production quickly after V-J Day. Hudson's output of 4735 cars in 1945 was enough for fifth place in this abbreviated calendar year. The firm hadn't held that slot since 1934—and would not hold it again.

The 1946-47 cars were slightly facelifted prewar mod-

1942 Commodore Eight four-door sedan

1942 Super Six convertible coupe

1946 Super Six convertible

1947 Super Six four-door sedan

1948 Super Six Brougham convertible

1948 Super Six club coupe

els. The engines were still sixes and eights; the wheelbase still 121 inches. There were three transmission options: overdrive, priced at $101; Drive-Master, $112; and Vacumotive Drive, $47. Vacumotive automatically engaged and disengaged the clutch; Drive-Master eliminated both clutch and gear lever motion. Hudson built over 90,000 of its 1946 models, two-thirds of which were Super Sixes.

The 1947s were unchanged except in details such as a new chrome nameplate on the trunk, right-hand as well as left-hand door locks, and a small lip around the center grille emblem housing. Again, Hudson produced around 90,000 cars, though its industry ranking changed. Ninth in production for 1946, Hudson dropped to 11th in '47, despite a 10 percent gain in actual volume. Other manufacturers were growing faster as all Detroit responded to the unprecedented seller's market. Hudson sales exceeded $120 million in 1946, and the firm made a profit of over $2.3 million. For 1948, Hudson had a brand-new car with a new engine, and made more money than it had at any other time after the war, netting $13.2 million on gross sales of $274 million.

The Step-down unit-body Hudson of 1948-49 (both models were identical except for serial numbers) was one of the great postwar designs. Low and sleek, it hugged the ground and handled well, thanks to a radically low center of gravity. The design team was led by Frank Spring, a fixture at Hudson and ahead of his time. The Step-down evolved from wartime doodling—sleek, aerodynamic forms modeled in quarter-scale clay and plaster. Like all Hudsons since 1932, it had a unit body and chassis that was extremely strong and rattle-free. The nickname Step-down referred to the dropped floorpan, which was completely surrounded by frame girders. It was probably the safest automotive package of its time, and perhaps one of the safest ever.

It was also beautiful in an understated way. The sides were clean, the grille was low and horizontal, the taillights were modest. The dashboard was flat and positioned upright in front of the driver. It contained a big speedometer and clock, warning lights for battery discharge and low oil pressure, and gauges for fuel and water temperature.

As the new Hudsons were introduced in mid-1948, dealers cheered. Here was precisely the formula they needed for good sales in those heady days when there were lots of eager customers. Four models, all riding a new 124-inch wheelbase, were offered: the Super Six and Eight, and the Commodore Six and Eight.

Violating an old Detroit rule about restyling and re-engineering in the same year, Hudson also brought out a new engine for '48: the 262-cid Super Six. It developed 121 bhp at 4000 rpm, only seven horsepower less than the eight. Although it had only four main bearings instead of five like the eight-cylinder unit, the six was a smooth-running, durable engine. By 1951, it had evolved into the 308-cid Hornet powerplant, the largest modern L-head six ever built. The Hornet was king of

stock-car racing from 1952 through 1954. Even in 1948 tune, the big six packed surprising power. The car could do 0 to 40 mph in 12 seconds using Drive-Master. Manual-shift cars were even faster. Hudsons had been adequate but not outstanding performers in 1946-47; the gutsy sixes made them some of the quickest, most roadable American cars for 1948-49.

There was one problem. In creating the beautiful Step-down, Hudson committed itself to a design that would be difficult and costly to change. Unit bodies are almost impossible to rework, and Hudson lacked the financial base to add new Step-down derivatives such as a station wagon, which probably would have sold well

**1950 Pacemaker four-door sedan**

**1951 Commodore Six Custom Hollywood hardtop coupe**

**1953 Super Wasp four-door sedan**

# Hudson

1954 Jet-Liner four-door sedan

1954 Hornet Special club coupe

1954 Super Wasp Hollywood hardtop coupe

Marshall Teague, AAA point leader, in '53

For too many years, each new Hudson would look too much like last year's model. This, combined with the natural decline of the seller's market after 1950, eventually destroyed the make in the mid-'50s. By 1952, production had dropped to well under 100,000 units. In early 1954, Hudson merged with Nash, forming American Motors. To a large extent, Hudson's problems were common to all independents after the war: they had too little money for really significant production, and too little depth for sufficient change and innovation to keep the public interested.

Roy D. Chapin, Jr., who was a Hudson sales executive in the 1950s, explained the situation this way: "If you don't have enough money to do something and do it right, and if you haven't learned to specialize in a given thing . . . sooner or later you find you just can't do everything. [Hudson was] usually reacting, rather than anticipating."

Nevertheless, the firm entered the '50s in fine fettle. It sold more than 143,000 cars in 1950, including more than 60,000 of its new Pacemaker. Generally priced under $2000, the Pacemaker used a destroked version of the flathead Super Six. Performance was as good as that of Nash's top-line Ambassador, and put it well ahead in its price class. The Super Six and Super Eight and the Commodore Six and Commodore Eight were carried over from 1948-49.

All models were available with overdrive, and Drive-Master or Supermatic Drive—two Hudson semi-automatics of repute. Drive-Master relieved the driver of the need to shift and declutch. The car was started by placing the shift lever in "High" and accelerating. The driver would ease up on the accelerator when the shift to regular drive was desired. With Supermatic, a high cruising gear was added; the shift to high occurred automatically at 22 mph when a dashboard button was engaged. In 1950, overdrive cost $95 extra; Drive-Master cost $105; Supermatic was priced at $199. None of these was a substitute for full automatic transmission, of course. When Hudson offered proprietary Hydra-Matic in '51 (at only $158 extra) Supermatic was dropped.

The Hudson Hornet, with its powerful six, was introduced in 1951 with four body styles, and was priced the same as the Commodore Eight. The Hornet powerplant produced only 145 bhp at 3800 rpm in stock form, but was capable of much more than that in the hands of precision tuners. The most famous of these, Marshall Teague, claimed he could get 112 mph from a Hornet certified as stock by AAA or NASCAR. He was helped by an enthusiastic cadré of Hudson engineers who developed "severe usage" options that were really thinly disguised racing parts. Twin H-Power, offered in 1953, consisted of twin carbs and dual manifold induction (the first dual manifold on a six) for greatly improved breathing. The "7-X" racing engine, which arrived in late 1953, used .020 overbored bylinders, special cam and head, larger valves, higher compression, Twin H-Power, and headers. Output was about 210 bhp.

1954 Italia sport coupe

1955 Hornet Custom Hollywood hardtop coupe

1955 Rambler Custom Cross Country station wagon

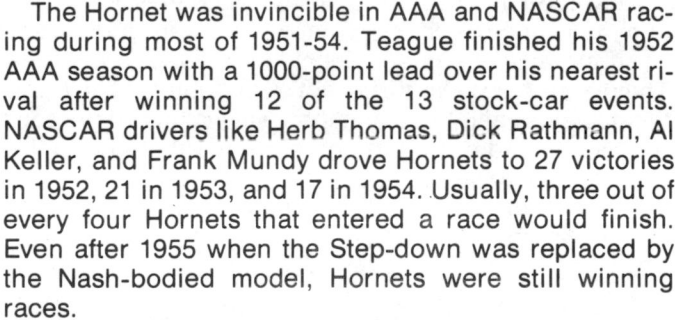

1956 Hornet Custom four-door sedan

The Hornet was invincible in AAA and NASCAR racing during most of 1951-54. Teague finished his 1952 AAA season with a 1000-point lead over his nearest rival after winning 12 of the 13 stock-car events. NASCAR drivers like Herb Thomas, Dick Rathmann, Al Keller, and Frank Mundy drove Hornets to 27 victories in 1952, 21 in 1953, and 17 in 1954. Usually, three out of every four Hornets that entered a race would finish. Even after 1955 when the Step-down was replaced by the Nash-bodied model, Hornets were still winning races.

But racing success wasn't enough to keep the Hudson ship afloat. Though the company kept adding and subtracting series through 1954, it was unable to add new body styles. The standard Pacemaker and the Super Eight were dropped for '51, when the Hornet and the Hollywood hardtop were added; the Wasp replaced the Super Six for '52. All the Commodores were discontinued for '53, and the line of big cars was cut. A lower-priced Hornet Special for '54 failed to spark sales. Throughout this period, Hudson could offer only two wheelbases and four basic body styles. Production dropped accordingly.

The Step-down cried for restyling in 1952, but Hudson couldn't afford it. The firm had sunk $12 million into a compact, the ill-fated Jet, in 1953. Using old Commodore Eight tooling, the Jet's 202-cid six produced 104 bhp. Twin H-power and a high-compression head were optional, and made for a speedy package. Jets were

roadable and well-built, but not very pretty. Over the objections of chief designer Spring, management had insisted on bolt-upright, slab-sided styling that failed to impress many customers. Hudson tried hard, adding a very cheap Family Club sedan and luxurious Jet-Liner models in 1954, but the car still sold poorly.

The Jet did spark a project that might have become the long-awaited and much-needed new Hudson: the Italia. This four-place *gran turismo* on the Jet chassis was designed by Spring and built by Carrozzeria Touring of Milan. Italias had wraparound windshields, doors cut into the roof, fender scoops that ducted cooling air to the brakes, flow-through ventilation, and form-fitting leather seats. They were 10 inches lower than the production '54 Hornet. Though powered by the 114-bhp Hornet engine, Italias weren't very fast, and the aluminum body was not very solid. But these were problems that might have been solved if Hudson only had money for a major commitment. The firm's conservative engineers held little hope for the wild European styling anyway. Only 25 "production" Italias, plus the prototype and a four-door derivative called X-161, were built. Roy D. Chapin, Jr., later AMC President, served as Italia sales manager. He shoved them out as fast as he could at $4800 a copy. "I got rid of them," he said, adding, "It wasn't one of my greatest accomplishments."

Late in 1953, rumors began circulating about a Hudson-Nash merger. Nash couldn't have come calling at a better time. Hudson sales were sinking: the books were

# Hudson

1957 Hornet Custom four-door sedan

1957 Hornet Custom Hollywood hardtop coupe

written in red ink. Between January 1, 1954 and the end of April when it closed as an independent company, Hudson had lost over $6 million on sales of only $28.7 million. Old-hat styling; the ugly, slow-selling Jet; a weak dealer network; and insufficient capital for development of new models were the reasons.

In merger talks, George Mason of Nash insisted on one big condition: the Jet had to go. Hudson President A. E. Barit fought this, but not for long. He was in a very poor position to bargain.

The merger was really a Nash takeover. Hudson's Detroit plant was soon shut down, and production was transferred to Kenosha, Wisconsin. Naturally, everybody recognized the all-new 1955 Hudson: it was a restyled Nash. It used Nash's unit-construction sedan and hardtop bodyshell, with a special eggcrate grille, distinct trim, and reworked rear end. The only link to previous Hudsons was the dashboard, which used the old 1954 instruments. Wasps were powered by the former 202 Jet engine; the big six was retained for the Hornet; the Hornet V8 used a 320 Packard mill of 208 bhp. Twin H-Power was available on the sixes, increasing Hornet and Wasp horsepower. A line of Metropolitans and Ramblers with Hudson emblems was also offered.

American Motors introduced its own 190-bhp V8 for 1956, replacing the Packard unit in mid-season for the Hornet Special. The small Wasp Six remained, as did the Hornet Six, along with the usual assortment of so-called Hudson Ramblers. "V-line Styling" was the way AMC described the horrendous chrome-plated nightmare created by Edmund E. Anderson. It was the ugliest Hudson in a generation. And the AMC V8 was far less powerful than the Packard unit. An anemic engine and terrible styling made for depressing sales. Only 10,671 non-Rambler Hudsons were peddled in '56. In the next year—Hudson's last—styling didn't improve, and only 3876 were sold, all V-8s. Rambler was listed as a separate make in 1957, but a rumor that Ramblers would diverge into very different 1958 Hudson and Nash models came to naught. There was no money for that.

AMC's decision to drop Hudson and Nash was only common sense. Said Roy Chapin, "We ran Hudson and Nash Metropolitans and Ramblers—it was a charade. They were basically the exact same automobiles, and the decision really was one that said we've got to spend our money and our effort and our concentration on the Rambler because we haven't got the dough to update the big Nashes and the big Hudsons."

# Hudson Specifications

## 1940

### 40-T Traveler (wb 113.0)*

|  | Wght | Price | Prod |
|---|---|---|---|
| cpe 3P | 2,800 | 670 | — |
| Victoria cpe 4P | 2,830 | 750 | — |
| sdn 2d | 2,895 | 735 | — |
| sdn 4d | 2,940 | 763 | — |

### 40-P Deluxe (wb 113.0)*

|  | Wght | Price | Prod |
|---|---|---|---|
| cpe 3P | 2,840 | 745 | — |
| Victoria cpe 4P | 2,865 | 791 | — |
| conv cpe | 2,860 | 930 | — |

|  | Wght | Price | Prod |
|---|---|---|---|
| sdn 2d | 2,930 | 775 | — |
| sdn 4d | 2,965 | 808 | — |
| conv sdn | 2,920 | 955 | — |

### 41 Super (wb 118.0)*

|  | Wght | Price | Prod |
|---|---|---|---|
| cpe 3P | 2,950 | 809 | — |
| Victoria cpe 4P | 2,980 | 860 | — |
| conv cpe | 2,980 | 995 | — |
| sdn 2d | 3,020 | 839 | — |
| sdn 4d | 3,050 | 870 | — |
| conv sdn | 3,020 | 1,030 | — |

| 43 Country Club (wb 125.0)* | Wght | Price | Prod |
|---|---|---|---|
| sdn 4d | 3,240 | 1,018 | — |
| Special sdn 4d | 3,240 | 1,044 | — |
| sdn 4d, 7P | 3,355 | 1,230 | — |

| 44 Eight (wb 118.0)* | Wght | Price | Prod |
|---|---|---|---|
| cpe 3P | 3,040 | 860 | — |
| Victoria cpe 4P | 3,075 | 942 | — |
| conv cpe | 3,065 | 1,087 | — |
| sdn 2d | 3,140 | 918 | — |
| sdn 4d | 3,185 | 952 | — |
| conv sdn | 3,130 | 1,122 | — |

| 47 Country Club Eight (wb 125.0)* | Wght | Price | Prod |
|---|---|---|---|
| sdn 4d | 3,285 | 1,118 | — |
| Special sdn 4d | 3,285 | 1,144 | — |
| sdn 4d, 7P | 3,400 | 1,330 | — |

| 48 Big Boy (wb 125.0)* | Wght | Price | Prod |
|---|---|---|---|
| Carry-all sdn 4d | 3,245 | 989 | — |
| sdn 4d, 7P | 3,140 | 1,095 | — |

*Total model year production: 87,915; Sixes: 77,295; Eights: 10,620.

| 1940 Engines | bore×stroke | bhp | availability |
|---|---|---|---|
| L6, 175.0 | 3.00×4.38 | 92 | S-40 |
| L6, 212.0 | 3.00×5.00 | 98 | S-48 |
| L6, 212.0 | 3.00×5.00 | 102 | S-41, 43 |
| L8, 254.0 | 3.00×4.50 | 128 | S-44, 47 |

# 1941

| 10-T Traveler (wb 116.0)* | Wght | Price | Prod |
|---|---|---|---|
| cpe 3P | 2,765 | 754 | — |
| club cpe 4P | 2,835 | 847 | — |
| sdn 2d | 2,870 | 824 | — |
| sdn 4d | 2,900 | 852 | — |

| 10-P Deluxe (wb 116.0)* | Wght | Price | Prod |
|---|---|---|---|
| cpe 3P | 2,840 | 870 | — |
| club cpe 4P | 2,880 | 917 | — |
| sdn 2d | 2,905 | 891 | — |
| sdn 4d | 2,945 | 925 | — |
| conv sdn | 3,085 | 1,132 | 140 est |

| 11 Super (wb 121.0)* | Wght | Price | Prod |
|---|---|---|---|
| cpe 3P | 2,925 | 956 | — |
| club cpe 4P | 2,995 | 1,011 | — |
| sdn 2d | 3,005 | 976 | — |
| sdn 4d | 3,040 | 1,007 | — |
| conv sdn | 3,145 | 1,230 | 300 est |
| wgn 4d | 3,315 | 1,298 | 100 est |

| 12 Commodore Six (wb 121.0)* | Wght | Price | Prod |
|---|---|---|---|
| cpe 3P | 2,970 | 1,028 | — |
| club cpe 4P | 3,045 | 1,090 | — |
| sdn 2d | 3,070 | 1,059 | — |
| sdn 4d | 3,135 | 1,087 | — |
| conv sdn | 3,160 | 1,297 | 200 est |

| 14 Commodore Eight (wb 121.0)* | Wght | Price | Prod |
|---|---|---|---|
| cpe 3P | 3,110 | 1,071 | — |
| club cpe 4P | 3,195 | 1,133 | — |
| sdn 2d | 3,200 | 1,096 | — |
| sdn 4d | 3,250 | 1,132 | — |
| conv sdn | 3,350 | 1,347 | 200 est |
| wgn 4d | 3,400 | 1,384 | 80 est |

| 15-17 Commodore Eight (wb 121–128)* | Wght | Price | Prod |
|---|---|---|---|
| cpe 3P, wb 121.0 | 3,185 | 1,162 | — |
| club cpe 4P, wb 121.0 | 3,235 | 1,225 | — |
| sdn 4d, wb 128.0 | 3,370 | 1,330 | — |
| sdn 4d, 7P, wb 128.0 | 3,440 | 1,537 | — |

| 18 Big Boy (wb 128.0)* | Wght | Price | Prod |
|---|---|---|---|
| sdn 4d, 7P | 3,155 | 1,223 | — |

*Total model year production: 91,769; Sixes: 82,051; Eights: 9,718.

| 1941 Engines | bore×stroke | bhp | availability |
|---|---|---|---|
| L6, 175.0 | 3.00×4.38 | 92 | S-10 |
| L6, 212.0 | 3.00×5.00 | 98 | S-18 |
| L6, 212.0 | 3.00×5.00 | 102 | S-11, 12 |
| L8, 254.0 | 3.00×4.50 | 128 | S-14, 15, 17 |

# 1942

| 20T Traveler (wb 116.0)* | Wght | Price | Prod |
|---|---|---|---|
| cpe 3P | 2,795 | 828 | — |
| club cpe 4P | 2,845 | 897 | — |
| sdn 2d | 2,895 | 878 | — |
| sdn 4d | 2,940 | 905 | — |

| 20P Deluxe (wb 116.0)* | Wght | Price | Prod |
|---|---|---|---|
| cpe 3P | 2,845 | 916 | — |
| club cpe 4P | 2,900 | 967 | — |
| sdn 2d | 2,935 | 946 | — |
| sdn 4d | 2,971 | 978 | — |
| conv sdn | 3,140 | 1,212 | — |

| 21 Super (wb 121.0)* | Wght | Price | Prod |
|---|---|---|---|
| cpe 3P | 2,950 | 1,036 | — |
| club cpe 4P | 3,010 | 1,090 | — |
| sdn 2d | 3,035 | 1,065 | — |
| sdn 4d | 3,080 | 1,093 | — |
| conv sdn | 3,200 | 1,332 | — |
| wgn 4d | 3,315 | 1,412 | — |

| 22 Commodore Six (wb 121.0)* | Wght | Price | Prod |
|---|---|---|---|
| cpe 3P | 2,995 | 1,115 | — |
| club cpe 5P | 3,090 | 1,175 | — |
| sdn 2d | 3,090 | 1,152 | — |
| sdn 4d | 3,145 | 1,182 | — |
| conv sdn | 3,280 | 1,402 | — |

| 24 Commodore Eight (wb 121.0)* | Wght | Price | Prod |
|---|---|---|---|
| cpe 3P | 3,130 | 1,156 | — |
| club cpe 5P | 3,205 | 1,215 | — |
| sdn 2d | 3,230 | 1,187 | — |
| sdn 4d | 3,280 | 1,224 | — |
| conv sdn | 3,400 | 1,451 | — |

| 25 Commodore Custom Eight (wb 121.0)* | Wght | Price | Prod |
|---|---|---|---|
| club cpe 4P | 3,235 | 1,311 | — |

| 27 Commodore Custom Eight (wb 128.0)* | Wght | Price | Prod |
|---|---|---|---|
| sdn 4d, 6P | 3,395 | 1,430 | — |

*Total model year production: 40,661; Sixes: 34,069; Eights: 6,592.

| 1942 Engines | bore×stroke | bhp | availability |
|---|---|---|---|
| L6, 175.0 | 3.00×4.38 | 92 | S-20 |
| L6, 212.0 | 3.00×5.00 | 102 | S-21, 22 |
| L8, 254.0 | 3.00×4.50 | 128 | S-24, 25, 27 |

# 1946

| 51 Super Six (wb 121.0)—61,787 built | Wght | Price | Prod |
|---|---|---|---|
| sdn 4d | 3,085 | 1,555 | — |
| Brougham sdn 2d | 3,030 | 1,511 | — |
| club cpe | 3,015 | 1,553 | — |
| cpe 3P | 2,950 | 1,481 | — |
| Brougham conv cpe | 3,195 | 1,879 | 1035* |

| 52 Commodore Six (wb 121.0)—17,685 built | Wght | Price | Prod |
|---|---|---|---|
| sdn 4d | 3,150 | 1,699 | — |
| club cpe | 3,065 | 1,693 | — |

| 53 Super Eight (wb 121.0)—3,961 built | | | |
|---|---|---|---|
| sdn 4d | 3,235 | 1,668 | — |
| club cpe | 3,185 | 1,664 | — |

| 54 Commodore Eight (wb 121.0)—8,193 built | | | |
|---|---|---|---|
| sdn 4d | 3,305 | 1,774 | — |
| club cpe | 3,235 | 1,760 | — |
| Brougham conv cpe | 3,410 | 2,050 | 140* |

*Estimated; total convertibles 1,177.

| 1946 Engines | bore×stroke | bhp | availability |
|---|---|---|---|
| L6, 212.0 | 3.00×5.00 | 102 | S-51, 52 |
| L8, 254.0 | 3.00×4.50 | 128 | S-53, 54 |

## 1947

| 171 Super Six (wb 121.0)—49,276 built | Wght | Price | Prod |
|---|---|---|---|
| sdn 4d | 3,110 | 1,749 | — |
| Brougham sdn 2d | 3,055 | 1,704 | — |
| club cpe | 3,040 | 1,744 | — |
| cpe 3P | 2,975 | 1,628 | — |
| Brougham conv cpe | 3,220 | 2,021 | 1,460* |

| 172 Commodore Six (wb 121.0)—25,138 built | | | |
|---|---|---|---|
| sdn 4d | 3,175 | 1,896 | — |
| club cpe | 3,090 | 1,887 | — |

| 173 Super Eight (wb 121.0)—5,076 built | | | |
|---|---|---|---|
| sdn 4d | 3,260 | 1,862 | — |
| club cpe | 3,210 | 1,855 | — |

| 174 Commodore Eight (wb 121.0)—12,593 built | | | |
|---|---|---|---|
| sdn 4d | 3,330 | 1,972 | — |
| club cpe | 3,260 | 1,955 | — |
| Brougham conv cpe | 3,435 | 2,196 | 360* |

*Estimated; total convertibles 1,823.

| 1947 Engines | bore×stroke | bhp | availability |
|---|---|---|---|
| L6, 212.0 | 3.00×5.00 | 102 | S-171, 172 |
| L8, 254.0 | 3.00×4.50 | 128 | S-173, 174 |

## 1948

| 481 Super Six (wb 124.0)—49,388 built | Wght | Price | Prod |
|---|---|---|---|
| sdn 4d | 3,500 | 2,222 | — |
| Brougham sdn 2d | 3,470 | 2,172 | — |
| club cpe | 3,480 | 2,219 | — |
| cpe 3P | 3,460 | 2,069 | — |
| Brougham conv cpe | 3,750 | 2,836 | 88* |

| 482 Commodore Six (wb 124.0)—27,159 built | | | |
|---|---|---|---|
| sdn 4d | 3,540 | 2,399 | — |
| club cpe | 3,550 | 2,374 | — |
| Brougham conv cpe | 3,780 | 3,057 | 48* |

| 483 Super Eight (wb 124.0)—5,338 built | | | |
|---|---|---|---|
| sdn 4d | 3,525 | 2,343 | — |
| club cpe | 3,495 | 2,340 | — |

| 484 Commodore Eight (wb 124.0)—35,315 built | | | |
|---|---|---|---|
| sdn 4d | 3,600 | 2,514 | — |
| club cpe | 3,570 | 2,490 | — |
| Brougham conv cpe | 3,800 | 3,138 | 64* |

*Estimated; total convertibles 200.

| 1948 Engines | bore×stroke | bhp | availability |
|---|---|---|---|
| L6, 262.0 | 3.56×4.38 | 121 | S-481, 482 |
| L8, 254.0 | 3.00×4.50 | 128 | S-483, 484 |

## 1949

| 491 Super Six (wb 124.0)—91,333 built | Wght | Price | Prod |
|---|---|---|---|
| sdn 4d | 3,555 | 2,207 | — |
| Brougham sdn 2d | 3,515 | 2,156 | — |
| club cpe | 3,480 | 2,203 | — |
| cpe 3P | 3,485 | 2,053 | — |
| Brougham conv cpe | 3,750 | 2,799 | 1,870* |

| 492 Commodore Six (wb 124.0)—32,715 built | | | |
|---|---|---|---|
| sdn 4d | 3,625 | 2,383 | — |
| club cpe | 3,585 | 2,359 | — |
| Brougham conv cpe | 3,780 | 2,952 | 655* |

| 493 Super Eight (wb 124.0)—6,365 built | | | |
|---|---|---|---|
| sdn 4d | 3,565 | 2,296 | — |
| Brougham sdn 2d | 3,545 | 2,245 | — |
| club cpe | 3,550 | 2,292 | — |

| 494 Commodore Eight (wb 124.0)—28,687 built | | | |
|---|---|---|---|
| sdn 4d | 3,650 | 2,472 | — |
| club cpe | 3,600 | 2,448 | — |
| Brougham conv cpe | 3,800 | 3,041 | 595* |

*Estimated; total convertibles 3,119.

| 1949 Engines | bore×stroke | bhp | availability |
|---|---|---|---|
| L6, 262.0 | 3.56×4.38 | 121 | S-491, 492 |
| L8, 254.0 | 3.00×4.50 | 128 | S-493, 494 |

## 1950

| 500 Pacemaker (wb 119.0)—39,455 built | Wght | Price | Prod |
|---|---|---|---|
| sdn 4d | 3,510 | 1,933 | — |
| Brougham sdn 2d | 3,475 | 1,912 | — |
| club cpe | 3,460 | 1,933 | — |
| cpe 3P | 3,445 | 1,807 | — |
| Brougham conv cpe | 3,655 | 2,428 | 1,100* |

| 50A Pacemaker Deluxe (wb 119.0)—22,297 built | | | |
|---|---|---|---|
| sdn 4d | 3,520 | 1,959 | — |
| Brougham sdn 2d | 3,485 | 1,928 | — |
| club cpe | 3,470 | 1,959 | — |
| Brougham conv cpe | 3,665 | 2,444 | 630* |

| 501 Super Six (wb 124.0)—17,246 built | | | |
|---|---|---|---|
| sdn 4d | 3,590 | 2,105 | — |
| Brougham sdn 2d | 3,565 | 2,068 | — |
| club cpe | 3,555 | 2,102 | — |
| Brougham conv cpe | 3,750 | 2,629 | 465* |

| 502 Commodore Six (wb 124.0)—24,605 built | | | |
|---|---|---|---|
| sdn 4d | 3,655 | 2,282 | — |
| club cpe | 3,640 | 2,257 | — |
| Brougham conv cpe | 3,840 | 2,809 | 700* |

| 503 Super Eight (wb 124.0)—1,074 built | | | |
|---|---|---|---|
| sdn 4d | 3,605 | 2,189 | — |
| Brougham sdn 2d | 3,575 | 2,152 | — |
| club cpe | 3,560 | 2,186 | — |

| 504 Commodore Eight (wb 124.0)—16,731 built | | | |
|---|---|---|---|
| sdn 4d | 3,675 | 2,366 | — |
| club cpe | 3,655 | 2,341 | — |
| Brougham conv cpe | 3,865 | 2,893 | 425* |

*Estimated; total convertibles 3,322.

| 1950 Engines | bore×stroke | bhp | availability |
|---|---|---|---|
| L6, 232.0 | 3.56×3.88 | 112 | S-500 |
| L6, 262.0 | 3.56×4.38 | 123 | S-50A, 501, 502 |
| L8, 254.0 | 3.00×4.50 | 128 | S-503, 504 |

# 1951

## 4A Pacemaker Custom (wb 119.0)— 34,495 built

| | Wght | Price | Prod |
|---|---|---|---|
| sdn 4d | 3,460 | 2,145 | — |
| Brougham sdn 2d | 3,430 | 2,102 | — |
| club cpe | 3,410 | 2,145 | — |
| cpe 3P | 3,380 | 1,965 | — |
| Brougham conv cpe | 3,600 | 2,642 | 430* |

## 5A Super Six Custom (wb 124.0)—22,532 built

| | Wght | Price | Prod |
|---|---|---|---|
| sdn 4d | 3,565 | 2,287 | — |
| Brougham sdn 2d | 3,535 | 2,238 | — |
| club cpe | 3,525 | 2,287 | — |
| Hollywood htp cpe | 3,590 | 2,605 | 1,100* |
| Brougham conv cpe | 3,720 | 2,827 | 280* |

## 6A Commodore Six Custom (wb 124.0)—16,979 built

| | Wght | Price | Prod |
|---|---|---|---|
| sdn 4d | 3,600 | 2,480 | — |
| club cpe | 3,585 | 2,455 | — |
| Hollywood htp cpe | 3,640 | 2,780 | 820* |
| Brougham conv cpe | 3,785 | 3,011 | 210* |

## 7A Hornet (wb 124.0)—43,656 built

| | Wght | Price | Prod |
|---|---|---|---|
| sdn 4d | 3,600 | 2,568 | — |
| club cpe | 3,580 | 2,543 | — |
| Hollywood htp cpe | 3,630 | 2,869 | 2,100* |
| Brougham conv cpe | 3,780 | 3,099 | 550* |

## 8A Commodore Eight Custom (wb 124.0)—14,243 built

| | Wght | Price | Prod |
|---|---|---|---|
| sdn 4d | 3,620 | 2,568 | — |
| club cpe | 3,600 | 2,543 | — |
| Hollywood htp cpe | 3,650 | 2,869 | 670* |
| Brougham conv cpe | 3,800 | 3,099 | 180* |

*Estimated; total convertibles 1,651; total hardtops 4,689.

| 1951 Engines | bore×stroke | bhp | availability |
|---|---|---|---|
| L6, 232.0 | 3.56×3.88 | 112 | S-Pacemaker |
| L6, 262.0 | 3.56×4.38 | 123 | S-Super & Commodore Six |
| L6, 308.0 | 3.81×4.50 | 145 | S-Hornet |
| L8, 254.0 | 3.00×4.50 | 128 | S-Commodore Eight |

# 1952

## 4B Pacemaker (wb 119.0)—7,486 built

| | Wght | Price | Prod |
|---|---|---|---|
| sdn 4d | 3,390 | 2,311 | — |
| Brougham sdn 2d | 3,355 | 2,264 | — |
| club cpe | 3,335 | 2,311 | — |
| cpe 3P | 3,305 | 2,116 | — |

## 5B Wasp (wb 119.0)—21,876 built

| | Wght | Price | Prod |
|---|---|---|---|
| sdn 4d | 3,485 | 2,466 | — |
| Brougham sdn 2d | 3,470 | 2,413 | — |
| club cpe | 3,435 | 2,466 | — |
| Hollywood htp cpe | 3,525 | 2,812 | 1,320* |
| Brougham conv cpe | 3,635 | 3,048 | 220* |

## 6B Commodore Six (wb 124.0)—1,592 built

| | Wght | Price | Prod |
|---|---|---|---|
| sdn 4d | 3,595 | 2,674 | — |
| club cpe | 3,550 | 2,647 | — |
| Hollywood htp cpe | 3,625 | 3,000 | 100* |
| Brougham conv cpe | 3,750 | 3,247 | 20* |

## 7B Hornet (wb 124.0)—35,921 built

| | Wght | Price | Prod |
|---|---|---|---|
| sdn 4d | 3,600 | 2,769 | — |
| club cpe | 3,550 | 2,742 | — |
| Hollywood htp cpe | 3,630 | 3,095 | 2,160* |
| Brougham conv cpe | 3,750 | 3,342 | 360* |

## 8B Commodore Eight (wb 124.0)—3,125 built

| | Wght | Price | Prod |
|---|---|---|---|
| sdn 4d | 3,630 | 2,769 | — |
| club cpe | 3,580 | 2,742 | — |
| Hollywood htp cpe | 3,660 | 3,095 | 190* |
| Brougham conv cpe | 3,770 | 3,342 | 30* |

*Estimated; total convertibles 636; total hardtops 3,777.

| 1952 Engines | bore×stroke | bhp | availability |
|---|---|---|---|
| L6, 232.0 | 3.56×3.88 | 112 | S-Pacemaker |
| L6, 262.0 | 3.56×4.38 | 127 | S-Wasp, Commodore Six |
| L6, 308.0 | 3.81×4.50 | 145 | S-Hornet |
| L8, 254.0 | 3.00×4.50 | 128 | S-Commodore Eight |

# 1953

## 1C Jet (wb 105.0)—21,143 built (includes Super Jet)

| | Wght | Price | Prod |
|---|---|---|---|
| sdn 4d | 2,650 | 1,858 | — |

## 2C Super Jet (wb 105.0)

| | Wght | Price | Prod |
|---|---|---|---|
| sdn 4d | 2,700 | 1,954 | — |
| sdn 2d | 2,695 | 1,933 | — |

## 4C Wasp (wb 119.0)—17,792 built (includes Super Wasp)

| | Wght | Price | Prod |
|---|---|---|---|
| sdn 4d | 3,380 | 2,311 | — |
| sdn 4d | 3,350 | 2,264 | — |
| club cpe | 3,340 | 2,311 | — |

## 5C Super Wasp (wb 119.0)

| | Wght | Price | Prod |
|---|---|---|---|
| sdn 4d | 3,480 | 2,466 | — |
| sdn 2d | 3,460 | 2,413 | — |
| club cpe | 3,455 | 2,466 | — |
| Hollywood htp cpe | 3,525 | 2,812 | 590* |
| Brougham conv cpe | 3,655 | 3,048 | 50* |

## 7C Hornet (wb 124.0)—27,208 built

| | Wght | Price | Prod |
|---|---|---|---|
| sdn 4d | 3,570 | 2,769 | — |
| club cpe | 3,530 | 2,742 | — |
| Hollywood htp cpe | 3,610 | 3,095 | 910* |
| Brougham conv cpe | 3,760 | 3,342 | — |

*Estimated; total hardtops 1,501.

| 1953 Engines | bore×stroke | bhp | availability |
|---|---|---|---|
| L6, 202.0 | 3.00×4.75 | 104 | S-Jet |
| L6, 202.0 | 3.00×4.75 | 106/114 | O-Jet |
| L6, 232.0 | 3.56×3.88 | 127 | S-Wasp |
| L6, 308.0 | 3.81×4.50 | 145 | S-Hornet |
| L6, 308.0 | 3.81×4.50 | 160 | O-Hornet |
| L6, 308.0 | 3.81×4.50 | 170 | O-Hornet (7-X) |

# 1954

## 1D Jet (wb 105.0)—14,224 built (includes Super Jet and Jet-Liner)

| | Wght | Price | Prod |
|---|---|---|---|
| sdn 4d | 2,675 | 1,858 | — |
| Utility sdn 2d | 2,715 | 1,837 | — |
| Family Club sdn 2d | 2,635 | 1,621 | — |

## 2D Super Jet (wb 105.0)

| | Wght | Price | Prod |
|---|---|---|---|
| sdn 4d | 2,725 | 1,954 | — |
| club sdn 2d | 2,710 | 1,933 | — |

## 3D Jet-Liner (wb 105.0)

| | Wght | Price | Prod |
|---|---|---|---|
| sdn 4d | 2,760 | 2,057 | — |
| club sdn 2d | 2,740 | 2,046 | — |

# Hudson

## 4D Wasp (wb 119.0)—11,603 built

| (includes Super Wasp) | Wght | Price | Prod |
|---|---|---|---|
| sdn 4d | 2,256 | 3,440 | — |
| club sdn 2d | 2,209 | 3,375 | — |
| club cpe | 2,256 | 3,360 | — |

### 5D Super Wasp (wb 119.0)

| | Wght | Price | Prod |
|---|---|---|---|
| sdn 4d | 3,525 | 2,466 | — |
| club sdn 2d | 3,490 | 2,413 | — |
| club cpe | 3,475 | 2,466 | — |
| Hollywood htp cpe | 3,570 | 2,704 | — |
| Brougham conv cpe | 3,680 | 3,004 | — |

### 6D Hornet Special (wb 124.0)—24,833 built (includes Hornet)

| | Wght | Price | Prod |
|---|---|---|---|
| sdn 4d | 3,560 | 2,619 | — |
| club sdn 2d | 3,515 | 2,571 | — |
| club cpe | 3,505 | 2,619 | — |

### 7D Hornet (wb 124.0)

| | Wght | Price | Prod |
|---|---|---|---|
| sdn 4d | 3,620 | 2,769 | — |
| club cpe | 3,570 | 2,742 | — |
| Hollywood htp cpe | 3,655 | 2,988 | — |
| Brougham conv cpe | 3,800 | 3,288 | — |

### Italia (wb 105.0)

| | Wght | Price | Prod |
|---|---|---|---|
| cpe | 2,710 | 4,800 | 20 |

| 1954 Engines | bore×stroke | bhp | availability |
|---|---|---|---|
| L6, 202.0 | 3.00×4.75 | 104 | S-Jet |
| L6, 202.0 | 3.00×4.75 | 106/114 | S-Italia; O-Jet |
| L6, 232.0 | 3.56×3.88 | 126 | S-Wasp |
| L6, 262.0 | 3.56×4.38 | 140 | S-Super Wasp |
| L6, 308.0 | 3.81×4.50 | 160 | S-Hornet |
| L6, 308.0 | 3.81×4.50 | 170 | O-Hornet (7-X) |

## 1955

### 54 Metropolitan (wb 85.0)—3,000* built

| | | Wght | Price | Prod |
|---|---|---|---|---|
| 1 | conv cpe 3P | 1,803 | 1,469 | — |
| 2 | htp cpe | 1,843 | 1,445 | — |

### 55 Rambler (wb 100.0)

| | | Wght | Price | Prod |
|---|---|---|---|---|
| 12 | Deluxe bus sdn | 2,400 | 1,457 | 34 |
| 14-1 | Super Suburban wgn 2d | 2,532 | 1,869 | 1,335 |
| 16-1 | Super club sdn | 2,450 | 1,683 | 2,970 |
| 17-2 | Custom Cntry Club htp cpe | 2,518 | 2,098 | 1,601 |

### 55 Rambler (wb 108.0)

| | | Wght | Price | Prod |
|---|---|---|---|---|
| 15 | Deluxe sdn 4d | 2,567 | 1,695 | 7,210 |
| 15-1 | Super sdn 4d | 2,570 | 1,798 | |
| 15-2 | Custom sdn 4d | 2,606 | 1,989 | |
| 18-1 | Super Cross Cntry wgn 4d | 2,675 | 1,975 | 12,023 |
| 18-2 | Custom Cross Cntry wgn 4d | 2,685 | 1,995 | |

### 3554 Wasp (wb 114.3)

| | | Wght | Price | Prod |
|---|---|---|---|---|
| 5-1 | Super sdn 4d | 3,254 | 2,290 | 5,561 |
| 5-2 | Custom sdn 4d | 3,347 | 2,460 | |
| 7-2 | Custom Hollywood htp cpe | 3,362 | 2,570 | 1,640 |

### 3556 Hornet 6 (wb 121.3)

| | | Wght | Price | Prod |
|---|---|---|---|---|
| 5-1 | Super sdn 4d | 3,495 | 2,565 | 5,357 |
| 5-2 | Custom sdn 4d | 3,562 | 2,760 | |
| 7-2 | Custom Hollywood htp cpe | 3,587 | 2,880 | 1,554 |

### 3558 Hornet V8 (wb 121.3)

| | | Wght | Price | Prod |
|---|---|---|---|---|
| 5-1 | Super sdn 4d | 3,806 | 2,825 | 4,449 |
| 5-2 | Custom sdn 4d | 3,846 | 3,015 | |
| 7-2 | Custom Hollywood htp cpe | 3,878 | 3,145 | 1,770 |

### Italia (wb 105.0)

| | Wght | Price | Prod |
|---|---|---|---|
| cpe | 2,710 | 4,800 | 5 |

*Estimated; total Nash & Hudson, 3,849.

| 1955 Engines | bore×stroke | bhp | availability |
|---|---|---|---|
| L4, 73.2 | 2.56×3.50 | 42 | S-Metropolitan |
| L6, 195.6 | 3.13×4.25 | 90 | S-Rambler |
| L6, 195.6 | 3.13×4.25 | 100 | S-Rambler fleet model |
| L6, 202.0 | 3.00×4.75 | 110 | S-Wasp |
| L6, 202.0 | 3.00×4.75 | 114 | S-Italia |
| L6, 202.0 | 3.00×4.75 | 120 | O-Wasp |
| L6, 308.0 | 3.81×4.50 | 160 | S-Hornet 6 |
| L6, 308.0 | 3.81×4.50 | 170 | O-Hornet 6 (Twin-H) |
| V8, 320.0 | 2.81×3.50 | 208 | S-Hornet V8 |

## 1956

### 54 Metropolitan (wb 85.0)—3,000* built

| | | Wght | Price | Prod |
|---|---|---|---|---|
| 1 | conv cpe 3P | 1,803 | 1,469 | — |
| 2 | htp cpe 3P | 1,843 | 1,445 | — |

### 56 Rambler DeLuxe (wb 108.0)—5,000 built (includes Super and Custom)

| | | Wght | Price | Prod |
|---|---|---|---|---|
| 15 | sdn 4d | 2,891 | 1,829 | — |

### 56 Rambler Super (wb 108.0)

| | | Wght | Price | Prod |
|---|---|---|---|---|
| 15-1 | sdn 4d | 2,096 | 1,939 | — |
| 18-1 | Cross Cntry wgn 4d | 2,992 | 2,233 | — |

### 56 Rambler Custom (wb 108.0)

| | | Wght | Price | Prod |
|---|---|---|---|---|
| 13-2 | Cross Cntry htp wgn 4d | 3,095 | 2,494 | — |
| 15-1 | sdn 4d | 2,929 | 2,059 | — |
| 18-2 | Cross Cntry wgn 4d | 3,110 | 2,329 | — |
| 19-2 | htp sdn | 2,990 | 2,224 | — |

### 3564 Wasp (wb 114.3)

| | Wght | Price | Prod |
|---|---|---|---|
| sdn 4d | 3,264 | 2,214 | 2,519 |

### 3565 Hornet Special (wb 121.3)

| | Wght | Price | Prod |
|---|---|---|---|
| sdn 4d | 3,467 | 2,405 | 1,528 |
| Hollywood htp cpe | 3,488 | 2,512 | 229 |

### 3566 Hornet 6 (wb 121.3)

| | Wght | Price | Prod |
|---|---|---|---|
| Super sdn 4d | 3,545 | 2,544 | 3,022 |
| Custom sdn 4d | 3,636 | 2,777 | |
| Hollywood htp cpe | 3,646 | 2,888 | 358 |

### 3568 Hornet V8 (wb 121.3)

| | Wght | Price | Prod |
|---|---|---|---|
| sdn 4d | 3,826 | 3,026 | 1,962 |
| Hollywood htp cpe | 3,026 | 3,159 | 1,053 |

*Estimated; total Nash & Hudson 7,645.

| 1956 Engines | bore×stroke | bhp | availability |
|---|---|---|---|
| L4, 73.2 | 2.56×3.50 | 42 | S-Metropolitan |
| L6, 195.6 | 3.13×4.25 | 120 | S-Rambler |
| L6, 202.0 | 3.00×4.75 | 120 | S-Wasp |
| L6, 202.0 | 3.00×4.75 | 130 | O-Wasp (Twin-H) |
| L6, 308.0 | 3.81×4.50 | 165 | S-Hornet 6 |
| L6, 308.0 | 3.81×4.50 | 175 | O-Hornet 6 (Twin-H) |
| V8, 320.0 | 3.81×3.50 | 208 | S-Hornet V8 (through 3/56) |
| V8, 250.0 | 3.50×3.25 | 190 | S-Hornet Special (3/56 on) |

## 1957—3,876 built

### 357-1 Hornet Super (wb 121.3)

| | Wght | Price | Prod |
|---|---|---|---|
| sdn 4d | 3,631 | 2,821 | — |
| Hollywood htp cpe | 3,655 | 2,911 | — |

### 357-2 Hornet Custom (wb 121.3)

| | Wght | Price | Prod |
|---|---|---|---|
| sdn 4d | 3,678 | 3,011 | — |
| Hollywood htp cpe | 3,693 | 3,101 | — |

| 1957 Engine | bore×stroke | bhp | availability |
|---|---|---|---|
| V8, 327.0 | 4.00×3.25 | 255 | S-all |

# Hupmobile

**Hupp Motor Car Corp.
Detroit, Michigan**

Hupmobile's best year ever was 1928, when the company recorded over 50,000 registrations. From there it was all downhill. After 1932, the company never produced more than 8000 cars annually. Ironically, the "Aerodynamic" series introduced in 1934 was among the better designs of the period. But buyers just didn't respond. Hupmobile closed down midway through 1936, reopened to produce a handful of 1937-38 models, then struggled on without much success into 1939.

Norman De Vaux, Hupmobile's general manager, had bought the body dies for the defunct front-drive Cord 810/812 Beverly sports sedan from Auburn. He then proposed to build a rear-drive derivation, and reportedly had 6000 orders. But Hupmobile was unable to get the reborn Cord into production beyond 35 handmade prototypes in 1939. De Vaux now approached Graham-Paige, which agreed to manufacture the bodies provided it could have its own version of the car. The deal gave Hupp a ready supplier and Graham had a new model to supplement its languishing "sharknose" design. This cooperation, said Hupp's president, J. W. Drake, "does not mean a merger of the two corporations. The Hupp-Graham contract is a most favorable one for both of us as careful checking of all production costs demonstrated that great savings could be made." Actually, it was a partnership of desperation.

Hupp's Cord-derived sedan was called the Skylark. Like Graham's Hollywood, it was identical with the Cord from the cowl back, but had a shorter hood and overall length. While the Hollywood used a double grille, the Skylark had a single, horizontal-bar design, not unlike the grille of the legendary Cord itself—except that the headlamps were freestanding, not hidden.

Each company used its own engine. In Hupp's case, this was an L-head six with four main bearings and a displacement of 245 cubic inches, as opposed to Graham's 217.8 cid. The Hupp powerplant was a bit livelier than the regular Graham engine, but the supercharged Hollywood had 120 bhp and was faster.

Bad luck plagued the Hupp-Graham operation from

1934 421-I "Aerodynamic" four-door sedan

1940 Skylark four-door sedan

the start. Graham took nine months to set up the assembly line, and production didn't begin until May 1940. By that time, most of the advance orders had been canceled, and sales were low for both companies. Graham grabbed the lion's share of publicity with its blown engine, and built six times as many cars as its partner. Hupp gave up in October 1940, only three weeks after 1941 model production had started. Just 319 of the '41 Skylarks had been built. Registrations were equally dismal: 211 in 1940; 103 in 1941.

Hupp recovered slightly during the war by way of defense contracts. After 1945, management elected not to return to the car business. Instead, the firm turned to making accessories for other auto companies.

# Hupmobile Specifications

## 1940

| R-015 Skylark Custom (wb 115.0) | | Wght | Price | Prod |
|---|---|---|---|---|
| RQK | sdn 4d | 3,000 | 1,145 | — |

| 1940 Engine | bore×stroke | bhp | availability |
|---|---|---|---|
| L6, 245.0 | 3.50×4.25 | 101 | S-all |

## 1941

| R-115 Skylark Custom (wb 115.0) | | Wght | Price | Prod |
|---|---|---|---|---|
| RQK | sdn 4d | 3,000 | 1,095 | — |

| 1941 Engine | bore×stroke | bhp | availability |
|---|---|---|---|
| L6, 245.0 | 3.50×4.25 | 101 | S-all |

# Imperial

**Chrysler - Imperial Division, Chrysler Corp.
Detroit, Michigan**

Imperial became a separate and distinct make in 1955, and remained as such through 1975. Long before that, it had been Chrysler's most luxurious model. Indeed, Imperial couldn't shake its image as a Chrysler, though it had some of its most successful years in the 1950s.

The beautiful 1955-56 models, based extensively on Virgil Exner's Parade Phaeton show cars and the Chrysler K-310, are recognized by many today as the most desirable Imperials of all. Wearing a distinctive split grille up front and elegantly trimmed inside and out, these big sedans and hardtops still look very good today. The infamous "gunsight" taillights were the only

Parade Phaeton show car of 1954-56

1955 Newport hardtop coupe

1955 Newport hardtop coupe

non-functional design feature, though the treatment was certainly distinctive. The '55s were powered by a 331 cubic-inch hemi-head V8; the '56 models used a bored-out version of the same engine.

The 1956s rode a longer wheelbase, which made them the longest Imperials. (Wheelbase shrank to 129 inches in 1957.) They were given tailfins, perhaps the only Chrysler product of the day to wear them as well. Styling was nicely integrated, and almost appeared to have been a ground-up design, rather than the quick facelift it was. The only significant optional extra for 1955-56 was air conditioning, priced at $567. The cars were comprehensively equipped, with PowerFlite transmission standard. Though not in the class of Chrysler's 300, Imperials were lively performers yet surprisingly economical. Imperials steadily won luxury-class laurels in the Mobilgas Economy Runs.

Crown Imperial long-wheelbase sedans or limousines were available in 1955-56. Built in Detroit, they replaced all previous Dodge, DeSoto, and Chrysler long-wheelbase cars. Though well styled along the lines of the standard Imperial, they sold slowly.

For 1957 came Exner's all-new Forward Look. Imperial sprouted huge tailfins and a full-width, complicated-looking grille. In an effort to surpass Lincoln, then second to Cadillac in the luxury field, Imperial added two new series, the Crown and LeBaron. More elaborately trimmed than standard cars, the Crown came as a sedan, two- and four-door hardtops, and a new convertible—the first soft-top Imperial since 1953. The LeBaron series was added in January and comprised a pillar sedan and four-door Southampton hardtop. Both new series were priced considerably higher than the basic models. TorqueFlite three-speed automatic transmission (new that year) and a 392 Hemi were standard for all.

From 1957 through 1965, Crown Imperial limousines were built by Ghia of Turin, Italy. Based on potential sales, Chrysler could no longer justify the time and space necessary to build such cars in Detroit. Against a potential $3.3 million tooling bill at home, Ghia offered to tool Crown Imperials for only $15,000, provided Chrysler could ship the basic "kit" to Torino.

Each Ghia limousine began as an unfinished two-door hardtop body mounted on a rigid convertible chassis, and was shipped with all body panels intact. Ghia cut the car apart, added 20.5 inches to the wheelbase, reworked the structure above the beltline, fitted and trimmed the luxurious interior, and finished off the exterior using 150 pounds of lead filler. Construction of each car took a month, and initial delays made the Crown Imperial a very late 1957 introduction, priced at a stratospheric $15,075. Sales were not impressive: only 132 Ghia Crowns had been built by the time the line ended in 1965, but all of them were impeccably tailored.

Imperial's best year ever was 1957. Nearly 38,000 cars were built, almost edging out Lincoln. Accordingly, the 1958 Imperial was changed only slightly. Circular parking lights and a complex mesh-and-eggcrate grille were the main styling features for this facelift. The model lineup was unchanged, but prices were marginally higher. Horsepower was boosted again. The year proved to be a poor one for Chrysler products in general; Imperial produced only about 16,000 units. In model years 1959 and 1960, Imperial finally outsold Lincoln, but these were the only times it did. Frustrating dealers, people still called the cars "Chrysler Imperials"—and a "Chrysler," though prestigious, didn't have the charisma of a Cadillac.

The basic 1957 styling was more extensively facelifted for '59, with a toothy grille and added brightwork along the sides. For the first time the standard series had its own model name, Custom. The lineup was otherwise unchanged. Offered again were Torsion-Aire front suspension, TorqueFlite automatic, and "Full-Time" power steering. Along with other Chrysler products, Imperial switched to the 413-cid wedge-head V8, which provided performance comparable to that of the Hemi, but was more economical to build and maintain.

Exner's heroically finned Imperials of the early '60s were the kind of cars that cause modern stylists to grimace, but they seemed perfectly valid at the time. They sold well, though not in record numbers. Imperial remained strictly an also-ran among luxury makes. Cadillac was the overwhelming choice among luxury-car buyers, Lincoln was a distant second, and Imperial was usually an even more distant third.

Imperial rode Chrysler's largest standard wheelbase, but unlike the firm's other 1960 products retained sep-

1956 Crown Imperial limousine

1957 four-door sedan

1956 four-door sedan

1958 LeBaron four-door sedan

1957 Crown convertible

D'Elegance show car from 1958

Styling clays under development, probably for 1958

1960 Crown Imperial limousine by Ghia

1959 Crown Imperial for Queen of England's Canadian tour

1961 Crown Southampton hardtop sedan

1960 Custom Southampton hardtop sedan

1961 LeBaron Southampton hardtop sedan

arate body-and-frame construction. This allowed greater insulation between body and frame, necessary in those days to achieve the level of smoothness and silence Imperial buyers demanded. The only engine available was held over from 1959, the wedge-head V8 that required premium fuel and had 10:1 compression.

The 1960 line was a repeat of '59. Three standard series were offered: Custom, Crown, and LeBaron, each separated by about $600. Custom-built Crown Imperial limousines were still available on the longer 149.5-inch wheelbase. Styling was again a facelift, with a new grille and a "wrapover" bright metal roof panel that extended all the way to the windshield. Comfort was the big feature for 1960, with a new high-back driver's seat padded in thick foam rubber, adjustable "spot" air conditioning, six-way power seat with single rotary-knob control, Auto-Pilot cruise control, and automatic headlamp dimmer. Customs were upholstered in pretty crown-pattern nylon. Crown upholstery was nylon and vinyl, wool, or leather. Wool broadcloth was used for LeBarons.

The 1961 model was altered considerably, though it used the 1960 shell. Fins were the most blatant ever to appear on an Imperial, and were accompanied by a new gimmick: freestanding headlamps pocketed in the curve of the front fenders. This was another idea from Exner, who was influenced by classic cars. Freestanding taillights suspended from the towering fins were also used. The strange-looking headlights survived through 1963, but rear styling was gradually improved during 1962 and '63. Custom, Crown, and LeBaron models were again offered, but the four-door pillared sedans were eliminated.

Before Exner left the corporation during 1961, he had envisioned a completely new, truncated Imperial for '62 as a companion for his downsized Dodges and Plymouths of that year. This didn't reach production, which is fortunate considering the failure of the cheaper makes. The production Imperial's small changes for '62 added up to a much improved appearance. The fins were shorn down to mere nubs of what they'd been. The new, elongated bullet taillights were

freestanding, but blended better with the rear fenders than the earlier "gunsight" versions. Predictably, sales were better than in '61.

Imperial received another mild facelift for 1963, which included a new grille composed of elongated rectangles, a crisp new roofline, and a restyled rear deck. Freestanding taillights were discontinued. The stylist responsible for much of this revision was Elwood Engle, who had replaced Exner in mid-1961. The lineup was unchanged, except for the Ghia Crown Imperial. Model year production totals were about the same as in '62.

Engle's styling completely replaced the old Exner silhouette for 1964. Imperial was now very reminiscent of the four-door Lincoln Continentals he had styled during his Ford days. Fenderlines were traced in brightwork, just like on the big Lincolns. A divided grille appeared, and the freestanding headlamps were replaced by integral units. The Custom had not sold well and was eliminated, along with the Southampton designation for pillarless body styles. This pared the line down to just five models. Sales were exceedingly good with over 23,000 units for the model year. This performance would not be approached until 1969.

Good sales and the big '64 redesign dictated a stand-pat lineup for the 1965 season. The only significant change was a new grille with glass-enclosed dual headlights. At the New York Automobile Show, Imperial displayed its exotic LeBaron D'Or show car, which used gold striping and embellishments, and was painted a special color, Royal Essence Laurel Gold. The usual range was again offered. Prices were about $100 to $200 higher than they'd been in 1964.

Ghia stopped building limousines in 1965, though 10 more Crown Imperials were constructed in Spain using grilles and rear decks from the '66 models. When Imperial finally went to unit body construction in 1967, Chrysler worked out a limousine program with Stageway Coaches of Fort Smith, Arkansas. Built from 1967 through 1971 at the rate of about six per year, the Stageway cars were called LeBarons rather than Crown Imperials. They were much longer than their predecessors, having an unbelievable 163-inch wheelbase, by far the longest in the American industry. Prices ranged from $12,000 to $15,000, depending on equipment.

Once more in 1966, the Engle-styled Crowns and LeBarons were offered with only detail changes. The grille was a cellular affair, each "cell" housing the familiar elongated rectangles. The rear deck was cleaned up by removing the fake spare tire cover, a throwback to the Exner years. Backup lights were inset in the rear bumper. The wedgehead V8 was bored out to 440 cubic inches and rated at 350 bhp. Model year production dropped considerably, however.

By 1967, Chrysler engineers had enough experience with unit construction to be satisfied with this approach for their most expensive product. Vast technological improvements had also occured, allowing computerized stress testing of any given shape before actual

1962 LeBaron Southampton hardtop sedan

1963 LeBaron Southampton hardtop sedan

1964 Crown Coupe hardtop

1965 LeBaron hardtop sedan

1966 Crown hardtop sedan

1967 Crown convertible

1968 Crown hardtop sedan

1969 LeBaron hardtop sedan

1970 LeBaron hardtop sedan

four-door pillar-type sedan returned without a series name. Other models were continued as before.

Volume dropped for 1968, and caused Chrysler to make a far-reaching decision: for 1969-70 and beyond, Imperial would share its sheetmetal with Chrysler. Among the casualties of this decision was the Crown convertible, which made its last appearance in 1968. The '68s were only slightly altered from the '67s. Changes included a new grille that extended around the front end to enclose the parking and cornering lights, dual moldings on the lower bodysides, and rear side marker lights (now required by the government). Narrow paint stripes were applied along the beltline on all models. The 440 V8 was still standard. Dual exhausts and twin-snorkel air cleaners were offered as an option.

The Chrysler-like cars of 1969-70 were certainly the cleanest Imperials in history. They had long, low "fuselage styling," a full-width eggcrate grille, concealed headlamps, and sequential turn signals set into the rear bumper. Ventless side glass was a feature of air-conditioned coupes. Although the 127-inch wheelbase was retained, the new styling stretched overall length by five inches, yet curb weight was about 100 pounds less. The engine, as before, was the 350-bhp 440 V8. A hardtop coupe and sedan were offered in both Crown and LeBaron trim, plus a pillared Crown sedan priced identically with the Crown hardtop. LeBaron was no longer the $7000 semi-custom it had been in past years. Its list price was slashed by about $800. Combined sales of the two LeBarons exceeded those of the Crown for the first time. This was a genuine boost to sales, which reached 22,183 units in 1969, the third best figure in Imperial history.

Unfortunately, Imperial's increasing resemblance to Chrysler during the early 1970s caused sales to drop rapidly. In 1975, its last year, only about 9000 were built. The "1976 Imperial" turned out to be a Chrysler New Yorker with a lower price. Sales improved temporarily, but were down by 50 percent in 1976. The Imperial name was absent until Chrysler reintroduced it for a super-luxury 1981 model.

construction. Unibody construction also cut weight by 100 pounds compared to 1966. As a result, the '67s were all-new and completely restyled. A new grille with a prominent nameplate was accompanied by sharp front fenders that housed the parking lights. Headlights were still integrated with the grille. There were vertical rear bumpers and horizontal "character lines" along the bodysides. Wheelbase contracted to 127 inches. The

# Imperial Specifications

## 1955

| C69 (wb 130.0) | Wght | Price | Prod |
|---|---|---|---|
| sdn 4d | 4,565 | 4,483 | 7,840 |
| Newport htp cpe | 4,490 | 4,720 | 3,418 |
| conv cpe (proto) | 4,600 | — | 1 |
| chassis | — | — | 1 |
| C70 Crown Imperial (wb 149.5) | | | |
| sdn 4d, 8P | 5,180 | 6,973 | 45 |

| | | Wght | Price | Prod |
|---|---|---|---|---|
| limo | | 5,230 | 7,095 | 127 |
| 1955 Engine | bore×stroke | bhp | availability | |
| V8, 331.0 | 3.81×3.63 | 250 | S-all | |

## 1956

| C73 (wb 133.0) | Wght | Price | Prod |
|---|---|---|---|
| sdn 4d | 4,575 | 4,832 | 6,821 |

| | | Wght | Price | Prod |
|---|---|---|---|---|
| | Southampton htp sdn | 4,680 | 5,225 | 1,543 |
| | Southampton htp cpe | 4,555 | 5,094 | 2,094 |

**C70 Crown Imperial (wb 149.5)**

| | | Wght | Price | Prod |
|---|---|---|---|---|
| | sdn 4d, 8P | 5,145 | 7,603 | 51 |
| | limo | 5,205 | 7,737 | 175 |

| 1956 Engine | bore×stroke | bhp | availability |
|---|---|---|---|
| V8, 354.0 | 3.94×3.63 | 280 | S-all |

## 1957

**IM1-1 (wb 129.0)**

| | | Wght | Price | Prod |
|---|---|---|---|---|
| | sdn 4d | 4,640 | 4,838 | 5,654 |
| | Southampton htp sdn | 4,780 | 4,838 | 7,527 |
| | Southampton htp cpe | 4,640 | 4,736 | 4,885 |

**IM1-2 Crown (wb 129.0)**

| | | Wght | Price | Prod |
|---|---|---|---|---|
| | sdn 4d | 4,740 | 5,406 | 3,642 |
| | Southampton htp sdn | 4,920 | 5,406 | 7,843 |
| | Southampton htp cpe | 4,755 | 5,269 | 4,199 |
| | conv cpe | 4,830 | 5,598 | 1,167 |

**IM1-4 LeBaron (wb 129.0)**

| | | Wght | Price | Prod |
|---|---|---|---|---|
| | sdn 4d | 4,765 | 5,743 | 1,729 |
| | Southampton htp sdn | 4,900 | 5,743 | 911 |

**Crown Imperial (wb 149.5)**

| | | Wght | Price | Prod |
|---|---|---|---|---|
| | limo | 5,960 | 15,075 | 36 |

| 1957 Engine | bore×stroke | bhp | availability |
|---|---|---|---|
| V8, 392.0 | 4.00×3.90 | 325 | S-all |

## 1958

**LY1-L (wb 129.0)**

| | | Wght | Price | Prod |
|---|---|---|---|---|
| 23 | Southampton htp cpe | 4,640 | 4,839 | 1,801 |
| 41 | sdn 4d | 4,590 | 4,945 | 1,926 |
| 43 | Southampton htp sdn | 4,795 | 4,945 | 3,336 |

**LY1-M Crown (wb 129.0)**

| | | Wght | Price | Prod |
|---|---|---|---|---|
| 23 | Southampton htp cpe | 4,730 | 5,388 | 1,939 |
| 27 | conv cpe | 4,820 | 5,729 | 675 |
| 41 | sdn 4d | 4,755 | 5,632 | 1,240 |
| 43 | Southampton htp sdn | 4,915 | 5,632 | 4,146 |

**LY1-H LeBaron (wb 129.0)**

| | | Wght | Price | Prod |
|---|---|---|---|---|
| 41 | sdn 4d | 4,780 | 5,969 | 501 |
| 43 | Southampton htp sdn | 4,940 | 5,969 | 538 |

**Crown Imperial (wb 149.5)**

| | | Wght | Price | Prod |
|---|---|---|---|---|
| | limo | 5,960 | 15,075 | 31 |

| 1958 Engines | bore×stroke | bhp | availability |
|---|---|---|---|
| V8, 392.0 | 4.00×3.90 | 345 | S-all exc Crown Imperial |
| V8, 392.0 | 4.00×3.90 | 325 | S-Crown Imperial |

## 1959

**MY1-L (wb 129.0)**

| | | Wght | Price | Prod |
|---|---|---|---|---|
| 612 | Southampton htp cpe | 4,675 | 4,910 | 1,743 |
| 613 | sdn 4d | 4,735 | 5,016 | 2,071 |
| 614 | Southampton htp sdn | 4,745 | 5,016 | 3,984 |

**MY1-M Crown (wb 129.0)**

| | | Wght | Price | Prod |
|---|---|---|---|---|
| 632 | Southampton htp cpe | 4,810 | 5,403 | 1,728 |
| 633 | sdn 4d | 4,830 | 5,647 | 1,335 |
| 634 | Southampton htp sdn | 4,840 | 5,647 | 4,714 |

| | | Wght | Price | Prod |
|---|---|---|---|---|
| 635 | conv cpe | 4,850 | 5,774 | 555 |

**MY1-H LeBaron (wb 129.0)**

| | | Wght | Price | Prod |
|---|---|---|---|---|
| 653 | sdn 4d | 4,865 | 6,103 | 510 |
| 654 | Southampton htp sdn | 4,875 | 6,103 | 622 |

**Crown Imperial (wb 149.5)**

| | | Wght | Price | Prod |
|---|---|---|---|---|
| | limo | 5,960 | 15,075 | 7 |

| 1959 Engines | bore×stroke | bhp | availability |
|---|---|---|---|
| V8, 413.0 | 4.18×3.75 | 350 | S-all exc Crown Imperial |
| V8, 392.0 | 4.00×3.90 | 325 | S-Crown Imperial |

## 1960

**PY1-L Custom (wb 129.0)**

| | | Wght | Price | Prod |
|---|---|---|---|---|
| 912 | Southampton htp cpe | 4,655 | 4,923 | 1,498 |
| 913 | sdn 4d | 4,700 | 5,029 | 2,335 |
| 914 | Southampton htp sdn | 4,760 | 5,029 | 3,953 |

**PY1-M Crown (wb 129.0)**

| | | Wght | Price | Prod |
|---|---|---|---|---|
| 922 | Southampton htp cpe | 4,720 | 5,403 | 1,504 |
| 923 | sdn 4d | 4,770 | 5,647 | 1,594 |
| 924 | Southampton htp sdn | 4,765 | 5,647 | 4,510 |
| 925 | conv cpe | 4,820 | 5,774 | 618 |

**PY1-H LeBaron (wb 129.0)**

| | | Wght | Price | Prod |
|---|---|---|---|---|
| 933 | sdn 4d | 4,860 | 6,318 | 692 |
| 934 | Southampton htp sdn | 4,835 | 6,318 | 999 |

**Crown Imperial (wb 149.5)**

| | | Wght | Price | Prod |
|---|---|---|---|---|
| | limo | 5,960 | 16,500 | 16 |

| 1960 Engine | bore×stroke | bhp | availability |
|---|---|---|---|
| V8, 413.0 | 4.18×3.75 | 350 | S-all |

## 1961

**RY1-L Custom (wb 129.0)**

| | | Wght | Price | Prod |
|---|---|---|---|---|
| 912 | Southampton htp cpe | 4,715 | 4,923 | 889 |
| 914 | Southampton htp sdn | 4,740 | 5,109 | 4,129 |

**RY1-M Crown (wb 129.0)**

| | | Wght | Price | Prod |
|---|---|---|---|---|
| 922 | Southampton htp cpe | 4,790 | 5,403 | 1,007 |
| 924 | Southampton htp sdn | 4,855 | 5,647 | 4,769 |
| 925 | conv cpe | 4,865 | 5,774 | 429 |

**RY1-H LeBaron (wb 129.0)**

| | | Wght | Price | Prod |
|---|---|---|---|---|
| 934 | Southampton htp sdn | 4,875 | 6,426 | 1,026 |

**Crown Imperial (wb 149.5)**

| | | Wght | Price | Prod |
|---|---|---|---|---|
| | limo | 5,960 | 16,500 | 9 |

| 1961 Engine | bore×stroke | bhp | availability |
|---|---|---|---|
| V8, 413.0 | 4.18×3.75 | 350 | S-all |

## 1962

**SY1-L Custom (wb 129.0)**

| | | Wght | Price | Prod |
|---|---|---|---|---|
| 912 | Southampton htp cpe | 4,540 | 4,920 | 826 |
| 914 | Southampton htp sdn | 4,620 | 5,106 | 3,587 |

**SY1-M Crown (wb 129.0)**

| | | Wght | Price | Prod |
|---|---|---|---|---|
| 922 | Southampton htp cpe | 4,650 | 5,400 | 1,010 |
| 924 | Southampton htp sdn | 4,680 | 5,644 | 6,911 |
| 925 | conv cpe | 4,765 | 5,770 | 554 |

**SY1-H LeBaron (wb 129.0)**

| | | Wght | Price | Prod |
|---|---|---|---|---|
| 934 | Southampton htp sdn | 4,725 | 6,422 | 1,449 |

# Imperial

| 1962 Engine | bore×stroke | bhp | availability |
|---|---|---|---|
| V8, 413.0 | 4.18×3.75 | 340 | S-all |

## 1963

| TY1-L Custom (wb 129.0) | | Wght | Price | Prod |
|---|---|---|---|---|
| 912 | Southampton htp cpe | 4,640 | 5,058 | 749 |
| 914 | Southampton htp sdn | 4,690 | 5,243 | 3,264 |

| TY1-M Crown (wb 129.0) | | Wght | Price | Prod |
|---|---|---|---|---|
| 922 | Southampton htp cpe | 4,720 | 5,412 | 1,067 |
| 924 | Southampton htp sdn | 4,740 | 5,656 | 6,960 |
| 925 | conv cpe | 4,795 | 5,782 | 531 |

| TY1-H LeBaron (wb 129.0) | | Wght | Price | Prod |
|---|---|---|---|---|
| 934 | Southampton htp sdn | 4,830 | 6,434 | 1,537 |

| Crown Imperial (wb 149.5) | | Wght | Price | Prod |
|---|---|---|---|---|
| | limo | 6,100 | 18,500 | 13 |

| 1963 Engine | bore×stroke | bhp | availability |
|---|---|---|---|
| V8, 413.0 | 4.18×3.75 | 340 | S-all |

## 1964

| VY1-M Crown (wb 129.0) | | Wght | Price | Prod |
|---|---|---|---|---|
| 922 | htp cpe | 4,950 | 5,739 | 5,233 |
| 924 | htp sdn | 4,970 | 5,581 | 14,181 |
| 925 | conv cpe | 5,185 | 6,003 | 922 |

| VY1-H LeBaron (wb 129.0) | | Wght | Price | Prod |
|---|---|---|---|---|
| 934 | htp sdn | 5,005 | 6,455 | 2,949 |

| Crown Imperial (wb 149.5) | | Wght | Price | Prod |
|---|---|---|---|---|
| | limo | 6,100 | 18,500 | 10 |

| 1964 Engine | bore×stroke | bhp | availability |
|---|---|---|---|
| V8, 413.0 | 4.18×3.75 | 340 | S-all |

## 1965

| AY1-M Crown (wb 129.0) | | Wght | Price | Prod |
|---|---|---|---|---|
| 922 | htp cpe | 5,075 | 5,930 | 3,974 |
| 924 | htp sdn | 5,015 | 5,772 | 11,628 |
| 925 | conv cpe | 5,345 | 6,194 | 633 |

| AY1-H LeBaron (wb 129.0) | | Wght | Price | Prod |
|---|---|---|---|---|
| 934 | htp sdn | 5,080 | 6,596 | 2,164 |

| Crown Imperial (wb 149.5) | | Wght | Price | Prod |
|---|---|---|---|---|
| | limo | 6,100 | 18,500 | 10 |

| 1965 Engine | bore×stroke | bhp | availability |
|---|---|---|---|
| V8, 413.0 | 4.18×3.75 | 340 | S-all |

## 1966

| BY3-M Crown (wb 129.0) | | Wght | Price | Prod |
|---|---|---|---|---|
| 23 | htp cpe | 5,000 | 5,887 | 2,373 |
| 27 | conv cpe | 5,315 | 6,164 | 514 |
| 43 | htp sdn | 4,990 | 5,733 | 8,977 |

| BY3-H LeBaron (wb 129.0) | | Wght | Price | Prod |
|---|---|---|---|---|
| 43 | htp sdn | 5,090 | 6,540 | 1,878 |

| 1966 Engine | bore×stroke | bhp | availability |
|---|---|---|---|
| V8, 440.0 | 4.32×3.75 | 350 | S-all |

## 1967

| CY1-M (wb 127.0) | | Wght | Price | Prod |
|---|---|---|---|---|
| 23 | Crown htp cpe | 4,780 | 6,011 | 3,235 |
| 27 | conv cpe | 4,815 | 6,244 | 577 |
| 41 | sdn 4d | 4,830 | 5,374 | 2,193 |
| 43 | Crown htp sdn | 4,860 | 5,836 | 9,415 |

| CY1-H LeBaron (wb 127.0) | | Wght | Price | Prod |
|---|---|---|---|---|
| 43 | htp sdn | 4,970 | 6,661 | 2,194 |

| LeBaron, Stageway body (wb 163.0) | | Wght | Price | Prod |
|---|---|---|---|---|
| | limo | | 15,000 | 6 |
| | | 6,300 | | |

| 1967 Engine | bore×stroke | bhp | availability |
|---|---|---|---|
| V8, 440.0 | 4.32×3.75 | 350 | S-all |

## 1968

| YM Crown (wb 127.0) | | Wght | Price | Prod |
|---|---|---|---|---|
| 23 | htp cpe | 4,660 | 5,722 | 2,656 |
| 27 | conv cpe | 4,795 | 6,497 | 474 |
| 41 | sdn 4d | 4,685 | 5,654 | 1,887 |
| 43 | htp sdn | 4,715 | 6,115 | 8,492 |

| YH LeBaron (wb 127.0) | | Wght | Price | Prod |
|---|---|---|---|---|
| 43 | htp sdn | 4,815 | 6,940 | 1,852 |

| LeBaron, Stageway body (wb 163.0) | | Wght | Price | Prod |
|---|---|---|---|---|
| | limo | 6,300 | 15,000 | 6 |

| 1968 Engines | bore×stroke | bhp | availability |
|---|---|---|---|
| V8, 440.0 | 4.32×3.75 | 350 | S-all |
| V8, 440.0 | 4.32×3.75 | 360 | O-all (dual exhaust) |

## 1969

| Crown (wb 127.0) | | Wght | Price | Prod |
|---|---|---|---|---|
| YL23 | htp cpe | 4,555 | 5,592 | 224 |
| YL43 | htp sdn | 4,690 | 5,770 | 823 |
| YM41 | sdn 4d | 4,620 | 5,770 | 1,617 |

| LeBaron (wb 127.0) | | Wght | Price | Prod |
|---|---|---|---|---|
| YM23 | htp cpe | 4,610 | 5,898 | 4,592 |
| YM43 | htp sdn | 4,710 | 6,131 | 14,821 |

| LeBaron, Stageway body (wb 163.0) | | Wght | Price | Prod |
|---|---|---|---|---|
| | limo | 6,300 | 16,000 | 6 est |

| 1969 Engine | bore×stroke | bhp | availability |
|---|---|---|---|
| V8, 440.0 | 4.32×3.75 | 350 | S-all |

## 1970

| YL Crown (wb 127.0) | | Wght | Price | Prod |
|---|---|---|---|---|
| 23 | htp cpe | 4,610 | 5,779 | 254 |
| 43 | htp sdn | 4,735 | 5,956 | 1,333 |

| YM LeBaron (wb 127.0) | | Wght | Price | Prod |
|---|---|---|---|---|
| 23 | htp cpe | 4,660 | 6,095 | 1,803 |
| 43 | htp sdn | 4,805 | 6,328 | 8,426 |

| LeBaron, Stageway body (wb 163.0) | | Wght | Price | Prod |
|---|---|---|---|---|
| | limo | 6,500 | 16,500 | 6 est |

| 1970 Engine | bore×stroke | bhp | availability |
|---|---|---|---|
| V8, 440.0 | 4.32×3.75 | 350 | S-all |

# Kaiser

**Kaiser-Frazer Corp.**
**Willow-Run, Michigan**

**Kaiser Motors Corp.**
**Toledo, Ohio**

Henry J. Kaiser and Joseph W. Frazer had a disagreement long before they went into business together. In 1942, Kaiser was experimenting with $400 to $600 plastic cars and suggesting that auto companies announce their postwar plans immediately. Frazer angrily replied: "I resent a West Coast shipbuilder asking us if we have the courage to plan postwar automobiles when the President has asked us to forego all work which would take away from the war effort. Kaiser has done a great job as a shipbuilder ... but I think his challenge to automobile men is as half-baked as some of his other statements . . . I think the public is being misled by all these pictures of plastic models with glass tops, done by artists who probably wouldn't want to sit under those tops in the summer and sweat."

After the two came together to form Kaiser-Frazer in July 1945, their relationship appeared amicable. Both sides compromised. Henry Kaiser was unable to build his cheap plastic car for the common man, but he had high hopes for a Kaiser with torsion-bar suspension and front-wheel drive.

The proposed front-drive Kaiser K-85 used a unit body/chassis based on the conventional Frazer, but its drivetrain and suspension, conceived by engineer Henry C. McCaslin, were very different. Its 85-horsepower engine, designed by Continental, drove the front wheels. Power was taken through a conventional three-speed transmission, routed to the front wheels by a helical-gear transfer case, and carried to the front-mounted differential by a universal joint. The torsion bar for each wheel was a 1.3-inch steel rod, 44.5 inches long, running the length of the car. The bars twisted to provide the springing. Unit construction was adopted, McCaslin said, because "we needed to use more of the operation in the plant. We had the welding equipment but lacked large dies and cranes. It was a compromise to get the car into production."

But the front-drive Kaiser never saw production. Huge problems developed—hard steering, gear whine, wheel shimmy. With so much weight over the front wheels, the K-85 needed power steering, which would have added $900 to its retail price. In May 1946, the decision was made to drop the project. Instead, K-F would build a conventional, rear-drive Kaiser similar to the Frazer but priced lower.

This Kaiser Special was introduced for 1947 at $1868, but the price quickly rose to over $2000. It shared the Frazer's body and 100-bhp six-cylinder engine. Kaiser used a multi-piece grille that was cheaper to produce than the Frazer's because the pieces were smaller. It was mundane inside, using conventional pin-striped upholstery. Late in the model year, a fancier model called the Kaiser Custom appeared, priced about $350 higher than the Special, $150 higher than the standard

Frazer, and about $250 less than the top-line Frazer Manhattan.

Willow Run, Ford's ex-bomber plant, was quickly converted for car production, and K-F was turning out finished vehicles by June 1946. The original plan had been to build two Kaisers for every Frazer, but in 1947 the company built about one to one to satisfy initial orders. The cars were basically unchanged for '48, but very few Customs were built. Both 1947 and 1948 were outstanding years for the young corporation. Profits were near $20 million in '47 and $10 million in '48. Combined output put K-F ninth in the industry, the best of any independent.

A facelift in 1949 gave Kaiser a broad horizontal grille

K-85 front-wheel-drive prototype, 1946

1947 Special four-door sedan

1947 Custom four-door sedan

233

and larger taillights. Several new models were added. Henry Kaiser had thought up the Traveler/Vagabond utility car—a conventional sedan with a double-door hatch cut into the rear section and a fold-down rear seat. The economical Traveler and the leather-upholstered Vagabond enabled the company to build a wagon-type model without the tooling expense normally required for a separate wood- or steel-bodied station wagon.

Two other new Kaisers for '49 were the Virginian four-door hardtop and the DeLuxe four-door convertible, the first postwar models to use those body styles. Both were lavishly upholstered, and offered excellent visibility because they had no steel "B" pillars. But they were as expensive as Cadillacs, and only a handful were produced. The ones that didn't sell in '49 were given new serial numbers for 1950.

A unique Kaiser-Frazer feature was a wide range of unusual colors, the work of color and fabric designer

1949-50 Deluxe convertible sedan

1949 Virginian (originally "Hard Top") sedan

1949 Deluxe Vagabond utility sedan

Carleton Spencer. He and K-F also worked with color research for home interiors with *House & Garden* magazine. The results were hues like Indian Ceramic (a vivid pink), Crystal Green, Caribbean Coral, and Arena Yellow. On Kaiser's DeLuxe sedan, the color name was written in chrome script on the front fenders. There were 150 different interior fabrics offered by the automobile industry in 1949, and K-F owned 62 of them. Of the 218 exterior colors offered that year, 37 were Kaiser-Frazer's.

Between 1948 and '49, Kaiser's dashboard changed dramatically. It had been an inexpensive unit with horizontal gauges in 1947-48. In '49, it became more ornate with a giant speedometer in front of the driver and a matching clock on the passenger's side. In Deluxe models, the dash sparkled with chrome, stainless steel, and a massive ivory steering wheel with a big semicircular chrome horn ring. The flashy interior design, colorful paint, and fashion upholstery did much to doll up what was basically an unaltered '47–'48 body.

Kaiser Customs were improved in performance with optional dual intake and exhaust manifolds that boosted horsepower to 112. This became standard on the 1949 DeLuxe, Vagabond, and Virginian. Kaiser had no automatic; its only transmission alternative was overdrive, priced at $80 extra.

Unfortunately, K-F sales plumeted in 1949. The main reason was the introduction of brand-new postwar designs by GM, Ford, and Chrysler, while K-F had a mere facelift. Joseph Frazer saw the onrush coming and warned against making too many '49s. New K-F designs were scheduled for release in early 1950, and Frazer's advice was to retrench until then. But Henry Kaiser wouldn't have it. "The Kaisers never retrench," he said. By this time, the influence of Kaiser's people was far greater than Frazer's, so Joe Frazer yielded the presidency to Kaiser's son Edgar, remaining on the board only for appearance's sake.

K-F tooled up for 200,000 units in '49, but built only some 101,000. About 20 percent of these couldn't be sold, and had to be given 1950 serial numbers. It is impossible to separate 1949 model year production from 1950's except to say that the '49s account for about 84 percent of the total.

By early 1950, the new '51 Kaiser was in production. Its debut was set for March of that year, six months ahead of normal introduction time. Sales rocketed. Close to 140,000 were sold, against about 15,000 of the 1950s. From a dismal 17th place in the industry in '49, Kaiser shot up to 12th—the highest it would ever achieve.

There was reason to be enthusiastic about the '51 Kaiser. From every angle it was unlike any other American car of the day. It offered 700 square inches more glass area than its nearest competitor, and a lower beltline than any Detroit car produced through 1956. Unique styling was complemented by an array of bright exterior colors and exciting interiors—again the work of color engineer Spencer.

Kaiser was probably the first company to really push safety. It advertised the new model's padded dash, recessed instruments, narrow windshield corner posts, outstanding visibility, and a windshield that popped out if struck with a force of more than 35 pounds per square inch. The engineering, too, was commendable. Engineers John Widman and Ralph Isbrandt shunned unit construction, but designed a very rigid separate body for a frame that weighed only 200 pounds. A low center of gravity gave Kaiser fine handling, yet curb weight was only about 3100 pounds. Many felt a V8 would have made the car unbeatable in the performance stakes. The lack of one would hurt Kaiser sales as the '50s wore on.

The facelifted '52s weren't quite ready by the end of 1951; in the interim, Kaiser offered the Virginian. About 5500 of these were built. They were nearly identical to the '51 design with similar body style offerings.

A smaller lineup and a mild facelift marked the "regular" '52 series. The most significant styling changes were "teardrop" taillights and a heavier-looking grille. Kaiser now called its top series Manhattan (the old Frazer model name) and the cheaper Special became the Deluxe. The later '52s are fairly rare: only 7500 Deluxes and 19,000 Manhattans were built in the short production run before the new-model changeover.

The 1953 Kaiser "Hardtop" Dragon sedan was the most luxurious Kaiser of all, inspired by Spencer's Dragon trim option from '51. Distinguished by gold-plated exterior trim (hood ornament, badges, script, and keyhole cover) the Dragon featured a padded top, usually made of "bambu" vinyl. This tough, oriental-style material also covered the dash and parts of the seats and door panels. Seat inserts were done in "Laguna" cloth, a fabric with an oblong pattern created by fashion designer Marie Nichols. The Dragon came standard with every possible option: tinted glass, Hydra-Matic drive, whitewalls, dual-speaker radio, and Calpoint custom carpeting on the floor and in the trunk. A gold medallion on the dash was engraved with the owner's name. The Dragon was a spectacular car, but its high price restricted sales. Only 1277 were built altogether, and the last few were almost given away.

Aside from the Dragon, changes for 1953 were slight. Kaiser offered a stripped Carolina model starting at $2313, but sold only a few copies. The company admitted the Carolina's chief purpose was to draw people into the showrooms. The two-door Travelers were eliminated, along with the club coupes. Engine output went up to 118 bhp, and power steering was offered late in the season as a $122 option.

Kaiser sales were plummeting in these years. The make had fallen again to its accustomed low standing in the production race, scoring only 32,000 units for 1952 and just 28,000 for '53. The Toledo-built '54 models were a last-ditch effort, cleverly facelifted by stylist Buzz Grisinger. The front end was much like the Buick XP-300 show car (one of Edgar Kaiser's favorite designs) with a wide, concave grille and "floating"

1951 Traveler four-door utility sedan

1951 Deluxe club coupe

1952 Manhattan four-door sedan

1953 "Hardtop" Dragon four-door sedan

1954 Special two-door sedan

headlights. Rear styling was set off by "Safety-Glo" taillights—big, rounded affairs with a lighted strip running up along the top of the fenders.

In an effort to wring more power out of its 226-cid six, Kaiser bolted a McCulloch centrifugal supercharger to Manhattan engines. Boosting power to 140 bhp, the blower went into full operation only when the accelerator was pressed to the floor. Alongside the two- and four-door Manhattans, K-F sold the unsupercharged Special in two models. The first series was a group of warmed-over 1953 Manhattans with '54 front ends—another effort to use up leftovers. The second was a genuine '54 with a wraparound rear window like the '54 Manhattan's. Neither version did well.

For 1955, Kaiser fielded Manhattans only, distinguished by a higher fin on the hood scoop and little else. Less than 300 genuine '55s were sold. About 100 were loaded on a ship bound for Argentina, where Kaiser Motors hoped to keep the model in production. It's a tribute to this design's durability that it was built there as the Kaiser Carabella through 1962.

Another memorable but unsuccessful experiment was the Kaiser Darrin sliding-door sports car of 1954, based on the 100-inch-wheelbase Henry J chassis. "Dutch" Darrin designed it in late 1952, and talked Henry Kaiser into marketing it for $3668. Only 435 were built before company operations wound down.

The fiberglass Darrin was beautifully styled, and still looks good today. In addition to the unique sliding doors, it featured a landau top with an intermediate half-up position. Full instrumentation was featured, and the car was usually fitted with a three-speed floorshift and overdrive, which gave economy of around 30 mpg. Yet, the Darrin could do the 0–60 mph sprint in about 13 seconds, and approach 100 mph flat out. The project was a big disappointment to Dutch Darrin. At the last minute, he bought about 100 leftovers from the factory, fitted some with Cadillac V8s, and sold them for $4350 each at his Los Angeles showroom. The Cadillac-powered cars were potent indeed, capable of about 140 mph at the top end.

**1954 Manhattan four-door sedan**

**1953 prototype for Darrin sports car**

**1954 Darrin roadster (production model)**

The Kaiser itself came to an end in America in 1955, after 10 years and a loss of $100 million. They were usually good cars, offering many innovative features, but they never seemed to make it with the public. Edgar Kaiser liked to say: "Slap a Buick nameplate on it, and it would sell like hotcakes."

# Kaiser Specifications

## 1947

### K100 Special (wb 123.5)

| | | Wght | Price | Prod |
|---|---|---|---|---|
| 1005 | sdn 4d | 3,295 | 2,104 | 65,062 |

### K101 Custom (wb 123.5)

| | | Wght | Price | Prod |
|---|---|---|---|---|
| 1015 | sdn 4d | 3,295 | 2,456 | 5,412 |

| 1947 Engines | bore×stroke | bhp | availability |
|---|---|---|---|
| L6, 226.2 | 3.38×4.38 | 100 | S-all |
| L6, 226.2 | 3.38×4.38 | 112 | O-Custom |

## 1948

### K481 Special (wb 123.5)

| | | Wght | Price | Prod |
|---|---|---|---|---|
| 4815 | sdn 4d | 3,295 | 2,244 | 90,588 |

### K482 Custom (wb 123.5)

| | | Wght | Price | Prod |
|---|---|---|---|---|
| 4825 | sdn 4d | 3,295 | 2,466 | 1,263 |

| 1948 Engines | bore×stroke | bhp | availability |
|---|---|---|---|
| L6, 226.2 | 3.38×4.38 | 100 | S-all |
| L6, 226.2 | 3.38×4.38 | 112 | O-Custom |

## 1949-50

### K491 Special (wb 123.5)

|      |                     | Wght  | Price | Prod    |
|------|---------------------|-------|-------|---------|
| 4911 | sdn 4d              | 3,311 | 1,995 | 29,000* |
| 4915 | Traveler util sdn 4d | 3,456 | 2,088 | 22,000* |

### K492 Deluxe (wb 123.5)

|      |                      | Wght  | Price | Prod    |
|------|----------------------|-------|-------|---------|
| 4921 | sdn 4d               | 3,341 | 2,195 | 38,250* |
| 4922 | conv sdn             | 3,726 | 3,195 | 54*     |
| 4923 | Virginian htp sdn    | 3,541 | 2,995 | 946*    |
| 4925 | Vagabond util sdn 4d | 3,501 | 2,288 | 4,500*  |

*1949-50 production combined by factory; approximate breakdown 84 percent 1949, 16 percent 1950. Estimates for body styles based on body numbers in extant vehicles. Actual 1949-50 production: 95,175.

### 1949-50 Engines

|            | bore×stroke | bhp | availability |
|------------|-------------|-----|--------------|
| L6, 226.2  | 3.38×4.38   | 100 | S-Special    |
| L6, 226.2  | 3.38×4.38   | 112 | S-Deluxe     |

## 1951

### K511 Special (wb 118.5)

|      |                      | Wght  | Price | Prod    |
|------|----------------------|-------|-------|---------|
| 5110 | Traveler util sdn 2d | 3,210 | 2,265 | 1,500*  |
| 5111 | sdn 4d               | 3,126 | 2,212 | 43,500* |
| 5113 | bus cpe              | 3,061 | 1,992 | 1,500*  |
| 5114 | sdn 2d               | 3,106 | 2,160 | 10,000* |
| 5115 | Traveler util sdn 4d | 3,270 | 2,317 | 2,000*  |
| 5117 | club cpe             | 3,066 | 2,058 | 1,500*  |

### K512 Deluxe (wb 118.5)

|      |                      | Wght  | Price | Prod    |
|------|----------------------|-------|-------|---------|
| 5120 | Traveler util sdn 2d | 3,285 | 2,380 | 1,000*  |
| 5121 | sdn 4d               | 3,171 | 2,328 | 70,000* |
| 5124 | sdn 2d               | 3,151 | 2,275 | 11,000* |
| 5125 | Traveler util sdn 4d | 3,345 | 2,433 | 1,000*  |
| 5127 | club cpe             | 3,111 | 2,296 | 6,000*  |

*Estimates based on extant vehicles. Actual total model year production: 139,452.

### 1951 Engine

|           | bore×stroke | bhp | availability |
|-----------|-------------|-----|--------------|
| L6, 226.2 | 3.38×4.38   | 115 | S-all        |

## 1952

### K521 Virginian Special (wb 118.5)*

|      |                      | Wght  | Price | Prod |
|------|----------------------|-------|-------|------|
| 5110 | Traveler util sdn 2d | 3,210 | 2,085 | —    |
| 5111 | sdn 4d               | 3,126 | 2,036 | —    |
| 5113 | bus cpe              | 3,061 | 1,832 | —    |
| 5114 | sdn 2d               | 3,106 | 1,988 | —    |
| 5115 | Traveler util sdn 4d | 3,270 | 2,134 | —    |

### K522 Virginian Deluxe (wb 118.5)*

|      |                      | Wght  | Price | Prod |
|------|----------------------|-------|-------|------|
| 5120 | Traveler util sdn 2d | 3,285 | 2,192 | —    |
| 5121 | sdn 4d               | 3,171 | 2,143 | —    |
| 5124 | sdn 2d               | 3,151 | 2,095 | —    |
| 5125 | Traveler util sdn 4d | 3,345 | 2,241 | —    |
| 5127 | club cpe             | 3,111 | 2,114 | —    |

### K521 Deluxe (wb 118.5)

|      |                      | Wght  | Price | Prod    |
|------|----------------------|-------|-------|---------|
| 5211 | sdn 4d               | 3,195 | 2,537 | 5,000** |
| 5214 | sdn 2d               | 3,145 | 2,484 | 2,000** |
| 5215 | Traveler util sdn 4d | 3,369 | 2,643 | ***     |
| 5217 | club cpe             | 3,045 | 2,296 | 500**   |

### K522 Manhattan (wb 118.5)

|      |          | Wght  | Price | Prod     |
|------|----------|-------|-------|----------|
| 5221 | sdn 4d   | 3,220 | 2,654 | 16,500** |
| 5224 | sdn 2d   | 3,185 | 2,601 | 2,000**  |
| 5227 | club cpe | 3,185 | 2,622 | 500**    |

*Total Virginian production: 5,579
**Estimates based on extant vehicles. Total Deluxe/Manhattan production: 26,552.
***Actual production questionable.

### 1952 Engine

|           | bore×stroke | bhp | availability |
|-----------|-------------|-----|--------------|
| L6, 226.2 | 3.38×4.38   | 115 | S-all        |

## 1953

### K530 "Hardtop" Dragon (wb 118.5)

|      |        | Wght  | Price | Prod  |
|------|--------|-------|-------|-------|
| 5301 | sdn 4d | 3,924 | 3,320 | 1,277 |

### K531 Deluxe (wb 118.5)

|      |                      | Wght  | Price | Prod   |
|------|----------------------|-------|-------|--------|
| 5311 | sdn 4d               | 3,200 | 2,513 | 5,800* |
| 5314 | sdn 2d               | 3,150 | 2,459 | 1,500* |
| 5315 | Traveler util sdn 4d | 3,315 | 2,619 | 1,000* |

### K532 Manhattan (wb 118.5)

|      |                      | Wght  | Price | Prod    |
|------|----------------------|-------|-------|---------|
| 5321 | sdn 4d               | 3,265 | 2,650 | 15,450* |
| 5324 | sdn 2d               | 3,235 | 2,597 | 2,500*  |
| 5325 | Traveler util sdn 4d | 3,371 | 2,755 | **      |

### K538 Carolina (wb 118.5)

|      |        | Wght  | Price | Prod   |
|------|--------|-------|-------|--------|
| 5381 | sdn 4d | 3,185 | 2,373 | 1,400* |
| 5384 | sdn 2d | 3,135 | 2,313 | 400*   |

### 1953 Engine

|           | bore×stroke | bhp | availability |
|-----------|-------------|-----|--------------|
| L6, 226.2 | 3.38×4.38   | 118 | S-all        |

*Estimates based on extant vehicles. Model year production:

| K531 | Deluxe    | 7,883  |
|------|-----------|--------|
| K532 | Manhattan | 17,957 |
| K538 | Carolina  | 1,182  |

**One example found; volume production questionable.

## 1954

### 161 Darrin (wb 100.0)

|     |       | Wght  | Price | Prod |
|-----|-------|-------|-------|------|
| 161 | rdstr | 2,175 | 3,668 | 435  |

### K542 Manhattan (wb 118.5)

|      |        | Wght  | Price | Prod   |
|------|--------|-------|-------|--------|
| 5421 | sdn 4d | 3,375 | 2,670 | 3,860* |
| 5424 | sdn 2d | 3,265 | 2,334 | 250*   |

### K545 Special (wb 118.5)**

|      |        | Wght  | Price | Prod   |
|------|--------|-------|-------|--------|
| 5451 | sdn 4d | 3,265 | 2,389 | 3,000* |
| 5454 | sdn 2d | 3,235 | 2,334 | 500*   |

### K545 Special, late (wb 118.5)

|      |        | Wght  | Price | Prod |
|------|--------|-------|-------|------|
| 5451 | sdn 4d | 3,305 | 2,389 | 800* |
| 5454 | sdn 2d | 3,265 | 2,334 | 125* |

### 1954 Engines

|            | bore×stroke | bhp | availability |
|------------|-------------|-----|--------------|
| L6, 161.0  | 3.13×3.50   | 90  | S-Darrin     |
| L6, 226.2  | 3.38×4.38   | 118 | S-Special    |
| L6, 226.2  | 3.38×4.38   | 140 | S-Manhattan  |

*Estimates based on extant vehicles. Model year production:

| K542 | Manhattan     | 4,110 |
|------|---------------|-------|
| K545 | Special**     | 3,500 |
| K545 | Special, late | 929   |

**Converted leftover 1953 Manhattans.

## 1955

### Manhattan (wb 118.5)

|       |                 | Wght  | Price | Prod  |
|-------|-----------------|-------|-------|-------|
| 51363 | sdn 4d (export) | 3,350 | —     | 1,021 |
| 51367 | sdn 4d          | 3,375 | 2,670 | 226   |
| 51467 | sdn 2d          | 3,335 | 2,617 | 44    |

### 1955 Engine

|           | bore×stroke | bhp | availability |
|-----------|-------------|-----|--------------|
| L6, 226.2 | 3.38×4.38   | 140 | S-all        |

# LaSalle

Cadillac Motor Car Division, General Motors Corp.
Detroit, Michigan

LaSalle was the result of GM President Alfred Sloan's desire to build "a car for every price and pocketbook." In the mid-1920s, Sloan detected a gap in the price structure between Buick and Cadillac, and assigned Cadillac Division the job of filling it. The magnificent 1927 LaSalle, designed by Harley Earl, amply fulfilled all its builders' hopes, and was the car that launched Earl on his illustrious 30-year career as the company's dean of design.

Throughout the 1930s, LaSalle provided the sales volume that helped Cadillac survive. Rarely did Cadillac/LaSalle production surpass Packard's, but LaSalle's share was usually substantial—and sometimes crucial. In the hard Depression year of 1933, the division's model year production slid to 6700 units: LaSalle accounted for more than half that total. In 1937, Cadillac Division built 46,000 cars: 32,000 of them were LaSalles.

Yet LaSalle sales never really satisfied GM managers, who wanted much more. They might have been happy with 50,000 in 1937, when the make received a new V8 engine, a longer wheelbase, and a more comfortable ride. Then came a recession in 1938, and nobody did very well. In 1939, LaSalle got a complete restyling, more glass, a shorter wheelbase, and an optional metal sunroof for sedans. Running boards were

1940 Series 52 Special four-door sedan

1940 Series 52 Special coupe

1940 Series 52 Special four-door sedan

1940 Series 52 Special convertible sedan

One of two prototypes for 1941 LaSalle never produced

Updated front-end styling of proposed '41 LaSalle

LaSalle II roadster, 1955 show car

LaSalle II hardtop sedan shown at 1955 Motorama

removed from all but the convertible (for which they were an option). But again, production was disappointing: only a few more than 20,000 were built that year.

The LaSalle V8, derived from the 1936 Cadillac Series 60, produced 130 horsepower at 3400 rpm. Its power, greater than that of the earlier straight eights, allowed lower axle ratios and smoother cruising. Top speed was close to 90 miles an hour.

The new styling for 1940 was one of the high points in the marque's 14-year history. Instead of Cadillac's free-standing headlamps, LaSalle's sealed-beams were integrated into the fenders. Lines were gently rounded, functional, and clean. Windows were large, and the interior spacious because of a wheelbase increase from 120 inches in 1939 to 123 for 1940. The trademark La-Salle grille had always been more narrow and delicate than Cadillac's. The 1940 rendition retained these characteristics and was flanked by "catwalk" openings (an idea of Earl's) built into the leading edges of the front fenders.

LaSalles for 1940 came in two series, the 40-50 and the plush 40-52 Special. The Special line was expanded at mid-year by a convertible and convertible sedan, the most elegant LaSalles that final season.

But the marque's exclusive price niche had disappeared by 1940. While the Cadillac nearest in price was the 62 at $1685, Buicks listed from as little as $895 up to $2199. LaSalle's original market position below Cadillac was being covered by a more popular GM make.

Cadillac Division did well in 1940. Out of about 37,000 cars, LaSalle accounted for 24,130. But the junior make ranked only slightly ahead of Lincoln, and remained far behind Packard. So, the most romantic of GM's "companion" cars was discontinued for 1941, its place taken by the new low-priced Cadillac 61.

In the long run, the decision to drop LaSalle was a correct one. Buyers could have a 1941 Cadillac for about $1300, and the magic of that name was important to dealers. Cadillac continued to price the 61 in luxury territory to prevent cheapening its image. Eventually, this would help Cadillac dominate the fine-car market.

LaSalle never really died in the minds of designers, though. To them it had always stood for distinction, refinement, and class. GM Styling had actually prepared a LaSalle design for 1941. A pretty car with the traditional narrow grille and "catwalk" fender inlets, it featured thin horizontal parking lights, spinner hubcaps, and a revival of the earlier LaSalle radiator badge—the "LaS" monogram in a circle. In 1955, Harley Earl's studio produced a four-door hardtop sedan and a two-seat roadster, both dubbed LaSalle II, for that year's Motorama. Interestingly, both these cars had grilles composed of vertical slats like that of their 1940 forebear, and the traditional LaSalle badge graced their hoods. In the early 1960s, the name was again considered for what became the Buick Riviera. And only at the last minute was LaSalle dropped in favor of Seville as the moniker for Cadillac's 1976 compact.

## LaSalle Specifications

### 1940

| 40-50 (wb 123.0) | | Wght | Price | Prod |
|---|---|---|---|---|
| 5011 | sdn 2d | 3,760 | 1,280 | 375 |
| 5019 | sdn 4d | 3,790 | 1,320 | 6,722 |
| 5027 | cpe, A/S | 3,700 | 1,240 | 1,527 |
| 5029 | conv sdn | 4,000 | 1,800 | 125 |
| 5067 | conv cpe | 3,805 | 1,395 | 599 |
| 50 | chassis | — | — | 1,032 |

| 40-52 Special (wb 123.0) | | | | |
|---|---|---|---|---|
| 5219 | sdn 4d | 3,900 | 1,440 | 10,250 |
| 5227 | cpe | 3,810 | 1,380 | 3,000 |
| 5229 | conv sdn | 4,110 | 1,895 | 75 |
| 5267 | conv cpe | 3,915 | 1,535 | 425 |

| 1940 Engine | bore×stroke | bhp | availability |
|---|---|---|---|
| V8, 322.0 | 3.38×4.50 | 130 | S-all |

# Lincoln

**Ford Motor Company, (Lincoln-Mercury Division from 1947)**
**Dearborn, Michigan**

For Lincoln, 1940 was the year of the Continental—one of the most stunning automotive designs of the decade, and perhaps of all time. The Continental was Edsel Ford's idea, styled by Bob Gregorie. Edsel had directed him to make it "thoroughly continental," complete with outside spare tire—hence the name.

Originally, this new Lincoln was a one-off custom for Edsel to use on his annual vacation in Palm Beach. But, everyone who saw it that winter of 1938-39 thought it was sensational. Scarcely a year later, the Lincoln-Zephyr Continental was on sale in Lincoln showrooms. A coupe and cabriolet were offered at about $2850 a copy, and brought customers into dealerships by the thousands. The marketing plan had been to attract all kinds of customers, and the Continental did just that.

The Lincoln-Zephyr, on which it was based, had first appeared in June 1935 as a 1936 model. The beautifully streamlined design by John Tjaarda employed a unit body/chassis to save weight, and was apparently quite aerodynamic. Although wind tunnel tests were never formally conducted, the prototype Zephyr—using an 80-horsepower rear-mounted V8—performed excellently, showing less than expected wind resistance at high speeds.

Production Zephyrs used a very different powertrain: a front-mounted L-head V12. With the exception of a few high-priced 1940 Lincolns that used a 414-cid V12, all 1940-48 models were powered by the smaller Zephyr V12. In 1940-41 form it produced 120 bhp at 3500 rpm.

The original Zephyr engine was a 75-degree cast-iron unit with four main bearings, steel pistons, and aluminum-alloy heads. It looked like a new design, but it actually relied heavily on the Ford V8. The two engines used many interchangeable parts and had identical strokes. But as a "stretched" V8, the V12 was severely criticized, and not without reason. Water passages, for example, were inadequate, causing overheating, bore warpage, and ring wear. Inadequate crankcase ventilation created oil sludge buildup. Poor oil flow was also a problem. In 1938, the engine was given hydraulic valve lifters, and had cast-iron heads from 1942, but it never lost its reputation for service difficulties. Had World War II not come along, this powerplant might have been completely re-engineered. In fact, it never was. Owners of many 1940s Lincolns discarded the V12 in favor of later L-heads or overhead-valve V8s.

The old 414-cid "K" series Lincoln was listed in early 1940, but only 133 were actually sold that model year. There were many styles to choose from, some built in quantities of one or two. Custom bodies by Willoughby, Brunn, LeBaron, and Judkins were offered. Prices started with the LeBaron sedan and ended with a Brunn cabriolet. The Ks were mounted on wheelbases ranging from 136 to 145 inches. Eight Customs (on a 138-inch wheelbase) were also built, powered by the Zephyr engine.

The Zephyr line was Lincoln's main sales hope in those days, but volume was low. In the early 1940s, sales dropped to around 20,000 units annually. Two Zephyr series were offered for 1940: the standard coupes, convertibles, and sedan, and custom-interior closed models. The latter group included a special five-passenger "town limousine" built by Briggs out of a four-door sedan. The Brunn Company also made four custom Zephyr town cars, three of which went to the Ford family. These were heavy-looking, with rooflines

Edsel Ford's original Continental, 1939

1940 Continental club coupe

1940 Continental club coupe

that didn't fit the chiseled lower body styling.

Continental became a separate model for 1941 instead of a Zephyr series, and production increased. The old Series K was dropped completely in favor of the Zephyr-engined, long-wheelbase Customs. The emphasis remained on Zephyr, though the town limousine was deleted. As in 1940, some were available with custom interiors. Prices increased slightly, but styling changes were slight on both Zephyr and Continental. Zephyrs can be identified by their fender-mounted parking lights; '41 Continentals have pushbutton exterior door knobs and directional signals combined with the parking lights.

The year 1942 was significant for both styling and engineering. Lincoln adopted a new 305-cid V12 that was more reliable than the engine it replaced. A flashy face-lift prefigured immediate postwar styling. All models now had longer, higher fenders, which increased the Continental's length by more than seven inches. Height on all models was reduced slightly, but weight went up. The front end acquired a bold grille of horizontal bars, and headlamps flanked by parking lights on either side.

Production in the years just before World War II had been steady, but hardly spectacular. The Zephyr had been Lincoln's low-priced key to survival in the Depression—comparable to the Packard One Ten/One Twenty and Cadillac's LaSalle. But Zephyr never sold well enough to put Lincoln in the same volume league as its rivals. In its best prewar year, 1937, the firm built barely one-fourth the number of cars Packard did, and reached only two-thirds the Cadillac/LaSalle figure. The last prewar Lincoln rolled out of the factory on February 10, 1942, and model year production was therefore slim.

1940 Zephyr three-passenger coupe

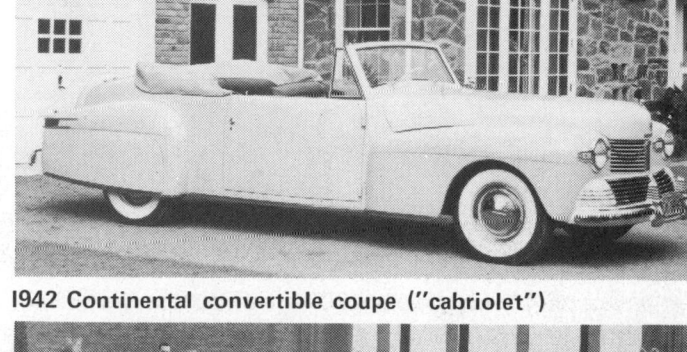

1942 Continental convertible coupe ("cabriolet")

1941 Continental convertible coupe ("cabriolet")

1947 convertible and Continental club coupe

1941 Continental club coupe

1948 four-door sedan

# Lincoln

During the war, Ford stylists were able to spend a little time devising postwar designs. The "bathtub" look, which would captivate manufacturers in the late '40s, evolved quickly. Dozens of scale models were built; hundreds of renderings were drawn. Lincoln concepts of these years were often grotesque: they looked, as one stylist put it, as if they'd been "carved out of a bar of soap." After V-J Day, civilian production resumed with 1942 dies. The first postwar cars were unchanged from 1946 through 1948 as presentation of an all-new Lincoln was put off until 1949.

Long-wheelbase offerings were dropped for 1946, along with several prewar styles, such as the three-passenger coupe. A sedan, club coupe, and convertible were fielded for 1946-48; closed models were available with custom interiors. Continentals came in prewar form—coupe and cabriolet. All Lincolns continued to use the 125-inch wheelbase and the V12, which then produced 125 bhp.

The grille was now composed of vertical and horizontal bars, with a Lincoln emblem in the upper segment. A winged globe was adopted for the hood ornament. The Continental's hood was low and clean. Body lines flowed back to a tapered rear deck and a protected spare tire mounting. Continentals were still good-looking cars, devoid of bright metal side moldings. The only name identification was a modest "Lincoln Continental" script at the rear edge of the hood. The metal tire cover was painted body color. For 1947, the Lincoln name appeared on hubcaps, pull-out door handles were used, interior armrests were "pocket" types, and the hood ornament received a longer "wing." No changes at all occured when the '47s became the '48s.

Lincoln considered a new Continental for 1949, but ultimately dropped the idea and concentrated on higher-volume models. Predictably, the '49 styling was of the bar-of-soap school, but was nevertheless a clean-looking design. Riding 121-inch and 125-inch wheelbases, the models were designated Lincoln and Lincoln Cosmopolitan, respectively. The base series comprised a sedan, coupe, and convertible. The costlier Cosmopolitan included these three body styles plus a town sedan. Lincoln now discarded the aged V12 and adopted an L-head V8 of 337 cid with 152 bhp at 3600 rpm. Overdrive was available for $96 extra.

For its time, the styling of the '49s was dignified. Fenders faded into the body on the base series, and were eliminated completely on the Cosmopolitan. Headlights and taillights were "frenched," and grilles were conservative. The Cosmopolitan used a curved one-piece (instead of two-piece) windshield, broad chrome gravel deflectors over the front wheelwells, and thin window frames. This basic styling would carry Lincoln through 1951. Model year volume for 1949 was a record 73,507 units.

The '50s would be a topsy-turvy decade for Lincoln. Its 1950-51 cars were posh, but bulky and slow. By 1952, they'd be transformed into the taut, powerful road machines that would reign supreme in their class at the

Clay model proposal for '49 styling

1949 Series 9EL sport Sedan

1950 Cosmopolitan Presidential convertible

Carrera Panamericana. The line was overhauled again for 1956. Lincoln changed dramatically into a very long, good-looking highway cruiser. From 1957 on, it grew fins, acquired some lamentable styling touches, and adopted the biggest engine in the business.

The 1950-51 Lincolns completed the three-year cycle for the '49 design. Easily distinguishable by their sunken headlamps (covered lights were intended first), they appear at first to be big Mercurys. As in 1949, the Cosmopolitan shared no body panels with Mercury, though the smaller Lincoln used Mercury panels from the cowl back.

The explanation lies in Ford's postwar planning. Originally, the 118-inch-wheelbase Mercury was to have been the '49 Ford, and the 121-inch-wheelbase Lincoln was to have been the '49 Mercury. What became the Cosmopolitan was, in fact, the proposed '49 Zephyr, which never materialized, of course. When Ford's policy committee, led by Ernest Breech and Harold Youngren, urged the adoption of a shorter, 114-

1950 Series 0EL Sport Sedan

1951 Series 1EL coupe

1952 Cosmopolitan four-door sedan

The 1951 grille was simplified, wheel covers were changed, and horsepower was increased. In both 1950 and 1951, special limited editions were offered with custom interiors and padded canvas tops. In the base Lincoln series the special was called Lido. Cosmopolitan offered the Capri. Not many of either were sold. For the completely restyled 1952 models, however, Capri became the name of the upper series, while the former ultra-luxurious Cosmopolitan became the lesser Lincoln.

Sales were up a little for 1952-54, but lagged miles behind Cadillac. Perhaps this was a result of dull uniformity: the same five models were offered in all three years. Cosmopolitan and Capri were both available as four-door sedans and two-door hardtops. Capri also was offered as a convertible. Styling was on the sedate side, which may have been another problem. Nevertheless, these were three of Lincoln's best years.

The most significant mechanical feature of 1952-54 was a new valve-in-head V8, a superior engine in many ways. The crankshaft, for example, had eight counterweights, rather than the usual six of its competitors. The intake valves were oversize, allowing better breathing, greater efficiency, and more output for every cubic inch. (In 1953, the Lincoln V8 produced 0.64 bhp per cubic inch, against 0.63 for Cadillac and 0.54 for the Chrysler Hemi.) There was also a deep-skirt crankcase, which extended below the crankshaft centerline to create an extremely stiff support for the shaft.

There was more to the story than the engine. In 1952, Lincoln introduced the first ball-joint front suspension. This very flexible, controllable system was a forerunner of suspensions used by most cars today. Recirculating-ball power steering, oversize drum brakes, an optional four-way power seat, and liberal sound deadening insulation were also incorporated. Models equipped with optional factory air conditioning offered flow-through ventilation when the compressor was turned off. Fabrics and leathers, fit and finish were of a quality that far exceeded conventional Ford products.

Despite a rather short 123-inch wheelbase, Lincolns of this period offered more room inside than preceding models did, and sometimes more than their successors would. Visibility was better than on any other contemporary car except Kaiser, and exterior trim was notably free of the era's excesses. The taillights were fluted, like those of a late-'70s Mercedes-Benz, which enabled them to shed water and dirt. Whether this was pure engineering or just a lucky styling idea, it functioned extremely well.

Lincoln's performance in Mexico was spectacular. In the second, third, and fourth Carrera Panamericana, the make had no rival in the International Standard Class. Lincolns took the top five places in 1952, the top four in 1953, and first and second in 1954. Major credit for the race preparation goes to Clay Smith, a gifted mechanic who was tragically killed in a pit accident in 1954. Smith had help from publicity-conscious Ford, which supplied him with "export" suspensions, Ford truck camshafts, mechanical valve lifters, special front wheel

inch-wheelbase Ford, the various designs were all moved down a notch and Zephyr was eliminated. The ex-Mercury Lincoln was thus a much cheaper car than the Cosmopolitan. The latter had heavy chrome moldings over the front wheelwells and a more complicated grille than the Lincoln. Both cars, however, used the same engine—a 336.7-cid L-head originally designed for Ford trucks.

From 1950 to 1954, Lincolns offered Hydra-Matic transmission (optional 1950-51) bought from arch-rival GM. While not known for performance, the Lincoln's specification was good enough for ninth place in the 1950 Mexican race. A high-geared Lincoln also won the Mobilgas economy run in '51 with a 25.5-mpg average.

The 1950 models featured a brand-new dashboard created by Tom Hibbard, then chief designer. An attractive, rolled affair with an oblong window covering the instruments, it was popular enough to remain in use as late as 1956. Longer rear fenders were adopted for '51, and upright taillights replaced the round 1949-50 units.

spindles and hubs, and a choice of two rear axle ratios. The higher one enabled a stock Lincoln to top 130 mph. The 1952 race winner, Chuck Stevenson, actually finished the 2000-mile grind from Juarez to the Guatemala border nearly an hour ahead of the Ferrari that had won the year before.

Lincoln wasn't ready for a total redesign in 1955, and its line that year was the most conservative in the indus-

1953 Capri four-door sedan

1954 Capri hardtop coupe

1955 Capri hardtop coupe

1956 Premiere hardtop coupe

try. The wraparound windshield was being used almost everywhere else, but Lincoln didn't have it yet—and as a result, was more practical. Wheelbase remained at 123 inches, but weight increased by 50 to 100 pounds. The company finally offered its own automatic transmission, called Turbo-Drive. Instead of Cosmopolitan, the bottom line was now called Custom; the Capri remained with the same three body styles as before. Styling was crisp, clean, and elegant. Interiors were a luxurious combination of quality fabrics and top-grain leather. Sales, unfortunately, were down for '55: Lincoln was one of the few makes to do better in 1954 than '55 because it wasn't "new" enough.

Drastic change occurred in 1956. "Unmistakably Lincoln," read the ads—but buyers had to look twice to see vestiges of the '55s in the newer edition. Gone were the short wheelbase and trim styling, replaced by a 126-inch-wheelbase chassis and a body seven inches longer and three inches wider. Capri became the lower series; the ultimate Lincoln was now called Premiere. Styling fit the new, enlarged body extremely well. The grille was clean, with peaked headlights and simple ornamentation; two-toning was confined to the roof; at the rear were rakish vertical taillights capping long exhaust ports and a "grille" motif duplicating the front design. The engine was as new as the styling, a 368-cid V8 with 285 bhp at 4600 rpm—"True power," the ads said, "that works for your safety at every speed." Despite their bulk, the cars didn't weigh much more than the 1955 models. As the only company that year with a major restyle instead of a mere facelift, Lincoln did well in '56. Over 50,000 cars were built for the 12 months. This was still only about a third of Cadillac's total, but was encouraging to Lincoln, nevertheless.

Among the changes for '57 was the first entirely new body style since 1951, a four-door hardtop dubbed the Landau. Lincoln's response to a popular Detroit trend, the Landau was offered in both the Capri and Premiere lines. The Premiere convertible, priced at $5381, was still the most expensive model. Tailfins sprouted, and four-lamp front-end styling was adopted a bit in advance of most competitors. With 10:1 compression, the 368 V8 delivered up to 300 bhp. Lincoln had a good year in '57, but not a great one. It sold slightly more cars than Imperial, and pinned its hopes for '58 on yet another totally new design.

Model year 1958 proved to be a bad one considering the millions invested in new tooling. The economy bottomed out, and car sales dropped by 50 percent or more from '57 levels. Elsewhere at Ford, the Edsel was beginning its rapid slide to nowhere, Mercury sales were running 40 percent behind 1957, and Ford was trailing Chevrolet by a quarter-million units. The new Lincolns were longer, lower, and wider at a time when luxury-car buyers were thinking about more compact dimensions. Model year production accordingly dropped to about 17,000.

At the bottom of this avalanche stood the 1958 Lincoln, longer by six inches than the '57, with a 131-inch

1956 Premiere four-door sedan

1957 Capri four-door sedan

Futura show car (left) and 1956 Premiere hardtop coupe

1958 Premiere hardtop coupe

1957 Premiere hardtop coupe

1961 Continental hardtop sedan

wheelbase. It was easily recognized, for there wasn't much else like it: sharp tailfins, pointed front fenders carrying four headlights in slanted recesses, a heavily chromed grille, and gigantic flared bumpers. Under the hood was the largest engine used in an American passenger car for 1958—the 430-cid Continental V8 of 375 bhp. It could be argued the Lincoln formula was nevertheless right. Recession or not, most buyers in this class were still demanding cars like this. Yet, Cadillac was attracting more people with a less radical facelift, and Imperial was garnering residual sales with its finned wonders. The two rivals had recently expanded with new series and body styles, and Cadillac's comparable models were priced several hundred dollars lower than Lincoln's. It was the 1958 debacle that ushered in Elwood Engle and a three-year styling program that culminated in the all-new, razor-edged look for 1961.

In the meantime, Lincoln returned for 1959 with the only thing it had: more of the same. The Premiere convertible had been eliminated in '58, and the lineup stayed the same for another year. (Up ahead in price

was the Continental, still a make on its own and available in a similar array of body styles.) Sales now slid to near-crisis levels. Only about 7800 each of Capri and Premiere were sold. For the first time in history, Imperial surpassed Lincoln in model year production; and would do so again in 1960. Mechanically, the '59 Lincolns were '58s with less horsepower. In desperation, Lincoln held prices to about where they'd been.

For 1960, the two-year-old bodyshell was facelifted with a revised grille and front bumper. The massive bumper guards were moved inward of the canted headlights. The deck was redesigned, with taillights and backup lights set into a "rear grille" panel, rather than in the rear edges of the fenders. The roof and rear window were reshaped, and a full-length bodyside molding was applied. Standard equipment on both Lincoln and Lincoln Premiere included Twin-Range Turbo-Drive automatic, self-adjusting power brakes, power steering, heater and defroster, whitewall tires, undercoating, clock, windshield washers, radio, remote-control outside mirror, padded instrument panel and sunvisors, backup lights, parking brake warning light, and full

wheel covers. Premieres also came with power seat, power windows, and a rear compartment reading light.

Better things were in the making for 1961. In fact, the generation of sedans, convertibles, and hardtops that began that year was one of the most memorable of the decade. A classically beautiful design was combined with superb engineering to create the most satisfying Lincolns since the prewar K series.

The chiseled styling was the work of seven Ford designers, who received the annual award of the Industrial Designers Institute in June 1961. They were Eugene Bordinant, Don DeLaRossa, Elwood P. Engle, Gayle L. Halderman, John Najjar, Robert M. Thomas, and George Walker. The IDI, which rarely gives prizes to automobile designers, called the '61 Lincoln an "outstanding contribution of simplicity and design elegance."

Although the new car—now called Lincoln Continental—looked unique, it shared tooling ahead of the cowl with that year's revamped Thunderbird. This cut tooling costs for two low-production automobiles in half. However, the Continental was a big four-door car on a 123-inch wheelbase, the T-Bird was a two-door on a wheelbase 10 inches shorter.

Styling of the 1961 and later Lincolns involved a smooth-lined body surface set off with bright metal fender strips that ran uninterrupted from stem to stern, plus a modest grille composed of horizontal and vertical elements. The fenderline emphasis made all four fenders easily visible from behind the wheel, which helped maneuverability. In front view, the windows sloped inward toward the roof for the greatest angle of "tumblehome" yet seen on a large American luxury car, and marked one of the first uses of curved side glass in regular production.

The Continental convertible, offered through 1967, was the first four-door convertible sedan since Kaiser-Frazer's abortive 1951 Frazer Manhattan. Unlike the Frazer's, the Lincoln's side glass and window frames slid completely out of sight. So did its convertible top, with the help of 11 relays connecting mechanical and hydraulic linkages.

Aside from styling, the 1961 and later Lincolns were renowned for quality of construction. The man chiefly responsible for this was Harold C. MacDonald, chief engineer of Ford's Car and Truck Group. MacDonald created no startling innovations, but refined and perfected techniques that were already known. The new Lincolns had the most rigid unit body and chassis ever produced, the best sound insulation and shock damping in mass production, extremely close machining tolerances for all mechanical components, an unprecedented number of long-life service components, a completely sealed electrical system, and superior rust and corrosion protection.

Finally, Continental received the most thorough product testing ever applied by Detroit. Each engine was tested on a dynamometer at 3500 rpm (equal to about 98 mph) for three hours. Then it was torn down for

1962 Continental convertible sedan

1963 Continental hardtop sedan

1964 Continental hardtop sedan

inspection and reassembled. Every automatic transmission was tested for 30 minutes before installation. Each finished car was road tested for 12 miles and had to pass nearly 200 individual categories. Then, black light was used to visualize a fluorescent dye in the cars' lubricants as a check for oil leaks. As proof of the Continental's invulnerability, Lincoln offered a two-year, 24,000-mile warranty.

Public response to the new line was immediate and satisfying. Sales of the 1961s exceeded 25,000 units, and put Lincoln ahead of Imperial for keeps. Styling changes for the second and third year were minimal, since Lincoln had declared its intention to make improvements only for function and not simply for the sake of change. The '62 had a cleaner grille than the 1961 with a narrower central crossbar. Headlamps were not sunk into the grille, and contours were removed from the front bumper. The '63 had a square-textured

Lehmann-Peterson limousine based on 1964 Continental

1967 Continental hardtop coupe

1965 Continental hardtop sedan

1968 Continental hardtop coupe

1967 Continental four-door sedan

1969 Continental four-door sedan

grille, a restyled back panel appliqué, and increased trunk space.

For 1964, Lincoln wheelbase was extended to 126 inches, a length retained into the 1970s. The basic styling theme, however, remained the same. A slightly convex grille with vertical bars, a wider roof, a broader rear window, and a low-contour convertible top were the only major alterations.

Convertibles had always accounted for just a small fraction of total sales, usually about 10 percent. Lincoln wanted a more popular body style, and added a two-door hardtop coupe for 1966. Prices were cut across the board, and sales moved sharply upward as a result. The model year total was more than 54,000 units. Although still only 25 percent of Cadillac's figure, this was a Lincoln record.

Also for 1966, the Continental V8 was bored and stroked to 462 cid and remained in this form as the stan-

dard (and only) Lincoln powerplant until 1968. At that point, the cars received the 460 V8 from the Continental Mark III with 365 bhp at 4600 rpm.

The 1965 Lincoln had a new horizontal grille, combination parking and turn signal lights housed in the front fenders, and ribbed taillights. For 1966, the hood was lengthened for an increase in overall length of about five inches. Rear wheel cutouts were enlarged, and a slight hop-up appeared in the rear beltline. A new grille and front bumper were applied; the latter wrapped all the way back to the front wheel cutouts. Another grille-and-taillight shuffle and a spring-loaded hood emblem distinguished the '67s. The convertible put in its last appearance that year and saw only 2276 copies.

During 1967-68, Lehmann-Peterson Company built special-order Continental limousines on a 160-inch wheelbase. Also, Lincoln delivered two custom convertibles to the U.S. Secret Service for official functions.

These incorporated a variety of classified features, and replaced two other cars that had been in service for a decade. They were equipped with a retractable platform for Secret Service riders. Their rear doors were designed in two sections to allow agents to enter the moving car from the running boards through a 15-inch-wide space. The tops were made of transparent vinyl. A rear-facing seat behind the front seat, advanced electronic communications systems, a PA speaker, a siren, and emergency flasher lights were all part of the specification.

In October 1968, Lincoln delivered a Presidential limousine to the White House. This custom had a glass enclosure over the passenger compartment with a hinged center section so the occupants could stand up during a parade. The rear bumper of this 21-foot Continental could be lowered like a tailgate and converted into a platform for Secret Service agents. The limousine had more advanced security, communications, and engineering features than any other automobile ever used by the White House.

Accompanied by the new Continental Mark III, the Lincoln Continental sedan and coupe were the offerings for 1968. One of the easiest things to change for model identification are the front and rear treatments, so the '68s got a new horizontal texture at both ends. Front fenders housed three-function lights for turn signals, parking, and front side markers. The rear lights had four functions; turn signals, brake lights, taillamps, and rear side markers. Their clean design blended well with the fenderlines and allowed Lincoln to avoid clumsy, separate side marker lights as a means to meet government mandates.

For 1969, there was a new, squarish grille, with a raised center section extending into the hood. A Town Car interior option for the sedan provided "unique, super-puff leather-and-vinyl seats and door panels, luxury wood-tone front seat back and door trim inserts, extra plush carpeting and special napped nylon headlining." Government-required safety equipment included a dual hydraulic brake system with warning light, four-way emergency flasher, day/night rearview mirror, and energy-absorbing steering column and instrument panel. Continentals retained the 126-inch wheelbase, but overall length had grown to 224.5 inches.

Aside from hidden headlights and a more horizontal grille design, the 1970 Lincoln was similar to the '69 version. Ventless side glass, concealed wipers, wider doors, and full-width taillights were the major differences. The 460-cid engine with appropriate emission controls remained the sole powerplant.

By the end of the '60s, the Lincoln Continental had grown appreciably in size, if not in weight. Sales continued at a respectable level, for the marque had made many friends among luxury-car buyers. The Continental had always been a good performer (0 to 60 mph in 11 seconds, top speed 117 mph). Clean design, careful attention to quality control, and conservative but thorough engineering had produced a highly desirable luxury automobile.

1969 Continental hardtop coupe

1970 Continental four-door sedan

1969 Continental four-door sedan

1970 Continental four-door sedan

# Lincoln Specifications

## 1940

### 06H Zephyr (wb 125.0)

| | | Wght | Price | Prod |
|---|---|---|---|---|
| 56 | Continental conv cpe | 3,740 | 2,916 | 54 |
| 57 | Continental club cpe | 3,850 | 2,783 | 350 |
| 72A | cpe 3P | 3,500 | 1,399 | 1,256 |
| 72A | cpe 3P, Custom interior | 3,500 | 1,506 | |
| 72B | cpe, A/S | 3,480 | 1,429 | |
| 73 | sdn 4d | 3,660 | 1,439 | 15,764 |
| 73 | sdn 4d, Custom interior | 3,660 | 1,547 | |
| 76 | conv cpe | 3,760 | 1,818 | 700 |
| 77 | club cpe | 3,590 | 1,439 | 3,500 |
| 77 | club cpe, Custom interior | 3,590 | 1,547 | |
| 22 | Custom Town Limousine | 3,700 | 1,787 | 4 |
| 26 | Custom Town Car | 3,650 | 1,750 | 4 |

### K Series (wb 136.0)*

| | | | | |
|---|---|---|---|---|
| 404A | sdn 4d | 5,735 | 4,905 | — |
| 406 | cpe, Willoughby | 5,615 | 5,926 | — |
| 408 | conv Victoria, Brunn | 5,530 | 5,926 | — |
| 410 | rdstr, LeBaron | 5,505 | 5,313 | — |
| 412 | stationary cpe, LeBaron | 5,415 | 5,313 | — |

### K Series (wb 145.0)*

| | | | | |
|---|---|---|---|---|
| 407A | sdn 4d, 7P | 5,880 | 5,109 | — |
| 407B | limo | 5,970 | 5,211 | — |
| 409 | cabriolet, Brunn | 6,010 | 6,947 | — |
| 411 | brougham 7P, Brunn | 6,120 | 7,049 | — |
| 413 | conv sdn, LeBaron | 5,670 | 5,823 | — |
| 415 | sdn limo 7P, Judkins | 5,950 | 6,334 | — |
| 417A | berline 2W, Judkins | 5,770 | 6,028 | — |
| 417B | berline 3W, Judkins | 5,840 | 6,130 | — |
| 419 | limo, Willoughby | 6,140 | 6,232 | — |
| 421 | spt sdn, Willoughby | 6,300 | 7,049 | — |
| 425 | cabriolet 2P, Brunn | 5,870 | 7,253 | — |

*Total K Series model year production: 133.

| 1940 Engines | bore×stroke | bhp | availability |
|---|---|---|---|
| V12, 292.0 | 3.88×3.75 | 120 | S-Zephyr |
| V12, 414.0 | 3.13×4.50 | 150 | S-K Series |

## 1941

### 16H Zephyr (wb 125.0)

| | | Wght | Price | Prod |
|---|---|---|---|---|
| 72A | cpe 3P | 3,560 | 1,478 | 972 |
| 72A | cpe 3P, Custom interior | 3,560 | 1,557 | |
| 73 | sdn 4d | 3,710 | 1,541 | 14,469 |
| 73 | sdn 4d, Custom interior | 3,710 | 1,641 | |
| 76 | conv cpe | 3,840 | 1,858 | 725 |
| 77 | club cpe | 3,640 | 1,541 | 178 |
| 77 | club cpe, Custom interior | 3,640 | 1,541 | |

### 16H Continental (wb 125.0)

| | | | | |
|---|---|---|---|---|
| 56 | conv cpe ("cabriolet") | 3,860 | 2,865 | 400 |
| 57 | club cpe | 3,890 | 2,812 | 850 |

### 168H Custom (wb 138.0)

| | | | | |
|---|---|---|---|---|
| 31 | sdn 4d, 8P | 4,250 | 2,704 | 355 |
| 32 | limo | 4,270 | 2,836 | 295 |

| 1941 Engine | bore×stroke | bhp | availability |
|---|---|---|---|
| V12, 292.0 | 2.88×3.75 | 120 | S-all |

## 1942

### 26H Zephyr (wb 125.0)

| | | Wght | Price | Prod |
|---|---|---|---|---|
| 72A | cpe 3P | 3,730 | 1,650 | 1,236 |
| 72A | cpe 3P, Custom interior | 3,730 | 1,735 | |

| | | Wght | Price | Prod |
|---|---|---|---|---|
| 73 | sdn 4d | 3,920 | 1,700 | 4,418 |
| 73 | sdn 4d, Custom interior | 3,920 | 1,795 | |
| 76 | conv cpe | 4,130 | 2,150 | 191 |
| 77 | club cpe | 3,810 | 1,700 | 253 |
| 77 | club cpe, Custom interior | 3,810 | 1,795 | |

### 26H Continental (wb 125.0)

| | | | | |
|---|---|---|---|---|
| 56 | conv cpe ("cabriolet") | 4,020 | 3,000 | 136 |
| 57 | club cpe | 4,000 | 3,000 | 200 |

### 268H Custom (wb 138.0)

| | | | | |
|---|---|---|---|---|
| 31 | sdn 4d, 8P | 4,380 | 2,950 | 47 |
| 32 | limo | 4,400 | 3,075 | 66 |

| 1942 Engine | bore×stroke | bhp | availability |
|---|---|---|---|
| V12, 305.0 | 2.94×3.75 | 130 | S-all |

## 1946

### 66H (wb 125.0)—16,179 built

| | | Wght | Price | Prod |
|---|---|---|---|---|
| 73 | sdn 4d | 3,980 | 2,337 | — |
| 73 | sdn 4d, Custom interior | 3,980 | 2,486 | — |
| 76 | conv cpe | 4,210 | 2,883 | — |
| 77 | club cpe | 3,380 | 2,318 | — |
| 77 | club cpe, Custom interior | 3,380 | 2,467 | — |

### 66H Continental (wb 125.0)

| | | | | |
|---|---|---|---|---|
| 56 | conv cpe ("cabriolet") | 4,090 | 4,474 | 201 |
| 57 | club cpe | 4,100 | 4,392 | 265 |

| 1946 Engine | bore×stroke | bhp | availability |
|---|---|---|---|
| V12, 292.0 | 2.88×3.75 | 125 | S-all |

## 1947

### 76H (wb 125.0)—19,891 built

| | | Wght | Price | Prod |
|---|---|---|---|---|
| 73 | sdn 4d | 4,015 | 2,554 | — |
| 73 | sdn 4d, Custom interior | 4,015 | 2,722 | — |
| 76 | conv cpe | 4,245 | 3,142 | — |
| 77 | club cpe | 3,915 | 2,533 | — |
| 77 | club cpe, Custom interior | 3,915 | 2,701 | — |

### 76H Continental (wb 125.0)

| | | | | |
|---|---|---|---|---|
| 56 | conv cpe ("cabriolet") | 4,135 | 4,746 | 738 |
| 57 | club cpe | 4,125 | 4,662 | 831 |

| 1947 Engine | bore×stroke | bhp | availability |
|---|---|---|---|
| V12, 292.0 | 2.88×3.75 | 125 | S-all |

## 1948

### 876H (wb 125.0)—6,470 built

| | | Wght | Price | Prod |
|---|---|---|---|---|
| 73 | sdn 4d | 4,015 | 2,554 | — |
| 73 | sdn 4d, Custom interior | 4,015 | 2,722 | — |
| 76 | conv cpe | 4,245 | 3,142 | — |
| 77 | club cpe | 3,915 | 2,533 | — |
| 77 | club cpe, Custom interior | 3,915 | 2,701 | — |

### 876H Continental (wb 125.0)

| | | | | |
|---|---|---|---|---|
| 56 | conv cpe ("cabriolet") | 4,135 | 4,746 | 452 |
| 57 | club cpe | 4,125 | 4,662 | 847 |

| 1948 Engine | bore×stroke | bhp | availability |
|---|---|---|---|
| V12, 292.0 | 2.88×3.75 | 125 | S-all |

## 1949

### 9EL (wb 121.0)—38,384 built

| | | Wght | Price | Prod |
|---|---|---|---|---|
| | cpe | 3,959 | 2,527 | — |
| | Sport Sedan 4d | 4,009 | 2,575 | — |
| | conv cpe | 4,224 | 3,116 | — |

# Lincoln

| 9EH Cosmopolitan (wb 125.0)—35,123 built | | Wght | Price | Prod |
|---|---|---|---|---|
| | cpe | 4,194 | 3,186 | — |
| | Sport Sedan 4d | 4,259 | 3,238 | — |
| | Town sdn 4d | 4,274 | 3,238 | — |
| | conv cpe | 4,419 | 3,948 | — |

| 1949 Engine | bore×stroke | bhp | availability |
|---|---|---|---|
| V8, 336.7 | 3.50×4.38 | 152 | S-all |

## 1950

| 0EL (wb 121.0) | | Wght | Price | Prod |
|---|---|---|---|---|
| L-72 | cpe | 4,090 | 2,529 | 5,748 |
| L-72C | Lido cpe | 4,145 | 2,721 | |
| L-74 | Sport Sedan 4d | 4,115 | 2,576 | 11,741 |

| 0EH Cosmopolitan (wb 125.0) | | | | |
|---|---|---|---|---|
| H-72 | cpe | 4,375 | 3,187 | 1,824 |
| H-72C | Capri cpe | 4,385 | 3,406 | |
| H-74 | Sport Sedan 4d | 4,410 | 3,240 | 8,341 |
| H-76 | conv cpe | 4,640 | 3,950 | 536 |

| 1950 Engine | bore×stroke | bhp | availability |
|---|---|---|---|
| V8, 336.7 | 3.50×4.38 | 152 | S-all |

## 1951

| 1EL (wb 121.0) | | Wght | Price | Prod |
|---|---|---|---|---|
| L-72B | cpe | 4,065 | 2,505 | 4,482 |
| L-72C | Lido cpe | 4,100 | 2,702 | |
| L-74 | Sport Sedan 4d | 4,130 | 2,553 | 12,279 |

| 1EH Cosmopolitan (wb 125.0) | | | | |
|---|---|---|---|---|
| H-72B | cpe | 4,340 | 3,129 | 2,727 |
| H-72C | Capri cpe | 4,360 | 3,350 | |
| H-74 | Sport Sedan 4d | 4,415 | 3,182 | 12,229 |
| H-76 | conv cpe | 4,615 | 3,891 | 857 |

| 1951 Engine | bore×stroke | bhp | availability |
|---|---|---|---|
| V8, 336.7 | 3.50×4.38 | 154 | S-all |

## 1952

| 2H Cosmopolitan (wb 123.0) | | Wght | Price | Prod |
|---|---|---|---|---|
| 60C | Spt htp cpe | 4,155 | 3,293 | 4,545 |
| 73A | sdn 4d | 4,125 | 3,198 | * |

| 2H Capri (wb 123.0) | | | | |
|---|---|---|---|---|
| 60A | htp cpe | 4,235 | 3,518 | 5,681 |
| 73B | sdn 4d | 4,140 | 3,331 | * |
| 76A | conv cpe | 4,350 | 3,665 | 1,191 |

*Combined sedan production: 15,854.

| 1952 Engine | bore×stroke | bhp | availability |
|---|---|---|---|
| V8, 317.5 | 3.80×3.50 | 160 | S-all |

## 1953

| 8H Cosmopolitan (wb 123.0) | | Wght | Price | Prod |
|---|---|---|---|---|
| 60C | Sport htp cpe | 4,155 | 3,322 | 6,562 |
| 73A | sdn 4d | 4,135 | 3,226 | 7,560 |

| 8H Capri (wb 123.0) | | | | |
|---|---|---|---|---|
| 60A | htp cpe | 4,165 | 3,549 | 12,916 |
| 73B | sdn 4d | 4,150 | 3,453 | 11,352 |
| 76A | conv cpe | 4,310 | 3,699 | 2,372 |

| 1953 Engine | bore×stroke | bhp | availability |
|---|---|---|---|
| V8, 317.5 | 3.80×3.50 | 205 | S-all |

## 1954

| Cosmopolitan (wb 123.0) | | Wght | Price | Prod |
|---|---|---|---|---|
| 60C | Sport htp cpe | 4,155 | 3,625 | 2,994 |
| 73A | sdn 4d | 4,135 | 3,522 | 4,447 |

| Capri (wb 123.0) | | | | |
|---|---|---|---|---|
| 60A | htp cpe | 4,250 | 3,869 | 14,003 |
| 73B | sdn 4d | 4,245 | 3,711 | 13,598 |
| 76A | conv cpe | 4,310 | 4,031 | 1,951 |

| 1954 Engine | bore×stroke | bhp | availability |
|---|---|---|---|
| V8, 317.5 | 3.80×3.50 | 205 | S-all |

## 1955

| Custom (wb 123.0) | | Wght | Price | Prod |
|---|---|---|---|---|
| 60C | Sport htp cpe | 4,185 | 3,666 | 1,362 |
| 73A | sdn 4d | 4,235 | 3,563 | 2,187 |

| Capri (wb 123.0) | | | | |
|---|---|---|---|---|
| 60A | htp cpe | 4,305 | 3,910 | 11,462 |
| 73B | sdn 4d | 4,245 | 3,752 | 10,724 |
| 76A | conv cpe | 4,415 | 4,072 | 1,487 |

| 1955 Engine | bore×stroke | bhp | availability |
|---|---|---|---|
| V8, 341.0 | 3.94×3.50 | 225 | S-all |

## 1956

| Capri (wb 126.0) | | Wght | Price | Prod |
|---|---|---|---|---|
| 60E | Sport htp cpe | 4,305 | 4,119 | 4,355 |
| 73A | sdn 4d | 4,315 | 4,212 | 4,436 |

| Premiere (wb 126.0) | | | | |
|---|---|---|---|---|
| 60B | htp cpe | 4,357 | 4,601 | 19,619 |
| 73B | sdn 4d | 4,347 | 4,601 | 19,465 |
| 76B | conv cpe | 4,452 | 4,747 | 2,447 |

| 1956 Engine | bore×stroke | bhp | availability |
|---|---|---|---|
| V8, 368.0 | 4.00×3.66 | 285 | S-all |

## 1957

| Capri (wb 126.0) | | Wght | Price | Prod |
|---|---|---|---|---|
| 57A | Landau htp sdn | 4,460 | 4,794 | 1,451 |
| 58A | sdn 4d | 4,349 | 4,794 | 1,476 |
| 60A | htp cpe | 4,373 | 4,649 | 2,973 |

| Premiere (wb 126.0) | | | | |
|---|---|---|---|---|
| 57B | Landau htp sdn | 4,538 | 5,294 | 11,223 |
| 58B | sdn 4d | 4,527 | 5,294 | 5,139 |
| 60B | htp cpe | 4,451 | 5,149 | 15,185 |
| 76B | conv cpe | 4,676 | 5,381 | 3,676 |

| 1957 Engine | bore×stroke | bhp | availability |
|---|---|---|---|
| V8, 368.0 | 4.00×3.66 | 300 | S-all |

## 1958

| Capri (wb 131.0) | | Wght | Price | Prod |
|---|---|---|---|---|
| 53A | sdn 4d | 4,799 | 4,951 | 1,184 |
| 57A | Landau htp sdn | 4,810 | 4,951 | 3,084 |
| 63A | htp cpe | 4,735 | 4,803 | 2,591 |

| Premiere (wb 131.0) | | Wght | Price | Prod |
|---|---|---|---|---|
| 53B | sdn 4d | 4,869 | 5,565 | 1,660 |
| 57B | Landau htp sdn | 4,880 | 5,565 | 5,572 |
| 63B | htp cpe | 4,820 | 5,318 | 3,043 |

| 1958 Engine | bore×stroke | bhp | availability | |
|---|---|---|---|---|
| V8, 430.0 | 4.30×3.70 | 375 | S-all | |

## 1959

| Capri (wb 131.0) | | Wght | Price | Prod |
|---|---|---|---|---|
| 53A | sdn 4d | 4,823 | 5,090 | 1,312 |
| 57A | htp sdn | 4,824 | 5,090 | 4,417 |
| 63A | htp cpe | 4,741 | 4,902 | 2,200 |

| Premiere (wb 131.0) | | Wght | Price | Prod |
|---|---|---|---|---|
| 53B | sdn 4d | 4,887 | 5,594 | 1,282 |
| 57B | htp sdn | 4,880 | 5,594 | 4,606 |
| 63B | htp cpe | 4,700 | 5,347 | 1,963 |

| 1959 Engine | bore×stroke | bhp | availability | |
|---|---|---|---|---|
| V8, 430.0 | 4.30×3.70 | 350 | S-all | |

## 1960

| (wb 131.0) | | Wght | Price | Prod |
|---|---|---|---|---|
| 53A | sdn 4d | 5,016 | 5,441 | 1,093 |
| 57A | Landau htp sdn | 5,012 | 5,441 | 4,397 |
| 63A | htp cpe | 4,917 | 5,253 | 1,670 |

| Premiere (wb 131.0) | | Wght | Price | Prod |
|---|---|---|---|---|
| 53B | sdn 4d | 5,064 | 5,945 | 1,010 |
| 57B | Landau htp sdn | 5,060 | 5,945 | 4,200 |
| 63B | htp cpe | 4,965 | 5,698 | 1,364 |

| 1960 Engine | bore×stroke | bhp | availability | |
|---|---|---|---|---|
| V8, 430.0 | 4.30×3.70 | 315 | S-all | |

## 1961

| Continental (wb 123.0) | | Wght | Price | Prod |
|---|---|---|---|---|
| 53A | htp sdn | 4,927 | 6,067 | 22,303 |
| 57C | htp sdn, special model | — | — | 4 |
| 74A | conv sdn | 5,215 | 6,713 | 2,857 |

| 1961 Engine | bore×stroke | bhp | availability | |
|---|---|---|---|---|
| V8, 430.0 | 4.30×3.70 | 300 | S-all | |

## 1962

| Continental (wb 123.0) | | Wght | Price | Prod |
|---|---|---|---|---|
| 53A | htp sdn | 4,966 | 6,074 | 27,849 |
| 74A | conv sdn | 5,370 | 6,720 | 3,212 |

| 1962 Engine | bore×stroke | bhp | availability | |
|---|---|---|---|---|
| V8, 430.0 | 4.30×3.70 | 300 | S-all | |

## 1963

| Continental (wb 123.0) | | Wght | Price | Prod |
|---|---|---|---|---|
| 53A | htp sdn | 4,936 | 6,270 | 28,095 |
| 74A | conv sdn | 5,340 | 6,916 | 3,138 |

| 1963 Engine | bore×stroke | bhp | availability | |
|---|---|---|---|---|
| V8, 430.0 | 4.30×3.70 | 320 | S-all | |

## 1964

| Continental (wb 126.0) | | Wght | Price | Prod |
|---|---|---|---|---|
| 82 | htp sdn | 5,055 | 6,292 | 33,969 |
| 86 | conv sdn | 5,393 | 6,938 | 3,328 |

| 1964 Engine | bore×stroke | bhp | availability | |
|---|---|---|---|---|
| V8, 430.0 | 4.30×3.70 | 320 | S-all | |

## 1965

| Continental (wb 126.0) | | Wght | Price | Prod |
|---|---|---|---|---|
| 82 | htp sdn | 5,075 | 6,292 | 36,824 |
| 86 | conv sdn | 5,475 | 6,938 | 3,356 |

| 1965 Engine | bore×stroke | bhp | availability | |
|---|---|---|---|---|
| V8, 430.0 | 4.30×3.70 | 320 | S-all | |

## 1966

| Continental (wb 126.0) | | Wght | Price | Prod |
|---|---|---|---|---|
| 82 | sdn 4d | 5,085 | 5,750 | 35,809 |
| 86 | conv sdn | 5,480 | 6,383 | 3,180 |
| 89 | htp cpe | 4,985 | 5,485 | 15,766 |

| 1966 Engine | bore×stroke | bhp | availability | |
|---|---|---|---|---|
| V8, 462.0 | 4.38×3.83 | 340 | S-all | |

## 1967

| Continental (wb 126.0) | | Wght | Price | Prod |
|---|---|---|---|---|
| 82 | sdn 4d | 5,049 | 5,795 | 33,331 |
| 86 | conv sdn | 5,505 | 6,449 | 2,276 |
| 89 | htp cpe | 4,940 | 5,553 | 11,060 |

| 1967 Engine | bore×stroke | bhp | availability | |
|---|---|---|---|---|
| V8, 462.0 | 4.38×3.83 | 340 | S-all | |

## 1968

| Continental (wb 126.0) | | Wght | Price | Prod |
|---|---|---|---|---|
| 81 | htp cpe | 4,883 | 5,736 | 9,415 |
| 82 | sdn 4d | 4,978 | 5,970 | 29,719 |

| 1968 Engine | bore×stroke | bhp | availability | |
|---|---|---|---|---|
| V8, 460.0 | 4.36×3.85 | 365 | S-all | |

## 1969

| Continental (wb 126.0) | | Wght | Price | Prod |
|---|---|---|---|---|
| 81 | htp cpe | 4,910 | 5,830 | 9,032 |
| 82 | sdn 4d | 5,005 | 6,063 | 29,258 |

| 1969 Engine | bore×stroke | bhp | availability | |
|---|---|---|---|---|
| V8, 460.0 | 4.36×3.85 | 365 | S-all | |

## 1970

| Continental (wb 126.0) | | Wght | Price | Prod |
|---|---|---|---|---|
| 81 | htp cpe | 4,669 | 5,976 | 9,073 |
| 82 | sdn 4d | 4,719 | 6,211 | 28,622 |

| 1970 Engine | bore×stroke | bhp | availability | |
|---|---|---|---|---|
| V8, 460.0 | 4.36×3.85 | 365 | S-all | |

# Mercury

**Ford Motor Company (Lincoln-Mercury Division from 1947)**
**Dearborn, Michigan**

Mercury was conceived largely by Edsel Ford, who saw a place for it in the market some time before his father did. It was announced in late 1938 as a '39 model. In price, Mercury was in the same field as the eight-cylinder Pontiac and somewhat below Oldsmobile, precisely where Edsel Ford wanted it—and where Ford Motor Company needed it. While Mercury never approached the volume of those popular GM makes, it did average about 80,000 cars per year in the early '40s. This put it in 12th or 13th place in the industry, and brought the corporation important sales in the market sector between Lincoln-Zephyr and Ford.

The engine introduced with the original Mercury remained in production through 1948. It was an L-head V8 slightly larger than the Ford V8/85, having the same bore but a longer stroke. Until 1942, it produced 95 horsepower at 3600 rpm; from 1942 through '48, output was 100 bhp at 3800 rpm. Mercury quickly gained a reputation for performance equal to its name. Well-tuned models in stock form were quicker than the V8/85, and were usually capable of turning close to 100 mph.

Mercury's wheelbase was not much longer than the more expensive Ford's, but it was sufficient to balance the lines and make the car look larger than the Ford. The dash was similar to Ford's, using strip-type instruments. Mercury exclaimed about its column-mounted gearlever.

The car's 1940 styling was Ford-like: a crisp, pointed nose; flush-mounted headlamps; and rounded lines that tapered to a beetle back. There were five body styles priced from $946 to $1212. The convertible sedan was a new addition for 1940: the heaviest and most expensive model in the line. But the convertible sedan's popularity had declined by the early '40s, so Mercury discontinued its version the following year after a run of only about 1000 units.

Sales were brisk in 1940, and Mercury looked for still greater success with its restyled '41 line. Seven different models were offered, including a 2/4-passenger coupe, business coupe, and station wagon. Styling, again in the Ford mold, was chunky and awkward. Longer, higher, squared-off fenders were accompanied by a divider-bar grille and fender-mounted parking lights.

Mercury tried harder in 1942 with a serious facelift, 100-bhp engines, and a clutchless transmission called Liquidmatic. But the war prevented a full model run. Chrome was "in," at least before government regulations restricted its use. The '42s wore a broad, glittery two-section grille composed of massive horizontal bars. Double chrome bands were applied to front and rear fenders, and a bright beltline molding ran completely around the hood. Parking lights were shifted inboard, but prominent chrome moldings remained on the tops of the front fenders. The general effect was busier than the '41 design, which had been busier than the 1940. Distinctly more elaborate styling seemed to be developing.

At the close of the war, when Henry Ford II returned from the Navy to run the firm, Ford Motor Company moved back quickly into civilian car production. Mercury reached tenth place in 1946, producing 86,808 units. Though plans had been laid for an all-new postwar design, the company decided to stay with its prewar model for a few years. The '46 Mercury was therefore quite similar to the '42. The inboard parking lights and two-band fender moldings remained, but the grille was reshaped with a vertical-bar motif, and the hood ornament was blended into the hood. The words "Mercury Eight" were prominently displayed front and center. Mechanically, the car was unchanged. A possible disadvantage was that it still shared its engine with the lower-priced Ford.

In 1946, the business coupe was replaced by the novel Sportsman convertible, comparable to Ford's Sportsman. Designated model 71, it was a convertible coupe with woodwork—maple or yellow birch framing mahogany inserts. The paneling was structural, not merely decorative. This created a problem at the rear, where the standard production fenders could not be fitted. To solve this, the company used 1941 sedan delivery fenders, and designed the wooden structure around them. The frame was constructed of solid wood, mitred together with beautiful craftsmanship and finished with multiple coats of varnish.

The Mercury Sportsman cost over $200 more than its Ford counterpart. Ford produced quite a few, but Mercury made only 205. Ford continued the Sportsman through 1948, but it was dropped from the Mercury lineup after '46.

An important corporate realignment in 1947 was the organization of Lincoln-Mercury Division. Up to that time, Lincoln and Mercury had been intrinsic parts of Ford, but Henry Ford II decided that the two makes could be more competitive as an autonomous operation, in the style of the various General Motors divisions. Lincoln-Mercury has remained a separate division ever since.

The 1947 Mercurys were proof that raw materials that had been scarce during World War II were now in greater supply: aluminum pistons and hood ornament, chrome-plated interior hardware, and a chrome grille frame rather than a painted one. Dashboard gauges were more legible than before, having silver letters on black backgrounds. The beltline molding no longer wrapped around the hood, but stopped just ahead of the cowl. Body styles decreased to five with the deletion of the Sportsman. Prices increased by about $150 model for model. Production of the glittery '47s didn't begin until February of that year, so model year output was

1940 convertible sedan

1941 Town Sedan

1942 convertible coupe

Wartime proposal for postwar front-end styling

1947 Town Sedan

1949 restyle taking shape on 1946 clay model

about the same as the year before.

No changes at all were recorded for 1948, and the only identification for these models was their serial numbers. Mercury offered the same body styles and prices (less the two-door sedan), and sold 1948-model cars from November 1947 until mid-April 1948, when the '49s appeared. As a result, 1948 production was the lowest for any postwar year.

Mercury was fully restyled for '49 with smooth, curving lines that made it appear much longer than before—though its 118-inch wheelbase was the same as before. In fact, it shared its bodyshell with the smaller 1949 Lincoln. Initial planning had called for a new Lincoln-Zephyr in this position. Mercury was to use a 116-inch wheelbase and Ford a shorter one. But management decided a smaller Ford was unnecessary, so the Zephyr was dropped in favor of the new Mercury. Styling was

good—clean, massive, streamlined. The new grille retained a resemblance to the '48 design, but was lower and wider, and had a faired-in cavity. A single piece of bright metal decorated the flanks. Overall, it was a pleasing style that still looks good today. The 1949 models quickly became hot items among customizers, who gave them special grilles, lowered bodies, and skirted rear fenders. The tail-dragging custom Merc, with cruiser skirts, foxtail, and fog lights, became a common sight around high schools in the '50s.

The 1949 Mercury also benefited from a heftier engine: the L-head had been stroked 0.25 inch for a displacement of 255.4 cubic inches, and delivered 110 bhp at 3600 rpm. Dual downdraft Holley carburetors were standard. Mercury thus became a genuine 100-mph car for the first time. Also introduced was an automatic overdrive option priced at $97, teamed up with a 4.27:1 rear

axle ratio instead of the standard 3.90:1. Mercury remained a one-series make. There were no "deluxe" versions until 1950.

The 1949-51 Mercury was an excellent value, considering it was styled like the Lincoln but had a lower price. Its V8 was about 12 percent larger than Ford's and offered 15 more horsepower. Many felt this made up for the Mercury's extra 300-some pounds in curb weight.

Essentially, the 1950-51 line consisted of only one series, but within it was a variety of new offerings. These included the Monterey, a low-production sport coupe with special trim and a padded top of either canvas or leather. Mercury would get a true hardtop, but somewhat later than its GM and Chrysler competitors. Monterey filled the gap in the meantime.

The 1950 and '51 models were very much alike. The

'51 had a semicircular crest and Mercury name above the grille, while the '50 had the name spelled out on a hood chrome strip and the crest was smaller. Parking light housings were larger on the '51, sweeping back to the front wheel wells. The '51s also used a different rear fender treatment—more upright, with rounded corners dropping straight down to the rear bumper. Mercury's V8 developed 100 bhp in 1950, 112 in 1951. And '51 was the first year for Merc-O-Matic, the two-speed automatic developed in cooperation with the Warner Gear Division of Borg-Warner. Mercury ran sixth in production in both 1949 and 1951.

Ford Motor Company was the only maker to introduce completely new styling for 1952, and Mercury received the same sort of tight, clean lines as that year's Lincoln. Wheelbase length was unchanged. The L-head V8 was retained, but power was boosted to 125

1949 eight-passenger station wagon

1951 Sport Sedan

1949 convertible

1952 Custom hardtop coupe

1950 coupe

1953 Monterey four-door sedan

bhp by means of a higher compression ratio.

For 1953, Mercury did some model shuffling, and emerged with two series. The Custom offered two- and four-door sedans and a hardtop. The Monterey became a separate series offering convertible, hardtop, wagon, and sedan. Monterey sedans were luxuriously upholstered in quality broadcloth; convertibles and hardtops used leather and vinyl. Solid colors were used for the sedan, but the hardtop came with two-tone paint standard. The dashboard was interesting, with aircraft-type toggle levers for heating and ventilation flanking a central gauge cluster. Sales fell along with those of the rest of the industry in 1952, partly because of Korean War restrictions on production. Yet the restyled line accounted for over 170,000 units, enough to put Mercury in eighth place. Business picked up in 1953 as Mercury built over 300,000 cars—though staying in eighth.

A significant engineering change was made for 1954 as Mercury joined Ford in a switch to the overhead-valve V8. Mercury's version was the same size as its previous L-head, but had squarer bore-and-stroke dimensions. With a low 3.9:1 rear axle ratio and standard transmission, the '54 was a fast car off the line. The new engine used a five-main-bearing crankshaft and came in standard form with a four-barrel carburetor. Another major mechanical change was the use of ball-joint front suspension. Styling was measurably improved by the addition of wraparound taillights and a clean grille. The model lineup stayed the same, except for the addition of one new model that is more famous today than it was then: the Monterey Sun Valley.

Ford's styling department had for some time experimented with plastic-topped cars: the Sun Valley (and the companion Ford Skyliner) was the result. In theory, it was sort of a cross between the airy convertible and the comfortable closed hardtop. In practice, it was something else. Though the plastic front half of the roof was tinted and a shade provided for really hot weather, customers complained the interior heated up like an oven. Predictably, sales weren't impressive. The '54 Sun Valley was the most attractive of this short-lived breed. It came in select color combinations of yellow or mint green to complement its dark green top. Embellished with gold-anodized fender script, it was a handsome automobile. The price, however, was forbidding. Mercury was more successful with the '54 Sun Valley than with the '55 version, which sold only 1787 copies. The glasstop was then dropped—to nobody's great surprise.

At 260,000 units, 1954 wasn't the greatest sales year ever, but there were high hopes for 1955. With all-new styling, a new V8, and the first wheelbase increase since 1941, the '55 couldn't miss, and over 329,000 were run up. It was the most appealing Mercury in years, offered in more models and series than ever before.

The line leader that season was the brand-new Montclair, offered as a four-door sedan, hardtop, convertible, and Sun Valley. Nicely styled, it used an evolutionary form of the '54 grille, and was distinguished by a thin color panel outlined in bright metal under the side windows. Next came the Monterey sedan, hardtop, and wagon, followed by the Custom series with the same body styles plus a two-door sedan. The standard Custom and Monterey engine was a 188-bhp 292-cid V8. For Montclair, and optional on other models, was a 198-bhp version with an 8.5:1 compression ratio, offered only with Merc-O-Matic transmission.

1954 Monterey hardtop coupe

1954 Monterey Sun Valley coupe

1955 Monterey four-door sedan

TV host Ed Sullivan announced the "Big M" line for '56, an ambitious expansion into somewhat uncharted territory. Prices were on the rise, so to stay competitive Mercury offered the cut-rate Medalist for the bottom-line buyer. There was a full range of body styles: two- and four-door hardtops and two- and four-door sedans. Unfortunately, inflation took its toll. The "low-priced" Medalist was actually more expensive than the previous year's Custom. At the same time, it wasn't priced far enough below the better-trimmed 1956 Custom. Although Lincoln-Mercury dealers pushed hard with the price-leading two-door sedan, a total of only 45,812 Medalists were sold. Customs, Montereys, and Montclairs all surpassed the Medalist by at least double its production, and the series was accordingly dropped for 1957. Curiously, it reappeared in '58, interfering in a price bracket that should have been sole territory for the new Edsel.

The '56 facelift was a useful update of the '55 styling. Side moldings were connected front-to-back in a sort of lightning-bolt motif that was attractive and looked new. Four-door hardtops now arrived in force in all four series. Known as Phaetons, they sold well, out-selling the standard four-door sedan in the Montclair series. Throughout the line, Mercury used an enlarged V8 that provided 210 bhp in standard form, up to 235 bhp for Monterey and Montclair. It was a downbeat year for the auto industry, but Mercury was an exception. Some 328,000 rolled off the lines, a bit below the '55 pace. Most promising was the Montclair, which managed to sell almost as well as it had in 1955. It was positioned in a higher price bracket than Monterey, however, and the junior model continued to be emphasized as Mercury's breadwinner.

In 1957, everyone's eyes were on the Turnpike Cruiser—a "dramatic expression of dream car design" offered as the top-of-the-line series in two- and four-door hardtop and convertible form. It had, Mercury thought, just about everything. There was the "skylight dual curve windshield" and a retractable, reverse-slanted rear window. There were dual air intakes over the windshield corners that housed little protruding radio antennae. There was even the creatively named "Seat-O-Matic" device, which automatically adjusted the driver's seat to any one of 49 preset positions at the twist of a dial. The Cruiser used pushbuttons like Chrysler's to control its Merc-O-Matic transmission. The convertible was a replica of the 1957 Indy pace car. Despite all the gadgetry, the Cruiser failed miserably. It was priced too high, for one thing. And while it could be said that today's kitsch was high style in the '50s, the Cruiser was too far out even then.

For the rest of the line, 1957 brought a major redesign on a new 122-inch-wheelbase chassis. A full range of Montereys and Montclairs was offered. Station wagons were made a separate series, with no fewer than six entries. There was a Colony Park four-door nine-seater, a Voyager in the same configuration along with a two-door version, and three Commuters with the various

1957 Monterey two-door sedan

1957 Turnpike Cruiser hardtop sedan

1957 Turnpike Cruiser convertible

1958 Park Lane Phaeton hardtop coupe

seat and door combinations. It was a complex lineup, but fairly successful. The Big M had grown a bit heavy-looking by '57, with big, oblong bumpers up front. The Turnpike Cruiser with its quad headlights looked even weightier. The V8 had grown commensurately, and now offered up to 290 bhp.

Similar, slightly quieter styling was offered for 1958, but the year was a disaster. From 286,000 units in 1957, production fell to 153,000. The Turnpike Cruiser was

1959 Monterey hardtop coupe

1962 Comet S-22 two-door sedan

1962 Meteor two-door sedan

1964 Comet Cyclone hardtop coupe

made an upper model in the Montclair series. The Medalist was back for a short encore, with two- and four-door sedans attempting to reach into the low-price field. Again, sales were disappointing: only 18,732. Up in the higher bracket above Montclair came the new Park Lane hardtops and convertible, ostensibly to replace the Turnpike Cruiser, with less outlandish looks and the 430-cid Lincoln V8. The same group of station wagons was offered, and a new automatic

called Multi-Drive made its debut.

What had happened was that the bottom had dropped out of the middle-priced market. This is evident from the fact that Mercury didn't lose its eighth place position in 1958, despite building only 40 percent of its '57 volume. But significantly, an independent from Kenosha had passed Mercury in sales and was gaining fast on Pontiac, Olds, and Buick. The Rambler revolution was underway. In its wake, Mercury would never be the same.

A little more of the same old stuff had to be cleared out before Mercury joined the rush to compacts and intermediates. Accordingly, the '59s were given a longer chassis that resulted in a more conventional full-width grille and an extension of the odd concave rear fender styling of 1957-58. The Medalist and Turnpike Cruiser were blessedly forgotten as the line thinned to four: Monterey, Montclair, Park Lane, and Station Wagon. Even these survivors were severely cropped. The Montclair went down from six models to just four, and there were only four varieties of wagons. Despite retrenchment, Mercury built 150,000 cars—hardly the improvement expected. A new engine for '58 was the 383-cid V8—same displacement as Chrysler's engine but with more oversquare dimensions. It was standard equipment for Montclair and station wagons.

In the '60s, Mercury evolved through a plethora of models, sizes, body types, and wheelbases, complicated by several changes in model names from year to year. This is perhaps symbolic of the make's mixed fortunes during the decade and its struggle to make improvements. Despite the confusion, many familiar names at the start of the decade were still around toward its end. Comet and Monterey spanned the entire 10 years; Montclairs and Park Lanes were still being offered in '68. Meteor, the long-time brand for a Canadian-made Mercury derivative, was seen on two different U.S. models between 1961 and 1963.

The first American Meteor appeared as a budget-priced version of the '61 full-size Mercury Monterey. 600 and 800 series were offered, powered by the 223-cid overhead-valve Ford six. Although Meteor actually outsold Monterey in '61, it was replaced the following year by a basic Monterey as the Meteor name went on Mercury's version of the intermediate Ford Fairlane.

Everything recorded about the Fairlane also applies to the 1962-63 Meteor. The cars shared the same body (although the Mercury's styling was busier) and came with an optional small-block 221-cid V8. This was supplemented in 1963 by an optional 260-cid small-block for the Meteor Custom and S-33 luxury hardtop. But the Meteor didn't sell as well as the Fairlane, and Mercury dropped it for 1964 to put its compact-car development funds into an extensively facelifted Comet.

The Comet arrived in 1960 as a companion of the Ford Falcon, and sold over 116,000 copies. Sales rose in '61 and were strong in '62. Except for station wagons,

Comet had a wheelbase five inches longer than Falcon. One of the reasons Meteor didn't sell is that Comet was comparably sized, yet priced lower. The decision to make Comet the only "small Mercury" after 1963 was a good one. Sales jumped by 55,000 units for '64 and remained high into '67.

Compared with the Falcon, Comet was better

1967 Comet Cyclone GT hardtop coupe

1969 Cyclone CJ428 fastback hardtop coupe

1970 Cyclone GT hardtop coupe

1960 Colony Park four-door station wagon

trimmed and more elaborately styled, but priced less than $100 higher. Several interesting models were offered. When it became obvious that people liked sporty compacts, Mercury introduced the $2300 bucket-seated S-22 two-door sedan in 1961. At the same time, all Comets became available with an optional 101-bhp six. For 1963, an S-22 hardtop and convertible were added. With the squarish facelift of 1964, the S-22 was renamed Caliente. By then, any Comet could be equipped with the outstanding 260-cid small-block. For all-out performance, there was a special Cyclone hardtop powered by the 210-bhp, 289-cid V8.

Comet received its first major overhaul in 1966, when it deserted the compact-car field and became an intermediate sharing that year's sleek new Fairlane bodyshell. This shift underlined a basic marketing decision: Mercury customers were assumed to be wealthier than Ford buyers, and would therefore probably be happier with a car larger than the Falcon. Comet retained this 116-inch-wheelbase platform through 1969, but experienced several lean years along the way as the name was gradually phased out. In 1967, for example, it appeared only on the very basic "Comet 202" model. The rest of the intermediate line consisted of the Capri, Caliente, Cyclone, and Station Wagon. For 1968, these were replaced by the luxurious Montego in three trim levels: the basic sedan and hardtop coupe; the MX sedan, hardtop coupe, convertible, and wagon; and the top-line MX Brougham four-door sedan and hardtop coupe. The MX was outfitted with high-quality cloth upholstery and other luxury details. The Comet name was retained for a price leader coupe, and disappeared after 1969.

The 1964-70 Cyclone and Montego intermediates were the basis for some of the most roadworthy Mercurys of the decade, including several champion race cars. After adopting the Fairlane shell in 1966, Mercury offered the Cyclone GT hardtop coupe and convertible. Powered by Ford's 335-bhp 390 V8, the Cyclone offered a variety of useful suspension options. The '67 edition was even more impressive with the optional 427-cid Ford V8, which provided 410–425 bhp. Similar street racers were available in 1968, though the 427 was detuned to 390 bhp that year.

An exciting pair of fastback hardtops, the Cyclone and Cyclone CJ, hit the streets for '69. Both had special identification, narrow racing paint stripes, and unique rear-end and taillight styling. Options included wide belted tires, turbine-style wheel covers, and racing-style outside mirrors. Both models had clean sides, no chrome, and a blacked-out grille. The CJ carried a functional hood scoop for its Ram-Air 428 Cobra-Jet engine. Although Ford was NASCAR Grand National Champion in 1968-69, the Cyclone turned in many notable performances. The best was Cale Yarborough's victory in the 1968 Daytona 500, at an average speed of 143.250 mph.

Mercury's most consistent and steady sales in the '60s came from its standard-size cars. Production levels

were usually around 100,000 units annually, except for those back-to-back record years of 1965 and '66. Of all the big Mercs, only Monterey spanned the entire decade. The upper-priced Montclair and Park Lane were dropped in 1961, revived for 1964-68, and dropped again in '69 to be replaced by the Marquis and Brougham.

The 1960 full-size line rode a 126-inch wheelbase. As before, the standard engine for Montclair and Park Lane was the Lincoln 430-cid V8. Montereys and Commuter wagons were available with a 312-cid unit, and a 383 V8 with 280 bhp was an option. Styling was a more modest rendition of '59: a short, concave, full-width grille; restyled taillights; a single bright metal side strip; and revised bumpers. The Monterey dominated sales.

For 1961, Mercury moved down into the market vacated by Edsel. Montclair and Park Lane were dropped, as were the high-priced Cruiser hardtops from the Monterey series, and the aforementioned six-cylinder Meteor was added. The 430 V8 was canceled, and a 292-cid engine was standard. Sales were not spectacular. Comet, however, had a record year with over 197,000 units sold.

Meteor was made an intermediate for '62, so the standard line now consisted of two Monterey series, plus Colony Park and Commuter wagons. There was another move up-market with the Monterey Custom series, which included a convertible. Joining the bucket-seat brigade at mid-year were the S-55 hardtop coupe and convertible. Styling was busier in '62, with tunnel-mounted taillights and a gaudy grille. The previous V8 lineup stayed intact, and a six was offered for the standard Monterey.

Once more, the Monterey and wagons made up the entire full-size line in '63. Mercury introduced "Breezeway Styling"—a reverse-slant rear window like that of the old Turnpike Cruiser, which dropped down for better ventilation. Monterey and Monterey Custom returned, and wagons were pared down to just the Colony Park. The S-55 notchback hardtop coupe and convertible were joined by a slopeback hardtop for 1963½, paralleling Ford's XL offerings.

By '64, tradition had returned. Mercury restored its old series lineup of Monterey, Montclair, Park Lane, and Commuter and Colony Park wagons. The first three included two-door and four-door hardtops, four-door sedans, and fastback "Marauder" hardtop sedans. The 390 V8 had become the standard powerplant in 1963, accompanied by an optional 427-cid engine for all models except wagons. Marauders with the 425-bhp version were awesome performers.

In record year 1965, the full-size Mercury shared a restyle with Ford. The wagons rode a 119-inch wheelbase; others had 123 inches. Breezeway and conventional four-door models were found in all series, with the usual line of 390 and 427 V8s. Mercury touted "Torque Box" body construction: frames tuned for each body style to minimize noise, vibration, and harshness.

1961 Colony Park four-door station wagon

1962 Monterey two-door sedan

1964 Montclair Marauder fastback hardtop sedan

1965 Park Lane Breezeway four-door sedan

1966 Montclair fastback hardtop coupe

For 1966, a new die-cast grille was adopted. Two-door models got a new "sweep-style roof" with concave backlight—a dramatic break with the Breezeway design. Styling was revised again on the '67s. The limited-production Marquis was announced: a two-door hardtop with broad rear roof pillars and vinyl top. Another newcomer was the vinyl-topped Park Lane Brougham, a hardtop sedan that was expanded into a complete series the following year. Marquis and Brougham replaced the long-running Montclair and Park Lane for 1969.

A high-performance, low-production '69 entry was the Marauder fastback hardtop, which accounted for 14,666 sales. Its sleek, clean bodywork featured the Marquis grille, concealed headlights, quad taillights, and ventless side windows. The 1970 lineup was a repeat of '69. All models sported new grilles, side ornamentation, rear trim, and taillights.

One of the more interesting and desirable Mercurys of the decade was the 111-inch-wheelbase Cougar, premiering as a hardtop for 1967 and joined by a convertible in '69. Based on the Mustang but riding a 3-inch longer wheelbase, it was a deluxe version of Ford's highly successful "ponycar," priced about $200 higher. While Mustang came with a six-cylinder engine as standard, Cougar's base engine was a 200-bhp V8. In 1969-70 the CJ 428 packing 335 bhp was available at extra cost.

The original Cougar was a dashing car, identified by its "electric-shaver" grille and hidden headlights. Sequential turn signals were a feature from the first. The vertical grille bars were blacked out for 1968, giving the car a more conventional look. For '69, the body was widened and lengthened. A full-length contour line, ventless curved side glass, die-cast grille, and full-width taillights were also featured. The '70 model adopted a divided grille with blacked-out section for the luxury XR-7. The best of the Cougar line, the XR-7 was equipped with a rich leather interior and comprehensive instrumentation set into a simulated walnut dashboard.

GT and GTE Cougars powered by the 427 V8 were available beginning in 1968, offered with a variety of handling and performance options. Though it never ap-

1968 Marquis hardtop coupe

1968 Cougar XR7-GTE hardtop coupe

1969 Marauder X-100 hardtop coupe

1969 Cougar hardtop coupe with "Eliminator" option

1970 Marquis Brougham hardtop sedan

1970 Cougar hardtop coupe with "Eliminator" option

proached the Mustang in sales, Cougar was a boost to Mercury. It was also more solid and luxurious than Mustang, but equally roadable. Among collectors, the appeal of the 1967-68 Cougars has long been acknowledged.

Cougar put the finishing touch on a decade that witnessed a complete reversal of Mercury's image. By 1967 the make was known for performance as well as luxury. By 1970, Mercury had again become the hot car it had been in the late '40s and early '50s.

# Mercury Specifications

## 1940

| Series 09A (wb 116.0)—01,128 built | | Wght | Price | Prod |
|---|---|---|---|---|
| | conv cpe | 3,107 | 1,079 | — |
| | sdn 2d | 3,068 | 946 | — |
| | cpe-sdn 2d | 3,030 | 987 | — |
| | Town Sedan 4d | 3,103 | 987 | — |
| | conv sdn | 3,249 | 1,212 | — |

*Estimate (see note below 1942).

| 1940 Engine | bore×stroke | bhp | availability |
|---|---|---|---|
| V8, 239.0 | 3.19×3.75 | 95 | S-all |

## 1941

| Series 19A (wb 118.0)—82,391* built | | Wght | Price | Prod |
|---|---|---|---|---|
| 67 | cpe, A/S | 3,049 | 936 | — |
| 70 | Tudor sdn | 3,184 | 946 | — |
| 72 | cpe-sdn 2d | 3,118 | 977 | — |
| 73 | Town Sedan 4d | 3,221 | 987 | — |
| 76 | conv cpe | 3,222 | 1,100 | — |
| 77 | cpe, 2P | 3,008 | 910 | — |
| 79 | wgn, 4d | 3,468 | 1,141 | — |

*Estimate (see note below 1942).

| 1941 Engine | bore×stroke | bhp | availability |
|---|---|---|---|
| V8, 239.0 | 3.19×3.75 | 95 | S-all |

## 1942

| Series 29A (wb 118.0)—22,816* built | | Wght | Price | Prod |
|---|---|---|---|---|
| 70 | Tudor sdn | 3,228 | 1,030 | — |
| 72 | cpe-sdn 2d | 3,148 | 1,055 | — |
| 73 | Town Sedan 4d | 3,263 | 1,065 | — |
| 76 | conv cpe | 3,288 | 1,215 | — |
| 77 | cpe, 3P | 3,073 | 995 | — |
| 79 | wgn, 4d, 8P | 3,528 | 1,260 | — |

*Estimate (see below).

Note: Factory records provide only calendar year production during 1940-41. Estimates are calculated by adding 25% of previous year's calendar production to 75% of current year's production. Model year production began in October each year.

| 1942 Engine | bore×stroke | bhp | availability |
|---|---|---|---|
| V8, 239.0 | 3.19×3.75 | 100 | S-all |

## 1946

| Series 69M (wb 118.0) | | Wght | Price | Prod |
|---|---|---|---|---|
| 70 | sdn 2d | 3,240 | 1,448 | 13,108 |
| 71 | Sportsman conv cpe | 3,407 | 2,209 | 205 |
| 72 | cpe-sdn 2d | 3,100 | 1,495 | 24,163 |
| 70 | Town Sedan 4d | 3,270 | 1,509 | 40,280 |
| 76 | conv cpe | 3,340 | 1,711 | 6,044 |
| 79 | wgn 4d | 3,540 | 1,729 | 2,797 |
| | chassis | — | — | 11 |

| 1946 Engine | bore×stroke | bhp | availability |
|---|---|---|---|
| V8, 239.0 | 3.19×3.75 | 100 | S-all |

## 1947

| Series 79M (wb 118.0) | | Wght | Price | Prod |
|---|---|---|---|---|
| 70 | sdn 2d | 3,268 | 1,592 | 34 |
| 72 | cpe-sdn 2d | 3,218 | 1,645 | 29,284 |
| 73 | Town Sedan 4d | 3,298 | 1,660 | 42,281 |
| 76 | conv cpe | 3,368 | 2,002 | 10,221 |
| 79 | wgn 4d | 3,571 | 2,207 | 3,558 |
| — | chassis | — | — | 5 |

| 1947 Engine | bore×stroke | bhp | availability |
|---|---|---|---|
| V8, 239.0 | 3.19×3.75 | 100 | S-all |

## 1948

| Series 89M (wb 118.0) | | Wght | Price | Prod |
|---|---|---|---|---|
| 72 | cpe-sdn 2d | 3,218 | 1,645 | 16,476 |
| 73 | Town Sedan 4d | 3,298 | 1,660 | 24,283 |
| 76 | conv cpe | 3,368 | 2,002 | 7,586 |
| 79 | wgn 4d | 3,571 | 2,207 | 1,889 |
| — | chassis | — | — | 34 |

| 1948 Engine | bore×stroke | bhp | availability |
|---|---|---|---|
| V8, 239.0 | 3.19×3.75 | 100 | S-all |

## 1949

| Series 9CM (wb 118.0) | | Wght | Price | Prod |
|---|---|---|---|---|
| 72 | cpe | 3,321 | 1,979 | 120,616 |
| 74 | Sport Sedan 4d | 3,386 | 2,031 | 155,882 |
| 76 | conv cpe | 3,591 | 2,410 | 16,765 |
| 79 | wgn 4d, 8P | 3,626 | 2,716 | 8,044 |
| — | chassis | — | — | 12 |

| 1949 Engine | bore×stroke | bhp | availability |
|---|---|---|---|
| V8, 255.4 | 3.19×4.00 | 110 | S-all |

## 1950

| Series OCM (wb 118.0) | | Wght | Price | Prod |
|---|---|---|---|---|
| M-72A | cpe (economy) | 3,345 | 1,875 | |
| M-72B | club cpe | 3,430 | 1,980 | 151,489 |
| M-72C | Monterey cpe, canvas top | 3,480 | 2,146 | |
| M-72C | Monterey cpe, vinyl top | 3,480 | 2,157 | |

# Mercury

| | | Wght | Price | Prod |
|---|---|---|---|---|
| M-74 | Sport Sedan 4d | 3,470 | 2,032 | 132,082 |
| M-76 | conv cpe | 3,710 | 2,412 | 8,341 |
| M-79 | wgn 4d, 8P | 3,755 | 2,561 | 1,746 |

| 1950 Engine | bore × stroke | bhp | availability | |
|---|---|---|---|---|
| V8, 255.4 | 3.19 × 4.00 | 110 | S-all | |

## 1951

| Series 1CM (wb 118.0) | | Wght | Price | Prod |
|---|---|---|---|---|
| M-72B | cpe | 3,485 | 1,947 | |
| M-72C | Monterey cpe, canvas top | 3,485 | 2,116 | 142,168 |
| M-72C | Monterey cpe, vinyl top | 3,485 | 2,127 | |
| M-74 | Sport Sedan 4d | 3,550 | 2,000 | 157,648 |
| M-76 | conv cpe | 3,760 | 2,380 | 6,759 |
| M-79 | wgn 4d, 8P | 3,800 | 2,530 | 3,812 |

| 1951 Engine | bore × stroke | bhp | availability | |
|---|---|---|---|---|
| V8, 255.4 | 3.19 × 4.00 | 112 | S-all | |

## 1952

| Series 2M (wb 118.0) | | Wght | Price | Prod |
|---|---|---|---|---|
| 60B | Monterey htp cpe | 3,520 | 2,225 | 24,453 |
| 60E | Sport Coupe | 3,435 | 2,100 | 30,599 |
| 70B | sdn 2d | 3,335 | 1,987 | 25,812 |
| 73B | sdn 4d | 3,390 | 2,040 | 83,475 |
| 73C | Monterey sdn 4d | 3,375 | 2,115 | |
| 76B | Monterey conv cpe | 3,635 | 2,370 | 5,261 |
| 79B | wgn 4d, 6P | 3,795 | 2,525 | 2,487 |
| 79D | wgn 4d, 8P | 3,795 | 2,570 | |

| 1952 Engine | bore × stroke | bhp | availability | |
|---|---|---|---|---|
| V8, 255.4 | 3.19 × 4.00 | 125 | S-all | |

## 1953

| 3M Custom (wb 118.0) | | Wght | Price | Prod |
|---|---|---|---|---|
| 60E | Sport Coupe | 3,465 | 2,117 | 39,547 |
| 70B | sdn 2d | 3,405 | 2,004 | 50,183 |
| 73B | sdn 4d | 3,450 | 2,057 | 59,794 |

| 3M Monterey (wb 118.0) | | Wght | Price | Prod |
|---|---|---|---|---|
| 60B | htp cpe | 3,465 | 2,244 | 76,119 |
| 73C | sdn 4d | 3,425 | 2,133 | 64,038 |
| 76B | conv cpe | 3,585 | 2,390 | 8,463 |
| 79B | wgn 4d, 8P | 3,765 | 2,591 | 7,719 |

| 1953 Engine | bore × stroke | bhp | availability | |
|---|---|---|---|---|
| V8, 255.4 | 3.19 × 4.00 | 125 | S-all | |

## 1954

| Custom (wb 118.0) | | Wght | Price | Prod |
|---|---|---|---|---|
| 60E | Sport htp cpe | 3,485 | 2,315 | 15,234 |
| 70B | sdn 2d | 3,435 | 2,194 | 37,146 |
| 73B | sdn 4d | 3,480 | 2,251 | 32,687 |

| Monterey (wb 118.0) | | Wght | Price | Prod |
|---|---|---|---|---|
| 60B | htp cpe | 3,520 | 2,452 | 79,533 |
| 60F | Sun Valley htp cpe | 3,535 | 2,582 | 9,761 |
| 73C | sdn 4d | 3,515 | 2,333 | 65,995 |
| 76B | conv cpe | 3,620 | 2,610 | 7,293 |
| 79B | wgn 4d, 8P | 3,735 | 2,776 | 11,656 |

| 1954 Engine | bore × stroke | bhp | availability | |
|---|---|---|---|---|
| V8, 256.0 | 3.62 × 3.10 | 161 | S-all | |

## 1955

| Custom (wb 119.0; wgn-118.0) | | Wght | Price | Prod |
|---|---|---|---|---|
| 60E | htp cpe | 3,480 | 2,341 | 7,040 |
| 70B | sdn 2d | 3,395 | 2,218 | 31,295 |
| 73B | sdn 4d | 3,450 | 2,277 | 21,219 |
| 79B | wgn 4d | 3,780 | 2,686 | 14,134 |

| Monterey (wb 119.0; wgn-118.0) | | Wght | Price | Prod |
|---|---|---|---|---|
| 60B | htp cpe | 3,510 | 2,465 | 69,093 |
| 73C | sdn 4d | 3,500 | 2,400 | 70,392 |
| 79C | wgn 4d | 3,770 | 2,844 | 11,968 |

| Montclair (wb 119.0) | | Wght | Price | Prod |
|---|---|---|---|---|
| 58A | sdn 4d | 3,600 | 2,685 | 20,624 |
| 64A | htp cpe | 3,490 | 2,631 | 71,588 |
| 64B | Sun Valley htp cpe | 3,560 | 2,712 | 1,787 |
| 76B | conv cpe | 3,685 | 2,712 | 10,668 |

| 1955 Engines | bore × stroke | bhp | availability |
|---|---|---|---|
| V8, 292.0 | 3.75 × 3.30 | 188 | S-Custom, Monterey |
| V8, 292.0 | 3.75 × 3.30 | 198 | S-Montclair; O-others |

## 1956

| Medalist (wb 119.0) | | Wght | Price | Prod |
|---|---|---|---|---|
| 57D | Phaeton htp sdn | 3,530 | 2,458 | 6,685 |
| 64E | Sport htp cpe | 3,545 | 2,389 | 11,892 |
| 70C | sdn 2d | 3,430 | 2,254 | 20,582 |
| 73D | sdn 4d | 3,500 | 2,313 | 6,653 |

| Custom (wb 119.0; wgn-118.0) | | Wght | Price | Prod |
|---|---|---|---|---|
| 57C | Phaeton htp sdn | 3,550 | 2,555 | 12,187 |
| 64D | Sport htp cpe | 3,560 | 2,485 | 20,857 |
| 70B | sdn 2d | 3,505 | 2,351 | 16,343 |
| 73B | sdn 4d | 3,520 | 2,410 | 15,860 |
| 76A | conv cpe | 3,665 | 2,712 | 2,311 |
| 79B | wgn 4d, 8P | 3,860 | 2,819 | 9,292 |
| 79D | wgn 4d, 6P | 3,790 | 2,722 | 8,478 |

| Monterey (wb 119.0; wgn-118.0) | | Wght | Price | Prod |
|---|---|---|---|---|
| 57B | Phaeton htp sdn | 3,800 | 2,700 | 10,726 |
| 58B | Sport Sedan 4d | 3,550 | 2,652 | 11,765 |
| 64C | Sport htp cpe | 3,590 | 2,630 | 42,863 |
| 73C | sdn 4d | 3,570 | 2,555 | 26,735 |
| 79C | wgn 4d, 8P | 3,885 | 2,977 | 13,280 |

| Montclair (wb 119.0) | | Wght | Price | Prod |
|---|---|---|---|---|
| 57A | Phaeton htp sdn | 3,640 | 2,835 | 23,493 |
| 58A | Sport Sedan 4d | 3,610 | 2,786 | 9,617 |
| 64A | Sport htp cpe | 3,620 | 2,765 | 50,562 |
| 76B | conv cpe | 3,725 | 2,900 | 7,762 |

| 1956 Engines | bore × stroke | bhp | availability |
|---|---|---|---|
| V8, 312.0 | 3.80 × 3.44 | 210 | S-Medalist, Custom 3spd |
| V8, 312.0 | 3.80 × 3.44 | 225 | S-Medalist, Custom auto, Mntclr |
| V8, 312.0 | 3.80 × 3.44 | 235 | S-Montclair; Monterey auto |

## 1957

| Monterey (wb 122.0) | | Wght | Price | Prod |
|---|---|---|---|---|
| 57A | Phaeton htp sdn | 3,915 | 2,763 | 22,475 |
| 58A | sdn 4d | 3,890 | 2,645 | 53,839 |
| 63A | Phaeton htp cpe | 3,870 | 2,693 | 42,199 |
| 64A | sdn 2d | 3,875 | 2,576 | 33,982 |
| 76A | Phaeton conv cpe | 4,035 | 3,005 | 5,033 |

| Montclair (wb 122.0) | | Wght | Price | Prod |
|---|---|---|---|---|
| 57B | Phaeton htp sdn | 3,925 | 3,317 | 21,567 |
| 58B | sdn 4d | 3,905 | 3,188 | 19,836 |
| 63B | Phaeton htp cpe | 3,900 | 3,236 | 30,111 |
| 76B | Phaeton conv cpe | 4,010 | 3,430 | 4,248 |

## Turnpike Cruiser (wb 122.0)

|  |  | Wght | Price | Prod |
|---|---|---|---|---|
| 65A | htp cpe | 4,005 | 3,758 | 7,291 |
| 75A | htp sdn | 4,015 | 3,849 | 8,305 |
| 76S | conv cpe | 4,125 | 4,103 | 1,265 |

## Station Wagon (wb 122.0)

|  |  | Wght | Price | Prod |
|---|---|---|---|---|
| 56A | Commuter 2d, 6P | 4,115 | 2,903 | 4,885 |
| 56B | Voyager 2d, 6P | 4,240 | 3,403 | 2,283 |
| 77A | Commuter 4d, 6P | 4,195 | 2,973 | 11,990 |
| 77B | Colony Park 4d, 9P | 4,165 | 3,677 | 7,386 |
| 77C | Commuter 4d, 9P | 4,155 | 3,070 | 5,752 |
| 77D | Voyager 4d, 9P | 4,280 | 3,570 | 3,716 |

| 1957 Engines | bore × stroke | bhp | availability |
|---|---|---|---|
| V8, 312.0 | 3.80 × 3.44 | 255 | S-all exc Turnpike Cruiser |
| V8, 368.0 | 4.00 × 3.66 | 290 | S-Turnpike Cruiser; O-others |

# 1958

## Medalist (wb 122.0)

|  |  | Wght | Price | Prod |
|---|---|---|---|---|
| 58C | sdn 4d | 3,875 | 2,617 | 10,982 |
| 64B | sdn 2d | 3,790 | 2,547 | 7,750 |

## Monterey (wb 122.0)

|  |  | Wght | Price | Prod |
|---|---|---|---|---|
| 57A | Phaeton htp sdn | 4,150 | 2,840 | 26,909 |
| 58A | sdn 4d | 4,160 | 2,721 | 28,892 |
| 63A | Phaeton htp cpe | 4,075 | 2,769 | 13,693 |
| 64A | sdn 2d | 4,080 | 2,652 | 10,526 |
| 76A | conv cpe | 4,225 | 3,081 | 2,292 |

## Montclair (wb 122.0)

|  |  | Wght | Price | Prod |
|---|---|---|---|---|
| 57B | Phaeton tp sdn | 4,165 | 3,365 | 3,609 |
| 58B | sdn 4d | 4,155 | 3,236 | 4,801 |
| 63B | Phaeton htp cpe | 4,085 | 3,284 | 5,012 |
| 65A | Turnpike Cruiser htp cpe | 4,150 | 3,498 | 2,864 |
| 75A | Turnpike Cruiser htp sdn | 4,230 | 3,577 | 3,543 |
| 76B | conv cpe | 4,295 | 3,536 | 844 |

## Park Lane (wb 125.0)

|  |  | Wght | Price | Prod |
|---|---|---|---|---|
| 57C | Phaeton htp sdn | 4,390 | 3,944 | 5,241 |
| 63C | Phaeton htp cpe | 4,280 | 3,867 | 3,158 |
| 76C | conv cpe | 4,405 | 4,118 | 853 |

## Station Wagon (wb 122.0)

|  |  | Wght | Price | Prod |
|---|---|---|---|---|
| 56A | Commuter 2d, 6P | 4,400 | 3,035 | 1,912 |
| 56B | Voyager 2d, 6P | 4,435 | 3,535 | 568 |
| 77A | Commuter 4d, 6P | 4,485 | 3,105 | 8,601 |
| 77B | Colony Park 4d, 6-9P | 4,605 | 3,775 | 4,474 |
| 77C | Commuter 4d, 9P | 4,525 | 3,201 | 4,227 |
| 77D | Voyager 4d, 6-9P | 4,540 | 3,635 | 2,520 |

| 1958 Engines | bore × stroke | bhp | availability |
|---|---|---|---|
| V8, 312.0 | 3.80 × 3.44 | 235 | S-Medalist only |
| V8, 383.0 | 4.30 × 3.30 | 312 | S-Monterey, Commuter |
| V8, 383.0 | 4.30 × 3.30 | 330 | S-Montclair, Voyager, Col Park |
| V8, 430.0 | 4.30 × 3.70 | 360 | S-Park Lane |

# 1959

## Monterey (wb 126.0)

|  |  | Wght | Price | Prod |
|---|---|---|---|---|
| 57A | htp sdn | 4,013 | 2,918 | 11,355 |
| 58A | sdn 4d | 3,985 | 2,832 | 43,570 |
| 63A | htp cpe | 3,932 | 2,854 | 17,232 |
| 64A | sdn 2d | 3,914 | 2,768 | 12,694 |
| 76A | conv cpe | 4,074 | 3,150 | 4,426 |

## Montclair (wb 126.0)

|  |  | Wght | Price | Prod |
|---|---|---|---|---|
| 57B | htp sdn | 4,234 | 3,437 | 6,713 |
| 58B | sdn 4d | 4,205 | 3,308 | 9,514 |
| 63B | htp cpe | 4,146 | 3,357 | 7,375 |

## Park Lane (wb 128.0)

|  |  | Wght | Price | Prod |
|---|---|---|---|---|
| 57C | htp sdn | 4,386 | 4,031 | 7,206 |

|  |  | Wght | Price | Prod |
|---|---|---|---|---|
| 63C | htp cpe | 4,311 | 3,955 | 4,060 |
| 76C | conv cpe | 4,455 | 4,206 | 1,254 |

## Station Wagon (wb 126.0)

|  |  | Wght | Price | Prod |
|---|---|---|---|---|
| 56A | Commuter 2d, 6P | 4,334 | 3,145 | 1,051 |
| 77A | Commuter 4d, 6P | 4,405 | 3,215 | 15,122 |
| 77B | Colony Park 4d, 6P | 4,535 | 3,932 | 5,929 |
| 77D | Voyager 4d, 6P | 4,483 | 3,793 | 2,496 |

| 1959 Engines | bore × stroke | bhp | availability |
|---|---|---|---|
| V8, 312.0 | 3.80 × 3.44 | 210 | S-Monterey |
| V8, 312.0 | 3.80 × 3.44 | 280 | O-Monterey |
| V8, 383.0 | 4.30 × 3.30 | 280 | S-Commuter |
| V8, 383.0 | 4.30 × 3.30 | 322 | S-Montclair, Voyager, Col Park |
| V8, 430.0 | 4.30 × 3.70 | 345 | S-Park Lane |

# 1960

## Comet (wb 114.0; wgn—109.5)

|  |  | Wght | Price | Prod |
|---|---|---|---|---|
| 54A | sdn 4d | 2,432 | 2,053 | 47,416 |
| 59A | wgn 2d | 2,548 | 2,310 | 5,115 |
| 62A | sdn 2d | 2,399 | 1,998 | 45,374 |
| 71A | wgn 4d | 2,581 | 2,365 | 18,426 |

## Monterey (wb 126.0)

|  |  | Wght | Price | Prod |
|---|---|---|---|---|
| 57A | Cruiser htp sdn | 4,011 | 2,845 | 9,536 |
| 58A | sdn 4d | 3,981 | 2,730 | 49,594 |
| 63A | Cruiser htp cpe | 3,931 | 2,781 | 15,790 |
| 64A | sdn 2d | 3,901 | 2,631 | 21,557 |
| 76A | conv cpe | 4,131 | 3,077 | 6,062 |

## Monclair (wb 126.0)

|  |  | Wght | Price | Prod |
|---|---|---|---|---|
| 57B | Cruiser htp sdn | 4,285 | 3,394 | 5,548 |
| 58B | sdn 4d | 4,255 | 3,280 | 8,510 |
| 63B | Cruiser htp cpe | 4,205 | 3,331 | 5,756 |

## Park Lane (wb 126.0)

|  |  | Wght | Price | Prod |
|---|---|---|---|---|
| 57F | Cruiser htp sdn | 4,380 | 3,858 | 5,788 |
| 63F | Cruiser htp cpe | 4,300 | 3,794 | 2,974 |
| 76D | conv cpe | 4,500 | 4,018 | 1,525 |

## Station Wagon (wb 126.0)

|  |  | Wght | Price | Prod |
|---|---|---|---|---|
| 77A | Commuter 4d, 6-9P | 4,301 | 3,127 | 14,949 |
| 77B | Colony Park 4d, 9P | 4,558 | 3,837 | 7,411 |

| 1960 Engines | bore × stroke | bhp | availability |
|---|---|---|---|
| L6, 144.3 | 3.50 × 2.50 | 90 | S-Comet |
| V8, 312.0 | 3.80 × 3.44 | 205 | S-Monterey, Commuter |
| V8, 383.0 | 4.30 × 3.30 | 280 | O-Monterey, Commuter |
| V8, 430.0 | 4.30 × 3.70 | 310 | S-Montclair, P Lane, Col Park |

# 1961

## Comet (wb 114.0; wgn-109.5)

|  |  | Wght | Price | Prod |
|---|---|---|---|---|
| 54A | sdn 4d | 2,411 | 2,055 | 85,332 |
| 59A | wgn 2d | 2,548 | 2,312 | 4,199 |
| 62A | sdn 2d | 2,376 | 2,000 | 71,563 |
| 62A | S-22 sdn 2d | 2,441 | 2,284 | 14,004 |
| 71A | wgn 4d | 2,581 | 2,355 | 22,165 |

## Meteor (wb 120.0)

|  |  | Wght | Price | Prod |
|---|---|---|---|---|
| 58A | 600 sdn 4d | 3,714 | 2,589 | 18,117 |
| 64A | 600 sdn 2d | 3,647 | 2,535 | |
| 54A | 800 sdn 4d | 3,762 | 2,767 | 35,005 |
| 62A | 800 sdn 2d | 3,680 | 2,713 | |
| 65A | 800 htp cpe | 3,694 | 2,774 | |
| 75A | 800 htp sdn | 3,780 | 2,839 | |

## Monterey (wb 120.0)

|  |  | Wght | Price | Prod |
|---|---|---|---|---|
| 54B | sdn 4d | 3,777 | 2,871 | 22,881 |
| 65B | htp cpe | 3,709 | 2,878 | 10,942 |
| 75B | htp sdn | 3,795 | 2,943 | 9,252 |
| 76A | conv cpe | 3,872 | 3,128 | 7,053 |

## Station Wagon (wb 120.0)

| | | Wght | Price | Prod |
|---|---|---|---|---|
| 71A | Commuter 4d, 6P | 4,115 | 2,924 | 8,945 |
| 71B | Colony Park 4d, 6P | 4,131 | 3,120 | 7,887 |
| 71B | Colony Park 4d, 9P | 4,171 | 3,191 | |
| 71C | Commuter 4d, 9P | 4,155 | 2,994 | 6 |

| 1961 Engines | bore × stroke | bhp | availability |
|---|---|---|---|
| L6, 144.3 | 3.50×2.50 | 85 | S-Comet |
| L6, 170.0 | 3.50×2.94 | 101 | O-Comet |
| L6, 223.0 | 3.62×3.60 | 135 | O-Meteor 600/800, Commuter |
| V8, 292.0 | 3.75×3.30 | 175 | S-all exc Comet |
| V8, 352.0 | 4.00×3.50 | 220 | O-all exc Comet |
| V8, 390.0 | 4.05×3.78 | 300 | O-all exc Comet |

## 1962

### Comet (wb 114.0; wgn-109.5)

| | | Wght | Price | Prod |
|---|---|---|---|---|
| 54A | sdn 4d | 2,457 | 2,139 | 70,227 |
| 54B | Custom sdn 4d | 2,648 | 2,226 | |
| 59A | wgn 2d | 2,626 | 2,396 | 2,121 |
| 59B | Custom wgn 2d | 2,642 | 2,483 | |
| 62A | sdn 2d | 2,420 | 2,084 | 73,880 |
| 62B | Custom sdn 2d | 2,431 | 2,170 | |
| 62C | S-22 sdn 2d | 2,458 | 2,368 | |
| 71A | wgn 4d | 2,662 | 2,439 | 16,759 |
| 71B | Custom wgn 4d | 2,679 | 2,526 | |
| 71C | Villager wgn 4d | 2,712 | 2,710 | 2,318 |

### Meteor (wb 116.5)

| | | Wght | Price | Prod |
|---|---|---|---|---|
| 54A | sdn 4d | 2,956 | 2,340 | 18,708 |
| 54B | Custom sdn 4d | 2,964 | 2,428 | 23,484 |
| 62A | sdn 2d | 2,922 | 2,278 | 11,550 |
| 62B | Custom sdn 2d | 2,930 | 2,366 | 9,410 |
| 62C | S-33 sdn 2d | 2,960 | 2,509 | 5,900 |

### Monterey (wb 120.0)

| | | Wght | Price | Prod |
|---|---|---|---|---|
| 54A | sdn 4d | 3,772 | 2,726 | 18,975 |
| 62A | sdn 4d | 3,695 | 2,672 | 5,117 |
| 65A | htp cpe | 3,712 | 2,733 | 5,328 |
| 75A | htp sdn | 3,781 | 2,798 | 2,691 |

### Monterey Custom (wb 120.0)

| | | Wght | Price | Prod |
|---|---|---|---|---|
| 54B | sdn 4d | 3,836 | 2,965 | 27,591 |
| 65B | htp cpe | 3,772 | 2,972 | 10,814 |
| 65C | S-55 htp cpe | 4,802 | 3,488 | 2,772 |
| 75B | htp sdn | 3,851 | 3,037 | 8,932 |
| 76A | conv cpe | 3,938 | 3,222 | 5,489 |
| 76B | S-55 conv cpe | 3,968 | 3,738 | 1,315 |

### Station Wagon (wb 120.0)

| | | Wght | Price | Prod |
|---|---|---|---|---|
| 71A | Commuter 4d, 6P | 4,120 | 2,920 | 8,389 |
| 71C | Commuter 4d, 9P | 4,132 | 2,990 | |
| 71B | Colony Park 4d, 6P | 4,186 | 3,219 | 9,596 |
| 71D | Colony Park 4d, 9P | 4,198 | 3,289 | |

| 1962 Engines | bore × stroke | bhp | availability |
|---|---|---|---|
| L6, 144.3 | 3.50×2.50 | 85 | S-Comet |
| L6, 170.0 | 3.50×2.94 | 101 | S-Meteor; O-Comet |
| L6, 223.0 | 3.62×3.60 | 138 | S-Monterey, Commuter |
| V8, 221.0 | 3.50×2.87 | 145 | O-Meteor |
| V8, 260.0 | 3.80×2.87 | 164 | O-Meteor |
| V8, 292.0 | 3.75×3.30 | 170 | S-Custom, Col Park; O-Mntry, Cmmtr |
| V8, 352.0 | 4.00×3.50 | 220 | O-all except Comet, Meteor |
| V8, 390.0 | 4.05×3.78 | 330 | O-all exc Comet, Meteor |

## 1963

### Comet (wb 114.0; wgn-109.5)

| | | Wght | Price | Prod |
|---|---|---|---|---|
| 54A | sdn 4d | 2,499 | 2,139 | 24,230 |
| 54B | Custom sdn 4d | 2,508 | 2,206 | 27,498 |
| 59A | wgn 2d | 2,644 | 2,440 | 623 |
| 59B | Custom wgn 2d | 2,659 | 2,527 | 272 |
| 62A | sdn 2d | 2,462 | 2,084 | 24,351 |

| | | Wght | Price | Prod |
|---|---|---|---|---|
| 62B | Custom sdn 2d | 2,471 | 2,171 | 11,897 |
| 62C | S-22 sdn 2d | 2,512 | 2,368 | 6,303 |
| 63B | Custom htp cpe | 2,572 | 2,605 | 9,432 |
| 63C | S-22 htp cpe | 2,613 | 2,635 | 5,807 |
| 71A | wgn 4d | 2,681 | 2,483 | 4,419 |
| 71B | Custom wgn 4d | 2,696 | 2,570 | 5,151 |
| 71C | Villager wgn 4d | 2,736 | 2,754 | 1,529 |
| 76A | Custom conv cpe | 2,784 | 2,557 | 7,354 |
| 76B | S-22 conv cpe | 2,825 | 2,710 | 5,757 |

### Meteor (wb 116.5; wgn-115.5)

| | | Wght | Price | Prod |
|---|---|---|---|---|
| 54A | sdn 4d | 3,025 | 2,340 | 9,183 |
| 54B | Custom sdn 4d | 3,031 | 2,428 | 14,498 |
| 62A | sdn 2d | 2,986 | 2,278 | 3,935 |
| 62B | Custom sdn 2d | 2,992 | 2,366 | 2,704 |
| 65A | Custom htp cpe | 3,010 | 2,448 | 7,565 |
| 65B | S-33 htp cpe | 3,030 | 2,628 | 4,865 |
| 71B | wgn 4d, 6P | 3,303 | 2,631 | 2,904 |
| 71D | Cus Cruiser wgn 4d, 6–9P | 3,319 | 2,886 | 1,485 |
| 71E | Custom wgn 4d, 6–9P | 3,311 | 2,719 | 3,636 |

### Monterey (120.0)

| | | Wght | Price | Prod |
|---|---|---|---|---|
| 54A | sdn 4d | 3,944 | 2,887 | 18,177 |
| 62A | sdn 2d | 3,854 | 2,834 | 4,640 |
| 65A | htp cpe | 3,869 | 2,930 | 3,879 |
| 75A | htp sdn | 3,959 | 2,995 | 1,692 |

### Monterey Custom (wb 120.0)

| | | Wght | Price | Prod |
|---|---|---|---|---|
| 54B | sdn 4d | 3,956 | 3,075 | 39,542 |
| 63B | Marauder fstbk htp cpe | 3,887 | 3,083 | 7,298 |
| 63C | S-55 Marauder fstbk htp cpe | 3,900 | 3,650 | 2,319 |
| 65B | htp cpe | 3,881 | 3,083 | 10,693 |
| 65C | S-55 htp cpe | 3,894 | 3,650 | 3,863 |
| 75B | htp sdn | 3,971 | 3,148 | 8,604 |
| 75C | S-55 htp sdn | 3,984 | 3,715 | 1,203 |
| 76A | conv cpe | 4,043 | 3,333 | 3,783 |
| 76B | S-55 conv cpe | 4,049 | 3,900 | 1,379 |

### Station Wagon (wb 120.0)

| | | Wght | Price | Prod |
|---|---|---|---|---|
| 71B | Colony Park 4d, 6P | 4,306 | 3,295 | 6,447 |
| 71D | Colony Park 4d, 9P | 4,318 | 3,365 | 7,529 |

| 1963 Engines | bore × stroke | bhp | availability |
|---|---|---|---|
| L6, 144.3 | 3.50×2.50 | 85 | S-Comet sdns |
| L6, 170.0 | 3.50×2.94 | 101 | S-other Comet, Meteor |
| V8, 221.0 | 3.50×2.87 | 145 | O-Comet, Meteor |
| V8, 260.0 | 3.80×2.87 | 164 | O-Meteor/Cus, S-33, Comet |
| V8, 390.0 | 4.05×3.78 | 250 | S-Monterey, Monterey Custom |
| V8, 390.0 | 4.05×3.78 | 300 | S-S-55; O-other Monterey |
| V8, 390.0 | 4.05×3.78 | 330 | O-Montereys, wagons |
| V8, 406.0 | 4.13×3.78 | 385 | O-Monterey, Monterey Custom |
| V8, 406.0 | 4.13×3.78 | 405 | O-Monterey, Monterey Custom |

## 1964

### Comet 202 (wb 114.0)

| | | Wght | Price | Prod |
|---|---|---|---|---|
| 01 | sdn 2d | 2,539 | 2,126 | 33,824 |
| 02 | sdn 4d | 2,580 | 2,182 | 29,147 |
| 32 | wgn 4d | 2,727 | 2,463 | 5,504 |

### Comet 404 (wb 114.0)

| | | Wght | Price | Prod |
|---|---|---|---|---|
| 11 | sdn 2d | 2,551 | 2,213 | 12,512 |
| 12 | sdn 4d | 2,588 | 2,269 | 25,136 |
| 34 | Custom wgn 4d | 2,741 | 2,550 | 6,918 |
| 36 | Villager wgn 4d | 2,745 | 2,734 | 1,980 |

### Comet Caliente (wb 114.0)

| | | Wght | Price | Prod |
|---|---|---|---|---|
| 22 | sdn 4d | 2,668 | 2,350 | 27,218 |
| 23 | htp cpe | 2,688 | 2,375 | 31,204 |
| 25 | conv cpe | 2,861 | 2,636 | 9,039 |

### Comet Cyclone (wb 114.0)

| | | Wght | Price | Prod |
|---|---|---|---|---|
| 27 | htp cpe | 2,860 | 2,655 | 7,454 |

| Monterey (wb 120.0) | | Wght | Price | Prod |
|---|---|---|---|---|
| 41 | sdn 2d | 3,895 | 2,819 | 3,932 |
| 42 | sdn 4d | 3,985 | 2,892 | 20,234 |
| 43 | htp cpe | 3,910 | 2,884 | 2,926 |
| 45 | conv cpe | 4,027 | 3,226 | 2,592 |
| 47 | Marauder fstbk htp cpe | 3,916 | 2,884 | 8,760 |
| 48 | Marauder fstbk htp sdn | 3,914 | 2,957 | 4,143 |

| Montclair (wb 120.0) | | | | |
|---|---|---|---|---|
| 52 | sdn 4d | 3,996 | 3,116 | 15,520 |
| 53 | htp cpe | 3,921 | 3,127 | 2,329 |
| 57 | Marauder fstbk htp cpe | 3,927 | 3,127 | 6,459 |
| 58 | Marauder fstbk htp sdn | 4,017 | 3,181 | 8,655 |

| Park Lane (wb 120.0) | | | | |
|---|---|---|---|---|
| 62 | sdn 4d | 4,035 | 3,348 | 6,230 |
| 63 | htp cpe | 3,960 | 3,359 | 1,786 |
| 64 | htp sdn | 4,050 | 3,413 | 2,402 |
| 65 | conv cpe | 4,066 | 3,549 | 1,967 |
| 67 | Marauder fstbk htp cpe | 3,966 | 3,359 | 1,052 |
| 68 | Marauder fstbk htp sdn | 4,056 | 3,413 | 4,505 |

| Station Wagon (wb 120.0) | | | | |
|---|---|---|---|---|
| 72 | Commuter 4d, 6P | 4,259 | 3,236 | 3,484 |
| 72 | Commuter 4d, 9P | 4,271 | 3,306 | 1,839 |
| 76 | Colony Park 4d, 6P | 4,275 | 3,434 | 4,234 |
| 76 | Colony Park 4d, 9P | 4,287 | 3,504 | 5,624 |

| 1964 Engines | bore × stroke | bhp | availability |
|---|---|---|---|
| L6, 170.0 | 3.50 × 2.94 | 101 | S-Comet |
| L6, 200.0 | 3.68 × 3.15 | 116 | O-Comet |
| V8, 260.0 | 3.80 × 2.87 | 164 | O-Comet |
| V8, 289.0 | 4.00 × 2.87 | 210 | S-Cyclone; O-other Comets |
| V8, 390.0 | 4.05 × 3.78 | 250 | S-all exc Comet, Park Lane |
| V8, 390.0 | 4.05 × 3.78 | 266 | O-all exc Comet, Park Lane |
| V8, 390.0 | 4.05 × 3.78 | 300 | S-Park Lane |
| V8, 390.0 | 4.05 × 3.78 | 330 | O-Park Lane |
| V8, 427.0 | 4.23 × 3.78 | 410 | O-Monterey, Montclair, P Lane |
| V8, 427.0 | 4.23 × 3.78 | 425 | O-Monterey, Montclair, P Lane |

# 1965

| Comet 202 (wb 114.0) | | Wght | Price | Prod |
|---|---|---|---|---|
| 01 | sdn 2d | 2,584 | 2,154 | 32,425 |
| 02 | sdn 4d | 2,624 | 2,210 | 23,501 |
| 32 | wgn 4d | 2,784 | 2,491 | 4,814 |

| Comet 404 (wb 114.0) | | | | |
|---|---|---|---|---|
| 11 | sdn 2d | 2,594 | 2,241 | 10,900 |
| 12 | sdn 4d | 2,629 | 2,294 | 18,628 |
| 34 | Custom wgn 4d | 2,789 | 2,578 | 5,226 |
| 36 | Villager wgn 4d | 2,789 | 2,762 | 1,592 |

| Comet Caliente (wb 114.0) | | | | |
|---|---|---|---|---|
| 22 | sdn 4d | 2,659 | 2,378 | 20,337 |
| 23 | htp sdn | 2,684 | 2,403 | 29,247 |
| 25 | conv cpe | 2,869 | 2,664 | 6,035 |

| Comet Cyclone (wb 114.0) | | | | |
|---|---|---|---|---|
| 27 | htp cpe | 2,994 | 2,683 | 12,347 |

| Monterey (wb 123.0) | | | | |
|---|---|---|---|---|
| 42 | Breezeway sdn 4d | 3,898 | 2,904 | 19,569 |
| 43 | sdn 2d | 3,788 | 2,767 | 5,775 |
| 44 | sdn 4d | 3,853 | 2,839 | 23,363 |
| 45 | conv cpe | 3,928 | 3,230 | 4,762 |
| 47 | htp cpe | 3,823 | 2,902 | 16,857 |
| 48 | htp sdn | 3,893 | 2,978 | 10,047 |

| Montclair (wb 123.0) | | | | |
|---|---|---|---|---|
| 52 | Breezeway sdn 4d | 3,933 | 3,137 | 18,924 |
| 57 | htp cpe | 3,848 | 3,135 | 9,645 |
| 58 | htp sdn | 3,928 | 3,210 | 16,977 |

| Park Lane (wb 123.0) | | Wght | Price | Prod |
|---|---|---|---|---|
| 62 | Breezeway sdn 4d | 3,988 | 3,369 | 8,335 |
| 65 | conv cpe | 4,013 | 3,599 | 3,006 |
| 67 | htp cpe | 3,908 | 3,367 | 6,853 |
| 68 | htp sdn | 3,983 | 3,442 | 14,211 |

| Station Wagon (wb 119.0) | | | | |
|---|---|---|---|---|
| 72 | Commuter 4d, 6P | 4,178 | 3,235 | 5,453 |
| 72 | Commuter 4d, 9P | 4,213 | 3,312 | 2,628 |
| 76 | Colony Park 4d, 6P | 4,228 | 3,434 | 6,910 |
| 76 | Colony Park 4d, 9P | 4,263 | 3,511 | 8,384 |

| 1965 Engines | bore × stroke | bhp | availability |
|---|---|---|---|
| L6, 200.0 | 3.68 × 3.15 | 120 | S-Comet |
| V8, 289.0 | 4.00 × 2.87 | 200 | S-Cyclone; O-other Comet |
| V8, 289.0 | 4.00 × 2.87 | 225 | O-Comet |
| V8, 390.0 | 4.05 × 3.78 | 250 | S-Monterey, Commuter |
| V8, 390.0 | 4.05 × 3.78 | 266 | S-Montclair, Colony Park |
| V8, 390.0 | 4.05 × 3.78 | 300 | S-Park Lane; O-all exc Comet |
| V8, 390.0 | 4.05 × 3.78 | 330 | O-all exc Comet |
| V8, 427.0 | 4.23 × 3.78 | 425 | O-all exc Comet |

# 1966

| Comet 202 (wb 116.0; wgn-113.0) | | Wght | Price | Prod |
|---|---|---|---|---|
| 01 | sdn 2d | 2,864 | 2,206 | 35,964 |
| 02 | sdn 4d | 2,908 | 2,263 | 20,440 |
| 06 | Voyager wgn 4d | 3,282 | 2,553 | 7,595 |

| Comet Capri (wb 116.0; wgn-113.0) | | | | |
|---|---|---|---|---|
| 12 | sdn 4d | 2,928 | 2,378 | 15,635 |
| 13 | htp cpe | 2,960 | 2,400 | 15,031 |
| 16 | Villager wgn 4d | 3,319 | 2,790 | 3,880 |

| Comet Caliente (wb 116.0) | | | | |
|---|---|---|---|---|
| 22 | sdn 4d | 2,930 | 2,453 | 17,933 |
| 23 | htp cpe | 2,966 | 2,475 | 25,862 |
| 25 | conv cpe | 3,228 | 2,735 | 3,922 |

| Comet Cyclone (wb 116.0) | | | | |
|---|---|---|---|---|
| 27 | htp cpe | 3,078 | 2,700 | 6,889 |
| 27 | GT htp cpe | 3,315 | 2,891 | 13,812 |
| 29 | conv cpe | 3,321 | 2,961 | 1,305 |
| 29 | GT conv cpe | 3,595 | 3,152 | 2,158 |

| Monterey (wb 123.0) | | | | |
|---|---|---|---|---|
| 42 | Breezeway sdn 4d | 3,966 | 2,917 | 14,174 |
| 43 | sdn 2d | 3,835 | 2,783 | 2,487 |
| 44 | sdn 4d | 3,903 | 2,854 | 18,998 |
| 45 | conv cpe | 4,039 | 3,237 | 3,279 |
| 47 | fstbk htp cpe | 3,885 | 2,915 | 19,103 |
| 48 | fstbk htp sdn | 3,928 | 2,990 | 7,647 |

| S-55 (wb 123.0) | | | | |
|---|---|---|---|---|
| 46 | conv cpe | 4,148 | 3,614 | 669 |
| 49 | fstbk htp cpe | 4,031 | 3,292 | 2,916 |

| Montclair (wb 123.0) | | | | |
|---|---|---|---|---|
| 54 | sdn 4d | 3,921 | 3,087 | 11,856 |
| 57 | fstbk htp cpe | 3,887 | 3,144 | 11,290 |
| 58 | fstbk htp sdn | 3,971 | 3,217 | 15,767 |

| Park Lane (wb 123.0) | | | | |
|---|---|---|---|---|
| 62 | Breezeway sdn 4d | 4,051 | 3,389 | 8,692 |
| 65 | conv cpe | 4,148 | 3,608 | 2,546 |
| 67 | fstbk htp cpe | 3,971 | 3,387 | 8,354 |
| 68 | fstbk htp sdn | 4,070 | 3,460 | 19,204 |

| Station Wagon (wb 119.0) | | | | |
|---|---|---|---|---|
| 72 | Commuter 4d, 6P | 4,280 | 3,240 | 3,970 |
| 72 | Commuter 4d, 9P | 4,331 | 3,336 | 2,877 |
| 76 | Colony Park 4d, 6P | 4,332 | 3,502 | 7,190 |
| 76 | Colony Park 4d, 9P | 4,383 | 3,598 | 11,704 |

# Mercury

| 1966 Engines | bore × stroke | bhp | availability |
|---|---|---|---|
| L6, 200.0 | 3.68 × 3.15 | 120 | S-Comet exc Cyclone |
| V8, 289.0 | 4.00 × 2.87 | 200 | S-Cyclone; O-other Comet |
| V8, 390.0 | 4.05 × 3.78 | 265 | S-Cyclone GT, full-size w/man |
| V8, 390.0 | 4.05 × 3.78 | 275 | S-full-size w/auto  Cyclone GT |
| V8, 390.0 | 4.05 × 3.78 | 335 | O-Cyclone GT |
| V8, 410.0 | 4.05 × 3.98 | 330 | S-Park Lane; O-other full-size |
| V8, 428.0 | 4.13 × 3.98 | 345 | S-S-55; O-other full-size |

| 1967 Engines | bore × stroke | bhp | availability |
|---|---|---|---|
| L6, 200.0 | 3.68 × 3.15 | 120 | S-Comet exc Cyclone |
| V8, 289.0 | 4.00 × 2.87 | 200 | S-Cougar, Cycl; O-other Comet |
| V8, 289.0 | 4.00 × 2.87 | 225 | O-Cougar |
| V8, 390.0 | 4.05 × 3.78 | 270 | S-Montclair, S Wgn; O-Comet |
| V8, 390.0 | 4.05 × 3.78 | 320 | S-Cycl/Cougar GT; O-Other Cougar |
| V8, 410.0 | 4.05 × 3.98 | 330 | S-P Lane, Brghm, Marquis; O-Monterey, Montclair |
| V8, 427.0 | 4.23 × 3.78 | 410 | O-Comet htps and 2d sedans |
| V8, 427.0 | 4.23 × 3.78 | 425 | O-Comet htps and 2d sedans |
| V8, 428.0 | 4.13 × 3.98 | 345 | S-S-55; O-other full-size |

## 1967

| Comet 202 (wb 116.0) | | Wght | Price | Prod |
|---|---|---|---|---|
| 01 | sdn 2d | 2,868 | 2,284 | 14,251 |
| 02 | sdn 4d | 2,906 | 2,336 | 10,284 |

| Comet Capri (wb 116.0) | | | | |
|---|---|---|---|---|
| 06 | sdn 4d | 2,940 | 2,436 | 9,292 |
| 07 | htp cpe | 2,970 | 2,459 | 11,671 |

| Comet Caliente (wb 116.0) | | | | |
|---|---|---|---|---|
| 10 | sdn 4d | 2,952 | 2,535 | 9,153 |
| 11 | htp cpe | 2,982 | 2,558 | 9,966 |
| 12 | conv cpe | 3,250 | 2,818 | 1,539 |

| Comet Station Wagon (wb 113.0) | | | | |
|---|---|---|---|---|
| 03 | Voyager 4d | 3,310 | 2,604 | 4,930 |
| 08 | Villager 4d | 3,332 | 2,841 | 3,140 |

| Comet Cyclone (wb 116.0) | | | | |
|---|---|---|---|---|
| 15 | htp cpe | 3,075 | 2,737 | 2,682 |
| 15 | GT htp cpe | 3,090 | 3,034 | 3,419 |
| 16 | conv cpe | 3,339 | 2,997 | 431 |
| 16 | GT conv cpe | 3,350 | 3,294 | 378 |

| Cougar (wb 111.0) | | | | |
|---|---|---|---|---|
| 91 | htp cpe | 2,988 | 2,851 | 116,260 |
| 91 | GT htp cpe | 3,000 | 3,175 | 7,412 |
| 93 | XR7 htp cpe | 3,015 | 3,081 | 27,221 |

| Monterey (wb 123.0) | | | | |
|---|---|---|---|---|
| 44 | sdn 4d | 3,798 | 2,904 | 15,177 |
| 44 | Breezeway sdn 4d | 3,847 | 2,967 | 5,910 |
| 45 | conv cpe | 3,943 | 3,314 | 2,673 |
| 46 | S-55 conv cpe | 3,960 | 3,837 | 145 |
| 47 | htp cpe | 3,820 | 2,985 | 16,910 |
| 48 | htp sdn | 3,858 | 3,059 | 8,013 |
| 49 | S-55 fstbk htp cpe | 3,837 | 3,511 | 570 |

| Montclair (wb 123.0) | | | | |
|---|---|---|---|---|
| 54 | sdn 4d | 3,863 | 3,187 | 5,783 |
| 54 | Breezeway sdn 4d | 3,881 | 3,250 | 4,151 |
| 57 | htp cpe | 3,848 | 3,244 | 4,118 |
| 58 | htp sdn | 3,943 | 3,316 | 5,870 |

| Park Lane (wb 123.0) | | | | |
|---|---|---|---|---|
| 61 | Brougham Breezeway sdn 4d | 3,980 | 3,896 | 3,325 |
| 62 | Brougham htp sdn | 4,000 | 3,986 | 4,189 |
| 64 | Breezeway sdn 4d | 4,011 | 3,736 | 4,163 |
| 65 | conv cpe | 4,114 | 3,984 | 1,191 |
| 67 | htp cpe | 3,947 | 3,752 | 2,196 |
| 68 | htp sdn | 3,992 | 3,826 | 5,412 |

| Marquis (wb 123.0) | | | | |
|---|---|---|---|---|
| 69 | htp cpe | 3,995 | 3,989 | 6,510 |

| Station Wagon (wb 119.0) | | | | |
|---|---|---|---|---|
| 72 | Commuter 4d, 6P | 4,178 | 3,289 | 3,447 |
| 72 | Commuter 4d, 9P | 4,297 | 3,384 | 4,451 |
| 76 | Colony Park 4d, 6P | 4,258 | 3,657 | 5,775 |
| 76 | Colony Park 4d, 9P | 4,294 | 3,752 | 12,915 |

## 1968

| Comet (wb 116.0) | | Wght | Price | Prod |
|---|---|---|---|---|
| 01 | htp cpe | 3,166 | 2,477 | 16,693 |

| Montego (wb 116.0; wgn-113.0) | | | | |
|---|---|---|---|---|
| 06 | sdn 4d | 3,062 | 2,504 | 18,492 |
| 07 | htp cpe | 3,138 | 2,552 | 15,002 |
| 08 | MX wgn 4d | 3,460 | 2,876 | 9,328 |
| 10 | MX sdn 4d* | 3,088 | 2,657 | 18,413 |
| 11 | MX htp cpe* | 3,162 | 2,676 | 25,827 |
| 12 | MX conv cpe | 3,374 | 2,935 | 3,248 |

| Cyclone (wb 116.0) | | | | |
|---|---|---|---|---|
| 15 | fstbk htp cpe | 3,407 | 2,768 | 6,165 |
| 15 | GT fstbk htp cpe | 3,430 | 2,936 | 6,105 |
| 17 | htp cpe | 3,361 | 2,768 | 1,034 |
| 17 | GT htp cpe | 3,380 | 2,936 | 334 |

| Cougar (wb 111.0)* | | | | |
|---|---|---|---|---|
| 91 | htp cpe | 3,134 | 2,933 | 81,014 |
| 93 | XR7 htp cpe | 3,174 | 3,232 | 32,712 |

| Monterey (wb 123.0) | | | | |
|---|---|---|---|---|
| 44 | sdn 4d | 3,895 | 3,052 | 30,727 |
| 45 | conv cpe | 3,977 | 3,436 | 1,515 |
| 47 | htp cpe | 3,854 | 3,133 | 15,845 |
| 48 | htp sdn | 3,892 | 3,207 | 8,927 |

| Montclair (wb 123.0) | | | | |
|---|---|---|---|---|
| 54 | sdn 4d | 3,897 | 3,331 | 7,255 |
| 57 | htp cpe | 3,882 | 3,387 | 3,497 |
| 58 | htp sdn | 3,907 | 3,459 | 4,008 |

| Park Lane (wb 123.0) | | | | |
|---|---|---|---|---|
| 64 | sdn 4d** | 4,019 | 3,552 | 6,408 |
| 65 | conv cpe | 4,122 | 3,822 | 1,112 |
| 67 | htp cpe | 3,955 | 3,575 | 2,584 |
| 68 | htp sdn** | 4,000 | 3,647 | 10,390 |

| Marquis (wb 123.0) | | | | |
|---|---|---|---|---|
| 69 | htp cpe | 3,987 | 3,685 | 3,965 |

| Station Wagon (wb 119.0) | | | | |
|---|---|---|---|---|
| 72 | Commuter 4d, 6P | 4,212 | 3,441 | 3,497 |
| 72 | Commuter 4d, 9P | 4,331 | 3,569 | 5,191 |
| 76 | Colony Park 4d, 6P | 4,259 | 3,460 | 5,674 |
| 76 | Colony Park 4d, 6P | 4,295 | 3,888 | 15,505 |

*Includes cars with Brougham trim option.
**Includes cars with GT and GTE package options.

| 1968 Engines | bore × stroke | bhp | availability |
|---|---|---|---|
| L6, 200.0 | 3.68 × 3.15 | 115 | S-Comet, Montego |
| V8, 289.0 | 4.00 × 2.87 | 195 | S-base Cougars; O-Comet |
| V8, 302.0 | 4.00 × 3.00 | 210 | S-Cougar Cyclone, O-Montego |
| V8, 302.0 | 4.00 × 3.00 | 230 | O-Cougar, Montego |
| V8, 390.0 | 4.05 × 3.78 | 265 | S-full-size w/man; O-Montego, Cyclone |
| V8, 390.0 | 4.05 × 3.78 | 280 | S-full-size w/auto; O-Cougar |

| | bore×stroke | bhp | availability |
|---|---|---|---|
| V8, 390.0 | 4.05×3.78 | 315 | S-P Lane, Brghm, Marquis; O-other full-size |
| V8, 390.0 | 4.05×3.78 | 325 | S-Cougar GT; O-Montego exc MX wgn, Cyclone, Cougar, XR7 |
| V8, 427.0 | 4.23×3.78 | 390 | S-Cougar GTE; O-Montego htps |
| V8, 428.0 | 4.13×3.98 | 340 | O-full-size only |

## 1969

**Comet (wb 116.0)**

| | | Wght | Price | Prod |
|---|---|---|---|---|
| 01 | htp cpe | 3,175 | 2,532 | 14,104 |

**Montego (wb 116.0; wgn-113.0)**

| | | Wght | Price | Prod |
|---|---|---|---|---|
| 06 | sdn 4d | 3,140 | 2,556 | 21,950 |
| 07 | htp cpe | 3,154 | 2,605 | 17,785 |
| 08 | MX wgn 4d | 3,504 | 2,979 | 10,590 |
| 10 | MX sdn 4d | 3,174 | 2,718 | 16,148 |
| 10 | MX Brougham sdn 4d | 3,198 | 2,808 | 1,590 |
| 11 | MX htp cpe | 3,186 | 2,736 | 23,160 |
| 11 | MX Brougham htp cpe | 3,210 | 2,826 | 1,226 |

**Cyclone (wb 116.0)**

| | | Wght | Price | Prod |
|---|---|---|---|---|
| 15 | fstbk htp cpe | 3,273 | 2,771 | 5,882 |
| 16 | CJ fstbk htp cpe | 3,634 | 3,224 | 3,261 |

**Cougar (wb 111.0)**

| | | Wght | Price | Prod |
|---|---|---|---|---|
| 91 | htp cpe | 3,219 | 3,016 | 66,331 |
| 92 | conv cpe | 3,343 | 3,382 | 5,796 |
| 93 | XR7 htp cpe | 3,221 | 3,315 | 23,918 |
| 94 | XR7 conv cpe | 3,343 | 3,595 | 4,024 |

**Monterey (wb 124.0, wgn 121.0)**

| | | Wght | Price | Prod |
|---|---|---|---|---|
| 44 | sdn 4d | 3,948 | 3,158 | 23,009 |
| 45 | conv cpe | 4,093 | 3,540 | 1,297 |
| 46 | htp cpe | 3,970 | 3,237 | 9,865 |
| 48 | htp sdn | 4,008 | 3,313 | 6,066 |
| 72 | wgn 4d, 6-9P | 4,277 | 3,536 | 5,844 |

**Monterey Custom (wb 124.0; wgn-121.0)**

| | | Wght | Price | Prod |
|---|---|---|---|---|
| 54 | sdn 4d | 4,013 | 3,377 | 7,103 |
| 56 | htp cpe | 3,998 | 3,459 | 2,898 |
| 58 | htp sdn | 4,023 | 3,533 | 2,827 |
| 74 | wgn 4d, 6-9P | 4,342 | 3,757 | 1,920 |

**Marauder (wb 121.0)**

| | | Wght | Price | Prod |
|---|---|---|---|---|
| 60 | htp cpe | 4,044 | 3,368 | 9,031 |
| 61 | X-100 htp cpe | 4,191 | 4,091 | 5,635 |

**Marquis (wb 124.0; wgn-121.0)**

| | | Wght | Price | Prod |
|---|---|---|---|---|
| 63 | sdn 4d | 4,226 | 3,857 | 16,787 |
| 63 | Brougham sdn 4d | 4,195 | 4,129 | 14,601 |
| 65 | conv cpe | 4,359 | 4,124 | 2,319 |
| 66 | htp cpe | 4,192 | 3,919 | 9,907 |
| 66 | Brougham htp cpe | 4,215 | 4,191 | 8,395 |
| 68 | htp sdn | 4,237 | 3,990 | 14,423 |
| 68 | Brougham htp sdn | 4,436 | 4,262 | 14,966 |
| 76 | Colony Park wgn 4d, 6-9P | 4,376 | 3,895 | 25,604 |

**1969 Engines**

| | bore×stroke | bhp | availability |
|---|---|---|---|
| L6, 250.0 | 3.68×3.91 | 155 | S-Comet, Montego |
| V8, 302.0 | 4.00×3.00 | 220 | S-Cyclone; O-Comet, Montego |
| V8, 351.0 | 4.00×3.50 | 250 | S-Coug; O-Montego, Comet, Cyc |
| V8, 351.0 | 4.00×3.50 | 290 | O-Coug, Comet, Cyc, Montego |
| V8, 390.0 | 4.05×3.78 | 265 | S-Mntry, Mrdr, SW w/man |
| V8, 390.0 | 4.05×3.78 | 280 | S-Mntry, Mrdr, SW w/man |
| V8, 390.0 | 4.05×3.78 | 320 | O-Coug, Montego, Cyc, Comet |
| V8, 428.0 | 4.13×3.98 | 335 | S-CJ; O-Cougar; Montego exc Brghm, SW, conv/sdns with 4spd |
| V8, 428.0 | 4.13×3.98 | 335 | O-Coug, Cyc, Cyc CJ (ram air) |
| V8, 429.0 | 4.36×3.59 | 320 | S-Marquis; O-other full-size |

| | bore×stroke | bhp | availability |
|---|---|---|---|
| V8, 429.0 | 4.36×3.59 | 360 | S- X-100; O-other full-size |

## 1970

**Montego (wb 117.0; wgn-114.0)**

| | | Wght | Price | Prod |
|---|---|---|---|---|
| 01 | htp cpe | 2,859 | 2,645 | 21,298 |
| 02 | sdn 4d | 3,208 | 2,631 | 13,988 |
| 06 | MX sdn 4d | 3,215 | 2,728 | 16,708 |
| 07 | MX htp cpe | 3,228 | 2,740 | 15,533 |
| 08 | MX wgn 4d, 6P | 3,653 | 3,091 | 5,094 |
| 10 | MX Brougham sdn 4d | 3,238 | 2,896 | 3,315 |
| 11 | MX Brougham htp cpe | 3,248 | 2,915 | 8,074 |
| 12 | MX Brougham htp sdn | 3,268 | 3,037 | 3,685 |
| 18 | MX Brghm wgn 4d, 6P | 3,668 | 3,304 | 2,682 |

**Cyclone (wb 117.0)**

| | | Wght | Price | Prod |
|---|---|---|---|---|
| 15 | htp cpe | 3,721 | 3,238 | 1,695 |
| 16 | GT htp cpe | 3,462 | 3,226 | 10,170 |
| 17 | Spoiler htp cpe | 3,773 | 3,759 | 1,631 |

**Cougar (wb 111.1)**

| | | Wght | Price | Prod |
|---|---|---|---|---|
| 91 | htp cpe | 3,285 | 3,114 | 49,479 |
| 92 | conv cpe | 3,382 | 3,480 | 2,322 |
| 93 | XR7 htp cpe | 3,311 | 3,413 | 18,565 |
| 94 | XR7 conv cpe | 3,408 | 3,692 | 1,977 |

**Monterey (wb 124.0; wgn-121.0)**

| | | Wght | Price | Prod |
|---|---|---|---|---|
| 44 | sdn 4d | 3,926 | 3,248 | 29,432 |
| 45 | conv cpe | 4,071 | 3,668 | 581 |
| 46 | htp cpe | 3,890 | 3,329 | 9,359 |
| 48 | htp sdn | 3,961 | 3,406 | 5,032 |
| 72 | wgn 4d, 6P | 4,235 | 3,682 | 1,657 |
| 72 | wgn 4d, 9P | 4,327 | 3,774 | 3,507 |

**Monterey Custom (wb 124.0)**

| | | Wght | Price | Prod |
|---|---|---|---|---|
| 54 | sdn 4d | 3,931 | 3,520 | 4,823 |
| 56 | htp cpe | 3,922 | 3,600 | 1,357 |
| 58 | htp sdn | 3,973 | 3,676 | 1,194 |

**Marauder (wb 121.0)**

| | | Wght | Price | Prod |
|---|---|---|---|---|
| 60 | htp cpe | 3,972 | 3,503 | 3,397 |
| 61 | X-100 htp cpe | 4,128 | 4,136 | 2,646 |

**Marquis (wb 124.0; wgn-121.0)**

| | | Wght | Price | Prod |
|---|---|---|---|---|
| 62 | Brougham sdn 4d | 4,166 | 4,367 | 14,920 |
| 63 | sdn 4d | 4,121 | 4,052 | 14,394 |
| 64 | Brougham htp cpe | 4,119 | 4,428 | 7,113 |
| 65 | conv cpe | 4,337 | 4,318 | 1,233 |
| 66 | htp cpe | 4,072 | 4,113 | 6,229 |
| 67 | Brougham htp sdn | 4,182 | 4,500 | 11,623 |
| 68 | htp sdn | 4,141 | 4,185 | 8,411 |
| 74 | wgn 4d, 6P | 4,347 | 3,930 | 959 |
| 74 | wgn 4d, 9P | 4,393 | 4,022 | 1,429 |
| 76 | Colony Park wgn 4d, 6P | 4,442 | 4,123 | 4,655 |
| 76 | Colony Park wgn 4d, 9P | 4,488 | 4,215 | 14,549 |

**1970 Engines**

| | bore×stroke | bhp | availability |
|---|---|---|---|
| L6, 250.0 | 3.68×3.91 | 155 | S-Montego |
| V8, 302.0 | 4.00×3.00 | 220 | O-Montego |
| V8, 302.0 | 4.00×3.00 | 290 | O-Cougar Eliminator |
| V8, 351.0 | 4.00×3.50 | 250 | S-Cyclone, Cougar; O-Montego |
| V8, 351.0 | 4.00×3.50 | 300 | S-Cgr Elmntr; O-Coug, Montego |
| V8, 390.0 | 4.05×3.78 | 265 | S-Monterey, Marauder, C. Park w/man |
| V8, 390.0 | 4.05×3.78 | 280 | S-above models w/auto |
| V8, 428.0 | 4.13×3.98 | 335 | O-Cougar |
| V8, 429.0 | 4.36×3.59 | 320 | S-Marquis exc Colony Park |
| V8, 429.0 | 4.36×3.59 | 360 | S-Cyc, Mrdr X-100; O-Montego exc Spoiler, Mntry, Mrdr, C Park |
| V8, 429.0 | 4.36×3.59 | 370 | S-Spoiler; O-Cyclone, GT* |
| V8, 429.0 | 4.36×3.59 | 375 | O-all Cyclone |
| V8, 429.0 | 4.36×3.59 | 375 | O-all Cyclone ("Boss") |

*Available in Ram-Air and non-Ram-Air versions.

# Nash

**Nash-Kelvinator Corp. (1940-53); Nash Division, American Motors Corporation (1953-57)**
**Kenosha, Wisconsin**

The first Nash appeared in 1918 and sold well. The company expanded in the 1920s, absorbing firms like Mitchell and Lafayette, and produced the low-priced, six-cylinder Ajax. Nash reintroduced the Lafayette as an inexpensive companion make in 1934. Selling for as little as $600, Lafayette established its builder's intention to pursue the low-to-middle-price market.

After bottoming out at 15,000 units in Depression year 1933, Nash sales steadily increased, reaching a record in 1937. A momentary downturn occurred the next year, but the company soon returned to high volume: 60,000-plus in 1939 and '40, 84,000 in 1941. In the late '30s, Nash and Lafayette combined production had ranked around 14th in the industry.

For Nash, 1940 marked the end of an era: the last Lafayette and the last use of separate body-and-chassis construction. The line consisted of the Lafayette Six and the Nash Ambassador with six-cylinder or straight-eight power. The six was a valve-in-head design, producing 99 horsepower in the Lafayette and 105 bhp in

the Ambassador. Having seven main bearings, it was an exceptionally quiet and smooth-running unit, if not exactly speedy off the line. The refined nine-main-bearing Ambassador eight was also a valve-in-head power-plant, with 115 bhp. For about $150 more than the Lafayette, the Ambassador Six offered a four-inch longer wheelbase and more horsepower. Looks were similar. Both used strong, vertical, peaked grilles and smooth, flowing lines complemented by nicely rounded fenders. Body styles in all three series were exactly the same. Nash and Lafayette combined output recorded 62,131 units for the model year.

The unit body/chassis 600 for 1941 was an important breakthrough for Nash. (The designation, incidentally, stood for 600 miles to a 20-gallon tankful.) Styling was similar to the 1940 line, but different enough to be accepted as entirely new. It was a handsome package on a 112-inch wheelbase and price was remarkable: just $805 for the fastback four-door sedan, less than the price of a Ford V8. *Time* called it "the only completely new car in 1941," and sales were high. The 600 engine

1940 Ambassador Eight four-door fastback sedan

1940 Ambassador with custom cabriolet coachwork

1941 "600" DeLuxe four-door sedan

1941 Ambassador Eight All-Purpose cabriolet

was a 172.6-cid six. Eight different models were offered with Special or Deluxe trim, all either sedans or coupes. Cabriolets (two-door convertibles) were listed in the high-priced Ambassador Six line, with the 234 engine and a 121-inch wheelbase, and the Ambassador Eight that shared this same body and chassis. Altogether, 1941 proved to be very profitable. Nash-Kelvinator closed the fiscal year with a $4.6 million profit.

Nash built only 31,780 cars for the short 1942 model year. They had distinctive styling, the result of a big facelift. Following a design trend of the day, Nash adopted a low, wraparound grille made up of three horizontal bars. This motif was repeated on the fenders. The tall '41 frontispiece was dropped in favor of a vertical nameplate and small upper grille of horizontal bars. Parking lights appeared atop the front fenders and a larger hood ornament was used. The three-model lineup—600, Ambassador Six and Eight—remained, but fewer body styles were offered.

During the war, Nash-Kelvinator manufactured $600 million worth of aircraft engines and parts, munitions, cargo trailers, and binocular cases.

Nash finished third in the first postwar production race. That was calendar year 1945, which amounted to only four months of civilian car building. But the firm resumed operations earlier than most, and actually built 6148 cars during that period—one Nash for every two Chevrolets. In 1946, the first full postwar model year, Nash produced about 94,000 cars and ranked eighth; in 1947-48, having produced 101,000 and 110,000 units, it ran 10th and 11th. These early postwar years were good ones for the company, and profits were high.

In June 1948, cigar-chomping Nash president George W. Mason succeeded the venerable Charles W. Nash as chairman of the board. Nash died that month at age 84. During the 1946 celebration of the industry's Golden Jubilee, he'd been one of a dozen industry pioneers still living to share in the honors. Among executives of independent companies, Mason was the most far-seeing. He knew the independents would eventually have to merge to survive, and hoped to put Nash together with Hudson, and ultimately with Studebaker and Packard as well.

Like most other automakers, Nash built slightly renovated versions of its 1942 models for 1946, '47, and '48. Management dropped the eight to concentrate on sixes, increasing the 600's horsepower to 82 and the Ambassador's to 112. Even though alterations were minor, styling appeared quite fresh.

The 600 series comprised three models in 1946-47: a

1942 Ambassador Eight four-door sedan

1942 "600" four-door sedan

1946 Ambassador four-door sedan

1946 Ambassador Suburban four-door sedan

two-door brougham and four-door sedans with trunk-back or fastback lines. The Ambassador Six offered those three plus the unique Sedan Suburban. Like the Chrysler Town & Country and Ford/Mercury Sportsman, it was lavishly trimmed with wood. Nash built 272 Sedan Suburbans in 1946; 595 in 1947; 130 in 1948. Because of the handwork involved, they were quite expensive, and were not fast sellers. But they played the same role as their Chrysler and Ford counterparts, attracting buyers to showrooms with the promise of something new. Suburbans were pretty cars, and ultimately became popular with collectors. Unfortunately, only about 10 to 15 are thought to exist today.

The 1946 styling was only slightly modified for '47. Nash had used inboard parking lights and a wide cen-

1947 Ambassador four-door sedan

1948 "600" Super four-door sedan

1949 Ambassador Super four-door sedan

tral grille in 1946. For '47, grilles were widened again, and new raised-center hubcaps were used. Then in 1948, the side molding below the beltline was eliminated, an inexpensive change that inadvertently made the cars appear higher and less streamlined than before.

The model line was expanded for 1948. Anticipating a significant upsurge in buyer demand, the company made the best of its prewar design, offering three styles of 600 and two of Ambassador. The price leader was the 600 DeLuxe business coupe. The usual assortment of sedans and broughams was offered in Super and Custom trim. Similarly, the Ambassador Super and Custom were listed. The Sedan Suburban was continued as a Super. The Custom included a new convertible—the first open Nash since the war. One thousand of these jaunty soft-tops were produced that year. (The company also built a limited number of trucks bearing sedan-type front ends beginning in 1947; most were exported.)

Nash officials knew they'd have to come up with an all-new car for 1949. Most of the company's independent rivals had restyled by then, and the Big Three were readying all-new designs that year. Nash's answer was the 1949-51 Airflyte. Though it looks positively awful now, it was one of the most advanced cars of its day, bristling with unusual features. Its shape was as purely aerodynamic as a postwar car ever had. Though all manufacturers had toyed with the "bathtub" look, only Nash actually put it into production. The Airflyte began during World War II. Nils Erik Wahlberg had been a Nash engineer ever since the company was formed in 1916. Ted Ulrich, who'd been a unit-body exponent since the '30s, had helped create the 1941 Nash while he was at Budd Inc., the body builders. The '41 was the first successful mass-produced unit-body car. Its success led to Wahlberg hiring Ulrich.

Actual styling of the Airflyte is claimed with some authority by Holden Koto, who, with partner Ted Pietsch, showed a small scale model very much like the eventual production version to Wahlberg in 1943. Wahlberg must have been interested because he had been experimenting with wind tunnel tests on streamlined bodies. The Airflyte's aerodynamics were superior: only 113 pounds of drag at 60 miles per hour, compared to as much as 171 pounds for the similar-looking '49 Packard.

All Airflytes had a one-piece curved windshield, "Uniscope" gauge cluster (a pod mounted atop the steering column), and fully reclining front seatbacks (pneumatic mattresses were sold as accessories). The seats, together with the Nash-Kelvinator "Weather-Eye" heating and ventilation system, made the new Nash the most habitable long-distance touring car in America.

Nash produced 135,000 cars for the 1949 model year, shooting into the industry's top 10. The Airflyte 600s and Ambassadors used the same wheelbases and powerplants that had been used the year before. Three body types were offered: a two-door sedan, a four-door

sedan, and a brougham (club coupe). Prices remained competitive: under $2000 for the 600s; about $2200 to $2400 for the Ambassadors.

At the height of the seller's market, these cars did very well: better, in fact, than any big cars in Nash history. For 1950, the figure was 172,000 units—an all-time company record, though it included about 58,000 Ramblers. The Statesman (nee 600) engine at 172.6 cid also powered the Rambler. Respected since its debut as an L-head in 1928, Nash's hardy old seven-main-bearing six had one of the longest production runs in history, and was not dropped until 1956.

Riding a 100-inch wheelbase, the little Rambler was the very antithesis of the huge Airflyte. Though there had been smaller cars long before World War II, the Rambler was really the first compact to sell in high volume. It was the progenitor of an entirely new breed of American automobile. Ford and Chevrolet had experimented with (and quickly discarded) compact-car designs right after the war, but their concepts were fundamentally different from Nash's. As former AMC President George Romney said, "It's one thing for a small company—a marginal firm—to pioneer a new concept like that and really push it. But it's another thing for people who already have a big slice to begin pushing something that undercuts their basic market."

Small cars fascinated George Mason. In addition to strength-through-mergers, Mason knew that independents needed cars the Big Three didn't offer. Together with chief engineer Meade Moore, Mason kept hammering away until the Rambler was a reality. It arrived just as the sell-anything era was coming to a close, and held Nash's head above water until the company merged with Hudson to become American Motors in 1954. AMC concentrated on Ramblers after 1957.

The first-generation Rambler spanned model years 1950-52. In its first season, it was sold as a two-door station wagon and an interesting convertible, on which the window frames were permanently fixed and only the top collapsed. A Country Club hardtop was added for '51, but most sales came from the practical, attractive wagons. In those early days of all-steel wagons, Ramblers accounted for 22 percent of total U.S. sales of that body type.

Road tester Tom McCahill admired Mason and Nash tremendously. They were, he said, "busier than a mouse in a barrel of hungry cats" with their many projects. Yet another of these endeavors was the Nash-Healey sports car.

Back where production really counted, Airflyte sales had slowed. Last of that type was the '51, easily recognizable by its prominent rear fenders (1949-50 cars had rounded bustle-backs). For his 1952 redesign, Mason went to Pininfarina and the result was much nicer-looking if less aerodynamic. The new, squared-off line included the Statesman and the larger Ambassador, both with unit construction.

The story was much the same for the 1953 models, identified by small chrome spacers on the cowl air-

1951 Ambassador Super four-door sedan

1952 Statesman Custom four-door sedan

1951 Rambler Greenbrier station wagon

scoop. The Statesman engine received a boost in output to 100 bhp. Ambassadors offered a "Le Mans" power option based on the latest Nash-Healey engine: 140 bhp at 4000 rpm through dual carburetors and a high-compression aluminum head.

An attractive new "floating" grille was adopted for 1954. The lineup, however, was much the same as it had been the previous two years. One difference was the deletion of two-door sedans from the two Custom series. Dual carbs and high compression had been successful on the Ambassador, so the Statesman got these modifications in '54. Its six was raised to 110 bhp, and the setup was known (with a furtive look to Chrysler) as "Dual Powerflyte." Nash probably got away with using that name (similar to Chrysler's PowerFlite transmission) only because sales were so dismal. From the heady years of 1950-51, they'd dropped steadily: 154,000 in 1952; 121,000 in 1953; 91,000 in 1954. And a growing portion was accounted for by Rambler. The latter had been facelifted for '53 with a cleaner front end.

# Nash

For 1955, the big Nash appeared with inboard headlights, an easy way to make the car look different, and a V8. Cooperation between newly formed American Motors and Studebaker-Packard put Packard's 320-cid V8 in the Ambassador Eight. It was much quicker than the six and cost $300 more. The Ambassador Six continued to use the six-cylinder engine with optional Le Mans power pack. The Statesman continued with its own L-head six. Each series came in two body styles.

After Hudson joined Nash, 1955-56 Ramblers were distributed to Hudson and Nash dealers alike with the appropriate grille badge. The model lineup grew to include the DeLuxe, Super, and Custom sedans, hardtops, and Cross Country or Suburban wagons. A completely revised model with a 108-inch wheelbase was added for '56. Initially, it was sold as a Nash, but became a separate make the following year. A boxy but practical design, the Rambler line significantly included a novel four-door hardtop (Cross Country) wagon and a hardtop sedan.

With all that, the big Nash was de-emphasized for '56. The last Statesman, a four-door sedan, appeared that year. Ambassadors used the Packard V8 early in the season, then switched to AMC's own 190-bhp, 327-cid V8 in April. Cars with the larger powerplant were called Ambassador Special.

For 1957, Nash moved the headlights back out to the fenders and fielded only two Ambassador models, Super and Custom. The latter was heroically overdecorated, and equipped with a more potent 327 V8, developing 255 bhp with the help of four-barrel carburetor, dual exhausts, and 9:1 compression ratio. The styling was pretty good by contemporary standards. Nash was among the first to offer four headlights as standard, (vertically stacked, no less), but the make was in its last year. AMC was only slowly recovering from the debts forced on it through the Hudson merger and subsequent reorganization. Romney, who became company president on Mason's death in 1954, pinned his hopes for the future solely on the Rambler.

Note: the Metropolitan, a Nash model in 1954-57, was a separate make from 1958 on. For convenience, Metropolitan is discussed under a separate heading.

*continued on page 289*

1953 Ambassador Custom Country Club hardtop coupe

1955 Ambassador Custom four-door sedan

1954 Rambler Custom convertible

1956 Ambassador Custom four-door sedan

1954 Ambassador Custom Country Club hardtop coupe

1957 Ambassador Custom Country Club hardtop coupe

Flashy styling
and high performance
dominate the mid-50s
to late 60s cars.

# COLOR
# SHOWCASE II

1955 Chrysler 300 hardtop coupe

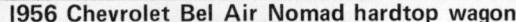

1956 Chevrolet Bel Air Nomad hardtop wagon

1956 Pontiac Star Chief Safari hardtop wagon

1957 Chrysler 300C convertible

1957 Ford Fairlane 500 Victoria hardtop sedan

1957 Chevrolet Bel Air convertible

1957 Mercury Turnpike Cruiser hardtop sedan

1957 Lincoln Premiere Landau hardtop sedan

1957 Continental Mark II hardtop coupe

1957 Cadillac Eldorado Brougham hardtop sedan

1958 Rambler Rebel V8 four-door sedan

1958 Plymouth Fury hardtop coupe

1958 Ford Thunderbird hardtop coupe

1959 Cadillac Eldorado Biarritz convertible

1960 Chrysler 300F convertible

1961 Chevrolet Corvette convertible roadster

1963 Studebaker Lark Daytona hardtop coupe

1963 Lincoln Continental four-door sedan

1963 Cadillac Eldorado Biarritz convertible

1965 Dodge Coronet 500 hardtop coupe

1964½ Ford Mustang hardtop coupe

1964½ Ford Mustang Indianapolis 500 Pace car

1967 Pontiac Grand Prix convertible

1969 Buick Electra 225 Limited hardtop sedan

1969 Imperial LeBaron hardtop coupe

1969 Pontiac GTO convertible

1970 AMC Hornet two-door sedan

1970 Plymouth GTX hardtop coupe

1970 Ford Torino Cobra fastback hardtop coupe

1970 Chevrolet Monte Carlo hardtop coupe

# Nash Specifications

## 1940—62,131 built

| Lafayette (wb 117.0) | | Wght | Price | Prod |
|---|---|---|---|---|
| 4010 | T/B sdn 4d | 3,280 | 875 | — |
| 4011 | All-Purpose cabriolet | 3,310 | 975 | — |
| 4012 | All-Purpose cpe | 3,190 | 850 | — |
| 4013 | fstbk sdn 2d | 3,235 | 845 | — |
| 4014 | bus cpe | 3,190 | 795 | — |
| 4018 | fstbk sdn 4d | 3,275 | 875 | — |

| Ambassador Six (wb 121.0) | | | | |
|---|---|---|---|---|
| 4020 | T/B sdn 4d | 3,305 | 985 | — |
| 4021 | All-Purpose cabriolet | 3,410 | 1,008 | — |
| 4022 | All-Purpose cpe | 3,295 | 960 | — |
| 4023 | fstbk sdn 2d | 3,350 | 955 | — |
| 4025 | bus cpe | 3,290 | 925 | — |
| 4028 | fstbk sdn 4d | 3,380 | 985 | — |

| Ambassador Eight (wb 125.0) | | | | |
|---|---|---|---|---|
| 4080 | T/B sdn 4d | 3,660 | 1,195 | — |
| 4081 | All-Purpose cabriolet | 3,640 | 1,295 | — |
| 4082 | All-Purpose cpe | 3,575 | 1,170 | — |
| 4083 | fstbk sdn 2d | 3,260 | 1,165 | — |
| 4085 | bus cpe | 3,555 | 1,135 | — |
| 4088 | fstbk sdn 4d | 3,655 | 1,195 | — |

| 1940 Engines | bore × stroke | bhp | availability |
|---|---|---|---|
| L6, 234.8 | 3.38×4.38 | 99 | S-Lafayette |
| L6, 234.8 | 3.38×4.38 | 105 | S-Ambassador Six |
| L8, 260.8 | 3.13×4.25 | 115 | S-Ambassador Eight |

## 1941—84,007 built

| 600 (wb 112.0) | | Wght | Price | Prod |
|---|---|---|---|---|
| 4140 | DeLuxe T/B sdn 4d | 2,655 | 880 | — |
| 4142 | DeLuxe bus cpe | 2,500 | 772 | — |
| 4143 | DeLuxe Brougham 2d | 2,575 | 835 | — |
| 4145 | Special bus cpe | 2,490 | 730 | — |
| 4146 | Special fstbk cpe | 2,630 | 765 | — |
| 4147 | Special fstbk sdn 4d | 2,615 | 805 | — |
| 4148 | DeLuxe fstbk sdn 4d | 2,630 | 837 | — |
| 4149 | DeLuxe fstbk sdn 2d | 2,640 | 797 | — |

| Ambassador Six (wb 121.0) | | | | |
|---|---|---|---|---|
| 4160 | T/B sdn 4d | 3,300 | 1,065 | — |
| 4161 | All-Purpose cabriolet | 3,430 | 1,130 | — |
| 4162 | bus cpe | 3,180 | 940 | — |
| 4163 | Brougham 2d | 3,235 | 1,009 | — |
| 4165 | Special bus cpe | 3,310 | 890 | — |
| 4167 | Special fstbk sdn 4d | 3,300 | 970 | — |
| 4168 | fstbk sdn 4d | 3,300 | 1,020 | — |
| 4169 | Special sdn 2d | 3,320 | 933 | — |

| Ambassador Eight (wb 121.0) | | | | |
|---|---|---|---|---|
| 4180 | T/B sdn 4d | 3,475 | 1,186 | — |
| 4181 | All-Purpose cabriolet | 3,580 | 1,250 | — |
| 4183 | DeLuxe Brougham 2d | 3,400 | 1,116 | — |
| 4187 | Special fstbk sdn 4d | 3,465 | 1,091 | — |
| 4188 | DeLuxe fstbk sdn 4d | 3,455 | 1,141 | — |

| 1941 Engines | bore × stroke | bhp | availability |
|---|---|---|---|
| L6, 172.6 | 3.13×3.75 | 75 | S-600 |
| L6, 234.8 | 3.38×4.38 | 105 | S-Ambassador Six |
| L8, 260.8 | 3.13×4.25 | 115 | S-Ambassador Eight |

## 1942—31,780 built

| 600 (wb 112.0) | | Wght | Price | Prod |
|---|---|---|---|---|
| 4240 | T/B sdn 4d | 2,655 | 918 | — |
| 4242 | bus cpe | 2,540 | 843 | — |
| 4243 | Brougham 2d | 2,580 | 883 | — |
| 4248 | fstbk sdn 4d | 2,650 | 893 | — |
| 4249 | sdn 2d | 2,605 | 873 | — |

| Ambassador Six (wb 121.0) | | | | |
|---|---|---|---|---|
| 4260 | T/B sdn 4d | 3,335 | 1,069 | — |
| 4262 | bus cpe | 3,200 | 994 | — |
| 4263 | Brougham 2d | 3,230 | 1,034 | — |
| 4268 | fstbk sdn 4d | 3,335 | 1,044 | — |
| 4269 | sdn 2d | 3,285 | 1,024 | — |

| Ambassador Eight (wb 121.0) | | | | |
|---|---|---|---|---|
| 4280 | T/B sdn 4d | 3,485 | 1,119 | — |
| 4283 | Brougham 2d | 3,385 | 1,084 | — |
| 4288 | fstbk sdn 4d | 3,485 | 1,094 | — |

| 1942 Engines | bore × stroke | bhp | availability |
|---|---|---|---|
| L6, 172.6 | 3.13×3.75 | 75 | S-600 |
| L6, 234.8 | 3.38×4.38 | 105 | S-Ambassador Six |
| L8, 260.8 | 3.13×4.25 | 115 | S-Ambassador Eight |

## 1946—94,000 built

| 600 (wb 112.0) | | Wght | Price | Prod |
|---|---|---|---|---|
| 4640 | T/B sdn 4d | 2,740 | 1,342 | — |
| 4643 | Brougham 2d | 2,685 | 1,293 | — |
| 4648 | fstbk sdn 4d | 2,780 | 1,298 | — |

| Ambassador (wb 121.0) | | | | |
|---|---|---|---|---|
| 4660 | T/B sdn 4d | 3,335 | 1,511 | — |
| 4663 | Brougham 2d | 3,260 | 1,453 | — |
| 4664 | Suburban sdn 4d | 3,470 | 1,929 | 272 |
| 4668 | fstbk sdn 4d | 3,360 | 1,469 | — |

| 1946 Engines | bore × stroke | bhp | availability |
|---|---|---|---|
| L6, 172.6 | 3.13×3.75 | 82 | S-600 |
| L6, 234.8 | 3.38×4.38 | 112 | S-Ambassador |

## 1947—101,000 built

| 600 (wb 112.0) | | Wght | Price | Prod |
|---|---|---|---|---|
| 4740 | T/B sdn 4d | 2,740 | 1,464 | — |
| 4743 | Brougham 2d | 2,685 | 1,415 | — |
| 4748 | fstbk sdn 4d | 2,780 | 1,420 | — |

| Ambassador (wb 121.0) | | | | |
|---|---|---|---|---|
| 4760 | T/B sdn 4d | 3,335 | 1,809 | — |
| 4763 | Brougham 2d | 3,260 | 1,751 | — |
| 4764 | Suburban sdn 4d | 4,664 | 2,227 | 595 |
| 4768 | fstbk sdn 4d | 3,360 | 1,767 | — |

| 1947 Engines | bore × stroke | bhp | availability |
|---|---|---|---|
| L6, 172.6 | 3.13×3.75 | 82 | S-600 |
| L6, 234.8 | 3.38×4.38 | 112 | S-Ambassador |

## 1948*

| 600 (wb 112.0) | | Wght | Price | Prod |
|---|---|---|---|---|
| 4840 | Super T/B sdn 4d | 2,786 | 1,587 | |
| 4842 | DeLuxe bus cpe | 2,635 | 1,478 | |
| 4843 | Super Brougham 2d | 2,731 | 1,538 | |
| 4848 | Super fstbk sdn 4d | 2,826 | 1,543 | |
| 4850 | Custom T/B sdn 4d | 2,786 | 1,776 | |
| 4853 | Custom Brougham 2d | 2,731 | 1,727 | |
| 4858 | Custom fstbk sdn 4d | 2,826 | 1,732 | |

# Nash

## Ambassador (wb 121.0)

| | | Wght | Price | Prod |
|---|---|---|---|---|
| 4860 | Super T/B sdn 4d | 3,387 | 1,916 | — |
| 4863 | Super Brougham 2d | 3,312 | 1,858 | — |
| 4864 | Super Suburban sdn 4d | 3,522 | 2,239 | 130 |
| 4868 | Super fstbk sdn 4d | 3,412 | 1,874 | — |
| 4870 | Custom T/B sdn 4d | 3,387 | 2,105 | — |
| 4871 | Custom cabriolet (conv) | 3,465 | 2,345 | 1,000 |
| 4873 | Custom Brougham 2d | 3,312 | 2,047 | — |
| 4878 | Custom fstbk sdn 4d | 3,412 | 2,063 | — |

*Model year registrations: 110,000.

| 1948 Engines | bore × stroke | bhp | availability |
|---|---|---|---|
| L6, 172.6 | 3.13 × 3.75 | 82 | S-600 |
| L6, 234.8 | 3.38 × 4.38 | 112 | S-Ambassador |

## 1949*

### 600 (wb 112.0)

| | | Wght | Price | Prod |
|---|---|---|---|---|
| 4923 | Super Special Brougham 2d | 2,960 | 1,846 | — |
| 4928 | Super Special sdn 4d | 2,950 | 1,849 | — |
| 4929 | Super Special sdn 2d | 2,935 | 1,824 | — |
| 4943 | Super Brougham 2d | 2,960 | 1,808 | — |
| 4948 | Super sdn 4d | 2,950 | 1,811 | — |
| 4949 | Super sdn 2d | 2,935 | 1,786 | — |
| 4953 | Custom Brougham 2d | 2,970 | 1,997 | — |
| 4958 | Custom sdn 4d | 2,985 | 2,000 | — |
| 4959 | Custom sdn 2d | 2,985 | 1,975 | — |

### Ambassador (wb 121.0)

| | | Wght | Price | Prod |
|---|---|---|---|---|
| 4963 | Super Brougham 2d | 3,390 | 2,191 | — |
| 4968 | Super sdn 4d | 3,385 | 2,195 | — |
| 4969 | Super sdn 2d | 3,365 | 2,170 | — |
| 4973 | Custom Brougham 2d | 3,415 | 2,359 | — |
| 4978 | Custom sdn 4d | 3,415 | 2,363 | — |
| 4979 | Custom sdn 2d | 3,400 | 2,338 | — |
| 4993 | Super Special Brougham 2d | 3,390 | 2,239 | — |
| 4998 | Super Special sdn 4d | 3,385 | 2,243 | — |
| 4999 | Super Special sdn 2d | 3,365 | 2,218 | — |

*Model year registrations: 135,328.

| 1949 Engines | bore × stroke | bhp | availability |
|---|---|---|---|
| L6, 172.6 | 3.13 × 3.75 | 82 | S-600 |
| L6, 234.8 | 3.38 × 4.38 | 112 | S-Ambassador |

## 1950*

### Rambler (wb 100.0)

| | | Wght | Price | Prod |
|---|---|---|---|---|
| 5021 | Custom Landau conv cpe | 2,430 | 1,808 | — |
| 5024 | Custom wgn 2d | 2,515 | 1,808 | — |

### Statesman (wb 112.0)

| | | Wght | Price | Prod |
|---|---|---|---|---|
| 5032 | DeLuxe bus cpe | 2,830 | 1,633 | — |
| 5043 | Super club cpe | 2,940 | 1,735 | — |
| 5048 | Super sdn 4d | 2,965 | 1,738 | — |
| 5049 | Super sdn 2d | 2,930 | 1,713 | — |
| 5053 | Custom club cpe | 2,965 | 1,894 | — |
| 5058 | Custom sdn 4d | 2,990 | 1,897 | — |
| 5059 | Custom sdn 2d | 2,950 | 1,872 | — |

### Ambassador (wb 121.0)

| | | Wght | Price | Prod |
|---|---|---|---|---|
| 5063 | Super club cpe | 3,335 | 2,060 | — |
| 5068 | Super sdn 4d | 3,350 | 2,064 | — |
| 5069 | Super sdn 2d | 3,325 | 2,039 | — |
| 5073 | Custom club cpe | 3,385 | 2,219 | — |
| 5078 | Custom sdn 4d | 3,390 | 2,223 | — |
| 5079 | Custom sdn 2d | 3,365 | 2,198 | — |

*Model year registrations: 171,782.

| 1950 Engines | bore × stroke | bhp | availability |
|---|---|---|---|
| L6, 172.6 | 3.13 × 3.75 | 82 | S-Rambler |
| L6, 184.0 | 3.13 × 4.00 | 82 | S-Statesman |
| L6, 234.8 | 3.38 × 4.38 | 112 | S-Ambassador |

## 1951*

### Rambler (wb 100.0)

| | | Wght | Price | Prod |
|---|---|---|---|---|
| 5114 | Super Suburban wgn 2d | 2,515 | 1,885 | — |
| 5121 | Custom conv cpe | 2,430 | 1,993 | — |
| 5124 | Custom wgn 2d | 2,515 | 1,993 | — |
| 5127 | Custom Cntry Club htp cpe | 2,420 | 1,968 | — |

### Statesman (wb 112.0)

| | | Wght | Price | Prod |
|---|---|---|---|---|
| 5132 | DeLuxe bus cpe | 2,835 | 1,841 | — |
| 5143 | Super club cpe | 2,935 | 1,952 | — |
| 5148 | Super sdn 4d | 2,970 | 1,955 | — |
| 5149 | Super sdn 2d | 2,930 | 1,928 | — |
| 5153 | Custom club cpe | 2,950 | 2,122 | — |
| 5158 | Custom sdn 4d | 2,990 | 2,125 | — |
| 5159 | Custom sdn 2d | 2,940 | 2,099 | — |

### Ambassador (wb 121.0)

| | | Wght | Price | Prod |
|---|---|---|---|---|
| 5163 | Super club cpe | 3,370 | 2,326 | — |
| 5168 | Super sdn 4d | 3,410 | 2,330 | — |
| 5169 | Super sdn 2d | 3,370 | 2,304 | — |
| 5173 | Custom club cpe | 3,395 | 2,496 | — |
| 5178 | Custom sdn 4d | 3,445 | 2,501 | — |
| 5179 | Custom sdn 2d | 3,380 | 2,474 | — |

*Model year registrations: 205,307.

| 1951 Engines | bore × stroke | bhp | availability |
|---|---|---|---|
| L6, 172.6 | 3.13 × 3.75 | 82 | S-Rambler |
| L6, 184.0 | 3.13 × 4.00 | 85 | S-Statesman |
| L6, 234.8 | 3.38 × 4.38 | 115 | S-Ambassador |

## 1952*

### Rambler (wb 100.0)

| | | Wght | Price | Prod |
|---|---|---|---|---|
| 5214 | Super Suburban wgn 2d | 2,515 | 2,003 | — |
| 5221 | Custom conv cpe | 2,430 | 2,119 | — |
| 5224 | Custom wgn 2d | 2,515 | 2,119 | — |
| 5227 | Custom Cntry Club htp cpe | 2,420 | 2,094 | — |

### Statesman (wb 114.3)

| | | Wght | Price | Prod |
|---|---|---|---|---|
| 5245 | Super sdn 4d | 3,045 | 2,178 | — |
| 5246 | Super sdn 2d | 3,025 | 2,144 | — |
| 5255 | Custom sdn 4d | 3,070 | 2,332 | — |
| 5256 | Custom sdn 2d | 3,050 | 2,310 | — |
| 5257 | Custom Cntry Club htp cpe | 3,095 | 2,433 | — |

### Ambassador (wb 121.3)

| | | Wght | Price | Prod |
|---|---|---|---|---|
| 5265 | Super sdn 4d | 3,430 | 2,557 | — |
| 5266 | Super sdn 2d | 3,410 | 2,521 | — |
| 5275 | Custom sdn 4d | 3,480 | 2,716 | — |
| 5276 | Custom sdn 2d | 3,450 | 2,695 | — |
| 5277 | Custom Cntry Club htp cpe | 3,550 | 2,829 | — |

*Model year registrations: 154,291.

| 1952 Engines | bore × stroke | bhp | availability |
|---|---|---|---|
| L6, 172.6 | 3.13 × 3.75 | 82 | S-Rambler |
| L6, 195.6 | 3.13 × 4.25 | 88 | S-Statesman |
| L6, 252.6 | 3.50 × 4.38 | 120 | S-Ambassador |

## 1953*

### Rambler (wb 100.0)

| | | Wght | Price | Prod |
|---|---|---|---|---|
| 5314 | Super Suburban wgn 2d | 2,555 | 2,003 | — |
| 5321 | Custom conv cpe | 2,590 | 2,150 | — |
| 5324 | Custom wgn 2d | 2,570 | 2,119 | — |
| 5327 | Custom Cntry Club htp cpe | 2,550 | 2,125 | — |

### Statesman (wb 114.3)

| | | Wght | Price | Prod |
|---|---|---|---|---|
| 5345 | Super sdn 4d | 3,045 | 2,178 | — |
| 5346 | Super sdn 2d | 3,025 | 2,143 | — |
| 5355 | Custom sdn 4d | 3,070 | 2,332 | — |
| 5356 | Custom sdn 2d | 3,050 | 2,310 | — |
| 5357 | Custom Cntry Club htp cpe | 3,095 | 2,433 | — |

| Ambassador (wb 121.3) | | Wght | Price | Prod |
|---|---|---|---|---|
| 5365 | Super sdn 4d | 3,430 | 2,557 | — |
| 5366 | Super sdn 2d | 3,410 | 2,521 | — |
| 5375 | Custom sdn 4d | 3,480 | 2,716 | — |
| 5376 | Custom sdn 2d | 3,450 | 2,695 | — |
| 5377 | Custom Cntry Club htp cpe | 3,550 | 2,829 | — |

*Model year registrations: 121,793.

| 1953 Engines | bore×stroke | bhp | availability |
|---|---|---|---|
| L6, 184.0 | 3.13×4.00 | 85 | S-Rambler manual |
| L6, 195.6 | 3.13×4.25 | 90 | S-Rambler automatic |
| L6, 195.6 | 3.13×4.25 | 100 | S-Statesman |
| L6, 252.6 | 3.50×4.38 | 120 | S-Ambassador |
| L6, 252.6 | 3.50×4.38 | 140 | O-Ambassador |

## 1954*

| Rambler (wb 100.0, 4d-108.0) | | Wght | Price | Prod |
|---|---|---|---|---|
| 5406 | DeLuxe sdn 2d | 2,425 | 1,550 | — |
| 5414 | Super Suburban wgn 2d | 2,520 | 1,800 | — |
| 5415 | Super sdn 4d | 2,570 | 1,795 | — |
| 5416 | Super sdn 2d | 2,425 | 1,700 | — |
| 5417 | Super Cntry Club htp cpe | 2,465 | 1,800 | — |
| 5421 | Custom conv cpe | 2,555 | 1,980 | — |
| 5424 | Custom wgn 2d | 2,535 | 1,950 | — |
| 5425 | Custom sdn 4d | 2,630 | 1,965 | — |
| 5427 | Custom Cntry Club htp cpe | 2,515 | 1,950 | — |
| 5428 | Custom Cross Cntry wgn 4d | 2,715 | 2,050 | — |

| Statesman (wb 114.3) | | | | |
|---|---|---|---|---|
| 5445 | Super sdn 4d | 3,045 | 2,158 | — |
| 5446 | Super sdn 2d | 3,025 | 2,110 | — |
| 5455 | Custom sdn 4d | 3,095 | 2,332 | — |
| 5457 | Custom Cntry Club htp cpe | 3,120 | 2,423 | — |

| Ambassador (wb 121.3) | | | | |
|---|---|---|---|---|
| 5465 | Super sdn 4d | 3,430 | 2,417 | — |
| 5466 | Super sdn 2d | 3,410 | 2,365 | — |
| 5475 | Custom sdn 4d | 3,505 | 2,600 | — |
| 5477 | Custom Cntry Club htp cpe | 3,575 | 2,735 | — |

*Model year registrations: 91,121.

| 1954 Engines | bore×stroke | bhp | availability |
|---|---|---|---|
| L6, 184.0 | 3.13×4.00 | 85 | S-Rambler 2dr manual |
| L6, 195.6 | 3.13×4.25 | 90 | S-Rambler 4dr, 2dr automatic |
| L6, 195.6 | 3.13×4.25 | 110 | S-Statesman |
| L6, 252.6 | 3.50×4.38 | 130 | S-Ambassador |
| L6, 252.6 | 3.50×4.38 | 140 | O-Ambassador |

## 1955*

| Rambler (wb 100.0, 4d-108.0) | | Wght | Price | Prod |
|---|---|---|---|---|
| 5512 | Fleet bus sdn 2d | 2,400 | — | — |
| 5514 | DeLuxe Suburban wgn 2d | 2,528 | 1,771 | — |
| 5514-1 | Super Suburban wgn 2d | 2,532 | 1,869 | — |
| 5515 | DeLuxe sdn 4d | 2,567 | 1,695 | — |
| 5515-1 | Super sdn 4d | 2,570 | 1,798 | — |
| 5515-2 | Custom sdn 4d | 2,606 | 1,989 | — |
| 5516 | DeLuxe sdn 2d | 2,432 | 1,585 | — |
| 5516-1 | Super sdn 2d | 2,450 | 1,683 | — |
| 5517-2 | Custom Cntry Club htp cpe | 2,518 | 1,995 | — |
| 5518-1 | Fleet Cross Cntry wgn 4d | 2,675 | — | — |
| 5518-2 | Cus Cross Cntry wgn 4d | 2,685 | 2,098 | — |
| 2504 | Fleet util wgn 2d | 2,500 | — | — |

| Statesman (wb 114.5) | | | | |
|---|---|---|---|---|
| 5545-1 | Super sdn 4d | 3,134 | 2,215 | — |
| 5545-2 | Custom sdn 4d | 3,204 | 2,385 | — |
| 5547-2 | Custom Cntry Club htp cpe | 3,220 | 2,495 | — |

| Ambassador Six (wb 121.3) | | Wght | Price | Prod |
|---|---|---|---|---|
| 5565-1 | Super sdn 4d | 3,538 | 2,480 | — |
| 5565-2 | Custom sdn 4d | 3,576 | 2,675 | — |
| 5567-2 | Cus Cntry Club htp cpe | 3,593 | 2,795 | — |

| Ambassador Eight (wb 121.3) | | | | |
|---|---|---|---|---|
| 5585-1 | Super sdn 4d | 3,795 | 2,775 | — |
| 5585-2 | Custom sdn 4d | 3,827 | 2,965 | — |
| 5587-2 | Custom Cntry Club htp cpe | 3,839 | 3,095 | — |

*Model year registrations: 121,261.

| 1955 Engines | bore×stroke | bhp | availability |
|---|---|---|---|
| L6, 195.6 | 3.13×4.25 | 90 | S-Rambler exc Fleet |
| L6, 195.6 | 3.13×4.25 | 100 | S-Rambler Fleet, Statesman man |
| L6, 195.6 | 3.13×4.25 | 110 | S-Statesman auto |
| L6, 252.6 | 3.50×4.38 | 130 | S-Ambassador Six |
| L6, 252.6 | 3.50×4.38 | 140 | O-Ambassador Six |
| V8, 320.0 | 3.81×3.50 | 208 | S-Ambassador Eight |

## 1956

| Rambler (wb 108.0)* | | Wght | Price | Prod |
|---|---|---|---|---|
| 5613-2 | Cus Cross Cntry htp wgn 4d | 3,095 | 2,494 | — |
| 5615 | DeLuxe sdn 4d | 2,891 | 1,829 | — |
| 5615-1 | Super sdn 4d | 2,906 | 1,939 | — |
| 5615-2 | Custom sdn 4d | 2,929 | 2,059 | — |
| 5618-1 | Super Cross Cntry wgn 4d | 2,992 | 2,233 | — |
| 5618-2 | Cus Cross Cntry wgn 4d | 3,110 | 2,329 | — |
| 5619-2 | Custom htp sdn | 2,990 | 2,224 | — |

| Statesman (wb 114.5)* | | | | |
|---|---|---|---|---|
| 5645-1 | Super sdn 4d | 3,134 | 2,139 | — |

| Ambassador Special (wb 121.3)—4,145 built* | | | | |
|---|---|---|---|---|
| 5657-1 | sdn 4d | 3,397 | 2,355 | — |
| 5657-2 | Country Club htp cpe | 3,418 | 2,462 | — |
| 5657-3 | Custom sdn 4d | 3,567 | 2,541 | — |

| Ambassador Six (wb 121.3)* | | | | |
|---|---|---|---|---|
| 5665-1 | Super sdn 4d | 3,555 | 2,425 | — |

| Ambassador Eight (wb 121.3)* | | | | |
|---|---|---|---|---|
| 5685-1 | Super sdn 4d | 3,748 | 2,716 | — |
| 5686-2 | Custom sdn 4d | 3,846 | 2,939 | — |
| 5687-2 | Cus Cntry Club htp cpe | 3,854 | 3,072 | — |

*Estimated Rambler production 10,000; total Statesman/Ambassador 14,352.

| 1956 Engines | bore×stroke | bhp | availability |
|---|---|---|---|
| L6, 195.6 | 3.13×4.25 | 120 | S-Rambler, Statesman |
| L6, 252.6 | 3.50×4.38 | 130 | S-Ambassador Six |
| L6, 252.6 | 3.50×4.38 | 140 | O-Ambassador Six |
| V8, 320.0 | 3.81×3.50 | 208 | S-Ambassador Eight |
| V8, 327.0 | 4.00×3.25 | 190 | S-Ambassador Special |

## 1957*

| Ambassador Super (wb 121.3) | | Wght | Price | Prod |
|---|---|---|---|---|
| | sdn 4d | 3,639 | 2,586 | — |
| | Country Club htp cpe | 3,655 | 2,670 | — |

| Ambassador Custom (wb 121.3) | | | | |
|---|---|---|---|---|
| | sdn 4d | 3,701 | 2,763 | — |
| | Country Club htp cpe | 3,722 | 2,847 | — |

*Approximate model year production: 5,000.

| 1957 Engine | bore×stroke | bhp | availability |
|---|---|---|---|
| V8, 327.0 | 4.00×3.25 | 255 | S-all |

# Nash Metropolitan

American Motors Corp., Kenosha, Wisconsin (via Longbridge, England)
Note: Nash model 1954-57; Hudson model 1955-57; separate make 1958-62

American Motors President George W. Mason loved small cars. The Rambler was his first, the Metropolitan followed. Unfortunately, Mason died in 1954 before the "Met" had met with its greatest success. A Nash model in its early days, the Metropolitan was also badge-engineered as a Hudson during a brief period before that make was discontinued. From 1958 on, Metropolitan was considered a separate AMC nameplate.

The car's origins go back to just after World War II, when Mason and Nash engineer Meade F. Moore accepted a design by independent stylist Bill Flajole. Based on a Fiat 500 chassis/drivetrain, the prototype was named NXI (Nash Experimental International). Mason's top assistant and heir-apparent, George Romney,

displayed the NXI at a variety of private showings in 1950, carefully sizing up public reaction before moving ahead with production. Reaction was favorable, but Mason still moved slowly: it wasn't until the end of 1953 that arrangements for volume production were complete. Bodies would be built in England by the well-known Birmingham manufacturers Fisher & Ludlow, Ltd. From there, they would be shipped to Austin at Longbridge, where the 42-horsepower A-40 four-cylinder engines were installed. The Metropolitan debuted in early 1954 in hardtop and convertible styles. All had loud two-tone paint schemes resembling, as one stylist put it, Neapolitan ice cream. Sales took off and Austin shipped 13,905 cars from late 1953 through '54.

Mid-year 1956 saw a more powerful 1500cc engine

**1954 Series 54 (1200) convertible**

**1954 Series 54 (1200) coupe**

**1957 Series 56 (1500) convertible**

**1959 Series 56 (1500) coupe**

**1961 Series 56 (1500) convertible**

with 52 bhp. The 1500s used different paint combinations, a larger clutch, and a new oval grille bearing Nash or Hudson emblems. The fake hood scoop that had adorned the original 1200 was dropped. Compared to about 70 mph for the earlier model, the 1500 would do close to 80, though not with sports-car efficiency. It was also higher priced.

Mid-year 1959 brought more refinements, though the 1500 designation remained. Metropolitans now received opening trunklids for the first time. (Before, cargo had to be pushed into the compartment from be-

hind the seats.) More comfortable seats, vent wings, and tubeless tires were other improvements. Prices had risen to over $1600, but Metropolitan nevertheless enjoyed its best year ever. With 20,435 built for calendar 1959, it ranked second only to Volkswagen among the "imports." On its 85-inch wheelbase, it was the smallest car sold by any domestic franchise.

Production ended in mid-1960, though leftovers accounted for 853 units sold in 1961 and another 412 in '62. Like many imports, Metropolitan was a victim of the compact onslaught from the Big Three in 1960.

# Nash Metropolitan Specifications

## 1954

### Series 54 (wb 85.0)—13,095* built

| | | Wght | Price | Prod |
|---|---|---|---|---|
| 541 | conv cpe 3P | 1,803 | 1,469 | — |
| 542 | cpe 3P | 1,843 | 1,445 | — |

*Includes 743 shipments in 1953. All production figures are calendar year shipments, including some destined for Canada.

| 1954 Engine | bore×stroke | bhp | availability |
|---|---|---|---|
| L4, 73.8 | 2.56×3.50 | 42 | S-all |

## 1955

### Series 54 (wb 85.0)—6,096 built

| | | Wght | Price | Prod |
|---|---|---|---|---|
| 541 | conv 3P | 1,803 | 1,469 | — |
| 542 | cpe 3P | 1,843 | 1,445 | — |

| 1955 Engine | bore×stroke | bhp | availability |
|---|---|---|---|
| L4, 73.8 | 2.56×3.50 | 42 | S-all |

## 1956—9,068 built

### Series 54 (wb 85.0)

| | | Wght | Price | Prod |
|---|---|---|---|---|
| 541 | conv 3P | 1,803 | 1,469 | — |
| 542 | cpe 3P | 1,843 | 1,445 | — |

### Series 56 "1500" (wb 85.0)

| | | Wght | Price | Prod |
|---|---|---|---|---|
| 561 | conv 3P | 1,803 | 1,551 | — |
| 562 | cpe 3P | 1,843 | 1,527 | — |

| 1956 Engines | bore×stroke | bhp | availability |
|---|---|---|---|
| L4, 73.8 | 2.56×3.50 | 42 | S-Series 54 (1200) |
| L4, 90.9 | 2.88×3.50 | 52 | S-Series 56 (1500) |

## 1957

### Series 56 "1500" (wb 85.0)—15,317 built

| | | Wght | Price | Prod |
|---|---|---|---|---|
| 561 | conv 3P | 1,803 | 1,591 | — |
| 562 | cpe 3P | 1,843 | 1,567 | — |

| 1957 Engine | bore×stroke | bhp | availability |
|---|---|---|---|
| L4, 90.9 | 2.88×3.50 | 52 | S-all |

## 1958

### Series 56 "1500" (wb 85.0)—13,128 built

| | | Wght | Price | Prod |
|---|---|---|---|---|
| 561 | conv 3P | 1,835 | 1,650 | — |
| 562 | cpe 3P | 1,875 | 1,626 | — |

| 1958 Engine | bore×stroke | bhp | availability |
|---|---|---|---|
| L4, 90.9 | 2.88×3.50 | 52 | S-all |

## 1959

### Series 56 "1500" (wb 85.0)—22,309 built

| | | Wght | Price | Prod |
|---|---|---|---|---|
| 561 | conv 3P | 1,835 | 1,650 | — |
| 562 | cpe 3P | 1,875 | 1,626 | — |

| 1959 Engine | bore×stroke | bhp | availability |
|---|---|---|---|
| L4, 90.9 | 2.88×3.50 | 52 | S-all |

## 1960

### Series 56 "1500" (wb 85.0)—13,103 built

| | | Wght | Price | Prod |
|---|---|---|---|---|
| 561 | conv 3P | 1,850 | 1,697 | — |
| 562 | cpe 3P | 1,890 | 1,673 | — |

| 1960 Engine | bore×stroke | bhp | availability |
|---|---|---|---|
| L4, 90.9 | 2.88×3.50 | 52 | S-all |

## 1961

### Series 56 "1500" (wb 85.0)—853 built

| | | Wght | Price | Prod |
|---|---|---|---|---|
| 561 | conv 3P | 1,850 | 1,697 | — |
| 562 | cpe 3P | 1,890 | 1,673 | — |

| 1961 Engine | bore×stroke | bhp | availability |
|---|---|---|---|
| L4, 90.9 | 2.88×3.50 | 52 | S-all |

## 1962

### Series 56 "1500" (wb 85.0)—412 built

| | | Wght | Price | Prod |
|---|---|---|---|---|
| 561 | conv 3P | 1,850 | 1,697 | — |
| 562 | cpe 3P | 1,890 | 1,673 | — |

| 1962 Engine | bore×stroke | bhp | availability |
|---|---|---|---|
| L4, 90.9 | 2.88×3.50 | 52 | S-all |

# Oldsmobile

**Olds Motor Works and Oldsmobile Division of General Motors Corp., Lansing, Michigan**

As the "experimental" division of General Motors, Oldsmobile produced some of the corporation's great innovations through the years. Two of these came into prominence during the 1940s—Hydra-Matic drive and the high-compression V8. Hydra-Matic was developed just before the decade began, the V8 at its end. Both strongly influenced industry thinking.

Hydra-Matic arrived late in the 1938 model year, but Oldsmobile had actually built a no-shift drive earlier. Its 1937 Automatic Safety Transmission used a conventional clutch while eliminating most gearshift actions. Hydra-Matic, however, was completely clutch-free, combining a torque converter with a fluid coupling. It was the first transmission that shifted for itself, and helped put Oldsmobile among Detroit's production leaders. Division volume, which had dipped below 100,000 units in recession year 1938, came back to nearly 160,000 in '39. In 1940 and '41, Olds produced a total of more than 400,000 cars, passing Dodge to reach sixth place in the industry—which it would surpass after World War II.

The Oldsmobile line for 1940 comprised three models, each having its own wheelbase. The Series 60 and 70 used a conventional six that produced 95 horsepower at 3400 rpm. The Series 90 L-head eight developed 110 bhp at 3600 rpm. Each line offered a range of body styles in keeping with its price category. The 60 included a wagon with a Hercules all-wood body. The larger and heavier 70 offered coupes, sedans, and convertibles. Series 90 styles included Oldsmobile's most expensive model, the convertible phaeton. Styling followed standard GM practice. Headlights were flush with the fenders, freestanding fenders were used all around, and roofs were "turret tops" with closed rear quarters.

The 1941 models took a step toward streamlining. The front fenders blended into the bodysides, but the rear fenders remained separate. This design change was accompanied by a model realignment: Oldsmobile now had new wheelbases—119 and 125 inches—in six different series. The six-cylinder engine was bored out slightly, boosting output to 100 bhp. Specials used the 119-inch wheelbase; other sixes used the 125. The eight powered the Special, Dynamic Cruiser, and Custom Cruiser Eights. Body styles were identical with either engine, except for the convertible phaeton, available only with the eight. It remained almost the same as it had been the year before, but only 119 copies were produced in its last year. Oldsmobile adopted new model names for '41 that would remain familiar for years: the previous 60, 70, and 90 series designations were altered to reflect the car's number of cylinders. For example, the Custom Cruiser Eight was called the 98; the Dynamic Cruiser Six became the 76. By 1952, names had given way to numerical disignations.

Olds built over 67,000 1942 models but slipped to seventh. A five-model lineup was offered, and the number of body styles was reduced in most series. A new Town Sedan with formal roofline was added to the 60 series. Styling was revised with "Fuselage Fend-

1940 Series 90 convertible coupe

1940 Series 90 four-door sedan

1941 Custom Cruiser 8 convertible coupe

1941 Special 8 four-door sedan

ers"—elongated pontoon types faired into the front doors. The rear fenders were longer, and tapered beyond the drop of the trunk deck. They were still bolt-on components.

During the war, Oldsmobile manufactured 350,000 precision aircraft engine parts, 175 million pounds of gun forgings, 140,000 machine guns, and millions of rounds of artillery ammunition. On January 1, 1942, the company acquired a new name: Oldsmobile Division of

1942 Sixty 8 four-door station wagon

1942 Ninety 8 convertible coupe

1946 Special 66 convertible

1947 Dynamic Cruiser 76 club sedan

General Motors. Its previous name, Olds Motor Works, had dated from the founding of the company by Ransom Eli Olds in 1896.

Oldsmobile ran seventh in the industry during 1946-47. Production of its warmed-over prewar cars was good: output had reached nearly 200,000 units annually by 1948. The '46 lineup now consisted of four different series, and models were considerably realigned. Six-cylinder cars used the 119-inch wheelbase; the most expensive Custom Cruiser 98 series rode the long 127-inch wheelbase. All other models continued on the prewar 125-inch wheelbase. The 100-bhp six and the 110-bhp eight were retained, and would remain unaltered through 1948. Oldsmobile continued to stress its popular Hydra-Matic, and produced more automatic-equipped cars as a percentage of total volume than any other company in the industry. In styling, the 1946-47 cars were only slightly changed from the '42 models. The gaudy, complicated prewar grille was replaced by four simple bars for 1946, and a shield-type hood medallion was devised. For 1947, a V-shaped plastic hood ornament appeared, and the nameplate on the fender moldings was enlarged. Strangely, Oldsmobile did not supply parking lights on these early postwar models.

Midway through 1948 model year came a memorable new design—the "Futuramic" 98. Appearing simultaneously with a similar new style from Cadillac, Futuramic was GM's first all-new postwar body design, created by Harley Earl's Art & Colour Studio, and influenced by the wartime Lockheed P-38 fighter aircraft. (The P-38 is well-known for having inspired Cadillac's tailfins.) The beautifully shaped 98s included sedan, club sedan, and convertible styles. The sedan and club sedan were offered with standard and deluxe trim, the convertible as a deluxe only. Prices ranged from $2078 for the standard club sedan to $2624 for the convertible. The 1948 series 66, 68, 76, and 78 retained previous styling, with detail changes only. Among these were a round hood medallion, "Oldsmobile" spelled out in block letters on the hood, the omission of fender nameplates, and the addition of full-length chrome strips to the rocker panels. The public responded to the new line, particularly the Futuramics, with excitement. By the close of the model year, over 60,000 98s had been sold, over half of them four-door sedans.

Another important innovation came in 1949 with the Rocket V8 engine, designed by Gilbert Burrell. It was an automotive landmark—one of the first two high-compression valve-in-head V8s. Cadillac also introduced an ohv V8 that year, but it was developed independently of Olds. Both divisions had been encouraged to compete with each other, and Cadillac actually raised the displacement of its V8 to exceed Oldsmobile's. The Rocket displaced 303 cubic inches; Cadillac had started with 309 cid, then increased it to 331.

The Rocket V8 was a five-main-bearing engine with oversquare bore-and-stroke dimensions, and developed 135 bhp at 3600 rpm. The 88's power-to-weight

1948 Futuramic 98 Deluxe four-door sedan

1949 Futuramic 76 Deluxe four-door station wagon

1949 Futuramic 98 Deluxe convertible

1950 Futuramic 88 convertible

1951 Super 88 convertible

ratio was about 22.5:1—quite good for the era. Torque was also impressive at 240 foot-pounds. Although it had a 7.25:1 compression ratio in 1949 form, Oldsmobile had designed the Rocket for ratios as high as 12:1. Engineers had anticipated the availability of high-octane fuel after the war, though octane levels never became high enough to make such ratios practical.

The best-known application of the new V8 was in the relatively light 88 body. Management had originally planned it for the 98 only, but then elected to drop it into a short-wheelbase model as well. The result was the Rocket 88, a car that soon began writing competition history. Though Oldsmobile didn't sponsor racing, stock-car drivers soon had 88s running and winning on oval tracks all around the country. Meanwhile, the 1949 Series 76 L-head engine was bored and stroked to 257.1 cid for 105 bhp at 3400 rpm. It remained in this form through its last year, 1950.

Two new body styles that predicted future trends were released for 1949. An all-steel station wagon, offered in the 76 and 88 series, was similar to wagons from Pontiac and Plymouth—and destined for tremendous popularity in the 1950s. For the 98 series, Olds introduced the Holiday two-door "hardtop convertible." Along with Buick's Riviera and Cadillac's Coupe deVille, the Holiday was the first pillarless hardtop in volume production.

Styling for 1950-51 could be traced back to prewar renderings and clay models, which first emerged (with Cadillac) in the 1948 model year. Smooth, low, and streamlined compared to the upright styles of the past, it was extremely well received, and soon influenced the entire GM line. Oldsmobile's "Futuramic" designation adequately described this outstanding shape. Olds restyled in 1951 and again in 1954, but the basic design concept—pronounced fenders and prominent grilles—remained through 1956.

After 1950, all Oldsmobiles were powered by V8s. The Rocket 88 engine continued to impress race-goers in the early '50s, and Oldsmobile was NASCAR racing champ from 1949 through 1951. Weighing 300–500 pounds less than the 98, the Rocket 88 was an obvious competitor, and it scored early. Of nine Grand National events held in 1949, 88s won six, with "Red" Byron the national champion. In 1950, an 88 broke the class speed record at Daytona with a two-way average of 100.28 mph. That same year, it won the first Mexican Road Race, besting such formidable competitors as Alfa Romeo, Cadillac, and Lincoln. On the ovals, Olds won 10 out of 19 races in 1950; the following year, 20 out of 41. Though displaced by the Hudson Hornet in 1952-54, 88s continued to show their ability in other competitions. Paul Frére, for example, won the 1952 Francorchamps stock car race in Belgium with one, and a 1950 88 nicknamed "Roarin' Relic" was still winning the occasional modified race as late as 1959.

Such goings-on naturally helped keep sales high after the seller's market began to shrink around 1950. Olds sold about 400,000 cars that year; during 1951-53

it did less well, but never fell below eighth place in production. By 1955 Olds was running fourth, and had even passed Plymouth. Interestingly, the division managed such sales triumphs with only three basic series, and didn't even offer a station wagon between 1951 and '56.

For 1950, with the 76 still in the lineup, there was only one 88 series. Standard and DeLuxe trim versions were offered for sedans, club coupe, Holiday hardtop, wagon, convertible, and the last of Olds' special "club sedans," a four-door fastback. The 98 also came in standard or DeLuxe form in notchback and fastback sedans, Holidays, and convertibles, All three '50 convertibles—the 76, 88, and 98—were curiously placed in the "standard" category; there were no DeLuxe versions.

For 1951, the Super 88 arrived on a new 120-inch wheelbase and with revised styling. The base 88 line shrank to sedans only, the 76 vanished, and the 98 was offered as four-door sedan, Holiday hardtop, and convertible. The all-steel wagons were dropped, possibly because they were ahead of their time. Styling was a bit gaudier than before, though the grille was formed by simple bars, side decoration was minimal, and taillights were built into little upright fins on the rear fenders. The same basic appearance was continued for '52, though the 88 moved up to the 120-inch wheelbase.

Along with Cadillac's Eldorado and Buick's Skylark, Oldsmobile offered a limited-production convertible for 1953. Selling for $5717, the Fiesta featured a custom leather interior, panoramic windshield, and a special 170-bhp version of the Rocket V8. Standard features included Hydra-Matic, power brakes and steering, and hydraulic servos for windows and seat. Fiesta's spinner wheel covers were soon copied by every accessory house in the business, and appeared on hot rods and custom cars from coast to coast. Only 458 Fiestas were produced, and the model was discontinued for 1954. But it did predict a host of styling features to come.

The 1954-55 period marked another styling generation, and some of the most attractive Oldsmobiles of the decade. Each series offered the same body styles in all three years, with the addition of four-door hardtops for 1955-56. A popular feature introduced for '54 was "Autronic Eye," GM's novel automatic headlight dimmer. Wheelbase was 122 inches for both the 88s and 126 for 98. A bored-out 324-cid V8 with 3.9×3.4-inch bore and stroke appeared, tuned to deliver 170 bhp for the basic 88, and 185 bhp for Super 88 and 98. As the horsepower race continued in '56, the figures were bumped up to 230 and 240 bhp.

Olds built a record number of cars in 1955, over 50 percent more than in '54, and improved its model year standing to fourth place. Model offerings and 1954's new bodyshell were retained, though styling was drastically facelifted with a new grille and two-tone color combinations. Together with Buick, Olds introduced the four-door hardtop, destined to be one of the most popular body styles of the late '50s. All GM divisions had it by 1956, having planned for it well in advance.

1953 Fiesta convertible

1953 Series 98 convertible

1953 Starfire show car

1954 Series 88 four-door sedan

1955 Series 98 Deluxe Holiday hardtop sedan

**1956 Series 88 Holiday hardtop coupe**

**Golden Rocket show car from 1956**

**1957 Golden Rocket 88 Holiday hardtop coupe**

**1957 Golden Rocket Super 88 convertible**

**F-88 rectractable-hardtop show car, 1959**

The rest of the industry hurried to put hastily contrived copies into production. Four-door hardtops generally were prone to let in rain and dust as the rubber window seals began to wear, but the idea of a four-door sedan with the airiness of a hardtop attracted buyers anyway.

There was yet another redo in 1956. Most of the changes were made up front, with a large gaping grille derived from the Starfire show car. The division did exceptionally well, producing some 485,000 vehicles.

Then came the '57s—an all-new design with an expanded model lineup, including a reborn station wagon. Once again Oldsmobile was innovative: some of its wagons were also four-door hardtops. The 88s were labeled Golden Rocket, after another show car; the 98 was called Starfire. Station wagons, dubbed Fiestas, came with and without B-pillars in the 88 line; pillarless only in Super 88 form. Standard horsepower was 277, but a popular option was the famous J-2 Rocket engine with three two-barrel carburetors and 300 bhp. The J-2 could propel an 88 from 0 to 60 mph in less than eight seconds.

For a '57 GM car, Olds was rather cleanly styled. The wide-mouth grille was only mildly reshaped; a broad, stainless-steel sweep-spear dropped down from the middle of the beltline, shooting straight back to the rear fenders to delineate the two-toning area. In the face of Virgil Exner's Forward Look at Chrysler, GM styling was beginning to seem a little old-fashioned, and the age of Harley Earl was coming to an end. Nevertheless, Olds built nearly 400,000 cars and finished fifth again.

In recession year 1958, most of the industry faltered, but Olds ran fourth and held production to near the 315,000 mark. Body offerings were as for '57 except that two-door sedans were now limited to the standard 88 series only. Styling, most observers concluded, was atrocious: Ford's Alex Tremulis satirized the four rear-fender chrome strips by drawing in a clef and a few notes of music. Indeed, the '58 Fords were better-looking than GM cars, and Chrysler's products were in another league entirely. But Oldsmobile still managed to sell well—aided, no doubt, by potent engines. A 371-cid V8 had been introduced in '57, and the hottest version produced 312 bhp for '58.

Behind the scenes in Detroit and Lansing, big changes were being contemplated. For the first time, corporate cross-pollination would occur: GM divisions would share basic bodyshells. A new greenhouse design using wide wraparound windows front and rear, plus narrow pillars, was devised for all makes. Inner panels were shared between Chevrolet and Pontiac, and between Oldsmobile and Buick. Chevys rode the shortest wheelbase, while Olds and Buick shared two chassis with wheelbase of 123 and 126 inches. Pontiac was slightly shorter. Only Cadillac retained its own individual panels. Exterior styling was devised to make each division's products look different from each other, though there was more resemblance between Olds and Pontiac than Olds management would have liked. Pontiac surged past Oldsmobile in '59 model year produc-

tion, something it hadn't done since 1953.

Body sharing had other repercussions. Chevrolet, for example, had to drop its 1958 tooling after only a year. Oldsmobile's previous bodyshell had only two years behind it. Still, it was an effective move because body sharing held production costs down, and the company was able to put that much more time and money into its forthcoming compacts. Oldsmobile would follow its peers into small-car territory with the F-85 in 1961.

The 59's, however, were big, roomy cars offering high performance and low mileage. Engines ranged from the 88's 371-cid unit with 270 or 300 bhp to the new 394 V8 for the Super 88 and 98 that provided 315 bhp with 9.75:1 compression ratio and four-barrel carburetor. Performance, of course, was an Olds tradition. Compared to Buick, Olds styling was sedate in '59. The grille was a rather simple dumbbell shape with four widely spaced headlights; the tail carried modest fins. The usual vast array of colorful interiors in vinyl and jacquard was offered.

As the innovator among GM divisions, Oldsmobile also led the way with its dream cars in the '50s. After the limited-edition Fiesta came a series of two-seaters. The '53 Starfire was Corvette-like. Its grille design, taken from the Air Force's Starfire jet fighter plane, eventually found its way onto 1956 production models. Perhaps the most exotic Olds show car was the 1956 Golden Rocket, a wild-looking aerodynamic coupe made of fiberglass and equipped with a 324-bhp Rocket engine. Features included gullwing roof panels that rose when the doors were opened, swivel seats, running lights mounted in stubby fins behind the doors, and a tilt steering wheel.

During the 1960s Oldsmobile continued to experiment—with its production models. The division introduced a variety of new models from compacts to full-size cars, new engines, new powertrains—and its product decisions were rarely mistaken. In annual volume, Oldsmobile never ranked below seventh place, often placed fourth, and averaged about fifth through the decade. From a model year output of about 350,000 cars in 1960, production rose to 635,000 in 1969.

Oldsmobile joined the compact wars in 1961. The F-85 and the Cutlass variations that followed set record after record; production through 1968 exceeded that of each previous model year. This success was due to Oldsmobile's correct matching of customer tastes with new products: compact V8s for 1961-62; larger compacts with V6 option for 1964-65; and the high-performance 4-4-2 series from 1964 on. Every year, Oldsmobile's smallest series seemed to offer a package that was right on the money. Its standard-size cars also consistently sold well.

The F-85 was part of GM's "second-wave" compact program for 1961. Buick, Oldsmobile, and Pontiac each developed its own version of the same basic car using a shared bodyshell and dimensions. Pontiac's Tempest, with its curved driveshaft and rear transaxle, was very radical; Olds took a more conventional route. The

1961 F-85 Cutlass sport coupe

1962 F-85 Jetfire sport coupe

1964 Cutlass Holiday hardtop coupe

1966 4-4-2 Holiday hardtop coupe

1967 4-4-2 Holiday hardtop coupe

F-85's V8 was built by Buick and developed 155 bhp. It provided good performance (0 to 60 mph in 13 seconds) and reasonable economy (18 mpg). Styling was clean and less busy than the Buick Special's. It had sculptured bodysides, a crisp roofline, and a simple vertical-bar grille.

Naming the F-85 had been a small problem. Starfire had been the original choice, but that seemed to denote

1968 4-4-2 Holiday hardtop coupe

1970 Cutlass Supreme Holiday hardtop coupe

1970 4-4-2 Holiday hardtop coupe

1966 Toronado hardtop coupe

a big sporty car. Rockette was suggested, but was thought to project an unwanted image of the Radio City Music Hall dancers. The numerical designation was inspired by an Olds show car called F-88. The number 85 was chosen because it suggested a family relationship with that experimental, yet was different enough from "88" to avoid confusion with the full-size cars. Initially, F-85s were offered in standard and deluxe form as sedans, coupes, and wagons. The Deluxe coupe with bucket seats and luxury trim was called Cutlass—a name that would supplant the F-85 moniker later on.

For 1962, the Cutlass came standard with a 185-bhp Power-Pack version of Buick's little 215 V8. Also offered was a new model, the turbocharged Jetfire. The turbocharger increased output to 215 bhp—one horsepower per cubic inch—but the engine suffered problems, including carbon buildup with certain grades of gasoline. Olds resorted to the unorthodox technique of water injection (actually, a mixture of water and alcohol) to cure these maladies. The car was remarkably fast (0 to 60 mph in 8.5 seconds with a top speed of 107 mph), but the injection system proved unreliable. In 1964, Oldsmobile gave up on turbocharging and settled on a new 330-cid engine, a conventional V8 that provided 230 to 290 bhp. The 225-cid Buick V6 was added as an option, and continued unchanged until 1966 when it was replaced by an inline six with the same horsepower.

The F-85 grew larger through these years, as the public kept insisting on more impressive "compacts." Wheelbase went from 112 to 115 inches for 1964, and to 116 (112 for two-doors) for 1968. Bodies grew longer and wider, but styling actually improved as time went on. The truncated '61–'62 original was greatly cleaned up for 1963, and was even cleaner for '64 after a facelift that gave it a closer identity with the full-size Oldsmobiles. In 1966, the straight beltline yielded to a more flowing contour, incorporating a "Coke-bottle" hump over the rear wheels. After 1968, styling began to get cluttered again, with a busier grille and deck and clumsy-looking vinyl tops. This trend culminated in 1970 with the all-new Cutlass Supreme Holiday coupe with notchback roofline.

The F-85 that offered the best performance was the exciting 4-4-2. The designation stood for four speeds (or after 1965, 400 cubic inches), four-barrel carburetor, and dual exhausts. The first 1964 edition came with a hot 330-cid V8, heavy-duty suspension, and a four-speed manual gearbox. In 1965, it was hotter still with a 400-cid V8, an under-bored version of the big 425 engine used in the full-size models. The 4-4-2 option package with four-speed cost only about $250 in 1965. It included heavy-duty wheels, shocks, springs, rear axle, driveshaft, engine mounts, steering and frame; stabilizer bars front and rear; fat tires; special exterior and interior trim; 11-inch clutch; and a 70-amp battery. Performance was sensational: 0 to 60 in 7.5 seconds, the quarter-mile in 17 seconds at 85 mph, and a top speed of 125 mph. The 4-4-2 proved, as *Motor Trend*

magazine said, "that Detroit can build cars that perform, handle and stop, without sacrificing road comfort. . . ."

Each successive 4-4-2 was eagerly awaited. The 400-cid engine was never pushed much beyond 350 bhp, but the cars continued to be good-looking, fast, and great fun to drive. The 1969s had big 4-4-2 numerals on the center grille divider, front fenders, and deck; twin, black horizontal grilles; and a unique "two-plateau" hood with special stripes in contrasting paint. They'd become a bit outlandish, perhaps, but were no less the performance cars than they'd been in the beginning.

In 1966, though, Cutlass and 4-4-2 were overshadowed by the intriguing new front-wheel-drive Toronado. Offered only as a hardtop coupe, this car represented a clean break with the past (and a commitment to front-wheel-drive that would become corporate-wide by 1980). It marked a big turnabout for a company that had once panned the front-drive Cord, but GM planned well: the Toronado worked, and worked beautifully.

The goal for this front-wheel-drive exercise was to combine traditional American big-car power with outstanding handling and traction. Toronado's 425-cid V8 was shared with the conventional full-size models, but was teamed with its own new transmission divided into two parts. The torque converter was mounted behind the engine, the gearbox was located remotely under the left cylinder bank, and both were connected by a chain drive and sprocket. The chain drive, virtually unbreakable yet flexible, was developed to save weight and cut costs. It also resulted in a very compact engine and

drivetrain package. Most previous front-drive systems had put the engine behind a front-mounted transmission. Toronado's split transmission enabled the engine to be placed directly over the front wheels. The result was a front/rear weight distribution of 54/46, excellent for a front-wheel-drive car.

Toronado's styling was as sophisticated as its engi-

1969 Toronado hardtop coupe

1970 Toronado hardtop coupe

1967 Toronado hardtop coupe

1968 Toronado hardtop coupe

1960 Super 88 convertible

1961 Super 88 Starfire convertible

# Oldsmobile

1962 Ninety Eight convertible

1963 Starfire hardtop coupe

1963 Ninety Eight convertible

1964 Jetstar 88 Celebrity four-door sedan

1965 Delta 88 Holiday hardtop sedan

1967 Ninety Eight Holiday hardtop coupe

1969 Ninety Eight Holiday hardtop coupe

1970 Delta 88 Custom Holiday hardtop sedan

neering. The C-pillars fell gently from the roof, there was no obvious beltline aft of the rear windows, and the roofline flowed down smoothly as a rakish fastback. The curved fuselage was set off by boldly flared wheel arches. The front and rear were clean and wrapped tightly underneath, as were the sides. Don Vorderman, then editor of *Automobile Quarterly* magazine, remarked: "A radically different look has been achieved with a minimum of fuss. There are no loose ends, no unresolved lines. . . The result is logical, imaginative, and totally unique."

The Toronado was a superb machine. It exhibited some understeer, but not much for a fwd car, and ran quietly even at 100 mph. It could do 135 mph when pressed, even with a "standard" rear axle ratio and automatic transmission. It was probably the most out-

standing single Olds model of the '60s. Although the 1968-70 versions were not as clean as the '66 and '67, the Toronado was a landmark creation.

While producing the interesting and exciting F-85, Cutlass, 4-2-2, and Toronado, Oldsmobile's mainstays were its conventional standard-size models. The 1960 lineup was traditional: Dynamic 88, the price leader; Super 88, the big-engined performance car of the group; and 98 (also called "Ninety Eight"), the luxury series. The lineup was expanded for 1964 when the Jetstar 88 arrived at the low end, along with the Jetstar I sports coupe (with concave backlight). To make room for the Jetstar, the Dynamic 88 moved up a notch on the price scale. In 1965, the Delta 88 replaced the Super; the Jetstar was replaced by the Delmont a year later. The Delmont's market territory was expanded in '67 by

eliminating the old Dynamic series. For 1968, the line reverted to a three-series range of Delmont, Delta, and 98. Then in 1969, the Delmont was dropped and Delta 88s were offered in standard, Custom, and Royale.

The broad range of body styles offered through most of the '60s included hardtop coupes and sedans, convertibles, the Vista Cruiser wagon (with transparent roof windows), and Fiesta wagons. The design was clean in 1960, cleaner in '61, and spectacularly handsome ("Straightaway Styling") in '62. Though facelifts brought rounder, fatter bodies in 1965, the full-size cars retained visual similarity to their predecessors throughout the decade. In 1968-70 the wide, square 1962-64 grille reappeared. In between was an era of broad, pointed noses; single-bar grilles; and prominent quad headlights. Styling continuity was preserved through the use of just two wheelbases, 123 and 126 inches, from 1960 to 1968. An inch was added to each chassis in 1969.

Oldsmobile entered the '60s with two V8s: a 371 for the Dynamic 88, and a 394 for the Super 88 and 98. The latter was the only big Olds engine for 1962-63. The low-priced '64 Jetstar shared the F-85's 330 engine. In 1965, the 394 was stroked out to 425 cid, and power gradually rose to 385 bhp for the 1966-67 Toronado. Outputs decreased slightly across the board in 1968-70 with the advent of emission controls. The Delmont started out in '67 with the F-85's 330-cid V8, which was bored out to 350 cid (250 bhp) for 1968.

The Starfire of 1961-66 and the Jetstar I of 1964-65 were Oldsmobile's flings in the market of bucket-seated performance cars. The Starfire debuted as a limited-edition item, but production was boosted to over 40,000 cars for the 1962 model year. Equipped with Olds' most powerful engines, Starfire hardtops and coupes featured individual styling, with broad sweeps of brushed aluminum on early models; bucket seats with center console; and luxurious interiors. The Jetstar I was the same idea at a more popular price. But it didn't catch on; production totaled only about 22,600 units over two model years. Although neither Starfire nor Jetstar met the true definition of a sports car (as Oldsmobile often referred to them), they handled well for their size and offered distinctive transportation.

# Oldsmobile Specifications

## 1940

### F-40 Series 60 (wb 116.0)

| | Wght | Price | Prod |
| --- | --- | --- | --- |
| bus cpe | 3,030 | 807 | 2,752 |
| club cpe | 3,015 | 848 | 7,664 |
| conv cpe | 3,110 | 1,021 | 1,347 |
| sdn 2d | 3,066 | 853 | 27,220 |
| sdn 4d | 3,100 | 899 | 24,422 |
| wgn 4d | 3,255 | 1,042 | 633 |

### G-40 Series 70 (wb 120.0)

| | Wght | Price | Prod |
| --- | --- | --- | --- |
| bus cpe | 3,100 | 865 | 4,337 |
| club cpe | 3,105 | 901 | 8,505 |
| conv cpe | 3,240 | 1,045 | 1,070 |
| sdn 2d | 3,170 | 912 | 21,486 |
| sdn 4d | 3,220 | 963 | 41,467 |

### L-40 Series 90 (wb 124.0)

| | Wght | Price | Prod |
| --- | --- | --- | --- |
| club cpe | 3,440 | 1,069 | 10,836 |
| conv cpe | 3,590 | 1,222 | 290 |
| sdn 4d | 3,555 | 1,131 | 33,075 |
| conv phaeton 4d | 3,750 | 1,570 | 50 |

### 1940 Engines

| | bore × stroke | bhp | availability |
| --- | --- | --- | --- |
| L6, 229.7 | 3.44 × 4.13 | 95 | S-60, 70 |
| L8, 257.1 | 3.25 × 3.88 | 110 | S-90 |

## 1941

### 66 Special 6 (wb 119.0)

| | Wght | Price | Prod |
| --- | --- | --- | --- |
| bus cpe | 3,145 | 852 | 6,433 |
| club cpe | 3,185 | 893 | 23,796 |
| conv cpe | 3,355 | 1,048 | 2,814 |
| sdn 2d | 3,190 | 898 | 30,475 |
| sdn 4d | 3,230 | 945 | 25,899 |
| Town Sedan 4d | 3,220 | 945 | 11,921 |
| wgn 4d | 3,565 | 1,176 | 604 |

### 68 Special 8 (wb 119.0)

| | Wght | Price | Prod |
| --- | --- | --- | --- |
| bus cpe | 3,260 | 893 | 188 |
| club cpe | 3,300 | 935 | 2,684 |
| conv cpe | 3,455 | 1,089 | 776 |
| sdn 2d | 3,305 | 940 | 499 |
| sdn 4d | 3,360 | 987 | 3,831 |
| Town Sedan 4d | 3,345 | 987 | 2,188 |
| wgn 4d | 3,660 | 1,217 | 95 |

### 76 Dynamic Cruiser 6 (wb 125.0)

| | Wght | Price | Prod |
| --- | --- | --- | --- |
| bus cpe | 3,260 | 908 | 353 |
| club sdn | 3,325 | 954 | 46,885 |
| sdn 4d | 3,390 | 1,010 | 40,719 |

### 78 Dynamic Cruiser 8 (wb 125.0)

| | Wght | Price | Prod |
| --- | --- | --- | --- |
| bus cpe | 3,360 | 944 | 51 |
| club sdn | 3,420 | 989 | 13,598 |
| sdn 4d | 3,500 | 1,045 | 15,580 |

### 96 Custom Cruiser 6 (wb 125.0)

| | Wght | Price | Prod |
| --- | --- | --- | --- |
| club cpe | 3,320 | 1,043 | 2,196 |
| conv cpe | 3,525 | 1,191 | 325 |
| sdn 4d | 3,410 | 1,099 | 4,196 |

### 98 Custom Cruiser 8 (wb 125.0)

| | Wght | Price | Prod |
| --- | --- | --- | --- |
| club cpe | 3,430 | 1,079 | 6,305 |
| conv cpe | 3,620 | 1,227 | 1,263 |
| conv phaeton 4d | 3,790 | 1,575 | 119 |
| sdn 4d | 3,500 | 1,135 | 22,081 |

# Oldsmobile

| 1941 Engines | bore × stroke | bhp | availability |
|---|---|---|---|
| L6, 238.1 | 3.50 × 4.13 | 100 | S-66, 76, 96 |
| L8, 257.1 | 3.25 × 3.88 | 110 | S-68, 78, 98 |

## 1942

| 66 "Sixty" 6 (wb 119.0) | Wght | Price | Prod |
|---|---|---|---|
| bus cpe | 3,230 | 915 | 1,026* |
| club cpe | 3,265 | 955 | 3,762* |
| conv cpe | 3,560 | 1,185 | 746* |
| club sdn | 3,270 | 970 | 9,744* |
| sdn 2d | 3,280 | 960 | 3,245* |
| sdn 4d | 3,315 | 1,005 | 7,086* |
| Town Sedan 4d | 3,320 | 1,005 | 3,421* |
| wgn 4d | 3,735 | 1,280 | 700* |

| 68 "Sixty" 8 (wb 119.0) | | | |
|---|---|---|---|
| bus cpe | 3,365 | 955 | 140* |
| club cpe | 3,405 | 995 | 501* |
| conv cpe | 3,715 | 1,225 | 102* |
| club sdn | 3,405 | 1,010 | 1,022* |
| sdn 2d | 3,410 | 1,000 | 443* |
| sdn 4d | 3,455 | 1,045 | 967* |
| Town Sedan 4d | 3,445 | 1,045 | 467* |
| wgn 4d | 3,890 | 1,320 | 95* |

| 76 "Seventy" 6 (wb 125.0) | | | |
|---|---|---|---|
| club sdn | 3,395 | 1,010 | 7,481* |
| Deluxe club sdn | 3,460 | 1,095 | 2,247* |
| sdn 4d | 3,465 | 1,065 | 6,507* |
| Deluxe sdn 4d | 3,510 | 1,150 | 2,414* |

| 78 "Seventy" 8 (wb 125.0) | | | |
|---|---|---|---|
| club sdn | 3,520 | 1,050 | 3,055* |
| Deluxe club sdn | 3,570 | 1,135 | 918* |
| sdn 4d | 3,580 | 1,105 | 2,659* |
| Deluxe sdn 4d | 3,640 | 1,190 | 986* |

| 98 "Ninety" 8 (wb 127.0) | | | |
|---|---|---|---|
| conv cpe | 3,955 | 1,450 | 216 |
| club sdn | 3,635 | 1,220 | 1,771 |
| sdn 4d | 3,715 | 1,275 | 4,672 |

*Estimates based on percentage distribution of known production of 66 (30,219), 68 (4,089), 76 (19,013) and 78 (7,803).

| 1942 Engines | bore × stroke | bhp | availability |
|---|---|---|---|
| L6, 238.1 | 3.50 × 4.13 | 100 | S-66, 76 |
| L8, 257.1 | 3.25 × 3.88 | 110 | S-68, 78, 98 |

## 1946

| F-46 Special 66 (wb 119.0) | Wght | Price | Prod |
|---|---|---|---|
| conv cpe | 3,605 | 1,681 | 1,409 |
| club cpe | 3,315 | 1,407 | 4,537 |
| club sdn 2d | 3,330 | 1,433 | 11,721 |
| sdn 4d | 3,350 | 1,471 | 11,053 |
| wgn 4d | 3,750 | 2,089 | 140 |

| G-46 Dynamic Cruiser 76 (wb 125.0) | | | |
|---|---|---|---|
| club sdn 2d | 3,460 | 1,497 | 30,929 |
| Deluxe club sdn 2d | 3,505 | 1,610 | 1,923 |
| sdn 4d | 3,510 | 1,568 | 18,425 |
| Deluxe sdn 4d | 3,555 | 1,678 | 2,179 |

| J-46 Dynamic Cruiser 78 (wb 125.0) | | | |
|---|---|---|---|
| club sdn 2d | 3,600 | 1,554 | 8,723 |
| Deluxe club sdn 2d | 3,630 | 1,666 | 2,188 |
| sdn 4d | 3,640 | 1,624 | 7,103 |
| Deluxe sdn 4d | 3,670 | 1,733 | 2,929 |

| L-46 Custom Cruiser 98 (wb 127.0) | | | |
|---|---|---|---|
| club sdn 2d | 3,680 | 1,762 | 2,459 |
| conv cpe | 4,025 | 2,040 | 874 |
| sdn 4d | 3,775 | 1,812 | 11,031 |

| 1946 Engines | bore × stroke | bhp | availability |
|---|---|---|---|
| L6, 238.1 | 3.50 × 4.13 | 100 | S-66, 76 |
| L8, 257.1 | 3.25 × 3.88 | 110 | S-78, 98 |

## 1947

| F-47 Special 66 (wb 119.0) | Wght | Price | Prod |
|---|---|---|---|
| club sdn 2d | 3,330 | 1,513 | 21,366* |
| club cpe | 3,325 | 1,488 | 10,723* |
| conv cpe | 3,605 | 1,845 | 3,949 |
| sdn 4d | 3,355 | 1,556 | 16,995* |
| wgn 4d | 3,770 | 2,456 | 968 |

| E-47 Special 68 (wb 119.0) | | | |
|---|---|---|---|
| club sdn 2d | 3,430 | 1,572 | 7,122* |
| club cpe | 3,420 | 1,546 | 3,574* |
| conv cpe | 3,710 | 1,903 | 2,579 |
| sdn 4d | 3,460 | 1,614 | 5,665* |
| wgn 4d | 3,885 | 2,514 | 492 |

| G-47 Dynamic Cruiser 76 (wb 125.0) | | | |
|---|---|---|---|
| club sdn 2d | 3,470 | 1,584 | 22,509* |
| Deluxe club sdn 2d | 3,515 | 1,705 | 3,951* |
| sdn 4d | 3,525 | 1,659 | 18,196* |
| Deluxe sdn 4d | 3,590 | 1,773 | 4,710* |

| J-47 Dynamic Cruiser 78 (wb 125.0) | | | |
|---|---|---|---|
| club sdn 2d | 3,590 | 1,643 | 15,643* |
| Deluxe club sdn 2d | 3,650 | 1,762 | 2,476* |
| sdn 4d | 3,655 | 1,717 | 12,645* |
| Deluxe sdn 4d | 3,705 | 1,830 | 3,184* |

| L-47 Custom Cruiser 98 (wb 127.0) | | | |
|---|---|---|---|
| club sdn | 3,715 | 1,865 | 8,475 |
| conv cpe | 4,075 | 2,307 | 3,940 |
| sdn 4d | 3,795 | 1,917 | 24,733 |

*Estimates based on percentage distribution of known production of 66 (55,610), 68 (17,956), 76 (49,711) and 78 (33,963).

| 1947 Engines | bore × stroke | bhp | availability |
|---|---|---|---|
| L6, 238.1 | 3.50 × 4.13 | 100 | S-66, 76 |
| L8, 257.1 | 3.25 × 3.88 | 110 | S-68, 78, 98 |

## 1948

| Dynamic 66 (wb 119.0) | Wght | Price | Prod |
|---|---|---|---|
| club sdn 2d | 3,285 | 1,634 | 15,071* |
| Deluxe club sdn 2d | 3,300 | 1,776 | 2,016* |
| club cpe | 3,240 | 1,609 | 5,923* |
| Deluxe club cpe | 3,255 | 1,749 | 792* |
| conv cpe | 3,550 | 2,003 | 1,801 |
| sdn 4d | 3,320 | 1,677 | 11,406* |
| Deluxe sdn 4d | 3,335 | 1,818 | 1,656* |
| wgn 4d | 3,620 | 2,614 | 840 |
| Deluxe wgn 4d | 3,635 | 2,739 | 553 |

| Dynamic 68 (wb 119.0) | | | |
|---|---|---|---|
| club sdn 2d | 3,420 | 1,693 | 5,861* |
| Deluxe club sdn 2d | 3,435 | 1,834 | 784* |
| club cpe | 3,355 | 1,667 | 2,303* |
| Deluxe club cpe | 3,370 | 1,808 | 308* |
| conv cpe | 3,660 | 2,061 | 2,091 |
| sdn 4d | 3,445 | 1,735 | 4,436* |
| Deluxe sdn 4d | 3,460 | 1,876 | 644* |
| wgn 4d | 3,770 | 2,672 | 760 |
| Deluxe wgn 4d | 3,785 | 2,797 | 554 |

| Dynamic 76 (wb 125.0) | | | |
|---|---|---|---|
| club sdn 2d | 3,425 | 1,726 | 9,984* |
| Deluxe club sdn 2d | 3,445 | 1,873 | 4,866* |
| sdn 4d | 3,500 | 1,801 | 7,342* |
| Deluxe sdn 4d | 3,535 | 1,947 | 7,199* |

| Dynamic 78 (wb 125.0) | Wght | Price | Prod |
|---|---|---|---|
| club sdn 2d | 3,545 | 1,785 | 6,939* |
| Deluxe club sdn 2d | 3,590 | 1,931 | 3,383* |
| sdn 4d | 3,625 | 1,859 | 5,102* |
| Deluxe sdn 4d | 3,665 | 2,005 | 5,003* |

| Dynamic/Futuramic 98 (wb 127.0/125.0)** | Wght | Price | Prod |
|---|---|---|---|
| club sdn 2d | 3,645 | 2,078 | 2,311 |
| Deluxe club sdn 2d | 3,685 | 2,182 | 11,949 |
| sdn 4d | 3,705 | 2,151 | 5,605 |
| Deluxe sdn 4d | 3,745 | 2,256 | 32,456 |
| Deluxe conv cpe | 4,035 | 2,624 | 12,914 |

*Estimates based on percentage distribution of known production of 66 (41,993), 68 (16,614), 76 (29,167) and 78 (20,651).
**Futuramic 98 introduced early 1948; weights and prices are for Futuramic, 98 production figures are for total Dynamic and Futuramic production.

| 1948 Engines | bore × stroke | bhp | availability |
|---|---|---|---|
| L6, 238.1 | 3.50 × 4.13 | 100 | S-66, 76 |
| L8, 257.1 | 3.25 × 3.88 | 110 | S-68, 78 |
| L8, 257.1 | 3.25 × 3.88 | 115 | S-98 |

# 1949

| Futuramic 76 (wb 119.5) | Wght | Price | Prod |
|---|---|---|---|
| club sdn 2d | 3,290 | 1,758 | 23,059 |
| Deluxe club sdn 2d | 3,355 | 1,900 | 8,960 |
| club cpe | 3,260 | 1,732 | 9,403 |
| Deluxe club cpe | 3,315 | 1,873 | 3,280 |
| conv cpe | 3,580 | 2,148 | 5,338 |
| Town Sedan 4d | 3,335 | 1,821 | 3,741 |
| Deluxe Town Sedan 4d | 3,400 | 1,963 | 2,725 |
| sdn 4d | 3,340 | 1,832 | 23,631 |
| Deluxe sdn 4d | 3,375 | 1,974 | 13,874 |
| Deluxe wgn 4d | 3,680 | 2,895 | 1,545 |

| Futuramic 88 (wb 119.5) | Wght | Price | Prod |
|---|---|---|---|
| club sdn 2d | 3,585 | 2,170 | 16,887 |
| Deluxe club sdn 2d | 3,615 | 2,301 | 11,820 |
| club cpe | 3,550 | 2,143 | 6,562 |
| Deluxe club cpe | 3,590 | 2,274 | 4,999 |
| conv cpe | 3,845 | 2,559 | 5,434 |
| Town Sedan 4d | 3,625 | 2,233 | 2,859 |
| Deluxe Town Sedan 4d | 3,665 | 2,364 | 2,974 |
| sdn 4d | 3,615 | 2,244 | 23,342 |
| Deluxe sdn 4d | 3,645 | 2,375 | 23,044 |
| Deluxe wgn 4d | 3,945 | 3,296 | 1,355 |

| Futuramic 98 (wb 125.0) | Wght | Price | Prod |
|---|---|---|---|
| club sdn | 3,835 | 2,426 | 3,849 |
| Deluxe club sdn | 3,840 | 2,520 | 16,200 |
| sdn 4d | 3,890 | 2,500 | 8,820 |
| Deluxe sdn 4d | 3,925 | 2,594 | 49,001 |
| Deluxe Holiday htp cpe | 4,000 | 2,973 | 0,000 |
| Deluxe conv cpe | 4,200 | 2,973 | 12,602 |

| 1949 Engines | bore × stroke | bhp | availability |
|---|---|---|---|
| L6, 257.1 | 3.53 × 4.38 | 105 | S-76 |
| V8, 303.7 | 3.75 × 3.44 | 135 | S-88, 98 |

# 1950

| Futuramic 76 (wb 119.5) | Wght | Price | Prod |
|---|---|---|---|
| club sdn 2d | 3,280 | 1,745 | 3,186 |
| Deluxe club sdn 2d | 3,285 | 1,813 | 1,919 |
| club cpe | 3,260 | 1,719 | 2,238 |
| Deluxe club cpe | 3,280 | 1,787 | 1,126 |
| conv cpe | 3,585 | 2,135 | 973 |
| Holiday htp cpe | 3,335 | 2,003 | 144 |
| Deluxe Holiday htp cpe | 3,385 | 2,108 | 394 |

| | Wght | Price | Prod |
|---|---|---|---|
| sdn 4d | 3,320 | 1,819 | 7,396 |
| Deluxe sdn 4d | 3,340 | 1,887 | 9,159 |
| sdn 2d | 3,290 | 1,761 | 3,865 |
| Deluxe sdn 2d | 3,295 | 1,829 | 2,489 |
| wgn 4d | 3,610 | 2,362 | 121 |
| Deluxe wgn 4d | 3,615 | 2,504 | 247 |

| Futuramic 88 (wb 119.5) | Wght | Price | Prod |
|---|---|---|---|
| club sdn 2d | 3,475 | 1,904 | 14,705 |
| Deluxe club sdn 2d | 3,486 | 1,982 | 16,388 |
| club cpe | 3,435 | 1,878 | 10,684 |
| Deluxe club cpe | 3,455 | 1,956 | 10,772 |
| conv cpe | 3,745 | 2,294 | 9,127 |
| Holiday htp cpe | 3,510 | 2,162 | 1,366 |
| Deluxe Holiday htp cpe | 3,505 | 2,267 | 11,316 |
| sdn 4d | 3,515 | 1,970 | 40,301 |
| Deluxe sdn 4d | 3,520 | 2,056 | 100,810 |
| sdn 2d | 3,485 | 1,920 | 23,889 |
| Deluxe sdn 2d | 3,500 | 1,998 | 26,672 |
| wgn 4d | 3,775 | 2,520 | 1,830 |
| Deluxe wgn 4d | 3,780 | 2,662 | 552 |

| Futuramic 98 (wb 122.0) | Wght | Price | Prod |
|---|---|---|---|
| club sdn 2d | 3,685 | 2,225 | 2,270 |
| Deluxe club sdn 2d | 3,705 | 2,319 | 9,719 |
| Deluxe conv cpe | 4,150 | 2,772 | 3,925 |
| Holiday htp cpe | 3,775 | 2,383 | 317 |
| Deluxe Holiday htp cpe | 3,840 | 2,641 | 7,946 |
| Town Sedan 4d | 3,710 | 2,267 | 255 |
| Deluxe Town Sedan 4d | 3,755 | 2,361 | 1,523 |
| sdn 4d | 3,765 | 2,299 | 7,499 |
| Deluxe sdn 4d | 3,775 | 2,393 | 72,766 |

| 1950 Engines | bore × stroke | bhp | availability |
|---|---|---|---|
| L6, 257.1 | 3.53 × 4.38 | 105 | S-76 |
| V8, 303.7 | 3.75 × 3.44 | 135 | S-88, 98 |

# 1951

| 88 (wb 119.5) | Wght | Price | Prod |
|---|---|---|---|
| sdn 4d | 3,542 | 2,111 | 22,848 |
| sdn 2d | 3,507 | 2,049 | 11,792 |

| Super 88 (wb 120.0) | Wght | Price | Prod |
|---|---|---|---|
| club cpe | 3,557 | 2,219 | 7,328 |
| sdn 4d | 3,636 | 2,328 | 90,131 |
| sdn 2d | 3,579 | 2,265 | 34,963 |
| conv cpe | 3,831 | 2,673 | 3,854 |
| Holiday htp cpe | 3,743 | 2,558 | 14,180 |

| 98 (wb 122.0) | Wght | Price | Prod |
|---|---|---|---|
| Deluxe sdn 4d | 3,787 | 2,610 | 78,122 |
| Holiday htp cpe | 3,762 | 2,545 | 3,914 |
| Deluxe Holiday htp cpe | 3,857 | 2,882 | 14,012 |
| Deluxe conv cpe | 4,107 | 3,025 | 4,468 |

| 1951 Engine | bore × stroke | bhp | availability |
|---|---|---|---|
| V8, 303.7 | 3.75 × 3.44 | 135 | S-all |

# 1952

| 88 Deluxe (wb 120.0) | Wght | Price | Prod |
|---|---|---|---|
| sdn 4d | 3,608 | 2,327 | 12,215 |
| sdn 2d | 3,565 | 2,262 | 6,402 |

| Super 88 (wb 120.0) | Wght | Price | Prod |
|---|---|---|---|
| club cpe | 3,597 | 2,345 | 2,050 |
| sdn 4d | 3,649 | 2,462 | 70,606 |
| sdn 2d | 3,603 | 2,395 | 24,963 |
| conv cpe | 3,867 | 2,853 | 5,162 |
| Holiday htp cpe | 3,640 | 2,673 | 15,777 |

# Oldsmobile

**98 (wb 124.0)**

|  | Wght | Price | Prod |
|---|---|---|---|
| sdn 4d | 3,765 | 2,786 | 58,550 |
| conv cpe | 4,111 | 3,229 | 3,544 |
| Holiday htp cpe | 3,874 | 3,022 | 14,150 |

| 1952 Engines | bore × stroke | bhp | availability |
|---|---|---|---|
| V8, 303.7 | 3.75 × 3.44 | 145 | S-88 |
| V8, 303.7 | 3.75 × 3.44 | 160 | S-Super 88, 98 |

## 1953

**88 Deluxe (wb 120.0)**

|  | Wght | Price | Prod |
|---|---|---|---|
| sdn 4d | 3,642 | 2,327 | 20,400 |
| sdn 2d | 3,603 | 2,262 | 12,400 |

**Super 88 (wb 120.0)**

|  | Wght | Price | Prod |
|---|---|---|---|
| sdn 4d | 3,673 | 2,462 | 119,317 |
| sdn 2d | 3,628 | 2,395 | 36,824 |
| conv cpe | 3,905 | 2,853 | 8,310 |
| Holiday htp cpe | 3,661 | 2,673 | 36,881 |

**98 (wb 124.0)**

|  | Wght | Price | Prod |
|---|---|---|---|
| sdn 4d | 3,779 | 2,786 | 64,431 |
| conv cpe | 4,119 | 3,229 | 7,521 |
| Holiday htp cpe | 3,893 | 3,022 | 27,920 |
| Fiesta conv cpe | 4,453 | 5,717 | 458 |

| 1953 Engines | bore × stroke | bhp | availability |
|---|---|---|---|
| V8, 303.7 | 3.75 × 3.44 | 150 | S-88 |
| V8, 303.7 | 3.75 × 3.44 | 165 | S-Super 88, 98 |

## 1954

**88 (wb 122.0)**

|  | Wght | Price | Prod |
|---|---|---|---|
| sdn 4d | 3,719 | 2,337 | 29,028 |
| sdn 2d | 3,699 | 2,272 | 18,013 |
| Holiday htp cpe | 3,721 | 2,449 | 25,820 |

**Super 88 (wb 122.0)**

|  | Wght | Price | Prod |
|---|---|---|---|
| sdn 4d | 3,780 | 2,477 | 111,326 |
| sdn 2d | 3,729 | 2,410 | 27,882 |
| conv cpe | 4,003 | 2,868 | 6,452 |
| Deluxe Holiday htp cpe | 3,775 | 2,688 | 42,155 |

**98 (wb 126.0)**

|  | Wght | Price | Prod |
|---|---|---|---|
| Deluxe sdn 4d | 3,895 | 2,806 | 47,972 |
| Holiday htp cpe | 3,851 | 2,826 | 8,865 |
| Deluxe Holiday htp cpe | 3,938 | 3,042 | 29,688 |
| Starfire conv cpe | 4,193 | 3,249 | 6,800 |

| 1954 Engines | bore × stroke | bhp | availability |
|---|---|---|---|
| V8, 324.3 | 3.88 × 3.44 | 170 | S-88 |
| V8, 324.3 | 3.88 × 3.44 | 185 | S-Super 88, 98 |

## 1955

**88 (wb 122.0)**

|  | Wght | Price | Prod |
|---|---|---|---|
| sdn 4d | 3,707 | 2,362 | 57,777 |
| sdn 2d | 3,688 | 2,297 | 37,507 |
| Holiday htp sdn | 3,768 | 2,548 | 41,310 |
| Holiday htp cpe | 3,707 | 2,474 | 85,767 |

**Super 88 (wb 122.0)**

|  | Wght | Price | Prod |
|---|---|---|---|
| sdn 4d | 3,762 | 2,503 | 111,316 |
| sdn 2d | 3,720 | 2,436 | 11,950 |
| conv cpe | 3,983 | 2,894 | 9,007 |
| Deluxe Holiday htp sdn | 3,825 | 2,788 | 47,385 |
| Deluxe Holiday htp cpe | 3,765 | 2,714 | 62,534 |

**98 (wb 126.0)**

|  | Wght | Price | Prod |
|---|---|---|---|
| sdn 4d | 3,864 | 2,833 | 39,847 |
| Starfire conv cpe | 4,159 | 3,276 | 9,149 |
| Deluxe Holiday htp sdn | 3,976 | 3,140 | 31,267 |
| Deluxe Holiday htp cpe | 3,924 | 3,069 | 38,363 |

| 1955 Engines | bore × stroke | bhp | availability |
|---|---|---|---|
| V8, 324.3 | 3.88 × 3.44 | 185 | S-88 |
| V8, 324.3 | 3.88 × 3.44 | 202 | S-Super 88, 98 |

## 1956

**88 (wb 122.0)**

|  | Wght | Price | Prod |
|---|---|---|---|
| sdn 4d | 3,748 | 2,487 | 57,092 |
| sdn 2d | 3,691 | 2,422 | 31,949 |
| Holiday htp sdn | 3,797 | 2,671 | 52,239 |
| Holiday htp cpe | 3,741 | 2,599 | 74,739 |

**Super 88 (wb 122.0)**

|  | Wght | Price | Prod |
|---|---|---|---|
| sdn 4d | 3,768 | 2,640 | 59,728 |
| sdn 2d | 3,717 | 2,574 | 5,465 |
| Holiday htp sdn | 3,869 | 2,881 | 61,192 |
| Holiday htp cpe | 3,771 | 2,808 | 43,054 |
| conv cpe | 4,033 | 3,031 | 9,561 |

**98 (wb 126.0)**

|  | Wght | Price | Prod |
|---|---|---|---|
| sdn 4d | 4,028 | 3,298 | 20,105 |
| Holiday htp sdn | 4,167 | 3,551 | 42,320 |
| Holiday htp cpe | 4,080 | 3,480 | 19,433 |
| Starfire conv cpe | 4,325 | 3,740 | 8,581 |

| 1956 Engines | bore × stroke | bhp | availability |
|---|---|---|---|
| V8, 324.3 | 3.88 × 3.44 | 230 | S-88 |
| V8, 324.3 | 3.88 × 3.44 | 240 | S-Super 88, 98 |

## 1957

**Golden Rocket 88 (wb 122.0)**

|  |  | Wght | Price | Prod |
|---|---|---|---|---|
| 3611 | sdn 2d | 3,942 | 2,733 | 18,477 |
| 3637 | Holiday htp cpe | 3,963 | 2,854 | 49,187 |
| 3639 | Holiday htp sdn | 4,052 | 2,932 | 33,830 |
| 3667TX | conv cpe | 4,232 | 3,182 | 6,423 |
| 3669 | sdn 4d | 4,000 | 2,798 | 53,923 |
| 3693 | Fiesta wgn 4d | 4,281 | 3,202 | 5,052 |
| 3695 | Fiesta htp wgn 4d | 4,314 | 3,313 | 5,767 |

**Golden Rocket Super 88 (wb 122.0)**

|  |  | Wght | Price | Prod |
|---|---|---|---|---|
| 3637SD | Holiday htp cpe | 4,010 | 3,180 | 31,155 |
| 3639SD | Holiday htp sdn | 4,117 | 3,257 | 39,162 |
| 3667DTX | conv cpe | 4,283 | 3,447 | 7,128 |
| 3669D | sdn 4d | 4,044 | 3,030 | 42,629 |
| 3695SD | Fiesta htp wgn 4d | 4,364 | 3,541 | 8,981 |
| — | sdn 2d | 4,001 | 2,968 | 2,983 |

**Starfire 98 (wb 126.0)**

|  |  | Wght | Price | Prod |
|---|---|---|---|---|
| 3037SDX | Holiday htp cpe | 4,296 | 3,937 | 17,791 |
| 3039SDX | Holiday htp sdn | 4,385 | 4,013 | 32,099 |
| 3067DX | conv cpe | 4,572 | 4,217 | 8,278 |
| 3069D | sdn 4d | 4,322 | 3,741 | 21,525 |

| 1957 Engine | bore × stroke | bhp | availability |
|---|---|---|---|
| V8, 371.1 | 4.00 × 3.69 | 277 | S-all |

## 1958

**Dynamic 88 (wb 122.5)**

|  |  | Wght | Price | Prod |
|---|---|---|---|---|
| 3611 | sdn 2d | 3,961 | 2,772 | 11,833 |
| 3637 | Holiday htp cpe | 3,972 | 2,893 | 53,036 |
| 3639 | Holiday htp sdn | 4,035 | 2,971 | 28,241 |
| 3667TX | conv cpe | 3,987 | 3,221 | 4,456 |
| 3669 | sdn 4d | 3,985 | 2,837 | 60,429 |
| 3693 | Fiesta wgn 4d | 4,258 | 3,284 | 3,249 |
| 3695 | Fiesta htp wgn 4d | 4,297 | 3,395 | 3,323 |

**Super 88 (wb 122.5)**

|  |  | Wght | Price | Prod |
|---|---|---|---|---|
| 3637SD | Holiday htp cpe | 4,000 | 3,262 | 18,653 |
| 3639SD | Holiday htp sdn | 4,073 | 3,339 | 27,521 |
| 3667DTX | conv cpe | 4,010 | 3,529 | 3,799 |
| 3669D | sdn 4d | 4,008 | 3,112 | 33,844 |
| 3695SD | Fiesta htp wgn 4d | 4,334 | 3,623 | 5,175 |

| 98 (wb 126.5) | | Wght | Price | Prod |
|---|---|---|---|---|
| 3037SDX | Holiday htp cpe | 4,329 | 4,020 | 11,012 |
| 3039SDX | Holiday htp sdn | 4,391 | 4,096 | 27,603 |
| 3067DX | conv cpe | 4,318 | 4,300 | 5,605 |
| 3069D | sdn 4d | 4,316 | 3,824 | 16,595 |

| 1958 Engines | bore × stroke | bhp | availability |
|---|---|---|---|
| V8, 371.1 | 4.00 × 3.69 | 265 | S-88 |
| V8, 371.1 | 4.00 × 3.69 | 305 | S-Super 88, 98 |
| V8, 371.1 | 4.00 × 3.69 | 312 | O-Super 88, 98 |

## 1959

| Dynamic 88 (wb 123.0) | | Wght | Price | Prod |
|---|---|---|---|---|
| 3211 | sdn 4d | 4,040 | 2,837 | 16,123 |
| 3219 | Celebrity sdn 4d | 4,130 | 2,902 | 70,995 |
| 3235 | Fiesta wgn 4d | 4,465 | 3,365 | 11,298 |
| 3237 | Scenic htp cpe | 4,085 | 2,950 | 38,488 |
| 3239 | Holiday htp sdn | 4,165 | 3,036 | 48,707 |
| 3267 | conv cpe | 4,120 | 3,286 | 8,491 |

| Super 88 (wb 123.0) | | | | |
|---|---|---|---|---|
| 3519 | Celebrity sdn 4d | 4,135 | 3,178 | 37,024 |
| 3535 | Fiesta wgn 4d | 4,485 | 3,669 | 7,015 |
| 3537 | Scenic htp cpe | 4,090 | 3,328 | 20,259 |
| 3539 | Holiday htp sdn | 4,185 | 3,405 | 38,467 |
| 3567 | conv cpe | 4,135 | 3,595 | 4,895 |

| 98 (wb 126.3) | | | | |
|---|---|---|---|---|
| 3819 | Celebrity sdn 4d | 4,390 | 3,890 | 23,106 |
| 3837 | Scenic htp cpe | 4,360 | 4,086 | 13,669 |
| 3839 | Holiday htp sdn | 4,450 | 4,162 | 36,813 |
| 3867 | conv cpe | 4,360 | 4,366 | 7,514 |

| 1959 Engines | bore × stroke | bhp | availability |
|---|---|---|---|
| V8, 371.1 | 4.00 × 3.69 | 270 | S-88 |
| V8, 371.1 | 4.00 × 3.69 | 300 | O-88 |
| V8, 371.1 | 4.00 × 3.69 | 315 | S-Super 88, 98 |

## 1960

| Dynamic 88 (wb 123.0) | | Wght | Price | Prod |
|---|---|---|---|---|
| 3211 | sdn 2d | 4,026 | 2,835 | 13,545 |
| 3219 | Celebrity sdn 4d | 4,091 | 2,900 | 76,377 |
| 3235 | Fiesta wgn 4d, 6P | 4,449 | 3,363 | 8,835 |
| 3237 | Sceni-Coupe htp | 4,049 | 2,956 | 29,368 |
| 3239 | Holiday htp sdn | 4,139 | 3,034 | 43,761 |
| 3245 | Fiesta wgn 4d, 8P | 4,470 | 3,471 | 5,708 |
| 3267 | conv cpe | 4,101 | 3,284 | 12,271 |

| Super 88 (wb 123.0) | | | | |
|---|---|---|---|---|
| 3519 | Celebrity sdn 4d | 4,128 | 3,176 | 35,094 |
| 3535 | Fiesta wgn 4d, 6P | 4,483 | 3,665 | 3,765 |
| 3537 | Sceni-Coupe htp | 4,086 | 3,325 | 16,464 |
| 3539 | Holiday htp sdn | 4,182 | 3,402 | 33,285 |
| 3545 | Fiesta wgn 4d, 8P | 4,506 | 3,773 | 3,475 |
| 3567 | conv cpe | 4,134 | 3,592 | 5,830 |

| 98 (wb 126.3) | | | | |
|---|---|---|---|---|
| 3819 | Celebrity sdn 4d | 4,360 | 3,887 | 17,188 |
| 3837 | Sceni-Coupe htp | 4,322 | 4,083 | 7,635 |
| 3839 | Holiday htp sdn | 4,431 | 4,159 | 27,257 |
| 3867 | conv cpe | 4,349 | 4,362 | 7,284 |

| 1960 Engines | bore × stroke | bhp | availability |
|---|---|---|---|
| V8, 371.1 | 4.00 × 3.69 | 240 | S-88 |
| V8, 371.1 | 4.00 × 3.69 | 260 | O-88 |
| V8, 394.0 | 4.13 × 3.69 | 315 | S-Super 88, 98 |

## 1961

| F-85 (wb 112.0) | | Wght | Price | Prod |
|---|---|---|---|---|
| 3019 | sdn 4d | 2,541 | 2,384 | 19,765 |
| 3027 | club cpe | 2,549 | 2,330 | 2,336 |
| 3035 | wgn 4d, 6P | 2,716 | 2,681 | 6,677 |
| 3045 | wgn 4d, 8P | 2,800 | 2,762 | 10,087 |

| F-85 Deluxe (wb 112.0) | | | | |
|---|---|---|---|---|
| 3117 | Cutlass spt cpe | 2,664 | 2,621 | 9,935 |
| 3119 | sdn 4d | 2,547 | 2,519 | 26,311 |
| 3135 | wgn 4d, 6P | 2,731 | 2,816 | 526 |
| 3145 | wgn 4d, 8P | 2,822 | 2,897 | 757 |

| Dynamic 88 (wb 123.0) | | | | |
|---|---|---|---|---|
| 3211 | sdn 2d | 3,966 | 2,835 | 4,920 |
| 3235 | wgn 4d, 6P | 4,354 | 3,363 | 5,374 |
| 3237 | Holiday htp cpe | 3,981 | 2,956 | 19,878 |
| 3239 | Holiday htp sdn | 4,074 | 3,034 | 51,502 |
| 3245 | wgn 4d, 8P | 4,428 | 3,471 | 4,013 |
| 3267 | conv cpe | 4,068 | 3,284 | 9,049 |
| 3269 | Celebrity sdn 4d | 4,031 | 2,900 | 42,584 |

| Super 88 (wb 123.0) | | | | |
|---|---|---|---|---|
| 3535 | wgn 4d, 6P | 4,382 | 3,665 | 2,761 |
| 3537 | Holiday htp cpe | 4,024 | 3,325 | 7,009 |
| 3539 | Holiday htp sdn | 4,099 | 3,402 | 23,272 |
| 3545 | wgn 4d, 8P | 4,445 | 3,773 | 2,170 |
| 3567 | conv cpe | 4,099 | 3,592 | 2,624 |
| 3569 | Celebrity sdn 4d | 4,065 | 3,176 | 15,328 |
| 3667 | Starfire conv cpe | 4,330 | 4,647 | 7,600 |

| 98 (wb 126.3) | | | | |
|---|---|---|---|---|
| 3829 | Holiday htp sdn | 4,269 | 4,021 | 13,331 |
| 3837 | Holiday htp cpe | 4,187 | 4,083 | 4,445 |
| 3839 | Sport Sedan (htp) | 4,319 | 4,159 | 12,343 |
| 3867 | conv cpe | 4,225 | 4,362 | 3,804 |

| 1961 Engines | bore × stroke | bhp | availability |
|---|---|---|---|
| V8, 215.0 | 3.50 × 2.80 | 155 | S-F-85 |
| V8, 394.0 | 4.13 × 3.69 | 250 | S-88 |
| V8, 394.0 | 4.13 × 3.69 | 325 | S-Super 88, 98; 0-88 |

## 1962

| F-85 (wb 112.0) | | Wght | Price | Prod |
|---|---|---|---|---|
| 3019 | sdn 4d | 2,599 | 2,457 | 8,074 |
| 3027 | club cpe | 2,607 | 2,403 | 7,909 |
| 3035 | wgn 4d, 6P | 2,780 | 2,754 | 3,204 |
| 3045 | wgn 4d, 8P | 2,852 | 2,835 | 1,887 |
| 3067 | conv cpe | 2,790 | 2,760 | 3,660 |

| F-85 Deluxe (wb 112.0) | | | | |
|---|---|---|---|---|
| 3117 | Cutlass spt cpe | 2,651 | 2,694 | 32,461 |
| 3119 | sdn 4d | 2,634 | 2,592 | 18,736 |
| 3135 | wgn 4d, 6P | 2,812 | 2,889 | 4,974 |
| 3167 | Cutlass conv cpe | 2,830 | 2,971 | 9,893 |
| 3147 | Jetfire spt cpe | 2,739 | 3,049 | 3,765 |

| Dynamic 88 (wb 123.0) | | | | |
|---|---|---|---|---|
| 3235 | wgn 4d, 6P | 4,392 | 3,460 | 8,527 |
| 3239 | Holiday htp sdn | 4,080 | 3,131 | 53,438 |
| 3245 | wgn 4d, 8P | 4,428 | 3,568 | 6,417 |
| 3247 | Holiday htp cpe | 3,992 | 3,054 | 39,676 |
| 3267 | conv cpe | 4,104 | 3,381 | 12,212 |
| 3269 | Celebrity sdn 4d | 4,038 | 2,997 | 68,467 |

| Super 88 (wb 123.0) | | | | |
|---|---|---|---|---|
| 3535 | Fiesta wgn 4d | 4,412 | 3,762 | 3,837 |
| 3539 | Holiday htp sdn | 4,117 | 3,499 | 21,175 |
| 3547 | Holiday htp cpe | 4,022 | 3,422 | 9,010 |
| 3569 | Celebrity sdn 4d | 4,069 | 3,273 | 24,125 |

| Starfire (wb 123.0) | | | | |
|---|---|---|---|---|
| 3647 | htp cpe | 4,213 | 4,131 | 34,839 |
| 3667 | conv cpe | 4,334 | 4,744 | 7,149 |

# Oldsmobile

| 98 (wb 126.0) | | Wght | Price | Prod |
|---|---|---|---|---|
| 3819 | Town Sedan 4d | 4,258 | 3,984 | 12,167 |
| 3829 | Holiday htp sdn | 4,306 | 4,118 | 7,653 |
| 3839 | Sport Sedan (htp) | 4,337 | 4,256 | 33,095 |
| 3847 | Holiday htp cpe | 4,231 | 4,180 | 7,546 |
| 3867 | conv cpe | 4,298 | 4,459 | 3,693 |

| 1962 Engines | bore × stroke | bhp | availability |
|---|---|---|---|
| V8, 215.0 | 3.50 × 2.80 | 155 | S-F-85 exc Cutlass/Jetfire |
| V8, 215.0 | 3.50 × 2.80 | 185 | S-F-85 Cutlass; O-F-85 |
| V8, 215.0 | 3.50 × 2.80 | 215 | S-F-85 Jetfire |
| V8, 394.0 | 4.13 × 3.69 | 280 | S-88 |
| V8, 394.0 | 4.13 × 3.69 | 330 | S-Super 88, 98 |
| V8, 394.0 | 4.13 × 3.69 | 345 | S-Starfire |

## 1963

| F-85 (wb 112.0) | | Wght | Price | Prod |
|---|---|---|---|---|
| 3019 | sdn 4d | 2,629 | 2,457 | 8,937 |
| 3027 | club cpe | 2,599 | 2,403 | 11,276 |
| 3035 | wgn 4d | 2,812 | 2,754 | 3,348 |

| F-85 Deluxe (wb 112.0) | | | | |
|---|---|---|---|---|
| 3117 | Cutlass club cpe | 2,679 | 2,694 | 41,343 |
| 3119 | sdn 4d | 2,659 | 2,592 | 29,269 |
| 3135 | wgn 4d | 2,833 | 2,889 | 6,647 |
| 3147 | Jetfire htp cpe | 2,774 | 3,048 | 5,842 |
| 3167 | Cutlass conv cpe | 2,858 | 2,971 | 12,149 |

| Dynamic 88 (wb 123.0) | | | | |
|---|---|---|---|---|
| 3235 | wgn 4d, 6P | 4,322 | 3,459 | 9,615 |
| 3239 | Holiday htp sdn | 4,059 | 3,130 | 62,351 |
| 3245 | wgn 4d, 8P | 4,354 | 3,566 | 7,116 |
| 3247 | Holiday htp cpe | 3,839 | 3,052 | 39,071 |
| 3267 | conv cpe | 4,039 | 3,379 | 12,551 |
| 3269 | Celebrity sdn 4d | 3,998 | 2,995 | 68,611 |

| Super 88 (wb 123.0) | | | | |
|---|---|---|---|---|
| 3535 | Fiesta wgn 4d | 4,347 | 3,748 | 3,878 |
| 3539 | Holiday htp sdn | 4,083 | 3,473 | 25,387 |
| 3547 | Holiday htp cpe | 3,966 | 3,408 | 8,930 |
| 3569 | Celebrity sdn 4d | 4,027 | 3,246 | 24,575 |

| Starfire (wb 123.0) | | | | |
|---|---|---|---|---|
| 3657 | htp cpe | 4,172 | 4,129 | 21,148 |
| 3667 | conv cpe | 4,293 | 4,742 | 4,401 |

| 98 (wb 126.0) | | | | |
|---|---|---|---|---|
| 3819 | Town Sedan 4d | 4,240 | 3,982 | 11,053 |
| 3829 | Luxury htp sdn | 4,362 | 4,332 | 19,252 |
| 3839 | Sport Sedan (htp) | 4,347 | 4,258 | 23,330 |
| 3847 | Holiday htp cpe | 4,215 | 4,178 | 4,984 |
| 3867 | conv cpe | 4,272 | 4,457 | 4,267 |
| 3947 | Custom htp cpe | 4,285 | 4,381 | 7,422 |

| 1963 Engines | bore × stroke | bhp | availability |
|---|---|---|---|
| V8, 215.0 | 3.50 × 2.80 | 155 | S-F-85 exc Cutlass/Jetfire |
| V8, 215.0 | 3.50 × 2.80 | 185 | S-F-85 Cutlass; 0-F-85 |
| V8, 215.0 | 3.50 × 2.80 | 215 | S-F-85 Jetfire |
| V8, 394.0 | 4.13 × 3.69 | 280 | S-88 |
| V8, 394.0 | 4.13 × 3.69 | 330 | S-Super 88, 98 exc Custom |
| V8, 394.0 | 4.13 × 3.69 | 330 | S-Starfire, 98 Custom |

## 1964

| F-85 (wb 115.0; Vista Crsr-120.0) | | Wght | Price | Prod |
|---|---|---|---|---|
| 3027 | club cpe | 2,980 | 2,343 | 16,298 |
| 3035 | wgn 4d | 3,274 | 2,689 | 4,047 |
| 3055 | Vista Cruiser wgn 4d, 2S | 3,652 | 2,938 | 1,305 |
| 3065 | Vista Cruiser wgn 4d, 3S | 3,729 | 3,072 | 2,089 |
| 3069 | sdn 4d | 3,025 | 2,397 | 12,106 |

| | | Wght | Price | Prod |
|---|---|---|---|---|
| 3127 | Del Sports Coupe | 2,824 | 2,537 | 6,594 |
| 3135 | Del wgn 4d | 3,304 | 2,797 | 909 |
| 3169 | Del sdn 4d | 3,055 | 2,505 | 7,428 |

| Cutlass (wb 115.0) | | | | |
|---|---|---|---|---|
| 3227 | Sports Coupe | 3,141 | 2,644 | 15,440 |
| 3237 | Holiday htp cpe | 3,180 | 2,784 | 36,153 |
| 3255 | Custom wgn 4d 2S | 3,714 | 3,146 | 3,320 |
| 3265 | Custom Wgn 4d, 3S | 3,781 | 3,270 | 7,286 |
| 3267 | conv cpe | 3,263 | 2,984 | 12,822 |

| Jetstar 88 (wb 123.0) | | | | |
|---|---|---|---|---|
| 3339 | Holiday htp sdn | 3,783 | 3,069 | 19,325 |
| 3347 | Holiday htp cpe | 3,701 | 2,992 | 14,663 |
| 3367 | conv cpe | 3,754 | 3,318 | 3,903 |
| 3369 | Celebrity sdn 4d | 3,729 | 2,935 | 24,614 |

| Dynamic 88 (123.0) | | | | |
|---|---|---|---|---|
| 3435 | wgn 4d, 2S | 4,286 | 3,468 | 10,747 |
| 3439 | Holiday htp sdn | 4,012 | 3,139 | 50,327 |
| 3445 | wgn 4d, 3S | 4,324 | 3,576 | 6,599 |
| 3447 | Holiday htp cpe | 3,924 | 3,062 | 32,369 |
| 3457 | Jetstar I spt cpe | 4,019 | 3,603 | 16,084 |
| 3467 | conv cpe | 3,996 | 3,389 | 10,042 |
| 3469 | Celebrity sdn 4d | 3,966 | 3,005 | 57,590 |

| Super 88 (wb 123.0) | | | | |
|---|---|---|---|---|
| 3539 | Holiday htp sdn | 4,069 | 3,486 | 17,778 |
| 3569 | Celebrity sdn 4d | 4,009 | 3,256 | 19,736 |

| Starfire (wb 123.0) | | | | |
|---|---|---|---|---|
| 3657 | htp cpe | 4,167 | 4,138 | 13,753 |
| 3667 | conv cpe | 4,253 | 4,753 | 2,410 |

| 98 (wb 126.0) | | | | |
|---|---|---|---|---|
| 3819 | Town Sedan 4d | 4,234 | 3,993 | 11,380 |
| 3829 | Luxury sdn 4d | 4,337 | 4,342 | 17,346 |
| 3839 | Sport Sedan (htp) | 4,323 | 4,265 | 24,791 |
| 3847 | htp cpe | 4,205 | 4,118 | 6,139 |
| 3867 | conv cpe | 4,255 | 4,468 | 4,004 |
| 3947 | Custom htp cpe | 4,271 | 4,391 | 4,594 |

| 1964 Engines | bore × stroke | bhp | availability |
|---|---|---|---|
| V6, 225.0 | 3.75 × 3.40 | 155 | S-F-85 |
| V8, 330.0 | 3.94 × 3.38 | 230 | S-Vista Crsr; O-F-85, Jetstar 88 |
| V8, 330.0 | 3.94 × 3.38 | 245 | S-Jetstar 88 |
| V8, 330.0 | 3.94 × 3.38 | 290 | S-Cutlass; O-F-85, Jetstar 88 |
| V8, 394.0 | 4.13 × 3.69 | 280 | S-88 |
| V8, 394.0 | 4.13 × 3.69 | 330 | S-Super 88, 98; 0-88 |
| V8, 394.0 | 4.13 × 3.69 | 345 | S-Jetstar I, Starfire, 98 Custom; O-Super 88, 98 |

## 1965

| F-85 (wb 115.0; Vista Crsr-120.0) | | Wght | Price | Prod |
|---|---|---|---|---|
| 3327 | club cpe, V6 | 2,940 | 2,344 | 5,289 |
| 3335 | wgn 4d, V6 | 3,252 | 2,689 | 714 |
| 3369 | sdn 4d, V6 | 2,991 | 2,398 | 3,089 |
| 3427 | club cpe, V8 | 3,146 | 2,415 | 7,720 |
| 3435 | wgn 4d, V8 | 3,457 | 2,760 | 2,496 |
| 3455 | Vista Crsr. wgn, 6P, V8 | 3,732 | 2,937 | 2,110 |
| 3465 | Vista Crsr. wgn, 8P, V8 | 3,809 | 3,072 | 3,335 |
| 3469 | sdn 4d, V8 | 3,174 | 2,469 | 5,661 |

| F-85 Deluxe (wb 115.0; Cus-120.0) | | | | |
|---|---|---|---|---|
| 3527 | Sports Coupe, V6 | 2,980 | 2,538 | 6,141 |
| 3535 | wgn 4d, V6 | 3,262 | 2,797 | 659 |
| 3569 | sdn 4d, V6 | 3,016 | 2,505 | 4,989 |
| 3635 | wgn 4d, V8 | 3,459 | 2,868 | 10,365 |
| 3669 | sdn 4d, V8 | 3,218 | 2,576 | 47,767 |
| 3855 | Cus wgn 4d, 6P, V8 | 3,762 | 3,146 | 9,335 |
| 3865 | Cus wgn 4d, 8P, V8 | 3,864 | 3,270 | 17,205 |

## Oldsmobile

### Cutlass (wb 115.0)

| | | Wght | Price | Prod |
|---|---|---|---|---|
| 3827 | Sports Coupe, V8 | 3,221 | 2,643 | 26,441 |
| 3837 | Holiday htp cpe, V8 | 3,245 | 2,784 | 46,138 |
| 3867 | conv cpe, V8 | 3,338 | 2,983 | 12,628 |

### Jetstar 88 (wb 123.0)

| | | | | |
|---|---|---|---|---|
| 5237 | Holiday htp cpe | 3,688 | 2,995 | 13,911 |
| 5239 | Holiday htp sdn | 3,775 | 3,072 | 15,922 |
| 5267 | conv cpe | 3,741 | 3,337 | 2,879 |
| 5269 | Celebrity sdn 4d | 3,726 | 2,938 | 22,725 |

### Jetstar I (wb 123.0)

| | | | | |
|---|---|---|---|---|
| 5457 | Sports Coupe | 3,982 | 3,602 | 6,552 |

### Dynamic 88 (wb 123.0)

| | | | | |
|---|---|---|---|---|
| 5637 | Holiday htp cpe | 3,873 | 3,065 | 24,746 |
| 5639 | Holiday htp sdn | 3,961 | 3,143 | 38,889 |
| 5667 | conv cpe | 3,946 | 3,408 | 8,832 |
| 5669 | Celebrity sdn 4d | 4,000 | 3,008 | 47,030 |

### Delta 88 (wb 123.0)

| | | | | |
|---|---|---|---|---|
| 5837 | htp cpe | 3,924 | 3,253 | 23,194 |
| 5839 | htp sdn | 4,010 | 3,330 | 37,358 |
| 5869 | Celebrity sdn 4d | 3,940 | 3,158 | 29,915 |

### Starfire (wb 123.0)

| | | | | |
|---|---|---|---|---|
| 6657 | htp cpe | 4,152 | 4,138 | 13,024 |
| 6667 | conv cpe | 4,247 | 4,778 | 2,236 |

### 98 (wb 126.0)

| | | | | |
|---|---|---|---|---|
| 8437 | htp cpe | 4,178 | 4,197 | 12,166 |
| 8439 | htp sdn | 4,286 | 4,273 | 28,480 |
| 8467 | conv cpe | 4,250 | 4,493 | 4,903 |
| 8469 | Town Sedan 4d | 4,186 | 4,001 | 13,266 |
| 8669 | Luxury sdn 4d | 4,285 | 4,351 | 33,591 |

### 1965 Engines

| | bore × stroke | bhp | availability |
|---|---|---|---|
| V6, 225.0 | 3.75 × 3.40 | 155 | S-F-85 6 |
| V8, 330.0 | 3.94 × 3.38 | 250/260 | S-F-85 V8 exc Cutlass /Jetstar 88 |
| V8, 330.0 | 3.94 × 3.38 | 315 | S-Cutlass |
| V8, 400.0 | 4.00 × 3.98 | 320 | O-Cutlass |
| V8, 425.0 | 4.13 × 3.98 | 310 | S-Delta 88, Dynamic 88; 0-98 |
| V8, 425.0 | 4.13 × 3.98 | 360 | S-98; O-other full-size |
| V8, 425.0 | 4.13 × 3.98 | 370 | S-Jetstar I. Starfire: O-full-size |

## 1966

### F-85 (wb 115.0)

| | | Wght | Price | Prod |
|---|---|---|---|---|
| 33307 | cpe, L6 | 2,951 | 2,348 | 6,341 |
| 33335 | wgn 4d, L6 | 3,246 | 2,695 | 508 |
| 33369 | sdn 4d, L6 | 3,001 | 2,401 | 2,862 |
| 33407 | cpe, V8 | 3,153 | 2,418 | 4,923* |
| 33435 | wgn 4d, V8 | 3,431 | 2,764 | 1,652 |
| 33469 | sdn 4d, V8 | 3,187 | 2,471 | 3,754 |

### F-85 Deluxe (wb 115.0)

| | | | | |
|---|---|---|---|---|
| 33517 | Holiday htp cpe, L6 | 2,990 | 2,513 | 2,974 |
| 33535 | wgn 4d, L6 | 3,273 | 2,793 | 434 |
| 33539 | Holiday htp sdn, L6 | 3,077 | 2,629 | 1,002 |
| 33569 | sdn 4d, L6 | 3,023 | 2,497 | 3,568 |
| 33617 | Holiday htp cpe, V8 | 3,196 | 2,583 | 13,141* |
| 33635 | wgn 4d, V8 | 3,453 | 2,862 | 8,058 |
| 33639 | Holiday htp sdn, V8 | 3,272 | 2,699 | 6,911 |
| 33669 | sdn 4d, V8 | 3,210 | 2,567 | 27,452 |

### Cutlass (wb 115.0)

| | | | | |
|---|---|---|---|---|
| 33807 | Sports Coupe | 3,219 | 2,633 | 13,518* |
| 33817 | Holiday htp cpe | 3,243 | 2,770 | 34,580* |
| 33839 | Supreme htp sdn | 3,296 | 2,846 | 30,871 |
| 33867 | conv cpe | 3,349 | 2,965 | 9,410* |
| 33869 | Celebrity sdn 4d | 3,240 | 2,673 | 9,017 |

### Vista Cruiser (wb 120.0)

| | | | | |
|---|---|---|---|---|
| 33455 | wgn 4d, 2S | 3,735 | 2,935 | 1,660 |

---

| | | Wght | Price | Prod |
|---|---|---|---|---|
| 33465 | wgn 4d, 3S | 3,806 | 3,087 | 1,869 |
| 33855 | Custom wgn 4d, 2S | 3,765 | 3,137 | 8,910 |
| 33865 | Custom wgn 4d, 3S | 3,861 | 3,278 | 14,164 |

### 4-4-2 (wb 115.0)

| | | | | |
|---|---|---|---|---|
| 33407 | cpe | 3,454 | 2,604 | 1,430* |
| 33617 | htp cpe | 3,502 | 2,769 | 3,827* |
| 33807 | spt cpe | 3,506 | 2,786 | 3,937* |
| 33817 | Holiday htp cpe | 3,523 | 2,923 | 10,053* |
| 33867 | conv cpe | 3,629 | 3,118 | 2,750* |

### Jetstar 88 (wb 123.0)

| | | | | |
|---|---|---|---|---|
| 35237 | Holiday htp cpe | 3,727 | 2,983 | 8,575 |
| 35239 | Holiday htp sdn | 3,823 | 3,059 | 7,938 |
| 35269 | Celebrity sdn 4d | 3,770 | 2,927 | 13,734 |

### Dynamic 88 (wb 123.0)

| | | | | |
|---|---|---|---|---|
| 35637 | Holiday htp cpe | 3,899 | 3,069 | 20,768 |
| 35639 | Holiday htp sdn | 3,982 | 3,144 | 30,784 |
| 35667 | conv cpe | 3,971 | 3,404 | 5,540 |
| 35669 | Celebrity sdn 4d | 3,930 | 3,013 | 38,742 |

### Delta 88 (wb 123.0)

| | | | | |
|---|---|---|---|---|
| 35837 | Holiday htp cpe | 3,944 | 3,253 | 20,857 |
| 35839 | Holiday htp sdn | 4,026 | 3,328 | 33,326 |
| 35867 | conv cpe | 4,010 | 3,588 | 4,303 |
| 35869 | Celebrity sdn 4d | 3,963 | 3,160 | 30,140 |

### Starfire (wb 123.0)

| | | | | |
|---|---|---|---|---|
| 35457 | htp cpe | 4,013 | 3,564 | 13,019 |

### 98 (wb 126.0)

| | | | | |
|---|---|---|---|---|
| 38437 | Holiday htp cpe | 4,165 | 4,158 | 11,488 |
| 38439 | Holiday htp sdn | 4,266 | 4,233 | 23,048 |
| 38467 | conv cpe | 4,233 | 4,443 | 4,568 |
| 38469 | Town Sedan 4d | 4,177 | 3,966 | 10,892 |
| 38669 | Luxury Sedan 4d | 4,271 | 4,308 | 30,123 |

### Toronado (wb 119.0)

| | | | | |
|---|---|---|---|---|
| 39487 | htp cpe | 4,311 | 4,617 | 6,333 |
| 39687 | Deluxe htp cpe | 4,366 | 4,812 | 34,630 |

*Production combined; numbers given are proportional to production of same models in F-85 and Cutlass lines. Total 4-4-2 production: 21,997.

### 1966 Engines

| | bore × stroke | bhp | availability |
|---|---|---|---|
| L6, 250.0 | 3.88 × 3.53 | 155 | S-F-85 6 |
| V8, 330.0 | 3.94 × 3.38 | 250 | S-F-85 V8, Vista Crsr; O-Jetstar 88 |
| V8, 330.0 | 3.94 × 3.38 | 260 | S-Jetstar 88 |
| V8, 330.0 | 3.94 × 3.38 | 310 | O-Cutlass, F-85, Vista Crsr |
| V8, 330.0 | 3.94 × 3.38 | 320 | S-Cutlass; O-Jetstar 88, F-85, Vst. Crsr |
| V8, 400.0 | 4.00 × 3.98 | 350 | S-442 |
| V8, 425.0 | 4.13 × 3.98 | 300 | O-Delta 88, Dynamic 88 |
| V8, 425.0 | 4.13 × 3.98 | 310 | S-Delta 88, Dynamic 88 |
| V8, 425.0 | 4.13 × 3.98 | 365 | S-98; O-Delta 88, Dynamic 88 |
| V8, 425.0 | 4.13 × 3.98 | 375 | S-Starfire; 0-98, Delta 88 |
| V8, 425.0 | 4.13 × 3.98 | 385 | S-Toronado |

## 1967

### F-85 (wb 115.0)

| | | Wght | Price | Prod |
|---|---|---|---|---|
| 33307 | club cpe, L6 | 3,014 | 2,410 | 5,349 |
| 33335 | wgn 4d, L6 | 3,295 | 2,749 | 2,749 |
| 33369 | Town Sedan 4d, L6 | 3,031 | 2,457 | 2,458 |
| 33407 | club cpe, V8 | 3,184 | 2,480 | 6,700 |
| 33435 | wgn 4d, V8 | 3,463 | 2,818 | 1,625 |
| 33469 | Town Sedan 4d, V8 | 3,469 | 2,527 | 5,126 |

### Cutlass (wb 115.0)

| | | | | |
|---|---|---|---|---|
| 33517 | Holiday htp cpe, L6 | 3,033 | 2,574 | 2,564 |
| 33535 | wgn 4d, L6 | 3,308 | 2,848 | 365 |
| 33539 | Holiday htp sdn, L6 | 3,125 | 2,683 | 644 |
| 33567 | conv cpe, L6 | 3,125 | 2,770 | 567 |

| | | Wght | Price | Prod |
|---|---|---|---|---|
| 33569 | Town Sedan 4d, L6 | 3,055 | 2,552 | 2,219 |
| 33617 | Holiday htp cpe, V8 | 3,216 | 2,644 | 29,799 |
| 33635 | wgn 4d, V8 | 3,473 | 2,917 | 8,130 |
| 33639 | Holiday htp sdn, V8 | 3,292 | 2,753 | 7,344 |
| 33667 | conv cpe, V8 | 3,306 | 2,839 | 3,777 |
| 33669 | Town Sedan 4d, V8 | 3,223 | 2,622 | 29,062 |

**Cutlass Supreme (wb 115.0)**

| | | Wght | Price | Prod |
|---|---|---|---|---|
| 33807 | Sports Coupe | 3,238 | 2,694 | 13,041* |
| 33817 | Holiday htp cpe | 3,262 | 2,831 | 41,344* |
| 33839 | Holiday htp sdn | 3,346 | 2,900 | 22,571 |
| 33867 | conv cpe | 3,867 | 3,026 | 7,793* |
| 33869 | Town Sedan 4d | 3,258 | 2,726 | 8,346 |

**4-4-2 (wb 115.0)**

| | | Wght | Price | Prod |
|---|---|---|---|---|
| 33807 | Sports Coupe | 3,540 | 2,788 | 5,215* |
| 33817 | Holiday htp cpe | 3,568 | 3,015 | 16,514* |
| 33867 | conv cpe | 4,047 | 3,210 | 3,104* |

**Vista Cruiser (wb 120.0)**

| | | Wght | Price | Prod |
|---|---|---|---|---|
| 33465 | wgn 4d, 3S | 3,836 | 3,136 | 2,748 |
| 33855 | Custom wgn 4d, 2S | 3,796 | 3,228 | 9,513 |
| 33865 | Custom wgn 4d, 3S | 3,907 | 3,369 | 15,293 |

**Delmont 88 "330" (wb 123.0)**

| | | Wght | Price | Prod |
|---|---|---|---|---|
| 35239 | Holiday htp sdn | 3,932 | 3,139 | 10,600 |
| 35269 | Town Sedan 4d | 3,867 | 3,008 | 15,076 |
| 35287 | Holiday htp cpe | 3,819 | 3,063 | 10,786 |

**Delmont 88 "425" (wb 123.0)**

| | | Wght | Price | Prod |
|---|---|---|---|---|
| 35639 | Holiday htp sdn | 4,007 | 3,202 | 22,980 |
| 35667 | conv cpe | 4,010 | 3,462 | 3,525 |
| 35669 | Town Sedan 4d | 3,968 | 3,071 | 28,690 |
| 35687 | Holiday htp cpe | 3,914 | 3,126 | 16,699 |

**Delta 88 (wb 123.0)**

| | | Wght | Price | Prod |
|---|---|---|---|---|
| 35839 | Holiday htp sdn | 4,053 | 3,386 | 21,909 |
| 35867 | conv cpe | 4,039 | 3,646 | 2,447 |
| 35869 | Town Sedan 4d | 3,986 | 3,218 | 22,770 |
| 35887 | Holiday htp cpe | 3,956 | 3,310 | 14,471 |

**Delta 88 Custom (wb 123.0)**

| | | Wght | Price | Prod |
|---|---|---|---|---|
| 35439 | Holiday htp sdn | 4,081 | 3,582 | 14,306 |
| 35487 | Holiday htp cpe | 3,994 | 3,522 | 12,192 |

**98 (wb 126.0)**

| | | Wght | Price | Prod |
|---|---|---|---|---|
| 38439 | Holiday htp sdn | 4,323 | 4,276 | 17,533 |
| 38457 | Holiday htp cpe | 4,221 | 4,214 | 10,476 |
| 38467 | conv cpe | 4,271 | 4,498 | 3,769 |
| 38469 | Town Sedan 4d | 4,242 | 4,009 | 8,900 |
| 38669 | Luxury Sedan 4d | 4,309 | 4,351 | 35,511 |

**Toronado (wb 119.0)**

| | | Wght | Price | Prod |
|---|---|---|---|---|
| 39487 | htp cpe | 4,310 | 4,674 | 1,770 |
| 39687 | Deluxe htp cpe | 4,362 | 4,869 | 20,020 |

*Production combined; numbers given are proportional to production of same models in Cutlass Supreme line. Total 4-4-2 production: 24,833.

| 1967 Engines | bore × stroke | bhp | availability |
|---|---|---|---|
| L6, 250.0 | 3.88 × 3.53 | 155 | S-F-85 6, Cutlass 6 |
| V8, 330.0 | 3.94 × 3.38 | 250 | S-F-85 V8, Cutlass V8, Vst. Crsr, Delm 88 man; O-Delm auto |
| V8, 330.0 | 3.94 × 3.38 | 260 | S-Delmont 88 w/auto |
| V8, 330.0 | 3.94 × 3.38 | 310 | O-Supreme, Cutls, F-85, VC |
| V8, 330.0 | 3.94 × 3.38 | 320 | S-Sprme; O-Delm, VC, F-85, Cutls |
| V8, 400.0 | 4.00 × 3.98 | 300 | O-Sprme cpe & conv |
| V8, 400.0 | 4.00 × 3.98 | 350 | O-Sprme cpe & conv |
| V8, 425.0 | 4.13 × 3.98 | 300 | S-all 88 man; O-all 88 auto |
| V8, 425.0 | 4.13 × 3.98 | 310 | S-all 88 automatic |
| V8, 425.0 | 4.13 × 3.98 | 365 | S-98; O-Delta 88, Delmont 425 |
| V8, 425.0 | 4.13 × 3.98 | 375 | O-98, Delta 88, Delmont 425 |

# 1968

**F-85 (wb 116.0; 2d-112.0)**

| | | Wght | Price | Prod |
|---|---|---|---|---|
| 33169 | Town Sedan 4d, L6 | 3,108 | 2,560 | 1,847 |
| 33177 | club cpe, L6 | 3,062 | 2,512 | 4,052 |
| 33269 | Town Sedan 4d, V8 | 3,304 | 2,665 | 3,984 |
| 33277 | club cpe, V8 | 3,255 | 2,618 | 5,426 |

**Cutlass (wb 116.0; 2d-112.0)**

| | | Wght | Price | Prod |
|---|---|---|---|---|
| 33535 | wgn 4d, 2S, L6 | 3,473 | 2,969 | 354 |
| 33539 | Holiday htp sdn, L6 | 3,193 | 2,804 | 265 |
| 33567 | conv cpe, L6 | 3,161 | 2,949 | 410 |
| 33569 | Town Sedan 4d, L6 | 3,143 | 2,674 | 1,305 |
| 33577 | Sports Coupe, L6 | 3,064 | 2,632 | 1,181 |
| 33587 | Holiday htp cpe, L6 | 3,108 | 2,696 | 1,492 |
| 33635 | wgn 4d, 2S, V8 | 3,649 | 3,075 | 9,291 |
| 33639 | Holiday htp sdn, V8 | 3,374 | 2,910 | 7,839 |
| 33667 | conv cpe, V8 | 3,342 | 3,055 | 13,667 |
| 33669 | Town Sedan 4d, V8 | 3,325 | 2,779 | 25,994 |
| 33677 | Sport Coupe, V8 | 3,271 | 2,738 | 14,586 |
| 33687 | Holiday htp cpe, V8 | 3,282 | 2,801 | 59,577 |

**Cutlass Supreme (wb 116.0; 2d-112.0)**

| | | Wght | Price | Prod |
|---|---|---|---|---|
| 34239 | Holiday htp sdn | 3,421 | 3,057 | 15,067 |
| 34269 | Town Sedan 4d | 3,372 | 2,884 | 5,524 |
| 34287 | Holiday htp cpe | 3,312 | 2,982 | 33,518 |

**4-4-2 (wb 112.0)**

| | | Wght | Price | Prod |
|---|---|---|---|---|
| 34467 | conv cpe | 3,580 | 3,341 | 5,142 |
| 34477 | Sports Coupe | 3,502 | 3,087 | 4,282 |
| 34487 | Holiday htp cpe | 3,512 | 3,150 | 24,183 |

**Vista Cruiser (wb 121.0)**

| | | Wght | Price | Prod |
|---|---|---|---|---|
| 34855 | Custom wgn 4d, 2S | 3,917 | 3,367 | 13,375 |
| 34865 | Custom wgn 4d, 3S | 4,027 | 3,508 | 22,768 |

**Delmont 88 (wb 123.0)***

| | | Wght | Price | Prod |
|---|---|---|---|---|
| 35439 | Holiday htp sdn | 3,928 | 3,278 | 21,056 |
| 35467 | conv cpe | 3,916 | 3,515 | 2,812 |
| 35469 | Town Sedan 4d | 3,873 | 3,146 | 24,365 |
| 35487 | Holiday htp cpe | 3,844 | 3,202 | 18,391 |

**Delta 88 (wb 123.0)***

| | | Wght | Price | Prod |
|---|---|---|---|---|
| 36439 | Holiday htp sdn | 4,038 | 3,525 | 30,048 |
| 36469 | Town Sedan 4d | 3,979 | 3,357 | 33,689 |
| 36487 | Holiday htp cpe | 3,950 | 3,449 | 18,501 |
| 36639 | Custom Holiday htp sdn | 4,059 | 3,721 | 10,727 |
| 36687 | Custom Holiday htp cpe | 3,982 | 3,661 | 9,540 |

**98 (wb 126.0)**

| | | Wght | Price | Prod |
|---|---|---|---|---|
| 38439 | Holiday htp sdn | 4,278 | 4,422 | 21,147 |
| 38457 | Holiday htp cpe | 4,185 | 4,360 | 15,319 |
| 38467 | conv cpe | 4,264 | 4,618 | 3,942 |
| 38469 | Town Sedan 4d | 4,197 | 4,155 | 10,584 |
| 38669 | Luxury Sedan 4d | 4,273 | 4,497 | 40,755 |

**Toronado (wb 119.0)**

| | | Wght | Price | Prod |
|---|---|---|---|---|
| 39487 | htp cpe | 4,322 | 4,750 | 3,957 |
| 39687 | Custom htp cpe | 4,374 | 4,945 | 22,497 |

*Factory records also indicate 54,794 Dynamic 88s, although other sources do not include these models.

| 1968 Engines | bore × stroke | bhp | availability |
|---|---|---|---|
| L6, 250.0 | 3.88 × 3.53 | 155 | S-F-85 6, Cutlass 6 |
| V8, 350.0 | 4.06 × 3.38 | 250 | S-Vista Crsr; O-Cutls, F-85 |
| V8, 350.0 | 4.06 × 3.38 | 310 | S-Supreme; O-F-85, Cutls, Vista Cruiser, Delmont 88 auto |
| V8, 400.0 | 4.00 × 3.98 | 290 | O-442 auto, Vista Cruiser auto |
| V8, 400.0 | 4.00 × 3.98 | 325 | S-442 auto; O-Vista Cruiser auto |
| V8, 400.0 | 4.00 × 3.98 | 350 | S-442 manual |
| V8, 400.0 | 4.00 × 3.98 | 360 | O-442 all |
| V8, 455.0 | 4.13 × 4.25 | 310 | S-Delta 88 & Custom; O-Delm |
| V8, 455.0 | 4.13 × 4.25 | 320 | 0-above models w/automatic |
| V8, 455.0 | 4.13 × 4.25 | 365 | S-98; O-all 88 w/automatic |

| | bore × stroke | bhp | availability |
|---|---|---|---|
| V8, 455.0 | 4.13 × 4.25 | 375 | S-Toronado |
| V8, 455.0 | 4.13 × 4.25 | 400 | O-Toronado |

## 1969

### F-85 (wb 116.0; 2d-112.0)

| | | Wght | Price | Prod |
|---|---|---|---|---|
| 33177 | Sports Coupe, L6 | 3,082 | 2,561 | 2,899 |
| 33277 | Sports Coupe, V8 | 3,281 | 2,672 | 5,541 |

### Cutlass (wb 116.0; 2d-112.0)

| | | Wght | Price | Prod |
|---|---|---|---|---|
| 33535 | wgn 4d, 2S, L6 | 3,537 | 3,055 | 180 |
| 33539 | Holiday htp sdn, L6 | 3,212 | 2,853 | 236 |
| 33567 | S conv cpe, L6 | 3,188 | 2,998 | 236 |
| 33569 | Town Sedan 4d, L6 | 3,155 | 2,722 | 137 |
| 33577 | S Sports Coupe, L6 | 3,093 | 2,681 | 483 |
| 33587 | S Holiday htp cpe, L6 | 3,118 | 2,745 | 566 |
| 33635 | wgn 4d, 2S, V8 | 3,736 | 3,165 | 8,559 |
| 33639 | Holiday htp sdn, V8 | 3,407 | 2,964 | 7,046 |
| 33667 | S conv cpe, V8 | 3,386 | 3,109 | 13,498 |
| 33669 | Town Sedan 4d, V8 | 3,356 | 2,833 | 24,521 |
| 33677 | S Sports Coupe, V8 | 3,293 | 2,792 | 10,682 |
| 33687 | S Holiday htp cpe, V8 | 3,316 | 2,855 | 66,495 |

### Cutlass Supreme (wb 116; 2d-112.0)

| | | Wght | Price | Prod |
|---|---|---|---|---|
| 34239 | Holiday htp sdn | 3,421 | 3,111 | 8,714 |
| 34269 | Town Sedan 4d | 3,361 | 2,938 | 4,522 |
| 34287 | Holiday htp cpe | 3,331 | 3,036 | 24,193 |

### 4-4-2 (wb 112.0)

| | | Wght | Price | Prod |
|---|---|---|---|---|
| 34467 | conv cpe | 3,580 | 3,395 | 4,295 |
| 34477 | Sports Coupe | 3,502 | 3,141 | 2,475 |
| 34487 | Holiday htp cpe | 3,512 | 3,204 | 19,587 |

### Vista Cruiser (wb 121.0)

| | | Wght | Price | Prod |
|---|---|---|---|---|
| 34855 | wgn 4d, 2S | 3,952 | 3,457 | 11,879 |
| 34865 | wgn 4d, 3S | 4,052 | 3,600 | 21,508 |

### Delta 88 (wb 124.0)

| | | Wght | Price | Prod |
|---|---|---|---|---|
| 35437 | Holiday htp cpe | 3,812 | 3,277 | 41,947 |
| 35439 | Holiday htp sdn | 3,901 | 3,353 | 42,690 |
| 35467 | conv cpe | 3,892 | 3,590 | 5,294 |
| 35469 | Town Sedan 4d | 3,859 | 3,222 | 49,995 |
| 36437 | Custom Holiday htp cpe | 3,927 | 3,525 | 22,083 |
| 36439 | Custom Holiday htp sdn | 4,009 | 3,600 | 36,502 |
| 36469 | Custom Town Sedan 4d | 3,962 | 3,432 | 31,012 |
| 36647 | Royale Holiday htp cpe | 3,935 | 3,836 | 22,564 |

### 98 (wb 127.0)

| | | Wght | Price | Prod |
|---|---|---|---|---|
| 38439 | Holiday htp sdn | 4,260 | 4,523 | 17,294 |
| 38457 | Holiday htp cpe | 4,150 | 4,461 | 27,041 |
| 38467 | conv cpe | 4,223 | 4,719 | 4,288 |
| 38469 | Town Sedan 4d | 4,150 | 4,255 | 11,169 |
| 38639 | Luxury Sedan (htp) | 4,288 | 4,692 | 25,973 |
| 38669 | Luxury Sedan 4d | 4,245 | 4,598 | 30,643 |

### Toronado (wb 119.0)

| | | Wght | Price | Prod |
|---|---|---|---|---|
| 39487 | htp cpe | 4,316 | 4,835 | 3,421 |
| 39687 | Custom htp cpe | 4,368 | 5,030 | 25,073 |

### 1969 Engines

| | bore × stroke | bhp | availability |
|---|---|---|---|
| L6, 250.0 | 3.88 × 3.53 | 155 | S- F-85, Cutlass |
| V8, 350.0 | 4.06 × 3.38 | 250 | S-Cutlass S/sdns/wgns, F-85, Delta 88, Vst Crsr; O-Supreme |
| V8, 350.0 | 4.06 × 3.38 | 310 | S-Supreme; O-Cutlass, Vst Crsr, F-85 |
| V8, 350.0 | 4.06 × 3.38 | 325 | O-Cutlass S, F-85 |
| V8, 400.0 | 4.00 × 3.98 | 325 | S-442 auto, Vista Cruiser auto |
| V8, 400.0 | 4.00 × 3.98 | 350 | S-442 manual |
| V8, 400.0 | 4.00 × 3.98 | 360 | O-442 |
| V8, 455.0 | 4.13 × 4.25 | 310 | S-Dlta 88 Cus/Royale; O-Delta |
| V8, 455.0 | 4.13 × 4.25 | 365 | S-98; O-all Delta 88 |
| V8, 455.0 | 4.13 × 4.25 | 375 | S-Toronado |

| | bore × stock | bhp | availability |
|---|---|---|---|
| V8, 455.0 | 4.13 × 4.25 | 390 | O-all Delta 88 |
| V8, 455.0 | 4.13 × 4.25 | 400 | O-Toronado |

## 1970

### F-85 (wb 116.0; 2d-112.0)

| | | Wght | Price | Prod |
|---|---|---|---|---|
| 33177 | Sports Coupe, L6 | 3,190 | 2,676 | 2,836 |
| 33277 | Sports Coupe, V8 | 3,401 | 2,787 | 8,274 |

### Cutlass (wb 116.0; 2d-112.0)

| | | Wght | Price | Prod |
|---|---|---|---|---|
| 33535 | wgn 4d, 2S, L6 | 3,630 | 3,234 | 85 |
| 33539 | Holiday htp sdn, L6 | 3,326 | 2,968 | 238 |
| 33569 | Town Sedan 4d, L6 | 3,257 | 2,837 | 1,171 |
| 33577 | S Sports Coupe, L6 | 3,201 | 2,796 | 484 |
| 33587 | S Holiday htp cpe, L6 | 3,238 | 2,859 | 729 |
| 33635 | wgn 4d, 2S, V8 | 3,807 | 3,044 | 7,686 |
| 33639 | Holiday htp sdn, V8 | 3,523 | 3,079 | 9,427 |
| 33669 | Town Sedan, V8 | 3,468 | 2,948 | 35,239 |
| 33677 | S Sports Coupe, V8 | 3,416 | 2,907 | 10,677 |
| 33687 | S Holiday htp cpe, V8 | 3,452 | 2,970 | 88,578 |

### Cutlass Supreme (wb 116; 2d-112.0)

| | | Wght | Price | Prod |
|---|---|---|---|---|
| 34239 | Holiday htp sdn | 3,558 | 3,226 | 10,762 |
| 34257 | Holiday htp cpe | 3,471 | 3,151 | 68,309 |
| 34267 | conv cpe | 3,510 | 3,335 | 11,354 |

### 4-4-2 (wb 112.0)

| | | Wght | Price | Prod |
|---|---|---|---|---|
| 34467 | conv cpe | 3,740 | 3,567 | 2,933 |
| 34477 | Sports Coupe | 3,667 | 3,312 | 1,688 |
| 34487 | Holiday htp cpe | 3,713 | 3,376 | 14,709 |

### Vista Cruiser (wb 121.0)

| | | Wght | Price | Prod |
|---|---|---|---|---|
| 34855 | wgn 4d, 2S | 4,064 | 3,636 | 10,758 |
| 34865 | wgn 4d, 3S | 4,166 | 3,778 | 23,336 |

### Delta 88 (wb 124.0)

| | | Wght | Price | Prod |
|---|---|---|---|---|
| 35437 | Holiday htp cpe | 3,900 | 3,590 | 33,017 |
| 35439 | Holiday htp sdn | 3,986 | 3,666 | 37,695 |
| 35467 | conv cpe | 3,985 | 3,903 | 3,095 |
| 35469 | Town Sedan 4d | 3,944 | 3,534 | 47,067 |
| 36437 | Custom Holiday htp cpe | 3,999 | 3,848 | 16,149 |
| 36439 | Custom Holiday htp sdn | 4,087 | 3,924 | 28,432 |
| 36469 | Custom Town Sedan 4d | 4,040 | 3,755 | 24,727 |
| 36647 | Royale Holiday htp cpe | 4,002 | 4,159 | 13,249 |

### 98 (wb 127.0)

| | | Wght | Price | Prod |
|---|---|---|---|---|
| 38439 | Holiday htp sdn | 4,329 | 4,582 | 14,098 |
| 38457 | Holiday htp cpe | 4,257 | 4,656 | 21,111 |
| 38467 | conv cpe | 4,289 | 4,914 | 3,161 |
| 38469 | Town Sedan 4d | 4,263 | 4,451 | 9,092 |
| 38639 | Luxury htp sdn | 4,400 | 4,888 | 19,377 |
| 38669 | Luxury sdn 4d | 4,356 | 4,793 | 29,005 |

### Toronado (wb 119.0)

| | | Wght | Price | Prod |
|---|---|---|---|---|
| 39487 | htp cpe | 4,331 | 5,023 | 2,351 |
| 39687 | Custom htp cpe | 4,386 | 5,216 | 23,082 |

### 1970 Engines

| | bore × stroke | bhp | availability |
|---|---|---|---|
| L6, 250.0 | 3.88 × 3.53 | 155 | S- F-85, Cutlass |
| V8, 350.0 | 4.06 × 3.38 | 250 | S- F-85/Cutlass V8, Vst Crsr; O-Supreme |
| V8, 350.0 | 4.06 × 3.38 | 310 | S-Supreme; O-Vst Crsr, F-85, Cutlass |
| V8, 350.0 | 4.06 × 3.38 | 325 | O-F-85, Cutlass S auto or 4 spd |
| V8, 455.0 | 4.13 × 4.25 | 310 | S-Delta 88 manual |
| V8, 455.0 | 4.13 × 4.25 | 320 | O-Cutlass w/automatic |
| V8, 455.0 | 4.13 × 4.25 | 365 | S-442, 98; O-Supreme, 88/Vst Crsr manual |
| V8, 455.0 | 4.13 × 4.25 | 370 | O-442 w/auto or close-ratio 4 spd |
| V8, 455.0 | 4.13 × 4.25 | 375 | S-Toronado |
| V8, 455.0 | 4.13 × 4.25 | 390 | O-Delta 88 |
| V8, 455.0 | 4.13 × 4.25 | 400 | O-Toronado |

# Packard

Packard was able to survive the Depression through clever marketing. Unlike Cadillac or Lincoln, this old independent company had no giant corporation to lean on when luxury car sales declined. Instead, it had to move down into the broader market with new models selling for less than any Packard ever had. Accordingly, the firm redesigned its production facilities for expanded volume, and in 1935 introduced the popular One Twenty—a straight eight that looked like a Packard, but sold for less than $1000. For 1937, there was a six-cylinder version priced even lower. From a rock-bottom 6000 units in 1934, production zoomed to 50,000 cars in 1935; 80,000 in 1936; and nearly 110,000 in 1937. Packard now ranked ninth in the industry—higher than ever before—and the dismal years of the early '30s were forgotten. Packard continued to rely on sixes and small eights into the 1940s, but never with the success of its '37 models.

The 1940-41 cars were among the most interesting and beautiful in the company's long history. The Packard Six was now designated One Ten and sold in an attractive price range. Six body styles were offered including five-passenger coupe and convertible coupe. The One Twenty series included five deluxe-trim coupes and sedans. One exception to this competitive price structure was the custom-built Darrin Victoria, listed at $3819. An exquisite sporting soft-top with cut-down doors and raked windshield, it was the work of stylist Howard "Dutch" Darrin, and is one of the few One Twentys accorded "Classic" status by the Classic Car Club of America (CCCA). The One Ten was the smallest Packard in a generation, and rode a 122-inch wheelbase. Its 100-horsepower six displaced 245.3 cubic inches. The One Twenty sat on a 127-inch wheelbase and was powered by a 282-cid eight.

Packard dropped its 12-cylinder cars for 1940, but retained an impressive line of Super and Custom Eights. Wheelbases ranged from 127 to 148 inches. Styling remained traditional: an upright, slope-shouldered radiator and chiseled hood. The shortest chassis was reserved for coupes, convertibles, and sedans. A touring sedan rode a 138-inch wheelbase, and a long sedan and limousine used the 148. Custom coachwork was offered for the highest-priced models, two Darrins: a Custom Eight Victoria (priced only about $800 higher than the One Twenty Darrin); and a sleek, four-door convertible sedan priced at $6332, making it the most expensive of all. Other specials were the Rollston all-weather cabriolet, $4473; and town car, $4599. But such exotic models accounted for only a fraction of total output. Of 98,000 cars, only 5662 were Super Eights and just 1900 were Customs. The rest were One Tens and One Twentys. Production was lower for 1941.

Packard's first big departure from traditional square-rigged styling came with the '41 Clipper. Designed by Darrin and modified by Packard's own Werner Gubitz, the Clipper had flowing fenders, hidden running boards, a tapered tail, and a narrow vertical grille. It came in only one body style, a four-door sedan priced at $1420—squarely between the One Twenty and One Sixty. The Clipper used a 127-inch wheelbase and 282-cid straight eight.

The same range of One Tens and One Twentys was placed at the lower end of the '41 line, while the Super Eight (now called One Sixty) and Custom Super (One Eighty) were the posher models. Again, Packard offered Darrin, Rollston, and LeBaron custom coachwork. LeBaron built long-wheelbase sedans and limousines and the beautifully formal Sport Brougham. An Electromatic Clutch, which eliminated the need to use the clutch pedal (but did require the driver to shift gears), was offered for only $37.50. Power for Supers and Customs came from a silky smooth straight eight, a 356-cid unit that developed 160 bhp at 3800 rpm. With nine main bearings and a crankshaft that weighed 105 pounds, the 356 was impressively quiet and powerful, capable of propelling some of the lighter models at well over 100 mph. It was used in Supers and Customs through 1947, in the Custom only through 1950, and was then dropped. Packard never built as large an engine again. The Clipper was popular, and over 16,000 sold in 1941. Accordingly, Packard converted almost entirely to Clipper styling for 1942. The only exceptions were the One Twenty convertible and some One Eighty models.

During the war, Packard built Rolls-Royce Merlin aircraft engines and other power units for military vehicles and PT boats. It was the only independent to emerge from the war completely free of debt. But then a significant decision was made—one that would adversely affect the company's future. Instead of reverting to luxury cars only, Packard continued to sell middle-price models in the One Twenty tradition. While such cars had been necessary before the war, they were not afterward and seriously damaged Packard's image. After 1945, Cadillac found it could sell anything on wheels, kept the cheaper LaSalle buried, and built high-priced cars only. Soon, it replaced Packard as the nation's premier luxury make.

The 1946 and '47 models were identical in all respects except for serial numbers. The low-priced '46 Clipper Six sedan and coupe looked exactly like the Clipper Eight series, which also included a DeLuxe sedan and club sedan. All used a 120-inch wheelbase. Clipper Supers and Customs—sedans and club sedans—rode the 127-inch wheelbase. The Custom series also offered a seven-passenger sedan and a limousine on the 148-inch wheelbase. Eights were

1940 One Eighty custom sport sedan by Darrin

1941 One Eighty Sport Brougham by LeBaron

1942 Custom Super Clipper (180) club sedan

1946 Clipper Eight four-door sedan

1946 Custom Super Clipper limousine

1948 Eight Station Sedan (wagon)

equipped with the prewar 282 engine, while Supers and Customs used the 165-bhp 356. Overdrive and Electromatic clutch were available as options. Customs were trimmed with plush broadcloth and leather upholstery, special carpeting, and beautiful imitation wood paneling. Dashboards in these years were symmetrical, as they'd been before the war. The speedometer was located at the left, minor gauges at the far left, clock at the right, and the radio and heater controls in the center. Packard moved out over 30,000 cars in 1946, and over 50,000 in 1947.

But the Clipper design was growing old. Packard replaced it with an extensively facelifted model for '48, based on a prewar show car known as the Phantom. The results were debatable. Management dictated heavy chunks of sheetmetal for a flow-through-fender effect, but this added about 200 extra pounds and made the new car look fat. "Pregnant elephant" was the term used by many to describe it. The styling wasn't helped by a short, squat grille—an eggcrate style on Customs and a bar-type on other models—that was far less elegant than the tall, narrow 1946-47 grille. Yet the 1948s sold well, and Packard produced some 92,000 of them.

In 1949 it did even better, building some 116,000 vehicles.

Chassis assignments remained unchanged for 1948, but the engine lineup was revised. Customs retained the 356 engine, but Supers were fitted with a new 327 straight eight with five main bearings. Standard Eights received a much squarer 288-cid engine. These power-plants were carried into 1949; horsepower on standards was raised to 135 bhp, Supers to 150.

The 1948 lineup included some familiar models: the standard and DeLuxe Eight in sedan and coupe form, and the sedan and coupe Super and Custom Eights. But some interesting additions were made: the novel Station Sedan in the standard Eight series, priced at $3425, and a pair of convertibles, one with the 127-inch wheelbase. The Station Sedan was made almost entirely of steel; its wooden body work was structural only at the tailgate. The Custom Eight convertible was the most luxurious standard-wheelbase American car and, at $4295, the most expensive. A 141-inch Super Eight wheelbase for two seven-passenger sedans and two limousines was also added, and a few long Custom chassis were created for commercial use. Packard built

1949 Custom Eight convertible

1952 300 four-door sedan

Scale model proposal for 1951 Packard styling

Pan American show car by Henney, 1952

1951 Patrician 400 four-door sedan

1953 Caribbean convertible

sixes only for taxi and export markets in 1948.

All Packard offerings were continued unchanged through May 1949, when a new series appeared. These were only slightly facelifted, mainly with a beltline spear. A new Super Deluxe series, using the Custom's eggcrate grille, was added to the lineup. The late '49s continued unchanged for 1950.

The big news was Ultramatic—the only automatic transmission developed by an independent without help from a transmission manufacturer. This shiftless drive combined a torque converter with multiple-disc and direct-drive clutches and forward/reverse bands. The car started from rest using the torque converter, then shifted into direct mechanical drive at about 15 miles an hour. Compared to Hydra-Matic, it was much smoother, but provided only leisurely acceleration. Frequent use of the low range for faster starts caused premature transmission wear.

Packard finally managed a total restyling for 1951, utilizing designer John Reinhart's praiseworthy shape on 122- and 127-inch wheelbases. But the firm per-

sisted with its less expensive models. Its 200 series even included a business coupe (the cheapest '51 Cadillac was $500 more expensive), plus two- and four-door sedans in basic and DeLuxe trim. The 200 really wasn't a Packard in the traditional sense of the word, and when the seller's market subsided it wasn't able to compete with established middle-priced rivals. Production was 71,000 cars in 1951, and less than 47,000 the following year.

The "real" Packard in 1951-52 was the 250, 300, and 400 line—all well-built, comfortable, high-speed road cars. The 250, on the shorter 122-inch wheelbase, included the Mayfair hardtop and 250 convertible, luxuriously trimmed, colorful, sporty cars that sold fairly well. The 300 and 400 were sedans, including the Patrician, Packard's highest-priced car in these years. The 356-cid straight eight was considered too expensive to build in light of potential sales, so the top engine for '51 was a 327 eight, also with nine bearings and almost the same output.

The '52 line was basically unchanged, though the 200

1953 Clipper DeLuxe four-door sedan

Balboa show car from 1953

1954 convertible (series 5431)

1055's Request show car

1955 Clipper Custom Constellation hardtop coupe

1956 Patrician four-door sedan

business coupe was dropped. Styling changes were minor: the most obvious was a different wing position on the pelican hood ornament. Colorful interiors in high-quality fabric and leather were done up by fashion designer Dorothy Draper. Power brakes were offered for the first time.

In May 1952, Packard's aging president, Hugh Ferry, announced the arrival of his successor, James J. Nance, and it was hoped that this market-wise promoter could invigorate the firm. By the time Nance arrived, the plant was working at only 50 percent of capacity. Incredibly, several long-time executives felt this was good enough. But Nance could see Packard was doomed at that level. Aggressively, he sought U.S. military business and laid out a vigorous new auto policy. Nance decreed the cheap 200 would henceforth be called Clipper and would eventually become a separate make. He also said Packard would go back to building nothing but luxury cars, returning to the long-wheelbase formal sedans and limousines it had neglected.

There was no time for a complete line-wide change for '53, but Nance did see to the inclusion of eight-passenger sedans and limousines. He even contracted with the Derham Body Company to build a few formal Patricians with leather-covered tops and tiny rear windows, priced at $6531 apiece. The glamorous Caribbean convertible was introduced, with handsome styling and a 180-bhp engine. Limited to 750 copies, it was well received and outsold Cadillac's comparable Eldorado. A colorful Clipper Sportster coupe was added at the bottom of the line.

Nance had hoped for all-new 1954 models, but time didn't permit this. Instead, a look-alike interim series was offered—outwardly distinguishable from the '53s by horn-rimmed headlamps and backup lights built into the taillight assemblies. The straight-eight Patrician engine was enlarged to 359 cid. Packard had been among the first to introduce air conditioning in 1940, and it was back in '54 for the first time since the war. But Packard had a terrible year, producing only about 30,000 cars. A revolutionary new model was on the way, but was de-

layed, partly because of the hubbub over the so-called Studebaker-Packard merger. Actually, Packard bought Studebaker. What Nance didn't know when he signed the papers was that Studebaker had huge productivity problems in its high-overhead South Bend plant, and that its break-even point was somewhere over 250,000 cars. Contrary to many accounts, Packard was still healthy at this time, but Studebaker was sinking and would drag Packard down with it.

As the '55s neared production, another smouldering problem burst into flame. Packard had given away its body business to Briggs in 1940. Briggs had sold out to Chrysler in 1954. Chrysler told Nance it would not continue Briggs' contract, and Packard had to settle for a cramped body plant on Conner Avenue in Detroit.

Never big enough, the plant caused big production line tie-ups and quality control problems. Though Packard built over 55,000 cars in prosperous 1955, the company would have done better to consign body building to its old but adequate main plant on Detroit's East Grand Boulevard.

Despite all these woes, the 1955 Packard was a technological wonder. Leading its list of features was Torsion-Level suspension, an interlinked torsion-bar setup operating on all four wheels. A complicated electrical system allowed the suspension to correct for load weight, and the interlinking of all four wheels provided truly extraordinary ride and handling. And there was more: the old-fashioned straight eights were superseded by powerful new V8s. These oversquare, very

Predictor show car by Ghia, 1956

Mock-up for '57 Clipper inspired by Predictor

Predictor-based steel prototype for 1957 senior series

1957 Clipper four-door Country Sedan (wagon)

1957 Clipper four-door Town Sedan

1958 Hawk hardtop coupe

powerful engines displaced 320 cid on Clipper DeLuxe and Super, and 352 cid on Clipper Customs and Packards. Ultramatic was also improved to deal better with the engines' higher torque outputs. With the V8, Ultramatic, and Torsion-Level suspension, Packard had a fine chassis. Caribbeans, with four-barrel 352s belting out 275 bhp, were impressively fast and roadable cars—real Packards in every sense of the word. Styling also was impressive. A clever facelift of the old 1951 body produced "cathedral" taillights, peaked front fenders, and an ornate grille. The Clipper was given its own special grille and 1954-style taillights.

Some problems at the Conner plant were finally licked, but not in time to save the 1956 models. Studebaker's desperate struggle was scaring customers away. Also, many people refused to buy a '56 because of the notorious quality and service problems of the '55s. Ironically, the '56s were better built. Ultramatic was given new electronic pushbutton control, and horsepower increased. The Clipper, as a separate make, was given the 352; the Packard engine was bored out to 374 cid. There was a hardtop as well as a convertible Caribbean. Both had unique reversible seat cushions—fabric on one side, leather on the other. In mid-year, an Executive appeared on the 122-inch wheelbase in sedan and hardtop form, bridging the gap between Packard and Clipper. Executives wore the Clipper's pointed taillights and Packard grilles. But none of this product shuffling helped, and only about 10,000 Packards were built for model year 1956.

No financial backer was found for an all-new 1957 line, and in August 1956, Nance resigned. Studebaker-Packard was picked up by Curtiss-Wright Corporation as a dalliance and/or a tax write-off, and C-W's Roy Hurley

began directing the firm's fortunes. Late in 1955, S-P decided to leave Detroit and to build Studebaker-based Packard cars in South Bend.

The 1957 Packard Clipper (or "Packardbaker," as detractors called it) was, despite it all, a very good Studebaker, though hardly in the image of the cars before it. A sedan and a station wagon were offered. A supercharged Studebaker 289 V8 provided 275 bhp, the same as some previous Packard V8s. Styling evoked Packard themes, and prices were higher than on comparable Studebakers. It was a charade, of course, and the public recognized it: only about 5000 '57 Clippers were built.

A big-Packard revival was still theoretically possible as the '58s were planned, so the firm again tried a holding action. This time, four Studebaker-based cars were marketed at prices up to $3995. On the shorter wheelbase came a two-door hardtop and wagon; a sedan and the Packard Hawk used the longer wheelbase. The latter, perhaps the most famous of this generation, was a more luxurious version of the Studebaker Golden Hawk. Featured were an all-leather interior and bizarre styling. In defense of stylist Duncan McRae, the Packard Hawk was really built only because of Roy Hurley, who demanded the long, bolt-on fiberglass nose and gaudy, gold mylar tailfins. McRae, however, takes credit for the car's outside armrests. McRae was also forced to create the other three '58 Packards—garish, finned affairs with hastily contrived four-headlight systems designed to keep up with the competition. Only the Hawk retained the supercharged engine. After '58, Packard vanished from the automotive scene, although the name was continued in the corporation's title until 1962.

# Packard Specifications

## 1940

### 1800 One Ten (wb 122.0) — 62,300 built

| | | Wght | Price | Prod |
|---|---|---|---|---|
| 1382 | sdn 4d | 3,200 | 996 | — |
| 1383 | wgn 4d, 8P | 3,380 | 1,200 | — |
| 1384 | sdn 2d | 3,190 | 964 | — |
| 1385 | club cpe | 3,165 | 940 | — |
| 1388 | bus cpe | 3,120 | 867 | — |
| 1389 | conv cpe | 3,200 | 1,104 | — |

### 1801 One Twenty (wb 127.0) — 28,138 built

| | | Wght | Price | Prod |
|---|---|---|---|---|
| 700 | conv vic by Darrin | 3,826 | 3,819 | — |
| 1392 | sdn 4d | 3,520 | 1,166 | — |
| 1393 | wgn 4d, 8P | 3,590 | 1,404 | — |
| 1394 | sdn 2d | 3,510 | 1,135 | — |
| 1395 | club cpe | 3,450 | 1,111 | — |
| 1396 | club sdn | 3,520 | 1,239 | — |

| | | Wght | Price | Prod |
|---|---|---|---|---|
| 1397 | conv sdn | 3,710 | 1,573 | — |
| 1398 | bus cpe | 3,340 | 1,038 | — |
| 1399 | conv cpe | 3,540 | 1,277 | — |
| DE1392 | Deluxe sdn 4d | 3,495 | 1,246 | — |
| DE1395 | Deluxe club cpe | 3,400 | 1,161 | — |
| DE1396 | Deluxe club sdn | 3,480 | 1,314 | — |
| DE1399 | Deluxe conv cpe | 3,470 | 1,318 | — |

### 1803 Super Eight One Sixty (wb 127.0) — 5,662 built (includes all One Sixtys)

| | | Wght | Price | Prod |
|---|---|---|---|---|
| 1372 | sdn 4d | 3,855 | 1,655 | — |
| 1375 | club cpe | 3,760 | 1,614 | — |
| 1376 | club sdn | 3,855 | 1,740 | — |
| 1377 | conv sdn | 4,000 | 2,075 | — |
| 1378 | bus cpe | 3,735 | 1,524 | — |
| 1379 | conv cpe | 3,825 | 1,797 | — |

# Packard

## 1804 Super Eight One Sixty (wb 138.0)

| | | Wght | Price | Prod |
|---|---|---|---|---|
| 1362 | sdn 4d | 4,165 | 1,919 | — |

## 1805 Super Eight One Sixty (wb 148.0)

| | | | | |
|---|---|---|---|---|
| 1370 | limo 7P | 4,500 | 2,179 | — |
| 1371 | sdn 4d, 7P | 4,425 | 2,051 | — |

## 1806 Custom Super Eight One Eighty (wb 127.0) — 1,900 built (includes all One Eightys)

| | | | | |
|---|---|---|---|---|
| 700 | conv vic by Darrin | 4,121 | 4,593 | — |
| 1356 | club sdn | 3,900 | 2,243 | — |

## 1807 Custom Super Eight One Eighty (wb 138.0)

| | | | | |
|---|---|---|---|---|
| 694 | A/W cabriolet by Rollston | 4,050 | 4,473 | — |
| 710 | conv sdn by Darrin | 4,050 | 6,332 | — |
| 1332 | form sdn | 4,210 | 2,855 | — |
| 1342 | sdn 4d | 4,210 | 2,422 | — |

## 1808 Custom Super Eight One Eighty (wb 148.0)

| | | | | |
|---|---|---|---|---|
| 695 | A/W town car by Rollston | 4,175 | 4,599 | — |
| 1350 | limo 7P | 4,585 | 2,683 | — |
| 1351 | sdn 4d, 7P | 4,510 | 2,554 | — |

## 1940 Engines

| | bore × stroke | bhp | availability |
|---|---|---|---|
| L6, 245.3 | 3.50 × 4.25 | 100 | S-One Ten |
| L8, 282.0 | 3.25 × 4.25 | 120 | S-One Twenty |
| L8, 356.0 | 3.50 × 4.63 | 160 | S-Super/Custom Super Eights |

# 1941

## 1900 One Ten (wb 122.0) — 34,700 built

| | | Wght | Price | Prod |
|---|---|---|---|---|
| 1482 | sdn 4d | 3,260 | 1,076 | — |
| 1483 | wgn 4d, 8P | 3,460 | 1,251 | — |
| 1484 | sdn 2d | 3,250 | 1,010 | — |
| 1485 | club cpe | 3,230 | 1,020 | — |
| 1488 | bus cpe | 3,190 | 927 | — |
| 1489 | conv cpe | 3,260 | 1,195 | — |
| 1463DE | Deluxe wgn 4d, 8P | 3,470 | 1,236 | — |
| 1482DE | Deluxe sdn 4d | 3,280 | 1,136 | — |
| 1484DE | Deluxe sdn 2d | 3,270 | 1,070 | — |
| 1485DE | Deluxe club cpe | 3,250 | 1,058 | — |
| 1489DE | Deluxe conv cpe | 3,280 | 1,229 | — |

## 1901 One Twenty (wb 127.0) — 17,000 built

| | | | | |
|---|---|---|---|---|
| 1473 | Deluxe wgn 4d, 8P | 3,730 | 1,541 | — |
| 1492 | sdn 4d | 3,535 | 1,291 | — |
| 1493 | wgn 4d, 8P | 3,720 | 1,466 | — |
| 1494 | sdn 2d | 3,525 | 1,260 | — |
| 1495 | club cpe | 3,470 | 1,235 | — |
| 1497 | conv sdn | 3,725 | 1,753 | — |
| 1498 | bus cpe | 3,360 | 1,142 | — |
| 1499 | conv cpe | 3,570 | 1,407 | — |

## 1951 Clipper (wb 127.0)

| | | | | |
|---|---|---|---|---|
| 1401 | sdn 4d | 3,725 | 1,420 | 16,600 |

## 1903 Super Eight One Sixty (wb 127.0) — 3,525 built (includes all One Sixtys)

| | | | | |
|---|---|---|---|---|
| 1472 | sdn 4d | 3,995 | 1,795 | — |
| 1475 | club cpe | 3,900 | 1,754 | — |
| 1477 | conv sdn | 4,140 | 2,225 | — |
| 1478 | bus cpe | 3,875 | 1,639 | — |
| 1479 | conv cpe | 3,965 | 1,937 | — |
| 1477DE | Deluxe conv sdn | 4,160 | 2,450 | — |
| 1479DE | Deluxe conv cpe | 3,985 | 2,112 | — |

## 1904 Super Eight One Sixty (wb 138.0)

| | | | | |
|---|---|---|---|---|
| 1462 | sdn 4d | 4,305 | 2,054 | — |

## 1905 Super Eight One Sixty (wb 148.0)

| | | | | |
|---|---|---|---|---|
| 1470 | limo 7P | 4,570 | 2,334 | — |
| 1471 | sdn 4d 7P | 4,495 | 2,206 | — |

## 1906 Custom Super Eight One Eighty (wb 127.0) — 930 built (inc all One Eightys)

| | | Wght | Price | Prod |
|---|---|---|---|---|
| 1429 | conv vic by Darrin | 4,040 | 4,595 | — |

## 1907 Custom Super Eight One Eighty (wb 138.0)

| | | | | |
|---|---|---|---|---|
| 794 | A/W cabriolet by Rollston | 4,075 | 4,695 | — |
| 1422 | spt sdn by Darrin | 4,490 | 4,795 | — |
| 1432 | form sdn | 4,350 | 3,090 | — |
| 1442 | sdn 4d | 4,350 | 2,632 | — |
| 1452 | Sport Brougham by LeBaron | 4,450 | 3,545 | — |

## 1908 Custom Super Eight One Eighty (wb 148.0)

| | | | | |
|---|---|---|---|---|
| 795 | A/W town car by Rollston | 4,200 | 4,820 | — |
| 1420 | limo 7P by LeBaron | 4,850 | 5,595 | — |
| 1421 | sdn 4d, 7P by LeBaron | 4,740 | 5,345 | — |
| 1450 | limo 7P | 4,650 | 2,913 | — |
| 1451 | sdn 4d, 7P | 4,590 | 2,769 | — |

## 1941 Engines

| | bore × stroke | bhp | availability |
|---|---|---|---|
| L6, 245.3 | 3.50 × 4.25 | 100 | S-One Ten |
| L8, 282.0 | 3.25 × 4.25 | 120 | S-One Twenty |
| L8, 282.0 | 3.25 × 4.25 | 125 | S-Clipper |
| L8, 356.0 | 3.50 × 4.63 | 160 | S-One Sixty, One Eighty |

# 1942

## 2000 Clipper 110 Special (wb 120.0) — 11,325 built (includes all 110s)

| | | Wght | Price | Prod |
|---|---|---|---|---|
| 1582 | sdn 4d | 3,435 | 1,232 | — |
| 1585 | club sdn | 3,415 | 1,199 | — |
| 1588 | bus cpe | 3,365 | 1,166 | — |

## 2010 Clipper 110 Custom (wb 120.0)

| | | | | |
|---|---|---|---|---|
| 1502 | sdn 4d | 3,460 | 1,299 | — |
| 1505 | club sdn | 3,440 | 1,266 | — |

## 2020 Clipper 110 (wb 122.0)

| | | | | |
|---|---|---|---|---|
| 1589 | conv cpe | 3,315 | 1,375 | — |

## 2001 Clipper 120 Special (wb 120.0) — 19,199 built (includes all 120s)

| | | | | |
|---|---|---|---|---|
| 1592 | sdn 4d | 3,560 | 1,275 | — |
| 1595 | club sdn | 3,540 | 1,241 | — |
| 1598 | bus cpe | 3,490 | 1,208 | — |

## 2011 Clipper 120 Custom (wb 120.0)

| | | | | |
|---|---|---|---|---|
| 1512 | sdn 4d | 3,585 | 1,341 | — |
| 1515 | club sdn | 3,565 | 1,308 | — |

## 2021 Clipper 120 (wb 127.0)

| | | | | |
|---|---|---|---|---|
| 1599 | conv cpe | 3,585 | 1,469 | — |

## 2003 Clipper One Sixty (wb 127.0) — 2,580 built (includes all One Sixtys)

| | | | | |
|---|---|---|---|---|
| 1572 | sdn 4d | 4,005 | 1,688 | — |
| 1575 | club sdn | 3,985 | 1,630 | — |

## 2023 Clipper One Sixty (wb 127.0)

| | | | | |
|---|---|---|---|---|
| 1579 | conv cpe | 3,905 | 1,786 | — |

## 2004 Clipper One Sixty (wb 138.0)

| | | | | |
|---|---|---|---|---|
| 1562 | sdn 4d | 4,090 | 1,893 | — |

## 2005 Clipper One Sixty (wb 148.0)

| | | | | |
|---|---|---|---|---|
| 1570 | limo 7P | 4,445 | 2,156 | — |
| 1571 | sdn 4d, 7P | 4,325 | 2,034 | — |

## 2055 Clipper One Sixty (wb 148.0)

| | | | | |
|---|---|---|---|---|
| 1590 | bus limo 7P | 4,435 | 2,010 | — |
| 1591 | bus sdn 4d, 7P | 4,315 | 1,888 | — |

## 2006 Clipper One Eighty (wb 127.0) — 672 built (includes all One Eightys)

| | | | | |
|---|---|---|---|---|
| 1522 | sdn 4d | 4,030 | 2,196 | |

| | | Wght | Price | Prod |
|---|---|---|---|---|
| 1525 | club sdn | 4,010 | 2,099 | — |
| 1529 | conv vic by Darrin | 3,920 | 4,519 | — |

### 2007 Clipper One Eighty (wb 138.0)

| | | Wght | Price | Prod |
|---|---|---|---|---|
| 894 | A/W cabriolet by Rollston | 4,075 | 4,792 | — |
| 1532 | form sdn | 4,390 | 3,011 | — |
| 1542 | sdn 4d | 4,280 | 2,440 | — |

### 2008 Clipper One Eighty (wb 148.0)

| | | Wght | Price | Prod |
|---|---|---|---|---|
| 895 | A/W town car by Rollston | 4,200 | 4,889 | — |
| 1520 | limo 7P by LeBaron | 4,850 | 5,690 | — |
| 1521 | sdn 4d, 7P by LeBaron | 4,740 | 5,446 | — |
| 1550 | limo 7P | 4,540 | 2,645 | — |
| 1551 | sdn 4d, 7P | 4,525 | 2,523 | — |

| 1942 Engines | bore × stroke | bhp | availability |
|---|---|---|---|
| L6, 245.3 | 3.50 × 4.25 | 105 | S-Clipper 110 |
| L8, 282.0 | 3.25 × 4.25 | 125 | S-Clipper 120 |
| L8, 356.0 | 3.50 × 4.63 | 165 | S-Clipper One Sixty, One Eighty |

## 1946

### 2100 Clipper Six (wb 120.0) — 15,892 built

| | | Wght | Price | Prod |
|---|---|---|---|---|
| 1682 | sdn 4d | 3,495 | 1,730 | — |
| 1685 | club sdn | 3,450 | 1,680 | — |

### 2101 Clipper Eight (wb 120.0)

| | | Wght | Price | Prod |
|---|---|---|---|---|
| 1692 | sdn 4d | 3,630 | 1,802 | 1,500 |

### 2111 Clipper Deluxe Eight (wb 120.0) — 5,714 built

| | | Wght | Price | Prod |
|---|---|---|---|---|
| 1612 | sdn 4d | 3,670 | 1,869 | — |
| 1615 | club sdn | 3,625 | 1,817 | — |

### 2103 Super Clipper (wb 127.0) — 4,924 built

| | | Wght | Price | Prod |
|---|---|---|---|---|
| 1672 | sdn 4d | 3,995 | 2,290 | — |
| 1675 | club sdn | 3,950 | 2,241 | — |

### 2106 Custom Super Clipper (wb 127.0) — 2,763 built (includes 148 wb)

| | | Wght | Price | Prod |
|---|---|---|---|---|
| 1622 | sdn 4d | 4,060 | 3,047 | — |
| 1625 | club sdn | 4,000 | 2,913 | — |

### 2126 Custom Super Clipper (wb 148.0)

| | | Wght | Price | Prod |
|---|---|---|---|---|
| 1650 | limo 7P | 4,900 | 4,496 | — |
| 1651 | sdn 4d, 7P | 4,870 | 4,332 | — |

| 1946 Engines | bore × stroke | bhp | availability |
|---|---|---|---|
| L6, 245.3 | 3.50 × 4.25 | 105 | S-Clipper Six |
| L8, 282.0 | 3.25 × 4.25 | 125 | S-Clipper Eight/DeLuxe Eight |
| L8, 356.0 | 3.50 × 4.63 | 165 | S-Super/Custom Super Clipper |

## 1947

### 2100 Clipper Six (wb 120.0) — 14,949 built

| | | Wght | Price | Prod |
|---|---|---|---|---|
| 2182 | sdn 4d | 3,520 | 1,937 | — |
| 2185 | club sdn | 3,475 | 1,912 | — |

### 2111 Clipper DeLuxe Eight (wb 120.0) — 23,855 built

| | | Wght | Price | Prod |
|---|---|---|---|---|
| 2112 | sdn 4d | 3,695 | 2,149 | — |
| 2115 | club sdn | 3,650 | 2,124 | — |

### 2103 Super Clipper (wb 127.0) — 4,802 built

| | | Wght | Price | Prod |
|---|---|---|---|---|
| 2172 | sdn 4d | 4,025 | 2,772 | — |
| 2175 | club sdn | 3,980 | 2,747 | — |

### 2106 Custom Super Clipper (wb 127.0) — 7,480 built (includes 148 wb)

| | | Wght | Price | Prod |
|---|---|---|---|---|
| 2122 | sdn 4d | 4,090 | 3,449 | — |
| 2125 | club sdn | 3,384 | 2,125 | — |

### 2126 Custom Super Clipper (wb 148.0)

| | | Wght | Price | Prod |
|---|---|---|---|---|
| 2150 | limo 7P | 4,920 | 4,668 | — |
| 2151 | sdn 4d, 7P | 4,890 | 4,504 | — |

| 1947 Engines | bore × stroke | bhp | availability |
|---|---|---|---|
| L6, 245.3 | 3.50 × 4.25 | 105 | S-Clipper Six |
| L8, 282.0 | 3.25 × 4.25 | 125 | S-Clipper Eight/DeLuxe Eight |
| L8, 356.0 | 3.50 × 4.63 | 165 | S-Super/Custom Super Clipper |

## 1948

### 2201 Eight (wb 120.0) — 12,782* built

| | | Wght | Price | Prod |
|---|---|---|---|---|
| 2292 | sdn 4d | 3,815 | 2,275 | — |
| 2293 | Station Sedan wgn 4d | 4,075 | 3,425 | — |
| 2295 | club sdn | 3,755 | 2,250 | — |

### 2211 DeLuxe Eight (wb 120.0) — 47,807 built

| | | Wght | Price | Prod |
|---|---|---|---|---|
| 2262 | sdn 4d | 3,840 | 2,543 | — |
| 2266 | club sdn | 3,770 | 2,517 | — |

### 2202 Super Eight (wb 120.0) — 12,921 built

| | | Wght | Price | Prod |
|---|---|---|---|---|
| 2272 | sdn 4d | 3,855 | 2,827 | — |
| 2275 | club sdn | 3,790 | 2,802 | — |

### 2222 Super Eight (wb 141.0) — 1,766 built

| | | Wght | Price | Prod |
|---|---|---|---|---|
| 2270 | DeLuxe limo 7P | 4,610 | 4,000 | — |
| 2271 | DeLuxe sdn 4d, 7P | 4,590 | 3,850 | — |
| 2276 | limo 7P | 4,525 | 3,650 | — |
| 2277 | sdn 4d, 7P | 4,460 | 3,500 | — |

### 2232 Super Eight (wb 120.0)

| | | Wght | Price | Prod |
|---|---|---|---|---|
| 2279 | conv cpe | 4,025 | 3,250 | 7,763 |

### 2206 Custom Eight (wb 127.0) — 5,936 built

| | | Wght | Price | Prod |
|---|---|---|---|---|
| 2252 | sdn 4d | 4,175 | 3,750 | — |
| 2255 | club sdn | 4,110 | 3,700 | — |

### 2226 Custom Eight (wb 148.0) — 230 built

| | | Wght | Price | Prod |
|---|---|---|---|---|
| 2250 | limo 7P | 4,880 | 4,868 | — |
| 2251 | sdn 4d, 7P | 4,860 | 4,704 | — |

### 2313 Custom Eight (wb 148.0)

| | | Wght | Price | Prod |
|---|---|---|---|---|
| — | chassis | — | — | 1,941 |

### 2233 Custom Eight (wb 127.0)

| | | Wght | Price | Prod |
|---|---|---|---|---|
| 2259 | conv cpe | 4,380 | 4,295 | 1,105 |

| 1948 Engines | bore × stroke | bhp | availability |
|---|---|---|---|
| L8, 288.0 | 3.50 × 3.75 | 130 | S-Eight, DeLuxe Eight |
| L8, 327.0 | 3.50 × 4.25 | 145 | S-Super Eight |
| L8, 356.0 | 3.50 × 4.63 | 160 | S-Custom Eight |

## 1949 First Series

### 2201 Eight (wb 120.0) — 13,553* built

| | | Wght | Price | Prod |
|---|---|---|---|---|
| 2292-9 | sdn 4d | 3,815 | 2,275 | — |
| 2293-9 | Station Sedan wgn 4d | 4,075 | 3,425 | — |
| 2295-9 | club sdn | 3,755 | 2,250 | — |

### 2211 DeLuxe Eight (wb 120.0) — 27,422 built

| | | Wght | Price | Prod |
|---|---|---|---|---|
| 2262-9 | sdn 4d | 3,840 | 2,543 | — |
| 2265-9 | club sdn | 3,770 | 2,517 | — |

### 2202 Super Eight (wb 120.0) — 5,879 built

| | | Wght | Price | Prod |
|---|---|---|---|---|
| 2272-9 | sdn 4d | 3,855 | 2,827 | — |
| 2275-9 | club sdn | 3,790 | 2,802 | — |

### 2222 Super Eight (wb 141.0) — 867 built

| | | Wght | Price | Prod |
|---|---|---|---|---|
| 2270-9 | DeLuxe limo 7P | 4,610 | 4,000 | — |
| 2271-9 | DeLuxe sdn 4d, 7P | 4,590 | 3,850 | — |
| 2276-9 | limo 7P | 4,525 | 3,650 | — |
| 2277-9 | sdn 4d, 7P | 4,460 | 3,500 | — |

### 2232 Super Eight (wb 120.0)

| | | Wght | Price | Prod |
|---|---|---|---|---|
| 2279-9 | conv cpe | 4,025 | 3,250 | 1,237 |

# Packard

| 2206 Custom Eight (wb 127.0) — 2,990 built | | Wght | Price | Prod |
|---|---|---|---|---|
| 2252-9 | sdn 4d | 4,175 | 3,750 | — |
| 2255-9 | club sdn | 4,110 | 3,700 | — |

| 2226 Custom Eight (wb 148.0) — 50 built | | Wght | Price | Prod |
|---|---|---|---|---|
| 2250-9 | limo 7P | 4,880 | 4,868 | — |
| 2251-9 | sdn 4d, 7P | 4,860 | 4,704 | — |

| 2213 Custom Eight (wb 148.0) | | Wght | Price | Prod |
|---|---|---|---|---|
| — | chassis | — | — | 220 |

| 2233 Custom Eight (wb 127.0) | | Wght | Price | Prod |
|---|---|---|---|---|
| 2259-9 | conv cpe | 4,380 | 4,295 | 213 |

## 1949 Second Series

| 2301 Eight (wb 120.0) — 53,168* built | | Wght | Price | Prod |
|---|---|---|---|---|
| 2362 | DeLuxe sdn 4d | 3,840 | 2,383 | — |
| 2365 | DeLuxe club sdn | 3,770 | 2,358 | — |
| 2392 | sdn 4d | 3,815 | 2,249 | — |
| 2393 | Station Sedan wgn 4d | 4,075 | 3,449 | — |
| 2395 | club sdn | 3,740 | 2,224 | — |

| 2302 Super Eight (wb 127.0) — 8,759 built | | Wght | Price | Prod |
|---|---|---|---|---|
| 2372 | DeLuxe sdn 4d | 3,925 | 2,919 | — |
| 2375 | DeLuxe club sdn | 3,855 | 2,894 | — |
| 2382 | sdn 4d | 3,870 | 2,633 | — |
| 2385 | club sdn | 3,800 | 2,608 | — |

| 2322 Super Eight (wb 141.0) — 4 built | | Wght | Price | Prod |
|---|---|---|---|---|
| 2370 | DeLuxe limo 7P | 4,620 | 4,100 | — |
| 2371 | DeLuxe sdn 4d, 7P | 4,600 | 3,950 | — |

| 2332 Super Eight (wb 127.0) | | Wght | Price | Prod |
|---|---|---|---|---|
| 2332 | DeLuxe conv cpe | 4,260 | 3,350 | 685 |

| 2306 Custom Eight (wb 127.0) | | Wght | Price | Prod |
|---|---|---|---|---|
| 2352 | sdn 4d | 4,310 | 3,750 | 973 |

| 2313 Custom Eight (wb 148.0) | | Wght | Price | Prod |
|---|---|---|---|---|
| — | chassis | — | — | 160 |

| 2333 Custom Eight (wb 127.0) | | Wght | Price | Prod |
|---|---|---|---|---|
| 2359 | conv cpe | 4,530 | 4,295 | 68 |

| 1949 Engines | bore × stroke | bhp | availability |
|---|---|---|---|
| L8, 288.0 | 3.50×3.75 | 135 | S-Eight, DeLuxe Eight |
| L8, 327.0 | 3.50×4.25 | 150 | S-Super/Super DeLuxe Eight |
| L8, 356.0 | 3.50×4.63 | 160 | S-Custom Eight |

## 1950

| 2301 Eight (wb 120.0) — 36,471* built | | Wght | Price | Prod |
|---|---|---|---|---|
| 2362-5 | DeLuxe sdn 4d | 3,840 | 2,383 | — |
| 2365-5 | DeLuxe club sdn | 3,770 | 2,358 | — |
| 2392-5 | sdn 4d | 3,815 | 2,249 | — |
| 2393-5 | Station Sedan wgn 4d | 4,075 | 3,449 | — |
| 2395-5 | club sdn | 3,740 | 2,224 | — |

| 2302 Super Eight (wb 127.0) — 4,528 built | | Wght | Price | Prod |
|---|---|---|---|---|
| 2372-5 | DeLuxe sdn 4d | 3,925 | 2,919 | — |
| 2375-5 | club sdn | 3,855 | 2,894 | — |
| 2382-5 | sdn 4d | 3,870 | 2,633 | — |
| 2385-5 | club sdn | 3,800 | 2,608 | — |

| 2332 Super Eight (wb 127.0) | | Wght | Price | Prod |
|---|---|---|---|---|
| 2379-5 | conv cpe | 4,110 | 3,350 | 600 |

| 2306 Custom Eight (wb 127.0) | | Wght | Price | Prod |
|---|---|---|---|---|
| 2352-5 | sdn 4d | 4,310 | 3,975 | 707 |

| 2313 Custom Eight (wb 148.0) | | Wght | Price | Prod |
|---|---|---|---|---|
| — | chassis | — | — | 244 |

| 2333 Custom Eight (wb 127.0) | | Wght | Price | Prod |
|---|---|---|---|---|
| 2359-5 | conv cpe | 4,530 | 4,520 | 77 |

| 1950 Engines | bore × stroke | bhp | availability |
|---|---|---|---|
| L8, 288.0 | 3.50×3.75 | 135 | S-Eight, DeLuxe Eight |
| L8, 327.0 | 3.50×4.25 | 150 | S-Super/Super DeLuxe Eight |
| L8, 356.0 | 3.50×4.63 | 160 | S-Custom Eight |

*Although Packard did not break down model year production by body style, some calendar year figures exist for the Station Sedan. These are: 126 in 1947, 3,266 in 1948, and 472 in 1949, for a total of 3,864. An estimated 75 percent were 1948 models.

## 1951

| 2401 200 (wb 122.0) | | Wght | Price | Prod |
|---|---|---|---|---|
| 2462 | DeLuxe sdn 4d | 3,660 | 2,616 | 47,052 |
| 2465 | DeLuxe club sdn | 3,605 | 2,563 | 47,052 |
| 2492 | sdn 4d | 3,665 | 2,469 | |
| 2495 | club sdn | 3,600 | 2,416 | 24,310 |
| 2498 | bus cpe | 3,550 | 2,302 | |

| 2401 250 (wb 122.0) — 4,640 built | | Wght | Price | Prod |
|---|---|---|---|---|
| 2467 | Mayfair htp cpe | 3,820 | 3,234 | — |
| 2469 | conv cpe | 4,040 | 3,391 | — |

| 2402 300 (wb 127.0) | | Wght | Price | Prod |
|---|---|---|---|---|
| 2472 | sdn 4d | 3,875 | 3,034 | 15,309 |

| 2413 300 (wb 127.0) | | Wght | Price | Prod |
|---|---|---|---|---|
| — | chassis | — | — | 401 |

| 2406 Patrician 400 (wb 127.0) | | Wght | Price | Prod |
|---|---|---|---|---|
| 2452 | sdn 4d | 4,115 | 3,662 | 9,001 |

| 1951 Engines | bore × stroke | bhp | availability |
|---|---|---|---|
| L8, 288.0 | 3.50×3.75 | 135 | S-Eight, DeLuxe Eight |
| L8, 327.0 | 3.50×4.25 | 150 | S-250/300 manual |
| L8, 327.0 | 3.50×4.25 | 155 | S-Patrician 400, 250/300 auto |

## 1952

| 2501 200 (wb 122.0) — 46,720 built | | Wght | Price | Prod |
|---|---|---|---|---|
| 2562 | DeLuxe sdn 4d | 3,685 | 2,695 | — |
| 2565 | DeLuxe club sdn | 3,660 | 2,641 | — |
| 2592 | sdn 4d | 3,680 | 2,548 | — |
| 2595 | club sdn | 3,640 | 2,494 | — |

| 2531 250 (wb 122.0) — 5,201 built | | Wght | Price | Prod |
|---|---|---|---|---|
| 2577 | Mayfair htp cpe | 3,805 | 3,318 | — |
| 2579 | conv cpe | 4,000 | 3,476 | — |

| 2502 300 (wb 127.0) | | Wght | Price | Prod |
|---|---|---|---|---|
| 2572 | sdn 4d | 3,380 | 3,116 | 6,705 |

| 2513 300 (127.0) | | Wght | Price | Prod |
|---|---|---|---|---|
| — | chassis | — | — | 320 |

| 2506 Patrician 400 (wb 127.0) | | Wght | Price | Prod |
|---|---|---|---|---|
| 2552 | sdn 4d | 4,100 | 3,797 | 3,975 |

| 1952 Engines | bore × stroke | bhp | availability |
|---|---|---|---|
| L8, 288.0 | 3.50×3.75 | 135 | S-Eight, DeLuxe Eight |
| L8, 327.0 | 3.50×4.25 | 150 | S-250/300 manual |
| L8, 327.0 | 3.50×4.25 | 155 | S-Patrician 400, 250/300 auto |

## 1953

| 2601 Clipper (wb 122.0) | | Wght | Price | Prod |
|---|---|---|---|---|
| 2692 | sdn 4d | 3,730 | 2,598 | 23,126 |
| 2695 | club sdn | 3,700 | 2,544 | 6,370 |

| 2697 | Sportster cpe | Wght | Price | Prod |
|------|---------------|------|-------|------|
| 2697 | Sportster cpe | 3,720 | 2,805 | 3,672 |
| — | chassis | — | — | 1 |

**2611 Clipper DeLuxe (wb 122.0)**

| 2662 | sdn 4d | 3,760 | 2,745 | 26,027 |
|------|--------|-------|-------|--------|
| 2665 | club sdn | 3,720 | 2,691 | 4,678 |

**2633 Clipper commercial (wb 122.0)**

| — | chassis (Henney bodies) | — | — | 380 |
|---|-------------------------|---|---|-----|

**2631 (wb 122.0)**

| 2677 | Mayfair htp cpe | 3,905 | 3,278 | 5,150 |
|------|-----------------|-------|-------|-------|
| 2678 | Caribbean conv cpe | 4,265 | 5,210 | 750 |
| 2679 | conv cpe | 4,125 | 3,486 | 1,518 |

**2602 Cavalier (wb 127.0)**

| 2672 | sdn 4d | 3,975 | 3,244 | 10,799 |
|------|--------|-------|-------|--------|

**2613 Packard commercial (wb 127.0)**

| — | chassis (Henney bodies) | — | — | 166 |
|---|-------------------------|---|---|-----|

**2606 Patrician (wb 127.0)**

| 2652 | sdn 4d | 4,190 | 3,740 | 7,456 |
|------|--------|-------|-------|-------|
| 2653 | form sdn by Derham | 4,335 | 6,531 | 25* |

**2626 (wb 149.0)**

| 2650 | Corporation limo 8P | 4,720 | 7,100 | 50 |
|------|---------------------|-------|-------|-----|
| 2651 | Executive sdn 4d, 8P | 4,650 | 6,900 | 100 |

**2602-2606-2631**

| — | chassis | — | — | 9 |
|---|---------|---|---|---|

*Constructed from finished Patricians.

| 1953 Engines | bore × stroke | bhp | availability |
|--------------|---------------|-----|--------------|
| L8, 288.0 | 3.50 × 3.75 | 150 | S-2601 |
| L8, 327.0 | 3.50 × 4.25 | 160 | S-2611 |
| L8, 327.0 | 3.50 × 4.25 | 180 | S-2602, 2631 (5 main bearing) |
| L8, 327.0 | 3.50 × 4.25 | 180 | S-2606, 2626 (9 main bearing) |

## 1954

**5400 Clipper Special (wb 122.0)**

| | | Wght | Price | Prod |
|---|---|------|-------|------|
| 5482 | sdn 4d | 3,650 | 2,594 | 970 |
| 5485 | club sdn | 3,585 | 2,544 | 912 |

**5401 Clipper DeLuxe (wb 122.0)**

| 5492 | sdn 4d | 3,660 | 2,695 | 7,610 |
|------|--------|-------|-------|-------|
| 5495 | club sdn | 3,950 | 2,645 | 1,470 |
| 5497 | Sportster cpe | 3,595 | 2,830 | 1,336 |

**5411 Clipper Super (wb 122.0)**

| 5462 | sdn 4d | 3,695 | 2,815 | 6,270 |
|------|--------|-------|-------|-------|
| 5465 | club sdn | 3,610 | 2,765 | 887 |
| 5467 | Panama htp cpe | 3,765 | 3,125 | 3,618 |

**5433 Clipper commercial (wb 122.0)**

| — | chassis (Henney bodies) | — | — | 120 |
|---|-------------------------|---|---|-----|

**5402 Cavalier (wb 127.0)**

| 5472 | sdn 4d | 3,955 | 3,344 | 2,580 |
|------|--------|-------|-------|-------|

**5413 Packard commercial (wb 127.0)**

| — | chassis (Henney bodies) | — | — | 205 |
|---|-------------------------|---|---|-----|

**5431 (wb 122.0)**

| 5477 | Pacific htp cpe | 4,065 | 3,827 | 1,189 |
|------|-----------------|-------|-------|-------|
| 5478 | Caribbean conv cpe | 4,660 | 6,100 | 400 |
| 5479 | convertible cpe | 4,290 | 3,935 | 863 |
| — | chassis | — | — | 1 |

**5406 Patrician (wb 127.0)**

| 5452 | sdn 4d | 4,190 | 3,890 | 2,760 |
|------|--------|-------|-------|-------|

**5426 (wb 149.0)**

| | | Wght | Price | Prod |
|---|---|------|-------|------|
| 5450 | Corporation limo 8P | 4,720 | 5,960 | 35 |
| 5451 | Executive sdn 4d, 8P | 4,650 | 5,610 | 65 |

| 1954 Engines | bore × stroke | bhp | availability |
|--------------|---------------|-----|--------------|
| L8, 288.0 | 3.50 × 3.75 | 150 | S-5400 |
| L8, 327.0 | 3.50 × 4.25 | 165 | S-5401, 5411 |
| L8, 327.0 | 3.50 × 4.25 | 185 | S-5402 |
| L8, 359.0 | 3.56 × 4.50 | 212 | S-5406, 5426, 5431 (9 mains) |

## 1955

**5540 Clipper (wb 122.0)**

| | | Wght | Price | Prod |
|---|---|------|-------|------|
| 5522 | DeLuxe sdn 4d | 3,680 | 2,586 | 8,039 |
| 5542 | Super sdn 4d | 3,670 | 2,686 | 7,979 |
| 5547 | Super Panama htp cpe | 3,700 | 2,776 | 7,016 |

**5560 Clipper Custom (wb 122.0)**

| 5562 | sdn 4d | 3,885 | 2,926 | 8,708 |
|------|--------|-------|-------|-------|
| 5567 | Constellation htp cpe | 3,865 | 3,076 | 6,672 |

**5580 (wb 127.0)**

| 5582 | Patrician sdn 4d | 4,275 | 3,890 | 9,127 |
|------|------------------|-------|-------|-------|
| 5587 | Four Hundred htp cpe | 4,250 | 3,930 | 7,206 |
| 5588 | Caribbean conv cpe | 4,755 | 5,932 | 500* |

*A very few 1955 Caribbean hardtops have been discovered.

| 1955 Engines | bore × stroke | bhp | availability |
|--------------|---------------|-----|--------------|
| V8, 320.0 | 3.81 × 3.50 | 225 | S-Clipper DeLuxe/Super |
| V8, 352.0 | 4.00 × 3.50 | 245 | S-Clipper Custom |
| V8, 352.0 | 4.00 × 3.50 | 260 | S-Packard exc Caribbean |
| V8, 352.0 | 4.00 × 3.50 | 275 | S-Caribbean |

## 1956

**5670 Executive (wb 122.0)**

| | | Wght | Price | Prod |
|---|---|------|-------|------|
| 5672 | sdn 4d | 4,185 | 3,465 | 1,784 |
| 5677 | htp cpe | 4,185 | 3,560 | 1,031 |

**5680 (wb 127.0)**

| 5682 | Patrician sdn 4d | 4,045 | 4,160 | 3,775 |
|------|------------------|-------|-------|-------|
| 5687 | Four Hundred htp cpe | 4,080 | 4,190 | 3,224 |

**5688 Caribbean (wb 127.0)**

| 5697 | htp cpe | 4,590 | 5,495 | 263 |
|------|---------|-------|-------|-----|
| 5699 | conv cpe | 4,960 | 5,995 | 276 |

| 1956 Engines | bore × stroke | bhp | availability |
|--------------|---------------|-----|--------------|
| V8, 352.0 | 4.00 × 3.50 | 275 | S-Executive |
| V8, 374.0 | 4.13 × 3.50 | 290 | S-Patrician, Four Hundred |
| V8, 374.0 | 4.13 × 3.50 | 310 | S-Caribbean |

## 1957

**57L (wb 120.5; wgn-116.5)**

| | | Wght | Price | Prod |
|---|---|------|-------|------|
| Y8 | Town Sedan 4d | 3,570 | 3,212 | 3,940 |
| P8 | Country Sedan wgn 4d | 3,650 | 3,384 | 869 |

| 1957 Engine | bore × stroke | bhp | availability |
|-------------|---------------|-----|--------------|
| V8, 289.0 | 3.56 × 3.13 | 275 | S-all |

## 1958

**58L (wb 120.5; wgn/htp-116.5)**

| | | Wght | Price | Prod |
|---|---|------|-------|------|
| J8 | sdn 4d | 3,505 | 3,212 | 1,200 |
| J8 | htp cpe | 3,480 | 3,262 | 675 |
| K9 | Hawk htp cpe | 3,470 | 3,995 | 588 |
| P8 | wgn 4d | 3,555 | 3,384 | 159 |

| 1958 Engines | bore × stroke | bhp | availability |
|--------------|---------------|-----|--------------|
| V8, 289.0 | 3.56 × 3.13 | 275 | S-Hawk |
| V8, 289.0 | 3.56 × 3.13 | 210 | S-Others |

# Plymouth

**Plymouth Division of Chrysler Corp.
Detroit, Michigan**

Walter P. Chrysler built his first Plymouth in 1928, hoping to give friend Henry Ford some strong competition in the low-price field. Plymouth never outsold Ford, but there were years when it came very close, often limited only by plant capacity. One of these was 1931 when Plymouth introduced its new PA model with Floating Power—rubber engine mounts. Walter Chrysler took one of the first PAs off the line and drove it to Dearborn, spent an hour with Henry and Edsel Ford, then left them with the keys and took a taxi home. Rumor has it that plans for an updated Model A were set aside after the Fords took their ride. Plymouth moved into third place in production that year, and usually

1940 DeLuxe four-door sedan

1941 DeLuxe club coupe

1942 Special DeLuxe convertible coupe

stayed there through the mid-1950s. The formula was conservative—a sturdy L-head six and a conventional suspension—but it was precisely right. Sound, built with quality, well engineered, and reliable as a Swiss watch, Plymouth was backed by a solid dealer network and the Mopar parts organization.

The 1940 models offered an improved body with "speedline" fenders. Sealed-beam headlamps appeared for the first time that year, and prices were as low as $645, just a few dollars higher than that of an equivalent Ford V8/60. The line comprised two series: Roadking and DeLuxe, both on a 117-inch wheelbase. Six models were offered in the Roadking series. The DeLuxe line comprised two- and five-passenger coupes, sedans, a convertible, and a wood-bodied eight-passenger station wagon. In addition, there was a special 137-inch-wheelbase chassis for the DeLuxe seven-passenger sedan and limousine. Long-chassis cars were a Chrysler specialty in those years, even on its low-price makes, but the Plymouth versions did not sell well.

The four-main-bearing 1940 six developed 84 horsepower at 3600 rpm. In no way did it rival the performance of the Ford V8, but it did provide reliable cruising at over 65 mph and was well known for its economy. (The original design dated back to 1933.) For 1941, horsepower was boosted to 87 bhp at 3800 rpm. It was bored out the year after that for 95 bhp at 3400 rpm. With the same displacement, output was raised to 97 bhp at 3600 rpm for 1949.

Plymouth gave its cars a facelift for '41. Model year production increased to 546,000, thanks mainly to heavy output in the closing months of 1940. Actual calendar year figures reflected the turn toward defense production a year later, running some 50,000 units behind Ford. The '41s were good-looking with a simple, almost heart-shaped horizontal grille, "speedline" fenders, and modest bright-metal side embellishments. Model lines increased to three: standard, Deluxe, and Special DeLuxe, the latter taking over from the 1940 DeLuxe. The longer wheelbase carried a seven-passenger sedan, but the slow-selling limousine was dropped after just 24 early-1941 examples were built. Other rarities among the '41s include the DeLuxe club coupe, the standard club coupe, utility sedan, and station wagon. New for all models was a Chrysler first, the Safety Rim wheel, designed to prevent tire loss during a blowout. The battery was moved under the hood for the first time, and Plymouth offered Powermatic shift, a vacuum transmission assist.

The 1942 line was revised with door sheetmetal extended to cover the running boards and a more massive horizontal grille. Plymouth retained its 117-inch standard wheelbase but dropped the 137. Only two lines

were fielded, DeLuxe and Special DeLuxe, and both used the more powerful engine. There were five DeLuxe models: three- and six-passenger coupes, two- and four-door sedans, and a two-door utility sedan. There were seven Special DeLuxe offerings: two coupes, two sedans, a convertible, a town sedan, and a station wagon. The town sedan was a new Chrysler style of the era, marked by a closed or "formal" rear roofline.

At the time World War II halted auto production, Plymouth's 1942 output was slightly more than 152,000 units. As a result, many models are very scarce today. Only 80 utility sedans were built, for example, along with just 1136 wagons and 2806 convertibles.

Plymouth manufactured munitions and military engines during the war, while stylists like A. B. Grisinger, John Chika, and Herb Weissinger worked on postwar car ideas whenever they could. Their designs took the form of most Chrysler prototypes in this period: rounded shapes with smooth fenders, thin door pillars, and wraparound grilles blended into the bodysides. When production resumed in late 1945, Plymouth fielded its prewar styles, and continued to do so until midway into the 1949 model year. The all-new postwar models that arrived in March were much squarer and more upright than the wartime prototypes had suggested. Production took a while to build up after V-J Day. Plymouth built only 770 cars before December 31, 1945. Volume quickly rose, however, exceeding a quarter-million units for 1946 and surpassing half a million in 1949.

The 1946 facelift consisted of a new grille with alternating thick and thin horizontal bars, rectangular parking lights located under the headlamps, wide front fender moldings, a new hood ornament, and reworked rear fenders. DeLuxe and Special DeLuxe series returned, but body choices were fewer than in '42. For 1947, DeLuxe prices stayed where they'd been, but Special DeLuxes ran as much as $250 higher than the year before. The formula was repeated for 1948, and again prices rose, this time by as much as $300. There were no styling changes at all, so the cars are identifiable as to year only by serial numbers. The '48s were continued as 1949 models starting in December 1948, while Plymouth readied its all-new design for spring introduction. In the meantime, there were a few engineering changes from prewar Plymouths, including a switch in tire and wheel size around January from 6.00×16s to 6.70×15-inch tires. Other chassis modifications resulted in a weight reduction of about 50 pounds.

By the time the "real" '49s arrived, styling wizards like Grisinger and Weissinger had departed for Kaiser-Frazer, and a new design philosophy had been established, influenced by Chrysler Corporation chairman K. T. Keller. Keller, who took over as president after Walter Chrysler died in 1940, didn't like low, torpedo-like shapes. Instead, he preferred what stylists called "three-box styling—one box on top of two others." His reasoning was that practicality should take priority over beauty, saying: "Cars should accommodate people

1946 DeLuxe club coupe

1947 Special DeLuxe four-door station wagon

1947 Special DeLuxe four-door sedan

Wartime proposal for postwar Plymouth

rather than the ideas of far-out designers." What he didn't realize was that after the war, people were *willing* to put up with cramped headroom and low ground clearance for the long, low look. In time, Keller's attitude would hurt Plymouth.

But in 1949 the seller's market was at its peak, and it didn't matter much what the cars looked like. Nonetheless, the new design was a very efficient package, comfortable and roomy with good visibility. Its chassis was

**1949 DeLuxe Suburban two-door station wagon**

**1950 DeLuxe club coupe**

**1950 XX-500 show car by Ghia**

**1951 Cranbrook four-door sedan**

slightly longer than before. Plymouth also offered a shorter 111-inch wheelbase for a two-door sedan, three-passenger coupe, and the new all-steel Suburban wagon.

Plymouth liked to take credit for this first "modern" station wagon, though Oldsmobile and Pontiac had all-steel wagons at the same time. Still, the Suburban cost only $1840, well under the GM makes, and therefore sold well. Nearly 20,000 were registered, convincing buyers that wagons didn't have to be made of wood.

Other Chrysler makes and the rest of the industry followed Plymouth's lead, and the "woody" soon vanished from the scene.

The longer-wheelbase models included the DeLuxe four-door sedan and coupe, priced in the $1500s; and the Special DeLuxe sedan, coupe, convertible, and wood-trimmed wagon, priced from about $1600 to $2400. The boxy body on all models carried a heavy grille extending under the headlamps, block letters spelling "Plymouth" on the hood, and an enlarged two-pane windshield. Quarter windows were eliminated for sedans, and both front and rear fenders continued as bolt-on units. Taillights were mounted high atop the rear fenders. A chrome nameplate and enameled crest were placed above the license plate on the decklid.

Plymouth's evolution in the '50s closely followed that of rival Chevrolet. It started the decade with economical, no-nonsense transportation, then fielded one of the industry's hot items in 1955. By the '60s, the division had an expanded line of increasingly luxurious and expensive models. Plymouths had no real style in 1950, but were among the best-looking cars in America after 1956.

The design and engineering revolutions of the '50s were prompted by Plymouth's declining fortunes in 1950-54. From 1931 up to that time, the division had never been challenged as the number-three producer behind Chevrolet and Ford, but Plymouth built fewer and fewer cars in the early '50s, dropping to fifth place in sales for calendar year 1954.

The 1950-54 models were well-engineered, solid and reliable—but not very fast and a little dull. All of them were powered by the same engine, Chrysler's smallest L-head six, which produced 97 bhp at 3800 rpm through 1952. Output was raised to 100 bhp for '53 (probably by the stroke of an ad writer's pen), and to 110 bhp the following season. This powerplant was capable of 20–23 miles per gallon, and perhaps 80 mph if pressed hard enough. (Interestingly, the long-lived L-head lasted through 1959, after which it was replaced by the modern overhead-valve slant six, but not before it had been boosted up to 132 bhp.)

In 1950, there were two lines—DeLuxe and Special DeLuxe. The Special outsold its stablemate by about seven to five. Two important innovations for the low-priced field were automatic electric choke and the combination ignition/starter switch.

Plymouth had built about 500,000 units in 1949 and some 600,000 in 1950. For 1951, it built 611,000 of a slightly modified design that was a little less blunt at the front end. New model names helped make the line seem fresh. There were Concord two-door sedans, coupes, and wagons; Cambridge four-door sedans and coupes; and Cranbrook sedans, coupes, hardtops, and convertibles. The hardtop, christened Belvedere, was Plymouth's first true pillarless style, and arrived a year behind Chevrolet's. It was distinguished from other models by a two-tone paint scheme.

Like other Chrysler Corporation cars, Plymouth re-

1952 Cranbrook Belvedere hardtop coupe

1953 Cambridge two-door sedan

1953 Cranbrook club coupe

Ghia's "Explorer" show car of 1954

1954 Belvedere four-door sedan

1954 Belvedere hardtop coupe

1955 Belvedere V8 four-door sedan

1955 Belvedere V8 Sport Coupe hardtop

mained essentially unchanged for 1952. The easiest way to tell the '52s from the '51s is by looking at the rear. The '52s have the Plymouth name integrated with the trunk handle assembly; the '51s spell it out in a separate piece of script. One important improvement on all 1951-52 models was the Oriflow shock absorber—a Chrysler hydraulic type designed to improve ride and handling. About 200,000 fewer cars rolled out of the factory than the year before, but the rest of the industry

also cut back production because of the Korean War and Plymouth remained number three.

Flow-through fenderlines and a one-piece windshield arrived with the redesigned 1953 models. A 114-inch wheelbase replaced the two chassis previously used. The Concord was dropped and the Cambridge expanded to include business coupes and wagons. A mid-year introduction was Hy-Drive, a combination manual transmission and torque converter that made

second-to-third shifts unnecessary—but the driver still had to use the clutch for first-gear getaways. Hy-Drive was a follow-up to overdrive, introduced the year before. The '54s would offer two-speed PowerFlite automatic, which was to prove very popular.

Plymouth, and Chrysler in general, suffered in 1954 as a result of uninspired styling. Fewer than 500,000 Plymouths were built, despite a rearranged model lineup. Plaza, Savoy, and Belvedere covered the price spread between $1600 and $2300.

These series would be offered again in 1955, but with a dramatic difference: Virgil Exner's all-new styling. Suddenly, Plymouth looked exciting, and with a brand-new polyspherical-head V8 it had performance to match.

The 260-cid "Hy-Fire" V8 was an excellent engine in the small-displacement generation that began with Studebaker's 232 in 1951. With a bore and stroke of $3.56 \times 3.25$ inches, it produced 167 bhp "standard" or 177 bhp with four-barrel carb and dual exhausts. Its outstanding features included lightweight aluminum pistons, an aluminum carburetor, and chrome-plated top piston rings for longer life and better oil control.

Other new mechanical features for 1955 were dashboard-controlled PowerFlite automatic, suspended foot pedals, tubeless tires, and front shocks enclosed within the coil springs. For the first time, air conditioning, power windows, and power front seats joined the options list. Brisk new pointed-end styling and neat two-toning characterized the three-series lineup. The Belvedere included a sporty hardtop and convertible, the latter available with V8 only from '55 through the end of the decade. "A great new car for the young in heart," it was called—a total departure from the past. Model year figures for 1955 are misleading. For the calendar year, Plymouth built 742,991 cars, a record that would still stand in the '70s.

For 1956, Virgil Exner formally announced The Forward Look (which meant tailfins) and Plymouth rose to fourth. The engineering department simultaneously brought forth pushbutton PowerFlite, a 12-volt electrical system, and an optional Highway Hi-Fi record player that used special records and a tone arm designed to stay in the groove. A new Suburban line covered four different wagons, a four-door hardtop was added to the Belvedere series, and a two-door hardtop was added to the Savoy.

The hottest performance news for '56 was the limited-production Fury—an attractive hardtop painted white with gold anodized body appliqués. It featured a 303-cid version of the V8 with a 9.25:1 compression ratio, solid lifters, stronger valve springs, dual exhausts, and Carter four-barrel carburetor. With its 240 bhp at 4800 rpm, the Fury approached 145 mph on test at Daytona Beach, and would do 0 to 60 mph in 10 seconds. Top speed in standard form was 111 mph. The Fury contributed greatly to Plymouth's growing performance image, and 4485 were sold—not bad for a car priced $600 higher than the Belvedere hardtop.

If 1955 had seen a victory with record production, 1957 was a second triumph. Over 655,000 cars were built during the calendar year. Exner's fresh new design prompted ad men to exclaim, "Suddenly it's 1960," and indeed, compared to the competition, Plymouth probably *was* three full years ahead. It had the lowest beltline, the most glass, the cleanest lines, and the highest tailfins in the field. It rode a 118-inch wheelbase (wagons were 122 inches) and was more powerful than ever. The old L-head six now ground out 132 bhp, the

**1956 Fury hardtop coupe**

**1957 Belvedere convertible**

**1957 Fury hardtop coupe**

**1957 Belvedere four-door sedan**

Hy-Fire V8 delivered up to 235 bhp, and the Fury's new 318 delivered 290 bhp. Like other Chrysler cars that year, torsion-bar front suspension was featured, with revised geometry that made for the best-handling Plymouth in history.

It's hard to remember how truly revolutionary the '57 Plymouths were at the time. The hardtop roofline, for example, was so clean and delicate-looking that it did not appear to serve any structural purpose. The grille, usually a large ornate object in those days, was slim

1958 Fury hardtop coupe

1958 Belvedere hardtop sedan

1959 Sport Fury hardtop coupe

1960 Fury hardtop sedan

and graceful. Grille height was reduced by a raised bumper that rode over a separate stone shield. At a time when rival cars were often garishly two-toned, Plymouth settled for a slim contrasting color spear along the sides painted to match the roof. Solid colors were also offered, or sometimes only the roof was done in a different hue. Traditional pillar sedans had huge glass areas; the convertible's windshield curved around at the top as well as the sides. By mid-year, there was a four-door hardtop in the Savoy as well as the Belvedere line. All hardtops had beautiful interiors trimmed in jacquard and vinyl. Dashboards grouped all instruments in a bolt-upright pod directly in front of the driver, with control knobs located safely out of the way. Suburbans saved load space by placing the spare tire vertically in the right rear fender—an idea first seen on the Plymouth Plainsman show car of 1956. The '57s were indeed memorable, but their tendency to rust (the design's major flaw) has made them rare finds today.

Plymouth's 1958 line was mostly a carryover, except for four headlamps and a new front stone shield without the vertical slots. The V8's output was up to at least 225 bhp, and as much as 315 in the high-performance Fury. Instant recognition at the rear was provided by round taillights, with the space above them filled by a piece of bright metal. Because of the recession, Plymouth built fewer '58s, but everyone else was affected, too. The division remained third overall in production.

Tailfins grew as big as they'd ever get in 1959 and were not very pretty. Front ends received a more garish eggcrate grille and a flatter hood, while the more-expensive models used anodized silver panels for side decoration. The Plaza line vanished, and other model names moved down a notch in price as Fury became a separate series offering four-door sedan and hardtop as well as two-door hardtop and convertible. Moving in as the new high-performance entry was the Sport Fury. Priced at around $3000–3200, this two-door hardtop and convertible was the top of the '59 line, equipped with a standard 260-bhp version of the 318 V8. For $87 extra, buyers could get a new 361 Golden Commando V8 with 305 bhp at 4600 rpm.

Plymouth show cars of the '50s were unique and interesting. The XX-500 of 1951 was a Ghia exercise—a very pretty sedan that won Exner's patronage for the Italian coachworks to build various show cars and limousines that followed. Ghia also did the Plymouth Explorer of 1954, a fast, smoothly styled grand tourer. A Briggs project was the 1954 Belmont, suggesting there might be a Plymouth two-seater (built by Briggs) to compete with Corvette and Thunderbird. Limited sales of the two American sports cars in '55 caused Plymouth to drop the idea. Two dream cars lending new features to production models were both wagons: Plainsman in 1956, Cabana in 1958. The Plainsman was marked by lots of glass like Chevrolet's Nomad, and donated the aforementioned concealed spare-tire compartment to the '57s. The Cabana sported even more glass and four-door hardtop styling. Neither saw production.

1960 Fury hardtop coupe

1960 Valiant V100 four-door station wagon

1960 Valiant V200 four-door sedan

1961 Fury hardtop coupe

1962 Valiant V200 four-door sedan

1962 Fury (Suburban) four-door station wagon

1963 Valiant Signet 200 hardtop coupe

1963 Fury hardtop sedan

Like the '50s, the '60s would be years of ups and downs for Plymouth. The division had barely recovered third place in production when it was knocked out by Rambler and Oldsmobile. A line of slow-selling intermediates and no standard-sized alternative dropped Plymouth to as low as eighth place in the early '60s. It recovered in 1963, but could not dislodge Pontiac from third place. These problems were of Plymouth's own doing. Time and again, management failed to gauge the market correctly. Plymouth had the right cars, but at the wrong time.

The difficulties began at the top of the line, with a garish, tailfinned line of Savoy, Belvedere, Fury, and Suburban models for 1960. Although Plymouth's new 225-cid slant-six engine was a good one, Rambler campaigned with conservative styling and more economical sixes, outproducing Plymouth by 2000 units for the calendar year. For 1961, Exner's drastically restyled bodyshell was marked by a strange, pinched grille and ponderous pod-like taillights, and was totally devoid of fins. The result was a fourth-place finish as Rambler swept by on the strength of its successful new compacts.

In 1962 came Plymouth's worst mistake of the decade. Anticipating a strong demand for compact "standard" cars, the company shaved up to eight inches from the wheelbase and 550 pounds from curb weight. The same model lineup was fielded on a shrunken 116-

1963 Fury convertible

Satellite II show car from 1964

1965 Fury I two-door sedan

1966 Satellite hardtop coupe

wheelbase (121 inches for station wagons). This new Fury line was offered in four series: Fury I, II, III, and Sport Fury. The largest Plymouths ever offered, they were greater in wheelbase, overall length, and width than the 1964 models, with greatly increased interior dimensions. Like all Plymouths since 1960, they used unitized body/chassis construction, but also had a bolt-on subframe to carry the engine and front suspension.

Plymouth had retained its 116-inch-wheelbase for its 1965 intermediate line, which was more in tune with buyer tastes. Designated Belvedere, it was styled to resemble the Fury with a squared-off roofline, clean sides, and a stamped grille. There were Belvedere I and II sixes and V8s, a Belvedere I Super Stock hardtop, and a top-line Satellite V8 hardtop and convertible. Standard on the Super Stock (and optional for other Belvederes and Furys) was a 426-cid wedge-head engine that developed 365 bhp and 470 pounds-feet of torque. The Super Stock had a special 115-inch wheelbase and weighed just 3170 pounds. Its mighty engine provided terrific performance: 120-mph top speed and 0 to 60 mph in eight seconds. Not cheap at a $4671 base price, the S/S was intended primarily for racing, and could be ordered with a hemi-head 426 as well as the wedge-head.

For 1966, the incredible 425-bhp Hemi was made available as an option on Belvedere II and Satellite. The result was the electrifying "Street Hemi," equipped as standard with heavy-duty suspension and oversize brakes. It was first offered with a four-speed gearbox, later with optional TorqueFlite automatic. Since the '66 Belvedere was shorter and lighter than the '65, the Street Hemi could be a docile tourer at low speeds and a demon when stirred up. Equipped with the proper tires and axle ratio, and correctly tuned, it could reach 120 mph in 12 or 13 seconds. Right off the floor it was ready for drag-race competition in A/Stock or AA/Stock classes, and along with Dodge's Coronet was allowed to run on NASCAR's shorter circuits in 1966—with predictable results. David Pearson won the '66 NASCAR championship for Dodge; Richard Petty won in '67 for Plymouth. Petty also won the 1964 Daytona 500 in a Plymouth. These were major breakups of Ford's otherwise tight stranglehold on NASCAR between 1965 and 1970.

The Satellites and Belvedere IIs were elegant-looking cars. When equipped with smaller V8s of 273, 318, and 361 cubic-inch displacement, they were among the best all-around Plymouths. Their crisp, chiseled styling was retained for 1967. In that year, the Hemi option was offered on the new Belvedere GTX, in addition to a 440-cid wedge-head V8 of 375 bhp. GTXs looked the part, with a silver-and-black grille and rear deck appliqués, simulated hood air intakes, sport striping, and dual exhausts.

In 1968, Plymouth restyled its intermediates with more rounded lines than before that looked just as pretty. The hottest model was ingenuously named Road Runner, available as a hardtop or coupe. The coupe was a European-looking machine with narrow pillars

inch wheelbase with Valiant-like styling. Plymouth's engines provided fine performance in these light cars, but that didn't make any difference. A public still hungry for large cars shunned Plymouth and looked to Ford or Chevrolet instead. Hasty facelifts took place. A more conventional grille, razor-edged fenders, and squared-off roof styling were devised for 1963; a Chevy-like grille and increased side decoration appeared for '64. These changes didn't help much, either. Plymouth's rebound to fourth place in 1963 was largely due to the success of its compact Valiant rather than any increased demand for its revamped standard models.

Plymouth's renaissance really began in 1965 when the division returned to the big-car fold with a 119-inch

1966 Barracuda hardtop coupe

1967 Belvedere GTX hardtop coupe

1967 Barracuda hardtop coupe

1967 Valiant Signet four-door sedan

1967 VIP hardtop sedan

and flip-out rear quarter windows. Road Runner nameplates and cartoon birds on the sides and rear, plus simulated hood scoops and racy wheels, identified it. Squeezed under the hood was either a 383-cid engine with a 440 intake manifold and heads, or a 426 Hemi. The GTX's beefy suspension and four-speed transmission options were also available for the Road Runner. On street or track, the car was dynamite. Extraordinary

as it seems, this finely tuned package of power and performance was available for only about $2800 to $3100.

In addition to the Road Runner, the GTX continued in hardtop and convertible form for 1968, along with the more mundane Belvedere, Satellite, and Sport Satellite sedans, coupes, and wagons. The lineup stayed mostly like this through 1970, but a Road Runner convertible was added for '69.

Full-size Plymouths continued on the 119-inch wheelbase through 1968 (wagons rode slightly longer spans). Fury I, II, and III models were offered with sixes and V8s. Sport Fury hardtops, convertibles, and fastbacks came with V8s in 1967-68. The top-of-the-line model in 1966 was the VIP, which had a "formal" roofline and conservative trim, in hardtop coupe or sedan form. Power options in 1965 included 361, 383, and 426 hemi engines. In 1966, a 440 wedge-head replaced the Hemi. From 1967 on, the optional big-blocks were the 383 and 440.

Plymouth's salvation in its poorer years of the '60s was the compact Valiant. The early 1960-62 models were ruggedly built, unit-body cars. Virgil Exner's styling included pronounced fenderlines, short decks, and square grilles, all on a 106-inch wheelbase. Elwood Engle's clean, square styling was featured on the same wheelbase for 1963-66. The line was completely redesigned again for '67, adopting a 108-inch wheelbase and four-square lines reminiscent of some middle-size European sedans. Valiant remained in this form, the top seller among Detroit compacts, until it was replaced by the Volaré in the mid-'70s.

One of Valiant's strong points was its robust slant-six engine. This powerplant was developed to give a low hoodline, but engineers also claimed certain manufacturing and operational efficiencies for the configuration. In stock form, the 170-cid version produced 101 bhp, though a four-barrel carburetor option for 1960-61 called Hyper-Pack raised output to 148 bhp. A larger, 225-cid unit was standard on larger Plymouths in 1960-61. From 1962 on, the 225 was optional for Valiant as well. A long-lived design of great durability, the 225 was still being used in the early '80s on some Plymouth models.

Valiant was straightforward in design with a conventional suspension. It was offered initially in two series—the V100 and V200, with sedans and wagons only in 1960. A hardtop was added the following year, and a bucket-seat Signet version answered the sporty compact challenge from Falcon and Corvair in '62. When Engle's styling took over for 1963, a Signet convertible was added.

The success of the Corvair Monza and the imminent arrival of Ford's Mustang prompted Plymouth to refocus its sights on the sporty-compact market. Accordingly, the Barracuda was launched in mid-1964 for the '65 model year. A hasty tooling revision carried out on the Valiant's upper body structure, it was a fastback coupe with a huge piece of curved glass forming part of a rakish roofline. Barracuda came standard with the 225

slant six, but a new V8 was optional, and desirable. A derivation of the Plymouth 318, it was a strong rival for Ford's excellent 260/289. It displaced 273 cubic inches and was oversquare (bore and stroke 3.62×3.31 inches). In base form, horsepower was 180, but a high-performance 235-bhp version was also offered. The 235 had a high-lift, high-overlap camshaft; dome-shaped pistons; solid lifters; dual-contact breaker points; an unsilenced air cleaner; and a sweet-sounding, low-back-pressure exhaust system. With Rallye Suspension (heavy-duty torsion bars and anti-sway bars up front, plus stiff rear leaf springs), Firm-Ride shocks, and a four-speed gearbox, the 235-bhp Barracuda would do 0 to 60 mph in eight seconds flat and the quarter-mile in 16 seconds.

Barracuda offered a combination of sporty looks, high performance, good handling, utility, and room for four. It was the most popular Plymouth model for 1965: almost 65,000 were built that year.

For 1966, Barracuda was facelifted with an eggcrate grille, then handsomely redesigned for '67: wheelbase was lengthened by two inches, overall length increased five inches. A sleek hardtop coupe and convertible joined the fastback. Plymouth's 383-cid V8 with four-barrel carb, detuned to 280 bhp, was now available. Although it gave better straightline performance, the 383 added up to 300 extra pounds, mostly over the front wheels, to the detriment of handling. The 273 was a better choice. Either V8 could be ordered with a Formula S package, which included heavy-duty suspension, tachometer, Goodyear Wide-Oval tires, and special identification.

Happily, Barracuda was not drastically changed for a few years. A vertical-bar grille appeared in 1968, and a checkered grille and redesigned taillights came along in '69. In both years beefy, big-block models, the 'Cuda 340 and 383, were offered. The former had 275 bhp; the latter 300 bhp in '68 and 330 bhp in 1969. Then came the completely redesigned 1970 model, sharing an all-new bodyshell with a Dodge double, the Challenger. Compared to previous models, the new Barracuda was shorter, wider, and somehow less distinctive. One of the more interesting variations was the mid-year AAR (All-American Racer) 'Cuda 340, quickly identifiable by its bold "strobe" tape stripes. Standard were a 340 V8 with Edelbrock intake manifold, special heads, and a modified block and valve train; heavy-duty suspension; wide tires; matte-black fiberglass hood with functional scoop; and functional rear spoiler. Only about 2800 were built.

Valiant underwent another of its periodic revivals with the 1970 debut of the semi-fastback Duster coupe, a pleasantly named little car of good quality that ran up nearly 200,000 sales. Among these were several thousand Gold Dusters, an option package consisting of gold trim on grille, body, and interior, plus bucket seats, whitewall tires, and special wheel covers. A racy derivation, the Duster 340, used a mechanical package similar to that of the AAR 'Cuda, which turned the inof-

fensive Valiant into a tiger. Equipment included a 275-bhp engine, three-speed floorshift, front disc brakes, wide-tread tires, and tuned suspension.

Among Plymouth's intermediates, 1970's most star-

1968 Barracuda fastback coupe

1968 GTX hardtop coupe

1968 Sport Fury convertible

1969 Valiant Signet four-door sedan

1969 Road Runner convertible

1969 'Cuda 383 fastback coupe

1970 Valiant Duster coupe

1970 Sport Fury S/23 hardtop coupe

1970 'Cuda hardtop coupe

tling newcomer was the Superbird (part of the Road Runner series), an evolution of Dodge's 1969 Charger Daytona. With a special "droop-snoot" front end, slippery bodywork, and huge tailfins carrying a stabilizer wing high above the rear deck, the Superbird looked fast—and it was. Over 220 mph was recorded by racing versions. The standard street drivetrain was the four-barrel 440 with TorqueFlite automatic, but a six-barrel 440, a racing 426 Hemi, and four-speed manual transmission were on the options list. After Dodge effortlessly built about 500 Charger Daytonas to qualify it as a "production" model for NASCAR events, the organization increased its minimum count to 1500. That was no problem for Plymouth, and 1920 Superbirds were built.

The Superbird's great moment came at Daytona when Pete Hamilton romped to victory at a near-150 mph average—ahead of every Dodge and every Ford. Of Chrysler's 38 Grand National wins in 1970, 21 were Superbird victories. NASCAR changed its regulations again in 1971, thus ending the Superbird's dominance on the high-speed ovals, but the aerodynamic lessons

learned from this car would later be applied in developing the fuel-efficient, ultra-slippery Plymouth Horizon TC3 coupe of 1979.

Even Plymouth's full-size cars were given the performance treatment in 1970. Most notable was the Sport Fury GT, with standard 440 engine, heavy-duty suspension, and long-legged rear axle ratios (as high as 2.76:1). Another Sport Fury package was the S/23, though it was not in the GT's league. Standard engine here was the 318 V8. Equipment also included a tuned suspension and "strobe tape." The luxury VIP was dropped that year, but in the spring Plymouth released the plush Gran Coupe, which offered almost every comfort and convenience feature except air conditioning for $3833, and included "air" for $4216.

The production figures in this chapter show numerous rarities, especially among Plymouth convertibles, many of which were produced in quantities of under 2000. Rarity coupled with high performance and good looks make late-'60s Plymouth convertibles—intermediates especially—prime candidates for future collectors.

# Plymouth Specifications

## 1940

| P9 Roadking (wb 117.0) | Wght | Price | Prod |
|---|---|---|---|
| bus cpe | 2,769 | 645 | 26,745 |
| sdn 2d | 2,834 | 699 | 55,092 |
| sdn 4d | 2,869 | 740 | 20,076 |
| util sdn | 2,769 | 699 | 589 |
| club cpe | 2,814 | 699 | 360 |
| wgn 4d | 3,089 | 925 | 80 |
| chassis | — | — | 907 |

| P10 DeLuxe (wb 117.0; 7P-137.0) | | | |
|---|---|---|---|
| bus cpe | 2,804 | 725 | 32,244 |
| sdn 2d | 2,889 | 775 | 76,781 |
| sdn 4d | 2,924 | 805 | 173,351 |
| util sdn | 2,824 | 775 | 4 |
| club cpe | 2,849 | 770 | 22,174 |
| conv cpe | 3,049 | 950 | 6,986 |
| wgn 4d | 3,144 | 970 | 3,126 |

|  | Wght | Price | Prod |
|---|---|---|---|
| sdn 4d 7P | 3,359 | 1,005 | 1,179 |
| limo 7P | 3,409 | 1,080 | 68 |
| chassis | — | — | 503 |

| 1940 Engine | bore×stroke | bhp | availability |
|---|---|---|---|
| L6, 201.3 | 3.13×4.38 | 84 | S-all |

## 1941

### P11 (wb 117.0)

|  | Wght | Price | Prod |
|---|---|---|---|
| bus cpe | 2,809 | 720 | 23,754 |
| sdn 2d | 2,859 | 769 | 46,646 |
| sdn 4d | 2,889 | 800 | 21,175 |
| util sdn | 2,794 | 760 | 468 |
| club cpe | 2,819 | 764 | 994 |
| wgn 4d | 3,139 | 1,006 | 217 |
| DeLuxe bus cpe | 2,839 | 760 | 15,862 |
| DeLuxe sdn 2d | 2,800 | 809 | 46,138 |
| DeLuxe sdn 4d | 2,924 | 845 | 32,336 |
| DeLuxe club cpe | 2,859 | 804 | 204 |
| DeLuxe util sdn | — | proto | 1 |
| chassis | — | — | 676 |

### P12 Special DeLuxe (wb 117.0; 7P-137.0)

|  | Wght | Price | Prod |
|---|---|---|---|
| bus cpe | 2,859 | 795 | 23,851 |
| sdn 2d | 2,934 | 845 | 84,810 |
| sdn 4d | 2,959 | 877 | 190,513 |
| util sdn | — | proto | 2 |
| club cpe | 2,934 | 842 | 37,352 |
| conv cpe | 3,166 | 1,007 | 10,545 |
| wgn 4d | 3,194 | 1,031 | 5,594 |
| sdn 4d, 7P | 3,379 | 1,078 | 1,127 |
| limo, 7P | 3,429 | 1,153 | 24 |
| chassis | — | — | 321 |

| 1941 Engine | bore×stroke | bhp | availability |
|---|---|---|---|
| L6, 201.3 | 3.13×4.38 | 87 | S-all |

## 1942

### P14S DeLuxe (wb 117.0)

|  | Wght | Price | Prod |
|---|---|---|---|
| bus cpe | 2,906 | 812 | 3,783 |
| sdn 2d | 2,961 | 850 | 9,350 |
| sdn 4d | 3,001 | 889 | 11,973 |
| util sdn | 2,906 | 842 | 80 |
| club cpe | 2,966 | 885 | 2,458 |
| chassis | — | — | 1 |

### P14C Special DeLuxe (wb 117.0)

|  | Wght | Price | Prod |
|---|---|---|---|
| bus cpe | 2,931 | 855 | 7,258 |
| sdn 2d | 2,996 | 895 | 24,142 |
| sdn 4d | 3,036 | 935 | 68,924 |
| Town Sedan | 3,061 | 980 | 5,821 |
| club cpe | 3,011 | 928 | 14,685 |
| conv cpe | 3,231 | 1,078 | 2,806 |
| wgn 4d | 3,371 | 1,145 | 1,136 |
| chassis | — | — | 10 |

| 1942 Engine | bore×stroke | bhp | availability |
|---|---|---|---|
| L6, 217.8 | 3.25×4.38 | 95 | S-all |

## 1946*

### P15S DeLuxe (wb 117.0)

|  | Wght | Price | Prod |
|---|---|---|---|
| bus cpe | 2,977 | 1,089 | — |
| sdn 2d | 3,047 | 1,124 | — |
| sdn 4d | 3,082 | 1,164 | — |
| club cpe | 3,037 | 1,159 | — |
| chassis | — | — | — |

### P15C Special DeLuxe (wb 117.0)

|  | Wght | Price | Prod |
|---|---|---|---|
| bus cpe | 2,982 | 1,159 | — |
| sdn 2d | 3,062 | 1,199 | — |
| sdn 4d | 3,107 | 1,239 | — |
| club cpe | 3,057 | 1,234 | — |
| conv cpe | 3,282 | 1,439 | — |
| wgn 4d | 3,402 | 1,539 | — |
| chassis | — | — | — |

| 1946 Engine | bore×stroke | bhp | availability |
|---|---|---|---|
| L6, 217.8 | 3.25×4.38 | 95 | S-all |

## 1947*

### P15S DeLuxe (wb 117.0)

|  | Wght | Price | Prod |
|---|---|---|---|
| bus cpe | 2,977 | 1,139 | — |
| sdn 2d | 3,047 | 1,164 | — |
| sdn 4d | 3,082 | 1,214 | — |
| club cpe | 3,037 | 1,189 | — |
| chassis | — | — | — |

### P15C Special DeLuxe (wb 117.0)

|  | Wght | Price | Prod |
|---|---|---|---|
| bus cpe | 2,982 | 1,209 | — |
| sdn 2d | 3,062 | 1,239 | — |
| sdn 4d | 3,107 | 1,289 | — |
| club cpe | 3,057 | 1,264 | — |
| conv cpe | 3,282 | 1,565 | — |
| wgn 4d | 3,402 | 1,765 | — |
| chassis | — | — | — |

| 1947 Engine | bore×stroke | bhp | availability |
|---|---|---|---|
| L6, 217.8 | 3.25×4.38 | 95 | S-all |

## 1948*

### P15S DeLuxe (wb 117.0)

|  | Wght | Price | Prod |
|---|---|---|---|
| bus cpe | 2,955 | 1,346 | — |
| sdn 2d | 2,995 | 1,383 | — |
| sdn 4d | 3,030 | 1,441 | — |
| club cpe | 3,005 | 1,409 | — |
| chassis | — | — | — |

### P15C Special DeLuxe (wb 117.0)

|  | Wght | Price | Prod |
|---|---|---|---|
| bus cpe | 2,950 | 1,440 | — |
| sdn 2d | 3,030 | 1,471 | — |
| sdn 4d | 3,045 | 1,529 | — |
| club cpe | 3,020 | 1,503 | — |
| conv cpe | 3,225 | 1,857 | — |
| wgn 4d | 3,320 | 2,068 | — |
| chassis | — | — | — |

| 1948 Engine | bore×stroke | bhp | availability |
|---|---|---|---|
| L6, 217.8 | 3.25×4.38 | 95 | S-all |

## 1949 First Series*

### P15S DeLuxe (wb 117.0)

|  | Wght | Price | Prod |
|---|---|---|---|
| bus cpe | 2,955 | 1,346 | — |
| sdn 2d | 2,995 | 1,383 | — |
| sdn 4d | 3,030 | 1,441 | — |
| club cpe | 3,005 | 1,409 | — |
| chassis | — | — | — |

### P15C Special DeLuxe (wb 117.0)

|  | Wght | Price | Prod |
|---|---|---|---|
| bus cpe | 2,950 | 1,440 | — |
| sdn 2d | 3,030 | 1,471 | — |
| sdn 4d | 3,045 | 1,529 | — |
| club cpe | 3,020 | 1,503 | — |
| conv cpe | 3,225 | 1,857 | — |
| wgn 4d | 3,320 | 2,068 | — |
| chassis | — | — | — |

| 1949(1) Engine | bore×stroke | bhp | availability |
|---|---|---|---|
| L6, 217.8 | 3.25×4.38 | 95 | S-all |

*Factory combined production figures for 1946 through 1949 First Series.

## Combined 1946–1949 First Series Production:

### P15S DeLuxe (wb 117.0)

| | Prod |
|---|---|
| bus cpe | 16,117 |
| sdn 2d | 49,918 |
| sdn 4d | 120,757 |
| club cpe | 10,400 |
| chassis | 10 |

### P15C Special DeLuxe (wb 117.0)

| | Prod |
|---|---|
| bus cpe | 31,399 |
| sdn 2d | 125,704 |
| sdn 4d | 514,986 |
| club cpe | 156,629 |
| conv cpe | 15,295 |
| wgn 4d | 12,913 |
| chassis | 5,361 |

## 1949 Second Series

### P17 DeLuxe (wb 111.0)

| | Wght | Price | Prod |
|---|---|---|---|
| bus cpe | 2,825 | 1,371 | 15,715 |
| sdn 2d | 2,951 | 1,492 | 28,516 |
| Suburban wgn 2d | 3,105 | 1,840 | 19,220 |
| chassis | — | — | 4 |

### P18 DeLuxe (wb 118.5)

| | Wght | Price | Prod |
|---|---|---|---|
| sdn 4d | 3,059 | 1,551 | 61,021 |
| club cpe | 3,034 | 1,519 | 25,687 |

### P18 Special DeLuxe (wb 118.5)

| | Wght | Price | Prod |
|---|---|---|---|
| sdn 4d | 3,079 | 1,629 | 252,878 |
| club cpe | 3,046 | 1,603 | 99,680 |
| conv cpe | 3,323 | 1,982 | 15,240 |
| wgn 4d | 3,341 | 2,372 | 3,443 |
| chassis | — | — | 981 |

| 1949(2) Engine | bore×stroke | bhp | availability |
|---|---|---|---|
| L6, 217.8 | 3.25×4.38 | 97 | S-all |

## 1950

### P19 DeLuxe (wb 111.0)

| | Wght | Price | Prod |
|---|---|---|---|
| bus cpe | 2,872 | 1,371 | 16,861 |
| sdn 2d | 2,946 | 1,492 | 67,584 |
| Suburban wgn 2d | 3,116 | 1,840 | 34,457 |
| Suburban Special wgn 2d | 3,155 | 1,946 | |
| chassis | — | — | 1 |

### P20 DeLuxe (wb 118.5)

| | Wght | Price | Prod |
|---|---|---|---|
| sdn 4d | 3,068 | 1,551 | 87,871 |
| club cpe | 3,040 | 1,519 | 53,890 |

### P20 Special DeLuxe (wb 118.5)

| | Wght | Price | Prod |
|---|---|---|---|
| sdn 4d | 3,072 | 1,629 | 234,084 |
| club cpe | 3,041 | 1,603 | 99,361 |
| conv cpe | 3,295 | 1,982 | 12,697 |
| wgn 4d | 3,353 | 2,372 | 2,059 |
| chassis | — | — | 2,091 |

| 1950 Engine | bore×stroke | bhp | availability |
|---|---|---|---|
| L6, 217.8 | 3.25×4.38 | 97 | S-all |

## 1951*

### P22 Concord (wb 111.0)

| | Wght | Price | Prod |
|---|---|---|---|
| bus cpe | 2,919 | 1,537 | — |
| sdn 2d | 2,969 | 1,673 | — |
| Savoy wgn 2d | 3,184 | 2,182 | — |
| Suburban wgn 2d | 3,124 | 2,064 | — |

### P23 Cambridge (wb 118.5)

| | Wght | Price | Prod |
|---|---|---|---|
| sdn 4d | 3,104 | 1,739 | — |
| club cpe | 3,059 | 1,703 | — |

### P23 Cranbrook (wb 118.5)

| | Wght | Price | Prod |
|---|---|---|---|
| sdn 4d | 3,109 | 1,826 | — |
| club cpe | 3,074 | 1,796 | — |
| conv cpe | 3,294 | 2,222 | — |
| Belvedere htp cpe | 3,182 | 2,114 | — |

| 1951 Engine | bore×stroke | bhp | availability |
|---|---|---|---|
| L6, 217.8 | 3.25×4.38 | 97 | S-all |

## 1952*

### P22 Concord (wb 111.0)

| | Wght | Price | Prod |
|---|---|---|---|
| bus cpe | 2,893 | 1,610 | — |
| sdn 2d | 2,959 | 1,753 | — |
| Savoy wgn 2d | 3,165 | 2,287 | — |
| Suburban wgn 2d | 3,145 | 2,163 | — |

### P23 Cambridge (wb 118.5)

| | Wght | Price | Prod |
|---|---|---|---|
| sdn 4d | 3,068 | 1,822 | — |
| club cpe | 3,030 | 1,784 | — |

### P23 Cranbrook (wb 118.5)

| | Wght | Price | Prod |
|---|---|---|---|
| sdn 4d | 3,088 | 1,914 | — |
| club cpe | 3,046 | 1,883 | — |
| conv cpe | 3,256 | 2,329 | — |
| Belvedere htp cpe | 3,105 | 2,216 | — |

| 1952 Engine | bore×stroke | bhp | availability |
|---|---|---|---|
| L6, 217.8 | 3.25×4.38 | 97 | S-all |

*Factory combined 1951 and 1952 production figures.

## Combined 1951–1952 Production:

### P22 Concord (wb 111.0)

| | Prod |
|---|---|
| bus cpe | 14,255 |
| sdn 2d | 49,139 |
| Savoy/Suburban wgn 2d | 76,520 |

### P23 Cambridge (wb 118.5)

| | Prod |
|---|---|
| sdn 4d | 179,417 |
| club cpe | 101,784 |

### P23 Cranbrook (wb 118.5)

| | Prod |
|---|---|
| sdn 4d | 388,785 |
| club cpe | 126,725 |
| Belvedere htp cpe | 51,266 |
| conv cpe | 15,650 |
| chassis | 4,171 |

## 1953

### P24-1 Cambridge (wb 114.0)

| | Wght | Price | Prod |
|---|---|---|---|
| bus cpe | 2,888 | 1,618 | 6,975 |
| sdn 2d | 2,943 | 1,727 | 56,800 |
| sdn 4d | 2,983 | 1,765 | 93,585 |
| club cpe | 2,950 | 1,725 | 1,050 |
| Suburban wgn 2d | 3,129 | 2,064 | 43,545 |

### P24-2 Cranbrook (wb 114.0)

| | Wght | Price | Prod |
|---|---|---|---|
| sdn 4d | 3,023 | 1,873 | 298,976 |
| club cpe | 2,971 | 1,843 | 92,102 |
| Belvedere htp cpe | 3,027 | 2,064 | 35,185 |
| conv cpe | 3,193 | 2,220 | 6,301 |
| Savoy wgn 2d | 3,170 | 2,207 | 12,089 |
| chassis | — | — | 843 |

| 1953 Engine | bore×stroke | bhp | availability |
|---|---|---|---|
| L6, 217.8 | 3.25×4.38 | 100 | S-all |

## 1954

### P25-1 Plaza (wb 114.0)

| | Wght | Price | Prod |
|---|---|---|---|
| bus cpe | 2,889 | 1,618 | 5,000 |
| club cpe | 2,950* | 1,700* | 1,275 |
| sdn 4d | 3,004 | 1,765 | 43,077 |
| sdn 2d | 2,943 | 1,727 | 27,976 |

| | Wght | Price | Prod |
|---|---|---|---|
| Suburban wgn 2d | 3,122 | 2,064 | 35,937 |
| chassis | — | | 1 |

**P25-2 Savoy (wb 114.0)**

| | Wght | Price | Prod |
|---|---|---|---|
| club cpe | 2,982 | 1,843 | 30,700 |
| sdn 4d | 3,036 | 1,873 | 139,383 |
| sdn 2d | 2,986 | 1,835 | 25,396 |
| Suburban wgn 2d | 3,165* | 2,172* | 450 |
| chassis | | | 3,588 |

**P25-3 Belvedere (wb 114.0)**

| | Wght | Price | Prod |
|---|---|---|---|
| sdn 4d | 3,050 | 1,953 | 106,601 |
| Sport Coupe htp | 3,038 | 2,145 | 25,592 |
| conv cpe | 3,273 | 2,301 | 6,900 |
| Suburban wgn 2d | 3,186 | 2,288 | 9,241 |
| chassis | — | — | 2,031 |

*Estimated.

| 1954 Engines | bore×stroke | bhp | availability |
|---|---|---|---|
| L6, 217.0 | 3.25×4.38 | 100 | S-all to engine #P25-243000 |
| L6, 230.2 | 3.25×4.63 | 110 | S-all from engine #P25-243001 |

## 1955

**P26-1 Plaza, L6 (wb 115.0)**

| | Wght | Price | Prod |
|---|---|---|---|
| sdn 4d | 3,129 | 1,781 | 68,826 |
| club cpe | 3,089 | 1,738 | 45,561 |
| Suburban wgn 2d | 3,261 | 2,077 | 23,319 |
| Suburban wgn 4d | 3,282 | 2,158 | 10,594 |
| bus cpe | 3,025 | 1,639 | 4,882 |

**P27-1 Plaza, V8 (wb 115.0)**

| | Wght | Price | Prod |
|---|---|---|---|
| sdn 4d | 3,246 | 1,884 | 15,330 |
| club cpe | 3,202 | 1,841 | 8,049 |
| Suburban wgn 2d | 3,389 | 2,180 | 8,469 |
| Suburban wgn 4d | 3,408 | 2,262 | 4,828 |

**P26-3 Savoy, L6 (wb 115.0)**

| | Wght | Price | Prod |
|---|---|---|---|
| sdn 4d | 3,154 | 1,880 | 93,716 |
| club cpe | 3,109 | 1,837 | 45,438 |
| chassis | — | — | 1 |

**P27-3 Savoy, V8 (wb 115.0)**

| | Wght | Price | Prod |
|---|---|---|---|
| sdn 4d | 3,265 | 1,983 | 69,025 |
| club cpe | 3,224 | 1,940 | 29,442 |

**P26-2 Belvedere, L6 (wb 115.0)**

| | Wght | Price | Prod |
|---|---|---|---|
| sdn 4d | 3,159 | 1,979 | 69,128 |
| club cpe | 3,129 | 1,936 | 19,471 |
| Sport Coupe htp | 3,330 | 2,113 | 13,942 |
| Suburban wgn 4d | 3,312 | 2,322 | 6,197 |

**P27-2 Belvedere V8 (wb 115.0)**

| | Wght | Price | Prod |
|---|---|---|---|
| sdn 4d | 3,262 | 2,082 | 91,856 |
| club cpe | 3,228 | 2,039 | 22,174 |
| Sport Coupe htp | 3,261 | 2,217 | 33,433 |
| conv cpe | 3,409 | 2,351 | 8,473 |
| Suburban wgn 4d | 3,475 | 2,425 | 12,291 |

| 1955 Engines | bore×stroke | bhp | availability |
|---|---|---|---|
| L6, 230.2 | 3.25×4.63 | 117 | S-all Sixes |
| V8, 241.0 | 3.44×3.25 | 157 | O-all V8 |
| V8, 260.0 | 3.56×3.25 | 167 | S-all V8 |
| V8, 260.0 | 3.56×3.25 | 177 | O-all V8 |

## 1956

**P28/29-1 Plaza (wb 115.0)**

| | Wght | Price | Prod |
|---|---|---|---|
| bus cpe | 3,100 | 1,784 | 3,728 |
| sdn 4d | 3,210 | 1,926 | 60,197 |
| club sdn | 3,175 | 1,883 | 43,022 |

**P28/29-2 Savoy (wb 115.0)**

| | Wght | Price | Prod |
|---|---|---|---|
| sdn 4d | 3,228 | 2,025 | 151,762 |
| club sdn | 3,190 | 1,982 | 57,927 |
| Sport Coupe htp | 3,200 | 2,130 | 16,473 |

**P28/29-3 Belvedere (wb 115.0)**

| | Wght | Price | Prod |
|---|---|---|---|
| sdn 4d | 3,248 | 2,109 | 84,218 |
| Sport Sedan htp | 3,343 | 2,281 | 17,515 |
| Sport Coupe htp | 3,243 | 2,214 | 24,723 |
| conv cpe | 3,435 | 2,478 | 6,735 |

**P28/29 Suburban (wb 115.0)**

| | Wght | Price | Prod |
|---|---|---|---|
| DeLuxe wgn 2d | 3,373 | 2,196 | 23,866 |
| Custom wgn 2d | 3,418 | 2,267 | 9,489 |
| Custom wgn 4d | 3,470 | 2,314 | 33,333 |
| Sport wgn 4d | 3,513 | 2,484 | 15,104 |

**P29-3 Fury (wb 115.0)**

| | Wght | Price | Prod |
|---|---|---|---|
| htp cpe | 3,650 | 2,866 | 4,485 |

| 1956 Engines | bore×stroke | bhp | availability |
|---|---|---|---|
| L6, 230.2 | 3.25×4.38 | 125 | S-all exc Fury, Belv conv |
| L6, 230.2 | 3.25×4.38 | 131 | O-all exc Fury, Belv conv |
| V8, 270.0 | 3.63×3.26 | 180 | O-Plaza, Savoy, Belvedere |
| V8, 277.0 | 3.75×3.13 | 187 | S-Belv conv; O-Belv, Savoy, Plaza |
| V8, 277.0 | 3.75×3.13 | 200 | O-all exc Fury |
| V8, 303.0 | 3.82×3.31 | 240 | S-Fury |

## 1957

**P30/31-1 Plaza (wb 118.0)**

| | Wght | Price | Prod |
|---|---|---|---|
| bus cpe | 3,235 | 1,899 | 2,874 |
| sdn 4d | 3,333 | 2,050 | 70,248 |
| sdn 2d | 3,245 | 2,009 | 49,137 |

**P30/31-2 Savoy (wb 118.0)**

| | Wght | Price | Prod |
|---|---|---|---|
| sdn 4d | 3,340 | 2,194 | 153,093 |
| Sport Sedan htp | 3,428 | 2,317 | 7,601 |
| sdn 2d | 3,263 | 2,147 | 55,590 |
| Sport Coupe htp | 3,335 | 2,229 | 31,373 |

**P30/31-3 Belvedere (wb 118.0)**

| | Wght | Price | Prod |
|---|---|---|---|
| sdn 4d | 3,373 | 2,310 | 110,414 |
| Sport Sedan htp | 3,428 | 2,419 | 37,446 |
| sdn 2d | 3,288 | 2,264 | 55,590 |
| Sport Coupe htp | 3,348 | 2,349 | 67,268 |
| conv cpe | 3,585 | 2,638 | 9,866 |

**P30/31 Suburban (wb 122.0)**

| | Wght | Price | Prod |
|---|---|---|---|
| DeLuxe wgn 2d | 3,620 | 2,330 | 20,111 |
| Custom wgn 2d | 3,668 | 2,440 | 11,196 |
| Custom wgn 4d, 6P | 3,753 | 2,494 | 40,227 |
| Custom wgn 4d, 9P | 3,800 | 2,649 | 9,357 |
| Sport wgn 4d, 6P | 3,748 | 2,622 | 15,414 |
| Sport wgn 4d, 9P | 3,795 | 2,777 | 7,988 |

**P31 Fury (wb 118.0)**

| | Wght | Price | Prod |
|---|---|---|---|
| htp cpe | 3,595 | 2,925 | 7,438 |

| 1957 Engines | bore×stroke | bhp | availability |
|---|---|---|---|
| L6, 230.2 | 3.25×4.63 | 132 | S-all exc Fury, Belv conv |
| V8, 277.0 | 3.75×3.13 | 197 | S-Plaza |
| V8, 277.0 | 3.75×3.13 | 235 | O-Plaza |
| V8, 301.0 | 3.91×3.13 | 215 | O-all exc Fury |
| V8, 301.0 | 3.91×3.13 | 235 | O-all exc Fury |
| V8, 318.0 | 3.91×3.31 | 290 | S-Fury |

## 1958

**LP1/2-L Plaza (wb 118.0)**

| | | Wght | Price | Prod |
|---|---|---|---|---|
| 21 | club sdn | 3,253 | 2,118 | 39,062 |
| 22 | bus cpe | 3,245 | 2,028 | 1,472 |

| | | Wght | Price | Prod |
|---|---|---|---|---|
| 41 | sdn 4d | 3,335 | 2,169 | 54,194 |

**LP1/2-M Savoy (wb 118.0)**

| | | Wght | Price | Prod |
|---|---|---|---|---|
| 21 | club sdn | 3,290 | 2,254 | 17,624 |
| 23 | Sport Coupe htp | 3,320 | 2,329 | 19,500 |
| 41 | sdn 4d | 3,310 | 2,305 | 67,933 |
| 43 | Sport Sedan htp | 3,393 | 2,400 | 5,060 |

**LP1/2-H Belvedere (wb 118.0)**

| | | | | |
|---|---|---|---|---|
| 21 | club sdn | 3,305 | 2,389 | 4,229 |
| 23 | Sport Coupe htp | 3,325 | 2,457 | 36,043 |
| 27 | conv cpe | 3,545 | 2,762 | 9,941 |
| 41 | sdn 4d | 3,343 | 2,440 | 49,124 |
| 43 | Sport Sedan htp | 3,425 | 2,528 | 18,194 |

**LP1/2 Suburban (wb 122.0)**

| | | | | |
|---|---|---|---|---|
| — | Deluxe wgn 4d | 3,660 | 2,486 | 15,535 |
| 25 | DeLuxe wgn 2d | 3,560 | 2,432 | 15,625 |
| 25 | Custom wgn 2d | 3,630 | 2,553 | 5,925 |
| 45A | Custom wgn 4d, 6P | 3,665 | 2,607 | 38,707 |
| 45B | Custom wgn 4d, 9P | 3,763 | 2,747 | 17,158 |
| 45A | Sport wgn 4d, 6P | 3,680 | 2,760 | 10,785 |
| 45B | Sport wgn 4d, 9P | 3,758 | 2,900 | 12,385 |

**LP2-H Fury (wb 118.0)**

| | | | | |
|---|---|---|---|---|
| 23 | htp cpe | 3,510 | 3,067 | 5,303 |

| 1958 Engines | bore×stroke | bhp | availability |
|---|---|---|---|
| L6, 230.2 | 3.25×4.63 | 132 | S-all exc Fury, Belv conv |
| V8, 318.0 | 3.91×3.31 | 225 | O-all exc Fury |
| V8, 318.0 | 3.91×3.31 | 250 | O-all exc Fury |
| V8, 318.0 | 3.91×3.31 | 290 | S-Fury |
| V8, 350.0 | 4.06×3.38 | 305 | O-all |
| V8, 350.0 | 4.06×3.38 | 315 | O-all (fuel injection) |

## 1959

**MP1/2-L Savoy (wb 118.0)**

| | | Wght | Price | Prod |
|---|---|---|---|---|
| 21 | club sdn | 3,333 | 2,222 | 46,979 |
| 22 | bus cpe | 3,130 | 2,143 | 1,051 |
| 41 | sdn 4d | 3,333 | 2,283 | 84,272 |

**MP1/2-M Belvedere (wb 118.0)**

| | | | | |
|---|---|---|---|---|
| 21 | club sdn | 3,310 | 2,389 | 13,816 |
| 23 | htp cpe | 3,318 | 2,461 | 23,469 |
| 27 | conv cpe | 3,580 | 2,814 | 5,063 |
| 41 | sdn 4d | 3,353 | 2,440 | 67,980 |
| 43 | htp sdn 4d | 3,335 | 2,525 | 5,713 |

**MP2-H Fury (wb 118.0)**

| | | | | |
|---|---|---|---|---|
| 23 | htp cpe | 3,435 | 2,714 | 21,494 |
| 41 | sdn 4d | 3,455 | 2,691 | 30,149 |
| 43 | htp sdn | 3,505 | 2,771 | 13,614 |

**MP2-P Sport Fury (wb 118.0)**

| | | | | |
|---|---|---|---|---|
| 23 | htp cpe | 3,475 | 2,927 | 17,867 |
| 27 | conv cpe | 3,670 | 3,125 | 5,990 |

**MP1/2 Suburban (wb 122.0)**

| | | | | |
|---|---|---|---|---|
| 25 | DeLuxe wgn 2d | 3,625 | 2,694 | 15,074 |
| 25 | Custom wgn 2d, 6P | 3,690 | 2,814 | 1,852 |
| 45A | DeLuxe wgn 4d | 3,675 | 2,761 | 35,086 |
| 45A | Custom wgn 4d, 6P | 3,678 | 3,881 | 35,024 |
| 45B | Custom wgn 4d, 9P | 3,775 | 2,991 | 16,993 |
| 45A | Sport wgn 4d, 6P | 3,760 | 3,021 | 7,224 |
| 45B | Sport wgn 4d, 9P | 3,805 | 3,131 | 9,549 |

| 1959 Engines | bore×stroke | bhp | availability |
|---|---|---|---|
| L6, 230.2 | 3.25×4.63 | 132 | S-Savoy, Belvedere, Suburb exc Cus 9P, Sports |
| V8, 318.0 | 3.91×3.31 | 230 | S-Fury; O-other exc Sport Fury |
| V8, 318.0 | 3.91×3.31 | 260 | S-Sport Fury; O-others |

| | bore×stroke | bhp | availability |
|---|---|---|---|
| V8, 361.0 | 4.12×3.38 | 305 | O-all |

## 1960

**V100 Valiant (wb 106.5)**

| | | Wght | Price | Prod |
|---|---|---|---|---|
| 110 | sdn 4d | 2,635 | 2,053 | 52,788 |
| 140 | wgn 4d, 6P | 2,815 | 2,365 | 12,018 |
| — | wgn 4d, 9P | 2,845 | 2,488 | 1,928 |

**V200 Valiant (wb 106.5)**

| | | | | |
|---|---|---|---|---|
| 130 | sdn 4d | 2,655 | 2,130 | 106,515 |
| 170 | wgn 4d, 6P | 2,855 | 2,443 | 16,368 |
| — | wgn 4d, 9P | 2,860 | 2,566 | 4,675 |

**PP1/2-L Savoy (wb 118.0)**

| | | | | |
|---|---|---|---|---|
| 21 | club sdn | 3,410 | 2,260 | 26,820 |
| 41 | sdn 4d | 3,433 | 2,310 | 51,384 |

**PP1/2-M Belvedere (wb 118.0)**

| | | | | |
|---|---|---|---|---|
| 21 | club sdn | 3,423 | 2,389 | 6,529 |
| 23 | htp cpe | 3,438 | 2,641 | 14,085 |
| 41 | sdn 4d | 3,448 | 2,439 | 42,130 |

**PP1/2-H Fury (wb 118.0)**

| | | | | |
|---|---|---|---|---|
| 23 | htp cpe | 3,465 | 2,599 | 18,079 |
| 27 | conv cpe | 3,630 | 2,967 | 7,080 |
| 41 | sdn 4d | 3,475 | 2,575 | 21,292 |
| 43 | htp sdn | 3,528 | 2,656 | 9,036 |

**PP1/2 Suburban (wb 122.0)**

| | | | | |
|---|---|---|---|---|
| 25 | DeLuxe wgn 2d | 3,375 | 2,721 | 5,503 |
| 45 | DeLuxe wgn 4d | 3,815 | 2,787 | 18,484 |
| 45 | Custom wgn 4d, 6P | 3,890 | 2,880 | 17,308 |
| 45 | Custom wgn 4d, 9P | 3,875 | 2,990 | 8,116 |
| 45 | Sport wgn 4d, 6P | 3,895 | 3,024 | 3,333 |
| 45 | Sport wgn 4d, 9P | 4,020 | 3,134 | 4,253 |

| 1960 Engines | bore×stroke | bhp | availability |
|---|---|---|---|
| L6, 170.0 | 3.40×3.13 | 101 | S-Valiant |
| L6, 170.0 | 3.40×3.13 | 148 | O-Valiant only |
| L6, 225.0 | 3.40×4.13 | 145 | S-full-size only |
| V8, 318.0 | 3.91×3.31 | 230 | S-full-size V8 (PP2) |
| V8, 361.0 | 4.12×3.38 | 305 | O-all full-size |

## 1961

**V100 Valiant (wb 106.5)**

| | | Wght | Price | Prod |
|---|---|---|---|---|
| 111 | sdn sdn 4d | 2,590 | 2,014 | 25,695 |
| 156 | wgn 4d | 2,745 | 2,327 | 6,717 |

**V200 Valiant (wb 106.5)**

| | | | | |
|---|---|---|---|---|
| 132 | htp cpe | 2,605 | 2,137 | 18,586 |
| 133 | sdn 4d | 2,600 | 2,110 | 59,056 |
| 176 | wgn 4d | 2,770 | 2,423 | 10,794 |

**RP1/2-L Savoy (2b 118.0)**

| | | | | |
|---|---|---|---|---|
| 211 | sdn 2d, L6 | 3,300 | 2,260 | 18,729 |
| 311 | sdn 2d, V8 | 3,440 | 2,379 | |
| 213 | sdn 4d, L6 | 3,310 | 2,310 | 44,913 |
| 313 | sdn 4d, V8 | 3,465 | 2,430 | |

**RP1/2-M Belvedere (wb 118.0)**

| | | | | |
|---|---|---|---|---|
| 221 | sdn 2d, L6 | 3,300 | 2,389 | 4,740 |
| 321 | sdn 2d, V8 | 3,450 | 2,508 | |
| 222 | htp cpe, L6 | 3,320 | 2,461 | 9,591 |
| 322 | htp cpe, V8 | 3,460 | 2,580 | |
| 223 | sdn 4d, L6 | 3,315 | 2,439 | 40,090 |
| 323 | sdn 4d, V8 | 3,470 | 2,559 | |

**RP1/2-H Fury (wb 118.0)**

| | | | | |
|---|---|---|---|---|
| 232 | htp cpe, L6 | 3,330 | 2,599 | 16,141 |
| 332 | htp cpe, V8 | 3,520 | 2,718 | |

| | | Wght | Price | Prod |
|---|---|---|---|---|
| 233 | sdn 4d, L6 | 3,350 | 2,575 | 22,619 |
| 333 | sdn 4d, V8 | 3,515 | 2,694 | |
| 234 | htp sdn, L6 | 3,390 | 2,656 | 8,507 |
| 334 | htp sdn, V8 | 3,555 | 2,775 | |
| 335 | conv cpe, V8 | 3,535 | 2,967 | 6,948 |

### RP1/2 Suburban (wb 122.0)

| | | Wght | Price | Prod |
|---|---|---|---|---|
| 255 | DeLuxe wgn 2d, L6 | 3,675 | 2,602 | 2,464 |
| 355 | DeLuxe wgn 2d, V8 | 3,845 | 2,721 | |
| 256 | DeLuxe wgn 4d, L6 | 3,715 | 2,668 | 12,980 |
| 356 | DeLuxe wgn 4d, V8 | 3,885 | 2,788 | |
| 266 | Custom wgn 4d, L6 | 3,730 | 2,761 | 13,553 |
| 366 | Custom wgn 4d, V8 | 3,885 | 2,880 | |
| 367 | Custom wgn 4d, 9P, V8 | 3,985 | 2,990 | |
| 376 | Sport wgn 4d, 6P, V8 | 3,890 | 3,024 | 2,844 |
| 377 | Sport wgn 4d, 9P, V8 | 3,995 | 3,134 | 3,088 |

| 1961 Engines | bore×stroke | bhp | availability |
|---|---|---|---|
| L6, 170.0 | 3.40×3.13 | 101 | S-Valiant |
| L6, 170.0 | 3.40×3.13 | 148 | O-Valiant only |
| L6, 225.0 | 3.40×4.13 | 145 | S-full-size only |
| V8, 318.0 | 3.91×3.31 | 230 | S-full-size eights (RP2) |
| V8, 318.0 | 3.91×3.31 | 260 | O-full-size with TorqueFlite |
| V8, 361.0 | 4.12×3.38 | 305 | O-full-size exc PowerFlite or air cond |
| V8, 383.0 | 4.25×3.38 | 330 | O-full-size exc PowerFlite or air cond |

## 1962

### SV1-L Valiant V100 (wb 106.5)

| | | Wght | Price | Prod |
|---|---|---|---|---|
| 111 | sdn 2d | 2,480 | 1,930 | 19,679 |
| 113 | sdn 4d | 2,500 | 1,991 | 33,769 |
| 156 | wgn 4d | 2,660 | 2,285 | 5,932 |

### SV1-H Valiant V200 (wb 106.5)

| | | Wght | Price | Prod |
|---|---|---|---|---|
| 131 | sdn 2d | 2,500 | 2,026 | 8,484 |
| 133 | sdn 4d | 2,510 | 2,087 | 55,789 |
| 176 | wgn 4d | 2,690 | 2,381 | 8,055 |

### SV1-P Valiant Signet (wb 106.5)

| | | Wght | Price | Prod |
|---|---|---|---|---|
| 142 | htp cpe | 2,515 | 2,230 | 25,586 |

### SP1/2-L Savoy (wb 115.0)

| | | Wght | Price | Prod |
|---|---|---|---|---|
| 211 | sdn 2d, L6 | 2,930 | 2,206 | 18,825 |
| 311 | sdn 2d, V8 | 3,080 | 2,313 | |
| 213 | sdn 4d, L6 | 2,960 | 2,262 | 49,777 |
| 313 | sdn 4d, V8 | 3,115 | 2,369 | |

### SP1/2-M Belvedere (wb 116.0)

| | | Wght | Price | Prod |
|---|---|---|---|---|
| 221 | sdn 2d, L6 | 2,930 | 2,342 | 3,128 |
| 321 | sdn 2d, V8 | 3,070 | 2,450 | |
| 222 | htp cpe, L6 | 2,945 | 2,431 | 5,086 |
| 322 | htp cpe, V8 | 3,075 | 2,538 | |
| 223 | sdn 4d, L6 | 2,960 | 2,399 | 31,263 |
| 323 | sdn 4d, V8 | 3,095 | 2,507 | |

### SP1/2-H Fury (wb 116.0)

| | | Wght | Price | Prod |
|---|---|---|---|---|
| 232 | htp cpe, L6 | 2,960 | 2,585 | 9,589 |
| 332 | htp cpe, V8 | 3,105 | 2,693 | |
| 233 | sdn 4d, L6 | 2,990 | 2,563 | 17,531 |
| 333 | sdn 4d, V8 | 3,125 | 2,670 | |
| 334 | htp sdn, V8 | 3,190 | 2,742 | 5,995 |
| 335 | conv cpe, V8 | 3,210 | 2,924 | 4,349 |

### SP2-P Sport Fury (wb 116.0)

| | | Wght | Price | Prod |
|---|---|---|---|---|
| 342 | htp cpe, V8 | 3,195 | 2,851 | 4,039 |
| 345 | conv cpe, V8 | 3,295 | 3,082 | 1,516 |

### SP1/2 Suburban (wb 116.0)*

| | | Wght | Price | Prod |
|---|---|---|---|---|
| 256 | Savoy wgn 4d, L6 | 3,225 | 2,609 | 12,710 |
| 356 | Savoy wgn 4d, V8 | 3,390 | 2,717 | |

| | | Wght | Price | Prod |
|---|---|---|---|---|
| 266 | Belvedere wgn 4d, 6P, L6 | 3,245 | 2,708 | 9,781 |
| 366 | Belvedere wgn 4d, 6P, V8 | 3,390 | 2,815 | |
| 367 | Belvedere wgn 4d, 9P, V8 | 3,440 | 2,917 | 4,168 |
| 376 | Fury wgn 4d, 6P, V8 | 3,395 | 2,968 | 2,352 |
| 377 | Fury wgn 4d, 9P, V8 | 3,455 | 3,071 | 2,411 |

*Due to factory numbering in 1962, model names such as "Savoy" were listed as body style names. This practice occurred in 1962 only.

| 1962 Engines | bore×stroke | bhp | availability |
|---|---|---|---|
| L6, 170.0 | 3.40×3.13 | 101 | S-Valiant |
| L6, 225.0 | 3.40×4.13 | 145 | S-SP1; O-Valiant |
| V8, 318.0 | 3.91×3.31 | 230 | S-all SP2 exc Sport Fury |
| V8, 318.0 | 3.91×3.31 | 260 | O-all SP2 exc Sport Fury |
| V8, 361.0 | 4.12×3.38 | 305 | S-Sport Fury; O-other SP2 exc w/PowerFlite or AC |

## 1963

### TV1-L Valiant V100 (wb 106.0)

| | | Wght | Price | Prod |
|---|---|---|---|---|
| 111 | sdn 2d | 2,515 | 1,910 | 32,761 |
| 113 | sdn 4d | 2,535 | 1,973 | 54,617 |
| 156 | wgn 4d | 2,700 | 2,268 | 11,864 |

### TV1-H Valiant V200 (wb 106.0)

| | | Wght | Price | Prod |
|---|---|---|---|---|
| 131 | sdn 2d | 2,515 | 2,035 | 10,605 |
| 133 | sdn 4d | 2,555 | 2,097 | 57,029 |
| 135 | conv cpe | 2,640 | 2,340 | 7,122 |
| 176 | wgn 4d | 2,715 | 2,392 | 11,147 |

### TV1-P Valiant Signet 200 (wb 106.0)

| | | Wght | Price | Prod |
|---|---|---|---|---|
| 142 | htp cpe | 2,570 | 2,230 | 30,857 |
| 145 | conv cpe | 2,675 | 2,454 | 9,154 |

### TP1/2-L Savoy (wb 116.0)

| | | Wght | Price | Prod |
|---|---|---|---|---|
| 211 | sdn 2d, L6 | 2,980 | 2,206 | 20,281 |
| 311 | sdn 2d, V8 | 3,200 | 2,313 | |
| 213 | sdn 4d, L6 | 3,020 | 2,262 | 56,313 |
| 313 | sdn 4d, V8 | 3,220 | 2,369 | |
| 256 | wgn 4d, 6P, L6 | 3,325 | 2,609 | 12,874 |
| 356 | wgn 4d, 6P, V8 | 3,475 | 2,717 | |
| 257 | wgn 4d, 9P, L6 | 3,375 | 2,710 | 4,342 |
| 357 | wgn 4d, 9P, V8 | 3,560 | 2,818 | |

### TP1/2-M Belvedere (wb 116.0)

| | | Wght | Price | Prod |
|---|---|---|---|---|
| 221 | sdn 2d, L6 | 3,000 | 2,342 | 6,218 |
| 321 | sdn 2d, V8 | 3,215 | 2,450 | |
| 222 | htp cpe, L6 | 3,025 | 2,431 | 9,204 |
| 322 | htp cpe, V8 | 3,190 | 2,538 | |
| 223 | sdn 4d, L6 | 3,020 | 2,399 | 54,929 |
| 323 | sdn 4d, V8 | 3,235 | 2,507 | |
| 366 | wgn 4d, 6P, V8 | 3,490 | 2,815 | 10,297 |
| 367 | wgn 4d, 9P, V8 | 3,585 | 2,917 | 4,012 |

### TP1/2-H Fury (wb 116.0)

| | | Wght | Price | Prod |
|---|---|---|---|---|
| 232 | htp cpe, L6 | 3,030 | 2,585 | 13,832 |
| 332 | htp cpe, V8 | 3,215 | 2,693 | |
| 233 | sdn 4d, L6 | 3,075 | 2,563 | 31,891 |
| 333 | sdn 4d, V8 | 3,265 | 2,670 | |
| 334 | htp sdn, V8 | 3,295 | 2,742 | 11,887 |
| 335 | conv cpe, V8 | 3,340 | 2,924 | 5,221 |
| 376 | wgn 4d, 6P, V8 | 3,545 | 2,968 | 3,304 |
| 377 | wgn 4d, 9P, V8 | 3,590 | 3,071 | 3,368 |

### TP2-P Sport Fury (wb 116.0)

| | | Wght | Price | Prod |
|---|---|---|---|---|
| 342 | htp cpe, V8 | 3,235 | 2,851 | 11,483 |
| 345 | conv cpe, V8 | 3,385 | 3,082 | 3,836 |

| 1963 Engines | bore×stroke | bhp | availability |
|---|---|---|---|
| L6, 170.0 | 3.40×3.13 | 101 | S-Valiant |
| L6, 225.0 | 3.40×4.13 | 145 | S-all TP1; O-Valiant |
| V8, 318.0 | 3.91×3.31 | 230 | S-all TP2 |
| V8, 361.0 | 4.12×3.38 | 265 | O-all TP2 |
| V8, 383.0 | 4.25×3.38 | 330 | O-all TP2 |

# Plymouth

## 1964

| VV1-L Valiant V100 (wb 106.0) | | Wght | Price | Prod |
|---|---|---|---|---|
| 111 | sdn 2d | 2,540 | 1,921 | 35,403 |
| 113 | sdn 4d | 2,575 | 1,992 | 44,208 |
| 156 | wgn 4d | 2,725 | 2,273 | 10,759 |

| VV1-H Valiant V200 (wb 106.0) | | | | |
|---|---|---|---|---|
| 131 | sdn 2d | 2,545 | 2,044 | 11,013 |
| 133 | sdn 4d | 2,570 | 2,112 | 63,828 |
| 135 | conv cpe | 2,670 | 2,349 | 5,856 |
| 176 | wgn 4d | 2,730 | 2,388 | 11,146 |

| VV1-P Valiant Signet 200 (wb 106.0) | | | | |
|---|---|---|---|---|
| 142 | htp cpe | 2,600 | 2,256 | 37,736 |
| 145 | conv cpe | 2,690 | 2,473 | 7,636 |
| 149 | Barracuda htp cpe | 2,740 | 2,365 | 23,443 |

| VP1/2-L Savoy (wb 116.0) | | | | |
|---|---|---|---|---|
| 211 | sdn 2d, L6 | 2,990 | 2,224 | 21,326 |
| 311 | sdn 2d, V8 | 3,205 | 2,332 | |
| 213 | sdn 4d, L6 | 3,040 | 2,280 | 51,024 |
| 313 | sdn 4d, V8 | 3,210 | 2,388 | |
| 256 | wgn 4d, 6P, L6 | 3,345 | 2,620 | 12,401 |
| 356 | wgn 4d, 6P, V8 | 3,495 | 2,728 | |
| 257 | wgn 4d, 9P, L6 | 3,400 | 2,721 | 3,242 |
| 357 | wgn 4d, 9P, V8 | 3,600 | 2,829 | |

| VP1/2-M Belvedere (wb 116.0) | | | | |
|---|---|---|---|---|
| 221 | sdn 2d, L6 | 3,000 | 2,359 | 5,364 |
| 321 | sdn 2d, V8 | 3,210 | 2,466 | |
| 222 | htp cpe, L6 | 3,010 | 2,444 | 16,334 |
| 322 | htp cpe, V8 | 3,190 | 2,551 | |
| 223 | sdn 4d, L6 | 3,065 | 2,417 | 57,307 |
| 323 | sdn 4d, V8 | 3,225 | 2,524 | |
| 366 | wgn 4d, 6P, V8 | 3,510 | 2,826 | 10,317 |
| 367 | wgn 4d, 9P, V8 | 3,605 | 2,928 | 42,107 |

| VP1/2-H Fury (wb 116.0) | | | | |
|---|---|---|---|---|
| 232 | htp cpe, L6 | 3,040 | 2,598 | 36,303 |
| 332 | htp cpe, V8 | 3,212 | 2,706 | |
| 233 | sdn 4d, L6 | 3,045 | 2,573 | 34,901 |
| 333 | sdn 4d, V8 | 3,230 | 2,680 | |
| 334 | htp sdn, V8 | 3,300 | 2,752 | 13,713 |
| 335 | conv cpe, V8 | 3,345 | 2,937 | 5,173 |
| 376 | wgn 4d, 6P, V8 | 3,530 | 2,981 | 3,646 |
| 377 | wgn 4d, 9P, V8 | 3,630 | 3,084 | 4,482 |

| VP2-P Sport Fury (wb 116.0) | | | | |
|---|---|---|---|---|
| 342 | htp cpe, V8 | 3,270 | 2,864 | 23,695 |
| 345 | conv cpe, V8 | 3,405 | 3,095 | 3,858 |

| 1964 Engines | bore×stroke | bhp | availability |
|---|---|---|---|
| L6, 170.0 | 3.40×3.13 | 101 | S-Valiant |
| L6, 225.0 | 3.40×4.13 | 145 | S-VP1; O-Valiant |
| V8, 273.0 | 3.62×3.31 | 180 | O-Valiant |
| V8, 318.0 | 3.91×3.31 | 230 | S-all VP2 |
| V8, 361.0 | 4.12×3.38 | 265 | O-all exc Valiant |
| V8, 383.0 | 4.25×3.38 | 330 | O-all exc Valiant |
| V8, 426.0 | 4.25×3.75 | 365 | O-all exc Valiant |

## 1965

| AV1-L Valiant 100 (wb 106.0)* | | Wght | Price | Prod |
|---|---|---|---|---|
| V11 | sdn 2d | 2,560 | 2,004 | 40,434 |
| V13 | sdn 4d | 2,590 | 2,075 | 42,857 |
| V56 | wgn 4d | 2,750 | 2,361 | 10,822 |

| AV1-H Valiant 200 (wb 106.0)* | | | | |
|---|---|---|---|---|
| V31 | sdn 2d | 2,570 | 2,127 | 8,919 |
| V33 | sdn 4d | 2,605 | 2,195 | 41,642 |

| | | Wght | Price | Prod |
|---|---|---|---|---|
| V35 | conv cpe | 2,695 | 2,437 | 2,769 |
| V78 | wgn 4d | 2,755 | 2,476 | 6,133 |

| AV-1P Valiant Signet (wb 106.0)* | | | | |
|---|---|---|---|---|
| V42 | htp cpe | 2,620 | 2,340 | 10,999 |
| V45 | conv cpe | 2,725 | 2,561 | 2,578 |

| AV1-P Barracuda (wb 106.0)* | | | | |
|---|---|---|---|---|
| V89 | htp cpe | 2,725 | 2,487 | 64,596 |

| Belvedere I (wb 116.0; SS-115.0) | | | | |
|---|---|---|---|---|
| R01 | Super Stock htp cpe | 3,170 | 4,671 | — |
| R11 | sdn 2d | 3,088 | 2,226 | 12,536 |
| R13 | sdn 4d | 3,153 | 2,265 | 35,968 |
| R56 | wgn 4d | 3,423 | 2,562 | 8,338 |

| Belvedere II (wb 116.0) | | | | |
|---|---|---|---|---|
| R32 | htp cpe | 3,123 | 2,378 | 24,924 |
| R33 | sdn 4d | 3,128 | 2,352 | 41,445 |
| R35 | conv cpe | 3,230 | 2,597 | 1,921 |
| R76 | wgn 4d, 6P | 3,425 | 2,649 | 5,908 |
| R77 | wgn 4d, 9P | 3,488 | 2,747 | 3,294 |

| Satellite (wb 116.0) | | | | |
|---|---|---|---|---|
| R42 | htp cpe | 3,220 | 2,649 | 23,341 |
| R45 | conv cpe | 3,325 | 2,869 | 1,860 |

| Fury I (wb 119.0; wgns-121.0) | | | | |
|---|---|---|---|---|
| P11 | sdn 2d | 3,518 | 2,376 | 17,294 |
| P13 | sdn 4d | 3,573 | 2,430 | 48,575 |
| P56 | wgn 4d | 4,030 | 2,776 | 13,360 |

| Fury II (wb 119.0; wgn-121.0) | | | | |
|---|---|---|---|---|
| P21 | sdn 2d | 3,525 | 2,478 | 4,109 |
| P23 | sdn 4d | 3,573 | 2,532 | 43,350 |
| P66 | wgn 4d, 6P | 4,135 | 2,948 | 12,853 |
| P67 | wgn 4d, 9P | 4,160 | 3,051 | 6,445 |

| Fury III (wb 119.0; wgns-121.0) | | | | |
|---|---|---|---|---|
| P32 | htp cpe | 3,563 | 2,691 | 43,251 |
| P33 | sdn 4d | 3,595 | 2,684 | 50,725 |
| P34 | htp sdn | 3,690 | 2,863 | 21,367 |
| P35 | conv cpe | 3,710 | 3,048 | 5,524 |
| P76 | wgn 4d, 6P | 4,140 | 3,090 | 8,931 |
| P77 | wgn 4d, 9P | 4,200 | 3,193 | 9,546 |

| Sport Fury (wb 119.0) | | | | |
|---|---|---|---|---|
| P42 | htp cpe | 3,715 | 2,960 | 38,348 |
| P45 | conv cpe | 3,755 | 3,209 | 6,272 |

*Factory quoted only V8 Valiant prices this year, which are given along with V8 weights. For sixes, deduct approximately $128.

| 1965 Engines | bore×stroke | bhp | availability |
|---|---|---|---|
| L6, 170.0 | 3.40×3.13 | 101 | S-Valiant |
| L6, 225.0 | 3.40×4.13 | 145 | S-Barracuda, Furys, Belv; O-Valiant |
| V8, 273.0 | 3.62×3.31 | 180 | S-Satellite; O-Valiant, Barracuda, Belvedere |
| V8, 273.0 | 3.62×3.31 | 235 | O-Valiant, Barracuda |
| V8, 318.0 | 3.91×3.31 | 230 | S-Furys; O-Belvedere, Satellite |
| V8, 361.0 | 4.12×3.38 | 265 | O-Belvedere, Satellite |
| V8, 383.0 | 4.25×3.38 | 270 | O-Belv, Satellite, Furys |
| V8, 383.0 | 4.25×3.38 | 330 | O-Belv, Satellite, Furys |
| V8, 426.0 | 4.25×3.75 | 365 | S-Belv I SS; O-Belvedere, Satellite, Furys |
| V8, 426.0 | 4.25×3.75 | 425 | O-Belvedere I Super Stock |

## 1966

| BV1/2-L Valiant 100 (wb 106.0) | | Wght | Price | Prod |
|---|---|---|---|---|
| 21 | sdn 2d | 2,700 | 2,025 | 35,787 |

| | | Wght | Price | Prod |
|---|---|---|---|---|
| 41 | sdn 4d | 2,725 | 2,095 | 36,031 |
| 45 | wgn 4d | 2,648 | 2,387 | 6,838 |

**BV1/2-H Valiant 200 (wb 106.0)**

| | | | | |
|---|---|---|---|---|
| 41 | sdn 4d | 2,728 | 2,226 | 39,392 |
| 45 | wgn 4d | 2,883 | 2,502 | 4,537 |

**BV1/2-H Valiant Signet (wb 106.0)**

| | | | | |
|---|---|---|---|---|
| 23 | htp cpe | 2,735 | 2,261 | 13,045 |
| 27 | conv cpe | 2,830 | 2,527 | 2,507 |

**BV1/2-P Barracuda (wb 106.0)**

| | | | | |
|---|---|---|---|---|
| 29 | htp cpe | 2,865 | 2,556 | 38,029 |

**BR1/2-L Belvedere I (wb 116.0; wgn-117.0)**

| | | | | |
|---|---|---|---|---|
| 21 | sdn 2d | 3,095 | 2,277 | 9,381 |
| 41 | sdn 4d | 3,125 | 2,315 | 31,063 |
| 45 | wgn 4d | 3,523 | 2,605 | 8,200 |

**BR1/2-H Belvedere II (wb 116.0; wgn-117.0)**

| | | | | |
|---|---|---|---|---|
| 23 | htp cpe | 3,123 | 2,430 | 36,644 |
| 27 | conv cpe | 3,200 | 2,644 | 2,502 |
| 41 | sdn 4d | 3,115 | 2,405 | 49,941 |
| 45 | wgn 4d, 6P | 3,525 | 2,695 | 8,667 |
| 46 | wgn 4d, 9P | 3,618 | 2,804 | 4,726 |

**BR2-P Satellite (wb 116.0)**

| | | | | |
|---|---|---|---|---|
| 23 | htp cpe | 3,255 | 2,695 | 35,399 |
| 27 | conv cpe | 3,320 | 2,910 | 2,759 |

**BP1/2-L Fury I (wb 119.0; wgn-121.0)**

| | | | | |
|---|---|---|---|---|
| 21 | sdn 2d | 3,518 | 2,426 | 12,538 |
| 41 | sdn 4d | 3,570 | 2,479 | 39,698 |
| 45 | wgn 4d | 4,048 | 2,836 | 9,690 |

**BP1/2-M Fury II (wb 119.0; wgn-121.0)**

| | | | | |
|---|---|---|---|---|
| 21 | sdn 2d | 3,530 | 2,526 | 2,503 |
| 41 | sdn 4d | 3,573 | 2,579 | 55,016 |
| 45 | wgn 4d, 6P | 4,145 | 2,986 | 10,718 |
| 46 | wgn 4d, 9P | 4,175 | 3,087 | 5,580 |

**BP1/2-H Fury III (wb 119.0; wgn-121.0)**

| | | | | |
|---|---|---|---|---|
| 23 | htp cpe | 3,578 | 2,724 | 41,869 |
| 27 | conv cpe | 3,720 | 3,074 | 4,326 |
| 41 | sdn 4d | 3,217 | 2,718 | 46,505 |
| 43 | htp sdn | 3,730 | 2,893 | 33,922 |
| 45 | wgn 4d, 6P | 4,155 | 3,115 | 9,239 |
| 46 | wgn 4d, 9P | 4,165 | 3,216 | 10,886 |

**BP2-P Sport Fury (wb 119.0)**

| | | | | |
|---|---|---|---|---|
| 23 | htp cpe | 3,730 | 3,006 | 32,523 |
| 27 | conv cpe | 3,755 | 3,251 | 3,418 |

**VP2-H VIP (wb 119.0)***

| | | | | |
|---|---|---|---|---|
| 23 | htp cpe | 3,700 | 3,069 | — |
| 43 | htp sdn | 3,780 | 3,133 | — |

*Included with Fury III.

| 1966 Engines | bore×stroke | bhp | availability |
|---|---|---|---|
| L6, 170.0 | 3.40×3.13 | 101 | S-Valiant |
| L6, 225.0 | 3.40×4.13 | 145 | S-Brcda, Belv exc Satellite, Fury sdns/wgns, Fury III 43; O-Val |
| V8, 273.0 | 3.62×3.31 | 180 | S-Sat; O-Belv, Brcda, Val |
| V8, 273.0 | 3.62×3.31 | 235 | O-Brcda, Valiant exc wgns |
| V8, 318.0 | 3.91×3.31 | 230 | S-VIP, Spt Fury, Fury II wgns, Fury III conv/htp/wgn; O-Fury, Belv |
| V8, 361.0 | 4.12×3.38 | 265 | O-Belvedere, Satellite |
| V8, 383.0 | 4.25×3.38 | 325 | O-VIP, Furys, Belv, Sat |
| V8, 426.0 | 4.25×3.75 | 425 | O-Belv, Sat exc wgns |
| V8, 440.0 | 4.32×3.75 | 365 | O-VIP, Furys |

## 1967

**CV1/2-L Valiant 100 (wb 108.0)**

| | | Wght | Price | Prod |
|---|---|---|---|---|
| 21 | sdn 2d | 2,738 | 2,117 | 29,093 |
| 41 | sdn 4d | 2,753 | 2,163 | 46,638 |

**CV1/2-H Valiant Signet (wb 108.0)**

| | | | | |
|---|---|---|---|---|
| 21 | sdn 2d | 2,765 | 2,262 | 6,843 |
| 41 | sdn 4d | 2,750 | 2,308 | 26,395 |

**CV1/2-P Barracuda (wb 108.0)**

| | | | | |
|---|---|---|---|---|
| 23 | htp cpe | 2,793 | 2,449 | 28,196 |
| 27 | conv cpe | 2,903 | 2,779 | 4,228 |
| 29 | fstbk cpe | 2,878 | 2,639 | 30,110 |

**CR1/2-E Belvedere (wb 117.0)**

| | | | | |
|---|---|---|---|---|
| 45 | wgn 4d | 3,543 | 2,579 | 5,477 |

**CR1/2-L Belvedere I (wb 116.0; wgn-117.0)**

| | | | | |
|---|---|---|---|---|
| 21 | sdn 2d | 3,095 | 2,318 | 4,718 |
| 41 | sdn 4d | 3,125 | 2,356 | 13,988 |
| 45 | wgn 4d | 3,553 | 2,652 | 3,172 |

**CR1/2-H Belvedere II (wb 116.0; wgn-117.0)**

| | | | | |
|---|---|---|---|---|
| 23 | htp cpe | 3,130 | 2,457 | 34,550 |
| 27 | conv cpe | 3,205 | 2,695 | 1,552 |
| 41 | sdn 4d | 3,118 | 2,434 | 42,694 |
| 45 | wgn 4d, 6P | 3,553 | 2,729 | 5,583 |
| 46 | wgn 4d, 9P | 3,595 | 2,836 | 3,968 |

**CR2-P Satellite (wb 116.0)**

| | | | | |
|---|---|---|---|---|
| 23 | htp cpe | 3,265 | 2,747 | 30,328 |
| 27 | conv cpe | 3,335 | 2,986 | 2,050 |

**CR2-P Belvedere GRX (wb 116.0)***

| | | | | |
|---|---|---|---|---|
| 23 | htp cpe | 3,545 | 3,178 | — |
| 27 | conv cpe | 3,615 | 3,418 | — |

**CP1/2-E Fury I (wb 119.0; wgn-122.0)**

| | | | | |
|---|---|---|---|---|
| 21 | sdn 2d | 3,493 | 2,473 | 6,647 |
| 41 | sdn 4d | 3,533 | 2,517 | 29,354 |
| 45 | wgn 4d | 4,000 | 2,884 | 6,067 |

**CP1/2-L Fury II (wb 119.0; wgn-122.0)**

| | | | | |
|---|---|---|---|---|
| 21 | sdn 2d | 3,490 | 2,571 | 2,783 |
| 41 | sdn 4d | 3,526 | 2,614 | 45,673 |
| 45 | wgn 4d, 6P | 4,045 | 3,021 | 10,736 |
| 40 | wgn 4d, 9P | 4,110 | 3,122 | 5,649 |

**CP1/2-M Fury III (wb 119.0; wgn-122.0)**

| | | | | |
|---|---|---|---|---|
| 23 | htp cpe | 3,535 | 2,872 | 37,448 |
| 27 | conv cpe | 3,670 | 3,118 | 4,523 |
| 41 | sdn 4d | 3,555 | 2,746 | 52,690 |
| 43 | htp sdn | 3,650 | 2,922 | 43,614 |
| 45 | wgn 4d, 6P | 4,080 | 3,144 | 9,270 |
| 46 | wgn 4d, 9P | 4,135 | 3,245 | 12,533 |

**CP2-H Sport Fury (wb 119.0)**

| | | | | |
|---|---|---|---|---|
| 23 | htp cpe | 3,630 | 3,033 | 28,448 |
| 23 | fstbk htp cpe | 3,705 | 3,062 | |
| 27 | conv cpe | 3,645 | 3,279 | 3,133 |

**CP2-P VIP (wb 119.0)**

| | | | | |
|---|---|---|---|---|
| 23 | htp cpe | 3,705 | 3,182 | 7,912 |
| 43 | htp sdn | 3,660 | 3,117 | 10,830 |

*Included with Satellite.

| 1967 Engines | bore×stroke | bhp | availability |
|---|---|---|---|
| L6, 170.0 | 3.40×3.13 | 115 | S-Valiant |
| L6, 225.0 | 3.40×4.13 | 145 | S-CR2 exc Sat/GTX, Fury sdns, Fury I wgn, Fury III htp, Brcda; O-Val |
| V8, 273.0 | 3.62×3.31 | 180 | S-CR2 exc GTX, Brcda, Val |
| V8, 273.0 | 3.62×3.31 | 235 | O-Valiant, Barracuda |

# Plymouth

| | bore×stroke | bhp | availability |
|---|---|---|---|
| V8, 318.0 | 3.91×3.31 | 230 | S-Furys; O-Belv exc GTX |
| V8, 383.0 | 4.25×3.38 | 270 | O-Furys; Belv exc GTX |
| V8, 383.0 | 4.25×3.38 | 280 | O-Barracuda |
| V8, 383.0 | 4.25×3.38 | 325 | O-Brcda, Furys, Belv exc GTX |
| V8, 426.0 | 4.25×3.75 | 425 | O-Belvedere GTX |
| V8, 440.0 | 4.32×3.75 | 350 | O-Fury wgns |
| V8, 440.0 | 4.32×3.75 | 375 | S-GTX; O-Furys exc wgns |

## 1968

### VL Valiant 100 (wb 108.0)*

| | | Wght | Price | Prod |
|---|---|---|---|---|
| 21 | sdn 2d | 2,733 | 2,254 | 31,178 |
| 41 | sdn 4d | 2,763 | 2,301 | 49,446 |

### VH Valiant Signet (wb 108.0)

| | | | | |
|---|---|---|---|---|
| 21 | sdn 2d | 2,745 | 2,400 | 6,265 |
| 41 | sdn 4d | 2,768 | 2,447 | 23,906 |

### VH Barracuda (wb 108.0)

| | | | | |
|---|---|---|---|---|
| 23 | htp cpe | 2,810 | 2,605 | 19,997 |
| 27 | conv cpe | 2,923 | 2,907 | 2,840 |
| 29 | fstbk cpe | 2,895 | 2,762 | 22,575 |

### RL Belvedere (wb 116.0; wgn-117.0)

| | | | | |
|---|---|---|---|---|
| 21 | cpe | 3,050 | 2,444 | 15,702 |
| 41 | sdn 4d | 3,080 | 2,483 | 17,214 |
| 45 | wgn 4d | 3,553 | 2,773 | 8,982 |

### RH Satellite (wb 116.0; wgn-117.0)

| | | | | |
|---|---|---|---|---|
| 23 | htp cpe | 3,070 | 2,594 | 46,539 |
| 27 | conv cpe | 3,188 | 2,824 | 1,771 |
| 41 | sdn 4d | 3,080 | 2,572 | 42,309 |
| 45 | wgn 4d, 6P | 3,605 | 2,891 | 12,097 |
| 46 | wgn 4d, 9P | 3,625 | 2,998 | 10,883 |

### RP Sport Satellite (wb 116.0; wgn-117.0)

| | | | | |
|---|---|---|---|---|
| 23 | htp cpe | 3,155 | 2,822 | 21,014 |
| 27 | conv cpe | 3,285 | 3,036 | 1,523 |
| 45 | wgn 4d, 6P | 3,610 | 3,131 | ** |
| 46 | wgn 4d, 9P | 3,685 | 3,239 | ** |

### RM Road Runner (wb 116.0)

| | | | | |
|---|---|---|---|---|
| 21 | cpe | 3,440 | 2,896 | 29,240 |
| 23 | htp cpe | 3,455 | 3,034 | 15,359 |

### RS GTX (wb 116.0)

| | | | | |
|---|---|---|---|---|
| 23 | htp cpe | 3,470 | 3,355 | 17,914 |
| 27 | conv cpe | 3,595 | 3,590 | 1,026 |

### PE Fury I (wb 119.0)

| | | | | |
|---|---|---|---|---|
| 21 | sdn 2d | 3,480 | 2,617 | 5,788 |
| 41 | sdn 4d | 3,653 | 2,660 | 23,208 |

### PL Fury II (wb 119.0)

| | | | | |
|---|---|---|---|---|
| 21 | sdn 2d | 3,488 | 2,715 | 3,112 |
| 41 | sdn 4d | 3,533 | 2,757 | 49,423 |

### PM Fury III (wb 119.0)

| | | | | |
|---|---|---|---|---|
| 23 | htp cpe | 3,538 | 2,912 | 60,472 |
| 23 | fstbk htp cpe "PX" | 3,528 | 2,932 | |
| 27 | conv cpe | 3,680 | 3,236 | 4,483 |
| 41 | sdn 4d | 3,545 | 2,890 | 57,899 |
| 43 | htp sdn | 3,635 | 3,067 | 45,147 |

### PH Sport Fury (wb 119.0)

| | | | | |
|---|---|---|---|---|
| 23 | htp cpe | 3,620 | 3,206 | 6,642 |
| 23 | fstbk htp cpe "PS" | 3,615 | 3,225 | 17,073 |
| 27 | conv cpe | 3,710 | 3,425 | 2,489 |

### PP VIP (wb 119.0)

| | | | | |
|---|---|---|---|---|
| 23 | fstbk htp cpe | 3,615 | 3,260 | 6,768 |
| 43 | htp sdn | 3,655 | 3,326 | 10,745 |

### DP Suburban (wb 122.0)

| | | Wght | Price | Prod |
|---|---|---|---|---|
| 45 | wgn 4d | 3,990 | 3,048 | 6,749 |
| 45 | Custom wgn 4d, 6P | 4,045 | 3,252 | 17,078 |
| 46 | Custom wgn 4d, 9P | 4,090 | 3,353 | 9,954 |
| 45 | Sport wgn 4d, 6P | 4,055 | 3,442 | 9,203 |
| 46 | Sport wgn 4d, 9P | 4,100 | 3,543 | 13,224 |

*Includes "Valiant 200" trim option.
**Sport Satellite wagon included with Satellite wagon.

### 1968 Engines

| | bore×stroke | bhp | availability |
|---|---|---|---|
| L6, 170.0 | 3.40×3.13 | 115 | S-Valiant |
| L6, 225.0 | 3.40×4.13 | 145 | S-Brcda, Belv, Sat, FI/II, FIII sdn, htps, Suburban; O-Val |
| V8, 273.0 | 3.62×3.31 | 190 | O-Val, Belv, Sat, Spt Sat wgn |
| V8, 318.0 | 3.91×3.31 | 230 | S-Spt Sat, Fury III; O-Val, Brcda, Belv, Sat, Spt Sat wgn |
| V8, 340.0 | 4.04×3.31 | 275 | S-Barracuda Formula S |
| V8, 383.0 | 4.25×3.38 | 290 | O-Belv, Sat, Spt Sat, Furys |
| V8, 383.0 | 4.25×3.38 | 300 | O-Barracuda Formula S |
| V8, 383.0 | 4.25×3.38 | 330 | O-Belv, Satellite, Furys, Suburbans |
| V8, 383.0 | 4.25×3.38 | 335 | S-Road Runner |
| V8, 426.0 | 4.25×3.75 | 425 | O-Road Runner, GTX |
| V8, 440.0 | 4.32×3.75 | 375 | S-GTX; O-Fury exc DP |
| V8, 440.0 | 4.32×3.75 | 350 | O-Suburban |

## 1969

### VL Valiant 100 (wb 108.0)*

| | | Wght | Price | Prod |
|---|---|---|---|---|
| 21 | sdn 2d | 2,740 | 2,094 | 29,672 |
| 41 | sdn 4d | 2,760 | 2,154 | 49,409 |

### VH Valiant Signet (wb 108.0)

| | | | | |
|---|---|---|---|---|
| 21 | sdn 2d | 2,740 | 2,253 | 6,645 |
| 41 | sdn 4d | 2,760 | 2,313 | 21,492 |

### VH Barracuda (wb 108.0)

| | | | | |
|---|---|---|---|---|
| 23 | htp cpe | 2,815 | 2,780 | 12,757 |
| 27 | conv cpe | 2,940 | 3,082 | 1,442 |
| 29 | fstbk htp cpe | 2,902 | 2,813 | 17,788 |

### RL Belvedere (wb 116.0; wgn-117.0)

| | | | | |
|---|---|---|---|---|
| 21 | cpe | 3,052 | 2,509 | 7,063 |
| 41 | sdn rd | 3,082 | 2,548 | 12,914 |
| 45 | wgn 4d | 3,540 | 2,879 | 7,038 |

### RH Satellite (wb 116.0; wgn-117.0)

| | | | | |
|---|---|---|---|---|
| 23 | htp cpe | 3,080 | 2,659 | 38,323 |
| 27 | conv cpe | 3,200 | 2,875 | 1,137 |
| 41 | sdn 4d | 3,087 | 2,635 | 35,296 |
| 45 | wgn 4d, 6P | 3,540 | 2,997 | 5,837 |
| 46 | wgn 4d, 9P | 3,612 | 3,106 | 4,730 |

### RP Sport Satellite (wb 116.0; wgn-117.0)

| | | | | |
|---|---|---|---|---|
| 23 | htp cpe | 3,156 | 2,883 | 15,807 |
| 27 | conv cpe | 3,276 | 3,081 | 818 |
| 41 | sdn 4d | 3,196 | 2,911 | 5,836 |
| 45 | wgn 4d, 6P | 3,596 | 3,241 | 3,221 |
| 45 | wgn 4d, 9P | 3,666 | 3,350 | 3,152 |

### RM Road Runner (wb 116.0)

| | | | | |
|---|---|---|---|---|
| 21 | cpe | 3,435 | 2,945 | 33,743 |
| 23 | htp cpe | 3,450 | 3,083 | 48,549 |
| 27 | conv cpe | 3,790 | 3,313 | 2,128 |

### RS GTX (wb 116.0)

| | | | | |
|---|---|---|---|---|
| 23 | htp cpe | 3,465 | 3,416 | 14,902 |
| 27 | conv cpe | 3,590 | 3,635 | 700 |

### PE Fury I (wb 120.0)

| | | | | |
|---|---|---|---|---|
| 21 | sdn 2d | 3,501 | 2,701 | 4,971 |
| 41 | sdn 4d | 3,533 | 2,744 | 18,771 |

| PL Fury II (wb 120.0) | | Wght | Price | Prod |
|---|---|---|---|---|
| 21 | sdn 2d | 3,506 | 2,813 | 3,268 |
| 41 | sdn 4d | 3,536 | 2,841 | 41,047 |

| PM Fury III (wb 120.0) | | Wght | Price | Prod |
|---|---|---|---|---|
| 23 | htp cpe | 3,516 | 3,000 | 44,168 |
| 27 | conv cpe | 3,704 | 3,324 | 4,129 |
| 29 | form htp cpe | 3,601 | 3,020 | 22,738 |
| 41 | sdn 4d | 3,541 | 2,979 | 72,747 |
| 43 | htp sdn | 3,643 | 3,155 | 68,818 |

| PH Sport Fury (wb 120.0) | | Wght | Price | Prod |
|---|---|---|---|---|
| 23 | htp cpe | 3,603 | 3,283 | 14,120 |
| 27 | conv cpe | 3,729 | 3,502 | 1,579 |
| 29 | form htp cpe | 3,678 | 3,303 | 2,169 |

| PP VIP (wb 120.0) | | Wght | Price | Prod |
|---|---|---|---|---|
| 23 | htp cpe | 3,583 | 3,002 | 4,740 |
| 29 | form htp cpe | 3,668 | 3,382 | 1,059 |
| 43 | htp sdn | 3,663 | 3,433 | 7,982 |

| EP Suburban (wb 122.0) | | Wght | Price | Prod |
|---|---|---|---|---|
| 45 | wgn 4d | 4,056 | 3,231 | 6,424 |
| 45 | Custom wgn 4d, 6P | 4,103 | 3,436 | 15,976 |
| 46 | Custom wgn 4d, 9P | 4,148 | 3,527 | 10,216 |
| 45 | Sport wgn 4d, 6P | 4,123 | 3,651 | 8,201 |
| 46 | Sport wgn 4d, 9P | 4,173 | 3,718 | 13,502 |

*Includes "Valiant 200" trim option.

| 1969 Engines | bore×stroke | bhp | availability |
|---|---|---|---|
| L6, 170.0 | 3.40×3.13 | 115 | S-Valiant |
| L6, 225.0 | 3.40×4.13 | 145 | S-Brcda, Belv, Sat, Fury I/II; O-Valiant |
| V8, 273.0 | 3.62×3.31 | 190 | O-Valiant |
| V8, 318.0 | 3.91×3.31 | 230 | S-Spt Sat, Fury III, Spt Fury, VIP, Suburban |
| V8, 340.0 | 4.04×3.31 | 275 | O-Barracuda |
| V8, 383.0 | 4.25×3.38 | 290 | O-Belv, Sat, Spt Sat, Furys, VIP |
| V8, 383.0 | 4.25×3.38 | 330 | O-Brcda, Belv, Sat, Spt Sat, Furys, VIP |
| V8, 383.0 | 4.25×3.38 | 335 | S-Road Runner |
| V8, 426.0 | 4.25×3.75 | 425 | O-Road Runner, GTX |
| V8, 440.0 | 4.32×3.75 | 375 | S-GTX; O-Furys exc EP |
| V8, 440.0 | 4.32×3.75 | 350 | O-Suburban |

## 1970

| VL Valiant (wb 108.0) | | Wght | Price | Prod |
|---|---|---|---|---|
| 29 | Duster htp cpe | 2,830 | 2,172 | 192,375 |
| 41 | sdn 4d | 2,835 | 2,250 | 50,810 |

| VS Valiant Duster 340 (wb 108.0) | | Wght | Price | Prod |
|---|---|---|---|---|
| 29 | htp cpe | 3,110 | 2,547 | 24,817 |

| BH Barracuda (wb 108.0) | | Wght | Price | Prod |
|---|---|---|---|---|
| 23 | htp cpe | 2,905 | 2,764 | 25,651 |
| 27 | conv cpe | 3,071 | 3,034 | 1,554 |

| BP Barracuda Gran Coupe (wb 108.0) | | Wght | Price | Prod |
|---|---|---|---|---|
| 23 | htp cpe | 3,015 | 2,934 | 8,183 |
| 27 | conv cpe | 3,090 | 3,160 | 596 |

| BS 'Cuda (wb 108.0) | | Wght | Price | Prod |
|---|---|---|---|---|
| 23 | htp cpe | 3,395 | 3,164 | 18,180 |
| 27 | conv cpe | 3,480 | 3,433 | 635 |

| RL Belvedere (wb 116.0; wgn-117.0) | | Wght | Price | Prod |
|---|---|---|---|---|
| 21 | cpe | 3,095 | 2,603 | 4,717 |
| 41 | sdn 4d | 3,130 | 2,641 | 13,945 |
| 45 | wgn 4d | 3,655 | 3,075 | 5,584 |

| RH Satellite (wb 116.0; wgn-117.0) | | Wght | Price | Prod |
|---|---|---|---|---|
| 23 | htp cpe | 3,105 | 2,765 | 28,200 |
| 27 | conv cpe | 3,225 | 3,006 | 701 |
| 41 | sdn 4d | 3,125 | 2,741 | 30,377 |
| 45 | wgn 4d, 6P | 3,637 | 3,101 | 4,204 |
| 46 | wgn 4d, 9P | 3,747 | 3,211 | 3,277 |

| RP Sport Satellite (wb 116.0; wgn-117.0) | | Wght | Price | Prod |
|---|---|---|---|---|
| 23 | htp cpe | 3,170 | 2,988 | 8,749 |
| 41 | sdn 4d | 3,205 | 3,017 | 3,010 |
| 45 | wgn 4d, 6P | 3,675 | 3,345 | 1,975 |
| 46 | wgn 4d, 9P | 3,750 | 3,455 | 2,161 |

| RM Road Runner (wb 116.0) | | Wght | Price | Prod |
|---|---|---|---|---|
| 21 | cpo | 3,450 | 2,896 | 15,716 |
| 23 | htp cpe | 3,475 | 3,034 | 24,944 |
| 23 | Superbird htp cpe | 3,785 | 4,298 | 1,920 |
| 27 | conv cpe | 3,550 | 3,289 | 824 |

| RS GTX (wb 116.0) | | Wght | Price | Prod |
|---|---|---|---|---|
| 23 | htp cpe | 3,515 | 3,535 | 7,748 |

| PE Fury I (wb 120.0) | | Wght | Price | Prod |
|---|---|---|---|---|
| 21 | sdn 2d | 3,603 | 2,790 | 2,353 |
| 41 | sdn 4d | 3,640 | 2,825 | 14,813 |

| PL Fury II (wb 120.0) | | Wght | Price | Prod |
|---|---|---|---|---|
| 21 | sdn 2d | 3,583 | 2,903 | 21,316 |
| 41 | sdn 4d | 3,643 | 2,922 | 27,694 |

| PM Fury III (wb 120.0) | | Wght | Price | Prod |
|---|---|---|---|---|
| 23 | htp cpe | 3,610 | 3,091 | 21,373 |
| 27 | conv cpe | 3,770 | 3,415 | 1,952 |
| 29 | form htp cpe | 3,645 | 3,333 | 12,367 |
| 41 | sdn 4d | 3,645 | 3,069 | 50,876 |

| PH Sport Fury (wb 120.0) | | Wght | Price | Prod |
|---|---|---|---|---|
| 23 | htp cpe | 3,630 | 3,313 | |
| 23 | S/23 htp cpe "PS" | 3,660 | 3,379 | 8,018 |
| 23 | GT htp cpe "PP" | 3,925 | 3,898 | |
| 29 | form htp cpe | 3,645 | 3,333 | 5,688 |
| 41 | sdn 4d | 3,680 | 3,291 | 5,135 |
| 43 | htp sdn | 3,705 | 3,363 | 6,854 |

| PL Fury Gran Coupe (wb 120.0) | | Wght | Price | Prod |
|---|---|---|---|---|
| 21 | cpe | 3,864 | 3,833 | * |

| FP Suburban (wb 122.0) | | Wght | Price | Prod |
|---|---|---|---|---|
| 45 | wgn 4d, 6P | 4,125 | 3,303 | 5,300 |
| 46 | wgn 4d, 9P | 4,205 | 3,518 | 2,250 |
| 45 | Custom wgn 4d, 6P | 4,155 | 3,527 | 8,898 |
| 46 | Custom wgn 4d, 9P | 4,215 | 3,603 | 6,792 |
| 45 | Sport wgn 4d, 6P | 4,200 | 3,725 | 4,403 |
| 46 | Sport wgn 4d, 9P | 4,260 | 3,804 | 9,170 |

*Included with Fury II sdn 2d.

| 1970 Engines | bore×stroke | bhp | availability |
|---|---|---|---|
| L6, 198.0 | 3.40×3.64 | 125 | S-Valiant, Duster |
| L6, 225.0 | 3.40×4.13 | 145 | S-Brcda, Belv, Sat, Fury I/II; O-Valiant, Duster |
| V8, 318.0 | 3.91×3.31 | 230 | S-Spt Sat, Fury III, Spt Fury, Gran Coupe, Suburban |
| V8, 340.0 | 4.04×3.31 | 275 | S-Duster 340; O-'Cuda |
| V8, 383.0 | 4.25×3.38 | 290 | O-all exc Valiant |
| V8, 383.0 | 4.25×3.38 | 330 | O-all exc Valiant |
| V8, 383.0 | 4.25×3.38 | 335 | S-Road Runner, 'Cuda |
| V8, 426.0 | 4.25×3.75 | 425 | O-RR, 'Cuda, GTX |
| V8, 440.0 | 4.32×3.75 | 350 | S-Spt Fury GT; O-other Fury |
| V8, 440.0 | 4.32×3.75 | 375 | S-GTX; O-'Cuda |
| V8, 440.0 | 4.32×3.75 | 390 | O-'Cuda, RR, GTX, PH23 |

# Pontiac

**Pontiac Division of General Motors Corp.
Pontiac, Michigan**

Of all the companion makes introduced in the 1920s by GM's various divisions, Pontiac alone survived. Buick's Marquette and Oldsmobile's Viking disappeared in the Depression; Cadillac's LaSalle lasted only until 1940. But Pontiac, offered by Oakland beginning in 1926, outsold its parent every year. In 1932, when GM decided to drop its slow sellers, Oakland was discontinued. Pontiac rolled on through the Depression, and was producing about a quarter-million cars a year by 1940. Pontiac usually ran fifth in production during the '40s, following Buick and the "low-priced three" (Chevrolet, Ford, and Plymouth). In model year 1950, its best up to that time, Pontiac produced over 466,000 units.

Although Pontiac had offered a V8 in 1932, it concentrated only on L-head engines from 1933 to 1954, selling six- and eight-cylinder models. In 1940 there were two lines for each engine: the six-cylinder Special and DeLuxe, and the eight-cylinder DeLuxe and Torpedo. Each series offered four-passenger coupes and four-door sedans. The lineup also included the Special six-cylinder business coupe and wagon, the DeLuxe six-cylinder "cabriolet" convertible, and the DeLuxe eight-cylinder cabriolet and business coupe. Pontiac engines were sturdy, smooth-running units delivering modest performance with reasonable economy.

Styling was typically GM: pontoon fenders; a rounded hood; a divided, horizontal-bar grille. The distinctive silver streak hood and deck trim were created by designer Virgil Exner, who would later help shape the 1947-49 Studebakers, and the Chrysler products of the 1950s. The streaks had arrived in the late '30s, and remained a Pontiac trademark through 1956.

In keeping with a corporate-wide restyle for 1941, Pontiac adopted higher, crisper fenders embellished with additional silver streaks. A new body style that year was a fastback sedan. Six separate series were offered: DeLuxe, Streamliner, and Custom Torpedos with six- or eight-cylinder engines. The DeLuxe Torpedo comprised the widest range of body styles, including a Metropolitan sedan with blind rear roof quarters that gave a formal appearance. The convertible was appealing, having clean, sleek lines and a soft top uninterrupted by rear side windows, a treatment reminiscent of earlier custom-bodied Packards.

Pontiac sales were good in 1940—217,000 for the model year. Sales were better yet the following year. The DeLuxe series, offering a wide range of body styles, accounted for 150,000 sales. Pontiac was seen as the next step up from Chevy, but was far less luxurious than Oldsmobile or Buick. Trimmed conservatively, it lacked exotic body styles, and was carefully built to a price. But that price was a competitive one: under $800 for the cheapest model in 1940 and just a little more than that in '41. The highest price in those

two years was $1250 for the wood-bodied Custom Torpedo station wagon.

For 1942, Pontiac built about 84,000 cars, all except 15,000 produced in the closing months of 1941. Again Pontiac followed GM styling practice: long front fenders blending into the front doors, rounded "drop-off"

1940 Torpedo Eight four-door sedan

1940 Torpedo Eight sport coupe

1941 Custom Torpedo Eight four-door sedan

1941 Custom Torpedo Eight Deluxe station wagon

rear fenders, and a gaudy grille. Considerable model shuffling occurred. The '42 line included only the Torpedo on the 119-inch wheelbase and Streamliner on the 122-inch wheelbase. Each was available with either a six- or eight-cylinder engine. Streamliner was broken down into standard and Chieftain sub-series, each of which offered a coupe, sedan, and wagon. Chieftains cost $50 more than the standard Streamliner, which was priced higher than the Torpedo. The eight-cylinder option cost only $25 more than the six. Production split

1941 Custom Torpedo Eight three-passenger coupe

1942 Torpedo Eight four-door sedan

1946 Torpedo Eight convertible

1946 Streamliner Eight Deluxe station wagon

about 50/50 between sixes and eights.

While marking time with prewar body styles for 1946-48, Pontiac stylists made each succeeding edition look a little different. The 1946s, which began rolling out of the plant in September 1945, were distinguished by triple chrome fender strips and a massive, full-width grille composed of vertical and horizontal bars. The grille was simplified for 1947, but became busy again for '48: vertical grille bars returned, and a small upper grille carried the Pontiac name. The 1948 was the first Pontiac to bear the Silver Streak nameplate, though the term had been used earlier in reference to styling. Despite name changes and minor appearance alterations, however, these early postwar models were entirely prewar in design and specifications. They used the same engines, the same conventional ladder chassis, the same suspension. Inexplicably, the eight was listed at 104 bhp in 1948 instead of 103, the only change from 1942 specifications.

Pontiac offered just four series in '46: the 119-inch wheelbase Torpedo and the 122-inch wheelbase Streamliner, each available with six- or eight-cylinder engines. There was no Chieftain sub-series as in '42, but body styles were the same as before. The eight cost $30 more than the six throughout the range. Torpedo styles included two- and four-door sedans, business and sport coupes, and the coupe sedan, a five-passenger fastback. Wagons had wooden bodies and were costly to build. All models came only with three-speed manual transmissions as Pontiac had decided to stay away from GM's popular Hydra-Matic for the time being.

All body styles were carried over for '47 except for a deluxe convertible added to the Torpedo line. For the 1948 model year, there was a model realignment. Without altering engine or chassis specifications, Pontiac offered most of its body styles with a choice of "standard" or "deluxe" trim. A deluxe sold for $90 to $120 extra. Chrome fender moldings, gravel guards, and wheel discs were part of the package. All models were available with either six or eight cylinders for a record 30 separate body/engine combinations. The division finally added Hydra-Matic as a $185 option in 1948, and this undoubtedly contributed to Pontiac's 235,000 sales that year. Hydra-Matic was especially important to eight-cylinder buyers who were gradually coming to dominate the ranks of Pontiac customers. Eight-cylinder sales surpassed the sixes in 1947, and were far ahead in '48. Only 50 percent of the sixes were equipped with Hydra-Matic, compared with 80 percent of the eights.

The increasing sales of Pontiac Eights indicated the division was moving away from the "big Chevy" class and toward the upper-medium-price bracket. In those days, strict market placement was still the rule: each GM make carved out its own price territory. Although Pontiac continued to build sixes until 1955, its eight-cylinder models had become the top sellers long before that. When the division switched to a new overhead-

1947 Torpedo Six four-door sedan

1950 Chieftain Eight Deluxe Catalina hardtop coupe

1948 Streamliner Eight coupe sedan

1950 Streamliner Eight coupe sedan

1949 Streamliner Eight Deluxe coupe sedan

1951 Chieftain Eight Super Catalina hardtop coupe

valve V8 in 1955, it simultaneously dropped its six-cylinder engine.

In the corporate-wide restyling of 1949 Pontiac fared extremely well. For the new 120-inch-wheelbase chassis, GM styling chief Harley Earl developed a smooth body for the Silver Streak Six and Silver Streak Eight, each offered in standard and deluxe form as Streamliners or Chieftains. The latter had notchback instead of fastback styling. Deluxe models had extra chrome, including side moldings, rear fender gravel guards, chrome wheel discs, chrome vent wings, and bright windshield trim. Engine displacement remained unchanged from 1948, but a new high-compression head boosted horsepower to 93 bhp for the six and 106 for the eight.

Styling was attractive. A full-width grille was bisected by a single bar and a row of little vertical teeth, a conservative "face" in the automotive world that year. Tradition dictated Exner's silver streaks would continue to adorn the deck and hood. However, the old pontoon-style fenders were replaced by free-flowing front fenders integral with the bodysides. Beltline and roofline were lower than those of any Pontiac that had gone before. Though the '49s looked lighter than the '48s,

they actually weighed a bit more. Performance stayed about the same, despite the small horsepower increase.

Inflation was an economic reality in the late '40s, and Pontiac prices rose considerably in 1949. The most expensive convertible model increased by nearly $200 over 1948. The woody wagon now exceeded $2600. The new metal-bodied station wagon was more practical than the woody though, and outsold it. Pontiac was a pioneer of this body style, along with Plymouth and Oldsmobile, and dropped its wood-bodied wagons after '49.

During the '50s, Pontiac usually built the right cars at the right time. When buyers began passing up six-cylinder medium-priced cars, Pontiac wisely switched to V8s only; at the height of the horsepower race, Pontiac brought out the Bonneville. For most of the decade, the division maintained competitive prices, which helped win sales, especially from Plymouth and Dodge.

Pontiacs of the early '50s still offered six- or eight-cylinder engines in the usual wide array of body styles. For 1950 there were two- and four-door sedans, business and club coupes, all-steel wagons, hardtops, convertibles, and two- and four-door Streamliner fastbacks. Styling was a facelift of the all-new '49

1952 Chieftain Eight Deluxe four-door sedan

1953 Chieftain Eight Custom Catalina hardtop coupe

1954 Star Chief Custom Catalina hardtop coupe

design. The illuminated countenance of Chief Pontiac was continued as a hood mascot. Optional Hydra-Matic drive was offered at $158. This was also the first year for a Pontiac hardtop, the Catalina, offered in four varieties. By the end of the year, Catalinas were accounting for some nine percent of total production.

Although 1951 proved less successful in sales volume, it was by no means disappointing to Pontiac. Output that year was the second-best in the division's history. (On August 11, the four-millionth Pontiac was built.) The Streamliner fastback two-door sedan, the sole holdover of that style from 1950, was dropped in the spring of '51. Other models were altered little from those of the year before, except for a new "V" grille motif.

Pontiac dropped its coupe bodies for 1952, reducing both Six and Eight series to sedans, four-door wagons, Catalinas, and convertibles. Within each line there were still three separate trim levels, standard, DeLuxe, and Super DeLuxe. This was the last year for the 1949 design, which would be replaced by a new Chieftain Six and Eight on a 122-inch wheelbase. Korean War restrictions and a nationwide steel strike slowed 1952 production to 271,000 cars, but Pontiac remained in fifth place.

Buying trends were clear as the 1953 models made their debut. Catalina hardtops, for example, were accounting for over 20 percent of volume, and Hydra-Matic installations had climbed to 84 percent. As a result, the '53s bore a distinct resemblance to earlier styles, but were larger in almost every dimension. New features were a kick-up rear fender line (Pontiac fenders had tapered downward in the past), a lower and more streamlined grille, upright-winged "chief" hood ornament, and a one-piece windshield. Mechanical improvements included optional power steering. Hydra-Matic models had an especially low rear axle ratio of 3.03.1, which gave smooth top-range performance. A fire in the Hydra-Matic plant in mid-1953 shortened supplies, however, so about 18,500 Pontiacs were fitted with Chevrolet's Powerglide in '53 and '54. Pontiac did extremely well for model year 1953, producing nearly 419,000 cars.

The 1954 models were facelifted '53s, with revised side moldings and a narrow scoop built into the central grille bar. The new top-line series that year was the luxury Star Chief in sedans, hardtop, and convertible form.

A big change was hinted at in early 1954: Pontiac's first modern overhead-valve V8. Known as the Strato Streak, it produced 180 bhp, or 200 bhp with optional four-barrel carburetor. Original displacement was 287.2 cubic inches, but it was capable of more and soon grew to over 300 cid. A lively, strong, conventional design with five main bearings, it was up to date, over-square, and ran on regular gas.

Of course, there was more for 1955 besides a new engine. Pontiac claimed 109 new features altogether, including extensively revised styling and an improved chassis. The lineup consisted of Chieftain and Star Chief series; both featured a wraparound windshield, cowl ventilation, new colors and two-tone combinations, tubeless tires, and a 12-volt electrical system. The 122-inch-wheelbase Chieftain comprised an 860 series of sedans and wagons, and an 870 line of sedans, wagons, and Catalina hardtop. Star Chief included an exotic new hardtop-styled Safari two-door wagon based on the Chevrolet Nomad. Carl Renner, Chevrolet stylist said: "When Pontiac saw [the Nomad] they felt they could do something with it . . . Management wanted it for the Pontiac line—so it worked out." Safaris retained this styling through 1957. They were priced higher than equivalent Nomads, of course, and sold in fewer numbers.

On balance, 1955 rated as a vintage year for Pontiac. The division built a record 553,000 cars. The lineup was a solid hit with both public and dealers. But Pontiac had some rough times in the later 1950s. The division didn't equal this volume again until 1963, after which it began setting new sales records. The reason was a change in the market. Buick's Special and Oldsmobile's standard 88 were more competitively priced than they'd been before, and demand for lower-medium-price cars was shrinking as import sales steadily increased. Pontiac did not tend to capture the enthusiasm of buyers in the

1956-58 period, even though its cars were certainly competitive in these years, and faster than ever.

A mild facelift and the addition of four-door hardtops marked 1956. Styling was less distinctive (Tom McCahill said the '56 looked like "it had been born on its nose"). Though the V8 had grown to 316.6 cid, it didn't pack an extraordinary amount of power—only 227 bhp maximum in the Star Chief. Unfortunately, too, the cars had picked up a reputation for a hard ride.

GM appointed Semon E. "Bunky" Knudsen as Pontiac general manager, told him to do what he could with the '55-'56 engineering, and hoped for the best in '57. Knudsen hustled. Though sticking with the same wheelbase, the '57s had very long rear springs mounted in rubber shackles. Ball-joint front suspension, adopted by other GM divisions, was not used, however. New 14-inch tires replaced the previous 15-inchers, and a foot pedal parking brake was instituted, along with an op-

1955 Star Chief convertible

1956 Star Chief Custom Safari station wagon

1957 Bonneville convertible

1957 Star Chief Custom four-door sedan

1958 Bonneville hardtop coupe

1959 Catalina Vista hardtop sedan

1959 Catalina Sport hardtop coupe

Bonneville Special show car of 1954

tional automatic antenna. The massive buck-toothed grille was revised, two-toning switched from its half-a-car 1956 pattern to a simpler sweep-spear motif, and Silver Streak exterior trim was banished. There was a new 347 V8—and Bunky had his day by creating the fast and flashy Bonneville.

Providing 300 bhp by way of fuel injection, hydraulic lifters, and racing cam, this $5782 convertible was the fastest Pontiac in history. It was even faster with optional Tri-Power (three two-barrel carbs). A fuel-injected Bonneville was timed at 18 seconds for the standing quarter-mile; one with Tri-Power did the same leap in 16.8. Though fuel injection never proved popular, Bonneville wasn't a hot seller mainly because of its price—only 630 were sold. But it did give the division a whole new performance image. Corporate racing was being played down, however. A few '57 Pontiacs raced with distinction in NASCAR, but were strictly private entries. Yet lack of race victories didn't affect sales. Chevy, Olds, and Buick all suffered downturns from 1956 (as Chrysler products filled the gap), but Pontiac built about 333,000 of its '57 cars and moved to within 51,000 units of Olds.

An all-new body should have brought added success in '58, but a recession set in and held the division's production to only 217,000 units. Compared to most GM products that year, Pontiac was really well-styled. A simpler, full-width grille was adopted, quad headlights appeared, and the side spear was wider and now concave. Bodies were lower, but not much longer or wider; wheelbases were unchanged. No fewer than seven Catalina hardtops were offered with two or four doors. Bonneville became a regular series with about 12,000 convertibles and hardtops sold.

For 1959, Pontiac shared inner body panels with Chevrolet, Buick, and Olds—and built some of the best-looking cars around. The first of the famous split grilles was introduced, along with modest twin-fin rear fenders and minimal side trim—plus the new Wide-Track chassis. The V8 was puffed up to 389 cid and delivered 315 bhp with Tri-Power. Pontiac also made a new Tempest 420E unit for economy-minded buyers, an engine that could deliver 20 miles per gallon if driven prudently. The old Chieftain and Super Chief were discontinued, replaced by the Catalina series on the 122 wheelbase; Star Chief and Bonneville shared a 124-inch chassis. Bonneville was a real hit, and some 82,000 were sold in '59.

During the '50s, Pontiac produced a number of interesting one-offs. The smooth-looking Strato Streak of 1954 was a harbinger of pillarless four-doors to come for '56. Also shown in '54 was the first Bonneville, a Corvette-like two-seater with a canopy-type cockpit and a 100-inch wheelbase. Both of these cars were fitted with straight eights. The Strato-Star of 1955 was a two-door, four-seat hardtop that previewed '56 styling. Metallic silver paint and a red leather and brushed aluminum interior were featured, as was flow-through ventilation and the new ohv V8. The wildest show car was the 1956 Club de Mer with "twin pod" seating and dual bubble windshields. Standing only 38.4 inches high, its anodized-aluminum body was painted Cerulean blue (Harley Earl's favorite color).

After being honored for its '59 line, Pontiac was named Car of the Year three more times by *Motor Trend* magazine in the 1960s. Some say that award is often breathlessly bestowed on ordinary cars or worse, but Pontiac truly deserved the title. Piloted by engineering-oriented general managers like Knudsen and Elliot M. (Pete) Estes (later to become GM president), Pontiac Division became the home of high performance. The early-'50s image of staid family cars vanished. Again and again, Pontiac introduced exciting automobiles: the unique '61 Tempest, the personal-luxury '62 Grand Prix, the swift and nimble '64 GTO, the singular '66 Tempest Sprint with its overhead-cam six, and the sporty '67 Firebird. All were interesting cars; some were great cars.

Most of Pontiac's revolutionary news was made by the compact Tempest, and the intermediate into which it later evolved. The original '61 version won the Car of the Year award for three reasons: GM's first postwar four-cylinder engine, a radical and unprecedented flexible driveshaft, and a transaxle (rear-mounted transmission and independent link-type rear suspension). *Motor Trend* said the new Tempest "sets many new trends and unquestionably is a prototype of the American car for the Sixties," a summary that was wrong on at least one count. Nobody copied its driveshaft or transaxle (unless we count the Porsche 928 of 18 years later), and not until the late 1970s was there a strong shift in Detroit to four-cylinder engines. The public bought many 1961-63 Tempests, but their more conventional successors did far better. The 195-cid four, created it by chopping one cylinder bank from the 389 V8, was abandoned in '64 for an inline six—practical, but hardly innovative.

The Tempest's driveshaft could be likened to a speedometer cable in that it transmitted rotary action through a bend, or at least a slight curve. It was a long torsion bar bent in an arc under the floor—thin, but lightly stressed. Mounted on bearings, it was permanently lubricated inside a steel case. The bent shaft eliminated the floor hump in the front, but not in the rear. It also eliminated universal joints and allowed for softer engine mounts giving better isolation of vibration from the interior.

The Tempest transaxle was a first for Detroit (if not the world). Aside from allowing for an ostensibly superior independent rear suspension, it made the Tempest less nose-heavy than its corporate cousins, the Olds F-85 or Buick Special. At the same time, the suspension made the car prone to oversteer, which could be especially alarming on wet roads. Yet the Tempest handled well generally, and tracked safely in mud and snow. Its unit body/chassis had a 112-inch wheelbase that was the standard B-O-P compact platform for 1961-63.

The four-cylinder engine came in several stages of

tune (regular or premium gas) and was available with manual and automatic transmission. Over its three-year-period, horsepower ranged from 110 to 166 bhp. The 1961-62 models were also offered with Buick's 155/185-bhp, 215 V8 as an option. A 260-bhp 326 debuted for '63, making Tempest a quick car, capable of 0–60 mph times of 9.5 seconds and a top speed of 115 mph. At first, there was only one series of two-door and four-door sedans and a Safari wagon. A coupe and convertible were added for '62 in deluxe and LeMans versions. A separate LeMans series was fielded for '63 with a bucket-seat coupe and convertible offering plusher interiors. Styling didn't change much during Tempest's early years. A twin semi-oval grille was used for 1961, a full-width three-section design for '62. The twin grille returned for 1963 along with squarer body lines. For '64, GM lengthened its compact wheelbase to 115 inches, and Pontiac redesigned the Tempest, using taut, geo-metric lines. Good styling and numerous high-performance models won Pontiac its second Car of the Year award in 1965.

Destined for greatness was a mid-1964 introduction, the Tempest GTO, the first of what soon became known as the "muscle cars." The nickname was well taken. Equipped with the proper options, a GTO could deliver unprecedented performance for a six-passenger automobile. Of course, it could be ordered in relatively mild-mannered form with automatic transmission, a 335-bhp engine, and so on. Enthusiasts, however, learned to use the option book wisely. The base was a Tempest LeMans coupe priced at $2500. The GTO package—floorshift, 389-cid engine, quick steering, stiff shocks, dual exhaust, and premium tires—cost about $300. The four-speed gearbox was $188 more. Another $75 bought a package comprising metallic brake linings, heavy-duty radiator, and limited-slip differential. And

1961 Tempest LeMans sport coupe

1964 Tempest GTO sport coupe

1966 LeMans sport coupe

1968 LeMans hardtop sedan

1969 GTO hardtop coupe

1970 GTO hardtop coupe

an additional $115 would buy a 360-bhp engine. At that point, all you needed was a lead foot and lots of gasoline.

Sports-car folk took umbrage at Pontiac's use of GTO (gran turismo omologato), an international term for production-class racing cars. *Car and Driver* magazine brazenly took issue with the critics by comparing Pontiac's GTO with Ferrari's. A good Pontiac, they said, would trim the Ferrari in a drag race and lose on a road course. But "with the addition of NASCAR road racing suspension, the Pontiac will take the measure of any Ferrari other than prototype racing cars . . . The Ferrari costs $20,000. With every conceivable option on a GTO, it would be difficult to spend more than $3800. That's a bargain."

The 115-inch-wheelbase LeMans and Tempest changed little in ensuing years. Vertical headlights and crisp styling for a three-inch-longer body appeared for 1966. "Coke-bottle" rear fenders and a divided vertical-bar grille were featured for '67. In 1968, the cars adopted GM's dual wheelbases of 116 inches for four-doors and 112 inches for two-doors, and borrowed styling themes from the big Pontiacs such as a large bumper/grille. The GTO's standard engine that year was a 400-cid V8 pumping out 350 bhp. It could also be ordered with 360 bhp by way of a Ram-Air hood scoop. The GTO featured an energy-absorbing front bumper made of Endura rubber that was neatly blended into the front-end styling. For performance mainly, Pontiac won its fourth Car of the Year award in 1968. Its 1969 intermediates were facelifted and cleaner than the '68s. The hottest GTO was now "The Judge" with a 366-bhp Ram-Air V8 and three-speed manual gearbox with Hurst shifter. The 1970s had all-new styling with changes at the front and rear, plus new bumpers and doors. The end result was a curvy, heavier-looking Tempest, GTO, LeMans, and LeMans Sport. Collectors have since tended to prefer the tidier 1964-69 models.

The 1964-65 Tempest's 140-bhp Oldsmobile six gave way to a surprise engine for '66: an overhead-cam six. The first performance six since the Hudson Hornet, and not in a league with hairier GTOs, the ohc was nevertheless satisfying. Typical acceleration for the Sprint version was 0 to 60 in 10 seconds flat and a top speed of 115 mph. With a capacity of 230 cid, it developed either 165 bhp standard or 207 in Sprint form (with Rochester Quadra-Jet carburetor, hotter valve timing, and double valve springs). The crankshaft had seven main bearings; the camshaft was driven by a fiberglass-reinforced notched belt rather than conventional chain or gear drive. The optional four-speed transmission, clean styling, and an interior that featured bucket seats and console gave the Sprint the look and feel of a true grand touring car. But its life span was short. By 1968, the Tempest had grown bulky, and by 1970, the engine had been emasculated by emission controls and detuning and was soon discontinued.

Since Pontiac had such a good reputation for performance and handling, division managers knew that

1967 Firebird hardtop coupe

1968 Firebird H.O. hardtop coupe

1969 Firebird convertible

1970 Firebird Formula 400 hardtop coupe

the Firebird "ponycar," based on the Chevrolet Camaro, had to be something special. Although it used the Camaro's bodyshell and 108-inch wheelbase, Firebird had its own divided grille and an optional 400-cid V8. Optional engines included the ohc six, which made it a sprightly yet economical performer. Changes were

1960 Catalina Vista hardtop sedan

1962 Catalina Vista hardtop sedan

1963 Bonneville convertible

1965 Bonneville convertible

1965 Catalina 2+2 convertible

1967 Catalina hardtop sedan

slight in subsequent model years. Side marker lights were added in 1968. The lower body and grille were revised, and a host of government-ordered safety features were added in '69. Convertibles continued to be offered until Firebird was redesigned with coupe-only bodywork for 1970. That styling, timeless and lovely, was still around 10 years later—albeit with much tamer performance than a decade before. In the 1967-70 period, before federal regulations took serious performance tolls, Firebirds rarely sold for more than $3500. They were performance cars designed to be enjoyed by good drivers.

Despite the publicity won by Pontiac's smaller models, its full-size cars were among the better-styled, better-handling standard-size cars of the decade. The public responded enthusiastically. Model year production for 1960 had been about 400,000. By 1969, the division

was building close to half a million full-size sedans, hardtops, convertibles, and wagons. In model year output, Pontiac ran third to Chevrolet and Ford from 1962 through 1970, and the big cars had a lot to do with this success.

Pontiac originally had a four-model lineup. The 1960-61 entries, from bottom to top, consisted of Catalina, Ventura, Star Chief, and Bonneville. In 1962, the Ventura was dropped; its place was taken by the bucket-seated, limited-edition Grand Prix. This elegantly tailored hardtop coupe, with crisp styling and svelte good looks, rapidly gained in popularity. By 1969, it was outselling all large Pontiac models except Catalina—with a single body style. (A convertible, offered in 1967 only, is now a collector's item since only 5,856 were built.)

Design of the standard-size cars kept improving, at

1968 Grand Prix hardtop coupe

1968 Catalina hardtop coupe

1969 Grand Prix Model J hardtop coupe

1969 Bonneville convertible

1970 Bonneville hardtop sedan

1970 Grand Prix Model SJ hardtop coupe

least through 1966. The distinctive split grille, first introduced in '59 and dropped for '60, was reintroduced in 1961. Clean machines with narrow, split grilles were the rule for 1963-64. The '65s were equally well executed, but had a prominent, bulging grille that was toned down slightly in 1966. Bulkier designs with heavy, curved rear fenders arrived in '67, and a huge bumper/grille was used in '68. The front end was greatly improved for 1969-70. Catalina and Grand Prix always rode the smaller Pontiac wheelbase. Bonnevilles, Star Chiefs, and Executives rode the longer one. Each model, separated from the others by a few hundred dollars, offered a comprehensive range of body styles.

Pontiac's big-car engines, though offered with numerous horsepower ratings, came in just two sizes throughout the '60s. The smaller was a 389-cid V8 (400

cid after 1966). Standard on all models, its horsepower ranged from 215 on up to 350, the latter version being standard on the 1967-70 Grand Prix. The larger engine, optional on most large Pontiacs, was a 421-cid unit in 1963-66, and 428 until 1970 when it was replaced by a 455. It began with 353 bhp in '63 and reached 376 by '67. A 421-cid, 427-bhp monster was offered in 1963-64 for a special drag racing Catalina with aluminum body panels, plastic side windows, and a drilled-out frame.

Pontiac engines never reached one horsepower per cubic inch as did GM's other divisions, but its big-block V8s were more than adequate to make suitably equipped models very fast. The Wide-Track chassis and taut suspensions combined to make them roadable as well.

Luxury, performance, comfort, and handling—full-size car, compact, or intermediate—nobody did it better than Pontiac between 1960 and 1970.

# Pontiac

## Pontiac Specifications

### 1940

**25HA Special Six (wb 117.0)—106,892 built**

|  | Wght | Price | Prod |
|---|---|---|---|
| cpe 3P | 3,060 | 783 | — |
| spt cpe 4P | 3,045 | 819 | — |
| sdn 2d | 3,095 | 830 | — |
| wgn 4d, 8P | 3,295 | 1,015 | — |
| sdn 4d | 3,125 | 876 | — |

**26HB DeLuxe Six (wb 120.0)—58,452 built**

|  | Wght | Price | Prod |
|---|---|---|---|
| cpe 3P | 3,115 | 835 | — |
| spt cpe 4P | 3,105 | 876 | — |
| cabriolet (conv) | 3,190 | 1,003 | — |
| sdn 2d | 3,170 | 881 | — |
| sdn 4d | 3,210 | 932 | — |

**28HA DeLuxe Eight (wb 120.0)—20,433 built**

|  | Wght | Price | Prod |
|---|---|---|---|
| cpe 3P | 3,180 | 875 | — |
| spt cpe 4P | 3,195 | 913 | — |
| cabriolet (conv) | 3,280 | 1,046 | — |
| sdn 2d | 3,250 | 919 | — |
| sdn 4d | 3,300 | 970 | — |

**29HB Torpedo Eight (wb 122.0)—31,224 built**

|  | Wght | Price | Prod |
|---|---|---|---|
| spt cpe 4P | 3,390 | 1,016 | — |
| sdn 4d | 3,475 | 1,072 | — |

| 1940 Engines | bore×stroke | bhp | availability |
|---|---|---|---|
| L6, 222.7 | 3.44×4.00 | 87 | S-Six |
| L8, 248.9 | 3.25×3.75 | 100 | S-Eight |

### 1941

**25JA DeLuxe Torpedo Six (wb 119.0)—117,976 built**

|  | Wght | Price | Prod |
|---|---|---|---|
| cpe 3P | 3,145 | 828 | — |
| sdn cpe | 3,180 | 864 | — |
| conv cpe | 3,335 | 1,023 | — |
| sdn 2d | 3,190 | 874 | — |
| sdn 4d | 3,235 | 921 | — |
| Metropolitan sdn 4d | 3,230 | 921 | — |

**26JB Streamliner Torpedo Six (wb 122.0)—82,527 built**

|  | Wght | Price | Prod |
|---|---|---|---|
| sdn cpe | 3,305 | 923 | — |
| Super sdn cpe | 3,320 | 969 | — |
| sdn 4d | 3,365 | 980 | — |
| Super sdn 4d | 3,400 | 1,026 | — |

**24JC Custom Torpedo Six (wb 122.0)—8,257 built**

|  | Wght | Price | Prod |
|---|---|---|---|
| sdn cpe | 3,260 | 995 | — |
| sdn 4d | 3,355 | 1,052 | — |
| wgn 4d, 8P | 3,650 | 1,175 | — |
| DeLuxe wgn 4d, 8P | 3,665 | 1,225 | — |

**27JA DeLuxe Torpedo Eight (wb 119.0)—37,823 built**

|  | Wght | Price | Prod |
|---|---|---|---|
| cpe 3P | 3,220 | 853 | — |
| sdn cpe | 3,250 | 889 | — |
| conv cpe | 3,390 | 1,048 | — |
| sdn 2d | 3,250 | 899 | — |
| sdn 4d | 3,285 | 946 | — |
| Metropolitan sdn 4d | 3,295 | 946 | — |

**28JB Streamliner Torpedo Eight (wb 122.0)—66,287 built**

|  | Wght | Price | Prod |
|---|---|---|---|
| sdn cpe | 3,370 | 948 | — |
| Super sdn cpe | 3,385 | 994 | — |
| sdn 4d | 3,425 | 1,005 | — |
| Super sdn 4d | 3,460 | 1,051 | — |

**29JC Custom Torpedo Eight (wb 122.0)—17,191 built**

|  | Wght | Price | Prod |
|---|---|---|---|
| sdn cpe | 3,325 | 1,020 | — |
| sdn 4d | 3,430 | 1,077 | — |
| wgn 4d, 8P | 3,715 | 1,200 | — |
| DeLuxe wgn 4d, 8P | 3,730 | 1,250 | — |

| 1941 Engines | bore×stroke | bhp | availability |
|---|---|---|---|
| L6, 239.2 | 3.56×4.00 | 90 | S-Six |
| L8, 248.9 | 3.25×3.75 | 103 | S-Eight |

### 1942

**25KA Torpedo Six (wb 119.0)—29,886 built**

|  | Wght | Price | Prod |
|---|---|---|---|
| cpe 3P | 3,210 | 895 | — |
| sdn cpe | 3,255 | 950 | — |
| spt cpe | 3,260 | 935 | — |
| conv cpe | 3,535 | 1,165 | — |
| sdn 2d | 3,265 | 940 | — |
| sdn 4d | 3,305 | 985 | — |
| Metropolitan sdn 4d | 3,295 | 985 | — |

**26KB Streamliner Six (wb 122.0)**

|  | Wght | Price | Prod |
|---|---|---|---|
| sdn cpe | 3,355 | 980 | 10,284 |
| sdn 4d | 3,415 | 1,035 | |
| wgn 4d, 8P | 3,810 | 1,265 | |
| Chieftain sdn cpe | 3,400 | 1,030 | 2,458 |
| Chieftain sdn 4d | 3,460 | 1,085 | |
| Chieftain wgn 4d, 6P | 3,785 | 1,315 | |

**27KA Torpedo Eight (wb 119.0)—14,421 built**

|  | Wght | Price | Prod |
|---|---|---|---|
| cpe dP | 3,270 | 920 | — |
| sdn cpe | 3,320 | 975 | — |
| spt cpe | 3,320 | 960 | — |
| conv cpe | 3,605 | 1,190 | — |
| sdn 2d | 3,325 | 965 | — |
| sdn 4d | 3,360 | 1,010 | — |
| Metropolitan sdn 4d | 3,355 | 1,010 | — |

**28KB Streamliner Eight (wb 122.0)**

|  | Wght | Price | Prod |
|---|---|---|---|
| sdn cpe | 3,430 | 1,005 | 15,465 |
| sdn 4d | 3,485 | 1,060 | |
| wgn 4d, 8P | 3,885 | 1,290 | |
| Chieftain sdn cpe | 3,460 | 1,055 | 11,041 |
| Chieftain sdn 4d | 3,515 | 1,110 | |
| Chieftain wgn 4d, 6P | 3,865 | 1,340 | |

| 1942 Engines | bore×stroke | bhp | availability |
|---|---|---|---|
| L6, 239.2 | 3.56×4.00 | 90 | S-Six |
| L8, 248.9 | 3.25×3.75 | 103 | S-Eight |

### 1946

**25LA Torpedo Six (wb 119.0)—26,636 built**

|  | Wght | Price | Prod |
|---|---|---|---|
| sdn 4d | 3,361 | 1,427 | — |
| sdn 2d | 3,326 | 1,368 | — |
| cpe sdn | 3,326 | 1,399 | — |
| spt cpe | 3,311 | 1,353 | — |
| cpe 3P | 3,261 | 1,307 | — |
| conv cpe | 3,591 | 1,631 | — |

**26LB Streamliner Six (wb 122.0)—43,430 built**

|  | Wght | Price | Prod |
|---|---|---|---|
| sdn 4d | 3,490 | 1,510 | — |
| cpe sdn | 3,435 | 1,438 | — |
| wgn 4d, 8P | 3,790 | 1,942 | — |
| DeLuxe wgn 4d, 8P | 3,735 | 2,019 | — |

**27LA Torpedo Eight (wb 119.0)—18,273 built**

|  | Wght | Price | Prod |
|---|---|---|---|
| sdn 4d | 3,436 | 1,455 | — |
| sdn 2d | 3,396 | 1,395 | — |
| cpe sdn | 3,391 | 1,428 | — |

| | Wght | Price | Prod |
|---|---|---|---|
| spt cpe | 3,376 | 1,381 | — |
| cpe 3P | 3,331 | 1,335 | — |
| conv cpe | 3,651 | 1,658 | — |

**28LB Streamliner Eight (wb 122.0)—49,301 built**

| | Wght | Price | Prod |
|---|---|---|---|
| sdn 4d | 3,550 | 1,538 | — |
| cpe sdn | 3,495 | 1,468 | — |
| wgn 4d, 8P | 3,870 | 1,970 | — |
| DeLuxe wgn 4d, 8P | 3,850 | 2,047 | — |

| 1946 Engines | bore×stroke | bhp | availability |
|---|---|---|---|
| L6, 239.2 | 3.56×4.00 | 90 | S-Six |
| L8, 248.9 | 3.25×3.75 | 103 | S-Eight |

## 1947

**6MA Torpedo Six (wb 119.0)—67,125 built**

| | Wght | Price | Prod |
|---|---|---|---|
| sdn 4d | 3,320 | 1,512 | — |
| sdn 2d | 3,295 | 1,453 | — |
| cpe sdn | 3,300 | 1,484 | — |
| spt cpe | 3,295 | 1,438 | — |
| cpe 3P | 3,245 | 1,387 | — |
| conv cpe | 3,560 | 1,811 | — |
| DeLuxe conv cpe | 3,560 | 1,853 | — |

**6MB Streamliner Six (wb 122.0)—42,336 built**

| | Wght | Price | Prod |
|---|---|---|---|
| sdn 4d | 3,450 | 1,598 | — |
| cpe sdn | 3,400 | 1,547 | — |
| wgn 4d, 8P | 3,775 | 2,235 | — |
| DeLuxe wgn 4d, 8P | 3,715 | 2,312 | — |

**8MA Torpedo Eight (wb 119.0)—34,815 built**

| | Wght | Price | Prod |
|---|---|---|---|
| sdn 4d | 3,405 | 1,559 | — |
| sdn 2d | 3,370 | 1,500 | — |
| cpe sdn | 3,370 | 1,531 | — |
| spt cpe | 3,360 | 1,485 | — |
| cpe 3P | 3,310 | 1,434 | — |
| conv cpe | 3,635 | 1,854 | — |
| DeLuxe conv cpe | 3,635 | 1,900 | — |

**8MB Streamliner Eight (wb 122.0)—86,324 built**

| | Wght | Price | Prod |
|---|---|---|---|
| sdn 4d | 3,515 | 1,645 | — |
| cpe sdn | 3,455 | 1,595 | — |
| wgn 4d, 8P | 3,845 | 2,282 | — |
| DeLuxe wgn 4d, 8P | 3,790 | 2,359 | — |

| 1947 Engines | bore×stroke | bhp | availability |
|---|---|---|---|
| L6, 239.2 | 3.56×4.00 | 90 | S-Six |
| L8, 248.9 | 3.25×3.75 | 103 | S-Eight |

## 1948

**6PA Torpedo Six (wb 119.0)—39,262 built**

| | Wght | Price | Prod |
|---|---|---|---|
| sdn 4d | 3,320 | 1,641 | — |
| sdn 2d | 3,280 | 1,583 | — |
| cpe sdn | 3,275 | 1,614 | — |
| spt cpe | 3,220 | 1,552 | — |
| bus cpe | 3,230 | 1,500 | — |
| DeLuxe sdn 4d | 3,340 | 1,731 | — |
| DeLuxe cpe sdn | 3,275 | 1,704 | — |
| DeLuxe spt cpe | 3,230 | 1,641 | — |
| DeLuxe conv cpe | 3,525 | 2,025 | — |

**6PB Streamliner Six (wb 122.0)—37,742 built**

| | Wght | Price | Prod |
|---|---|---|---|
| sdn 4d | 3,450 | 1,727 | — |
| cpe sdn | 3,365 | 1,677 | — |
| wgn 4d, 8P | 3,755 | 2,364 | — |
| DeLuxe sdn 4d | 3,455 | 1,817 | — |
| DeLuxe cpe sdn | 3,370 | 1,766 | — |
| DeLuxe wgn 4d, 6P | 3,695 | 2,442 | — |

**8PA Torpedo Eight (wb 119.0)—35,300 built**

| | Wght | Price | Prod |
|---|---|---|---|
| sdn 4d | 3,395 | 1,689 | — |
| sdn 2d | 3,360 | 1,630 | — |
| cpe scn | 3,340 | 1,661 | — |
| spt cpe | 3,295 | 1,599 | — |
| bus cpe | 3,295 | 1,548 | — |
| DeLuxe sdn 4d | 3,395 | 1,778 | — |
| DeLuxe cpe sdn | 3,340 | 1,751 | — |
| DeLuxe spt cpe | 3,305 | 1,689 | — |
| DeLuxe conv cpe | 3,600 | 2,072 | — |

**8PB Streamliner Eight (wb 122.0)—123,115 built**

| | Wght | Price | Prod |
|---|---|---|---|
| sdn 4d | 3,525 | 1,775 | — |
| cpe sdn | 3,425 | 1,724 | — |
| wgn 4d, 8P | 3,820 | 2,412 | — |
| DeLuxe sdn 4d | 3,630 | 1,864 | — |
| DeLuxe cpe sdn | 3,455 | 1,814 | — |
| DeLuxe wgn 4d, 6P | 3,765 | 2,490 | — |

| 1948 Engines | bore×stroke | bhp | availability |
|---|---|---|---|
| L6, 239.2 | 3.56×4.00 | 90 | S-Six |
| L8, 248.9 | 3.25×3.75 | 104 | S-Eight |

## 1949

**6R Streamliner Six (wb 120.0)—69,654 built (includes 6R Chieftain)**

| | Wght | Price | Prod |
|---|---|---|---|
| sdn 4d | 3,385 | 1,740 | — |
| cpe sdn | 3,360 | 1,689 | — |
| wgn 4d, 8P wood body | 3,745 | 2,543 | — |
| wgn 4d, 8P metal body | 3,650 | 2,543 | — |
| DeLuxe sdn 4d | 3,415 | 1,835 | — |
| DeLuxe cpe sdn | 3,375 | 1,784 | — |
| DeLuxe wgn 4d, 6P wood body | 3,730 | 2,622 | — |
| DeLuxe wgn 4d, 6P metal body | 3,580 | 2,622 | — |

**6R Chieftain Six (wb 120.0)**

| | Wght | Price | Prod |
|---|---|---|---|
| sdn 4d | 3,385 | 1,761 | — |
| sdn 2d | 3,355 | 1,710 | — |
| cpe sdn | 3,330 | 1,710 | — |
| bus cpe | 3,280 | 1,587 | — |
| DeLuxe sdn 4d | 3,415 | 1,856 | — |
| DeLuxe sdn 2d | 3,360 | 1,805 | — |
| DeLuxe cpe sdn | 3,345 | 1,805 | — |
| DeLuxe conv cpe | 3,600 | 2,138 | — |

**8R Streamliner Eight (wb 120.0)—235,165 built (inc 8R Chieftain)**

| | Wght | Price | Prod |
|---|---|---|---|
| sdn 4d | 3,470 | 1,808 | — |
| cpe sdn | 3,435 | 1,758 | — |
| wgn 4d, 8P wood body | 3,835 | 2,611 | — |
| wgn 4d, 8P metal body | 3,690 | 2,611 | — |
| DeLuxe sdn 4d | 3,500 | 1,903 | — |
| DeLuxe cpe sdn | 3,445 | 1,853 | — |
| DeLuxe wgn 4d, 6P wood body | 3,800 | 2,690 | — |
| DeLuxe wgn 4d, 6P metal body | 3,640 | 2,690 | — |

**8R Chieftain Eight (wb 120.0)**

| | Wght | Price | Prod |
|---|---|---|---|
| sdn 4d | 3,475 | 1,829 | — |
| sdn 2d | 3,430 | 1,779 | — |
| cpe sdn | 3,390 | 1,779 | — |
| bus cpe | 3,355 | 1,656 | — |
| DeLuxe sdn 4d | 3,480 | 1,924 | — |
| DeLuxe sdn 2d | 3,430 | 1,874 | — |
| DeLuxe cpe sdn | 3,415 | 1,874 | — |
| DeLuxe conv cpe | 3,670 | 2,206 | — |

| 1949 Engines | bore×stroke | bhp | availability |
|---|---|---|---|
| L6, 239.2 | 3.56×4.00 | 90 | S-Six |
| L6, 239.2 | 3.56×4.00 | 93 | O-Six |
| L8, 248.9 | 3.25×3.75 | 104 | S-Eight |
| L8, 248.9 | 3.25×3.75 | 106 | O-Eight |

# Pontiac

## 1950

### 6T Streamliner Six (wb 120.0)—
### 115,542 built (includes 6T Chieftain)

| | Wght | Price | Prod |
|---|---|---|---|
| fstbk sdn 4d | 3,414 | 1,724 | — |
| fstbk cpe sdn | 3,379 | 1,673 | — |
| wgn 4d, 8P | 3,714 | 2,264 | — |
| DeLuxe fstbk sdn 4d | 3,419 | 1,819 | — |
| DeLuxe fstbk cpe sdn | 3,399 | 1,768 | — |
| DeLuxe wgn 4d, 6P | 3,649 | 2,343 | — |

### 6T Chieftain Six (wb 120.0)

| | Wght | Price | Prod |
|---|---|---|---|
| sdn 4d | 3,409 | 1,745 | — |
| sdn 2d | 3,384 | 1,694 | — |
| cpe sdn | 3,359 | 1,694 | — |
| bus cpe | 3,319 | 1,571 | — |
| DeLuxe sdn 4d | 3,414 | 1,840 | — |
| DeLuxe sdn 2d | 3,389 | 1,789 | — |
| DeLuxe cpe sdn | 3,364 | 1,789 | — |
| DeLuxe Catalina htp cpe | 3,469 | 2,000 | — |
| DeLuxe conv cpe | 3,624 | 2,122 | — |
| Super Catalina htp cpe | 3,469 | 2,058 | — |

### 8T Streamliner Eight (wb 120.0)—330,887 built (inc 8T Chieftain)

| | Wght | Price | Prod |
|---|---|---|---|
| fstbk sdn 4d | 3,499 | 1,792 | — |
| fstbk cpe sdn | 3,464 | 1,742 | — |
| wgn 4d, 8P | 3,799 | 2,332 | — |
| DeLuxe fstbk sdn 4d | 3,509 | 1,887 | — |
| DeLuxe fstbk cpe sdn | 3,469 | 1,837 | — |
| DeLuxe wgn 4d, 6P | 3,739 | 2,411 | — |

### 8T Chieftain Eight (wb 120.0)

| | Wght | Price | Prod |
|---|---|---|---|
| sdn 4d | 3,494 | 1,813 | — |
| sdn 2d | 3,454 | 1,763 | — |
| cpe sdn | 3,444 | 1,763 | — |
| bus cpe | 3,399 | 1,640 | — |
| DeLuxe sdn 4d | 3,499 | 1,908 | — |
| DeLuxe sdn 2d | 3,464 | 1,858 | — |
| DeLuxe cpe sdn | 3,454 | 1,858 | — |
| DeLuxe Catalina htp cpe | 3,549 | 2,069 | — |
| DeLuxe conv cpe | 3,704 | 2,190 | — |
| Super Catalina htp cpe | 3,549 | 2,127 | — |

### 1950 Engines

| | bore×stroke | bhp | availability |
|---|---|---|---|
| L6, 239.2 | 3.56×4.00 | 90 | S-Six |
| L8, 268.4 | 3.38×3.75 | 108 | S-Eight |

## 1951

### 6U Streamliner Six (wb 120.0)—
### 53,748 built (includes 6U Chieftain)

| | Wght | Price | Prod |
|---|---|---|---|
| fstbk cpe sdn | 3,363 | 1,824 | — |
| wgn 4d, 8P | 3,718 | 2,470 | — |
| DeLuxe fstbk cpe sdn | 3,378 | 1,927 | — |
| DeLuxe wgn 4d, 6P | 3,638 | 2,556 | — |

### 6U Chieftain Six (wb 120.0)

| | Wght | Price | Prod |
|---|---|---|---|
| sdn 4d | 3,388 | 1,903 | — |
| sdn 2d | 3,358 | 1,848 | — |
| cpe sdn | 3,338 | 1,848 | — |
| bus cpe | 3,308 | 1,713 | — |
| DeLuxe sdn 4d | 3,388 | 2,006 | — |
| DeLuxe sdn 2d | 3,358 | 1,951 | — |
| DeLuxe cpe sdn | 3,343 | 1,951 | — |
| DeLuxe Catalina htp cpe | 3,458 | 2,182 | — |
| DeLuxe conv cpe | 3,603 | 2,314 | — |
| Super Catalina htp cpe | 3,468 | 2,244 | — |

### 8U Streamliner Eight (wb 120.0)—316,411 built (inc 8U Chieftain)

| | Wght | Price | Prod |
|---|---|---|---|
| fstbk cpe sdn | 3,458 | 1,900 | — |
| wgn 4d, 8P | 3,813 | 2,544 | — |
| DeLuxe fstbk cpe sdn | 3,463 | 2,003 | — |
| DeLuxe wgn 4d, 6P | 3,743 | 2,629 | — |

### 8U Chieftain Eight (wb 120.0)

| | Wght | Price | Prod |
|---|---|---|---|
| sdn 4d | 3,478 | 1,977 | — |

| | Wght | Price | Prod |
|---|---|---|---|
| sdn 2d | 3,443 | 1,922 | — |
| cpe sdn | 3,418 | 1,922 | — |
| bus cpe | 3,388 | 1,787 | — |
| DeLuxe sdn 4d | 3,488 | 2,081 | — |
| DeLuxe sdn 2d | 3,448 | 2,026 | — |
| DeLuxe cpe sdn | 3,433 | 2,026 | — |
| DeLuxe Catalina htp cpe | 3,543 | 2,257 | — |
| DeLuxe conv cpe | 3,683 | 2,388 | — |
| Super Catalina htp cpe | 3,548 | 2,320 | — |

### 1951 Engines

| | bore×stroke | bhp | availability |
|---|---|---|---|
| L6, 239.2 | 3.56×4.00 | 102 | S-Six |
| L8, 268.4 | 3.38×3.75 | 122 | S-Eight |

## 1952

### 6W Chieftain Six (wb 120.0)—19,809 built

| | Wght | Price | Prod |
|---|---|---|---|
| sdn 4d | 3,403 | 2,014 | — |
| sdn 2d | 3,378 | 1,956 | — |
| wgn 4d, 8P | 3,718 | 2,615 | — |
| DeLuxe sdn 4d | 3,403 | 2,119 | — |
| DeLuxe sdn 2d | 3,378 | 2,060 | — |
| DeLuxe Catalina htp cpe | 3,483 | 2,304 | — |
| DeLuxe conv cpe | 3,603 | 2,444 | — |
| DeLuxe wgn 4d, 6P | 3,653 | 2,699 | — |
| Super Catalina htp cpe | 3,493 | 2,370 | — |

### 8W Chieftain Eight (wb 120.0)—251,564 built

| | Wght | Price | Prod |
|---|---|---|---|
| sdn 4d | 3,503 | 2,090 | — |
| sdn 2d | 3,458 | 2,031 | — |
| wgn 4d, 8P | 3,813 | 2,689 | — |
| DeLuxe sdn 4d | 3,503 | 2,194 | — |
| DeLuxe sdn 2d | 3,458 | 2,136 | — |
| DeLuxe Catalina htp cpe | 3,568 | 2,380 | — |
| DeLuxe conv cpe | 3,683 | 2,518 | — |
| DeLuxe wgn 4d, 6P | 3,758 | 2,772 | — |
| Super Catalina htp cpe | 3,573 | 2,446 | — |

### 1952 Engines

| | bore×stroke | bhp | availability |
|---|---|---|---|
| L6, 239.2 | 3.56×4.00 | 102 | S-Six |
| L8, 268.4 | 3.38×3.75 | 122 | S-Eight |

## 1953

### 6X Chieftain Six (wb 122.0)—38,914 built

| | Wght | Price | Prod |
|---|---|---|---|
| sdn 4d | 3,506 | 2,015 | — |
| sdn 2d | 3,466 | 1,956 | — |
| wgn 4d, 6P | 3,713 | 2,450 | — |
| wgn 4d, 6P (woodgrain) | 3,713 | 2,530 | — |
| wgn 4d, 8P | 3,791 | 2,505 | — |
| wgn 4d, 8P (woodgrain) | 3,791 | 2,585 | — |
| DeLuxe sdn 4d | 3,521 | 2,119 | — |
| DeLuxe sdn 2d | 3,481 | 2,060 | — |
| DeLuxe Catalina htp cpe | 3,546 | 2,304 | — |
| DeLuxe conv cpe | 3,696 | 2,444 | — |
| DeLuxe wgn 4d, 6P | 3,751 | 2,590 | — |
| DeLuxe wgn 4d, 6P (woodgrain) | 3,751 | 2,670 | — |
| Custom Catalina htp cpe | 3,546 | 2,370 | — |

### 8X Chieftain Eight (wb 122.0)—379,705 built

| | Wght | Price | Prod |
|---|---|---|---|
| sdn 4d | 3,581 | 2,090 | — |
| sdn 2d | 3,546 | 2,031 | — |
| wgn 4d, 6P | 3,811 | 2,525 | — |
| wgn 4d, 6P (woodgrain) | 3,811 | 2,605 | — |
| wgn 4d, 8P | 3,881 | 2,580 | — |
| wgn 4d, 8P (woodgrain) | 3,881 | 2,660 | — |
| DeLuxe sdn 4d | 3,596 | 2,194 | — |
| DeLuxe sdn 2d | 3,561 | 2,136 | — |
| DeLuxe Catalina htp cpe | 3,621 | 2,380 | — |
| DeLuxe conv cpe | 3,751 | 2,518 | — |
| DeLuxe wgn 4d, 6P | 3,841 | 2,664 | — |
| DeLuxe wgn 4d, 6P (woodgrain) | 3,841 | 2,744 | — |
| Custom Catalina htp cpe | 3,621 | 2,446 | — |

| 1953 Engines | bore×stroke | bhp | availability |
|---|---|---|---|
| L6, 239.2 | 3.56×4.00 | 115 | S-Six man |
| L6, 239.2 | 3.56×4.00 | 118 | S-Six auto |
| L8, 268.4 | 3.38×3.75 | 118 | S-Eight man |
| L8, 268.4 | 3.38×3.75 | 122 | S-Eight auto |

## 1954

### 6Z Chieftain Six (wb 122.0)—22,670 built

| | Wght | Price | Prod |
|---|---|---|---|
| Special sdn 4d | 3,391 | 2,027 | — |
| Special sdn 2d | 3,331 | 1,968 | — |
| Special wgn 4d, 8P | 3,691 | 2,419 | — |
| Special wgn 4d, 6P | 3,601 | 2,364 | — |
| DeLuxe sdn 4d | 3,406 | 2,131 | — |
| DeLuxe sdn 2d | 3,351 | 2,072 | — |
| DeLuxe Catalina htp cpe | 3,421 | 2,316 | — |
| DeLuxe wgn 4d, 6P | 3,646 | 2,504 | — |
| Custom Catalina htp cpe | 3,421 | 2,382 | — |

### 8Z Chieftain Eight (wb 122.0)—149,986 built

| | Wght | Price | Prod |
|---|---|---|---|
| Special sdn 4d | 3,451 | 2,102 | — |
| Special sdn 2d | 3,396 | 2,043 | — |
| Special wgn 4d, 8P | 3,771 | 2,494 | — |
| Special wgn 4d, 6P | 3,676 | 2,439 | — |
| DeLuxe sdn 4d | 3,466 | 2,206 | — |
| DeLuxe Catalina htp cpe | 3,491 | 2,392 | — |
| DeLuxe wgn 4d, 6P | 3,716 | 2,579 | — |
| Custom Catalina htp cpe | 3,491 | 2,458 | — |

### 8Z Star Chief (wb 124.0)—115,088 built

| | Wght | Price | Prod |
|---|---|---|---|
| DeLuxe sdn 4d | 3,536 | 2,301 | — |
| DeLuxe conv cpe | 3,776 | 2,630 | — |
| Custom sdn 4d | 3,536 | 2,394 | — |
| Custom Catalina htp cpe | 3,551 | 2,557 | — |

| 1954 Engines | bore×stroke | bhp | availability |
|---|---|---|---|
| L6, 239.2 | 3.56×4.00 | 115 | S-Chieftain Six man |
| L6, 239.2 | 3.56×4.00 | 118 | S-Chieftain Six auto |
| L8, 268.4 | 3.38×3.75 | 122 | S-Chftn 8/Star Chief man |
| L8, 268.4 | 3.38×3.75 | 127 | S-Chftn 8/Star Chief auto |

## 1955

### 860 Chieftain (wb 122.0)

| | Wght | Price | Prod |
|---|---|---|---|
| sdn 4d | 3,511 | 2,164 | 65,155 |
| sdn 2d | 3,476 | 2,105 | 58,654 |
| wgn 4d, 8P | 3,686 | 2,518 | 6,091 |
| wgn 2d, 6P | 3,626 | 2,434 | 8,620 |

### 870 Chieftain (wb 122.0)

| | Wght | Price | Prod |
|---|---|---|---|
| sdn 4d | 3,511 | 2,268 | 91,187 |
| sdn 2d | 3,476 | 2,209 | 28,950 |
| Catalina htp cpe | 3,521 | 2,335 | 72,608 |
| wgn 4d, 6P | 3,676 | 2,603 | 19,439 |

### Star Chief (wb 124.0)

| | Wght | Price | Prod |
|---|---|---|---|
| sdn 4d | 3,556 | 2,362 | 44,800 |
| conv cpe | 3,791 | 2,691 | 19,762 |
| Custom sdn 4d | 3,557 | 2,455 | 35,153 |
| Custom Catalina htp cpe | 3,566 | 2,499 | 99,629 |
| Custom Safari wgn 2d, 6P | 3,636 | 2,962 | 3,760 |

| 1955 Engine | bore×stroke | bhp | availability |
|---|---|---|---|
| V8, 287.2 | 3.75×3.25 | 180 | S-all |

## 1956

### 860 Chieftain (wb 122.0)

| | Wght | Price | Prod |
|---|---|---|---|
| sdn 4d | 3,512 | 2,298 | 41,987 |
| Catalina htp sdn | 3,577 | 2,443 | 35,201 |
| sdn 2d | 3,452 | 2,240 | 41,908 |
| Catalina htp cpe | 3,512 | 2,370 | 46,335 |
| wgn 4d, 9P | 3,707 | 2,653 | 12,702 |
| wgn 2d, 6P | 3,612 | 2,569 | 6,099 |

### 870 Chieftain (wb 122.0)

| | Wght | Price | Prod |
|---|---|---|---|
| sdn 4d | 3,512 | 2,413 | 22,082 |
| Catalina htp sdn | 3,577 | 2,534 | 25,372 |
| Catalina htp cpe | 3,512 | 2,840 | 24,744 |
| wgn 4d, 6P | 3,657 | 2,749 | 21,674 |

### Star Chief (wb 124.0)

| | Wght | Price | Prod |
|---|---|---|---|
| sdn 4d | 3,577 | 2,527 | 18,346 |
| conv cpe | 3,797 | 2,857 | 13,510 |
| Custom Catalina htp sdn | 3,647 | 2,735 | 48,035 |
| Custom Catalina htp cpe | 3,567 | 2,665 | 43,392 |
| Custom Safari wgn 2d, 6P | 3,642 | 3,129 | 4,042 |

| 1956 Engines | bore×stroke | bhp | availability |
|---|---|---|---|
| V8, 316.6 | 3.94×3.25 | 205 | S-Chieftains |
| V8, 316.6 | 3.94×3.25 | 227 | S-Star Chief |

## 1957

### Chieftain (wb 122.0)

| | Wght | Price | Prod |
|---|---|---|---|
| sdn 4d | 3,560 | 2,527 | 35,671 |
| Catalina htp sdn | 3,635 | 2,614 | 40,074 |
| sdn 2d | 3,515 | 2,463 | 21,343 |
| Catalina htp cpe | 3,555 | 2,529 | 51,017 |
| Safari wgn 4d, 9P | 3,835 | 2,898 | 11,536 |
| Safari wgn 2d, 6P | 3,690 | 2,841 | 2,934 |

### Super Chief (wb 122.0)

| | Wght | Price | Prod |
|---|---|---|---|
| sdn 4d | 3,585 | 2,664 | 15,153 |
| Catalina htp sdn | 3,640 | 2,793 | 19,758 |
| Catalina htp cpe | 3,570 | 2,735 | 15,494 |
| Safari wgn 4d, 6P | 3,765 | 3,021 | 14,095 |

### Star Chief (wb 124.0; wgn-122.0)

| | Wght | Price | Prod |
|---|---|---|---|
| sdn 4d | 3,630 | 2,839 | 3,774 |
| conv cpe | 3,860 | 3,105 | 12,789 |
| Custom sdn 4d | 3,645 | 2,896 | 8,874 |
| Custom Catalina htp sdn | 3,710 | 2,975 | 44,283 |
| Custom Catalina htp cpe | 3,640 | 2,901 | 32,864 |
| Custom Safari wgn 2d, 6P* | 3,750 | 3,481 | 1,292 |
| Custom Safari wgn 4d, 6P | 3,810 | 3,636 | 1,894 |

### Bonneville (wb 124.0)

| | Wght | Price | Prod |
|---|---|---|---|
| conv cpe | 4,285 | 5,782 | 630 |

*All Pontiac wagons were called Safaris in 1957. The model indicated is the hardtop-styled Safari, first offered in 1955 and discontinued after 1957.

| 1957 Engines | bore×stroke | bhp | availability |
|---|---|---|---|
| V8, 347.0 | 3.94×3.56 | 252 | S-Chieftain |
| V8, 347.0 | 3.94×3.56 | 270 | S-Super Chief, Star Chief |
| V8, 347.0 | 3.94×3.56 | 290 | O-all exc Bonneville |
| V8, 347.0 | 3.94×3.56 | 300+ | S-Bonneville (fuel injection) |

## 1958

### Chieftain (wb 122.0)

| | | Wght | Price | Prod |
|---|---|---|---|---|
| 2567 | conv cpe | 3,850 | 3,019 | 7,359 |
| 2731 | Catalina htp cpe | 3,650 | 2,707 | 26,003 |
| 2739 | Catalina htp sdn | 3,785 | 2,792 | 17,946 |
| 2741 | sdn 2d | 3,640 | 2,573 | 17,394 |
| 2749 | sdn 4d | 3,735 | 2,638 | 44,999 |
| 2793 | Safari wgn 4d, 6P | 4,025 | 3,019 | 9,701 |
| 2794 | Safari wgn 4d, 9P | 4,070 | 3,088 | 5,417 |

### Super Chief (wb 124.0)

| | | Wght | Price | Prod |
|---|---|---|---|---|
| 2831D | Catalina htp cpe | 3,690 | 2,880 | 7,236 |
| 2839D | Catalina htp sdn | 3,810 | 2,961 | 7,886 |
| 2849D | sdn 4d | 3,770 | 2,834 | 12,006 |

### Star Chief Custom (wb 124.0)

| | | Wght | Price | Prod |
|---|---|---|---|---|
| 2793SC | Safari wgn 4d, 6P | 4,065 | 3,350 | 2,905 |
| 2831SD | Catalina htp cpe | 3,735 | 3,122 | 13,888 |
| 2839SD | Catalina htp sdn | 3,850 | 3,210 | 21,455 |
| 2849SD | sdn 4d | 3,825 | 3,071 | 10,547 |

# Pontiac

| Bonneville Custom (wb 122.0) | | Wght | Price | Prod |
|---|---|---|---|---|
| 2547SD | htp cpe | 3,710 | 3,481 | 9,144 |
| 2567SD | conv cpe | 3,925 | 3,586 | 3,096 |

| 1958 Engines | bore×stroke | bhp | availability |
|---|---|---|---|
| V8, 370.0 | 4.06×3.56 | 240 | S-Chieftain/Super Chief man |
| V8, 370.0 | 4.06×3.56 | 255 | S-Star Chief/Bonneville man |
| V8, 370.0 | 4.06×3.56 | 270 | S-Chieftain/Super Chief auto |
| V8, 370.0 | 4.06×3.56 | 285 | S-Star Chief/Bonneville auto |
| V8, 370.0 | 4.06×3.56 | 300 | O-all (Tri-Power) |
| V8, 370.0 | 4.06×3.56 | 310 | O-all (fuel injection) |

## 1959

| Catalina (wb 122.0) | | Wght | Price | Prod |
|---|---|---|---|---|
| 2111 | Sport sdn 2d | 3,870 | 2,633 | 26,102 |
| 2119 | sdn 4d | 3,955 | 2,704 | 72,377 |
| 2135 | Safari wgn 4d, 6P | 4,345 | 3,101 | 21,162 |
| 2137 | Sport htp cpe | 3,900 | 2,768 | 38,309 |
| 2139 | Vista htp sdn | 4,005 | 2,844 | 45,012 |
| 2145 | Safari wgn 4d, 9P | 4,405 | 3,209 | 14,084 |
| 2167 | conv cpe | 3,970 | 3,080 | 14,515 |

| Star Chief (wb 124.0) | | Wght | Price | Prod |
|---|---|---|---|---|
| 2411 | Sport sdn 2d | 3,930 | 2,934 | 10,254 |
| 2419 | sdn 4d | 4,005 | 3,005 | 27,872 |
| 2439 | Vista htp sdn | 4,055 | 3,138 | 30,689 |

| Bonneville (wb 124.0; wgn-122.0) | | Wght | Price | Prod |
|---|---|---|---|---|
| 2735 | Custom Safari wgn 4d, 6P | 4,370 | 3,532 | 4,673 |
| 2837 | Sport htp cpe | 3,985 | 3,257 | 27,769 |
| 2839 | Vista htp sdn | 4,085 | 3,333 | 38,696 |
| 2867 | conv cpe | 4,070 | 3,478 | 11,426 |

| 1959 Engines | bore×stroke | bhp | availability |
|---|---|---|---|
| V8, 389.0 | 4.06×3.75 | 215 | O-all auto |
| V8, 389.0 | 4.06×3.75 | 245 | S-Catalina/Star Chief man |
| V8, 389.0 | 4.06×3.75 | 260 | S-Bonneville auto |
| V8, 389.0 | 4.06×3.75 | 280 | S-Catalina/Star Chief auto |
| V8, 389.0 | 4.06×3.75 | 300 | S-Bonneville auto |
| V8, 389.0 | 4.06×3.75 | — | O-all (4bbl) |
| V8, 389.0 | 4.06×3.75 | 310 | O-all (Tri-Power) |

## 1960

| Catalina (wb 122.0) | | Wght | Price | Prod |
|---|---|---|---|---|
| 2111 | Sport sdn 2d | 3,835 | 2,631 | 25,504 |
| 2119 | sdn 4d | 3,935 | 2,702 | 72,650 |
| 2135 | Safari wgn 4d, 6P | 4,310 | 3,099 | 21,253 |
| 2137 | Sport htp cpe | 3,850 | 2,766 | 27,496 |
| 2139 | Vista htp sdn | 3,990 | 2,842 | 32,710 |
| 2145 | Safari wgn 4d, 9P | 4,365 | 3,207 | 14,149 |
| 2167 | conv cpe | 3,940 | 3,078 | 17,172 |

| Ventura (wb 122.0) | | Wght | Price | Prod |
|---|---|---|---|---|
| 2337 | Sport htp cpe | 3,865 | 2,971 | 27,577 |
| 2339 | Vista htp sdn | 3,990 | 3,047 | 28,700 |

| Star Chief (wb 124.0) | | Wght | Price | Prod |
|---|---|---|---|---|
| 2411 | Sport sdn 2d | 3,910 | 2,932 | 5,797 |
| 2419 | sdn 4d | 3,995 | 3,003 | 23,038 |
| 2439 | Vista htp sdn | 4,040 | 3,136 | 14,856 |

| Bonneville (wb 124.0; wgn-122.0) | | Wght | Price | Prod |
|---|---|---|---|---|
| 2735 | Custom Safari wgn 4d, 6P | 4,360 | 3,530 | 5,163 |
| 2837 | Sport htp cpe | 3,965 | 3,255 | 24,015 |
| 2839 | Vista htp sdn | 4,065 | 3,331 | 39,037 |
| 2867 | conv cpe | 4,030 | 3,476 | 17,062 |

| 1960 Engines | bore×stroke | bhp | availability |
|---|---|---|---|
| V8, 389.0 | 4.06×3.75 | 215 | O-all auto |
| V8, 389.0 | 4.06×3.75 | 245 | S-Star Chief/Cat/Vent man |
| V8, 389.0 | 4.06×3.75 | 260 | S-Bonneville man |

| | bore×stroke | bhp | availability |
|---|---|---|---|
| V8, 389.0 | 4.06×3.75 | 283 | S-Star Chief/Cat/Vent auto |
| V8, 389.0 | 4.06×3.75 | 303 | S-Bonneville auto |
| V8, 389.0 | 4.06×3.75 | 318 | O-all (Tri-Power) |

## 1961

| Tempest (wb 112.0) | | Wght | Price | Prod |
|---|---|---|---|---|
| 2117 | Custom spt cpe | 2,795 | 2,297 | 7,455 |
| 2119 | sdn 4d | 2,800 | 2,167 | 22,557 |
| 2120 | Custom sdn 4d | 2,810 | 2,351 | 40,082 |
| 2127 | spt cpe | 2,785 | 2,113 | 7,432 |
| 2135 | wgn 4d | 2,980 | 2,438 | 7,404 |
| 2136 | Custom wgn 4d | 2,990 | 2,622 | 15,853 |

| Catalina (wb 119.0) | | Wght | Price | Prod |
|---|---|---|---|---|
| 2311 | Sport sdn 2d | 3,650 | 2,631 | 9,846 |
| 2335 | Safari wgn 4d, 6P | 4,135 | 3,099 | 12,595 |
| 2337 | Sport htp cpe | 3,680 | 2,766 | 14,524 |
| 2339 | Vista htp sdn | 3,785 | 2,842 | 17,589 |
| 2345 | Safari wgn 4d, 9P | 4,175 | 3,207 | 7,783 |
| 2367 | conv cpe | 3,805 | 3,078 | 12,379 |
| 2369 | sdn 4d | 3,725 | 2,702 | 38,638 |

| Ventura (wb 119.0) | | Wght | Price | Prod |
|---|---|---|---|---|
| 2537 | Sport htp cpe | 3,685 | 2,971 | 13,297 |
| 2539 | Vista htp sdn | 3,795 | 3,047 | 13,912 |

| Star Chief (wb 123.0) | | Wght | Price | Prod |
|---|---|---|---|---|
| 2639 | Vista htp sdn | 3,870 | 3,136 | 13,559 |
| 2669 | sdn 4d | 3,840 | 3,003 | 16,024 |

| Bonneville (wb 123.0) | | Wght | Price | Prod |
|---|---|---|---|---|
| 2735 | Custom Safari wgn 4d | 4,185 | 3,530 | 3,323 |
| 2837 | Sport htp cpe | 3,810 | 3,255 | 16,906 |
| 2839 | Vista htp sdn | 3,895 | 3,331 | 30,830 |
| 2867 | conv cpe | 3,905 | 3,476 | 18,264 |

| 1961 Engines | bore×stroke | bhp | availability |
|---|---|---|---|
| L4, 194.5 | 4.06×3.75 | 110 | S-Tempest man |
| L4, 194.5 | 4.06×3.75 | 130 | S-Tempest auto |
| V8, 215.0 | 3.50×2.80 | 155 | O-Tempest |
| V8, 389.0 | 4.06×3.75 | 215 | S-Star Chief/Cat/Vent man |
| V8, 389.0 | 4.06×3.75 | 230 | O-all auto exc Tempest |
| V8, 389.0 | 4.06×3.75 | 235 | S-Bonneville man; O-other man |
| V8, 389.0 | 4.06×3.75 | 267 | S-Catalina/Ventura auto |
| V8, 389.0 | 4.06×3.75 | 283 | S-Star Chief auto |
| V8, 389.0 | 4.06×3.75 | 287 | O-Catalina/Ventura auto |
| V8, 389.0 | 4.06×3.75 | 303 | S-Bonneville auto; O-Star Chief auto |
| V8, 389.0 | 4.06×3.75 | 318 | O-all exc Tempest (Tri-Power) |

## 1962

| Tempest (wb 112.0)* | | Wght | Price | Prod |
|---|---|---|---|---|
| 2117 | spt cpe | 2,800 | 2,294 | 51,981 |
| 2119 | sdn 4d | 2,815 | 2,240 | 37,430 |
| 2127 | cpe | 2,785 | 2,186 | 15,473 |
| 2135 | Safari wgn 4d | 2,995 | 2,511 | 17,674 |
| 2167 | conv cpe | 2,955 | 2,564 | 20,635 |

| Catalina (wb 120.0; wgn-119.0) | | Wght | Price | Prod |
|---|---|---|---|---|
| 2311 | Sport sdn 2d | 3,705 | 2,725 | 14,263 |
| 2335 | Safari wgn 4d, 6P | 4,180 | 3,193 | 19,399 |
| 2339 | Vista htp sdn | 3,825 | 2,936 | 29,251 |
| 2345 | Safari wgn 4d, 9P | 4,220 | 3,301 | 10,716 |
| 2347 | Sport htp cpe | 3,730 | 2,860 | 46,024 |
| 2367 | conv cpe | 3,855 | 3,172 | 16,877 |
| 2369 | sdn 4d | 3,765 | 2,796 | 68,124 |

| Star Chief (wb 123.0) | | Wght | Price | Prod |
|---|---|---|---|---|
| 2639 | Vista htp sdn | 3,925 | 3,230 | 13,882 |
| 2669 | sdn 4d | 3,875 | 3,097 | 27,760 |

| Bonneville (wb 123.0) | | Wght | Price | Prod |
|---|---|---|---|---|
| 2735 | Custom Safari wgn 4d | 4,255 | 3,624 | 4,527 |
| 2839 | Vista htp sdn | 4,005 | 3,425 | 44,015 |
| 2847 | Sport htp cpe | 3,900 | 3,349 | 31,629 |
| 2867 | conv cpe | 4,005 | 3,570 | 21,582 |

| Grand Prix (wb 120.0) | | | | |
|---|---|---|---|---|
| 2947 | Sport htp cpe | 3,835 | 3,490 | 30,195 |

*Tempest includes DeLuxe and LeMans trim options. Factory records include the following production breakdowns:

| | std | DeLuxe | LeMans |
|---|---|---|---|
| cpe | 15,473 | — | — |
| spt cpe | — | 12,319 | 39,662 |
| sdn 4d | 16,057 | 21,373 | — |
| wgn 4d | 6,504 | 11,170 | — |
| conv cpe | — | 5,076 | 15,660 |

| 1962 Engines | bore×stroke | bhp | availability |
|---|---|---|---|
| L4, 194.5 | 4.06×3.75 | 110 | S-Tempest man |
| L4, 194.5 | 4.06×3.75 | 115 | S-Tempest auto |
| V8, 215.0 | 3.50×2.80 | 185 | O-Tempest |
| V8, 389.0 | 4.06×3.75 | 215 | S-Catalina/Star Chief man |
| V8, 389.0 | 4.06×3.75 | 230 | O-all full-size |
| V8, 389.0 | 4.06×3.75 | 235 | S-Bonn man; O-Cat/S Chf man |
| V8, 389.0 | 4.06×3.75 | 267 | S-Catalina auto |
| V8, 389.0 | 4.06×3.75 | 283 | S-Star Chief auto |
| V8, 389.0 | 4.06×3.75 | 303 | S-Bonn auto, GP; O-others |
| V8, 389.0 | 4.06×3.75 | 318 | O-all full-size (Tri-Power) |
| V8, 389.0 | 4.06×3.75 | 333 | O-all full-size (4bbl) |
| V8, 389.0 | 4.06×3.75 | 348 | O-all full-size (Tri-Power) |

# 1963

| Tempest (wb 112.0) | | Wght | Price | Prod |
|---|---|---|---|---|
| 2117 | DeLuxe spt cpe | 2,820 | 2,294 | 13,157 |
| 2119 | sdn 4d (incl DeLuxe) | 2,835 | 2,241 | 28,221 |
| 2127 | cpe | 2,810 | 2,188 | 13,307 |
| 2135 | wgn 4d (incl DeLuxe) | 2,995 | 2,512 | 10,135 |
| 2167 | DeLuxe conv cpe | 2,980 | 2,564 | 5,012 |

| Tempest LeMans (wb 112.0) | | | | |
|---|---|---|---|---|
| 2217 | spt cpe | 2,865 | 2,418 | 45,701 |
| 2267 | conv cpe | 3,035 | 2,742 | 15,957 |

| Catalina (wb 120.0, wgn-119.0) | | | | |
|---|---|---|---|---|
| 2311 | Sport sdn 2d | 3,685 | 2,725 | 14,091 |
| 2335 | Safari wgn 4d, 6P | 4,175 | 3,193 | 18,446 |
| 2339 | Vista htp sdn | 3,815 | 2,934 | 31,256 |
| 2345 | Safari wgn 4d, 9P | 4,230 | 3,300 | 11,751 |
| 2347 | Sport htp cpe | 3,725 | 2,859 | 60,795 |
| 2367 | conv cpe | 3,835 | 3,179 | 18,249 |
| 2369 | sdn 4d | 3,755 | 2,795 | 79,961 |

| Star Chief (wb 123.0) | | | | |
|---|---|---|---|---|
| 2639 | Vista htp sdn | 3,915 | 3,229 | 12,448 |
| 2669 | sdn 4d | 3,885 | 3,096 | 28,309 |

| Bonneville (wb 123.0; wgn-119.0) | | | | |
|---|---|---|---|---|
| 2835 | Safari wgn 4d, 6P | 4,245 | 3,623 | 5,156 |
| 2839 | Vista htp sdn | 3,985 | 3,423 | 49,929 |
| 2847 | Sport htp cpe | 3,895 | 3,348 | 30,995 |
| 2865 | conv cpe | 3,970 | 3,568 | 23,459 |

| Grand Prix (wb 120.0) | | | | |
|---|---|---|---|---|
| 2957 | Sport htp cpe | 3,915 | 3,489 | 72,959 |

| 1963 Engines | bore×stroke | bhp | availability |
|---|---|---|---|
| L4, 194.5 | 4.06×3.75 | 115 | S-Tempest |
| L4, 194.5 | 4.06×3.75 | 120 | O-Tempest man |
| L4, 194.5 | 4.06×3.75 | 140 | O-Tempest auto |
| L4, 194.5 | 4.06×3.75 | 166 | O-Tempest |

| | bore×stroke | bhp | availability |
|---|---|---|---|
| V8, 326.0 | 3.72×3.75 | 260 | O-Tempest |
| V8, 389.0 | 4.06×3.75 | 215 | S-Catalina/Star Chief man |
| V8, 389.0 | 4.06×3.75 | 230 | O-all full-size auto |
| V8, 389.0 | 4.06×3.75 | 235 | S-Bonn man; O-Cat/ Star Chief man |
| V8, 389.0 | 4.06×3.75 | 267 | S-Catalina man |
| V8, 389.0 | 4.06×3.75 | 283 | S-Star Chief man |
| V8, 389.0 | 4.06×3.75 | 303 | S-GP, Bonn auto; O-SC/Cat auto |
| V8, 389.0 | 4.06×3.75 | 318 | O-all full-size (Tri-Power) |
| V8, 421.0 | 4.09×4.00 | 353 | O-all full-size |
| V8, 421.0 | 4.09×4.00 | 370 | O-all full-size |

# 1964

| Tempest (wb 115.0) | | Wght | Price | Prod |
|---|---|---|---|---|
| 2027 | spt cpe | 2,930 | 2,259 | 6,365 |
| 2035 | Safari wgn 4d | 3,245 | 2,605 | 6,834 |
| 2069 | sdn 4d | 2,970 | 2,313 | 19,427 |
| 2127 | Custom spt cpe | 2,955 | 2,345 | 25,833 |
| 2135 | Custom Safari wgn 4d | 3,260 | 2,691 | 10,696 |
| 2167 | Custom conv cpe | 3,075 | 2,641 | 7,987 |
| 2169 | Custom sdn 4d | 2,990 | 2,399 | 29,948 |
| 2227 | LeMans spt cpe | 2,975 | 2,491 | 31,317 |
| 2237 | LeMans htp cpe | 2,995 | 2,556 | 31,310 |
| 2267 | LeMans conv cpe | 3,125 | 2,796 | 17,559 |

| Tempest G.T.O. (wb 115.0) | | | | |
|---|---|---|---|---|
| 2227 | spt cpe | 3,000 | 3,200 | 7,384 |
| 2237 | htp cpe | 3,020 | 3,250 | 18,422 |
| 2267 | conv cpe | 3,150 | 3,500 | 6,644 |

| Catalina (wb 120.0; wgn-119.0)* | | | | |
|---|---|---|---|---|
| 2311 | sdn 2d | 3,695 | 2,735 | 12,480 |
| 2335 | Safari wgn 4d, 6P | 4,190 | 3,203 | 20,356 |
| 2339 | Vista htp sdn | 3,835 | 2,945 | 33,849 |
| 2345 | Safari wgn 4d, 9P | 4,235 | 3,311 | 13,140 |
| 2347 | Sport htp cpe | 3,750 | 2,869 | 74,793 |
| 2367 | conv cpe | 3,825 | 3,181 | 18,693 |
| 2369 | sdn 4d | 3,770 | 2,806 | 84,457 |

| Star Chief (wb 123.0) | | | | |
|---|---|---|---|---|
| 2639 | Vista htp sdn | 3,945 | 3,239 | 11,200 |
| 2669 | sdn 4d | 3,885 | 3,107 | 26,453 |

| Bonneville (wb 120.0; wgn-119.0) | | | | |
|---|---|---|---|---|
| 2835 | Safari wgn 4d | 4,275 | 3,633 | 5,844 |
| 2839 | htp sdn | 3,995 | 3,433 | 57,630 |
| 2847 | htp cpe | 3,920 | 3,358 | 34,769 |
| 2867 | conv cpe | 3,985 | 3,578 | 22,016 |

| Grand Prix (wb 120.0) | | | | |
|---|---|---|---|---|
| 2957 | Sport htp cpe | 3,930 | 3,499 | 63,810 |

*Includes models equipped with 2+2 option package.

| 1964 Engines | bore×stroke | bhp | availability |
|---|---|---|---|
| L6, 215.0 | 3.75×3.25 | 140 | S-Tempest exc GTO |
| V8, 326.0 | 3.72×3.75 | 250 | O-Tempest |
| V8, 326.0 | 3.72×3.75 | 280 | O-Tempest |
| V8, 389.0 | 4.06×3.75 | 230 | O-all full-size auto |
| V8, 389.0 | 4.06×3.75 | 235 | S-Catalina/Star Chf man |
| V8, 389.0 | 4.06×3.75 | 267 | S-Catalina/Star Chf auto |
| V8, 389.0 | 4.06×3.75 | 283 | S-Cat 2+2 option; O-Cat/SC auto |
| V8, 389.0 | 4.06×3.75 | 303 | S-GP/Bonn auto; O-Cat/SC auto |
| V8, 389.0 | 4.06×3.75 | 306 | S-GP/Bonn man; O-Cat/SC man |
| V8, 389.0 | 4.06×3.75 | 325 | S-GTO; O-Tempest |
| V8, 389.0 | 4.06×3.75 | 330 | O-full-size |
| V8, 389.0 | 4.06×3.75 | 348 | O-GTO |
| V8, 421.0 | 4.09×4.00 | 350 | O-full-size |
| V8, 421.0 | 4.09×4.00 | 370 | O-full-size |

## 1965

### 233 Tempest (wb 115.0)

| | | Wght | Price | Prod |
|---|---|---|---|---|
| 27 | spt cpe | 2,930 | 2,260 | 18,198 |
| 35 | Safari wgn 4d | 3,220 | 2,605 | 5,622 |
| 69 | sdn 4d | 2,975 | 2,313 | 15,705 |

### 235 Tempest Custom (wb 115.0)

| | | | | |
|---|---|---|---|---|
| 27 | spt cpe | 2,975 | 2,346 | 18,367 |
| 35 | Safari wgn 4d | 3,215 | 2,619 | 10,792 |
| 37 | htp cpe | 2,975 | 2,411 | 29,906 |
| 67 | conv cpe | 3,080 | 2,641 | 8,346 |
| 69 | sdn 4d | 2,980 | 2,400 | 25,242 |

### 237 Tempest LeMans (wb 115.0)

| | | | | |
|---|---|---|---|---|
| 27 | spt cpe | 3,020 | 2,491 | 18,881 |
| 27 | G.T.O. spt cpe | 3,468 | 2,751 | 8,319 |
| 37 | htp cpe | 3,030 | 2,556 | 60,548 |
| 37 | G.T.O. htp cpe | 3,478 | 2,816 | 55,722 |
| 67 | conv cpe | 3,115 | 2,797 | 13,897 |
| 67 | G.T.O. conv cpe | 3,563 | 3,057 | 11,311 |
| 69 | sdn 4d | 3,020 | 2,551 | 14,227 |

### 252 Catalina (wb 121.0)*

| | | | | |
|---|---|---|---|---|
| 11 | sdn 2d | 3,695 | 2,734 | 9,526 |
| 35 | Safari wgn 4d, 6P | 4,165 | 3,202 | 22,399 |
| 37 | Sport htp cpe | 3,750 | 2,868 | 92,009 |
| 39 | Vista htp sdn | 3,855 | 2,945 | 38,814 |
| 45 | Safari wgn 4d, 9P | 4,210 | 3,309 | 15,110 |
| 67 | conv cpe | 3,815 | 3,196 | 18,347 |
| 69 | sdn 4d | 3,750 | 2,805 | 78,853 |

### 256 Star Chief (wb 124.0)

| | | | | |
|---|---|---|---|---|
| 39 | htp sdn | 3,925 | 3,238 | 9,132 |
| 69 | sdn 4d | 3,860 | 3,106 | 22,183 |

### 262 Bonneville (wb 124.0; wgn-121.0)

| | | | | |
|---|---|---|---|---|
| 35 | Safari wgn 4d | 4,310 | 3,632 | 6,460 |
| 37 | Sport htp cpe | 3,890 | 3,357 | 44,030 |
| 39 | htp sdn | 3,990 | 3,433 | 62,480 |
| 67 | conv cpe | 3,950 | 3,594 | 21,050 |

### 266 Grand Prix (wb 121.0)

| | | | | |
|---|---|---|---|---|
| 57 | Sport htp cpe | 3,940 | 3,498 | 57,881 |

*Includes models equipped with 2+2 option package.

| 1965 Engines | bore×stroke | bhp | availability |
|---|---|---|---|
| L6, 215.0 | 3.75×3.25 | 140 | S-Tempest exc GTO |
| V8, 326.0 | 3.72×3.75 | 250 | O-Tempest |
| V8, 326.0 | 3.72×3.75 | 285 | O-Tempest |
| V8, 389.0 | 4.06×3.75 | 256 | S-Cat/SC man; O-other full-size |
| V8, 389.0 | 4.06×3.75 | 290 | S-Catalina/Star Chf auto |
| V8, 389.0 | 4.06×3.75 | 325 | S-Bonn/Grand Prix auto |
| V8, 389.0 | 4.06×3.75 | 333 | S-Bonn/Grand Prix man |
| V8, 389.0 | 4.06×3.75 | 335 | S-GTO |
| V8, 389.0 | 4.06×3.75 | 360 | O-GTO |
| V8, 421.0 | 4.09×4.00 | 338 | S-Cat 2+2; O-other full-size |
| V8, 421.0 | 4.09×4.00 | 356 | O-all full-size |
| V8, 421.0 | 4.09×4.00 | 376 | O-all full-size |

## 1966

### 233 Tempest (wb 115.0)

| | | Wght | Price | Prod |
|---|---|---|---|---|
| 07 | spt cpe | 3,040 | 2,278 | 22,266 |
| 35 | wgn 4d | 3,340 | 2,624 | 40,095 |
| 69 | sdn 4d | 3,075 | 2,331 | 17,392 |

### 235 Tempest Custom (wb 115.0)

| | | | | |
|---|---|---|---|---|
| 07 | spt cpe | 3,060 | 2,362 | 17,182 |
| 17 | htp cpe | 3,075 | 2,426 | 31,322 |
| 35 | wgn 4d | 3,355 | 2,709 | 7,614 |
| 39 | htp sdn | 3,195 | 2,547 | 10,996 |
| 67 | conv cpe | 3,170 | 2,665 | 5,557 |
| 69 | sdn 4d | 3,100 | 2,415 | 23,988 |

### 237 LeMans (wb 115.0)

| | | Wght | Price | Prod |
|---|---|---|---|---|
| 07 | spt cpe | 3,090 | 2,505 | 16,654 |
| 17 | htp cpe | 3,125 | 2,568 | 78,109 |
| 39 | htp sdn | 3,195 | 2,701 | 13,897 |
| 67 | conv cpe | 3,220 | 2,806 | 13,080 |

### 242 Tempest G.T.O. (wb 115.0)

| | | | | |
|---|---|---|---|---|
| 07 | spt cpe | 3,445 | 2,783 | 10,363 |
| 17 | htp cpe | 3,465 | 2,847 | 73,785 |
| 67 | conv cpe | 3,555 | 3,082 | 12,798 |

### 252 Catalina (wb 121.0)

| | | | | |
|---|---|---|---|---|
| 11 | sdn 2d | 3,715 | 2,762 | 7,925 |
| 35 | wgn 4d, 6P | 4,250 | 3,217 | 21,082 |
| 37 | htp cpe | 3,835 | 2,893 | 79,013 |
| 39 | htp sdn | 3,910 | 2,968 | 38,005 |
| 45 | wgn 4d, 9P | 4,315 | 3,338 | 12,965 |
| 67 | conv cpe | 3,860 | 3,219 | 14,837 |
| 69 | sdn 4d | 3,785 | 2,831 | 80,483 |

### 254 2+2 (wb 121.0)*

| | | | | |
|---|---|---|---|---|
| 37 | htp cpe | 4,005 | 3,298 | — |
| 67 | conv cpe | 4,030 | 3,602 | — |

### 256 Star Chief Executive (wb 124.0)

| | | | | |
|---|---|---|---|---|
| 37 | htp cpe | 3,920 | 3,170 | 10,140 |
| 39 | htp sdn | 3,980 | 3,244 | 10,583 |
| 69 | sdn 4d | 3,920 | 3,114 | 24,489 |

### 262 Bonneville (wb 124.0; wgn-121.0)

| | | | | |
|---|---|---|---|---|
| 37 | htp cpe | 4,020 | 3,354 | 42,004 |
| 39 | htp sdn | 4,070 | 3,428 | 68,646 |
| 45 | wgn 4d, 3S | 4,390 | 3,747 | 8,452 |
| 67 | conv cpe | 4,015 | 3,586 | 16,299 |

### 266 Grand Prix (wb 121.0)

| | | | | |
|---|---|---|---|---|
| 57 | htp cpe | 4,015 | 3,492 | 36,757 |

*Included in Catalina production figures.

| 1966 Engines | bore×stroke | bhp | availability |
|---|---|---|---|
| L6, 230.0 | 3.88×3.26 | 165 | S-Tempest, LeMans |
| L6, 230.0 | 3.88×3.26 | 207 | O-Tempest, LeMans |
| V8, 326.0 | 3.72×3.75 | 250 | O-Tempest, LeMans |
| V8, 326.0 | 3.72×3.75 | 285 | O-Tempest, LeMans |
| V8, 389.0 | 4.06×3.75 | 256 | S-Cat/SC man O-other full-size |
| V8, 389.0 | 4.06×3.75 | 290 | O-Catalina, Star Chief |
| V8, 389.0 | 4.06×3.75 | 325 | S-Bonn/GP auto; O-Cat, Star Chief |
| V8, 389.0 | 4.06×3.75 | 333 | S-Bonn/GP man, GTO |
| V8, 389.0 | 4.06×3.75 | 360 | O-GTO |
| V8, 421.0 | 4.09×4.00 | 338 | S-2+2; O-other full-size |
| V8, 421.0 | 4.09×4.00 | 356 | O-all full-size |
| V8, 421.0 | 4.09×4.00 | 376 | O-all full-size |

## 1967

### 223 Firebird (wb 108.1)

| | | Wght | Price | Prod |
|---|---|---|---|---|
| 37 | htp cpe | 2,955 | 2,666 | 67,032 |
| 67 | conv cpe | 3,247 | 2,903 | 15,526 |

### 233 Tempest (wb 115.0)

| | | | | |
|---|---|---|---|---|
| 07 | cpe | 3,110 | 2,341 | 17,978 |
| 35 | wgn 4d | 3,370 | 2,666 | 3,495 |
| 69 | sdn 4d | 3,140 | 2,388 | 13,136 |

### 235 Tempest Custom (wb 115.0)

| | | | | |
|---|---|---|---|---|
| 07 | cpe | 3,130 | 2,437 | 12,469 |
| 17 | htp cpe | 3,140 | 2,494 | 30,512 |
| 35 | wgn 4d | 3,370 | 2,760 | 5,324 |
| 39 | htp sdn | 3,240 | 2,608 | 5,493 |
| 67 | conv cpe | 3,240 | 2,723 | 4,082 |
| 69 | sdn 4d | 3,145 | 2,482 | 17,445 |

| 237 LeMans (wb 115.0) | | Wght | Price | Prod |
|---|---|---|---|---|
| 07 | cpe | 3,155 | 2,586 | 10,693 |
| 17 | htp cpe | 3,155 | 2,648 | 75,965 |
| 39 | htp sdn | 3,265 | 2,771 | 8,424 |
| 67 | conv cpe | 3,250 | 2,881 | 9,820 |

| 239 Tempest Safari (wb 115.0) | | Wght | Price | Prod |
|---|---|---|---|---|
| 35 | wgn 4d | 3,390 | 2,936 | 4,511 |

| 242 Tempest G.T.O. (wb 115.0) | | Wght | Price | Prod |
|---|---|---|---|---|
| 07 | cpe | 3,425 | 2,871 | 7,029 |
| 17 | htp cpe | 3,430 | 2,935 | 65,176 |
| 67 | conv cpe | 3,515 | 3,165 | 9,517 |

| 252 Catalina (wb 121.0)* | | Wght | Price | Prod |
|---|---|---|---|---|
| 11 | sdn 2d | 3,735 | 2,807 | 5,633 |
| 35 | wgn 4d, 6P | 4,275 | 3,252 | 18,305 |
| 39 | htp sdn | 3,960 | 3,020 | 37,256 |
| 45 | wgn 4d, 9P | 4,340 | 3,374 | 11,040 |
| 67 | conv cpe | 3,910 | 3,276 | 10,033 |
| 69 | sdn 4d | 3,825 | 2,866 | 80,551 |
| 87 | htp cpe | 3,860 | 2,951 | 77,932 |

| 256 Executive (wb 124.0; wgn-121.0) | | Wght | Price | Prod |
|---|---|---|---|---|
| 35 | wgn 4d, 6P | 4,290 | 3,600 | 5,903 |
| 39 | htp sdn | 4,020 | 3,296 | 8,699 |
| 45 | wgn 4d, 9P | 4,370 | 3,722 | 5,593 |
| 69 | sdn 4d | 3,955 | 3,165 | 19,861 |
| 87 | htp cpe | 3,925 | 3,227 | 6,931 |

| 262 Bonneville (wb 124.0; wgn-121.0) | | Wght | Price | Prod |
|---|---|---|---|---|
| 39 | htp sdn | 4,110 | 3,517 | 56,307 |
| 45 | wgn 4d, 9P | 4,415 | 3,819 | 6,771 |
| 67 | conv cpe | 4,010 | 3,680 | 8,902 |
| 87 | htp cpe | 3,975 | 3,448 | 31,016 |

| 266 Grand Prix (wb 121.0) | | Wght | Price | Prod |
|---|---|---|---|---|
| 57 | htp cpe | 4,005 | 3,549 | 37,125 |
| 67 | conv cpe | 4,040 | 3,813 | 5,856 |

*Includes models equipped with 2+2 option package.

| 1967 Engines | bore×stroke | bhp | availability |
|---|---|---|---|
| L6, 230.0 | 3.88×3.26 | 165 | S-Firebird, LeMans, Temp exc GTO |
| L6, 230.0 | 3.88×3.26 | 215 | O-Firebird, LeMans, Temp exc GTO |
| V8, 326.0 | 3.72×3.75 | 250 | O-Firebird, LeMans, Temp exc GTO |
| V8, 326.0 | 3.72×3.75 | 285 | O-Firebird, LeMans, Temp exc Tempest Safari wgn |
| V8, 400.0 | 4.12×3.75 | 255 | O-GTO auto |
| V8, 400.0 | 4.12×3.75 | 265 | S-Cat/Vent/Exec man; O-auto |
| V8, 400.0 | 4.12×3.75 | 290 | S-Cat/Vent/Exec auto |
| V8, 400.0 | 4.12×3.75 | 325 | S-Bonn auto, Firebird 400 O-Catalina, Ventura, Exec |
| V8, 400.0 | 4.12×3.75 | 333 | S-Bonn man; O-Cat, Vent, Exec |
| V8, 400.0 | 4.12×3.75 | 335 | S-GTO |
| V8, 400.0 | 4.12×3.75 | 350 | S-Grand Prix |
| V8, 400.0 | 4.12×3.75 | 360 | O-GTO |
| V8, 428.0 | 4.12×4.00 | 360 | S-2+2; O-Cat, Exec, Bonn, Grand Prix |
| V8, 428.0 | 4.12×4.00 | 376 | O-Catalina, Exec, Bonn, Grand Prix |

# 1968

| 223 Firebird (wb 108.1) | | Wght | Price | Prod |
|---|---|---|---|---|
| 37 | htp cpe | 3,061 | 2,781 | 90,152 |
| 67 | conv cpe | 3,346 | 2,996 | 16,960 |

| 233 Tempest (wb 116.0; 2d-112.0) | | Wght | Price | Prod |
|---|---|---|---|---|
| 27 | spt cpe | 3,242 | 2,461 | 19,991 |

| 233 Tempest (wb 116.0; 2d-112.0) | | Wght | Price | Prod |
|---|---|---|---|---|
| 69 | sdn 4d | 3,309 | 2,509 | 11,590 |

| 235 Tempest Custom (wb 116.0; 2d-112.0) | | Wght | Price | Prod |
|---|---|---|---|---|
| 27 | spt cpe | 3,252 | 2,554 | 10,634 |
| 35 | wgn 4d | 3,667 | 2,906 | 8,253 |
| 37 | htp cpe | 3,277 | 2,614 | 40,574 |
| 39 | htp sdn | 3,384 | 2,728 | 6,147 |
| 67 | conv cpe | 3,337 | 2,839 | 3,518 |
| 69 | sdn 4d | 3,297 | 2,602 | 17,304 |

| 237 LeMans (wb 116.0; 2d-112.0) | | Wght | Price | Prod |
|---|---|---|---|---|
| 27 | spt cpe | 3,287 | 2,724 | 8,439 |
| 37 | htp cpe | 3,302 | 2,786 | 110,036 |
| 39 | htp sdn | 3,407 | 2,916 | 9,002 |
| 67 | conv cpe | 3,377 | 3,015 | 8,820 |

| 239 Tempest Safari (wb 116.0) | | Wght | Price | Prod |
|---|---|---|---|---|
| 35 | wgn 4d | 3,677 | 3,107 | 4,414 |

| 242 Tempest G.T.O. (wb 112.0) | | Wght | Price | Prod |
|---|---|---|---|---|
| 37 | htp cpe | 3,506 | 3,101 | 77,704 |
| 67 | conv cpe | 3,590 | 3,227 | 9,980 |

| 252 Catalina (wb 121.0) | | Wght | Price | Prod |
|---|---|---|---|---|
| 11 | sdn 2d | 3,839 | 2,945 | 5,247 |
| 35 | wgn 4d, 6P | 4,327 | 3,390 | 21,848 |
| 39 | htp sdn | 4,012 | 3,158 | 41,727 |
| 45 | wgn 4d, 9P | 4,408 | 3,537 | 13,363 |
| 67 | conv cpe | 3,980 | 3,391 | 7,339 |
| 69 | sdn 4d | 3,888 | 3,004 | 94,441 |
| 87 | htp cpe | 3,943 | 3,089 | 92,217 |

| 256 Executive (wb 124.0; wgn-121.0) | | Wght | Price | Prod |
|---|---|---|---|---|
| 35 | wgn 4d, 6P | 4,378 | 3,744 | 6,195 |
| 39 | htp sdn | 4,077 | 3,439 | 7,848 |
| 45 | wgn 4d, 9P | 4,453 | 3,890 | 5,843 |
| 69 | sdn 4d | 4,022 | 3,309 | 18,869 |
| 87 | htp cpe | 3,975 | 3,371 | 5,880 |

| 262 Bonneville (wb 124.0; wgn-121.0) | | Wght | Price | Prod |
|---|---|---|---|---|
| 39 | htp sdn | 4,171 | 3,660 | 57,055 |
| 45 | wgn 4d, 9P | 4,485 | 3,987 | 6,926 |
| 67 | conv cpe | 4,090 | 3,800 | 7,358 |
| 69 | sdn 4d | 4,122 | 3,530 | 3,499 |
| 87 | htp cpe | 4,054 | 3,592 | 29,598 |

| 266 Grand Prix (wb 121.0) | | Wght | Price | Prod |
|---|---|---|---|---|
| 57 | htp cpe | 4,075 | 3,697 | 31,701 |

| 1968 Engines | bore×stroke | bhp | availability |
|---|---|---|---|
| L6, 250.0 | 3.88×3.53 | 175 | S-Firebird, LeMans, Tempest exc GTO |
| L6, 250.0 | 3.88×3.53 | 215 | S-Frbrd Sprint; O-as above exc wgns |
| V8, 350.0 | 3.88×3.75 | 265 | S-Frbrd 350; O-Tempest exc GTO, LeMans |
| V8, 350.0 | 3.88×3.75 | 320 | S-Frbrd HO; O-Temp, LeM exc wgns |
| V8, 400.0 | 4.12×3.75 | 265 | O-GTO, all full-size |
| V8, 400.0 | 4.12×3.75 | 290 | S-Catalina, Ventura, Exec |
| V8, 400.0 | 4.12×3.75 | 330 | S-Firebird 400 |
| V8, 400.0 | 4.12×3.75 | 335 | O-Firebird 400 (Ram-Air) |
| V8, 400.0 | 4.12×3.75 | 340 | S-Bonn; O-Cat, Vent, Exec |
| V8, 400.0 | 4.12×3.75 | 350 | S-Grand Prix, GTO |
| V8, 400.0 | 4.12×3.75 | 360 | O-GTO |
| V8, 428.0 | 4.12×4.00 | 375 | O-Cat, Vent, Exec, Bonn, GP |
| V8, 428.0 | 4.12×4.00 | 390 | O-Cat, Vent, Exec, Bonn, GP |

# 1969

| 223 Firebird (wb 108.0) | | Wght | Price | Prod |
|---|---|---|---|---|
| 37 | htp cpe | 3,080 | 2,821 | 76,059 |
| 67 | conv cpe | 3,330 | 3,045 | 11,649 |

### 233 Tempest (wb 116.0; 2d-112.0)

| | | Wght | Price | Prod |
|---|---|---|---|---|
| 27 | spt cpe | 3,180 | 2,510 | 17,181 |
| 69 | sdn 4d | 3,250 | 2,557 | 9,741 |

### 235 Tempest Custom (wb 116.0; 2d-112.0)

| | | | | |
|---|---|---|---|---|
| 27 | spt cpe | 3,210 | 2,603 | 7,912 |
| 35 | wgn 4d | 3,595 | 2,956 | 6,963 |
| 37 | htp cpe | 3,220 | 2,663 | 46,886 |
| 39 | htp sdn | 3,315 | 2,777 | 3,918 |
| 67 | conv cpe | 3,265 | 2,888 | 2,379 |
| 69 | sdn 4d | 3,235 | 2,651 | 16,532 |

### 237 LeMans (wb 116.0; 2d-112.0)

| | | | | |
|---|---|---|---|---|
| 27 | spt cpe | 3,225 | 2,773 | 5,033 |
| 37 | htp cpe | 3,245 | 2,835 | 82,817 |
| 67 | conv cpe | 3,290 | 3,064 | 5,676 |
| 69 | htp sdn | 3,360 | 2,965 | 6,475 |

### 239 Tempest Safari (wb 116.0)

| | | | | |
|---|---|---|---|---|
| 36 | wgn 4d | 3,690 | 3,198 | 4,115 |

### 242 Tempest G.T.O. (wb 112.0)

| | | | | |
|---|---|---|---|---|
| 37 | htp cpe | 3,503 | 3,156 | 64,851 |
| 67 | conv cpe | 3,553 | 3,382 | 7,436 |

### 252 Catalina (wb 122.0)

| | | | | |
|---|---|---|---|---|
| 36 | wgn 4d, 6P | 4,455 | 3,519 | 20,352 |
| 37 | htp cpe | 3,925 | 3,174 | 84,006 |
| 39 | htp sdn | 4,005 | 3,244 | 38,814 |
| 46 | wgn 4d, 9P | 4,520 | 3,664 | 13,393 |
| 67 | conv cpe | 3,985 | 3,476 | 5,436 |
| 69 | sdn 4d | 3,945 | 3,090 | 84,590 |

### 256 Executive (wb 125.0; wgn-122.0)

| | | | | |
|---|---|---|---|---|
| 36 | wgn 4d, 6P | 4,475 | 3,872 | 6,411 |
| 37 | htp cpe | 3,970 | 3,456 | 4,492 |
| 39 | htp sdn | 4,065 | 3,525 | 6,522 |
| 46 | wgn 4d, 9P | 4,545 | 4,017 | 6,805 |
| 69 | sdn 4d | 4,045 | 3,394 | 14,831 |

### 262 Bonneville (wb 125.0; wgn-122.0)

| | | | | |
|---|---|---|---|---|
| 37 | htp cpe | 4,080 | 3,688 | 27,773 |
| 39 | htp sdn | 4,180 | 3,756 | 50,817 |
| 46 | wgn 4d, 9P | 4,600 | 4,104 | 7,428 |
| 67 | conv cpe | 4,130 | 3,896 | 5,438 |
| 69 | sdn 4d | 4,180 | 3,626 | 4,859 |

### 276 Grand Prix (wb 118.0)

| | | | | |
|---|---|---|---|---|
| 57 | htp cpe | 3,715 | 3,866 | 112,486 |

| 1969 Engines | bore×stroke | bhp | availability |
|---|---|---|---|
| L6, 250.0 | 3.88×3.53 | 175 | S-Frbrd, LeMans, Tempest exc GTO |
| L6, 250.0 | 3.88×3.53 | 230 | S-Frbrd Sprint; O-LeMans, Tempest exc GTO |
| V8, 350.0 | 3.88×3.75 | 265 | S-Frbrd 350; O-Tempest, LeMans |
| V8, 350.0 | 3.88×3.75 | 325 | S-Firebird 350 HO |
| V8, 350.0 | 3.88×3.75 | 330 | O-Frbrd, Tpst, LeMans exc wgns/GTO |
| V8, 400.0 | 4.12×3.75 | 265 | O-GTO/full-size auto |
| V8, 400.0 | 4.12×3.75 | 290 | S-Catalina, Ventura, Exec |
| V8, 400.0 | 4.12×3.75 | 330 | S-Firebird 400 |
| V8, 400.0 | 4.12×3.75 | 335 | O-Firebird 400 (Ram Air) |
| V8, 400.0 | 4.12×3.75 | 345 | O-Firebird 400 (Ram Air) |
| V8, 400.0 | 4.12×3.75 | 350 | S-GTO, Grand Prix |
| V8, 400.0 | 4.12×3.75 | 366 | O-GTO (Ram Air) |
| V8, 400.0 | 4.12×3.75 | 370 | O-GTO (Ram Air) |

## 1970

### 223 Firebird (wb 108.0)

| | | Wght | Price | Prod |
|---|---|---|---|---|
| 87 | htp cpe | 3,140 | 2,875 | 18,874 |
| 87 | Formula 400 htp cpe | 3,470 | 3,370 | 7,708 |

| | | Wght | Price | Prod |
|---|---|---|---|---|
| 87 | Trans Am htp cpe | 3,550 | 4,305 | 3,196 |
| 87 | Esprit htp | 3,435 | 3,241 | 18,961 |

### 233 Tempest (wb 116.0; 2d-112.0)

| | | | | |
|---|---|---|---|---|
| 27 | cpe | 3,225 | 2,623 | 11,977 |
| 37 | htp cpe | 3,250 | 2,683 | 20,883 |
| 69 | sdn 4d | 3,295 | 2,670 | 9,187 |

### 235 LeMans (wb 116.0, 2d-112.0)

| | | | | |
|---|---|---|---|---|
| 27 | cpe | 3,240 | 2,735 | 5,656 |
| 35 | wgn 4d | 3,585 | 3,092 | 7,165 |
| 37 | htp cpe | 3,265 | 2,795 | 52,304 |
| 39 | htp sdn | 3,385 | 2,921 | 3,872 |
| 69 | sdn 4d | 3,315 | 2,782 | 15,255 |

### 237 LeMans Sport (wb 116.0; 2d-112.0)

| | | | | |
|---|---|---|---|---|
| 27 | cpe | 3,265 | 2,891 | 1,673 |
| 36 | wgn 4d | 3,775 | 3,328 | 3,823 |
| 37 | htp cpe | 3,290 | 2,953 | 58,356 |
| 39 | htp sdn | 3,405 | 3,083 | 3,657 |
| 67 | conv cpe | 3,330 | 3,182 | 4,670 |

### 242 G.T.O. (112.0)*

| | | | | |
|---|---|---|---|---|
| 37 | htp cpe | 3,641 | 3,267 | 36,366 |
| 67 | conv cpe | 3,691 | 3,492 | 3,783 |

### 252 Catalina (wb 122.0)

| | | | | |
|---|---|---|---|---|
| 36 | wgn 4d, 6P | 4,517 | 3,646 | 16,944 |
| 37 | htp cpe | 3,952 | 3,249 | 70,350 |
| 39 | htp sdn | 4,042 | 3,319 | 35,155 |
| 46 | wgn 4d, 9P | 4,607 | 3,791 | 12,450 |
| 67 | conv cpe | 4,027 | 3,604 | 3,686 |
| 69 | sdn 4d | 3,997 | 3,164 | 84,795 |

### 256 Executive (wb 125.0; wgn-122.0)

| | | | | |
|---|---|---|---|---|
| 36 | wgn 4d, 6P | 4,552 | 4,015 | 4,861 |
| 37 | htp cpe | 4,042 | 3,600 | 3,499 |
| 39 | htp sdn | 4,132 | 3,669 | 5,376 |
| 46 | wgn 4d, 9P | 4,632 | 4,160 | 5,629 |
| 69 | sdn 4d | 4,087 | 3,538 | 13,061 |

### 262 Bonneville (wb 125.0; wgn-122.0)

| | | | | |
|---|---|---|---|---|
| 37 | htp cpe | 4,111 | 3,832 | 23,418 |
| 39 | htp sdn | 4,226 | 3,900 | 44,241 |
| 46 | wgn 4d, 9P | 4,686 | 4,247 | 7,033 |
| 67 | conv cpe | 4,161 | 4,040 | 3,537 |
| 69 | sdn 4d | 4,181 | 3,770 | 3,802 |

### 276 Grand Prix (wb 118.0)

| | | | | |
|---|---|---|---|---|
| 57 | htp cpe | 3,784 | 3,985 | 65,750 |

*Includes models equipped with "The Judge" option.

| 1970 Engines | bore×stroke | bhp | availability |
|---|---|---|---|
| L6, 250.0 | 3.88×3.53 | 155 | S-Tempest, LeMans, Firebird |
| V8, 350.0 | 3.88×3.75 | 255 | S-Firebird Esprit; O-above models, Cat exc conv and wgns |
| V8, 400.0 | 4.12×3.75 | 265 | O-all auto exc GTO, Bonn |
| V8, 400.0 | 4.12×3.75 | 290 | S-Cat conv/wgn, Exec; O-other Cat |
| V8, 400.0 | 4.12×3.75 | 330 | S-Frbrd 400; O-Tpst/LeM/ Cat/Exec auto |
| V8, 400.0 | 4.12×3.75 | 345 | S-Frbrd Trans Am; O-Tpst/ LeMans man |
| V8, 400.0 | 4.12×3.75 | 350 | S-GTO, Grand Prix |
| V8, 400.0 | 4.12×3.75 | 366 | S-GTO Judge; O-GTO (Ram Air) |
| V8, 400.0 | 4.12×3.75 | 370 | O-GTO (Ram Air); O-GTO Judge |
| V8, 455.0 | 4.15×4.21 | 360 | S-Bonn; O-Cat, Exec, GTO |
| V8, 455.0 | 4.15×4.21 | 370 | S-Grand Prix SJ; O-GP J, Cat, Exec, Bonn |

# Rambler
**American Motors Corp.**
**Kenosha, Wisconsin**

When George Romney succeeded George Mason as president of American Motors, he turned his full attention to the Rambler and soon forgot about Mason's merger plans (see Nash), including a link-up with Studebaker-Packard. The Rambler was AMC's most successful car, and developed a whole new market.

Retaining the 108-inch wheelbase unit body/chassis introduced in '56, AMC removed ostensible Nash and Hudson parentage to make Rambler a separate nameplate for the 1957 model year. The car was solidly built, reliable, and perfectly attuned to the burgeoning market for economy cars. By 1961, its successors had brought Rambler to third place in the industry.

All but forgotten today is the fact that AMC introduced the industry's first four-door hardtop wagon: the 1956 (Nash and Hudson) Rambler Cross Country. This neat, airy, roomy wagon featured a 33 percent increase in cargo space over that of the '55s, and a roll-down tailgate window that eliminated the clumsy upper hatch. "We just rolled with those cars," said former AMC Board Chairman Roy D. Chapin, Jr. "We couldn't get enough." There was nothing like the luxurious little Cross Country, and the public responded accordingly.

In 1957, with the big Hudson and Nash destined for oblivion, American Motors built 118, 990 cars; 114,084

of them were Ramblers. The overhead-valve six was raised in horsepower, while a lively new oversquare V8 was offered with 190 hp at 4900 rpm. It was available only on the upper-priced cars—Custom and Super sedan and wagon. An interesting new Custom model was the specially trimmed Rebel, a four-door hardtop announced at mid-year with an even larger V8, the new AMC 327. The Rebel had Gabriel shocks, an anti-roll bar, heavy-duty springs, power steering, and power brakes. All that and 255 bhp from the V8s 9.5:1 compression ratio transformed Rambler's image. During tests at Daytona Beach, a Rebel flew from 0 to 60 mph (and 50 to 80) in scarcely more than seven seconds. Unfortunately, it just didn't appeal to the Rambler market, and only 1500 were built. Rebel was the most expensive '57 offering, and that may have contributed to its low sales.

Economy cars were continuing to set sales records, so AMC brought back its old 100-inch '55 models for 1958. Called Rambler American and fitted with a new mesh-type grille, it was priced very low. It couldn't help but sell, and over 42,000 Americans were registered for the 12 months. Larger Ramblers received more than 100 changes for '58, and were outwardly quite different from their predecessors. The grille was made more massive

1957 Custom hardtop sedan

1957 DeLuxe four-door sedan

1957 Custom Cross Country hardtop wagon

1957 Rebel Custom hardtop sedan

and square, dual headlamps were used, fashionable little fins appeared at the rear, and a pedal-type parking brake was adopted. The six-cylinder Super Cross Country wagon was the top seller that year. The Rebel name was retained for top-line models powered by the 250-cid V8. But Rambler did not revive its fancy,

**1958 Rebel Custom four-door sedan**

**1958 Rebel Custom Cross Country station wagon**

**1959 Rebel Custom Country Club hardtop sedan**

**1959 American Super two-door sedan**

limited-edition Rebel hardtop. Instead, it created a new 117-inch wheelbase for a separate line powered by the 327 V8 and named Ambassador.

Actually, Ambassador styling had been predicted in mid-1957, when it was thought that these cars would bear separate Nash and Hudson identification. In essence, they were stretched versions of the roomy, squarish Rambler unit body/chassis, available as four-door sedans and wagons, with or without roof pillars. The Ambassador hardtop wagon was the only one of its type in the '58 line, and only 294 were sold. In fact, sales overall were quite disappointing—just 1340 for the model year. Ambassador was entering a field of heavy competition and decreasing demand, and AMC did much better with its smaller Ramblers. Registrations of all 1958 models climbed in a year that was generally a disaster for other manufacturers. After four years of losses, AMC turned the corner, making a profit of $26 million on sales of $470 million.

For 1959, it was the same formula again. This time, the company netted $60 million in profits and built nearly 364,000 cars for an all-time record. The same models and powertrains were fielded, but horsepower wasn't raised. Unlike its competitors, AMC had apparently decided enough was enough.

A two-door wagon was revived for the Rambler American DeLuxe and Super lines, helping rack up 90,000 sales for the '59 junior series. The 108-inch-wheelbase cars were mildly facelifted with thin "color sweep" side moldings and simplified grilles. As in 1958, Rambler V8s were called Rebels and used the 250-cid engine. The Ambassador Super and Custom continued as before on the longer wheelbase and with a more ornate grille.

At the beginning of the '60s, everything looked rosy. Led by hard-driving president Romney, Rambler could do no wrong. In 1960 it almost beat Plymouth for third place in production, with nearly half a million cars, and did in 1961. This was the highest sales volume ever recorded for an independent. But Rambler's success triggered an avalanche of compacts from the Big Three—and formidable new competition. A downward slide began in 1962, when Rambler was passed by Pontiac. By 1967, AMC as a whole was in 12th place.

Perhaps Romney saw the handwriting on the wall, because he left the company in 1962. Replacing him was Roy Abernethy, who began a program of product diversification that tried to meet the opposition on every front. It didn't work, and Abernethy was succeeded by Roy D. Chapin, Jr. in 1966. Chapin became AMC board chairman in 1967, and William V. Luneberg became president. The Chapin-Luneberg administration ordered new makes like the Javelin, and dropped the Rambler name completely after 1969.

For 1960, the 108-inch-wheelbase unibody Rambler acquired less cluttered lines, little tailfins, and a full-width grille. Facelifts occurred in 1961 and '62 as the cars became known as Rambler Classics. A lower hoodline for '61 was accompanied by an eggcrate

1960 American Super two-door station wagon

1961 Classic Custom four-door station wagon

1961 Ambassador Custom four-door sedan

1961 American Custom convertible

grille. In 1962, the crate held larger eggs, the fins were cropped, and the side sweep-spear was moved higher. An interesting option was the E-stick, a combination automatic and clutch transmission that cost $60. But it was too complex to sell really well. It was similar in concept to the twin-stick manual gearbox of the 1979 Dodge Colt FF and Plymouth Champ made by Mitsubishi of Japan.

Richard A. Teague joined the American Motors design staff in 1961, and the first cars he was able to influence were the '63 Classic and Ambassador. Teague used a longer (112-inch) wheelbase, a lower silhouette than before, a concave grille, sculptured body panels, and curved side glass to create a smooth new shape. Although still chunky, the new Rambler was at least cleanly styled. The Classic retained this basic body shape throughout its life span. Teague made further refinements to the design over the next few years. The 1964s had a new flush grille and stainless-steel-trimmed rocker panels. Two hardtop coupes were added to the line, which until then had consisted of two- and four-door sedans and four-door Cross Country station wagons. The 1965s received a new grille, a squared-off hood, and wraparound taillights. The '66s featured a new roof with convertible-like accents, a revised roof and tailgate for station wagons, and more sharply creased lines from front to rear.

For 1967, the Classic was renamed Rebel. From 1968 on, Rebel was listed as a separate make (see the American Motors chapter), the Rambler name reserved only for the smaller American line. The '67 Rebel had a two-inch longer wheelbase. Its all-new styling comprised a floating rectangular grille flanked by horizontal dual

headlamps and squarish front fenders that flowed into a curved rear fenderline. The rear end displayed large, canted taillights blended into the fenders.

Rambler started the '60s with two engines, a six and a V8. The six, a holdover from Nash days, developed 127 or 138 bhp, and was standard on Classics through 1964. The V8 had been designed for use by Hudson and Nash in the mid-1950s. In its 1960-61 form, it developed either 200 or 215 bhp.

The '61 Classic V8 scored well for both performance and economy. When equipped with the optional Flash-omatic (Borg-Warner) automatc transmission, it could spring from 0 to 60 mph in ten seconds, and delivered 16 to 20 miles per gallon. But the V8 was heavier than the six, so that no less than 57 percent of the car's curb weight was over the front wheels. Sales were not high. When the Ambassador was made smaller for 1962-63, the V8 Classic was temporarily dropped.

In 1964, it returned with 198 bhp. For 1965, a 270-bhp version was available. For the 1967 Rebel, the engine was stroked for 200 bhp. A larger V8, the Ambassador 327, was also offered for the '66 Classic. For the 1967 Rebel, it was enlarged by boring and stroking to 343 cid, which gave 235 or 280 bhp depending on tune.

As an option to the Classic's standard six, Rambler brought out a new oversquare engine for 1964, the Torque Command or Typhoon six, which yielded 145 bhp. About 2500 special Typhoon hardtops, painted yellow and black, were released to celebrate the occasion.

At the lower end of the size and price scale was the Rambler American. In 1960 form, it was an anachronism with its old Pininfarina styling and an ancient Nash L-

1962 Classic Custom two-door sedan

1962 American Super four-door station wagon

1963 American 330 four-door sedan

1963 Ambassador 990 two-door sedan

1964 Ambassador 990H hardtop coupe

head six. Convinced that the American was marketable, AMC restyled it for 1961. The new model also got a new overhead-valve engine that had actually appeared in mid-1960 on the larger Ramblers. Available with either 90 or 125 bhp, it gave the American fuel mileage in the middle 20s, plus adequate performance. The styling, created by Edmund Anderson, was something else again: boxy and truncated, with odd, concave side sculpturing. Sedans, business coupes, two- and four-door wagons, and a convertible were offered in three series. Although they were genuine economy cars and provided a fair amount of interior room, they were anything but beautiful. Teague decided to change them at all costs for 1964.

The revamped design sat on a longer 106-inch wheelbase, as the Classic had already gone from 108 to 112. It was a clean car with curved glass and modest brightwork—quite in keeping with its function. The styling was so good, in fact, that it wasn't significantly altered for the rest of the decade. By 1968, the American had a specially trimmed hardtop derivative, the Rogue. In 1969, the base American was still listed under $2000. A post-introduction decision was to offer AMC's new 290-cid V8 as an option. This led to a limited-edition Rogue, equipped with an even larger 315-bhp 390 engine and Hurst shifter, called the SC/Rambler. "Scramblers" were sold to a handful of buyers. Though hardly in keeping with the traditional Rambler image, they were impressive performers.

Teague hastily conjured up a bucket-seat fastback for 1965 to do battle with Mustang and Barracuda. The result was the Marlin, a Rambler model in 1965 and a make in its own right thereafter. The Marlin was basically a Rambler Classic reworked above the beltline with a sweeping glassed-in greenhouse. When equipped with the 327 V8, a Marlin would do 0 to 60 mph in 12 seconds and the standing quarter-mile in 18 seconds at 76 mph—not earthshaking, but performance of a sort. And that was the goal: to turn Rambler's image around by making cars that appeared sporty and fun to drive, instead of just dull and economical.

The 1960-61 Ambassador was a continuation of the '58 original, with increasingly luxurious interiors and slightly excessive ornamentation. The price leader in both years was the Deluxe four-door sedan. In addition, there were Super and Custom four-doors, and wagons with either six or eight seats. In 1961, a posh Custom 400 sedan with the highest-quality trim and standard automatic was added. The 327 V8 was standard power. But before the end of the '50s, AMC managers had decided the large Ambassador V8s were not salable. For 1962, therefore, the 117-inch wheelbase was dropped, and Ambassador shared the Classic body and chassis. The V8 was dropped from the Classic's option list and was restricted to Ambassador only.

For 1963, Teague planned to restyle the Classic, which, of course, meant a restyled Ambassador as well. Again, both cars shared the same wheelbase. From a distance, Classics and Ambassadors looked almost

1965 Ambassador 990 convertible

1966 American 440 convertible

1965 Classic 770 convertible

1967 Rebel SST hardtop coupe

1965 Marlin fastback hardtop coupe

1968 American 440 four-door station wagon

1969 Rogue hardtop coupe

identical—and they *were* similar, except for power-plants. For 1964, Classic was offered with an optional small V8. Ambassador was then restricted to one 327-powered 990 series. There was a sedan, a Cross Country wagon, and two hardtop coupes called the 990 and 990H. The 990H was the only Ambassador with the 270-bhp engine standard.

The 1964 lineup wasn't particularly successful, so the game plan was changed again for '65. Ambassador now returned its own (116-inch) wheelbase (the Classic stayed with the 112), and in standard form had the 232-cid six. There were almost no changes for '66, except that the name was registered as a separate make.

The styling of the '65 Rambler Ambassador was prob-

ably the best it had ever been. Teague's four-square de-sign resulted in an intermediate comparable in size to the Ford Fairlane, but with distinctive looks and more interior space. The lineup comprised the 880 two-door and four-door sedan and wagon; the luxury 990 four-door sedan, wagon, and hardtop; and the 990H hardtop and convertible.

AMC made a play for the soft-top market in 1965: there was a convertible in every line—American, Clas-sic, and Ambassador. Unhappily, they tended to leak because of the curved side windows, and did not sell well. Soft-top production in '65 consisted of 3882 Amer-icans, 4953 Classics, and 3499 Ambassadors. The Ambassador convertible was dropped after 1967.

# Rambler

## Rambler Specifications

### 1957*

**Six (wb 108.0)**

| | | Wght | Price | Prod |
|---|---|---|---|---|
| 5715 | DeLuxe sdn 4d | 2,911 | 1.961 | — |
| 5715-1 | Super sdn 4d | 2,914 | 2,123 | — |
| 5715-2 | Custom sdn 4d | 2,938 | 2,213 | — |
| 5718-1 | Super Crss Cntry wgn 4d | 3,042 | 2,410 | — |
| 5718-2 | Custom Crss Cntry wgn 4d | 3,076 | 2,500 | — |
| 5719-1 | Super htp sdn | 2,936 | 2,208 | — |

**V8 (wb 108.0)**

| | | Wght | Price | Prod |
|---|---|---|---|---|
| 5723-2 | Custom Crss Cntry htp wgn 4d | 3,409 | 2,715 | — |
| 5725-1 | Super sdn 4d | 3,223 | 2,253 | — |
| 5725-2 | Custom sdn 4d | 3,259 | 2,343 | — |
| 5728-1 | Super Crss Cntry wgn 4d | 3,359 | 2,540 | — |
| 5728-2 | Custom Crss Cntry wgn 4d | 3,392 | 2,630 | — |
| 5729-2 | Custom htp sdn | 3,269 | 2,428 | — |
| 5739-2 | Custom Rebel htp sdn | 3,353 | 2,786 | 1,500 |

*Total model year registrations: 91,469.

| 1957 Engines | bore×stroke | bhp | availability |
|---|---|---|---|
| L6, 195.6 | 3.13×4.25 | 135 | S-Six |
| V8, 250.0 | 3.50×3.25 | 190 | S-V8 exc Rebel |
| V8, 327.0 | 4.00×3.25 | 255 | S-Rebel |

### 1958*

**American (wb 100.0)**

| | | Wght | Price | Prod |
|---|---|---|---|---|
| 5802 | bus sdn 3P | 2,439 | 1,775 | — |
| 5806 | DeLuxe sdn 2d | 2,463 | 1,789 | — |
| 5806-1 | Super sdn 2d | 2,475 | 1,874 | — |

**Six (wb 108.0)**

| | | Wght | Price | Prod |
|---|---|---|---|---|
| 5815 | DeLuxe sdn 4d | 2,947 | 2,047 | — |
| 5815-1 | Super sdn 4d | 2,960 | 2,212 | — |
| 5815-2 | Custom sdn 4d | 2,968 | 2,327 | — |
| 5818 | DeLuxe wgn 4d | 3,050 | 2,370 | — |
| 5818-1 | Super Crss Cntry wgn 4d | 3,069 | 2,506 | — |
| 5818-2 | Custom Crss Cntry wgn 4d | 3,079 | 2,621 | — |
| 5819-1 | Super Ctry Club htp cpe | 2,983 | 2,287 | — |

**Rebel V8 (wb 108.0)**

| | | Wght | Price | Prod |
|---|---|---|---|---|
| 5825 | DeLuxe sdn 4d | 3,287 | 2,177 | — |
| 5825-1 | Super sdn 4d | 3,300 | 2,342 | — |
| 5825-2 | Custom sdn 4d | 3,313 | 2,457 | — |
| 5828-1 | Super Crss Cntry wgn 4d | 3,410 | 2,636 | — |
| 5828-2 | Custom Crss Cntry wgn 4d | 3,418 | 2,751 | — |
| 5829-2 | Custom Ctry Club htp cpe | 3,328 | 2,532 | — |

**Ambassador (wb 117.0)—1,340 built (inc 294 model 5883-2)**

| | | Wght | Price | Prod |
|---|---|---|---|---|
| 5883-2 | Custom Crss Cntry htp wgn 4d | 3,586 | 3,116 | — |
| 5885-1 | Super sdn 4d | 3,456 | 2,587 | — |
| 5885-2 | Custom sdn 4d | 3,462 | 2,732 | — |
| 5888-1 | Super Crss Cntry wgn 4d | 3,544 | 2,881 | — |
| 5888-2 | Custom Crss Cntry wgn 4d | 3,568 | 3,026 | — |
| 5889-2 | Custom Ctry Club htp sdn | 3,475 | 2,822 | — |

*Total model year registrations: 186,227.

| 1958 Engines | bore×stroke | bhp | availability |
|---|---|---|---|
| L6, 195.6 | 3.13×4.25 | 90 | S-American |
| L6, 195.6 | 3.13×4.25 | 127 | S-Six |
| L6, 195.6 | 3.13×4.25 | 138 | O-Six |
| V8, 250.0 | 3.50×3.25 | 215 | S-Rebel |
| V8, 327.0 | 4.00×3.25 | 270 | S-Ambassador |

### 1959*

**American (wb 100.0)—90,000 built**

| | | Wght | Price | Prod |
|---|---|---|---|---|
| 5902 | bux scn 3P | 2,435 | 1,821 | — |
| 5904 | DeLuxe wgn 2d | 2,554 | 2,060 | — |
| 5904-1 | Super wgn 2d | 2,554 | 2,145 | — |
| 5906 | DeLuxe sdn 2d | 2,476 | 1,835 | — |
| 5906-1 | Super sdn 2d | 2,492 | 1,920 | — |

**Six (wb 108.0)**

| | | Wght | Price | Prod |
|---|---|---|---|---|
| 5915 | DeLuxe sdn 4d | 2,934 | 2,098 | — |
| 5915-1 | Super sdn 4d | 2,951 | 2,268 | — |
| 5915-2 | Custom sdn 4d | 2,956 | 2,383 | — |
| 5918 | DeLuxe Crss Cntry wgn 4d | 3,047 | 2,427 | — |
| 5918-1 | Super Crss Cntry wgn 4d | 3,082 | 2,562 | — |
| 5918-2 | Custom Crss Cntry wgn 4d | 3,097 | 2,677 | — |
| 5919-1 | Super Ctry Club htp sdn | 2,961 | 2,343 | — |

**Rebel V8 (wb 108.0)**

| | | Wght | Price | Prod |
|---|---|---|---|---|
| 5925 | DeLuxe sdn 4d | 3,283 | 2,228 | — |
| 5925-1 | Super sdn 4d | 3,287 | 2,398 | — |
| 5925-2 | Custom sdn 4d | 3,295 | 2,513 | — |
| 5928-1 | Super Crss Cntry wgn 4d | 3,398 | 2,692 | — |
| 5928-2 | Custom Crss Cntry wgn 4d | 3,407 | 2,807 | — |
| 5929-2 | Custom Ctry Club htp sdn | 3,338 | 2,588 | — |

**Ambassador (wb 117.0)**

| | | Wght | Price | Prod |
|---|---|---|---|---|
| 5983-2 | Custom htp wgn 4d | 3,591 | 3,116 | — |
| 5985-1 | Super sdn 4d | 3,428 | 2,587 | — |
| 5985-2 | Custom sdn 4d | 3,437 | 2,732 | — |
| 5988-1 | Super Crss Cntry wgn 4d | 3,546 | 2,881 | — |
| 5988-2 | Custom Crss Cntry wgn 4d | 3,562 | 3,026 | — |
| 5989-2 | Custom Ctry Club htp sdn | 3,483 | 2,822 | — |

*Total model year registrations: 363,372.

| 1959 Engines | bore×stroke | bhp | availability |
|---|---|---|---|
| L6, 195.6 | 3.13×4.25 | 90 | S-American |
| L6, 195.6 | 3.13×4.25 | 127 | S-Six |
| L6, 195.6 | 3.13×4.25 | 138 | O-Six |
| V8, 250.0 | 3.50×3.25 | 215 | S-Rebel |
| V8, 327.0 | 4.00×3.25 | 270 | S-Ambassador |

### 1960*

**American (wb 100.0)**

| | | Wght | Price | Prod |
|---|---|---|---|---|
| 6002 | DeLuxe bus sdn 3P | 2,428 | 1,781 | — |
| 6004 | DeLuxe wgn 2d | 2,527 | 2,020 | — |
| 6004-1 | Super wgn 2d | 2,549 | 2,185 | — |
| 6004-2 | Custom wgn 2d | 2,606 | 2,235 | — |
| 6005 | DeLuxe sdn 4d | 2,474 | 1,844 | — |
| 6005-1 | Super sdn 4d | 2,490 | 1,929 | — |
| 6005-2 | Custom sdn 4d | 2,551 | 2,059 | — |
| 6006 | DeLuxe sdn 2d | 2,451 | 1,795 | — |
| 6006-1 | Super sdn 2d | 2,462 | 1,880 | — |
| 6006-2 | Custom sdn 2d | 2,523 | 2,010 | — |

**Six (wb 108.0)**

| | | Wght | Price | Prod |
|---|---|---|---|---|
| 6015 | DeLuxe sdn 4d | 2,912 | 2,098 | — |
| 6015-1 | Super sdn 4d | 2,930 | 2,268 | — |
| 6015-2 | Custom sdn 4d | 2,929 | 2,383 | — |
| 6018 | DeLuxe wgn 4d | 3,051 | 2,427 | — |
| 6018-1 | Super wgn 4d, 6P | 3,054 | 2,562 | — |
| 6018-2 | Custom wgn 4d, 6P | 3,057 | 2,677 | — |
| 6018-3 | Super wgn 4d, 8P | 3,117 | 2,687 | — |
| 6018-4 | Custom wgn 4d, 8P | 3,137 | 2,802 | — |
| 6019-2 | Custom htp sdn | 2,981 | 2,458 | — |

**Rebel V8 (wb 108.0)**

| | | Wght | Price | Prod |
|---|---|---|---|---|
| 6025 | DeLuxe sdn 4d | 3,252 | 2,217 | — |
| 6025-1 | Super sdn 4d | 3,270 | 2,387 | — |
| 6025-2 | Custom sdn 4d | 3,278 | 2,502 | — |

| | | Wght | Price | Prod |
|---|---|---|---|---|
| 6028-1 | Super wgn 4d, 6P | 3,391 | 2,681 | — |
| 6028-2 | Custom wgn 4d, 6P | 3,395 | 2,796 | — |
| 6028-3 | Super wgn 4d, 8P | 3,446 | 2,806 | — |
| 6028-4 | Custom wgn 4d, 8P | 3,447 | 2,921 | — |
| 6029-2 | Custom htp sdn | 3,319 | 2,577 | — |

**Ambassador (wb 117.0)**

| | | Wght | Price | Prod |
|---|---|---|---|---|
| 6083-2 | Custom htp wgn 4d | 3,583 | 3,116 | — |
| 6085 | DeLuxe sdn 4d | 3,384 | 2,395 | — |
| 6085-1 | Super sdn 4d | 3,395 | 2,587 | — |
| 6085-2 | Custom sdn 4d | 3,408 | 2,732 | — |
| 6088-1 | Super wgn 4d, 6P | 3,521 | 2,881 | — |
| 6088-2 | Custom wgn 4d, 6P | 3,538 | 3,026 | — |
| 6088-3 | Super wgn 4d, 8P | 3,581 | 3,006 | — |
| 6088-4 | Custom wgn 4d, 8P | 3,592 | 3,151 | — |
| 6089-2 | Custom htp sdn | 3,465 | 2,822 | — |

*Total model year registrations: 422,273.

| 1960 Engines | bore×stroke | bhp | availability |
|---|---|---|---|
| L6, 195.6 | 0.13×4.25 | 90 | S-American |
| L6, 195.6 | 3.13×4.25 | 127 | S-Six |
| L6, 195.6 | 3.13×4.25 | 138 | O-Six |
| V8, 250.0 | 3.50×3.25 | 200 | S-Rebel |
| V8, 250.0 | 3.50×3.25 | 215 | O-Rebel |
| V8, 327.0 | 4.00×3.25 | 250 | S-Ambassador |
| V8, 327.0 | 4.00×3.25 | 270 | O-Ambassador |

## 1961*

**American (wb 100.00)**

| | | Wght | Price | Prod |
|---|---|---|---|---|
| 6102 | DeLuxe bus sdn 2d | 2,454 | 1,831 | — |
| 6104 | DeLuxe wgn 2d | 2,549 | 2,080 | — |
| 6104-1 | Super wgn 2d | 2,556 | 2,165 | — |
| 6104-2 | Custom wgn 2d | 2,617 | 2,295 | — |
| 6105 | DeLuxe sdn 4d | 2,523 | 1,894 | — |
| 6105-1 | Super sdn 4d | 2,530 | 1,979 | — |
| 6105-2 | Custom sdn 2d | 2,557 | 2,060 | — |
| 6106 | DeLuxe sdn 2d | 2,490 | 1,845 | — |
| 6106-1 | Super sdn 2d | 2,499 | 1,930 | — |
| 6106-2 | Custom sdn 2d | 2,557 | 2,060 | — |
| 6107-2 | Custom conv cpe | 2,712 | 2,369 | — |
| 6108 | DeLuxe wgn 4d | 2,595 | 2,129 | — |
| 6108-1 | Super wgn 4d | 2,602 | 2,214 | — |
| 6108-2 | Custom wgn 4d | 2,660 | 2,344 | — |

**Classic Six (wb 108.0)**

| | | Wght | Price | Prod |
|---|---|---|---|---|
| 6115 | DeLuxe sdn 4d | 2,905 | 2,098 | — |
| 6115-1 | Super sdn 4d | 2,923 | 2,268 | — |
| 6115-2 | Custom sdn 4d | 2,863 | 2,413 | — |
| 6118 | DeLuxe wgn 4d | 3,037 | 2,437 | — |
| 6118-1 | Super wgn 4d, 6P | 3,046 | 2,572 | — |
| 6118-2 | Custom wgn 4d, 6P | 2,984 | 2,717 | — |
| 6118-3 | Super wgn 4d, 8P | 3,087 | 2,697 | — |
| 6118-4 | Custom wgn 4d, 8P | 3,023 | 2,842 | — |

**Classic V8 (wb 108.0)**

| | | Wght | Price | Prod |
|---|---|---|---|---|
| 6125 | DeLuxe sdn 4d | 3,237 | 2,227 | — |
| 6125-1 | Super sdn 4d | 3,255 | 2,397 | — |
| 6125-2 | Custom sdn 4d | 3,262 | 2,512 | — |
| 6128-1 | Super wgn 4d, 6P | 3,372 | 2,701 | — |
| 6128-2 | Custom wgn 4d, 6P | 3,378 | 2,816 | — |
| 6128-3 | Super wgn 4d, 8P | 3,408 | 2,826 | — |
| 6128-4 | Custom wgn 4d, 8P | 3,420 | 2,941 | — |

**Ambassador (wb 117.0)**

| | | Wght | Price | Prod |
|---|---|---|---|---|
| 6185 | DeLuxe sdn 4d | 3,343 | 2,395 | — |
| 6185-1 | Super sdn 4d | 3,361 | 2,537 | — |
| 6185-2 | Custom sdn 4d | 3,380 | 2,682 | — |
| 6188-1 | Super wgn 4d, 6P | 3,493 | 2,841 | — |

| | | Wght | Price | Prod |
|---|---|---|---|---|
| 6188-2 | Custom wgn 4d, 6P | 3,495 | 2,986 | — |
| 6188-3 | Super wgn 4d, 8P | 3,560 | 2,966 | — |
| 6188-4 | Custom wgn 4d, 8P | 3,566 | 3,111 | — |

*Total model year registrations: 370,685.

| 1961 Engines | bore×stroke | bhp | availability |
|---|---|---|---|
| L6, 195.6 | 3.13×4.25 | 90 | S-American exc Custom |
| L6, 195.6 | 3.13×4.25 | 125 | S-American Custom |
| L6, 195.6 | 3.13×4.25 | 127 | S-Classic Six |
| L6, 195.6 | 3.13×4.25 | 138 | O-Classic Six |
| V8, 250.0 | 3.50×3.25 | 200 | S-Classic V8 |
| V8, 250.0 | 3.50×3.25 | 215 | O-Classic V8 |
| V8, 327.0 | 4.00×3.25 | 250 | S-Ambassador |
| V8, 327.0 | 4.00×3.25 | 270 | O-Ambassador |

## 1962*

**American (wb 100.0)**

| | | Wght | Price | Prod |
|---|---|---|---|---|
| 6202 | DeLuxe bus sdn 2d | 2,454 | 1,832 | — |
| 6204 | DeLuxe wgn 2d | 2,555 | 2,081 | — |
| 6204-2 | Custom wgn 2d | 2,565 | 2,141 | — |
| 6205 | DeLuxe sdn 4d | 2,500 | 1,895 | — |
| 6205-2 | Custom sdn 4d | 2,512 | 1,958 | — |
| 6205-5 | 400 sdn 4d | 2,585 | 2,089 | — |
| 6206 | DeLuxe sdn 2d | 2,480 | 1,846 | — |
| 6206-2 | Custom sdn 2d | 2,492 | 1,909 | — |
| 6206-5 | 400 sdn 2d | 2,558 | 2,040 | — |
| 6207-5 | 400 conv cpe | 2,735 | 2,344 | — |
| 6208 | DeLuxe wgn 4d | 2,573 | 2,130 | — |
| 6208-2 | Custom wgn 4d | 2,600 | 2,190 | — |
| 6208-5 | 400 wgn 4d | 2,692 | 2,320 | — |

**Classic (wb 108.0)**

| | | Wght | Price | Prod |
|---|---|---|---|---|
| 6215 | DeLuxe sdn 4d | 2,888 | 2,050 | — |
| 6215-2 | Custom sdn 4d | 2,898 | 2,200 | — |
| 6215-5 | 400 sdn 4d | 2,853 | 2,349 | — |
| 6216 | DeLuxe sdn 4d | 2,866 | 2,000 | — |
| 6216-2 | Custom sdn 2d | 2,876 | 2,150 | — |
| 6216-5 | 400 sdn 2d | 2,841 | 2,299 | — |
| 6218 | DeLuxe wgn 4d, 6P | 3,014 | 2,380 | — |
| 6218-2 | Custom wgn 4d, 6P | 3,024 | 2,492 | — |
| 6218-4 | Custom wgn 4d, 8P | 3,094 | 2,614 | — |
| 6218-5 | 400 wgn 4d | 2,985 | 2,640 | — |

**Ambassador (wb 108.0)**

| | | Wght | Price | Prod |
|---|---|---|---|---|
| 6285 | DeLuxe sdn 4d | 3,249 | 2,336 | — |
| 6285-2 | Custom sdn 4d | 3,259 | 2,464 | — |
| 6285-5 | 400 sdn 4d | 3,283 | 2,605 | — |
| 6286 | DeLuxe sdn 2d | 3,227 | 2,282 | — |
| 6286-2 | Custom sdn 2d | 3,237 | 2,410 | — |
| 6286-5 | 400 sdn 2d | 3,261 | 2,551 | — |
| 6288 | DeLuxe wgn 4d | 3,375 | 2,648 | — |
| 6288-2 | Custom wgn 4d | 3,385 | 2,760 | — |
| 6288-5 | 400 wgn 4d, 6P | 3,408 | 2,901 | — |
| 6288-6 | 400 wgn 4d, 8P | 3,471 | 3,023 | — |

*Total model year registrations: 423,104.

| 1962 Engines | bore×stroke | bhp | availability |
|---|---|---|---|
| L6, 195.6 | 3.13×4.25 | 90 | S-American |
| L6, 195.6 | 3.13×4.25 | 125 | O-American |
| L6, 195.6 | 3.13×4.25 | 127 | S-Classic |
| L6, 195.6 | 3.13×4.25 | 138 | O-Classic |
| V8, 327.0 | 4.00×3.25 | 250 | S-Ambassador |
| V8, 327.0 | 4.00×3.25 | 270 | O-Ambassador |

## 1963*

**American (wb 100.0)**

| | | Wght | Price | Prod |
|---|---|---|---|---|
| 6302 | 220 bus sdn 2d | 2,446 | 1,832 | — |

# Rambler

| | | Wght | Price | Prod |
|---|---|---|---|---|
| 6304 | 220 wgn 2d | 2,528 | 2,081 | — |
| 6304-2 | 330 wgn 2d | 2,539 | 2,141 | — |
| 6305 | 220 sdn 4d | 2,485 | 1,895 | — |
| 6305-2 | 330 sdn 4d | 2,500 | 1,958 | — |
| 6305-5 | 440 sdn 4d | 2,575 | 2,089 | — |
| 6306 | 220 sdn 2d | 2,472 | 1,846 | — |
| 6306-2 | 330 sdn 2d | 2,484 | 1,909 | — |
| 6306-5 | 440 sdn 2d | 2,556 | 2,040 | — |
| 6307-5 | 440 conv cpe | 2,743 | 2,344 | — |
| 6308 | 220 wgn 4d | 2,549 | 2,130 | — |
| 6308-2 | 330 wgn 4d | 2,561 | 2,190 | — |
| 6308-5 | 440 wgn 4d | 2,638 | 2,320 | — |
| 6309-5 | 440 htp cpe | 2,550 | 2,136 | — |
| 6309-7 | 440H htp cpe 4P | 2,567 | 2,281 | — |

## Classic (wb 112.0)

| | | Wght | Price | Prod |
|---|---|---|---|---|
| 6315 | 550 sdn 4d | 2,729 | 2,105 | — |
| 6315-2 | 660 sdn 4d | 2,740 | 2,245 | — |
| 6315-5 | 770 sdn 4d | 2,686 | 2,349 | — |
| 6316 | 550 sdn 2d | 2,720 | 2,055 | — |
| 6316-2 | 660 sdn 2d | 2,725 | 2,195 | — |
| 6316-5 | 770 sdn 2d | 2,663 | 2,299 | — |
| 6318 | 550 wgn 4d | 2,893 | 2,435 | — |
| 6318-2 | 660 wgn 4d, 6P | 2,890 | 2,537 | — |
| 6318-4 | 660 wgn 4d, 9P | 2,885 | 2,609 | — |
| 6318-5 | 770 wgn 4d | 2,828 | 2,640 | — |

## Ambassador (wb 112.0)

| | | Wght | Price | Prod |
|---|---|---|---|---|
| 6385 | 800 sdn 4d | 3,140 | 2,391 | — |
| 6385-2 | 880 sdn 4d | 3,145 | 2,519 | — |
| 6385-5 | 990 sdn 4d | 3,158 | 2,660 | — |
| 6386 | 800 sdn 2d | 3,110 | 2,337 | — |
| 6386-2 | 880 sdn 2d | 3,116 | 2,465 | — |
| 6386-5 | 990 sdn 2d | 3,132 | 2,606 | — |
| 6388 | 800 wgn 4d | 3,270 | 2,703 | — |
| 6388-2 | 880 wgn 4d | 3,275 | 2,815 | — |
| 6388-5 | 990 wgn 4d, 6P | 3,298 | 2,956 | — |
| 6388-6 | 990 wgn 4d, 9P | 3,305 | 3,018 | — |

*Total model year registrations: 428,346.

| 1963 Engines | bore×stroke | bhp | availability |
|---|---|---|---|
| L6, 195.6 | 3.13×4.25 | 90 | S-American 220/330; 0-440 |
| L6, 195.6 | 3.13×4.25 | 125 | S-American 440; 0-220/330 |
| L6, 195.6 | 3.13×4.25 | 127 | S-Classic |
| L6, 195.6 | 3.13×4.25 | 138 | S-American 440H; O-Classic |
| V8, 327.0 | 4.00×3.25 | 250 | S-Ambassador |
| V8, 327.0 | 4.00×3.25 | 270 | O-Ambassador |

# 1964*

## American (wb 106.0)

| | | Wght | Price | Prod |
|---|---|---|---|---|
| 6405 | 220 sdn 4d | 2,527 | 1,964 | — |
| 6405-2 | 330 sdn 4d | 2,526 | 2,057 | — |
| 6405-5 | 440 sdn 4d | 2,572 | 2,150 | — |
| 6406 | 220 sdn 2d | 2,506 | 1,907 | — |
| 6406-2 | 330 sdn 2d | 2,504 | 2,000 | — |
| 6407-5 | 440 conv cpe | 2,752 | 2,346 | — |
| 6408 | 220 wgn 4d | 2,661 | 2,240 | — |
| 6408-2 | 330 wgn 4d | 2,675 | 2,324 | — |
| 6409-5 | 440 htp cpe | 2,596 | 2,133 | — |
| 6409-7 | 440H htp cpe 5P | 2,617 | 2,292 | — |

## Classic (wb 112.0)

| | | Wght | Price | Prod |
|---|---|---|---|---|
| 6415 | 550 sdn 4d | 2,755 | 2,116 | — |
| 6415-2 | 660 sdn 4d | 2,758 | 2,256 | — |
| 6415-5 | 770 sdn 4d | 2,763 | 2,360 | — |
| 6416 | 550 sdn 2d | 2,732 | 2,066 | — |
| 6416-2 | 660 sdn 2d | 2,736 | 2,206 | — |
| 6416-5 | 770 sdn 2d | 2,740 | 2,310 | — |
| 6418 | 550 wgn 4d | 2,915 | 2,446 | — |
| 6418-2 | 660 wgn 4d | 2,916 | 2,548 | — |
| 6418-5 | 770 wgn 4d | 2,921 | 2,651 | — |
| 6419-5 | 770 htp cpe | 2,789 | 2,397 | — |
| 6419-7 | Typhoon htp cpe | 2,818 | 2,509 | — |

## Ambassador 990 (wb 112.0)

| | | Wght | Price | Prod |
|---|---|---|---|---|
| 6485-5 | sdn 4d | 3,204 | 2,671 | — |
| 6488-5 | wgn 4d | 3,350 | 2,985 | — |
| 6489-5 | htp cpe | 3,213 | 2,736 | — |
| 6489-7 | 990H htp cpe | 3,255 | 2,917 | — |

*Total model year registrations: 379,412.

| 1964 Engines | bore×stroke | bhp | availability |
|---|---|---|---|
| L6, 195.6 | 3.13×4.25 | 90 | S-American 220/330; 0-440 |
| L6, 195.6 | 3.13×4.25 | 125 | S-American 440; 0-220/330 |
| L6, 195.6 | 3.13×4.25 | 127 | S-Classic |
| L6, 195.6 | 3.13×4.25 | 138 | S-American 440H; O-Classic exc Typhoon |
| L6, 232.0 | 3.75×3.50 | 145 | S-Typhoon; O-other Classic |
| V8, 287.0 | 3.75×3.25 | 198 | O-Classic |
| V8, 327.0 | 4.00×3.25 | 250 | S-Ambassador exc 990H |
| V8, 327.0 | 4.00×3.25 | 270 | S-Amb 990H; O-Other Amb |

# 1965*

## American (wb 106.0)

| | | Wght | Price | Prod |
|---|---|---|---|---|
| 6505 | 220 sdn 4d | 2,518 | 2,036 | — |
| 6505-2 | 330 sdn 4d | 2,522 | 2,129 | — |
| 6505-5 | 440 sdn 4d | 2,580 | 2,222 | — |
| 6506 | 220 sdn 2d | 2,492 | 1,979 | — |
| 6506-2 | 330 sdn 2d | 2,490 | 2,072 | — |
| 6507-5 | 440 conv cpe | 2,747 | 2,418 | 3,882 |
| 6508 | 220 wgn 4d | 2,684 | 2,312 | — |
| 6508-2 | 330 wgn 4d | 2,682 | 2,396 | — |
| 6509-5 | 440 htp cpe | 2,596 | 2,205 | — |
| 6509-7 | 440H htp cpe | 2,622 | 2,327 | — |

## Classic (wb 112.0)

| | | Wght | Price | Prod |
|---|---|---|---|---|
| 6515 | 550 sdn 4d | 2,987 | 2,192 | — |
| 6515-2 | 660 sdn 4d | — | — | — |

## Classic 550 (wb 112.0)

| | | Wght | Price | Prod |
|---|---|---|---|---|
| 6515 | sdn 4d | 2,987 | 2,192 | — |
| 6516 | sdn 2d | 2,963 | 2,142 | — |
| 6518 | wgn 4d | 3,134 | 2,522 | — |

## Classic 660 (wb 112.0)

| | | Wght | Price | Prod |
|---|---|---|---|---|
| 6515-2 | sdn 4d | 3,016 | 2,332 | — |
| 6516-2 | sdn 2d | 2,991 | 2,282 | — |
| 6518-2 | wgn 4d | 3,155 | 2,624 | — |

## Classic 770 (wb 112.0)

| | | Wght | Price | Prod |
|---|---|---|---|---|
| 6515-5 | sdn 4d | 3,029 | 2,436 | — |
| 6517-5 | conv cpe | 3,169 | 2,696 | 4,953 |
| 6518-5 | wgn 4d | 3,180 | 2,727 | — |
| 6519-5 | htp cpe | 3,063 | 2,436 | — |
| 6519-7 | 770H htp cpe | 3,089 | 2,548 | — |

## Marlin (wb 112.0)

| | | Wght | Price | Prod |
|---|---|---|---|---|
| 6559-7 | htp cpe | 3,234 | 3,100 | 10,327 |

## Ambassador (wb 116.0)

| | | Wght | Price | Prod |
|---|---|---|---|---|
| 6585-2 | 880 sdn 4d | 3,120 | 2,565 | — |
| 6585-5 | 990 sdn 4d | 3,151 | 2,656 | — |
| 6586-2 | 880 sdn 2d | 3,087 | 2,512 | — |
| 6587-5 | 990 conv cpe | 3,265 | 2,955 | 3,499 |
| 6588-2 | 880 wgn 4d | 3,247 | 2,879 | — |
| 6588-5 | 990 wgn 4d | 3,268 | 2,970 | — |

| | | Wght | Price | Prod |
|---|---|---|---|---|
| 6589-5 | 990 htp cpe | 3,168 | 2,669 | — |
| 6589-7 | 990H htp cpe | 3,198 | 2,837 | — |

*Total model year registrations: 324,669.

| 1965 Engines | bore×stroke | bhp | availability |
|---|---|---|---|
| L6, 195.6 | 3.13×4.25 | 90 | S-American 220/330 |
| L6, 195.6 | 3.13×4.25 | 125 | S-American 440/440H |
| L6, 199.0 | 3.75×3.00 | 128 | S-Classic 550 |
| L6, 232.0 | 3.75×3.25 | 145 | S-Classic 660/770/770H, Marlin; O-Amb, American |
| L6, 232.0 | 3.75×3.25 | 155 | S-Amb; O-Classic |
| V8, 287.0 | 3.75×3.25 | 198 | O-Classic, Marlin, Amb |
| V8, 327.0 | 4.00×3.25 | 270 | O-Classic, Marlin, Amb |

## 1966*

### American 220 (wb 106.0)

| | | Wght | Price | Prod |
|---|---|---|---|---|
| 6605 | sdn 4d | 2,574 | 2,086 | — |
| 6606 | sdn 2d | 2,554 | 2,017 | — |
| 6608 | wgn 4d | 2,740 | 2,369 | — |

### American 440 (wb 106.0)

| | | | | |
|---|---|---|---|---|
| 6605-5 | sdn 4d | 2,582 | 2,203 | — |
| 6606-5 | sdn 2d | 2,562 | 2,134 | — |
| 6607-5 | conv cpe | 2,782 | 2,486 | — |
| 6608-5 | wgn 4d | 2,745 | 2,477 | — |
| 6609-5 | htp cpe | 2,610 | 2,227 | — |

### Rogue (wb 106.0)

| | | | | |
|---|---|---|---|---|
| 6609-7 | htp cpe | 2,630 | 2,370 | — |

### Classic 550 (wb 112.0)

| | | | | |
|---|---|---|---|---|
| 6615 | sdn 4d | 2,885 | 2,238 | — |
| 6616 | sdn 2d | 2,860 | 2,189 | — |
| 6618 | wgn 4d | 3,070 | 2,542 | — |

### Classic 770 (wb 112.0)

| | | | | |
|---|---|---|---|---|
| 6615-5 | sdn 4d | 2,905 | 2,337 | — |
| 6617-5 | conv cpe | 3,070 | 2,616 | — |
| 6618-5 | wgn 4d | 3,071 | 2,629 | — |
| 6619-5 | htp cpe | 2,935 | 2,363 | — |

### Rebel (wb 112.0)

| | | | | |
|---|---|---|---|---|
| 6619-7 | htp cpe | 2,950 | 2,523 | — |

*Total model year registrations: 265,712.

| 1966 Engines | bore×stroke | bhp | availability |
|---|---|---|---|
| L6, 199.0 | 3.75×3.00 | 128 | S-American, Rogue |
| L6, 232.0 | 3.75×3.50 | 145 | S-Classic, Rebel |
| L6, 232.0 | 3.75×3.50 | 155 | O-all |
| V8, 287.0 | 3.75×3.25 | 198 | O-Classic, Rebel |
| V8, 327.0 | 4.00×3.25 | 250 | O-Classic, Rebel |
| V8, 327.0 | 4.00×3.25 | 270 | O-Classic, Rebel |

## 1967*

### American 220 (wb 106.0)

| | | Wght | Price | Prod |
|---|---|---|---|---|
| 6705 | sdn 4d | 2,621 | 2,142 | — |
| 6706 | sdn 2d | 2,591 | 2,073 | — |
| 6708 | wgn 4d | 2,767 | 2,425 | — |

### American 440 (wb 106.0)

| | | | | |
|---|---|---|---|---|
| 6705-5 | sdn 4d | 2,613 | 2,259 | — |
| 6706-5 | sdn 2d | 2,586 | 2,191 | — |
| 6708-5 | wgn 4d | 2,769 | 2,533 | — |
| 6709-5 | htp cpe | 2,643 | 2,283 | — |

### American Rogue (wb 106.0)

| | | | | |
|---|---|---|---|---|
| 6707-7 | conv cpe | 2,821 | 2,611 | — |
| 6709-7 | htp cpe | 2,663 | 2,426 | — |

### Rebel 550 (wb 114.0)

| | | Wght | Price | Prod |
|---|---|---|---|---|
| 6715 | sdn 4d | 3,055 | 2,319 | — |
| 6716 | sdn 2d | 3,089 | 2,294 | — |
| 6718 | wgn 4d | 3,287 | 2,623 | — |

### Rebel 770 (wb 114.0)

| | | | | |
|---|---|---|---|---|
| 6715-5 | sdn 4d | 3,053 | 2,418 | — |
| 6718-5 | wgn 4d | 3,288 | 2,710 | — |
| 6719-5 | htp cpe | 3,092 | 2,443 | — |

### Rebel SST (wb 114.0)

| | | | | |
|---|---|---|---|---|
| 6717-7 | conv cpe | 3,180 | 2,872 | — |
| 6719-7 | htp cpe | 3,109 | 2,604 | — |

*Total model year registrations: 237,785.

| 1967 Engines | bore×stroke | bhp | availability |
|---|---|---|---|
| L6, 199.0 | 3.75×3.00 | 128 | S-American |
| L6, 232.0 | 3.75×3.25 | 145 | S-Rebel; O-American |
| L6, 232.0 | 3.75×3.25 | 155 | O-American, Rebel |
| V8, 290.0 | 3.75×3.28 | 200 | O-American, Rebel |
| V8, 290.0 | 3.75×3.28 | 225 | O-American |
| V8, 343.0 | 4.08×3.28 | 235 | O-Rebel |
| V8, 343.0 | 4.08×3.28 | 280 | O-Rebel |

## 1968*

### American (wb 106.0)

| | | Wght | Price | Prod |
|---|---|---|---|---|
| 6805 | sdn 4d | 2,638 | 2,024 | — |
| 6806 | sdn 2d | 2,604 | 1,946 | — |

### American 440 (wb 106.0)

| | | | | |
|---|---|---|---|---|
| 6805-5 | sdn 4d | 2,643 | 2,166 | — |
| 6808-5 | wgn 4d | 2,800 | 2,426 | — |

### Rogue (wb 106.0)

| | | | | |
|---|---|---|---|---|
| 6809-7 | htp cpe | 2,678 | 2,244 | — |

*Total model year registrations: 259,346

| 1968 Engines | bore×stroke | bhp | availability |
|---|---|---|---|
| L6, 199.0 | 3.75×3.00 | 128 | S-American |
| L6, 232.0 | 3.75×3.50 | 145 | S-Rogue; O-American |
| V8, 290.0 | 3.75×3.28 | 225 | O-American, Rogue |

## 1969*

### American (wb 106.0)

| | | Wght | Price | Prod |
|---|---|---|---|---|
| 6905 | sdn 4d | 2,638 | 2,076 | — |
| 6906 | sdn 2d | 2,604 | 1,998 | — |

### American 440 (wb 106.0)

| | | | | |
|---|---|---|---|---|
| 6905-5 | sdn 4d | 2,643 | 2,218 | — |
| 6908-5 | wgn 4d | 2,800 | 2,478 | — |

### Rogue (wb 106.0)

| | | | | |
|---|---|---|---|---|
| 6909-7 | htp cpe | 2,678 | 2,296 | — |

### SC/Rambler-Hurst (wb 106.0)

| | | | | |
|---|---|---|---|---|
| 6909-7 | htp cpe | 3,160 | 2,998 | — |

*Total model year registrations: 239,937.

| 1969 Engines | bore×stroke | bhp | availability |
|---|---|---|---|
| L6, 199.0 | 3.75×3.00 | 128 | S-American |
| L6, 232.0 | 3.75×3.50 | 145 | S-Rogue; O-American |
| V8, 290.0 | 3.75×3.28 | 200 | O-Rogue, American 440 |
| V8, 290.0 | 3.75×3.28 | 225 | O-Rogue |
| V8, 390.0 | 4.17×3.57 | 315 | S-SC/Rambler-Hurst |

# Shelby

**Shelby Automotive, Ionia, Michigan**
**Ford Motor Co., Dearborn, Michigan**

Carroll Shelby, who retired from racing for health reasons in 1960, settled down to become America's most charismatic manufacturer of specialty cars. Between 1962 and 1970 he built or contributed to many blindingly fast, raceworthy classics: the AC Cobra, Sunbeam Tiger, Cobra 427, Ford GT40, and Ford Mark IV. He helped bring Ford to its racing pinnacle, the winning of Le Mans.

Shelby's most popular project from the standpoint of sales was the GT-350, a super-tuned version of the Ford Mustang. Built by Shelby American in 1965-66, it was an uncompromising, potent grand touring car equally at home on road or track. Later models, built by Ford from 1967 through 1970, were not quite what their predecessors had been, but were good examples of what talented specialists could do with a stock package like the Mustang.

The 1965 GT-350 was aimed primarily at the B-Production racing class of the Sports Car Club of America

(SCCA). (It was B-Production champion in 1965-67.) Shelby began with a blue-striped white Mustang fastback powered by the high-performance version of Ford's 289 cubic-inch V8. He added a high-rise manifold, a big four-barrel carburetor, and free-flow exhaust headers. This brought horsepower up to 306 at 6000 rpm. All Shelbys came with a Borg-Warner T-10 four-speed gearbox, a regular Mustang option. Instead of the Mustang's Falcon-based rear axle, GT-350s used a stronger unit from the Fairlane station wagon. Other significant component revisions included metallic-lined rear brakes, Koni shock absorbers, and extra-heavy-duty front disc brakes with metallic pads. Steering was made quicker by relocating the front suspension mounting points. Connecting the tops of the front shock absorbers to each other with a length of steel tubing prevented shock flex under hard cornering. Shelby used its own 15-inch cast-aluminum road wheels shod with high-performance Goodyear bias-ply

1965 GT-350 fastback coupe

1968 GT-500 convertible

1968 GT-500 convertible

1968 GT-500 fastback coupe

1968 GT-500KR fastback coupe

1968 GT-500KR fastback coupe

tires. The result of all this chassis tuning was nearly neutral handling instead of the stock Mustang's strong understeer.

Externally, the stock Mustang's steel hood was replaced with a fiberglass one containing a prominent scoop and held down by NASCAR hood pins. The galloping horse emblem was removed from the grille, and the simulated side scoops were opened up to admit cool air to the rear brakes. For 1966, the fastback's stock rear-quarter air extractor vents were replaced by plastic windows. Internally, the only changes consisted of competition-style three-inch seatbelts and a mahogany-rimmed steering wheel. GT-350s also came without the stock Mustang's rear seat, with the spare tire lashed down in the vacated space. Shelby offered a kit so the buyer could put the spare back in the trunk and install a new rear seat. The stock front seats were left alone, and all interiors were solid black.

For the racing version of the GT-350, Shelby achieved 350 bhp—an astounding 1.21 horsepower per cubic inch. This engine was basically the same one used in the racing Cobra 289. Its four-speed gearbox had an aluminum case to save weight. The interior was stripped and a racing seat was installed along with a roll bar and safety harness. Competition tires and an extra-heavy-duty suspension were fitted. A special fiberglass nose eliminated the front bumper and provided a rudimentary air dam with a central slot as an additional air intake. The ultimate racing GT-350 had four-wheel disc brakes, a 400-bhp engine, and wide tires under flared fenders.

Hertz Rent-A-Car got into the act in 1966 when it ordered 936 Shelbys painted black with gold stripes. Hertz called it the GT-350H, and would rent one for $17 a day and 17 cents a mile. It was a stock GT-350, aside from the special paint job and a three-speed automatic transmission instead of the stock four-speed manual. Hertz inevitably rented some of these to weekend racers, and a few of them performed successfully on SCCA tracks.

In 1967, when Ford Motor Company offered Mustang with a 390-cid V8, Shelby went one better and tossed in a huge 428. The result was the GT-500, sold as a linemate to the GT-350. Its advertised horsepower was 335, but the real figure was probably closer to 400. The GT-350 was advertised at its usual 306 bhp, but the ac-

**1969 GT-500 fastback coupe**

**1969 GT-500 convertible**

**1969 GT-500 fastback coupe**

**1969 GT-500 convertible**

**1969 GT-500 fastback coupe**

**1969 GT-500 convertible**

tual rating was below 300 because the '67 did not have steel-tube exhaust headers like the '66 model.

The '67 Shelby now had its own fiberglass front end to distinguish it from production Mustangs, plus other styling modifications and minor chassis refinements. It also bore a new emblem: a coiled cobra in anodized gold. The interior featured a huge, black-painted roll bar, to which were affixed inertia-reel seatbelts instead of the three-inch harness. Over 3000 cars were built, and they were priced lower than the 1965-66 models.

In 1968, the 350 and 500 were again offered with only a wider hood scoop for identification. Interiors were lifted from the stock Mustang with few alterations. A Stewart Warner oil pressure gauge and ammeter were mounted on the central console. A convertible was added to each line, priced about $100 higher than the fast-back. Also new was the GT-500KR ("King of the Road"), which had Ford's Cobra Jet 428 block, extra-large heads and intake manifold, and a Holley 735-cfm four-barrel carburetor. The KR sold for $4473 as a fast-back and $4594 as a convertible.

Mechanically, the 1969 GT-350 and GT-500 were more closely related to the production Mustang than their predecessors had been (the Mustang was all-new that year). There were now air scoops in the fiberglass front fenders, and side stripes were relocated midway up the bodysides. Although a few 1969s were reserialed for 1970, Shelby production effectively ended in '69. A combination of government regulations and spiraling insurance rates (the cars' accident record was staggering) prompted Carroll Shelby to ask the then-president of Ford, Lee Iacocca, to cancel the program.

# Shelby Specifications

## 1965

### GT-350 (wb 108.0)

|  | Wght | Price | Prod |
|---|---|---|---|
| fstbk cpe | 2,800 | 4,547 | 562 |

| 1965 Engine | bore×stroke | bhp | availability |
|---|---|---|---|
| V8, 289.0 | 4.00×2.87 | 306 | S-all |

## 1966

### GT-350 (wb 108.0)

|  | Wght | Price | Prod |
|---|---|---|---|
| fstbk cpe | 2,800 | 4,600 | 2,378 |

| 1966 Engine | bore×stroke | bhp | availability |
|---|---|---|---|
| V8, 289.0 | 4.00×2.87 | 306 | S-all |

## 1967

### GT-350 (wb 108.0)

|  | Wght | Price | Prod |
|---|---|---|---|
| fstbk cpe | 2,800 | 3,995 | 1,175 |

### GT500 (wb 108.0)

|  | Wght | Price | Prod |
|---|---|---|---|
| fstbk cpe | 3,000 | 4,195 | 2,050 |

| 1967 Engines | bore×stroke | bhp | availability |
|---|---|---|---|
| V8, 289.0 | 4.00×2.87 | 290 | S-GT350 |
| V8, 428.0 | 4.13×3.98 | 400* | S-GT500 |

*Estimated; advertised bhp lower.

## 1968

### GT-350 (wb 108.0)

|  | Wght | Price | Prod |
|---|---|---|---|
| fstbk cpe | 3,000 | 4,117 | 1,253 |
| conv cpe | 3,100 | 4,238 | 404 |

### GT-500 (wb 108.0)

|  | Wght | Price | Prod |
|---|---|---|---|
| fstbk cpe | 3,100 | 4,317 | 1,140 |
| conv cpe | 3,200 | 4,439 | 402 |

### GT-500KR (wb 108.0)

|  | Wght | Price | Prod |
|---|---|---|---|
| fstbk cpe | 3,200 | 4,473 | 933 |
| conv cpe | 3,300 | 4,594 | 318 |

| 1968 Engines | bore×stroke | bhp | availability |
|---|---|---|---|
| V8, 302.0 | 4.00×3.00 | 250 | S-GT350 |
| V8, 302.0 | 4.00×3.00 | 350 | O-GT350 (supercharged) |
| V8, 390.0 | 4.05×3.78 | 335 | S-GT500 |
| V8, 428.0 | 4.13×3.98 | 360 | S-GT500 |
| V8, 428.0 | 4.13×3.98 | 400* | S-GT500KR |

*Estimated; advertised bhp lower.

## 1969

### GT-350 (wb 108.0)

|  | Wght | Price | Prod |
|---|---|---|---|
| fstbk cpe | 3,000 | 4,434 | 1,085 |
| conv cpe | 3,100 | 4,753 | 194 |

### GT-500 (wb 108.0)

|  | Wght | Price | Prod |
|---|---|---|---|
| fstbk cpe | 3,100 | 4,709 | 1,536 |
| conv cpe | 3,200 | 5,027 | 335 |

| 1969 Engines | bore×stroke | bhp | availability |
|---|---|---|---|
| V8, 351.0 | 4.00×3.50 | 290 | S-GT350 |
| V8, 428.0 | 4.13×3.98 | 400* | S-GT500 |

*Estimated; advertised bhp lower.

## 1970

### GT-350 (wb 108.0)

|  | Wght | Price | Prod |
|---|---|---|---|
| fstbk cpe | 3,000 | 4,500* | 315 |
| conv cpe | 3,100 | 4,800* |  |

### GT-500 (wb 108.0)

|  | Wght | Price | Prod |
|---|---|---|---|
| fstbk cpe | 3,100 | 4,800* | 286 |
| conv cpe | 3,200 | 5,100* |  |

*Estimated.

| 1970 Engines | bore×stroke | bhp | availability |
|---|---|---|---|
| V8, 351.0 | 4.00×3.50 | 290 | S-GT350 |
| V8, 428.0 | 4.13×3.98 | 375* | S-GT500 |

*Estimated; advertised bhp lower.

# Studebaker

Studebaker Corp. (Studebaker-Packard Corp., 1954-62)
South Bend, Indiana and Hamilton, Ontario, Canada

Studebaker was the oldest company in the transportation field as of 1940, having built cars since 1902 and horse-drawn wagons since 1852. The firm had first run into trouble in the late 1920s when it introduced the low-priced Erskine, which did not sell as well as anticipated. The company's financial situation worsened as the stock market crashed in 1929. In 1931-33 came another failure, the Rockne (named for Notre Dame's football coach). The company went into receivership in 1933, but was eventually rescued by two energetic executives, Paul Hoffman and Harold Vance, who streamlined management, brought new life to products and dealerships, and slowly put Studebaker back on its feet.

The recovery was complete by 1939. In that year, Studebaker fielded the Champion, a good-looking economy car styled by Raymond Loewy. More economical to run than Fords, Chevrolets, or Plymouths, the Champion was quite popular. Studebaker sales doubled, and for the first time since 1928, the company produced more than 100,000 units in 1940. The model line that year consisted of three series: the Champion, Commander, and President. The Champion, then in its second year, was by far the most important. This cleanly styled compact employed a conventional ladder-type chassis with a 110-inch wheelbase. Like other Studebakers, it offered "planar" independent front suspension, transverse front leaf springs with upper and lower links, and Delco tubular shock absorbers. It was powered by a 164.3 cubic-inch L-head six, a peppy engine with the highest rpm limit in the industry, yet economical to operate. Studebaker claimed the Champion's mileage was 10 to 25 percent better than that of Ford, Chevrolet, or Plymouth. The car weighed 500 to 650 pounds less than the low-priced three, which helped both economy and performance. Maximum speed was close to 80 mph, against 75 for Chevrolet, 78 for Plymouth, and 90 for the Ford V8/85. Studebaker's favorite performance quote was 10–65 mph acceleration in 19.6 seconds, versus 19.8 for Chevrolet and 22.3 for Ford. The Ford, of course, could handily outperform the Champion in all other categories, but Studebaker's statistics made for a good sales pitch.

Champions came in four body styles for 1940; three- and five-passenger coupes, and two- and four-door sedans. Standard and DeLuxe trim were offered. The Champion's price range of $660 to $785 made it a formidable competitor for the Big Three makes, and 1940 volume rose to more than 66,000 units.

The middle-priced 1940 Studebaker was Commander offered in three body styles on a 116.5-inch wheelbase: a three-passenger coupe, and two- and four-door sedans. Commanders used a 226-cid six with 90 bhp at 3400 rpm, and differed from the Champion in styling. The Commander had a sharply creased nose and a latticework grille, more like Ford's than the Champion's rounded lines.

The company continued to offer the President, equipped with a smooth, nine-main-bearing straight eight delivering 110 bhp at 3600 rpm. Prices were roughly $125 higher than for the equivalent Commander. Presidents rode a 122-inch wheelbase, were offered in the same three body styles as Commander, and had similar styling.

Raymond Loewy had earned his high standing at Studebaker on the strength of the Champion. For 1941, he reworked the entire line with more formal, elegant styling. A new body style, the Land Cruiser (with closed rear roof quarters), was developed for the Commander and President. Loewy pioneered the first bodyside two-toning, consisting of a color sweep just below the beltline. Engines were reworked. The Champion unit was stroked out to four inches for 169.6 cid and 80 bhp. The Commander powerplant was raised to 94 bhp, while the President's silky straight eight was increased to 117.

The 1941 facelift brought additional trim levels to all three lines. For the Champion, these were Custom, Custom DeLuxe, and Delux-Tone trims available for all body styles. Commanders were offered in Custom, DeLux-Tone, and Skyway versions. The Skyway was a very richly trimmed, fender-skirted series that went into production in March 1941. There was also a Skyway President. South Bend had another excellent year in '41. Nearly 85,000 Champions were built; Commander

**1940 President four-door Cruising Sedan**

**1941 President Skyway Land Cruiser four-door sedan**

# Studebaker

production reached nearly 42,000 units. (Presidents traditionally sold in much smaller quantities.)

Before the war put an end to civilian auto production in 1942, Studebaker built about 50,000 units—sufficient to keep the company in eighth place. Then the factory turned to defense work, building trucks, airplane engines, and Weasel personnel carriers. Styling generally ground to a halt at most auto companies during wartime as skeleton design crews could spend only a fraction of their time on civilian projects. But Studebaker was different. Its car styling was being handled by Loewy As-

1942 President Skyway club sedan

1946 Skyway Champion five-passenger coupe

1947 Commander DeLuxe five-passenger coupe

sociates, an outside consultant firm not entirely occupied with defense contracts. As a result, Studebaker was able to introduce an all-new postwar design in the spring of 1946—well ahead of everyone else.

Earlier that year, the company offered a handful of Skyway Champions, slightly facelifted versions of the 1942 model. The alterations were indeed modest: the upper grille molding was extended under the headlamps, the side hood moldings were eliminated, and parking lamps were placed atop the fenders. The usual four body styles—three- and five-passenger coupes, two- and four-door sedans—were offered. Only 19,275 were built before production changed over.

The appealing new 1947 Studebaker was mainly the product of the Loewy Studios. Virgil M. Exner, who had left Pontiac to join Loewy before the war, had directed the '47 design at first, but split with Loewy before introduction time. Engineer Roy Cole supported Exner with staff and equipment for a home studio outside South Bend. His design was based on shapes that Loewy had developed earlier, and was officially accepted over Loewy's own proposal. Exner's influence on it was mostly from the cowl forward—a shorter hood and a more blunt, chrome-laden front end. This basic look was retained, except for detail changes, through 1949, followed by Loewy Studio's novel "bullet-nose" facelift for 1950-51.

The Commander and Champion series returned for '47, but the Skyway designation didn't. A special 123-inch wheelbase carried the Commander Land Cruiser, Studebaker's luxury sedan. Among standard-wheelbase Commanders, the usual four closed body styles were offered in DeLuxe and Regal DeLuxe trim, the latter priced about $120 higher. A new Regal convertible also debuted. The Champion followed the same pattern on a 112-inch wheelbase, and was nearly identical mechanically with its prewar counterpart.

One reason Studebaker styling didn't change much from 1947 to '52 was because the Loewy/Exner design—low profile, large glass area, and flow-through fenders—was so far ahead of the competition. Instant recognition of the '48s was provided by a winged hood medallion. The 1949 Commander was a continuation of the '48, while that year's Champion had a new grille composed of horizontal and vertical louvers forming three rows of rectangular openings. The most significant change in 1947-49 was mechanical. The Commander engine's stroke was lengthened to 4.75 inches for a displacement of 245.6 cubic inches and an even 100 bhp.

Studebaker's model offerings remained the same in 1948-49 as in '47. Commander coupes and sedans in DeLuxe and Regal DeLuxe trim, a Regal DeLuxe convertible, and long-wheelbase Land Cruiser; plus a similar Champion lineup minus the Land Cruiser. The big selling point continued to be styling, despite certain jokes ("Which way is it going?"). The design was an innovation, eliminating the bolt-on fenders of prewar models. The envelope body allowed for an increase of

six inches in front seat width and 10 in the rear, providing excellent interior room, too. Even after the major manufacturers restyled in 1949, Studebaker's shape remained one of the most advanced on the road.

The company enjoyed its best year ever in 1950, and many grand predictions were made about its upcoming "second century." But United States operations came to an end some 14 years later, and the Hamilton, Ontario branch built the last Studebaker automobile two years after that.

The story of how this happened is complex, but it can be summarized as follows: (1) Studebaker's productivity was lower than the rest of the industry, even though its work force was highly paid; (2) the firm's old South Bend plant suffered from high overhead and was more isolated from component suppliers than Detroit factories; and (3) the Big Three, competing with each other, caused casualties among the independents (an example is the Ford and Chevrolet price wars, which Studebaker dealers could not match because of their lower volume).

The product itself probably had less to do with the firm's failures than these commercial factors. Though Studebaker styling was controversial, it usually featured ideas adopted later by other manufacturers. Although the bullet-nose front end of 1950-51 wasn't really copied by anyone else, it did suggest the strong central grille styling that would appear later in different form on Edsels and Pontiacs. The 1950 models also offered Studebaker's excellent automatic transmission, designed in cooperation with the Detroit Gear Division of Borg-Warner.

Studebaker fielded a short-wheelbase Champion in three trim variations for 1950. Commanders rode a longer wheelbase and continued to offer a larger six-cylinder engine. The long-wheelbase Land Cruiser was still part of this series, available as a four-door sedan only. The Champion engine was continued for 1951, while the Commander received Studebaker's first V8.

Displacing 232.6 cubic inches, this new powerplant developed 120 bhp at 4000 rpm. Its engineering was fairly conventional, though overhead cams and hemispherical combustion chambers had been considered. The 232 and its successors have been called heavy for their size, but such statements were made on the basis of comparisons with engines developed much later. In fact, Studebaker's V8 was the first in a long line of robust, efficient small-blocks of less than 300 cid. Those that followed from Dodge, Ford, Chevrolet, and Plymouth certainly benefited from its technology. The 232's greatest contribution, perhaps, was that it closed the power gap between popular-priced cars and luxury machines. As a result, the V8 would become the engine design favored by automakers and buyers alike.

The '51 Studebaker line was essentially the same as in 1950. The main difference was body size: Commanders now shared the 115-inch wheelbase with Champions, while the Land Cruiser shrank from 124 to 119 inches. Prices went up slightly, but buyers seemed

**1946 Champion Regal DeLuxe convertible**

**1949 Champion Regal DeLuxe convertible**

**1950 Champion Custom four-door sedan**

**1951 Commander State five-passenger coupe**

happy to pay the difference for the lively V8, which increased Commander sales considerably. The 232 was no powerhouse, but it did give 90-mph performance. As time would tell, it was capable of considerably more displacement and horsepower.

# Studebaker

Styling changes for '51 were slight. The bullet-nose was refined with a second chrome ring, the prominent air vents above the grille were deleted, and model names were spelled out on the leading edges of the hood. Whatever can be said about its styling now, the bullet-nose Studebaker was popular when new.

With 222,000 unit sales for calendar 1951, Studebaker fell far below its 1950 record, though this was more a result of Korean War restrictions than decreased demand. The firm's market share actually increased, from 4.02 to 4.17 percent.

The company's centenary was marked in 1952. Though all-new styles weren't ready, that year's facelift was acceptably different. The bullet-nose was replaced by a low, toothy grille that some stylists called the "clam digger." The model lineup stayed the same, with the addition of a new hardtop, the Starliner. But production was much lower throughout the industry, and Studebaker built fewer cars. Optimistically, management looked on the upcoming '53s with more enthusiasm.

The now-legendary "Loewy coupes"—Commander and Champion Starliner hardtop and Starlight pillar coupe—were actually designed by Robert E. Bourke, chief of the Loewy Studios at South Bend. Originally envisioned only as a special show car, Loewy sold the design as a production model to Studebaker's management. These coupes were truly magnificent. Mounted on the new 120.5-inch Land Cruiser wheelbase rather than the sedans' 116.5-inch span, they were perfect from every angle. Not a line or a detail was out of place. They were hailed at the time as the "new European look." Today, they're considered by many as the finest American automotive styling of the entire decade.

Sadly, the changeover to the new design delayed production, which was disappointly low. Further problems surfaced when demand for coupes began running four times higher than for the sedans (which had the same general lines but were shorter, higher, and more ungainly). Management had planned just the reverse, and time was lost in switching around.

The same lineup was offered for 1954 (an eggcrate grille was the most obvious change), but production was even lower. By now, the company's weaknesses were becoming apparent: the cost of building each car was frightening. As an experiment, Bourke "priced out" a Commander Starliner using the General Motors cost structure, and found Chevrolet could have sold it for about $1900. Meanwhile, the Ford Blitz was on, as Dearborn waged a price war with GM. Neither giant damaged the other, but both wreaked havoc on the independents. Just when things looked blackest, Packard bought Studebaker and announced a bold new effort to create "the industry's Big Four."

Unable to justify new styling so soon, Studebaker hung a lot of chrome on the old bodies for '55 and adopted a wraparound windshield in mid-year. The model line was shaken up, with Champions (excluding the coupes) still placed on the shorter wheelbase. The

longer chassis now served a separate series, the revived President. The Champion six was raised to 101 bhp. For more economy, the firm shrank the Commander V8 to 224.3 cid, which resulted in 140 bhp. Presidents, in turn, used a larger V8: 259.2 cid and 175 bhp. The top of the line was the wildly two-toned President Speedster hardtop, with special "quilted" vinyl interior, tooled metal dash, and color combinations like pink and black or "lemon and lime." At $3253, the Speedster was not a big seller, and neither were its linemates. In a year when nearly every company was setting new sales records, Studebaker produced only about 116,000 cars. Soon it was determined the company needed to sell about 250,000 cars a year just to break even.

While Studebaker-Packard president James Nance shopped for financing (eventually leading to a takeover by Curtiss-Wright), the firm gamely restyled for 1956. Retaining the old wheelbases and bodyshells, styling became more upright and squared off, with larger, mesh-type grilles. A cheap two-door called the sedanet was offered in the Commander and Champion series. The long-wheelbase chassis was now reserved for the top-line President Classic sedan and the sporty new Hawks.

The Hawks were the last Studebakers of the '50s designed by Loewy's team, and were good-looking, exciting to drive, competent on the curves, and impressive on the straightaways. There were four altogether. The Power (V8) and Flight (six) Hawks were descendents of the pillar-type Starlight coupe. Based on the old Starliner hardtop were the Sky Hawk and Golden Hawk, the latter with the 352-cid Packard engine. Styling was keyed to a square classic-style grille, freestanding parking lights, and deluxe interiors with engine-turned dash like the '55 Speedster's. The Flight Hawk was priced under $2000, while the Golden Hawk listed at only $3061, so they were good buys. Unfortunately, they were all peripheral models that appeared mainly to enthusiasts, while the bread-and-butter family cars continued to sell slowly. Only 70,000 vehicles were turned out at South Bend in 1956, and things would continue to get worse. In 1957 and '58, Studebaker and Packard combined couldn't produce more than 70,000 cars a year.

This was the period when none of the plant's employees knew from one day to the next whether they were working their last shift. With so little money to alter the '56 design, there was nothing else to do but try a facelift. Accordingly, a full-width grille appeared for 1957, and grew more massive in 1958, when Studebakers also got hastily developed quad headlight systems and ungainly tailfins. The Scotsman—a naked, bargain-priced line of sedans and a station wagon—did not spark sales. Neither did the nice-looking Starlight hardtop with its DeSoto-like roof.

Mechanical changes were beneficial, however. The '56 Golden Hawk's huge Packard engine had made it embarrassingly front-heavy, so the 1957-58 edition

1952 Commander State Starliner hardtop coupe

1953 Commander Regal Starliner hardtop coupe

1954 Commander Regal Conestoga station wagon

1955 President Speedster hardtop coupe

1956 President Classic four-door sedan

1956 Golden Hawk hardtop coupe

1956 Sky Hawk hardtop coupe

1957 President Classic four-door sedan

used a 289 V8 with Paxton supercharger. This arrangement developed the same 275 bhp, but in a more efficient way: the blower freewheeled economically until the accelerator was floored. The other Hawks were replaced by a single fixed-pillar Silver Hawk with plainer trim and an unblown 289 developing 210 bhp. The Golden Hawk and Silver Hawk were fine road machines, capable of carrying four people comfortably over long distances at high speed in true *gran turismo* style. As "personal cars," their appeal was limited, however, especially in 1958 when Studebaker hit bot-

tom. Fewer than 45,000 cars were built that year.

The end might have come right there had not the firm succeeded with the compact 1959 Lark. Though the Lark used many body panels and mechanical components from earlier '53–'58 models, stylist Duncan McRae had done enough to the exterior to make it look considerably different. The boxy, practical styling found a market among compact-conscious buyers, and people flocked to Studebaker dealerships in droves. The turnaround was astounding. Compared to 18,850 four-door sedans built for '58, a total of 48,459 four-door

'59 Larks rolled off the lines. The Lark was also offered as a two-door sedan, two-door wagon, and two-door hardtop, all on a 108.5-inch wheelbase. Six-cylinder models still used the old 169.6-cid L-head, detuned to 90 bhp. The V8 versions were fitted with the 259, rated at 180 bhp, or 195 with four-barrel carburetor. In V8 form, the Lark was lively, yet surprisingly easy on gas. The Hawk was also continued for '59, but only the Silver Hawk was issued. As a result of all this, Studebaker made its first profit in six years, building over 126,000 cars. But the Lark would provide only a temporary reprieve.

For 1960, Lark was changed only mildly from the introductory model, receiving a new grille composed of thick and thin horizontal bars, and small alterations in script and medallions. The Hawk was carried over virtually unaltered. It sold for $2650 and was worth it. Equipped with functional white-on-black instruments and semi-bucket seats, it was a unique "family sports car" offering good performance. But scant advertising, plus emphasis on the Lark, hampered its sales.

For 1961, Lark was modestly facelifted. The six-cylinder engine was converted to overhead-valve design, yielding 112 bhp. One new model was the Lark Cruiser, outfitted with rich upholstery and riding the wagon wheelbase for extra rear seat room. It could be ordered with the Hawk's 289 V8, available with a power pack consisting of four-barrel carburetor and dual exhausts that raised output to 225 bhp. The Hawk itself was slightly revised for 1961, receiving two-tone color panels just below the fins and an optional four-speed gearbox.

When Sherwood Egbert became company president in early 1961, he asked Milwaukee stylist Brooks Stevens to help redesign the Lark and Hawk on a six-month crash basis. Randall Faurot, Studebaker's head of styling, willingly stepped back. Stevens adopted the longer 113-inch wheelbase for all four-door models, then developed elongated rear quarters, large round taillights, and a Mercedes-like rectangular grille (Studebaker was distributing Mercedes-Benz cars at the time). A new entry with either six or V8 power was the sporty Lark Daytona, which had bucket seats, bright new interiors, and an optional 289 engine.

In reworking the Hawk, Stevens reskinned the old Loewy-styled coupe to create a true hardtop with a Thunderbird-like rear roofline. He eliminated the large tailfins, which had become dated by 1960, and restyled the dashboard, which retained its full complement of purposeful gauges. Christened Gran Turismo, the result was a remarkable piece of expeditious redesign. The GT's optional 225-bhp engine provided a 120-mph top speed and a 0–60 sprint of less than 10 seconds. Although heavy, the 289 V8 was incredibly strong, capable of performance far greater than its displacement suggested. Sales picked up in 1962, when about 8400 Gran Turismos were built.

For 1963, Stevens reworked the Lark's body above the beltline. He improved visibility by using more glass

1957 Golden Hawk hardtop coupe

1957 Silver Hawk coupe

1957 President Broadmoor four-door station wagon

1958 President Starlight hardtop coupe

and thinner upper door frames. The grille was revised slightly. The dashboard was completely new, fitted with needle gauges, rocker-type control switches, and a "vanity" style glove compartment containing a makeup case and pop-up mirror. For utility-car buyers, Stevens came up with a great innovation: the Wagonaire, with a sliding rear roof panel.

Stevens gave the 1963 GT Hawk a new grille similar

1959 Lark Regal hardtop coupe

1960 Lark Regal convertible

1961 Hawk coupe

1962 Gran Turismo Hawk hardtop coupe

1963 Lark Daytona hardtop coupe

1963 Gran Turismo Hawk hardtop coupe

1963 Lark Daytona Wagonaire station wagon

1964 Commander four-door sedan

to the Lark's, round amber parking lights, a wood-like dash, and pleated vinyl seats. Both Lark and Hawk were available by mid-year with the R1 (240 bhp) and R2 (290 bhp) Avanti engines, priced at $210 and $372 respectively. The R2 Super Hawk exceeded 140 mph at Bonneville, and an R2 Super Lark did over 132 mph.

Studebaker's greatest achievement of the decade was undoubtedly the Avanti, introduced for 1963. This brilliantly conceived grand touring car was created by Raymond Loewy and a team of talented designers— John Ebstein, Robert Andrews, and Tom Kellogg. Like Stevens, Loewy had been hired by Sherwood Egbert. While Stevens attended to emergency restyling, Egbert asked Loewy for an exotic sports-type car that would revitalize the company's image. It was the first assignment Loewy had been given by Studebaker since his

old contract lapsed following completion of the 1956 Hawks. In haste and in complete secrecy, he gathered his team at a rented house in Palm Springs, California.

The car they developed had a Coke-bottle shape, a large rear window, and a built-in roll bar. Front fenders were razor-edged, and swept back into curved rear fen-

**1964 Daytona Wagonaire station wagon**

**1964 Avanti sport coupe**

**1965 Daytona two-door sport sedan**

**1965 Cruiser four-door sedan**

ders, then flowed into a jacked-up tail. Avoiding a conventional grille. Loewy designed an air scoop under a thin front bumper. An asymmetrical hump in the hood directed the driver's vision forward and added character to the front-end shape. Inside, ample crash padding was combined with four slim-section vinyl bucket seats and an aircraft-style control panel. The whole design was accepted for production with very little change from Loewy's original quarter-scale model.

Fiberglass was chosen as the body material for reasons of cost and time, and chief engineer Eugene Harding chose a Lark convertible frame, shortened and highly modified, fitted with front and rear anti-sway bars and rear radius rods. The Bendix disc brakes used on the Avanti (as well as on some Larks and Hawks) were the first caliper discs in domestic production. The engine was, of course, the 289 V8. In standard (R1) form, it developed 240 bhp, thanks to a Paxton supercharger, ¾-race high-lift cam, dual-breaker distributor, four-barrel carburetor, and dual exhausts. Andy Granatelli and Paxton also developed a supercharged R2 version with 290 bhp, followed by a bored-out 304.5-cid version in three higher states of tune, the R3, R4, and R5. The experimental R5 had two Paxton superchargers, one for each cylinder bank, along with magneto ignition and Bendix fuel injection. It developed an incredible 575 horsepower, but was not a production option.

The Avanti had a remarkably slippery shape, even though Loewy had not had time for wind tunnel tests—he'd just guessed. In late 1962, Granatelli broke 29 Bonneville speed records with an R3, traveling faster than anyone ever had in an American stock car.

Unfortunately, Studebaker failed to get Avanti production going immediately after announcement. Unexpected distortion during fiberglass curing accounted partly for the delay. As a result, the firm was forced to add its own fiberglass body facility. By the time all the bugs were out, most of the customers who'd placed advance orders had given up on the Avanti and bought Corvettes. Fewer than 4600 were produced during 1963 and 1964. Production had already ceased by the time Studebaker stopped building Larks in December 1963.

The car was revived, however, by a pair of South Bend dealers. Equipped with a Corvette engine, it was still being produced in the 1980s (see Avanti II).

Despite the Avanti's obvious showroom appeal, Studebaker sales plunged in 1963. Model year output fell short of 70,000 units. The company ranked 12th in production, ahead of only Lincoln and Imperial among the major makes. Egbert, who'd been hospitalized repeatedly, entered the hospital again in November 1963 and did not return to the company. (He died of cancer in 1969.) Byers Burlingame replaced him as president. A month later, after desperate last-ditch attempts to obtain backing for future models, Burlingame announced the closure of the South Bend factory. Operations were transferred to the assembly plant in Hamilton, Ontario, where management hoped to con-

tinue production at the rate of 20,000 a year. After '64, all Studebakers were Canadian-built.

The 1964 models were the most attractive of the decade. Brooks Stevens had created more new styling for the Cruiser, Daytona, and Lark: a crisp, squared-off body, six inches longer than the 1963 version; a broad, horizontal grille integrated with the headlights; and a pointed upper tail section housing backup lights and taillamps. A stripped Challenger line was added at around $2100, and a still more powerful R3 engine was announced for the Super Lark and Super Hawk. (The Super Lark could do 0 to 60 mph in 7.3 seconds.) The '64 GT Hawk had a landau-style roof with partial vinyl top (optional), a smoothed-off deck, and a matte-black dash. A test driver pushed an R2 Hawk to 90 mph in 13.8 seconds and estimated its top speed at 150-plus mph. All the high-performance specials were dropped after the move to Canada.

The 1965 models were unchanged in appearance. However, without the South Bend engine plant, Hamilton had to find another powerplant. Ultimately, the source was Chevrolet, which provided its solid 120-bhp, 194-cid six and its excellent 283-cid V8 with 195 bhp. A six-cylinder Cruiser was available along with Commander two- and four-door sedans and a four-door Wagonaire (with or without sliding roof). The V8 was offered for Commander sedans and wagon, the Daytona Sport sedan and wagon, and the Cruiser.

The Hamilton plant almost met its 20,000-unit quota for 1965. But the lack of facilities for advanced research and development meant production simply couldn't last. The last Studebaker—the '66—had new front-end

1966 Cruiser four-door sedan

1966 Daytona two-door sedan

styling with two dual-beam headlights instead of quads, a revised grille with rectangular panels, new bodyside moldings, and air-extraction ports in the rear panel. But production numbered only 8947 units. Despite rescue attempts by Stevens and others, Studebaker was doomed. Its range of prototypes (from economy cars to a revived Packard) never saw the light of day.

# Studebaker Specifications

## 1940

| 2G Champion (wb 110.0)—66,264 built | Wght | Price | Prod |
|---|---|---|---|
| cpe 3P | 2,290 | 660 | — |
| cpe 5P | 2,335 | 696 | — |
| club sdn | 2,360 | 700 | — |
| Cruising Sedan 4d | 2,390 | 740 | — |
| DeLuxe cpe 3P | 2,315 | 705 | — |
| DeLuxe cpe 5P | 2,360 | 740 | — |
| DeLuxe club sdn | 2,385 | 745 | — |
| DeLuxe Cruising Sedan 4d | 2,415 | 785 | — |
| **LOA Commander (wb 116.5)—34,477 built** | | | |
| Custom cpe 3P | 3,055 | 895 | — |
| club sdn | 3,135 | 925 | — |
| Cruising Sedan 4d | 3,180 | 965 | — |

| 6C President (wb 122.0)—6,444 | Wght | Price | Prod |
|---|---|---|---|
| cpe 3P | 3,280 | 1,025 | — |
| club sdn | 3,370 | 1,055 | — |
| Cruising Sedan 4d | 3,420 | 1,095 | — |

| 1940 Engines | bore×stroke | bhp | availability |
|---|---|---|---|
| L6, 164.3 | 3.00×3.88 | 78 | S-Champion |
| L6, 226.2 | 3.31×4.38 | 90 | S-Commander |
| L8, 250.4 | 3.06×4.25 | 110 | S-President |

## 1941

| 3G Champion (wb 110.0)—84,910 built | Wght | Price | Prod |
|---|---|---|---|
| Custom cpe 3P | 2,370 | 710 | — |
| Custom Opera cpe | 2,410 | 750 | — |
| Custom club sdn | 2,450 | 755 | — |
| Custom Cruising Sedan 4d | 2,480 | 795 | — |
| Custom DeLuxe cpe 3P | 2,395 | 745 | — |
| Custom DeLuxe Opera cpe | 2,425 | 780 | — |
| Custom DeLuxe club sdn | 2,470 | 785 | — |
| Custom DeLuxe Cruising Sdn 4d | 2,500 | 825 | — |
| DeLux-Tone cpe 3P | 2,400 | 780 | — |
| DeLux-Tone Opera cpe | 2,430 | 815 | — |
| DeLux-Tone club sdn | 2,470 | 820 | — |
| DeLux-Tone Cruising Sedan 4d | 2,500 | 860 | — |

| 11A Commander (wb 119.0)—41,996 built | Wght | Price | Prod |
|---|---|---|---|
| Custom sdn cpe | 3,160 | 990 | — |
| Custom Cruising Sedan 4d | 3,210 | 1,010 | — |
| Custom Land Cruiser sdn 4d | 3,230 | 1,055 | — |
| DeLux-Tone Cruising Sedan 4d | 3,225 | 1,075 | — |
| DeLux-Tone Land Cruiser sdn 4d | 3,245 | 1,120 | — |
| Skyway sdn cpe | 3,200 | 1,080 | — |
| Skyway Cruising Sedan 4d | 3,240 | 1,100 | — |
| Skyway Land Cruiser sdn 4d | 3,260 | 1,130 | — |

| 7C President (wb 124.5)—6,994 built | | | |
|---|---|---|---|
| Custom Cruising Sedan 4d | 3,450 | 1,140 | — |
| Custom Land Cruiser sdn 4d | 3,475 | 1,185 | — |
| DeLux-Tone Cruising Sedan 4d | 3,475 | 1,205 | — |
| DeLux-Tone Land Cruiser sdn 4d | 3,500 | 1,250 | — |
| Skyway sdn cpe | 3,440 | 1,210 | — |
| Skyway Cruising Sedan 4d | 3,500 | 1,230 | — |
| Skyway Land Cruiser sdn 4d | 3,520 | 1,260 | — |

| 1941 Engines | bore×stroke | bhp | availability |
|---|---|---|---|
| L6, 169.6 | 3.00×4.00 | 80 | S-Champion |
| L6, 226.2 | 3.31×4.38 | 94 | S-Commander |
| L8, 250.4 | 3.06×4.25 | 117 | S-President |

# 1942

| 4G Champion (wb 110.0)—29,678 built | Wght | Price | Prod |
|---|---|---|---|
| Custom cpe 3P | 2,415 | 744 | — |
| Custom Double Dater cpe 5P | 2,455 | 769 | — |
| Custom club sdn | 2,495 | 774 | — |
| Custom Cruising Sedan 4d | 2,520 | 804 | — |
| DeLuxstyle cpe 3P | 2,435 | 779 | — |
| DeLuxstyle Double Dater cpe 5P | 2,470 | 804 | — |
| DeLuxstyle club sdn | 2,520 | 809 | — |
| DeLuxstyle Cruising Sedan 4d | 2,545 | 839 | — |

| 12A Commander (wb 119.0)—17,500 built | | | |
|---|---|---|---|
| Custom sdn cpe | 3,195 | 1,025 | — |
| Custom Cruising Sedan 4d | 3,265 | 1,045 | — |
| Custom Land Cruiser sdn 4d | 3,290 | 1,080 | — |
| DeLuxstyle sdn cpe | 3,210 | 1,070 | — |
| DeLuxstyle Cruising Sedan 4d | 3,280 | 1,090 | — |
| DeLuxstyle Land Cruiser sdn 4d | 3,305 | 1,125 | — |
| Skyway sdn cpe | 3,240 | 1,105 | — |
| Skyway Cruising Sedan 4d | 3,300 | 1,125 | — |
| Skyway Land Cruiser sdn 4d | 3,315 | 1,160 | — |

| 8C President (wb 124.5)—3,500 built | | | |
|---|---|---|---|
| Custom sdn cpe | 3,440 | 1,141 | — |
| Custom Cruising Sedan 4d | 3,485 | 1,161 | — |
| Custom Land Cruiser sdn 4d | 3,510 | 1,196 | — |
| DeLuxstyle sdn cpe | 3,455 | 1,186 | — |
| DeLuxstyle Cruising Sedan 4d | 3,500 | 1,206 | — |
| DeLuxstyle Land Cruiser sdn 4d | 3,515 | 1,241 | — |
| Skyway sdn cpe | 3,470 | 1,221 | — |
| Skyway Cruising Sedan 4d | 3,540 | 1,241 | — |
| Skyway Land Cruiser sdn 4d | 3,540 | 1,276 | — |

| 1942 Engines | bore×stroke | bhp | availability |
|---|---|---|---|
| L6, 169.6 | 3.00×4.00 | 80 | S-Champion |
| L6, 226.2 | 3.31×4.38 | 94 | S-Commander |
| L8, 250.4 | 3.06×4.25 | 117 | S-President |

# 1946

| 5G Skyway Champion (wb 110.0) | Wght | Price | Prod |
|---|---|---|---|
| cpe 3P | 2,456 | 1,002 | 2,465 |
| cpe 5P | 2,491 | 1,044 | 1,285 |
| club sdn | 2,541 | 1,046 | 5,000 |
| Cruising Sedan 4d | 2,566 | 1,097 | 10,525 |

| 1946 Engine | bore×stroke | bhp | availability |
|---|---|---|---|
| L6, 169.6 | 3.00×4.00 | 80 | S-all |

# 1947

| 6G Champion (wb 112.0)—105,097 built | Wght | Price | Prod |
|---|---|---|---|
| DeLuxe sdn 4d | 2,735 | 1,478 | — |
| DeLuxe sdn 2d | 2,685 | 1,446 | — |
| DeLuxe cpe 5P | 2,670 | 1,472 | — |
| DeLuxe cpe 3P | 2,600 | 1,378 | — |
| Regal DeLuxe sdn 4d | 2,760 | 1,551 | — |
| Regal DeLuxe sdn 2d | 2,710 | 1,520 | — |
| Regal DeLuxe cpe 5P | 2,690 | 1,546 | — |
| Regal DeLuxe cpe 3P | 2,620 | 1,451 | — |
| Regal DeLuxe conv cpe | 2,875 | 1,902 | — |

| 15A Commander (wb 119.0; LC-123.0)—56,399 built | | | |
|---|---|---|---|
| DeLuxe sdn 4d | 3,265 | 1,761 | — |
| DeLuxe sdn 2d | 3,230 | 1,729 | — |
| DeLuxe cpe 5P | 3,210 | 1,755 | — |
| DeLuxe cpe 3P | 3,140 | 1,661 | — |
| Regal DeLuxe sdn 4d | 3,280 | 1,882 | — |
| Regal DeLuxe sdn 2d | 3,245 | 1,850 | — |
| Regal DeLuxe cpe 5P | 3,225 | 1,877 | — |
| Regal DeLuxe cpe 3P | 3,155 | 1,782 | — |
| Regal DeLuxe conv cpe | 3,420 | 2,236 | — |
| Land Cruiser sdn 4d | 3,340 | 2,043 | — |

| 1947 Engines | bore×stroke | bhp | availability |
|---|---|---|---|
| L6, 169.6 | 3.00×4.00 | 80 | S-Champion |
| L6, 226.2 | 3.31×4.38 | 94 | S-Commander |

# 1948

| 7G Champion (wb 112.0)—99,282 built | Wght | Price | Prod |
|---|---|---|---|
| Deluxe sdn 4d | 2,720 | 1,636 | — |
| DeLuxe sdn 2d | 2,675 | 1,604 | — |
| DeLuxe cpe 5P | 2,670 | 1,630 | — |
| DeLuxe cpe 3P | 2,590 | 1,535 | — |
| Regal DeLuxe sdn 4d | 2,725 | 1,709 | — |
| Regal DeLuxe sdn 2d | 2,685 | 1,678 | — |
| Regal DeLuxe cpe 5P | 2,690 | 1,704 | — |
| Regal DeLuxe cpe 3P | 2,615 | 1,609 | — |
| Regal DeLuxe conv cpe | 2,865 | 2,060 | — |

| 15A Commander (wb 119.0; LC-123.0)—85,711 built | | | |
|---|---|---|---|
| DeLuxe sdn 4d | 3,195 | 1,956 | — |
| DeLuxe sdn 2d | 3,165 | 1,925 | — |
| DeLuxe cpe 5P | 3,150 | 1,951 | — |
| DeLuxe cpe 3P | 3,080 | 1,856 | — |
| Regal DeLuxe sdn 4d | 3,215 | 2,078 | — |
| Regal DeLuxe sdn 2d | 3,175 | 2,046 | — |
| Regal DeLuxe cpe 5P | 3,165 | 2,072 | — |
| Regal DeLuxe cpe 3P | 3,095 | 1,978 | — |
| Regal DeLuxe conv cpe | 3,385 | 2,431 | — |
| Land Cruiser sdn 4d | 3,280 | 2,265 | — |

| 1948 Engines | bore×stroke | bhp | availability |
|---|---|---|---|
| L6, 169.6 | 3.00×4.00 | 80 | S-Champion |
| L6, 226.2 | 3.31×4.38 | 94 | S-Commander |

# 1949

| 8G Champion (wb 112.0)—85,604 built | Wght | Price | Prod |
|---|---|---|---|
| DeLuxe sdn 4d | 2,745 | 1,689 | — |
| DeLuxe sdn 2d | 2,720 | 1,657 | — |
| DeLuxe cpe 5P | 2,705 | 1,683 | — |
| DeLuxe cpe 3P | 2,645 | 1,588 | — |
| Regal DeLuxe sdn 4d | 2,750 | 1,762 | — |
| Regal DeLuxe sdn 2d | 2,725 | 1,731 | — |
| Regal DeLuxe cpe 5P | 2,725 | 1,757 | — |
| Regal DeLuxe cpe 3P | 2,650 | 1,652 | — |
| Regal DeLuxe conv cpe | 2,895 | 2,086 | — |

## 16A Commander (wb 119.0; LC-123.0)—43,694 built

| | Wght | Price | Prod |
|---|---|---|---|
| DeLuxe sdn 4d | 3,240 | 2,019 | — |
| DeLuxe sdn 2d | 3,215 | 1,988 | — |
| DeLuxe cpe 5P | 3,200 | 2,014 | — |
| DeLuxe cpe 3P | 3,130 | 1,919 | — |
| Regal DeLuxe sdn 4d | 3,245 | 2,141 | — |
| Regal DeLuxe sdn 2d | 3,220 | 2,109 | — |
| Regal DeLuxe cpe 5P | 3,205 | 2,135 | — |
| Regal DeLuxe cpe 3P | 3,135 | 2,041 | — |
| Regal DeLuxe conv cpe | 3,415 | 2,468 | — |
| Land Cruiser sdn 4d | 3,325 | 2,328 | — |

| 1949 Engines | bore×stroke | bhp | availability |
|---|---|---|---|
| L6, 169.6 | 3.00×4.00 | 80 | S-Champion |
| L6, 245.6 | 3.31×4.75 | 100 | S-Commander |

# 1950

## 9G Champion (wb 113.0)—270,604 built

| | Wght | Price | Prod |
|---|---|---|---|
| Custom sdn 4d | 2,730 | 1,519 | — |
| Custom sdn 2d | 2,695 | 1,487 | — |
| Custom cpe, 5P | 2,690 | 1,514 | — |
| Custom cpe 3P | 2,620 | 1,419 | — |
| DeLuxe sdn 4d | 2,750 | 1,597 | — |
| DeLuxe sdn 2d | 2,720 | 1,565 | — |
| DeLuxe cpe 5P | 2,705 | 1,592 | — |
| DeLuxe cpe 3P | 2,635 | 1,497 | — |
| Regal DeLuxe sdn 4d | 2,755 | 1,676 | — |
| Regal DeLuxe sdn 2d | 2,725 | 1,644 | — |
| Regal DeLuxe cpe 5P | 2,715 | 1,671 | — |
| Regal DeLuxe cpe 3P | 2,640 | 1,576 | — |
| Regal DeLuxe conv cpe | 2,900 | 1,981 | — |

## 17A Commander (wb 120.0; LC-124.0)—72,562 built

| | Wght | Price | Prod |
|---|---|---|---|
| DeLuxe sdn 4d | 3,255 | 1,902 | — |
| DeLuxe sdn 2d | 3,215 | 1,871 | — |
| DeLuxe cpe 5P | 3,215 | 1,897 | — |
| Regal DeLuxe sdn 4d | 3,265 | 2,024 | — |
| Regal DeLuxe sdn 2d | 3,220 | 1,992 | — |
| Regal DeLuxe cpe 5P | 3,220 | 2,018 | — |
| Regal DeLuxe conv cpe | 3,375 | 2,328 | — |
| Land Cruiser sdn 4d | 3,355 | 2,187 | — |

| 1950 Engines | bore×stroke | bhp | availability |
|---|---|---|---|
| L6, 169.6 | 3.00×4.00 | 85 | S-Champion |
| L6, 245.6 | 3.31×4.75 | 102 | S-Commander |

# 1951

## 10G Champion (wb 115.0)—144,286 built

| | Wght | Price | Prod |
|---|---|---|---|
| Custom sdn 4d | 2,690 | 1,667 | — |
| Custom sdn 2d | 2,670 | 1,634 | — |
| Custom cpe 5P | 2,650 | 1,662 | — |
| Custom cpe 3P | 2,585 | 1,561 | — |
| DeLuxe sdn 4d | 2,715 | 1,759 | — |
| DeLuxe sdn 2d | 2,690 | 1,716 | — |
| DeLuxe cpe 5P | 2,675 | 1,744 | — |
| DeLuxe cpe 3P | 2,610 | 1,643 | — |
| Regal sdn 4d | 2,720 | 1,833 | — |
| Regal sdn 2d | 2,690 | 1,800 | — |
| Regal cpe 5P | 2,675 | 1,828 | — |
| Regal cpe 3P | 2,615 | 1,727 | — |
| Regal conv cpe | 2,890 | 2,157 | — |

## H Commander (wb 115,0; LC-119.0)—124,280 built

| | Wght | Price | Prod |
|---|---|---|---|
| Regal sdn 4d | 3,065 | 2,032 | — |
| Regal sdn 2d | 3,045 | 1,997 | — |
| Regal cpe 5P | 3,030 | 2,026 | — |
| State sdn 4d | 3,070 | 2,143 | — |
| State sdn 2d | 3,045 | 2,108 | — |
| State cpe 5P | 3,030 | 2,137 | — |
| State conv cpe | 3,240 | 2,381 | — |
| Land Cruiser sdn 4d | 3,165 | 2,289 | — |

| 1951 Engines | bore×stroke | bhp | availability |
|---|---|---|---|
| L6, 169.6 | 3.00×4.00 | 85 | S-Champion |
| V8, 232.6 | 3.38×3.25 | 120 | S-Commander |

# 1952

## 12G Champion (wb 115.0)—101,390 built

| | Wght | Price | Prod |
|---|---|---|---|
| Custom sdn 4d | 2,695 | 1,769 | — |
| Custom sdn 2d | 2,655 | 1,735 | — |
| Custom cpe 5P | 2,660 | 1,763 | — |
| DeLuxe sdn 4d | 2,720 | 1,862 | — |
| DeLuxe sdn 2d | 2,685 | 1,828 | — |
| DeLuxe cpe 5P | 2,675 | 1,856 | — |
| Regal sdn 4d | 2,725 | 1,946 | — |
| Regal sdn 2d | 2,690 | 1,913 | — |
| Regal cpe 5P | 2,695 | 1,941 | — |
| Regal Starliner htp cpe | 2,860 | 2,220 | — |
| Regal conv cpe | 2,870 | 2,273 | — |

## 3H Commander (wb 115.0; LC-119.0)—84,849 built

| | Wght | Price | Prod |
|---|---|---|---|
| Regal sdn 4d | 3,085 | 2,121 | — |
| Regal sdn 2d | 3,040 | 2,086 | — |
| Regal cpe 5P | 3,030 | 2,115 | — |
| State sdn 4d | 3,075 | 2,208 | — |
| State sdn 2d | 3,055 | 2,172 | — |
| State cpe 5P | 3,025 | 2,202 | — |
| State Starliner htp cpe | 3,220 | 2,488 | — |
| State conv cpe | 3,230 | 2,548 | — |
| Land Cruiser sdn 4d | 3,155 | 2,365 | — |

| 1952 Engines | bore×stroke | bhp | availability |
|---|---|---|---|
| L6, 169.6 | 3.00×4.00 | 85 | S-Champion |
| V8, 232.6 | 3.38×3.25 | 120 | S-Commander |

# 1953

## 14G Champion (wb 116.5; cpes-120.5)—93,807 built

| | Wght | Price | Prod |
|---|---|---|---|
| Custom sdn 4d | 2,710 | 1,767 | — |
| Custom sdn 2d | 2,690 | 1,735 | — |
| DeLuxe sdn 4d | 2,735 | 1,863 | — |
| DeLuxe sdn 2d | 2,700 | 1,831 | — |
| DeLuxe Starlight cpe | 2,695 | 1,868 | — |
| Regal sdn 4d | 2,745 | 1,949 | — |
| Regal sdn 2d | 2,715 | 1,917 | — |
| Regal Starlight cpe | 2,700 | 1,955 | — |
| Regal Starliner htp cpe | 2,760 | 2,116 | — |

## 4H Commander (wb 116.5; LC/cpes-120.5)—76,092 built

| | Wght | Price | Prod |
|---|---|---|---|
| DeLuxe sdn 4d | 3,075 | 2,121 | — |
| DeLuxe DeLuxe sdn 2d | 3,055 | 2,089 | — |
| DeLuxe Starlight cpe | 3,040 | 2,127 | — |
| Regal sdn 4d | 3,095 | 2,208 | — |
| Regal Starlight cpe | 3,040 | 2,213 | — |
| Regal Starliner htp cpe | 3,120 | 2,374 | — |
| Land Cruiser sdn 4d | 3,180 | 2,316 | — |

| 1953 Engines | bore×stroke | bhp | availability |
|---|---|---|---|
| L6, 169.6 | 3.00×4.00 | 85 | S-Champion |
| V8, 232.6 | 3.38×3.25 | 120 | S-Commander |

# 1954

## 15G Champion Six (wb 116.5; cpes-120.5)—51,431 built

| | Wght | Price | Prod |
|---|---|---|---|
| Custom sdn 4d | 2,735 | 1,801 | — |
| Custom sdn 2d | 2,705 | 1,758 | — |
| DeLuxe sdn 4d | 2,765 | 1,918 | — |
| DeLuxe sdn 2d | 2,730 | 1,875 | — |
| DeLuxe Starlight cpe | 2,740 | 1,972 | — |
| DeLuxe Conestoga wgn 2d | 2,930 | 2,187 | — |
| Regal sdn 4d | 2,780 | 2,026 | — |
| Regal sdn 2d | 2,745 | 1,983 | — |
| Regal Starlight cpe | 2,750 | 2,080 | — |

| | Wght | Price | Prod |
|---|---|---|---|
| Regal Starliner htp cpe | 2,825 | 2,241 | — |
| Regal Conestoga wgn 2d | 2,950 | 2,295 | — |

### 5H Commander (wb 116.5; LC/cpes-120.5)—30,499 built

| | Wght | Price | Prod |
|---|---|---|---|
| DeLuxe sdn 4d | 3,105 | 2,179 | — |
| DeLuxe sdn 2d | 3,075 | 2,136 | — |
| DeLuxe Starlight cpe | 3,085 | 2,233 | — |
| DeLuxe Conestoga wgn 2d | 3,265 | 2,448 | — |
| Regal sdn 4d | 3,120 | 2,287 | — |
| Regal Starlight cpe | 3,095 | 2,341 | — |
| Regal Starliner htp cpe | 3,175 | 2,502 | — |
| Regal Conestoga wgn 2d | 3,265 | 2,556 | — |
| Land Cruiser sdn 4d | 3,180 | 2,438 | — |

| 1954 Engines | bore×stroke | bhp | availability |
|---|---|---|---|
| L6, 169.6 | 3.00×4.00 | 85 | S-Champion |
| V8, 232.6 | 3.38×3.25 | 120 | S-Commander |

## 1955

### 16G Champion (wb 116.5; cpes-120.5)—50,368 built

| | Wght | Price | Prod |
|---|---|---|---|
| Custom sdn 4d | 2,790 | 1,783 | — |
| Custom sdn 2d | 2,740 | 1,741 | — |
| DeLuxe sdn 4d | 2,805 | 1,885 | — |
| DeLuxe sdn 2d | 2,780 | 1,841 | — |
| DeLuxe cpe | 2,790 | 1,875 | — |
| DeLuxe wgn 2d | 2,980 | 2,141 | — |
| Regal sdn 4d | 2,815 | 1,993 | — |
| Regal cpe | 2,795 | 1,975 | — |
| Regal htp cpe | 2,865 | 2,125 | — |
| Regal wgn 2d | 2,985 | 2,312 | — |

### 6G Commander (wb 116.5; cpes-120.5)—58,792 built

| | Wght | Price | Prod |
|---|---|---|---|
| Custom sdn 4d | 3,065 | 1,919 | — |
| Custom sdn 2d | 3,105 | 1,873 | — |
| DeLuxe sdn 4d | 3,075 | 2,014 | — |
| DeLuxe sdn 2d | 3,045 | 1,969 | — |
| DeLuxe cpe | 3,065 | 1,989 | — |
| DeLuxe wgn 2d | 3,265 | 2,274 | — |
| Regal sdn 4d | 3,080 | 2,127 | — |
| Regal cpe | 3,065 | 2,094 | — |
| Regal htp cpe | 3,150 | 2,282 | — |
| Regal Conestoga wgn 2d | 3,274 | 2,445 | — |

### 6H President (wb 120.5)

| | Wght | Price | Prod |
|---|---|---|---|
| DeLuxe sdn 4d | 3,165 | 2,311 | 22,451 |
| State sdn 4d | 3,220 | 2,381 | |
| State cpe | 3,210 | 2,270 | |
| State htp cpe | 3,175 | 2,456 | |
| Speedster htp cpe | 3,301 | 3,253 | 2,215 |

| 1955 Engines | bore×stroke | bhp | availability |
|---|---|---|---|
| L6, 185.6 | 3.00×4.38 | 101 | S-Champion |
| V8, 224.3 | 3.56×2.81 | 140 | S-Commander |
| V8, 259.2 | 3.56×3.25 | 175 | S-President exc Speedster |
| V8, 259.2 | 3.56×3.25 | 185 | S-President Speedster |

## 1956

### 56G Six (wb 116.5; Hawk-120.5)—28,918* built

| | Wght | Price | Prod |
|---|---|---|---|
| Champion sdn 4d | 2,835 | 1,996 | — |
| Champion sdn 2d | 2,800 | 1,946 | — |
| Champion sedanet | 2,780 | 1,844 | — |
| Pelham wgn 2d | 3,000 | 2,232 | — |
| Flight Hawk cpe | 2,780 | 1,986 | — |

### 56B V8, 259 (wb 116.5; Hawk-120.5)—30,654* built

| | Wght | Price | Prod |
|---|---|---|---|
| Commander sdn 4d | 3,140 | 2,125 | — |
| Commander sdn 2d | 3,110 | 2,076 | — |
| Commander sedanet | 3,085 | 1,974 | — |
| Parkview wgn 2d | 3,300 | 2,354 | — |
| Power Hawk cpe | 3,095 | 2,101 | — |

### 56H V8, 289 (wb 116.5; Classic/Hawk-120.5)

| | Wght | Price | Prod |
|---|---|---|---|
| President sdn 4d | 3,210 | 2,235 | 18,209 |
| President sdn 2d | 3,180 | 2,188 | |
| President Classic sdn 4d | 3,295 | 2,489 | |
| Pinehurst wgn 2d | 3,395 | 2,529 | |
| Sky Hawk htp cpe | 3,215 | 2,477 | 3,610 |

### 56J V8, 352 (wb 120.5)

| | Wght | Price | Prod |
|---|---|---|---|
| Golden Hawk htp cpe | 3,360 | 3,061 | 4,071 |

*Includes 11,484 Flight Hawks and Power Hawks.

| 1956 Engines | bore×stroke | bhp | availability |
|---|---|---|---|
| L6, 185.6 | 3.00×4.38 | 101 | S-Champion, Flight Hawk, Pelham |
| V8, 259.2 | 3.56×3.25 | 170 | S-Commander, Power Hawk, Parkview |
| V8, 259.2 | 3.56×3.25 | 185 | O-Champ, Comm, Power/Flight Hawk, Wgns |
| V8, 289.0 | 3.56×3.63 | 195 | S-President, Pinehurst |
| V8, 289.0 | 3.56×3.63 | 210 | S-President Classic, Sky Hawk |
| V8, 289.0 | 3.56×3.63 | 225 | O-President, Pinehurst, Sky Hawk |
| V8, 352.0 | 4.00×3.50 | 275 | S-Golden Hawk |

## 1957*

### 57G Six (wb 116.5; Hawk-120.5)

| | Wght | Price | Prod |
|---|---|---|---|
| Scotsman sdn 4d | 2,725 | 1,826 | — |
| Scotsman club sdn | 2,680 | 1,776 | — |
| Scotsman wgn 2d | 2,875 | 1,995 | — |
| Champion Custom sdn 4d | 2,785 | 2,049 | — |
| Champion Custom club sdn | 2,755 | 2,001 | — |
| Champion DeLuxe sdn 4d | 2,810 | 2,171 | — |
| Champion DeLuxe club sdn | 2,780 | 2,123 | — |
| Pelham wgn 2d | 3,015 | 2,382 | — |
| Silver Hawk cpe | 2,790 | 2,142 | ** |

### 57B V8, 259 (wb 116.5)

| | Wght | Price | Prod |
|---|---|---|---|
| Commander Custom sdn 4d | 3,105 | 2,173 | — |
| Commander Custom club sdn | 3,075 | 2,124 | — |
| Commander DeLuxe sdn 4d | 3,140 | 2,295 | — |
| Commander DeLuxe club sdn | 3,100 | 2,246 | — |
| Provincial wgn 4d | 3,355 | 2,561 | — |
| Parkview wgn 2d | 3,310 | 2,505 | — |

### 57H V8, 289 (wb 116.5; Classic/Hawks-120.5)

| | Wght | Price | Prod |
|---|---|---|---|
| President Classic sdn 4d | 3,270 | 2,539 | — |
| President sdn 4d | 3,205 | 2,407 | — |
| President club sdn | 3,170 | 2,358 | — |
| Broadmoor wgn 4d | 3,415 | 2,666 | — |
| Silver Hawk cpe | 3,185 | 2,263 | ** |
| Golden Hawk htp cpe | 3,185 | 3,182 | 4,356 |

*Total 1957 production: 74,738.
**Silver Hawk only: 15,318.

| 1957 Engines | bore×stroke | bhp | availability |
|---|---|---|---|
| L6, 185.6 | 3.00×4.38 | 101 | S-Scotsman, Champ, Silver Hawk, Pelham |
| V8, 259.2 | 3.56×3.25 | 180 | S-Commander & 57B Wagons |
| V8, 259.2 | 3.56×3.25 | 195 | O-Commander & 57B Wagons |
| V8, 289.0 | 3.56×3.63 | 210 | S-President, Silver Hawk, 57H Wagons |
| V8, 289.0 | 3.56×3.63 | 225 | S-President Classic; O-Silver Hawk, 57H Wgn |
| V8, 289.0 | 3.56×3.63 | 275 | S-Golden Hawk |

## 1958

### 58G Six (wb 116.5; Hawk-120.5)

| | Wght | Price | Prod |
|---|---|---|---|
| Silver Hawk cpe | 2,810 | 2,291 | * |

| | Wght | Price | Prod |
|---|---|---|---|
| Scotsman sdn 4d | 2,740 | 1,874 | |
| Scotsman sdn 2d | 2,695 | 1,795 | 20,870 |
| Scotsman wgn 2d | 2,870 | 2,055 | |
| Champion sdn 4d | 2,835 | 2,253 | 10,325 |
| Champion sdn 2d | 2,795 | 2,189 | |

**58B V8, 259 (wb 116.5)—12,249 built**

| | Wght | Price | Prod |
|---|---|---|---|
| Commander sdn 4d | 3,185 | 2,378 | — |
| Commander Starlight htp cpe | 3,270 | 2,493 | — |
| Provincial wgn 4d | 3,420 | 2,664 | — |

**58H V8, 289 (wb 120.5; Starlight htp-116.5)**

| | Wght | Price | Prod |
|---|---|---|---|
| President sdn 4d | 3,365 | 2,639 | 10,442 |
| President Starlight htp cpe | 3,355 | 2,695 | |
| Silver Hawk cpe | 3,210 | 2,352 | * |
| Golden Hawk htp cpe | 3,470 | 3,282 | 878 |

*Total Silver Hawk: 7,350

| 1958 Engines | bore×stroke | bhp | availability |
|---|---|---|---|
| L6, 185.6 | 3.00×4.38 | 101 | S-Scotsman, Champion, Silver Hawk |
| V8, 259.2 | 3.56×3.25 | 180 | S-Commander, Provincial |
| V8, 289.0 | 3.56×3.63 | 210 | O-Silver Hawk |
| V8, 289.0 | 3.56×3.63 | 225 | S-President; O-Silver Hawk |
| V8, 289.0 | 3.56×3.63 | 275 | S-Golden Hawk |

## 1959

**59S Lark VI (wb 108.5; Regal wgn-113.0)—98,744 built**

| | Wght | Price | Prod |
|---|---|---|---|
| DeLuxe sdn 4d | 2,605 | 1,995 | — |
| DeLuxe sdn 2d | 2,577 | 1,925 | — |
| DeLuxe wgn 2d | 2,805 | 2,295 | — |
| Regal sdn 4d | 2,600 | 2,175 | — |
| Regal htp cpe | 2,710 | 2,275 | — |
| Regal wgn 2d | 2,815 | 2,455 | — |

**59V Lark VIII (wb 108.5; wgn-113.0)—32,334 built**

| | Wght | Price | Prod |
|---|---|---|---|
| Regal sdn 4d | 2,924 | 2,310 | — |
| Regal htp cpe | 3,034 | 2,411 | — |
| Regal wgn 2d | 3,148 | 2,590 | — |

**59S/59V Silver Hawk (wb 120.5)**

| | Wght | Price | Prod |
|---|---|---|---|
| cpe, L6 | 2,795 | 2,360 | 2,417 |
| cpe, V8 | 3,140 | 2,495 | 5,371 |

| 1959 Engines | bore×stroke | bhp | availability |
|---|---|---|---|
| L6, 169.6 | 3.00×4.00 | 90 | S-Lark VI, Silver Hawk 6 |
| V8, 259.2 | 3.56×3.25 | 180 | S-Lark VIII, Silver Hawk 8 |
| V8, 259.2 | 3.56×3.25 | 195 | O-Lark VIII, Silver Hawk 8 |

## 1960

**60S Lark VI (wb 108.5; wgns-113.0)—70,153 built**

| | Wght | Price | Prod |
|---|---|---|---|
| DeLuxe sdn 4d | 2,592 | 2,046 | — |
| DeLuxe sdn 2d | 2,588 | 1,976 | — |
| DeLuxe wgn 4d | 2,792 | 2,441 | — |
| DeLuxe wgn 2d | 2,763 | 2,366 | — |
| Regal sdn 4d | 2,619 | 2,196 | — |
| Regal htp cpe | 2,697 | 2,296 | — |
| Regal conv cpe | 2,961 | 2,621 | — |
| Regal wgn 4d | 2,836 | 2,591 | — |

**60V Lark VIII (wb 108.5; wgns-113.0)—57,562 built**

| | Wght | Price | Prod |
|---|---|---|---|
| DeLuxe sdn 4d | 2,941 | 2,181 | — |
| DeLuxe sdn 2d | 2,921 | 2,111 | — |
| DeLuxe wgn 4d | 3,161 | 2,576 | — |
| DeLuxe wgn 2d | 3,138 | 2,501 | — |
| Regal sdn 4d | 2,966 | 2,331 | — |
| Regal htp cpe | 3,033 | 2,431 | — |
| Regal conv cpe | 3,315 | 2,756 | — |
| Regal wgn 4d | 3,183 | 2,726 | — |

**60V Hawk (wb 120.5)**

| | Wght | Price | Prod |
|---|---|---|---|
| cpe | 3,207 | 2,650 | 3,939 |

| 1960 Engines | bore×stroke | bhp | availability |
|---|---|---|---|
| L6, 169.6 | 3.00×4.00 | 90 | S-Lark VI |
| V8, 259.2 | 3.56×3.25 | 180 | S-Lark VIII |
| V8, 259.2 | 3.56×3.25 | 195 | O-Lark VIII |
| V8, 289.0 | 3.56×3.63 | 210 | S-Hawk |
| V8, 289.0 | 3.56×3.63 | 225 | O-Hawk |

## 1961

**61S Lark VI (wb 108.5; wgns-113.0)—41,035 built**

| | Wght | Price | Prod |
|---|---|---|---|
| DeLuxe sdn 4d | 2,065 | 1,935 | — |
| DeLuxe sdn 2d | 2,661 | 2,005 | — |
| DeLuxe wgn 4d | 2,865 | 2,370 | — |
| DeLuxe wgn 2d | 2,836 | 2,290 | — |
| Regal sdn 4d | 2,692 | 2,155 | — |
| Regal htp cpe | 2,770 | 2,243 | — |
| Regal conv cpe | 3,034 | 2,554 | — |
| Regal wgn 4d | 2,836 | 2,520 | — |

**61V Lark VIII (wb 108.5; Crsr/wgns-113.0)—25,934 built**

| | Wght | Price | Prod |
|---|---|---|---|
| DeLuxe sdn 4d | 2,941 | 2,140 | — |
| DeLuxe sdn 2d | 2,921 | 2,070 | — |
| DeLuxe wgn 4d | 3,183 | 2,505 | — |
| DeLuxe wgn 2d | 3,112 | 2,425 | — |
| Regal sdn 4d | 2,956 | 2,290 | — |
| Regal htp cpe | 3,074 | 2,378 | — |
| Regal conv cpe | 3,315 | 2,689 | — |
| Regal wgn 4d | 3,183 | 2,655 | — |
| Cruiser sdn 4d | 3,001 | 2,458 | — |

**61V Hawk (wb 120.5)**

| | Wght | Price | Prod |
|---|---|---|---|
| cpe | 3,205 | 2,650 | 3,340 |

| 1961 Engines | bore×stroke | bhp | availability |
|---|---|---|---|
| L6, 169.6 | 3.00×4.00 | 112 | S-Lark VI |
| V8, 259.2 | 3.56×3.25 | 180 | S-Lark VIII |
| V8, 259.2 | 3.56×3.25 | 195 | O-Lark VIII |
| V8, 289.0 | 3.56×3.63 | 210 | S-Hawk |
| V8, 289.0 | 3.56×3.63 | 225 | O-Hawk |

## 1962

**62S Lark Six (wb 113.0; 2d-109.0)—54,397 built**

| | Wght | Price | Prod |
|---|---|---|---|
| DeLuxe sdn 4d | 2,760 | 2,040 | — |
| DeLuxe sdn 2d | 2,655 | 1,935 | — |
| DeLuxe wgn 4d | 2,845 | 2,405 | — |
| Regal sdn 4d | 2,770 | 2,190 | — |
| Regal wgn 4d | 2,875 | 2,555 | — |
| Regal htp cpe | 2,765 | 2,218 | — |
| Regal conv cpe | 3,075 | 2,589 | — |
| Daytona htp cpe | 2,765 | 2,308 | — |
| Daytona conv cpe | 3,075 | 2,679 | — |

**62V Lark Eight (wb 113.0; 2d-109.0)—38,607 built**

| | Wght | Price | Prod |
|---|---|---|---|
| DeLuxe sdn 4d | 3,015 | 2,175 | — |
| DeLuxe sdn 2d | 2,925 | 2,070 | — |
| DeLuxe wgn 4d | 3,115 | 2,540 | — |
| Regal sdn 4d | 3,025 | 2,325 | — |
| Regal wgn 4d | 3,145 | 2,690 | — |
| Regal htp cpe | 3,015 | 2,353 | — |
| Regal conv cpe | 3,305 | 2,724 | — |
| Daytona htp cpe | 3,015 | 2,443 | — |
| Daytona conv cpe | 3,305 | 2,814 | — |
| Cruiser sdn 4d | 3,030 | 2,493 | — |

**62V Gran Turismo Hawk (wb 120.5)**

| | Wght | Price | Prod |
|---|---|---|---|
| htp cpe | 3,230 | 3,095 | 8,388 |

# Studebaker

| 1962 Engines | bore×stroke | bhp | availability |
|---|---|---|---|
| L6, 169.6 | 3.00×4.00 | 112 | S-Lark Six |
| V8, 259.2 | 3.56×3.25 | 180 | S-Lark Eight |
| V8, 259.2 | 3.56×3.25 | 195 | O-Lark Eight |
| V8, 289.0 | 3.56×3.63 | 210 | S-GT Hawk; O-Lark Cruiser |
| V8, 289.0 | 3.56×3.63 | 225 | O-GT Hawk, Lark Cruiser |

## 1963

### 63S Lark Six (wb 113.0; 2d-109.0)—74,201 built (includes 63V)

| | Wght | Price | Prod |
|---|---|---|---|
| Standard sdn 4d | 2,775 | 2,040 | — |
| Standard sdn 2d | 2,650 | 1,935 | — |
| Standard wgn 4d | 3,285 | 2,430 | — |
| Regal sdn 4d | 2,790 | 2,160 | — |
| Regal sdn 2d | 2,665 | 2,055 | — |
| Regal wgn 4d | 3,200 | 2,550 | — |
| Custom sdn 4d | 2,800 | 2,285 | — |
| Custom sdn 2d | 2,680 | 2,180 | — |
| Daytona wgn 4d | 3,245 | 2,700 | — |
| Daytona htp cpe | 2,795 | 2,308 | — |
| Daytona conv cpe | 3,045 | 2,679 | — |

### 63V Lark Eight (wb 113.0; 2d-109.0)

| | Wght | Price | Prod |
|---|---|---|---|
| Standard sdn 4d | 2,985 | 2,175 | — |
| Standard sdn 2d | 2,910 | 2,070 | — |
| Standard wgn 4d | 3,435 | 2,565 | — |
| Regal sdn 4d | 3,000 | 2,295 | — |
| Regal sdn 2d | 2,925 | 2,190 | — |
| Regal wgn 4d | 3,450 | 2,685 | — |
| Custom sdn 4d | 3,010 | 2,420 | — |
| Custom sdn 2d | 2,940 | 2,315 | — |
| Daytona wgn 4d | 3,490 | 2,835 | — |
| Daytona htp cpe | 3,035 | 2,443 | — |
| Daytona conv cpe | 3,265 | 2,814 | — |
| Cruiser sdn 4d | 3,065 | 2,595 | — |

### 63V Gran Turismo Hawk (wb 120.5)

| | Wght | Price | Prod |
|---|---|---|---|
| htp cpe | 3,280 | 3,095 | 4,634 |

### 63R Avanti (wb 109.0)

| | Wght | Price | Prod |
|---|---|---|---|
| spt cpe | 3,140 | 4,445 | 3,834 |

| 1963 Engines | bore×stroke | bhp | availability |
|---|---|---|---|
| L6, 169.6 | 3.00×4.00 | 112 | S-Lark 6 |
| V8, 259.2 | 3.56×3.25 | 180 | S-Lark V8 |
| V8, 259.2 | 3.56×3.25 | 195 | O-Lark V8 |
| V8, 289.0 | 3.56×3.63 | 210 | S-Hawk, Cruiser; O-Lark V8 |
| V8, 289.0 | 3.56×3.63 | 225 | O-Hawk, Lark V8, Cruiser |
| V8, 289.0 | 3.56×3.63 | 240 | S-Avanti; O-Hawk, Lark V8 (R1) |
| V8, 289.0 | 3.56×3.63 | 290 | O-Avanti, Hawk, Lark V8 (R2) |

## 1964

### 64S Six (wb 113.0; 2d-109.0)—44,184 built (includes 64V)

| | Wght | Price | Prod |
|---|---|---|---|
| Challenger sdn 4d | 2,780 | 2,048 | — |
| Challenger sdn 2d | 2,660 | 1,943 | — |
| Challenger wgn 4d | 3,230 | 2,438 | — |
| Commander sdn 4d | 2,815 | 2,168 | — |
| Commander sdn 2d | 2,695 | 2,063 | — |
| Commander Special sdn 2d | 2,725 | 2,193 | — |
| Commander wgn 4d | 3,265 | 2,558 | — |
| Daytona sdn 4d | 2,790 | 2,318 | — |
| Daytona conv cpe | 3,040 | 2,670 | — |
| Daytona wgn 4d | 3,240 | 2,708 | — |

### 64V Eight (wb 113.0; 2d-109.0)

| | Wght | Price | Prod |
|---|---|---|---|
| Challenger sdn 4d | 3,010 | 2,183 | — |
| Challenger sdn 2d | 2,910 | 2,078 | — |
| Challenger wgn 4d | 3,480 | 2,573 | — |
| Commander sdn 4d | 3,045 | 2,303 | — |
| Commander sdn 2d | 2,945 | 2,198 | — |
| Commander Special sdn 2d | 2,975 | 2,328 | — |
| Daytona sdn 4d | 3,055 | 2,453 | — |
| Daytona htp cpe | 3,060 | 2,451 | — |
| Daytona conv cpe | 3,320 | 2,805 | — |
| Daytona wgn 4d | 3,555 | 2,843 | — |
| Cruiser sdn 4d | 3,120 | 2,603 | — |

### 64V Gran Turismo Hawk (wb 120.5)

| | Wght | Price | Prod |
|---|---|---|---|
| htp cpe | 3,120 | 2,966 | 1,767 |

### 64R Avanti (wb 109.0)

| | Wght | Price | Prod |
|---|---|---|---|
| spt cpe | 3,195 | 4,445 | 809 |

| 1964 Engines | bore×stroke | bhp | availability |
|---|---|---|---|
| L6, 169.6 | 3.00×4.00 | 112 | S-Challenger/Commander/Daytona 6 |
| V8, 259.2 | 3.56×3.25 | 180 | S-Challenger/Commander/Daytona 8 |
| V8, 259.2 | 3.56×3.25 | 195 | O-Challenger/Commander/Daytona 8 |
| V8, 289.0 | 3.56×3.63 | 210 | S-Hawk, Cruiser; O-other V8 |
| V8, 289.0 | 3.56×3.63 | 225 | O-all V8 exc Avanti |
| V8, 289.0 | 3.56×3.63 | 240 | S-Avanti; O-other V8 (R1) |
| V8, 289.0 | 3.56×3.63 | 290 | O-all (R2) |
| V8, 304.5 | 3.65×3.63 | 335 | O-all (R3) |
| V8, 304.5 | 3.65×3.63 | 280 | O-Avanti (R4) |

## 1965—19,435 built

### C-1 Six (wb 113.0; 2d-190.0)

| | Wght | Price | Prod |
|---|---|---|---|
| Commander sdn 4d | 2,815 | 2,230 | — |
| Commander sdn 2d | 2,695 | 2,125 | — |
| Commander wgn 4d | 3,265 | 2,620 | — |
| Cruiser sdn 4d | 2,820 | 2,470 | — |

### C-5 Eight (wb 113.0; 2d-109.0)

| | Wght | Price | Prod |
|---|---|---|---|
| Commander sdn 4d | 2,995 | 2,370 | — |
| Commander sdn 2d | 2,895 | 2,265 | — |
| Commander wgn 4d | 3,465 | 2,760 | — |
| Daytona Sport sdn 2d | 2,970 | 2,565 | — |
| Daytona wgn 4d | 3,505 | 2,890 | — |
| Cruiser sdn 4d | 3,070 | 2,610 | — |

| 1965 Engines | bore×stroke | bhp | availability |
|---|---|---|---|
| L6, 194.0 | 3.56×3.25 | 120 | S-Commander 6, Cruiser 6 |
| V8, 283.0 | 3.88×3.00 | 195 | S-Commander/Cruiser V8, Daytona |

## 1966—8,947 built

### Six (wb 113.0; 2d-109.0)

| | Wght | Price | Prod |
|---|---|---|---|
| Commander sdn 4d | 2,815 | 2,165 | — |
| Commander sdn 2d | 2,695 | 2,060 | — |
| Wagonaire wgn 2d | 3,246 | 2,555 | — |
| Daytona sdn 2d | 2,755 | 2,405 | — |
| Cruiser sdn 4d | 2,815 | 2,405 | — |

### Eight (wb 113.0; 2d-109.0)

| | Wght | Price | Prod |
|---|---|---|---|
| Commander sdn 4d | 2,991 | 2,305 | — |
| Commander sdn 2d | 2,891 | 2,200 | — |
| Wagonaire wgn 2d | 3,501 | 2,695 | — |
| Daytona sdn 2d | 3,006 | 2,500 | — |
| Cruiser sdn 4d | 3,066 | 2,545 | — |

| 1966 Engines | bore×stroke | bhp | availability |
|---|---|---|---|
| L6, 194.0 | 3.56×3.25 | 120 | S-Commander/Cruiser/Daytona 6 |
| V8, 283.0 | 3.88×3.00 | 195 | S-Commander/Cruiser/Daytona V8 |

Postwar Studebaker production includes cars manufactured in South Bend and Hamilton, Ontario for U.S., Canadian, and export sale.

# Willys

**Willys-Overland Motors (Kaiser-Willys Sales Division 1954-55), Toledo, Ohio**

In the years before World War I, Willys-Overland ranked second only to Ford in annual production. The company founded by John North Willys occupied sixth place in the early '20s, rose to third in 1928 with help from its low-priced Whippet model, then lost ground in the Depression. From 1933 through 1937, Willys-Overland was in receivership and built only one model, the four-cylinder "77." Slowly, sales recovered. Joseph W. Frazer took over as president and general manager in January 1939, bringing along several production and marketing men from Chrysler, where he'd worked since 1924. The first evidence of Frazer's presence was seen on 1940 emblems, where he eliminated the name Overland in favor of just Willys.

The new line, designated Series 440 (four cylinders, 1940) was powered by the firm's 61-bhp L-head four, which displaced 134.2 cubic inches and delivered 25 miles per gallon. It remained the standard Willys powerplant through the decade, though horsepower increased (to 63) in 1941. In 1949 it was converted by engineer Barney Roos to F-head, overhead-valve configuration. The chassis was a conventional ladder design with an X-braced center and a 102-inch wheelbase. There were five body styles in two series. Calendar and model year production, which had dipped to 16,000 in

1938, was up to 21,418 for 1940.

For the '41 Series 441, Frazer and his team made further improvements. The new line was named Americar, providing patriotic appeal, and got more horsepower and a longer wheelbase. It came in three series: the Speedway coupe and sedan; the DeLuxe coupe, sedan, and wagon; and the top-line Plainsman coupe and sedan. Styling was Ford-like with faired-in headlamps on the front fenders, and a sharply pointed nose over a small vertical-bar grille.

Production for 1942 was cut short earlier than for most automakers since Willys had begun building Jeeps for the Army. The '42 Americars were the same as the '41s—three models and seven body styles. Prices rose slightly, ranging from $695 to $978. The original Jeep was conceived mainly by American Bantam, but Willys-Overland produced a similar design in vast quantities through 1945.

During the war, Frazer left to take over Graham-Paige, while Chairman Ward Canaday planned postwar activities around Jeep-like vehicles.

A truck-type all-steel station wagon using the L-head four and the 104-inch wheelbase was announced for 1946-47. It was significant in that it was the first true all-steel wagon, though for purposes of the industry and

**1941 Series 440 DeLuxe station wagon**

**1948 Jeepster phaeton convertible**

**1943 Army Jeep**

**1950 Jeepster phaeton convertible**

this book it was considered more of a truck than a car. It was Willys' main civilian product in those two years, priced at $1495 in 1946 and $1625 in '47.

In 1948, Willys-Overland continued the wagon (now listed at $1645) and added two new vehicles: the four-cylinder Jeepster "phaeton" priced at $1765, and the six-cylinder Station Sedan, which went for $1890. The Jeepster was a pleasant little touring car designed during the war by Brooks Stevens, who borrowed its lines from the Jeep. It had a big open compartment behind

1952 Aero-Eagle hardtop coupe

1953 Aero-Ace two-door sedan

1954 Aero-Ace four-door sedan

the cowl and a mechanically operated soft top. The six-cylinder Station Sedan was a luxury version of the four-cylinder wagon, with a larger body and wider seats. Together with the Jeepster, it helped keep Willys-Overland alive.

For 1949, Willys offered a new 104.5 inch-wheelbase wagon priced at $1895, plus the regular wagon and two Jeepsters in its four-cylinder lineup. The second series Jeepster appeared in January, powered by the firm's first F-head engine. The company continued to sell the six-cylinder Station Sedan and wagon, and debuted a six-cylinder Jeepster at $1530. Conversion to overhead-valve engines was completed for all models by 1950. Over 10,000 Jeepsters were sold for 1948. In 1950, however, only 4066 fours and 1778 sixes were sold. Some leftovers were registered as 1951s.

The 1952 Aero-Willys was a unit-body car styled by Phil Wright and engineered by Clyde Paton. Returning Willys to the passenger-car field, it was a clean design, providing good comfort and handling. Four separate models were offered. The Aero-Lark used the older 161-cid, 75-bhp L-head six; the Wing, Ace, and Eagle hardtop used the overhead-valve version. The 161 was small, but a good performer, providing economy on the order of 25 mpg. The biggest problem for these cars was their list prices. The Eagle hardtop, for example, carried a $2155 price tag; a Chevrolet Bel Air hardtop cost $150 less. Willys-Overland dealers were hard pressed—not only to explain how builders of Jeeps could produce a smooth, comfortable family car, but also why they had to charge so much for it. Production was good, but not great. For the '52 model year, about 31,000 Aeros were built. About 23 percent were base-line Larks, while seven percent were Eagle hardtops.

Willys expanded the Aero line for 1953 and made only minor appearance changes, including red-painted wheel cover emblems and a gold-plated "W" in the grille to symbolize the firm's 50th anniversary. About 500 Larks were fitted with an F-head four-cylinder engine. The Aero-Wing was replaced by the Aero-Falcon, and a new four-door sedan was developed for the Lark, Falcon, and Ace. Again, the hardtop Eagle was priced on the high side. Willys-Overland had another modestly good year, selling about 42,000 units.

In 1954, Willys-Overland was purchased by Henry Kaiser, who combined it with his ailing Kaiser-Frazer Corporation to form the Toledo-based Kaiser-Willys Sales Corporation. The K-F plant at Willow Run was sold to General Motors, and Kaiser production was shifted to the old Willys plant.

At first, the new '54 Aero appeared to be the same as the '53 with larger taillights and revised interiors. But in March 1954, the company made the 226-cid L-head six available as an option for the Ace and Eagle. To further complicate matters, there were Ace and Eagle Customs—the designation merely indicating the presence of a "continental" spare tire. With the Kaiser 226, the Aero was relatively fast. Though its 85-mph top speed was little higher than the Willys-engine models, it was

1955 Bermuda hardtop coupe

Proposal for 1955 hardtop wagon (not produced)

geared for good acceleration: A typical 0–60 mph time was 14 seconds. As an experiment, a few cars were fitted with the 140-bhp supercharged Manhattan engine, which engineers say gave pickup comparable to that of contemporary V8s.

The 1954 Aero also handled much better than before. A new front end was adopted using threaded trunions adjustable for wear. The kingpins and coil springs were longer, shocks and A-arms were stronger, and the steering idler arm was lengthened. A cross-member connected left and right front suspension assemblies to eliminate lateral torque and reduce tow-in variations. The Aero-Willys was thus one of the best combinations of ride and handling offered by a domestic manufacturer in the '50s. The Eagle hardtop in particular was an attractive car, though price was still a problem: the '54 version sold for close to $2600 with Hydra-Matic. Sales dropped to around 12,000 units.

By early 1955, Kaiser-Willys had decided to abandon passenger cars, but not before selling some 6500 of the '55 models. No longer called Aeros, the line was divided into the Custom two- or four-door sedans and the Bermuda hardtop (plus a handful of Ace sedans). Engine options included 161- and 226-cid sixes. Prices were cut drastically in an effort to spark sales, and the Bermuda was advertised as the nation's lowest-priced hardtop. But only 2215 were built, most powered by the 226 engine.

Styling for '55 was much busier than before, and no designer takes credit for it. A clumsy attempt at two-toning involved complicated side trim; the grille was no longer a simple bar, but a garish expanse of concave, vertical bars. In contrast to this glitter, a neat hardtop-wagon had been planned for '55 and a very sleek face-lift was scheduled for 1956. Neither materialized.

The Aero did get a new lease on life in South America. Its dies were eventually shipped to the former Kaiser subsidiary, Willys do Brasil, where a cleaned-up '55 model without the busy side molding was built with F-head Willys power through 1962. In all, the Aero actually lasted over 10 years—which attests to its basically good design.

# Willys Specifications

## 1940

### 440 (wb 102.0)—26,698 built

| | Wght | Price | Prod |
|---|---|---|---|
| Speedway cpe | 2,146 | 529 | — |
| Speedway sdn 4d | 2,238 | 596 | — |
| DeLuxe cpe | 2,190 | 641 | — |
| DeLuxe sdn 4d | 2,255 | 672 | — |
| DeLuxe wgn 4d | 2,124 | 830 | — |

| 1940 Engine | bore×stroke | bhp | availability |
|---|---|---|---|
| L4, 134.2 | 3.13×4.38 | 61 | S-all |

## 1941

### 441 American (wb 104.0)*

| | Wght | Price | Prod |
|---|---|---|---|
| Speedway cpe | 2,116 | 634 | — |
| Speedway sdn 4d | 2,230 | 674 | — |
| DeLuxe cpe | 2,135 | 685 | — |
| Deluxe sdn 4d | 2,265 | 720 | — |
| DeLuxe wgn 4d | 2,483 | 916 | — |
| Plainsman cpe | 2,175 | 740 | — |
| Plainsman sdn 4d | 2,305 | 771 | — |

| 1941 Engine | bore×stroke | bhp | availability |
|---|---|---|---|
| L4, 134.2 | 3.13×4.38 | 63 | S-all |

## 1942

### 442 American (wb 104.0)*

| | Wght | Price | Prod |
|---|---|---|---|
| Speedway cpe | 2,142 | 695 | — |
| Speedway sdn 4d | 2,261 | 745 | — |
| DeLuxe cpe | 2,184 | 769 | — |
| DeLuxe sdn 4d | 2,295 | 795 | — |
| DeLuxe wgn 4d | 2,512 | 978 | — |
| Plainsman cpe | 2,242 | 819 | — |
| Plainsman sdn 4d | 2,353 | 845 | — |

| 1942 Engine | bore×stroke | bhp | availability |
|---|---|---|---|
| L4, 134.2 | 3.13×4.38 | 63 | S-all |

*Total 1941-1942 Americar production: 28,935.

## 1948

| 463 Four (wb 104.0) | | Wght | Price | Prod |
|---|---|---|---|---|
| Jeepster phtn conv | | 2,468 | 1,765 | 10,326 |

| 1948 Engine | bore×stroke | bhp | availability |
|---|---|---|---|
| L4, 134.3 | 3.13×4.38 | 63 | S-all |

## 1949

| 463 Four (wb 104.0)—2,307 built (includes VJ-3 Four) | Wght | Price | Prod |
|---|---|---|---|
| Jeepster phtn conv | 2,468 | 1,495 | — |

| VJ-3 Four (wb 104.5) | Wght | Price | Prod |
|---|---|---|---|
| Jeepster phtn conv | 2,468 | 1,495 | — |

| VJ-3 Six (wb 104.0) | Wght | Price | Prod |
|---|---|---|---|
| Jeepster phtn conv | 2,392 | 1,530 | 653 |

| 1949 Engines | bore×stroke | bhp | availability |
|---|---|---|---|
| L4, 134.3 | 3.13×4.38 | 63 | S-463 Four |
| L4, 134.3 | 3.13×4.38 | 72 | S-VJ3 Four (F-head) |
| L6, 148.5 | 3.00×3.50 | 72 | S-Six |

## 1950

| 473 Four (wb 104.0)—4,066 built (includes VJ-3) | Wght | Price | Prod |
|---|---|---|---|
| Jeepster phtn conv | 2,459 | 1,390 | — |

| VJ-3 Four (wb 104.0) | Wght | Price | Prod |
|---|---|---|---|
| Jeepster phtn conv | 2,468 | 1,495 | — |

| 673VJ Six (wb 104.0) | Wght | Price | Prod |
|---|---|---|---|
| Jeepster phtn conv | 2,485 | 1,490 | 1,778 |

| 1950 Engines | bore×stroke | bhp | availability |
|---|---|---|---|
| L4, 134.2 | 3.13×4.38 | 63 | S-Four, 1st series, L-head |
| L4, 134.2 | 3.13×4.38 | 72 | S-Four, 2nd series, F-head |
| L6, 148.5 | 3.00×3.50 | 72 | S-Six, 1st series, L-head |
| L6, 161.0 | 3.13×4.38 | 75 | S-Six, 2nd series, F-head |

## 1951

| 473-VJ Four (wb 104.0)* | Wght | Price | Prod |
|---|---|---|---|
| Jeepster phtn conv | 2,459 | 1,426 | — |

| 673-VJ Six (wb 104.0)* | Wght | Price | Prod |
|---|---|---|---|
| Jeepster phtn conv | 2,485 | 1,529 | — |

*Combined with 1950 totals; includes 1950 leftovers sold as '51s.

| 1951 Engines | bore×stroke | bhp | availability |
|---|---|---|---|
| L4, 134.2 | 3.13×4.38 | 72 | S-Four |
| L6, 161.0 | 3.13×4.38 | 75 | S-Six |

## 1952

| 652-K Aero-Lark (wb 108.0) | | Wght | Price | Prod |
|---|---|---|---|---|
| KA2-675 | sdn 2d | 2,487 | 1,731 | 7,474 |

| 652-L Aero-Wing (wb 108.0) | | Wght | Price | Prod |
|---|---|---|---|---|
| LA1-685 | sdn 2d | 2,570 | 1,989 | 12,819 |

| 652-M Aero- (wb 108.0) | | Wght | Price | Prod |
|---|---|---|---|---|
| MA1-685 | Ace sdn 2d | 2,584 | 2,074 | 8,706 |
| MC1-685 | Eagle htp cpe | 2,575 | 2,155 | 2,364 |

| 1952 Engines | bore×stroke | bhp | availability |
|---|---|---|---|
| L6, 161.0 | 3.13×4.38 | 75 | S-Lark |
| L6, 161.0 | 3.13×4.38 | 90 | S-Wing, Ace, Eagle |

## 1953

| 653-K Aero-Lark (wb 108.0) | | Wght | Price | Prod |
|---|---|---|---|---|
| KA1-675 | sdn 2d | 2,487 | 1,646 | 8,205 |
| KB1-675 | sdn 4d | 2,509 | 1,732 | 7,692 |

| 653-M Aero- (wb 108.0) | | Wght | Price | Prod |
|---|---|---|---|---|
| MA1-685 | Ace sdn 2d | 2,584 | 1,963 | 4,988 |
| MB1-685 | Ace sdn 4d | 2,735 | 2,038 | 7,475 |
| MC1-685 | Eagle htp cpe | 2,575 | 2,157 | 7,018 |

| 653-P Aero-Falcon (wb 108.0) | | Wght | Price | Prod |
|---|---|---|---|---|
| PA1-675 | sdn 2d | 2,507 | 1,760 | 3,054 |
| PB1-675 | sdn 4d | 2,529 | 1,861 | 3,117 |

| 1953 Engines | bore×stroke | bhp | availability |
|---|---|---|---|
| L4, 134.2 | 3.13×4.38 | 72 | S-Lark 4 |
| L6, 161.0 | 3.13×4.38 | 75 | S-Lark 6, Falcon |
| L6, 161.0 | 3.13×4.38 | 90 | S-Ace, Eagle |

## 1954

| 654-K Aero-Lark (wb 108.0) | | Wght | Price | Prod |
|---|---|---|---|---|
| KA2 | sdn 2d, (226) | 2,740 | — | 59 |
| KB2 | sdn 4d, (226) | 2,730 | — | 282 |
| KA3-685 | sdn 2d | 2,623 | 1,737 | 1,370 |
| KA3-685 | Custom sdn 2d | 2,678 | 1,798 | 1,132 |
| KB3-685 | sdn 4d | 2,661 | 1,823 | 1,482 |
| KB3-685 | Custom sdn 4d | 2,722 | 1,878 | 548 |

| 654-M Aero- (wb 108.0) | | Wght | Price | Prod |
|---|---|---|---|---|
| MA1 | Ace DeLuxe sdn 2d (226) | 2,751 | — | 1,195 |
| MA1 | Ace DeLuxe Custom sdn 2d (226) | 2,806 | — | 7 |
| MB1 | Ace DeLuxe sdn 4d (226) | 2,778 | — | 1,498 |
| MB1 | Ace DeLuxe Custom sdn 4d (226) | 2,833 | — | 9 |
| MA2-685 | Ace sdn 2d | 2,682 | 1,892 | 2 |
| MA2-685 | Ace Custom sdn 2d | 2,737 | 1,947 | 586 |
| MB2-685 | Ace sdn 4d | 2,709 | 1,968 | 1,380 |
| MB2-685 | Ace Custom sdn 4d | 2,764 | 2,023 | 611 |
| MC1 | Eagle htp cpe (226) | 2,847 | — | 660 |
| MC1 | Eagle Custom htp cpe (226) | 2,904 | — | 11 |
| MC2 | Eagle Special htp cpe (226) | — | — | 302 |
| MC3-685 | Eagle DeLuxe htp cpe | — | 2,222 | 84 |
| MC3-685 | Eagle DeLuxe Custom htp cpe | — | 2,411 | 499 |

| 1954 Engines | bore×stroke | bhp | availability |
|---|---|---|---|
| L4, 134.2 | 3.13×4.38 | 72 | S-Lark 4 |
| L6, 161.0 | 3.13×4.38 | 90 | S-Lark 6, Ace, Eagle |
| L6, 226.2 | 3.31×4.38 | 115 | O-Lark 6, Ace, Eagle |

## 1955

| 522/6 Ace (wb 108.0) | | Wght | Price | Prod |
|---|---|---|---|---|
| 52367 | sdn 4d (226) | — | — | 659 |

| 523/4 Custom (wb 108.0) | | Wght | Price | Prod |
|---|---|---|---|---|
| 52367 | sdn 4d (226) | 2,778 | 1,795 | 2,822 |
| 52462 | sdn 2d (161) | — | — | 2 |
| 52467 | sdn 2d (226) | 2,751 | 1,725 | 288 |

| 525 Bermuda (wb 108.0) | | Wght | Price | Prod |
|---|---|---|---|---|
| 52527 | htp cpe (161) | — | — | 59 |
| 52567 | htp cpe (226) | 2,831 | 1,997 | 2,156 |

| 1955 Engines | bore×stroke | bhp | availability |
|---|---|---|---|
| L6, 161.0 | 3.13×4.38 | 90 | S-Custom, Bermuda |
| L6, 226.2 | 3.31×4.38 | 115 | S-Ace; O-Custom, Bermuda |

Willys production does not include steel-bodied station wagons manufactured from 1946 through 1961, or Wagoneers (wagons) manufactured from 1960 onward. Aero production does not include export or taxi models.

# Model Year Production

1940-1970
(*calculated or estimated)
(1,000 or more units)

## 1940

| | | |
|---|---|---|
| 1. | Chevrolet | 764,616 |
| 2. | Ford | 541,896 |
| 3. | Plymouth | 423,155 |
| 4. | Buick | 278,784 |
| 5. | Pontiac | 217,001 |
| 6. | Dodge | 195,505 |
| 7. | Oldsmobile | 185,154 |
| 8. | Studebaker | 107,185 |
| 9. | Packard | 98,020 |
| 10. | Chrysler | 92,419 |
| 11. | Hudson | 87,915 |
| 12. | Mercury | 81,128* |
| 13. | DeSoto | 65,467 |
| 14. | Nash | 62,131 |
| 15. | LaSalle | 24,130 |
| 16. | Lincoln | 21,765 |
| 17. | Willys | 21,418* |
| 18. | Cadillac | 13,043 |
| 19. | Graham | 2,000* |

## 1941

| | | |
|---|---|---|
| 1. | Chevrolet | 1,008,976 |
| 2. | Ford | 691,455 |
| 3. | Plymouth | 545,811 |
| 4. | Buick | 374,196 |
| 5. | Pontiac | 330,061 |
| 6. | Oldsmobile | 265,864 |
| 7. | Dodge | 237,002 |
| 8. | Chrysler | 161,704 |
| 9. | Studebaker | 133,900 |
| 10. | DeSoto | 97,497 |
| 11. | Hudson | 91,769 |
| 12. | Nash | 84,007 |
| 13. | Mercury | 82,391* |
| 14. | Packard | 72,855 |
| 15. | Cadillac | 66,130 |
| 16. | Willys | 22,102* |
| 17. | Lincoln | 18,244 |
| 18. | Crosley | 2,289 |

## 1942

| | | |
|---|---|---|
| 1. | Chevrolet | 254,885 |
| 2. | Ford | 160,432 |
| 3. | Plymouth | 152,427 |
| 4. | Buick | 92,573 |
| 5. | Pontiac | 83,555 |
| 6. | Dodge | 68,522 |
| 7. | Oldsmobile | 67,783 |
| 8. | Studebaker | 50,678 |
| 9. | Hudson | 40,661 |
| 10. | Chrysler | 36,586 |
| 11. | Packard | 33,776 |
| 12. | Nash | 31,780 |
| 13. | DeSoto | 24,015 |
| 14. | Mercury | 22,816 |
| 15. | Cadillac | 16,511 |
| 16. | Lincoln | 6,547 |
| 17. | Crosley | 1,029 |

## 1946

| | | |
|---|---|---|
| 1. | Ford | 468,022 |
| 2. | Chevrolet | 398,028 |
| 3. | Plymouth | 264,660* |
| 4. | Dodge | 163,490* |
| 5. | Buick | 153,627 |
| 6. | Pontiac | 137,640 |
| 7. | Oldsmobile | 117,623 |
| 8. | Nash | 94,000* |
| 9. | Hudson | 91,030 |
| 10. | Mercury | 86,608 |
| 11. | Chrysler | 83,810* |
| 12. | DeSoto | 66,900* |
| 13. | Packard | 30,793 |
| 14. | Cadillac | 29,214 |
| 15. | Studebaker | 19,275 |
| 16. | Lincoln | 16,645 |
| 17. | Crosley | 4,999 |

## 1947

| | | |
|---|---|---|
| 1. | Chevrolet | 671,546 |
| 2. | Ford | 429,674 |
| 3. | Plymouth | 382,290* |
| 4. | Buick | 272,827 |
| 5. | Dodge | 243,160* |
| 6. | Pontiac | 230,600 |
| 7. | Oldsmobile | 193,895 |
| 8. | Studebaker | 161,496 |
| 9. | Chrysler | 119,260* |
| 10. | Nash | 101,000* |
| 11. | Hudson | 92,083 |
| 12. | DeSoto | 87,000* |
| 13. | Mercury | 85,383 |
| 14. | Kaiser | 70,474 |
| 15. | Frazer | 68,775 |
| 16. | Cadillac | 61,926 |
| 17. | Packard | 51,086 |
| 18. | Lincoln | 21,460 |
| 19. | Crosley | 19,344 |

## 1948

| | | |
|---|---|---|
| 1. | Chevrolet | 696,449 |
| 2. | Ford | 430,198 |
| 3. | Plymouth (+'49 First Series) | 412,540* |
| 4. | Dodge (+'49 First Series) | 243,340* |
| 5. | Pontiac | 235,419 |
| 6. | Buick | 213,599 |
| 7. | Studebaker | 184,993 |
| 8. | Oldsmobile | 172,852 |
| 9. | Chrysler (+'49 First Series) | 130,110* |
| 10. | Hudson | 117,200 |
| 11. | Nash | 110,000* |
| 12. | DeSoto (+'49 First Series) | 98,890* |
| 13. | Packard | 92,251 |
| 14. | Kaiser | 91,851 |

| | | |
|---|---|---|
| 15. | Cadillac | 52,706 |
| 16. | Mercury | 50,268 |
| 17. | Frazer | 48,071 |
| 18. | Crosley | 29,094 |
| 19. | Lincoln | 7,769 |

## 1949

| | | |
|---|---|---|
| 1. | Ford | 1,118,308 |
| 2. | Chevrolet | 1,010,013 |
| 3. | Plymouth (+'49 Second Series) | 520,385 |
| 4. | Buick | 324,276 |
| 5. | Pontiac | 304,819 |
| 6. | Mercury | 301,319 |
| 7. | Oldsmobile | 288,310 |
| 8. | Dodge (+'49 Second Series) | 256,857 |
| 9. | Hudson | 159,100 |
| 10. | Nash | 135,328* |
| 11. | Studebaker | 129,298 |
| 12. | Chrysler (+'49 Second Series) | 124,218 |
| 13. | Packard | 116,248 |
| 14. | DeSoto (+'49 Second Series) | 94,201 |
| 15. | Cadillac | 92,554 |
| 16. | Kaiser | 79,947* |
| 17. | Lincoln | 73,507 |
| 18. | Frazer | 21,223* |
| 19. | Crosley | 7,431 |

## 1950

| | | |
|---|---|---|
| 1. | Chevrolet | 1,498,590 |
| 2. | Ford | 1,208,912 |
| 3. | Buick | 667,826 |
| 4. | Plymouth | 610,954 |
| 5. | Pontiac | 466,429 |
| 6. | Oldsmobile | 407,889 |
| 7. | Dodge | 341,797 |
| 8. | Studebaker (US) | 320,884 |
| 9. | Mercury | 293,658 |
| 10. | Chrysler | 179,299 |
| 11. | Nash | 171,782 |
| 12. | DeSoto | 133,854 |
| 13. | Hudson | 121,408 |
| 14. | Cadillac | 103,857 |
| 15. | Packard | 42,627 |
| 16. | Lincoln | 28,190 |
| 17. | Kaiser | 15,228* |
| 18. | Crosley | 6,792 |
| 19. | Frazer | 3,700* |

## 1951

| | | |
|---|---|---|
| 1. | Chevrolet | 1,229,986 |
| 2. | Ford | 1,013,381 |
| 3. | Plymouth | 611,000* |
| 4. | Buick | 592,511 |
| 5. | Pontiac | 370,159 |
| 6. | Mercury | 310,387 |

| | | |
|---|---|---|
| 7. Dodge | 290,000* | |
| 8. Oldsmobile | 285,612 | |
| 9. Studebaker (US) | 246,195 | |
| 10. Nash | 205,307 | |
| 11. Chrysler | 163,613 | |
| 12. Kaiser | 139,452* | |
| 13. Hudson | 131,915 | |
| 14. Cadillac | 110,340 | |
| 15. DeSoto | 106,000* | |
| 16. Packard | 100,713 | |
| 17. Henry J | 81,942 | |
| 18. Lincoln | 32,574 | |
| 19. Frazer | 10,214 | |
| 20. Crosley | 6,614 | |

**1952**

| | |
|---|---|
| 1. Chevrolet | 818,142 |
| 2. Ford | 671,733 |
| 3. Plymouth | 396,000* |
| 4. Buick | 367,760 |
| 5. Pontiac | 271,373 |
| 6. Oldsmobile | 213,419 |
| 7. Dodge | 206,000* |
| 8. Mercury | 172,087 |
| 9. Studebaker (US) | 167,662 |
| 10. Nash | 154,291 |
| 11. Cadillac | 90,259 |
| 12. Chrysler | 87,470* |
| 13. DeSoto | 88,000* |
| 14. Hudson | 70,000 |
| 15. Packard | 62,921 |
| 16. Kaiser | 32,131 |
| 17. Willys | 31,363 |
| 18. Henry J | 30,585 |
| 19. Lincoln | 27,271 |
| 20. Crosley | 2,075 |
| 21. Allstate | 1,566 |

**1953**

| | |
|---|---|
| 1. Chevrolet | 1,346,475 |
| 2. Ford | 1,247,542 |
| 3. Plymouth | 650,451 |
| 4. Buick | 486,812 |
| 5. Pontiac | 418,619 |
| 6. Oldsmobile | 334,462 |
| 7. Dodge | 320,008 |
| 8. Mercury | 305,863 |
| 9. Chrysler | 170,006 |
| 10. Studebaker (US) | 151,576 |
| 11. DeSoto | 130,404 |
| 12. Nash | 121,793 |
| 13. Cadillac | 109,651 |
| 14. Packard | 90,252 |
| 15. Hudson | 66,143 |
| 16. Willys | 42,057 |
| 17. Lincoln | 40,762 |
| 18. Kaiser | 27,652* |
| 19. Henry J | 16,672 |

**1954**

| | |
|---|---|
| 1. Ford | 1,165,942 |
| 2. Chevrolet | 1,143,561 |
| 3. Plymouth | 463,148 |

| | |
|---|---|
| 4. Buick | 442,903 |
| 5. Oldsmobile | 354,001 |
| 6. Pontiac | 287,744 |
| 7. Mercury | 259,305 |
| 8. Dodge | 154,648 |
| 9. Chrysler | 105,030 |
| 10. Cadillac | 96,680 |
| 11. Nash | 91,121 |
| 12. DeSoto | 76,580 |
| 13. Studebaker (US) | 68,708 |
| 14. Hudson | 50,670 |
| 15. Lincoln | 36,993 |
| 16. Packard | 31,291 |
| 17. Willys | 11,856 |
| 18. Kaiser | 8,539 |
| 19. Henry J | 1,123* |

**1955**

| | |
|---|---|
| 1. Chevrolet | 1,704,667 |
| 2. Ford | 1,451,157 |
| 3. Buick | 737,035 |
| 4. Oldsmobile | 583,179 |
| 5. Pontiac | 553,808 |
| 6. Plymouth | 401,075 |
| 7. Mercury | 329,808 |
| 8. Dodge | 276,936 |
| 9. Chrysler | 152,777 |
| 10. Cadillac | 140,777 |
| 11. Nash | 126,000* |
| 12. Studebaker (US) | 116,333 |
| 13. DeSoto | 114,765 |
| 14. Packard | 55,247 |
| 15. Hudson | 46,000* |
| 16. Lincoln | 27,222 |
| 17. Imperial | 11,432 |
| 18. Willys | 6,565 |
| 19. Kaiser | 1,291 |

**1956**

| | |
|---|---|
| 1. Chevrolet | 1,567,117 |
| 2. Ford | 1,408,478 |
| 3. Buick | 635,158 |
| 4. Plymouth | 552,577 |
| 5. Oldsmobile | 485,458 |
| 6. Pontiac | 405,429 |
| 7. Mercury | 327,943 |
| 8. Dodge | 240,686 |
| 9. Cadillac | 154,577 |
| 10. Chrysler | 128,322 |
| 11. DeSoto | 110,418 |
| 12. Nash | 83,420 |
| 13. Studebaker (US) | 69,593 |
| 14. Lincoln | 50,322 |
| 15. Hudson | 35,671* |
| 16. Clipper | 18,482 |
| 17. Imperial | 10,684 |
| 18. Packard | 10,353 |
| 19. Continental | 1,325 |

**1957**

| | |
|---|---|
| 1. Ford | 1,676,449 |
| 2. Chevrolet | 1,505,910 |
| 3. Plymouth | 762,231 |
| 4. Buick | 404,049 |

| | |
|---|---|
| 5. Oldsmobile | 384,390 |
| 6. Pontiac | 333,473 |
| 7. Dodge | 287,608 |
| 8. Mercury | 286,163 |
| 9. Cadillac | 146,841 |
| 10. Chrysler | 124,675 |
| 11. DeSoto | 117,514 |
| 12. Rambler | 91,469 |
| 13. Studebaker (US) | 63,101 |
| 14. Lincoln | 41,123 |
| 15. Imperial | 37,593 |
| 16. Nash | 20,317 |
| 17. Packard | 4,809 |
| 18. Hudson | 3,876 |

**1958**

| | |
|---|---|
| 1. Chevrolet | 1,142,460 |
| 2. Ford | 987,945 |
| 3. Plymouth | 443,799 |
| 4. Oldsmobile | 314,374 |
| 5. Buick | 240,659 |
| 6. Pontiac | 216,982 |
| 7. Rambler | 186,227* |
| 8. Mercury | 153,271 |
| 9. Dodge | 137,861 |
| 10. Cadillac | 121,778 |
| 11. Chrysler | 63,681 |
| 12. Edsel | 63,110 |
| 13. DeSoto | 49,445 |
| 14. Studebaker (US) | 44,759 |
| 15. Lincoln | 17,134 |
| 16. Imperial | 16,133 |
| 17. Metropolitan | 13,128 |
| 18. Continental | 12,550 |
| 19. Packard | 2,622 |

**1959**

| | |
|---|---|
| 1. Chevrolet | 1,462,140 |
| 2. Ford | 1,450,953 |
| 3. Plymouth | 458,259 |
| 4. Pontiac | 382,940 |
| 5. Oldsmobile | 382,864 |
| 6. Rambler | 363,372* |
| 7. Buick | 284,248 |
| 8. Dodge | 156,385 |
| 9. Mercury | 149,987 |
| 10. Cadillac | 142,272 |
| 11. Studebaker (US) | 126,156 |
| 12. Chrysler | 69,970 |
| 13. DeSoto | 45,724 |
| 14. Edsel | 44,891 |
| 15. Metropolitan | 22,309 |
| 16. Imperial | 17,269 |
| 17. Lincoln | 15,780 |
| 18. Continental | 11,126 |

**1960**

| | |
|---|---|
| 1. Chevrolet | 1,653,168 |
| 2. Ford | 1,439,370 |
| 3. Plymouth | 447,724 |
| 4. Rambler | 422,273* |
| 5. Pontiac | 396,179 |
| 6. Dodge | 367,804 |
| 7. Oldsmobile | 347,142 |

| | | |
|---|---|---|
| 8. Mercury | 271,331 | |
| 9. Buick | 253,807 | |
| 10. Cadillac | 142,184 | |
| 11. Studebaker (US) | 120,465 | |
| 12. Chrysler | 77,285 | |
| 13. DeSoto | 25,581 | |
| 14. Imperial | 17,719 | |
| 15. Lincoln | 13,734 | |
| 16. Metropolitan | 13,103 | |
| 17. Continental | 11,086 | |
| 18. Checker | 6,980* | |
| 19. Edsel | 3,008 | |

**1961**

| | |
|---|---|
| 1. Ford | 1,338,790 |
| 2. Chevrolet | 1,318,014 |
| 3. Rambler | 370,685* |
| 4. Plymouth | 350,285 |
| 5. Pontiac | 340,248 |
| 6. Oldsmobile | 317,548 |
| 7. Mercury | 317,351 |
| 8. Buick | 276,754 |
| 9. Dodge | 269,367 |
| 10. Cadillac | 138,379 |
| 11. Chrysler | 96,454 |
| 12. Studebaker (US) | 59,713 |
| 13. Lincoln | 25,164 |
| 14. Imperial | 12,258 |
| 15. Checker | 5,683 |
| 16. DeSoto | 3,034 |

**1962**

| | |
|---|---|
| 1. Chevrolet | 2,072,000* |
| 2. Ford | 1,476,031 |
| 3. Pontiac | 521,437 |
| 4. Oldsmobile | 428,853 |
| 5. Rambler | 423,104 |
| 6. Buick | 399,526 |
| 7. Mercury | 341,366 |
| 8. Plymouth | 339,814 |
| 9. Dodge | 240,484 |
| 10. Cadillac | 160,840 |
| 11. Chrysler | 128,921 |
| 12. Studebaker (US) | 89,318 |
| 13. Lincoln | 31,061 |
| 14. Imperial | 14,337 |
| 15. Checker | 8,173 |

**1963**

| | |
|---|---|
| 1. Chevrolet | 2,148,000* |
| 2. Ford | 1,525,404 |
| 3. Pontiac | 589,294 |
| 4. Plymouth | 488,448 |
| 5. Oldsmobile | 476,753 |
| 6. Buick | 457,818 |
| 7. Dodge | 446,129 |
| 8. Rambler | 428,346* |
| 9. Mercury | 301,581 |
| 10. Cadillac | 163,174 |
| 11. Chrysler | 128,937 |
| 12. Studebaker (US) | 69,555 |
| 13. Lincoln | 31,233 |
| 14. Imperial | 14,121 |
| 15. Checker | 7,050 |

**1964**

| | |
|---|---|
| 1. Chevrolet | 2,308,700* |
| 2. Ford | 1,594,053 |
| 3. Pontiac | 738,317 |
| 4. Plymouth | 596,221 |
| 5. Buick | 510,490 |
| 6. Dodge | 501,781 |
| 7. Oldsmobile | 493,991 |
| 8. Rambler | 379,412* |
| 9. Mercury | 298,609 |
| 10. Cadillac | 165,909 |
| 11. Chrysler | 153,319 |
| 12. Studebaker (US/Canada) | 36,697 |
| 13. Lincoln | 36,297 |
| 14. Imperial | 23,295 |
| 15. Checker | 6,310 |

**1965**

| | |
|---|---|
| 1. Chevrolet | 2,372,900* |
| 2. Ford | 2,170,795 |
| 3. Pontiac | 801,357 |
| 4. Plymouth | 721,234 |
| 5. Buick | 600,145 |
| 6. Oldsmobile | 591,701 |
| 7. Dodge | 489,065 |
| 8. Mercury | 346,751 |
| 9. Rambler | 324,669* |
| 10. Chrysler | 206,089 |
| 11. Cadillac | 182,435 |
| 12. Lincoln | 40,180 |
| 13. Studebaker (Canada) | 19,435 |
| 14. Imperial | 18,409 |
| 15. Checker | 6,136 |

**1966**

| | |
|---|---|
| 1. Ford | 2,212,415 |
| 2. Chevrolet | 2,206,200* |
| 3. Pontiac | 830,778 |
| 4. Plymouth | 683,879 |
| 5. Dodge | 632,658 |
| 6. Oldsmobile | 578,385 |
| 7. Buick | 553,870 |
| 8. Mercury | 343,149 |
| 9. Rambler | 265,712* |
| 10. Chrysler | 264,848 |
| 11. Cadillac | 196,685 |
| 12. AMC | 76,239 |
| 13. Lincoln | 54,755 |
| 14. Imperial | 13,742 |
| 15. Studebaker (Canada) | 8,947 |
| 16. Checker | 5,761 |
| 17. Shelby | 2,378 |

**1967**

| | |
|---|---|
| 1. Chevrolet | 2,193,100* |
| 2. Ford | 1,730,224 |
| 3. Pontiac | 782,734 |
| 4. Plymouth | 636,893 |
| 5. Buick | 562,507 |
| 6. Oldsmobile | 548,390 |
| 7. Dodge | 465,732 |
| 8. Mercury | 354,923 |
| 9. Rambler | 237,785* |
| 10. Chrysler | 218,742 |
| 11. Cadillac | 200,000 |
| 12. AMC | 65,160 |
| 13. Lincoln | 45,667 |
| 14. Imperial | 17,620 |
| 15. Checker | 5,822 |
| 16. Shelby | 3,225 |

**1968**

| | |
|---|---|
| 1. Chevrolet | 2,131,200* |
| 2. Ford | 1,753,334 |
| 3. Pontiac | 910,482 |
| 4. Plymouth | 747,237 |
| 5. Buick | 651,823 |
| 6. Dodge | 627,533 |
| 7. Oldsmobile | 562,459 |
| 8. Mercury | 360,467 |
| 9. Chrysler | 264,853 |
| 10. Rambler | 259,346* |
| 11. Cadillac | 230,003 |
| 12. AMC | 187,435 |
| 13. Lincoln | 39,134 |
| 14. Imperial | 15,367 |
| 15. Continental | 7,770 |
| 16. Checker | 5,477 |
| 17. Shelby | 4,451 |

**1969**

| | |
|---|---|
| 1. Chevrolet | 2,106,500* |
| 2. Ford | 1,826,777 |
| 3. Pontiac | 870,081 |
| 4. Plymouth | 720,209 |
| 5. Buick | 665,422 |
| 6. Oldsmobile | 635,241 |
| 7. Dodge | 611,645 |
| 8. Mercury | 398,262 |
| 9. Chrysler | 260,773 |
| 10. Rambler | 239,937* |
| 11. Cadillac | 223,237 |
| 12. AMC | 173,106 |
| 13. Lincoln | 38,290 |
| 14. Continental | 23,088 |
| 15. Imperial | 22,103 |
| 16. Checker | 5,417 |
| 17. Shelby | 3,150 |

**1970**

| | |
|---|---|
| 1. Ford | 2,096,184 |
| 2. Chevrolet | 1,456,574 |
| 3. Pontiac | 690,953 |
| 4. Plymouth | 684,975 |
| 5. Buick | 666,501 |
| 6. Oldsmobile | 633,981 |
| 7. Dodge | 543,019 |
| 8. Mercury | 324,716 |
| 9. AMC | 276,000* |
| 10. Cadillac | 238,744 |
| 11. Chrysler | 180,777 |
| 12. Lincoln | 37,695 |
| 13. Continental | 21,432 |
| 14. Imperial | 11,822 |
| 15. Checker | 5,500* |

# Minor Makes

Compiled by R. Perry Zavitz and Alden Jewell

## NOTES TO THE READER

What follows is a compilation of all American-built automobiles in the 1940-1970 period not listed in the preceding "Major Makes" section. The vast majority of these saw very limited production; some never proceeded beyond the prototype stage; a rare few were sold for several years. The facts about some of them are, unfortunately, completely elusive, or at best sketchy.

Several rules were adopted in compiling this section. To keep the list within the scope of the book, all unsubstantiated, experimental, racing, and Canadian cars were omitted, as were products designed only for children. Though a number of prototypes are included, they fall within the primary qualification adopted: evidence of *serious intent to manufacture in complete form*. Vehicles sold as kits ("kit cars") are included only where fully assembled models were available from the manufacturer or a dealer.

Each entry is dated as accurately as possible, and builder or factory locations are stated where known. Where only one year is shown (1965-?) the editors were unable to determine exactly when "production" ceased. When "c." (circa) is shown, it was not possible to determine the precise date production started and/or terminated.

Since no list of this scope can possibly be complete, the editors welcome additions to the roster and updated information on the makes listed. Contributions should be addressed to: R. Perry Zavitz, 460 Ridgewood Crescent, London, Ontario, N6J 3H5, Canada; or to CONSUMER GUIDE® magazine, 3841 W. Oakton Street, Skokie, Illinois 60076.

## AEROCAR (1948-c.1970)

Aerocar Inc. of Longview, Washington had been building combination car/planes since 1948, but only seven had been constructed through 1970. Moulton P. Taylor developed the Aerocar; airworthiness certification was first received from the Civil Aeronautics Authority in 1954. The earliest models used a 100-bhp Franklin engine for both ground and air propulsion. Top speed on the ground was 50 mph, 110 in the air. As a plane, the Aerocar had a 300-mile range. It needed 655 feet for take-off and only 300 feet for landing. At least

one prototype had semi-retractable landing gear. Conversion from car to airplane or vice-versa took just five minutes for one person with a wrench. In car form, the wings and propeller assembly were carried in a 14-foot trailer. The main section measured 124 inches long overall, and wheelbase was 78 inches. Gross flying weight was 1750 pounds. Aerocar was to have been priced starting at $3995, but listed for $7500 in 1954. By the early 1970s its price was well into five figures.

An Aerocar International Corp. of Fort Worth, Texas reportedly planned production in 1961. Sufficient orders were apparently on hand to make this feasible, but the effort failed. It is unknown whether any were built, but it seems unlikely. The relationship of this firm to Aerocar Inc. is also a mystery. It is not clear whether it was an independent contractor or a subsidiary of the Washington firm.

## AEROMOBILE (1958)

Aeromobile was built in 1958 by Waldo Dean Waterman of San Diego, California. It was a car/plane, but little information about it is available. It was reported to have had no tail.

## AIRCAR (1970-c.1973)

The Aircar, from Advanced Vehicle Engineers of Van Nuys, California, revived the "flying auto" idea in a somewhat different form. Instead of being purposely designed, the Aircar was an aeronautical conversion. Control surfaces from a Cessna Skymaster were attached to an ordinary production car. Pontiac Firebirds were most commonly used, but some heavier cars were also given wings and used more powerful turbo-prop engines. Development continued until at least 1973, at which time a Pinto was being test-flown under the name Mizar.

## AIRPHIBIAN (1946-52)

Mass production of flying autos never got off the ground—but it wasn't because nobody tried. Robert E. Fulton, Jr. was one of many who saw great possibilities for the car/plane in the postwar market. His Airphibian was first shown in 1946, under the aegis of Continental, Inc., Danbury,

Connecticut, of which Fulton was president. The Airphibian's passenger compartment (or cockpit) was made of aluminum. As a plane, it could be converted to a two-passenger, four-wheeled car by detaching wings, propeller, and fuselage (a five-minute exercise). In the air it could reach 120 mph. Top speed on the highway was a modest 45 mph. A six-cylinder, 150-horsepower air-cooled engine provided the power. When ready for flying, the Airphibian weighed 2200 pounds and could travel 400 miles on 30 gallons of gasoline. Highway mileage was 25 mpg. In 1952, Fulton was still trying to get production started.

## AIRSCOOT (1947)

You've just arrived at your local airport in your private plane. How do you get home? Simply pull your folded-up Airscoot out of the baggage compartment and prepare it for the road. After you've unfolded this vehicle's two seats and two-suitcase luggage rack (in front of the seats), you fire up the one-cylinder, 2.6-horsepower engine and drive away at speeds up to 25 mph.

The three-wheeled Airscoot was made of lightweight tubing, which accounts for the toteable weight of only 72 pounds. The gas tank on this midget commuter held only three-tenths of a gallon; a full gallon would take you 60 miles. Overall length was 37 inches. Aircraft Products Company of Wichita, Kansas apparently was never able to get their unique little folding auto into production.

## AIRWAY (1948-50)

At least two Airway "vicinity car" prototypes were built, but they were not very similar in appearance. The 1948-49 version had a very plain fastback two-door sedan body. The 1950 Airway was a notchback-style coupe. Under the skin, the cars were much more alike. A 10-horsepower air-cooled aluminum engine transmitted power through a fluid drive. Both cars were 2- to 3-seaters, and had space for packages behind the single seat. The first prototype weighed 600 pounds and had an aluminum body. The 1950 car weighed 775 pounds with its body

of aluminum alloy and plastic. Wheelbase on both was 100 inches. Top speed was 45-50 mph.

The T. P. Hall Engineering Corporation of San Diego developed the designs and licensed Airway Motors, Inc. to manufacture them. Prices were expected to be in the $500-$750 range. It is doubtful any were sold.

## AMITRON (1967-?)

Amitron was a co-operative effort by Gulton Industries of Metuchen, New Jersey and American Motors in Detroit. It was a three-passenger electric car, powered by lithium-nickel fluoride batteries, which are about 10 times more powerful than the lead-acid type. Two batteries weighing 75 pounds each were used along with two nickel-cadmium batteries. The car could accelerate from 0 to 50 mph in about 20 seconds. Range was some 150 miles, even at speeds up to 50 mph. The wedge-shaped Amitron featured vinyl bumpers in an off-white color.

## APACHE (1966-?)

Apache was similar to European economy cars in overall size, engine displacement, and seating, although further details about it are unavailable. Its most unusual feature was a collapsible roof, which transformed it from a fastback coupe to an open convertible. Production of 500 to 1000 cars a year was predicted in 1966 by John G. Zullo, president of Interco Development Corporation of New York City. Volume never reached that figure though.

## APOLLO (1962-65)

Newt Davis and Milt Brown, a pair of enthusiastic entrepreneurs from Oakland, California, conceived the interesting Apollo. They formed International Motor Cars, Inc., designed a chassis, bought a batch of 215-cid Buick aluminum V8s, and planned a sleek fastback body. The somewhat dated styling was created by designer Ron Plescia, with modifications by Franco Scaglione of Turin, Italy. Frank Reisner's Carrozzeria Intermecannica, also of Turin, contracted to build the bodies.

Final assembly took place in

Oakland. The cars were painstakingly built at a rate of four a month.

The chassis, designed by Brown, combined a ladder-type tubular-steel frame with a beefed-up Buick Special suspension. Bendix disc brakes were later offered as an option. A three-speed manual gearbox was standard, but Borg-Warner's T-10 four-speed and Buick's Turbo Hydra-Matic were available.

Since the Apollo GT weighed only 2400 pounds, the unmodified Buick V8 provided ample performance. A 0–60 mph sprint took just 8 seconds.

International Motor Cars soon added an Apollo cabriolet, and in 1964 brought out an additional series, the 5000 GT, which used Buick's 300-cid V8. The 5000 could run 0 to 60 mph in 7.5 seconds, and had a claimed top speed of over 150 mph.

Davis and Brown were serious about their project, intent on offering good value for the dollar. But their company had fallen apart by 1966. The Apollo was never advertised nationally, and the firm lacked a sufficient dealer network. The operation was also sidetracked at one point by the distress sale of a score of Apollo bodies to a Dallas firm that assembled them under the name Vetta Ventura. International Motors was renamed Apollo International in 1965, and moved from Oakland to Pasadena—a last-ditch recapitalization effort. Total Apollo production was 77 coupes and 11 convertibles, plus one experimental 2+2.

## ARGONAUT (1959-63)

A large and very ambitiously designed luxury car, the Argonaut appeared in 1959. It was made by the Argonaut Motor Machine Co. of Cleveland, Ohio. There were seven models planned, ranging from a two-passenger sports coupe, sometimes referred to as the Steed, to a limousine. Another model was dubbed Smoke.

Frames were made of five-inch seamless steel tubing. Wheelbases were 126½ to 154 inches, while total length ran from 218 to 258 inches. The aluminum bodies were made in the United States or Italy. Interiors were trimmed to owner specifications.

An air-cooled, overhead-cam, aluminum V12 was used. This was thought to be a military engine. After some hesitation, the company revealed this powerplant developed an astonishing 1020 horsepower. Yet fuel consumption was a surprisingly good 13 mpg. A top speed in excess of 240 mph was claimed. A manual transmission with overdrive was standard, but a three-speed automatic was optional.

Prices were targeted at $25,150 up to $36,000. The cars would have been sold directly from the factory, and servicing would be done either at factory depots or the owner's home. Twice-a-year inspection by factory engineers was also planned. Production ended by 1963.

## ARNOLT (1952-63)

S. H. "Wacky" Arnolt was a sportsman from Warsaw, Indiana and first made money by building marine engines during World War II. After the war, he expanded into allied industries. Because he liked automobiles, one of his early interests was a foreign-car dealership in Chicago.

His first creation was the Arnolt-MG, of which 65 were built. Arnolt had found a Bertone body at the Turin Auto Show in 1952. He contracted to buy 100 copies, and went to MG for mechanicals. The $3195 Arnolt-MG resembled contemporary MGs only in its narrow, upright grille.

He soon discovered a much hotter engine than the MG—Bristol's BSI Mark II, a 220.3-cid four developing 130 horsepower. But it was a curious affair. Horizontal pushrods ran across the head, so the engine was very tall. Bertone, to whom Arnolt again turned for styling, had to design a body around it. Even so, the Arnolt-Bristol was one of the finest shapes ever to be carried on four wheels. Three distinct models were listed. The Bolide—originally priced at $3995, later at $4250—was topless, designed for sunny days or race tracks. A Deluxe model—first $4765, then $4995—had a top, but didn't look half as nice. A coupe with roll-up windows and a luxurious interior was offered at $5995. Typical performance figures were: 0–60 mph in 8.7 seconds, 0–90 mph in 21.3 seconds; standing quarter-mile in 17 seconds at 82 mph; top speed 110 mph.

In 1955 and '56, Arnolt entered three cars in the Sebring 12 Hours, and finished 1-2-4 in the two-liter production category both years. Interestingly, they were all street-stock: they had not been modified for racing. Alas, Sebring '57 was one race too many. One of Arnolt's drivers, blinded by the setting sun, rolled his car and was killed instantly. Arnolt took the crash hard, blaming himself, and never raced cars again. When he died of a heart attack in 1963, the Arnolt-Bristol died with him.

## ARROWBILE (c. 1937- c.1958)

Initially known as Arrowbile, and later Aerobile, this series of flying autos by Waldo D. Waterman was perhaps this country's first serious attempt to get such a vehicle into production. A 1937 effort using a Studebaker Commander six-cylinder engine almost reached full production: five or six vehicles were built in Santa Monica, California. Studebaker was to sell the Arrowbile through selected dealers, but backed out because of a downturn in the economy.

A report in December 1940 showed a drawing of an Aerobile three-wheeled "torpedo-shaped" car with detachable wings, by a Dayton, Ohio inventor and manufacturer. The final Aerobile was apparently put together in San Diego during the '50s. It was powered by a horizontally opposed, water-cooled Franklin six-cylinder engine.

## ASARDO (1959)

The name Asardo stems from the initials of its builder, the Amer-

Airphibian

Asardo

Apollo GT

Arnolt-MG

Bassons Star

Bobbi-Kar

# Minor Makes

ican Special Automotive Research & Design Organization, in North Bergen, New Jersey. The car had a tubular space-frame with an 88-inch wheelbase. A 195-pound fiberglass sport coupe body was used, as well as an aluminum belly pan. Overall length was 150 inches, and total weight was some 1350 pounds.

The engine was a four-cylinder 91.3 cubic-inch Alfa Romeo unit, tuned to develop 135 horsepower. A four-speed transmission was standard. The car's 0–60 mph acceleration time averaged 6.4 seconds, and a top speed of 135 mph was claimed. The price, including Borrani wire wheels, was $5875.

## ASCOT (1955)

Ascot was made by the Glass-par Co. of Santa Ana, California. Not surprisingly, its roadster body was made of fiberglass. It had butterfly-type fenders, free-standing headlights, a square grille, and external deck-mounted spare tire. Originally, the car was designed for a 172 cubic-inch Ford industrial engine, but various other units were tried, including a Studebaker six. Wheelbase for this 1770-pound car was 94 inches. Height with the top up was just 48 inches. Production apparently took place only during 1955.

## ASTRO-GNOME (1956)

Astro-Gnome, designed by the Richard Arbib Co. Inc. in New York, was a futuristic prototype. (Richard Arbib had a hand in the facelift for the 1956 Hudson, and also created the 1952 Packard Pan American.) Andrew Mazzard carried out the custom body work. The Astro-Gnome's side panels were made of ribbed anodized aluminum, offered in a choice of colors. They were easily replaceable. The car's bubble top provided unobstructed vision and was high enough so passengers could walk in. Leather was used for the upholstery, interior trim, and floor. Matching leather luggage was also supplied. The Astro-Gnome was only 13½ feet long, but comparatively wide at six feet. The unusual styling also featured an integrated full-perimeter bumper.

## AUBURN (1967-date)

In 1966, Glenn Pray left the Cord Automobile Company he had formed several years earlier. He had made some mistakes, but had learned a great deal about making replicas of classic automobiles.

Now it was time to start a new venture. This time it would be a revival of the Auburn 851/852 Speedster of 1935-36. The new model would be known as the 866. Unlike the 8/10-scale Cord, the 866 was a full-size replicar. The 127-inch wheelbase of its modified Ford Galaxie frame was identical to the original's. Overall weight was considerably less, however: 3100 pounds versus the 851's 3850. The big 428 cubic-inch Thunderbird V8 engine turned out 365 horsepower. The body was made of fiberglass, like those of most other revivals. Some of the hardware was reported to be new old stock from the original Auburn factory. Top speed was estimated to be in the neighborhood of 130 mph. Many stories were told about vintage-car enthusiasts being fooled into believing the 866 was an original. Pray had obviously done his homework well. And the price of $8450 was certainly less than you would expect to pay for a mint-condition original — if you could find one. The only options were the customer's choice of upholstery materials and paint colors.

Other Auburn replicas would follow from Pray's company and a spate of others. The 866 was later joined by Model 874, a dual-cowl phaeton that was an interesting variation, even though it had no counterpart in the '30s. These cars continued in limited production through the early 1980s.

## AURORA (1954)

Aurora was a one-off safety car prototype designed by Father Alfred A. Juliano of Branford, Connecticut. It was based on a 1954 Buick Roadmaster chassis, but could accommodate Cadillac, Lincoln, or Chrysler engines. The fiberglass body was topped by a transparent plastic roof. Its bubble-shaped windshield was raked forward.

Only one prototype was built at a cost of $30,000. It was hoped that interest in the design would be high enough to make limited production commercially feasible, in which case the car would have cost an estimated $15,000. Sales profits would have been used for further research in car safety.

## AUTO CUB (1956)

Auto Cub was the creation of Randall Products of Hampton, New Hampshire. It was a small, single-passenger runabout with tiller steering, and was only 51 inches long. The car reached a top speed of 15 mph with a 1.6-

horsepower Briggs & Stratton or Clinton engine mounted at the rear. Fuel consumption for this 115-pound mite was 75 mpg. Its price was $169.50 complete. The Auto Cub appears to have been the economy mate to the Daytona.

## AUTOETTE (1952-57)

Autoette was produced for approximately five years beginning in 1952 by Autoette Electric Car Co., Long Beach, California. A small, electric shopping-type car for two passengers, it was a three-wheeler with a single wheel at the front. The body was made of steel. A set of four heavy-duty 6-volt batteries supplied power to a 24-volt DC motor. Prices ranged from $775 to $950 in 1954 and three models were available.

## BASSONS STAR (1956)

One wheel in front, two in the rear, a low-slung two-passenger open fiberglass body, and a single-cylinder, two-cycle engine—that was the Bassons Star. Gil D'Andrea designed it for Bassons Industries Corporation of Bronx, New York. Bassons intended their creation for use as a low-cost, short-haul delivery car. Other suggested customers for this $1000 vehicle were commuters, farmers, and families needing an economical second car. The unenclosed storage space over the rear wheels could carry up to 500 pounds. The 10-horsepower, one-cylinder, two-cycle German J.L.O. engine was mounted between the passengers and the storage area. The Star could cruise at 40 mph, top speed was 70. The entire vehicle weighed only 400 pounds. It was 33 inches high, 49 inches wide, and 125 inches long.

Bassons also showed an enclosed reinforced plastic-bodied delivery van called Stationette in 1955. This was an update of the earlier wooden-bodied Stationette. Both of these three-wheelers were designed by James V. Martin (see Martinette).

## BAYMONT (1955)

Simple, safe, convenient transportation at an operating cost of 3 cents a day—average operating costs of less than $1.00 a month. What else but an electric car? This one was made by Baymont Company in Redwood City, California. Most of the electrics in the 1950s were golf carts modified for local running on city streets. The Baymont Suburban Model 240 was no exception. It had sufficient

space for two passengers, and room in the rear for several bags of groceries. Factory equipment included a single headlight, taillight, and horn. Six color choices were available. For a few extra dollars, the customer could add a windshield or a top. The company claimed the Suburban had sufficient power under full load to climb any paved road in America. Speeds up to 20 mph were said to be easy to achieve. The driving range was as high as 60 miles per day.

## BEARCAT (1956)

Bearcat was an unusual little car, built by the American Buckboard Corp. of Los Angeles. It had five wheels: the extra one, located at the rear, was connected by chain to the rear-mounted two-cylinder engine and served as the drive wheel.

Wheelbase, excluding the fifth wheel, was only 70 inches, and the car was just 120 inches long overall. Its fiberglass sports body was formed in one piece. A claimed 50 mpg was achievable by this $1000 vehicle.

## BEECHCRAFT PLAINSMAN (1948)

The Plainsman was a prototype for a possible venture into the automobile business by the Beech Aircraft Co. of Wichita, Kansas. Unit construction was used with an aluminum frame and body panels. For better visibility and entry/exit, the windshield and door openings were cut into the roof.

The Plainsman's drive system was quite unorthodox. A four-cylinder Franklin air-cooled engine was used to drive an electric generator which, in turn, drove four electric motors—one at each wheel. Although the gas-electric system was never installed in this four-wheel-drive car, it was successfully tested in some military trucks. The Plainsman had a very large six-passenger body. Riding comfort was enhanced by an all-independent suspension system featuring a rubber air bag and an air-filled shock absorber at each wheel.

The price was optimistically pegged at $5000, but the car certainly would have cost more than that to produce.

## BERGERMOBILE (1949)

Bergermobile, named after its inventor Joseph M. Berger, was a prototype built by the Berger Air-Turbine Car Co. of Mount Vernon, New York. Basically, it was a con-

verted Chevrolet. The engine was removed and replaced by a 30-gallon air tank and an Ingersoll-Rand air turbine. A 24-volt airplane-type storage battery supplied electrical power to drive the compressed-air turbine and also powered the electrical system. A simple forward/reverse lever controlled both speed and drive direction.

## B. M. C. (1952)

B. M. C. Sports got its name from the British Motor Car Co. of San Francisco, which built it in 1952. BMCC president, Kjell H. Quale, was one of its designers. The vehicle had no connection with the British Motor Corporation, and in fact used components from the rival Rootes Group of Britain. The car was designed around the chassis and engine of the production Singer 1500. The B. M. C. used a one-piece fiberglass body with much different styling, however. The project was terminated after only a few months, despite plans to produce 400 units a year.

## BOBBI-KAR (1945-47)

S. A. Williams was a shrewd promoter who began as a dishwasher in 1936 and ultimately found prosperity in the restaurant business. Attracted by a car-hungry market at the end of World War II, he bankrolled the Bobbi Motor Car Corporation in San Diego. The

resulting "aero-engineered" lightweight was named Bobbi-Kar, after Williams' son. The original prototype, affectionately dubbed the "Iron Monster," had a four-cylinder, 25-horsepower rear engine. Top speed was an unspectacular 55 miles an hour. Overall length was 132 inches; wheelbase was 80 inches. Projected price for the tiny two-place roadster was around $500. A plastic body and four-wheel independent "Torsilastic" suspension were publicized features. The suspension was developed by B. F. Goodrich. It used the torsion-bar principle with rubber bushings bonded to steel at the control points.

Subsequent convertible and station wagon prototypes were much larger than the original, although they retained the same styling themes. Length was now up to 152 inches and the wheelbase became 92 inches. Optimistic advertising brochures showed sketches of other proposed body styles; sedan, urban sedan (a wood-bodied two-door), coupe, and the Bobbi-Wagon package car (without doors). The grand plan called for production in an unused Consolidated Vultee aircraft plant.

Following investigations of his stock-selling schemes, revelation of his prison record, and a hasty move of operations to Birmingham, Alabama, Williams sold out and returned to California. He

later became involved in at least two more automobile ventures, the Towne Shopper and the Elektrakar. The Bobbi-Kar became the Keller, and the story continues under that heading.

## BOLIDE (1969-?)

Bolide came from the Bolide Motor Car Corp. of Huntington, New York, but the name graced two quite different models. Both were built by Andrew J. Griffith, Jr. who was associated earlier with the Griffith operation. The fiberglass-bodied Can-Am 2 was designed for use on street or track. It had a wheelbase of 105 inches, and used a Ford 351 V8 located amidships. This model was priced at $3500.

Another model called XJ002 was a four-wheel-drive Jeep-style two-passenger sports car. Designed for on- or off-road use, it was powered by a 225 cubic-inch 160-bhp V6.

## BOSLEY (1955-66)

Richard Bosley of Mentor, Ohio spent nearly three years and $9000 building his first car, the Bosley Mark I. The attractive fiberglass-bodied sports coupe could easily have come from Torino. The specially built frame supported a 1952 Chrysler V8 with a Cunningham intake manifold. With the 225 horsepower produced by this combination, the car could reach a top speed of 160 mph. With

long-distance races in mind, Bosley installed a 55-gallon fuel tank.

In late 1966, a second car was shown, the Bosley Mark II Interstate. Again, the styling had a distinct Italian flavor. This time, power was provided by a 345-bhp Pontiac V8. The fiberglass body rested on a reinforced Corvette chassis with a 102-inch wheelbase. Gas tank capacity was now a mere 35 gallons.

## BROGAN (1946-50)

Brogan was one of several small-car designs from the B & B Specialty Co. of Rossmoyne, Ohio. Some models were also known as Broganette and the B & B Three Wheel.

A three-wheeler with a single wheel in front, this car had a 60-inch wheelbase. The top of its windshield stood less than four feet above ground. Total weight was a mere 450 pounds. Its air-cooled two-cylinder engine produced 10 horsepower and was rear-mounted. No clutch was required. Mileage claims of 65–70 mpg were made, and top speed was 45 mph. The smaller Broganette scored up to 85 mpg, but its top speed was scarcely 40 mph.

By 1951, the Brogan name was phased out and considerable changes were made to the Broganette. It was still a three-wheeler, but the lone wheel was moved to the rear. Overall length

Californian

Convaircar

Crofton Bug

Cunningham C-4RK

Darrin

Davis

was now about 10 feet, but width was a narrow 52 inches. A roof was provided on the deluxe version of this two-seat design.

With its air-cooled 10-bhp Onan engine and three-speed transmission, the Broganette could reach 50 mph. Fuel consumption was in the 55–60 mpg range. Price was $550.

Some models in 1947 were apparently sold under the name B & B Three Wheel. However, not more than 30 of them were built.

## BRYAN (1949-72)

Leland (Dewey) Bryan, a General Motors Proving Grounds employee, built at least three flying automobiles. Several different names for his vehicles have been reported by the press: Bryan, Bry-Car, and Roadaplane. Bryan's design differed from most others by utilizing permanently attached folding wings rather than detachable wings. The third version (Bryan III, 1972) had wings that folded electrically in 35 seconds. The unusual craft was licensed as an automobile by the state of Michigan. All Bryan's inventions used pusher props mounted at the rear of the fuselage. Maximum road speed of the several versions varied from 50 to 70 mph; top air speed ranged from 60 to 80 mph. The second version had a 75-horsepower A-75 Continental engine.

## BUCKAROO (1957)

Buckaroo was built in Cleveland, Ohio by an unidentified manufacturer. It was very small, and its air-cooled engine was capable of providing a top speed of only 18 mph. Very little else is known about this $400 vehicle.

## BUCKBOARD (1956)

An Ariel "Square-4" motorcycle engine, mounted amidships on a Renault 4CV frame, powered this modern cycle car by Don Bruce of Bronx, New York. Bruce first displayed the car at an auto show in Hartford, Connecticut, and offered construction plans for do-it-yourselfers. It is not known if he built more than the one car.

The unusual body was constructed of 3/8-inch marine plywood with oak stringers and mahogany strips. The light weight of 738 pounds combined with the 43- (later reported as 61-) horsepower engine enabled the Buckboard to reach speeds in excess of 90 mph. It had retractable headlights controlled from the driver's seat (the right headlight turned

with the wheels). The car was 143 inches long overall, and had a 94-inch wheelbase.

## BUGETTA (c.1968-?)

Bugetta was made by Bugetta Inc. of Costa Mesa, California. Its fiberglass body would seat two to four passengers. A fiberglass or fabric top was available. It was a mid-engine design powered by a Ford 302 V8. Prices started at $3695. Some off-road type vehicles were also made.

## BUSHMASTER (1968-?)

Bushmaster was built by the Bushmaster Co. of Austin, Texas. Production began in 1968 and apparently lasted into the early '70s.

## CALIFORNIAN (1945-46)

This three-wheeler was the predecessor of the Davis. The prototype was built by Frank Kurtis. Although its size and general shape were similar to the Davis, the Californian differed in several respects. Its grille was in front, with the headlights mounted behind it. The Davis had hidden lights and no grille. It also used separate rear fenders, while the Davis had flush side panels. And the Californian was a convertible; the production Davis was a hardtop. The Californian's 58-horsepower engine helped it reach a 100-mph hour top speed while returning 40 mpg.

In 1945, publicity referred to Warner Manufacturing Company of Glendale, California, but 1946 reports indicated the maker as Californian Motor Car Company of Los Angeles.

## CANNON (1955)

Cannon was a product of Cannon Engineering Co., North Hollywood, California. Although it definitely existed, its design details have been lost to researchers.

## CHADWICK (1960)

Chadwick was an open shopper from the Chadwick Engineering Works, Pottstown, Pennsylvania. A 58-inch-wheelbase tubular chassis was used, with independent suspension at the front and quarter-elliptic leaf springs at the rear. Four-wheel hydraulic brakes were featured. A single-cylinder 13-horsepower air-cooled BMW engine was connected to a four-speed BMW transmission with enclosed chain drive. Overall length was 87 inches and weight was only 680 pounds. Radio, head-

lights, fixed windshield and top, and a speedometer were available as options. The Chadwick was built only in 1960.

## CHARLES TOWN-ABOUT (1958-59)

Charles Town-About was a product of the Stinson Aircraft Tool & Engineering Corporation of San Diego, California. Stinson's vice-president, Dr. Charles H. Graves, was responsible for the design as well as the name.

The vehicle was an electric, using two 3.2-horsepower motors, one for each rear wheel. A 48-volt electrical system was used. The car had a 77-mile range between charges, and a top speed of 58 mph.

The Town-About used a modified VW Karmann-Ghia body. Behind its tubular, loop front bumper was a dummy grille. At the back, DeSoto fins and taillights were grafted on. Suspension was by torsion bars. Despite the heavy batteries, the car weighed just 90 pounds more than a standard Karmann-Ghia.

Van-About was Graves' name for his utility model. At the back, it had a protruding cargo box, like the coupe-pickups of the 1930s. Production of both models was limited to 1958 and 1959.

## CHICAGOAN (1952-54)

The Chicagoan came from Triplex Industries Ltd. of Blue Island, Illinois. A two-passenger fiberglass sports car, it used a six-cylinder Willys engine. It's likely no more than 15 cars were built from 1952 to 1954, and the name was probably changed to Triplex around 1954.

## COLT (1958)

According to one source, the Colt was made by Colt Manufacturing Company of Milwaukee. But a catalog names the Colt Motors Corporation of Boston as the maker. A change in location and manufacturer might explain this discrepancy.

The Colt was a small 700-pound two-passenger economy model. Its single-cylinder four-cycle engine was a 23 cubic-inch Wisconsin air-cooled unit capable of 60 mpg, even with automatic transmission, which was standard. The fiberglass Colt had a top speed of 50 mph, and its price was $995.

## COMET (i) (c.1946-48)

Comet (i) was built by General Developing Company of Ridgewood, New York. A three-wheeler

with a tubular frame and plastic body, it measured only 114 inches in length. The single wheel was mounted at the front while the engine was located at the rear. With a modest 4.5 horsepower, the Comet's fuel economy was a claimed 100 mpg.

## COMET (ii) (1951-55)

Micro-midget race cars were the mainstay of Comet Manufacturing Company's production in the early '50s. In 1951, however, it advertised a special roadster that could be assembled by the buyer, or bought fully assembled and ready to drive. The Sacramento, California firm claimed its Comet Roadster was the world's lowest-priced transportation, and could be driven for 50 cents a week. The sleek little open two-seater came equipped with a 6-horsepower engine, automatic drive, heavy-duty brakes, and oversize balloon tires. Ratings of 60 mpg and 40 mph were touted.

## CONVAIRCAR (1941-48)

Convaircar, occasionally spelled ConVaircar or ConvAircar, was a car/plane made by the Consolidated-Vultee Aircraft Corporation of San Diego. The prolific Ted Hall headed the Convaircar project after he had designed the Roadable.

For road use, the vehicle got its power from a 26.5-horsepower Crosley engine. It had a second engine for flying, a 190-bhp Lycoming. The Convaircar had a four-seat fiberglass body, with a long sloping back and considerable rear overhang. The airframe, with its 34½-foot wing span, was attached to the roof at three points. Portable aluminum jacks supported the airframe section during attachment.

The Convaircar had made three successful trial flights before it ran out of fuel and crashed in late 1947. Development work continued, however, and by 1950 the car was known as the Hall Flying Auto, with a price tag of $20,000.

## CORD (1964-66; 1968-70)

This mid-'60s replicar revived one of the all-time greats: the 1936-37 Cord 810/812. It was built by the Cord Automobile Co. of Tulsa, Oklahoma (registered as a Delaware corporation) under the aegis of Glenn Pray, a former school teacher. Gordon Buehrig, who had designed the original, styled the revival too, and kept its lines faithful to the original's. Pray's car was about 80 percent of

the 1936-37 model in size, so it was designated the Cord 8/10.

U.S. Rubber, now Uniroyal, had developed a plastic material in the early '60s called Royalex, and this was chosen for the 8/10 body. Maintaining tradition, the new Cord retained front-wheel drive. Power came from the Chevrolet Corvair air-cooled flat six that developed 110 horsepower from 164 cubic inches.

Available only as a two-passenger convertible, the Cord 8/10 was priced at $4000 in 1964. This rose to nearly $6000 by the time production ended in 1966. A total of 91 Cords were built, excluding prototypes.

Despite several attempts by company president Wayne McKinley to keep the firm solvent, the Cord Automobile Company went into receivership. (Glenn Pray was no longer part of the organization by then.) A bankruptcy sale was held in March 1967.

In 1967-68, the firm was owned briefly by Elfman Motors Inc. of Philadelphia. Exactly what took place during that time is hazy, though it seems certain no cars were produced during the Elfman regime. Then in 1968, the car was taken over by the Sports Automobile Manufacturing Company of Mannford, Oklahoma.

SAMCO, as the company was more commonly known, produced a much different car than the previous version. Since the Corvair was being phased out, a new powerplant was sought and two were finally adopted. The Ford 302-cid V8 was selected as the standard engine and Chrysler's 440 Magnum V8 was offered optionally. SAMCO phased out Royalex and reverted to conventional fiberglass body construction. The styling was also revised. Its retractable headlights were now fixed in the open position, and front-wheel drive gave way to rear drive.

Two models were offered: the Warrior, on a 108-inch wheelbase, and the Royal, on a 113-inch wheelbase. (The original Cord's wheelbase was 125 inches, and that of Pray's revival was 100 inches.) SAMCO prices were $7300 and up. Production ended in the spring of 1970.

### CORTEZ (c.1947-c.1950)

Though the Cortez does not appear to have reached production, this full-size car was intended for volume sale at $1000 a copy. An October 1950 news clipping indicated that a new $40 million corporation was to introduce a new light car to the public "next year, providing military production does not interfere." The company, North American Motors, Inc., was located in Dallas, Longview, or Grand Prairie, Texas, depending upon which report you read. Perhaps the company moved frequently during its short life span. Various reports were consistent, however, in stating that well-known automotive designer John Tjaarda (of Lincoln-Zephyr fame) was involved in the Cortez project. A wheelbase of 100 inches, weight of about 1000 pounds less than a standard car, and fuel consumption of 45 miles per gallon were all part of the grand plan.

### CROFTON (1959-61)

The Crofton, or Crofton Bug, was built by Crofton Marine Engine Company of San Diego. Crofton acquired the rights to the Crosley engine after that car went out of production. A 35-horsepower version of this engine went into a Jeep-style vehicle, an on- or off-road machine that weighed 1100 pounds. Wheelbase was 63 inches, overall length 111 inches.

Crofton's price was $1350, but for an extra $450 a "Brawny Kit" was available. This consisted of a six-speed transmission, limited-slip differential, crash pan, 9.00×10 tires (5.30×12s were standard), and deluxe seats.

Approximately 200 Croftons were built from 1959 until production terminated in 1961.

### CRUE-CUT (1966-date)

Missouri (Sugar Creek and Kansas City) and later Kansas (Gardner) have been the home for hundreds of half-scale cars made by Crue-Cut Manufacturing Company since 1966. Starting with the Tin Lizzie formerly made by McDonough Power Equipment, Inc., this firm has added Ford Lotus, Stutz Bulldog, GM touring car, and Chrysler replicas to its line over the years. The Model T roadster also provided the basis for a fire engine version with "real wood ladders." These "magnificent minis" apparently serve well in sales promotions, fund-raising events, and advertising. All are powered by 3-horsepower engines that can take them up to 12 mph.

### CUBSTER (1949)

Osborn Wheel Company of Doylestown, Pennsylvania wasn't content to sell just wheels. In 1946, you could buy its Model A racer chassis (with a 12-inch steering wheel and 10×0.175 Goodyear semi-pneumatic tires) mounted on, of course, Osborn ball-bearing steel wheels. Customers added a body and engine to suit. In 1949, the Model D chassis was available for $299.50, complete with 6.6-horsepower engine, or $159.50 without engine. Osborn now offered a kit for its Cubster body that fit nicely on the Model D chassis. Company advertising made no mention of what material was used for the body, but it was a 118-inch long, two-passenger ("any age") roadster of modern fenderless style. The ads did claim 35 mph was attainable.

### CUNNINGHAM (1953-55)

Many car enthusiasts dream of building their own automobiles. Wealthy sportsman Briggs Swift Cunningham did just that from 1951 to 1955, producing the fastest cars in America and very nearly winning Le Mans with one of them. The prototype of the series was the 1951 C-1, which rode a 105-inch wheelbase. Beautifully styled by Cunningham and his team, it was fully instrumented and sumptuously upholstered with leather over comfortable bucket seats. The C-2R series followed, using both open and closed body styles. Both series were powered by the Chrysler hemi-head V8, which produced 180 horsepower in stock form. Cunningham got

Die Valkyrie

Duesenberg (ii)

Edwards (hardtop prototype)

Electric Shopper

El Morocco

Eshelman Sportabout

much more out of it than that: as much as 300 bhp. The C-2Rs failed at Le Mans in 1951, however.

The C-3 of 1953-55 was Cunningham's ''production'' car. This $10,000 grand tourer used its predecessors' tubular frame and race-proven suspension. Its coupe body was styled by Giovanni Michelotti, then a designer with the Vignale coachbuilding firm of Italy.

Back at Le Mans for 1952, Cunningham entered three copies of his new C-4R. Lighter than the C-2R by 1000 pounds, it rode a 100-inch wheelbase and was powered by a 325-bhp Hemi. Two of the three cars entered eventually dropped out, but Cunningham himself drove the third to a fourth-place overall finish. In 1953, two of the C-4Rs were back, along with the new C-5R. The latter was an aggressive-looking roadster with torsion-bar suspension, Hallibrand knock-off wheels, and Al-Fin 17-inch-diameter brake drums. It was timed at 156 mph. The two C-4Rs placed seventh and tenth.

Cunningham raced a Ferrari in 1954 while his C-6R was being built. Its debut the following year was anticlimactic. Powered by a 3-liter Offenhauser engine, it lacked sufficient endurance for the 24-hour race, and Cunningham did not finish. After that, he quit designing and campaigning his own race cars.

## CURTISS-WRIGHT AIR-CAR (1959-60)

Curtiss-Wright introduced their own car in 1959, and it was unlike any other. This one had no wheels. The Air-Car traveled on a cushion of low-pressure, low-velocity air at a height of 6 to 12 inches over land, water, swamps, or mud. Production of the 300-horsepower Model 2500 Air-Car was scheduled for November, 1959 in South Bend, Indiana. The odd-looking, four-passenger vehicle was said to have a top speed of about 60 mph. A January 1960 press photo showed an Air-Car on display in New York's Rockefeller Plaza with the caption stating production was then underway. How many were produced is not known. Other versions planned were an Air- Bus and Air-Car pickups and trucks.

## CUSHMAN (1945-date)

Cushman was a shopper-type car from Cushman Motor Works Inc. of Lincoln, Nebraska. Cushman is best known for its motor scooters and golf carts, but it has made some car-like runabouts over the years. With a low-power, one-cylinder air-cooled engine, the Cushman is small and very economical. Electric models have also been occasionally available. Around 1969, the Town & Fairway model was offered. It could be converted from a four-passenger minicar to a golf cart or carry-all.

## CUSTER (1959-60)

The Custer Specialty Company of Dayton, Ohio entered the automobile business earlier than most. Custer had built an electric car in 1898 or 1899. It again offered cars from 1920 to 1946, and in 1959 made another try at the business.

This latest effort was a two-passenger ''buckboard'' vehicle, with either a Custer Special electric motor, or a 6-horsepower four-cycle gasoline engine. The electric motor had two forward and two reverse speeds, and gave a top speed of 18 mph. The gas model could reach 40 mph. Wheelbase of either model was 70 inches, and overall length was 93 inches. Custer left the automobile business permanently in 1960.

## DARRIN (1946-47)

A prewar designer of custom coachwork, Howard A. ''Dutch'' Darrin made a bid for the volume market with an intriguing convertible in 1946. One of the first cars designed expressly for fiberglass body construction, this five-seater was vaguely reminiscent of Darrin's styling for the production 1947 Kaiser and Frazer: the grille was horizontal like the Frazer's, and the overall look was rounded with slab sides. But there the similarities ended: mechanically, the Darrin was unique. An elaborate hydraulic system provided power for the car's convertible top, power front seat, four-wheel jacking system, and hood-raising mechanism. The Darrin's hood and front fenders pivoted up as a unit to expose the entire engine and front suspension. The rectangular frame was of box-section steel. Wheelbase was 115 inches, overall length 185 inches. Power was derived from a 100-bhp Kaiser six of 226 cubic inches.

Darrin hoped to build up to 30,000 of these cars a year. After constructing a running prototype, he attempted to interest financial backers in production. The most promising opportunity appeared in the form of Lehman Brothers, the New York financial house, which had simultaneously been approached by Kaiser interests to help underwrite K-F. Possibly because of Lehman's inability to reach a deal with Kaiser and because of Darrin's association with K-F, neither arrangement ever materialized.

## DAVIS (1947-49)

The Davis is perhaps the best-known postwar three-wheeler made in the U.S. Its maker was the Davis Motor Co. of Van Nuys, California, headed by Glenn Gordon ''Gary'' Davis. It is said his idea for a ''tricycle'' car came from none other than Howard Hughes.

A seven-passenger sedan and an 11-passenger station wagon were planned, but only a four-place, single-seat coupe was actually built. Its 64-inch bench seat was supposed to hold four people.

The body consisted of nine aluminum panels, each attached by twist bolts for easy removal or replacement. The metal top was detachable. Doors opened by means of external pushbuttons instead of conventional handles. Styling was simple and sleek. A single wheel was mounted at the front, the prow was quite pointed, and the headlights were hidden.

A Continental engine was used in the first few cars built, but most had a four-cylinder, 133 cubic-inch 60-horsepower Hercules unit. A top speed of 116 mph was claimed. If true, that would make the Davis the fastest U.S. car of 1947.

The Davis was intended to sell for $995, and production of 40,000 units was anticipated for 1949. Actually, just 17 cars were completed, all prototypes, which were never formally sold. Gary Davis was convicted of fraud in the financing of his firm, though he claimed innocence.

## DAYTONA (1956)

Daytona was made by Randall Products of Hampton, New Hampshire. Priced at $495, this was the rich-man's version of the Auto Cub. The Daytona was bigger, heavier, and more substantial. It was 72 inches long and weighed 235 pounds. A steel chassis was used for this two-passenger runabout. Unusually, body panels were made of Formica. A rear-mounted 2-horsepower Briggs & Stratton engine gave the car a top speed of 18 mph and fuel economy of 75 mpg.

## DEBONNAIRE (1955)

Although contemporary accounts of the Debonnaire indi-cated it was available with top for about $1800, it is unclear whether this was a complete car or just a body kit ready to mount on the chassis of your choice. It is clear, however, that the fiberglass body was designed for the 1941-48 Ford platform. Replac Corporation of Euclid, Ohio was the maker.

## DELCAR (1947-49)

Delcar was produced by American Motors Inc. of Troy, New York. The company's name is coincidentally similar to that of the Wisconsin automaker formed by the Nash/Hudson merger a few years later.

Delcars were built from 1947 to 1949. Most were small delivery trucks, but at least one station wagon was built. It was a very boxy vehicle with no hood. The front-mounted four-cylinder engine was situated under the front floor. The station wagon was roomy enough for six people, yet it had a very short 60-inch wheelbase, a 102-inch overall length, and stood 78 inches tall.

## DEL MAR (1949)

Del Mar Motors Inc. of San Diego completed only a few prototypes of a neat-looking subcompact. The engine was a four-cylinder, 160 cubic-inch, 63-horsepower Continental. With its three-speed Warner transmission, 80 mph was possible. Fuel consumption was as high as 30 mpg. Wheelbases varied between 100 and 104 inches. The suspension used Ford transverse leaf springs front and rear, although some examples had semi-elliptic rear springs. Monroe aircraft-type rubber-filled shock absorbers were installed.

The body was a combination of aluminum, plastic, and steel. Styling was not unlike that of the British Hillman introduced at about the same time. The Del Mar's projected price was around $1200, and production of two-door sedans, business coupes, and convertibles was planned at the rate of 600 per day.

## DEVIN (1957-64)

Bill Devin owned Devin Motors in Los Angeles, California where he and partner Ernie McAfee sold exotic cars like Siatas and Ferraris to wealthy racers. Devin received a particularly pretty Ermini 1100 that he sold to racer Jim Orr. But before he did, he made a fiberglass mold of the Ermini's aluminum Scaglietti body. Devin then invented a system of

modular molds that would enable him to alter the dimensions of the Scaglietti design to fit a wide variety of chassis and drivetrains.

Soon after Devin got into the kit-car business, he received an intriguing order from an Irish engineer named Malcolm MacGregor. MacGregor wanted a body kit to fit a chassis he was building around the Corvette V8.

MacGregor's chassis was state-of-the-art in 1957. Steel tubing, three inches in diameter, was formed into a ladder-type frame with tubular loops at the cowl and behind the seats. Rear suspension was fully independent, including De Dion tube, coil springs, dual parallel trailing arms, and huge 11-inch Girling disc brakes mounted inboard next to the differential. At the front were parallel A-arms with coil springs and tubular shock absorbers, along with another pair of Girling discs. The Devin chassis was one of the first to offer all-independent suspension and four-wheel disc brakes.

Rolling chassis were shipped to El Monte, California where Devin and his crew completed assembly. A stock Corvette 283-cid V8, fitted with a special low-profile manifold and carburetor so it would fit under the low hood, was bolted in along with the Corvette's Borg-Warner T-10 four-speed transmission. The result was dubbed Devin SS. It could run 0 to 60 mph in 4.8 seconds, and 0 to 100 in 12 seconds. Top speed was over 140 mph.

Yet the cars didn't sell. Production lasted from early 1958 through the end of '61, during which time exactly 15 were sold.

Devin had other irons in the fire.

In 1959, he restyled his original body, giving it a high trunk into which a Volkswagen engine fit like hand in glove. He built a frame of square tubing and bonded it to a fiberglass undertray. This was planned to take stock VW suspension components. The interior was fitted with bucket seats. The car, called the Devin D, was available as a kit for only $1495 or completely assembled for just $2950. It was pretty, reliable, and surprisingly sophisticated. Hundreds were sold along with a derivative Devin C—the same chassis but with a Chevy Corvair powerplant.

Unfortunately for Devin, that smooth, Scaglietti-styled body for which his cars were famous had come to look old-fashioned by the mid-1960s. His kits had been fairly profitable in their day, but the SS, C, and D were too costly to produce for their limited market. Eventually, Devin got out of the car business completely.

### DIEHLMOBILE (1962-64)

The Diehlmobile three-wheeler was made by the H. L. Diehl Co. of South Willington, Connecticut. Its unique feature was that it could be folded up flat, and fit into the trunk of a normal car. With wire wheels and 3-horsepower Briggs & Stratton engine, it weighed 225 pounds. Its price was only $299.50.

### DIE VALKYRIE (1952)

In 1952, Brooks Stevens was commissioned by a Cleveland syndicate to create a low-volume, special-order car on a contemporary Cadillac chassis. The Die Valkyrie show prototype, built by the Spohn bodyworks of Ravensburg, West Germany, was the result. It created some interest at that year's Paris Auto Salon, but production did not materialize.

Stevens emphasized the car's V8 power by a strong "V" frontal motif. The long-hood/short-deck body configuration prefigured that of several forthcoming luxury cars, notably the Continental Mark II. Die Valkyrie also evidenced Stevens' first use of what he called the "Washington coach door line." This allowed rear seat entry and exit in a two-door without materially disturbing the front passengers. This feature later appeared on the Gaylord.

### DOUGHERTY (1955-56)

Dougherty was made by Frazer Dougherty of Sierra Madre, California in 1955 and 1956. No information about its design is available.

### DOW ELECTRIC (1960)

Dow Electric came from the Dow Testing Laboratory Inc. of Detroit. It's possible this is another name for a car called the D.T.L. made by Detroit Testing Laboratory Inc. at about the same time.

Douglas Dow, former research chief of the Detroit Edison Co., designed this two-passenger electric. Two 0.3-horsepower motors were used. Power came from three 12-volt and four 2-volt batteries. Top speed was about 15 to 20 mph and the range was 30 miles. Operating costs of $\frac{1}{4}$ cent to $\frac{1}{2}$ cent per mile were claimed. Rear disc brakes were a feature of this 447 pound, 74-inch-long vehicle.

Dow tried to get his electric car produced but couldn't find a company willing to take it on. If it had been produced, the Dow car was expected to sell for around $500 to $800.

### DUAL-GHIA (1956-61)

Most exotic cars are the products of a single imaginative individual. The Dual-Ghia produced by Dual Motors Corp., Detroit, Michigan was no exception. In this case, the individual was Eugene Casaroll, owner of Automobile Shippers, Inc., a Detroit trucking firm.

In 1952, Chrysler stylist Virgil Exner had teamed up with Ghia coachworks in Italy to produce the Dodge Firearrow. When Dodge Division president William Newberg announced the Firearrow wouldn't be produced, Casaroll approached him for the design rights. Casaroll recruited designer Paul Farrago to work with Ghia.

The production car did not emerge until mid-1956. By then, its name was Dual-Ghia, and it featured the faddish wraparound windshield of '56 Chrysler production models. Price was $7650. It was available with two engines. Standard was the 230 horsepower, 315-cid Dodge Red Ram V8. Optional at $100 extra was a 260-bhp engine in D-500 tune. A "Stage 2" Firebomb engine could also be ordered with 285 bhp. PowerFlite automatic transmission with floorshift was standard equipment, coupled to a "performance" 3.54:1 axle ratio. Power steering and brakes were optional. The suspension was set up for stable handling. The chassis, a stock Dodge modified by Ghia's chief

Ferrer GT

Formacar

Gaylord (Brooks Stevens at wheel)

Fitch Sprint (and John Fitch)

Gadabout

Graham

engineer Giovanni Savonuzzi, measured 115 inches in wheelbase and had a "step-down" floor like that of the Hudson Hornet. To hold costs down, the stock chassis was sent to Turin, where it was modified and the smooth sports-car body fitted to it. Each partially finished car was shipped back to Detroit for installation of engine, transmission, and interior trim.

Unfortunately, Casaroll was unable to produce more than a fraction of his planned output. Between 1956 and '58, his factory turned out only 117 cars—102 convertibles, two special hardtops, and 13 various prototypes. The problem wasn't lack of orders; the real hang-up was the time it took to put the cars together. Casaroll was also not charging enough to cover costs, Dual Motors was now faced with the choice of building a new model or giving up.

Its decision appeared in August 1960, the new and beautiful L6.4. It had a smooth deck, semi-outrigger taillights, and a neat crease along the bodysides. The grille, defined by a strong hood bulge, retained a resemblance to previous models with a rounded, oblong shape and single horizontal bar. The roofline was semi-fastback; the glass began just behind the C-pillar and tapered cleanly into the deck.

Lacking a stock platform to work with, Ghia was forced to design the L6.4's chassis from scratch. Wheelbase was 115 inches as before, but overall length grew by seven inches to 210. Unlike the first-generation D-Gs, which used body parts from every Chrysler division, the L6.4 was made up of few stock components. A Chrysler convertible windshield was the most obvious. Ultimately, the L6.4 listed at $13,000 in Italy, or $15,000 f.o.b. Detroit. By 1960, Chrysler had abandoned its hemi-head V8, so Casaroll switched to the 383-cid wedge-head engine with 325 bhp. No performance options were available. The chassis was more softly sprung than the previous Dual-Ghia.

Only 26 L6.4s were built between 1961 and '63. After that, Dual Motors collapsed. Casaroll died in the late '60s, leaving a planned third-generation Dual-Ghia stillborn.

## DUESENBERG (i) (1959)

Duesenberg (i) was a hybrid built by Mike Kollins of Detroit. Based on a 1950 Packard chassis, it was powered by the famous Duesenberg straight eight, rebored to yield a displacement of 435 cubic inches and 400 horsepower. The steel and aluminum roadster body was hand-formed. Only one example is believed to have been built.

## DUESENBERG (ii) (1966)

Duesenberg (ii) was one of several attempts made in the '60s to revive famous nameplates of the past. The Duesenberg Corp. of Indianapolis was formed with Fred "Fritz" Duesenberg as chairman of the board. Fritz was the son of August and a nephew of Fred, the famous brothers who built the original Duesenbergs.

The revived Duesenberg was not a replica of the classic 1930s model, but rather an all-new super-luxury sedan—a latter-day Duesie in the modern idiom. Its styling was the work of Virgil Exner, former styling chief at Chrysler Corp. The body was made by Ghia in Italy.

Naturally, it had to be big. The wheelbase was 137½ inches, and overall length was 245 inches. That was a half an inch more than a contemporary Cadillac limousine. Legroom was a generous 42½ inches in front, and 44 inches in back. The hood was a massive 80 inches long. Under it was a 440 cubic-inch, 425-horsepower Chrysler V8.

Production never progressed beyond one prototype. But the Duesenberg's general design was adopted in 1970 for a similar Stutz revival, which continues in production today.

## DYNAMO JR. (1959)

Dynamo Jr. was an electric from Dynamo Electric Co. of Los Angeles. It was little more than a fiberglass-bodied golf and shopping cart.

## EDWARDS (1949-55)

Sterling H. Edwards built this car under the auspices of his Edwards Engineering Co., in South San Francisco, California. The first Edwards Special appeared in 1949 as a four-seat convertible with hardtop and windshield that could be quickly removed for racing.

Edwards' "production" car, the America, was announced in late 1953. A slab-sided, good-looking four-seat convertible, it had a large rectangular eggcrate grille and 1952 Mercury taillights. Greater rigidity was provided by a Mercury station wagon chassis, sectioned to a wheelbase of 107 inches.

By 1955, an Edwards cost over $7800. All models came standard with electric window lifts, Hydra-Matic transmission, and Kelsey-Hayes wire wheels. The high price kept demand extremely low.

## ELECTRA KING (1961-date)

Electra King is made by the B & Z Electric Car Co. in Long Beach, California. The firm was founded by Messrs. Billard and Zarpe in 1961. Zarpe withdrew shortly after the company was founded, while Billard sold out in 1972 because of poor health. The present owner is Robert E. McCoy, who has a background in electrical engineering.

Originally, a 1-horsepower DC electric motor was used and gave the car a 45-mile range. A modest cruising speed of 18 mph was advertised. Usually, five 6-volt batteries were provided, but some examples had 24-, 30-, and 36-volt electrical systems. A two-passenger car only 88 inches long, the Electra King is available with either three or four wheels. The single wheel is at the front of the tricycle model. Tire size is 4.00×8. With a fiberglass top, total weight is only 675 pounds. The interior is carpeted, as is the seven cubic-foot trunk.

Electra King remains in production with choice of four motors, ranging from 1 to 3.5 horsepower. Several types of battery packs are also offered, so performance and range vary depending on the motor/battery selection. Speeds run from 16 to 29 mph, and range from 18 to 36 miles between charges.

Styling has not changed greatly over the years, but prices have risen. The 1974 models sold for $2270 to $2900.

## ELECTRICAR (1950-c.1966)

Electricar was made by the Boulevard Machine Works of North Hollywood, California. Established in 1949, this firm made a vehicle known by its initials, B.M.W. But in 1950, the firm moved to North Hollywood, and its product was renamed Electricar. Three models were announced, each a small open runabout.

The Boulevard model was a two-seater, 106 inches long. It had four ⅙-horsepower electric motors, one to drive each wheel. The Cutie, a single-passenger version, had two such motors, one driving a front wheel and the other a rear wheel. Its top speed was 25 mph. The Cutie Junior had just one motor, and its top speed was only 10 mph.

How long production continued is uncertain. There were reports of a 1966 model that could reach 70 mph.

## ELECTRIC SHOPPER (c.1956-?)

Made by the Electric Car Co. of Long Beach, California, this vehicle was just what its name implied: an electrically powered shopping car. Its lifespan is open to question, however. One source says the car was built from about 1960 to 1973, while another lists the period as 1956 to 1962. All agree that it was a fiberglass three-wheeler, 86 inches long on a wheelbase of 61 inches. The price was $945, although a metal-bodied model was also sold for $750. The motor was a 24-volt DC series-wound unit, rated at just 1.5 horsepower. The car could reach speeds up to 18 mph in either forward or reverse. Range was 30–35 miles between charges.

## ELECTRO MASTER (1962-?)

Electro Master, from Nepa Manufacturing Co. of Pasadena, was an electric shopping car with a fiberglass body. Its 2-horsepower motor was connected to six 6-volt batteries. Top speed was 20 mph and range was 40 miles. Weight was just 680 pounds. Production began in 1962 and reportedly ended in 1964, but may have continued longer.

## ELECTROBILE (1951)

Two enterprising gentlemen from Chicago thought they had the answer to burgeoning suburban transportation problems. Their Electrobile design was a three-wheeled fiberglass-bodied runabout for shopping and running errands. This 300-pound electric was expected to travel 25–35 miles on a recharge. A high-speed DC motor and a built-in charger were included in the proposed price of $350. The fiberglass body consisted of several molded sections mounted over an aluminum frame. Press releases showed only sketches of the Electrobile. It is doubtful even a prototype was ever built.

## ELECTRONIC (1955)

Electronic was an unusual car planned in 1955 by the Electronic Motor Car Corp. of Salt Lake City, Utah. A sedan, station wagon, and panel truck were proposed, as

well as a sports car to be available with or without a hardtop. Overall length was 210 inches, and wheelbase was 110 inches.

A gasoline or diesel engine provided power to an 80-cell battery pack, which was connected to a "Dual-Torque" electric motor located within the rear axle housing. Also incorporated was the "Electro-Magnetic Differential," an electric device that was supposed to act like a limited-slip differential.

Only the prototype Electronic was built. Production had been planned for either Detroit or Oxford, Michigan.

## EL MOROCCO (1956-57)

El Morocco was a Chevrolet conversion designed by Reuben Allenden of Detroit. The car was basically a 1956 or 1957 Chevrolet hardtop or convertible with somewhat altered styling. Revisions were made to the grille, bumpers, side trim, and fins. The result looked very much like the contemporary Cadillac Eldorado. In spite of all the work involved, the converted car cost about as much as a standard Chevrolet. It is believed that about 30 El Moroccos were built over a two-year period.

## ESHELMAN (c.1954-date)

Cheston L. Eshelman of Baltimore, Maryland and now Miami, Florida has built quite a variety of vehicles over the years. All of his early cars were very tiny ones— some for children, and slightly larger ones for one or two adults.

In the mid-to-late '60s, Eshel-man began selling franchises for his Golden Eagle line of automobiles. These were various Chevrolet models with large Eagle emblems and nameplates in place of the standard badges. Apparently there were no other modifications. At this writing, Eshelman sells Golden Eagle Prestige Car accessory kits (emblems and nameplates) and experimental rights to his electric car and/or his 30-mph crash absorber.

## FERGUS (1949)

Fergus, from Fergus Motors Inc. of New York City, was that firm's second attempt at car making. Its first effort lasted from 1915 to 1922. The second endeavor was a car based on the Austin A40 from Britain. It used the A40 engine and its styling somewhat resembled that of the relatively uncommon Austin A40 Sports. Development did not progress beyond the prototype stage, however.

## FERRER (1966)

The Ferrer GT was made by Ferrer Motors Corp. of Miami, although one source names the manufacturer as Bottier Engineering of Camden, New Jersey. This car had a sleek steel-reinforced fiberglass body, similar in appearance to Ford's GT of the mid-'60s. The ubiquitous Volkswagen Beetle provided the chassis, with a wheelbase of 94.5 inches. Overall, the Ferrer was 158 inches long, 60 inches wide, and 42 inches high. It was sold as a basic kit for $990 and as a more complete deluxe kit for $1750. However, the buyer could have a fully assembled car with 50-horsepower engine for $2950. An optional VW engine reworked to put out 70 bhp could boost price to $3800.

Ferrer claimed their standard model would cruise at a 90-mph top speed, and was capable of 29 mpg at a steady 68 mph. The 0-60 mph run could be accomplished in 12.5 seconds.

## FINA (1953-c.1955)

Perry Fina, a New York City importer of European cars and a connoisseur of fine automobiles, backed development of the Fina Sport. Based on a 115-inch wheelbase Ford chassis, its overall length was 188 inches. The bodies, convertible or hardtop, were built by Vignale of Italy. A floating U-bar was the main feature of the grille design. Standard engine was the contemporary 210-horsepower Cadillac V8, but a hopped-up version with 300 bhp was also available. The car could be fitted with any other V8 to special order. The transmission was a General Motors Dual-Range Hydra-Matic.

Despite the high $10,000 price, Fina deliveries were said to be running about five months behind at one point. Evidently, the market was quickly saturated.

## FITCH (1949; 1961-69)

The first car called Fitch was made by Sports and Utility Motors Inc. of White Plains, New York. It was designed for both competi-tion and general road use, but the emphasis was largely on the sports side. Its originator was John Fitch, a famous race driver, sports-car promoter/builder, and safety expert. Only one prototype was built in 1949.

The Fitch Type B (the prototype was Type A), used the 96-inch-wheelbase Fiat 1100 chassis. Its engine was the small 60-horsepower Ford V8, souped up to yield 105 bhp. This was wrapped in a greatly modified Crosley Hot Shot body. Dry weight was only 1520 pounds. This excellent power-to-weight ratio gave the Fitch a 0–50 mph acceleration time of 6.3 seconds. Top speed was 120 mph.

John Fitch and Co. Inc. at Falls Village, Connecticut started turning out customized Corvairs bearing the name Fitch Sprint beginning in 1961. Performance, handling, and appearance alterations turned the standard 1960-64 Corvair coupe into an outstanding GT. The modifications could be carried out on an existing car or on a brand-new one ordered through Fitch.

The engine kit, costing only $29.00 installed, raised output of the Corvair flat six to 155 bhp. That was good enough for a 0-60 mph time of only 9.5 seconds. Other modifications were available for suspension and steering.

On 1965 and later Corvairs, the Sprint package included a "tunnel" fastback roof, created by attaching a "blade" on each side of the rear window.

An entirely different concept was the Fitch Phoenix, which

Gregory

Griffith

Imp

Jetmobile

Keen Steamliner

King Midget

appeared in 1966. Illustrator Coby Whitmore helped design the body, which has been described as "wickedly beautiful." Body construction was done in Turin, Italy by Frank Reisner's Intermeccanica company. The Phoenix used Corvair running gear, and featured an integrated "targa" rollbar. The front part of the roof was removable. A spare tire was mounted in each front fender, which was humped to clear it. Two spares were needed because the car used two different tire sizes: the fronts were 175×14 while the rears were 185×14. Flying-buttress roof styling was used although the Phoenix was really a notchback. Its reverse-slant rear window could be raised or lowered electrically.

The Phoenix's 2150-pound weight was about 300 pounds lighter than the comparable Corvair. Its wheelbase was 95 inches, total length 174 inches. A modified Corvair engine was used and produced 170 bhp. The car could cruise at 100 mph, but top speed was in excess of 130 mph. Acceleration from 0 to 60 mph took only 7.5 seconds.

A production run of 500 was planned, but the Phoenix project was halted because of the expense involved in meeting federal safety standards, which went into effect for 1968. Only one prototype was built.

## FLETCHER (1954)

The Fletcher Flair was built by Fletcher Aviation Corp. of Rosemead, California. It was a four-wheel-drive, Jeep-type vehicle with an unlikely powerplant—a Porsche 1500cc engine. Riding a 78-inch wheelbase, the Fletcher had an overall length of 126 inches, which could be shortened to 115 by body alterations.

## FLINTRIDGE-DARRIN (1957)

This car, sometimes known as Flintridge Darrin-DKW or Flintridge-DKW, was made by the Flintridge Motor Manufacturing Corp. of Los Angeles. Howard "Dutch" Darrin, who had designed the 1946 Darrin and the Kaiser-Frazer cars, did the styling.

The Flintridge-Darrin was based on the chassis of a German D.K.W. four-door sedan. Darrin's rear-end treatment was unique: concave, with a scalloped decklid lip. The body, supplied by Woodill, was made of fiberglass and made the Flintridge 10 inches longer and 6.5 inches lower than

the D.K.W. It weighed 1870 pounds, about 200 pounds less than the D.K.W. Its price was $3195, compared to $2275 for the D.K.W. sedan. Some 15 of these cars had been made when problems at Woodill cut off delivery of the bodies.

## FORD 1901 REPLICA (1968)

The Ford 1901 Replica was built by the Horseless Carriage Corp. of Ft. Lauderdale, Florida. It was said to be "a ¾-scale replica of a 1901 Ford," but since the first production Ford wasn't built until 1903, this description was obviously inaccurate. Specifications of this replicar, including the engine it used, are not known. Production lasted only a few months.

## FORMACAR (c. 1968)

Marbon Division of Borg-Warner Corp., Washington, West Virginia, built this prototype to demonstrate a new lightweight plastic material called Cycoloc for automotive use. The Formacar's total weight was 2200 pounds. Its 290 cubic-inch, 198-horsepower V8 and transmission accounted for over a third of that. The GT-type body design had a 90-inch wheelbase and a 162-inch overall length. Formacar never reached production.

## FRICK (1955)

The Frick, sometimes called Frick Special, was one of several cars built by Bill Frick Motors of Rockville Centre, New York. Already established as an expert in dropping Cadillac motors into various production cars (see Studillac), Frick decided to build a complete car from the ground up. For it, he devised a box-channel chassis with a 110-inch wheelbase. The independent front suspension consisted of coil springs with unequal-length wishbones. At the rear, semi-elliptic leaf springs were used. Not surprisingly, the engine was a Cadillac and a supercharger was planned. Dual-Range Hydra-Matic transmission completed the drivetrain. The coupe body, not unlike a Ferrari in appearance, was made by Vignale in Italy. The car's all-up weight was 3000 pounds.

## GADABOUT (1945)

The Gadabout was designed and built by industrial designer Ray Russell in his Grosse Pointe Park, Michigan home workshop. The relatively small three-passenger roadster had a wheelbase of

only 80 inches. His prototype consisted of a modern-style "duraluminum" body mounted on an MG chassis and powered by the original British four-cylinder engine. This accounted for its right-hand drive, though production models were to have conventional left-hand drive. An unobtrusive steel tube surrounded the body at bumper height as a crash protection measure. Front or rear engine placement was to be at the customer's option. The lightweight body helped keep the total weight to 1100 pounds, which contributed to claimed mileage of 50 mpg. Maximum speed was 50 mph. The car probably never got beyond the prototype stage.

## GASLIGHT (1960-61)

From Gaslight Motors Corp. of Detroit came this replica of the 1902 Rambler. Weighing 640 pounds, the car had a 77-inch wheelbase. Power was provided by a single-cylinder, 4-horsepower, air-cooled engine. The price was about $1495. Production is believed to have ended sometime around 1961. The Gaslight may have been a successor to the 1902 Rambler Replica.

## GAYLORD (1955-57)

Gaylord Cars Ltd., Chicago, Illinois, was founded by Edward and Jim Gaylord to build an exclusive luxury two-seater. Brooks Stevens of Milwaukee was hired to create the design. Jim Gaylord's concept involved a modern envelope body with classic overtones. Stevens suggested the body be built by his associates at the Spohn Company in Ravensburg, Germany. The Gaylords hoped to introduce a finished prototype at the 1955 Paris Salon.

The Gaylord's retractable roof was ingenious. With the push of just one button, the decklid lifted on a pair of electric supports, then the top was pulled back into the trunk by a chain drive. The roof itself contained a recessed rear window and extractor vents for stale air. Ford stylists took many photos of this system, but the later Ford retractable was much more complicated than the Gaylord.

Jim Gaylord designed the very strong chrome-molybdenum tubular chassis, using coil springs and A-arms for the front suspension and a beam axle with leaf springs at the rear. The suspension made extensive use of rubber; the passenger compartment was absolutely impervious to shock over rough surfaces. The original

engine was a 365-cid Chrysler Hemi V8. Although it scaled close to 4000 pounds, the Gaylord behaved like a 2000-pound sports car. Runs from 0 to 60 mph averaged about eight seconds. Top speed was an easy 120 mph.

Yet the Gaylord failed. It was extremely expensive—the target production price was $17,500—but that wasn't the real problem. Jim Gaylord was a perfectionist, and drove himself to a breakdown during the car's production engineering phase. Gaylord Motors also got into a dispute over quality control with the firm that was to build production models, Luftschiffbau Zeppelin in Freidreichshaven, West Germany. By 1957, the project had been abandoned. Three production chassis were built. Two of them are on display at the Early American Museum in Orlando, Florida.

## GLASCAR (1956)

Glascar was built by Bob Tucker of Richmond, Indiana. The fiberglass body panel molds were made from altered Corvette panels. The grille was different from the Corvette's and incorporated the headlights. A vee'd windshield was used, and there were fins at the rear. The prototype carried an Oldsmobile V8, but a modified flathead Ford V8 was planned for production models. With a 100-inch wheelbase, the Glascar was to have sold for $2500. Whether actual production ever took place is not clear.

## GLASSIC (1966-75)

Jack Faircloth and his son Joel began Glassic Industries Inc. in West Palm Beach, Florida by building fiberglass-bodied cars on International Scout chassis. The Scout's 93.5-horsepower four was retained. Styling was deliberately in the image of the Model A Ford phaeton. Later, a Model-A-styled roadster with rumble seat was also offered. Price was around $3800 when the car first appeared in 1966. However, this rose considerably, reaching $10,000 by the time production ended. In 1967, the Glassic was sold by the famous New York department store of Abercrombie and Fitch under the name Abercrombie Runabout, priced at $5200.

In 1972, Fred Pro bought the business and moved it to larger facilities. The firm's name changed to Glassic Motor Car Co. Changes were made to the cars as well. They switched to the 210-bhp Ford 302 V8 and were available with

Ford automatic transmission. Cruising speed was increased to 70 mph. Sometime in 1976 or 1977 the name was changed to Replicar, and production was continued under that name.

## GOFF (1956)

Charles Goff of Texarkana, Texas offered this $600 kit car—a five-passenger sports model. It used a stock 1939 Ford engine, and a rebuilt '39 Ford chassis. The body consisted of five fiberglass panels. A plastic top was also available. Fully assembled, the car cost $1500. Other engines could be installed at extra charge.

## GORDON (c.1947-48)

Gordon Diamond was a very unusual car built by H. Gordon Hansen of San Lorenzo, California. The name "Diamond" refers to the car's wheel placement: a diamond pattern with one wheel at the front, one at the back, and one on each side. Wheelbase between the front and back wheels was 156 inches, with the side wheels situated halfway in between.

Several advantages were claimed for this unorthodox arrangement. The middle wheels "created a smoother ride." Because the front and rear wheels steered, the Gordon could be pivoted on its middle wheels, resulting in a 12-foot turning circle, extremely short for the car's 214-inch overall length. Whether it managed to stay upright on twisty roads is not known, but a tubular body cage provided protection in case of rollover. A 100-horse-power Ford truck V8 located just ahead of the rear wheel provided power to the middle wheels. The car was capable of 95 mph, which was good for a 3750-pound car and was undoubtedly exciting given the unusual chassis.

Hansen sought financial backing for regular production. Although some interest was expressed, no firm commitment was ever secured.

## GRAHAM (1967)

This replicar effort was intended to bring the 1940 Graham Hollywood back to life. However, it appears the project died soon after the prototype was built. The prototype was shown at a Fort Wayne, Indiana shopping center and, according to maker Bob Gerig, hundreds of inquiries and scores of orders resulted. Even a price was established: $5200 at the factory.

The original Graham Hollywood was made from modified 1937 Cord dies. As is true of many replicars, the new Graham took a bit of license with the original design. Although all production Hollywoods were sedans, the revival was the convertible Graham and Hupp originally hoped to build, but didn't. The revival's body was made of fiberglass and mounted on a Kaiser Jeep chassis. The former freestanding headlight pods were sunk into the fenders, but were not covered as on the original Cord. The grille was from a 1948-50 Packard. The powerplant was a 160-horsepower V6. A removable top was standard equipment.

## GREEN MINI BUG (1968)

Green Mini Bug was made by the Green Leaf Cycle Co., and also by Green Motors Inc., of Livonia, Michigan for a short time in 1968. No description of this car is available.

## GREGORY (1948; 1952-?)

Ben F. Gregory of Kansas City, an avid fan of front-wheel drive, had designed and built cars with this layout between 1918 and 1922. Interestingly, his 1948 design had a rear-mounted engine.

The Gregory was quite small, just 153 inches in overall length. Wheelbase was 94 inches, weight 1800 pounds.

The Gregory's engine was a flat-four Continental rated at 40 horsepower. It was removable by one man in an hour, the company claimed. Only one prototype of this unusual car was built, but Gregory made another try in 1952. This one was a sports car built on a contemporary Porsche chassis and using its 1600cc, 70-bhp engine. Gregory now transplanted the engine to the front of the car, to drive the front wheels. Weight was 1925 pounds, wheelbase 80 inches. The body on production models would have been made of either aluminum or fiberglass.

## GRIFFITH (1964-66)

The first Griffith appeared in 1964 from Griffith Motors of Syosset, New York, which was succeeded by the Griffith Motor Car Co. of Plainview, New York the following year. One-time Ford dealer Jack Griffith designed this car's tubular chassis, then dropped in a Ford 289 V8 with 200 horsepower. The fiberglass body of the British TVR was used.

With a four-speed Ford manual transmission, the Griffith Series 200 could really go: acceleration from 0 to 60 mph took less than four seconds. Its weight was 1850 pounds. The 138-inch-long, two-passenger coupe sold for $3995, but the price later jumped to at least $4800.

Some 285 Griffiths had been made when body deliveries were cut off because the British supplier was going through a reorganization. At about the same time, Griffith acquired the manufacturing rights to the Vetta Ventura.

Consequently, a new model called the GT was introduced, using a body supplied by Intermeccanica of Italy. A new engine was fitted, too. Griffith switched from Ford power to the fairly new 273 cubic-inch Plymouth V8. The hot 235-bhp version was chosen, along with a three-speed Torque-Flite automatic transmission. A four-speed manual gearbox was optional. Other options included leather upholstery instead of vinyl, and air conditioning. Base price for the Griffith GT was $6095. After 1966, this model was known as the Omega. (See Omega.)

## HENNEY (1960-date)

The Henney Kilowatt was an electric car made by the Henney Motor Co. of Canastota, New

Kurtis

Lost Cause

Marketeer

Marketour

Merry Olds

Mohs Ostentatienne

York. It was designed by C. Russell Feldman. Feldman had become chairman of the board and president of National Union Electric Corp., which made Exide batteries. The Henney Motor Co., a division of National Union, was well-respected for its custom limousines and funeral coaches.

The Kilowatt was a very different sort of vehicle. Its body was that of the French-built Renault Dauphine, outfitted with 12 6-volt batteries that powered a 7-horsepower electric motor. A normal 12-volt battery provided power for lights, horn, and windshield wipers. The Kilowatt ran at up to 40 mph, though 30 mph was recommended in order to extend range to 40 miles. The batteries could be charged in eight hours from a conventional 115-volt 30-amp source. Curb weight was 2250 pounds, some 750 pounds heavier than the regular Dauphine, and didn't promise much performance. By the end of 1961, some 47 Kilowatts had been sold, mainly to utility companies across the country. Further development, testing, and production continued until around 1964. Although Henney had ordered 100 Renault bodies, the number of cars it actually built is not known. It seems safe to assume that more Kilowatts were made than any other single U.S. electric car since the first electrics of the early 1900s. Interestingly, they were still available in 1980 from Robert Steven Witkoff of Glen Cove, New York for $5995. These were believed to be leftovers from the Henney production run.

## HONEY BEE (1959)

Honey Bee was made by the Swift Manufacturing Company of El Cajon, California. The same company made several mini-replicars under the name Swift. The Honey Bee was a very small three-wheeler, with one wheel in front and four-cycle Briggs & Stratton 1½-horsepower engine in the rear. The fiberglass body had a teardrop shape, with a low, rounded nose and an open cockpit. Priced at $195 ready to run, the Honey Bee was advertised as "designed for kids between 7 and 77."

## HOPPENSTAND (1948-49)

Hoppenstand Motors Inc. of Greenville, Pennsylvania built this rather odd-looking, two passenger open economy car. A coupe and convertible were also proposed. The design featured a 90-inch wheelbase, with all-inde-

pendent coil suspension, and an overall length of 162 inches. The car's aluminum body kept weight to just 684 pounds.

The Hoppenstand "Firebug" engine was an air-cooled flat twin. Displacement was 21.4 cubic inches for an output of 8.5 horsepower. It was located in the chassis just ahead of the rear axle. An automatic torque converter was also included. The Hoppenstand's base price was around $1000. Top speed was 50 mph, but fuel economy was said to be 35 mpg.

## HUMMINGBIRD (1946)

Hummingbird was the name Talmadge Judd of Kingsport, Tennessee gave to the small car he designed and built in 1946. Only 85 inches long, his two-passenger convertible weighed just 1350 pounds. The body was made of 8-gauge steel, instead of the usual 20-gauge. The four-cylinder engine gave up to 50 mpg and provided a top speed of 70 mph. Despite Judd's ambitious efforts to interest backers in regular production, only the prototype was built.

## HYDRAMOTIVE (c. 1960)

The novel Hydramotive was built by the Hydramotive Corp. of Charlotte, North Carolina, and designed by Durward Willis of that city. The car was the crux of a stock fraud investigation involving more than a million shares. In 1961, the Securities and Exchange Commission uncovered a prototype as part of its investigation. It had no transmission, universal joints, driveshaft, differential, axles, or brakes. These had been promoted as features the Hydramotive would not need. The car did have a diesel engine and was supposed to sell for $1200, but production never got going.

## HYDRO-IMP (1948)

The Hydro-Imp was a buckboard-type vehicle from Centerscope Products Inc. of Glendale, California. A description of this car is lacking. There is a possibility this car is related to the Imp.

## IMP (1948-51)

Although many new small cars were introduced in the late '40s, few were as tiny as the Imp. Several different models were produced over a span of four years, but all held to the original concept of a midget convertible. International Motor Products (whose initials apparently inspired the

name) of Glendale, California intended this little car as transportation for teenagers or as a second car for the family. R. Stanley Griffin, the firm's president, hoped to sell it for $500.

The production prototype of 1949 was powered by a 7½-horsepower Gladden 75 engine, mounted at the rear of the 63-inch-wheelbase chassis. The open, doorless fiberglass-laminate body was supported by a tubular-steel frame. The whole thing weighed only 475 pounds, and was 120 inches long overall. The 3-gallon gas tank provided a range of 180–240 miles. Maximum speed was 35 mph. A tubular bumper completely encircled the car. The 1951 version was even smaller, with a 108-inch overall length. Although styling differed from earlier models, the Imp remained a two-passenger car, using the same powerplant as the 1949 prototype. The price, however, did change—it was now $795.

## INMAN (1946)

Inman was made by Frank Inman of Goose Creek, Texas. Details on this car are not available.

## JETMOBILE (1952)

Jetmobile was an eye-catching three-wheeler, a flight of fancy of Richard Harp in Frederick, Maryland. It was a missile-shaped, single-passenger car made out of an aircraft fuel tank. The odd wheel was at the front, and the engine was at the rear. Originally, a 75-horsepower Lycoming engine provided the Jetmobile with a 110-mph top speed, but later a 60-bhp Ford V8 was used. The builder had plans to add folding rotors so the Jetmobile could become airborne, but that idea (like the car itself) never got off the ground.

## JOHNSONMOBILE (1959)

The Johnsonmobile was a product of Horton Johnson Inc. in the Chicago suburb of Highland Park. A replica of an antique car circa 1904, it had a two-passenger body made of plywood. Only one prototype was built. It was powered by an air-cooled 3-horsepower Clinton engine.

## JOMAR (c.1954-60)

The Jomar appeared about 1954 from the Manchester, New Hampshire firm of Saidell Sports Racing Cars, headed by racing enthusiast Ray Saidell. This was basically a marriage of the British-made TVR

chassis and a specially designed aluminum body (the TVR body was fiberglass). The standard engine was the 71.5 cubic-inch Ford Anglia four-cylinder unit. Various optional engines were offered, including a supercharged version of the Anglia engine and at least three different Coventry-Climax powerplants. Depending on the engine selected, prices ranged from $2995 to $4595.

## KEEN STEAMLINER (c.1955-c.1968)

The original Keen Steamliner was a shortened, modified Plymouth of 1946-48 vintage, converted to steam power. It was the brainchild of Charles F. Keen of Madison, Wisconsin.

Sometime between 1955 and 1968, Keen produced a second car, this one with a modern fiberglass convertible body. In fact, it was the same Victress bodyshell as used for the Williams steamer, often leading to the mistaken belief that they were one and the same. The Keen car had its engine in the rear and the boiler up front, just the reverse of the Williams brothers' design. It also had different style bumpers. The second Steamliner could build up sufficient steam from a cold start for a smooth, powerful takeoff in less than 30 seconds. Conflicting reports mentioned top speeds of 60 mph and 100 mph. The rear-mounted engine was a V4 of unknown origin, and reportedly operated on any distillate fuel, such as kerosene.

By 1968, Thermal Kinetics Corporation of Rochester, New York had acquired Keen's interests. It is unlikely any additional cars were produced by that firm.

## KELLER (1948-50)

Bobbi Motor Car Corporation was reorganized as the Dixie Motor Car Corp. in July 1947. It was at this point that George D. Keller took over. Keller was a respected former general sales manager for Studebaker. The company was reorganized again in November 1947 as Keller Motors Corp. It moved to Huntsville, Alabama, and the car's name was changed to Keller.

The Keller retained the Bobbi-Kar's front-end styling with its low horizontal grille, along with its Torsilastic suspension. Overall length for both convertible and station wagon models was now 171 inches. A choice of a fabric or metal top was offered for the convertible. The Keller featured more

powerful engines than the Bobbi-Kar. A 133-cid 47-bhp Hercules unit or a 162-cid 58-bhp Continental could be ordered. Both body types were offered in two series—the Chief, and the more deluxe Super Chief. The Hercules engine powered the Chief; the Super Chief used the Continental. Fuel consumption of 35.6 mpg was claimed. The three-passenger convertible was available either front- or rear-engined, but the station wagon had its powerplant up front. The wagon was a two-door model, and weighed 2100 pounds. The convertible was 300 pounds lighter. Plastic-fabric upholstery material was used. Base prices started at $895 for the Chief convertible. A double bed was optional for the station wagon.

In 1948, Keller claimed to have a dealer network totaling 1150. Production was supposed to reach an annual rate of 150,000—volume almost as high as Mercury's at the time. But a mere 18 cars had been built by 1949, and the company went bankrupt in the spring of 1950. That was the end of Keller in the United States, although there was an attempt in the early '50s to build a restyled version in Belgium.

### KING MIDGET (1946-69)

Midget Motors Supply Co. later changed its name to Midget Motors Corp. of Athens, Ohio. Its King Midget was one of the more successful new American makes introduced in the postwar period. This tiny economy model was developed by Claud Dry and Dale Orcutt. The earliest 1946 versions were available only as kits. When assembled, the King Midget

looked like a slightly modernized buckboard. At first, a manual transmission was used, but Dry and Orcutt soon produced their own automatic transmission, which then became standard.

In 1951, a redesigned King Midget was offered. Its appearance was more car-like than the original model, and its two-passenger carrying capacity was 100 percent greater. The second-generation model continued through early 1957. A third series was then introduced, and it looked even more conventional.

Until 1966, Wisconsin one-cylinder engines powered the King Midget, rated at 7.3 to 8.5 horsepower. After that, Kohler engines of 9.3 to 12 bhp were fitted. Throughout its history, fuel economy was the King Midget's strongest selling point: it could get up to 60 mpg.

Like Detroit cars, the King Midget grew over the years. Overall length stretched from 96 inches to 117. Yet, the wheelbase was still only 76.5 inches for the third series, which was the largest model. The King Midget also put on weight as it grew older, from around 400 pounds to almost 700. Naturally, prices kept pace—from a low of near $350, rising to just over $1000.

The King Midget came to an end in 1969 after 23 years, a phenomenal run for such a car in the American auto industry. Production over the years amounted to approximately 5000 units.

### KNUDSEN (1948)

The Knudsen was a prototype made by the Knudsen Manufacturing & Design Co. Inc. of Buffalo,

New York. Descriptive details are unavailable.

### KRIM-GHIA (1966)

Krim-Ghia originated at the Krim Car Import Co. of Detroit. Krim designed two different models. Bodies for both were supplied by the famous Ghia coachbuilding house of Italy. A sports model, the 1500 GT was based on the Fiat 1500 and used its 86-horsepower four-cylinder engine. The other model was a roadster based on the Plymouth Barracuda chassis, powered by a 245-bhp Plymouth V8. Production lasted only a few months in 1966.

### KRUEGER (1947)

In 1947, you could order a new Krueger for $15,000 if production had gotten underway as planned. Although that was a whopping sum of money then, consider what you might have had: a sleek, low-slung, boattail roadster with a classic upright grille, rakish windshield, full fender skirts, and a 225-horsepower Marmon V16 powerplant. The chassis was Duesenberg, with a wheelbase of 106 inches. Top speed was said to be 140 miles per hour.

The car began life in 1933-34 in the Los Angeles area, with a Duesenberg Model A straight-eight engine. Some of the other parts were from production cars of that era. It appears Mr. Krueger acquired the car during or after the war and, following a few modifications, had thoughts about selling duplicates of it. It is doubtful any additional cars were produced.

### KURTIS (1948-49)

Racing-car builder Frank Kurtis

claims to have produced America's first postwar sports car, built by his Kurtis-Kraft firm of Glendale, California. From the 1920s through 1948, Kurtis made a name for himself with highly competitive stock-car-based racers—particularly midgets. This vast competition experience accounted for the light, strong, and deceptively simple Kurtis Sport Car. Although 95 percent of its mechanical pieces were stock production-car items, they were carefully packaged for maximum performance.

The Kurtis had a 100-inch wheelbase, measured 68 inches wide and 169 inches long, and weighed only 2300 pounds. Chassis and body were integral. Ten smooth but bulbous body panels were built over this supporting structure. The body was mainly aluminum, with steel doors and a fiberglass hood and deck.

Into this tuned body/chassis Frank Kurtis first installed a supercharged Studebaker Champion engine. The small L-head did not respond as well as he had hoped, so he experimented with a variety of V8s. Ford flatheads with 110 horsepower were used in some cars; others employed the new short-stroke 160-bhp Cadillac engine.

Kurtis' small factory was incapable of high production. Only a handful—estimates are between 20 and 34—were built before he sold out to Earl "Madman" Muntz for $200,000. Later in the '50s Frank Kurtis again built a street/track sports car, the 500S. Based on his tubular-frame Indy racers, it had a spartan, Allard-like body. Kurtis sold about 25 at about $5000 in 1954-55, before

Navajo

Multiplex

Muntz

Nic-L-Silver (Pioneer)

Omega

Panther

dropping them to concentrate on all-out competition machines. A few more cars with smooth fiberglass bodies and Ford V8 power were sold as the Kurtis 500M.

## LAHER (1960-1963)

The Laher was made by the Laher Spring & Electric Car Corp. of Oakland, California and Memphis, Tennessee. It was a two-passenger, three-wheeled, open electric with a single front-mounted wheel. It was little more than a golf cart.

## LARSON (1966-?)

Larson was built by the Larson Boat Works, of Little Falls, Minnesota. Although limited production began in 1966, the car reportedly continued into the '70s. There is little other available information about it.

## LA SAETTA (1955)

During the '50s, there were many cars with bodies made of that new wonder material, fiberglass. The Testaguzza brothers of Detroit joined the parade with their La Saetta (The Thunderbolt). Typical of most fiberglass-bodied cars, it was basically a two-passenger roadster. At least 15 were built, but no two were alike. They differed in engines (primarily Olds 88 and Hudson), windshields, grilles, taillights, dashboards, and other components. Wheelbase was around 110 inches; overall length ranged from 200 to 210 inches. Late in 1955 a linkup was formed with Electronic Motor Car Corporation of Salt Lake City. The result was a turbo-electric called Electronic.

## LAWLER (1948-50)

James H. Lawler of Huntington Park, California was the inventor of this steam-powered conversion of a 1938 Terraplane. There is some indication he carried out similar conversions of other cars at nearby South Gate. Whatever base was used, all conversions were dubbed Lawler Steamobile.

## LOST CAUSE (1963-64)

Lost Cause was the unlikely name of what was actually a Corvair modified by the famous Derham Body Co. of Rosemont, Pennsylvania. It was sold by Charles Farnsley, former mayor of Louisville, Kentucky, and proprietor of Lost Cause Motors.

The car's roof and seats were covered with black leather, and wire wheels were fitted. Most of the special equipment was found inside. The dash panel included an altimeter, compass, and clock, as well as a full complement of rally and racing instruments. The dash, steering wheel, and door panels were finished in hand-rubbed Kentucky burl walnut. Other items included lap robes, fitted luggage, and a picnic hamper. Proclaimed as "the world's most expensive small car," the Lost Cause carried a $23,200 price tag. The only option was an engine modified by John Fitch (see Fitch), which lifted top speed to nearly 120 mph.

## LUPEAR (1963)

George Lupear from Walled Lake, Michigan was formerly with the Ford Motor Company. He had invented jet-propelled water skis and a portable magnetic drill press. His car, an 8-passenger utility vehicle, was constructed with the assistance of Rocco Pugliese. A 6000-pound winch was one of its features. Top speed was 60 mph, and it could get a claimed 40 mpg.

## MK III (1968)

MK III seems to be Fiberfab's Valkyrie with some variations. The Portland, Oregon firm of Auto Craft Northwest marketed this car with either a mid- or rear-engine setup. The buyer had a choice between Chevrolet 327 or 427 cubic-inch V8s for the mid-engine model. The rear-engine version mounted the 164-cid Corvair flat six. Prices were $4600 (rear-engine), $7500 (327 V8), and $12,500 (427 V8). MK III was offered as a limited-production sports car personally built to owner specifications. The interior featured full instrumentation and naugahyde bucket seats flanking a center console. Leather upholstery was an option. MK IIIs were also available in a variety of kits at prices ranging from $895 to $4850.

## MARKETEER (1954-date)

Marketeer was a two-passenger shopping car from Electric Marketeer Manufacturing Co. of Redlands, California. As the name suggests, it was powered by six 6-volt batteries that ran a 3-horsepower electric motor. A range of 30–35 miles between charges was normal. This was a three-wheeler with its single wheel at the front. The top was made of fiberglass. Operating costs of only $1 per month were claimed by the man-

ufacturer. A 1956 Californian model sold for $735. Marketeer electric vehicles are still produced in Redlands by Nordco Electric Vehicle Division.

## MARKETOUR (1964)

Marketour was built in Long Beach, California by Marketour Electric Cars. It was a two-passenger, three-wheel electric with the single wheel at the front. Six heavy-duty batteries, specially engineered for electric cars, provided power for its 36-volt motor. The car had four forward speeds and one reverse. Operating range was 35–40 miles on a single charge. This boxy vehicle had a steel body with a removable leatherette-covered top. Overall length was 84 inches, wheelbase 64 inches. A ¼-ton pickup model was also built.

## MARKETTE (1967-68)

Westinghouse Electric Corp. built this boxy electric. It was 116 inches long and had a 45-horsepower motor. Twelve 6-volt batteries accounted for about half the 1730-pound curb weight. A retractable electric cord for battery recharging was supplied. The batteries were good for at least two years, and could be replaced for about $300. Range was 50 miles, and top speed was 25 mph. Although this was a prototype, production cars were planned to sell for less than $2000. It is believed production did not actually get underway, probably due to lack of buyer interest. The Markette is sometimes confused with the Marketeer because it was made by the Marketeer Division of Westinghouse.

## MARQUIS (1954)

The chassis of this two-door fastback sports coupe was a Renault, presumably the 4CV model. Marquis was to be a rather luxurious small car with a proposed selling price of $3100. The prototype's body was made of aluminum, but production models were to be of "plastic," perhaps fiberglass. The developer was Plasticar of Doylestown, Pennsylvania. The name Plasticar has erroneously been applied to this car.

## MARS II (1966-c.1970)

Mars II, from Electric Fuel Propulsion Inc. of Ferndale, Michigan, was an electric car based on the Renault 10 body.

Power was provided by four 3-

volt battery packs, each consisting of five lead-cobalt batteries. The battery packs alone weighed 1900 pounds, accounting for almost half the car's 4160-pound weight. Dynamic braking charged the batteries during coasting and braking, so the driving range was 60–120 miles between charges. Five-year or 50,000-mile battery life was claimed. Replacement cost for the power packs was around $600. This electric had a top speed of 68 mph, but cruising speed was around 45 to 55 mph. It took just 12 seconds to accelerate from 0 to 40 mph.

## MARTINETTE (1954)

Martinette was built by Martin Development Laboratories in Rochelle Park, New York. James Vernon Martin, an innovative designer, sketched out a three-wheeler in 1932. After many experiments, false-starts, and revisions, a prototype was completed in 1948.

By 1954, Martin's company had been reorganized as the Commonwealth Research Corp. of New York City. Under Commonwealth's auspices a few cars were produced. Like the prototype, they were two- or three-passenger vehicles of teardrop shape, all three-wheelers with the single wheel at the rear. The body was 114 inches long and made by Biehl Autobody. It had wood paneling like a station wagon, hence the new name Stationette (or sometimes, Martin Stationette). Suspended on rubber, the Stationette used no springs, shock absorbers, axles, driveshaft, universal joints, or differential. Its magnetic fluid drive made a clutch unnecessary. The rear-mounted engine was a 24-bhp Hercules four. Maximum speed was between 40 and 45 mph, fuel consumption 60 to 70 mpg. An unknown number of Stationettes were built and sold for $1000 each. One was a panel delivery produced in 1955 based on Martin's designs. The designer sold his business to Bassons Industries Corp. sometime around 1955 or '56. His car was then renamed the Bassons Star.

## MAVERICK (1953-55)

This Maverick was not connected with the Ford Motor Company. Rather, it was made by Maverick Motors of Mountain View, California.

For a three-passenger car, it was quite large. Mounted on a Cadillac chassis, it had a wheelbase of 122 to 128 inches, and its length was 16 feet. The sleek

fiberglass body was available with one, two, or no doors.

A spun-copper instrument panel incorporated a Stewart-Warner vacuum gauge/tachometer, and 160-mph speedometer, among others. Plastic was used for the upholstery. Although the floor was made of half-inch marine plywood, it was impregnated with special resin, then coated with sound-deadening material. A Cadillac engine with Borg-Warner overdrive was used. Only about seven cars had been completed when production came to an end in 1955.

## MCDONOUGH (1959-65)

McDonough, Georgia was the home of the Tin Lizzie and the Buckboard, small cars made primarily for youngsters by McDonough Power Equipment, Inc. The Tin Lizzie Model T-10 Torpedo was a half-scale replica of a 1910 Ford Model T. A 3-horsepower engine propelled the fiberglass-and-steel-bodied car up to 10 miles per hour on driveways, parks, etc. (it was not intended for road use). Although built for youngsters, it had "ample power and strength for hauling two adults." Fully assembled, the Tin Lizzie sold for $353.00; in kit form, minus engine, the price was $249.50.

## MERCURY SPECIAL (1946)

Mercury Special was built by

Paul Omohundro of Los Angeles, who put an aluminum sports-car body on a Mercury chassis. Though Omohundro contemplated using Cadillac power, the original Mercury engine was retained. Hopes of getting this car into production were dashed by postwar material shortages.

## MERRY OLDS (1958-62)

Merry Olds was billed as the car with "the backward look" (contrasting with Chrysler Corporation's "forward look" slogan of that time). It emulated the original curved-dash Olds of 1903 and was built by American Air Products, a Fort Lauderdale, Florida firm. Construction was of plywood and steel. Power came from a Clinton 4-horsepower air-cooled single, which drove the left rear wheel by chain. The car had two forward speeds and one reverse, plus an automatic clutch. Top speed was 35 mph, fuel economy an astonishing 67 mpg.

## MERRY RUNABOUT (c.1960)

The Merry Runabout, from Greg-San Klassic Kars of Glendale, California, was a half-scale replica of the curved-dash 1903 Olds. A Lawson 2.5-horsepower four-cycle engine was used. Top speed was 15 mph. A two-passenger novelty vehicle, it was only 65 inches long and weighed a mere 190 pounds.

## MIDGET (date unknown)

Midget was built by Greenfield-Lippman in Buffalo, New York and may be related to the Playboy. However, no other information about this car is available.

## MIGHTY MITE (1953)

Once again, front-wheel drive advocate Ben F. Gregory presented a new vehicle design. This time, however, it was a full-time four-wheel-drive Jeep-like vehicle. Mid-America Research Corporation of Wheatland, Pennsylvania had great hopes for getting this small, versatile vehicle into production with a wide range of body types. The combination of a light engine, aluminum body, and small size (64-inch wheelbase, 96-inch length) made this lightweight (1496-pound) vehicle ideal for the Marines as a transport vehicle for airborne assaults. The prototype's air-cooled Porsche engine was to be replaced in production versions by a modified Lycoming 65-horsepower aircraft engine.

## MINICAR (1969)

Minicars Inc. of Goleta, California designed this small three-passenger machine with big-car features like automatic transmission and air conditioning. In spite of its short dimensions, it had 40 inches of legroom. Overall length was a modest 108 inches. A 164-cid air-cooled six was

used. The anticipated price of $2500 was based on production volume of 25,000 units annually, but it's doubtful the project ever went beyond the 1969 prototype.

## MOBILETTE (c.1965)

The Mobilette was made by Mobilette Electric Cars, Long Beach, California. There is no description of this car available, other than the fact that it was an electric runabout.

## MOHS (1967-78)

The first Mohs car was not built until 1967, though Bruce Baldwin Mohs' Madison, Wisconsin company dates back to 1948.

The monstrous Ostentatienne Opera Coupe tipped the scales at 5740 pounds, and measured 246 inches long and 69 inches high. Overhang was considerable, since the wheelbase was only 119 inches.

International Harvester supplied the chassis to Mohs specifications, as well as a 304-cubic-inch V8 with 193 horsepower. Optional were a huge 549-cid V8, which developed 250 bhp, and a five-speed manual transmission. The larger engine was claimed to give the car a top speed of 115 mph; with the smaller engine, 100 mph was the maximum.

Here are just a few items from the Ostentatienne's long list of equipment: quartz-iodine headlights, sealed-beam taillights,

Playboy (station wagon prototype)

Powell

Rockefeller Yankee

Rollsmobile

Rowan Electric

Ruger

wide whitewall 7.50×20 tires by Denman (the inner tubes filled with pure nitrogen), water-cooled automatic transmission, removable skylight, butane furnace-heater, 24-karat gold inlaid walnut-covered instrument panel, 3/4-inch Ming Dynasty-style carpet with 3/8-inch pad, and velvet upholstery. All this cost $19,600 in the late '60s, with the 549 V8 priced at $25,600.

Understandably, the demand for such an expensive, unorthodox package was extremely limited, and production generally ran to about three or four cars per year. Nevertheless, the model was ostensibly in production through 1978, at least. An additional model, the Safarikar, was introduced in 1971. It was described as a dual-cowl phaeton with metal top, and sold for $14,500.

## MOTA (1953)

Mota came from Banning Electric Products Corp. Automotive Division of New York City. It had a fiberglass body and was a gas-electric hybrid.

## MOTORETTE (1947-48)

At first glance, it appeared to be a motor scooter. Its two-passenger capacity and three wheels, however, took it out of the scooter class—barely. Raising the rear hood exposed a 4.1-horsepower, one-cylinder air-cooled engine. Power was transmitted to the left rear wheel by chain drive. Luggage was stored under the bench seat or in a front storage compartment under a tiny hinged lid. In place of a steering wheel was a sort of handlebar. Total weight was 380 pounds. Overall length was only 90 inches, and wheelbase was just 60 inches. Tires were 4.00×8. Motorette Corporation of Buffalo, New York sold it complete with pushbutton starter, horn, lights, mechanical brakes, and 6-volt battery for only $495. The company is said to have gone bankrupt in 1948.

## MULTIPLEX (1952-54)

Multiplex was built by the Multiplex Manufacturing Co. of Berwick, Pennsylvania. From 1912 to 1915, this firm built a very good car, but production was limited to scarcely more than a dozen units. Multiplex tried for a second time after World War II (its primary business was the manufacture of Crispin air valves).

The postwar Multiplex was a two-passenger sports model made from proprietary compo-nents. Willys F-head four- and six-cylinder engines were used, modified to develop 87 and 124 horsepower, respectively. The car's frame was a tubular truss-type. A transverse spring and wishbones made up the independent front suspension.

Only three cars were built from 1952 to 1954.

## MUNTZ (1949-54)

Earl "Madman" Muntz had been a promoter since the age of 12, when he bought old Model Ts, fixed them up, and sold them at a profit. He opened a used-car lot in his hometown of Elgin, Illinois in the early '30s. Later he began selling car radios. Through 1940, Muntz rapidly built a small sales empire. When Frank Kurtis decided to quit the auto business, the Madman bought him out. The Muntz Car Company built 28 Muntz Jets in Glendale before moving to Evanston, Illinois. There another 366 Jets were built between 1950 and 1954.

As a two-seater, the Kurtis lacked broad appeal, so wheelbase was increased in the transformation to Muntz. Cars built in Glendale measured 113 inches, those built in Evanston 116 inches, compared to the 100-inch wheelbase of the Kurtis. As quickly as he could, Muntz switched body construction from aluminum to steel, which was not only more durable but cheaper. The Jet sold for $5000-$6000.

Muntz also changed the running gear. Kurtis had been using a 3.73:1 rear axle ratio, which Muntz said "would just unravel" the Cadillac V8. So, he installed a 3.24:1 rear axle that made the Jet a bit slower off the line than the Kurtis, but faster at the top end. According to Muntz, a Jet would do 128 mph. After the move to Illinois, Muntz switched to the flathead 336.7-cid Lincoln V8 with 154 horsepower. These heavy engines had an adverse effect on handling, and later Jets were hardly the ground huggers the Kurtis had been. However, the Jet was by no means unexciting to drive. Acceleration from 0 to 60 mph took 9–12 seconds; top speed was around 110 mph.

Muntz stopped building his sports car for the same reason as a lot of other custom car producers. He was losing money—about $1000 per car, he said—through lack of volume.

## MURENA (1969-70)

The Murena was a luxury two-door sports station wagon con-ceived by Joseph Vos, an importer of British cars for Murena Motors Ltd. of New York City. The cars were built by Intermeccanica of Turin, Italy. A 360-horsepower, 429 cubic-inch Ford V8 provided the power. The vehicle was 205 inches long on a 118-inch wheelbase. Weight was approximately 3770 pounds. An indication of the car's luxury was its $14,950 price.

## MUSTANG (1948)

The Mustang was designed by Roy C. McCarty of the Mustang Engineering Corp. in Seattle. Earlier, McCarty had been service manager of the Ford Motor Company's Lincoln Division. With its flat front, the Mustang looked much like a bus in the head-on view. It also had a sloping rear end.

The 59-horsepower rear-mounted Hercules four was accessible by a door on the left side. A tubular-steel frame with a 102-inch wheelbase was used, and the body was aluminum. The Mustang had room for six people: two in front and four in the back. It was expected this unusual car would sell for $1235, but volume production was not achieved.

## NASH-HEALEY (1950-55)

George Mason, president of Nash-Kelvinator Corporation, Kenosha, Wisconsin, met English rally driver and car designer Donald Healey in 1949. Their conversation naturally led to cars, and soon an idea hatched: why not build a Nash-based two-seater, powered by the big 235 cubic-inch Nash six? The result was one of the first Anglo-American hybrids.

The overhead-valve Nash six was a strong, modern unit capable of a fair amount of "hotting up," as Healey quickly found. He fitted it with a pair of British SU carburetors, a hot cam, and an 8:1 compression aluminum cylinder head. The result was a healthy 125 horsepower at 4000 rpm. Healey combined the three-speed Nash transmission with Borg-Warner overdrive, hammered out a racing body—a smooth envelope with a large headrest—and entered the car in Italy's Mille Miglia endurance race. It finished ninth in its class. For Le Mans, two N-Hs were entered. One finished fourth overall behind two Talbots and a Jaguar. A year later, a lone N-H was sixth overall, and fourth in class.

With performance and durability established, Mason and Healey worked toward putting the car into production. Aluminum bodies were built by Panelcraft Ltd. in England. Healey's company in Warwickshire did the rest of it. Onto the British roadster styling, a Nash grille, badge, headlights, bumpers, and other trim parts were bolted on. Production began in mid-1950. By early 1951, Healey was shipping 10 cars a week to the United States. The '51 model listed for $4063. Wheelbase was 102 inches, and curb weight was around 2700 pounds. Nash sold 104 for the model year.

Mason didn't care much for Healey's slab-sided aluminum body with its two-piece, flat-pane windshield. So for 1952, he called in Pininfarina. Headlights were mounted inboard, a two-bar grille between them; the windshield was one-piece and slightly curved; the rear fenders had a pronounced bulge, which broke up the slab-sided look. The body was now all-steel—cheaper and easier to repair than aluminum. By careful engineering, curb weight was actually reduced. The 1952 version sold for much more—$5868—but production increased to 150 units for the model year. In late 1952, Nash fitted a larger 4.1-liter (253-cid) engine that developed 135 bhp at 4000 rpm. This was fitted to most cars for 1953 and later.

For the 1953 model year, 162 Nash-Healeys were produced and a coupe model was added on a longer 108-inch wheelbase, probably the prettiest in the series. Prices were now $5444 for the convertible and $5899 for the coupe. The '53 convertible weighed 2700 pounds, the coupe 2970.

Hardtop models proved relatively popular, so the convertible was dropped for '54. The coupe was modified with a three-piece wraparound rear window instead of the one-piece backlight, and the rear side glass was raked back at the top. A total of 90 coupes were built for '54. Some leftovers were registered as 1955 models. In the end, volume was not sufficient to sustain the project.

## NAVAJO (c.1954)

The Navajo was made by Navajo Motor Car Co. of New York City. One source names the maker as Jim Craig of Rumson, New York.

The Navajo was a three-passenger sports car. Bucket seats had not yet made much impression on Americans, so it had a simple bench seat. A Mercury flathead V8 tweaked up to 130 horsepower was used. A 0–60 mph acceleration time of 7.8 seconds was quoted. The car's most striking

feature was its styling, a close copy of the Jaguar XK-120.

## NORVELL (1946)

The Norvell was named for its builder, Jack Norvell of Los Angeles. A description of this car is not currently available.

## NU-KLEA (1959-60)

Despite its name, the Nu-Klea, from Nu-Klea Automobile Corp. of Lansing, Michigan, was a small electric and not an atomic-powered car. Each rear wheel was driven by a separate motor. The steel chassis carried a fiberglass body in either convertible or hard-top style. A range of 75–85 miles per charge was claimed. This two-passenger car was suspended by leaf springs at the rear and coil springs in front.

## OLDS 1901 REPLICA (1968)

The Olds 1901 Replica came from the Horseless Carriage Corp. of Fort Lauderdale, Florida. It was a ¾-scale facsimile of the early curved-dash Olds runabout.

## OMEGA (1967-68)

The stillborn 1966 Griffith GT was given new life in 1967 as the Omega. The car was taken over by Suspensions International Corporation of Manhasset, New York, though actual construction was carried out by Holman and Moody of Charlotte, North Carolina. Steve Wilder, former technical editor of *Car and Driver* magazine, was the head of Suspensions International. The only major change made by the new firm was a switch from the Griffith's Plymouth V8 to a Ford 289 V8 engine and driveline. The price was $8250. For 1968, the 302 Ford V8 was listed as a factory-installed option for $400. Base price had now risen to $8950. As before, the steel bodies were made by Intermeccanica in Turin, Italy.

After this point, the car continued in production for several years as the Torino, Italia, and IMX. All were presumably assembled by Intermeccanica.

## PANDA (1955-56)

The Panda, from Small Cars Inc. of Kansas City, was a $1000, two-passenger vehicle built on a 70-inch wheelbase. A fiberglass roadster body styled like a child's pedal car was mounted on a frame of the manufacturer's own design. The top was a two-piece plastic affair, which could be stored in the trunk. A choice of a 44 cubic-inch

Aerojet four-cylinder engine or a 67-cid Kohler flat twin was announced for 1956 (the 1955 prototype sported a Crosley engine).

## PANKOTAN (1940)

Paul Pankotan of Miami, Florida is the only reference to this vehicle, aside from a 1940 build date. Specifications are not currently available.

## PANTHER (1962-c.1963)

The Panther Automobile Co. in Bedford Hills, New York made this two-passenger fiberglass sports car of very sleek appearance. Two models were available, each using a 157.4 cubic-inch Daimler V8 that developed 145 horsepower. In the deluxe model M, higher compression and twin carburetors raised output to 190 bhp. The M could hit 150 mph, and the standard model 130 mph.

Coil springs were used for the independent front suspension, while semi-elliptic leaf springs and radius rods were employed at the rear. The Bendix brakes were self-adjusting. A 94-inch wheelbase was used for both models. Prices were $4250 for the standard version and $4995 for the M.

## PAXTON (1951-54)

Sometimes known as the Paxton Phoenix, this was a five-passenger car from Paxton Engineering Co. of Los Angeles. This was the same firm that supplied superchargers to Studebaker in the early '60s. Brooks Stevens did the styling for the fiberglass hardtop body. The top was designed to open and close electrically: when open, it moved backwards and rested on the rear deck. A "torque-box" frame weighing 160 pounds was used. Wheelbase was 118 inches.

At least two possible engines were considered. The more interesting of these was a 120-horsepower three-cylinder steamer. A compound six-cylinder steam engine was also under development. Much of this engine work was done by none other than Abner Doble, who had created the advanced Doble steam cars of 1914-1931.

Despite the Paxton's top-notch technical backing, it ultimately didn't run on steam. A rear-mounted Porsche 1500 engine was fitted instead. Production costs convinced builder Robert Paxton McCulloch not to pursue the program, which ended in 1954.

## PECO BUCKAROO (1957)

Another of the "buckboard" type vehicles, the Buckaroo was produced by Production Engineering Company (PECO) of Austell, Georgia. This small, inexpensive off-road "fun" car was powered by a 3-horsepower rear-mounted engine. The basic white-ash frame, steel fenders, and fiberglass cowling (with the "smart continental look") rode on 12-inch wheels, and a 57⅜-inch wheelbase. A top speed of 18 miles per hour was attainable in this 185-pound car.

## PERRYMOBILE (1942-45)

The Perrymobile Company of Los Angeles and a build date of 1942-45 are the only pieces of information currently available about this vehicle. The time span would suggest a small runabout designed to run on miniscule quantities of rationed gasoline, or powered by electricity.

## PIONEER (1959-c.1960)

Pioneer, Lippencott Pioneer, and Nic-L-Silver are names that have been variously applied to this electric model made by the Nic-L-Silver Battery Co. of Santa Ana, California. Whatever the name, the design featured twin motors to drive the rear wheels. By flipping a simple toggle switch, the driver could put the car in forward or reverse. Depending on driving conditions, load, and speed, range was 40–100 miles between battery charges. The batteries could be charged overnight from 110- or 220-volt outlets.

Offered in sport coupe, hardtop, and station wagon styles, the Pioneer used fiberglass body construction. Proprietary production-car wheels, axles, and brakes were incorporated. Suspension was of the trailing-arm, torsion-bar type. Overall length was 157 inches and curb weight was 1800 pounds. Production ended in late 1959 or early 1960.

## PIRANHA (1967)

Piranha was made by AMT Corp. of Phoenix, Arizona with essentially the same lower body styling as the 1964 experimental CRV. Cycolac plastic was used for the body, which had hidden headlights and gullwing doors. A tilt-type steering wheel was also featured. By mid-1967, only five or six cars had been constructed. The project ended shortly thereafter. Price for this two-passenger car was to have been around $6000.

## PLAYBOY (1947-51)

Playboy was the much-publicized minicar of the Playboy Motor Car Corp. of Buffalo, New York.

Former Packard salesman Louis Horowitz was president of the Playboy company. The vice-president was Charles D. Thomas, formerly of Pontiac. Experimental work on the car had begun before U.S. entry into World War II. A prototype appeared as early as 1940. Although Horowitz expected production to reach 100,000 cars annually, just 90–97 were built over the make's short four-year lifetime.

The Playboy was a three-passenger convertible, with a factory-undercoated unit body. A normal fabric top was found on some of the very first examples, but the famous folding steel top soon became a Playboy trademark. It could be opened or closed by hand from within the car.

A Hercules 40-horsepower four was used in most Playboys, although some had a Continental engine of similar displacement. The manufacturer claimed fuel consumption of 25 mpg for city driving, and 30 mpg for the country. Two of the car's more noteworthy mechanical features were a three-speed Warner Gear automatic transmission and self-adjusting brakes. On a 90-inch wheelbase, the 2035-pound Playboy had an overall length of 155 inches.

## POWELL (1954-56)

The Powell Sport Wagon was unusual in several ways. Although registered and sold as new, it incorporated remanufactured Plymouth parts. It was a full-sized model, selling initially for only $998. The Powell concept of a relatively low-slung pickup on a passenger-car chassis was later popularized by Ford's Ranchero and Chevrolet's El Camino. Though not unattractive, the Sport Wagon's appearance was rather boxy and plain, contributing to the ease and low cost of building it. The body was steel, except for a fiberglass nose panel. The rebuilt chassis and 90-horsepower engine were from Plymouths of the '40s and '50s. Overall length was 14 feet 9 inches, wheelbase was 117 inches, height was 5 feet 8 inches.

Powell Manufacturing Company (brothers Channing and Hayward) of Compton, California had been a motor scooter manufacturer before switching to larger

vehicles. By 1956, the price of the Sport Wagon (pickup) had reached $1195 (standard) and $1295 (deluxe), and a station wagon ($1525) had been added to the line. Approximately 2200 pickups and 200 station wagons were sold through a very limited dealer network.

## POWER CAR (1953-67)

Although designed mainly for children, some of these little vehicles were promoted as adult fun cars. The 1953 Power Car Jr. was powered by a modified starter motor from a Ford V8. In appearance it resembled a miniature tractor with wheels. The distributor was Mystic River Sales Company of Mystic, Connecticut. The Power Car Company, also of Mystic, was the maker of the electric powered Thunderbird Jr. from 1955 to 1957. The 1957 version and a miniature '57 Mercury (Big M Junior) were available with a 2-cycle, 2-horsepower gasoline engine at extra cost. In 1965, the Thunderbird Jr. and Mustang Jr. were available in children's models with electric power, or with either 20-mph gasoline engines or 5-mph electric motors for "adult fun."

## PUBLIX (1947-48)

The Publix was announced in 1947 by the Publix Motor Car Co., which claimed to have factories in Buffalo, New York, and across the river in Canada at Fort Erie, Ontario. It was a two-passenger three-wheeler with a choice of fabric or plexiglass top. The single wheel was at the front. An aluminum tube frame was used, along with an aluminum body. Aluminum engines ranging from 1.7 to 10.4 horsepower were considered. A feather-light vehicle, Publix weighed only 150 to 250 pounds. On a 50-inch wheelbase, its overall length was 72 inches.

The steering wheel could be positioned for driving on either side of the car. The starter was the simple pull-type and a belt-drive transmission was used. Speeds of 40-60 mph were attainable, depending on the engine, and claimed fuel economy was in the 70-90 mpg range.

One B. de H. McCloskey designed the Publix, and planned to build 1000 a week, mostly for export. However, there's reason to believe not everything was right about the company. Company offices were said to be located in Newark, New Jersey and Wilmington, Delaware, but the Newark address was nothing more than a mailbox.

## PUP (1948-49)

Two quite differently styled cars were proposed under the Pup nameplate. One was a very basic open two-seat roadster with four separate fenders and no doors or top. The other, presumably a later design, was an enclosed coupe with slab-sided styling. Features included side curtains and a full-perimeter rubber bumper. Both models were to be available with an automatic clutch and choice of a 7.5-horsepower single-cylinder Briggs & Stratton engine, or a 10-bhp two-cylinder unit. The bodies of both were of wood; varying reports indicated plywood or pressed-wood construction. Fuel consumption was in the 50-60 mpg range, top speed was 35-40 mph, and prices were $500-$600. The maker was Pup Motor Car Company of Spencer, Wisconsin.

## QUANTUM (1962-63)

The Quantum was a rebodied Saab, built by Quantum Corp. of Rockland, Massachusetts. Mechanical components, including the 42-horsepower three-cylinder, two-stroke engine and front-wheel drive, were naturally of Saab origin. The Quantum was 150 inches long, eight inches less than the Saab; its 85-inch wheelbase was a foot shorter. Curb weight was a light 900 pounds. The car was distributed through individual Saab dealers in the U.S.

## RAMBLER 1902 REPLICA (c.1959-60)

The Rambler 1902 Replica was another old-time revival of American Air Products of Fort Lauderdale, Florida (see Merry Olds). In 1960, production was taken over by Gaslight Motors Corp. of Lethrup Village, Michigan. In view of this, it seems reasonable to assume the Rambler Replica was a predecessor of the 1960 Gaslight.

## RIK-MOBILE (1948)

Rik as in rickshaw, mobile as in motorized transportation tells the story. China Engineering Corporation of San Francisco must have seen a market for a three-place, three-wheeled motor scooter to replace the venerable rickshaw. The first model was shipped to China for demonstration purposes. Steering was controlled by handlebars, the throttle by a right-hand grip. Clutch and brake pedals were conventionally positioned on the floorboard. Top speed was only 35 miles per hour.

Fuel consumption was a thrifty 80 miles per gallon.

## ROADABLE (1946)

Roadable, from the Southern Aircraft Division, Portable Products Corp. of Garland, Texas was a car/plane combination designed and built by Ted Hall. Only one example is thought to have been constructed.

A three-wheel design, the Roadable had its single wheel mounted at the front. The two rear wheels and the propeller aided in take-off. When airborne, the wheels disengaged from the drive, and ailerons and elevators were controlled by the steering wheel. A Franklin 130-horsepower engine powered this machine, which could cruise at about 110 mph in the air with a range of 600 miles. Only five minutes were required to remove the wings, twin-boom tail section, and propeller in converting the vehicle for road use. Such items might then, presumably, be left at the airport. On the highway, the Roadable could travel at speeds up to 60 mph.

## ROADPLANE (1945)

Roadplane was designed by Norman Davidson, an engineer with Consolidated Aircraft Co. in San Diego. Consolidated was not involved with this project, although as the name implies this vehicle could be driven as a car or flown as a plane. The 36-foot wings and other airplane controls were detachable. A 75-horsepower air-cooled engine powered this three-wheeler. There is some indication the prototype may not have been completed.

## ROAD RUNNER (1963)

Road Runner was made by the Cyclone Sales Co. of Los Angeles. No further description is obtainable at present.

## ROCKEFELLER YANKEE (1953)

A tough, durable body of fiberglass and Vibrin was the main feature of this four-passenger sports car. Designer Warren Shiber had a liking for Ford products, hence the Ford V8 engine, clutch, gearbox, rear end, and springs. Even the frame was modified Ford. For $2500 you would get a 2000-pound car that could do 100 miles per hour tops, and 0 to 60 mph in 12 seconds. And if you should damage the body (molded by Lunn Laminates of Long Island) a repair kit was provided so you

could fix it up in a hurry. Dimensionally, the car had a 100-inch wheelbase, 66-inch width, and 14-foot overall length. The Yankee featured full Stewart-Warner instrumentation, including a tachometer. The tires were 6.00 × 16. Rockefeller Sports Car Corp. of Rockville Centre, New York expected this car to get 25 miles or more per gallon.

## ROCKET (1948)

The Rocket car, from Hewson Pacific Corp. of Los Angeles, was a three-passenger model riding a 106-inch wheelbase, with a 161-inch overall length. Two engines were available, either a 65-horsepower four or a 95-bhp six. With either engine, a torque-converter automatic transmission was standard. Top speed was 75 mph for the four and 95 mph for the six. The body consisted of ten aluminum panels, and the styling was simple and attractive. Price was around $1500. Very few of these cars were made.

## ROLLSMOBILE (1958-c.1961)

Rollsmobile was a replicar from Fort Lauderdale, Florida. It was made by Starts Manufacturing Co. from 1958 to around 1960, then by the Horseless Carriage Corp. for a short time. Two models were offered, each slightly smaller than the original that inspired them. One was based on the 1901 Olds, the other on the "1901" Ford. (Since the first production Ford appeared in 1903, the latter designation is incorrect.) Power came from an air-cooled 3-horsepower Continental engine, and top speed was 30 mph. Gas consumption was a commendable 100 mpg.

## ROWAN (1967-69)

The tiny Rowan electric was built by Rowan Controller Co. of Westminster, Maryland, and/or Oceanport, New York. It was a closed electric runabout with a pleasant-looking Ghia body. Some of its mechanical parts were from DeTomaso. The car used the dynamic-braking method of generating power during coasting and deceleration. Its range was a remarkable 200 miles between charges.

## RSL (c. 1969-?)

The RSL came from RSL Corporation of Cleveland. Although it seems to have been made for a number of years starting in 1969, there is no available data on the car's specifications.

## RUGER (1969-c.1972)

The Ruger was built by Sturm Ruger & Co. Inc. of Southport, Connecticut, the famous gun maker. A replica, it was inspired by the 4.5-liter Bentley tourer. The Ruger used fiberglass body panels covered with naugahyde to imitate the leather-covered Bentley body. Semi-elliptic leaf springs were used all around. The wheelbase was 131 inches, overall length was 186 inches. The engine was a 427 cubic-inch, 425-horsepower Ford V8, which gave 0–60 mph acceleration of about 7.7 seconds—very good for a 3535-pound car. A maximum speed of 110 mph was claimed. The price was $13,000. Production continued into the early 1970s.

## RUSSELL (1946)

Raymond Russell of Detroit, a former Ford Motor Co. employee, was behind this mechanically unusual car. It used hydraulic four-wheel drive: the main engine pumped oil through a motor at each wheel. There were seven to 15 forward speeds. The car was claimed to be smoother-running than a steamer, and to have more power in low gear than any other car. Braking was accomplished by slowing the oil flow, or reversing it. There was no need for a transmission or driveshaft. A plywood body on an experimental chassis helped keep total weight to around 2000 pounds. A year earlier, Russell had built the Gadabout.

## SAVAGE (1968-69)

If you had a yen for a Plymouth Barracuda but wanted something hotter than the factory could provide, and perhaps a customized appearance as well, Auto Craft Company was happy to oblige. The Fond du Lac, Wisconsin company equipped convertibles or coupes with 343, 383, or 440 Magnum engines with carburetor and manifold modifications. The suspension was stiffened up a bit. The GT image was aided by the addition of custom aluminum wire wheels, special grille, custom fiberglass hood and decklid (with integral spoiler), and exposed chrome exhausts below the rocker panels. The interior was not overlooked, either. The real wood dashboard contained full instrumentation, and the steering wheel was also wood. An all-vinyl bucket-seat interior was standard, complete with wall-to-wall loop-pile carpeting.

## SAVIANO (1960)

Saviano Scat was built by Saviano Vehicles Inc. in Warren, Michigan. "Scat" was an acronym for Saviano Cargo and Touring, and was apt for this vehicle: a go-anywhere two-door, four-passenger Jeep-type car. The rear seats could be folded down for additional cargo space. The frame was made of welded rectangular tubing. The body used 16-gauge steel, twice the thickness of that commonly used. The doors were easily removable. Steel or canvas tops were optional, and could also be removed. The engine was an air-cooled 25-horsepower Kohler unit teamed with a three-speed Borg-Warner transmission. This 1700-pound vehicle had an 80-inch wheelbase, and was priced at $1395.

## SCOOTER CAR (1947)

The Scooter Car, the product of an unknown manufacturer, was a two-passenger vehicle available in several forms. One 5-horsepower model lacked a conventional body and was fitted only with angular mud guards. A 7.5-bhp model had a full body, while a third variation had only front-end body panels. Production lasted only a few months.

## SCOOTMOBILE (c.1946; 1952)

Scootmobile was the result of efforts by three Corunna, Michigan men: Norman Anderson, Vernon Servoss, and Lester Sworthwood. Their car made use of many aircraft parts. The body was a modified auxiliary fuel tank that rolled on airplane wheels, two in front and one at the rear. Top speed was a moderate 40 mph, although 70 mph was claimed. Production plans for this $350 car, which included automatic transmission, never materialized.

Anderson moved to Owasso, Michigan, and made another Scootmobile in 1952. Like the first version, this was a three-wheeler with the lone wheel at the back. A 12-horsepower two-cycle engine was also rear-mounted. Overall length of this torpedo-shaped roadster was about 108 inches.

## SEAGRAVE (1960)

Seagrave was a stab at the growing compact-car market made by Seagrave Fire Apparatus Co. in Columbus, Ohio. Three prototypes were built, all on a 93-inch wheelbase. Two had fiberglass bodies, while the third was made of aluminum. A four-cylinder Continental engine gave the 1700-pound car a top speed of 75-80 mph. Seagrave hoped to sell it for under $3000, but the car never saw production.

## SKORPION (1952-54)

The Skorpion, made by the Wilro Co. of Pasadena, California, was a pleasant looking, low-priced, fiberglass sporty car that received rather wide publicity in its day. It was sold as a kit for just $445, or fully assembled for $1200. The Skorpion was designed to accept several different chassis and engines. The best combination was the Crosley Hot Shot chassis and the Ford flathead V8/60. On this 80-inch wheelbase, the little car tipped the scales at just over 1000 pounds. A Super Skorpion with opening doors instead of cut-down sides was advertised for $640.

## SKYLINE (c.1953)

Skyline was produced by Skyline Inc. of Jamaica, New York. Skyline was a two-passenger hardtop-convertible. Its L-head, 85-horsepower six, along with its chassis and most lower body panels, were shared with the Henry J. The grille resembled that of the 1951 Nash. At the push of a button, the top swung completely out of sight. Many safety features were incorporated. The instrument panel was leather-covered, and all knobs and switches were located on a console between the seats. High-back seats and safety belts with shoulder harnesses were standard. The Skyline was intended to sell for less than $3000.

Seagrave

Skorpion

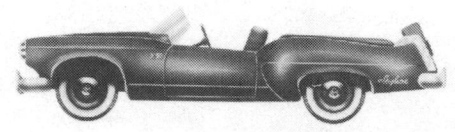

Skyline

Stout Project Y

Stutz

Swift-T

# Minor Makes

## SPOOK ELECTRIC (1968)

"Charge Now—Drive Later" was Dynamic Development's advertising slogan for its version of the small electric town car. The Pasadena, California firm touted it as the first modern production electric. It was, in fact, typical of many such designs that did not succeed. A 36-volt DC ball-bearing motor was connected to the rear wheels by a chain drive. Six 6-volt batteries completed the power package. The steel-and-fiberglass body rested on a steel-channel frame. The car weighed only 750 pounds, and was 99 inches long and 41 inches high. The suspension was by coil springs, with all four wheels independently sprung. Tires were 500×8s.

## STAR DUST (1953)

Star Dust was made in Los Angeles, presumably by the Grantham Motor Car Co. There was a close connection between the Grantham kit car and the Star Dust. The latter was possibly the assembled version. Star Dust used an altered Ford chassis with a 110-inch wheelbase. The engine was also Ford, but located five inches lower and 19 inches farther back in the chassis than normal. Weight was 2650 pounds. Estimated price was $3750.

## STARLITE (c.1959-?)

Starlite, manufactured by Kish Industries Inc. of Lansing, Michigan, may also have been known as the Kish. It was an electric sports model, with an 82-inch wheelbase and an overall length of 148 inches. A soft-top version was produced, and a clear-plastic hardtop model was planned. Prices were around $3000.

## STORM (1954)

Storm was a short-lived product of Sports Car Development Corp. in Detroit. Details are quite sketchy. It had a two-passenger Bertone body and 250-horsepower Dodge V8, but little other information about it is available.

## STORY (1950)

The Story was constructed by Tom Story of Portland, Oregon. It was a sports model, based on a frame made of 10-gauge Chrome-Moly channel steel, to which Willys front suspension, rear axle, and springs were attached. The steering gear was from a Mercury. The engine was basically a Ford V8/60 but with Offenhauser 10.5:1 compression heads, twin carbure-tors, and dual manifolds, which boosted output to 113 horsepower. Top speed was 105 mph. To give good balance and improved rear traction, the engine was located 16 inches farther back than normal. Wheelbase was 97 inches, and the car weighed 2080 pounds. Probably only one car was made, though Story intended to produce more copies for sale at about $3500 apiece.

## STOUT PROJECT Y (1946)

Beginning in 1936, the brilliant inventor-engineer William B. Stout produced unique streamlined cars called Scarabs in his Detroit factory. The design was taken largely from John Tjaarda's experimental Sterkenbergs, which had themselves evolved into the prewar Lincoln-Zephyr. Stout quoted a price of $5000 for his rear-engined fastbacks, and a handful were built through 1941. In June 1945, Graham-Paige President Joseph W. Frazer acquired Stout's services to develop a proposal for the postwar car he hoped to build. After Frazer joined with Henry Kaiser to form Kaiser-Frazer Corporation, Stout continued to experiment at K-F's factory in Willow Run, Michigan.

Stout's prototype was called "Project Y," and differed in detail from his prewar Scarabs. Instead of a Ford V8, the new design used a 95-bhp Mercury V8—though this would have obviously been replaced by a K-F engine on production models. The body was fiberglass—along with the 1946 Darrin, one of the first uses of this material for body construction. Like the Scarabs, Project Y featured a vast open space behind the front seat in which a 74-inch-wide rear seat, cargo platform, or even a small desk might be installed at the owner's whim.

K-F abandoned Project Y in late 1946 because it was too radical and too expensive. The price was also forbidding: Stout estimated a production version might cost $10,000. Project Y was fortunately saved for posterity, and may be seen today at the Detroit Historical Museum.

## STUART (1962)

The Stuart was a two-passenger fiberglass-bodied electric made by Stuart Motors in Kalamazoo, Michigan. Overall length was 115 inches, width 64 inches, height 56 inches. Eight 6-volt batteries supplied current to the 4-horsepower motor. The Stuart had a 40-mile range when driven at 35 mph. The 1200-pound vehicle was available in a passenger version for $1600, or as a commercial for $1500.

The six-year-old company had produced a predecessor in 1960, the Voltaram electric. Neither car seems to have gotten beyond the prototype stage, however.

## STUDILLAC (1953-55)

The Studillac conversion was built by Bill Frick Motors of Rockville Centre, New York. Around 1953, Frick began installing Cadillac engines in Studebaker hardtops. This was a great combination: a production body of outstanding beauty coupled with a high-performance Cadillac V8. Acceleration from 0 to 60 mph took just 8.5 seconds, and top speed was 125 mph. The Studillac conversion added some $1500 to the Studebaker's cost, so the total package price in 1954 was $3695 with three-speed manual transmission, or $4195 with Dual-Range Hydra-Matic.

## STUTZ (1969-date)

The Stutz, built by Stutz Motor Car of America Inc., New York City, is another revival, but in name only. The car itself is modern, quite similar in appearance to the 1966 Duesenberg (ii). Indeed, Virgil Exner styled both cars.

Based on the Pontiac Grand Prix chassis with a 116-inch wheelbase, Stutz offered two-door hardtop, convertible, and limousine body styles, and, briefly, a ceremonial parade car. The bodies were supplied by Carrozzeria Padana of Italy. The Pontiac 400 cubic-inch V8 was used originally; later a 455-cid V8 was installed, followed by a 403 V8. Prices, depending on model, have ranged from $22,500 to over $100,000.

## STUTZ BEARCAT (1969)

The legendary Stutz Bearcat was considered *the* sports car of its day. Howard D. Williams of Tulsa, Oklahoma was certain its name and image still spelled magic in 1968. Late that year he began road testing a bright yellow prototype of a new Bearcat. Williams, a member of the Oklahoma House of Representatives, had chosen the chassis and engine of the International Scout as the basis for his replicar. The standard 198 cubic-inch four-cylinder Scout engine produced 111 horsepower—enough to move the new car at speeds up to 100 mph. The transmission was a three-speed manual. Included in the $4950 price were a "monocle" (round) windshield, a temperature gauge on the radiator cap, and a choice of wire-spoked or disc wheels.

## SUPER KAR (1946)

The Super Kar prototype was created by Louis R. Elrod of Cleveland, Ohio. Information about it is limited. It was a three-wheeler powered by an air-cooled 15-horsepower engine.

## SUPER STATION WAGON (1954)

The Super Station Wagon was a conversion by the Henney Motor Co. of Freeport, Illinois. It was based on the contemporary 1954 Packard Cavalier sedan. A 12-passenger station wagon, it featured an observation lounge arrangement with a three-passenger curved rear seat and a table. Packard's 359 cubic-inch, 212-horsepower straight-eight engine was retained. Though production was intended, the car's price of around $7500 precluded many orders.

## SURREY (c.1960)

The Surrey, made by the E. W. Bliss Co. of Canton, Ohio, was an antique replica, duplicating the appearance of the early curved-dash Olds. The standard engine was rated at 4.8 horsepower, but an 8-bhp air-cooled Cushman unit was optional. Other mechanical features were semi-automatic clutch and chain drive. The car rode on 12-spoke wooden wheels. Top speed was 35 mph and mileage was a claimed 65 mpg. The base model was priced at $1045; the DeLuxe model was $100 more. The Surrey was also available in kit form for $895.

## SWIFT (1959)

The Swift was first built by Swift Manufacturing Co. in El Cajon, California, then by W. M. Manufacturing Co. in San Diego. Three different ⅝th-scale replica models were offered. All used the same basics—a single-cylinder air-cooled Clinton engine and belt drive. The Swift-T looked like a 1910 Model T Ford. The Stutz Bearcat was mirrored by the Swift-Cat, while the Swifter was similar to the first 1903 Cadillac. Top speed was hardly swift at 27 mph. Prices were in the vicinity of $795. (See also Honey Bee.)

## TASCO (1948)

Tasco is an acronym for The

414

American Sports Car Company of Hartford, Connecticut, organized by members of the Sports Car Club of America (SCCA) to build an American sports car. Designed by Gordon Buehrig (see Cord), the prototype was constructed by the Derham Body Co. of Rosemont, Pennsylvania, a firm well-known for its custom bodywork in the '30s. The Tasco has been described as "a wingless cockpit on wheels." The front as well as the rear wheels were enclosed by cycle-type fenders. The front fenders turned with the wheels as the car was steered. Removable plastic roof panels prefigured a popular feature adopted by the industry some 25 years later. The engine was a modified Mercury V8. Had it been produced, the Tasco would have cost $7500, too high to attract many buyers in 1948.

## TAYLOR-DUNN (1949-68)

Taylor-Dunn was an electric built by the Taylor-Dunn Manufacturing Co. of Anaheim, California. Taylor and his son-in-law Dunn left Pacific Telephone and Telegraph to produce electric industrial trucks. Some cars were produced over the years as well.

The cars were built with three or four wheels. The three-wheelers had a 98-inch wheelbase, while four-wheelers had an inch-longer wheelbase and were three inches longer overall. Passenger capacity varied from two to four, depending on model. These electrics could reach a speed of 12 mph and had a range of 30 miles between charges.

The company began building electric cars in 1949. Around 1959 or 1960, they were sold under the name Trident.

## THORNE (1945)

The Thorne Tiger came from Thorne Engineering Co. in Los Angeles. Not much is known about this car, except that it was designed by Art Sparkes. Apparently, it was a forerunner of the Californian.

## THRIF-T (1947-55)

Tri-Wheel Motor Corporation of Oxford, North Carolina (later Springfield, Massachusetts) tried for several years to get their three-wheel delivery vehicles into serious production. Body types included a pickup, an enclosed delivery, and an open utility model. The power source was a 10-horsepower, 62.6 cubic-inch Onan flat twin. The most notable feature of the $800 Thrif-T was that its powerplant was mounted on a detachable cradle under the rear deck. The entire unit could be detached and rolled away on the rear wheels in about 30 minutes. The idea, of course, was to speed engine repairs or replacement. Curb weight was about 900 pounds, and payload was 500 pounds. Top speed was 35–40 miles per hour. The wheelbase was a very compact 85 inches, and overall length a mere 126 inches. The company optimistically expected to produce 500 vehicles per month, although it indicated a more modest 50 units monthly in the early stages of production. It is doubtful even that rate was ever achieved.

## TOWNE SHOPPER (1948)

The Towne Shopper was developed by the International Motor Car Company of San Diego. It was a tiny two-passenger model designed for shopping and urban use. Overall length of the prototype was only 116 inches, wheelbase was 63 inches. Considerable use was made of aluminum in the car's construction, helping to keep weight down to 600 pounds. The car's most unique mechanical feature was a combination starter-generator-flywheel. A two-cylinder Onan 10.5-horsepower engine gave a top speed of 50 mph and fuel consumption of 50 mpg. Tire size was 4.00×8. The announced price was $595, based on planned production of 100 units per day. The company collapsed in 1948, however.

In September 1948, the Carter Motor Corporation issued publicity sheets on a Town Shopper (note the different spelling of Town) with considerably different specifications. Overall length was now 130 inches and wheelbase 79 inches. Weight was listed as 1000 pounds. The body and frame were to be made of steel. It is not known whether this was a revised design by a reorganized company, or a totally different car by a different company.

## TRI-CAR (1955)

The Tri-Car was a three-wheeler with two wheels in front and one in the rear. Sources disagree on who manufactured it: either Lycoming Division of the Avco Corp. in Williamsport, Pennsylvania or the Tri-Car Co. in Wheatland, Pennsylvania.

The Tri-car used a closed three-passenger fiberglass body mounted on Goodrich rubber suspension. A Lycoming vertical twin connected to a Westinghouse-Schneider torque converter drove the single rear wheel. Top speed was said to be 65 mph, and fuel consumption of 41.5 mpg was reported. Overall length of this rear-engined shorty was just 117 inches.

## TRIPLEX (c.1954-55)

Triplex was a product of Ketchem's Automotive Corp. of Chicago. It was a two-passenger sports car with a one-piece fiberglass body and a box-section frame. Almost any American engine could be used, but the chassis was primarily designed to accept a contemporary Ford V8. Sometimes referred to as the Triplex Lightning, this car was derived from the earlier Chicagoan.

## TUCKER (1948-50)

Preston Tucker, a Chicago engineer who had helped design Miller racing cars in the prewar years, was driven by a desire to build his own automobile. Tucker leased a former Dodge aircraft plant in Chicago where he planned to build a radical new design based on a 1946 prototype called the Torpedo.

The Tucker was like no other car ever made. Its engine was a 335 cubic-inch aluminum-alloy flat six, mounted in the rear for what was claimed to be excellent weight distribution. The frame dropped below the center line of the wheels, the wheelbase was a full 128 inches long, and four-wheel independent suspension was featured. There was a central headlight that turned with the front wheels, a "safety dashboard" with instruments and controls grouped under the steering wheel, a "storm cellar" ahead of the front seat in which occupants were supposed to take shelter in event of a collision, doors cut into the roof for ease of entry, gloveboxes built into the door panels, and a windshield designed to pop out if the car was struck with a certain minimum force. The whole package was supposed to sell for $2485.

The engine used in all "production" Tuckers was an air-cooled Franklin six modified by Aircooled Motors of Syracuse, New York. In tests, it propelled a Tucker from 0 to 50 mph in 7.5 seconds, 0 to 60 in 10 seconds, and 0 to 100 in 33 seconds. Top speed was also what Tucker claimed—120 mph at the very least. One car actually averaged 131.64 mph in three runs on the Bonneville Salt Flats in 1950.

Alex Tremulis, a respected designer who had worked for many years at Auburn-Cord-Duesenberg and the Briggs Body Company, created the Tucker's styling. The four-door six-window fastback sedan had pontoon-like front fenders that tapered into a reverse curve on the front doors. The rear fenders started behind the rear doors and contained engine air scoops in their leading edges.

Preston Tucker sold $15 million worth of common stock, but no genuine production materialized

Towne Shopper

Thrif-T

Tucker

despite two years of heavy promotion. Only 51 cars were built, yet the company claimed a production line was in operation. The enterprise foundered when the Securiities and Exchange Commission began a fraud investigation. Tucker and seven colleagues were tried in 1950. Tucker was found not guilty.

Ever the optimist, Tucker continued to promote his unusual automotive ideas. Tremulis designed a beautiful "second generation" model in the early '50s. Named the Talisman, it was a very clean sedan with superb aerodynamics. In 1955, Tucker gave up hopes of a U.S. venture and moved to Brazil. He was planning a sporty economy model when he died in 1956.

## U.S. MARK II (1956)

The U.S. Mark II was built by the U.S. Fiberglass Co. of Norwood, New Jersey. Its fiberglass convertible body spanned a wheelbase of 110 to 118 inches. The car was available in kit form or completely assembled. It is not known how long production continued.

## VALKYRIE (1967-69)

For years, Fiberfab has been one of the best-known producers of fiberglass bodies, mostly designed for the Volkswagen Beetle chassis. One of these designs, the Valkyrie, was available for a time fully assembled for the rather outlandish price of $12,500. This sum bought the Valkyrie body wrapped around a Chevrolet 427 V8 mounted at the rear of a special ladder-type chassis. The 450-horsepower engine and five-speed ZF transaxle resulted in a claimed 0–60 mph time of 3.9 seconds. Top speed was said to be in excess of 180 mph. Conspicuously a drag chute was provided.

## VETTA VENTURA (1964-66)

An Apollo by any other name is a Vetta Ventura. They were one and the same. For a time, it appears, they were produced simultaneously. The Apollo seems to have been phased out during 1965, while the Vetta was still being marketed in May 1966. Coupe and convertible models were listed at that time at $6897 and $7237, respectively. The body was built in Turin, Italy by Intermeccanica and shipped to Dallas, Texas, where Vanguard Motors Corporation completed final assembly. When Vanguard took on the Vetta Ventura project, it postponed development of the Warrior sports car. (See Apollo.)

## VIKING (1966)

The Viking, produced by the Viking Corp. of Miami, had a brief existence in 1966. Details about its design are unavailable.

## VOLTRA (c.1962)

Voltra Inc. of New York City built this electric car powered by a General Electric DC motor. With a wheelbase of 106 inches, the Voltra was 170 inches long and weighed 1600 pounds, which was quite light for an electric. Maximum speed was about 45 mph.

## WAGON DE VILLE (1965)

Wagon De Ville was a conversion from Cadillac Wagons Limited of Linden, New Jersey. On the contemporary Cadillac body and chassis, the Wagon De Ville could seat up to nine passengers. It featured an electrically operated sunroof and a rooftop luggage rack. Its price was $14,950.

## WARRIOR (1964)

The Warrior I was built by Vanguard Products Inc., a maker of air conditioners in Dallas. It was a two-passenger sports car featuring a removable one-piece roof panel. When in place, the panel fastened to the windshield and a built-in rollbar. With the panel removed, the car had an appearance much like the open "T-bar" roofs of a decade later, but without that design's longitudinal brace. The fiberglass body was mounted on a 94-inch-wheelbase chassis made up of rectangular tubing. Power came from a rear-mounted V4 engine from Ford of Germany.

There was no connection between the builders of this car and Vanguard Motors Inc., producers of the Vetta Ventura, although both firms were building cars in Dallas at about the same time.

## WILLIAMS (1957-69)

Williams was a steam car from the Williams Engine Co. Inc. of Ambler, Pennsylvania. Since the early 1940s, Calvin Williams and his sons had been trying to develop a practical steam-powered car. Eventually, they entered the market in 1957. Most of these cars used conventional gasoline engines converted to steam operation. A 1963 model had an S-4 body from Victress, the kit-car manufacturer, and sold for $7000.

Another model—a converted 1966 Chevrolet Chevelle—carried a $10,250 price tag. The high cost of maintaining such low-volume production forced the firm to abandon car making in 1968.

## WOODILL (1952-56)

Woodill Motor Company of Downey, California gets credit for the first production fiberglass sports car. Its Wildfire arrived in 1952, a year or so before the Corvette and Kaiser-Darrin. But only a few were sold as complete cars off the floor; most were kits.

The Wildfire was conceived by B. R. "Woody" Woodill, a Downey Dodge-Willys dealer, and most were built around Aero-Willys components.

The Wildfire frame was constructed on a 101-inch wheelbase by hot rodder Shorty Post. It featured a very low driveshaft tunnel and a passenger compartment/firewall built into the frame. The Willys engine produced 90 horsepower and came with three-speed overdrive transmission as standard. Woodill offered no fewer than nine rear axle ratios, ranging from a stump-pulling 5.88 to a less frantic 3.88:1. Post reduced the steering ratio to only 2.5 turns lock-to-lock. The price of the assembled car was $2900, and Woodill recruited a network of Willys dealers to sell the Wildfire across the nation.

Woodill was market-wise, and soon realized the conservative little Willys six would not be enough for some drivers. So he had Post redesign the frame to accept the Ford V8 drivetrain. The V8 version was apparently not considered a Wildfire.

Glasspar's body was the Wildfire's best feature. It had a low, crouching silhouette, and a large oval radiator opening that accepted various grilles.

The Woodill Wildfire received tremendous publicity. The car came close to volume production. Willys-Overland was interested, and negotiations were well along when Kaiser-Frazer bought Willys. K-F went on to build the Darrin, and Woody Woodill went on selling Wildfires himself—assembled and in kit form. Prices for the fully assembled cars rose to $3263, and finally to $4500. Between 1953 and '56, Woodill says he produced 300 cars, of which only 15 were "factory assembled."

## WORTHINGTON (1957)

The Worthington was made by Worthington Motor Co., Strouds-burg, Pennsylvania. Little information survives as to its design or production history.

## X-RAY SPECIAL (1955)

The X-Ray Special was built by X-Ray Inc. of Highland Park, Michigan. Details about the car are not available.

## YANK (1950)

The Yank, from Custom Auto Works of San Diego, was a two-passenger, aluminum-bodied sports car with a 100-inch wheelbase. A top speed of 78 mph was claimed for its Willys four-cylinder engine. The price was $1000.

## YANKEE CLIPPER (1953-54)

The Yankee Clipper was produced by the Strassberger Motor Co., Menlo Park, California. The firm used a lightweight, 101-inch-wheelbase chassis of its own design, fitted with a Glasspar G-2 body (see Woodill). A completely assembled car, it stood only 37 inches tall and weighed 1900 pounds. Many 1954 Ford Components were used, including a 130-horsepower V8 engine. Early plans called for production of 40 units per month and a selling price of $3400.

## YENKO (1965-69)

Yenko Sportscars Inc. of Cannonsburg, Pennsylvania, was operated by Don Yenko, a Chevrolet dealer. In essence, Yenkos were Corvair Corsa coupes modified for high-performance work, mainly racing. Five Yenko "Stinger" models were offered, ranging in horsepower from 160 to 240 bhp. All used the 164-cid Corvair flat six, except the 240-bhp version, which had a slightly overbored 176-cid powerplant with 1.36 bhp per cubic inch. The Yenko won the D production national championship in Sports Car Club of America (SCCA) competition in 1967.

Two Camaro-based Yenko models were listed for 1969, with engines of 435 and 450 bhp. Production ended in 1969, after 185 Yenko conversions had been completed, including both Corvair- and Camaro-based models. In 1971, Yenko announced his Turbo Stinger, a turbocharged version of the Vega, to be available through selected Chevrolet dealers. It is not known how many of these were produced if, indeed, the project ever got past the prototype stage.